THE DOCTORS OF
REVOLUTION

SHLOMO BARER

THE DOCTORS OF
REVOLUTION

19th-Century Thinkers
Who Changed the World

Thames & Hudson

For Karen, who bore the brunt of it all, with love

© 2000 Shlomo Barer

First published in hardcover in the United States of America
in 2000 by Thames & Hudson Inc.,
500 Fifth Avenue, New York, New York 10110

Library of Congress Catalog Card Number 99-65583
ISBN 0-500-01884-7

Printed and bound in Singapore by
Kyodo Printing Co (S'pore) Pte Ltd.

Contents

ACKNOWLEDGMENTS

In reviewing some of the vast 20th-century literature on the so-called 'doctors of revolution' and the kings, emperors and institutions against whom they rose, I have learned much from each of the works quoted or mentioned in the text and listed in the Bibliography. I owe thanks to all the authors, translators and publishers without whose work I would hardly have been able to bring to life in authentic detail a bunch of unusually controversial characters – so controversial that of one author's ten friends and colleagues who had read his draft chapter on Marx, 'one or more suffered a mild form of apoplexy'. I hope that my treatment of Marx will have no such drastic effect, though it may come as a shock to some people that Marx, the 'infallible' man of science, also had a demonstrably irrational streak in him.

I have greatly benefited from conversations with the University of Michigan's late Arthur P. Mendel on the double life of the Anarchist Bakunin, as exposed by him in the biography published in 1981. I had further illuminating talks with Maximilien Rubel, the late editor of the French Pléiade edition of Marx's works, and with A. Yassour of Haifa University on a variety of subjects, but I hasten to stress that all opinions expressed in this book are entirely my own.

To organize and synchronize the biographies of seven philosophers of world revolution moving and acting against a wide panorama of political and social events in a continually developing plot seemingly stage-managed by history itself – as it will appear in hindsight – was no simple task. I was lucky to have Stanley Baron as an editor. Undaunted by a growing mass of material confronting him, he was patient and forbearing, and his always cogent as well as considerate advice did much to give this narrative history of two centuries its present form.

I could not have completed my research into Marx's ancestry without the help of Dr Paul J. Jacobi, a lawrer and former vice-mayor of Jerusalem. A kinsman of Johann Jacoby of Königsberg, whose trial on charges of high treason for publishing Four Questions to the King of Prussia is one of the episodes related in this book, Dr Jacoby spent 45 years of his life turning genealogy into a handmaiden of history.

I would further like to thank Peter Halban, who has been in on this project from the very beginning; Dr Dan Simon, the Director of the Tel Aviv University Library, and his staff; Stanley Broza, who has always been ready to help with research, as were Liliane Busscher and Herzliya Tsameret; and my daughter Naomi Keren; and Lina, Ami and L.D. for their encouragement during what turned out to be a long haul.

Finally, the editors and translators of the MECW (Marx-Engels Collected Works) deserve credit for providing an authoritative English-language version of their writings. So does Paul Draper for his monumental volume containing *The Complete Poems of Heinrich Heine* (CPHH) in English. And I gained greatly in understanding from Arnold Künzli's in-depth study of Marx's persona and works.

PREFACE

'Only an idiot can really believe in Marxism,' Alexander Tsipko, a philosopher at the Institute of Economic and Political Studies in Moscow, told Elisabeth Tucker of *Newsweek* in July 1990. Gorbachev's policy of *perestroika* had just won the day at the 28th and last Congress of the Communist Party in the USSR when Tsipko raised the question whether the Bolshevik Revolution had been 'worth 60 or 70 million lives'. Discussing the problems which led to the disintegration of the Soviet empire and society, Tsipko traced them to the very fundamentals of Marxism. Marx, he said, 'saw only those historical problems that fit into his scheme. Those that didn't, he didn't see.' Tsipko confessed that, like many Western liberals, he too had once admired the 'early' humanist Marx who wanted to save man from his 'alienation', only to realize that the 'early' Marx was in fact more frightening than the mature Marx who talked about class struggle:

> What he saw as forms of alienation – the family, government, nation,
> private property, and religion – these are the very foundations of civi-
> lization... He was a thinker of genius, but his soul was dead.

There had been no end of controversy and polemics about Marx's vision of a proletarian kingdom to come, but few had questioned the range and power of his rational mind. Only six years before Tsipko quipped that the idiocy of Marxism appeared 'crystal clear' in the first three pages of *Das Kapital*, a redoubtable American historian had ranked Marx as the founder of a 'great', albeit 'secular religion' on a par with Jesus, Buddha and Muhammad.

An extraordinary new dispute about Marx's very personality seemed, paradoxically, to be in the offing even as Marxism was collapsing. At this point I happened to conclude an investigation of Marx's family history which I hoped might help to resolve the one great remaining mystery of his otherwise well-documented life, the conflict between his atheist philosophy and his genes.

The Swiss philosopher and psychiatrist Arnold Künzli, in a thorough study, has come close to the inner drama that drove the Jewish-born but baptized young man to adopt the suffering proletariat as a class 'entrapped in a "Jewish fate" with whom he could identify ... while remaining a non-Jew or even an anti-Jew.' My discovery that Marx was the scion of nearly 30 generations of rabbinical scholars, lawgivers, captains of finance and community leaders gave me a whole new perspective on the secular saviour of the proletariat. Casting light where there were only dim shadows, it helped me to see how – plagued by 'the tradition of all these dead generations' weighing heavily on his brain – he may have found that stamping it out, erasing his genes, was the nightmarish price he had to pay for becoming Germany's premier modern philosopher and ultimately the Marx of history.

8

Besides turning him against himself, this inner drama may have been intensified by the conflict between his rational rejection of all transcendental beliefs and the hubris which made him claim practically divine foreknowledge of the universal role history had 'incontrovertibly' and 'in advance' assigned to the proletariat. No wonder that Heine, while becoming Marx's best friend in Paris, called him a 'godless self-god'. Heine himself reflected all the dilemmas of the 'jagged modern soul'. Although half-blind, he early foresaw that Communism, speaking a 'universal language as elementary as hunger and death', was destined to play a formidable role in history. He feared that it endangered civilization, but dreaded even more a nationalist outbreak of Teutonic 'berserk fury' such as the world had never seen.

Moses Hess and Ferdinand Lassalle were two men who could not bow to what the former called Marx's demand for 'personal subjection' or stand the intrigues of Engels, his 'co-prophet'. Lassalle had the same *a priori* knowledge of the process of history as Marx. With it he combined a will of steel and the oratorical skill of a people's tribune. Because of Marx's jealousy of him, Communism and Social Democracy were to come into the world as two distinct movements. Hess, having been the 'bellwether' of both, was to have the unique distinction of also becoming the apostle of yet a third, that of modern political Zionism.

Bakunin, after years of inner torment alternating with grand heroic gestures, surfaced from Siberia to assail Marx and publicly dispute his thesis that the world-saving revolution would come first in the economically most advanced countries of Western Europe, arguing on the contrary that it might erupt in non-civilized Russia, China or other parts of Asia. Indeed, a new generation of young radicals did not see why Russia, having no bourgeoisie, should import capitalism and wait for millions of peasants to form a proletariat strong enough to revolt, when – as Bakunin felt before he died in 1876 – there were other means 'to drag them into the millennium by the scruff of their necks'. And Marx, before he closed his eyes in 1883, may have realized that it was Russia, and not industrialized England, that would show the other 'the image of its future'.

Most of the 'doctors of revolution', with their wives and/or mistresses, knew the bitterness of exile as they struggled mightily against the monarchs and powers of their time. Figures larger than life, they will for ever be the subject of controversy.

My principle has been not to judge, but to let the reader gauge the extent to which each of these visionaries and world reformers measured up to Sir Isaiah Berlin's description of the great man as one who has taken 'a large step beyond the normal capacities of men', and achieved 'something unlikely to be brought about by the mere force of events.'

As I write this at the dawn of the new millennium, all theories of 'an end to history' have proved as illusory as sundry promises of 'a new world order'. The controversial NATO 'bombing for peace' air campaign in Kosovo – 'the good little war', as it has been called, fought not for land but ostensibly for humanitarian reasons – had hardly ended when Russia began her less telegenic but equally destructive war in Chechnya. Only time will tell what consequences the bombing of a sovereign state to solve an ethnic conflict will ultimately have elsewhere and how the USA and a politically frustrated Russia in the throes of economic crisis will repair their strained relations. Or will these two different wars, whose common feature was the indiscriminate victimization of civilians, merely have provided the last bangs to remind us that the 20th century was to its very end one of the most violent in history?

This book was in fact written for those who remember the clash of ideas and interests that made it so, as well as for those who are too young to know. In the new century man is sure to continue the robotic exploration of the planet Mars. Hope springs eternal. Yet how is one to forget the recent statement by James Wolfensohn, the President of the World Bank, that we are entering the third millennium with a global population of 6 billion, 3 billion of whom live on $2 a day, and 1.3 billion on $1.

In the opening chapter of this volume the workers of Paris in 1796 are chanting the revolutionary song of Bastille days about 'the people dying of hunger, dying of cold.' With starvation now rampant around half the globe, my narrative seems to have come full circle.

SHLOMO BARER
23 December 1999

There is a solidarity of the generations that succeed each other, yea, even [of] the nations that follow each other into the arena… and in the end the whole of mankind is held accountable for the collective assets and liabilities of the past. In the Valley of Joshaphat the great Debt Register will be destroyed, unless perhaps before that in a universal bankruptcy.

Heinrich Heine, *Memoirs*

Men make their own history, but not spontaneously, under conditions they have chosen for themselves… The tradition of all dead generations weighs like a heavy alp on the brain of the living.

Karl Marx, *The Eighteenth Brumaire of Louis Bonaparte*

1

Babeuf, Buonarroti and the 'conspiracy of the equals'

The year was 1796, and the French Revolution was in its last gasps. The population of Paris was beginning to exceed half a million. It was the fourth year since the proclamation of the Republic, and the second since the Directory of Five, led by the indolent and profligate ex-viscount Barras, was trying to hold bankrupt France together.

Gone was the high excitement of the days of the Bastille. The feudal system had been destroyed, but France was tired of bloody strife between Royalists, Jacobins, Girondins, *patriotes* and *enragés*, tired of terror and mob rule. Robespierre's Committee of Public Safety had been dissolved, Jacobin clubs had been closed and *sans-culotte* violence seemed to have spent itself.

But the troops of the Republic were deployed in Belgium, parts of Holland and along the Rhine, and what with all the internal upheavals and external wars, the French economy was in a ruinous state beginning to resemble that of 1789. Although the revolutionary fervour had gone out of the people, many remembered that, at the time of the storming of the Bastille too, they had thought with the Duke of Dorset that they had witnessed 'the greatest revolution we know of… effected with the loss of very few lives', only to be shaken within days by the spectacle of a mixed mob of hungry Parisians, military deserters and armed cut-throats from the provinces stringing up the food contractor and short-lived Minister of Finance, Foulon, on a lantern outside the Hôtel de Ville. Then they had carried his disfigured head – and that of his son-in-law Berthier de Sauvigny – on the ends of pikes to the Palais Royal. Foulon's mouth had been stuffed with hay, to make him expiate his reputed remark, 'if they have no bread, let them eat hay.'[1]

Those days with their cannibal excesses were gone. In reaction to all the violence, the Terror and the spartan impositions of Robespierre's 'Republic of Virtue', Paris seemed to have gone wild. 'Balls and spectacles and fireworks have replaced prisons and revolutionary committees,' wrote Talleyrand, who arrived there in September 1796, after 4 years spent as an émigré in England and America. 'Next to money, everyone in Paris loves, adores, idolizes dancing,' noted another observer, 'and every class, rich or poor, high or low, dances everywhere.'[2]

While part of the population hungered, the Directory of 'the Five' (Barras, Lazare Carnot, J.F. Ruebell and two men of lesser stamp), often described as the most corrupt regime which ever ruled France, were amassing huge fortunes in gifts and bribes from foreign powers – 8 million francs from Portugal were divided among them and Talleyrand (who by the following year had become Foreign Minister) for negotiating peace with that country; a million and a half went into their pockets from Spain; and more millions from others. At the same time, a new class of nouveaux-riches engaged in an extravagant spree of gambling, dancing and carousing. The reaction to all the recent violence and convulsions expressed itself both in their dress and in their entertainments. Abandoning the austere costumes of the 'Republic of Virtue', their women wore a flimsy *robe en chemise* of white muslin and Greek length, but so transparent that the effect was of semi-nudity, heightened by their bare or sandaled feet with rings on the toes. These women set the pace of the new society. Dictating its tone and exercising no small political influence were three of the *merveilleuses* – the marvellous ladies who, in Talleyrand's words, 'took the place of the vanished ladies of the court and who, like the latter, were imitated by sluts competing for the prize in luxury and extravagance.'[3]

Foremost among them was the 'divine-looking', 23-year-old wife of Jean-Lambert Tallien, a friend of Robespierre's who had eventually led the attack against him. It was from the window of this lovely woman's house that the painter David is said to have made his cruel but magnificent sketch of Marie Antoinette sitting with upright Habsburg disdain in the cart carrying her to her beheading. After Robespierre and the 'Robespierrists' had suffered the same fate at the hands of the 'Thermidorians', the spirited Mme Tallien (née Thérèse Cabarrus) became known as 'Our Lady of Thermidor' for helping to persuade the new executioners that there had been enough bloodshed, and rushing around Paris to free prisoners.

Currently the mistress of Barras, the leading Director and actual ruler of France, Mme Tallien presided at his gambling parties and revelries, where she and other prominent *merveilleuses* danced with politicians and rich bankers. It was one of these extravagant, luxury-loving women that Bonaparte had just married: Joséphine, the luscious Creole who had seen her husband, the Vicomte de Beauharnais, dragged to the guillotine, had herself spent a long and terrible period in jail, and had since been the mistress of General Hoche and of Barras himself.

The flamboyant *jeunesse dorée* who set the new vogue may have been a numerical minority, but they and the cupidity of the new rulers were conspicuous at a time of economic distress. The regular provision of bread, meat and groceries at a time of unrest, civil war and chaotic roads had defied the cleverest leaders of the Revolution and even the most ruthless measures had failed. Bread-cards, meat-cards, laws against hoarding and the famous maximum price-control act had been introduced in 1793, and transgressors had been sent to the guillotine.

The maximum had been abolished, reimposed and abolished again. Neither the requisitioning of stocks, nor all the police bureaux and control organs established to regulate the production, supply and distribution of food and to supervise prices, nor even the beheading in a single month of 55 assorted shopkeepers, *cultivateurs*, innkeepers, grocers – and 35 other 'enemies of the people' accused of hoarding[4] – had worked even when these measures were in force. The black market in Paris had flourished all the time.

It was against the background of rising unemployment and the gnawing new famine that Babeuf staged the revolt of 'the Equals' in May 1796.

No more unlikely world reformer can be imagined. A hopeless idealist, he was neither a philosopher nor a charismatic leader of men. The son of an army deserter who, since his return under an amnesty, barely eked out a miserable existence as a day labourer, Babeuf had to start work at the age of 12 as a canal digger to help support the family. At 17, he was apprenticed to a surveyor and *commissaire à terrier*, a man looking after the accounts of the estates of noblemen and the clergy, and keeping track of their feudal rights over the peasants. In one of the houses of the rich he now frequented, he met an illiterate chambermaid, Marie-Anne Langlais, whom he married. Three years older than he, she was to give him 4 (some say 5) children, of whom three survived.

On his father's death, Babeuf, with two families to support, suffered great hardship and was often destitute. At times he hired himself out as a domestic servant. Eventually he set up as an independent *feudiste*, a kind of lawyer or notary who kept the manorial archives containing the *aveux*, or declarations, recording the type of each peasant's tenure and his obligations to the seigneur.

Through reading the classics and Rousseau, Babeuf developed literary aspirations. Proceeding from the idea that 'in the natural state all men are equal', he began to write a book, *Le Cadastre perpetuel*, in which he proposed that the government – by way of legally redressing the existing inequalities between 15 million landless peasants and 9 million landowners – should divide all arable land in France equally between all families, giving each an area approximating 14 acres.

The outbreak of the Revolution found him destitute but busily writing and distributing political reform propaganda at Roye in Picardy. A righteous little man, consumed by big ideas, he was irresistibly drawn to Paris, where he found the walls plastered with inscriptions of L'EGALITE OU LA MORT. The fall of the Bastille was living proof to him that the 'transformation of the entire world' was no wild utopia but within the realm of possibility.

He was confident that the practical blueprint he was offering France's new rulers in the *Cadastre perpetuel* would make a great stir, especially as the storming of the Bastille was followed by actual and rumoured food shortages, fear of famine and riots in both Paris and the countryside.

On 4 August 1789, while his book was still being printed, the alarmed National Assembly rushed through a decree proclaiming the 'complete abolition of the feudal system', an end to serfdom, to the tithe paid to the nobles, to seigneurial hunting, fishing, judicial and tax privileges. The landowners, however (as Babeuf, the ex-*feudiste*, immediately realized), had been deprived only of their personal rights. Other feudal dues – including those arising from the concession of land in perpetuity to the peasants, all land rents, and certain manorial labours and corvées – would have to be repurchased in cash according to details to be worked out by a committee of lawyers. In the meantime, these taxes were to be collected. 'Never', one authority on feudal legislation was later to write, 'have laws let loose a more lively indignation.'[5]

France's peasants, the majority of her population – only 5 million Frenchmen lived in cities at the time – felt instinctively that the feudal system 'hung together', and that they had been swindled. For though they were now free to hunt hares and partridges, the privileges given up by the landlords represented only a quarter of their income, while the total compensation for those to be redeemed – as eventually worked out by what has been called a 'soviet of lawyers' – imposed on the peasantry a burden estimated at nearly 350 million pounds sterling.[6] The peasants, however, drove off the tax collectors and went on burning castles to destroy the feudal deeds of their indebtedness. The tax revolt was to become the recurring plague of the revolutionary regime.

In October, burning with a 'unique vocation' to serve as a 'defender of the oppressed', Babeuf rushed back to Roye where he launched a newspaper in which he violently attacked the remaining feudal taxes in speeches and pamphlets. Before long, in speeches and pamphlets, he was threatening to lead armed resistance if the government sent troops to enforce tax collection.

Denounced by the mayor of Roye for his incendiary activities, Babeuf was arrested in May and transported in chains to the Conciergerie prison in Paris. From there he sent out such a stream of petitions and protests against the Cour des Aides prosecuting him that Marat took up his case in the National Assembly. He was granted a conditional release and in August he returned to a hero's welcome in Roye. Once there, he promptly resumed his incitement.

Although Roye was a conservative town which in July 1792 refused to celebrate Bastille Day, his popularity grew to the point where, upon his renewed arrest, none of the witnesses called would testify against him, and he had to be released.

On 17 September of that turbulent year, he was elected to the 36-man Council-General of the Somme Departement. While his wife was barely supporting herself and their 4 children by sewing shirts for the army, he saw himself becoming 'the Marat of the Somme', and hoped to be elected to the National Convention. Just then, however, the historic battle of Valmy set the Revolution on a new course.

On 25 July the Duke Charles Ferdinand of Brunswick – in command of a coalition of Austro-Prussian troops – had issued a manifesto threatening to raze Paris if the slightest harm was done to the French royal family. A philosopher-prince and gentleman-warrior, Brunswick had opposed the barbarous tone of the manifesto, but both Prussia's King Friedrich Wilhelm II and Austria's Emperor Francis II – a nephew of Marie Antoinette – had insisted on driving terror into the hearts of the French.

On 10 August, a Paris mob invaded the Tuileries, massacring the Swiss Guard. On the 13th, the French Royal family was imprisoned. Louis XVI, whom the manifesto was meant to save, had from the beginning cautioned the Austrian and Prussian monarchs, through his agents, not to enter France as conquerors, but as armed mediators. Nevertheless, the invasion had started in August, and by 2 September the Prussians had taken Verdun. Yet in the midst of all the anarchy and panic in Paris, a rabble-like French army consisting largely of volunteers – roused by Danton to a patriotic *levée en masse* – had rushed to the front and not only saved Paris and the Revolution, but stupefied the world by routing Prussia's war machine and the Austrian forces in the battle of Valmy, in the Champagne district of France.

'Here and today begins a new epoch in the history of the world,' Goethe observed after the famous French cannonade from the ridge of Valmy on 20 September 1792. The Duke of Weimar had taken him along as a sightseer to watch Brunswick make his triumphal entry into Paris. It was raining, and some of the Prussian troops suffered from dysentery. 'You will bear witness', Brunswick said to Goethe, 'that I have been defeated by the elements.'[7]

But the fact was that the Prussian army, which had not been modernized since the days of Frederick the Great, had become tactically a museum piece, whereas the French at Valmy inaugurated new tactics of warfare.

Defending the Revolution and *la patrie* against Brunswick's forces and their pathetic ally – the 'Army of the Princes' of French Royalist émigrés (some of whom had arrived in their carriages to be equipped with obsolete Prussian muskets against their own compatriots) – was the future King of the French, Louis-Philippe, son of the Duke of Orléans and at that time a 19-year-old colonel of dragoons. Cited in dispatches for his bravery, the young prince turned Jacobin returned to Paris two days after the battle to find a city reeling under the shock of the 'September massacres' perpetrated by the Jacobins in the capital's prisons; and while he was en route from Valmy, the monarchy had been abolished and France turned into a republic.

During the few days he spent in Paris, Louis-Philippe was promoted to the rank of lieutenant-general, and invited for a private talk by Danton, the Minister of Justice and man of the hour. Danton, the fiery tribune with the bovine, pockmarked face, had hoped to save 'the prisoner of the Temple', Louis XVI, from the threat of being executed for treason. Following Brunswick's manifesto, he had, by his sheer energy and defiance – and against the wish of his colleagues to abandon Paris – saved France. Now he shocked Louis-Philippe by his brutally frank admission that it was he, too, who had ordered the 'September massacres'. To the horrified prince, he explained that the rush of volunteers to the Champagne district had left the leaders of the Revolution defenceless in Paris. The prisons were full of aristocrats and 'conspirators who were only waiting for the approach of the enemy to rise and cut our throats. That I had to prevent.' He added another reason for having ordered the massacre in the prisons: 'I could not risk the sudden changes of mood which in times of crisis swing from patriotic enthusiasm to panic and even treason. I wanted the whole *jeunesse* of Paris heading for the Champagne to arrive there with blood on their hands, which would be for us the gauge of their loyalty. I had to put a river of blood between them and the émigrés.'

Louis-Philippe could not contain his indignation. How could one justify besmirching the noble cause of liberty with the blood of thousands of victims slaughtered without trial?

'And who are these victims whose fate you deplore?' Danton replied.

> They were the most fanatical enemies of your father, of yourself, of
> your family, and of us all. Don't you know that they were the accom-
> plices of the émigrés?... I suppose you have seen, as I have, the dread-
> ful roll published at Coblenz [the headquarters of the émigrés] on
> which my name was listed together with that of your father and all
> those who took part in the Revolution and its assemblies. You cannot
> have failed to notice that each name on this list was marked with
> one of the three initials E. R. P., designating those who were to be
> écartelé, rompu vif ou pendu [quartered, torn alive or hanged,
> respectively] according to the degree of guilt attributed to them.[8]

Louis-Philippe interposed that the authenticity of the list was at least doubtful.

'Listen carefully,' said Danton. 'You may be a lieutenant-general, but you are
still very young and I want to give you a piece of serious advice. I appreciate
your candour, but you must learn, and the sooner the better, to keep your
tongue and not talk about anything you happen to dislike or disapprove of. For
in a revolution one often finds oneself an accomplice to acts one may not have
wanted to commit, nor would have dared undertake by oneself.' Cultured,
leisurely, less virtuous and doctrinaire than Robespierre and not above taking
bribes, Danton, the grand seigneur of *sans-culottisme*, praised Louis-Philippe
for his devotion to the Revolution and his courage at the front.

'It is a good *mise en scène* and preparation for the long career perhaps awaiting
you. Remember, you will always be more closely watched than your father. It
will always be on you, rather than on him, that all eyes and public attention will
be fixed. Try, therefore, to contain your indignations.'

'But my conscience!' cried Louis-Philippe.

'It is not a question of your conscience. Nobody is asking you to take anything upon your conscience, only not to judge that of others. Keep strictly to
your soldier's métier, do not meddle with our actions, and stay out of politics.'

It was in the course of this strange conversation, here condensed, that
according to one account Danton told the astonished young prince: 'This
republic we have just proclaimed won't last. Much more blood will be shed.'
France might one day be restored to the monarchy, 'but not to that of the old
regime, which is finished... A democratic monarchy will be established. France
will never put up with the elder branch of the family, while you, who have
fought under the tricolour, you will have a great chance of reigning...'

And so it was to be, nearly 40 years later.

Before he returned to the Northern Army, which was about to invade
Belgium, Louis-Philippe pleaded with his father, the Duke of Orléans, to stay

away from the forthcoming trial of his cousin King Louis XVI and urged him to emigrate to America. But the Duke (to be known as 'Philippe Egalité') refused for fear of having 'to live with blacks' and missing the opera. He half-promised that he would have no part in his royal cousin's undoing, but in January 1793 allowed himself to be fetched to the Convention and there morosely cast the fatal ballot which, as it turned out, produced the one-vote majority dispatching the King to the guillotine.

Seized by the horror of his own action, the Duke was later found sitting on the steps of his palace, mumbling that he didn't know 'how they made me do it.' Before the end of 1793, during the Terror, he was to pay for his foolishness and frivolities when he was in his turn carted to the guillotine, but to face his death with dignity and the words: '*Dépêchez-moi vite.*'

In Belgium, Louis-Philippe's superior, General Dumouriez, hard pressed by the enemy, signed an armistice with Austria and decided to march his troops on Paris and overthrow the bloodthirsty Convention which was making 'everyone in Europe our enemy'. His plans, however, were intercepted and a letter from Louis-Philippe expressing similar sentiments was actually read out in the Convention. The Minister of War and a number of Jacobins were sent to Belgium to bring Dumouriez to his senses or to arrest him and Louis-Philippe. A prolonged argument about what was good for France ensued, which Dumouriez cut short by delivering the whole delegation into the hands of the Austrians.

His young French volunteer soldiers, refusing his plan to march on Paris, Dumouriez then escaped to the Austrian camp. Louis-Philippe had little choice but to follow him. On 5 April, not yet 20 but much sobered by his recent experiences both at home and at the front, he crossed the lines together with two other officers. To the Royalist émigrés he remained 'Général Egalité', a soldier of the Revolution and the son of a regicide; to France's revolutionary leaders, on the other hand, he was not only a deserter, but a prince 'born near the throne', who had treasonably conspired with the Austrians and Dumouriez to restore the monarchy; to the Legitimist supporters of the Bourbon Pretender, Louis XVIII, he was a potential claimant to the crown who might be supported by other Royalist cliques. He was to spend the next 37 years under this cloud of double and treble suspicion.

In Austria, where he arrived without money, the young prince had the good sense to refuse a commission in the Austrian army. Instead, he went to Switzerland under the assumed name of Monsieur Chabos.

At the beginning of 1793, Babeuf was elected to the post of administrator of the Montdidier district, and seemed to settle down to a quiet and secure existence. He was in charge of the sequestration of the lands of émigré nobles. He toned down his social agitation and seemed quietly to relish the task of doing away with the vestiges of feudalism in the area.

He had hardly set about it when a negligent entry he made in the auction record of the *biens nationaux* fired a dispute between two land speculators about a large plot of church land and led to charges of fraud against him.

Suspended pending trial, Babeuf fled to Paris, claiming that he could trust no jury in Montdidier to give him a fair hearing. Arriving without a penny, he first fell in with the most extreme *sans-culotte* elements. Working as a salaried propagandist for Claude Fournier, the 'wild American' who wanted to form an élite corps of 'revolutionary super-patriots', he called for the execution of the 'faithless' deputies of the Convention who were protecting the profiteering rich, and in an access of zealotry, he even turned against Marat, the man who had once got him out of prison. With France now declaring war on Britain and Holland in February, and Marat calling for a march to the frontier, Babeuf wrote a pamphlet *Où en sommes nous?* in which he demanded a law to reward the *sans-culottes* with land for their service in protecting the property of the rich in war. Any agitation for social revolution and the division of land had, however, been prohibited by the Convention on pain of death. When Marat blocked Fournier's appointment as commander of a force of 12,000 volunteers, Babeuf lost his salary and for a time was reduced to utter privation.

His fortunes underwent a miraculous transformation when he met Sylvain Maréchal, the atheist poet, playwright and author of the famous *Révolutions de Paris*, who was soon to write the liturgy for Robespierre's cult of the Goddess of Reason. Maréchal introduced Babeuf to Anaxagoras Chaumette, the *procureur* of the Paris Commune, who was to play an important part in the Jacobin take-over. Chaumette felt that Babeuf, with his *sans-culotte* philosophy, could be of use in combatting the wave of popular discontent, and before the end of May appointed him Secretary of the all-important and embattled Food Administration. An exultant Babeuf, about to move into the Champs-Elysées, wrote to his wife: 'My friends are the most important people in Paris: Chaumette, the *procureur* of the Commune; Pache, the mayor; Garin, the chief Food Administrator; Robespierre; Sylvain Maréchal...' As the right-hand man of Garin, the ex-baker in charge of the Food Administration, he was propelled to the centre of events in the stormiest year of the Revolution. Civil strife between the revolutionary factions and reverses abroad, added to recurrent food shortages and *sans-culotte* insurrections soon led to the breakdown of all authority in Paris. With Marat calling the people to arms against the Girondins, the Girondins impeaching him, the *tribunal extraordinaire* acquitting him, and his Jacobin minority thereupon staging the bloodless *coup* of 2 June 1793 – when 80,000 *sans-culottes* and National Guard men surrounded the Convention of the Tuileries with 60 cannon and the Girondin deputies were arrested – the way was clear for Robespierre's 'Republic of Virtue'.

The mass *levée* of 300,000 men added to the food crisis of that hectic summer. While France was going through a paroxysm of 'patriotic' as well as 'revolutionary' fervour, Paris demanded to be fed. Babeuf, working with several score officials under him, had his hands full and realized that his agrarian law rewarding *sans-culottes* returning from war with land would have to wait.

He now lived in an apartment in the rue Saint-Honoré put at his disposal by Garin, and his wife and children had joined him. As cries for bread began to be mixed with loud demands for purging 'traitors from within', Marat – who was to be murdered in July – blamed Garin and his Administration for the flour and bread shortage. Garin and the Ninister of the Interior Garat began a pamphlet war in which each laid responsibility for the crisis at the other's door. Babeuf, def ending his boss and benefactor, had the streets of Paris plastered with placards accusing Garat of starving Paris. He further informed the Jacobin Evêché Committee – which met at the episcopal palace near Notre Dame – that not only Garat, but the Mayor Pache as well as the prominent Bertrand Barère and Robespierre's 'whole Committee of Public Safety' were involved in a counter-revolutionary plot to starve Paris.[9]

Some time in August, in the midst of the tumults caused by the referendum on Robespierre's new Constitution and the Committee of Public Safety's subsequent announcement of 'the Reign of Terror' – '*la terreur est à l'ordre du jour*' – both Garat and Garin were sacrificed: the Minister dismissed, the ex-baker and his deputy placed under arrest. It is not known how Babeuf escaped the purge. Unknown to him, the Criminal Court of the Somme *département* had sentenced him *in contumaciam* on 23 August to 20 years in irons for bolting justice after tampering with the auction record of Montdidier. Unaware of this heavy sentence hanging over him and to pursue him with a vengeance, Babeuf remained in Paris and soon even landed a better post as Secretary of the Comité des Subsistances et Approvisionnements. This consisted of three food commissioners who – in an attempt to save the economy – were given wide powers to establish a countrywide price-schedule for France's 750 districts, to stock 'national granaries', keep Paris fed and requisition supplies for the army. At an undreamt-of salary of 4,000 *livres*, it was the highest ranking position Babeuf had so far achieved in his up-and-down career as a revolutionary, and of late as an official of the Republic.

But where in all this was Babeuf the *sans-culotte* agitator? Since he had joined Garin's Food Administration and become an official of the regime he could not, except for agitating from within, but abide by the 1793 Constitution. At the same time, for all its faults, the Constitution affirmed the people's right to 'subsistence' by work or the dole, and consecrated at least one principle that engraved itself upon Babeuf's mind: 'When the government violates the rights of the people, insurrection is... the most sacred of its rights and the most indispensable of its duties.'[10]

No matter that the new constitution with its high rhetoric was quickly abandoned, postponed *sine diem*, in fact buried, by the decree of 10 October 1793 (giving Robespierre's provisional government 'revolutionary' – i.e. dictatorial – control of France 'until the peace'), the above principle was to fire Babeuf's later actions and to justify them morally in his eyes.

By then Babeuf's time in Paris was running out. He had hardly assumed his post on the Comité des Subsistances, which was set up a week after the execution of Queen Marie Antoinette ('the widow Capet') on 16 October when he was taken from his apartment straight to a Paris jail. The 20-year sentence imposed on him *in absentia* by the Criminal Court of the Somme département had finally caught up with him. The influential Sylvain Maréchal and Babeuf's friends and protectors in the Paris Commune and the Food Administration managed to prevent his transfer to the Somme département. Claiming that he was the victim of a plot hatched by some ex-aristocrats at Montdidier, they tried to turn his case into a political trial before the revolutionary tribunal, but failed. He was held for two months in the dank Abbaye jail. Then he was transferred to the Saint-Pélagie prison in the Paris area while his case was shunted from one authority to another, before it was eventually referred to the high Cour de Cassation. And while he languished in jail, the Revolution proceeded to its climactic phase.

Shortly before Babeuf's arrest in October, Barras, Fouché, Tallien, Fréron and other Jacobin deputies had been sent out from Paris with orders to subdue the rebellious provinces. Lyons was half-destroyed by Fouché and his team, adding machine-guns to the guillotine to keep up the rate of executions. Tallien, who ordered 'only' 300 executions at Bordeaux, later had to defend himself against charges of having been bribed into laxity. At Marseilles, Barras and Fréron had whole *quartiers* destroyed, and would have wiped out the town if Robespierre had not stopped. These towns had not only rebelled against the Jacobin takeover in Paris but had collaborated with the British, Spanish and other invading enemies, such as Admiral Hood's fleet at Toulon. Eight hundred people were executed in that city – where Barras, the future leader of the Directory, first met the young artillery captain Bonaparte, who was to unseat him – before he and Fréron were recalled to Paris.

Robespierre had launched the 'Reign of Terror' for the lofty aim of enacting Rousseau's ideas of 'virtue' and 'the general will'. Restless, unhappy, a social misfit, Rousseau, revolting against the injustices of 18th-century society, had attacked the rationalist trend of the Enlightenment *philosophes*. Reason alone, Rousseau argued, was incapable of changing society. 'Conscience', the feeling or instinct which enabled even a simple, uneducated man to distinguish between right and wrong, was the 'infallible judge of good and evil... The promptings of the heart are more to be trusted than the logic of the mind.

When Rousseau had published his two famous books, *Emile* and *Du Contrat Social*, he was execrated throughout Europe – 'I was called an infidel, an atheist, a lunatic, a madman, a wild beast, a wolf'[11] – and no wonder. His appeal to the passions was seen as a revolutionary attack on absolutism, as was his vision of a Golden Age in which everyone would 'put his person and his power under the supreme direction of the general will', implying that general will was sovereign, and that government not based on the consent of the people was illegitimate. Thus Rousseau, the pacifist and recluse, had sounded the clarion call of revolution, and by the time he died in 1778 his writings, previously burned in both Paris and Geneva, had become the bible of Europe's intellectuals. Robespierre and Saint-Just, like Rousseau, felt that it was the vices of the social institutions that corrupted man. But how, asked Robespierre, could 'venal souls' be turned into virtuous men? Force and intimidation would have to be used.

Indeed, Rousseau's theory that the 'general will' was 'always what it ought to be' – that is, absolute – could be taken to mean not only that the minority had to bow to it in principle but that each individual had to surrender 'the totality of his rights to the community as a whole.' It could also be taken as a licence to destroy all opposition. Rousseau at his Ermitage may never have dreamt of such ruthless rationalizations. Yearning for an idyllic life and a harmonious society in accord with nature, he may have inspired the Revolution, but through certain ambiguous passages in his writings he also unwittingly became the spiritual father of the Terror and 'laid himself open to the charge of totalitarianism.'[12]

In a raging fury, righteous Frenchmen between October 1793 and the following summer slaughtered 20,000 of their compatriots with or without trial. Robespierre styled himself 'one of the most suspicious and melancholy of patriots'. While he was determined to purify France by fire – always, it is said, hoping that 'the next execution would be the last' – the savagery that marked the Terror could not have taken place but for the paranoid fear of the Jacobins that, with France divided and beset by enemies from without, *their* republic was threatened on all sides. Although the Terror did not, as in Russia after the Bolshevik Revolution, become a permanent institution, it was opprobrious because of its brutal instincts and the fanatical trampling of elementary justice sanctioned by Saint-Just when – indicting Danton – he exalted love of *la patrie* as something terrible, sacred and 'so exclusive that it sacrifices everything to the public interest, without pity, without fear, without respect for the human individual.'[13]

Nature, Robespierre claimed, 'is the true priest of the Supreme Being, the universe is His Temple.' Calling a halt to the reckless attacks on Christianity, he offered Frenchmen an enlightened but water-down state religion free of priests and superstition. Although new ceremonies and public observances were instituted in honour of such abstract generalities as 'liberty and equality', 'modesty', 'paternal devotion' and the like, Robespierre's admission that 'belief in God' and even Catholicism were part of France's popular moral values gained him praise abroad.

At home, however, his 'Republic of Virtue' and the forceful transformation of the whole life of France met with no small opposition. Babeuf was still in jail when, on 23 March 1794, the so-called 'Hébertistes' were executed as part of a struggle between moderates and extremists within the ruling coalition itself. Even Danton, enriched by graft and temperamentally opposed to the Terror, was under suspicion of plotting against the ruling triumvirate – Robespierre, Saint-Just, Couthon – and before the month was out, Saint-Just was accusing Danton before the Convention of being a Royalist at heart, of conspiring to overthrow the government, and every other crime under the sun.

'Better a hundred times to be guillotined than to guillotine,' Danton cried defiantly. To the executioner about to decapitate him as well as Camille Desmoulins and several dozen of their supporters on 5 April, he said, 'Don't forget to show my head to the people: it is worth it.' With the opposition destroyed, Robespierre's dictatorial rule seemed safe. But it was now based on fear. His gradual suppression of the *sans-culotte* societies and the execution of their spokesman in the Commune – Chaumette, the *procureur* and Babeuf's protector, had been guillotined together with the 'Hébertistes' – lost him his popular support. Yet for the middle class he was too radical.

On 8 June, at a ceremonial Festival of the Supreme Being in the Tuileries Gardens stage-managed by the artist David, Robespierre formally inaugurated the new religion by setting fire to statues symbolizing Vice, Atheism and Folly; as they collapsed, a victorious statue of Wisdom emerged in their place. As the day happened to coincide with Whit Sunday, Catholics in some parts of the country took the opportunity to observe the new religious-patriotic festival by celebrating Mass. The French, it has been observed, seemed ready to accept the Republic, but refused to be reformed.[14]

On the day after the Festival, the Cour de Cassation at last revised Babeuf's case. Setting aside the verdict on a technical flaw, it referred the case to the tribunal of Laon in the Aisne département, but did not quash the sentence. Babeuf was marched on foot to Laon, where the tribunal found that the case had been mishandled at all levels – including that of the Cour de Cassation – and ordered Babeuf to be released on bail pending a new review by the Commission de Tribunaux. In the third week of July he set out on the road back to Paris, accompanied by his 9-year-old son Emile.

On 26 July Robespierre, fully aware that a plot against him was in progress, delivered his last speech and 'testament'. Refusing to avert his fall by defending himself in the Convention and/or resorting to force, he denounced the conspiracy against him without naming the conspirators and defiantly reaffirmed his faith in the ideal Rousseauist republic, founded on virtue. 'In peacetime', he had said in February, 'the mainspring of popular government is virtue,' but 'in a revolution it is at once virtue and terror... without which virtue is powerless and impotent.' Now, reiterating his lofty credo, he said that virtue 'exists, I swear... this profound horror of tyranny, this compassionate zeal for the oppressed, this sacred love of mankind... it exists, that generous ambition to found on Earth the first republic of the world.'

The next day he was met in the Convention with cries of 'Down with the tyrant!' Robespierre had indeed transformed France and propelled her into the future ahead of any other European country, had made her people free even if not, as he had hoped, 'happy' or even socially equal. A new French army, forged and equipped in the very midst of the Revolution, was beginning to gather victories abroad. In this sense it may be said that Robespierre left the stage having saved his country, though not before dispatching in daily batches another 1,400 real or alleged 'enemies of the people' by the guillotine – under a decree issued on the morrow of the Festival of the Supreme Being – until heads seemed to 'fall like slates from the roof', 47 of them even on the 27th when he was not allowed to finish his speech in the Convention.

On the 28th, Robespierre, Saint-Just and Couthon were executed, and during the next few days more than 100 of their supporters met with the same fate.

That summer, his second in Switzerland, Louis-Philippe of Orléans was preparing to make himself scarce in embarrassing circumstances. During his first summer, tramping in the Swiss mountains with a faithful servant, the young prince has sometimes slept in barns, homeless and otherwise reduced to penury. In October 1793 he had found a job as a language and mathematics teacher in a village boarding school for boys. There, in November, a month after his 20th birthday, he learned of his father's execution, the incarceration of other members of his family and the confiscation of its vast properties.

He was now titular Duke of Orléans, but continued under the name of Chabos. In the summer of 1794 he succumbed to the charms of the school's cook and – upon the discovery that he had fathered a child on her – he left for Germany, from where he was eventually, under another alias, to depart for America.

Babeuf, reaching Paris from Laon at the end of July, found a changed world. The surviving members of the Committee of Public Safety were in disrepute. The Commune had been outlawed, and Chaumette was gone. Exploiting the popular tide of revulsion inspired by the Terror, the newly installed Thermidorians – so called after the date of the coup, 27 July being the 9th Thermidor (of the Year II) in the Revolutionary calendar – proclaimed freedom of the press, especially for publications attacking the tyranny of the previous regime. Babeuf had not been long in Paris when Tallien and Fréron offered him the editorship of a new *Journal de la liberté de la presse*. This journal gave Babeuf full scope for the role of publicist that he had always dreamed of. At last, he had a platform for unfolding his skill at political propaganda, the importance of which he had early realized. On 3 September, he joined in the violent chorus against Robespierre's dictatorship and the surviving diehard Jacobins, but his alliance with the 'Thermidorian reaction' was short-lived.

Barras, Fréron, Fouché, Tallien and the other organizers of the Thermidor coup were practical men. Yet they also felt threatened by surviving Robespierrists, *sans-culottes* and various anarchists of the Left. Having no intention to relinquish power, they first played off one faction against the other. By October 1794 they felt strong enough to arrest the leaders of the *sans-culottes*. The Jacobin club in Paris was attacked by ruffians, and in November it was closed by the authorities. The maximum price control had been abolished and a new issue of *assignats* devalued the currency further at the start of an extremely harsh winter.

At the beginning of October, sensing that Tallien and Fréron were out to abolish the people's sovereignty by 'delegating' it to the Convention, Babeuf had renamed the journal *Le Tribun du Peuple* and began to publish it clandestinely. A new tyranny, he wrote, was on the point of 'overthrowing the republican system'.

For the first time he styled himself 'Gracchus' Babeuf, after the stoic Roman tribune Caius Gracchus, who was killed in an uprising in 121 BC. With his brother, who later met with the same fate, he had agitated for an agrarian law against the aristocracy's snatching most of the lands conquered by the Roman soldiery.

'I became myself again,' Babeuf wrote as he broke with the Thermidorians. The poor had so far gained little from the Revolution, and there had been much crime, bloodshed and profiteering. But the Revolution had shown that the fantasy he had entertained as a *feudiste* of a world transformed (which had seemed to belong to some distant future) was now within the realm of 'reasonable possibility'. The Revolution had brought about an electrifying and 'unexpected disposition of things'. It had 'fired souls with the necessary courage' to realize that the theories of a few *philosophes*, which only a short time before had seemed utopian, were 'practicable'. Babeuf now felt he had a unique vocation as propagandist of liberty and defender of the oppressed. An historic force produced 'the great revolution predicted in the Book of Time and Destiny' and he, 'Gracchus' Babeuf, like his eponymous hero, was called upon to bring about the inevitable 'overturn in the system of property' and to lead the 'revolt of the poor against the rich which has become an invincible necessity.'[15]

As soon as he started to attack the Thermidorians in his paper during October 1794, he was arrested. Released after a few days, he went into hiding, but continued to publish *Le Tribun du Peuple* clandestinely, keeping up a barrage of anti-government propaganda. The government issued a new warrant for his arrest, but it was not until 7 February 1975 that Babeuf, who now called himself the leader of a 'plebeian party' and the spokesman of the poor, the underpaid workers, the starving unemployed and the whole hungry '*classe des sans-culottes*', was apprehended by the police. For the next 8 months he was kept in various prisons, first in Paris, then in Arras, and then in Paris again. By the time he released on 18 October, the outlawed Girondins had been re-admitted to the Convention; the deputies of the Left had been expelled and arrested on the pretext of having incited bread riots; and the Thermidorian majority had submitted the new 1795 Constitution (under which France was to be governed by a Directory with the help of two legislative bodies) and had also passed the so-called 'Two-thirds Decree'. To assure themselves victory against both Royalists and the extreme Left, the 'Two-thirds Decree' provided that two-thirds of the new legislative bodies – the 'Council of Five Hundred' and the 'Council of Ancients' – must be members of the outgoing Convention, and that those not re-elected would be automatically co-opted as 'perpetuals'. Whereas the new Constitution had been endorsed by a majority of the voters, the 'Two-thirds Decree' had been overwhelmingly defeated in the referendum. The Convention, however, with the help of the army vote, went ahead and proclaimed elections for the legislative bodies.

During his long months in various prisons, Babeuf had gradually conceived the idea of a classless society which would put an end to 'the barbaric law of capital' that enabled landlords, merchants and speculators to deprive farmers, weavers and other actual producers of essential goods of the value of their labour while themselves growing rich and swimming in gold. In prison, among the fanatical Jacobins, dedicated revolutionaries and leaders of the Terror jailed by the Thermidorians, he also met his future comrades-in-arms and allies in conspiracy – men like Augustin Darthé, the public prosecutor in Arras during the Terror; Lebon, the town's ruthless ex-mayor; and Jean-François Baby, another commissar of the Terror. They were all to become Babeuf's aides, with Darthé in a prominent role.

Held in another of the 7 prisons in Arras was Charles Jean-Antoine Germain, a 25-year-old former lieutenant of Hussars, who wrote poetry and had wide intellectual interests. It was through arguments exchanged in correspondence with Germain, smuggled from prison to prison,[16] that Babeuf arrived at the idea of establishing a 'common storehouse' (*le magasin commun*) central clearing-house, where the nation's total production would be redistributed in equal portions to every citizen. People would no longer be driven to accumulate private wealth. Property, competition, money – between them representing the root of all evil – would be eliminated and 'perfect equality' achieved.

From these prison speculations was to develop the 'Conspiracy of the Equals' and the eventual framework for a 'Supreme Administration' that would plan and regulate national production, distribution and work quotas. The idea of classifying people into useful and unproductive or not useful citizens to be deported to labour or concentration camps was already present in a letter from Babeuf to Germain containing the sentence: 'He who does not work, neither shall he eat.'

After much argument and discussion, his the group of conspirators was to reach the conclusion that the 'perfect', yet state-controlled equality would have to be imposed on the people from above by an élite of courageous, determined and far-sighted men, and by means of a dictatorship. But how to stage a revolution? This question too came up in Babeuf's prison correspondence with young Germain. Germain was for a shattering, cataclysmic operation destroying 'in a single night at a fixed hour... the pernicious and false institutions that justice commands us to overturn.'[17] Babeuf was more cautious and thought of establishing 'a republican Vendée' in some part of France, whence the revolution would spread gradually by propaganda and guerilla tactics. In this respect too, things were to take a different turn.

On 10 September 1795, about a month before the elections for the Council of Five Hundred and the Council of Ancients, Babeuf was transferred to the Le Plessis prison in Paris. Crowded at the time with nearly 2,000 dedicated revolutionaries and former Jacobin officials, Le Plessis was a breeding ground of conspiracies.

It was there that Babeuf met Philippe Michèle Buonarroti, a 34-year-old Italian nobleman, a great-nephew several times removed of Michelangelo, whose enthusiasm for the French Revolution had incurred the disfavour of the Grand Duke of Tuscany. He was sent into exile on Corsica, but his instigation of revolutionary activities there had caused his expulsion. Upon his arrival in Paris he was warmly received, and in 1793 the National Convention rewarded him with French citizenship. Becoming a personal friend of Robespierre, he had been entrusted with various political missions, but after the execution of the Robespierrists he was charged with abuse of power and imprisoned at Le Plessis.

Babeuf was a self-taught man who had pulled himself up from the ranks of the destitute. He and his family had suffered severe destitution, for which he held a grudge against society. Buonarroti, on the other hand, was a man of the world who had received an excellent education. He was an early member of the Italian cloak-and-dagger movement called 'Charcoal Burners', the famous Carbonari. This 'brotherhood', with its mysterious rituals, had connections with various Masonic lodges, and gave Buonarroti easy access to important personalities in Paris. Moreover, he knew Bonaparte from the days of his exile on Corsica. A born conspirator who had abandoned the society to which he belonged to become a firm believer in universal equality, he was also a man of imagination. Although, on the face of it, he and Babeuf had little in common other than a few principles, their meeting was to give the ideas of the new-fangled 'people's tribune' a new impetus.[18]

Buonarroti and other Jacobin prisoners, including Bertrand, the former mayor of Lyons, had been planning action against the Thermidorians and their new Constitution before Babeuf's arrival. The referendum vote for the endorsement of the 'Two-thirds Decree' and election of the members of the Council of Five Hundred and the Council of Ancients had been set for 12 October 1795. Before it took place, more than 20,000 Royalists prepared to march against the Tuileries and attack the Convention. Barras, who was in charge of defending it, had only 4,000 loyal soldiers at his disposal. He hastily armed a number of 'patriots of 1789' and ex-terrorists; and there was a feeling among the imprisoned Jacobins, sans-culottes and republican leaders that they too might soon be released.

Barras turned for help to the young artillery captain Bonaparte, whom he had met at Toulon, and whose coup d'oeil in espying the right hill which made Admiral Hood's fleet vulnerable had driven the British Navy from that port. In making Bonaparte his second in command, Barras chose well. Bonaparte decided that if he fired blanks at the mass of Royalists and others investing the Tuileries on 6 October, the noise would frighten them, but they would 'pluck up their spirits' and 'become twice as insolent'. He ordered his troops to fire cannon balls into the crowd. At Le Plessis, hearing ominous gunfire, Babeuf and a few other prisoners rushed a petition to Barras, asking to be armed and offering to save the Convention. It was, however, Bonaparte with his 'whiff of grapeshot' who became its saviour at the start of his rise to fame. After Toulon, he had been promoted from captain to general at the age of 24. Now he was to command the Army of the Interior.

On or about 10 October, within days of dispersing the attack on the Convention, he used his influence to arrange for Buonarroti's release from Le Plessis. At the same time Barras, feeling he might need the support of Jacobins and ex-terrorists for the unpopular new Constitution, was considering a political amnesty. On 18 October, a week before it was to be declared, he ordered Babeuf and a number of other prisoners to be set free. Three weeks later, the Directory of Five – Barras, Carnot, Reubell, Barthélemy and La Révellière-Lepaux – became the executive government of France under the new Constitution.

Events now began to move rapidly towards a climax. 'To wage active war upon Royalists, stimulate patriotism, crush all factions, extinguish partisan feelings and all desires for vengeance,' was the Directory's announced programme. Four of the 5 Directors were regicides. Some were more competent than others – Carnot was an engineer with modern ideas on armaments. All were practical men who, by their wits and inflexibility of principle, had survived all the upheavals of the Revolution. In a sense they were its receivers and beneficiaries, having accumulated power as well as personal riches through it.

All the same, while the Directory's official aim was to pacify France and restore national concord, it felt threatened on all sides. It wanted only to keep the boat from being rocked, but it continued to fear Royalist plots as much as attacks from the poor, the discontented and various anarchists of the Left. Following the general amnesty of 26 October, Paris had filled up with *sans-culotte* militants, Jacobins, former *enragés* and ex-terrorists. The new Constitution had done away with the universal suffrage granted by that of 1793, restricting the vote to wealthy taxpayers and to soldiers who had fought for the republic.

Immediately upon arriving in Paris and seeing his family, Babeuf walked through the working-class quarters of Saint-Marceau and Saint-Antoine, where he found the populace hungry but apathetic. The economy was experiencing stupendous inflation. The Directory's paper money – nearly 40 billion francs of *assignats* in circulation – was becoming practically worthless. While the extravagantly dressed *incroyables* and bankers, profiteers and other new 'men of talent', who had become rich by purchasing public land and buildings in deferred and depreciated payments, were on a spree, bands of deserters, vagrants, marauders and thugs roamed the streets of Paris. Playing up the Royalist danger, the Directory was keen to enlist the support of the released

Jacobins and ex-terrorists in order to help it maintain order. Some allowed themselves to be persuaded and entered government service.

Babeuf, Buonarroti, Germain and a hard core of several dozen 'Irreconcilables', who had discussed and made plans of their own in the prisons of Arras and Le Plessis, refused to cooperate. As early as the first week of November, Babeuf had taken the initiative and decided to start direct agitation. The Directory having learned that he was about to resume publication of the *Tribun du Peuple*, allegedly offered him – through Fouché, who came personally to see him – a bribe to toe the line. Babeuf refused, and that same month, in Nos. 34 and 35 of his paper, began openly to call for civil war, declaring that this was preferable to letting people die of hunger. Attacking the tyranny of the Directory in a phrase prefiguring Bakunin's later anarchist credo, he wrote: 'Let there be chaos, for out of chaos a new and regenerated world will arise.' The fundamentals of his egalitarian, Communist-type society – nationalizing production and obliging everyone to work and to deliver 'the fruit of his labours to the *magasin commun*', from which his spartan share of essential goods would be returned 'to his domicile' – was now clear in his mind and he promised to lead a social revolution that would free everyone from want. He was thinking in the grand manner of a man about to 'regenerate' society. He would 'abolish frontiers, fences, hatred, wars, door locks, disputes, lawsuits, theft, assassination, all the crimes, the tribunals, the prisons, the gallows, punishments, and the despair caused by all these calamities.' France had got rid of the *ancien régime*; now the remaining evils of property, of landlords and merchants who robbed the consumers, and the government which taxed the poor, had to be done away with.

Babeuf's impassioned tone appealed not only to the hungry, but also to salaried employees and even government officials whose pay bought less and less. Nor was there enough bread and meat to supply the population. Babeuf's own children were starving and his bitter personal experiences were reflected in his formulation that his society would put an end to 'anxiety, the perpetual, general but individually felt anxiety gnawing each of us like a worm, anxiety about our fate tomorrow, next month, next year, about our old age, about our children and their children.'

At the beginning of December the Directory ordered his arrest, but he managed to escape and for the next 4 months, from various hideouts, went on publishing the *Tribun*. Through Germain he kept in touch with the Jacobins, Hébertists, and ex-terrorists of the recently formed Panthéon Society, a group tolerated by the Directory, whose headquarters was a convent's former refectory near the Panthéon. As the refectory had been turned into a dance hall, parties of revellers sometimes forced the Republican diehards to move their plottings against the Directory to a torchlit subterranean vault where (as Buonarroti put it) the shadows and hollow echoes of their voices impressed on them 'the perils of their enterprise and the courage and prudence it required.' For the sake of prudence, the Panthéon Society outwardly played along with the Directory and at one point, in January 1796, declared its support of the new Constitution.

Babeuf himself continued as the chief spokesman of radicalism, and his anti-government articles were being read and discussed at the Café Chrétien, the Bains Chinois, and some 10 other Paris cafés frequented, as the police noted, by soldiers and workers. In March 1796 he began to join Buonarroti, Darthé, Germain and others at secret meetings in private apartments which the ex-prisoners of Arras and Le Pléssis had started without him, their object being the formation of an Insurrectional Committee to plan the overthrow of the Directory. Among those taking part in the discussions were Robert Lindet, the former Minister of Supplies and member of Robespierre's Committee of Public Safety; Jean-Baptiste Amar and M.G. Vadier, of the Comité de Sûreté Générale which had conducted the Terror; Antonelle, a former marquis who had sat on the jury that condemned the Girondins; Félix Le Peletier, another high-born and wealthy nobleman. Elsewhere, J.B. Drouet, a member of the Council of the Five Hundred, and a couple of ex-generals were being drawn into the conspiracy, including Fyon, Massey and Général Rossignol, the conqueror of the Bastille.

The leaders of the plot were divided between those who were satisfied with a return to the Jacobinism of 1793 and those who wanted an all-out revolution that, succeeding where Robespierre had failed, would draw the social and economic lessons of that failure and build a full-fledged Communist society, as proposed by Babeuf and Buonarroti. Even such well-situated men as Lindet, Le Peletier, Antonelle and Amar eventually agreed that half-measures against private property were not enough and that 'common property' was the fundamental solution; though some had reservations as to whether it could be achieved without excessive and endless bloodshed. For military support, the conspirators fomented agitation in the 7,000-strong Légion de Police, a force originally formed by the Directory for its own protection but now disaffected by rumours of being sent to the front.

When the Directory failed to track Babeuf down, they had his wife arrested. This provoked a protest from the Panthéon Society. The Directory had allowed the singing of the revolutionary Ça ira and the Marseillaise, and had tolerated the Panthéon Society – mainly in order to infiltrate it with its agents – but by the end of February they felt that things had gone too far. On the 27th, General Bonaparte was ordered by the Director Carnot to close the Society. Swooping down on it with some of his cavalry units, Bonaparte, himself an ex-Jacobin, was not too happy to find Buonarroti presiding over a meeting at which Darthé was reading a text by Babeuf.

But Babeuf's paper continued to appear clandestinely, and there was a new ferocity to its tone. Although he had earlier denounced the September massacre of 1792, No. 40 of the *Tribun* caused a sensation when he called the Directory a government of 'bloodsuckers, tyrants, hangmen and mountebanks', and suggested that a new 'September' was needed to get rid of them. He regretted that Robespierre had not wiped out 'the totality of starvation-mongers... One cannot govern democratically' without 'terrorizing [*terrifier*] those evilly disposed, the Royalists, Papists and starvers of the public.' Privately he wrote that Robespierre's policy was 'devilishly well conceived' and that even if the rivals whom he had executed had been innocent, the happiness of 25 million men by far outweighed the fate 'of a few shady individuals'.

On 4 April 1796 the Directory received an alarming report that 500,000 'indigent' people in Paris were in need of relief – an extraordinary figure, considering that the city's population 4 years later was no more than 550,000. Whatever the Directory's achievements in solving some of the enormous problems it had inherited after years of anarchy and war, its inability to provide the mere means of subsistence to the populace – coupled with the panic created by plans to divide the recipients of relief into classes – conjured up the spectre of a return to mob-rule and created a propitious field for Babeuf's seditious incitement. On the 11th, the walls of Paris were plastered with placards headed *Analyse de la doctrine de Babeuf*. They were torn down, put up again, and a 'poster war' began with the police. On the 24th, Babeuf was no longer able to print the *Tribun*, but he had started producing a new sheet, *L'Eclaireur du peuple, ou Le Défenseur de 25 million d'opprimés*, which was distributed in the streets. Crowds gathered and in some places the army was unable to control them. In the cafés they were singing Maréchal's song, 'Dying of hunger, dying of cold...' to general applause. On the 28th there was a mutiny in the Légion de Police, and three battalions had to be disbanded.

Babeuf, Buonarroti and their fellow-conspirators had decided that the Communist republic they envisioned would have to be imposed by military force and a *coup d'état*. According to Buonarroti, they counted on altogether 17,000 supporters, including 6,000 members of the disintegrating Légion de Police, 3,000 soldiers from other units and 2,000 purged Jacobin officials and ex-officers. To the sound of the tocsin and trumpets to rouse the people, the military part of the insurrection was to be carried out by three 'divisions'. Significantly, each 'division', commanded by a general, was to be accompanied by a political commissar. The five Directors, all the ministers, the Commander of the Army of the Interior (Bonaparte) and his headquarters staff were to be seized and executed. So were all the members of the Council of Five Hundred and the Council of Ancients. Besides the Luxembourg Palace, the Ministries and the army headquarters, other targets to be occupied were the military camps at Grenelle and Vincennes, the Feuillants arsenal with its weapons, the artillery camp at Meudon and the optical telegraph terminals at the Louvre and on the heights of Montmartre.

The takeover of power was to be turned into a 'Day of the People'. Once the objectives had been captured, the mutineers were to display to the people 'the heads of their enemies' and to incite them to revolt. It was to be a day of wrath; the populace would be let loose and encouraged to vent their fury on the oppressors. The happiness to be brought to 'the majority of the people', Babeuf was later to tell his judges, justified the necessary evil of terrorism after centuries of oppression. Darthé, one of his chief associates, felt that implicating the people in the bloodletting was the best way of binding it to the revolution. Food hoarders, recalcitrant bakers as well as foreigners found in the street were to be strung up from the nearest 'lanterne', as in the stormy days of the Bastille. Commissars were to be dispatched to the provinces to stir up the people and spread the revolution, and, where necessary, organize terror à la Robespierre.

The seizure of power was to be followed by the establishment of a provisional *'dictature de l'insurrection'*. All the institutions established since the overthrow of Robespierre were to be declared illegal and the Constitution of 1793 – which granted universal suffrage, but had remained on paper – was to be enacted. The object was 'the re-establishment of popular sovereignty', but, as Buonarroti was to put it, one could not, at the start of a revolution, busy one's self with 'collecting the votes of a nation'. Tyranny had to be brought down first.

To make sure of success and lend a semblance of democratic legality to the transitional dictatorship, the people of Paris, makers of the original Revolution, were to elect a new national Convention. This was to be filled with a majority of the 'Equals'. Even a provisional dictatorship, however, needs to have all legislative and executive powers concentrated in its hands in order to assume command and exact its writ swiftly and effectively in order to avert being overthrown. Vadier and other Jacobin deputies expelled from the previous Convention protested that they were its only legal heirs and that a Convention formed by a snap election in Paris alone was an infringement of the principle of 'the people's sovereignty'. They were overruled.

This was to be 'the last revolution', a vast design rarely conceived in the history of the world, discussed in trembling whispers by a few philosophers and

33

'men of genius', a social transformation never before put into motion, to which 1789 had been the mere forerunner. So wrote Sylvain Maréchal in the text of the Manifesto of the Equals which was to be released at the start of the insurrection. A combination of 'wisdom and authority', in Buonarroti's words, was required, and after much discussion it was decided to propose that the new 'popular' Convention divest itself of its legislative functions and leave them, together with all executive power, in the hands of the Insurrectional Committee itself.

Georges Grisel, an ex-captain who had become one of the secret Insurrectional Committee's military experts, had to rewrite Babeuf's ideological leaflets when it was found that the peasant conscripts in the Légion de Police, besides being largely illiterate, cared little about politics. All they wanted, Grisel reported, was to go home, and they would gladly 'give the republic away for a piece of village gateau.' The only way to attract them, he said, was to offer them 'wine and the hope of pillage.' With all its plans ready, the Insurrectional Committee was bothered by one question. How many militants from among the civilian population and the rabble in the slums would actually respond to the summons? The Committee's agents had quietly instructed *sans-culottes* and other disaffected elements in the various arrondissements to collect pikes and firearms and hold themselves in readiness. But there were conflicting reports on the number and reliability of these adherents, and the quantity of weapons actually available.

On 9 May 1796, the Insurrectional Committee fixed a meeting for the 10th in an apartment in the rue Papillon to finalize the date of the uprising. This might now be launched any day, possibly on the 11th. The Committee hoped in any case to capture enough arms in the military camps; *faute de mieux*, the civilians might resort to bricks and cauldrons of boiling water against the government troops.

Since the beginning of May, however, the government had detailed information – through the same Grisel, who had turned informer – of the plot in the offing. Grisel gave the details to Carnot, Barras's rival in the Directory, on 4 May. Ahead of him, Barras, in a typical move of his own, had in April made an overture to the 'Equals' and sent his carriage to fetch Germain to the Luxembourg Palace. There, in his office, he had asked for their support against the Royalists and Carnot's leanings towards the bourgeois centre. Professing his sympathy and good faith, he had even offered 'to put himself, with his staff, at the head of the insurrection or, failing that, to place himself as a hostage in the Faubourg Saint-Antoine.'[19]

When Carnot received Grisel's report, he summoned him to the Luxembourg Palace to repeat the details to the other Directors, except Barras. As

Grisel did not know the date of the insurrection the Directory were in a quandary about acting immediately or letting the conspiracy ripen; but finally they decided to order the arrest of the plotters. Barras also signed the order, but sent his silver into the country and took the precaution of not sleeping at home.

On the morning of 10 May, the day the Insurrectional Committee was to hold its last meeting, the headquarters of the conspiracy was raided by the police. Sixty-five of the conspirators were arrested, including Lindet, Amar, Vadier, Drouet and Darthé. Babeuf and Buonarroti were discovered in another apartment in the process of putting the final touches to the victory Manifesto of the Equals. Grisel was paid altogether 50,000 francs for his service to the Directory.

In the midst of tension and unrest in Paris, preparations were afoot for the trial of Babeuf, Buonarroti, Darthé – 47 conspirators altogether – before a specially constituted High Court. 'Gracchus' Babeuf was transported in a cage to Vendôme at the end of August. The families of some of the prisoners – including Babeuf's pregnant wife, his 10-year-old son, and Buonarroti's mistress, Thérèse – made the 150-kilometre journey on foot in the wake of the heavily guarded wagons. At Vendôme, 1,000 infantry, 100 cavalry and two cannon were on hand to guard the monastery converted into a prison and courtroom. The legal formalities, presided over by 5 judges of the Cour de Cassation, and the selection of 16 jurors out of a panel of 87, took months. The trial finally opened on 23 February 1797. Most of the accused chose to deny 'conspiracy' and to keep silent. Only Babeuf, Buonarroti, Antonelle and Germain made statements of principle.

Babeuf made the most spirited defence, pointing out that the Manifesto of the Equals had never been published; that the 'national community of goods' they had planned to institute upon seizing power was in the best tradition of Mably and Diderot, who had long preached that property and the inequality of wealth were the root of all evil; and that one of the charges against him actually concerned a passage written by Rousseau almost half a century earlier. Accusing the Directory of having turned the republic into a worse tyranny than the monarchy, he told the court that one of his children had died of starvation while he was in jail and concluded: 'I am leaving you slaves, and this thought alone will torture my soul in its final moments.' Then, sentenced to death after a trial lasting three months, he stabbed himself before being guillotined on 27 May 1797. Darthé was beheaded together with him.

Buonarroti, Germain and three others were sentenced to deportation. The rest of the defendants were acquitted. Buonarroti, by far the most important figure among the conspirators, was imprisoned for the next 4 years on the island of Oléron, and held for another 6 under surveillance at Sospel. Expelled to Switzerland in 1806, he went underground, lived for a time in Geneva, reappeared for a while in France, and then spent 15 years in Belgium (1815–30). Although kept under police surveillance everywhere, he remained in touch with the heads of the 'universal democratic' but highly secretive Carbonari movement, and during the 1820s conducted a vast network of conspiratorial activities in Italy, France and Spain.

Returning to Paris in 1830, after the July Revolution, this living bearer of Robespierre's legacy and the embodiment of selfless idealism, with an aura of Romantic mystery and of clandestine activities on behalf of 'liberty and equality' – became a hallowed figure to a new generation of revolutionaries in several countries. In France, his two main disciples were the Socialists Louis Blanc and Auguste Blanqui, who became the chief protagonist of proletarian insurrection.

Of the other people involved in the 1796 'Conspiracy of the Equals', the most prominent was Jean Baptiste Drouet. He was the energetic postmaster and excavalryman who, galloping after an imposing carriage with an eight-in-hand team, had stopped and arrested Louis XVI and Marie Antoinette at Varennes, and brought them back in triumph to Paris. He had become a member of the Council of Five Hundred, and it was because of his status as a legislator that the whole trial had to take place before a special High Court. Drouet, however, had made his escape with the Directory's connivance before the trial opened. Though Babeuf was not the sole or even the principal leader of the conspiracy, his making the most of his vocation as a propagandist during the trial played into the hands of the Directory, which was only too glad to present the whole plot as a 'plebeian' affair and at the same time to indicate that the period of mob upheavals – in fact, of popular revolution – was over, because the Directory was a government of law and order.

Through his sincerity and martyrdom, however, Babeuf – with the help of Buonarroti's book – entered history. Communism as an idea had existed long before him. The conspiracy that took its name from him was the first attempt to convert a country by force into a classless, egalitarian society, and to consolidate its ideological conquest by means of a dictatorship.

After Babeuf, Communism remained a highly amorphous and vague concept for decades. But everything pertaining to the 'conspiracy' was intensely studied by the succeeding makers of Socialist, Anarchist and Communist risings in Europe – not only Blanqui and others in France in the 1830s, but also Marx and Engels, who mentioned Babeuf's writings in *The Communist Manifesto*, by the 'Democratic' revolutionaries of 1848, the Communards of 1870–71 and down to Jaurès, Lenin and Trotsky. For these 19th- and 20th-century revolutionaries were to be preoccupied by many of the questions over which the members of the Insurrectional Committee, especially Babeuf and Buonarroti, had searched their hearts and brains – questions such as to what extent the end justified the means; what was to happen on the morrow of the takeover of Paris as a central power base; how to legalize violence and bloodshed and square the contradiction between an élitist 'vanguard' imposing its will on the nation without consulting it, and all in the name of democracy, 'the general will' and 'the people's sovereignty'?

2

From the Imperial Purveyor of Coin and Capital to Heine and Karl Marx

In February 1796, Heinrich Heine's future mother, Betty van Geldern, at that time an unmarried virgin, wrote from her native Düsseldorf to her friend Helen Israel Jacob in neighbouring Wesel: 'Hopes of peace have disappeared here entirely.'

In November 1794, Düsseldorf, rising prettily on the east bank of the Rhine, with its palatial Schloss set in beautiful gardens, a theatre in the market-place and an art academy, had been shelled from across the river and set on fire by French revolutionary troops under Count Bernadotte. By September of the next year its fortified walls had been stormed by a French column, which crossed the Rhine and marched into the town under General Kleber. In October, 5 months before Betty was writing, her father, the distinguished physician Gottschalk van Geldern, had died. Her mother had died much earlier, and during the winter Betty had sought comfort with Helen's family in Wesel. Still grieving upon her return to Düsseldorf, she was appalled by the renewed sight of her ravaged home-town and in her letter to her friend gave vent to mournful feelings:

> My favourite spot, lying at the end of the Palace garden, is practi-
> cally in ruins. All the lovely trees which gave such welcome shade
> even in the fiercest midday heat have been felled. In future there will
> be no cool spot anywhere in the neighbourhood, except the grave. Do
> not reproach me for deliberately picking on such dismal matters.
> Whatever I should choose to write about would fill heart and mind
> with inexhaustible grief . . . I fear the flames of war will not be extin-
> guished save in tears and blood!

Although Max Brod was to refer to the passage above as 'patriotic lamentation' and to cite it as 'an example of the characteristic style of Heine's mother', the fact is that her presentiment was correct: Europe was to have no peace, and to experience seemingly endless war, blood and tears, for the next 21 years.

Betty van Geldern was 25 in 1796. Born into one of Düsseldorf's oldest families, and a remarkable young lady in her own right, she had an intellectual bent

and had been educated in the spirit of Rousseau. She played the flute, read the literature of the Enlightenment – including German and French poetry, as well as some in English – and had often helped her father by reading for him 'Latin dissertations and other learned writings'. It was only natural that she had taken a keen interest in the medical studies of her elder brother, Joseph van Geldern, who, though only 31, had recently been appointed personal physician to the Prince-Elector of Bavaria. The product of a rationalist age, yet capable of strong emotions, she was petite and had a deceptively fragile-looking figure which hid unexpected resources of energy, as she was presently to prove. She also had an independent mind. At a time when much stress was laid on artificial etiquette and the conventions of social behaviour, when men and women culti-vated 'sensibility', Betty van Geldern, not long after the death of her father, wrote: 'Only the weak depend for support on the shaky reed of etiquette. Although my plain face goes with an ordinary figure and an ordinary mind, I feel I have the strength to rise above fanciful conceptions, prejudices, conven-tion and etiquette.' She could forgive 'a little reverie and Schwärmerei', but detested the 'so-called fashionable sensibility' in which there was little real heart.

Before the end of April 1796, within 5 months of her father's death, Betty van Geldern suffered another personal blow. Her brother Joseph, the doctor, succumbed to a wartime epidemic. Under the impact of her double bereave-ment, Betty was writing in June 1796 to her friend in Wesel: 'When my father died I was inconsolable. When my brother followed him I thanked God that my father had not lived to see his death. It is, of course, the depth of despair that turns one's past misfortune into one's present consolation.'

Some time at the height of that grievous summer, a good-looking young man with the air of a gentleman and a passion for horses turned up in Düsseldorf. Blond and blue-eyed, Samson Heine wore his long, soft hair in a queue sup-ported by a small, hidden hair-pad and held together at the back by a tortoise-shell clasp. Born in Bückeburg in north Germany, he was in his early thirties and had spent most of his adult life in the Hanover dragoons. After going through the Flanders campaign on the staff of Duke Ernest of Cumberland, son of King George II of Hanover and England, he had been discharged in 1795, when that two-year-long campaign against the French revolutionary armies came to an inglorious end.

'My late father', Heinrich Heine was to write of him many years later, 'arrived in Düsseldorf as a complete stranger.' He depicted Samson Heine as an easygoing, artless man who 'thought less with his head than with his heart' and impressed everyone by his uncomplicated manner – 'With his mental antennae he felt at once that which clever people only realized after long reflection' – and by his natural charm and gallantry. The father emerges as a rather shallow-minded, vain but likeable man whose powdered hair and 'elegant' hands exuded a scent of almonds and who was as happy as a child whenever he was called out to parade through town with Düsseldorf's uniformed Civil Guard. He had an eye for the ladies, and a weakness for wine, gambling and other sporting pastimes which he had apparently picked up in the Duke of Cumberland's entourage. As an *officier de bouche* in charge of supplying victuals to the troops and catering to the officers' mess, he had been – or so the son was to write – a favourite of the Duke, who much later became King Ernest Augustus of Hanover.

Samson Heine had arrived in Düsseldorf with a coach and 12 fine horses, a groom and a number of hunting dogs. Since, for all his good looks and impeccable character, he had neither a profession nor a penny to his name and could hardly afford the upkeep of so large an equine establishment – indeed, because of the expense of the fodder, the horses soon had to be given up – it is believed by some that Heine may have embellished things to emphasize his father's lightheaded extravagance.

But whether he did or not, he wrote that when, as a boy, he once asked his father about his grandfather, Samson Heine brushed him off half-angrily and half in jest with the cryptic answer: 'Your grandfather was a little Jew with a long beard.' In an otherwise loving portrayal in his Memoirs he described his father as a plump, 'monosyllabic' man whose handsome face had 'something too soft, characterless, almost feminine' about it and 'lacked well-cut distinctiveness, blurring into haziness.' This 'blur' of a portrait contrasts so strongly with the sharp delineation of his mother's character and personality (and the amount of space given to her and her family in his writings) that Heine himself, aware of the disparity, and elaborating on the theme of his father's being a 'stranger' and uncommunicative, recognized the disparity and claimed that he never knew much about his antecedents.

This is rather curious, for Heine's paternal grandfather had not been exactly an obscure 'little Jew'. The Heines of Bückeburg, established in that town since the end of the 17th century, were court bankers and suppliers to the Counts of Schaumburg-Lippe-Bückeburg. The grandfather in question had married a wealthy Hamburg banker's daughter, Eva Popert, of whose extraordinary beauty, gleaned in a painting of her he saw as an adolescent, Heine himself was to give a rapturous description. Heine saw the painting at the splendid house of his father's more famous brother, Salomon Heine, and was to remark that 'the little Jew' must have had something to him to have carried off the celebrated beauty and 'only daughter of a Hamburg banker famed far and wide for his wealth.'

Not only that, but in his famous *Deutschland, ein Wintermärchen* ('Germany, A Winter's Tale'), Heine was to include the verse

Half the Duchy of Bückeburg
Sticks to my boots . . . At Bückeburg I stopped in town
To gaze at the ancestral castle
Where my grandfather was born,

though he supposedly had no idea who his grandfather was.

But such dissimulation or the hazy portrait of his father are only minor enigmas compared to the mystery surrounding the circumstances of his parents' marriage and the date of his birth. For no sooner had Betty van Geldern, some time in the summer of 1796, decided to marry Samson Heine, than she came up against some unexpected opposition. By November she was angrily complaining to her friend: 'Would you really believe I could make so many enemies through my engagement?' Well into the mid-20th century it was assumed that the opposition came from members of her own family; that it had to do with their fear that Samson Heine, the impecunious ex-dragoon, was 'paying court to her only in order to gain admission into the family and with their support to set himself up in the town.' Indeed, the Van Gelderns were an old-established family whose history and fortunes since the Thirty Years War had been intimately connected with those of Düsseldorf itself. Betty's relatives, especially two spinster aunts, often evoked 'the great palaces, Persian wall-carpets and massive gold and silver plate' they had possessed in times past.

Although those fabulous riches had by now evaporated, the Van Gelderns were a prominent family and it was thought that Betty's relatives prevailed upon the municipal authorities to refuse residence to the swashbuckler Samson Heine, and that, to save Betty from the hands of this handsome charmer, they further persuaded the rabbi of Düsseldorf not to marry the couple.

Betty and Samson were eventually married, but it is not known when and how they overcame the obstacles to the match – whether the resourceful Betty forced the issue by defying convention and one day showing herself in the street 'in an advanced state of pregnancy', or resorted to other means to have her way. On 13 December 1797 (or so it is usually declared), Betty gave birth to a son, though that date is not absolutely sure. No one, of course, would have cared, had not the life and writings of the son provoked more controversy and outright feuds than those of any author and artist of world rank, with the possible exception of Karl Marx and Richard Wagner.

Heine himself was an incorrigible jester. Having put in the mouth of one of his characters the phrase, 'He is one of the first men of our century', he so enjoyed the double meaning that in order to call himself 'the first man of the century' he told a French writer and journalist that he was born in the year 1800.

Though every facet of Heine's work and personality, every incident of his life, has by now been explored and he is the subject of a considerable and continually growing literature,[1] he remains a contradictory and enigmatic character. As a person he was elusive, as a writer allusive, often covering up his meanings, sometimes in order to elude the Prussian censorship which reacted to his provocative sallies by treating him practically as the public enemy of Germany's political-social institutions. Solitary and distrustful by nature, always on the watch against attacks from both the Right and the Left, Heine was, in short, a great mystifier by temperament as well as necessity.

Besides stating that he was born in 1800, on various and successive occasions Heine gave the year of his birth as 1799, 1779 (which may have been a slip of the pen for 1797), 1798, then again 1799. Once he wrote that his birthdate was 13 December 1799; another time, 31 December 1799; then he reverted to 13 December 1799.

To compound matters, his younger brother Maximilian, who became a Russian army doctor and settled in St Petersburg, wrote that their parents' wedding had taken place on 6 January 1798. The consensus being that Heine was born in December 1797, Maximilian may have realized the implications of the wedding date and fabricated Heine's 1799 birthdate, which has given rise to the so-called illegitimacy theory. Even more curious is the fact that Heine's father at one point indicated that Heine had been born in 1802.

In July 1853, three years before his death, Heine instructed his younger sister Charlotte by letter how to fill out a questionnaire which had apparently reached her from the editor of a biographical encyclopaedia. In this letter he remarked that 'all our family papers were destroyed in the fire in Altona and Hamburg', which was true.

> I observe to you that, according to my certificate of baptism, I was born on 13 December 1799. The date of my birth in the Düsseldorf archives cannot be correct; for reasons that I do not wish to mention, the above date is the only authentic one, in any case more authentic than the recollections of my mother, whose ageing memory cannot replace lost papers. In this connection I observe to you, dear Lottchen, that you are perhaps much younger than mother thinks, since you came into the world many years after I did.

Obviously referring to some secret which, whether his sister was a party to it or not, he did not wish to put on paper, he was directing her in a roundabout way to maintain his fictitious birth date and mislead posterity. As if that were not enough, Heine had recently cautioned Saint-René Taillandier, a French writer about to devote an article to him in the *Revue des Deux Mondes* – and preparing another for the *Biographie Universelle* about 'the most original German poet since Goethe' – that the biographical notices so far published about him, some of which had been inspired by himself, were full of inexactitudes, and delivered himself of the following odd piece of information: 'Between you and me these inexactitudes seem [*sic!*] to stem from deliberate errors which were committed in my favour at the time of the Prussian wars in order to spare me service to His Majesty the King of Prussia.'

As Jeffrey Sammons has pointed out, Heine 'was never old enough to be drafted into Prussian service during the Napoleonic Wars,' and by the time he became eligible for military service he lived in the independent city-state of Hamburg, not in Prussia, and Napoleon was long gone.

The illegitimacy theory has been circulating since the end of the 19th century. In 1958 Philipp F. Veit, a Milwaukee scholar, finally demonstrated that the obstacles that held up Betty van Geldern and Samson Heine's marriage derived from 'the restrictive laws against Jewish marriages in force throughout the German principalities'. Referring to the so-called *Familiantenrecht*, a body of legislation designed to keep down the number of Jewish families, he cited among its 'obnoxious features' the fact that prospective Jewish couples were issued a marriage licence 'only when "vacancies" existed for the establishment of yet another Jewish family'. Indeed, ever since 1727, when the Habsburg Emperor Charles VI promulgated a law known as the *Familiantengesetz*, only a fixed quota of Jewish men – who were given numbers and whose names were entered in a special register, the so-called *Familiantenbuch* – were permitted to marry and establish a family in each Austrian province. Upon the death of the *Familiant*, his number was inherited by his eldest son when he reached the age of 24, or by a younger son – but not a daughter – if the elder brother had died.

Between 1750 and 1812 Prussia allowed even its small class of 'protected Jews' to marry off only a single son or daughter, and the *Familianten* law was not to be abolished until the middle of the next century; thus the *numerus clausus* on Jewish marriages was, at the relevant 1796–97 juncture, in force in all the German and Austrian lands from Silesia in the east to the Rhine in the west. The Duchy of Jülich-Berg was no exception. As far as Düsseldorf's tiny Jewish community of 150 to 300 souls was concerned, this meant that each couple's marriage licence postponed another couple's marriage 'vacancy'. Samson Heine, moreover, came from Hanover and was a 'foreigner'. Though there was no ghetto in Düsseldorf, Jews still required a ducal 'protection letter' before they were allowed to settle there. In other words, Samson Heine needed a residence permit in addition to a marriage licence. In the Duchy of Jülich-Berg, both these documents, before being approved by the authorities, required the formal endorsement of the Jewish community elders.

The French forces occupying Düsseldorf since 1795 had not abolished these regulations, as the Duchy had not been annexed to France. It was in fact to be returned a few years later (though only temporarily, as it turned out) to the Bavarian Prince-Elector.

It was the elders of the Jewish community, rather than the Van Geldern family or the rabbi, who obstructed Betty's marriage. Samson Heine had no means to set up a family. The elders, besides feeling that a residence permit to the 'foreign' Samson jeopardized the wedding chances of a local man, were in no hurry to grant him one for fear that he and Betty might become a financial burden on the tiny community. For by 1796 all that remained of the once considerable Van Geldern fortune was little more than those legends and stories of a fabulous past which Heine heard over and over again as a child and which struck him, as he was to recall in his Memoirs, like tales from *The Thousand and One Nights*.

Other than her two maiden aunts, Betty's only close relative in Düsseldorf was another brother, Simon, an eccentric 28-old bibliophile, who lived like a recluse with his books and an angora cat, and though amiable was hardly a great provider. Thus the elders' doubts about Betty's financial prospects if she married the penniless Samson Heine were not entirely unfounded. But it was Betty's own strong-headedness that ultimately aroused the enmity of the community leaders.

As Philipp Veit convincingly pointed out, it was the *dating* of the residence permit that became the crux of the conflict between her and them. For the elders eventually agreed to recommend the issuance of a residence permit to Samson Heine valid from the date of his wedding. The far-sighted Betty, however, insisted on an immediate and unconditional permit, meaning in effect – as she explained on 8 November 1796 in a letter to her friend Helen – that in case she died before the wedding took place, Samson's residence should remain irrevocable. When the community elders refused this, Betty remained adamant.

'I have triumphed over my enemies!' she proudly announced in the same letter. According to Walter Wadepuhl, writing in 1974, she achieved her will by appealing over the heads of the community to the French authorities. Ludwig Rosenthal argues that she took her case not to the French but to the local ducal officials. In a nation still impressed by titles, the latter may indeed have been more susceptible than the French to the family's standing in town, seeing that Betty's recently deceased brother had had the impressive old German Empire title of Aulic Councillor conferred on him by the Bavarian Prince-Elector Karl Theodor.

Finally, in another essay published in 1962, Philipp Veit established, on the basis of certain documents, that Heine's parents were married on 1 February 1797. Though questioning the son's birth date of 13 December 1797, officially registered in the Düsseldorf Archives and commonly accepted, and moving it forward to 8 February 1798, Veit was still able to demolish the illegitimacy theory.[2] Nonetheless, Walter Wadepuhl, another and quite redoubtable Heine specialist, was still firmly upholding that theory in 1974. By 1979, however, Jeffrey L. Sammons, in his *Heinrich Heine, A Modern Biography*, was again dismissing it. Accepting the marriage date given by Veit, he declared Heine legitimate by any reckoning.

What does it matter when and under what circumstances Heine was born? The main thing, after all, is that he was born. Yet we know how much Alexander Herzen, the wealthy Russian revolutionary, was affected by the discovery of *his* illegitimate birth. Emile de Girardin, the French deputy and press baron, went to court some 50 years after Heine was born to force his father, a general, to recognize him as legitimate. Richard Wagner was plagued all his life by his well-founded assumption that he was the illegitimate son of the actor-playwright Ludwig Geyer, and not of his legal father. He went to great lengths of mystification both to cloud the question and to create one of the famous 'mysteries of history', while at the same time turning the subject of uncertain paternity, and of false or unknown fathers, into a cosmic theme running through the whole body of his music dramas.

We know that Cosima and the whole Wagner family closed ranks to maintain this mystery for a full century with a ruthless diligence comparable only to that with which Marxist stalwarts late into this century suppressed the fact that Karl Marx found time during the starkest period of his London misery to father an illegitimate son by his housekeeper.

Obviously, Heine too had something to hide, something that must have mattered very much to the whole family, or else they would not have assisted in creating and keeping up the so-called 'birth date riddle' that, generating the 'draft dodger' and 'illegitimacy' theories – not to mention an appendix to the latter, the 'Oedipus complex theory' (according to which Heine never forgave his father for seducing his mother before their marriage and casting obloquy on his own name) – has befuddled countless experts for nearly a century. It is important to note that Heine's problem was unlike Girardin's or any of the others mentioned. That Samson Heine was his father was never in doubt. But Jeffrey Sammons – who has compared Heine to Henry James as a literary man confronting his biographer 'with the most elaborate and most organized game of hide-and-seek or hunt-the-author ever conceived'[3] – has observed that Heine

45

apparently had a reason for creating an issue which would hardly exist 'if he had not made one of it', and that it 'may have been a fairly serious one in his own mind.'

Commenting tersely that 'no one has been able to discover what it was', Sammons concluded his enlightening summary with a conjecture of his own: 'I think it is at least possible that he [Heine] actually did not know when he was born.' But this still leaves open the question why others in his family joined in creating the whole mystery.

It is possible to maintain that Heine was indeed illegitimate, but only in the sense of *premature* birth before his parents' formal wedding took place or before it could be registered. In a letter written to his brother Maximilian on 29 August 1837, Heine complained furiously about remarks made about his birth by a Professor Wurm. The editor of a Hamburg review which had belittled one of Heine's prose works, Wurm was one of his known detractors. To the poet's great annoyance, Wurm and his fiancée Fräulein Speckter frequented his uncle Salomon's house. When Heine heard from his publisher of certain things said about him at his uncle's table, he wrote his explosive letter:

> A miserable *Wurm* ['worm' in German], this doctor who has most
> vulgarly attacked and maligned me from the side of my birth *[von
> Seiten der Geburt]* was, I am told, entertained to dinner by my uncle;
> and to think that old Fräulein Speckter... got her trousseau from my
> uncle.[4]

These few lines are the only indication from Heine's own pen that he was bothered by rumours surrounding his birth. Though they helped to launch the 'illegitimacy theory', they do not prove it. The true facts will probably never be known, but the premature birth theory does at least provide a *motive* for all the cover-up attempts made so assiduously by so many of Heine's family, starting with himself, during his life and after.

'Earliest beginnings', Heine was to write in his Memoirs, 'explain latest phenomena.' As S.S. Prawer has pointed out in the latest of his masterly Heine studies, this maxim can be inverted: that is, 'late phenomena' in Heine's development at the time of writing governed his 'selection' of what he chose to share with posterity about his 'earliest beginnings'.

Besides playing hide-and-seek with his biographers, Heine undisguisedly announced in the short fragment of his Memoirs that he would 'loyally reveal' only what he thought 'characteristic and significant' for the development of his being. Prawer, while noting those aspects of his childhood and education which Heine left out, has remarked about his portrayal of his mother that one of the features he highlighted was her descent from 'a family once favoured by one of the Electors (*Kurfürsten*) of the Holy Roman Empire.' Though most scholars believe that Heine heightened her stature by various stratagems, Prawer in 1983 recognized that what Heine did 'in recounting the history of his mother's family is very important', for he was 'consciously dispelling simplistic notions – current even in our own day – of the lack of contact between Jews and Gentiles before the age of legal emancipation.'

Heine was well aware of his place in German literature. 'Goethe himself', he wrote to his friend Varnhagen, 'will not be able to prevent it that his name shall frequently be mentioned in the same breath with that of H. Heine'; at the same time, the more famous he became in his self-chosen Paris exile, the more acutely he felt the anti-Jewish bias he attracted in Germany, an emotional bias that in 1911, long after his death, was to make Adolph Bartels, a staid professor of German literature, wish 'to jump at the scoundrel's throat'.

Concerned as Heine may have been to stress his family's ancient roots in Germany, scholarly investigation has by now confirmed that ever since the Thirty Years War, when Düsseldorf consisted of a castle, a couple of churches and fewer than a dozen streets, his Van Geldern ancestors – as official bankers, purveyors and treasurers to the ruler of the Duchy of Jülich-Berg – had dealt on a daily basis with any number of German counts, barons and other nobles; that they had lived in style, and that one of them had travelled more of the world, met with more adventure and seen more of Europe's princely courts than most of his contemporary German knights and aristocrats. In short, the 'old family legends' which 'the female bards of the clan kept relating with epic monotony', and to which as a child he listened in awestruck wonder – not insignificantly, he called his Memoirs 'the fairy-tale of my life' (*das Märchen meines Lebens*) were not fables.

The founder of the clan, Jacob van Geldern, had arrived in Düsseldorf in 1628, in the midst of the Thirty Years War. Coming from the vicinity of the Dutch town of Geldern – hence his name – he purchased a 'letter of protection' allowing him to join the 5 Jewish families permitted to reside in Düsseldorf at the time. The prolonged war ruined Germany for generations. But each of the several hundred princes, dukes, counts and landgraves emerged from it as the absolute sovereign of his petty territory, with the right to maintain his own standing army. To raise the necessary cash and credits, the Palatine Count of the Rhine who ruled over the Duchy appointed one of Jacob's sons as his 'Court Factor' and financial adviser.

Two generations later, in 1690, Heine's great-great-grandfather, Joseph 'Juspa' van Geldern, was holding the same position when the Palatine Prince-Elector Johann Wilhelm inherited the Duchy and his family's rise to fame and fortune began. Johann Wilhelm, besides being Lord High Treasurer of the Holy Roman Empire, was the Emperor's twofold brother-in-law – they had married each other's sister – and lived in suitably lavish style. Joseph 'Juspa' van Geldern's role was to finance his architectural improvements and artistic requirements. He also, in the midst of the War of the Spanish Succession (1701–13), helped the Prince-Elector establish his own currency bank and supplied his troops with all their wheat requirements.

In return for Joseph van Geldern's charging him only 6 per cent interest on the sums advanced – sometimes running as high as a quarter of a million Thaler – the Prince exempted his 'Court Jew' and his family, employees and entire household from wearing the identifying yellow badge and paying the equally humiliating poll-tax; he also provided him with passports for unhindered travel and granted him some other precious, though to himself inexpensive, favours. In 1712 he permitted Van Geldern to build a house in Düsseldorf's new quarter and to erect the small town's first synagogue – a rare privilege at a time when the theological faculty and merchant guilds of Frankfurt-on-the-Oder were demanding the expulsion of 'Christ-haters' and the mere talk of 'a cursed synagogue' opening in Halberstadt caused a public outcry.

'Juspa' van Geldern's splendid new house, completed a few years later, was designed by the Prince's own architect, and he eventually owned a castle at Gravenberg. The tiny Jewish community of Düsseldorf he presided over enjoyed the protection afforded them by his standing at court. Basking in the princely favours accorded him, they rejoiced, rather prematurely as it turned out, at the building of the synagogue. 'This was no paper protection affording the right of stay for a limited period. This – or so it seemed in the bliss of that first enthusiasm – was a monument, rooted firmly in the soil and reaching proudly to heaven, symbolizing a right accorded to the whole religious community to reside permanently in a land they could call their own.' So David Kaufmann, writing in 1896, summed up their feelings in the first scholarly investigation of Heine's ancestry.

In 1716, Juspa's 21-year-old son, Lazarus – who was to succeed him in his office as Court Factor to the next ruler of Jülich-Berg – married the daughter of Simon Michael, Purveyor to the Court, the Mint and the Treasury Bank of three successive rulers of the Holy Roman Empire.

Since Karl Marx was also a direct descendant of the same Imperial Purveyor Simon Michael – a fact unearthed only in the 1970s after more than a century of assiduous but curiously unsuccessful research into Marx's exact ancestry – it is of some interest to pause briefly and consider his career, which had begun to flourish about the time the Turks were being beaten back from the gates of Vienna in 1683, or shortly afterwards.

Between 1687 and 1700, during the fighting which led to the final eviction of the Turks from Hungary and Transylvania, Simon Michael, who lived in Pressburg (now Bratislava) had supplied 2.4 million pounds of flour and quantities of barley to the Habsburg troops in Budapest (Ofen) and several other fortresses, thereby (in the language of an official document) 'preventing them from starving and surrendering to the enemy.' During the same period he had also lent Vienna's Imperial Chancellery 64,000 guilders, had travelled through what the document called 'rebellion-troubled' areas, and had further supplied the Vienna Mint with 'a substantial quantity of silver'.

A residence permit issued in 1693, shortly after the 'personal' union between Hungary and Austria under the Habsburgs was proclaimed at Pressburg, allowed him to live in that city, though only in the outskirts. Curiously enough, the permit bore the recommendation of Cardinal Archbishop Kollonitsch, who only some 20 years before had prevailed upon the Emperor Leopold I to expel the Jews from Vienna, confiscate their properties and turn Vienna's Great Synagogue into the Catholic 'Leopoldskirche'. In 1693, however, in order to repair Habsburg finances, a few rich Jews had been readmitted to the Austrian capital as 'tolerated subjects', in exchange for a payment of 300,000 florins and a high annual tax.

In 1705 Simon Michael, henceforth known as 'the Mint Jew' Simon of Pressburg – or Simon Pressburg for short – likewise obtained a special 'tolerance and protection' permit, signed by the new Emperor Joseph I, to settle in the Austrian capital. As Austria-Hungary joined the ranks of the great powers, Simon suggested to the authorities in 1715 that the opening of a bank in Pressburg would facilitate trade between the two hyphenated parts of the empire. Though Simon himself, who continued to purvey gold and silver to the Mint in Vienna under the next emperor, Charles VI, died in Vienna in 1719, the success of the family's rising fortune – like that of the Rothschilds later, though on a smaller scale – was assured by his having 6 sons.

While the two eldest remained in Pressburg and another moved to Prague, the youngest son became one of the 10 richest of the several hundred Jews permitted to reside in Vienna during the 1730s.[5] This son, Samuel Pressburg, had by that time facilitated certain contacts between Vienna and St Petersburg, and by a decree of 30 March 1731 had been appointed by 'Anne, Empress and Autocrat of all the Russias', to be her personal financial agent in Vienna.

A brother of Samuel's, Jehiel Pressburg, became Court Factor to the Margrave of Anhalt, Karl Wilhelm Friedrich, who was the brother-in-law of Frederick the Great. A sister, Semelle Pressburg, married Wolff Isaac Liebmann, who was a financial agent for the Imperial Russian Court in London.

Simon Pressburg, the 'Mint Jew', was still alive in 1716 when Juspa van Geldern's son Lazarus married his youngest daughter, Sarle. Lazarus, who was

49

Heine's great-grandfather, thus entered a family that had even wider court and commercial connections in some of Europe's most important capitals than the Düsseldorf-based House of Van Geldern. At the same time the marriage, solemnized in Vienna, represented – as is known today – an alliance between Heine's ancestors and those of Karl Marx, for Simon Pressburg, as we shall see, was the great-great-great-grandfather of the future Marx.

Lazarus was not to take his young wife home to Düsseldorf until 1721. He worked with his father-in-law, but even as powerful a Jew as Simon Pressburg was unable to get him a residence permit in Vienna, so Lazarus figured during his 5-year stay there as a clerk and bookkeeper in the firm of Marx's forefather. The 'Mint Jew's' own original permit had been extended to 1726, but when he died in 1719 it could be inherited only by 'one son chosen and substituted by him'. That son was Samuel, who greatly increased his father's fortune.

But the new permit acquired by Samuel Pressburg and issued by Charles VI in 1727 was valid for 10 years only. It was also in 1727 that the Emperor promulgated the law restricting the number of Jewish men permitted to marry (the *Familiantengesetz*), which Lazarus's granddaughter, Betty van Geldern, later had to overcome before marrying Heine's father.

Some time in the mid-1770s a grandson of the Viennese Samuel Pressburg – Isaac Pressburg by name – turned up in the Dutch town of Nijmegen. According to some, he became its rabbi, but in municipal papers he figures as a 'merchant and lottery collector'. Like many of the Pressburgs before him, he may have had a rabbi's education and title, but was otherwise a businessman. In 1785, at the age of 35, he married a younger woman, Nanette Cohen. Their daughter, Henriette Pressburg, born in 1788, later married the lawyer Heinrich Marx and was to become the mother of Karl Marx.

Ten years after Marx's death in 1883, his daughter Eleanor wrote: 'Strange that my father's semi-Dutch parentage should be so little known. My grandmother's family name was Pressburg and she belonged by descent to an old Hungarian Jewish family. This family, driven by persecution to Holland, settled down in that country and became known, as I have said, by the name Pressburg – really the town from which they came.'

Stranger still, it took another 80 years before it was revealed that these two rebellious men of genius, Heinrich Heine and Karl Marx – the one a prince of poets, the other an angry world reformer, both haunted all their lives by money worries and the general 'demony of money' – had a common ancestor in Simon Michael Pressburg, supplier of coin and capital to the Habsburgs and founder of a family which, under his son Samuel, joined the 8 or 10 constituting what Heinrich Schnee – in *Die Hoffinanz und der moderne Staat* – has called the 'core of Viennese high and court finance' that kept the complicated economic mechanism of the Austrian Empire going.

To this day, it is not known whether Marx and Heine themselves, who at one time met almost daily in Paris, were aware of the fact that Heine's mother Betty was a second cousin of Marx's grandfather, Isaac Pressburg; or that some time after the Russian intervention in the War of the Polish Succession led to the 'preliminary peace' of Vienna in 1835, Samuel Pressburg, having paid out the Russian army, arrived in Düsseldorf to attend the festive betrothal of a son of his brother Jehiel Pressburg to Hanna van Geldern, the eldest daughter of Lazarus.

The ancestors of Heine and Marx were thus doubly related, and there were frequent contacts between the two families in the next generation.

The Van Gelderns' decline from wealth to comparative poverty by the time of Heine's birth began as early as 1716, the very year Lazarus married in Vienna. That year the free-spending Prince-Elector Johann Wilhelm died, owing Juspa van Geldern substantial amounts of money. His successor, Prince Karl Phillip, was in no hurry to settle the debt. For all the opulence he had achieved in Düsseldorf, Juspa now faced financial ruin. He could hardly have recourse to justice against Karl Phillip; like every other Court Jew employed by Europe's monarchs, he was entirely at the ruler's mercy, depending not only on the latter's fortunes and good or bad policies but on his good will, whims and caprices.

Fearing he would die insolvent, the ageing Juspa recalled Lazarus from Vienna in 1721. The dowry of 40,000 Reichsthaler that Lazarus had received from Simon Pressburg gave a new impetus to the Van Gelderns' business with the Court before Juspa died in 1727 at the age of 74. In the next decade, however, Lazarus, investing in long-term contracts to supply grain to the army, lost 55,000 Reichsthaler as a result of bad harvests. His wife Sarle, forced to sell her jewelry, had to make a personal plea to Prince Karl Phillip in Mannheim before Lazarus obtained a minor refund and got new contracts, only to have his replenished stores sealed by officials on the pretext that he was in debt to the treasury. Though an inquiry commission eventually found a balance in his favour, the grain had meanwhile been supplied by others, and Lazarus lost most of his capital.

In this period, the Duchy of Jülich-Berg passed into the hands of another branch of Palatine princes. Its new ruler Karl Theodor confirmed Lazarus as his Court Factor, but favoured other purveyors. Lazarus was gradually reduced to fulfilling whatever contracts were thrown his way by his brother-in-law, Samuel Pressburg.

Still, Lazarus van Geldern, who had 4 sons and 6 daughters, lived in comparative splendour in Düsseldorf's Neubrückstrasse. He frequented Count Hatzfeld, the Prince-Elector's governor in Düsseldorf, and other princely and ducal officials on business as well as socially, and entertained courtiers and knights passing through town with their ladies. In Düsseldorf, the Jews were not, as they were in neighbouring Bonn or in Frankfurt, immured in a ghetto but free to live where they pleased. Lazarus had refined tastes, kept a large library and collected rare books and illuminated manuscripts. Though the Van Gelderns were observant Jews, they moved in Gentile society and were familiar with European developments and currents of thought. As early as 1739 a brother of Lazarus was studying medicine in Heidelberg, and two other Van Gelderns, Gottschalk (Heine's grandfather) and Joseph (his uncle), were to follow in his footsteps.

Lazarus gave his offspring a traditional Jewish upbringing, but he also saw to it that they received an education suitable to the society of the day. His children mixed with those of the local officialdom and all were taught German, French, Latin and mathematics. They were given dancing lessons and the 4 boys learned to fence and to ride horses.

On his mother's side, Heine thus came of a family which, compared to the rest of Germany's segregated Jews, belonged to a privileged few who – much earlier than the rest of that mass which was to erupt on the scene only after the French Revolution – absorbed German influences and developed a penchant for European culture.

This is the 'very important' thing Heine, in Prawer's phrase, was doing by driving home the notion, in his highly selective Memoirs, that Jews, including his own family, had been open to Gentile culture even before Moses Mendelssohn, in the second half of the 18th century, began to pave the way for the Jews' entry into the modern world, a process Heine himself was in a sense to complete by helping to prod the world into modernity.

All this, needless to say, hardly helped Heine's complicated problem later, when – becoming a German poet in the most natural way – he was to find his credentials disputed.

When Heine was still a child, he often played in an old attic filled with discarded household junk and dusty crates containing his grandfather Gottschalk's medical books and various Latin texts. One day he came upon 'the best and most precious find I ever made.' It was the diary of Lazarus's eldest son, Simon van Geldern, who called himself 'the Chevalier', but whom the 'female bards', who normally sang the praises of the clan, described as the black sheep of the family. They intimated that this great-uncle had spent a great deal of time in North Africa, where a warring Bedouin tribe had chosen him to be its sheikh. From 'an unknown oasis in the North African sands' he had led the tribe's raids on the caravan routes. He was also supposed to have had a vision on

Jerusalem's Mount Moriah. The Chevalier's notebook was written in Arabic, Syriac and Coptic (or so the boy thought), interspersed 'strangely enough with French quotations, for example, very often the verse: *Ou l'innocense périt c'est un crime de vivre.*'

Young Heine was able to decipher only parts of the diary – most of which was actually in Hebrew, with frequent Aramaic words – and the tales he heard from the family only added 'an air of mystery' to the figure of the so-called Chevalier.

On the one hand, he gathered that 'my late great-uncle, the pious visionary from the Holy Mount Moriah, was a robber captain' with a marauding African tribe. On the other, the old great-aunts shook their heads and dropped many a hint that the Chevalier had been a dashing ladies' man, a Don Juan who had to flee 'court and country' on his horse to escape death after a gallant intrigue with 'a very illustrious lady', and that he had also been a 'necromancer' and Kabbalist. Late in life, Heine was to describe the curious effect these stories had on him:

> Everything that I was told about him made an ineradicable impression on my young mind, and I plunged so deeply into his peregrinations and vicissitudes that I often had the queer feeling in broad daylight that I myself was my late great-uncle and that my life was only a continuation of his life who had died so long ago!
>
> At night the same thing happened in my dreams. In these dreams I identified myself completely with my great-uncle. It was a weird sensation, feeling that I was someone else and that I belonged to another age! I found myself in places I had never seen before and in situations I had never conceived of.

In his Memoirs he wrote that, though he became 'quite one with myself again', this year left behind 'secret traces' in his soul. In a striking observation, he attributed many of his own 'peculiarities' and irrational actions, seemingly contrary to his own nature, to the strange dream-time 'when I was my own great-uncle' – striking, because Heine did not know half his great-uncle's story. Much of what he heard about him was fanciful. More of the Chevalier's diary, as well as his address book and a mass of other papers, were discovered by scholars and literary investigators in 1905, more during the 1930s, and some were only found – in, among other places, the estate of the Grand Duke Ludwig I of Hesse-Darmstadt (1806–30) – as late as the 1970s.[6] And yet, the life story of the Chevalier van Geldern, pieced together and reconstructed on the basis of research over a period of some 170 years (interrupted by two World Wars and other conflagrations) since a wide-eyed boy in an attic first held part of his diary in his hands, has led several of Heine's latest biographers to trace certain 'genetically conditioned' affinities, as well as 'conspicuous' parallels, between his character and that of the mysterious Chevalier, parallels which Heine seems to have sensed when he attributed some of his irrational actions in maturity to the year-long period when he identified himself with the Chevalier.

Whatever the nature of these dreams or tricks of his over-active imagination (if that is what they were), Heine's extraordinary powers of intuition, his ability to see through complex situations and relationships, has of course long been known from his political prose and poetry. But these powers were never so curiously manifest as in his prescient self-identification with the fantasy-figure of his ancestor. Though greatly puzzled by him, Heine devoted a large section of his Memoirs to the Chevalier, surmising that 'he must have led one of those colourful existences which were only possible in the beginning and in the middle of the 18th century.'

As it turned out, Heine's amazing intuition permitted him to come close to the truth as it is today known.

In 1748, Montesquieu, writing of a 10-year-old Jewish girl burned at the stake by the Inquisition, had castigated Europe's inhumanity towards the Jews, observing in his famous *L'Esprit des Lois*: 'You complain that the Emperor of Japan is having all the Christians in his realm roasted on a slow fire. But he could say to you: "We treat you... as you treat those who do not believe as you do."' If anyone, he added, should in future claim that 'the nations of Europe were cultured', generations to come would condemn them on the basis of their acts as 'barbarians.'

This and other pleas for tolerance were eventually to have their effect. But in 1749, when Gottfried Lessing, then only 20 years old, wrote the play *Die Juden*, for the first time featuring a decent and noble-hearted Jew, who saves a Christian aristocrat's life at the risk of his own, thereby putting the Christian's prejudice to shame, this was so unusual, not to say sensational, that Göttingen's Professor J.D. Michaelis, expressing his doubt that so 'noble a character' could really exist among the Jews, publicly insinuated that virtue and honesty were in any case rare among them. This had elicited an equally sensational protest from a shy, hunchbacked young man: How, asked Moses Mendelssohn, could any decent man 'have the cheek to deny to a whole nation the likelihood or the ability of producing a single honest man?' Was it not enough that the Jews were exposed to 'the ridicule and contempt of the world' and made to feel its hatred 'in many a cruel fashion. Must these injustices we suffer be justified by further calumny?... Do not, at least, totally deny us virtue, the only comfort of the oppressed.'

Like Lessing, Moses Mendelssohn was 20 at the time. He had made his way on foot from Dessau to Berlin when he was 14, a nervously stammering boy with a slight spinal deformity, who knew no German or any other language but Hebrew, and had in fact come to join his rabbi. In Berlin he took up the study of German, Latin, English, French and mathematics. Before long he was reading Plato and Aristotle and publishing his first philosophical treatise. At 33 he was to win the first prize of the Berlin Academy of Sciences – in an essay competition in which Kant achieved only an honorary second – but it was to take another three decades or so before Mendelssohn became the first Jew to win the admiration and respect of the German intelligentsia.

Frederick the Great's Charter or 'General-Privilegium und Reglement' for the Jews, promulgated in 1750, had divided the 266 family-heads permitted to reside in Berlin into 203 'Regular Protected Jews', who had to make an irrevocable decision which son or daughter would inherit their residence right, this child being the only one allowed to marry; and a new category of 63 'Extraordinary Protected Jews' merely tolerated during their lifetime and 'not authorized to settle a child nor to marry off a child.' The 2,100 Jewish families living in Prussia were similarly divided: upon coming of age, all young Jews, bar one son or daughter of those in the first category, had to buy their residence right and 'protection' writ anew. Those not possessing the financial means were threatened, 'under penalty of expulsion, in no wise to dare to set up a business for themselves but must either work for other licensed Jews or go away and seek to be accepted somewhere else.'

Cynical, sophisticated and 'enlightened', Frederick, for all his frivolities, was a most perspicacious and capable administrator. He prohibited foreign Jews from settling 'in our land at all', but stipulated that any of them having a fortune of 10,000 Reichsthaler were to be referred to the sovereign himself, who would fix the fee for admission.

Like every other potentate at the time, Frederick resorted to the services of Court Jews, but these, for all their contact with ruling circles, never became part of court society. By excluding them from all but a few manual crafts and most professions, and by forcing the privileged ones chiefly to deal in 'money-exchange', he prevented the formation of a middle class among the Jews and perpetuated their medieval stigma as money-lenders and pawnbrokers, while actually turning the vast majority of them into pedlars. The language of his edict drove home the point that the Jews were an obnoxious and contemptible people, non-citizens and second-rate subjects, to be supervised, rendered harmless and milked at the same time in the interest of the state.

Prussia's cultured despot was as meticulous in listing occupations permitted to Jews – such as trading with 'gold-cloth, silver-cloth', fabrics, ribbons, snuff, used furniture and kitchen utensils, old clothes, old pocket watches as well as 'feathers, wigs, hair' – as he was in fixing the number of 'tolerated' communal Jewish officials in Berlin at 6 grave-diggers, one cemetery guard, three bakers, one restaurant-keeper, one physician and 'one fattener of fowl and cattle', or in specifying that 'the basses and sopranos' assisting the cantor must not be married.

Perhaps the most humiliating squeeze applied to the Jews was the medieval poll-tax or 'body tax' they were forced to pay – usually at a rate corresponding to the toll per head of imported cattle – not only at every turnstile between the several hundred German States, petty principalities and dukedoms, but practically everywhere on the Continent, including France.[7]

It was Moses Mendelssohn who was eventually able to reconcile Judaism with the rationalist trend of the age. Over the opposition of the rabbis, he pointed out that the Covenant of Sinai was a binding historic experience in the form of 'revealed law' – and not as revealed dogma – and that there was neither miracle nor mystery nor anything in Judaism to contradict reason. At the same time he realized that if German society was to give up its prejudices, the Jews must come out of their isolation and learn to speak good German instead of their foreign-sounding Yiddish jargon. In this way he hoped to build a bridge between the two hitherto exclusive communities, the dominant and the despised.

Mendelssohn became such a fervent champion of the German language that he dared publicly to criticize Frederick the Great's predilection for versifying in French. Denounced to the monarch and summoned to Sans Souci palace, he got away unpunished – reputedly by making the simple plea that 'he who makes verses plays at nine-pins' and, 'be he monarch or peasant, must be satisfied with the judgment of the boy in charge of the bowls'. But the king later vetoed Mendelssohn's election to Prussia's Royal Academy of Sciences.

In 1785 the Royal Society of Arts and Sciences in Metz announced an essay competition on the question: 'Are there possibilities of making the Jews more useful and happier in France?' Before the prizes were to be awarded two years later, Mirabeau went on a state visit to Berlin in 1786. There Moses Mendelssohn's philosophic works, his advocacy of the separation of state and religion, his championship of religious plurality – expressed in his appeal to 'the regents' of the earth to allow every righteous man 'to speak as he thinks fit, to pray to God after his own fashion... and to seek eternal salvation where he thinks he may find it' – had by now won him not only the admiration of Kant, Herder and other German intellectuals, but acknowledgment as Europe's 'Jewish Socrates'. Mirabeau was so impressed by the 'humanity and truth' of Mendelssohn's philosophy that on his return to France he wrote a book, *Sur*

Moses Mendelssohn, sur la réforme politique des Juifs, advocating the civic equal-ization of the Jews.

With the all-European debate for and against the emancipation of the Jews coming to a head in Alsace, whose Jews happened to be the most oppressed minority of all on the Continent,[8] the Abbé Grégoire decided to take part in the Metz essay competition. His 260-page *Essai sur la régénération physique, morale et politique des Juifs*, with its reasoned arguments for integrating the Jews in French society, became the basis for the emancipation debate which was to occupy the Assembly, off and on, for a full two years. Besides meeting with the opposition of several archbishops, the radical abbé's proposition – reflecting enlightened intellectual opinion – that the Jews were not irremediably corrupt, but capable of being 'regenerated', i.e., reformed, once freed by the new France from segregation and the anomalous condition of their lives, aroused such riotous protests in Alsace that according to one view, but for these violent pas-sions, the act of emancipation might never have gone through, or not at the time when it did.

Once married, Samson and Betty Heine settled down in an oblong, red-shin-gled two-storey house in Düsseldorf that has survived. It was at the back of No. 602 Bolkerstrasse (today No. 53, though not the front building which bears the plaque).

Although the story of the 12-horse equipage with which Samson Heine had arrived in town is generally regarded as an attempt by the son to invest his father with the allure of a gentleman of extravagant habits, Samson – as a for-mer supply officer to the Duke of Cumberland's troops – may well have brought a carriage and a couple of horses with him. Anyhow, the practical Betty, with her no-nonsense mind, had no difficulty convincing her husband that they could ill afford to keep up a stable and a groom. Once the horses had been sold Betty also got rid of Samson's hunting dogs, all except one ugly-looking animal called Jolly. In a vignette illuminating the contrast between his realistic, strong-willed mother and his compliant father, Heine was to write in his Memoirs that Jolly became a 'loyal and virtuous house-dog', and that it and his resigned father sometimes exchanged 'significant glances, my father sighing "Jolly, Jolly", and the dog wagging its tail sadly.'

About the turn of the century, weaned by his wife away from his fondness for gambling and other expensive pastimes, Heine's father set up shop as a silk and cloth merchant. Though much less brainy than his spouse, he was a soft-tempered man with a nice way of treating people. His courtesy and dry humour endeared him to the ladies who came to Bolkerstrasse for their hose and finery. Because of its proximity to the Dutch border, Düsseldorf, with its theatre, its art gallery, its fairs and its flourishing river trade with the Low Countries and the English Channel, normally teemed with visitors and a constant traffic of coaches, freight carts and Rhine barges. Though the town was under French occupation since 1795, and times at the dawn of the 19th century were hardly normal, Samson Heine, trading in silk serge, imported English velvets and other fabrics, prospered for a decade or so before Napoleon's Continental blockade and his own lack of business acumen combined to work his eventual ruin.

Betty bore and raised their 4 children. Whether the first-born, Heinrich Heine, came into the world on 13 December 1797 or at the beginning of February 1798 (to take the two most commonly accepted dates), he was born within a year of Babeuf's execution, and only 4 years or so after the beheading of Louis XVI. His life, character and very soul were to reflect not only the different temperaments of his parents and other contradictory influences, but all the conflicts of a new age.

3

Heine's Childhood

'In my cradle lay my marching orders for the rest of my life,' Heine was to observe many years later. Late in life, describing his mother's dominant influence on his early development, he wrote that she had 'her plans for my education ready even before my birth.' But though he was far ahead of his time in perceiving a genetic factor, and even ascribed some of his own conflicting character traits to his unknown great-uncle Simon, Heine did not forget, in a different but related context, to emphasize that 'time and place are also of importance: I was born at the end of the sceptical 18th century, in a town which was governed, during my childhood, not only by Frenchmen, but also by the French mind and spirit.'

In these and other passages, he implicitly, and sometimes explicitly, impressed upon posterity his self-image of a man whose destiny was affected from birth by the interplay of heredity and external circumstances – environment, wars, and the continual upheaval and confusion caused by the frequent changes of government in his native Düsseldorf as a result of the struggle between the revolutionary armies of France and the rest of absolutist Europe.

The French occupation of Düsseldorf lasted until May 1801. Heine was nearly 4 that year, when the town reverted to Bavarian rule. It was only 5 years later when, following the Battle of Austerlitz, the French returned in force, and Düsseldorf was annexed to Napoleon's empire. Nor was that the end of it. Seven years later Russian troops temporarily occupied the town, and when the whole of the Rhineland became part of Prussia, Heine, barely out of his teens, underwent yet another change of nationality without having moved from his birthplace.

Much to his joy, in 1806 a French tambour was billeted on the Heine household. A short lithe figure with a fierce-looking black moustache and fiery darting eyes, 'Monsieur LeGrand' took great pride in his resplendent silver-embroidered waistcoat and spent a great deal of time on his military appearance. Heine, a lively boy who sometimes 'polished his buttons until they shone like mirrors and helped him whiten his vest with pipe-clay', later wrote that LeGrand never picked up more than a few essential German expressions – the words for 'bread, kiss, honour' – but that he was very clever in the use of his drum as a means of communication. To convey to the boy what the word *liberté* meant, he raised his batons and drummed the rousing rhythm of the *Marseillaise*.

'I understood him,' Heine said of the little French drummer in his *Ideas. The Book of LeGrand*. 'I did not, of course, understand the words, but as he kept drumming while he spoke, I nevertheless grasped the meaning.' M. LeGrand 'knew exceedingly well how to make himself understood with his drum... When I did not know the meaning of the word égalité, he drummed the march Ça ira! ça ira... les aristocrates à la lanterne – and I understood him.' To bring alive to the boy the events of the French Revolution, LeGrand used 'the best teaching method' – his drum – and played for him the 'Red March of the Guillotine' to which music king, queen and various 'highnesses and their spouses' had been led to the beheading machine. The lugubrious march sent shivers down the boy's spine. But he became very attached to the French drummer who, if he is to be believed, taught him more of 'modern history' than mere words could.

'The history of the storming of the Bastille, of the Tuileries, etc. cannot be properly understood,' Heine wrote, 'until we know how the drumming was done on such occasions.' Evoking the figure of LeGrand in 1826, a little over a decade after Düsseldorf and the whole Rhineland had been annexed by Prussia, Heine used him, in a passage sensational for its time, to deplore the servility of his German compatriots under their new masters. LeGrand, he wrote, 'once wished to explain to me the word l'Allemagne, so he drummed that primitive, primordial melody – dum, dum, dum – to which dogs are made to perform on market days. I was annoyed, but I understood him.'

Without going into the much-discussed question whether and how much Heine's imagination had its source in experience or was fictional, we must not forget that the horrors of the French Revolution were still real during his childhood. Ludwig Börne (1786–1837), Germany's greatest political writer before Heine, recalled that as a child in Frankfurt he had an émigré French tutor who

> heaped on Voltaire every possible curse and damnation, completely forgetting in his fury that he was speaking to an eight-year-old boy...
> I had heard older children's nurses speaking a lot about decapitation, and decapitation and revolution became a synonym in my mind. I built myself a guillotine out of cards and beheaded many an aristocratic fly caught stealing sugar.

Heine was younger than Börne, but with the ongoing wars fought in the name, and sometimes by the veterans, of *liberté* and *égalité*, images of the 'guillotine', of 'decapitation' and 'headless' figures were to appear again and again in the most varied connections in his poetry and prose. As he reached puberty, his first love was the executioner's daughter, Josepha or 'Red Sefchen', whose hair was 'red as blood'. She was the first of a whole series of archetypal women, culminating in the figure of Salome, whom Heine was to conjure up in a manner suggesting an association between eroticism and fatal danger or death. In a splendid metaphor inspired by this early love, he was to write that he kissed her lips not only out of tenderness, but 'to mock the old society and all its dark prejudices; in that instant there flared up in me the first flames of the two passions of my later life, the passion for beautiful women and the passion for the French Revolution,' suggesting an additional association between eroticism and politics.

Obviously, Heine's childhood recollections were coloured by his poetic imagination and the uses to which he put his witty pen. But figurative or not, and however mixed with fancy the facts might have become, the story of the French tambour LeGrand and the things he taught the boy help to bring home how close in time to the events set in motion by the French Revolution and its spirit Heine grew up.

Heinrich Heine had been named Chayyim at birth, but his father called him Harry in honour of a Liverpool business associate from whom he imported English velveteen. Harry was what he remained to his family and friends before he became Heinrich at the age of 27. Though he grew up to be one of the greatest poet-rebels of all time, Harry's childhood was relatively carefree and happy. His blond, blue-eyed father may have had a poor head for business under his massive powdered chignon, but he was apparently the first merchant to import soft, lustrous English velveteen into the Duchy of Jülich-Berg, and was frankly, artlessly assiduous in pleasing his customers. Treating everyone, young and old, rich or poor, with equal deference, he was able before long to move his family into a larger house across the street. This had its main entrance at No. 655 (later 42) Bolkerstrasse, and a garden at the rear.

Betty employed a cook and a maid, and the Heine children's room had an English fireplace. It was on the door of this room that Harry, around the age of 4, was taught by his mother to scrawl the alphabet with a piece of white chalk – or so his sister Charlotte, who was born three years after him, was to recall. In the autumn of 1801, he had for unknown reasons become the only boy in a kindergarten for little girls run by a Frau Hindermans. He quickly learned to read, but was often punished by Frau Hindermans for his lack of interest in the games and activities she organized for the children. The lady's method of discipline would not matter had it not caused little red-haired Harry to retaliate by pouring ink into a milk-pot she had on her desk. Many years later he was to evoke his kindergarten days in a long-suppressed or bowdlerized poem, *Citronia*, a humorous, erotically tinged fantasy reading in which he described Frau Hindermans using a birch rod on offending girls.

If Frau Hindermans whipped little Harry in the same manner in front of the girls, his violent reaction – according to his sister, he mixed sand into the woman's snuff-box, and did everything to annoy her – is easier to understand. He eventually told the bewildered teacher to her face, 'I cannot stand you,' with the result that some time in 1803, before he was 5, he was transferred to a boys' school, where he felt more comfortable.

In 1804 or 1805 Harry's brother Gustav was born. Next, some time between 1805 and 1807,[1] came Maximilian. Gustav, after a varied career, was to become an influential newspaper editor in Vienna, Maximilian a distinguished physician in St Petersburg. Of all his siblings it was to Charlotte, Lotte or 'Lottchen' – who married a Hamburg merchant and was to live to the age of 99 – that Harry was most closely attached. In a poem dedicated to her, he lovingly recalled how as children they would crawl into the hen house, hide under the hay, and crow like cocks whenever somebody passed on the road; and how, after the 'great freight cars' had unloaded their father's ware, they would paper up the empty boxes left about the courtyard to make a 'splendid house', and played at domesticity.

From the age of 8 Harry played rhyming games with Lottchen. An exceptionally bright and articulate child, he helped her with her school work. Once, when he wrote an essay or story for her, the schoolmaster was so impressed that he showed it to two of his colleagues. As they all agreed that it was 'a masterpiece', Lottchen was forced to confess in a small voice that it was the work of her brother Harry (who was 10 years old at the time).

Betty Heine gave her children a strict upbringing. Among other proprieties, she taught them that when eating in public they must not greedily empty the sugar box or reach for the last piece of food on the table. They must always leave something out of 'respect' for others. Once, when the family had coffee out of town, little Maximilian could not resist temptation and furtively put the last piece of sugar into his mouth as they rose to leave. 'Mama', Harry called, 'Max has eaten up the respect.'

Besides being admired by his siblings, Harry was also his parents' favourite and the object of their loving care. Although he was to write that in effect his handsome father was no deep thinker, he was careful to stress his lovable qualities. Samson Heine may have had little to give Harry intellectually, but he passed on to him his cheerful, good-humoured disposition and warmth of feeling, his optimism and joy of life. An uncomplicated man who did not break his head about the problems of the world, Harry's father, in the words of the son, treated life as if it was a permanent fair: 'There was always the sound of violins about him.' Proud to be the first Jew to be appointed – some time after the Napoleonic annexation of Düsseldorf in 1806 – official Almoner for the district, he would periodically spend some night-hours meticulously dividing the contents of the poor-box into small bags, adding to some of them from his own purse, and distribute them to the beggarly figures of every description crowding his doorstep before sunrise. But he enjoyed ceremonial and festivities, and was happiest when, becoming an officer in the town's newly formed Civil Guard, he had occasion to parade about the streets at the head of his column in a three-cornered, plumed hat and dark-blue uniform, saluting smartly as he led it past his proudly blushing wife at the window of the house in the Bolkerstrasse. With the same mixture of gravity and flourish, he loved to preside over a festive Sabbath meal when he returned from the synagogue.

As for Harry's education, he left that to his wife. Unlike her, Samson Heine never tried to push his son in any particular direction. He was a man of few words, and the influence he exerted on Harry was more by example than by preaching. In an effort to counteract some of the less flattering things he had written about him, Heine may in his Memoirs have idealized his father's gallantry, charm and goodness of heart. But he was certainly sincere when he wrote: 'He was of all people the one I loved most of all on this earth.' More than 25 years after his father's death, he was to evoke his figure in a moving recollection: 'When I awake in the morning, often I still think I hear the sound of his voice, as if echoing in a dream. And then I feel I must dress quickly and hurry down to my father in the big parlour as I used to do as a boy.'

Betty Heine was not only a more resolute and ambitious character than her happy-go-lucky husband, but, having read Rousseau's *Emile*, she thought of herself as an expert educator. Besides being familiar with much of the advanced Enlightenment literature, she had, until her marriage, spent most of her time in the company of her cultured father and brother. Her husband could not offer her similar intellectual companionship, and she concentrated all her energy and frustrated aspirations on her bright son. Harry later made no bones about the unfortunate consequences of the way she programmed his studies and his future.

'Not from her', he was to write, 'did I inherit my love of the imaginative and the romantic.' Indeed, the rationalist Betty, feeling that Harry was highly impressionable, given to day-dreaming and much too imaginative, tried to curb this bent. She snatched novels from his hands, with the result that, wrapped in a fur jacket against the cold in winter, he sat up late at night reading stealthily by the light of wax candles supplied by the cook. Betty Heine forbade him to attend the theatre or to mix with urchins and the crowds watching clowns and other popular spectacles on market-days and during fairs. She scolded the maids when she caught them exchanging in his presence gruesome old German folk tales and ghost stories – all the thrilling Gothic material that would later be grist to his poetic mill. In short, 'she did all she could', Heine wrote, 'to keep superstition and poetry from me.'

Instead, having seen the decline of the Van Gelderns from riches to comparative poverty, and dreading the prospect of Harry's ending up as a starving versifier or ragged troubadour, she made him study mathematics, science and other subjects completely foreign to his nature. The old order was collapsing. All around her, under the impact of the French Revolution and Napoleon's advances, new administrations were springing up. While Harry's father lived in a rosy world made up of the small pleasures of life, Betty Heine sensed the winds of change, the promise and opportunities of a new world.

Determined as she was to prepare her son for one of the many new careers gradually becoming open to capable men of all creeds, she dreamt first of his becoming a top administrator in Napoleon's growing empire; then, when the empire collapsed, she made him study 'foreign languages, especially English, geography, bookkeeping and all the sciences connected with the land and sea trade', so that he might apply his excellent head to becoming a prince of finance à la Rothschild or his Uncle Salomon in Hamburg. When this failed, she conceived the idea that he must absolutely study law.

By that time, as Harry was humorously to observe, she had correctly noticed that in England and France, as well as in Germany, 'lawyers versed in public speaking were playing the babbling chief roles and rising to the highest offices in the state.' Obviously, she always aimed only for the highest for her talented boy. The trouble was her conviction that if Harry, being so exceptional, only studied the right things and used his head, he could master any situation and fit any role, regardless of his natural vocation.

Though Heine later dealt lucidly with his mother's lack of understanding for his temperament and inner needs, he was fully aware of her well-intentioned motives, her honest, forthright character and utter devotion. The portrait he gave of her, and especially the poems he devoted to her, and the regular letters he kept writing to her after he left Germany – hiding from her the fatal illness that was to confine him for years to a 'mattress grave' – leave no doubt that he loved her very much. He always praised her good sense, and though her misconceived insistence on guiding his destiny with a firm hand was to have untoward consequences, it is important to note that he had a relatively happy childhood.

Bright and naughty, he was adored by everyone. He did not grow up in fear of repressive parents. Though they set bounds, they made him feel their love and care. Nor was he afraid to express himself freely, usually getting everyone's attention by the striking way in which he did so. 'He always says whatever comes into his mind,' the cook once complained to his father. His two elderly great-aunts doted on him. And when things at home were too dull or his mother pestered him, he could always escape to the quaint little old house known as 'Noah's Ark' – after a representation of the ark chiselled into the wall over the entrance – that belonged to his maternal uncle, Simon.

This Simon van Geldern was as unlike his legendary namesake – the 'Chevalier' Simon van Geldern – as possible, but in his own way no less eccentric. Both loved and collected books, but whereas the other had travelled the world adventurously, this younger Simon, after studying humanities at the local Jesuit college, had retired to the seclusion of 'Noah's Ark', to explore the world reflected in the books of his huge library. A small, quaint figure, he was only 32 at the turn of the century, but clung to every old-fashioned dress- and hair-style, wearing short breeches, white silk stockings, buckled shoes, and his hair looped up in a long pigtail. He lived alone with an angora cat, and besides his bibliomania indulged his other compulsive hobby, which was to follow and comment furiously on all topical questions in a ceaseless stream of learned political and philosophical articles he kept pouring out for publication in minor newspapers and obscure periodicals. A gentle soul, he liked to have Harry about him, and reacted only with feigned dismay at the disrespect of the young when the child would tug his pigtail like a bell-pull while he sat writing or reading his gazette.

He let Harry play and rummage freely in his cobwebbed attic, filled with discarded old wigs, stuffed birds, broken porcelain and assorted family junk. It was a veritable treasure-house transformed by the rays of the skylight – in Harry's eyes – into a 'splendid fairy palace'. He spent whole days up there, inspecting the ornamental sword of his late grandfather, Doctor Gottschalk van Geldern, studying his ancient maps, globes and astronomical charts with 'marvellous pictures of the planets'. It was there, too, that Harry pored over anatomical drawings and leafed through Nettesheim's 16th-century *Philosophia Occulta* and the works on alchemy by Paracelsus.[2] And, as he tells us, he discovered in the attic part of the diary of his great-uncle, the 'Chevalier'.

Far from being an uprooted, oppressed or deprived child estranged from his environment, Harry had playmates, both Jewish and Christian. Coming from a family that had ancient roots in Düsseldorf, he grew up with a sense of belonging to the place. When he later entered Düsseldorf's Lyceum, its Catholic principal, Schallmeyer, turned out to have been a patient both of his grandfather Gottschalk (who on one occasion is said to have saved his life) and of Harry's late uncle Joseph, the personal physician to the Prince-Elector of Bavaria.

Harry grew up by the Rhine, which flowed majestically not far from where he lived. The water, the ships, the barges and the traffic of goods that he watched for hours, the bands of foreign sailors embarking and disembarking, all widened his horizon and carried his thoughts to distant lands. If the phantom image of his exotic ancestor gave the boy a strong feeling of family continuity and helped his self-definition, Harry was to acknowledge that the living Simon of 'Noah's Ark' greatly stimulated his intellectual progress by giving him 'beautiful, precious' books as gifts and free use of his large classical and modern library.

The attention lavished on him from all sides may have prepared him poorly for the struggle and vicissitudes of life, making him rather vulnerable to criticism, but left him no great reason to rebel against his parents. There were more complex reasons for his becoming Heinrich Heine, the singer and seer to whom the human condition and the man-made afflictions of his day gave a permanent 'toothache in the heart', but whose refrain nevertheless tolled the end of the old society and divined the new. The mutual interplay of external events and inner happenings of the soul, as he termed it – 'die Wechselwirkung äusserer Begebenheiten und innerer Seelenereignisse' – that shaped his being cannot be traced exactly or in precise order. But when his persona is peeled of the mystifications, dissembling, and assertive self-esteem of a more than ordinarily embattled genius, the very factors that caused Heine's Zerrissenheit, or confusion of mind and alienation – a mood shared by many of his contemporaries as a result of 'the great rip in the world' produced by the new century's clashing forces – appear in hindsight also to have been the source from which he ultimately drew the strength to become a cultural hero who was not simply a rebellious poet or enfant terrible, but the herald of a humanist society, a champion of progress defying the powers of his day, inspiring successive generations, and transcending time as one of the great visionaries of modernity.

Equality, equality, everyone wanted liberty and equality. The philosophers of the Enlightenment had prepared the ground for it. Rousseau thought that human nature could be changed to bring it about. Babeuf, who was executed the year Heine was born, was so obsessed with it that, when he discovered that even in a society of 'absolute equality' someone would have to be in authority, he was in such haste to establish it that he was ready to base it on forced labour and concentration camps.

Are all men really equal? This was one of the questions the French Revolution posed to people everywhere in Europe during the 1790s, not excluding Prussia and all those picturesque, sleepy, politically retarded German lands and diminutive 'states' with their swarm of princes, dukes, barons and knights still reigning supreme from their medieval castles and baroque manors. Revolution had succeeded in America. Was Europe – nay, humanity, as some intellectuals claimed – now stirring to life and liberty, peace, democracy and brotherhood?

Friedrich von Schiller, Germany's greatest dramatist, had early sent a 'kiss to the whole world' and proclaimed 'all men are brothers', in recognition of which the revolutionary Paris Assembly, in 1792, had solemnly voted to make him an honorary French citizen (though misspelling his name as Gille in the protocol). The German Count Stolberg, who raved so violently against 'tyrants' that he was said to be 'wading' in their blood, had predicted the Revolution in 1755, long before it happened. Hegel, who was 19 when it did happen and a student in the dank old cloister of Tübingen's Evangelical Theological Seminary, felt (or so he recalled later) that 'it was a glorious sunrise', and he was 'thrilled... as if the Divine had now made peace with the world.' Indeed, one German scholar wrote at the time that 'the angels must be singing Te Deum in heaven' and the poet Klopstock wished to 'sing hymns to the triumph of liberty.'

A journal edited by C.F. Moser – long-time chief minister of the Landgraves of Hesse-Darmstadt – had actually greeted the outbreak of the Revolution with a front-page picture of the 'sun rising in all its glory' on the French side of the Rhine, and above it the caption: 'At last...'[3]

In Prussia, too, the death of Frederick the Great in August 1786, three years before the storming of the Bastille, had raised expectations of a new dawn. The accession to the throne of his nephew, Friedrich Wilhelm II, was greeted with high hopes that he would alleviate the severity of Frederick's militaristic rule, which had lasted nearly half a century and, for all its glories, was beginning to strike enlightened circles as nothing less than 'baroque tyranny'.

Moreover, Mirabeau had gone to Berlin and advised the new king immediately after his accession to abolish 'military slavery' in Prussia and to ease the lot of his subjects by granting 'freedom to emigrate, freedom to acquire the estates of the nobility, freedom to industry, freedom of the press'; in short, to save his absolutist monarchy by emancipating his people, including the serfs.

But the impulsive and mystically inclined, though good-natured Friedrich Wilhelm II – whose chief repute so far rested on a protracted liaison with the wife of his chamberlain, Madame Ritz, on his spiritualist seances and on his 'lefthanded' marriage with a Fräulein von Voss – was not the man to carry out such sweeping reforms. Under the influence of a clique of bigoted advisers, headed by J.R. von Bischoffswerder, a former army major, and J.C. von Wöllner, an ex-theologian – two Rosicrucians who surrounded the King with pious cant, encouraged his orthodoxy and conducted mystic rites at court – he launched Prussia upon a course disastrous to herself and fateful to Europe.

One of the first acts of Von Wöllner as Minister of Justice, Privy Councillor of Finance, and in fact chief Minister, was to issue the notorious Edict on religious affairs. This extolled the King's partiality to 'freedom of conscience', but in the next breath threatened dire punishment to anyone propagating the erroneous and 'untimely crotchets of the Enlightenment'. As censorship was tightened, teachers, professors, preachers – and even government ministers – who were known free-thinkers were in fact advised that, whatever their private opinions, they must toe the official line in public.

Wöllner's Edict was to serve as a model for the censorship restrictions and variegated devices of thought-control instituted in the countries of the 'Holy Alliance' after Napoleon's downfall. It is one of the small ironies of history that Heine – who more than Marx or any of his literary confrères was to be involved in a life-long fight with these restrictions – had no idea that both Wöllner and Bischoffswerder were one-time members of the occult Order of the 'Knights of the Strict Observance' led by the swindler Gugomos, the order with whom Heine's great-uncle, the 'Chevalier', had been involved in his most bizarre adventure.[4]

While Wöllner institutionalized Prussia's state hypocrisy, Bischoffswerder had persuaded the malleable King not only to join Austria in the War of the First Coalition, but to prevail upon the Duke of Brunswick to issue the manifesto threatening nothing less than the destruction of Paris.[5] When the hesitant Brunswick signed that ill-conceived manifesto, he was not only unwittingly sealing the fate of Louis XVI, but thwarting Danton's hopes of saving the peace. In provoking, at Valmy, a French cannonade that continued to reverberate 'around the world', Brunswick had in a sense signed the first 'marching orders' Heinrich Heine and his generation were to receive in their cradles.

Although the Terror in France somewhat cooled enthusiasm for the Revolution in Germany, some of her best minds, young and old, continued to uphold its principles. In 1793 the Duke of Württemberg was alarmed to hear that students at the Tübingen Theological Seminary, where Hegel was about to complete his fifth and final year, had not only publicly justified the execution of the French King but had demonstratively planted a 'Liberty Tree'. At the 300-year-old cloister of the Tübingen Stift, seminarists wore dark monkish cassocks and lived in narrow cells, studying official Church doctrine and Gospel interpretation on stipends provided by the Duke Charles Eugene ('Serenissimus', as he was referred to in the annals of the Stift) against a written pledge that they would seek no employment other than as evangelical priests or as school teachers. Studying that year were three young seminarists who were to make their lasting mark on German thought. They were Hegel and Schelling, later to contend for the title of Germany's premier philosopher; and the poet Hölderlin.

'Nowhere else', Hegel wrote a few years later, was 'the old system so well and truly reproduced [*fortgepflanzt*]' as at the Stift with its dogmatic teaching, its clerical hierarchy, cloistered way of life, prayer meetings and fixed, monotonous routine. In spite of their seclusion from the events raging in the outside world, many of the students had read Rousseau and Voltaire on the sly. Schelling, who was 18 and one of the top students, had translated the words of the recently composed *Marseillaise*, and the German version had been sung with great fervour at a public concert. One student had actually run away to France to join the Republican army.

The Duke paid several visits to the Stift to investigate the situation in person. On one occasion, accompanied by the Duchess, courtiers and the Danish Ambassador, he reminded the staff – in the presence of the students assembled in the refectory – that their task was to produce 'loyal shepherds' to Württemberg's 600,000 souls. In the course of another visit, in May 1793,[6] the Duke asked the Ephor (a Spartan-derived title for Rector) whether it was true that some of the students had formed a political or 'parliamentary' debating society on the model of the Jacobin clubs. The Ephor, C.F. Schnurrer, paled visibly but made light of the 'club' by assuring 'Serenissimus' that it was nothing but a sort of 'ragging' society. As for the famous 'Liberty Tree' – famous for Hegel's supposed involvement in an outright pro-revolutionary demonstration – one of the many and conflicting versions sums up what happened as follows: 'A bust of Liberty was placed upon a balcony between busts of Brutus and Demosthenes. The room resounded with patriotic speeches. Two young student-members of the club got up and went to the outskirts of the town, to plant a Liberty Tree: their names were Schelling and Hegel.'

According to another version, the tree was 'set up in the market-place', with the poet Hölderlin as Hegel's accomplice in a public gesture of solidarity with the French fight for liberty.[7] Though the tree-planting is sometimes placed in the spring, it apparently took place – if at all – on 14 July 1793, to mark the fourth anniversary of the Fall of the Bastille.[8] Whether based on fact or not, the myth of the 'Liberty Tree' planted by Hegel reflected the fact that many of the Tübingen students had caught what Schnurrer privately called the infectious bug of 'freedom dizziness'. Some of the Gospel-cramming seminarists were in touch with officers and men of General Custine's armies on the Rhine stationed at Mainz, and obtaining revolutionary literature from them. Although most of the agitation was verbal, there was enough of it to worry the Duke. For in Paris heads had rolled in the dust, and as Hegel soon tersely observed in a letter to Schelling, even the heads of the surviving 'oppressors and gods of the earth' had lost their 'halo'.

In this letter, written from republican Switzerland[9] in April 1795, Hegel – stating that once philosophy had demonstrated man's dignity 'the people will learn to feel it and will not merely demand their rights, which have been trampled in the dust, but will themselves take and appropriate them' – sounded one of the foremost themes that were to preoccupy Heine, Marx and a good many other members of the intelligentsia in the first half of the 19th century, particularly in Germany and in Russia.

As late as 1798 Kant hailed the Revolution for its discovery in human nature of 'a possibility of moral progress' hitherto unsuspected by statesmen. France had by then been at war with Prussia, Austria, England, Spain, Portugal, and had invaded the Netherlands. Yet Kant felt that for all its horrors and 'tremendous cost', so terrible a revolution by a civilized people aroused in the minds of all spectators 'a desire to participate almost verging on enthusiasm', which could only stem from 'a moral faculty in mankind'. Given that hidden potential, Kant, foreseeing the universal effect of the Revolution, concluded that, whether it failed or succeeded, it was an event too great to be easily forgotten 'if favourable circumstances should make new experiments of this kind possible.' The admired philosopher Johann Gottlieb Fichte, too, like Hegel, held at this time that 'the hopes and very existence of mankind' hung on the hoped-for 'victory of the French Republic'.

In 1801, Tsar Alexander I ascended the throne of the Russian Empire. Three years earlier, Bonaparte had driven the Austrians to within 160 kilometres of Vienna, the French annexed Geneva, occupied Berne and Rome, and carried off the Pope. Then on 9 November 1799, having returned from the Battle of the Nile and the siege of Acre, Bonaparte overthrew the Directory in a military coup and became Consul, then (in 1802) First Consul for life, and eventually named himself Emperor. Faced with these dizzying events, few could say whether they were still part of the revolutionary 'war of the peoples against the kings' which Paris had promised to stir up – on the morally defensible grounds of safeguarding the Revolution and her natural frontiers – in answer to the 'war of the kings' who had sent their armies to invade France. Did Bonaparte's actions prove the triumph of that 'liberty' which the Revolution had promised to bring to all the 'oppressed nations', or did they signal the fact that the Moloch of Revolution, spitting fire in endless battles of conquest and aggrandizement abroad, represented some form of divine retribution for Europe's collective sins?

It could be asked why the 'most famous statesmen' had made so many mistakes and the 'best generals' been defeated, and 'how the most criminal of all men could triumph over the whole world' – unless God had decided to punish France and the whole of Europe for abandoning religion and morality. This was the reactionary view propagated in Switzerland and Russia by Count Joseph de Maistre, a French émigré who ended up as Sardinia's envoy to the Imperial Court in St Petersburg. On the basis that man's nature was innately sinful and wicked, De Maistre held that mankind, unless it was to fall into anarchy, had to pass through the periodic purgatory of war according to some suprarational, divine scheme.

The start of the 19th century, coinciding with Harry Heine's childhood, was thus a time of crisis, of promise as well as great confusion. Less than a quarter-century after the American Revolution, the old world with all its familiar traditions was breaking down in Europe.

The boy who became Heinrich Heine was a born nonconformist. Whatever the mix of genetic and environmental factors that went into the making of his personality, he was no child prodigy at school, but a boy set apart by his original way of thinking, his extraordinary sensitiveness and poetic imagination. His mother's constant harping on his ability to achieve distinction and influence in this or that field may have strengthened Harry's feeling that he was meant for great things. But it had the disastrous effect of creating a conflict between the rationalist approach she tried to instil in him and his own inclinations and emotional needs. As if that and the contradictory influence of his easy-going but basically unrealistic father were not enough, the three changes of government he experienced in Düsseldorf before he was 10 influenced his schooling and affected his environment.

In September 1807, a year and a half after the town became part of the Grand Empire, Harry Heine entered the first of the two preparatory classes of the Lyceum, which shortly afterwards – under a decree signed by Napoleon – was organized on the model of the French lycée. The Lyceum was situated in the former Jesuit college, and though Napoleon's educational reforms are a matter of controversy, he did take the church out of the schools and established the principle of lay education for all. Compared to what it had been under the Jesuits, the Lyceum, staffed by a motley group of Franciscan monks, Jesuits and French émigrés, was opened up to new ideas. In a tribute to its headmaster, the 'respected' Rector Agidius Schallmeyer, Heine was to write that this liberal-minded and rationalist Catholic priest acquainted him with 'all the systems of the freethinkers', demonstrating – 'without the slightest neglect of his sacerdotal duties' – that religion and scepticism could 'co-exist peacefully and without hypocrisy.'

Harry, however, was nearly 15 by the time he was promoted to Schallmeyer's philosophy class, and up to then he had been exposed to a disconcerting jumble of conflicting influences. In 1804, when he was only 7, he started his primary education at a Catholic public school, while at the same time attending a communal Jewish school, run by a man named Rintelsohn, in Düsseldorf's Ratinger-strasse. Little is known of either school, except that the primary one was situated in a 'musty Franciscan cloister', while Rintelsohn's was of the traditional *heder* or

'Talmud Torah' type common until World War II in every European *shtetl*. In these schools the boys first learned to recite the Torah in singsong fashion in Hebrew, according to certain cantillation accents called *shalsheleth*. In one of the most famous of his 'Hebrew Melodies',[10] combining a variety of themes with the purported life-story of the medieval philosopher-poet Yehuda Halevi but containing obvious autobiographical elements, Heine was to reproduce a child's impression not only of the strange-looking Torah script – 'lovely, picturesquely hieroglyphic, old Chaldean squared-off letters, derived out of the childhood of the world' – but the thrill to his tongue of reciting 'this ancient text, the book of God', in gurgling, cantillating fashion:

> And with loving care he gurgled
> > Those fat gutturals right gladly,
> > > And the quaver, the Shalsheleth,
> > > > He trilled like a feathered warbler...

Harry was to attend Rintelsohn's school until he was 13 – i.e., he continued to warble the Old Testament even as he went through the Catholic primary school. And from the age of 8 or 9, he and the other boys at Rintelsohn's, sitting in pairs, would rehearse the dialectical method of Talmudic disputation, questioning and challenging each other on subtle points of religious law, or Halacha – e.g., whether 'an egg laid on the Sabbath' may or may not be consumed – discussed in the Babylonian Talmud.

> Yes, his father early led him
> > To the pages of the Talmud,
> > > And thereby he laid before him
> > > > The Halacha, that prodigious
> School of fencing, where the greatest
> > Of the dialectic athletes
> > > In the Babylonian contest
> > > > Used to carry on their war games.

In this wide-ranging poem, in which he substituted his father for Rintelsohn, Heine suggested that by these intellectual 'fencing' exercises he learned to 'master every art and science of polemic'.[11] At the same time, while speaking of Yehuda Halevi, he indicated his own predilection as a child for the poetic parables and legends of the non-legal part of the Talmud – the so-called Aggada: when his heart felt 'dry and dusty' from the hair-splitting debates about 'the plaguy egg that a hen laid on a feast day', or about 'some equally profound' question, he fled for solace of the spirit 'to the blossom-filled Aggada'. Comparing its old fables, myths and legends, 'festive songs and wise old sayings, droll exaggerations also', yet bubbling and sparkling with 'faith's old power' and fire, to that 'eighth wonder of the world', the hanging gardens of Babylon, he wrote that his childish fancy

> Was enraptured by the sweetness,
>> Wild and wonderful adventure,
>>> And the strangely aching gladness,
>>>> And the fabled thrills and shivers
>>>>> Of that blissful secret world,
>>>>>> Of that mighty revelation
>>>>>>> Which we title poesy.

To commute from the 'blissful secret world' of Talmudic lore and legend which stirred his poetic imagination to the different atmosphere of the Catholic cloister school must, on the face of it, have been an unsettling experience for an impressionable boy – for more reasons than one. For one thing, the Franciscan headmaster of the primary school, Padre Dickerscheit, was not the type of liberal-minded and rationalist clergyman Harry was later to meet in Schallmeyer at the Lyceum. For another, the Bavarian edict of 18 June 1804 – which for the first time admitted Jewish children to the public schools – contained the typical observation that 'the liberal principles of unrestricted tolerance' could not be applied to the Jews 'without detriment to the civic society'.

There has been a century-long and still continuing discussion about how much Jewish tradition Harry really picked up at Rintelsohn's school. The opinions expressed range from 'probably not much', through the more balanced observation that 'Jewishness remained a significant factor in his thought and feeling even after his formal acceptance into the Protestant Church', to the view that his 'rootedness in the Jewish tradition is the key to Heine's work.' Fruitless attempts have been made to establish the exact quality of Jewish life Heine imbibed at home as a child, and the debate has included quibbling about how much of Hebrew and its grammar he really knew, as though Harry Heine was to become a Hebrew scholar, and not a German poet.[12]

The fact is that Hebrew at the time was a 'holy language' reserved for Bible study and prayer. It was not a living or spoken language, which it became only upon the birth of Zionism, and the probability is that at Rintelsohn's Harry received no instruction in Hebrew at all, for – as Margarita Pazi has pointed out – it was not studied as a special discipline, and its use in everyday life was frowned upon 'almost as blasphemy'. Harry was introduced to the Old Testament and some Talmud texts in the original, but each sentence chanted by the pupils was translated by the teacher into German or Yiddish. Harry's Jewish education stopped in his thirteenth or bar-mitzvah year, and though he later supplemented it from other sources for his symbolic treatment of Yehuda Halevi and other historic figures and themes, he reproduced in the poem under review, accurately and in a manner reflecting his own childhood experience at Rintelsohn's, both the curriculum and the traditional method of Torah and Talmud study still in use today in schools of this type.[13]

Whereas the parallel debate about Heine's firm or loose attachment to Judaism – which has not been helped by the frequent and befuddling changes of his own attitude towards it – is in itself significant, the issue of the profundity of his Jewish learning is in a way pointless. For Heine became neither a Judaist nor a Hebraist. In his mid-twenties he delved into, and was greatly impressed by, Israel's glorious and tragic long history. But what has been said of the portraits of Jews in his work is even truer of the Jewish subjects he treated: 'They form only one strain in a most varied tapestry.' And his approach to them, as to all others, was so multi-faceted and rich in combining past and present, facts and symbols, that in the midst of discussing the intellectual and poetic inspiration purportedly found in the Talmud by his medieval hero, Yehuda Halevi, Heine, suddenly and not untypically, delivered himself of his view of the poet's ideal, sovereign position above the multitude, as a 'star and beacon for his age, light and lamp among his people', a position he himself aspired to in the imperfect society of his day.

But Heine's childhood experiences are important for their influence on the development of his character and personality. The very language of the Bavarian edict admitting him to the Catholic primary school – the only primary school in town – is enough to show that even in tolerant Düsseldorf he was made aware at an early age that to be Jewish meant at best to be accepted on sufferance. Although his mother, raised on the watered-down deism of the Enlightenment, took no great interest in religion, his father Samson, whether from piety or genuine love of tradition – not to mention his capacity as president of Düsseldorf's 'Society for the Practice of Philanthropy and the Recital of Psalms' – adhered to a simple orthodoxy. Harry grew up in a traditional, if not excessively strict, Jewish atmosphere, observing the various commandments – on one occasion, according to his childhood friends, refusing to help put out a fire on the Sabbath – and his explicable and occasional later difficulties with complicated Hebrew or Judaic matters notwithstanding, he was sufficiently familiar with the synagogue prayer service, with some of the terminology and thematics of the Talmud, and the ritual of the Passover seder, the Feast of Tabernacles and other feast-days to infuse some of his prose, and more especially his poems, with their authentic flavour.[14]

74

In short, as a child he accepted his Jewishness so naturally that on the occasion when his 'monosyllabic' father one Sunday told him that his grandfather had been 'a little Jew with a long beard,' Harry hastened 'to impart this important news to my classmates' next morning, before class had started at 'the musty Franciscan cloister school'. As some of the boys grimaced and jumped about in a parody of the little Jew, Padre Dickerscheit came rushing into the room. Red with anger, he started an interrogation, but as no culprit came forward, he decided that Harry was to blame for starting it all and gave him a hiding.

'The hollow cane with which I was beaten was yellow, the stripes it left on my back were dark blue. I have never forgotten them,' Heine was to write in his Memoirs. 'As atrocities go', it has been remarked, the incident 'does not weigh very heavily', but little 'Red Harry' – the satirist who was mercilessly to mock and flay men and situations – seems to have smarted with a sense of unjust humiliation strong enough to make him recall it nearly 50 years later. Proud and sensitive, he was a vulnerable boy. One other childhood experience he chose to record concerned the 'misfortune' of being called Harry, a foreign-sounding name to German ears. Harry liked his name well enough until, at an early age, his playmates, not without malice, began to tease him and made him wince by calling him 'Harruh', the cry with which the local *Dreckmichel*, the scavenger who collected the refuse piled up every morning in front of the houses, whipped up his donkey.

'My homonymity with the mangy, long-eared quadruped turned my life into a nightmare. Big boys would pass me shouting "Harruh!" Small ones greeted me in the same fashion, but at a respectful distance.' The cry of 'Harruh' even followed him to the Franciscan primary school. On his final sickbed in Paris, 'bereft of any further hope of ever reappearing in society, and unfettered by personal vanity', Europe's great cosmopolitan, born Chaim, to be baptized Christian Johann Heinrich – Henry to the French, Enrico to the Italians, yet for a long time Harry to most people – was to confess that the stinging, rankling ridicule attracted by his name 'poisoned and embittered' the best years of his childhood and youth.

To be sure, Harry had friends, both at the Franciscan primary school and at the Lyceum in the Jesuit College: Joseph Neunzig, Christian Sethe, son of the presiding judge of Berlin's Court of Appeals, to whom he became particularly attached, and Samuel Prag. Nor was Harry a helpless or wholly innocent boy. The quick-witted stratagems he resorted to from kindergarten age to puberty in order, first, to get himself transferred from Frau Hinderman's 'birdcage' of trilling little girls to Riltensohn's more interesting boys' school, and next, to get rid of the series of unwanted private teachers imposed on him by his mother, show that he knew how to fend for himself. Though based on family anecdotes, the tactics he used in his childhood, when taken together, add up almost to a paradigm prefiguring the defensive-aggressive style that was to become characteristic of him. He was an imaginative boy with a lively mind and cheerful disposition, but emotionally high-strung, and reacted with anger, sometimes irrationally and spitefully, when hurt.

Though his mother did not take his 'Harruh' trouble very seriously – when he complained to her 'all she said was that I should try to learn more and be clever and then no one would be able to mistake me for a donkey' – it taught him something about xenophobia with a mildly anti-Semitic tinge. Whether or not the sensitiveness he developed about his first name had anything to do with his later signing his first published poem with the atrocious pseudonym Sy Freudhold Riesenhalf – an anagram made up by the transposition of the letters Harry Heine, Düsseldorf – it certainly did not increase his inner security or his trust in people.

The rise of Napoleon Bonaparte and his conquests had kindled his mother's idea that her son must have the type of education fitting him for a suitably high post in the administration of the waxing French empire. This self-defeating pragmatism – Harry later ascribed the sense of frustration induced in him by her setting him objectives in which, for all his striving, he was by nature destined to fail – added to the contradictory pulls exerted on the boy's spirit. Although Heine was to write that 'this, more than all world-events, determined my future', the momentous developments leading to the collapse of Prussia and the Habsburg empire were critical to his immediate environment, and as reflected in his work, affected him in many more ways than those related to his schooling.

In September 1804, Georg Wilhelm Friedrich Hegel, 32 years old and at that time a Privatdozent, or unsalaried lecturer (receiving only the students' fees), at the University of Jena, had asked Goethe to put in a word on his behalf if and when the university's 'most serene benefactors should decide on new professorial appointments'. The most august of these benefactors was that bohemian prince and patron of the arts, His Serene Highness the Duke of Sachsen-Weimar, who employed Goethe as his chief Minister. Hegel eventually submitted a 'most obedient application' for the post of an assistant professor; but it was to take time before this was granted.

In March 1804 Bonaparte had ordered a raid into the neutral Duchy of Baden, where his troops kidnapped the duc d'Enghien, a prince of the blood, and brought him to France for trial by a military court. This followed upon the discovery by Fouché of a plot on the life of the First Consul – involving, among others, a royalist émigré, Cadoutal, who had landed in France with British help.

As Cadoutal confessed that the aim of the conspiracy was to restore the monarchy under 'a French prince of the ancien régime', Bonaparte – deciding that the innocent duc d'Enghien was the prince referred to – expressly arranged to have him summarily sentenced and shot. The judicial outrage shocked even some of his own supporters, including Joséphine. Bonaparte justified his act by saying that the Bourbons at the time had 'sixty paid assassins in Paris' hired to kill him. His worry that if he fell to a bullet his regime would collapse was shared by all those who had taken part in the Revolution or profited by it. 'The regicides, the bourgeoisie and the peasants who now enjoyed the nationalized lands of the Church' all felt that if that happened 'they were threatened with a return to Jacobin anarchy or a Bourbon restoration.'

The plot and the public sympathy it created were exploited by Napoleon to have the Senate proclaim him hereditary Emperor of the French Republic – as it still was – but he bore that strange title only for some months until, ordering Pope Pius VII to Paris for 2 December 1804, he had himself anointed by His Holiness at Notre Dame and then, picking up the circles of golden laurel leaves from the altar, crowned himself (and afterwards the kneeling Joséphine) with his own hands, as though to indicate that his power stemmed from no heavenly source via the Church, but from his own person embodying the people's will.

'Now he will be the most famous of tyrants in history,' raged the young, recently installed Tsar Alexander I (as did Beethoven in practically the same words, striking out his dedication of the Eroica Symphony to Napoleon in protest against the 'tyrant'). Since the Tsar's wife was a princess of Baden, where the murdered duc d'Enghien had been abducted in violation of its territory, he had strongly protested the double illegality. Talleyrand had sent back a cynical note – dictated by Bonaparte when he was still First Consul – alluding to the murder of Tsar Paul and suggesting that a person implicated in the assassination of his own father had better not ask questions concerning an execution which had been necessary for the peace and stability of France. The Tsar had thereupon broken off relations with France.

Now Talleyrand hastened to assure the European powers that Napoleon's coronation signified 'an end to the Revolution'. France, he declared, had a government in keeping with the traditions which it had maintained for 'fourteen centuries and had abandoned only to lose herself in idealistic byways...' At the same time he added that the anointing and the coronation had rendered the Emperor 'sacred'.

While his elevation upset all Europe's sovereigns by its threat to the balance of power, none was more alarmed than the Habsburg Emperor Francis II, head of the ramshackle but 1,000-year-old 'Holy Roman Empire of the German Nation' established by Charlemagne. There could be only one Emperor wearing that hallowed crown. Some of the petty German states belonging to it had already been abolished by Napoleon, or had moved over into his camp. Francis II, with the suavity of a Habsburg survivalist, had therefore quietly begun to style himself by a second, more modest title – Emperor of Austrian Possessions – as though foreseeing that he would soon have to make room for Napoleon to pose as Charlemagne's successor.

In June, after having himself ceremoniously crowned King of Italy in Milan Cathedral, Napoleon had annexed Genoa to France. These two high-handed acts became the last straw. 'The man is insatiable: he is the scourge of the world,' Tsar Alexander complained. 'He wants war, he will get it.' Indeed, in April England had joined Russia, Austria and Sweden in the Third Coalition designed to rid Europe of the Corsican menace. William Pitt the Younger's hopes soared that summer. Austria promised to field an army of 250,000 men and was to strike at Napoleon's forces in Italy, immobilizing them south of the Alps. British and Swedish troops were to liberate Hanover and Holland. A Russian army 200,000 strong was to link up with the bulk of the Austrian army north of the Alps and thrust across the Upper Rhine into France.

Prussia had refused to join, but with half a million men, as Pitt hoped, due to strike at Napoleon from several flanks, he had 'sanguine expectations' of success. Britain was to contribute 50,000 men and a huge annual sum for the upkeep of every 100,000 put into the field by her allies.

Indeed, by August 1805, Talleyrand was warning Napoleon that an army of 225,000 under Austria's General Mack was about to invade Bavaria and cross it in the direction of the Rhine. Bavaria was in the French camp, its ruler having allied himself with Napoleon.

Dictating his changed campaign plans in 6 hours, Napoleon – who was at Boulogne with 100,000 men lined up and waiting for his fleet to launch the oft-postponed invasion of England – wrote to Talleyrand: 'They have no idea how quickly I can make 200,000 men march.' He could be on the Rhine in 20 days. General Mack, thinking it would take him at least 80, began to pour his Austrian troops into Bavaria on 11 September. But Napoleon had set out from Boulogne at the end of August, and before Mack knew it, he had been surrounded in the fortress of Ulm and had to capitulate with 50,000 troops.

Napoleon's fleet, blocked by Nelson at Cadiz, had never reached Boulogne. Having moved 190,000 men across the Rhine, Napoleon was launching 7 columns in forced marches into the heart of Europe. By mid-November he was in Vienna. The Emperor had fled with his court to Bohemia. With Napoleon installed in Maria Theresa's castle at Schönbrunn, the first performance of *Fidelio* conducted by Beethoven at the Theater an der Wien took place on 25 November before a house full of French officers.

In September, to guard his flank against Prussia, Napoleon had offered her an alliance. In October the Tsar, assuming the name of comte du Nord, travelled personally to Berlin for the other side. William Pitt, realizing that, in spite of Nelson's victory at Trafalgar that month, 'the destiny of Europe' depended on Prussia's resolve, sent Lord Harrowby. But Prussia's weak, vacillating King Friedrich Wilhelm III – suspecting that Austria might sign a separate peace, and fearing the Russian embrace as much as the French – kept wavering and trying to guess which side would win, while negotiating with both. Napoleon did not wait. Gambling on the fact that Friedrich Wilhelm was no Frederick the Great, he sent some of his columns through 'neutral' Prussia and by the time the Russians had lined up a sizable army in Moravia his Grande Armée was waiting for them. Prussia began to have second thoughts.

Conducting the Tsar into the torchlit vault containing the Hohenzollern tombs, Friedrich Wilhelm had at last agreed at the beginning of November to join in the war against Napoleon, insisting that he and Alexander seal their secret pact in a macabre scene over the casket of Frederick the Great. Even so, Lord Harrowby was incensed when he belatedly heard of its terms. In return for Prussia's help the Tsar, like Napoleon before him, had promised her Hanover, of which England's King George III was also Elector; and she would under no circumstances act before 15 December – if by then Napoleon had rejected a Prussian peace plan for Europe, to be sent in terms of an 'ultimatum'. In the meantime the Allied armies were to play for time by diverting Napoleon.

As usual, he anticipated them. On 2 December, at Austerlitz, 73,000 soldiers of his Grande Armée beat a 90,000-strong Austro-Russian combination after he had allowed the Allies to believe that they were outflanking him only to strike at and break the centre of their front, inflicting heavy casualties. Achieved in a single day – at the end of which the proud young Tsar, seeing most of his army 'cut up or dispersed' and some of them drowning in frozen lakes, sat under an apple tree and cried, while Austria's Francis II was riding away under cover of darkness – Napoleon's victory in the 'Battle of the Three Emperors' was not only the most brilliant of his career, but placed Europe at his feet, signalling the defeat of the last British-backed coalition on the Continent.

Indeed, Pitt was so shaken by the collapse of his earlier hope that with some Prussian exertion they might 'still see Bonaparte's army either cut off or driven back to France, and Holland recovered before Christmas' that, declaring himself 'hit at Austerlitz', he died 7 weeks later.

In Heine's native Düsseldorf, capital of the Duchy of Berg, a proclamation went up in March 1806 on the door of the town hall. Harry, who was 8 years old at that time, later evoked the scene. 'A dull anxiety, a funereal air' hung over the town. People crept silently to the market-place, expecting the worst. The tailor Kilian, having shuffled up in his Nanking jacket, 'which he normally wore only in the house, stood with his blue woollen stockings hanging down, so that his bare legs peeped out mournfully, and his thin lips trembled as he mumbled to himself the words on the long paper placard.' An old war pensioner in a faded uniform shed tears that trickled down his scarred, loyal old soldier's face and hung glistening on his white moustaches.

'I stood beside him', Heine went on, 'and cried with him, then asked him why we were weeping. For an answer he read out aloud: "The Prince-Elector thanks his subjects for their proven loyalty, and releases them from their oath of allegiance", and at these words he sobbed even more bitterly...'

The Prince-Elector was Maximilian Joseph of Bavaria. The Duchy's previous ruler, Karl Theodor of Bavaria and the Palatinate, had lost it – and much larger chunks of land besides – in 1792 when, backing the wrong horse, he had joined the first Austro-Prussian coalition against the French. France's revolutionary armies, occupying Düsseldorf in 1795, had stayed until the Peace of Lunéville in 1801. By that time, Karl Theodor having died without issue, Maximilian Joseph had made good his predecessor's mistake and recovered the Duchy by moving over into Napoleon's camp. For this, at the 'Great Paris Auction' of 1803, he had been further rewarded with several cities and sundry bishoprics added to the territory of Berg.

On 15 March 1806, Napoleon issued an imperial decree simultaneously enlarging the Duchy and annexing it to France. In exchange for ceding it to him, Maximilian Joseph was obtaining the Austrian province of Tyrol. It was one of the many changes and transactions effected by the Emperor in the wake of his victory at Austerlitz. What's more, for troops and services supplied to Napoleon in that battle and previous campaigns, Bavaria was to be raised to the rank of a kingdom, and Maximilian Joseph was to wear its crown.

The scene recalled by Heine actually took place a week later, on 21 March. Maximilian Joseph had ruled the Duchy by proxy. The proclamation which went up on the town hall at 11 a.m. was a well-meant farewell signed on his behalf by his regent – Wilhelm, Duke of Bavaria – who had left Düsseldorf's castle with his family on the 20th. The French were expected to enter the town on the morrow of the scene witnessed by Heine. His account of that morning went on: 'Everything became so frighteningly desolate, as if we expected the very sun to be eclipsed. The town councillors moved about with an air of having been dismissed, and even the mighty Constable looked as if his days of authority were over' and watched indifferently as the town idiot stood grimacing on one leg and 'crackled out the names of French generals, while drunken, deformed Gumpertz rolled in the gutter, singing 'Ça ira, ça ira.'

The previous year, in July 1805, Hegel's 'most obedient application' to take up the post of an assistant professor at Jena University had finally been granted. Twelve students registered for his lectures in logic. Now, in June 1806, an edict from Weimar fixed his salary at 100 Thaler per annum. By July, however, in the wake of Austria's defeat at Austerlitz, the Holy Roman Empire of the German Nation was falling apart, and August brought a surprise development: Prussia had decided to mobilize against Napoleon, and with the Emperor on the rampage again, Hegel lost his job and presently had this to report to his friend Niethammer:

> Jena. Monday, 13 October, 1806, the day the French occupied Jena and the Emperor Napoleon entered its gates.
>
> Yesterday, towards sundown, I watched the French patrols firing simultaneously from Gempenbachthal and the Winzeria. During the night the Prussians were driven out of the latter... This morning between 8 and 9 the French tirailleurs, and an hour later the regular troops, made their entry. It was a fearful hour... I saw the Emperor – this world soul – ride through the town and out on reconnaissance... It is a marvellous feeling to see such a personality, concentrated in one point, en-croaching upon the world and dominating it from horseback.

By sundown on the 14th a scene of carnage stretched from Jena to Auerstadt 13 miles to the north, Napoleon and his generals having practically annihilated Prussia's army of 171,000, her pride and glory since the days of Frederick the Great. Scores of thousands of Prussians, whole battalions that had marched into battle in rigid formations, 'with bands playing and colours flying, as if on parade ground', lay dead. From his vantage point just outside Jena, Napoleon, according to General Savary, 'could see [part of] the Prussian army in full flight' and the French cavalry slashing into them, 'taking thousands of prisoners.'

With Hegel's house wrecked in the French destruction, with Jena University closed and his subsistence gone, one might have expected him to be shocked by Prussia's collapse. Quite to the contrary, he saw Napoleon's victory as the triumph of the new over the old. 'We stand at the gates of an important epoch,' he had told his students in September, 'a time of ferment, when spirit moves forward in a leap...' What leaped forward on that embattled 14th of October at Jena was a French column which rode into Weimar before nightfall. Hegel, however, had come to regard philosophy as 'the queen of the sciences'. Ever since he had so called it – two years before he saw Napoleon in the distance – he hoped to find in it the supreme key for an understanding of political and historical reality. Napoleon and the havoc at Jena helped him towards the conclusion which he put on paper three months after the bloody battle, shortly before he was to find a job as a newspaper editor in Bamberg: 'Spirit, through consciousness, intervenes in the way the world is ruled... Then there are bayonets, cannon, bodies.' These were as necessary as 'the cogs and wheels in a clock', but in themselves they did not rule events. 'Spirit that subordinates matter to its laws' was the real ruler. An epic like the *Iliad* 'is not thrown together at random, neither is a great deed composed of bayonets and cannon. It is spirit that is the composer', just as a clockwork has time for its 'soul'.

Groping for the system whereby he would dominate German and much European thought from the quiet concentration of his study, Hegel could not but admire Napoleon's new order. When he had spoken in 1804 of philosophy as 'the queen' or 'soul' of the sciences, he meant of course his own philosophy. Indirectly comparing himself on that occasion to Luther, who had translated the Bible into German, he unabashedly announced his intention to 'teach philosophy to speak German. If I succeed, it will henceforth be more difficult for the superficial to pose as profundity.' In Germany, he felt, 'nothing happens spontaneously and as a consequence of one's own judgement. For where is that to be found? And so it will have to be decreed by the will of Heaven, that is to say by the Emperor's will...'

For reasons that will become apparent, Hegel saw in Napoleon the great 'teacher of constitutional law' ('*der grosse Staatsrechtslehrer*') who would modernize politically mindless, stagnant Prussia. 'Concepts and bonds linking our world together are dissolving and collapsing like a dream picture. A new phase of the spirit is preparing itself,' he had told his students in his September 1806 lecture (his last before the Battle of Jena), adding that philosophy had to welcome its appearance.

In his preface to *The Phenomenology of the Spirit*, the first great work he had by then completed and sent to the printer, he had written: 'As in the birth of a child', whose silent and gradual growth in size in the womb 'is suddenly cut short by the first breath drawn – a break in the process, a qualitative change – and the child is born,' so in this period of transition 'the spirit of the time' was slowly ripening to its new form without completely losing 'the general look of the previous world' it was fragmenting in the process – until 'the sunrise in a flash and single stroke' suddenly revealed 'the form and structure of the new world.'

Thus by the autumn of 1806 Hegel would be philosophically contemplating the birthpangs of the new world. In Düsseldorf, on the eve of the French entry that spring, the population had been mourning the passage of the old in an atmosphere of gloom heavy with forebodings.

The night after he watched the old war pensioner and the tailor Kilian reacting to the Bavarian regent's farewell proclamation, Harry, who had been agitated all afternoon, had a terrible dream in which the world was coming to an end. Although his mother made rational efforts to minimize all the talk of doomsday, 'I knew what I knew and would not let myself be talked out of it...' Besides, he had been born in the age of the guillotine. Heads had actually rolled, and not only in Gothic tales; and some of Europe's cleverest men had nightmares that spring of 1806, fearing developments that might lead the whole of Europe to its grave.

The Tsar's armies were retreating to the east in March, and Napoleon was hurling threats at any European ruler who ever again summoned the Russian 'barbarians' to his aid. He promised peace, but he was on the march – against whom? He had defeated every coalition of British-backed forces on the Continent. After Austerlitz, Prussia was the only one of the Big Five – other than France – that still had an army worth speaking of. But Prussia at the time was still feigning 'neutrality' and there was a frightening possibility that Napoleon might secretly conspire with the Tsar and make a pact with him. Friedrich Gentz had early and perspicaciously warned that such a development would be the consummation of the final and most terrible of evils, 'a union of robbers... between the Despot of the East and the Despot of the West' which was sure to spell the end of 'security and peace in Europe, save for the peace of the grave'. With the two tyrants able to divide Asia and Africa between them, they were sure to bring down the British Empire and to achieve dominion over most of the known world.

Thus, whether Harry really had that apocalyptic dream, or dreamed it up later to illustrate the funereal mood in Düsseldorf on that day, it was a perfect satirical-political metaphor in more than one sense. It was a time when a number of princes in what was left of the Holy Roman Empire of the German Nation were in various states of dread or high spirits, according to which side they had put their troops and money on. Some were fleeing with their courts. Others were returning. Ambassadors of the various powers rumbled in carriages on the choked roads, trying to deliver anxious messages or to get out.

'In those days', Harry was to write of the Bavarian regent's farewell, 'princes were not yet the worried people they are today. Their crowns sat as firmly on their heads as though they had been glued there. At bedtime they pulled their nightcaps over them and slept peacefully, and peacefully at their feet slumbered the people.

'In the morning the people would say, "Good morning, Father," and the princes answered, "Good morning, dear children!"'

The morning after his dream, Harry woke up to the sound of drums in the street. The sun was shining, and he was quickly out of bed. In the living room his father was talking to the wigmaker and putting on a white smock before having his hair powdered. Samson Heine clung to this daily ritual long after powdered hair had gone out of fashion.

Harry walked up to his father and kissed his hand. It tickled his nose with a clean fragrance of almond powder. Samson Heine, who did not always look up from his desk when accepting the hand-kiss on other mornings, took him between his knees.

'I hear you had a bad dream,' he said in a pleasant voice. 'I want to tell you that I had a very nice one about you. I'm very satisfied with you, son,' he added with a smile in his blue eyes. 'I want you to know that, dear Harry.' The boy, who admired his handsome father, felt secure in his tenderness and was to remember the long, golden hair brushing his face as being of a softness comparable only to that of Chinese floss silk.

Having put the boy at ease, Samson Heine gave himself over to the attentions of the wigmaker, who in the manner of hairdressers kept up a newsy tattle as he worked. He related that the new Grand Duke Joachim Murat was going to be sworn in at the town hall, 'that he was from one of the best families, had married the Emperor Napoleon's sister, was really very refined, wore his beautiful black hair in curls, would make his entrance into town any minute, and would surely find favour with all the ladies. Meanwhile the drumming outside continued, and I went out in front of the house and watched the French troops marching in.'

The French entry into Düsseldorf, led by General Dupont de l'Etang, actually took place on 23 March 1806, a day later than Heine was to recall. But he did see Napoleon's 'happy soldiers of glory who marched across the world singing and playing', making their entry along the Bolkerstrasse, 'the serio-comic faces of the grenadiers, the bearskin caps, the tricoloured cockades, the glittering bayonets, the gay voltigeurs', marching full of spirit and *point d'honneur* and the giant, silverembroidered drum-major 'tossing his gold-knobbed baton as high as the first floor', while rolling his eyes 'up to pretty girls filling the windows of the second.'

It was on the very same day, to Harry's great joy (and his mother's dismay), that the French tambour LeGrand was billeted on the Heine household. No matter how much of his own fancy and barbed wit Harry was later to mix with the facts in *The Book of LeGrand*, there is little doubt that the little Frenchman with the fierce moustache was the hero of his childhood and strongly stimulated his imagination.

On the next day, Marshal Joachim Murat, the son of an innkeeper and Napoleon's brother-in-law, arrived to assume the office and regalia of Duke of Berg. Harry hurried to the market-place. With other boys he climbed up on the equestrian statue of the late Prince-Elector Jan Wilhelm, and over the heads of the crowd of burghers and soldiers filling the square, he watched the public homage to the new masters. 'It was as if the world had been freshly painted. A new coatof-arms hung on the town hall; the iron banisters on its balcony were draped in embroidered velvet; French grenadiers stood guard; the old town councillors had put on new faces and wore their Sunday jackets and looked at each other in French and said "bon jour".' At last, to the sound of trumpets, Murat made his appearance and took his place among the notables on the balcony. The lord mayor, conspicious in a red coat, could be seen gesticulating as he welcomed the French in a speech 'that stretched in length like India rubber... I could distinctly understand many of the phrases, for instance that "they want to make us happy", and at these last words the trumpets were blown, the banners waved, the drums beaten and the people shouted Vivat!'

What Harry was hearing was Murat's proclamation of the new liberties – free trade, and an end to the petty customs limitations among the former German states; civic equality, an end to aristocratic privileges, and a chance for the bourgeoisie – hitherto without influence at court, though recognized as one of the three estates, by the side of the nobility and the clergy – to have a say in the conduct of affairs. And there was to be justice and deliverance for those so far considered unfit even to be reckoned among the classes of the existing social order – the peasants, still treated practically as serfs, and the Jews.

Murat that day actually did vow to make 'the people happy', later repeating this pledge before the Duchy's officials. When Heine evoked the scene in the market-place 20 years later he wrote that while he was himself shouting 'Vivat' he had to cling for dear life to the metal horse's high-flung neck, for he suddenly felt dizzy – 'The people seemed to me to be standing on their heads, and the world whirling and turning about' – thus encapsulating in a few words the whirlwind events and changes that marked the world of his childhood.

Murat, however, did not stay long in Düsseldorf, being too busy with Napoleon's campaigns. By the autumn of 1806, even as he was being elevated to the rank of Grand Duke of the enlarged territory of Berg and Cleves, he was taking part in the battle of Jena and before nightfall the same day he was riding at the head of his cavalry into Weimar, and on to Erfurt and Berlin.

On 24 October 1806, before entering Berlin, Napoleon stopped for three days at Potsdam. He stayed at Sans-Souci, Frederick the Great's pleasure palace on a hill. From its colonnaded balustrade he looked down on the vista of oak and maple forests and 6 garden terraces leading down between fountains, obelisks and pavilions to a river.

Napoleon, who found Sans-Souci 'very agreeable', also went down to the Hohenzollern vault to pay his respects to the military and administrative genius who had raised Prussia – once the land of the heathen Pruzzi, or Borussi – from a thinly inhabited bog of marshes and Baltic forests to a European power.

'Hats off, gentlemen,' he is reported to have said to his officers as he stood before the tomb of Frederick the Great. 'If he was still alive, we should not be here.'

Indeed, in the two decades since Frederick the Great's death Prussia had pursued an unreliable course, defecting from the War of the First Coalition, then keeping Europe on tenterhooks by staying put and finally staggering back and forth between contradictory alliances. Since letting her Russian and Habsburg partners go down at Austerlitz she had, in spite of the compact sworn by Friedrich Wilhelm III with Tsar Alexander in that same vault, allied herself with Napoleon in exchange for being allowed to keep Hanover, which belonged to England. It was only on learning in the summer of 1806 that Napoleon, with equal duplicity, was offering to return Hanover to England that the wavering Friedrich Wilhelm III – giving in to the promptings of the vivacious Queen Luise and 'the war party' among his quarreling advisers – had rashly, without waiting for Russian help, decided to teach Napoleon a lesson and sent his troops to disaster in the battle of Jena.

Now, a bare 10 days since that battle – on the eve of which Hegel had caught a glimpse of the emperor on horseback – Prussia lay shattered, her once-proud army practically demolished, its myth gone, its aging commanders dead or humiliated. On the eve of the battle, Prussia's 71-year-old generalissimo, the Duke Ferdinand of Brunswick, had sorrowfully complained to Friedrich Gentz: 'I can hardly answer for myself, and now I am required to be responsible for others.' Shot through both eyes at Jena, he died shortly afterwards. The King's handsome and unhappy but heroic brother, Prince Louis Ferdinand of Prussia, had been killed in the battle. Schmettau, the infantry commander, had been mortally wounded; Marshal von Mollendorf was a prisoner in French hands; Prince von Hohenlohe had fled to Stettin, on the river Oder. Within a matter of three weeks since Jena, however, the Prussian fortresses of Magdeburg, Kustrin, Spandau and finally Stettin, too, surrendered one after another. Lieutenant-General Gebhard Leverecht von Blucher tried to fight his way from the Oder to the neutral port of Lübeck in the hope of escaping to Sweden, but Murat and his cavalry soon caught up with him and took him prisoner together with his remaining 6,000 men.

Prussia's entire general staff had been wiped out or captured, and 140,000 of her soldiers were in French hands. Released on his *parole d'honneur* and presently exchanged for a French general, Blucher was yet to take his revenge on Napoleon.

Upon entering Berlin in triumph on 27 October, Napoleon began dictating his terms for peace, which were so harsh for Prussia that its dispossessed King, who had fled to East Prussia, at first refused to accept them. Napoleon also proclaimed the 'Continental System', which closed all European ports, including those of the neutral countries (which were implicitly threatened with invasion if they disobeyed), to British shipping.

By 15 December, passing through the Prussian part of Poland, Napoleon was entering Warsaw, into which the dashing Murat had led a French contingent before the end of November. Far from contemplating 'the supreme folly' of restoring the Polish kingdom – and drawing fire from both Austria and Russia, the two other beneficiaries of its repeated partitions – he encouraged the upsurge of Polish hopes sufficiently to gain him not only the favours of the beautiful and patriotic Countess Marie Walewska but food for his troops as well as volunteer contingents of splendid Polish cavalry. A Russian army, however, was on the move against him. Originally dispatched to help Prussia, it threatened the French flank and Napoleon's communications with Berlin. One more battle was required to impose peace on Russia and make her join the blockade against England.

It turned out, however, that he had miscalculated. At Eylau, at the beginning of February 1807, Napoleon and three of his famous marshals – Soult, Augereau and Murat – fought a calamitous and indecisive battle. With Soult's and Augereau's troops mowed down in the blinding snowstorm by Russian guns, and at one point by their own, Murat prevented a complete defeat, but Napoleon lost 23 generals and 18,000 to 25,000 men, more than the Russians. Though Napoleon claimed victory, the Grande Armée had fared badly in its first encounter with blizzards and the rigours of winter warfare. Vulnerable and no longer invincible, it was forced to fall back and lick its wounds in East Prussia.

If Tsar Alexander I saw this as a good opportunity for a new coalition – the fourth – to defeat Napoleon, he had reckoned without Napoleon's resourcefulness. In April, while the Tsar rushed to Memel to prop up the disconsolate Friedrich Wilhelm with a promise to help him drive the French out of Prussia, Napoleon made preparations for a summer campaign with an army reinforced by fresh conscripts. By mid-June, having crushed the Russians at Friedland and achieved a victory which he termed 'as decisive as Austerlitz, Marengo and Vienna', a jubilant Napoleon and a chastized but imperturbable-looking Alexander made highfalutin 'peace' overtures to one another which led to their historic, and brilliantly stage-managed, 'summit' meeting at Tilsit, on the river Niemen.

The Tilsit treaty of 9 July 1807, ostensibly designed 'to assure the happiness and tranquillity of the globe', in fact divided Europe between the two emperors, the west and centre becoming Napoleon's recognized preserve, the east, from Finland down to Turkey, going to Alexander. Publicly the Tsar was to mediate a peace between England and France. In secret clauses, however, Alexander, knowing that Whitehall would never accept Napoleon's outrageous terms, had agreed to declare war on England and to join the blockade against her, thus changing sides and losing much important trade into the bargain. In exchange, Napoleon undertook to 'mediate' in the war he had incited Turkey to declare on Russia, promising that within three months of failure he would join the Tsar's forces against the Sultan.

Under the treaty, Alexander was given a free hand to wrest Finland from Sweden, another ex-ally, so that 'the belles of St Petersburg' should no longer be perturbed by 'the roar of Swedish guns' (Napoleon). Besides Sweden, the Tsar had undertaken to force Denmark to join in the alliance against Britain, all for the avowed purpose of coercing the latter to make peace. The British reaction was the bombardment of Copenhagen and the seizure of the large Danish fleet in September. Ingeniously Napoleon got the Tsar to withdraw his naval forces from the Mediterranean and to return the Ionian Islands to French sovereignty by making Alexander believe that they might in any case eventually divide Turkey between themselves. He had, however, no intention of letting Alexander have Constantinople and strategic 'control of the whole world' at the Dardanelles. An unexpected result of the vision of an Eastern Empire he dangled before the eyes of his new ally was that Alexander – who had never dreamed of it – suddenly woke up to the fact that Constantinople was as vital to Russia as 'the key to my house'.

As for Prussia, Napoleon cut up the territory of this 'nasty nation with its nasty army, a power which has betrayed everyone', to carve out of it the Grand Duchy of Warsaw in the east. All western Prussia went to create the Kingdom of Westphalia, Napoleon at the same time making good his vow to remove the rapacious Prince Wilhelm IX of Hesse-Cassel by joining his dominions to the new Westphalian creation. The Prince, who was a Prussian Fieldmarshal, had fled to Schleswig and Denmark, and Napoleon, having laid hands on his palaces and some of his hidden treasures, was trying to confiscate his assets all over Europe. Brunswick, too, was incorporated into Westphalia. Danzig became a 'free city' but with a French garrison. Altogether, Napoleon deprived Prussia of half her territories and more than 4 million of her 9 million people. In despair at the 'frightful terms' imposed on his country, the tongue-tied Friedrich Wilhelm III sent Queen Luise to soften the Emperor's heart. Napoleon received her in his study with the brusque question: 'How did you dare to make war against me, Madame, with such feeble means at your disposal?' The Queen, a sad but charming and dignified figure, replied that they had been 'blinded by the glory of the great Frederick' into misjudging 'the true state of Prussia's strength.' Talleyrand thought this a superb reply. Napoleon, however, was stung by the implied hint that glory was transitory. To Joséphine he wrote that Queen Luise's 'coquetry' left him unmoved. 'I am an oilcloth on which all that sort of thing runs off.' Anyhow, truncated Prussia was further made to bear the cost of the war by a heavy indemnity of 140 million francs, pending payment of which some of her fortresses were to be garrisoned by French troops.

When the two emperors left Tilsit in different directions on 9 July, Napoleon had once more changed the map of Europe to show his imperial sway extending from the border of Denmark and Lübeck on the Baltic to the straits of Messina in the south. The Kingdom of Naples was ruled by his brother Joseph Bonaparte; Holland by his brother Louis; in the centre the German states which had formed the Confederation of the Rhine depended on him as their suzerain and were under his direct control; so, between the Rhine and the Elbe, was the new Kingdom of Westphalia, where a month after Tilsit his youngest brother, Jérôme, was created king. Prussia, or what was left of it, was now his compulsory ally, as was the reduced Austrian Empire to the south. And from Saxony, across a sausage-like strip of Prussia, the Grand Duchy of Warsaw – placed under the rule of the newly elevated Saxon King Frederick Augustus, who had opportunely defected to his side three days after the battle of Jena – protruded right to the Russian border.

Since the entry of his 'soldiers of Liberty' into Düsseldorf at the end of March 1806, Napoleon had thus become the direct or indirect master of practically the entire Continent. With his invasion of Portugal before the end of 1807, and the occupation of Spain to follow, his dominion soon extended from the Atlantic to the Vistula and the Niemen. And with Alexander ruling from the Niemen to the Pacific, it seemed for a moment that the two of them might indeed divide the world.

Having got a free hand at Tilsit to strike at England's ally Portugal, Napoleon decided to kill two birds with one stone and to conquer Spain as well, ousting the Bourbons from its throne, as he had vowed to do shortly after the occupation of Berlin. The 'Spanish affair', which he lived to regret, is of interest not only because it sparked the first national revolt against the mighty conqueror, but because it provided evidence of the level of degeneracy to which some of the Bourbons had sunk and the degree of trickery and deceit Napoleon was capable of adding to his sheer bullying.

In order to occupy Spain 'without striking a blow' while ostensibly concerned only with punishing recalcitrant Portugal for not adhering to the blockade of

England, Napoleon concluded in October 1807 a secret treaty with the infamous Manuel de Godoy, promising this unscrupulous premier of Spain to make him king of southern Portugal.

Even before signing this treaty, Napoleon had sent an army under Marshal Junot to advance through Spain on Portugal. It reached Lisbon before the end of November, only to find that the Portuguese royal family had sailed for their colony of Brazil under the protection of a British squadron. As Napoleon nevertheless went on pouring 40,000 troops under Marshal Dupont into northern and western Spain, King Carlos – to whom Napoleon had promised the northern tip of Portugal and half of its overseas colonies – realized too late that he was being swindled out of his own country. Prince Ferdinand was being held prisoner in the Escorial for having plotted against Godoy, and the rift within the royal family came as a Godsend to Napoleon just when the collapse of Portugal deprived him of any further pretext for keeping troops in Spain. He was quick to exploit it.

By 3 March 1808, when Marshal Murat entered Madrid as over-all French commander, Napoleon was holding all the cards, and the divided Bourbons had no alternative but to curry his favour. Prince Ferdinand was writing to solicit the hand of a Bonaparte princess, and King Carlos was sending him missives denouncing Ferdinand. The Spanish populace, who at first welcomed the French as liberators – thinking they had come to overthrow the hated Godoy and install Ferdinand on the throne – realized that they had been sold out and became restive.

In the end, the Spanish Bourbons were dethroned, an event which frightened Europe's rulers, as Napoleon hoped it would. When his brother Louis, King of Holland, refused the vacant throne, he ordered his youngest brother Joseph from the Kingdom of Naples to Bayonne, and there, on 15 June 1808 – in the presence of a number of Spanish notables summoned to lend the proceedings a semblance of legality – he proclaimed him 'Don José I, by the Grace of God King of Castille, Aragon, the Two Sicilies, Jerusalem and Navarre', or in short, of Spain and its colonies.

Many years later, on St Helena, Napoleon admitted, 'I embarked very badly on the Spanish affair. The immorality of it was too shocking, the injustice too cynical.' But his deceit aside, the 'affair' marked Napoleon's first military fiasco. Joseph, or Don José, had hardly spent 11 days in Madrid when he had to flee the city in the face of a general revolt. With the Spaniards engaging in a new type of guerrilla warfare, and British troops under Sir Arthur Wellesley, later Duke of Wellington, intervening, the sure-fire Spanish gamble was to involve Napoleon in the prolonged Peninsular War and to contribute to his eventual downfall.

To deter Austria from attacking his flank in Central Europe while he was engaged in Spain, Napoleon – surrounded by three German kings and a host of vassal-princes specially summoned to display the extent of his dominance and power – held another meeting with Tsar Alexander I. Alexander was to be impressed, indeed 'dazzled', into agreeing to intervene against Austria if she started war with France, and to join in the firm enforcement of the Continental blockade of England. The conference which opened at Erfurt on 28 September 1808 has gone down in history chiefly for the way the two emperors and nominal allies deceived each other, while Talleyrand, playing the most daring of his games so far, betrayed his master and secretly conspired with the Tsar on ways to curtail his own sovereign's excessive military sway in Europe.

As the throne of Naples and Sicily remained vacant, Napoleon created 'our dear and beloved brother-in-law Prince Joachim Napoleon' – who was none other than Marshal Murat, the absentee Grand Duke of Berg and Cleves, whose installation Harry Heine had witnessed only two years earlier – 'to be King of Naples and Sicily from 1 August 1808'.

Napoleon now assigned the Grand Duchy of Berg to his 5-year-old nephew, Napoleon-Louis, but took personal control of its affairs. For the small Duchy on the Rhine was a staging-post on the road to Prussia and the east. Unbelievable as it may sound, with the Emperor as regent, his capable stand-in governor, Count Jacques-Claude Beugnot, was to fulfil Murat's promise to make the people 'happy' as far as humanly possible. The French parcelled the estates of the aristocrats who had fled, bought up some of the large church domains, and distributed or sold farming plots to the landless peasants. Serfdom and feudal obligations were abolished, the inheritance laws disadvantaging daughters and younger sons were changed, and trial by jury was introduced.

This was, of course, only one side of the picture. Napoleon exacted from the Duchy men and money for his armies, but before this drain grew heavy enough to produce dissatisfaction, the middlemen dealing with the land sales grew rich, while a public works programme launched by the energetic Beugnot pumped new life into the economy. Builders, artisans, entrepreneurs and industrialists began to flourish. Coins, weights and measures were unified, the administration was simplified, the French currency introduced. With Napoleon 'intermixing nations' and frontier and customs barriers falling, corn prices soaring and an unhindered flow of capital, prosperity for a time became such that peasants gathering at country inns were reliably reported to be 'throwing dice for stakes of kronentalers or even gold'.

Between 1807 and 1809, while continuing to warble the Old Testament at Rintelsohn's school, Harry went through the two preparatory classes of the newly reorganized Lyceum. Now that careers were open to everyone, his mother, in her wish to see him become an imperial 'strategist' or high official – especially since 'a friend of hers, the daughter of a local ironmonger, had become a duchess' – made him take private lessons in 'geometry, statics, hydrostatics, hydraulics and so forth', although his head 'was already swimming in logarithms and algebra' at school.

The truth in this embroidery of fact that appears in the Memoirs was that the wife of Napoleon's well-known general, Marshal Soult, was a native of Düsseldorf, and in 1808 Napoleon had created the couple Duke and Duchess of Dalmatia. But Betty Heine's ambitions for her boy aside, the private lessons she arranged for him to receive in French, mathematics and algebra had to do with the fact that at the start of the school year in the autumn of 1809 Harry – being not yet 12 – was too young to be admitted to the Lyceum proper; they were meant to help him catch up with the curriculum when he entered its lowest class in April 1810.

While his father relished his turns as duty-officer 'in charge of the town's security' at the Civil Guard post, and happily led his fellow-officers in prolonged 'skirmishes with whole batteries' of Rudesheimer and other Rhine wines of the best vintage, Harry at the Lyceum now studied German under Rector Schallmeyer, as well as Greek, Latin, French and mathematics. In spite of his mother's hectoring and her attempts to forbid him poetry, ghost stories, novels in general, the theatre, etc., he spent every free minute reading books. In May 1810, in Düsseldorf's lovely palace garden, where his mother in 1796 had first lamented 'the flames of war' engulfing the town, the budding satirist in him was devouring Cervantes's *Don Quixote* and Swift's *Gulliver's Travels*.

There was at this time no pronounced German national feeling in the former Duchy of Berg or the many German states allied in the Confederation of the Rhine controlled by Napoleon. Napoleon's rule from Paris was absolutist but cosmopolitan in character, and most leading German intellectuals could not but applaud the speed and simplicity with which his Code Napoléon – abolishing the caste system and making everyone equal before the law – overhauled Europe's archaic legal and civic structure, while respecting property rights. Napoleon, who was now actually the lawgiver of much of Europe, instructed his brother Jérôme to make the new kingdom of Westphalia a model for the rest of Germany: 'Your people must enjoy a liberty, an equality unknown in the rest of Germany.' Although for every of Napoleon's reforms countless acts of repression – including summary executions at the slightest suspicion of revolt – could be cited, new constitutions were gradually enacted in Westphalia, Württemberg and Bavaria, guaranteeing to all citizens 'freedom of conscience and of the press' and 'equal access to all offices, ranks and benefices'.

Hegel hailed the new Bavarian press freedom as the 'conversation of the government with the people' and in February 1808 called Napoleon 'the great teacher of constitutional law' from whom Germany had much to learn. As far as the Duchy of Berg was concerned, Hegel had already written in 1807: 'In Berg the Diet still exists. When it was abolished in Württemberg, Napoleon said severely to the Württembergian Minister, "I have made your master a sovereign, not a despot"; German princes have not yet grasped the concept of a free monarchy or attempted its realization. Napoleon will have to organize it all.'

Goethe so admired Napoleon that when the latter was maligned in his presence, he said: 'Please, leave my emperor alone.' At one of the many glittering soirées held during the Erfurt 'summit', Napoleon conspicuously singled out Goethe for conversation and conferred the Légion d'Honneur on him. Long before this piece of Napoleonic flattery, Goethe had advised the Germans: 'In vain you hope to constitute yourselves into a nation. Train yourselves instead to become freer human beings.'

In 1808, the year of Erfurt, Goethe was actually observing to Friedrich von Muller: 'The German nation is nothing, but the individual German is something, and yet they imagine the opposite to be true.' They 'should be dispersed throughout the world', he often said, 'like the Jews, for they could best develop all the good there is in them for the benefit of mankind without a common fatherland.'[15]

If it is difficult for the modern reader to appreciate 'the almost total absence of national feeling in Germany in early Napoleonic times'.[16] Heine himself was later to stress – as a further manifestation of the 'French spirit' prevailing in Düsseldorf during his childhood – the unusual atmosphere of religious tolerance in which he grew up. Recalling the philosophy course given by the Lyceum's 'genuinely liberal' Rector Schallmeyer, he wrote that this respected Jesuit 'candidly and unreservedly set forth the Greek systems of free thought', no matter how glaringly they contrasted with Catholic dogma, and then smoothly and without any pangs 'celebrated Mass in his priestly vestments, just like his brother priests.' Harry concluded that religion and scepticism could co-exist peacefully 'without hypocrisy'.

But Heine had yet to enter Schallmeyer's philosophy class when, in the autumn of 1811, he beheld Napoleon in person. No phantasm or figment of his imagination this, but an unforgettable experience – the Emperor in the flesh, Hegel's 'World-Spirit on horseback', riding through Düsseldorf's palace garden on a white charger.

Napoleon arrived in Düsseldorf on 2 November 1811. Riding at the head of 'a cortège proudly seated on snorting steeds laden with golden, bejewelled -

93

trappings,' he entered the town, to the sound of trumpets and the roll of drums, through an arch of triumph erected in his honour in the market-place. Whether Heine actually witnessed his entry, or only saw Napoleon on his way to inspect his troops the following day, it was a great moment in the life of a 13-year-old boy. He was to evoke the scene 16 years later in *The Book of LeGrand*:

> As I pressed through the gaping crowd, I thought of the exploits and battles that Monsieur LeGrand had drummed for me; my heart beat the call to arms... The Emperor with his cortège rode straight down the avenue. The shuddering trees bowed toward him as he passed, the sun's rays quivered fearfully and inquisitively through the green leaves, and floating visibly in the blue heaven above was a golden star. The Emperor was wearing his plain green uniform and his small, historic hat. He rode a little white horse... His face had the colour that we find in marble Greek and Roman busts; its features were also nobly proportioned like those of the ancients, and on his face stood written: 'Thou shalt have no other gods before me'...

It may have been November, but to magnify the boyhood thrill, and the impression itself, of his glimpse of Napoleon, Heine first called up the memory of 'flowering lindens' lining the avenue, of 'singing nightingales, rustling waterfalls' and flowerbeds full of tulips, lilies and 'tipsy red roses...' This lyrical introduction has given rise to the erroneous impression that he moved the event 'for poetic effect' into the spring.

This most famous passage in *The Book of LeGrand*, published 6 years after Napoleon's death, was to get Heine into everlasting hot water, with furious Germans then and later accusing him of unpatriotic behaviour towards the 'fatherland' in fostering a cult of Napoleon. How, indeed, could he eulogize the military tyrant whose stride left such a trail of blood and untold suffering across Germany and the Continent? When Napoleon arrived in Düsseldorf he was already contemplating war with Russia, Tsar Alexander I having capped his refusal to close Russian ports to 'neutral' ships carrying British goods by a ukase imposing high duties on French products. Napoleon had written to the King of Württemberg that if the Tsar, 'without wanting war, fails to stop the movement towards it, he will be dragged into it against his will... my experience of the past reveals the future. It is all like a scene at the opera, with the English in the wings...'

Napoleon was 44. At his birthday reception at the Tuileries on 15 August of that year he had delivered an ominous attack on the Tsar in the hearing of the Russian Ambassador. Although Alexander did not respond to the calculated affront, by mid-December, within 6 weeks of his visit to Düsseldorf, Napoleon was asking the Imperial Librarian for books 'best worth consulting on the topography of Russia, and especially of Lithuania', as well as for 'the most detailed account of the Polish and Russian campaigns of Charles XII' of Sweden (whose march on Moscow had come to a disastrous end at Poltava one icy winter a century earlier).

Even in our own times, Heine's practical deification of Napoleon, describing his entry into Düsseldorf as if he were Jesus entering Jerusalem, has led some to accuse Heine of 'Caesarism,'[17] although no similar charges have been brought against either Hegel or Goethe, both of whom – defying the patriotic fervour and nationalist excitement which seized Germany's youth and some of her intellectuals after Napoleon's defeat – continued to venerate the French Emperor to the end of their lives. Goethe, in fact, translated Manzoni's ode on the death of Napoleon, 'Il Cinque Maggio', and so identified with the feelings expressed in it that when on an August day in 1822 he read to the Court at Weimar the lines

> Was this true glory? let succeeding time
> That arduous question ask;
> Ours be the simpler task
> Before the mighty Maker's throne to bow,
> Who in that towering genius deigned to show
> Of His Creator Spirit an image, how sublime!

his eyes burned 'with an inner fire' and he 'seemed transfigured'.[18] Heine was thus in good company. Nor were the patriotic fervour and anti-French hostility 'so general as German historians and publicists later wished to make it appear'.[19] Many Germans, especially in the Rhineland, 'continued to admire Napoleon for decades' after his downfall, finding it hard to accept 'the strict discipline of the Prussian bureaucratic and military state-machine' that superseded the French rule, which for all its heavy tax-load and intolerable troop levies had swept away Germany's entire antiquated feudal structure, including the medieval prohibition on marriages between aristocrats and commoners.[20]

Although Heine's paean to Napoleon is couched in the emotional tones suiting the evocation of a boyhood experience, he knew quite well what he was doing. He shared Hegel's view of Napoleon as a world-historical figure who, by putting an end to feudalism and the dominance of the church, inaugurated a new epoch; that Napoleon was the 'mortal body' and human 'incarnation' of the French Revolution, the man of destiny implementing its principles.

In fact, considering that *The Book of LeGrand* appeared 12 years after the Congress of Vienna, Heine's homage to Napoleon actually represented an

audacious attack on Metternich's and the Prussian King's attempt to stamp out
the infectious libertarian ideas that had gained ground on the Continent since
the French Revolution and to set Europe's clock back, politically and socially,
under the aegis of the restored conservative aristocracy. This, indeed, lent the
book its sensational aspect. Heine was soon to clarify the limits of his admiration of Napoleon in the third volume of his *Travel Pictures* (*Reisebilder* III), by
writing during his 1828 Italian journey from the battlefield of Marengo:

> I beg thee not to take me for an absolute Bonapartist; it is not the
> man's actions I admire, but his genius, whether the man's name be
> Alexander, Caesar, or Napoleon. My absolute love for the latter does
> not go beyond the 18th Brumaire, when he betrayed liberty. Nor did
> he betray it out of necessity, but out of a secret predilection for the
> aristocracy. Napoleon Bonaparte was an aristocrat, a nobleman who
> was an enemy of civil equality, and it was a colossal misunderstand-
> ing that led the aristocracy of Europe, represented by England, to
> fight him to the death.

In an earlier but related prose piece, 'The North Sea III' (*Die Nordsee* III),
written on the island of Nordeney, Heine had hailed Goethe as one of those
rare individuals of genius and 'archetypal intellect' who have the intuitive
faculty to grasp the spirit of the times, and to use and 'cajole' it. Goethe, in one
of his essays, had quoted a passage from Kant on the intuitive (as opposed to
the discursive) type of archetypal intellect. Elaborating on this passage, Heine
wrote, 'Yes, what takes us slow cogitation and elaborate conclusions to recognize, their minds have gone over and perceived in a single moment.' One such
man, in Heine's view, was Napoleon. Another was Goethe himself, whose
extraordinary powers of perception and healthy unity of 'thought and feeling'
Heine contrasted with the *Zerrissenheit*, the inner disarray and 'sickly, disjointed Romantic feelings' of his own generation in an alienated world. As
Nigel Reeves observed in 1974, 'Napoleon was a man of action, who employed
his archetypal intellect to make history. What Napoleon tried to achieve is still a
possibility, Heine implies.'[21] In 'North Sea III', giving the Romantic malaise of
Zerrissenheit a subtle political connotation that escaped the censor's vigilance,
Heine had otherwise ridiculed the new order established after Napoleon's
defeat. All it had achieved, he wrote sarcastically, was to redivide Germany into
three-score states and tiny principalities, with consequent 'trading of souls'
across new borderlines, and 'bewildered people reduced to celebrating the
national glories of Hildburghausen, or Meiningen or Altenburg...'

But Heine's lament about this 'bleeding *Zerrissenheit*' of the German fatherland should not be confused with the cries of the nationalists who had begun to

dream of building a new German Reich. By 1829, when his reflections on the battlefield of Marengo appeared in print, they contained his declaration of faith not in nationalism, but in the universality of European civilization. Noting that new 'intellectual interests' seemed to be replacing material ones, he wrote:

> It really appears as if world history is no longer to be a history of robbers, but a history of minds. The main lever which ambitious and greedy princes were able to set in motion so effectively for their private ends, namely nationalism, with its vanity and its hatred, has become worn and brittle; foolish national prejudices are disappearing more and more every day, all sharp disparities are becoming merged in the universality of European civilization, *there are no longer nations in Europe, but only parties*, and it is marvellous to see how well these, despite their great diversity of colours, recognize one another and how well, despite the numerous differences of language, they get on together.

Only one year later, in speaking to Eckermann of a future state of civilization he hoped for, Goethe expressed his vision in terms akin to Heine's. 'There is a stage of civilization', he said, 'in which it is not possible to hate one's neighbours, where one stands, so to speak, above nations, and feels the weal or woe of a neighbouring people as if it were one's own. This is the stage of civilization that I long for.' Goethe was 80 and had only two more years to live. Heine, watching the sun rise over the battlefield of Marengo, where (as he wrote) Napoleon had become so intoxicated with success that 'he only sobered up on St Helena', not only signalled the developing conflict of ideas but, with the optimism and combativeness of a man at the start of his thirties, announced the great task of the age – emancipation not merely of the Irish, Greeks, Jews, West Indian Blacks and 'suchlike oppressed people', but

> the emancipation of the whole world, particularly of Europe, which has now come of age and is wrenching itself free from the iron leading-strings of the privileged aristocracy. A few philosophical renegades of freedom may adduce subtle arguments to prove that millions of human beings have been created to be beasts of burden for a few thousand privileged knights; nevertheless, they will fail to convince us until, as Voltaire says, they can also demonstrate that the former came into the world with saddles on their backs and the latter with spurs at their heels.

Napoleon now appeared to Heine as 'perhaps the last of the conquerors'. The sunrise over the battlefield from which all military glory had faded suggested

97

to him the dawn of a new and glorious world of freedom, in which 'a new generation' conceived in liberty and subject neither to aristocratic abuse nor to the mind-control of 'intellectual customs men' would be able freely to exchange ideas and feelings, of which his own generation of 'slaves' had no inkling. And although he himself might not live to see the day, he asked that instead of a poet's laurel wreath 'a sword be placed upon my coffin, for I was a brave soldier in the war for the liberation of mankind.'

Heine may have been in an exuberant mood when, figuratively composing his own epitaph, he deprecated his poetry in favour of militancy in a universal cause, but he was also making a political commitment. He was serious, but his weapons were light, elegant but biting. In *The Book of LeGrand*, besides extolling Napoleon he ingeniously mocked the practice of Metternich's censors of marking excisions by a series of dashes. Chapter XII of *LeGrand*, as written by Heine, consisted of 96 dashes and 4 words. When printed, it looked like this:

Chapter XII

The German censors –
– –
blockheads –

In December 1810, at Napoleon's behest, all English wares and manufactured goods in the Duchy of Berg had been burned in public bonfires. Harry's father, a dealer in imported English velveteen, was one of the first of the many victims of Napoleon's Continental blockade. The year when Heine had his star-crossed view of Napoleon coincided with the beginning of Samson Heine's material and physical decline, ultimately leading to his mental collapse in somewhat mysterious circumstances.

But this long drawn-out tragedy lay in the future. For the time being, the disastrous end of Napoleon's march on Russia marked a turning point in young Harry's life, as it did in the history of Europe. In 1813, the 'French spirit' abruptly vanished from Düsseldorf. By the summer of 1815, when the Congress of Vienna formally concluded its deliberations, Heine, who had grown up in an atmosphere remarkably free of nationalism and religious intolerance, woke up with a shock to the fact, as he put it, that 'the whole of Europe became one St Helena, and Metternich was its Sir Hudson Lowe.'

4

Tsar Alexander, Young Harry Heine and Marx's Father

Alexander the Great, Napoleon remarked to one of his intimates in Paris early in 1812, 'was as far from Moscow when he marched to the Ganges. I have said this to myself ever since St Jean d'Acre.' His interlocutor, Count Louis de Narbonne, was stunned. 'What a man! What ideas! What dreams!' he mused to himself. 'Where is the keeper of this genius? It was halfway between Bedlam and the Pantheon.'

In 1811 Napoleon had told the Abbé de Pradt: 'In five years I will be ruler of the world.' He had even earlier confided to General Wrede his intention of becoming nothing less than the master of the universe.

But now it was 1814, and Napoleon in defeat was about to be banished to Elba. Towards noon on 31 March, a glorious spring day and otherwise 'a day unexampled in history (as it struck some eye-witnesses), Tsar Alexander I of All the Russias, preceded by broad rows of cavalcading red-coated Cossacks and lancers and hussars of the Imperial Guard, entered Paris in triumph. Alexander had chosen a light-grey horse called Eclipse for the ride. Flanking him were Prussia's King Friedrich Wilhelm III and Austria's Prince Schwarzenberg. They were followed by a suite of more than 1,000 Russian, Prussian, Austrian and other generals and staff-officers of the multi-national Allied coalition. Columns of Austrian grenadiers, the Russian grenadier corps and Horse Guards, the footguards, and three divisions of Russian cuirassiers with artillery closed the impressive military display.

But Parisians crowding the boulevards had eyes only for the handsome 34-year-old Tsar, a majestic-looking figure in his general's uniform with golden epaulettes glistening in the sun. Men wearing white cockades doffed their hats, women waved white scarves, and windows were hurriedly decked with white draperies, the populace mistaking the white bands on the Russian uniforms for a sign that they were coming in the cause and under the banner of the Bourbons. Crowds exhausted by years of war and glory pressed around the Tsar's horse. 'I come to you not as an enemy, but as a friend,' Alexander said in a loud voice. 'I bring you peace.' Paris responded with cries of 'Vive la paix!'

Before dawn, the Tsar had dispatched his trusted Foreign Minister, Count Nesselrode, to Talleyrand's house in the rue St-Florentin to ascertain the situation in Paris. Surprised at his toilette with 'his hair only half done', Talleyrand rushed to meet Nesselrode, covering him 'with powder from head to foot'. While Alexander reviewed the troops in the Champs-Elysées and the two statesmen were drafting a proclamation to the French people, a Russian officer brought word of reports that the Elysée Palace – where the Tsar was supposed to stay – had been mined. Talleyrand expressed doubt about the reports, but is believed to have planted them himself. Next, the Tsar showed up in the rue St-Florentin, where he accepted Talleyrand's 'humble' offer of hospitality, as promptly as it was made.[1] To have Alexander, the arbiter of Europe, under his roof was a masterstroke which brought the 60-year-old ex-bishop, super-diplomat and arch-intriguer back into the centre of events. Reaping the fruits of his daring, if duplicitous, gamble in helping the Tsar to outplay Napoleon, he was able to settle the fortunes of France according to his own designs, and to play a leading part in the future of Europe.

Alexander was opposed to the restoration of the Bourbon Pretender, the Count of Provence. He sincerely wished to give the French the government they – or rather, as he put it, their 'most estimable men' – wanted, but relied entirely on his host to ascertain their wishes. Talleyrand, as Vice Grand Elector of the Empire, a position he owed to Napoleon, was one of the few high dignitaries of defeated France who had not left Paris during the crisis. While the Count of Provence was awaiting developments at Hartwell, not far from London, Talleyrand, deftly manipulating the Royalist minority and the depleted Senate, set up a provisional government headed by himself. He fed Alexander false reports on the popularity of the Bourbons and played successfully upon the principle of legitimacy. Thus he prevailed on the Tsar to let the Pretender (who styled himself Louis XVIII, but whom no one in France had seen for the last 25 years) occupy the throne of his executed brother Louis XVI.

The Tsar remained in France long enough to make sure that Louis XVIII, a short, obese but dignified figure, did not enter Paris before pledging to sign the new liberal constitution prepared by Talleyrand. On Easter Sunday (10 April 1814) he stunned Paris by leading his troops to the Place de la Concorde – formerly the Place de la Révolution, where Louis XVI (and 2,800 others) had been executed – for a religious service, described by some as an unusual Requiem chanted by Russian priests, according to the rites of the Orthodox Church, for the repose of the unfortunate Catholic king, and by others as a solemn *Te Deum*.[2] The high-minded Tsar retained much of the idealism of his youth and the libertarian notions instilled in him by his humanist tutor, La Harpe. Among other plans, he toyed with the idea of establishing 'a democratic republic' in

France – but under the pressure of the trials of 1812 he had developed a mystic strain.

'The fire of Moscow', he was later to say, 'lit up my soul. I got to know God and became another man.' In the course of that terrible year he had what is believed to have been his first religious transport when, during a visit to his friend Prince Alexander Golitsyn, the latter happened to drop a volume of the Bible. It fell open at the page containing the 19th Psalm. Golitsyn, himself a mystic, convinced the troubled Tsar that its verses – 'I will say of the Lord, He is my refuge and fortress... He shall cover thee with His feathers, and under His wings shalt thou trust' – were a sign from God.

The troubled Alexander then had his own palace library searched for a copy of the Bible, but none being found, surprised his wife, the Empress Elisabeth Alexeyevna, by asking for her French copy, which he began to devour: 'Its words poured an unknown peace into my heart and quenched the thirst of my soul.' Previously unfamiliar with the Bible, Alexander henceforth made it a practice to study it twice a day, marking passages which seemed to apply to the events and problems he faced. He became convinced that miraculous forces had saved Russia from the scourge of Napoleon.

Haunted by the night in 1801 when he had connived in the murder of his father Paul, he took 1812 as a warning, but 'felt that the Almighty was not forcing him yet to expiate his blood.' He found the prophecies of Jeremiah, Isaiah and Ezekiel in the Old Testament astonishing revelations of the truth. From then on he would devote himself to the triumph of everything that was sacred: truth, justice, and the fear of God. The words of Isaiah were like a solemn and mysterious pledge: 'The Almighty Jehovah punishes impious kings.'[3]

At the end of December 1812 – shortly after Napoleon, leaving the remnant of the Grande Armée in Russia under the command of Murat, had decamped for Paris – General Yorck von Wartenburg, despite the fact that Prussia was formally allied to Napoleon, had declared the neutrality of his Prussian troops, who were supposed to fight the Russians. The military convention of Tauroggen that Yorck signed, forcing the French to retreat to the Vistula and enabling the Russians to occupy East Prussia, has been compared to 'a flash of lightning that transformed the entire horizon' of Europe. It was indeed the first of a feverish series of multilateral alliances, conventions and open or secret treaties – altogether 19 during the next 15 months – by means of which Russia, Prussia and Austria, with British support from the sidelines, somehow managed, in spite of their conflicting interests and designs, to work out and sustain the grand military-political strategy for breaking Napoleon's armed might, unmaking his alliances with most of Europe's sovereigns and undoing his empire.

By the end of March 1813, Prussia's faint-hearted King, having at last summoned the courage to declare war on Napoleon, a Russo-Prussian force occupied Dresden, forcing the King of Saxony to flee to Bohemia. Britain had signed the Stockholm Treaty, giving the Swedes £1,000,000 for a Swedish army to operate in Germany. On 8 May, however, Napoleon, having crossed the Rhine, was driving the Allies from Dresden and the King of Saxony returned to his capital.

In the very midst of the patriotic fervour accompanying Prussia's 'War of Liberation', Prince Metternich of Austria – whose country was still allied with Napoleon, and who was moreover the son-in-law of the Austrian Emperor Francis – engaged in a diplomatic game that was too complicated to be understood even in Vienna. Trusting the Tsar as little as he did Napoleon, Metternich wanted Prussia restored to sufficient strength to hold Russia in check; but he did not want a united Germany, which Tsar Alexander had promised in a proclamation after signing the Treaty of Kalish with Prussia. While the Allied setback at Bautzen in May made the Prussian King tremble at the thought of being exiled to Baltic Memel again, Metternich, in a complicated piece of covert diplomacy, conducted negotiations with England and at the same time assumed the role of 'armed mediator' between Napoleon and the Tsar.

Heine's relatively tranquil childhood now lay behind him, and to the confusions and perturbations of adolescence were added the drama and confusion loose in Europe. In German Düsseldorf under French rule, and in the dual world of Talmudic and Franciscan schools, he had early absorbed a multitude of contradictory influences – French versus German, Jewish versus Catholic, religious traditionalism versus rational and revolutionary ideas, Napoleonic *grandeur* and its price in bloodshed, to mention but a few – and had digested them without untoward effect on his development. If they had created a certain ambivalence in him, they had also immensely widened his mental horizon.

Now Schallmeyer's critique of philosophy opened a new world to him. Impressed by the Jesuit headmaster's fashionably rationalist combination of Catholicism and free-thinking, Harry developed an eye for the beauty of Catholic rites. But until he was replaced in May 1813, Schallmeyer, carrying his ambitious curriculum to excess, lectured his young pupils at great length on 'the affirmations of the supranaturalists, naturalists, deists and pantheists, sceptics and critics'. This profusion of different viewpoints of religious philosophy was apt to confuse more mature minds. Coming on top of an onslaught of antagonisms and inconsistencies which Heine had been too young to resolve completely, it had the effect of producing in him 'not just unbelief, but the most tolerant indifference.'

His father was warning him against 'atheism' and telling him: 'My dear son! Your mother sends you to Rector Schallmeyer to study philosophy. That is her affair. I for my part do not like philosophy as it is nothing but superstition.' This, said at a time when Schallmeyer seems to have suggested to the boy's mother that Harry might be sent to a theological seminary in Rome (with the notion, as he playfully wrote later, that he might there become a high-ranking prelate, perhaps even a cardinal), affords a glimpse of more divergent parental influences added to those already contending in his young soul.

To compound matters, his father's business had never recovered from Napoleon's Continental blockade. Gone were the days when an advertisement in Berg's 'Grand-Ducal Weekly News' brought the ladies to Samson Heine's store to finger his stock of fine 'Damask tablecloths, chintz, muslin, satins, levontins, velvets, crêpe in all colours, taffetas, Madras and cashmere shawls' and he was able to pay 11,200 Reichsthaler for the house at 655 Bolkerstrasse. In the summer of 1813, while Britain undertook by the Treaty of Reichenbach to provide £2,000,000 to be divided between Prussia and Russia – not before Lord Castlereagh had made sure that they would adjust their grandiose peace plans to British interests on the Continent – the Duchy was in the throes of economic crisis and widespread unemployment. Samson Heine was trying to redress his financial situation by taking over the Berg lottery agency for the Düsseldorf *arrondissement*

Wellington's victory in Spain was perhaps Britain's most important contribution to the effort against Napoleon. As Wellington crossed the border into France, the campaigns raging since August in Silesia, Saxony and Bohemia were coming to a head, and Napoleon was about to lose his second great army in a year in 'the Battle of the Nations' at Leipzig. The immediate consequence of the Austro-Prusso-Russian victory on 19 October was that the Confederation of the Rhine, with its 16 monarchs allied to Napoleon, fell apart.

Düsseldorf was evacuated by the French before the month was over. On 10 November, Russian dragoons entered the town. Three days later a new governor, Justus von Gruner, arrived to establish a provisional Prussian administration in the Grand Duchy of Berg. By that time Samson Heine, unable to pay his promissory notes, was on the brink of insolvency.

Upon Napoleon's downfall, Harry's mother dreamed up another 'brilliant' career for him, or so Harry was to write. Instead of an empire-builder he was to become a banker. Watching the fabulous rise of the 'house of Rothschild, whose chief my father knew', and the success of 'other princes of banking and

103

industry in our vicinity, my mother declared that this was the time when a man of outstanding intelligence could achieve extraordinary things in the mercantile sphere and attain the highest pinnacle of worldly power.' The nearest 'prince of banking' in the vicinity was Harry's uncle, Salomon Heine (1766-1844). Unlike his brother Samson in Düsseldorf, Salomon Heine was a financial genius. From a boy-apprentice in a bank belonging to his mother's family, he had worked his way up to the position of governor of the Heine & Heckscher Bank in Hamburg. Presently to found his own prominent banking house and to become reputedly the richest man in all of Germany, he was the financial mainstay of the Heines in Düsseldorf in times of trouble. Thus he, rather than the Rothschilds, was always in their minds.

Harry was soon to meet Uncle Salomon and his two beautiful daughters in Hamburg. But his hope of graduating from the Lyceum in 1813 had been dashed in May of that year, when the ailing Schallmeyer had been replaced as rector by A.W. Kortum. A strict disciplinarian, Kortum considered Harry, who thanks to his private lessons had indeed jumped a class, too young to be allowed to graduate. Thus Harry continued for another year in the senior class, but by January 1814 Kortum – in reorganizing the school from a French Lyceum to a German Gymnasium – extended the senior class to two years. This meant that none of its 13 pupils would graduate before the autumn of 1815. Whether his parents, having three other children to educate, found it financially hard to keep Harry in school for that length of time, or because of the uncertainty of their being able to send him to the university and his mother's new plans to make a banking magnate out of him, Harry left the Gymnasium in the course of 1814 without graduating.

Transferred that same year to Vahrenkapf's Business School in Düsseldorf to study commerce and foreign languages, Harry acquired some English. But in a typical reaction, he indicated his disdain for the study of bookkeeping and the intricacies of commerce by translating Homer's *Iliad* and some verses of Ovid into Yiddish. He lampooned certain friends from the Lyceum in good-natured verse, read every book he could find, flirted with girls who were to make fleeting appearances in his Memoirs under such names as Gertrude, Catherine and Hedviga, and lived an intense emotional life, plagued by the uncertainties of adolescence, personal frustration and the general insecurity of the times.

In 1812 and 1813, Harry was not yet fully conscious of any general or personal 'Jewish problem' about to befall him and others of his generation. He had grown up under 'the French spirit', which had granted equal citizenship rights to the Jews back in 1791, and he had no idea that the emancipation which the countries conquered by Napoleon had been induced to grant the Jews would come to an end with the Emperor's downfall.

The shock of it, when it came, may have had something to do with his life-long cult of Napoleon, a cult he developed not because the emperor had brought the Jews the Rights of Man, but in spite of his double-edged policy towards them. Heine never mentioned Napoleon's three dramatic attempts to change the course of Jewish history. The first of these had occurred in Palestine in 1799, on Napoleon's way from Egypt to Syria. Camping after a victorious battle at the foot of Mount Tabor, he conceived the idea of advancing on Constantinople in order – as he told Bourienne – to 'overthrow the Turkish empire and found a great new empire in the East which will fix my name in the annals of posterity.'[4] Whether General Bonaparte, as he was at the time, already dreamed of emulating Alexander the Great, the idea of cutting the British trade route to India was tempting and he wrote to Tippo Sahib of Mysore that he was burning with the desire to 'deliver you from the yoke of England.'[5]

In a little-known episode, Bonaparte also sent a dispatch to Paris in April, announcing that he had issued a 'Proclamation to the Jews'. Published in the official *Le Moniteur Universel* on 22 May 1799, the dispatch said that Bonaparte 'invites all the Jews of Asia and Africa to gather under his flag in order to re-establish the ancient Jerusalem. He has already given arms to a great number, and their battalions threaten Aleppo.' The Proclamation itself, issued on 19 April at Mount Tabor, but datelined the 20th and purporting to come from 'General Headquarters, Jerusalem' (which he felt confident of capturing without effort), called on the Jews 'to claim the restoration of your rights among the populations of the universe which have been shamefully denied you for thousands of years,' with a view to resuming 'your political existence as a nation among the nations.' Lacing his phrases with such Biblical prophecies as 'the ransomed of the Lord shall return, and come with singing into Zion' and invoking the 'Providence [which] has sent me hither', Bonaparte urged the Jews to take over 'Israel's patrimony' and promised them the French Republic's 'warranty and support to maintain it against all comers.'

In the event, Napoleon never got beyond Acre, nor did he enter Jerusalem. The original Proclamation has never been found, but a German translation of it, addressed to the 'Rightful Heirs of Palestine', was discovered in 1940 in Vienna. Though accepted by some historians, the authenticity of this document is in doubt; but the fact remains that the Proclamation was mentioned in the *Gazette de France* and twice in *Le Moniteur*. Napoleon himself, harking back to his dream of an eastern empire, later often remarked: 'I missed my destiny at St Jean d'Acre'; in the memoirs he dictated on St Helena he claimed that, had Acre fallen, 'I would have changed the face of the world'; and to his Irish physician, O'Meara, he said in another context that he had hoped the Jews would 'consider me like Solomon or Herod, to be the head of their nation.'[6]

Napoleon's transparent attempt to enlist the support of the Jews for his abortive eastern expedition was to be followed by a sharp turn of policy towards them after he became emperor. Seeing in them a 'nation', he proceeded to stage nothing less than a replica of the Sanhedrin – the assembly of 71 sages who, sitting in the Chamber of Hewn Rock on Jerusalem's Temple Mount, had in glorious ancient times acted as the combined parliament and supreme court of the extinct kingdom of Israel – by summoning an assembly of 71 leading rabbis and notables from all over Western and Central Europe to convene in Paris in February 1807.

This time, however, the underlying idea was precisely to end the role of Europe's Jews as a 'nation within the nations' by persuading them in subtle ways to redefine their status as a religion like other religions. Like his earlier hint of a plan to restore Palestine to Jewish rule, this move too mixed bold conception with historic associations, Napoleonic *grandeur* and ulterior motives. This was all couched in terms that virtually made the Emperor out to be a messianic 'Liberator' for the first time in history inviting a representative body of Jews to a political-religious conference.

Hard on the heels of the Sanhedrin, in 1808 Napoleon issued his 'Infamous Decree', which, besides retroactively cancelling certain debts owed to the Jews, imposed such discriminatory restrictions on them as to make a mockery of the equality only recently granted them in the fervour of the Revolution. The edict caused such an outcry – besides hurting the economy – in France itself that a third of its départements soon stopped enforcing it. But it remained on the books, its spirit – ironically – obscuring the fact that Napoleon, tackling time-forgotten, festering old ills of intolerance and injustice in the heart of Europe, everywhere released the Jews from the ghettos, abolished the special 'Jew taxes' and the yellow badge in places where it was still obligatory.

In Düsseldorf, except for some limitations, the 'Infamous Decree' was not enforced. Harry Heine was a child when it and the spectacular Sanhedrin followed each other in short order. To him, Napoleon remained the great emancipator and unifier of Europe. The only thing he would not forgive the Emperor was 'his faithlessness to his mother, the Revolution'. Harry had never experienced actual persecution. In 1814, when he was transferred to a commercial school, he probably could not, even after the arrival of Prussian soldiers in a Düsseldorf swept by the 'War of Liberation' fever, imagine a situation in which he would be deprived of the rights enjoyed by other men.

This was not true of the Marx family in Trier, on the Moselle river, a short distance south of Düsseldorf. There Samuel Marx (uncle of the future Karl), who had attended the debates of 'the representatives of the heads of the Jewish nation' – as Napoleon had styled the Sanhedrin in a note on its terms of reference – had since been appointed Grand Rabbi of the newly created départements of Sarre and Sambre et Meuse. He was thus actually in charge of implementing the decisions of the Sanhedrin in that area. In this task he was helped for a time by a younger brother, Heschel, or Hechel (as the French spelled it). Sometimes called Henry Marx, he was a 37-year-old bachelor and more than familiar with Napoleon's shifting policies, from his acts of legislation treating the Jews as equal citizens to the discriminations of the 'Infamous Decree'.

But the tide had turned. The Emperor was on Elba, and it was Tsar Alexander I who, since his triumphal entry into Paris, was 'the sovereign among sovereigns, the "Agamemnon", the "new sun",' in the eyes of most of Europe. It was Alexander who had insisted after the Battle of Leipzig that the Allies cross the Rhine and pursue Napoleon to his lair; and he, too, who had pressed for the 'indispensable capitulation' of Paris so that 'Napoleon standing amidst Moscow in flames' should be followed in future chronicles by a page 'where Alexander appears in the midst of Paris'.[7] He was the 'Liberator of Europe, the *restitutor orbis*', as he was hailed in London when he arrived there on 7 June 1814. The Tsar, who now believed that 'Divine Providence' was guiding his idealistic mission 'to return to every nation the possibility of enjoying its rights and institutions' – as he had written to La Harpe – had left Paris in a huff. He was sincere when promising France peace without revenge, but felt he had been tricked by Louis XVIII, who, contrary to his pledge of a constitution making him King of France by the will of the people, had formally passed through the Senate a Charter that, albeit not undemocratic, was presented as a 'gift' to the people by Louis XVIII, 'in the nineteenth year of his reign', counting from his executed brother's heir (Louis XVII), who had died in 1795 at the age of 10. The righteous Tsar fumed even more at Talleyrand's acquiescence in this betrayal.

Startling changes of administration began to take place as Napoleon's grand empire was being dismantled. On 5 January 1814 the French began to evacuate Trier. The next morning they were gone, and 'Royal' Prussian troops marched into the town which, called Trèves by the French, resumed its German name. The Rhinelanders placed their hopes in the Prussian King's promise to grant them a constitution. The Jews expected the abrogation of the 'Infamous Decree', which in Trier, Bonn, Cologne and throughout most Rhenish districts – except Düsseldorf – had remained in force until the last day of French rule. Both expectations, however, failed to materialize.

On 13 June 1815, some two months after Prussia formally annexed the Rhenish provinces, Heinrich Marx – as his recently Germanized name appeared on a roster of legal staff at the Appellate Court of Trier – raised his voice in a public protest against the injustice and illegality of Prussia's continued enforcement of the 'Infamous Decree'. Far from sharing Heine's view of Napoleon, he attacked his 1808 edict, 'the like of which no tyrant had ever drawn up', and in a sarcastic passage wrote to the newly installed Prussian Governor-General of the Lower Rhineland: 'Who in this nineteenth century would think of preaching intolerance against the Jews? And why? Perhaps because they are circumcised and eat unleavened bread at Easter?'

Marx was writing just 4 days after the Vienna Congress, among its many resolutions, had adopted one so phrased that, while sanctimoniously 'guaranteeing the confessors of the Jewish faith the enjoyment of civil rights' in all the 36 states and several 'free cities' of the new German Bund or Confederation, actually enabled each to rescind the full or partial emancipation forced on them from the outside as a result of the French Revolution. In the interval since the entry of the Prussian troops, Marx had become a family man. He had married in November 1814 and his wife was expecting a child. The new development meant that he might lose his post – but on the basis of some new evidence, this seems not to have been the only reason for his making his protest to the Governor.

Its contents would hardly be of interest – he was, as he wrote himself, a person of 'no significance', indeed a nonentity in the European scheme of things – had he not been destined soon to father a son who was described in 1987 as 'indirectly responsible for nothing less than the entire socio-political complexion of the world today.'[8]

Very little is known about the life and personality of Karl Marx's father, much less than about his remote ancestors. Until late into the 20th century, even the subject of where his father had studied law remained a mystery. He was 20 when Trier's own university had been closed by French revolutionary troops. It was only in 1975 that an entry in the register of student admissions of the one-time French Law School in Coblenz, under the date of 31 January 1813, was published. It read in part: 'Henry Marx, né dans le mois d'avril de l'an mil sept cent soixante dix sept à Sarrelouis... s'inscrit pour suivre pendant le second trimêstre de l'année classique 1812/1813 les cours du Code Napoléon et dela procédure. Coblenz le 31 Janvier 1813. H. Marx.'

Published along with it was another document found in 1974 in the Archives Nationales in Paris. This was a list of students prepared by one of the Law School's deans, Lassaulx, on 1 September 1813. It contained a note saying that the 'Henry Marx' who had enrolled for the courses in 'the Code Napoléon and procedure' intended to sit for qualification as a lawyer some time after the start of the new school year at the end of September 1813.[9]

Since the law studies lasted three years, it is believed that Marx had started them in September 1810. Why he did so as late as the age of 33 can only be surmised. The Law School established by Napoleon at Coblenz, situated at the confluence of the Rhine and the Moselle rivers, and formerly part of the Archbishopric of Trier, had opened its doors a few years before. Marx, named Joshua Heschel at birth, Hechel or Henry to the French, issued a passport in the name of Heinrich in June 1814, yet again called Henry on 7 August – when his marriage banns were published in French, 7 months after the Prussian occupation of Trier – solved the difficulties created by his name and the political changes and administrative take-over confusions of the time by scribbling 'H. Marx' on the altogether three extant documents (all from the period between 1810 and 1818) that bear his signature, the 'H' each time standing for a different variant of his given name. He duly travelled to Holland, and after marrying Henriette Pressburg, a daughter of Rabbi Isaac Pressburg of Nijmegen, returned with her to Trier. As is known, he eventually converted his entire family to Christianity in halting stages, starting with his own baptism at some unknown date between 1816 and 1819. In 1820, with the obstacle to his career removed, he was offered work as an Advokatanwalt, or barrister-at-law, at the High Court of Appeals in Trier.

After an interval, in 1824, while his brother Samuel continued as the town's rabbi, he led his 6-year-old son Karl and 6 other offspring to the font of Trier's Lutheran church.[10] Their mother, Henriette Marx, stayed away; her own baptism took place a year or so later. Thereafter, no doubt partly or perhaps entirely due to his talent, his rise was fairly rapid and he obtained the coveted title of Justizrat, equivalent to King's Counsel in England. The serial baptisms in which he figured, to the embarrassment of his brother and numerous kin, especially the public mass ceremony involving his children, caused something of a small-town stir. Yet surprisingly, for a man whose well-known and old-established maternal family had provided almost all the rabbis of Trier since the 17th century, a man, moreover, who became head of the bar in Trier, and thus one of its prominent citizens, no family papers relating to his life and activities have turned up or been published – aside from some 18 letters written by him to Karl, and one or two legal briefs by his hand.

Karl Marx himself wrote nothing about his father, but his youngest daughter, Eleanor, wrote after his death that 'he was never tired of talking about him' in the privacy of his home. Eleanor Marx-Aveling, unlike her father, felt a keen urge to provide posterity with some information about his personal life and background. Since she was born and lived in London and never met her grandfather, it is accepted that whatever she wrote about him can only have come from Karl Marx himself.

She stressed his deep attachment to his father: 'He always carried an old daguerrotype photograph of him. But he would never show it to strangers because, he said, it was so unlike the original. I thought the face very handsome, the eyes and brow were like those of his son but the features were softer about the mouth and chin.' But that photograph, too, is gone. Discovered with two others in Marx's breast pocket when he died, Engels laid it in his coffin. No other likeness of Marx's father exists, only Eleanor's impression that he looked 'definitely Jewish, but beautifully so'.[11]

Most of Marx's biographers have tended to depict his father as a man of 'gentle, timid and accommodating temper', a 'timorous lawyer' and compromiser. He is presented as a well-educated liberal humanist with 'a touching family sense' and a sense of duty, but also as 'a born placator', submissive, even 'servile'. His weak character and 'craven' attitude towards the Prussian authorities are said to have kindled in the son 'a smouldering sense of resentment, which later events fanned into a flame'.[12] Indeed, the adult Karl Marx cited 'servility' as the vice he detested most. Asked about his 'favourite virtue' in man, he answered: 'Strength'. The bourgeoisie he described in contemptuous terms of Christian 'meekness' and compliance, the proletariat as proud, independent men of courage, possessed of his own attributes and that bellicose spirit which made him describe his idea of happiness in two words: 'to fight'.

A writer in 1978, however, commented that 'Marx's father was not soft internally; in iron will and determination he and his son were alike. Each was girded for personal battle against odds, with the crucial difference that Heschel was cautious and diplomatic, while his son Karl came to be dogmatic and ruthless.'[13] Heinrich Marx adored, even idolized, his son Karl. Recognizing early the potential genius in Karl, but also what struck him as some 'Faust-like' element, he treated him with great understanding, trying to moderate his youthful tempestuousness and tendency to excess, but never bullying him. Of the struggles which marked his own life, the elder Marx left only a few cryptic hints in his surviving letters to the son, alluding to some early estrangement from his parents. When the prospect of Karl Marx's attaining a professorship was broached, the normally reserved father made a rare wistful remark in his letter: 'For you it is not anywhere as difficult as it was for your papa to become a lawyer.'

We do not always know much about the fathers of great men, nor do we always care. But most biographers of Karl Marx acknowledge that his father exerted a far-reaching and 'definite influence' – second to none but Hegel's – 'on his son's intellectual development.' He implanted in him 'the principles of philosophical rationalism', thereby, in the view of one eminent scholar, inoculating him against accepting supernatural causes, visionary fantasies or the metaphysical systems of the Romantics;[14] along with the belief of France's enlightened philosophers in a perfectible world 'in which democratic freedom and the rule of reason were taken as virtually synonymous.' The father is also said to have instilled into the son a love for French culture and lucid argument.[15]

Conversely, Heschel-Heinrich Marx's 'pathetic attempt at assimilation', involving his estrangement from his own culture and the loss of his self-esteem, is now seen as having accentuated in Karl Marx a feature described by some as self-contempt, and by others as outright *Selbsthass*, self-hate. What the father accomplished 'was to establish a sense of shame in his son – both for his parents' Jewishness and for the servile aspect of the father's attempt to escape from it.'[16]

Whereas Franz Mehring, author of the first great, but now outdated, biography of Marx, launched the view that his father's conversion was an act of faith which actually spared his son the problems of joining the mainstream culture which Heine and others had to solve for themselves, the modern claim is that the father transferred his own alienation to Karl Marx, the 'alienated man par excellence'. This finds some support in two documents, one by the father and the other by the son. The first is the above-mentioned petition or memorandum addressed by Heschel-Heinrich Marx to the Prussian Governor-General, Privy Councillor von Sack, in June 1815. The only document, other than his letters, in which Marx's father speaks to us in his authentic voice, it is remarkable less for the several explosions into bitter sarcasm by this cautious 'placator' than for the reasoned tone in which he protested Prussia's arbitrary extension of Napoleon's 'Infamous Decree' on legal as well as moral grounds. It is even more significant for a passage in which he forecast his son's alienation.

Attacking the wholesale exclusion of his Jewish 'co-religionists' from the arts and sciences, from the legal and other professions as a 'breach of fundamental state law', he concluded what may be described as his 'human rights' plea with a warning that 'robbing the fathers of their livelihood' and honour 'without the commonest formality', could not but kindle anti-social 'feelings of revenge in the hearts of their children'. It was bound to lead to the spiritual alienation of that generation from the society that dispossessed and humiliated their fathers.

This premonitory observation was to be echoed by the son in a striking passage of his school-leaving examination essay. Karl Marx, putting down at the age of 17 his 'Reflections of a Young Man on the Choice of a Profession' and dwelling at considerable length on the crucial importance of making the right choice – for making the wrong one and missing one's true vocation can 'frustrate' a man's plans and 'destroy his whole life' – listed every kind of circumstance, obstacle, temptation and deficiency that a young man has to consider in making this grave decision. Self-deception, 'false inspiration', the 'demon of ambition', can all deflect him from his true and proper vocation, and drive him to adopt a profession for which he is unfit.

The experience of 'our parents', he wrote, 'who have already encountered the vicissitudes of fate', may help their sons avoid the many pitfalls with which the choice is fraught. But that is not enough. For 'we cannot always attain the position to which we are called; our relations in society have to some extent already begun to be established before we are in a position to determine them.'

Writing in 1984, Bruce Mazlish asked what the young student had in mind. 'Is he thinking of his own position as a bourgeois in a stratified society? Or is he thinking of his own position as a converted Jew, with all the bars that might place around him?'[17]

Early biographers of Marx, as well as theological Marxists, have hailed those youthful lines of his as 'the germ of the materialist conception of history, unconsciously conceived.' But this theory has been dismissed on the grounds that 'the materialist conception' can hardly have sprung full-blown into Marx's adolescent mind – 'it would be surprising' if it had done so even in 'germ', David McLellan observed in 1973 – at a time when the concept of social strati-fication in bourgeois society was still largely unknown in Germany. Noting that the idea of human activity's being circumscribed 'by the prestructured environ-ment' is at least as old as the Enlightenment, McLellan remarks drily: 'Marx here merely means that when choosing a career one should consider one's cir-cumstances.'[18]

Others, of course, have been quick to relate the circumstances young Marx had in mind to the 'conversion conflict' between his parents, the assumption being that during his childhood he must have heard echoes of this conflict – though born a Jew, he was not baptized until he was 6 – and that afterwards the tension created at home by his mother's remaining a Jew at heart, even after her conversion, fed his growing resentment of her. In 1966, in fact, Arnold Künzli went as far as to suggest that the father's baptism actually 'predetermined the intellectual path of Karl Marx before his birth, with ultimate after-effects that were to transform the world.'[19]

But the most curious passage in Marx's justly famous school-leaving essay, in which he idealistically proclaimed that 'man can attain his own perfection only by working for the perfection and welfare of his fellow-men', is in the lines in which he conjured up the nemesis awaiting anyone choosing a profession for which he does not have the talent:

> If we have chosen a profession for which we do not possess the talent, we can never exercise it worthily, we shall soon realise with shame our own incapacity and tell ourselves that we are useless created beings... Then the most natural consequence is self-con-tempt and what feeling is more painful and less capable of being

cured by anything the outside world may offer? Self-contempt is a serpent that ever gnaws at one's breast, sucking the life-blood from one's heart and mixing it with the poison of misanthropy and despair.

An illusion about our talents for a profession which we have closely examined is a fault which takes its revenge on us ourselves. Even if it does not meet with the censure of the outside world it gives rise to more terrible pain in our hearts than such censure could inflict.

Bruce Mazlish asks how Marx as teenager had learned about self-contempt? Portraying him as 'a youth in turmoil and strife', obviously wrestling 'with acute problems of self-esteem', Mazlish ascribes the youngster's perplexing anxiety about 'self-contempt' and his early alienation 'from his self' to the father's accusing him, shortly after his departure for the university, of spending money extravagantly and of being more than an ordinary 'egoist'. It is this that early on makes Marx vulnerable, 'as a Jew, though a Christian, to the criticism of anti-Semites that Jews were self-interested hucksters.'[20]

The 'conversion conflict' is not mentioned by Mazlish. Marx's father, this scholar suggests, 'seems to have suffered no pain' in his baptism of convenience. Not so Murray Wolfson, who, writing only shortly before Mazlish, found it 'inconceivable' that the adolescent Marx's fear of self-contempt in the passage quoted 'is unrelated to the frustrations and humiliation' suffered by his father 'in the course of his assimilation'. What is the worst that can happen if the young man chooses wrongly? 'Failure. Self-hatred. Self-contempt. By the very stress that Karl Marx puts on the words it is clear that he is no stranger to their meaning,' Wolfson wrote.

> This most recent of many controversies on the subject has of course to do with the fact that, within less than 10 years of his school-leaving essay, the student – in his Economic and Philosophic Manuscripts of 1844 (or 'The Paris Manuscripts', as they are called) – was to work the various forms of human 'alienation' in a capitalist society ruled by 'money-greed' and competition into a key concept of his social and political philosophy and entire world conception.

The publication of the Paris Manuscripts shortly before World War II led, in the decades immediately following it, to a much-debated reappraisal of conceptions about Karl Marx that had been taken for granted. Within the wider aim of tracing the correspondence between his life and thought, the search was on for the 'human' Marx of the formative years, for the roots of his personal alienation and its relation to that of the proletariat. Though in some of the literature on the subject his father appears only as a name, it is not without significance that the two scholars already mentioned, Mazlish and Wolfson – approaching Marx from different and sometimes startling angles in the 1980s, 150 years after he wrote his school-leaving essay – both attached considerable importance to his father's influence, not only on his development but far into his mature theories.

Wolfson, analyzing Marx's writings up to *The Communist Manifesto*, shows him grappling with all the dilemmas faced by his father's generation, to end up with a monistic theory of salvation that – reflecting 'the deeper Jewish ideological heritage which his father had passed on despite himself' – failed as a science 'because its historical form was too close to the Old Testament original', though it succeeded as a religion of the oppressed.

Mazlish sees 'the heaviest incubus inherited by the young man' in what he paraphrases as the 'Jewish guilt' instilled in him by his father: 'Karl was to spend the rest of his life sacrificing self, wife and children, in a material sense, to disprove his father's charge of egoism.' The father's contradictory admonitions, feeding his ego and lofty ambitions while accusing him of selfishness, 'are a shadow over the later dialectical solutions worked out by the mature thinker, Marx.'[21]

Whatever the real nature of the alienation problem Karl Marx inherited from his father, he was of course not the product of parental influence alone. Through the history of the Marx family, even prior to Karl's father, we may – applying Heine's dictum, 'Earliest beginnings explain latest phenomena' – not only reach the roots of the alienation problem but gain a new and comprehensive view of the elements that went into the making of the future Marx of history, the Marx of world importance.

Joshua Heschel Marx was born on 8 April 1777 at Sarrelouis, today's Saarlautern in Germany, but at that time a small French fortress-town on the Sarre or Saar river. He was the second son of Mordecai Halevi (the Levite), who was the rabbi of Sarrelouis. The French spelled the rabbi's name Lévy, and did not call him Mordecai but Marc. 'Le rabbin Marc Lévy' is how he figured in a census carried out at Sarrelouis in 1788. This grandfather of Karl Marx was born around 1740 in Bohemia, but some time after the mid-century he had turned up in Trier, where in 1774 he married Hayya Lvov, the daughter of Trier's rabbi Moses Lvov.

In 1788, when his father-in-law died, Mordecai or Marc Lévy was called to succeed him as rabbi of Trier, which – though only some 50 kilometres south of Sarrelouis – was ruled by Archbishop Clement Wenceslas, who was a Prince-Elector of the then German Holy Roman Empire. Rabbi Mordecai and his wife

Hayya already had three children, Samuel, Joshua Heschel and Esther; a fourth, Moses, was born either in Sarrelouis or in Trier; a fifth, Babette, followed in 1789. The family's name was still Lévy.

The origin of the name Marx is entirely a matter of conjecture. Indeed, conjecture has ranged from 'Marx is a shortened form of Mordecai' to the observation that 'Marx is a German form of Mark, the New Testament apostle'. But it is now established that, some time after his arrival in Trier, Marx's grandfather began to call himself Marx-Levy, and that the first member of the family to be called Marx at birth was his sixth child, Jacob or Jacobus Marx, as reported on behalf of his parents by the midwife who delivered him on 16 June 1800, and so entered in his birth certificate. To confound matters and confuse later researchers, the Trier population census in 1802 continued to feature Marx's grandfather as Marx-Levy; the Coblenz Law School entry, made years after his death, referred to him as 'Marcus Samuel Levy'; and the name of Karl Marx's grandmother Hayya appears in some documents as Hayen Moyses, in others as Cain, and in the Coblenz entry as Eve Moses.[22] Moses was actually the first name of her father, Moses Lvov, but most of Europe's Jews, with some exceptions – Heine is a case in point – had no family names at the time. They were known by their first name, followed by their father's first name.

Karl Marx's grandfather became 'Marcus Samuel Levy' by a similar coupling of his own and his father's names. His real name – as inscribed on his tombstone in Trier – was 'Mordecai Halevi, son of Samuel of Poselburg'. Poselburg was identified in 1973 as Bosenberg in Bohemia, also called Postelberg in German. In Czech it is called Postoloprti, and German researchers have unearthed a single Samuel registered in that place in 1735, who may well have been Karl Marx's great-grandfather.

The name that was one day to resound around the world thus developed by stages from Mordecai-Marc-Marcus-Marx-Levy to Marx. The original Mordecai, however, never had any personal papers in the name of Marx. He died before Napoleon in 1808 ordered the Jews in his territories to adopt family names for the purpose of facilitating their conscription into the army. Joshua Heschel's elder brother Samuel thereupon formally and officially adopted the name Marx in his own behalf and that of all his siblings.

Marx's father, Heschel Marx-Levy by name at the time, was 11 years old when Rabbi Mordecai and his family moved from Sarrelouis to Trier. This was a circumvallated city, with an overwhelmingly Catholic population that, between then and 1815, apparently never exceeded 9,000.[23] Its small number of Protestant families had been expelled in 1738, but a few had since been readmitted as 'tolerated' inhabitants. Conquered from the Treveri by Julius Caesar in 56 BC and later fortified by Augustus, it was Germany's oldest city. Its Jewish community, too, was the oldest in Germany after Worms, which together with Coblenz belonged to the same Trier church-state. With the number of Jews throughout the sovereign archbishopric limited since 1723 to 165 families, only a dozen or so lived in Trier itself.[24] Besides a yearly lump sum to the prince-archbishop's court treasury for the right of residence, they paid – on penalty of expulsion – 'New Year's money' and *Schutzgeld* ('protection money') to the cathedral chapter, and were too few to support their rabbi in style.

The Marx-Levys settled down in an old two-storey building at 183 Weberbachstrasse, in the rear garden of which a converted summer-house served as a synagogue. The front building had 6 rooms, which they shared with another family, the house having two kitchens, two pantries and a cellar. Karl Marx's grandparents eventually had 6 sons – not counting one who died as a baby – and two daughters; they kept two maids, and the part of the ramshackle building they inhabited in the Weberbachstrasse became uncomfortably crowded.

Marx's father thus grew up in straitened circumstances, not to say in penury. Trier, rising picturesquely on the Moselle, presided over a fertile valley ringed by lovely wine-producing hills. Besides boasting an amphitheatre built around AD 100, a huge 4th-century Roman gateway black with age and called Porta Nigra, and other monuments of its past glory as Augusta Treverorum, Trier had some pretty red sandstone houses set between orchards and gardens. But it was also a stifling city, for within its ancient walls it was – as Goethe described it in 1793 – 'burdened, nay, oppressed' with medieval 'churches and chapels and cloisters and colleges and buildings dedicated to chivalrous and religious orders, to say nothing of the abbacies, Carthusian convents and institutions investing, nay, blockading it from without.'

Yet in popish-looking Trier – *sancta civitas Trevirorum*, once famous for its piety and monastic learning and still teeming with nearly 1,000 ecclesiastics – the boy who was to become Marx's father also landed in a place close to the Rhine, whose burghers were among the first to sense the intellectual currents in France on the eve of the Revolution. Although politically governed from Coblenz, Trier's town council was dominated by a coalition of bourgeois patricians, important merchants and professors of its ancient university. In March 1785, three years before the arrival of the Marx-Levys, the governor of Trier had reported to Coblenz that the local citizenry was beginning to harbour 'strong republican' feelings and showing an 'indomitably libertarian spirit'.[25]

The decisive events that were to affect the life of Heschel Marx-Levy were, of course, the French Revolution and, in its aftermath, the emancipation of the Jews on 28 September 1791, when the National Assembly in Paris unanimously adopted a resolution making France the first country – other than the

USA – to grant its Jews equality and the rights of full 'active' citizenship. The Revolution brought a growing stream of Royalist French émigrés to Trier, swelling its population by 10 per cent. Soon Condé's Royalist troops could be seen exercising in the territory of the archbishopric by permission of its ruler. The insolence and carousing in town of these young aristocratic sports, coupled with fear of retaliation by the new leaders of France, caused friction between the citizenry and the Archbishop before the adolescent Heschel was to see the so-called 'Army of the Princes' retreating in disarray through Trier from the terrible artillery drubbing at Valmy.

As for the emancipation of the French Jews, Heschel was a little over 14 when this epochal event of wider than Jewish significance occurred. For the first time since their dispersal in antiquity, when they had been carried off into captivity in such numbers that the price of slaves in the Roman Empire had dropped, Jews were to be admitted, however slowly and gradually, into the mainstream of European life. 'The metric system and the pioneer emancipation of the Jews' were ranked by the historian E.J. Hobsbawm as the two 'most striking international results' and lasting achievements of the French Revolution.[26] Yet a century or so after the event, Max Nordau, one of the principal speakers at the First Zionist Congress held in Switzerland in 1897, was to charge that in practice the emancipation was a sham precisely because it had been granted on the basis of a purely rationalist, mathematically abstract principle and not out of any fraternal sentiment.

Indeed, the National Assembly's resolution of September 1791 had only been adopted after many adjournments, several stormy debates and much foot-dragging. The readmission into the Gentile world of a shadow-people excluded from it for nearly two millennia confronted the fathers of the Revolution with unprecedented problems and a terrible dichotomy between their principles and their feelings. On the one hand, they could not deny the Jews equality on theological grounds, the Declaration of the Rights of Man having expressly stipulated that no person could be deprived of equal rights or 'molested for his opinions, even such as are religious'; on the other, the Abbé Grégoire, Mirabeau and other advocates of emancipation shared with its opponents the collective negative image of the Jews, popularized by Voltaire, as an 'uncivilized' horde. But whereas Marat and Desmoulins simply ridiculed the idea of equalizing the Jews, and such violent anti-emancipation spokesmen as the Abbé J.S. Maury, the later cardinal of Paris, and the Alsatian deputy Reubell (a future member of the Directory) referred to them, respectively, as 'aliens' and 'Africans', the Abbé Grégoire blamed their 'vices' on their long servitude and argued that their character could be 'regenerated', i.e., reformed for the better by ending their disabilities.

The battle for and against emancipation went on for more than 21 months in and outside the Assembly, to the accompaniment of a pamphlet war between the two camps. Its drama turned chiefly on the fate of some 32,000 Ashkenazi Jews of Alsace and Lorraine. Unlike France's remaining 6,000 or so Sephardi or 'Portuguese' Jews of Bordeaux, Bayonne and Avignon – whose forefathers had arrived as 'new Christian' refugees of the Inquisition, and who had since adopted French manners and customs – those of Alsace (which had become French only in 1648) had never assimilated. The acculturated Sephardi minority, who were well-to-do and had ancient letters-patent, had been allowed to vote for the States General and to serve in the national militia. The Ashkenazi Jews of Alsace, excluded from the cities and most professions, were largely observant. They petitioned the National Assembly for elementary human rights and an end to discrimination, but asked to maintain the communal autonomy which since the Middle Ages had allowed their rabbinical judges and administrators to run their internal affairs so long as they paid their oppressive taxes. This was something the new French nation-state – having just abolished the corporate body of the Church – was hardly prepared to contemplate.

The National Assembly's way of dealing with its dilemmas was to enfranchise only the Sephardi-Portuguese minority in January 1790. The bulk of French Jewry in Alsace was left in limbo. At the same time citizenship was granted to the Negro freemen in the French Antilles. It was only after Adrien Duport, a leading Jacobin and one of the founders of the Club des Trentes, reminded the Assembly that 'Muslims and men of all sects enjoy political rights in France' that the deputies, fearful of betraying the Revolution's own principles, had conferred equality on the Jews. The decision had provoked riots, especially in Alsace. Overnight, as one of France's Jewish intellectuals rejoiced, a people who only yesterday 'seemed doomed to remain forever in bondage and abasement' were awakened to 'a sense of happiness by the liveliest emotion of the purest joy.'[27] Something of the same emotion must have gripped the Marx-Levys in 1794 when the emancipation came to them upon Archbishop Clement Wenceslas's taking flight before the victorious troops of the French Revolution, who occupied the main Rhineland cities.

The Jews were not the only ones to receive the French with enthusiasm. In Bonn, German 'democrats' helped to smash the gate of the ghetto with axes. During the short-lived 'Mainz Republic', Jewish members of the city's 500-strong 'Jacobin' Club were given a prominent part in the ceremonial planting of a 'Liberty Tree' to signal the new era of equality. In Trier, too, where the French 'freed the intelligentsia from the tutelage of the priests, men danced round their "tree of freedom" just like the inhabitants of Mainz. They had their own Jacobin Club.'[28]

In Trier, the French – besides demanding 60,000 bottles of wine to be supplied to them daily – imposed a levy of 1.5 million *livres*, requisitioned everything from hemp, hides and foodstuffs to steel, timber and building materials, turned the cathedral into a storage centre and dismantled the lead roof of one of the churches. But after the Peace of Campo Formio (in which they were secretly promised the left bank of the Rhine in a future settlement), they relaxed their heavy hand. By the end of 1797 all officials, teachers, judges and municipal councillors had taken the French oath of loyalty. All burghers wore the tricoloured *cocarde*, and early in 1798 Trier celebrated the end of feudal privileges, peasant servitude and the grant of 'all the benefits of the French Republic', with two-day ceremonies, processions and the solemn planting – to the mixed sound of church bells and salvos from 50 cannon – of a second 'Liberty Tree' in the cathedral square.

Trier became the government centre, and starting with the Peace of Lunéville in 1801, the official capital of the Departement de la Sarre. It was to remain that for another 13 years until Napoleon's downfall. Karl Marx's father thus spent two uninterrupted decades, from 1794 to 1814 – the decisive period of his passage to maturity from a 17-year-old to a full-grown man of 37 – under the same egalitarian 'French spirit' which Heine experienced in Düsseldorf up to his adolescence.

According to the oral family tradition transmitted by Eleanor Marx-Aveling, her grandfather was 'steeped in the eighteenth century's free French ideas on politics, religion, life and art'.[29] It is something of a mystery, though, what education he received, and where, before he started his law studies when he was past 30. Until 1794 Trier had only Catholic schools, and it is doubtful that Rabbi Mordecai Marx-Levy would send his son to one.[30] It may be assumed that his chief boyhood tuition was in the Bible and the Talmud, though he was not trained for the rabbinate, as were two of his brothers, the elder Samuel and a younger one, Moses.

A more intriguing question is when he became estranged from his family, or what caused the process of alienation which he supposedly passed on to his son Karl. His veiled remark, years later, to Karl that he had 'got nothing' from his family but his 'mother's love, and for that I had to struggle and to suffer in order not to hurt her', would seem to indicate some rift with his father, Rabbi Mordecai, and a better, though not a smooth, relationship with his mother. The precise nature of what went on in the family is unknown. All that can be said for certain is that once Heschel's interest in the general secular culture had been aroused, he began to devour the rationalist literature of the Enlightenment and the fashionable works of Voltaire and Rousseau; and that, in this or that order, he also familiarized himself with the philosophic ideas of Kant and the scientific ones of Newton and Leibniz. There is internal evidence to show that he was a fervent

119

admirer of John Locke, and saw the philosopher as the handmaiden of science employed 'in clearing the ground a little and removing some of the rubbish that lies on the way to knowledge'; and ultimately he was to become, in the words of his son's brother-in-law, 'a Protestant à la Lessing.'[31]

Although the next great turning-point in Heschel's life was to come in 1804, when Rabbi Mordecai died and Napoleon visited Trier, no appreciation of his intellectual development and tortuous life can ignore a trend of major significance which became evident at the end of the 18th century among the several hundred unemancipated Jewish families rich enough to have bought 'protected' status and residence permits in Berlin. For some, if not all, the reasons that were ultimately to propel Heschel Marx-Levy towards baptism were being prefigured in the Prussian capital. There, even as Schiller, Goethe, Kant, Fichte, Hölderlin, Novalis and other poets and thinkers were in the 1790s producing the finest flowers of German culture, the historic rapprochement – and eventually veritable 'symbiosis' – between enlightened German and Jewish minds had started in Moses Mendelssohn's circle.

Berlin in 1797, when Friedrich Wilhelm III ascended the Prussian throne, was a city tense and agog with the wars and other after-effects of the French Revolution, but otherwise one of the most boring capitals in Europe. The social life of Prussia's aristocratic civil and military officials, who hardly ever read a book, was confined to 'court festivities and levees, and at carnival time there were routs organized according to prescription' for the high functionaries.[32]

Scholars usually met at taverns, without their wives or mistresses. Before he died in 1786, Moses Mendelssohn was practically the only intellectual who kept open house for friends and visitors. At the same time, the drawing-rooms of several extraordinary Berlin Jewish women had become the most brilliant and sought-after meeting places, next to the court, of the cream of the capital's society and enlightened intelligentsia, both Christian and Jewish.

The first and most famous was that of Henriette Herz, a cultured young beauty and the wife of Marcus Herz, a distinguished physician and former philosophy student, whom Kant himself had chosen to be his 'advocate' when arguing his dissertation in Königsberg. King Friedrich Wilhelm III, when still Crown Prince, had often come to the Herz drawing-room with his tutor to hear Marcus Herz expound Kant's philosophy. Doctor Herz, who had wide-ranging extramedical interests, also read papers on physics 'illustrated by experiments' which attracted numbers of Prussian courtiers, young aristocratic intellectuals, and distinguished foreign visitors.

Wilhelm von Humboldt, the budding scholar and statesman, who at 20 had attended sessions of the National Assembly in Paris, was so bored at his family castle in Tegel that he dated his letters from 'Castle Ennui'. Soon he found his way to the Herz house, as did his brother Alexander, the later explorer of Venezuela and the Orinoco River and world-famous natural scientist. In the Herz drawing-room, and a little later in the 'garret-salon' of their friend Rahel Levin, they would find the philosopher Fichte and the leader of the new Romantic movement, Friedrich von Schlegel, as well as the poets and writers Jean Paul Richter, Clemens Brentano and Ludwig Tieck, the co-translator of Shakespeare together with Schlegel's brother August. Schiller was sometimes present, and Madame de Staël, whenever she visited Berlin. There would be Mendelssohn's two daughters, Dorothea and Henriette, and several other beautiful, well-educated young women familiar with Voltaire and the fashionable French and English literature.[33]

In the Herz drawing-room, after food and wine, guests danced the new 'Queen's minuet', or played party games. There were reading-circles, and sometimes lawn tennis. At Rahel Levin's, on the top floor of her father's house in the Jaegerstrasse, the atmosphere was more bohemian. There the King's eccentric younger brother Louis Ferdinand – the Prince of Prussia by his court style, destined to die while leading the Prussian vanguard against Napoleon in the Battle of Jena – would climb the stairs to her 'garret' late at night to discuss the mysteries of existence in the light of the new philosophical and Romantic ideas with Heinrich von Kleist, the Humboldt brothers, the Schlegel brothers, Prince Radziwill, Friedrich Gentz – who translated Edmund Burke's *Reflections on the French Revolution* and was to become Metternich's right-hand man at the Vienna Congress – and the Reverend Schleiermacher, who preached a new rationalist Christianity. Within less than 10 years of Mendelssohn's death, this small German-Jewish elite had developed a degree of intimacy that made Rahel Levin's home the only place where the unfortunate Prince of Prussia felt free to play the piano and sing out his fantasies 'through the open window in all the stillness of a winter night.'[34] Against the sombre background of the times, the women not only provided intellectual stimulation and a refuge, in an atmosphere free of convention rare in Germany, to some of her best young minds, but also set the cultural and literary tone in Berlin at the turn of the century.

'She was the first to understand and recognize me,' Goethe said of Rahel Levin. Indeed, after reading his *Wilhelm Meisters Lehrjahre* and several meetings with him she proclaimed him – at a time when Goethe and the whole 'Weimar school' were being attacked for snobbishness, paganism and profligacy – 'divine', and continued to be the prime mover in the launching of the Goethe cult in Germany. Hers was a sure literary flair that recognized the imaginative talent of Jean Paul Richter, the novelist who was to be acclaimed as the 'German Dostoyevsky', just as many years later she detected an 'exceptional' talent in young Harry Heine and became his patron and literary mentor when he was still quite unknown. Many of her famous contemporaries tried to capture in words the ineluctable quality which made the fragile, unprepossessive and melancholy-looking Rahel Levin not only a great inspirer and consoler of men, but the centre and 'quintessence, as it were, of all the spiritual life of her time'.[35]

The remarkable thing about these 'clever Jewesses' of Berlin who, in the words of Golo Mann, rapidly became 'partners in the literary life of Germany, in fact, even helped to make it', is that they did so while one Jew only – the court banker Daniel Itzig – had so far exceptionally been granted full citizenship rights in Prussia. The self-emancipated Berlin women, like the rest of the city's small but educated Jewish community – now allowed to own 70 houses, but still subject to marital, occupational and other medieval-type restrictions – were all the more acutely conscious of the indignity of their inferior status as the French emancipation had now reached the Jews of the Rhineland. So painful was this feeling that in 1795 Rahel Levin, at the age of 24, cried out: 'I imagine that just as I was being thrust into the world a supernatural being plunged a dagger into my heart with these words: "You shall have feeling, see the world as only a few see it. You shall be great-hearted and noble... restless and given to incessant thought... But with one reservation: You shall be Jewish." And now my whole life is a continual bleeding...'

Moses Mendelssohn's new definition of Judaism, postulating that certain of its ancient laws had become obsolete with the destruction of the Temple in Jerusalem, when God ceased to be the sovereign of the Jewish state, had seemingly resolved its conflict with the rationalist age. As far as the Sinai revelation was concerned, he had – in his main philosophical work, *Jerusalem, or On Religious Might and Judaism* – limited himself to presenting it as a divine law or 'constitution' handed down to the Jews in a unique empirical-historic occurrence witnessed and accepted by a whole people, and therefore to be seen as a *vérité de fait*. The moral imperatives of this code were binding only on those who wished to obey it, and those of its commandments that remained valid were only the Jews' prescribed way of serving God. Writing in Christian Prussia before the advent of the national state, Mendelssohn affirmed that a man's beliefs were a private matter between himself and his conscience. Moreover, since the Jewish religion claimed no miracles unacceptable to reason, its adherents were entitled to a place in the civil society of the enlightened state, which had no right to coerce religious convictions. Already during his lifetime, however, Mendelssohn's subtle philosophical transformation of the God of Sinai into the God of Reason involved him in sharp controversy not only with orthodox rabbis but with conservative Christian theologians.

Challenged by the latter either to convert or to refute Christianity, Mendelssohn – whose vision was of a plurality of religions respecting and enriching each other within a universal humanist civilization – had before his death rushed to explain 'the difference between the Old and the New Testament, as I see it. The first harmonizes with my philosophical convictions or at least does not contradict them; the latter asks for a belief that I am unable to accept.' And in an allegory refuting the argument that Judaism was only the herald of Christianity, he wrote that 'even if the Jewish faith were, as claimed, the lower basement upon which Christianity rests as the upper floor, no one would expect anyone to tear down the basement in order to take up residence on the upper floor.'

Mendelssohn, who died before the French Revolution, had hoped that tolerance and reason would gradually put an end to prejudice and discrimination. While he set Judaism on the road towards modernity, he had no way of foreseeing that his break with historic tradition, though inevitable in the long run, would lead his own family tragically far from his intentions. For now his own daughters and the other 'clever Jewesses' of Berlin, who in Henriette Herz's words had been educated without 'any link to tradition such as perpetuates itself from generation to generation yet keeps pace with the spirit of the age', were like 'absolutely virgin soil' to every fashionable secular current. Breaking the barrier of their formal non-emancipation, dazzled by the ferment which in 1799 made the Romantic poet Novalis speak of 'a new and better civilization' being born from the intellectual renaissance in Germany – even as the rest of Europe was absorbed in war – they had got the idea that much of Judaism with its discardable old 'superstitions' was no longer a religion fit for 'educated' people and were irresistibly attracted by what Heine was to call 'the very enlightened Christianity... which could be had in Berlin's churches at that time without even the divinity of Christ, like turtle soup without turtle.'

Dorothea Mendelssohn, the philosopher's eldest and highly sophisticated daughter, went completely overboard when she fell in love with Friedrich Schlegel, the great aesthete of the Romantic school. In 1798 she divorced her banker husband Simon Veit, left their two children, and defying public opinion, went to live with Schlegel. Following him to Jena and Paris, where they were married in 1804, Dorothea converted to Protestantism, and a few years later in Vienna went over with her husband to Catholicism. Dorothea's younger sister, Henriette, was independently to be baptized into the Catholic Church while tutoring the daughter of a French general in Paris. Only one of Mendelssohn's sons remained Jewish, while two others – including the father of Felix Mendelssohn, the composer – converted to Protestantism. So, after waiting until her mother died, did the 'beautiful Circassian', Henriette Herz. The melancholy

Rahel Levin, after two prolonged and disappointing engagements with a Prussian count and a Spanish legation secretary, was to break with her family at the age of 43 when – marrying Varnhagen von Ense, a liberal Prussian diplomat 14 years her junior – she, too, became a Protestant.

It has been said of these women that they were deluded by the humanist voice of Friedrich von Schiller, and in trying to build a bridge to the Germans they had found 'the wrong address'. For Schiller, the anti-nationalist poet of freedom and universal brotherhood, was not truly representative of Germany. Alternately, the enthusiasm with which they stimulated the gestation, within a most select Berlin circle, of the singular German-Jewish 'symbiosis' which in the 19th century was to produce some brilliant as well as bitter fruit has been ascribed to their intoxication with 'the things of the spirit', with 'great thoughts and philosophies and art' in a way which made them 'soar beyond the confines of actual everyday reality.'[36] Indeed, in prosaic reality, neither Schlegel nor Fichte nor Friedrich Gentz nor any of Germany's rising young men who frequented the salons of these women would have accepted them had they not so easily succumbed to the teaching of the elegant and suave Reverend Schleiermacher – whom Henriette Herz called 'our bijou' – that Judaism was a 'moaning', mummified religion.

Goethe, the idol of Rahel's salon and himself a freethinker, admired the Jews for having produced 'so many gifted men in art and science'. But for all the detestable 'wrangling and partisanship' he saw in Christianity, he felt that it offered the only common ground for generating some truly humanist religion, and vehemently opposed granting the Jews equality. Wilhelm von Humboldt, on the other hand, was to advise the Prussian King in favour of it as the best way of converting the Jews. Friedrich Gentz made Rahel Levin the life-long confidante of his many love-affairs but considered the Jews damned 'unto the ten thousandth generation' for their 'purblind, wanton intellectuality', one of the very qualities that made her attractive to him and others. Kant, whose philosophy found an early expositor in Henriette Herz's husband – and the most brilliant one, by Kant's own admission, in Solomon Maimon, another habitué of her salon – disparaged Judaism as a religion. While praising Maimon in one place, Kant, as only recently discovered, privately maligned him in 1798 and strongly disparaged the Jews.[37]

And Fichte, the idealist philosopher who called Solomon Maimon 'one of the greatest thinkers of our period' and in another context confessed that Dorothea Mendelssohn undermined his belief 'that no good can come out of this nation', declared in an article in the 1790s that the only way of protecting Germany from the Jews – short of 'chopping off all their heads in a single night and screwing fresh ones on their shoulders from which any Jewish idea has been expurgated' – was 'to conquer their Promised Land for them and ship the lot off there.'[38]

Shortly after Prussia's defeat at Jena, Fichte was invited to give a series of morale-boosting lectures in Berlin. In these famous 'Addresses to the German Nation' (*Reden an die Deutsche Nation*) – delivered in a capital teeming with Napoleon's troops and bayonets, and to have an extraordinary effect on the youth of a dejected country – Fichte launched the theory that 'according to one of the particular laws of development of the Divine', the Germans were an unadulterated *Urvolk*, a 'primal' and superior 'people of peoples'.[39] At the same time, he took the occasion to put the Jews beyond the pale as an 'inimical nation', inferior yet hostile to and menacing 'all the human species'. Appointed the first rector of Berlin University on its foundation in 1810 by Wilhelm von Humboldt, Fichte, the theorist of 'might is right', was to become Germany's national philosopher and the godfather of its 19th-century chauvinist and racially minded tendencies.

Heschel Marx-Levy's life, once Trier was restored to Prussia, was to be affected by this nascent current and by the reactionary policies carried out by such men as Friedrich Gentz and one or two other friends of the 'clever Jewesses' of Berlin. He was not a party to, though he may have known of, the frustration which in 1799 moved the leader of Berlin's educated Jews, David Friedlaender, to make a bold and rather desperate announcement, in an anonymously published *Open Letter to the Right Reverend Church Councillor and Provost Teller in Berlin*. What Friedlaender's Letter said was that, if granted citizenship and exempted from having to accept the divinity of Jesus, a group of 'householders' was ready to undergo baptism in a kind of merger between Judaism and Protestantism based on the principle of monotheism common to both beliefs.

Politely rejected, Friedlaender's attempt to obtain from the Church – by means of 'dry baptism', as his idea was ridiculed in Jewish and Christian circles alike – the civil rights that the state refused to grant was motivated by a combination of eagerness to prove his genuine love of Germany and German culture and an anxiety which made his hair 'bristle at the thought that our sons will first abandon Judaism and then convert to Christianity.' Friedlaender, who was a rich and respected community leader, a disciple of Kant and Mendelssohn, next proposed the replacement of Talmud study by secular German subjects, and was to become one of the founders of modern Reform Judaism.

Friedlaender's father-in-law was that Daniel Itzig, who, for his services to Prussia since the Seven Years War, had been singled out for the special 'benefaction' of citizenship and 'the same rights as all Christian families'. This included the spouses of his children as well as their descendants, but only of the male line. While Friedlaender had thus become a citizen, his own children remained, in the language of Itzig's patent, 'common Jews', adding personal fuel to his continuing struggle for emancipation by means of speeded-up 'Germanization'. Itzig himself, who died in 1798 – the year before Friedlaender sent up his 'dry baptism' trial balloon – was so alarmed by the rapid 'assimilationist' trend unwittingly launched by his old friend Mendelssohn that he inserted a stipulation in his will disinheriting any of his descendants who converted.

At this time, Heschel Marx-Levy, far from being reduced to any such straits, enjoyed civil rights under the French emancipation act of 1791. No one in Trier was trying to make his enjoyment of them dependent on his submitting to any state-approved faith or the majority religion. His interest in Voltaire and the other Enlightenment philosophers, including Mendelssohn, had estranged him from his father, Rabbi Mordecai, and there was some tension in the family. But one could be a follower of Mendelssohn, read Voltaire, Rousseau and all the secular literature and yet remain, like Mendelssohn himself, faithful to Judaism. Mendelssohn had even coined a famous dictum – 'Be a Jew at home and a man outside' – encapsulating all it required. Anyhow, Heschel's rift with his father, possibly aggravated by differences of temperament, family disputes or other conceivable reasons, ended on 24 October 1804, when Rabbi Mordecai died.

By that time, however, the emancipation had given rise to its own host of political, legal, socio-economic and cultural as well as psychological problems – some of them foreseen and others undreamt-of – bedevilling both the emancipators and the emancipated. Napoleon was about to take them in hand and cut through the whole complex knot in one clean sweep. It was this imperial intervention and its consequences that were to preoccupy Heschel even as his father's death freed him to live as he pleased.

Napoleon arrived in Trier on a three-day visit on 6 October 1804. The newly anointed Emperor, on a tour of his northern departements since the end of August, arrived from Coblenz, after having stopped at Aix-la-Chapelle, Cologne, Bonn and Mainz. At Coblenz he received the local rabbi, Emanuel Deutz, and was favourably impressed by him. (Deutz was later to become Chief Rabbi of Paris.) Napoleon is known to have met other rabbis and Jewish notables in the course of this tour, but there is no knowing whether he also received Rabbi Mordecai Marx-Levy, who, less than three weeks from his death, may have been too ill to wait upon the Emperor.

'As for the Jews', Napoleon Bonaparte had told the Conseil d'Etat in 1801, 'they are a nation apart, the sect of which does not mix with any other. We shall have ample time to deal with it later on.' The Council was discussing the Concordat with the Papacy, according to which ecclesiastics were henceforth to be appointed by the government and merely to be confirmed by the Pope. In presenting the new law which by 1802 was to regulate the functioning of the Protestant church as well, Portalis – Bonaparte's Director of Cults – explained rather cynically why the Jews could wait: 'They are less a religion than a nation... The government wishes to respect the eternity of this people which has survived to this day... and which, so far as its priesthood and cult are concerned, regards it as one of its greatest privileges to have only God as its lawgiver.'[40]

This pointed reference to the unique historical character of the Jews as both a religion and a nation since antiquity touched upon an aspect which the fathers of the Revolution had disregarded when they emancipated the Jews in 1791 and offered them legal and social integration into 'the common culture of Europe'. In the supranational ardour of the Enlightenment, they had dismissed it as irrelevant, or had brushed it aside by the argument that the Jews were anyway 'only the debris of a destroyed nation'. Taking a great leap forward, they had emancipated the Jews as individuals but had abolished the autonomy which had enabled their rabbis, rabbinical judges and syndics not only to administer their religious life and ceremonies but to settle internal lawsuits, collect the taxes and run the social and educational affairs of their communities. This autonomy, coupled with their voluntary discipline, was one of the elements which had made it possible for the Jews to maintain an extraordinary inner cohesion and to survive under the most precarious conditions.

By 1804, nothing had yet been substituted for this type of quasi-political self-government. The prefect of the Moselle departement reported that year to the Minister of Cults in Paris 'a state of anarchy in nearly all the [Jewish] communes of the departement'. The rabbis, he wrote, no longer had 'any power to maintain religious discipline or to assess the taxes needed for the religion's expenses.' Similar reports were coming in from all parts of the empire. During the Terror, synagogues, like the churches, had been closed or turned into clubs or 'temples of Reason', occasionally into stables. With people not only leaving the ghettos, but free to move to other towns, and the voluntary tax-system in disarray, there was in 1804 no institution authorized to finance charities, hospitals and Torah schools, or even to pay the rabbis' salaries. The Jewish religion, although not outlawed, had been left without a legal basis on which to function.

Rabbi Mordecai Marx-Levy, who in 1804 was 55 years old, was an orthodox rabbi to whom preserving the theology, values and customs of Judaism was as important as the right to vote. The Talmudic principle that 'the law of the land is the law' – another of the elements which, enabling the Jews to adjust to any external national framework, had ensured their survival over vast stretches of history – meant in practice that there was no religious obstacle to their taking the civic oath to the French Republic. The emancipators, however, brought up by the Enlightenment *philosophes* to deprecate all history that had gone before their own superior age, hardly regarded the Jews as a people with a history. Convinced in some degree or other that their character needed to be 'regenerated' and reformed, they had undertaken to cure the Jews of their 'vices' in the expectation that equality would make them conform to the customs and way of life of the surrounding society.

To Rabbi Mordecai, who had lived to see the holy Sabbath abolished (together with the Sunday day of rest), this meant accepting the norms of the society that had so long oppressed his people. To his son Heschel it was the new open society, inviting, alluring and full of opportunities. Due to the small number of Jews in Trier, Rabbi Mordecai was never well off. Now he had problems with his salary and the subsistence of his large family. By 1804, moreover, groups of Jews keen to restore synagogues and resume communal activities were requesting government approval for sundry schemes of 'interior policing', voluntary or obligatory fundraising, the appointment of rabbis, and so forth. Unhappy with their inviting 'government intervention' in the organization of religious life, Marx's grandfather resented the loss of his authority, the fact that he could no longer marry couples unless a civil ceremony had taken place first, and the disorganization of his community. Perhaps most of all, he frowned at the new possibility of mixed marriages.[41]

Thus the tremendous and sudden change in the Jews' relation to society wrought by the French emancipation, adding its own stress to the generation gap and increasing gulf between Heschel's widening horizons and Rabbi Mordecai's narrow world conception and constricting orthodoxy, had already had a disrupting effect on Karl Marx's paternal family during the last years of his grandfather's life. Nevertheless, Karl's father – as seems clear from recent research – remained Jewish enough after Rabbi Mordecai's death and Napoleon's reforms to serve for two years as secretary of the newly created Synagogue Consistory for the Sarre Departement. Even before that, as the kith and kin of both Trier's late and new rabbi – his brother Samuel – Heschel was familiar with the state of affairs which induced Napoleon by 1806 to assemble what he termed the 'States General' of the Jews – commonly known as the Assembly of Notables – in Paris, and in short order to call a Great Sanhedrin.

In the third week of January 1806, fresh from the triumph at Austerlitz, Napoleon stopped for two days at Strasbourg before going on to Paris. In March he ordered the Minister of Justice to examine the possibility, nearly 15 years after the emancipation, of depriving the Jews of their citizenship. The discussions which followed in the Conseil d'Etat during the next few months were to culminate in a report by Louis Mathieu Molé – a young count, who became Prime Minister of France 30 years later – to the effect that 'the code of the Jews includes at the same time the religion, the political and the civil laws, the habits, the manners and all of the customs of life. These diverse things, which everywhere else are separated, are here mixed in the same code.'

This discovery, at any rate, put an end to the ambiguity evident in such loose previous definitions of Judaism as a 'sect', 'religion', 'less of a religion than a nation', etc. But even as it showed up the full complexity of the subject, Napoleon now heaped abuse on the Jews and, short of expelling them, seemed determined to take 'exceptional' measures against them – to the consternation of the jurists on the Conseil d'Etat, who felt that there was no legal basis for discriminating between citizens, whatever their religion.

In the background of Napoleon's volte-face towards the Jews lurked an economic problem with political implications. Extending to Trier and the Rhine and Moselle departements which Napoleon had visited in 1804, it was of anarchic proportions in Alsace, where it had been festering since the 'forged receipts' case of the 1770s. Three of the counterfeiters had been hanged, which only increased endemic anti-Jewish feelings in Alsace, but the peasants had never repaid the debts involved in the swindle, and starting in 1801, court decisions in favour of the Jewish lenders led to increasing charges of usury against them. There were old debts and mortgages and new debts; between September 1800 and December 1802, Alsatian peasants officially borrowed no less than 12,296,000 francs, though not from Jews alone. At the same time, the emancipation had found the Jews owing large sums to Christians, which they had borrowed to pay their heavy communal taxes but found hard to collect and repay following the dissolution of their communities.[42] The French had refused to nationalize these communal debts as they had done in the case of the other religious corporations dissolved in the course of the Revolution.

During his stop-over in Strasbourg on 22–23 January 1806, Napoleon heard from the prefect and other Alsatian leaders exaggerated reports of Jewish usury. He left with the impression that 'whole villages' were mortgaged to Jews and that unless something was done the peasants, being in a murderous mood since the worsening economic crisis of 1805, might riot and massacre their creditors. The Jews of Alsace and the Rhine and Moselle departements, faced with similar charges, asked the prefects to be heard before being indiscriminately condemned. But while these pleas and the Jews' requests for a statute ordering their religious affairs were ignored, the Alsatians established a powerful lobby in Paris. Although one of its virulent pamphlets was impounded by the police, copies of it evidently influenced the discussions in the Conseil d'Etat in the spring of 1806, making some of its members feel that while France alone had 'incorporated the Jewish nation without any conditions into all the rights and benefits of its social order', the Jews had somehow not kept their end of the bargain. And by that time the arch-conservative philosopher Louis de Bonald, who considered the whole Revolution to have been a terrible mistake, was declaring in the *Mercure de France* that the Jews had become the new feudal 'seigneurs of Alsace', and openly demanding that their citizenship rights should be revoked.[43]

With the Abbé Grégoire and several other liberal writers publishing out-raged ripostes in other journals, the whole emancipation debate seemed to be flaring up anew, even as the discussions in the Conseil d'Etat reached their climax. The most dramatic session of the full Conseil took place on 30 April 1806. It had originally ruled that it was impossible 'to enact a particular law for the Jews', as there was no fixed rate of interest on private or commercial loans. Noting that there was usury in regions uninhabited by Jews – and that it was in fact so widespread as to be curable only by a law 'common to the whole Empire' – the Conseil held that until such legislation was enacted, any usury blamed on the Jews had to be dealt with by the courts. Napoleon, however, worked through Molé, who belonged to Louis de Bonald's reactionary circle. Repeating the opinion of that theoretician of the *ancien régime* that the misfor-tunes of the Jews were divine retribution for their crimes, Molé placed before the Conseil on 30 April a long report recommending drastic exceptional mea-sures against them. The Conseil then heard Jean-Claude Beugnot, a middle-aged liberal, who said in substance that the Jews could either be reformed or expelled, but that 'exceptional' measures against them would be 'a lost battle on the battlefields of Justice'.

At this, according to an eyewitness, the Emperor flew into a rage: 'He rep-eated the unhappy phrase about the lost battle, and, in steadily growing excite-ment, he began to swear, something which, to my knowledge, never happened to him in the Conseil d'Etat.'[44] Beugnot, who was to serve as Minister after Napoleon's downfall, was stunned.

Napoleon silenced all further discussion, ordered Molé's report to be pub-lished in the *Moniteur*, and a few days later received its young author in private audience. On 7 May he informed the Conseil of his decision. 'The Jewish nation', he said, 'has been constituted since Moses, usurious and oppressive.' Metaphysics had misled Beugnot 'to prefer a violent measure of deportation to a more effective and milder remedy.' Neither abstract 'metaphysical laws' nor the tribunals would solve the problem in Alsace. What was needed were 'simple laws, laws of exception'. To expel the Jews would be a sign of weakness, their reform an act of strength. But he would not act in an arbitrary manner. 'The law needs a foundation. It is necessary to assemble the *états généraux* of the Jews in Paris and to hear them. I wish that a General Synagogue be held in Paris on 15 June.'[45]

This led to the so-called Assembly of Jewish Notables which, after some delays, finally held its opening session on 26 July 1806 in a hastily redecorated chapel of the former church of Saint-Jean-en-Grève behind the Hôtel de Ville. The 111 delegates from France, Italy and the Rhineland chosen by the prefects to attend had no idea of Napoleon's intentions. Several omens, though, boded ill for the Jews. In spite of the absence of a credit law making it impossible to ascertain the actual extent of Jewish usury, the Emperor in his Proclamation summoning the Assembly suspended for a year all mortgages held by Jews in 8 departements in and around Alsace before their illegality had been proved. He also insisted that the Assembly open on a Sabbath, as if to show that France did not recognize it as a religious holiday.

In Trier, Heschel Marx-Levy and his elder brother, Samuel, who had now been the town's rabbi for almost two years, knew even less what was on Napoleon's mind. All they knew was that on the left bank of the Rhine, including the Sarre departement and Trier itself, the Jews had since medieval times been restricted to petty commerce, cattle trading and money-lending; and that this area was now included in the 'suspension of all executions of judgment and bond-obligations by farmers in favour of Jews.' Some of them faced financial ruin and the rabbi was powerless to help them; the French – having inspected the books of the former Archbishopric and discovered that during the War of the First Coalition the Jews had not paid two years' cathedral and 'protection' taxes – were now tabulating these arrears and preparing to claim them from the community, with the interest since 1792.

In Paris, Molé, one of three commissars appointed by the Emperor to the Assembly of Notables, informed the Jews that Napoleon was inviting them to cooperate in fixing their fate. As 'the first Prince in the annals of Christianity' to do so, he hoped they would prove themselves worthy of the title of Frenchmen. It was only when asked to formulate answers to 12 questions, ranging from usury to polygamy and including some doctrinal ones, that they realized that Judaism and its legitimacy as a religion compatible with French civil law was to be probed. Etienne Pasquier, later president of the Chamber of Peers and Chancellor of France, who was one of the three commissars soon descried two camps among the delegates: 'the philosophers' and the rabbis. The former were mostly Portuguese or Italian lay syndics, wealthier, less religious and readier to assimilate than the minority of 15 or so rabbis. Differences of opinion did indeed develop between the two camps, but by the middle of August the Assembly, solving some of the dilemmas posed by their desire to be accepted as Frenchmen without being false to their faith, had all their answers ready.

A showdown over the question of mixed marriages was avoided by the formulation that they were not expressly forbidden but that 'the rabbis of this Assembly would be no more inclined to bless the wedding of a Christian woman with a Jew, or of a Jewess with a Christian, than Catholic priests themselves would be disposed to sanction unions of this kind.'[46] To the question whether Jewish citizens would patriotically defend France, the delegates responded spontaneously, 'Yes, unto death!' On the thorny issue of usury the Assembly, with many Bible quotations, declared that the Mosaic law forbade interest on loans to the needy but distinguished between these and 'commercial operations, where the lender runs some of the risk of the borrower and is entitled to a share of his profit.' Stating that all the Talmud 'doctors' had allowed such lawful interest even among themselves, the Assembly rejected claims that Jews charged higher interest from Gentiles. If individuals did so, would it not be 'injustice to lay the same imputation on all Christians because some of them are guilty of usury?'

Although the commissars were dissatisfied with some of the replies, both Molé and Pasquier were impressed by the rabbis. Pasquier later wrote in his Memoirs: 'One found oneself in the presence of men who were very superior to the rabble they had been identified with. Very carefully taught in their religion and in its principles, they were strengthened in their attachment to it by the reproof it attracted to them: their very cultured minds were estranged from no human knowledge.' Contrary to the commissars, the Minister of the Interior, Champagny, advised the Emperor on 20 August that the Jews had sincerely done their utmost 'to comply with Your Majesty's intentions' without prejudicing their religion.

Three days later, Napoleon decided to take in hand a new 'organization of the Jewish people' and by 18 September the summons went out for convening a Great Sanhedrin in Paris. It is not known who gave the Emperor the idea of resuscitating on French soil – nearly 19 centuries after the Romans had burned, razed and finally ploughed up Jerusalem – a dubious form of the once-august body which, eventually moving to Babylon, had gone out of the world in AD 432. The symbolism inherent in his observation that no assembly like it had met 'since the fall of the Temple' may have constituted its very attraction, bolstered by the realization – according to Pasquier – that only firm endorsement by a representative group of rabbis could lend the decisions of the 'Notables' the spiritual authority and legal sanction to make them binding on Europe's Jews.

And so Karl Marx's uncle, Samuel Marx-Levy, set out for Paris in time for the solemn opening – on 4 February 1807 – of the great conclave. Heralded as 'a miraculous turn in the history of the world', the event made Metternich, at that time Vienna's consul in Paris, call for counter-measures lest Napoleon's 'messianic' ploy beguile the Jews of Poland to help him 'liberate' that country. Indeed Napoleon, who between summoning the Sanhedrin the previous autumn and its actual opening had crushed Prussia at Jena and entered Warsaw, is said to have been well aware of the fact that, according to Jewish lore, 'the reconstitution of the Sanhedrin is associated with the coming of the Messiah.'[47]

Samuel Marx-Levy was one of 30 rabbis chosen to join the 17 already in Paris. The statutory membership of the traditional Sanhedrin being 71, the most distinguished of the Assembly of Notables were picked to bring up the number to the full complement. They were seated in a semicircle, as of old. Napoleon, however, did nothing by halves. For greater effect, though unwittingly giving away something of its character as a travesty, special costumes had been designed for the Sanhedrin's members – for the President, a tall, fur-lined two-cornered hat and a long magisterial robe with long white Geneva bands which gave Strasbourg's distinguished Rabbi Sintzheim the stern look of a Swiss Calvinist; for the rabbis, black short silk capes and Geneva bands; the laymen wore capes without Geneva bands, but were equipped with side-swords.

Although the Assembly of Notables had finished its business almost 5 months earlier, Napoleon, before leaving Paris for the wars, had ordered it not to disband. Its full plenum of more than 100 delegates – including those not involved in the proceedings of the Sanhedrin – were to remain on hand in Paris, to serve as 'the basis of the operation', the object of which was to elicit a clear statement that the French civil code took precedence over Judaic law. They were, in short, to help persuade the rabbis that any other attitude might, in the Emperor's words, lead to 'the expulsion of the Jewish people'.[48]

Since many of the delegates chosen by the prefects for their reputations as learned men hardly had the means to afford such a long stay while leaving their families unprovided for, the government agreed that they were entitled to an indemnity, but decided that it was to be raised from the Jewish communities in the form of a special tax.

The Great Sanhedrin, faced with the exigency of adjusting Judaism to the new era and a changed society, met twice a week and performed its task both expeditiously and with an air of dignity. It refused to sanction mixed marriages, but endorsed most of the answers already given to the other questions. Its main affirmation was that Judaic law contained religious as well as political principles. While the religious ones were timeless and 'by their very nature absolute and independent of the circumstances of the age', the Great Sanhedrin ruled that the political ones applied only when Israel 'possessed its own kings, pontiffs and magistrates' in its own land. It emphasized the continuity of Jewish history by stressing that its 'inalienable right to legislate according to the needs of the situation' was derived from ancient and sacred law, but enjoined on all 'obedience to the State in all matters civil and political.' In short, the Sanhedrin, acting on the Talmudic precept that 'the law of the land is the law', conceded that the Jews were not a functioning nation. It had in fact no other alternative. Napoleon was about to engage the Tsar's armies at Eylau and Friedland, and the shadow of the invincible Emperor hung over Poland and Russia, which at that time contained the largest Jewish settlement.

The proceedings of the Great Sanhedrin, which ended on 9 March 1807, were immediately published in Paris, and shortly afterwards in English translation in London and in German at Hamburg.[49] Having finished its main business in a matter of 4 weeks, the Sanhedrin expected to be consulted on the future 'organization' and legal status of the Jewish religion. But no sooner had it issued its doctrinal resolutions than it was dissolved as suddenly as it had been called. For reasons that will become apparent, Molé and the commissars preferred to discuss the future of the Jewish cult with the more enlightened leaders of the Assembly of Notables. The abrupt disbanding of the Great Sanhedrin may or may not also have been prompted by the desire to assuage the growing annoyance in some Catholic circles at Napoleon's making such a fuss about a 'detestable sect'. In fact the Sanhedrin generated more excitement in Christian circles than among the Jewish masses in Russia. There, as in Austria, the Jews continued to be treated like a rabble unfit to grace the cities, and the authorities feared that Napoleon was out to incite them against the Tsar. While Moscow's Holy Synod pronounced Napoleon's Sanhedrin an outright 'debasement of the Church', ultra-reactionary Catholic circles in Paris reputedly complained to the Pope that Napoleon was plotting an unholy alliance with world Jewry.[50]

Of the part played by Rabbi Samuel Marx-Levy in the Sanhedrin discussions, nothing is known. Letters written by its President and other members have been preserved, but none by Karl Marx's uncle has come to light. The upshot of it all is, however, known. In May 1807, the date for the suspended repayment of the loans owed to the Jews was indefinitely extended. In Rabbi Samuel's departement of the Sarre the Jews protested at having to pay the new tax imposed on them to defray the expenses of the Assembly of Notables – whose stay in Paris lasted a full 10 months – while not getting their own money back from their debtors. In Paris the chairman of the Assembly of Notables pled that 45,000 Jews in the 8 departements affected by the suspension of the debts could not be held responsible for perhaps a score of usurers who had only to be prosecuted. But the French representatives kept saying that nothing could be done while the Emperor was away.

Still, Rabbi Samuel may be assumed to have shared the general optimism of the Jewish leaders. The Sanhedrin having done its best to satisfy the new Caesar, they felt confident that it was only a question of time before he would respond with a fair solution to the problem of the loans and put an end, too, to the limbo in which the status of their cult had been left. They did not know that at the end of January, on the eve of the Sanhedrin's opening, the Emperor had sent the Minister of the Interior certain instructions, and that he had judged and condemned them long before it convened.

Napoleon's secret instructions – sent from his headquarters in Poland and received in Paris on 16 February – detailed the aims he wished to see achieved. They showed that nothing had changed in his mind since his declaration in the Conseil d'Etat in May of the previous year that the Jews were a nation 'usurious' by their very nature. His principal aim, according to the new instructions, was to save 'the countryside and some departements from the disgrace of having become vassals to the Jews.' This evil had to be stopped. He realized that it might 'not be possible to proceed by means of the law.' But he had other remedies. 'The blood of the Jews will lose its particular character when, out of every three marriages, one is between Jew and Frenchman.' Mixed marriages were so important in the Emperor's determination to assimilate the Jews by hook or by crook that 'measures must be taken to instruct, to encourage, to command in order to reach this aim.' Napoleon was far from any racial or Wagnerian ideas, but he felt that the blood of the Jews was vitiated, and 'a mass of vitiated blood can be improved only through time', just as 'good is produced slowly...' For the rest, the Mosaic law had to be purged of any national or other connotations beyond pure religious worship. As for the *modus operandi*, 'political results' could be achieved through 'civil measures', a circumlocution for administrative coercion and the 'exceptional' steps he had in mind all along.[51]

To get round the illegality of discriminating between citizens, a way had to be found to persuade the Jews themselves to ask the authorities to look into their affairs – for such purposes, say, as absolving them from the wholesale charge of usury and moral misbehaviour – thus opening the way to government intervention. Since the measures contemplated were sure to 'frighten' the rabbis, the Grand Sanhedrin had been sent home. The Assembly of Notables, in which the so-called 'philosophers' – led by the chairman, A. Furtado, a respected liberal politician, disciple of Voltaire and former vice-mayor of Bordeaux – predominated, was considered more amenable. Its members were especially sensitive to the usury issue. Having no idea that they were puppets in a larger game of Napoleon's, and with his commissars denying that he had any intention of applying special legislation to the Jews at large, they fell for the trick, and at their final session on 6 April 1807, after much heart-searching, adopted a motion in the sense desired of them. Still, the unconstitutional nature of the planned regulations caused some government hesitation, and it was not before the following spring that the blow fell.

On 17 March 1808, Napoleon signed an imperial edict barring Jews from engaging in trade without an annual certificate of 'morals' from a magistrate and a special permit. It restricted their movement across the Rhine, advised them to take up 'useful' crafts, and stopped newcomers from entering France unless they went into agriculture. While ostensibly lifting the moratorium on the debts owed to the Jews, it hedged their repayment with so many conditions and legal complexities as to practically cancel them, for the courts usually sided with the debtors. The decree also retroactively cancelled all debts owed by women, soldiers and officers to Jews if they swore they had borrowed the money without the knowledge of their husbands, officers, or commanding officers, respectively. Altogether, the decree meant practically 'an annulment of monetary obligations'.[52] It was signed by Napoleon for 10 years. Putting the Jews on probation, he expressed the pious hope that 'by virtue of these regulations, no difference whatever would [by then] remain between the Jews and the other citizens', or else the edict would be extended.

This was the 'Infamous Decree', issued 10 years before Karl Marx's birth, which his father-to-be was presently to attack. However, Heschel Marx-Levy owed his later profession as a lawyer to the fact that Napoleon had opened the doors of the universities to the Jews; paradoxically, too, his officers and administrators were at this very time engaged in running battles with various German authorities to make them concede to the Jews even the kind of 'equality' with a difference now prescribed by the Emperor. Not before he made Frankfurt a Grand Duchy in 1810 did that 'free city' abolish its ill-famed ghetto or grant its Jews a modicum of equality, and then only after it had exacted a lump sum of 440,000 florins in 'protection tax' revenue for 20 years ahead.

Napoleon's own contradictory-looking policy towards the Jews, for which he was to be compared to a man who 'began like Julius Caesar but ended like Caligula', was inspired by a genuine, if calculated, desire to ease the lot of the peasants of Alsace at somebody else's expense. He had a general aversion to merchants and financiers, regarding them all as usurers. He knew few of his Jewish subjects, and learned only later – as he was to acknowledge in a little-known letter to a Jew in Danzig – that many of them served in his armies: 'Dear sir, I love your nation,' he wrote in 1812. 'On the battlefields of Italy and the fields of Spain many a Jew gave his life for France's greatness. I entirely favour your aspiration to be given rights in Prussia too.'[53]

But there was a discernible dichotomy which Napoleon was unable to overcome. This was between his having grown up with the Enlightenment's fixed contemptible image of the Jews and his statesmanlike wish, once he recognized their vitality, to absorb them into the French nation and integrate them into his new organization of Europe. For this purpose they not only had to be re-educated, taught agriculture and useful crafts, but denationalized. With the Great Sanhedrin itself subtly conveying that Jerusalem could be rebuilt in France, Napoleon – on the same day of 17 March 1808 – issued a second decree containing his long-expected new Law for Judaism and its religious organization. The accompanying aura of a messianic 'Liberator' and 'Lawgiver' – contemporary illustrations indeed depicted the Emperor holding a copy of his reformed version of 'The Laws Given to Moses', with his other hand raising a woman representing the Jewish people, her arm on the Ten Commandments, the Temple candelabrum behind her, with admiring rabbis prostrated at his feet and Mount Sinai in the distant background – made this an ambitious imperial scheme grandiose enough for Napoleon to follow its progress in detail throughout the eventful period of his campaigns between Jena and Tilsit.

Ironically, it was under the illiberal Bourbons that France was to drop the provisions of the 'Infamous Decree'. But in 1808 Napoleon's influence extended to the Grand Duchy of Warsaw and the edict humiliated the Jews everywhere. Besides the economic damage inflicted on them – it has been estimated that 'at least one-half, if not three-fourths, of the debts due to the Jews were never paid back'[54] – their leaders felt that they had been deceived. In the event, after it was found that only 4 of the more than 2,500 Paris Jews were at all suspected of petty usury, most of the other provisions of the decree were gradually allowed to lapse into abeyance in parts of France. But the stain remained.

The form in which Napoleon 're-established' the Jewish religion had an immediate effect on the Marx-Levy family in Trier. Within a month of the two Napoleonic decrees, Rabbi Samuel Marx became *grand rabbin*, or regional chief rabbi, of the Sarre and Sambre et Meuse departements. By April of the following year, he was appointed a member of the new 'Synagogue Consistory' for the same region, one of the first 13 such consistories (together with Bordeaux, Marseilles and Turin, among others) established by Imperial Decree in December 1808, to which, by 1812, Napoleon's conquests were to add those of Florence, Rome, Amsterdam and Hamburg. Trier's 'Consistorial Synagogue' was actually the old synagogue in the garden house at the rear of 183 Weberbachstrasse.

In 1809 there was a change among the occupants of the house in front. Rabbi Samuel's widowed mother Hayya left for Amsterdam, where in September of that year she married Rabbi Moses Saul Loewenstamm. She took the youngest of her children, 9-year-old Jacob or Jacobus, with her. The house, however, did not become less crowded, or not for long. The same autumn Rabbi Samuel, at the age of 34, married Michele Marianne Brisac, the daughter of a book printer of Lunéville, and brought her back to Trier. One of Samuel's brothers, Moses, had died in 1808 at the age of 20, but Heschel, who in 1809 was 32, and three other siblings – including Esther, aged 23; Babette, 20; and Cerf (French for

Hirsch), 19 – continued to share what had been their parental home since 1788. And within a year of their marriage, Samuel's wife presented him with the first of 5 daughters.

As prescribed by Napoleon, Trier's regional Consistory comprised three laymen besides Rabbi Samuel. His brother Heschel, however, acted as its official secretary until his departure in 1810 to study law at Coblenz. One of the members of the Consistory was the physician Lion Berncastel, who later bought a vineyard in partnership with Heschel-Heinrich, and also seems to have been the family doctor. (When Karl Marx was a student in Bonn and needed a medical certificate, his father advised him, 'I can send you one by Herr Berncastel, who has been treating you.')

A Central Consistory had been established in Paris. Its members, like the Catholic prelates, took the oath of loyalty to the Emperor. The regional consistories represented the Jews with the departmental authorities. They were expected to report any 'evil' or unauthorized acts, such as private prayer services; to provide annual lists of prospective conscripts; to collect, administer and account for the taxes needed for their religious expenses; and 'by every means to encourage the Israelites' to take up 'useful professions'.

Some of the prefects saw in Rabbi Samuel Marx and other regional chief rabbis personages akin to bishops. But the government's promise to pay the rabbis' salaries, as it did those of the Catholic clergy, was not kept, and the salaries devolved on the Jewish taxpayers. Within the centralized, hierarchic and controlled consistorial system, the rabbis' role – besides conducting religious ceremonies, officiating at weddings and pronouncing divorces – was to supervise the orderly and moral behaviour of their flock and to preach submission to the laws of the Empire and to its invincible ruler.

Already in the summer after his return from the Great Sanhedrin, Rabbi Samuel Marx had conducted a service in honour of Napoleon's birthday. There was nothing remarkable about this, as eulogies to the Emperor were read in all the churches, except that Rabbi Samuel took the occasion, in line with Napoleon's wishes, to call on young Jews to learn and take up farming and manual crafts or devote themselves to the sciences.

It is a curious fact that, whereas one of Samuel's younger sons was to top his rabbinical studies with a doctorate in philosophy, his eldest son, Marc, was from the beginning trained to become a gardener. This may or may not have been Rabbi Samuel's way of setting an example to the 3,500 or so Jews living at the time in the Sarre département. More intriguing, in retrospect, is the case of Rabbi Samuel's and Heschel's second-youngest brother, Cerf Marx. Starting in 1803, when he was 13, his name had appeared regularly every year in the local 'Herald' (the *Trierer Ankündiger*) as a prize-winning pupil. For 6 years running, until he finished high school in 1808, he won first prize either in 'living languages', French, mathematics, algebra and/or natural science. This young uncle of Karl Marx – he was only 18 years older than Karl – appears, on the face of it, to have been intellectually the most gifted of his relatives. Yet, shortly after finishing high school, he was rather abruptly apprenticed to a watchmaker. He is known to have spent some time in England and France before he settled down at Aix-la-Chapelle (Aachen). In 1820 he married Henriette Meter. In 1831 the two of them, together with their 5 young daughters, converted to the Catholic faith.

In 1975, the Karl Marx Study Centre in Trier reprinted in one of its publications the text of a report on 'The Baptism of a Jew-Family on the Eve of the Holy Pentecost Feast 1831 in the Main Parish Church of St Nicholas in Aachen'. Written by the Catholic padre who had baptized Cerf Marx and his family and originally published in July of the same year, the report described the three-hour-long ceremony, emphasizing Cerf Marx's rabbinical ancestry and his scholarly potential in both 'genuine Talmudic' and secular subjects, and went on to say: 'On the advice of his family, however, he abandoned a learned career, choosing instead to practice the watchmaker's art. He did so, in that era so full of hope for his race, principally in order to disprove – as the grandson, son and brother of distinguished rabbis – the accusation that the Jews are averse to learning manual crafts and that they deal only in trade.'[55]

Karl Marx's father was thus not the only one of the family to convert. Leaving aside the 'triumphalist' tone of the report quoted, it should be noted that Cerf Marx did not convert – nor, incidentally, did Samuel's son Marc (born in 1812) become a gardener – under Napoleon, but after reactionary Prussia put an end to what, in spite of everything, had indeed been an era full of hope not only for the Jews but for other long-suffering classes in Europe. The only other thing known about Cerf Marx is that he lived impecuniously in Aachen. In 1823 he appealed to the municipality to reduce a tax of 8 Thaler, declaring that his earnings as a watchmaker hardly covered the upkeep of his family and that he was reduced to giving up his house and taking rented lodgings.[56]

In 1808, when Cerf finished high school, his brother Samuel had not been getting a regular salary for several years; he was, as far as is known, the only earner among 5 children. It is no rash assumption that Cerf's switch to watchmaking may have been dictated by financial need; or it may have been connected with his suffering, like Karl Marx himself, from a 'weak chest', as tuberculosis ran in the family. Cerf Marx died in 1831, apparently shortly after his conversion, at the age of 41.

Life went on amidst all the bloodshed, even as the tide in Europe turned and events moved to their climax in 1814. Between 13 August 1810, when Heschel witnessed a document in Trier with the signature 'H. Marx, Secrétaire du consistoire', and the first week of January 1814, his sister Esther married; Rabbi Samuel's wife gave birth to three children; and on 4 January 1814 Heschel Marx, attesting the birth certificate of the third, his niece Caroline, for the first time affixed to his name the professional designation *avoué*, lawyer. He had completed almost three and a half years of study, including his final examination, at the French law school in Coblenz, and was back in Trier.

The first document he witnessed, on 13 August 1810, was the marriage certificate of his sister Esther, who married a Bavarian-born Jew, Gabriel Kosel. Samuel Marx's first two children were a daughter, Malka, and Marc (German: Markus); the day his second daughter, Caroline, was born coincided with the French evacuation of Trier. The chief of the prefecture, Dagereau, headed with his staff for Luxembourg early next morning, followed in the afternoon by the last French troops.

The Prussian, Hessian and Russian soldiery that occupied the town or were temporarily quartered in it imposed a new and heavy burden on a populace already squeezed to the bone by the French. The Prussian commander demanded an immediate contribution of 25,000 francs for the care of his wounded, threatened to execute the mayor, and confiscated the municipal fund for the poor. In two reports, on 28 February and 10 April, Justus Grüner, the first Prussian Governor, reported 'extreme bitterness' in Trier at the brutality of Prussian and Hessian soldiers and at the requisitioning of 'enormous' quantities of food at a time of great shortage – including old Moselle wines, ham and assorted victuals for the table of the Prince of Hesse. Grüner's appeal for army volunteers met with little success, and he later blamed the behaviour of the military for alienating the Rhineland from Prussia.[57]

While the Rhineland and much of Europe were waiting to have their political future settled at the Congress of Vienna, Heschel Marx, who had turned 37, was preparing to marry. On 16 June, in the midst of the administrative confusion still reigning in Trier during this period of provisional government, he obtained a passport in which he figured for the first time as Heinrich Marx. As municipal publications, however, continued to appear in French, the marriage banns published on 7 and 14 August were to call him Henry again. Some time afterwards he left for Holland, where, on 21 September, at Nijmegen, he and his bride Henriette Pressburg signed a marriage contract before a notary.[58] The two were married on 22 November 1814 in a civil ceremony in the same Dutch town, followed by a religious wedding.

Henriette Pressburg was 26. Her father Isaac, a well-to-do and respected businessman, came of the Pressburg family of financiers, rabbis and communal leaders once headed by Simon Pressburg – the court purveyor to three Habsburg emperors – into which Heine's great-grandfather Lazarus van Geldern had married almost a century before. On her mother's side, Henriette Pressburg came from a long line of rabbis in Amsterdam and other parts of Europe. Her sister Sophie later married the banker Lion Philips, whose family were the founders of the bulb factory and latter-day Philips electronics corporation. In every respect, Heinrich Marx married into a 'good' family. Henriette's dowry was a substantial 8,100 Dutch guilders, though much of it remained tied up in Holland in the form of real estate or shares, later to be prudently administered by the banker Philips.

Heinrich Marx returned with his wife to Trier in the winter of 1814, to find a town in which, according to a complaint sent by its mayor to the Vienna Congress, 'indescribable misery' reigned as a result of the heavy burden of billeting and feeding an endless stream of troops. Other official reports soon noted that the influential part of the populace longed for Napoleon's civil code, if not for Napoleon himself.[59]

Some time at the beginning of 1815, Heinrich Marx obtained a lawyer's post at the Rhenish Appellate Court in Trier. He had not been there long, dealing with penal cases, when, on 13 June 1815, he sent to Privy Councillor von Sack, the newly appointed Governor-General of the Lower Rhineland, the document – known as his *Eingabe*, or petition – attacking Napoleon's 'Infamous Decree'. This document is presented in practically all the literature on the subject as being directly inspired by his fear of losing his post, or of being forbidden to practise law at all, on the grounds of his religion. Although this is not at all sure, the threat developed soon enough; and the three or four years that followed, in the course of which his second son, Karl, was to be born, were to turn into one long nightmare for him.

Prussia, severely truncated after the military catastrophe at Jena but since recovered through the reforms introduced by Stein and Hardenberg, had been induced at last in 1812 to follow the French example and emancipate its 30,000 Jews – after a fashion. Granted civil rights, they were to be conscripted into the army, though excluded from the officer corps; they could settle in the towns, no longer had to pay special taxes and were henceforth allowed to hold 'academic school-teaching and municipal posts'; as things turned out, however, this did not include university professors. Article 9 of the emancipation decree created another ambiguity by postponing the admission of Jews 'to other public service and government offices' to some future 'regulation by law.' Unfortunately for Heinrich Marx, lawyers fell into this wide-open category, although his personal case was to lead to some embarrassed discussions in high Prussian circles.

The background to Prussia's whole policy in the matter was a tendency to inflate to its extremity a trend already inherent in the way France had emancipated her Jews two decades earlier. There they had finally been given full equality partly on the idea, half-openly propagated by the Abbé Grégoire and shared by Mirabeau, that their emancipation would ultimately lead to their conversion. In Prussia this proposition was explicitly expressed by Wilhelm von Humboldt, the famous scientist and founder of Berlin University, while temporarily in charge of cults and education. Besides advocating emancipation on the grounds of law, he recommended a policy of 'justifiable tolerance' as best fitted to 'weaken the bonds' and 'foster schisms' among the Jews to the point where 'the Jewish hierarchy will fall apart of itself', causing its followers to 'turn towards the Christian faith'.[60]

This particular argument of the liberal Humboldt appealed to Prussia's deeply religious King Friedrich Wilhelm III and had enabled Hardenberg to 'wrest' the 1812 emancipation decree from his otherwise reluctant monarch. What the French merely hoped for and encouraged became in the 'German-Christian' state of Prussia public policy and undisguised pressure. The state let its new citizens know that they were now equal, but if they wanted to be officers, judges, lawyers or university professors, they would have to be baptized.

It is worth noting, however, that when Heinrich Marx sent his *Eingabe* to Governor von Sack no one in the Rhineland, or anywhere for that matter, knew that Prussia's king was never to keep his promise to grant a constitution. Less than a month before, on 22 May, Friedrich Wilhelm III actually repeated this pledge (which he had first made in 1810). Nor was it known that Prussia would withhold the benefits, such as they were, of its emancipation decree of 1812 from the Jews of the Rhineland. As late as May of the following year the Prussian Minister of Justice still seemed to think that it would in fact be extended to the Rhineland, or at least wrote so. It emerged only later that Prussia, the largest of the German states represented at the Vienna Congress, would deny civil rights to the Polish Jews acquired by the annexation of the Posen (Poznan) territory in the east. And the Prussian King, circumventing the government and acting through 'Royal Cabinet Orders', was arbitrarily to strip Jews in the Rhineland of the rights conferred on them by the French. Far from abrogating Napoleon's 'Infamous Decree', Prussia would in 1818 reimpose its restrictions (even as they lapsed into oblivion in France) for an indefinite time – to last, as it turned out, until 1848.

It is all the more remarkable that as early as 13 June 1815 Heinrich Marx was drawing Governor Von Sack's attention to the existence on the books of this humiliating Napoleonic decree. His letter went on to say that he found it impossible to fathom that it was 'the will' of so enlightened a king as Friedrich Wilhelm 'to permit any legal verdict' to be based on the clauses of so draconian a decree conceived by a 'tyrant'.

His *Eingabe* was not, as it is most often presented, a 'petition' pleading to be allowed to keep his post. It consisted of his letter and an attached memorandum titled 'Some Observations on the Napoleonic Decree of 17 March 1808', which he wished to publish. Before sending it to the printer he was, as was customary for a public official, requesting the Governor's approval to do so. His letter, though, contained a significant sentence saying that he would be only too 'happy' to help in any way with the process of integrating his 'co-religionists' as 'useful and worthy citizens of His Serene Majesty'. This, he submitted, could only be done by a 'paternal government', and not by discrimination. For the rest, he offered to answer any questions 'objectively and without bias'.

The memorandum itself was another matter. It was a reasoned, in places sarcastic, thesis, showing that the various clauses of the 'Infamous Decree' contradicted every principle of justice, law, morality and humanity. He was not, he wrote, submitting a formal treatise in defence of the Jews, for that 'would mean an apology'. He admitted that there might have been wrong-doers among them, but castigated the illegality of condemning the many for the faults of a few and the hypocrisy inherent in the decree – and implicitly in any Prussian intention to keep it – at a time when 'human welfare and civic-mindedness are on the tongue of every villain who has enriched himself at the expense of helpless widows and orphans, plunging decent hard-working families into misery'. And in what has been called a 'Marxist' interpretation, he wrote that it was these 'wolves in sheep's clothing', pretending to wish nothing but to 'reform' the Jews, who were 'most prejudiced against the descendants of Jacob because here and there they ran across some Jewish good-for-nothings and in all probability had to share their loot with them.'

The exact circumstances that prompted Heinrich Marx to address the Prussian Governor-General are not known. He did warn that depriving the fathers of their livelihood would ultimately turn their sons into social misfits or rebels. But there was no mention of his own job. He was in a fix, for he must have been conscious of the fact that if, as the Jews expected, Prussia extended its 1812 emancipation decree to the Rhineland, article 9 would place his post in jeopardy. There is no evidence that he had been told he was going to be dismissed – that question, ultimately to be decided by several Prussian Cabinet ministers, was to hang fire until the summer of 1816.

Indeed, his memorandum burned with a tone of moral indignation long suppressed, perhaps since the days when the Jews, including his brother Samuel, had found themselves deceived by Napoleon. At the Coblenz Law School, Heinrich Marx had specialized in the Code Napoléon. Sensitive to the moral stigma of usury placed on the Jews by the 'Infamous Decree', he could also, from his experience as secretary of the Consistory for the Sarre Departement, quote chapter and verse on the abuses of the law – such as courts delaying the repayment of debts in cases where no usury was alleged, and petty municipal 'despots' indirectly inciting the countryside by summoning its peasants to state their 'objections' to the renewal of each merchant's good-conduct certificate – which accompanied it in practice.

Heinrich Marx may have been brooding over his memorandum during the very months since October 1814 when the fate of the Jews, not only in Prussia, but in each of the states and 'free cities' about to form the German *Bund* or Confederation, had first come up for discussion among their delegates to the Congress of Vienna. The legislation applying to Jews in these states ranged from the medieval to French-imposed emancipation, and their future depended on the uniform constitution to be adopted by the new *Bund*. Hardenberg, Humboldt and Metternich generally favoured a progressive initiative, while Bavaria, Saxony and the four 'free cities' – Bremen, Frankfurt, Hamburg and Lübeck – led the anti-Jewish camp.

The Vienna Congress held its closing session on 9 June 1815. The *Bund* of German states, which emerged from it within the new settlement of Europe, set up a Federal Diet at Frankfurt. But since its member-states remained autonomous, it left to the discretion of each individual sovereign the granting of a constitution to his subjects. In a mockery of liberalism, Germany was thus restored to the rule of reactionary, or at best, conservative monarchs strengthened by working in concert.

On 10 June, paragraph 16 devoted to the Jews in the constitution of the new German Confederation was resolved. The paragraph charged the Federal Diet to consider their 'civic improvement, and in particular ways of securing to them the enjoyment of civic rights' in return for accepting civic duties. There followed a crucial phrase: 'Until then the members of this religion will have safeguarded for them the rights which have already been granted to them by the individual states of the Confederation.'

Three days later – less than a week, as it happened, before the Battle of Waterloo – Heinrich Marx sent off his *Eingabe*. There is no knowing whether he had any idea that in the original version adopted by the Congress the last line of the above paragraph read 'in the individual states of the Confederation'; or that at the last minute Friedrich von Gentz, the capable but corruptible Secretary of the Congress or 'Secretary of Europe', had fraudulently substituted 'by' for 'in'. By these means he provided a loophole for all but three of the more than 30 German states now federated in the Bund to postpone or revoke Jewish equality on the grounds that, even where they enjoyed it under Napoleon, it had not been granted by their own governments.

Gentz is said to have worked in cahoots with Bremen's Senator Smidt; and Metternich and the other leaders of the Congress are believed to have over-looked his machinations because of their wish not to delay the final resolutions.[61] The result was that the lot of the Jews, instead of being 'improved', was actually worsened in most parts of Germany. The city of Hamburg hastened to curtail the Jews' previous rights; Lübeck actually expelled all its Jewish families; and the King – notwithstanding the fact that his country was one of the three (besides Baden and Mecklenburg) which of their own initiative had proclaimed Jewish civil rights – found ways of withdrawing with one hand what he had given with the other.

Prussia entered the new age with 18 different statutes for its 124,000 Jews in the various parts of its newly aggrandized territory. It was not fully to emancipate them before 1869, and the other German states – now comprising between them 300,000, or 1.25 per cent of the Bund's total population of 24 million – did not act at all before the foundation of the Reich in 1871.

In September 1815, while Heinrich Marx's professional future remained uncertain pending a survey of the judicial personnel in the Rhineland, Harry Heine travelled with his father to Frankfurt, the nastiest of the 4 'free cities' in its treatment of the Jews, a number of whom, registered as bankers or 'merchants dealing in money exchange', had helped to turn the city into Germany's chief trading centre. Now Frankfurt was trying to herd them back into the ghetto; but as the Federal Diet opposed the move, the City Senate excluded them from certain quarters, restricted their occupations and otherwise hampered their lives at every step. Because of the general economic crisis and the fact that his father was virtually bankrupt, Harry Heine, at the age of 17, was apprenticed to the reputable banking house of B.N. Rindskopf, where he lasted only three weeks. Next, he unenthusiastically went to work in a large grocery store. He loved the odours of the various spices, but was dismissed after a month for day-dreaming over acc-ounts and exchange bills. His impression of the famous Frankfurt Fair was to be summed up in the remark that in 'the big stores, Christian as well as Jewish, you buy ten per cent below factory price and are cheated just the same.'

In a reading-room in Frankfurt, Harry caught a glimpse of Ludwig Börne, his admired counterpart and later rival among German political writers. Börne came from an old-established and influential banking family. His grandfather, among other services to the Empress Maria Theresa, had been instrumental in helping one of her sons to be appointed Prince-Elector of the Archbishopric of Cologne, and his father had represented the Frankfurt Jews at the Vienna Congress. Börne held a doctorate in political science, having studied at Halle, Heidelberg and

Giessen universities. Since 1811, he had worked as an actuary in Frankfurt's police department, but wrote theatre reviews and *feuilletons* which had made him famous enough to be pointed out to Harry by his father.

About the time Heine saw him, Börne was dismissed from his post in the police. In 1818 he launched *Die Waage*, a periodical written mostly by himself, in which – in a genre new to Germany – he infused his essays on art and literature with such biting social and political criticism that he became the scourge of Metternich's reactionary policies. In May 1819 Gentz declared *Die Waage* to be 'the wittiest material written since the days of Lessing',[62] and Metternich, the most powerful man in Central Europe, secretly tried to entice Börne (through his father) to settle in Vienna on attractive terms: Börne was to be granted the rank and income of an Imperial Councillor, without any strings attached. Free to write whatever he pleased, he was to be his own and only censor. Börne's father urged him to 'go to Vienna at my expense at last for a few months' experiment and not to miss the chance of your life...'[63]

Börne, however, would not hear of it. Besides raging against Metternich, the 'prince of darkness' who was blocking the emancipation of Germany, of Austria's oppressed national minorities and of the destitute lower classes, Börne raved at the Rothschilds for financially backing the monarchs, and mocked Goethe for his self-indulgent life as a courtier and his 'indifferentism' to the monstrous social and political conditions of the age.

In 1818, in order to remove any suspicion that his championship of human freedom was in any way motivated by self-interest, Börne converted to Lutheranism. But with his enemies constantly reminding him of his origin, he never forgot the *ungeheurer Judenschmerz* ('the great Jewish sorrow') caused by 18 centuries of persecution. In 1821, under mounting pressure from the authorities, Börne was forced to give up *Die Waage*. Later he moved to Paris, where he became the leader of the German political émigrés and a revolutionary 'tribune', returning to Germany on only one occasion, to address a huge political rally. A man of unbending character, outwardly cool but inwardly seething with a passion against tyranny – and a burning, if naive, hope that America, the melting-pot of nations, would show Europe the way towards a world in which all differentiation between man and woman, serf and lord, poor and rich, Jew and Christian, would disappear[64] – his *Letters from Paris* and other writings were to make him the idol of Germany's radical intelligentsia and to have an impact on German political literature for which the ghetto street where he lived as a child would one day be renamed Börnestrasse.

Harry Heine returned to Düsseldorf after an absence of two months. He had proved to his mother that he had no head for business, but at 18 he was a somewhat confused youth on the verge of manhood, troubled and uncertain about his future. Later on, he was to have new experiences in Hamburg and to dine at his Uncle Salomon's house with Fieldmarshal Blucher of Waterloo fame.

But it was to take a couple of years more and the chauvinist agitation launched by two Teutomaniac professors, Ruhs of Berlin and Fries of Heidelberg – culminating in the latter's proto-Nazi demand to extirpate the Jews 'root and branch' – for young Heine fully to grasp that he might be personally affected by the outcome of the first international discussion of the 'Jewish Question' at the Vienna Congress.

Heine was to write little about Frankfurt. But as that city's patrician Senate continued to permit only 15 Jewish marriages a year and to enforce other medieval regulations well into the 19th century, it is little wonder that he was later to place the 'Frankfurt Jews' next to the Irish, Greeks and West Indian Blacks as a pointed epitome of the situation of the world's oppressed peoples awaiting the most urgent task of the age: emancipation.

On 13 October 1815 Heinrich Marx's wife Henriette bore a son who was given the name Maurice David. The family lived at No. '55 1/2' in Trier's Liebfrauenstrasse, and Heinrich Marx had yet to receive an answer to his *Eingabe*. There is no record of his ever receiving one, or permission to print his memorandum. Its text was only to be published, together with his letter, more than a century later.[65]

In or before April 1816, he was personally interviewed by Christoph Wilhelm Sethe, President of the Provincial Supreme Court in Düsseldorf. At the time, Sethe was heading a Royal Commission in charge of introducing the Prussian legislation in the Rhineland, and stopped in Trier on a tour of inspection of all Rhenish judicial institutions and personnel. On 23 April, he reported to the Minister of Justice that the judicial personnel included three Jewish individuals: 'The first is the lawyer Heinrich Marx.' The two others were a bailiff and a court clerk in two different regions. Of Marx, Sethe mentioned that both the president and the chief prosecutor of Trier's Appellate Court had 'high praise' for him and that his personal file characterized him by the following attributes: 'wide-ranging erudition; very industrious; eloquent; absolute integrity.' Sethe himself had been 'favourably' impressed by him. Since then, he had read a paper submitted by the lawyer Marx to the governor's office in Aachen. It showed 'erudition and a good head.'

Sethe, who was later to become President of the High Court of Appeals in Berlin, then delivered himself of a piece of legal reasoning. Under French law the three Israelites concerned had been eligible for public office. Assuming as he did 'with certainty' that the Prussian emancipation decree of 1812 would be instituted in the Rhineland, he could not disregard their disqualification from such office under Article 9. 'But these three Israelites obtained their posts legally. When they chose their profession they trusted the law which did not exclude them from state offices; to deprive them of their vocation will render them breadless.' Sethe also did not hesitate to mention that His Prussian Majesty had 'unreservedly given his royal word' that all officials whose conduct was without blemish would be left in their posts. Noting that there had never been a complaint against the three persons involved, 'on the contrary all official certificates speak highly of them', he carefully suggested a 'decree of exception which must come from his Majesty.' In his actual recommendations he singled out Heinrich Marx, proposing a decree appointing him a *Justizkommissarius*, or attorney-at-law.

Sethe's intercession on behalf of Marx was to be of no avail. On 4 May 1816 the Prussian Minister of the Interior, von Schuckmann, declared that the Jews in the former French territories could 'not be considered fit for public office', and that the latter term included lawyers. Concurring with him, the Minister of Justice, von Kircheisen, wrote to Sethe on the same day that he wished 'to settle this affair without attracting public attention, but within the framework of the law.' The claim of the three individuals concerned to eligibility for state office only held good so long as the French law applied. As it was sure to be replaced by the laws of Prussia, including its 1812 emancipation decree, he could not see his way to exempting the three from the disqualification in Article 9 of that edict.[66]

Since in the event the emancipation decree was not to be extended to cover the Rhenish Jews, the practical result was that, while they were denied its benefits (i.e., civil rights), its restrictions were applied to them.

Heinrich Marx was now in a corner, under threat not only of losing his post but his livelihood as well. The possibility that stared him in the face was that Prussia would not allow him to practice at all unless he changed his religion. But it is not known whether he was actually ever dismissed, or when. Nor is the date of his conversion to Protestantism known. In 1816 Trier's tiny Protestant population numbered no more than 161 souls and its baptisms were performed by Catholic priests. It was only in July 1817, a year or so after the arrival of a Prussian regimental chaplain, that they joined some army personnel to found Trier's first Evangelical church community. Its baptismal register, started in 1818, has no record of Heinrich Marx's baptism, only an entry made in 1824 – on the occasion of the baptism of his 6-year-old son Karl and his 6 other children – mentioning that their father had 'previously' converted.

It was long thought that Heinrich Marx was baptized by the regimental chaplain Mühlenhoff some time between May 1816 and August 1817. However, on the basis of certain documents discovered in the 1960s and 1970s, it is now believed that his conversion may have taken place as late as the second half of 1819. The question of how to give legal form to the unwillingness of Prussia's ruler to grant the Jews in the newly acquired territories civil rights, or to admit even those of old Prussia to public office, preoccupied its statesmen and officials for an exceedingly long time. 'Due to the state's aspiration to lead the Jews into the Christian fold', their condition was to a large extent decided by arbitrary means 'outside the sphere of formal law'.[67] Thus, with few exceptions, none was admitted to the legal profession or allowed to lecture at universities, long before the paragraph permitting Jews to hold 'academic school-teaching posts' in the King's own 1812 emancipation decree was revoked in 1822 and they were simultaneously excluded from serving as judges, lawyers or pharmacists.

As for Heinrich Marx and the two other Jewish lawyers on the staff of the courts in the Rhineland, it would seem that they were kept in limbo for an excruciating 4 years, since the day in 1815 when Marx, rightly reading the omens, had sent off his *Eingabe*.

President Sethe's 1816 report on Heinrich Marx strikingly anticipated the oral family tradition and all later testimonies portraying him as a highly cultured man and a talented, dedicated lawyer. Born in French Sarrelouis, and later studying law under the French at Coblenz, Marx had broken out of the confining rabbinical world of the 'synagogue house' in the Weberbachgasse, situated in Trier's former ghetto, and had obtained his 'entry ticket to European culture' much earlier than Heine, whose senior he was by some 20 years. Under the influence of the French Enlightenment and its beginnings in Germany during the last quarter of the 18th century, he had come to believe in a rationalist world of tolerance, humanism, justice, equality and scientific progress. Racine, Rousseau and Voltaire, Lessing, Kant and Schiller, Leibniz and Newton were his favourite authors, not to forget John Locke, who as early as 1689 had declared that no one ought to be denied civil rights 'because of his religion'.

Whether or not the philosophy of the Enlightenment 'took the place of the Torah and the Talmud in his life', as has been colourfully suggested,[68] one is struck by the fact that his adoption of the secular culture went hand in hand with a deep and prolonged involvement in Jewish communal affairs. His memorandum against Napoleon's 'Infamous Decree' bristled here and there with practically Voltairean shafts against the abuses of power and the illegalities and 'inhumanity' inspired by sheer prejudice. But it was also, in spite of his denials, a *plaidoyer* for his 'co-religionists'. It was in their name that he wrote: 'Thanks to the Almighty, we have, in spite of everything, remained men. We never sank down to the level of helots.' And without mentioning the word 'Jews', he added that a people that 'did not degenerate after such long oppression carries the unmistakable stamp of noble humanity; in its bosom it harbours ineradicable

149

seeds of virtue, and its spi–rit is animated by a divine spark.' In other ways, the memorandum was the work of a man with a distinct social conscience and a developed feeling of communal responsibility.

Familiar as he was with the ups and downs of the Jewish condition at every frenzied stage since the French Revolution, Heinrich Marx could justly write in the short letter accompanying his *Eingabe*: 'Through bitter experience in my not altogether easy career, I have learned the true origin of many a deep-rooted prejudice.' Yet for all his experience, there was something he simply could not fathom. He could not imagine that Friedrich Wilhelm III – who in 1815, after making a public promise that army volunteers would be entitled to certain civil benefits irrespective of their religion, refused pensions to Jewish war widows – had no intention of 'paternal government' for Prussia, certainly not as far as the Jews were concerned; or that von Schuckmann – one of the three Ministers in charge of deciding their future after the Vienna Congress – would declare that he personally knew 'some Jews who are upright and respectable', but that collectively their character was nevertheless one of 'cunning knavery', and 'no self-respecting people with a pronounced national spirit' like the Germans 'can accept them as their equals.'

Nor, and perhaps least of all, could Marx, with his legalistic mind, conceive of Prussia's adopting a state policy based, in the words of another of these Ministers, Wohlfart, on 'facilitating the conversion of the Jews to the Christian religion, and with this all civil rights are tied up.' Wolfahrt explained that he would prefer 'not to have any Jews in the country at all, but since we have them, we must be tireless in our efforts to make them harmless.'[69]

This was the brute reality that confronted Heinrich Marx during the lengthening years of mixed hope and despair before all avenues bar conversion were finally closed in his face. It must have been a traumatic time for a gentle but ambitious man. He may have felt bitter at the thought that the Jews, having been the first to settle in the towns built by the Romans in the Rhineland, had been in Trier before the Germans. But, except for the general circumstances, no document has been preserved to reveal the depth of his feelings or how painfully he wrestled with his conscience. The only thing that can be safely said is that he converted neither out of atheism nor out of his free will. Although he eventually had his entire family baptized, he seems, according to the register of the Trier's Protestant community, to have attended holy communion only once.[70]

His only significant reference to religion shows the strong influence of the Enlightenment's shallow deism and its belief in man's intrinsic goodness, morality and reason: 'A great support for morality', he was to write to his son Karl in a typical Enlightenment vein, 'is pure faith in God... There are moments in life when even the atheist is involuntarily drawn to worship the Almighty... for what Newton, Locke and Leibniz believed, everyone... can submit to.' While this was written long after his conversion under duress, the question of what, if any, elements of 'self-contempt' or 'self-hate' arising from 'Jewish guilt' – in short, elements of his personal alienation – he passed on to his son is more complex. Besides the phrase already mentioned that hints at his estrangement from his own father, Heinrich Marx left only one other pointer in his extant papers. In the winter of 1816–17, he submitted to the Royal Commission, headed by President Sethe, a proposal for the establishment of commercial courts in the Rhineland. When the Commission recommended its publication, he requested that his name and any details identifying him as its author be removed.

'Unfortunately', he explained,

> my circumstances are such that as a paterfamilias I am compelled to be rather careful. The sect to which nature has chained me is, as known, not held in particularly high esteem. Nor is the local province renowned for its tolerance. Having had to swallow many a bitter pill and almost entirely exhausted my modest fortune waiting for people to find it possible to believe that even a Jew may have some talent and integrity, I hope it will not be held against me that I have become rather wary of my steps.[71]

This offers a glimpse of the local atmosphere, added to the pressure of Prussia's anti-Jewish policy, under which Heinrich Marx finally caved in. It shows a touch of the old sarcasm, but also a torn and intimidated man, his pride bent or broken, reduced by concern for his livelihood to caution and faint-hearted petty diplomacy.

5

The Leaders of Europe after the Congress of Vienna; Heine in Love; Saint-Simon and Other Utopians

On 4 June 1815, Tsar Alexander I established his headquarters at Heilbronn, a small town in Württemberg. It was 5 days before the Congress of Vienna closed, but the Tsar had left the diplomats to draft the resolutions to be embodied in its Final Act. The battle of Waterloo lay two weeks ahead. But Russian troops, advancing in all haste from the far end of Prussia, still had a long way to go to reach the position on the Rhine assigned to them.

'My first action', the Tsar later confessed to Countess Edling, the Tsarina's lady in waiting, 'was to open the Holy Book which I have always with me, but my mind could not grasp the sense of what I was reading. My thoughts were incoherent, my heart was oppressed. I put the book aside and started to think what a relief it would have been for me at such a time to have a real talk with a person who would be in spiritual unity with me. This thought made me recall you and what you told me about Madame de Krüdener as well as my desire communicated to you to meet her. "Where is she?" I asked myself, "and how could I meet her? Probably never!"'

At that moment there was a knock at the door and Prince Volkonsky announced a lady who insisted on seeing the Tsar. 'He said it was Madame de Krüdener,' Alexander recalled years later. 'Imagine my surprise! I thought I was dreaming... I received her immediately and she addressed me, as if she were reading my very soul, with strong and consoling words, which calmed the troubled thoughts that had been torturing me for ever so long. Her appearance proved to be a real benefit to me and I promised myself to continue this acquaintance, which was of such obvious importance to me.'

If Alexander felt a sudden need for her spiritual company, the Baltic-born Baroness Barbara Juliana von Krüdener had known for some time that 'the Lord' would grant her 'the joy of seeing the Emperor', for she had a multitude of things to tell him about himself and his 'mission'.

Alexander had arrived at Heilbronn weary from the pomp and glitter and political bargaining over the spoils of war at the Congress of Vienna. Napoleon's flight from Elba, followed by his triumphal reception in Paris in March 1815 at the start of the 'Hundred Days', had spurred the Congress –

which had been 'dancing, but not advancing' for months – to speed up its business.

Talleyrand had found the Tsar much less 'affectionate' in Vienna than he had been the previous year in liberated Paris. Indeed, a change seemed to have come over the usually diplomatic Alexander. He had danced with inimitable charm at the nightly balls and fetes in Vienna, but was shockingly high-handed in his discussions with his allies. He was fully determined to reunite Poland and to grant it a constitution under his personal sovereignty, not only because he had promised – or because his one-time Swiss tutor, La Harpe, and his Polish friend, Prince Czartoryski, were among the advisers he had brought to Vienna – but because he felt he was in justice entitled to some reward for all he had done to rid Europe of the scourge of Napoleon. He also felt that Prussia, having suffered so much, should be given Saxony, which had backed the Corsican. His overbearing and irascible manner enabled Talleyrand, a wizened figure stooping about the Congress on 'crooked legs', to drive a wedge between the allies.

'The coalition is destroyed,' France's master-diplomat triumphantly reported to Paris. Playing on England's and Austria's fears that a restored Poland under the Tsar's sovereignty would greatly increase his power, he had indeed got them to sign a secret treaty against Russia. Napoleon, finding its text in the Tuileries – King Louis XVIII forgot it on his desk in his hasty flight – promptly sent it to the Tsar. Alexander fumed, but gritted his teeth. Firm in his resolve to give Europe's 'evil genius' no quarter, he showed the document to Metternich in the presence of a witness, tore it up and addressed the embarrassed Chancellor with the words: 'Metternich, as long as we live neither of us shall mention this. Napoleon has returned, and our alliance must be stronger than ever.'

And so in the end the Tsar, after more haggling in Vienna, had to be satisfied with getting only the larger part of the Grand Duchy of Warsaw. As Cracow became an independent republic, and another piece went to Prussia, Poland was again partitioned. Austria regained Lombardy and Venetia. Prussia got a large chunk of Saxony as well as the Rhineland. Spain and the Two Sicilies were restored to their two Bourbon kings.

At Heilbronn, Alexander, the frustrated 'saviour of Europe', smarting from the way his promises, plans and ambitions had been foiled by his treacherous allies, may have been nervous at the thought that his army would be too late for Waterloo and the final contest with Napoleon. But already during his triumphal visit to Paris in 1814, the Tsar had vainly sought peace for his 'tortured' mind by visiting Jung-Stilling, 'the high priest of pietist occultism', who had high-placed followers all over Europe. Ever since the fire of Moscow had 'lit up' his soul, Alexander was a prey to religious fervour and read the Bible twice a day, but had no peace of mind. It has been calculated that during a 10-year period the Tsar dined with Prince Alexander N. Golitsyn, another mystic, '3,635 times, which is almost every day', and as one of his own generals was to observe not long after his meeting with the Baroness Krüdener, his thoughts, even when he was dancing, seemed to wander to 'objects far removed' from the women who had 'captured his attention'.[1]

Baroness von Krüdener (1764–1824) is known to us by an Angelika Kauffmann portrait in the Louvre, depicting her and her son as 'Venus disarming Cupid'. In 1790 she had abandoned her husband, who was the Russian Ambassador to Copenhagen and later Berlin, for a French cavalry officer. Widowed at the age of 38, widely travelled, acquainted with Europe's best society, she had lived extravagantly before her 'conversion' by an occultist shoemaker who was a member of the Moravian Brethren. Initiated into the mysteries by Jung-Stilling himself, whose influence had spread from the court of Baden to those of St Petersburg and Stockholm (the Tsar's wife Elisabeth Alexeyevna was a Baden princess, as was that of Sweden's Gustav Adolph IV), Madame Krüdener had spent a decade or so travelling across the Continent from one pietist visionary and prophet of the millennium to another – the peasant Adam Müller at Königsberg, Pastor Fontaines in the Vosges, the mystic draper Weggelin at Strasbourg, Pastor Oberlin at Waldbach, Empeytaz at Geneva and other miracle-makers – until she felt that she herself was one of 'the elect' through whom the Second Coming of Christ would be announced. Not only Russia's, Sweden's and Baden's ruling families, but Prussia's Friedrich Wilhelm III and many of Europe's other princes were – or had, in reaction to the prolonged wars, become – believers in the millennium, feeling that Napoleon was the Antichrist. The appearance of a comet in 1811 was taken as a sign that the days were near when he would be destroyed by a man arising 'from the north... from the rising of the sun', according to Isaiah XLI:25.

During the Congress of Vienna, Baroness Krüdener, who knew Princess de Sturdza, a sister of the Tsarina's Rumanian lady-in-waiting, told her that she had much to tell the Tsar about his destiny. Indeed, for 11 years the Baroness had been sitting on the secret – first revealed to her by Adam Müller – that Isaiah's prophecy was about to be fulfilled. At the beginning of 1815 she moved to Baden, at a time when the Tsarina was in Karlsruhe with her family. The pietist Tsarina thought that the prophetess's spiritual powers might well help to calm the Emperor's troubled mind. But with Napoleon on the loose after Elba, no interview could be arranged. On the day in June 1815 when Alexander arrived at Heilbronn, Madame Krüdener was at Schlüchtern nearby. That very night she presented herself at his residence. To the Tsar, brooding over the Bible, she appeared to be sent by Providence.

She talked to him for three hours. Speaking as one who had been a great sinner herself but now had a sacred duty, she told him that he had to humble himself more before Christ, quoted amply from Scripture, and otherwise, according to all reports, raised his spirit with such 'magic' or appropriate words that the agitated Tsar was moved to tears. He asked to see more of her and a week later, at his new headquarters in Heidelberg, spent most of his evenings unburdening his soul to her.

On 7 July the Allies made their second entry into Paris; King Louis XVIII, following 'in their baggage', as it were, returned to the Tuileries next day; and while the Tsar this time took up his residence at the Elysée Palace, Baroness Krüdener was lodged at the adjoining Hôtel Montchenu, enabling him to slip through a private connecting door to the prayer-meetings she held every evening.

Alexander's army had been too late for Waterloo, but once Napoleon finally took up residence in Saint Helena in August, the Tsar marked his part in the Corsican's undoing in a twofold manner. On 10 September, in a huge demonstration of his military power, more than 100,000 Russian infantrymen paraded in perfect step past the Austrian Emperor, the King of Prussia and an admiring Wellington; and on the 11th – in the same open valley near the Marne across which Cossack regiments had thundered the day before – an Orthodox Te Deum was celebrated before the massed troops, the fervour of the chanting rising to heaven from 7 altars touching the emotions of all beholders. Present on both occasions was Madame Krüdener, whose religious seances in Paris, conducted with the assistance of two other evangelists and a female oracle, Marie Kummer, now attracted Chateaubriand, Madame Récamier, Benjamin Constant and other Paris celebrities. It was in this atmosphere that Alexander suddenly felt an urge for that 'act of adoration', as he described it to Madame Krüdener, which led to the birth of the Holy Alliance. Having drafted this unprecedented diplomatic document, establishing a pact among monarchs under the sign of the Gospels, he reputedly showed it to her and explained that he wished the Emperor of Austria and the King of Prussia to join him in a public act that would make it clear for all to see 'that we, like the Eastern Magi, confess the supreme power of God the Saviour.'[2]

Dismissed by Castlereagh as 'a piece of sublime mysticism and nonsense', the document, to which the Prussian King enthusiastically and the Austrian Emperor somewhat reluctantly added their signatures on 26 September 1815 (other European sovereigns, with three exceptions, signed it later), declared that the monarchs and princes undertook to be guided solely, both internally and in their foreign affairs, by 'the precepts of holy religion, namely, the rules of Justice, Christian Charity and Peace'. Britain's Prince Regent, the future

George IV, concurred in the 'sacred maxims' expressed, but withheld his signature on constitutional grounds; Pius VII declared that the Papacy 'needed no new interpretation' of Christian truths; and the Sultan, not being Christian, was excused for not signing.

'A sort of new code of international law' had been in Alexander's mind for at least 11 years. As early as 1804, when discussing the Third Coalition with Pitt, the idealistic young Tsar had proposed that once 'the tyrant' was brought down, the liberated nations of Europe should join in a compact committing themselves to preserve peace and 'to begin no war without exhausting every means of mediation by a third power'. Precisely how this idea became transmuted into a 'brotherhood of monarchs' invoking God, the Holy Trinity, 'the Word of the Most High, the Word of Life' for a structure mixing internal as well as external government policies with religion has never been determined. Although scholarly opinion is divided as to the extent of Baroness Krüdener's influence on the Tsar – some authors hold that it has been exaggerated, others that it was 'considerable'[3] – Europe's mightiest monarch had been relying for months on her moral support and spiritual sustenance, and the religious hothouse atmosphere she provided may well have bred his impulse to invest a major project like the Holy Alliance with that divine sanction which he now increasingly sought for all his acts.

When Krüdener overplayed her hand, however, claiming that she had inspired the whole idea, Alexander politely got rid of her. He gave her a passport to Russia and she left Paris for Switzerland in mid-October 1815. Five years later, when she turned up in St Petersburg and began to prophesy a new mission for the Tsar 'on behalf of Christendom', Alexander refused to receive her, and she never saw him again.

The Tsar had asked that the Holy Alliance be kept secret for the moment. The Allies signed the Second Peace of Paris on 20 November 1815, and on the same day laid the seed for the birth of the 'Concert of Europe' by concluding the Quadruple Alliance. Designed to enforce the temporary occupation of France and to prevent any further attempts to unseat the Bourbons (after the lesson of the Hundred Days), this new treaty between victorious Russia, Austria, Prussia and Britain contained an innovative article providing for the sovereigns of the 4 powers to congregate at fixed intervals in order to discuss 'the most salutary' measures for 'the maintenance of peace in Europe'. This was to breed the new diplomacy of the 'Congress System'.

Finally, the Tsar chose Christmas Day 1815 – 6 January 1816 by the Russian calendar – to announce his Holy Alliance in a resounding manifesto proclaiming in gist that the truths and 'wisdom of God, made known in his revelation', henceforth assured the peace and prosperity of nations. Five weeks earlier, on

27 November, Alexander, having kept his promise to restore the Kingdom of Poland, had entered Warsaw in triumph and approved a liberal constitution granting individual freedom, press freedom and full independence under his own rule. The Polish standard went up on the royal castle to the ringing of bells and great outpourings of popular enthusiasm. In 1816 the Tsar emancipated the Estonian serfs, and when the rest of the Baltic provinces followed suit and released their peasants, he praised them for 'setting an example that ought to be imitated'.

As for Russia's own serfs, Alexander had spoken of liberating them ever since 1807, when he had said that serfdom kept his country in a 'state of barbarism', adding grandiloquently that 'if civilization were more advanced, I would abolish this slavery even if it were to cost my head.'[4] He continued to cherish the idea, and even commissioned several plans for abolishing serfdom, but did nothing to implement them. Unable to overcome the autocratic tradition to which he was heir, he dismissed the voluntary proposal of a group of noblemen to ease the lot of the serfs on the grounds that he was the empire's 'sole legislator'. He made countless utterances in favour of constitutional government – at one point, in Warsaw, even holding up the Polish Diet as a model for 'showing my own country what I have long been preparing for it' – but seemed incapable of mustering the necessary resolve for applying in his own retrograde empire what he preached abroad.[5]

The Tsar was now a weary man. As he later told two leading English Quakers, William Allen and Stephen Grellet, who visited him in St Petersburg, he had conceived the Holy Alliance after spending 'many sleepless nights grieving over the innumerable calamities and misfortunes caused by war.' Unburdening his soul to the two Friends after praying and meditating with them for several hours, he said that he had jumped from bed to draft the document, 'possessed' by the idea of abolishing bloodshed forever. This anxiety, coupled with his view of Russia's imperial interests, made Alexander from 1816 onwards devote whatever energy he had left from his mystic preoccupations to securing the peace of the Continent, which – with student unrest in Germany, and revolts brewing in Spain and Portugal, and soon in Naples and Sardinia – was indeed precarious.

On 18 October 1817, some 500 students from 8 German universities converged on Wartburg Castle, where Luther had taken refuge from his persecutors. The rally was intended to celebrate the fourth anniversary of the liberation of the 'fatherland' from the yoke of Napoleon at the Battle of Leipzig, but 1817 also marked the third centenary of the Reformation. Marching through the town of Eisenach – where they later attended a church service and staged a gymnastic display – the students went up to the castle and listened to various addresses. Jena's Professor J.F. Fries, speaking in the ancient Knights' Hall, launched the slogan: 'One God, one German sword, one German spirit for honour and justice.' The rally culminated in a torchlight procession and an auto-da-fé at which the Code Napoléon as well as the Vienna Congress Act establishing the German Bund and a multitude of other books and pamphlets were thrown into the flames.

It was a patriotic outburst by young people, some of them ex-soldiers of the 'War of Liberation', ardent with the desire to wipe out the shame of Germany's having succumbed for so long to foreign domination. Many in the so-called *Burschenshaften*, or student fraternities, were followers of the famous *Turnvater* Jahn, an obscure peasant who, preaching a return to the old Teutonic virtues, had fashioned a huge nationalist youth movement cultivating 'physical fitness' in thousands of gymnastic clubs. Romanticism, anti-French ideas, anti-Semitism and what the historian Treitschke called a perennial German yearning 'for the simplicity of primitive life' had combined to make 'the sons of a cultured people worship a barbarian as their master'. Not only the sons, but the fathers, too – for the Universities of Jena and Kiel conferred on Jahn (who, among other things, proposed to keep Germany safe from foreign influences by surrounding her with an impenetrable forest housing starving wild beasts) the degree of doctor *honoris causa*.

Other students, fired by the ideas of Moritz Arndt and by Fichte's message that the Germans were a superior 'primal people' (*Urvolk*) destined for great things, dreamed of a 'mighty fatherland' and the glories of a reconstituted German empire. The rest were a heterogeneous lot, including progressive libertarian and even cosmopolitan enthusiasts who wanted a change in line with the times, away from the former provincialism of Germany's petty states. Uniting them all was a deep dissatisfaction with the way the sovereigns and diplomats at the Vienna Congress had left Germany fragmented – 5 kingdoms, 8 grand duchies, 9 duchies, 11 princedoms and 4 free cities, not counting the Austrian empire – under the cover of a sham federation which was actually a pact in which Austria had confirmed the sovereignty of the rulers of these units, but not the sovereignty of their peoples.

The students burned the Vienna Congress Act in imitation of Luther's burning of a Papal bull, but also because hardly any of the German states had granted the constitutions provided for in Article 13 of the Act, and the few that had done so had promulgated 'antediluvian' charters favouring the nobility and the clergy. 'A gigantic fraud', the writer Joseph Görres raged at the Vienna settlement. He and a number of intellectuals recalled that Alsace and Lorraine had once been German and felt bitter that Prussia, instead of taking up the cause of

German nationalism and *Lebensraum*, had allowed Russia in Poland and Britain in Hanover 'to drive a sharp wedge into Germany'. The Austrian-led German Bund, Görres felt, seemed more concerned with assuring the peace of France and 'the rebirth of Africa' than with 'the rebirth of its own fatherland'. France had indeed been admitted to the Quadruple, now the Quintuple, Alliance, but this – Friedrich von Gentz answered Görres in an article – had not been done 'from any false tenderness, but from obvious self-interest'. The common welfare of Europe required self-control, restraint and sometimes sacrifices. This, he declared, was a mature approach, and anything that undermined the striving for 'perpetual peace' was an obstacle to be removed.

Gentz, who like Talleyrand had collected quite a few bribes at the Vienna Congress, and on the same principle (accepting them only when the intercessions demanded of them did not conflict with their own views), was a highly perspicacious observer. The Holy Alliance, he remarked, was a farce, but it might prove 'more valuable than so many other farces of our time that have led to nothing but disasters.' Nor had it taken him long to realize that there was more to Jahn's 'physical fitness' slogan than mere gymnastics. Jahn's youth movement attracted boys from the aristocracy who ate, exercised and otherwise mixed with the sons of commoners. This in itself was an intolerable breach of the social order. 'Gymnastics is a suppurating abscess,' Gentz declared. 'It has to be removed before undertaking a thorough cure.'

The sensational Wartburg auto-da-fé prompted Metternich, the architect of the policy of 'equilibrium' – a concept, of which Gentz was the theorist, implying that any unrest, commotion, change, move or even any new idea threatening to upset the national or international balance must be nippped in the bud – to intervene with the government of Weimar. Inquiry followed upon inquiry, and eventually an Austrian investigation commission was sent to Weimar and Jena. With proceedings instituted against some of the students and censorship introduced at the universities – amidst much talk about 'subversion of the public order' – the Wartburg affair assumed a dimension quite beyond its intrinsic gravity and led to the prohibition by Prussia of all student associations.

It was in this atmosphere of official suspicions and resentful students – more of whom now made it a point of honour to grow long hair and beards in old Teuton fashion – that the Tsar at the Aachen Congress of the Quadruple Alliance in 1818 brought up what he saw as the menace represented by the German universities. In Russia, not long after his return, people who had studied abroad found it difficult to gain admission to universities.

Metternich, increasingly convinced that Europe's monarchs would not survive unless they acted, individually and in concert, against any threat to the system, continued to smell conspiracies, subversion and revolution in the slightest disorder. Although he often made mountains out of molehills, there was actually in this 1817–18 period one conspiratorial German student fraternity whose radical militancy did not stop short of contemplating revolution.

They were the 'Blacks' of Giessen, a small university town in Hesse, who dressed in that austere 'old-German' colour to show their contempt for anything smacking of lively 'Frenchified' fashions. Their leader, Karl Follen, who in 1818 obtained a doctor's degree in law, was a charismatic personality. He had made a detailed study of the French Revolution and developed an ideology mixing extreme Jacobin and 'terrorist' methods with Romantic-mystic and Teutomaniac notions for the national and social regeneration of the German fatherland. Follen's personal magnetism, his earnestness, zeal and intellectual superiority made him appear as nothing less than a national 'saviour' to growing ranks of fervent admirers. Together with his brother Adolf August Ludwig Follen, he worked out a constitution for a new German-Christian Empire. This vested 'the sovereignty of the people' in a popularly elected Reichstag, which was to hold its meetings in a cathedral, but combined this democratic feature with the xenophobic and totalitarian ideas of Fichte, providing for the exclusion of every foreign influence and the baptism or expulsion of all Jews. In the autumn of 1818, even as the Aachen Congress was dispersing, Karl Follen became a tutor at Jena University, where J.F. Fries – who had spoken at the Wartburg rally – and two other Teutomanic professors had already propagated similar ideas. The Blacks of Giessen, who wore daggers at their secret meetings, saw themselves as an elite ready to die as martyrs in the cause of saving Germany from the tyranny of her 'princes and their lackeys'. There was dire poverty and unemployment in Hesse and the Follen brothers meant to rouse the masses. A revolutionary 'Great Hymn' composed by them in 1818, and soon recited in some Hessian villages, rang with such vehement calls 'Draw the knife of liberty… Drive the dagger through the throat!'

Five months after the Aachen Congress a young man, Karl Ludwig Sand, intoxicated by these slogans, went on foot from Jena to Mannheim and stabbed August von Kotzebue, a minor but well-known playwright to death with the words, 'Here, traitor to the fatherland.' Kotzebue had attacked several of the Teutomanic professors and was, moreover, suspected of being a spy for the Tsar, to whom he had indeed been sending occasional reports. Sand had been at the Wartburg rally and later met Karl Follen at Jena. Convinced that his deed would awaken Germany's patriots, he knelt down and stabbed himself in the breast, but not deeply enough to escape arrest and eventual trial.

'Sand is a splendid fellow,' Metternich wrote to Gentz. For the stir caused by the political assassination of Kotzebue provided the Austrian Chancellor, who was beginning to see himself as 'the physician in the great hospital of the world', with the hoped-for opportunity to proceed with the 'thorough cure' contemplated by Gentz. While Sand was to be publicly executed two years later, Metternich set off immediately for Bohemia to see the Prussian King, who was taking the baths at Teplitz. Metternich was worried by the latter's appointment of Wilhelm von Humboldt as 'Minister in charge of the constitution', but upon being reassured that the King had no intention of redeeming his pledge to grant one, he called a conference of the 9 most important member-states of the Federal German Bund.

The so-called Karlsbad Decrees they adopted were – in the words of Humboldt, who resigned together with two other ministers – 'disgraceful' and 'calculated to enrage a thinking people'. Ratified by the Federal Diet, they dissolved all student fraternities in Germany; instituted strict supervision of schools and universities; abolished freedom of the press and subjected all books and publications of 'fewer than twenty-one sheets', or 320 pages, to preliminary censorship. The most powerful instrument placed in Metternich's hands by these Decrees was the appointment of a Central Investigation Commission composed of Austrian, Prussian, Hessian and other high officials. Operating from Mainz, the Commission was charged with putting an end to any kind of agitation aimed at 'subverting the monarchic principle in any of the member-states of the German Bund', and was given wide powers to root out all 'demagogic' elements in public and academic life.

At Giessen and elsewhere, students had their rooms ransacked and many were arrested. No evidence was found that Karl Follen had instigated the murder of Kotzebue, but as harassment continued he escaped to France and a couple of years later emigrated to the United States. His brother was imprisoned for two years in Berlin pending trial. The examining magistrate, who happened to be the Bohemian E.T.A. Hoffmann, already famous for his 'Devil's Elixir' and other Gothic tales, released him on sworn bail, whereupon Follen made his escape to Switzerland just before being sentenced to 10 years in a fortress. He became the wealthy Follen of Zurich, patron of the growing colony of intellectual refugees from Germany. Joseph Görres fled to Strasbourg. *Turnvater* Jahn was to spend many years at Spandau, Küstrin and other fortresses, before being banished for life to Freiburg-an-der-Unstrut. Ernst Moritz Arndt was deprived of his chair at Bonn and many other academics were entangled in long investigations.

The very words 'Germany' or 'republic' were given an incriminating character. Paradoxically, the Holy Alliance, which was not even a treaty, was to serve Metternich better than the formal Quadruple Alliance. The latter, after the suppression of the Naples and Spanish revolts, was gradually to fall apart because of the rival political interests of the powers and Britain's reluctance to subscribe to the right claimed by her eastern partners of policing the Continent and 'indiscriminately' interfering in the affairs of other states. In the Holy Alliance, Metternich – a cool but often frightened rationalist – had the united support of the mystic and reactionary rulers of both Prussia and the Russian Empire for a policy of quenching any new social ideas or germinating nationalist sentiments.

In the Karlsbad Decrees, followed by more repressive measures whenever the growing liberal middle class or the now clandestine *Burschenschaften* tried to raise their heads, he laid the foundation for an elaborate spy, police and 'thought control' system which – covering the press, theatre, lecture hall and every existing public forum – was over the next three decades to result in the periodic dismissal of more academic teachers; the hounding, and often the years-long incarceration in fortresses, of journalists, *Burschenschaftler* and other dissenters; the banning of the works of individual as well as whole groups of writers. And this created that mentally stifling atmosphere which was to drive such diverse characters as Börne, Heine, Büchner, Weitling, Hess, Marx, Herwegh, Engels – some of them hardly or not yet born when the Karlsbad Decrees were promulgated in 1819 – from Germany, and most of her thinking people, idealists and realists, liberal patriots as well as a number of conservatives, to despair.

Heine had been in Hamburg for a year and a half when the Wartburg Festival took place. Recalling the ships he sometimes watched setting sail from the great northern port, he was to write: 'Such a harbour in the spring greatly resembles the heart of a young man who is going out in the world, and plunges for the first time into the stormy sea of life. His thoughts are still beflagged with multi-coloured bunting, rashness fills the sails of his desires. Heave-Ho!...'

It was in some such mood that Harry had departed for Hamburg in June 1816. 'A golden star draws me northwards', he wrote in an early poem. A metropolis of some 150,000 inhabitants compared to little Düsseldorf, the flourishing, fastgrowing 'free' city-state of Hamburg offered many worldly attractions to young men in search of a career. But shining bright and drawing Harry was the image of his cousin Amalie, the fair-haired daughter of his uncle Salomon Heine, rather than the prospect of making his start in the world as a junior clerk in Hamburg's Heckscher & Heine Bank, of which his uncle was the governor. He had first met Amalie, nicknamed Molly, when she was 14, during one of her father's visits to Düsseldorf. Whatever youthful flirtation had passed between them, this delicate angel-minx with her disturbing bluish-green 'all-knowing eyes' and enigmatic smile, had filled his dreams in the two years since and become the object of his pining. She was not in Hamburg when Harry arrived, but on 6 July he exulted in a letter to his friend Christian Sethe in Düsseldorf: 'Rejoice, rejoice: Four weeks from now I shall be seeing Molly.'

He settled down in rented quarters, worked at the bank under the strict supervision of one of his uncle's accountants, and in the evenings, dressed in a yellow frock coat, went strolling along Hamburg's elegant Jungfernstieg ('The Virgin's Walk'). It was not long before he detected the city's two faces, the façade of high respectability maintained by its business community, and its underside of hypocrisy. 'A pretty foul commercial dump', he reported his first impressions to Sethe. 'Whores in plenty, but no Muses. Many a German bard has sung himself into a consumption here.'

Forlorn among uninspiring bank clerks, he was waiting for Molly – 'with her returns my Muse' – but there was much to distract him on visits to his uncle's beautiful old Château Rainville, on a hill at Ottensen overlooking the Elbe. Its gardens boasted a marble fountain adorned with sphinxes, there were statues and stone benches, flowerbeds and avenues of trees, and beyond them rose a terrace from which one could gaze far out to the North Sea. The château's interior was sumptuous, but its salons were tastefully furnished.

In that magnificent setting, Heine was by mid-September dining with the hero of Germany's 'Liberation Wars', Fieldmarshal Blücher – a 'Homeric' figure, Heine found him – and otherwise mingling with 'the whole mob of the diplomatic world, millionaires, senators', bankers and members of Hamburg's high society. Molly had returned, more ladylike now, a full-grown debutante of 16. With her came her friends, bejewelled girls and young businessmen and sons of her father's friends. There were picnics and outings, dancing parties and garden fêtes. Heine was 19, a young man in the flush of his first infatuation. Pale but elegant, awkward but clever and witty, he was, both as the nephew of the great Salomon Heine and to some extent in his own right, the object of some interest. Bosoms rose and good-looking girls sent him provocative glances, watched by their calculating mothers. His inspiration returned, and it was in Hamburg that he became a published poet. But, alas, all was not well with the world or with him.

'She loves me not! You must, dear Christian, pronounce this last monosyllable very softly. The first three words promise eternal heavenly bliss, but the last is eternal living hell.' This, from Heine's second letter to Christian Sethe, dated 27 October 1816 but not sent before 20 November, might have been the end of what Jeffrey Sammons has called 'one of the most celebrated love-affairs in all literature' – only to declare it, a little later in the same paragraph, 'almost entirely a creation of literary historians'. But it was only the beginning of the youthful Heine's amorous tribulations. In page after page of this second letter to Sethe, which for its sheer uncontrolled emotion has been compared by some to Goethe's letters to Kate Schönkopf, while others have found in it echoes of Schiller's *Sturm und Drang* period,[6] Heine poured out his hurt to his only friend and confidant. He has had 'the most irrefutable proofs' that cousin Molly does not requite his love – 'proofs that even Rector Schall-meyer would admit were absolutely logical and would not hesitate to put at the head of his system'. But all the same, his heart refuses to bend to the force of logic: 'What has your logic to do with me, I have my own logic. – I have seen her again. – I am a fanatical chess player. I've lost my queen on my first move, and yet I still play. I play for the queen!'

In a postscript, he informed Sethe, who had meanwhile moved to Göttingen, that he now bore his pain in a much 'manlier' fashion. 'But I am dying in-wardly... O M[olly], you exact a high price! – ... over my naked breast hangs a black iron chain, and affixed to it precisely over my heartbeats is a black iron cross with many sharp edges: in it lies a lock of M...'s hair. Ooh! How that burns.' Heine knows what he is letting himself in for: 'O Christian! It's enough to send the purest and most pious of minds into a frenzy of wild demented god-lessness.' But, 'coute ce que coute, here I am and here I remain.'

And so Harry Heine, fully aware of the folly of his misplaced love, was to spend a full three years in Hamburg, tossed between 'demented godlessness' and a sudden urge 'to drug' his senses and submerge his pain 'in the infinite depths of mysticism. How pitiable knowledge seems to me now in its beggar's rags.'

His second letter to Sethe included the following lines: 'Has Heine gone mad? you will exclaim. Nevertheless, I must have a Madonna. Will the heavenly replace the earthly Madonna for me?' Other than the two 1816 letters to his boyhood friend, Heine left hardly a direct reference to the personality of his cousin, or his actual experiences with her. But in one of his first ballads, pub-lished in 1817, he is transported to a forest chapel, where the heavenly Virgin herself – by 'a hairraising marvel' transformed into a charming, smiling maiden – offers him 'a lock of golden hair' in reward for his 'blindly trusting love's devotion'. In two more of his youthful poems Heine alluded to the lock of Amalie's hair he supposedly wore on his breast. Heine's *Book of Songs* – espe-cially in the sections 'Youthful Sorrows', 'Fresco Sonnets to Christian S.' and 'Lyrical Intermezzo' – abounds with images and scenes, some of them night-marish and macabre in Romantic fashion, of the grief, torments and fatality of deceitful love. The faithless Amalie-Molly is, however, nowhere named, and as so often in the case of Heine, much scholarly investigation and biographical speculation have been spent on unravelling the truth of the affair from its fictional elements, and his real feelings from Romantic literary attitudinizing. The famous lines

> And when the heart within the breast is broken,
> All slashed to bits, all shivered and all shattered –
> What's left is laughter, shrill and ringing laughter

in one of his sonnets were actually part of a letter he wrote in 1821, after a return visit to Hamburg, to a new friend of his, Straube. This letter contains a lengthy description of the madness that nearly drove him to suicide when he stood under Amalie's window – 'It was getting on for midnight when I betook myself to the house of my Dulcinea' – which was to be echoed the following year in a poem evoking the ghostly night when 'I stood before your house and stared up from the street below, and stared up at your window,' etc. But does this mean that Heine is in each case speaking of a real experience?

In 1961 William Rose pointed out that Heine's early poems, for all the correspondence of the recurring 'lock of hair' or other images to things he related to Sethe or Straube, were written after 'some considerable lapse of time' since Harry had last seen Amalie and could not provide a solid enough basis for identification. Jeffrey Sammons, noting that clearly 'something happened' between young Heine and his cousin – and further that he did have a 'capacity for carrying emotional pain intact in his memory for many years' – observed that his poetry is 'not narrative' but an evolving state of mind, with the female figures 'functional and thematic in a fictionalized drama of the self', rather than recognizable persons. And Ritchie Robertson commented that 'for Heine, disillusionment as a literary attitude is not the result of experience; it precedes experience. He knows in advance that reality will disappoint his expectation.'[7]

The intensity of Heine's feelings for Amalie will probably never be known. Molly in Hamburg was not the prim, shy, elfin 14-year-old he had briefly met in Düsseldorf. In her own social milieu at Rainville, she was the princess of the château. Surrounded by friends and suitors, she tried out her charms on the love-sick Harry and kept him in a tantalizing frenzy with her bewitching eyes and coquettish smiles, only to mock him with her cold indifference. Worse, as a mortified Harry confessed to Sethe in the aforementioned letter, 'she has run down my beautiful poems in a galling and despicable manner, poems which I wrote only for her.' She and her friends, in fact, cruelly humiliated him by laughing at his verses. But this was not Harry's only humiliation in Hamburg. In a poem called '*Affrontenburg*' – 'The Castle of Affront' – published only two years before his death, he evoked the many snubs and indignities he suffered at the château in Ottensen, with its old battlements, its weathercock and its magnificent but 'accursed garden'.

He was certainly referring here to his treatment by his uncle, Salomon Heine (1766–1842). A commanding figure, Salomon was at this time about to buy out his partner and found one of Germany's leading banks under his own name. He presided over his business, his town mansion on the Jungfernstieg and his château with what Harry was to represent as the growling imperiousness of a hyberborean bear. Although the Heine ancestors had been financiers, Salomon was a self-made man who as a boy had been running about Hamburg delivering bills from house to house. At Harry's age he was already set on the course which was to make him perhaps the richest man in Germany, and a philanthropist noted for his public charities. He had helped set up Harry's father in business and was presently to bail him out of financial catastrophe. He was also prepared to do a lot for Harry, recognizing his brightness, but he had no more under-standing for his nephew's intellectual bent and poetic vein than the rest of the hard-nosed Hamburgers – of whom Harry remarked that all they knew about poetry was 'doggerel written to order for weddings and christenings' – and did not see how he was going to make a living by his pen. By the banker's practical lights, the best way to launch Harry in life was to give him a businessman's training under his own supervision.

Harry had a good deal of admiration for his uncle. Compared to his own father, who lived in the clouds, Uncle Salomon represented money and power, and in 1825 Harry was to call him 'a redoubtable man who, despite great faults, also has great qualities.' In fact, he found that, 'by nature and in character, we are much alike: the same obstinate daring, the same bottomless capacity for affection, the same unpredictable folly. Only Fortune has made of him a mil-lionaire and of me a pauper, that is to say a poet, and for this reason our views on life and our modes of living are very different.'[8]

Neither of them was ready to accept the other's values. Harry's Hamburg period marked the start of the ambivalent relationship between Salomon, who felt that if Harry 'had only learned something he would not have to write books', and the nephew who – beginning to see his benefactions as the nabob's tribute to genius – made himself dependent on his financial support, a depen-dence which was increasingly to prey on his mind as his needs grew and ulti-mately to consume much of his energy in the famous 'money war' with his Hamburg family.

After only 4 months in Hamburg, Harry wrote in his second letter to Sethe that Uncle Salomon, dissatisfied with his lack of progress at the bank, wanted to send him home to Düsseldorf; and that while rubbing shoulders with sena-tors and high society at his uncle's château, he felt 'entirely isolated'. There was much 'decorous formality' at the château, but he was asserting 'the poet's inde-pendent spirit' by often 'sinning against etiquette'. Indeed, besides visiting brothels and trying to make Amalie jealous by courting a Mlle Charaux until her father forbade him the house, Harry reacted to Amalie's indifference and the barbs he suffered in his uncle's house by showing off his wit. Enjoying the luxury, but a poor relation at the feast, he assumed a superior, mocking pose and developed a defensive-aggressive attitude. At the same time, he assured Sethe – the only person he could confide in – that he was writing more poetry than ever. His verses, he felt, were becoming gentler and 'sweeter, like pain dipped in honey'.

Heine was also swept along by the patriotic fervour of Germany's youth. Two years before the Wartburg rally, he had written the poem 'Deutschland', extolling Germany's glory and her Teuton heroes and virtues, from Arminius down to her fair women bending over the 'sacred wounds' of the soldiers 'bleed-ing for the Fatherland'. Some of his older schoolmates had returned from the wars against Napoleon. It was a topsy-turvy world, a time of disorientation and Romantic mysticism, and Harry, a gauche young man beset by many anxieties, had yet to find his bearings. He had grown up on German folk-songs. He was going to be a German poet but, adding to his other troubles, he was perturbed by the anti-Semitic atmosphere in Hamburg. The Jungfernstieg, where Harry's uncle had his town house, was an area normally forbidden to Jewish residents. However, in spite of his numerous charities and public services to the city – cul-minating in his saving it from financial ruin after the 'great fire' of 1842 by con-tributing a fifth of his fortune to its rehabilitation loan, waiving the insurance on his demolished town house, and preventing speculation by discounting bills at the normal bank rate – he was denied citizenship and admission to the Cham-ber of Commerce. (Salomon Heine's proviso that Hamburg's Jewish hospital, which he founded, would admit Gentiles when the Jews were granted civil rights was not to be fulfilled before 1864, 20 years after his death.) But already in 1816, his nephew observed to Sethe that there was 'a rather sticky tension' in the city – which was indeed to explode before long in anti-Jewish riots to the old cry of Hep! Hep! (*Hierosolyma est perdita*) – and expressed his fear that 'Christian love will not leave unmolested the love-songs of a Jew', making it difficult for him to publish his poetry.

There is no definite answer to the question why Harry, frustrated in love and feeling generally unhappy in uncongenial Hamburg – 'the beautiful cradle of my sorrows' – stayed on there for three years; whether it was from indolence, indecision or sheer inertia, or some hope (as he told Sethe) of still winning Amalie's heart, or possibly because he had no profession and no future else-where. The post-Napoleonic period had left his father with a large stock of assorted textile goods at his silk-and-cloth store, while England, the Nether-lands and France started dumping custom-free textiles at cut-throat prices into the Rhineland. By 1817 the price of cotton merchandise had sunk so low that Samson Heine could only sell below cost. Increasingly indebted, and with 5 other mouths to feed, Harry's parents may well have considered it best to have him provided for by his powerful uncle.

Heine's first poems began to appear in print in February 1817, starting with *'Die Weihe'* ('The Boon'), which featured his cousin as a blond German Madonna handing an adoring youth a lock of her hair. It was a sign of his insecurity that, whether in order not to antagonize his uncle or to make sure that his poems would not be rejected because of his being Jewish, he signed them with the atrocious pseudonym 'Sy Freudhold Riesenharf' (an anagram formed of the letters 'Harry Heine, Düsseldorf'). It also showed his distraction that he had thoughtlessly offered the poems to the editor of the *Hamburger Wächter*, only to learn from Sethe after their publication that this was 'an anti-Semitic rag' whose editor never thought that their author could be a Jew.

On New Year's Day 1818, at the château, Harry presented Amalie with a red leatherbound volume of a verse-tragedy by Adolf Müllner. Her reaction was a curt 'Write something like that', to which Harry responded that he would write 'better things';[9] but it seems that at this point he definitely realized that she did not love him.

He continued to work in the bank until May, when his uncle, who made all the decisions for him, suddenly set him up as a linen-draper in a firm of his own – Harry Heine & Co. – specializing in English cloth. Harry dutifully tended the shop, which was in vaulted cellar rooms. He may well have thought that he was helping to rehabilitate his father's business in Düsseldorf, as some of the merchandise came from the surplus stock of the latter's store. At that, Harry now had enough time on his hands to frequent the theatre, cafés and dancing halls, although he did not dance.

That autumn, out of the blue, he was presented with a demand to pay a promissory note drawn by his father in Düsseldorf on Harry Heine & Co. in Hamburg. Assuming there had been a mistake somewhere, Harry refused payment, not knowing that the demand marked the beginning of a family drama that was to end in tragedy. It has long been known that the banker Heine not only bankrupted Harry's father but brought an action to have him declared mentally incompetent. The exact circumstances of the affair, however, remained shrouded in mystery until 1974 when Klaus Schulte came up with a detailed study of all promissory notes circulated by Harry's father between 1808 and 1818, showing that he had increasingly been playing the credit system to the limit.[10]

It was common and legal business practice at that time for merchants to buy goods against promissory notes drawn on third or fourth parties, who redeemed them at a discount on the sole security of the original drawer's integrity and good standing in the business community. Such notes sometimes circulated from hand to hand for years. But once a promissory note bounced and its last holder 'protested' it before a notary, the 'drawer' who failed to pay up faced official proceedings and a stain on his name worse than death.

Until the summer of 1818, Harry's father, according to the records of several Düsseldorf notaries, had been able to obtain deferments on a large number of 'protested' notes. Between August and mid-September, hard-pressed as his own clients defaulted on payments, he drew 8 or 9 notes on Harry Heine & Co. and on his brother Salomon's associates in the Heckscher bank, and thereby precipitated his own ruin. When the notes were presented in Hamburg in November, Salomon Heine was about to dissolve the Heckscher partnership and establish his own bank. With other creditors beginning to 'protest' Samson's notes, Salomon Heine was determined to have his name kept out of his brother's bankruptcy affair. He ordered his trusted factotum, an accountant by the name of Hirsch (who was Harry's financial supervisor at Harry Heine & Co.), to honour only one of the notes. Placed in the impossible position of humiliating his father by refusing to redeem the others, Harry tried to make himself scarce. On three separate occasions, creditors were told that he had moved or gone on an 8-day trip. These evasive tactics, however, did not prevent the unpaid notes from being protested.

In Düsseldorf a curious intermezzo had taken place on 12 November. Its unexpected protagonist was Harry's maternal uncle Simon van Geldern, the eccentric, pigtailed bachelor and bookworm of 'Noah's Ark'. Claiming to act on behalf of Salomon, he obtained from Harry's father a statement that he owed his brother in Hamburg the sum of 85,218 Reichsthaler and was therefore making over to him merchandise and outstanding debts to the same value. In return Simon van Geldern authorized Harry's father to carry on business on behalf of his brother until further notice from the latter. Whether or not Salomon was behind this move, Samson saw in it a glimmer of hope. On 16 December, however, Hirsch arrived in Düsseldorf with different orders. By early January – even as Salomon Heine's new bank was opening in Hamburg – Hirsch, having spent 7,166 Reichsthaler to pay off Samson's most pressing creditors, had him sign over part of his merchandise and consigned it to Harry Heine & Co. in Hamburg. With the immediate danger of a financial scandal averted, the banker's next move, according to Schulte, was motivated by his fear that if his brother continued in business he might draw more notes on Harry Heine & Co. or otherwise embarrass him.

In the first week of February, Hirsch started the liquidation of Samson's firm by putting in a demand – in the name of his brothers Salomon and Henry

Heine, both of them bankers in Hamburg – to 'interdict' him on the grounds of mental incompetence. He submitted a certificate by Düsseldorf's district medical officer saying that Samson had been suffering epileptic fits for the last 5 years, and that for the last two he appeared to be suffering from softening of the brain. As for Simon van Geldern's having licensed Samson to carry on business, Hirsch denied that Salomon Heine had ever authorized this.

Samson Heine's reaction was to go to Hamburg. He spent two days there, but it is not known whether he confronted his brother, or even whether he saw Harry. On 4 March he declared before a Hamburg notary that he no longer felt bound by his acknowledgment of a debt of 85,218 Reichsthaler to his brother. He was, however, powerless to stop the forces mobilized against him. The drama reached a climax on 28 April when – the Düsseldorf court having ordered a family council to be heard on the motion for 'interdiction' – this council of 6 people returned a recommendation that Samson be placed under a guardian.

There is no evidence as to whether Samson himself was or was not in Düsseldorf at the time. All that is known is that, for reasons and purposes unexplained, he set out for Hamburg again some time after 6 March, this time 'accompanied' by Hirsch. In Düsseldorf the court had yet to adjudicate the demands of his two Hamburg brothers when their lawyer moved that the whole case be transferred to Hamburg. When the court rejected this motion – prompted, in the opinion of some, by the likelihood that in Düsseldorf people might have attested that Samson was far from being mentally incapacitated – the lawyer produced a certificate signed by two Hamburg doctors, revealing that Samson was actually in that city, and unable to travel. In the face of this, the court, at an undated hearing, agreed that Samson be interrogated in Hamburg.

The Hamburg hearing took place on 2 November 1819, when Samson Heine appeared before a magistrate by the name of Sillem. Shortly after it began he had an epileptic fit, followed by another after the motion for his 'interdiction' was read. The hearing was broken off, and Sillem sent the minutes to the court in Düsseldorf. The court added them to the file; but by the time Schulte ended his researches in 1974 no proof had been found that the court ever acted on the Hamburg motion. Schulte's conclusion was that at some point during the wearisome proceedings, Harry's father fell in with the role assigned to him by his brothers, though he played it 'not like a loser, but rather like a man intent on making it transparent that he is taking part in a farce.'[11]

Farce or no farce, Samson's store and house in Düsseldorf were to be auctioned off the following year. But even before Harry's father's complete undoing – he was eventually to be packed off with his wife for a prolonged 'cure' in the salt-baths of Oldesloe in Holstein – the crass affair brought their son's stay in Hamburg to a traumatic end. Heine was, not surprisingly, even more reticent about it than about his 'great love affair'. In the absence of any information on the activities of his family during its protracted course, his own role in the episode remains unclear. Uncle Salomon's treatment of his father certainly added venom and a vengeful element to his relationship with the mighty banker, and very likely magnified that distaste for the money world and its practices he first felt in Hamburg – 'It is not foul Macbeth, but Banko who reigns here,' he wrote – even as his dependence on his uncle increased. For Salomon now took over financial responsibility for Harry's entire family – for his father Samson, until he lived out his days in melancholy retirement at Lüneburg; for Harry's mother, who was to survive her husband by 31 years; and for their 4 children, including the university education of their 3 sons.

The Hamburg firm of Harry Heine & Co. had been dissolved in March 1819 because of looming bankruptcy. Harry had not particularly exerted himself to succeed in this third attempt by his family to make a businessman out of him. Whether Salomon Heine wanted to get rid of him or gave in to Harry's mother's entreaties, it was decided after a time that he should study law at the newly founded Bonn University on a generous 400 Thaler a year provided by the uncle.

Frustrated in love and disillusioned with the world, Heine left Hamburg in mid-June 1819. 'My secret inner life', he was to write of the Hamburg period, 'sank in an abyss of dreams whose obscurity was relieved only by fitful lightning flashes; in my other, external life, I became mad, dissipated, cynical, and disgusting.' It was in Hamburg that he consciously adopted an outward persona designed 'to be the opposite of my inner life, lest the latter should destroy all the rest.' Possibly he did so also to protect his inner self. He became the odd man out, vulnerable but mocking, aggressively witty, and wearing a thousand masks.

But it was in Hamburg that he found his vocation as a poet and stuck to it through all his heartbreaks and the pressures on him. With his Muse for his only friend and consolation, he had started translating his great contemporary, Byron, the poet of unhappy love, Romantic gloom and *Weltschmerz*.

After the family council which had declared his beloved father incompetent, he spent the summer of 1819 in Düsseldorf. The circumstances he found at home and the emotions they engendered in him are a complete blank. All we know is that, never having finished high school, he studied with a private tutor for a special examination to gain admission to the university. But among the poems he wrote that summer was one that was to go around the world: *'Die Grenadiere'* (The Grenadiers).

At the beginning of October, he left for Bonn, where he found the student body agitated by the banning of the *Burschenschaft* fraternities and the Federal Diet's adoption of the Karlsbad Decrees.

In Trier, a short distance south of Bonn, Heinrich Marx rented a house at No. 664 Brückengasse in April 1818. Built in 1727, it was a baroque middle-class house into which he moved with his pregnant wife and their two children: Maurice (Moritz) David, who was two and a half, and 18-months-old Sophie. Maurice had been born at 'No. 55 1/2' in Liebfrauenstrasse, where Marx – registered since 1815 as a 'lawyer at the Rhenish Court of Appeals' – had settled down with his wife some time after their marriage. His first office was at the same address. Sophie was born either there or at No. 485 Nagelstrasse, where the Marxes seem to have lived, between 1816 and the end of March 1818.[12]

The house to which they now moved was of the type inhabited by wealthy middle-class citizens and higher officials. It had two rooms on the ground floor and three on the first floor, besides a basement room and garrets. It was in one of the upstairs rooms on 5 May 1818 that Henriette Marx gave birth to a boy whose birth certificate, registered two days later, recorded his name as 'Carl', although he himself later spelled it Karl.

It was only in 1904 that this house was identified as Marx's birthplace. Bought and renovated by the German Social Democratic Party in 1928, it was – due to the rise of the Nazis – not until the end of World War II that it was turned into a memorial and study centre. Nowadays 10 Brückenstrasse, it was – after the study centre was transferred to a new building in the vicinity – dedicated as a 'Marx Museum' in 1983, on the centenary of his death.

Marx was born nearly three years after the signing of the Holy Alliance effectively put an end (as it turned out) to all liberal aspirations of the post-Napoleonic era; and some 14 months before the adoption of the Karlsbad Decrees. By the time he was born, Henri de Saint-Simon, the French theorist of the class conflict and tireless prophet of the industrial age, was finding powerful supporters for his long-neglected ideas. After a short spell in the madhouse of Charenton, he had, about the time of the Congress of Vienna, published his *De la réorganisation de la société européenne*, outlining an economically and politically united European Community of Nations. And after the fall of Napoleon, Saint-Simon's insistence that 'the whole of society rests on industry', which is 'the sole guarantee of its existence', could not but impress the French bourgeoisie, faced as it was with the aristocracy's push to recover vested positions of influence along with its huge estates.

By 1818 he was once more a society figure, on intimate terms with Baron Ternaux the 'textile king', with Lafitte and several regents of the Banque de

France, and frequenting the salons of leading industrialists and financiers – men of the very elite he deemed capable of creating a world of plenty based on 'productivity' and 'scientific' distribution in the best interest of mankind. With their help, Saint-Simon launched a series of periodical publications – *L'Industrie*, *Le Politique* and *L'Organisateur* – extolling the merits of bourgeois enterprise. His industrial friends, however, hardly became converts to his notion that improving the lot of the poorest and 'most numerous class', i.e. the proletariat, was not against the interest of the rich, but would increase their own happiness as well. Before long, the breadth of Saint-Simon's vision and his Faust-like temperament proved too much for them. For when he spoke of 'terrestrial morality', they feared a confrontation with the Catholic Church; and a piece he published in *L'Organisateur* landed him in deep trouble.

The piece was Saint-Simon's famous 'Parabole', in which he brazenly declared that if the King of France and all the princes, marshals, cardinals, bishops, ministers, judges, government officials and high-born landowners – in short, 30,000 Frenchmen considered most important – were suddenly to perish, France would be aggrieved, but would 'suffer no political harm', because they could be easily replaced by other worthy courtiers, clerics and administrators, without damage to the French genius; whereas, if France suddenly lost 30,000 of her best physicists, chemists, mathematicians, doctors, surgeons, pharmacists, civil and military engineers, architects, miners, locksmiths, mechanics, plumbers, watchmakers, shipbuilders, or for that matter, her foremost poets, painters, musicians and writers – 'the flower of French society' – then France would lose her prosperity, her place among the nations and her very 'soul' for at least a generation.

Saint-Simon's 'Parabole' was his way of appealing to King Louis XVIII to become France's 'First Industrialist', that is, to take the lead in creating and promoting the new century's Industrial Society. It was his way of solving 'the frightful crisis involving the whole of Europe', of overhauling its political and social system and adjusting the Continent to the industrial age without war or revolu-tion and the resulting anarchy. But it was provocatively phrased, and the Bour-bon king was the wrong addressee for such visionary plans. In February 1820, Louis XVIII's nephew, the duc de Berry – son of the future King Charles X – was assassinated. Saint-Simon, the humanist who envisioned a World Parliament and had spent a lifetime racking his fertile brain to devise a system that would eliminate national as well as class conflicts and abolishing the causes of violence, was charged with 'morally' instigating the crime.

Profoundly humiliated, abandoned during his prosecution by the bourgeoisie and almost everyone, he emerged from the affair unpunished but once again a pauper at 60. The admirable crackpot who in former times used to have

173

his valet wake him with the words, 'Time to get up, monsieur le comte, you have important things to do,' literally had to collect alms to keep body and soul together. He tried to shoot himself. Rescued and recovering, he set about providing a synthesis between a reformed, socially oriented 'brotherly' Christianity and the spiritual needs of the age of technology, and died (7 years after Marx's birth) confident that he had 'the idea that would save the human species'.

Saint-Simon's demonstration of the influence of social and economic factors on the process of history was to provide rich, if divisive, inspiration to the new generation of social theorists and militants born at the height of the Napoleonic era or immediately afterwards. As for his whole utopian vision of the development of the industrial world, in our own time it has indeed become a reality, with our dependence on the efforts of supra-national scientists, financial corporations and technocratic administrators such as he proposed to place in charge of affairs in order to ensure 'the association of all men on the surface of the globe'.

'The frightful crisis' which Saint-Simon meant to solve was depicted in stark terms by that other eccentric, not to say mad French visionary, Charles Fourier. In the 7 years between 1808 and 1815, he observed at the time of the Vienna Congress, France alone had lost 'more than 1,200,000 men in battle, not counting the victims of the revolutionary plagues.' As early as 1803, Fourier had proposed to First Consul Bonaparte the introduction of a 'decent minimum wage' in order to abolish poverty and social unrest. In 1808, he published his *Théorie des quatre mouvements et des destinées générales* in two volumes; out of fear of being plagiarized, he gave Leipzig as the place of publication, although they were printed in Lyons. In this dissertation he had placed before the world his system of 'universal Harmony', based on the theory that Newton's principle of attraction or harmony among material bodies had its equivalent in the mutual attraction or 'harmony' between the natural passions of men. Their repression and stultification by the false values, restraints and pharisaic morality of 'civilization' led to all the ills and conflicts of the social organism.

Fourier, with his elaborate blueprint for a happy humanity living in communal 'phalansteries', carefully designed for the maximum satisfaction of each individual's 12 'fundamental passions' (i.e., economic, social, cultural and psychological needs), would one day be hailed by André Breton as a forerunner of surrealism. His forecast of a planet inhabited by five billion people would be fulfilled only in 1988, but in the ravings of this monomaniac against the state and its 'political wisdom' expressed in 'bayonets', against the kings who posed as 'infallible divine beings' and against the Catholic Church (which banned his writings), the future rebels were to find a ready textbook of all the 'crimes', vices, hypocrisy and oppression practised by the various establishments of the 'civilized' world, from the exploitation of cheap labour to the endemic chaos of economic crises, from the rat-race and destruction of family life in the urban centres to the wretchedness and alienation of the hungry and the dispossessed.

In England, Byron in 1812 had spoken in the House of Lords in defence of the Nottingham workers who had smashed the new industrial machines or 'stocking-frames' for producing cheap cotton calicoes which made them jobless. Never, 'in the most oppressed provinces of Turkey', said Byron, 'did I behold such squalid wretchedness as I have in the very heart of a Christian country.' By 1817, Robert Owen had demonstrated at his New Lanark Mills in Scotland that England's textile workers could be turned from drunken wretches into orderly men. The revolutionary social amenities established by Owen for his workers and their children had made New Lanark an internationally famous industrial community, a showplace visited by some of Europe's rulers and leading statesmen, including Tsar Alexander's brother and later successor Nicholas.

Less than a year before Marx's birth, Owen (supported by the Duke of Kent, father of Queen Victoria) was on the way to becoming the leading Socialist reformer of the age by launching his 'cooperative villages' when, in August 1817, at a meeting in the City of London Tavern, he spoke out against the 'gross errors' of all received forms of religion. Owen, whose plan initially had the cautious blessing of the Archbishop of Canterbury, was dropped by the establishment just as Saint-Simon was dropped by the bourgeoisie for his remarks about 'terrestrial morality'. Owen had started his social experiment at New Lanark in the first decade of the 19th century. In that period of Napoleon's expanding conquests – in which Hegel had produced his *Phenomenology of the Spirit* – Fourier and Saint-Simon had both developed their separate social theories. To the glory and madness of the times, the two 'prophets of Paris' opposed their own highly idiosyncratic vistas of peace and human happiness. They went on propagating them through the economic slump that spread poverty and unemployment at the end of the Napoleonic wars. Although their message was not lost on the next generation, they were like men crying in the wilderness.

In June 1817, Heinrich Marx – while still anxiously waiting to see whether Prussia would force him out of his profession unless he changed his faith – was appointed a member of an official 'Commission for the Regulation of the Jewish Debts in the former Archbishopric of Trier'. The Commission dealt with arrears in 'protection' money, residential permits and other taxes owed by the Jews to the former Archbishop of Trier for two years between 1792 and 1794, when his feudal-clerical state had gone out existence. Since then, coming under French sovereignty, its frontiers had been twice changed. The Prussians changed them again. In 1817, for a start, the debts carried over from the Archbishopric were claimed, together with interest, from Jews who had lived in the original territory, or from their descendants; from others who had since moved into different provinces; and still others who had only recently been 'annexed' to it.

Though individual Jews protested both the injustice of the state's argument – which was that the 'communal' debt concerned them no matter whether they had been involved in contracting it – and the sums demanded of them, the matter was frequently held up by appeals to the courts, with the result that the settlement of these debts was to drag on until 1836.

From June 1817 until April 1819, it was the task of Marx and two other Jewish members of the Commission to fix the individual quotas to be paid by the debtors. It was an onerous job, for the Jews, forbidden public office, teaching posts, crafts, trades and farming, fared worst in the economic depression. Around 2,800 Jews altogether lived in the new Prussian government district of Trier, only about 250 in the town itself. With the exception of some cattle-dealers and a few doctors, 'they were, if anything, even more destitute than the Christian poor', and reduced to 'the meanest and most degrading peddling'.[13]

Their plight is perhaps best illustrated by the fact that since 1813 they had been unable to collect their rabbi's salary. The rabbi was Heinrich's brother Samuel, who continued to live in the crowded and dilapidated old 'synagogue house' in the Weberbachgasse. In March 1815 Rabbi Samuel complained to the authorities that he had not received his salary – which under the French had been 3,000 francs, but had since been halved – for the past 17 months. Karl Marx thus came of a family which had long known poverty, for even his grandfather Rabbi Mordecai had never been able to make ends meet. His own father, though, had married a woman of some means. But it may be assumed that the privation Heinrich had known in his youth, the spreading pauperism around him and his fear of being bereft of his profession and unable to provide for his family, was to be a factor in his ultimate decision to convert.

In 1975 the publication of a 439-page collection of documents[14] discovered in Trier's municipal library showed that when Heinrich Marx and two other 'conscientious' and fair-minded Jews were co-opted to the Commission, they asked 'to consult their community'. None of its members objected to Heinrich's presence on the grounds that he had 'defected' from the community by conversion, indicating that his baptism may have taken place later than was previously thought.

In January 1819, Jewish functionaries in the Rhineland and Westphalia were beginning to be officially dismissed. There is no document concerning the fate of Heinrich Marx, except that he continued his work on the Debts Commission. But another of the three lawyers whom President Sethe had interviewed during his inspection of the Rhineland's legal institutions and their staff – Benedict Philipp, a bailiff at Heinsberg, appointed under the French – was informed by Prussia's Chancellor Hardenberg that since religion was one of 'the principles governing the qualification of public officials, and as these principles apply throughout the entire state, no one of the Israelite confession can hold a state post.'[15]

On 15 April 1819, the Marxes' first son Maurice David, a sickly child, died at the age of 3. His death was notified to the authorities on behalf of 'the lawyer Heinrich Marx' by a representative of the Jewish community. This is taken as another indication that Marx had not yet been baptized. So is the fact that a Jewish debtor, who about this time strongly contested Heinrich Marx's membership of the Commission, did so only on the grounds that his own name – Marx's – nowhere appeared on the list of debtors. The answer given by another member was that Heinrich Marx had spent so much time and effort on the Commission's work without remuneration that it was thought only 'a small recompense' to exempt him from his rate of the debt. The provincial government, however, thought otherwise. On 14 May, Mayor Haw, as president of the Commission, was informed that its members, least of all those dealing with the list of debtors, deserved no special consideration, as it had from the beginning been instituted on a 'voluntary' basis.

It is assumed that Marx resigned in the wake of this criticism and that he finally accepted baptism some time later in 1819.[16] This also fits in with the sequence of official measures against the Jews which, in the absence of other information, is the only record to go by; and with the fact that the Divisional Chaplain Mühlenhoff, mentioned at a later date in the baptismal register as the pastor who performed the act, was only promoted to that rank in 1819.

Whatever the date of the conversion, what really matters is the possible effect of the father's break with his roots on 'Fortune's child' – the 'Glückskind' Karl – as his parents called him.

As Edmund Wilson pointed out, Karl Marx was descended on his father's side from an 'unbroken succession of rabbis, some of them distinguished teachers of the fifteenth and eighteenth centuries.' Friedrich Heer[17] named Marx's two best-known 16th-century ancestors: 'Joseph ben Gershon Cohen, Rabbi of Cracow', and 'Meir Katzenellenbogen, who died as Rabbi of Padua in 1565' and was regarded by the university there 'as one of the most illustrious minds of his age.' Even the best of the more up-to-date biographies and studies of Marx published since – some of them as late as the 1983 centenary of his death or after – trace Marx's genealogy no further than to an earlier 15th-century rabbi of Padua.

Marx's paternal ancestry, however, goes much further back, to RASHI, the 11th-century sage and greatest Jewish Bible and Talmud commentator of all time. The line leading from RASHI to Karl Marx across nearly 800 years makes for a ramified family tree, which – both on its own, and due to Marx's maternal descent from 'the Exalted Rabbi' Judah Loew (the legendary Golem-maker of Prague) – came to be decorated with whole clusters of famous scholars, rabbinical judges, community leaders as well as bankers and court financiers all over Europe. Among these previously unknown ancestors are to be found some of the greatest Talmudists and rabbinical 'law-givers' of the last thousand years.

6

Heine's Three Universities

On the first day of October 1819, Heinrich Marx bought, and shortly afterwards moved with his family into, a house at No. 1070 in Trier's Simeongasse. Although the new house was smaller than the previous one, it had 8 rooms on the two main floors and three small garrets in the roof. According to the contract, it also comprised 'a small courtyard, a laundry room and a small garden'. By this time the Marxes had three small children, Sophie, Karl and two-months-old Hermann; but as they were to produce 5 more children in almost as many years, the house was eventually occupied by a family of 10. It was in this house that Karl Marx was to spend his childhood and adolescence. A plaque on the house – since converted into a mixed residential and commercial building at what is today No. 8 Simeonstrasse – commemorates the fact that he lived there until he left to go to university at the age of 17. His father bought the house from a Privy Councillor, Peter Schwarz, for 3,650 Thaler, making a down payment of 1,050 Thaler, probably with money from his wife's dowry. The rest was to be paid in three installments over the next 6 years at 5 per cent interest, all of it (including the interest) in 'hard cash in any legal currency' at the prevailing Thaler rate in Trier.

Following his baptism, Heinrich Marx was appointed on 3 July 1820 an *Advokatanwalt*, or barrister-at-law, at the High Court of Appeals in Trier. As a simple *Advokat* his practice had been limited to penal cases, and in others he had had to hire the services of an *Anwalt*, or solicitor, but now his practice was unlimited. Little is known about the detailed stages of his professional rise to the esteemed rank of *Justizrat*, or the type of cases he handled. The only indication that his income soon increased is that within less than a decade he bought, like most bourgeois families in the wine-blessed Moselle area, a small vineyard at Kurenz, just outside Trier. While this may have been meant primarily for his family's private consumption, he was eventually to prosper enough to acquire another vineyard, worth 3,000 Thaler, apparently as a property investment.

The only extant documents pertaining to his legal activities show that he represented Trier's Lord Mayor Wilhelm Haw in a case brought against him before the Court of Appeals. There is a similar dearth of authentic information about Karl Marx's childhood before the start of his grammar-school education at Trier's Gymnasium. The only recorded events in the lives of either the son or the father in the period between 1819 and 1825 are the boy's baptism in 1824, and the start of the hearings in the appeal against Mayor Haw the following year.

During the same period, Harry Heine attended three universities in a row. Each of them left its imprint on him, starting with Bonn University, which he entered about the same week in October 1819 when the Marx family moved into their new house. Almost immediately he felt the sting of the Karlsbad Decrees, promulgated only some weeks earlier. On 18 October, when he was almost 22, but still, in student slang, a 'mule' (a freshman who still had to pass a university entrance examination), he joined a torchlight procession of students to the Kreuzberg to celebrate the anniversary of the Battle of Leipzig. On the hilltop, around a bonfire, they listened to speeches and sang songs to freedom.

When the fire died down, they returned to their beds, and the demonstration would have had no further consequences had not Bonn's *Allgemeinheit* student fraternity – so named to stress its 'general' character and accessibility to all, in the hope of evading the ban on the old, exclusivist *Burschenschaften* with their rigorous code and *esprit de corps* – shortly afterwards published a radical leaflet. This brought the Prussian police to the campus. Several student leaders were arrested, and all who had been on the Kreuzberg had to appear before a university court of two professors. Heine's turn came on 26 November. Asked whether there had been any cheers for the *Burschenschaften*, Heine said there had been only two cheers, one for Blücher, and one for German freedom. As to the common theme of the speeches, he declared: 'In the first speech I was able to discern no coherent theme at all; as for the second, I am unable to say, for I cannot remember what it was about.'

Fending off all 16 questions in this vague, half-amused manner, he pricked the pompousness of the interrogation, and a week later passed his entrance examination. The examiners found him weak in Latin and mathematics, but could not help seeing that his German essay, 'although written in an unusual style', showed 'a remarkable aptitude for satire'.

That very aptitude, of course, expressed itself in his whole bearing. All accounts of him speak of his 'sardonic smile', and Adolph Strodtmann, later to become Heine's first biographer, noted that he seldom joined in companionable conversation, and then only to interject a flash of wit or some jocular remark. Highly reticent about his inner life, 'good-natured and soft to excess, he seemed almost ashamed of his sensibility.' The fact is that Heine was by nature a self-absorbed loner, and the sad circumstances which led, that winter, to the liquidation of his father's business in Düsseldorf preyed on his mind, aggravating the insecurity which had made him publish his first verses under a pseudonym. One day in Bonn he showed the 'Riesenharf' poems, as printed in a Hamburg newspaper, to J.B. Rousseau, himself an aspiring poet who had been assigned to coach Harry in Latin. Pretending that the author was a friend of his, Harry declared them to be execrable and waited anxiously for Rousseau's opinion. 'When I unsuspectingly said that they were the work of a genius', Rousseau was to write, 'he fell about my neck, tearful and jubilant.'[1]

Heine felt at home in Bonn, a city only slightly larger than Düsseldorf, where the same easy-going Rhineland spirit prevailed. Bonn University – where Karl Marx was to start his studies 16 years later – was in 1819 Germany's youngest *alma mater*, having opened, or rather reopened, only the year before (the original university founded in 1786 having been closed by Napoleon). But it was about to become famous as the 'fortress of Romanticism', thanks to the presence on its academic staff of August Wilhelm Baron von Schlegel, the panjandrum of German literature and leader of the Romantic School.

At the insistence of both his mother and his uncle Salomon, Harry had enrolled as a law student. The law, however, especially Roman Law, bored him. He preferred to attend the lectures on ancient German history given by Ernst Moritz Arndt – until Arndt was suspended for his political views in February 1820 – and by the rector of the university, Karl D. Hullmann. But his inclination drew him most to the hall in which Schlegel lectured on German literature, on the *Nibelungenlied*, and on metrics and prosody.

An elegant, cosmopolitan, rather fastidious-looking figure of 52, Schlegel, before coming to Bonn, had spent 14 years abroad, most of them – but for a two-year interval as secretary to the Crown Prince of Sweden – on Madame de Staël's famous Swiss estate at Coppet. He had accompanied her on all her travels, and had met almost every European personality worth knowing.

'With the exception of Napoleon', Heine wrote later, 'he was in those days the first great man I had ever seen, and I shall never forget his impressive appearance.' It took some courage for him to show the great man his poetry, but Schlegel recognized his talent and took the trouble to go over his verses, correcting his metrics and showing how to achieve simplicity of style. Harry exulted when Schlegel invited him to coffee and returned his manuscripts with detailed pencil marks in the text and in the margin. He spent hours perfecting them accordingly, and Schlegel's influence is evident in Heine's poetry at the time, especially in the 'Fresco Sonnets' to Christian Sethe.

Shortly after the demonstration on the Kreuzberg, Heine had written a second 'Deutschland' ode. Still sharing the disappointment of Germany's patriotic youth at being robbed by Metternich of the fruits of the 'War of Liberation', and

181

possibly under the influence of Schlegel's Romanticism, he contrasted the 'pygmy nation', hyprocrisy and false values he saw around him with the strong Germany of old castles, 'knightly' men and fair ladies of sterling virtue. He also joined the *Allgemeinheit* fraternity, and became friends with a number of kindred spirits among its members. Besides Rousseau and Strodtmann, these included Joseph Neunzig, a future physician and prominent liberal; Johann F. Dieffenbach, who became a famous surgeon in Berlin; Karl Simrock and Hoffmann von Fallers-leben, two future prominent poets. Since two others in this group, Heinrich Straube and Fritz von Beughem, likewise wrote or had an interest in poetry, it became known as 'the lyrical half-dozen'.

In June 1820 Heine moved from Bonn to Beuel, a quiet village on the oppo-site bank of the Rhine. There, during the summer vacation, he acknowledged his debt to Schlegel by dedicating to him three sonnets which were published the following year.

There is no doubt that the young Heine genuinely admired Schlegel, who had translated Shakespeare, Dante, Cervantes and other masters of world lit-erature. But it is the fate of many 'masters' to be overtaken, and sometimes demolished, by their most talented pupils. Thirteen years later Heine wrote *Die romantische Schule* ('The Romantic School'), in which he killed off two birds with one stone, the double title signalling that he intended both to challenge most of Madame de Staël's ideas in her famous book on Germany – ideas which had been directly inspired by Schlegel – and to administer the *coup de grâce* to Schlegel's conception of Romanticism. In 1837, Heine was further to wound Schlegel by referring to him as 'the eternal dandy', while calling Goethe 'the eternal youth'. By that time, others too were taking jibes at Schlegel's vanity and affectations. What is remarkable is that as early as 1820 the grateful Heine of the sonnets already saw himself superseding the great master. 'You greedy man', he apostrophized Schlegel, advising him to be content with his hoard of riches and to 'think of spending now, not of accumulating more.'

Remarkably, too, during that summer vacation at Beuel, Heine also wrote a short essay in which, while defending Schlegel's Romanticism, he moved slightly away from him. To attack Romanticism, he wrote, was to wound the German language itself, 'the German word which is our most precious posses-sion'. Although he was still a long way from his later statement that the medieval 'thousand-year-old empire of Romanticism is dead, and I myself was its last and fabulous king', he observed that 'Christianity and chivalry', the two great Romantic influences,

> were only a means of bringing Romanticism to the fore; its flame has
> long been burning on the altar of our poesy; no priest needs to tend

its lamp with holy oil, and no knight needs to keep armed watch over it any longer. Germany is free now; no cleric can imprison German minds any longer, no petty aristocratic tyrant can whip German bodies into socage-service any longer, and therefore let us see to it that the German Muse becomes a freely blossoming, unaffected, honest German girl again and no languishing nun, and no pedigree-ridden damsel beholden to her knight.

In this essay, titled 'Die Romantik' and published in August 1820 shortly after it was written, an uncertain Heine was groping his way towards a conception of Romantic art no longer confined to the satisfying world of the imagination but seeking points of contact with the political and other realities of the modern world. The balance between subjective imagination and objective reality, and the question of art-for-art's-sake versus relevant or committed art, were beginning to preoccupy the young artist.

Near the end of September 1820, Heine was hiking through Westphalia, heading for Göttingen University in the Kingdom of Hanover. It had been decided that it was time for him to start 'swotting' in earnest for a lawyer's degree at Göttingen's Georgia Augusta University, which had the reputation of being Germany's Bologna for learning without Bologna's distractions.

Leaving the village solitude of Beuel, where he had started work on his first tragedy, *Almansor*, Harry had gone to Bonn in mid-August to settle his ex-matriculation. On or about 20 September he left for Düsseldorf. His parents were no longer there and he did not stay more than a day, after which he set out on foot for Göttingen, some 240 kilometres away. He broke his journey twice in Westphalia, 'the magic land' of ham, pumpernickel and pig beans. At Hamm he met the editors of the *Rhenish-Westphalian Advertiser*, which had published 'Die Romantik'; at Soest he had a joyful reunion with his long-time friend and soul-mate, Christian Sethe, who was now a junior barrister. Then he took the post-chaise as far as the next town, rested overnight, and went on walking. Guided, as he put it, by the 'Spirit of Swotting' which pointed inexorably in the direction of the 'towers of Georgia Augusta', he reached Göttingen after a 10-day journey.

He had not been long in the small town when, in short and increasingly grotesque order, he had an argument in a tavern and challenged a fellow-student to a pistol duel. The duel never took place, but occasioned a prolonged faculty wrangle, at the end of which, after a stay of only 4 months, Heine was abruptly sent down by order of the university's royal trustees; and almost simultaneously the student *Burschenschaften* threw him out, on the grounds, since discredited, of having violated its 'vows of chastity'.

In the *Harz Journey*, written 4 years after his arrival, Heine was to give a merciless picture of Göttingen, 'famous for its sausages and university', and to stigmatize the place as inhabited by 'students, professors, philistines and livestock – four classes which are, however, anything but strictly separable. The livestock are the most important class.' Most of Göttingen's 1,300 students were aristocratic young sparks and sons of Hanoverian Junkers. Snobbish fops and conceited dandies, they brought their valets to the town, rode, strutted about or roamed the streets in hordes, duelled daily amongst themselves, talked of nothing but their dogs, horses and their noble ancestors, and treated the servile local burghers, who relied upon them for their living, with the insolence of provincial lords of creation.

Heine had yet to witness the scene he was to describe in *The North Sea III* (1826), of a group of them on horseback cruelly chasing a hired sprinter as if he were an animal:

> It was an oppressively hot, humid Sunday, and the poor fellow was already pretty well exhausted with the running he'd done, when some Hanoverian Junkers – students of the humanities, mark you – offered him a few thalers to run over the course again; and the fellow ran, and he was deathly white and wore a red jacket, and close behind him, raising a cloud of dust, galloped the well-fed aristocratic youths on their tall steeds. Every now and then the horses' hooves prodded the gasping, hunted fellow; and he was a human being.

His own forebears, Heine was to observe, had not been hunters. 'They were very much hunted, and my blood rises at the thought of taking aim at the descendants of their colleagues.' Confronted with a living example of feudal days, 'when human beings were the game in a grand hunt', Heine could not but be repelled by Göttingen's 'sportsmen', and identified with their quarry.

Thrown together for the first time with the scions of 'old' Germany's loyal knights and fair ladies he had celebrated in his two 'Deutschland' poems, Heine reacted to their boorish behaviour in the flesh by spending most of his first fortnight at Göttingen in his lonely rooms, working on *Almansor*. Then, deciding to make the best of the absence of any cultural life in 'this learned nest', he wrote the famous quatrain 'Swot, German youth' and registered for courses in philosophy, German history and medieval German literature. He began to dine at Göttingen's 'English' tavern (the 'Hoff von England'); and at three o'clock, on 4 afternoons a week, he religiously attended the lectures on old High German poetry given by one of Göttingen's few distinguished professors, Georg Friedrich Benecke (1762–1844), to whom Schlegel had given him a laudatory letter of introduction. By 9 November, an amazed Harry was exclaiming in a letter to his friend Fritz von Beughem: 'Can you imagine, dear Fritz, only 9 students, literally nine, attend the course in High German or take the slightest interest in the spiritual life and heritage of their forefathers! Oh Germany! Land of oaks and stupidity!'

He, of course, was most interested in old High German poetry and was to put Benecke's lectures to good use. He also, oddly enough, joined the *Burschenschaft* – for, although he seems to have met some literati among Göttingen's boisterous students, he was describing them to von Beughem on 9 November as dull, 'watery prose writers' and summing up the whole '*Burschenschaft personnel*' as 'pomaded stallions in patent leather shoes.'

The fact is that in 1820 the *Burschenschaft* situation was highly confused in the immediate aftermath of the Karlsbad Decrees. Students entertaining the French libertarian ideas that animated Harry and his friends in the Bonn fraternity shared with French-hating Teutomaniacs and *Turnvater* Jahn's chauvinist 'gymnasts' the dream of an undivided Germany, and all were precariously united in opposition to Metternich's policies. In Hanover, dynastically united with Britain, the spirit of the common 'great German fatherland' – in the interests of which the students had in 1818 broken up the different fraternities and formed the national *Allgemeine Burschenschaft* Association – had not yet taken root. Göttingen's students were still feudally organized in *Landsmannschaften*, and their rude old code and duelling spirit prevailed. It was only late in 1820 that a *Burschenschaft* of the new, politically radical type was formed by students arrived from other parts of Germany. Whether Heine joined out of idealism, or to relieve the tedium, the latest studies show him to have been one of its first members.[2]

The newcomers brought with them echoes of the two-year-long student agitation before the new national Association had managed to impose its views, years during which fraternities at several universities had taken to vilifying, and even boycotting each other. It was actually the stand Heine took on this issue that was to land him in trouble.

It was the end of November, three weeks after he had declared to his 'dear Fritz' that he was determined to swot and 'achieve something this winter'. Besides Benecke's lectures and a course in logic, he enjoyed being introduced to the 'consolations of history' by Baron Georg Sartorius, a professor who invited him to his home some evenings, and whom he was to single out as an open-hearted man sensitive to 'the joys and sorrows of all races, the cares of beggars and kings ... a bright star in these dark days.' Otherwise Harry had finished the third act of *Almansor*; sent off a slim parcel of poems to the publisher Brockhaus; and spent a great deal of time in Göttingen's magnificent library, where a quarter of a million volumes were ranged 12 rows high, reading

Shakespeare and London's literary *Monthly Review*, among other things. Strangely, or typically, his attendance record shows no lectures on law, and he seems to have cultivated his mind and his Muse rather than the *corpus juris*.

During a lunch-time argument at the 'English' tavern, Heine was vehemently condemning mutual denunciations between fraternities, and declared that an incident at Heidelberg showed that such warfare was bound to degenerate into one big, ill-famed 'Schweinerei'. A certain Wilhelm Wiebel jumped to his feet and shouted that for anyone who had not been at Heidelberg to say so was in itself a 'Schweinerei'. This, under the formal code of the *Burschenschaften*, was so grave an insult that the next day Heine – who had already duelled with sabres at Bonn – challenged Wiebel to a pistol duel. The time and place had been set by Wiebel's second (Baron Ranzau) with Heine's second (Vallender) when the pro-rector got wind of the affair. On 3 December both Heine and Wiebel were placed under *Stubenarrest* (confined to their rooms). Next, they were interrogated by the prorector, who ruled that Wiebel was to retract the offensive remark. But Heine insisted he should also state that he had uttered it 'in the heat of argument'. Wiebel agreed, but next day proclaimed loudly at table that, though he was being forced to retract, he had meant every cool word he had said. Thereupon a university court of 6, headed by the pro-rector and including one of the syndics, held 4 sessions on 4, 6, 7 and 8 December. According to the minutes of the proceedings,[3] Wiebel was caught lying on three points.

He claimed that Heine had challenged him personally while they were still at the tavern, not to a pistol duel but to sabres, and denied that his second had fixed the time and venue. Under pressure, and after various confrontations, he admitted the truth of Heine's version of events. Wiebel remained adamant, however, in his refusal to keep his promise to the pro-rector and declare in public that he had uttered the insult 'in the heat of argument'. After more discussion and persuasion he agreed to say so before the court. Heine declared himself satisfied, and the two were forbidden to duel on penalty of rustication.

This, however, was not the end of the matter. In January the academic authorities met to consider a weighty point raised by Wiebel's *Landsmannschaft*: had the duel which never took place been stopped by outside 'intervention' or a genuine 'reconciliation'? Pistol duels having been forbidden by law, the university heads, unsure of their ground, sought the Hanover government's advice. The matter had meanwhile become public, and after solemnly debating it for a while the trustees of Georgia Augusta University – on the government's advice – adopted the harsher interpretation and ruled 'intervention'. By their sentence of 27 January 1821, Wiebel was to be rusticated, not before spending a fortnight in the university prison, and Heine was sent down for 6 months.

'Where shall I go now?' he wrote to his friend Steinmann on 4 February. He was penniless and waiting for money from home. He kept to his room 'because only by pretending to be sick have I been allowed to remain a few days longer.' Wiebel had got the severer punishment, but Heine feared his family's reaction to the news of his expulsion, and a worse blow that had befallen him shortly before the New Year: the decision of the *Burschenschaft* to expel him from the society.

He was accused of unchastity, but what had he committed? Rape? Orgies? Debauchery? No such accusation bothered the young man himself at the time. It was only in 1881, long after his death, that the literary historian Karl Goedeke launched the allegation that Harry's 'pretended' illness was not only real but venereal, a sexual affliction 'proving that he had violated the *Burschenschaft*'s vows of chastity.' Goedeke's claim, soon embroidered by a story that Heine had been caught at a prostitute's 'Knallhütte' outside Göttingen, has haunted the literature on Heine for almost a century. The mystery surrounding the unknown reason for his ouster from the *Burschenschaft* generated a number of wild theories, none of them substantiated.

In 1972 Dr Eberhard Galley, the director of the Heine Institute in Düsseldorf, uncovered a clue to the original sin for which the fraternity decreed Heine's expulsion. On 29 September 1820, about the time he was arriving in Göttingen, the *Burschenschaften*, meeting at a secret national convention in Dresden, had adopted a charter stressing the 'Christian-German' character of the Association. The charter described Jews as people 'who have no fatherland and can have no interest in ours', and declared them to be inadmissible to its ranks unless they were ready to be integrated 'in our Christian-German *Volk*'. Dr Galley, who noted that the then nascent Göttingen fraternity had sent an observer to Dresden who brought back the resolutions, was joined at the 1972 International Heine Congress by Professor Pierre Grappin of Paris, who told a large gathering of scholars that these resolutions at last made clear the 'actual reason' behind the fraternity ouster.[4]

But Heine already had his answer – and a fatherland – at hand. His essay, 'Die Romantik', published in August 1820 – some 6 weeks before the secret Dresden resolutions – had contained a passage comparing 'the German word' and language to 'a liberty bell' that no foreign despot could silence. Into it he had worked a remarkable statement: 'And this word – "the German word" – is our highest possession... a fatherland even to him whom stupidity and malice deny a fatherland.'

They could ostracize him or expel him, but they could not silence his tongue nor take away his talent. The word, the German language, would be his refuge. 'Present circumstances', he had written to the publisher Brockhaus, 'force me to suppress any poem to which political meaning could be imputed,' explaining why he was offering only a slim collection of 'mostly erotic' verse (which Brock-haus rejected). But henceforth, as soon he had made a name for himself, the artistry of his language would turn his pen, his poet's tool, into a sharp sword. From early youth he had immersed himself in German lore and folksong. It was the genuine folksong he had in mind when, in 'Die Romantik', he called for a return to the 'honest' German Muse.

In a single phrase unrelated to the theme of that short article, he gave notice that he was a sovereign of the spirit, the proud possessor of an exalted realm, a *sui generis* fatherland knowing no frontiers and requiring no one else's arrogant approval. That Heine should have served this notice so early in his life – long before his books would be banned in Germany – was another instance of his uncanny sense of the direction of events.

The hep-hep riots in Hamburg had of course told Heine which way the wind was blowing before the Dresden *Burschenschaft* ever convened; and already at Bonn he had fought a duel over an anti-Semitic remark. There, however, he had moved among kindred spirits. Most of its fraternity was composed of Rhenish students belonging to the 'progressive', liberal wing of the *Burschenschaften* and he had been less exposed to the hate propaganda against anything and anyone 'foreign' to their 'Teutonist' wing. At Göttingen he found that chauvinist line had been adopted as policy by the supposedly 'democratic' fraternities, too – his own liberal friends, as it were.

'They and no others', in Grappin's view, 'declared the Jews to be fatherland-less' and despicable and 'chased Heine from their midst... His exclusion on the grounds of his Jewishness, even if camouflaged, must have been a very hard blow to Harry Heine.'[5]

Years later, a more mature Heine, looking back on the *Burschenshaft*'s 'com-mon struggle for German unity', was to observe that its numerically stronger liberal wing lacked the semi-religious fanaticism of the 'regenerated Teutonist' minority, whose catchwords – 'Fatherland', 'Germany', 'faith of our ancestors' – were always sure to 'electrify the masses' more effectively than appeals to reason or cosmopolitan ideas of humanity, truth and reason.

But at the beginning of 1821, the hurt of his expulsion from the fraternity went all the deeper as in his two 'Deutschland' poems he had made himself the spokesman of the high hopes and disillusion of Germany's youth. He had felt like a German then. Now, at 23, he was an outcast, an expatriate in the land of his birth. To add to all his miseries, during his last week in Göttingen he received, together with the money enabling him to depart, the news that Amalie, his beloved 'damosel', had become engaged to another man.

Rejected on all sides – it was enough to drive a young man to despair. Yet he kept his despondency to himself and most of his letter of 4 February to Steinmann dealt with literary matters. Three days later, having arranged and packed his papers, he turned his back on inhospitable Göttingen.

Although he was not unhappy to leave the pompous little citadel of 'Teuton stupidity', there is no doubt that his humiliation at Göttingen enhanced Heine's cynicism, his mockery and whole defensive-aggressive attitude towards life. Though Amalie was engaged to Jonathan Friedländer, a wealthy East Prussian landowner, it was straight to Hamburg, the 'city of hucksters', that Heine went from Göttingen. He expected the worst as far as his amatory feelings went, but he was forced to settle his future with Uncle Salomon. With him travelled his pen and his manuscripts, including the nearly final draft of *Almansor*. His play dealt with the forcible conversion to Christianity of the Moors in Spain, but into this social drama on the oppression of a minority in the name of Christian 'love' he had also poured the bitterness of his love for Amalie and 'my paradoxes, my wisdom, my love, my hate and all my craziness.'

Just before he left, he realized with some horror that *Almansor* was – as often happens with the most genuine outpourings – not quite the great tragedy that had swum before his eyes. Nonetheless, he was sure that because of its 'topical' subject, *Almansor* would be seen as an allegory of Prussia's treatment of the Jews and would make 'a great stir'. It did. It was to be hissed and booed on its opening night, though not for the reasons he imagined.

Amalie was now an elegant young lady – a smartly done-up 'Sunday doll', as Heine described her in March 1821 to his friend Straube; 'the celestial maker who fashioned her surpassed himself'. A dazzling beauty with a glitter of diamonds, she showed little sympathy for his feelings – of whose depth she may have been unaware – but her puzzling, 'icy' eyes continued both to lure him and to put him in his place. Four years earlier he had realized that she was beyond his reach – 'I lost my queen on the first move.' Yet, as he now confided to Straube, she remained his madness, the hard 'rock on which my reason has foundered and to which, nevertheless, I cling... It is an old story.'

In February he spent only a fortnight in Hamburg before going on to Oldesloe. There he was upset to find his father in a pitiful state of melancholia. His mother suffered from migraine, and Harry himself was in an overwrought mood. It is a little-known fact that, although Göttingen University had relegated him for 6 months, a proviso in its archives – not included in the university court's sentence – left open the possibility of readmitting him for the summer semester starting in April.[6] But his dismissal from the *Burschenschaft* made him feel that he had been placed outside the pale. It was from Oldesloe that he wrote Straube the incoherent letter about his midnight hallucinations under the window of his Dulcinea, the 'Sunday doll'.

Straube was the editor of a literary journal, himself woefully lovestruck at the time, and thus a friend with whom Heine could share both his poetic interests and his heart's sorrows; but the letter also contained the famous passage in which Heine wondered, 'How will the book of my life end? And did the divine author mean to write it as a tragedy or a comedy?' He answered his own question: 'Thank God, I also have something to say about that. On my will depends the denouement... What do I care whether the gallery whistles or applauds? Let the stalls, too, hiss, I laugh... And if the heart in the body is torn, pierced, stabbed and cut, there still remains laughter loud and clear! Yes, if the gaping wide death wound in my heart could speak, it would speak: I laugh.'

After a depressing 10 days in Oldesloe, he went back to Hamburg to obtain from his uncle the means to continue his studies. Conscious of his fledgling power but still highly vulnerable, he was soon off towards sensational success as well as new challenges, returning to the war of Germany's chauvinists. Crying, 'I was provoked to the battle,' he would fight back in the manner of a solitary knight with 'the German word' and his lance-like wit for his chief weapons, and laughter the armour to hide his scars.

Berlin University, where Heine arrived in mid-April 1821, impressed him as 'a splendid edifice', but in an expurgated section of the first of his 'Letters from Berlin' he was to write that most of the lecture rooms were gloomy. Some of the windows overlooked the Opera House across the square, and for students condemned to listen to some boring afternoon lecture while their eyes kept wandering to the tantalizing spectacle of 'smart coaches, military men and fleet-footed, sporting nymphs' on their way to the opera, it was 'like sitting on live coals.'[7]

The University had been founded as recently as 1810 by Wilhelm von Humboldt, who after Prussia's debacle at Jena had told King Friedrich Wilhelm III that 'the state must replace by intellectual force what it has lost in physical force.' Besides reforming Prussia's entire school system, Humboldt brought to Berlin some of Germany's most illustrious minds – Fichte to teach philosophy, Schleiermacher to lecture on theology, Friedrich Karl von Savigny as professor of Roman Law, to mention but a few of the distinguished faculty. But if von Humboldt, the famous philologist and natural scientist – and brother of the even more famous Alexander – had created the brightest jewel in Prussia's educational crown, it was Hegel's agreement in 1818 to leave Heidelberg and fill the chair of philosophy vacated by Fichte's death which – in the resigned forecast of Heidelberg's prorector, Karl Daub – was to put 'the crown' itself on Berlin's academic renown.[8]

Hegel usually lectured at 4 or 5 o'clock in the afternoon. But on the stroke of 6 he would no more than finish his sentence and hurry across the square to hear the famous Spontini, Berlin's 'Royal Music Director', conduct one of Gluck's operas, or his own spectacular but shallow Italian-style *Olympie*, first performed shortly after Heine arrived at the University. Heine was to write feelingly about 'the poor student with sixteen pennies burning in his pocket', envious of the people flocking to the Opera House. At the beginning of his stay in Berlin, his uncle indeed kept him short of funds, but music historians were to single out the young Heine, along with E.T.A. Hoffmann and 13-year-old Felix Mendelssohn, among the brilliant audience that within a month of *Olympie* attended the premiere of Weber's *Der Freischütz*. Heine was to write at some length about the 'battle' that followed between the aristocratic devotees of Spontini and the bourgeois admirers of Weber's first Romantic 'German' opera, pointing out that 'this violent party strife' was not 'of a political nature between liberals and ultra- conservatives, such as we see in other capitals. Such political strife cannot break to the surface here because of the mediating non-partisan Royal power,' he wrote, but went on to compare the Spontini-Weber musical battle with that which had divided Paris between the followers of Gluck and those of Piccini towards the end of the *ancien régime*. It was Heine's veiled way of suggesting that, with strict censorship prevailing in the Prussian capital, the live elephants produced by Spontini on stage, no less than the serious music-making that went on at the *Singakademie* under Mendelsssohn's teacher Zelter, and the general public craze for 'the opera, theatre, concerts, assemblees, balls, teas (both dansant and médisant), masquerades large and small',[9] filled the vacuum created by the suppression of all political and social issues.

University lectures were in fact politically supervised and professors had to stick to their approved lecture plans. Books were confiscated. *Wilhelm Tell* and *The Prince of Homburg* could not be performed, and lending libraries were checked for 'subversive' material. Hegel may have been at the height of his fame in 1821 as 'the living culmination of the revolution in thought initiated by Kant',[10] but not everyone in Berlin had welcomed his appointment. Daub of Heidelberg expected Hegel to clash 'like a cuirassier armed to the teeth' with the Reverend Schleiermacher, whom he compared to an 'Uhlan on a nimble horse'. Indeed, Schleiermacher soon complained that Hegel was ridiculing Christian obedience by declaring 'dogs to be the best Christians'; and Professor Savigny, an arch-conservative with high connections in government circles, criticized Hegel not only for his 'arrogance', but for 'disseminating doubts on every subject in the world, leading his enthusiastic pupils to abandon all religious ties.' Savigny found Hegel's 'absolutely crooked, confused talk about non-scientific matters' particularly objectionable in view of 'the university's rather difficult position vis-à-vis the government, on which there is only one voice among all the other professors.'[11]

Hegel, however, proved to be a very resourceful personality. In his opening lecture he had declared that 'man cannot think highly enough of the power of the mind' and that 'the closed essence of the universe has no intrinsic power to resist man's cognition, but must open up and reveal its riches and depths to him.' Schleiermacher might privately fume at Hegel's allegedly accusing him 'of animal ignorance of God', but Hegel continued to lecture to crowded halls, to take a lively interest in the opera and theatre, to applaud the various prima donnas appearing at the Schauspielhaus, and to express enthusiasm at the acting of Ludwig Devrient in the role of Tartuffe. Oddly dressed in a blue tailcoat and yellow trousers, Hegel would be seen in a carriage with Moritz Gottlieb von Saphir, publisher-editor of Berlin's *Theatre Almanac* and its *Fast Literary, Theatre and Social Mail* (*Berliner Schnellpost für Literatur, Theater und Gesellig-keit*), for the latter of which he also wrote a regular theatre review. And while continuing to affirm his 'faith in reason and truth', Hegel managed both to remain Germany's most prominent philosopher and to retain his government professorship. This was a remarkable achievement in the Prussia of his day, when the King alone ultimately decided what was truth and what could be published. For example, when the *Vössische Zeitung* reported a 'double anniversary' celebration staged by Hegel's admirers in honour of his 56th (and of Goethe's coincidental 77th) birthday, a Royal order instructed the *Ober-Zensur* that reports of such 'private festivities' were henceforth to be kept out of the press.

Hegel's influence on Heine is one of the contentious questions that exercise scholars to this day. However, as Jeffrey Sammons has pointed out, 'Heine's life outside the university was fully as important as his academic experiences.'[12] On 7 May 1821, not long after his arrival in Berlin, *Der Gesellschafter*, a serious local magazine edited by F.W. Gubitz, a professor at the Academy of Arts, began to publish Heine's poems. By the beginning of July about a dozen of them had appeared, including the sonnets dedicated to Schlegel and Christian Sethe. At the same time a number of his essays appeared in another periodical, *Der Zuschauer* ('The Spectator'), followed by his translation of the Spirit choruses in Byron's *Manfred*.

Remarkably, within a month or so of his arrival, Heine had been introduced to the salon of the famous Rahel Levin, now Rahel von Varnhagen, who once again presided over Berlin's intellectual elite. Rahel's husband had recommended him to Professor Gubitz, who later related how a pale, negligently dressed young Heine had approached him: '"I am absolutely unknown to you," he said, "but hope that you will make me known." "Willingly," I laughed, "if it is possible."'

Gubitz asked him to polish some of his verses and emend a few passages that 'went too far for the censor'. He noted that Heine, although slightly peeved,

'revised very skilfully', and later Heine dubbed the professor's editorial meti-
culousness 'gubitzing'. Gubitz also helped to smoothe relations between Heine
and his millionaire uncle. Arranging with a banker of his acquaintance to meet
Salomon Heine on his next visit to Berlin, Gubitz told the millionaire that poets
were not always in touch with reality and that 'such an uncle ought not to abandon' so talented a nephew. 'I never intended to,' Salomon Heine replied. 'But
he has to learn that a man must make proper use of his money, whatever his
occupation.' He then turned to their host, the banker Leonard Liepke, and
said: 'The gentleman here says that a great genius is in danger of being stunted.
I hope he is right about the genius. Please pay my nephew 200 Thaler now, and
then 500 annually for three years. After that – we'll see.'

In November 1821, Gubitz's paper serialized a dozen scenes from Heine's
Almansor; and on 20 December the publisher and bookseller Friedrich Maurer –
whose printing press produced Gubitz's magazine – issued a slim volume of
Poems by 'H. Heine'. It included the early verses which had appeared in
Hamburg under a pseudonym, the newer ones published in Berlin, and a translation of Byron's 'Fare Thee Well' and two songs from *Childe Harold's Pilgrimage*. A week after his 24th birthday, Heine found himself, like Byron, famous
overnight.

The analogy, which Heine (while stressing the affinity he felt for 'my cousin
Lord Byron') had the good sense to dissociate himself from, was not entirely
without foundation. Blond, pale, and now sporting an ivory-topped cane and
elegant suit, he was in fact acclaimed as the 'German Byron' by Baroness Elise
von Hohenhausen – Byron's German translator and a distinguished literary
hostess – at one of her Tuesday afternoon tea parties.

After the final defeat of Napoleon, who died on St Helena in May 1821, Berlin was a bustling capital. It was, however, as Heine noted, a new capital, lacking
character or tradition. In this stolid 'Biedermeyer' period there was a certain
amount of social razzle-dazzle, but the various strata – 'the court and the ministers, the diplomatic corps, civil servants, merchants, officers' – each had their
separate entertainments. Like guilds, Heine observed, they never mixed, and
even 'the noble class' at its fetes 'aspired to imitate court affairs or princely
balls.'

Unlike those exclusivist, caste-like groups, the parties of the beautiful Elise
von Hohenhausen – who was only 33 when Heine read some of his poems and
fragments of his *Ratcliff* tragedy to her circle – included such figures as the
elderly mathematician and Kantian philosopher Lazarus Bendavid mingling
freely with the Romantic writer Adalbert von Chamisso, the publisher Eduard
Hitzig, the poetess Helmine von Chezy, the rising painter Wilhelm Hensel, and
other young artists and trend-setters.

Even more important to Heine's future was the influence of Rahel von Varn-hagen. At her new salon in the Französische Strasse, Heine met Berlin's most cultured and sophisticated society – Alexander von Humboldt, August von Schlegel (his teacher at Bonn) and Schlegel's brother Friedrich; Ludwig Tieck, the Romantic poet, and Baron de la Motte-Fouqué; the Reverend Schleierma-cher; Henriette Herz and Dorothea Mendelssohn (now Schlegel) – two of the original trio of 'clever Jewesses' – and Pauline Wiesel, the mistress of that favourite of Rahel's pre-war 'garret' soirées, Louis Ferdinand, 'Prince of Prussia' and nephew of Frederick the Great, who had fallen in the Battle of Jena.

If at first Heine was shy and awkward in the company of these veteran, worldly-wise social figures, some of whom – like Humboldt, Friedrich von Schlegel and the younger Varnhagen – had attended the Congress of Vienna in various official capacities, Rahel gently put him at ease and taught him social graces almost without his noticing it. Elise von Hohenhausen sometimes brought her young friends to the Varnhagens, in whose circle Heine also met Dr Johann Koreff, physician, poet, diplomat, and Spontini's librettist; Rahel's brother, the poet and literary editor Ludwig Robert; Eduard Gans, Hegel's foremost disciple, no older than Heine but already a university lecturer on his way to an early professorship and to becoming Hegel's heir-presumptive; and occasionally Hegel himself, although not a habitué of Rahel's salon, would put in an appearance.

Rahel's personal magnetism, the devotion and influence she brought to her self-chosen, successful task of publicly restoring the septuagenarian Goethe to his position as Germany's greatest mind, have been ascribed by the Danish lit-erary historian Georg Brandes to her intuitive grasp of the mysterious *Zeitgeist*, which others were to take years to analyze. With her fine antennae, Rahel was quick to recognize the talent and originality of 'our little Heine' as well as some contrariety in his character. She called him 'a ne'er-do-well favoured by the Graces', praised him generously, but was not afraid to criticize immature, crude or over-sentimental elements in his poetry. 'I'd let nothing slip by if I saw his manuscript before it went to the press,' she was to write Gentz, the 'Secretary of Europe', with whom she continued to correspond in spite of his reactionary policies. She made Heine appreciate Goethe's harmony, with one reservation: young Heine could not be deterred from feeling, and presently announcing, that Goethe's *Kunstperiode*, with its aesthetic indifference to political and social issues, would soon have to yield its dominion to fresh minds animated by the 'new ideas of a new age'.[13]

The Varnhagen couple had a civilizing influence on Heine. No ordinary patrons, they were sincerely concerned for his literary development. To her husband, Rahel remarked: 'Heine must become *wesentlich*' (i.e., must go to the essence of things). The husband helped to launch Heine by writing a favourable review of his little book of poems.

In February 1822 his 'Letters from Berlin' began to appear in the 'art and science' section of the *Rhenish-Westphalian Advertiser*. Heine was now a regular visitor to the theatre and concerts, missed no opera premiere, whether Koreff's *Aucassin and Nicolette* or Spontini's new offering, *Nurmahal or the Cashmere Rose Festival*; and late at night he was to be seen hobnobbing at the Café Royal and other bohemian hangouts with members of yet a third circle – the actor Ludwig Devrient, E.T.A. Hoffmann, Dietrich Grabbe, the frustrated dramatist and 'drunken Shakespeare' (as Heine called him), and various actors, actresses and singers who dropped in after their performances.

In July, the 'Letters from Berlin' were abruptly broken off, apparently for censorship reasons. As they were written for a provincial audience and published anonymously, the fact that many readers identified Heine as the author testified to his early established personal style. The 'Letters' were remarkable for the lighthanded way in which the young writer, flitting 'by the association of ideas' from a masked ball at the Opera House to street scenes, from bemedalled high officials and military men to liveried servants, laundresses, coachmen, barbers and landladies, and back again to society gossip and the taste of truffles-and-ice-cream, conjured up a picture of socially sparkling, comically pompous, politically muzzled Berlin – in which even press criticism of Spontini's music was prohibited by Royal order. The censors may have disliked his outrageous way of introducing, in the midst of reporting on a grandiose Royal wedding, the scene of an angry musician suddenly muttering, 'guillotines, lanterns... O Saint Marat! O Danton! Robespierre!...' and by other allusions to forbidden themes.

Most of August and September 1822 Heine spent in the Prussian part of Poland as the guest of a fellow-student, Count Eugen von Breza. On his return to Berlin he looked for new lodgings, fought a duel and was slightly injured, but wrote or revised more poems – 16 of which appeared during October in Gubitz's *Gesellschafter* and other journals – and began to write down his travel impressions.

That winter he wrote a no longer extant opera libretto called *The Batavians* and, after successful discussions with the publisher Dummler, also polished the material for a new volume. The result was *Tragedies*, with a 'Lyrical Intermezzo', issued in April 1823. Inserted between the two tragedies, *Almansor* and *Ratcliff*, was the 'Intermezzo' of 66 poems dedicated to Rahel von Varnhagen, including many that – set to music and more than metaphorically borne 'on wings of song' – were to make him world-famous.

With so much extracurricular activity, the question arises of his Berlin studies, and inevitably that of his relations with Hegel. Heine later claimed to

195

have been acquainted with Hegel – indeed, to have been initiated into the abstruse 'scholastic secrets' of German philosophy by Hegel himself, 'my great teacher'. A famous passage in Heine's *Confessions* reads:

> One beautiful starlight night, Hegel stood with me at an open window. I, being a young man of twenty-two, and having just eaten well and drunk coffee, naturally spoke with enthusiasm of the stars, and called them abodes of the blest. But the master muttered to himself: 'The stars! Hm! hm! the stars are only a brilliant eruption on the firmament.' 'What!' cried I; 'then there is no blissful spot above, where virtue is rewarded after death?' But he, glaring at me with his dim eyes, remarked, sneering: 'So you want a tip because you have supported your sick mother and not poisoned your brother?'

Thus Heine supposedly learned that presiding over the heavens was no one but an old spinster, 'Necessity'. But the *Confessions* were written late in his life, and as so often with Heine, the degree of veracity that may or may not be hidden in his allegories and metaphors is in dispute. A number of scholars doubt that he personally knew or even studied under Hegel, let alone that he understood what he called Hegel's 'spider's web of dialectic'.

These doubts apply even more strongly to other passages in the *Confessions*, in which he wrote that he 'could easily prophesy what songs would one day be whistled and chirped in Germany', for he had seen Hegel, 'with his almost comically serious face, like a sitting hen brooding over the fatal eggs', hatching 'the birds that later gave tone to the new school of songs.' And then the climax of his intimacy with Hegel:

> I stood behind the maestro when he composed [this music] in his obscure symbols and flourishes, so that only the initiated should be able to decipher it – I could sometimes see him looking anxiously about, for fear that he might be understood. He liked me very much, being sure that I would not betray him; I even thought him very servile at the time. When I once questioned his phrase: 'All that exists is rational,' he observed with a strange smile that it could also be construed 'All that is rational must be.'

Heine was here referring, though in somewhat distorted form, to Hegel's oracular dictum, 'What is rational is actual and what is actual is rational.' This famous formula was first thought by everyone, including Heine, to express Hegel's servile acquiescence in Prussia's reactionary *status quo*, until its potential as a formula for revolution – when turned round, in the manner suggested by

Heine, to read 'What is rational shall be' – was realized. But the scene of Heine looking over Hegel's shoulder and 'the maestro' decoding his cryptic sentence for him, was not included in the *Confessions*. It was published only after Heine's death and is considered by many to be merely a 'significant' but dubious anecdote.

Heine wrote that scene at the beginning of 1844, 20 years after his Berlin studies. During the intervening years he not only realized that the political implications of German philosophy were apt to breed revolution, but in an article published in mid-June 1843 – before he had ever met Karl Marx – he revised his opinion about Hegel's servility, suggesting that 'the great man' had simply camouflaged his 'most liberal' philosophy, enciphering it, as it were, in conservative-sounding cryptograms to protect it from being nipped in the bud by the government or the Church. Recalling this transitional period before Marx turned Hegel 'upside down' and produced his materialist dialectic of history, Engels wrote: 'What neither the government nor the liberals realized was foreseen as early as 1833 by at least one man, and his name was Heinrich Heine.'

Taking up this thesis in our own times, Georg Lukàcz, the Marxist philosopher and literary historian, declared in a lengthy essay on Heine that Hegel's influence on him was 'the strongest' of all, to the point where it 'determined' Heine's 'entire conception of history' as well as his 'entire theory of art'.[14]

On 1 December 1823, while Heine was staying with his parents at Lüneburg, he asked his friend Moser to obtain his ex-matriculation papers from Berlin University. He named three professors whose attendance certificates Moser was to get, 'one certificate from Hegel (!!!), one from Hasse and another from Schmalz.' Heine put in the three exclamation marks because Moser – a bank clerk, but otherwise a highly educated '*Privatgelehrter*' – was so ardent a 'Hegelian' that Heine had humorously written him of 'a most terrible nightmare' which dissolved only when 'you suddenly materialized and you comforted me by saying not to fear because I was only an Idea, to prove which you reached for Hegel's Logic.'

The 'Idea' (*Idee* in German) was a Hegelian concept, subsuming the constant dynamic movement of the Spirit or the Absolute in history towards its ultimate fulfilment. Hegel spoke of the *Idee* in his lectures on logic, and again in his course on 'The Philosophy of World History' delivered in the 1822–23 winter semester – lectures which Heine definitely attended.

In 1823 Heine described Hegel as 'the profoundest of German philosophers'. But he gave Hegel's *Idee* an interpretation of his own. He saw in it a revolutionary principle, for the movement of history meant change, away from censorship, oppression, 'stagnation, lethargy and yawning';[15] and when, in 1825, he described to Moser his disappointing visit to Goethe in Weimar, he affirmed his adherence to the *Idee* from an aesthetic viewpoint too. Characterizing Goethe as an epicurean who sometimes played with but never really understood the *Idee*, he wrote: 'I, on the other hand, am a born enthusiast... ready to sacrifice my life for the sake of the *Idee*.' He clarified what he meant when he alluded to the end of Goethe's *Kunstperiode* of uncommitted art:

> Present-day art is condemned to die because it is rooted in the decrepit old regime of the Holy Roman Empire of the past. Like all the wilted remnants of that past it represents a stark contradiction to the present. It is this contradiction, and not the flux of time [Zeitbewegung], that is injurious to art; on the contrary, the flux of time ought to favour it, as once in Athens and Florence art flourished most splendidly in the midst of wars and violent party strife.

Of course, he went on with a stab at Goethe, 'those Greek and Florentine artists did not lock themselves up with their idly poeticizing souls in egoistic isolation, hermetically shutting out the great pains and joys of their time; on the contrary, their works were the dreaming mirror reflection of their age, and they themselves were whole men... they did not divorce their art from the politics of the day.'[16]

This was Heine writing in 1828. Although he was later to rank Goethe with Napoleon among the rare 'archetypal intellects' capable of intuitively 'cajoling' the spirit of their age into an emancipatory direction, he felt strongly that the new age required a new art form. We know that Heine was eventually to find it both in poetry and in prose, but in 1820s Berlin he was torn between contradictory pulls and undecided about which mode best suited his personal need for realism and involvement.

His inner struggle reflected what had become one of the great literary-philosophical issues in Germany in the last phase of Romanticism – the question whether subjective poetry sprung from the artist's imagination could properly deal with the problems of the post-Napoleonic world. At the sound of Napoleon's guns even Schlegel, the high priest of Romanticism, had privately wondered for a moment whether 'dreamy' poetry ought not to yield its place to 'elocution'; and Hegel, in his lectures on Aesthetics – begun in Heidelberg and continued in Berlin during the 1820s – deprecated the ability of contemporary poetry and, to a lesser degree, prose to encompass the complex reality and contradictory truths of the modern world in the manner in which Homer and the ancient Greeks had fused beauty, truth, sensuous nature and reflective reason.

Heine, however, determined as he was already in 1822 to fight with his pen 'against inveterate injustice, the dominant foolishness, and evil',[17] read into this a challenging call – corresponding to his own search – for a new relevant art form; and when he came to formulate it in the passage on the end of Goethe's *Kunstperiode* he did so in terms consonant both with Hegel's method and with his theory of the movement of history ('the flux of time'). The passage has been cited by Nigel Reeves as 'an example [of] how Heine pushes Hegel's thought in a new direction, a Left Hegelian direction.'[18]

Heine had made a name for himself, but fame did not bring him happiness. The reasons were many and complex. But their gist was that between 1822 and 1825 the writer of bitter-sweet songs felt unbearably 'provoked' and assaulted from all sides; and the result – given Heine's temperament and sensibility – was to cast him while still young into the mould of the mocking, cynical poet-rebel and embattled political writer that was to become his persona and his hallmark.

Fame meant exposure, and Heine soon felt the envy aroused by an original talent. His friend Grabbe asked Heine to help him place one of his wild dramas. Heine argued with the publisher Gubitz that in spite of his coarseness Grabbe was not a madman, but a genius. Failing to convince Gubitz, he showed the manuscript to Rahel von Varnhagen, who promptly returned it with the remark that she could 'get no sleep while that thing is in the house'. Grabbe repaid Harry's efforts by publicly insulting him in a café. Bawling that Heine's success was a flash in the pan, and that 'the Christian Muse' had left him because 'our little friend has never known how to satisfy a woman', he threw Harry out of the door. Heine knew that Grabbe was a poor gaoler's son from Düsseldorf, and understanding his friend's frustration and jealousy, he let the incident pass.

For once justifying J.B. Rousseau's recollection that he was at heart 'a most loyal and good-natured fellow', he bore his assailant no rancour. In sober moments Grabbe continued to show respect for Heine's talent, but more than a decade later still boasted of having 'thrown him down the stairs'. In his Memoirs Heine exonerated Grabbe's mother of the charge that she was responsible for her son's alcoholism and wrote in a moving epitaph that Grabbe had drunk himself to death because of the misery of his existence.[19]

But Heine was dismayed by the hypocrisy of some of his suaver friends. In June 1822 he was appalled when an anonymous reviewer who had ridiculed both his Poems and his first 'Letter from Berlin' in the capital's *Conversazions-blatt* turned out to be one of his coffee-house companions, the poet Karl Kochy. Then he found to his annoyance that his essay 'On Poland' had been 'gubitzed' by his editor and publisher, who had deleted passages and substituted his own 'surrogate' jokes; and the censors had further tampered with the text. To make matters worse, some of the things Heine had written about the Poles infuriated the German barons and landowners living in Prussia's eastern province, with the result that the local newspapers had heaped abuse on his essay.

Whereas Heine welcomed (or so he claimed) informed and reasoned criticism, he was disgusted by self-interested or simply malicious pen-pushers posing as literary critics. Hungry for recognition at the start of his career, he had been 'nearly moved to tears' in May 1822 when the playright Karl Immermann published a sensitive review of the Poems. Immermann lived in Magdeburg, and when Heine learned that he was looking for a publisher he enlisted Varnhagen to recommend him to Brockhaus. At the same time he warned Immermann that, even if successful, a new writer's path was not strewn with roses: 'After the publisher's scorn and the spitting-in-the-face comes the tea-party scourging, the thorn-crowning of stupidly clever praise, the literary-magazine crucifixion between two critical thieves – it would be unbearable if one didn't think of the final ascension!'[20]

But behind these inevitable vexations lay something else, something that, as early as April 1822, had caused Heine's vehement outburst to Christian Sethe, his oldest and best friend: 'I shall always love you,' he wrote, 'it's something that doesn't depend on me... But friends we can no longer be.' And: 'Tell Klein, and let Klein tell his brother and the whole clique, and may the latter tell Berlin and let Berlin tell the whole of Germany.'

Tell them what? 'I would never have believed that these beasts whom one calls Germans could be so stupid a race and so malicious at the same time.' What had happened was that Klein and a number of Heine's Bonn fellow-students, now studying in Berlin and named in the letter, had heard from those in Göttingen and were spreading the nastiest tales about his ouster from Georgia Augusta University and the *Burschenschaft*. 'Everywhere I hear my name whispered,' he wrote, 'followed by mocking laughter... This miserable gang has been doing its best to poison the air of Berlin for me.'

Heine had apparently tried to join Berlin's student fraternity, but by 1822, as Eberhard Galley has pointed out,[21] the *Burschenschaft* no longer accepted Jews. Göttingen had ejected Heine, and this new rebuff – aggravated by Sethe's quietly acquiescing in it and failing to defend him against the malign gossip – caused Heine to explode: 'I detest everything German. Everything German makes me want to vomit, the German language splits my ears, my own poems disgust me when I see they are written in German.'

It was the beginning of Heine's love-hate relationship with Germany. He could no more help writing in German (even in Paris) than he could help loving Sethe, with whom – after Sethe left Berlin – he resumed correspondence within less than a year of the dramatic rupture. He might have overcome the hurt of his 'expatriation' by the *Burschenschaft* if the students had not displayed their Jew-hatred, as the historian Treitschke was to write, 'with a ferocity which strongly recalled the times of the Crusaders.' For the rest, with Hardenberg's approaching death in 1822, Prussian policy took a more pronounced reactionary turn and between then and 1824 everything conspired to remind Heine that he was not a German.

Six weeks before he wrote his violent letter to Sethe, a 'Society for the Conversion of Jews' was founded in Berlin; and in the interval it took Heine to attend an Opera masquerade and several concerts at the Schauspielhaus, he learned that members of the Polish student fraternity had been arrested and his friend Breza – who was later his host in Poland – had been expelled from Berlin. Grabbe called Heine an impotent little Jew, but even before that an anti-Semitic student insulted him. As in Bonn, Heine challenged the offender to a duel, this time with mallets, and sustained a slight leg injury. Next, a love-tryst he had with a young baroness among the trees of the Tiergarten ended in his discomfiture when, between kisses, she unsuspectingly began to make anti-Jewish remarks. Heine was to sublimate the Tiergarten contretemps by transferring the scene to Spain in his ballad 'Donna Clara', in which she keeps spouting curses on the Jews while swearing love to a handsome knight, only to learn when they part that he is 'the son of the distinguished and learned Rabbi Israel of Saragossa'.[22]

Duelling and literary sarcasm, however, were of no avail against two shocks Heine suffered in 1822. In his letter to Sethe, he had affirmed his devotion to the French Revolution and human rights, but also to Lessing, Herder, Schiller. Herder with his love of folk-songs struck a chord of affinity in him; Lessing fortified his own humanism, Schiller his love of liberty. But along with these German classics, Heine had also been reading the violent anti-Semitic diatribes of Berlin University's historian Christian Rühs and of the philosopher Jakob Fries. He had heard of Rühs and Fries, for their books and pamphlets, marking the wave of xenophobia which swept Germany after Napoleon's final defeat, were popular among the students.

From an impulse to go to the source of the students' hostility towards him, Heine read Fries's professorial arguments why the Jews, no less than the French, were responsible for Germany's sufferings under Napoleon and why 'the whole lot' should be either deported or exterminated *mit Stumpf und Stiel* – root and branch.

Rühs, who professed to have started out as a tolerant humanitarian, was more moderate. His view was that, since it would be cruel to expel the Jews wholesale, it was necessary to render them harmless by imposing a ceiling on their birthrate, reinstituting the compulsory yellow badge of the Middle Ages and otherwise excluding them from society.[23]

As it happened, on 18 August 1822, while Heine was in Poland, King Friedrich Wilhelm III issued a cabinet order which – repealing paragraph 8 of his own Emancipation Decree of 1812 – excluded Jews from academic posts, the magistrature or the practice of law and a number of other professions. The measure, which was actually illegal,[24] represented open pressure on the Jews to convert. On his return to Berlin, Heine began to attend meetings of a Society for the Culture and Science of the Jews. This organ, originally founded in 1819, had been reactivated by Eduard Gans and a number of intellectuals for the declared purpose of freeing the Jews from the constraints of 'medieval rabbinism' and ending their alienation from European culture. The Society had an educational programme, but Gans objected to having 'religion' included as one of the subjects.

'On God, immortality, etc., philosophy gives us sufficient information', he declared, 'and by its light everyone can form his own subjective religion.' A minority of the Society's members, who were never more than 50 all told, disagreed with this but there was general consent that Judaism was to be placed 'on the scientific plane on which European life is lived'; and that the Jews were to be integrated in modern society, while maintaining their identity. It was in three lectures to this circle that Gans – elaborating on Hegel and drawing an impressive picture of Europe as the final result of 'reason and the Spirit working in world history for four thousand years' since monotheism – developed the approach that Heine adopted in his report on Poland. Gans, however, was speaking of the Jews, expressing the view that their early contribution to civilization not only lived on in history, but that now, after centuries of being confined to commerce, they had the chance to contribute in other capacities to Europe's history and to enrich it without losing their own 'substance'. He believed that 'Integration does not mean dissolution.'[25] Hence, by transposition, Heine's observation that the Poles need not fear extinction, his stress on their youth's appreciating Hegel's greatness and the importance of 'science', and other remarks that brought down on his head all the savage attacks by the German newspapers of Posen.

The King's cabinet order regarding the Jews showed that Gans's and the Society's idea of a world based on reason, science and philosophy was a case of wishful thinking. It was a particularly severe blow to Heine's self-esteem, he who had already announced himself as Schlegel's 'heir' and secretly hoped to be ranked one day with no one less than Goethe, to be placed into a special category and to have his right to call himself a German poet denied.

'Ill, isolated, and surrounded by hostility, incapable of enjoying life, such is my existence here,' he wrote on 21 January 1823, adding in another letter at the beginning of February that he was ill-humoured and 'living in inner discord, error and struggle.'[26] For the King's order confronted him with a double dilemma between his *Deutschtum* (Germanness) and his Jewishness, and between the hatred of 'everything German' he had angrily expressed to Sethe and the deep attachment to Germany that two years later was to make him declare that he was himself 'one of the most German beasts in existence... I love everything German more than anything else in the world. My breast is an archive of German feelings just as my two books are an archive of German songs.'[27]

From his years spent in Hamburg in late adolescence, Heine had come away with a lasting impression of that city's anti-Semitism, but he had also mocked Hamburg's bourgeois Jews who, in their attempt to melt into the environment, had 'reformed' ancient synagogue rituals to make them resemble Protestant church ceremonial. 'They make a prayer-shawl out of the wool of the lamb of God, a vest out of the feathers of the Holy Ghost, and underpants out of Christian love,' he wrote in April 1823. He raged against Christianity for oppressing the Jews for 1,800 years, and declared that it was going bankrupt in Europe and doomed to disappear (except perhaps in Africa and Asia) within 'a few centuries', along with the Jewish 'Reform faction'.[28]

As for his own attachment to Judaism, he wrote to his brother-in-law in May that it was 'rooted merely in a deep antipathy to Christianity. I who detest all positive religions may even one day adopt the most extreme rabbinism as the most effective antidote'; and a few months later he again suggested that if he clung to his Judaism it was chiefly out of 'tender emotions, obstinacy, and to maintain an antidote.'[29]

Things, however, were more grievously complex, and Heine's frequent, sometimes inconsistent utterances on the subject during this and the next year show him to be desperately struggling and thrashing about in all directions, impaled on the horns of an identity problem, in which all the choices were equally abhorrent to him.

Three times in April and May 1823, even as the poems of the 'Lyrical Intermezzo' appeared in print and were about to make his name a household word in Germany, he announced his intention to move to France. First he thought he would do so 'after the conclusion of my studies', but two days later he wrote: 'This autumn I shall be in Paris. I shall continue to study for some time, and then take up a diplomatic career.' A couple of weeks later he declared that he would 'spend many years in Paris', and besides studying, he was going to work 'actively for the spread of German literature'.[30]

On 19 May, he left Berlin on an extended visit to his parents in melancholy Lüneburg. Although plagued by nervous headaches of which he had been complaining for some time, he wrote some of the famous poems of the *Heimkehr* (Homecoming) cycle. But his personal as well as the general situation of the Jews gave him no rest, and on 18 June he poured out his feelings to his friend Moser in Berlin:

Has the Old Baron of Sinai and Sole Ruler of Judea become enlightened, abjured His nationality, given up His claims and abandoned his
adherents in favour of a few cosmopolitan ideas? I fear the Old Gentleman has lost his head and the little Jew of Amsterdam [Spinoza]
has every right to whisper in his ear: entre nous, Monsieur, vous
n'existez pas. But what about us? Do we exist?

For Heine had come to realize that the elitist attempt by Moser, Gans and the
handful of highbrow intellectuals of the Jewish Society to solve the problem of
the Jews through philosophy was a hopeless undertaking. In his report on
Poland he had written with mixed cultural shock and admiration of the mass of
ragged eastern Jews who lived there in filth and poverty, fulfilling the functions
of a 'third estate between the peasant and the nobility' whose châteaux he had
visited in Breza's company. Impressed by the way they always 'pored over their
Hebrew books of learning' and by the steadfastness and fortitude with which
they upheld their ancient values, he had concluded that in spite of their 'barbarous' appearance these Polish Jews were more 'homogeneous' in character,
more authentic and 'whole' than some of Berlin's sophisticated but spineless
Jews who flirted with Christianity out of weakness and sheer convenience.

One of the most distinguished members of the Society was David Friedlaender. Heine respected this wealthy, cultured man who had known Moses Mendelssohn. But he could not forget Friedlaender's fatuous proposal that the Jews
accept 'dry baptism', and privately he wrote that Friedlaender's assimilationist
faction – no longer having 'the strength to wear a beard, to fast, to hate and to
endure'[31] – covered up their impotence by glorifying rationalism, while Israel
was 'bleeding to death'. In a letter to Moser on 25 October 1824, he asked, 'Will
God be strong in the weak?'

In his Polish essay, Heine had taken public issue with Freidlaender, writing
that he had no good idea of 'the merits and moral importance of the rabbis'.
But this only complicated his own dilemma in the summer of 1823 – for while
he criticized the westernized 'reformers' he was himself far from being an
orthodox Jew, nor one who lived in a Polish ghetto.

At Lüneburg he felt a sudden urge, as he informed Moser in his letter of 18
June, 'to write an essay on "the Great Jewish Sorrow (as Börne calls it)"' for the
Society's journal, and between reading Gibbon's *Decline and Fall* and Montesquieu's *L'Esprit des lois*, he began a serious study of Judaism. In the French
original of Jacques Basnage's 5-volume *History and Religion of the Jews from the
Time of Jesus Christ to the Present* – a work published in Rotterdam in 1706–11
by a Huguenot priest who made an honest attempt to free himself of theological prejudice and be scholarly and impartial – Heine for the first time came

across a detailed compendium of the long martyrdom epitomized in 'the Great Jewish Sorrow'. What he learned from Basnage and other sources filled him with anger at God, but also with awe at the 'miracle' of the Jews' survival through all disasters. But with their future looking bleak, he turned to the past and was to evoke their destiny in a colourful 15th-century setting in his unfinished novel *The Rabbi of Bacherach*.

On 6 July he left Lüneburg, not for Paris, but to discuss his future with Salomon Heine in Hamburg. His uncle was about to leave on a journey, and Heine was left for 3 weeks in the hated city. He had ostensibly overcome his jilting by Amalie, and had since referred to her as 'a feminine shadow who now lives only in my poems.' But now the trauma was revived. 'The old passion breaks out again in me,' he wrote to Moser on 11 July. And as though to bedevil the situation, Amalie's younger sister, Therese, bore an uncanny likeness to her. 'The little one resembles the beloved, especially when she laughs,' he was to write in a poem. 'She has the same eyes that made me so miserable.' Whether, as has been surmised, Heine was 'bewitched' by her fortune, or really had a fancy for her, he realized with perfect self-perception that this was 'new folly grafted on old'.

Heine was determined to free himself 'as soon as possible' of his dependence on his uncle. By 1823 he had made quite a name for himself. No reviewer treated him with indifference, and some important journals had variously praised his 'originality', his 'powers of observation' and his 'sharp style'. His tragedy *Almansor* had recently been accepted for performance in Braunschweig. Heine had seen to it that reports of all this should reach his uncle's ears, in the hope of convincing him that he had prospects of a literary career. But everything had gone wrong. 'I should never have come to Hamburg. I am in the toils of an evil genius,' he wrote to Moser on 11 July, alluding to the effect on him of Therese, a nymph of gentler temperament than her cool sister. Angry with himself and the world, disliking Hamburg's burghers, Christians and Jews with equal intensity, Heine was so irritable that he quarreled with everyone – including the innocent Varnhagen who was on a visit to the city – before he left Hamburg temporarily to cure his headaches at a seaside resort near Cuxhaven.

There, even as he was collecting the impressions that were to go into *The North Sea*, the poet who that autumn was to write the immortal 'Loreley' opened his heart just enough to give an inkling of the traumatic issue that had been exacerbating his sundry vexations for more than a year: 'If I were a German – and I am not a German, see Rühs and Fries passim', he informed Moser, then he would have to go into long narrations of 'great emotional' turmoil. Writing from the seaside on 23 August, he declared himself, once again, 'the born enemy of all dogmatic religions.' But he would champion the rights of the Jews and their civic equality 'and in bad times, which are inevitable, the

Germanic mob will hear my voice resounding in German beer-halls and palaces.'
As for his plans, he did not know where he would spend the winter. Though fed
up with living on the moods and 'munificence' of his uncle, he was still dependent on him for the moment and would have to go back to Hamburg to see him.
'I am a man who does not know today what he will live on the day after tomorrow.'

Even as he wrote, his expectations of the theatrical version of *Almansor* had
suffered shipwreck. As early as 1820 he had worked into this tragedy on the
destruction of the 15th-century Moorish kingdom in Spain the crux of the
problem that preoccupied him now. *Almansor*, which had its premiere on 20
August, showed the ruthless conquest of Granada by its Christian neighbours,
but also satirized those of the Moors who crawled to the cross like some of Berlin's unheroic Jews and professed a new faith with the ease of people changing
into new fashionable clothes. The Braunschweig theatre director, E.A. Klingemann – who was later to stage the first performance of Goethe's *Faust* – thought
that *Almansor*, though no masterpiece, showed sparks of 'genius'. Heine secretly hoped that the King's *Kabinetsordre*, openly sanctioning discrimination of
the unbaptized, might heighten 'topical' interest in his Spanish allegory. But
rumours that the play attacked Christianity itself – which Heine vainly protested as a misrepresentation – led to the first performance's being stopped in a
hissing uproar. 'A few rowdy idiots last night drummed *Almansor* off the stage,'
the embarrassed Klingemann wrote to a fellow theatre director in Hamburg.[32]
But other performances elsewhere did not fare better.

The denouement of Heine's personal affairs followed quickly upon this
fiasco. In Hamburg, Uncle Salomon was not overjoyed to see his nephew
becoming a troublemaker. For the rest, Salomon – who 'owns millions', Harry
complained, 'but is pernickety about every penny' – erroneously thought that
Harry had overdrawn his allowance. Once this was cleared up, Uncle Salomon
graciously entertained Harry at his castle and praised him to everyone. But he
would not hear of his going to Paris, insisting that Harry continue his studies
and obtain his law degree within a year. Used to getting his way with people, the
banker in fact made this a condition for granting him 100 louis d'or for the year
1824. But how was Harry to make a career in a profession from which Jews had
been excluded?

'Baptism', Harry reported to Moser on 27 September – a fortnight after his
return from Hamburg to Lüneburg – 'came up for discussion. No one in my
family is against it, but I am. And it is a very headstrong I.' He went on to say
that he was 'indifferent' to the act of baptism,[33] adding that its only effect on
him would be to make him devote himself 'all the more staunchly to the defence
of the rights of my unfortunate co-religionists. Nevertheless, I find it beneath

my dignity and honour to be baptized in order to obtain employment in Prussia – in this dear Prussia!!!'

Defeated by his uncle's ultimatum regarding his financial support, Heine found himself in an impasse. 'I am at a loss to know what to do,' he wrote to Moser in the same letter. 'My vexation will in the end drive me to embrace Catholicism and hang myself. But enough of this fatal theme... we live in sad times; villains are becoming the elite and the elite must become villains.'

Whether Harry Heine was morbidly sensitive or a young man who felt intolerably provoked to battle, his expulsion from the *Burschenschaften*, combined with the hate propaganda conducted by professors Rühs and Fries and capped by the *Kabinetsordre* which turned him into a second-class citizen in the Germany of his birth, had a cumulative effect on him. This, added to the strain of holding his own in an unequal contest with his uncle, unable either to flatter the nabob on whom he depended for his bread or to cut loose from him, turned him into the mocking cynic and rebel against society that was to become his persona.

His early inclination to anticipate disaster became more pronounced even as his fame spread. When de la Motte-Fouqué in 1823 praised him in verse, Harry reacted by saying: 'He will be sorry for having written these verses the day he sees my genealogical tree'; and a favourable review drew his comment that it would be 'contrary both to custom and to human nature' if those who now cheered him 'to the skies' would not one day drag him 'through the mud'.

Yet in all the turmoil and exasperation of this period Heine had several assets on his side. He was confident of his talent, and like 'the coachman Pattensen' – in *The Book of Legrand* – 'who knows how to find his way at night or in fog across the broad Lüneburg Heath' – he knew his vocation and his path, except that the coachman of the story was an uncomplicated character, and Heine would have to find his way through a maze of contradictions. But it was in his nature that the more obstacles, opposition and resistance he met, the more defiant and contemptuous he became. 'Ill, sour, sulky and unbearable', as he described himself in 1823, feeling like an outcast, with hardly an ally and few friends among either Germans or Jews, he became the 'wounded knight' some time during this period – possibly as early as the 1822 declaration to Sethe, 'I detest everything German.' He was highly vulnerable, but with his fine antennae, his lance-like wit and lucid perceptions, his unsettling effrontery and elegant feints, he would sometimes appear to be an army complete unto himself, moving with flying banners all over the field to flay, mock and savage his enemies. In the summer of 1820 he had declared 'the German word' to be his fatherland. It became his realm, his sceptre and his greatest 'good' and asset. His way with language, thoughts, images and emotions was stunning, original, often disarming; combined with his biting wit it would make a formidable weapon.

He spent the remaining months of 1823 at Lüneburg, 'the residence of boredom', trying to catch up on his neglected law studies. To lighten this exercise, and to please Rahel Varnhagen, he read most of Goethe's works. 'Muzzling' his own literary urge as much as he could, but angry at Uncle Salomon, he began to make the first notes for his Memoirs – most of which were unfortunately to be suppressed during his 'inheritance war' with the banker's son – and also wrote more of the poems of the *Homecoming* cycle. More mature than the 'Lyrical Intermezzo' which had brought him acclaim as the 'poet of the bleeding heart', the 88 poems of this cycle, including the famous '*Du bist wie eine Blume*', were to consolidate his fame.

His main distraction during the altogether 8 months he spent in Lüneburg may have been to lament his intimate troubles to Moser, to keep in touch with a number of friends and acquaintances or to turn for comfort to the Varnhagens – 'I have met with so little true kindness in my life and have already become the subject of so much mystification,' he had written to them in June, thanking them for standing by him in his moody hours. But now he seemed bereft of illusions, bent on a realistic course and set on obtaining his doctor's degree in law.

He had no alternative to setting out again for Göttingen, which had thrown him out three years before. But during this interval he had become so well-known that even the buxom waitress at one of the beer gardens came over to his table and, offering him her cheek, said: 'Sir, I have seen your poems. How beautiful they are! You may kiss me in front of all these gentlemen, if you wish, but you must go on writing those lovely verses.' Heine embraced her with moist eyes. 'This is the happiest moment of my life,' he declared, according to one of those present. Welcomed by his two quondam professors, Baron Sartorious and Bennecke, but 'determined to earn my own bread instead of my uncle's food of mercy',[34] he spent most of the time swotting law under the guidance of the faculty dean and famous jurist, Gustav Hugo.

Between Göttingen's library and its English tavern, he lived a comparatively ascetic life, but not enough to prevent him from boasting that he was 'no longer a monotheist in love'. He now loved, he wrote, 'the Medici Venus decorating the library as well as Councillor Bauer's beautiful cook. Alas, the first is made of plaster and the second is venereal. Or is that mere calumny? I am going to find out.' He added, affecting a new coarseness, that he had bought half a dozen condoms (Heine wrote 'gondons') of violet silk.[35]

He made some new literary friends at Göttingen, including Wedekind and Eckermann, and shocked them – especially the latter, who was later to become Goethe's secretary and confidant – by outlining plans to write a *Faust* in which Mephisto would have the commanding role. For the moment, however, he stuck doggedly to his law books (he was later to write a different *Faust* as a ballet scenario), drank beer and went on picnics with other students, and generally seemed healthier than heretofore.

In April 1824 he went to Berlin and was surprised to find himself a celebrity, for 33 of the *Homecoming* poems had appeared serially in Berlin's *Gesellschafter* during the last week of March. He renewed contacts with old acquaintances, celebrated Passover with his Jewish friends, apologized to Varnhagen for his irritation in Hamburg and re-established his relationship with the couple. Rahel, always his severest critic, warned him 'not to become a Brentano', that is, to break away from the conservative Romanticism of traditional folksongs and chivalrous old ballads canonized by Clemens von Brentano and Achim von Arno in their famous anthology *Des Knaben Wunderhorn* (The Boy's Magic Horn). Although this was not to hinder Heine from praising the anthology, he had already worked a miracle with Brentano's 'Lorelei' ballad, whose golden-haired heroine, unhappy in love and about to be confined to a nunnery, jumps from a high rock into the waters of the Rhine. By ingeniously turning her into a fatal temptress whose siren-song sends passing boatmen crashing to the depths while she combs her golden hair, Heine created one of Germany's most famous legends, which became so much a part of German lore that even Hitler did not dare to erase it from schoolbooks, though his minions substituted for its Jewish author the attribution 'unknown'.

Rahel wrote to Gentz that she 'frequently understood' Heine, 'and he me, where others did not understand. This won him over to me and he accepted me as his patroness.' Heine, for his part, was so devoted that he wrote, 'I should like to have engraved on my collar the words "I belong to Rahel Varnhagen."' Hannah Arendt has ascribed the special affinity between the young poet and the society lady who could have been his mother to the fact that Rahel, in spite of her baptism and her marriage to Varnhagen, suffered all her life from the same problem of 'fraudulent' identity that was now troubling Heine.[36] Indeed, within a couple of weeks of his return to Göttingen, he was deep into Jewish history again, reading more of Basnage's volumes as well as such assorted old chronicles as the famous travel book of Benjamin of Tudela[37] – a 12th-century Spanish Jew whose account of life in Provence, Rome, Corfu, Constantinople, Palestine, Egypt, Baghdad, Persia and China is a primary medieval source-book – or a history of Frankfurt, scene of a 15th-century Passover feast he lovingly described that summer in *The Rabbi of Bacherach*.

On 25 June 1824, having completed one-third of *The Rabbi*, he wrote to Moser that reading these 'sad annals', partly 'also because of an inner need', he had gained a moving as well as illuminating 'insight into the spirit of Jewish history, and this armour will stand me in good stead in the future.' At the same time he was going on with his law studies, and once or twice mentioned his hope of obtaining a professorship in literature or some other official post. Baptism was thus on his mind, but he continued to regard it as a kind of betrayal and the nearer the day came when he would have to make a decision, the more he seems to have felt an urge to assert his Jewishness, assuring Moser that he had not forgotten 'our brethren', repeatedly asking him for news of the Jewish Society, and writing such things as 'May my right hand wither if I forget thee, Jerusalem.'

On 18 August 1824, Jewish professors still holding posts at German universities were fired.

In mid-September Heine set out on the walking tour that was to result in the *Harzreise* (Journey in the Harz). During this 4-weeks ramble he first walked north, visited the Hanover silver mines and, after stopping in various places, climbed the Brocken – legendary scene of the Walpurgis Night witches' dance – and then down to Ilsenburg in the Ilse River valley and uphill again on the steep path leading to the Ilsenstein, an enormous granite cliff named after the Princess Ilse, a fabled water nixie said to be living in a palace in the cliff. Then, through forests and valleys, he worked his way to Halle, Jena and Weimar. There he paid his respects to Goethe, to whom he had letters of introduction from Varnhagen. He had been greatly looking forward to this meeting, but no warmth developed between the flustered student who hoped for a word of encouragement about his poetry and Weimar's revered old man, who had to be addressed as 'Your Excellency'. Heine was to write little about what took place but, increasingly annoyed at Goethe for engaging him in trivial conversation (such as the quality of plums growing between Jena and Weimar), he reputedly spoiled the visit by blurting out that he was 'working on a Faust', whereupon he was curtly dismissed.

In spite of this incident, Heine returned to Göttingen greatly refreshed after his hike of 350 kilometres. In October and November, even though the 'ghost of jurisprudence' was breathing down his neck, he finished a section of the *Harzreise*, which was printed a few months later in the *Gesellschafter* in 'gubitzed' form and otherwise multilated by censorship; but other circumstances were to delay the publication of the entire work for nearly two years. This proved beneficial to Heine's first major prose work, a travel book of a new genre in Germany, for during this interval he was able – possibly as a result of reading Laurence Sterne's *Tristram Shandy* (he was already familiar with *A Sentimental Journey*) – to improve the text. Whatever the degree of Sterne's influence, Heine presented reality in this book by the same capricious-seeming but well-organized 'sequential association of ideas' that he had used in his 'Letters from Berlin'. Coupled with its rambling, conversational style and comic touches, the *Harzreise* was so novel and pungent a piece that – not unlike *Tristram Shandy* –

it 'stimulated the blood circulation' of readers and was immediately recognized by some of the critics as a work of 'modernity'.

At the beginning of 1825 Heine had to ask his uncle for another half year's support. Between January and April he laboured, with increasing headaches, on 'the chrestomathy of pandect law' and subjects related to his doctoral examination. Even then he went on working sporadically on his Memoirs and found the time to send off three sonnets to Friederike Robert, Rahel's sister-in-law, whom ever since his Berlin days he admired as 'Europe's most beautiful woman'. Law didn't suit Heine; he complained that 'what the most ordinary people are capable of grasping will not enter my head.' He was terrified of the examination, and greatly relieved when he passed it with a C on 3 May, but his formal promotion still required a Latin disputation to be held in the third week of July.

It was during this interval that Heine finally acted. He went about his baptism stealthily, entreating the Protestant pastor of nearby Heiligenstadt on 24 May not to divulge his intention to anyone. The pastor, J.L. Grimm, told him that he required the permission of the Erfurt Consistory, which was granted on the 31st on condition that the applicant be examined in the Catechism. During the next fortnight Heine commuted several times to Heiligenstadt to be instructed by Grimm in the new faith, and then announced that he was ready. The religious examination took place on the morning of 28 June in the presence of another cleric, and the baptism was performed immediately afterwards by Pastor Grimm at his house, with the second cleric acting as godfather. When it was over, the new proselyte was invited to lunch with the two pastors, who observed that he took little part in the conversation, or no more than required by politeness, but sat half-absorbed in thought, 'his face showing his inner excitement'. Shortly afterwards he begged to take his leave.

Heine returned to Göttingen as a Christian, Johann Heinrich Heine, though he was never to use both the given names, calling himself merely Heinrich Heine or simply H. Heine. On 20 July, after holding a Latin disputation on 5 theses, he was formally promoted *Doctor juris* and on the same evening Professor Hugo, the dean of the faculty – not knowing that Heine had lived in terror of him, or that he was to satirize him in the *Harzreise* – hosted him to dinner and, being in high spirits, declared in a Latin oration that he was not only a great jurist but a great poet comparable to Goethe.

The present consensus – with some exceptions – about the motive behind Heine's baptism is that, having resisted as long as he could, he resorted to it for the sake of a career that would assure him of a living. He soon expressed his 'regret' at the act, which brought him nothing but 'enemies among both the Christians and the Jews', and made the famous statement that 'if the law had allowed me to steal silver spoons, I would not have converted.'

Curiously for a new convert, but characteristically for Heine, less than half a year after undergoing the ceremony at Heiligenstadt he attended a synagogue service in Hamburg and on 14 December 1825 wrote to Moser how much he had 'enjoyed Dr Salomon's sermon against baptized Jews, especially his cutting remarks about those abandoning their faith "merely in the hope of obtaining some post".' There was more than ironic self-torture in this. For, his own inconstancy notwithstanding, Heine both privately and in his literary work continued to express the same contempt for submissive conversion for the sake of expediency which he had earlier ridiculed in his allegory on the baptized Moors in *Almansor*.

In the *Harzreise* he turned his ascent to the iron cross on the summit of the Ilsenstein into a metaphor illustrating his precarious position at the time of his baptism. Advising anyone reaching the towerlike tip of the Ilsenstein to think of nothing 'but his own feet', he wrote:

> As I stood there, lost in thought, I suddenly heard the subterranean music of the enchanted palace, and I saw the mountains all around stand themselves on their heads, and the red-tiled roofs of Ilsenburg began to dance, and the green trees flew about in the blue air until everything went green and blue before my eyes. Overcome by giddiness, I would surely have plunged in the abyss if I had not, in my soul's dire need, clung fast to the iron cross. For doing this in the awkward position in which I found myself no one, surely, will blame me.

But he blamed himself, and henceforth he would have to live with a residue of self-contempt, however much he sublimated it – not so much for abandoning Judaism as a religion, as for having given in to the duress of circumstances against which he revolted. His attachment to the Jewish people or 'race', as it was called at the time, grew all the stronger; and in the draft of a planned continuation of the *Harzreise* he wrote bitterly, 'How much we owe to the Jews! I will not here mention that we owe Christianity itself' to the Jews, 'but the invention of bills of exchange, commercial premiums and the Cross! Is not our deepest gratitude due to them? And yet – their German stepfatherland won't even allow them to become barristers or advocates in Prussia as a change from dealing in cast-off trousers.'

There was the rub: the German 'stepfatherland'. Heine had hoped against hope that baptism and Varnhagen's influence would help him to attain nothing less than a professorship in literature at Berlin University. There was a certain naiveté in this, or in his alternative plan of setting up as an attorney in Hamburg. At the same time one cannot help noting that he was more realistic than his uncle in assessing his own future in Germany, and setting his heart on Paris from the beginning; for baptism was not to help him and the suffocating atmosphere in Germany was in the end to make him seek the free air of the French capital. He also correctly assessed the hopelessness of the Society's hopeful premise that once the Jews were elevated to the level of European 'science' and philosophy, antiSemitism would disappear. It is noteworthy that in some lectures at a small 'school' established by the Society, Heinrich Heine, then still Harry, advised young Jews to emigrate to England or America, 'where nobody asks for your beliefs and everyone may be happy after his own fashion.'

Much has been written about the irony of the baptized Heine denouncing Gans, as president of the Society, for 'preaching Christianity' at a time when Gans had not yet converted. 'If he does so out of conviction he is a fool; if out of hyprocrisy, he is a scoundrel,' Heine wrote in December 1825. Behind his frequent mockery of Gans and 'Ganstown' lay a fundamental difference of approach. In 1822 the Society had given serious consideration to the project of the former American Consul to Tunis and later New York County Sheriff, Manuel Noah (1785–1851), to establish a Jewish colony on Grand Island in the Niagara River near Buffalo. When Gans was appointed as Noah's representative in Germany, Heine had humorously suggested the name Ganstown for the capital of the new Jewish 'homeland', but Gans gave only lukewarm support to the project.

About 1823, while Gans was away in France and England, Heine, knowing of his intention to convert, became ambivalent towards him. By that time nearly 1,250 of Berlin's Jews – about half the members of the community – had accepted baptism. Heine saw Gans as the 'captain' about to abandon the Society – which indeed fell apart, much to Heine's regret. For even at the time of his baptism he thought that its developing a non-rabbinical 'science of Judaism' would serve as a 'source' for the history of the glorious and tragic destiny of the Jews, one that he still hoped to write in *The Rabbi of Bacherach*. 'I often think of him when I do not want to think of myself,' Heine wrote of Gans in a letter in 1826, and as if to confirm that the grudge he bore was a grudge against himself, he wrote to Gans – who shortly after his baptism had been appointed associate professor at Berlin University, where he was later to be one of Karl Marx's teachers – that 'it offends me to the depths of my soul to think that our books are no longer sources; because of this I am angry with you and I am angry with myself.' But he was also mockingly to list Gans among those who meekly turned the other cheek when attacked, adding: 'I am different, and that is a good thing. It is good if the wicked find the right man for once, the man who will ruthlessly and unsparingly take revenge for himself and others.'

'Madame, c'est la guerre!' he was to write in *The Book of LeGrand*. 'I am by no means one of the reasonable and rational men, but I have joined their party, and for 5,588 years we have been at war with the party of fools.' At the time of his writing (in 1827), 5,588 was the Jewish calendar year. He was beginning to let everybody know that, in spite of his baptism, he remained a Jew. He had early developed a social conscience and, castigating the spineless rich Jews as severely as their bigoted Christian counterparts, he would sublimate particular anger by making himself the spokesman of all oppressed humanity. On 9 June 1827 he declared to Moser: 'I now have a resounding voice that is heard far and wide. In years to come you will often hear it thunder against the policing of men's thoughts and the suppression of their fundamental rights. I shall obtain a quiet extraordinary professorship in the university of the intellectual and spiritual elite.'

And so it was to be.

7

The Decembrist Revolution that Failed

Michael Bakunin, the future anarchist, was not yet 12 when news of the so-called Decembrist rebellion first reached his father's estate at Premukhino, in the province of Tver. For months thereafter the quiet of Premukhino was upset by the 'horror' that gripped Russia following the seizure of nearly 600 men representing the cream of Tsarist society – mostly senior Guards officers, besides writers and intellectuals, all of them members of the upper class – who were to stand trial for the bloody events which had shaken St Petersburg on 14 December 1825. The boy's parents, Count Alexander Bakunin and his wife Varvara, had reason for particular alarm. She was a born Muraviev, of that clan of aristocrats who, then and later, were among Russia's leading 19th-century generals, 'imperial proconsuls, high civil and judicial officials, ambassadors, as well as famous rebels.'[1] And now five of them were in a dungeon for having plotted, abetted, or taken leading parts in, the armed attempt – three weeks after the mysterious death at Taganrog of Tsar Alexander I, the 'Liberator of Europe' – to overthrow the youngest of his two brothers, Nicholas I, on the day of his accession.

Two cousins in particular, Captain of the Imperial Guards Nikita Muraviev and Lieutenant Colonel Sergei Muraviev-Apostol, were deeply implicated and in danger of paying with their heads for the activities of which they stood accused. These included instigating the mutiny of troops in Petersburg and elsewhere and conspiring to kidnap, and if necessary, kill Nicholas; planning a revolution with the aim of turning Russia into a constitutional monarchy under his elder brother, the Grand Duke Constantine; and contemplating even worse things.

'We want Constantine!' and 'Constantine and Konstitutsia!' had been the chant of 3,000 Guards officers and men in Peterburg's Senate Square on that fateful day. Tsar Alexander having died without leaving an heir (or not a legitimate one), Constantine, as the brother next in age, was actually the heir-presumptive. Fortysix years old and well-liked by the people, he was at that time Viceroy of Poland. His succession being taken for granted, portraits of 'our beloved new Emperor Constantine' had actually gone up in shops all over Petersburg.

Constantine, however, had in a private act of abdication known only to him and the defunct Alexander, and kept as a 'palace secret' from all but two people, renounced his rights to the throne nearly 4 years earlier. The original document lay in the Uspensky Cathedral and a copy had been deposited in each of three places, the State Council, the Senate and the Holy Synod. The sealed envelopes, to be opened only after Alexander's death, also contained a 'manifesto' with his instructions for proclaiming Nicholas Tsar. Strangely, Alexander had mentioned to Nicholas that he might be called upon to rule Russia, but had never told him of Constantine's abdication; and even Constantine had been left in ignorance of the procedure laid down for passing the crown to Nicholas. Only Archbishop Philaret, who had written Alexander's undisclosed 'manifesto' for him, and Prince Alexander Golitsyn, who had copied and deposited the papers in secret, were aware of the manner in which the succession was to be made public.

The result, on Alexander's death, was utter confusion, with the sealed envelopes opened only in one place (the Senate) but not in the others, and State Councillors, Senators as well as Archbishop Philaret all swearing allegiance to Constantine. Constantine, who was in Warsaw, at the same time proclaimed Nicholas to be the Tsar; and Nicholas, who was 17 years his junior and feared a mutiny of the Petersburg garrison if he did otherwise, proclaimed Constantine.

'History knows no similar example of two brothers so magnanimously tossing a crown from one to the other like a ball,'[2] wrote Countess Nesselrode, the wife of Russia's Foreign Minister, as the succession crisis mounted and frantic, courier-borne messages kept crossing each other between Petersburg and Warsaw. Constantine, abandoned by his princely wife, Anna Juliana of the Saxe-Coburg line, had formally renounced his rights in return for permission to marry a Catholic Polish countess. And he had long ago, upon the murder in 1801 of his father Tsar Paul I, declared that 'if the throne ever comes to me I shall certainly not accept it.' From this decision he did not budge. Nor, for that matter, would he budge from Warsaw to help Nicholas put things straight in Petersburg by showing his face there for so much as a few days and announcing his abdication in person. Nicholas, who was practically unknown to the Russian people – and disliked as a martinet by the entire Army – pleaded with his brother to do so. But Constantine would not hear of it and at one point sent back a warning that rather than 'hastening my departure for St. Petersburg', he would, if further pressed, 'leave Warsaw only to retire to some greater distance' from the capital.

On 12 December, after three tense weeks of uncertain interregnum, Nicholas decided to act. The assembled dignitaries of the land heard in some bewilderment his announcement that he was their Tsar and about to assume the emperorship: having taken the oath to Constantine – as he had himself – they learned that they and all state officials and military personnel were now to swear allegiance to him. The ceremonies were to take place on the morning of the 14th, but some of the dignitaries doubted the legality of this act – which only confounded the confusion.

Learning of this on the 13th, Nikita Muraviev and his fellow-conspirators in Petersburg, including Colonel Prince Trubetskoy, the poet Ryleyev and the writer Alexander Bestuzhev – between them heading a secret 'Northern Society' which had been planning an uprising for the following summer – decided to strike forthwith. Throughout the day and night of the 13th, they revised existing plans, improvised new ones and made hectic preparations to forestall Nicholas's 'tsarification'. They finally resolved on several moves – to occupy the Senate building in the morning, to seize the Winter Palace, to arrest Nicholas and his family, to force the Senators to adopt a revolutionary proclamation they had drafted, and more. Nicholas, too, prepared for the morrow. One of the rebel officers had felt in duty bound to warn him of a possible insurrection by the Guards in the capital. This precious tip-off enabled Nicholas to take his measures. By that time he had also had intelligence reports of a revolt brewing in the Second Army in the Ukraine.

On the morning of the 14th, with the capital's garrison drawn up at various points, rebel officers began to rush around and spread a false story that Nicholas was holding the beloved Constantine, their lawful tsar, captive. They managed to whip up sufficient anger against him, mostly among their own troops, for some 3,000 men to refuse him the oath and march off with drums and banners to the Senate Square. There, by 11 o'clock, incomplete units of Grenadier Guards, Marine Guards and the Moscow Guards Regiment (stationed in Petersburg) were drawn up in battle formation.

Surrounded by growing crowds of the idle and the curious, they waited a long time for instructions. But Prince Trubetskoy, the over-all commander of the rebellion, was nowhere to be seen. Its chief-of-staff, Lieutenant Prince Obolensky, had no idea where he was, nor why any of the senior conspirators had failed to appear. He knew that an officer from the Caucasus had been placed in charge of storming the Winter Palace and arresting Nicholas.

Instead, early in the afternoon, Nicholas was seen approaching the Senate Square at the head of a loyal battalion of the Horse Guards. The rebel soldiers, egged on by two or three dozen junior officers, growled 'Usurper!' in his direction. Holding their ground, they went on stomping their feet in the freezing cold, as they had for hours. Nicholas, on his side, was unwilling to start his reign with a bloodbath. He was holding frantic consultations with his generals and aides, and for a while the two camps confronted each other in the tense knowledge that, one way or the other, the situation was bound to come to a head soon, before Petersburg's early winter dark obscured the square.

In the Ukraine, another conspiratorial group, the so-called 'Southern Society', led by Colonel Pavel Pestel and Lieutenant Colonel Sergei Muraviev-Apostol, had likewise been planning a rebellion for the following year. It and the 'Northern Society' had been in touch with each other for years, but the two plots, conceived in haste due to the turn of events precipitated by Alexander's death, had not been co-ordinated. Not only that, but the Petersburg conspirators had no idea that Colonel Pestel had in fact been arrested on the 13th; and for lack of safe and speedy communications, compounded by sheer ineptitude, the remaining 'southerners' under Sergei Muraviev-Apostol were to learn only 10 days later of the events that took place in the capital on the 14th.

There General Count Mikhail Miloradovich, a hero of the war against Napoleon, and an impressive figure on horseback, had arrived in the Senate Square. At his appearance, the jeering rebels, who had refused all earlier appeals to surrender, fell silent. They were in fact surrounded, Nicholas having used the interval to reinforce the Horse Guards with more loyal troops that closed off the square, mob and all, on every side. Facing the mutinous soldiers, General Miloradovich addressed them in a paternal tone. Drawing from its sheath a sword which he declared had been given him by 'my friend, the Grand Duke Constantine', he held it aloft for all to see and assured them that he too wished Constantine had accepted to be 'our Emperor', and went on to say: 'But if he refuses the throne, what can we do? I have seen his abdication with my own eyes.'

This was the first the soldiers heard of the document in the sealed envelopes. Nor had Nikita Muraviev and his friends told them that Constantine was in Warsaw, or briefed them even vaguely about any plan of action. The soldiers were to be used merely as pawns, and the conspirators had not seen fit to share with them the secret goals and true aim of their revolution. Many of the Guardsmen clamouring for 'Konstitutsia' are in fact said to have thought that this was the name of Constantine's wife, and there were other grotesque touches to the Decembrist drama about to unfold.

Miloradovich had finished speaking and was turning his horse about when a hot-headed young ex-lieutenant drew his pistol and fired, and the expected clash and inevitable horror suddenly became real. The General dropped dead from his horse; tension was at fever pitch as Nicholas approved, then cancelled, orders to open fire, while the rebels threw stones at his troops. The Archbishop pled with them to surrender; then the Horse Guards attacked, their animals slipping and falling on the ice, and the leaderless, suddenly cocksure mutineers fell over them with bayonets, repelling the charge and pelting them with snowballs. Finally, just before the onset of darkness, Nicholas reluctantly ordered 4 cannon to fire at the mass of 3,300 insurgents.

By nightfall or shortly afterwards, with 80 or more Guardsmen dead in the snow and the rest dispersed in all directions, it was all over bar the epilogue – a belated rising by several infantry detachments in the Ukraine. Led by Muraviev-Apostol and a stripling officer of 22, Bestuzhev-Ryumin, it was easily suppressed at the beginning of January. With another 100 or so men killed, soldiers in the regiments involved were lashed – 'in a number of cases twelve thousand strokes (incredibly some survived)' were administered – and/or transferred to the Caucasus.

There followed the interrogation of altogether 570 suspected conspirators, most of them noblemen or Guards officers, or both, first by the Tsar, who had some of them hauled before him, and then for days, weeks and months amid rumours and whispered reports of torture, before a secret 5-man Inquiry Commission. Then, the following summer, there was the summary trial of 121 of them before a specially appointed Tribunal. The death sentence pronounced 5 weeks later on scores of Guards officers ('the corporate essence of the Russian nobility') and some prominent civilians caused shock-waves to course throughout Russia. Not all, however, were to be executed. Prince Trubetskoy and 115 others, stripped of their titles, estates and civil rights, had their sentences commuted to exile with hard labour for life in Siberia.

Then came the night of 12 July 1826. Colonel Pavel Pestel, son of a former Govenor-General of Siberia – hanged; Lieutenant Colonel Sergei Muraviev-Apostol – hanged; the poet Kondraty Ryleyev – hanged; Kakhovsky, who had fired the fatal shot – hanged; Bestuzhev-Ryumin – hanged before he was even 23. Before they were all led to the scaffold in the courtyard of the Peter-and-Paul Fortress at 4 a.m., each of the 100-odd officers who were exiled to Siberia had to prostrate himself on his knees before his regiment. One by one their swords were broken over their heads, their epaulets torn off, and their uniforms exchanged for prison garb.

After the ceremonial humiliation of the Guards officers, and not long after the others had been strung up on the gallows at the 'curtain-wall' of Petersburg's notorious fortress – across the Neva from the Imperial Palace – Nicholas's family and his ministers attended a solemn Thanksgiving service in Moscow. 'Cannon roared from the heights of the Kremlin', while inside the Metropolitan Philaret led the festive Te Deum. And the added pathos of it all as Princess Trubetskoy, Princess Volkonsky and several dozen of Russia's highest society ladies – confronted with a cruel choice between never seeing their men again or life-long exile for themselves – left their families and their grand houses and set out nobly in the wake of their chained convict-husbands on the long hard journey taking them for the rest of their lives to the icy wastes beyond Lake Baikal. There the Decembrist men were to be employed chopping wood or digging salt in Siberian forests and mines until they died. Only 29 of them survived until the day when they would be amnestied upon the coronation of the next Tsar, 30 years later.

Count Fyodor Vasilevich Rostopchin, one-time Commander-in-Chief and Military Governor of Moscow, could not believe his ears when he heard of the aims pursued by the two rings of nobles. Summing up the most striking feature of what was to become known variously as the Decembrist 'uprising', 'revolt', 'coup d'état', or 'the conspiracy of officers and poets' (or of 'officers and gentlemen') – he is said to have observed: 'Hitherto revolutions have been made by peasants who wanted to become gentlemen. Now gentlemen are trying to make a revolution so as to become cobblers.'[3] For the leaders of the two societies had been secretly planning to give Russia not only a Constitution, but to liberate her millions of serfs. What's more, they had decided to free the peasants 'with land' – the land to be provided by the nobility giving up part of their large estates.

The leaders of the two conspiracies had been hatching their plans for nearly 10 years. Nikita Muraviev's 'Northern' and Muraviev-Apostol's 'Southern' Societies were twin outgrowths of the same tiny Union of Salvation founded in 1816 – by another highly distinguished Colonel Muraviev – when it had become clear that Alexander I had abandoned whatever reforms he had entertained, or merely talked about, in his more liberal days. Hundreds of senior officers who had been to France with him had been appalled to see the 'Liberator of Europe' and its mightiest monarch fall, first, under the occult spell of the 'seer' Madame von Krüdener and, when she was gone, under the influence of his reactionary Minister and police chief, Arakcheyev. On their return, the officers, seeing Russia with Western eyes and resenting the tightened censorship, the spying, the floggings and other cruelties in Arakcheyev's 'military colonies', had started noticing other things, too: the petty bureaucracy, the general corruption, the intolerable condition and humiliation of the serfs, and the sullen hatred in their eyes. The peasants on the private estates paid the landlord taxes, extra taxes and cash dues. They had to do *corvées* of unpaid labour for him. The lives of each of his serfs belonged to him.

In due course the Union of Salvation had transformed itself into the Union of Welfare, which, with its membership grown to several hundred, hovered for a time between those supporting a moderate programme designed to modernize Russia and gradually educate her people, and radical designs for a republic by those who were beginning to feel that nothing less than a violent shake-up of the whole tsarist structure from the top down had a chance of curing Russia of her ills. Spying in the Army, though ostensibly abolished under Alexander, had actually been intensified – with the result that two of his Generals-in-Waiting had successively warned the 'Liberator', years before his death, that certain officers were engaging in liberal talk and conspiring to subvert the monarchy. But Alexander was by then in a brooding mood of religious reflection, lassitude and remorse. He is said to have told the officer commanding the Corps of Guards, Prince Ilarion Vasilchikov: 'You who have been in my service since the start of my reign, you know that I shared and encouraged these illusions and aberrations.' After a long pause he added: 'It is not for me to come down on them with a heavy hand.'[4]

By 1821 the members of the Union of Salvation were agreed on the need for a revolution, but divided to the point of deadlock about its political aims and aftermath. As it had meanwhile been infiltrated by spies, the Union resolved early that year to disband – in order to escape further attention by the authorities – only to re-form secretly in the shape of the 'Northern' and 'Southern' Societies. Each included revolutionaries of every sort, but the main rift between liberal monarchists and radical republicans continued to cut across both. Not daring to strike against Alexander, the leaders juggled and discussed various ideas, waiting for favourable 'circumstances'. By the time these arose with his death nearly 5 years later, no joint or definite plan had been communicated to members – many of whom were young officers bristling for any kind of action – but two different programmes had crystallized: Nikita Muraviev and Prince Trubetskoy in Petersburg's 'Northern Society' were for replacing Nicholas with a constitutional monarch and integrating Russia's nationalities into a federal system – on the model of what was then still the infant United States – complete with Western-type institutions and parliamentary checks, including such British features as a House of Lords. Colonel Pestel and Sergei Muraviev-Apostol of the 'Southern Society' were for abolishing the monarchy altogether, and Pestel had prepared plans for a republic.

Though neither faction, nor any of the Decembrist gentlemen-officers, had the remotest intention of rousing the masses or involving the people in what was to be strictly a 'palace revolution', they were united on the need, if not the details, of a vast land reform. Nikita Muraviev and Trubetskoy favoured the division of the estates. Pestel and Muraviev-Apostol were for confiscating them and abolishing all aristocratic privileges.

Heated debates had taken place on the question of serfdom. Some of the would-be rebels were afraid that the sudden emancipation of 20 or so million serfs would lead to disorder and unrest. The future of the common land worked by the village collectives, which assured the Russian peasant of a modicum of subsistence, was seriously considered. Nikita Muraviev proposed splitting it up in the general land reform; Pestel feared that partitioning it into small plots would impoverish the villagers.

Pestel's republican plans were supported by some of the Petersburg leaders, such as the poet Ryleyev and the writer Alexander Bestuzhev: they were 'left-wingers' against what might be called Nikita Muraviev's 'right wing' of conservative but enlightened monarchists. And the radical Pestel had other far-reaching plans, so subversive that Nicholas I had them suppressed, and they were to remain unknown for many decades.

The Decembrists were high-minded idealists, young counts and princes inspired by the noblest sentiments of liberty and ready to die 'a glorious death' in its cause. But after all the plotting and planning, the endless talk and arguments pursued for years at private champagne dinners – or at vodka-borscht-and-singing parties in Ryleyev's flat – they had not only been caught unprepared, but had performed so poorly as to invite disaster.

Trubetskoy, for one, had got cold feet at the last moment and spent the crucial hours of the 14th walking the streets, immersed in second thoughts. A gallant officer who by virtue of his rank and prestige with the Guardsmen had been chosen to proclaim the Constitution, he was later discovered hiding at the house of the Austrian Ambassador (who happened to be his brother-in-law). Many others had dropped out even earlier. Here were men of varied persuasions and inclinations – royalists and republicans, officers and poets, conservatives and radicals – who had long schemed to start the immense task of attuning Russia to modernity. The very phenomenon of so many nobles and big landowners joining forces to overthrow the autocracy, attack the feudal system and abolish serfdom was an unprecedented one. It stunned Tsarist society, threatening as it did to disrupt its very structure as well as the vast fabric of Russia's rural life and economy. It seems also to have overwhelmed the conspirators themselves, numbers of whom had lost heart, and recoiling at the magnitude of the enterprise and the risks involved had withdrawn on the eve or at the last minute.

In the end, the Petersburg insurrection had been hastily improvised and launched by no more than 60 or so impatient members of the conspiracy, and more as a desperate gesture of defiance than with any conviction of success. For these, too, were beset by last-minute doubts. Their discouragement at the depletion of their ranks, coupled with the slapdash planning and the reckless, fatalistic, come-what-may spirit in which they approached the venture, resulted in a series of disorganized, erratic moves and in so many snags and omissions as to make the whole operation look inexplicably amateurish.

Started without popular support, the conspiracy had floundered from a combination of false expectations, faulty reckoning and illusory hopes, in miserable and stark contrast to the grandiose aims and plans of the officers and gentlemen.

Nor was there among the Petersburg Decembrists a single resolute and purposeful leader who possessed the audacity, will and cool organizational ability to
mount a rebellion, supervise its details and see it through to the end. It was
perhaps significant that, though 50 of the ringleaders were officers, the strategy
as well as the operational moves of the military putsch had been largely master-
minded by a civilian – the poet Kondraty Ryleyev. He was the poorest of them
all but had a charismatic personality as well as the zeal and temperament of a
revolutionary. It was he who, during the critical few days before the 14th, had
kept up and fired the spirit of the others and racked his brain to devise solutions
and forestall contingencies.

'Our soldiers are good, simple folk. They don't think much,' was the reasoning of the leaders of the rising in the Ukraine (according to one of their associates).[5] Both they and the Petersburg conspirators relied on the obedience of the
rankand-file and on the sheer enthusiasm for action of the junior officers. The
latter had simply promised the soldiers a better life – including the reduction of
the length of army service to 15 instead of 25 years – and the leaders, for reasons of secrecy and the good of their cause, had not revealed their full goals to
either. In Petersburg they had practised outright deception, misinforming and
inciting the troops to mutiny on a fraudulent pretext. Adam B. Ulam, writing in
1981, called this 'the most morally dubious aspect of the uprising'. At no point
in their investigation, he remarked, 'were the Decembrists asked how they
could justify the gross deception they used on their soldiers in stirring them to
rebellion. Nor did any of the main actors of the drama see fit then or subsequently to express contrition for the hoax.'[6]

Not only Nicholas had hesitated before allowing fire to be opened. It was a
measure of the awesome authority associated in the Russian mind with the Tsar's
inviolate person – as it was of the Decembrists' wavering faith in the legitimacy
of their deed – that, although they had considered killing Nicholas, no one during the long confrontation fired a shot at him. 'Patriotism drove them toward
revolution, patriotism kept them from carrying it out.'[7] Rebels with a cause but
novice revolutionaries, they had not yet reached the self-supporting belief of the
professionals and desperadoes of a later breed that all means were justified to
achieve their end, or that anarchy was a prelude to creation.

Many of the Decembrists had only a hazy idea of the effect of their contemplated reforms on nearly 50 million Russians, or of the best way to run Europe's
largest and most populous empire. In the West the Industrial Revolution had
turned 'those poor wretches, the English, French and American workers' – as
one Russian Minister had recently called them – into jobless proletarians. The
leading Decembrists had long debated how to make sure that the same fate did
not befall the millions of serfs to be turned loose on the economy, with ruinous

effect to it and themselves; and Nikita Muraviev in the 'Northern Society' and Colonel Pestel in the 'Southern' one had each finally come up with fairly detailed, if divergent, plans setting out the kind of social and political regime they wished to establish. Nikita Muraviev's draft Constitution provided for equality before the law, trial by jury and freedom of speech. Pestel seems to have picked up outright egalitarian, pre-socialist ideas similar to those circulated by Babeuf in France and embodied them in a Russian Law, An Instruction for the Supreme Provisional Government, that was to run his post-revolutionary republic.

Pestel had made a brilliant career before he was executed at the age of 33. Trying to adapt French ideas to local conditions, he had found himself in a basic dilemma: his wish to assure the minimum means of existence to Russia's peasants clashed with his realization that in order to 'create plenty' Russia needed immense agricultural development, which in turn required 'great expense', i.e., capital. Where was this to come from? Babeuf had meant to abolish all property. Pestel, realizing that only the bigger landowners were capable of investing, felt that 'the man who agrees to make this expense should own the land as his private property,' just as the man who 'farms its different products must have exclusive right of possession.'[8]

To solve this problem, Pestel eventually opted for confiscating half the estates of the biggest landowners without compensation, and distributing the land to their private serfs. His Russian Law proposed to divide all arable land into two categories: 'Common land will belong collectively to the entire community of each district... Private land will belong either to the state or to private persons who will own it in complete freedom and will have the right to do with it as they please.' Pestel, in other words, upheld both private enterprise and property rights but was anxious to preserve the ancient framework of the village collectives and peasant communes: by granting ownership of a plot to every peasant family willing to work, these were to help assure 'the needs of life to all citizens without exception'.

But Pestel's plan, remarkable for its attempt to solve the potentially explosive peasant problem by means of village collectives – anticipating by half a century the violent debate between the Narodniks (Populists) and Russia's first Marxists, the former seeing in the peasant communes, or *obschina*, the best breeding-ground for revolution, the latter arguing in the name of 'scientific Socialism' that they were an 'archaic form condemned by history to perish' – had other, less altruistic and more unsavoury features. He and the Southern Decembrists were in touch with the Swiss branch of the Carbonari. Filippo Michele Buonarroti, after serving his sentence in France for taking part in Babeuf's 'Conspiracy of the Equals' – and before being expelled from Switzerland in

1824 – is known to have set up a number of secret Swiss societies connected with that Italian-French-Spanish cloak-and-dagger movement. The Decembrists are believed by some Russian writers to have had contact with Buonarroti, who passed on to them some of Babeuf's ideas.[9] But whether he did or not, Pestel's egalitarian republic, like Babeuf's 'Republic of the Equals', was to be a centralized state: Pestel shared with Babeuf a fierce desire – common to more than one later revolutionary – to protect his new regime by means of an all-embracing spy system, rigorous censorship and other drastic methods suitable to a totalitarian and police state.

'All private societies... public or secret' were to be banned in Pestel's future republic. Babeuf, contemplating a nation of 'good' citizens spying on those not 'useful to the fatherland', had proposed – all in the name of equality and 'the happiness of all' – to confine the latter in forced-labour and virtual concentration camps. Pestel planned to suppress all opposition by manning 'ministries, military commands' and all senior posts with adherents of the regime and by establishing a pervasive police department that, besides being secret and above the law, was to spy on both officials and private citizens, and to be called the Department of Order and Benevolence.

Though of German origin, Pestel was a fanatic Russian nationalist. To russify the empire's various nationalities – except for the unassimilable Poles and Jews – he was ready to go to such extremes as eradicating the very name Ukrainian from the vocabulary and forcibly 'resettling' the Caucasian peoples in distant areas. The Poles were to be granted independence, but Poland, in Pestel's plan (anticipating a tendency that was to become reality after World War II) was to be placed under Russian 'protection' and control as a virtual puppet state.

Pestel's ideas for getting rid of Russia's Jews were highly intriguing; he had a plan, briefly described in one of the latest accounts of the Decembrist rising, 'to push them through the Turkish frontier' – and elsewhere 'to deport them to Asia Minor and help them establish a Jewish State there.' Terse, though not untruthful, these cryptic versions[10] sacrifice to brevity the question of how two or so million Jews were in practice to be 'pushed' into Turkey and then 'helped' to appropriate one of the Sultan's provinces. The question of liberating these Jews, who were deprived of civic rights and most of whom were restricted to living from hand to mouth in a 'Pale of Settlement' in the eastern and Polish provinces, had been raised by a Jewish-born (though converted) Decembrist, who proposed resettling them as a 'unified nation' in the Crimea or the Orient.

Pestel probably had little personal contact with Jews, few of whom were permitted to reside in the cities, and he shared the general anti-Semitism of Russian society and its bogey-image of the strange Jewish rabble, with its foreign customs and religion, as an alien element inspiring both fear and hatred. He was, on the other hand, struck by the way they clung to their rabbis, observed their own laws and kept up their separate Talmudic schools – so much so that he actually and without conscious cynicism complained that they enjoyed 'more rights' than the Russians. While about to emancipate the downtrodden serfs, he was no more ready to grant civic equality to the persecuted Jews than Nicholas I, who 20 years later was still declaring their emancipation to be 'inconceivable, and such a thing shall not pass as long as I am alive.' Pestel remained obsessed by the spectacle of their 'excessive unity' and by their faith in 'awaiting the Messiah who will return them to their kingdom of old,' but after some study, he included in his Russian Law a twofold proposal.[11] The first, reminiscent of Napoleon's Sanhedrin convocation, was to call an assembly of rabbis and Jewish sages to discuss measures ostensibly designed to end their isolation and reduce Christian hostility – though actually meant to break up their 'harmful' cohesion – 'if Russia is not to expel the Jews.' The second was to expel and push them out, but in a *sui generis* manner including an offer of some armed assistance to help them establish 'their own exclusive state somewhere in Asia Minor.' His practical suggestion was to designate 'an assembly area for the Jewish people... If all the Jews of Russia and Poland were concentrated in one place', he reasoned, 'such a mass, exceeding two million' and assisted in raising an army from its midst, would 'not find it difficult to sweep away all Turkish obstacles.' Traversing or fighting its way through 'all of European Turkey', it was to 'reach Asiatic Turkey, there to seize an area sufficient for its numbers and to establish its Jewish State.'[12]

Nikita Muraviev, on the other hand, proposed to grant the Jews full equality in Russia. It is difficult to say whether Pestel's radical plan was a sincere attempt to solve an obstreperous problem that all Tsarist governments allowed to fester (and their Soviet successors were to try to suppress for 60 more years thereafter) or a calculated stratagem to lend the wholesale expulsion of the Jews a constructive-looking, statesman-like air. For all its anti-Semitic inspiration, Pestel himself, the all-out reformer, may have regarded it as a humane plan. Before the end of the 19th century, at any rate, with the Russian Jews savaged by a wave of pogroms, Konstantin Pobedonostsev, a high dignitary and adviser to a the last two Tsars, was to come up with a more notorious solution to the problem of the unemancipated Jews: 'to let one third of them die, expel another third, and convert the rest.'[13]

If Babeuf came to be regarded, though not universally, as a 'totalitarian democrat', Pestel, too, was to be seen by some 20th-century historians as standing 'first in the long line of revolutionaries who were both activists and theorists – the tradition which would one day produce Lenin.'[14] Yet this dictatorially inclined and methodical man, who had thought of everything, collapsed under interrogation, gave away all his comrades and cringingly appealed for mercy to the 'Sacred Person' of the Tsar whom he, for one, had meant not only to depose, but to massacre with his entire family. Ryleyev, on the other hand, singled out by the Inquiry Commission as the main organizer and 'chief catalyst' of the Petersburg insurrection, behaved with great dignity and assumed full responsibility for his part in it.

'Liberty has never been gained without victims,' he had written, aware (as he said in another line) that 'a cruel fate awaits those who first rise against the oppressors of the people.'[5] Paradoxically, it was the defiant spirit expressed in these lines, rather than the fiasco of the amateurish Decembrist attempt to seize the helm of an empire, that was to imprint itself deeply, hauntingly, on the mind of Russian society.

Giving rise to a growing saga of heroic courage and 'martyrdom', the very quixotism of their improvident but selfless gesture was to have striking after-effects long after 'the Five', as they became known, were hanged. In the end, this was to become the most remarkable single aspect of the politically inept, deplorably executed and impulsive revolution that failed.

The new Tsar's repression of the rebellious movement was ferocious. Almost directly after the execution of 'the Five', he entered Moscow in festive procession and proceeded with his own coronation. Alexander Herzen, who was 14 when he watched him riding past on horseback, was to recall that he looked 'handsome, but there was a coldness about his looks'. Herzen's boyhood impression that the new Tsar's face bespoke 'iron will and feeble intelligence', his eyes being 'entirely without warmth, without a trace of mercy, wintry eyes', was to be strikingly confirmed by high-placed Westerners during Nicholas's visit to London nearly 20 years later.

Nicholas I was 30, and looked impressive in his imperial regalia when he formally mounted the throne. He had, indeed, met the Decembrist challenge with cool courage in the face of personal danger. He had a highly developed sense of duty, took his new tasks very seriously, and went to great lengths to discover the motives of the insurgents. He knew some of them or their families, personally conducted the first night-long interrogation of their leaders immediately after their capture, and made every effort to understand them. Many of them went on sending him letters from prison, earnestly explaining their ideas. Nicholas read their letters and made a painstaking record of their recommendations.

Having been born to absolute power, he took it and unquestioning obedience to himself for granted, and though he carefully studied the evidence gathered by the Inquiry Commission, as well as Pestel's Russian Law and the confessions, letters and ideas for reform submitted by the other Decembrist leaders, the chief – if not the only – conclusion he drew from the insubordination of so many officers was that liberalism was dangerous.

'Dear, dear Constantine! Your will has been done, I am Emperor' – he had written to his brother in Warsaw the night after the Petersburg revolt was quelled – 'but great God, at what a price! At the price of my subjects' blood!'[16] But he could not bring himself to commute the death sentence of 'the Five', which should not have been pronounced in the first place, for capital punishment had been abolished in Russia, and there had been no executions for half a century. Though the sentences were handed down by a Special Tribunal of 72 judges, who went through the whole trial procedure involving 121 accused in a matter of 5 weeks (without hearing them or any defence pleas), 'it was Nicholas who was in fact the judge, the court expressing his will in legal formulas.'

With his coronation in the offing, there was widespread expectation that Nicholas would inaugurate his rule with an act of clemency. Instead, he insisted that the hangings be carried out as a deterrent; declared he would never again set eyes on those sent into exile, which meant that the deportees must remain in Siberia to the end of their lives, or his, whichever came first; and further broke up their families by allowing only those of their wives and children to accompany them who undertook never to return.

At the beginning of July 1826 he appointed General Alexander Benckendorff to be his Chief of Gendarmes, heading the new 'Higher' or Political Police. Ten days later Benckendorff, who since the Decembrist insurrection had become the person closest to Nicholas, attended the ceremonial execution of 'the Five' – which did not go off without a hitch. First, at the end of the formal and sombre rites in the courtyard of the Peter-and-Paul Fortress, young Bestuzhev-Ryumin broke down and had to be dragged up to the scaffold. Then the ropes of three others, who mounted the scaffold without fuss, broke and they fell alive or half-alive into the ditch. Having faced death with dignity, they had to wait for heavier ropes to be brought and to go through the whole procedure again before their necks were finally broken. Benckendorff, who had been a member of the Tsar's secret Inquiry Commission – and is said to have both recommended and supported his stringent measures against the conspirators – wrote that he was not 'attracted' to the gruesome spectacle 'by mere curiosity, but by sympathy', and went on to say of the Decembrists:[17] 'These were mostly young persons, noblemen of good families; many had served with me, and some of them such as, for instance, Prince Volkonsky, had been my immediate companions. My heart ached.' He regretted, too, the tragedy caused to 'so many families' (such as, for one cruel instance, that of his friend Volkonsky, whose new-born son, left behind when the princess chose to share her husband's exile, died shortly afterwards).

Benckendorff was a man whose highest virtue, and chief distinction, was absolute devotion to the dynasty. Any sympathy he felt for his former companions soon gave way to 'disgust' with these well-born but 'unfortunate' young men whose subversive plans and shocking action he could only ascribe to profound 'moral deterioration'.

Nicholas himself found it hard to fathom how trusted gentlemen and senior Guards officers charged, among other things, with the protection of the palace – and, moreover, destined by birth, rank and abilities to ease his burden and help him govern a vast empire – could have sunk to the level of committing treason against Russia in his, the Tsar's, person. After signing the death sentences he spent solitary hours in prayer. To his mother he wrote: 'I feel extreme anguish and at the same time gratitude to God who has allowed me to bring this horrible case to an end... Only the idea of a terrible duty permits me to endure such martyrdom.'[18]

Having started his reign under these circumstances, Nicholas was to become Europe's worst and most notorious despot. His first step was to set up the so-called 'Third Section'. Operating within his Imperial Chancellery, and thus under his personal control, the Third Section was charged with the political surveillance of all 'sects and dissenting movements'; with 'the exile, disposal and accommodation of suspicious and harmful persons'; and with the supervision of 'all places of confinement'. Another of its chief tasks was to provide information and reports on all events 'without exception'. Comprising a special gendarmerie wearing green uniforms with white stripes and known as the 'Higher Police' – to distinguish it from the 'Lower Police' in charge of normal police work – the Third Section also established a country-wide network of informers and was placed under the direction of General Benckendorff, who was accountable to no one but Nicholas.

There was a certain logic to this appointment, for Benckendorff had already 4 years earlier seen the need for a secret political police, and had submitted a detailed plan for its establishment to the late Alexander I.[19] Interestingly, he was the second General-in-Waiting to have warned the 'Liberator' that Pestel, the Muravievs, Prince Trubetskoy and the other Decembrist leaders were conspiring against the throne. Alexander had paid little heed to Benckendorff, but Nicholas, shaken by events and determined never to be surprised again and to suppress all opposition in germ, was all the more ready to listen to him as Benckendorff had not only proved his foresight but had acted with remarkable sang-froid on the day of the rebellion itself. He had, in the words of a French historian, 'had his eye on everything', had 'multiplied himself', as it were, 'bearing down with remarkable precision on all points of the insurrection.'

'A man most close and loyal to the Tsar', a man who 'should be the Tsar's eye, a faithful eye... fearing none but God and His Imperial Majesty', was how another Russian, a century earlier, had described the chief quality that would be required of the director of a special Chancellory of the Tsar's which he proposed to establish. As for the powers to be vested in him, he had stipulated it as essential that 'he should be supreme above judges and officials and should maintain an all-powerful surveillance over all authorities.'[20] General (and later Count) Alexander Khristoforovich Benckendorff, as it happened, fitted the prescription and its specifications perfectly. His loyalty to the Tsar was absolute, to the point where he was 'incapable of separating the duty of personal attachment [to the Tsar] from his duty to his country' – as one of his antagonists put it – 'even though that country was not his own.' And Nicholas did indeed vest in Benckendorff discretionary powers that made him the most influential and feared man in the empire, second only to himself. Benckendorff, who was 42 when he became head of the Third Section in July 1826, would sit in on all meetings of the Tsar's Ministers, and in time was to be described as 'actually a kind of Prime Minister'.

He also saw Nicholas daily. It was Benckendorff's 'duty', as the Countess Nesselrode soon observed, to inform the Tsar 'of everything said in society that might damage his reputation.' Benckendorff's spy-system, its secret agents recruited 'from all walks of life, including schoolchildren', penetrated all strata of Russian society. This, and his having the Tsar's ear – coupled with the fact that the Third Section, in Herzen's words, operated 'outside and above the law' – was, for the next 20 years, to place an extraordinary concentration of power in the hands of Nicholas's new confidant.

Benckendorff had high connections which had stood him well since his youth. His mother was a friend of the Russian Queen-Mother Maria Feodorovna. His sister was the famous Princess Lieven. Reputed to have been Metternich's mistress, Madame Lieven had for the last 14 years been presiding over the Russian Embassy in London. By dint of her intelligence, social aplomb, diplomatic intrigues and sumptuous parties, she had turned it into 'the most exclusive house' in the British capital, while she herself, outshining her ambassador-husband, and 'feared, respected, cultivated and courted' by Britain's office-holders and high society, had come to be regarded as the late Alexander's, and now Nicholas's, actual 'ambassadress' to the Court of St James.

Brave as well as 'lucky in war' as in peace, Benckendorff had fought in all the Russian as well as most Allied campaigns against Napoleon from Moscow to the crossing of the Rhine, and had survived to become a Lieutenant-General and Chief of Staff to the Corps of Guards. The Countess Nesselrode described him shortly before his appointment to the Third Section as 'amazingly frivolous'.

She thought he had a 'poor head' but an 'enthusiasm for good', and declared that 'anyone else' so close to the new Tsar 'might make things much worse.'[21] For Benckendorff was the type of urbane person who could inflict evil on a large scale and yet appear protective and the soul of amiability to some of his victims; and sometimes he would intercede with Nicholas to reduce a particularly harsh sentence.

Baron Koreff, however, who sat with him at various official meetings for more than a decade, later portrayed him as an uneducated mediocrity 'whose goodness was negative', a man immoderately devoted to women who 'learned nothing, read nothing', lacked 'personal initiative' and any natural talent other than his pleasant manners and 'that chivalrous something in his tone...' An apathetic, sleepy-looking person, Benckendorff stupefied Koreff by his incredible 'forgetfulness and perpetual absent-mindedness' – to the point where he would sit through meetings without knowing what had been decided, or praise a Minister's speech without realizing that the speaker had opposed his own view.[22]

Another official dismissed him as 'this empty-headed creature'. Stories of Benckendorff's profligacy persisted, and Herzen later wondered how many innocents 'perished through his lack of attention', or because of his gallant preoccupations. 'In his hands lay the fortunes, the liberty and the lives of all the inhabitants of Russia,' a French chronicler of Nicholas's reign was to sum up Benckendorff's extraordinary position.[23] He may have been 'empty-headed' and intellectually shallow, but by the testimony of the same official Benckendorff 'would have cut himself into pieces' for Nicholas's sake, and therein lay the basis of the Tsar's trust in him and the ultimate source of his power and ascendancy.

Remote from his people, ruling by means of a vast bureaucracy and with the mind of an 'imperial sergeant-major', Nicholas suppressed free speech and all 'western' ideas, personally censored Pushkin's *Boris Godunov*, forbade its printing for several years, and exiled the poet Lermontov. He invited other intellectuals and noblemen suspected of holding 'subversive' ideas to harangue them at the palace, and unless they 'repented' would send them off into the Army or to Siberia.

In the Army, soldiers recruited by levy and quota from the village communes, or supplied by the landowners from among their serfs, continued to serve for 25 years. Cruelty and floggings continued, too, with even aristocratic cadets punished for a cigarette with 'a thousand blows with birch rods' and offending plain soldiers beaten senseless or dead while made to run a gauntlet of two facing ranks of 1,000 men armed with knouts.

Under a new Censorship Law every newspaper article had to be approved 'by two separate censors, supervised by a third controlling official, who spied on both of them.' With censorship departments in every university and every

Ministry, with a new Education Minister, Count Sergei Uvarov, openly proclaiming that it was his object to 'consolidate in the hands of the government the control of all intellectual resources', anything not conforming to his three cherished principles – 'Orthodoxy, autocracy and nationality' – was stamped out of textbooks and general books.

'Teachers of logic had simultaneously to convince their pupils that the laws of reason did not exist, and history teachers had to prove that Greece and Rome were never republics, but absolute monarchies,' Alexander Nikitenko, a conservative liberal who himself served as a censor at St Petersburg University and then as a professor, noted in his diary.[24] But as the young were irrepressible and could not be entirely muzzled or their ideas effectively controlled, Nicholas gradually reduced the size of schools and universities and limited the number of those allowed to attend them. With widespread fear of denunciations, and people afraid of falling into the hands of the 'white straps' (the gendarmes of the Third Section), Russians learned to hide their thoughts, officials adopted a mask of servil-ity, and the whole of Russian society became infested with a phenomenon best described as 'cultivated hypocrisy', making for a stifling atmosphere in which thinking people felt degraded.

For the next 30 years, in short, Nicholas I not only did his best to hamper Russia's intellectual development but turned his empire and its eventually 70 million subjects into a 'land of silence' or sanctimonious lies. The land problem 'always remained present in his mind'.[25] Indeed, he kept on his desk a full list of the 570 Decembrist insurgents as well as a record of their ideas for social reform. He was aware of 'the flagrant evil of serfdom' and as Russia's peasant problem worsened with her growing population, he appointed one secret commission after another to recommend solutions – but carried out only the most timid and limited reforms. Afraid of losing the remaining support of the nobility whose brightest heads he had eliminated, he was encouraged by Benckendorff's Third Section to believe that in case of 'war, diseases, famine... giving freedom to the nobles' peasants may easily provoke grave disturbances.'[26] And having concealed Pestel's Russian Law even from Bludow – the author of his own Inquiry Commission's report – Nicholas had it locked up. Pestel's plan had been found by digging up some earth beneath which he had buried his incriminating papers. Now it was sealed and buried in some secret archive, to be discovered and published only 70 years after the execution of 'the Five'.

But long before that, the shock caused by the hangings and the brutal repression that followed had generated an extraordinary and undying saga of Decembrist 'suffering' and 'self-sacrifice' of mythic power and proportions. The failure of the dilettantish insurrection was dimmed and outshone by the sheer desperate bravura of the rebels in flinging themselves against superior might and impossible odds for the sake of an ideal. Many of the gentlemen-officers had expressed contrite repentance, but their depositions and pleas to the Tsar were unknown. What was remembered was the dignity with which most of them, having willingly risked instant execution or slow death in Siberia, had accepted and borne their fate. Already in 1826 the British envoy to St Petersburg, in a report on the abortive revolution, had stated that for all its 'lack of management' and 'head to direct it', and though it was 'too premature to answer any good purpose... the seeds have been sown which one day must produce important consequences.'[27]

And so they did, in the sense that to increasingly restless, continually oppressed, generations of Russians, the executed as well as the exiles, and the noble wives who kept faith with them (later celebrated in Nekrasov's poem, 'The Decembrist Women') appeared as selfless and magnificent heroes, heroines and 'martyrs' of the struggle for freedom from tyranny, inspiring thousands of the young to engage in revolutionary activities.

In time to come, 20th-century Soviet historians were to present the Decembrist rebellion as the beginning of a prolonged revolutionary process that culminated in the October Revolution; and even Western historians proclaimed it as 'the first act' in a continuous drama that led to the 1917 Bolshevik take-over. Of late, however – and but for the figure of Pestel, whom a Harvard historian in 1981 rightly singled out as, 'of all the Decembrists', the one 'closest to being a precursor of Bolshevism' – the idea of a direct link between the limited officers' insurrection of 1825 and the events of 1917 has been dismissed as a mixture of fact and fiction.[28]

In considering the Decembrist myth, it must be kept in mind that all subsequent 19th-century attempts to stir up a popular revolt in Russia and overthrow tsardom failed. It was only the disorganization and the defeat of the Russian armies at the start of World War I, coupled with the shortage of bread and other basic products, which reduced the Tsarist Empire to anarchy and impotence, and for the first time created a truly revolutionary situation that brought the masses out into the streets and led in March 1917 to the abdication of Russia's last Tsar. Such, however, is the power of myth that as recently as 1988 a couple of serious scholars found it necessary to bring back to memory the fact that the first attempt 'to establish a democratic regime in Russia' – in the elections for the Constituent Assembly, which gave the Socialist parties more than 62 per cent of the vote – was 'suppressed before it began' when the Bolshevik minority, led by Lenin and Trotsky, dispersed the Constituent Assembly with machine guns on the morrow of its first meeting.[29]

But this all lay in the distant future when Pestel and his associates were hanged on 13 July 1826.

233

8

Fathers and Sons: Herzen and Bakunin in Their Youth

At Premukhino, a few hundred kilometers northwest of Moscow, Michael Bakunin celebrated his 12th birthday at the end of May 1826. A tall boy, soon to grow 'strong as an ox' and one day to become, physically as well as figuratively, the towering apostle and hero of international Anarchism – the first Russian to preach total revolution and a 'tornado of destruction' to set the whole world aflame as the only way of purging it of evils, imperfections and injustice – he was absorbed in the carefree summer joys of childhood when, some time in mid-July, horrifying news reached his parents. A second cousin of his mother, Lieutenant Colonel Sergei Muraviev-Apostol, had been executed as one of 'the Five', hanged on the crosspiece of the gallows like a common criminal.

Michael Bakunin grew up in an idyllic setting. His father's estate at Premuk-hino was comparatively small by Russian standards at the time, but beautifully situated in the pastoral part of Tver, today the district of Kalinin. The comfortable one-storey Bakunin house, with its garden and lawns, presided from a wooded hillside over the village of Premukhino – whose chief landmark was a large church built in memory of the boy's grandfather – and over more woods stretching down to the quiet-flowing Ossuga river. In May the cherries blossomed, and July brought the scent of wild roses. There was a little island where Michael and the other Bakunin children had their sport by day, when not playing hide-and-seek among the trees or exploring secret groves; there were magic summer evenings and moonlight picnics, and early winter nights when their father, Count Alexander Bakunin, would read *The Swiss Family Robinson* to his large family gathered round the fire.

The previous winter, however, a heavy pall of dread and suspense had descended on Premukhino. One by one, Captain Nikita Muraviev, a first cousin of the Countess Varvara Bakunin, and then the now-executed Sergei Muraviev-Apostol, his brother Mattei and Michael Nikolayevich Muraviev, to count only her more prominent relatives, had all been imprisoned in the Peter-and-Paul Fortress. The Muraviev clan were among Russia's largest landowners. Varvara Bakunin belonged to it through her late father (her stepfather was an equally noble Poltoratsky). Back in 1816 Alexander Nikolayevich Muraviev, then a

23-year-old colonel and war-hero, had founded the original Union of Salvation. Michael Nikolayevich Muraviev, a senior officer on his way to a generalship, was a brother of his. He and Sergei Muraviev-Apostol, who were the same age, had barely turned 20 when they secretly enrolled among the Union's first 6 members.

Few of Russia's great families had done more than the Muraviev clan to foster the revolutionary tendencies which suddenly erupted in the two Decembrist insurrections. At the same time, nothing better reflected the crushing political as well as inner difficulties and dilemmas which these aristocratic and intensely patriotic Russians had to overcome before deciding to attack a century-old autocracy – and to exchange the role of rulers for that of rebels – than the fact that Alexander Nikolayevich, the dashing young colonel and 'founder', had shortly afterwards taken flight into religion, turned mystic, and severed his subversive connections.

In addition, Michael Nikolayevich was now to provide in his person a crass example of these contrary pulls dividing whole families into fervent reformers and brutal oppressors. He strenuously denied his involvement in the Decembrist affair and managed to exculpate himself before the Inquiry Commission. Then he switched sides.

'There are the Muravievs who hang, and those who are hanged,' he declared – making it clear that he belonged to the former – after he became a general and suppressed the Polish 1830–31 rebellion. For his brutal methods then and later, he was to be known as 'Muraviev the Hangman'. Another Muraviev was later to extend Russia's hold along the Amur as far as the Pacific, and yet another to serve as Foreign Minister.

Sergei Muraviev-Apostol, on the other hand, who was second-in-command of the Chernohov Regiment in the Ukraine when he was hanged, was a sincere, if over-impulsive idealist. Placed under house-arrest after Pestel's seizure, he had escaped together with his brother Mattei and on 29 December – when he already knew of the collapse of the revolt in St Petersburg – had advanced with 800 mutineers in the direction of Kiev, a reckless decision which did much to inspire the legend of Decembrist 'self-sacrifice' and courageous martyrdom. Severely wounded in the artillery bombardment which put an end to his venture, Muraviev-Apostol had now, in July 1826, been hanged twice, the first time falling blindfolded into the ditch when the rope around his neck broke.

'What a wretched country!' he is said to have exclaimed, 'They don't even know how to hang properly.'[1] But the defiance he showed to the last and bequeathed to future revolutionaries as part of the Decembrist 'spirit' did not lessen the terror inspired at the time by his frightening end. Nor did it lighten the atmosphere at Premukhino, any more than did the fact that his St Petersburg kinsman, Captain Nikita Muraviev, who had drafted pamphlets against

Tsarist absolutism, had often visited his cousin Varvara at Premukhino. Her husband, Count Alexander Bakunin, a former diplomat, is believed to have been a member of the defunct Union of Welfare. With the remotest ramifications of the Decembrist plot continuing to be stringently investigated, this alone was enough to render him suspect. Worse, the vengeful Tsarist retribution visited upon the more prominent Decembrists often extended to entire families, and Michael Bakunin's father, though not actively involved in either the Northern or the Southern insurrection, felt doubly and trebly exposed for, besides his marital ties with the Muraviev rebels, several of them had actually aired their subversive plans for years in his own drawing-room.

The Count had been raised in Italy from the age of 9. Happening to be in Paris in 1789, he had witnessed the French Revolution, and according to the memoirs of one of his sons, participated in the siege of the Bastille.[2] This did not mean that he was or became a revolutionary himself. But on his return home at the start of the century, after serving for years at the Russian Legations in Florence and Turin, this highly cultured man – who held a doctorate in philosophy from Padua University and had been elected to the Academy of Turin – impressed the provincial gentry of Tver with his liberal Western ideas. Eventually, in 1810, when he was 42, he met Varvara Muraviev – a vivacious beauty who could have been his daughter (she was only 18) – and after a *coup de foudre* summer romance married her the same autumn.

The couple left for Tver, where the Grand Duchess Catherine, Tsar Alexander's sister, had set up her court for the winter. The Grand Duchess was an arrogant and very sharp-tongued lady – during the Tsar's 1814 London visit she was to stop the band playing at a Carlton House dinner with the Prince-Regent 'because music always makes me vomit'[3] – but Alexander and Varvara Bakunin honeymooned there over the winter in resplendent company. It was the young woman's last great social fling, for after she returned to Premukhino at the beginning of 1811, she bore no fewer than 11 children between then and 1824. The last-born died at the age of two in 1826, the year of the Decembrist executions, leaving the Bakunins with 4 daughters and 6 sons. Although their father's liberal ideas had been shaken by Napoleon's brutal invasion of Russia, he remained a humanist. In love with the countryside, he had settled down to a squire's sedate life and had spent the decade and a half during which his wife was busy childbearing quietly improving his estate, turning it – with its park-like setting, its flower gardens, fruit orchards, lawns, pond, river and woodland – into a charming 'nobleman's nest'. A man of scholarly inclinations, he kept a well-stocked library and some of Tver's intelligentsia gathered in his drawing-room for musical soirées, or to discuss local politics, the latest changes in Europe, Russian and French literature and German philosophical ideas.

Premukhino's intellectual ambience and serene rustic setting have led at least one modern historian to compare it to Madame de Staël's famous retreat at Coppet. Obviously it would not have aroused any special interest if Michael Bakunin had not emerged from this splendid natural setting and ideal playground as a prophet of universal conflagration.

Michael's childhood was a perfectly happy one. Nothing predicted the fact that he would become a firebrand agitator and master-conspirator, the first Russian 'to conceive social revolution in cosmic terms and on an international scale.'[4] Whether because of their father's stories of sunlit Italy, or because of the carefree life they enjoyed at Premukhino, with its ancient ivy, its sawmill, its meandering river and serene flow of seasons, the Bakunin children felt (as Michael's brother Paul later declared) that they 'grew up in Russia, but under a clear Italian sky. Everything about us breathed a happiness such as is difficult to find on earth.'[5]

Michael himself was later to write an extraordinary testimonial to his father, praising him for having inculcated in his children 'a feeling for the good and the beautiful', a love for truth, a 'feeling of proud independence and freedom. You did it because you loved us, and we were devoted to you heart and soul.'[6] Indeed, Alexander Bakunin always found time to listen to the chatter of his young brood, to take his older children on long strolls, to chat with them about nature, make them look for rare plants, tell them historical anecdotes and awaken sundry interests in them. When Michael was 23 he was to put down on paper what it meant to him to bask in his father's loving care: 'Yes, dear father, memories about you and the love for you, about the Premukhino house, the garden and all its surroundings, about the love of nature and the pleasures of nature, and about our childhood – all this is merged in one, all this comprises our inalienable treasure and the best period of our family life.[7]

There were some 500 serfs on the Bakunin estate. Michael's father, on his return from abroad imbued with progressive Western ideas, had offered them a kind of charter or 'constitution'. But they would not hear of it. Like other Russian intellectuals disappointed with some of the things they had seen in Western Europe, Count Bakunin began to feel that hurried imitation of the West might do Russia more harm than good. And those of his liberal ideas that survived the Napoleonic invasion had gradually given way to an intense Russian patriotism. He and Captain Nikita Muraviev had often discussed the tricky question of Russia's serfs and her land problem, which between them had no parallel in the world. He thus knew something about the long-nursed ideas of the Decembrists. But as a former diplomat he was wary of illegality, and with a large family to consider, he had been doubly careful to stay out of any adventurous conspiracies.

Whatever part he had played in the storming of the Bastille, his adventurous days were over and his temperament, age, training and the tranquil happiness of his environment had all inclined him to advocate prudence to his wife's hot-headed cousins. Nor had Nikita or any of the other Muravievs given him notice when, on the spur of the moment, they had decided to strike in St Petersburg and the Ukraine.

His wife, affected by the fate of her Muraviev relatives and still relatively young, clung to her husband and fervently supported his new attitude. For all her child-bearing, she remained a good-looking, attractive woman. Besides greatly enjoying her loving attentions, the count was delighted to watch the nymph-like grace of his two demure adolescent daughters, Lyubov, approaching 16, and Varvara 14 – henceforth, to distinguish her from her mother, to be called by her pet-name, Varinka. He took pleasure in hearing the house ringing with the giggles, cries and bustle of the rest of his girls and boys. Giving himself over entirely to the charm of his rustic retreat and the pleasures of family life, he declared in a lyrical prose poem, 'When, at the evening hour, the whole family is gathered together like a swarm of bees, then I am happier than a king.'

He went on collecting the *obrok* the serfs had to pay their master – in money or kind, in lieu of giving him their labour – but, cultured aristocrat that he was, he took time off from his affairs to supervise the education of his children. Like Heine's mother, Count Bakunin was a believer in Rousseau, but having less reason to be anxious about the future of his offspring, had decided early in his marriage to educate them not by parental authority, but by means of 'tenderness, affection and indulgence', through 'advice, example and reason';[8] and he personally taught his children history, geography, natural science and religion, devoting special attention to his eldest boy.

At 12, Michael Bakunin was also being privately tutored in Russian, French and German. He had teachers for other subjects, and was receiving some English lessons as well. He learned to play the violin, was taught to draw (and at 16 and 17 did two accomplished self-portraits). His sisters had piano or harp lessons and the elder children often played, hummed or sang together.

By Michael's own later testimony, his father rarely scolded him or the other children and hardly ever punished them. As far as humanly possible, Count Bakunin was, or tried to be, the ideal father. Yet, permissive to a degree, he instilled in them his own sense of duty, and, presiding over his family like a gentle but firm patriarch, tried to impart to them his belief in the virtues of honesty and industrious work harmonized with the enjoyment of life.

Because his eldest son Michael was later to praise 'the glory' of the Decembrist 'heroes, martyrs of our liberty, prophets of our future... our salvation, our light, source of our inspiration',[9] it was sometimes to be claimed that the events of 1825–26 represented the boy's 'revolutionary baptism'. In fact, neither the wholesale persecution of hundreds of Decembrist families, nor the impact of the hanging of his mother's cousin and the deportation of other Muravievs, aroused in Michael any adolescent impulse to identify with the victims. In the new atmosphere at Premukhino he felt no particular sympathy for the rebels. His grandfather had been a violent man of giant stature. Holding the minor rank of state councillor under Catherine the Great, he had once, in a fit of rage, bodily lifted a coachman from his box and thrown him into the river. Michael, who inherited his strong physique, showed no such tendencies. He was, on the contrary, a boy of gentle disposition, sensitive to beauty, the arts and the softer, spiritual values now being cultivated by his father in Premukhino.

The Bakunin family was deeply religious. On his father's side, Michael had three extremely devout maiden aunts and his father, too, strictly observed all Russian Orthodox Church rituals. Michael later referred to the indelible impact made on him by the fervour and pathos of the 'ineffable, glorious' Holy Week ceremonies: 'These incidents seem insignificant, but they penetrated deeply into our souls.'[10]

He was loved by all his siblings, and nothing at this stage suggested to them or to his parents that they were nursing in their midst no mere future atheist and rebel, but a 'mutineer of the pure will and act', an apostle of destruction who – when not in fetters, awaiting execution or the Tsar's pardon in Siberia – would spread subversion wherever he went and launch such incendiary visions as having 'the whole of Europe, with Petersburg, Paris and London, transformed into a giant rubbish-heap.'

Not until he was 19 did young Bakunin show any rebellious instincts, and then he would direct them against his father.

But already in 1826, immediately after the hanging of 'the Five', another, only slightly older, boy had sworn to avenge the 'murdered' Decembrists. He did so at the Kremlin, while kneeling with his father among prostrated ranks of high dignitaries at the solemn Thanksgiving Service held in Moscow to celebrate the new Tsar's victory over the impractical insurgents

'In the midst of the Kremlin', he was to recall, 'the Metropolitan Philaret thanked God for the murders. The whole of the Royal Family' – except Nicholas I himself, who had yet to arrive in the city for his festive coronation – 'took part in the service, near them the Senate and the Ministers and in the immense space around, packed masses of the Guards knelt bareheaded; they also joined in the prayers. Cannon roared from the walls of the Kremlin.'[11]

The boy listening to the service was 14 years old. He came from the Yakovlev clan of nobles, whose ancestry went back to the 15th century when the Grand

Duke and first 'Tsar' Ivan III and his Greek-born wife Zoe-Sophia, adopting Byzantine pageantry at the court of the new-born Russian Empire and proclaiming Moscow to be 'the third and last Rome' (after the fall of both the first and the second – Constantinople), had built the Kremlin Square with the cathedral in which the 1826 service took place.[12] On the spot, 'before that altar defiled by bloody rites', the boy dedicated himself 'to the struggle with that throne, with that altar, with those cannon.'

The Yakovlevs were also distantly related to the Romanov dynasty which had occupied 'that throne' since 1613 and was to be in charge of Russia's destinies for altogether 300 years until the Bolshevik Revolution. In the 18th century the boy's grandfather, Alexis Alexandrovich Yakovlev, married to a Princess Meshchersky, had been president of the College of Justice and director of the Imperial Mint. The boy's father, Ivan Yakovlev, had retired from the famous Izmaylovsky Guards with the rank of captain at the age of 31, and a few years later – in 1801 – had left Russia and spent the next 10 years moving leisurely 'from one country to another', while Napoleon's armies were invading them all. Part of the time he had travelled in the company of the beautiful and notorious Olga Zherebtsov – a sister of Catherine the Great's last lover Platon Zubov – and had otherwise mingled with the best society in Italy, France and Germany, where his brother Lev was the Tsar's ambassador to King Jérôme of Westphalia.

Before going abroad, Ivan Yakovlev had fathered a sickly illegitimate boy called Yegor by a serf-girl on one of his estates. When he finally returned home late in 1811, aged 45, he brought back with him a pregnant 16-year-old mistress, Luisa Haag, whom he had met at his brother's Russian embassy in Cassel. The runaway daughter of a minor German official, she had, in unknown circumstances, been given 'asylum' from her parents at the ambassador's residence, against 'the nominal duty of pouring the morning coffee.'[13]

Ivan Yakovlev was an unemotional man who, in 10 years, had shown not the slightest interest in the son he had left behind in Russia. But with Napoleon in full flow across the Continent, he reluctantly gave in to the girl's pleadings and smuggled her across the Russian frontier disguised as a boy.

In Moscow, he temporarily installed Luisa Haag in the house of his eldest brother, Alexander Yakovlev, who had once held the post of Procurator of Russia's Holy Synod, but had been dismissed from this high position and banished from St Petersburg after creating a disturbance and actually coming to blows with another dignitary at an official dinner. In Moscow he presided over a 'great library' and a 'regular harem of serf-girls' in separate wings of a large house, and when not busy terrorizing the peasants on his estates, amused himself playing games with a collection of bought medals and 'decorations he might have received'.

It was in April 1812, in the sprawling establishment of this queer and lecherous character of uncontrolled temper – believed to have inspired Dostoyevsky's portrait of Fyodor Pavlovich in *The Brothers Karamazov* – that Luisa Haag gave birth to Ivan Yakovlev's second son. Whether Ivan Yakovlev had married her in Germany and chose for whatever reasons not to repeat the marriage ceremony in Russian Church style, or whether he in fact never married her at all, she never became his wife, legally or socially, in Russia.[14]

Ivan Yakovlev's second son, like the first, therefore remained illegitimate. He was the boy 'in the midst of the Kremlin' in 1826, who was to become that celebrated and wealthy godfather of 19th-century Russian Socialism, Alexander Ivanovich Herzen, one of the most fascinating personalities of his age. The patronymic Ivanovich may have indicated his father's intention to adopt him as his ward.[15] The name Herzen, derived from the German word for 'heart' – which his father also gave to his half-brother Yegor – may have been a private joke alluding to the momentary sentiment in which he had unintentionally begotten them. For Ivan Yakovlev, who cared little for his first son but was to give the second whatever affection he was capable of, was also a sarcastic man with a caustic sense of humour.

Alexander Herzen's stormy life was marked from the outset by adventure. He was barely 5 months old when Napoleon entered Moscow with his armies and the 'great fire' which was to devour three-quarters of the city began. Ivan Yakovlev and Luisa Haag, with the baby and several servants, set out from the burning house of Ivan's aunt, the Princess Meshchersky, and moved between crackling trees on the Tverskoye Boulevard towards that of his brother-in-law, Golokhvastsov, only to find it too on fire. In the garden behind the house they were attacked by a mob of soldiers, one of whom struck Golokhvastsov in his face with a sword.

Another grabbed the child from the arms of his nurse and tore off his babyclothes to search them for hidden diamonds. A fight between a drunken servant who had got hold of a sabre and a French dragoon who was about to steal a horse ended with the servant pushing the dragoon alive into a lime pit. Fleeing for their lives, the party, 'masters and servants all together', finally sat down in a corner of the Tverskoye Square and the baby spent the cold night, opaque with smoke, wrapped in 'a piece of green baize' torn from a billiard table.

In the morning more fires raged and the very air of Moscow became 'insufferably hot'. But in the midst of more dreadful scenes, that day brought the great moment in the life of Herzen's father which resulted in his meeting Napoleon face to face and being given the curious mission which was to earn 'Captain Yakovlev' brief mention in two places in Tolstoy's *War and Peace*.[16] Yakovlev heard from an Italian officer that one of Napoleon's commanders in

Moscow was Marshal Mortier, whom he had met during his stay in Paris. Speaking to the Italian in his native tongue, he asked him to inform Mortier of his family's plight. The upshot, as Herzen was to hear it described over and over again during his childhood, was that the whole famished Yakovlev party huddling in Tverskoye Square were taken into a shop where masters and servants fed on 'dates, figs, and almonds' as well as 'the choicest tea'; and next they were given 'a room in the Governor-General's house', whose maître d'hôtel 'even sent us wine.'

For Marshal Mortier had found the opportunity to inform Napoleon, and Ivan Yakovlev was summoned to his presence. As Herzen was to evoke the scene decades later, his father, 'who worshipped decorum', made his appearance in the throne room of the Kremlin Palace 'without his wig, in high boots that had not been cleaned for several days, with dirty linen and unshaven chin.' Napoleon gave him a long speech, expounding on his magnanimity and peaceful inclinations, and made Yakovlev engage himself upon his honour to try and cross the Russian lines and deliver a personal message from the Emperor to the Tsar. In return, he was given a safe-conduct for his family to leave the smoking city. 'At four o'clock one morning', Mortier sent an adjutant 'to summon my father to the Kremlin... Napoleon took a sealed letter that was lying on the table, handed it to him, and said, bowing him out: "I rely on your word of honour." On the envelope was written: "*A mon frère, l'Empéreur Alexandre.*"

'The permit given to my father has survived... An open wagonette was given us for the wounded old man [Yakovlev's brother-in-law], my mother and my nurse; the others walked. A few Uhlans escorted us on horseback as far as the Russian rearguard... A minute later the Cossacks surrounded the strange refugees.' Yakovlev, with a dragoon escort provided by one of the Russian generals, set out for St Petersburg. There he was to spend weeks under house arrest at the home of the War Minister, Arakcheyev, awaiting the Tsar's decision whether to punish him for contact with the enemy.

Nothing came of the mission entrusted to him by Napoleon. The Tsar refused to receive the former 'Captain Yakovlev' or to reply to Napoleon's message, which had been passed on to him by Arakcheyev. Its only result was that it enabled Yakovlev, who, for 15 years after leaving his regiment and for another 34 until the day he died, never did a normal day's work, to save his family and some of his household from perishing in the fire of Moscow.

Seventeen-year-old Luisa Haag, her infant and the rest of Yakovlev's relatives and servants had been taken to one of his villages at Yaroslavl, where they settled down in a peasant hut. There his brother-in-law, Golokhvastov, died of a stroke, and his baby son slept on a cold bench partly covered with snow that kept drifting in through a crack in a window.

Ivan Yakovlev himself, ordered to retire to the country until further notice, joined them there before the end of October 1812. He moved them to another of his estates, where he had a house, and about a year after the 'great fire' was allowed to return to Moscow.

Herzen, looked after by two nurses, grew up in a mansion staffed by some 60 male and female house-serfs – maids, laundresses, married couples, besides boys and girls 'being trained in their duties' – and then educated by a string of private Russian and French tutors. On his birthdays the ballroom doors were thrown open and to the sound of music 'serf-boys dressed up as Turks' entered with trays of sweets. He was presented with toys and costly presents, then a puppet show was put on for his entertainment. On summer visits to one of the large Yakovlev estates at Vasilevskoye, the village headman, 'the priest, his wife, the church-servitors, the house-serfs,' etc., were always on hand to greet the family's arrival. The village was surrounded by forests and vast quivering corn fields, and little Herzen spent enchanted summers playing and romping about, building dams on a nearby river or reading under a lime tree, and every evening he was allowed to fire a small but real cannon.

He was pampered by his father, by his mother, and by his uncle Lev Yakovlev. Upon his return to Moscow, this former ambassador to the dissolved court of Westphalia was elected to the Senate and moved into his brother's mansion. But the boy's father, his mother and the Senator all lived in separate apartments of the great house. And 'Captain' Ivan Yakovlev, who in his smart young days had turned many a lady's head with his intelligence, wit and sarcastic charm, became increasingly, morbidly preoccupied with his real or imaginary illnesses. Idle, discontented, given to a peculiar blend of hypochondriacal self-pity and irascibility, and a great stickler for etiquette, he exasperated his family and his huge household staff with his barbed remarks and his mocking way of putting everyone in the wrong.

The boy's mother was barely 21 when Ivan turned 50. A stranger to Russia in spite of now being called Luisa Ivanovna, she bore the brunt of his spleen. Weak-willed, gentle, dominated by his superior education and worldliness as much as by his age – and irregulaly positioned between the serfs, who regarded her as the titular mistress of the household, and Ivan, who treated her as something like a concubine-cum-nurse – she lived in a kind of formal and legal limbo, suffered his criticism and his crotchets, and ministered to his needs and wants with cheerful resignation, having little alternative or perhaps not knowing better.

On solemn occasions, the boy was taken to his father's 80-year-old maiden aunt, the Princess Meshchersky, a noble, wax-like figure whose youth passed away before the days of Catherine the Great. The entire milieu in which he grew up seemed invented by a writer of grotesque fiction. His uncle, who held various honorific appointments – including that of 'Court Chamberlain' to Moscow's non-existent court – kept tirelessly, artificially busy, hurrying from the Senate to committee meetings of various benevolent societies and then home and to the English Club, or a French play, or to some ball, dinner, reception or other function, whether of 'a medical or fire insurance society, or of the Society of Natural Philosophy.' The Senator and his brother could barely stand each other. Their elder sister, the Princess Khovansky, was a formidable-looking woman, but all three of them were afraid of their malevolent brother, Alexander Yakovlev, the one-time Procurator of the Holy Synod. This vindictive old man, who amused himself with endless lawsuits (one, over a violin, went on for 30 years), kept his bastard children separate from their mothers in the 'harem', allowing them to see each other only on holidays.

None of the three Yakovlev brothers ever formed any lasting human attachment, marital or otherwise. The Senator – the only one in whom the boy sensed 'some degree of human feeling and a certain warmth of heart' – remained a life-long bachelor, rousting about town to a ripe old age. Herzen's father, on the other hand, hardly ever went out; but, unlike the fierce former Procurator, who relieved his 'solitary' retirement with a whole troop of serf-women, veteran paramours and younger 'odalisques', enjoying every minute of his quarrelsome and debauched life, Ivan Yakovlev spent his days in an atmosphere of contagious gloom and ill-temper, which eventually caused the Senator to move into a house of his own. After that, Herzen's father, too, bought a new house, but every house the family lived in soon came to reflect his morose personality: 'The walls, the furniture, the servants, everything bore a look of discontent and suspicion.... The unnatural stillness, the whispers and cautious footsteps of the servants, did not suggest attentive solicitude, but oppression and terror.'[17]

The *Moscow News* Ivan Yakovlev read with his morning coffee had to be warmed to take out the dampness before he touched it; then he would use every farcical pretext to berate his staff, quarrel with his valet, or criticize the cook's purchases or his proposed menu. Except for some hours it took him to go over his accounts, send instructions to his villages, see his doctor or receive occasional visitors for tea, he had the rest of the day free for his household tyranny, which went on unabated until it was time for his nightly routine of 'washings, fomentations and medicines'; and he was so fussy over his health that he allowed no books or furniture to be moved in his bedroom, 'nor the windows opened for years.'

One day Alexander overheard a Russian general talking to his father about 'your young man' and pricked up his ears: they were discussing his future. Hearing a reference to his 'false position', the 8-year-old boy suddenly realized that there was some mystery about his birth. He became increasingly aware of his father's capricious temper, and things which up to then had seemed to him normal, such as that everyone, including his mother, should be afraid of his father, began to appear in a new light. Listening with a new ear to stray, commiserating remarks by the servants about their young mistress's poor fate, he gathered in almost no time – without asking a single question, and keeping his shock to himself – sufficient information to comprehend both his mother's lack of regular marital status, and therefore of any status in society, and the fact of his own illegitimate birth.

Ivan Yakovlev was painfully aware of his own peevish nature, hated the world, distrusted everyone and was dissatisfied with himself. The more conscious he was of the chill he exuded, the more helplessly cold and mocking became his manner. If he had originally placed the young Luisa Haag in a separate apartment because of her ambiguous status, the division of the living quarters also satisfied Yakovlev's desire to be left alone and the misanthropic inclinations he shared with his brothers. Many years later, Herzen was to realize that 'the old man's heart was more open to love and even tenderness' than he thought as a boy. Nevertheless, he was an estranged, lonely child, nursing what was to grow into a hidden resentment against his father for neglecting to legitimize him.

His elder half-brother, Yegor, had an incurable disease and was 'always in the hands of the surgeons'. Herzen, growing up without playmates, began to play 'with the house-serf boys, which was strictly forbidden.' But he felt he owed less filial obedience than a legitimate son. The servants' hall, in the part of the house occupied by his mother, became his refuge from his father's cheerless carping and acrimonious presence. There he could behave with complete liberty and enjoy himself. Mixing in the discussions of the maids and manservants, he got to know 'all their intimate affairs', joined the domestic guerilla tactics they sometimes employed against his father, and never dropped 'a word in the drawing-room about the secrets of the servants' hall.'

The Yakovlev house-serfs were flogged only in rare and extreme instances. But they could be punished by being sent off as soldiers for 20 years, and when this happened there were tragedies. In the servants' hall Herzen gained an invaluable insight into the 'downstairs' reality beneath the surface of Tsarist society with its gilded drawing-rooms and patriarchal estates. Coupled with his later political imprisonment, this was to enable him to give the Western public – or the interested section of it – an unexcelled and at that time unknown picture of 19th-century conditions in Russia. As a bastard child he was perhaps more sensitive than others to injustice, and on one occasion, seeing an agent of his father's beating an old peasant in the courtyard, he was so furious that he 'clutched him by the beard and fainted.' In the servants' hall, in short, he developed 'an invincible hatred for every form of slavery and every form of tyranny.'

He found another refuge and distraction in books. His father, who had a huge library and in his own crotchety way was trying to do his best for him, encouraged him to read. From French books and Schiller's writings – not to mention his tail-coated, guardedly revolutionary French tutor, Bouchot – he began to discover the ideas of liberty and equality.

When the Decembrists struck in the winter of 1825 Herzen was among the first in Moscow to hear of the revolt in Senate Square from a friend of his father's, General Komarovsky, who dropped in with details of the bloody suppression of the uprising. This and the mass arrests, trial, hangings and deportations which followed affected him deeply. There was a rebellious fire in him, and though at 14 he had only a vague idea of what it all meant politically, he perceived the action of the rebels as a high-minded gesture of protest against a vast, pervading wrong – thus grasping instinctively that idealistic feature of the event which was to impress itself with the force of a myth on the minds of most cultured Russians. The hanging of 'the Five' shook him for ever out of his 'childish dreams' of liberty, equality, and so forth: his life, indeed, was to prove that he meant every word of the youthful oath he took in the midst of the packed Thanksgiving ser-vice at the Kremlin.

Unable to communicate his new ideas to his father, and having no close friends to discuss them with, the adolescent Herzen mentioned them to a young prince of his acquaintance. The latter, hearing of Bouchot's verdict that Louis XVI had been justly executed as a 'traitor to his country', was scandalized. 'But you know, he was God's anointed!' he blandly closed the argument, whereupon Herzen dropped him. Finally confiding in his Russian tutor, he was surprised when this man began to give him 'much-soiled', handwritten copies of Ryleyev's poems and Pushkin's 'Ode to Freedom' which were being passed from hand to hand – the way the *samidzat* writings of Soviet dissidents would be a century and a half later – and read in secret.

Then Herzen met Nicholas ('Nick') Ogarev, a gentle boy who was likewise reading Pushkin's and Ryleyev's unpublished poems. Ogarev was 15 years old in 1828 when, accompanied by his German tutor, he happened to be visiting Alexander Herzen. Ivan Yakovlev, in a rare show of spontaneity, invited them all for an after-dinner drive into the country. After an hour or so, the party left the carriage at Luzhniki and crossed the Moskva river in a boat. While Herzen's father walked slowly with the German, the two boys raced ahead and ran up to the top of the Sparrow Hills. Below, stretched a unique view of Moscow, its cupolas glittering in the sunset. There they joined in a solemn oath and 'vowed in sight of all Moscow to sacrifice our lives to the struggle' begun by the Decembrists.

Nick Ogarev, a rich landowner's son, was another lonesome boy. His mother had died young. His father, who was an invalid, had retired to one of his estates in the province of Penza, leaving the German to look after the boy in a general way. Like Herzen, Nick had private tutors and a personal valet and had grown up surrounded by servants. Shy, sensitive, a budding poet and highly impressionable, he suffered pangs of conscience at the sight of the iniquities and inequality around him, and though he later gave up one of the family estates as soon as he inherited it, the idea that he lived in wealth and comfort on the sweat of others never ceased to plague him. 'What is a man to do', he once exclaimed, 'who feels overcome by grief at his own position, brought about by heredity and not through work?'

Ogarev, in short, was ashamed of being rich and hated the injustice inherent in his feudal privileges and luxurious upbringing. Drawn by common sympathies and a common cause, the two boys played games together, smoked cigars when alone in Herzen's room and sometimes got drunk on punch and Pushkin's poetry in Ogarev's large, and largely empty, house.

Starting in 1829, Herzen, followed by a footman, walked every day to Moscow University. He was nearly 18, but his father insisted that the footman, after sitting through lectures in the corridor of the Mathematics and Physics Department, escort his son home or wherever he went. Not until he was 21 was Herzen allowed to be out after 10:30 in the evening. Ogarev enrolled at the university shortly afterwards and these two inseparable companions, sworn to the Decembrist 'struggle', immediately began to look for sympathizers.

Moscow's 700 students – all wearing uniforms, though no longer swords, as in the past – were strictly supervised, and anyone suspected of carrying on 'criminal conversations' was liable to be seized at night and disappear. Nicholas I regarded the university as a 'hotbed of depravity'. He would personally interrogate students guilty of lampooning his regime or his person and send them off to atone indefinitely in the army, or beyond the Urals, where they often died before he got round to reviewing their cases.

Ogarev and a friend of his sang the *Marseillaise* outside a Moscow theatre and were placed under police surveillance. Herzen had spent nearly a week in prison when he was only 17. Sungurov, an older student who tried to organize a political society, was sentenced to hard labour in Siberia, from where he never returned. His two small estates were confiscated and his wife was kept for 6 months in jail, where one of her babies died. Sungurov's fate frightened the students.

Herzen and Ogarev, having only vague political ideas, could not have formed a subversive organization even if they had wanted to. But gradually they became the leaders of a small, informal group of youngsters who circulated manuscript copies of prohibited poems, argued in favour of a constitution and a republic, drank to the success of the July Revolution and engaged in small gestures 'against tyranny'.

'The first to raise their heads were children,' Herzen later recalled. 'The savage punishment inflicted on boys of sixteen and seventeen served as a stern lesson' of the dangers of 'playing at conspiracy', but children were unable to look silently 'at the hundreds of Poles clanking their fetters in Vladimir road, at serfdom, at the soldiers flogged in the Khodynsky Field...'

With a Censorship Department and secret police surveillance at every university, there was little young students and *lycée* boys could do by way of organized opposition. But the very act of braving the authorities by singing the *Marseillaise* or discussing Schiller and passing around copies of Pushkin and Ryleyev made them proud and defiant as the guardians of a cowed generation. Indeed, until the 'conspiracy' for which Dostoyevsky ran afoul of the authorities nearly 20 years later, the small, youthfully reckless voice of Herzen's coterie of 'children' was to be the only one to disturb the compliance and general servility with which Russian society submitted to Tsar Nicholas's increasingly heavy-handed rule in the aftermath of the Decembrist rebellion.

At 19 Herzen fell in love. It was, one might say, almost natural that his feelings should blossom for a girl who shared his devotion to the 'struggle'. Ludmilla Passek, whose father had once been deported to Siberia and forgotten there for more than 20 years, had spent most of her young life in hunger and deprivation. Victims of an earlier Tsar's arbitrariness, her whole family knew the kind of persecution that was now the lot of the Decembrists and their sympathizers. Herzen described their youthful first love: 'We dreamed together of the future – of exile, of prison, for she was ready for anything... and I used to fancy how she would accompany me to the Siberian mines.'

Ironically, what so impressed these and later would-be martyrs – i.e., the bravura gesture of the Decembrist noblemen in risking their lives and all for the sake, among others, of liberating the serfs – had hardly caused a stir or hopes of salvation among the vast millions of Russia's peasantry. The peasants believed, on the contrary, that the Tsar was on their side and only biding his time to overcome the machinations of the nobility, the clergy, his Ministers and all the ranks of the bureaucracy – down to the village police – who stood between them and the remote throne before he would abolish their forced labour and set them completely free.

To Herzen and Ogarev, on the other hand, the same gesture augured the liberation of the Russian people. They regarded themselves as 'sons of the Decembrists'. This was not the case with young Michael Bakunin. In later years, he was to inveigh against the evils of 'law and order', attack inherited wealth and pro-claim that 'over the whole surface of the civilized world' governments were employing 'base and criminal means to fleece their peoples and keep them per-manently enslaved.' But as an adolescent in 1828 he felt no pangs about the hun-dreds of serfs slaving at Premukhino to produce the wealth which afforded him the comforts and pleasures he enjoyed. Unlike Herzen, a rebel at 14, absorbed 'day and night' by political dreams, Bakunin was disturbed in his puberty by no such preoccupations. Nor was he bothered by any early stirrings of social con-science, such as would make Ogarev cry out that he did not wish to be rich, but yearned 'to turn to the people' and work with them for their salvation.

At 14, after an untroubled childhood, Michael Bakunin was enjoying a lei-surely, happy boyhood – studying, playing the violin, browsing in his father's library, roaming the fields and orchards, singing *Au clair de la lune* with his sisters and brothers on enchanted evenings, picnicking in the woods or by the Ossuga river, and otherwise disporting himself in the idyllic country paradise of Premukhino. He was an intelligent, wide-awake and lusty boy, loved, listened to and admired by the four sisters closest to him in age – Lyubov (16), Varinka (15), Tatyana (13) and Alexandra (12) – while his five young brothers, born in a row and ranging in age from 10 to 5 (Nicholas, Ilya, Paul, Alexander and Alexis) looked up to him.

Besides being a natural leader, Michael enjoyed the double advantage of being not only the eldest son in the family but the only male among 4 adolescent girls. He was thus, in Edmund Wilson's phrase, able 'to dominate his sisters by his sex' – with consequences which will be seen – and his brothers 'by his age'.[18] The Bakunin girls were well-read. Romantically preoccupied with matters of 'the soul' and apparently modelling themselves on their three pious maiden aunts, they made 'a cult of their inner life'. Michael, emotionally sensitive and mentally as well developed as he was physically, became their fellow-explorer in the search and 'striving towards unattainable truth'.[19] Eventually he was to dominate their minds completely.

In autumn 1828 he was due to leave for the Tsar's Artillery School in St Petersburg. Unlike Herzen, who lost any enthusiasm for uniforms and medals he had felt as a child, there was no question in Michael's mind that, as the eldest son of a nobleman, he was destined for a military career.

After a year's preliminary training, he became an artillery cadet in St Peters-burg. The letters he sent home were as patriotic as his father could have wished. They resounded with love of the 'fatherland'; but at the same time were harping constantly on his terrible loneliness. Away from his large family, out of the lovely 'nobleman's nest' and into the rigours of military discipline, he felt frightfully unhappy. In letter after letter this young man, who was later to jump from one European revolution to another, bewailed his fate and – even as he was assuring his parents that the Russians 'love their fatherland, revere their Tsar, his will is their law' – swore to his sisters that he was ready to forgo 'forever the chance of seeing any capital in the world' in exchange for being back in Premukhino.[20]

A couple of years later the future hero of the Dresden revolt and would-be 'leader of an international rebel army' was to write to his father point-blank that he absolutely lacked 'that heroism, that courage, that leads one to seek danger.'[21] The fact was that in St Petersburg he underwent one long crisis and found out several things about himself.

'Pure and virginal' in soul and imagination, 'untainted by any evil', this is how (as he put it later) he had left Premukhino. 'In the Artillery School I quickly came to know all the dark, filthy, vile side of life.' Though he managed 'not to fall into the vices' of which he was a 'frequent spectator... I soon got into the habit of lying,' which was not considered dishonourable by the cadets.[22]

Young Bakunin was sexually impotent, as he discovered to his dismay when he was 16 or 17. At the Artillery School he was thrown together with young males who relieved the harsh discipline by taking more than a healthy interest in drinking and whoring; 'wine, cards and other occupations which modesty does not permit me to mention,' he wrote to his parents, were their chief pastime and 'only subjects of conversation'. Doubly shocked by their 'vices' and his own inadequacy, he 'kept completely apart' from the other cadets and in the end became so accustomed to their ways that 'they no longer disgusted or even surprised me.'[23] But he was lonely and frustrated. Thrown back on himself, he was never to recover, but to seek – and find after many years – other outlets for his immense energy.

Ogarev at the same age had another problem, which he described as follows: 'At sixteen my passionate imagination impelled me to fall in love,' but he met with disillusionment. 'At seventeen I desired to possess a woman, and I satisfied my desire without love on either side – a shameful commercial transaction between an inexperienced youth and a public prostitute. This was my first step on the road to vice...'[24]

Ogarev's lifelong predicament was only beginning when he wrote this. He loathed physical sex without love, but was seldom able to resist a woman, whether a serf-girl or a lady. At the same time, when he was in love he needed to reconcile it, as was the Romantic fashion, with 'universal love', with God and the 'world feeling'. Otherwise he felt an egoist, and in either case he suffered torments of remorse.

Bakunin's impotence, with its long-range consequences, has been ascribed to his being in love with his sister Tatyana, who was only one year younger than he. Edmund Wilson, for one, termed (not to say diagnosed) it 'a case of sexual inhibition based on the incest taboo.'[25] E.H. Carr attributed it to the psychological effect of his 'hatred of a dominating mother', but he, too, noted 'the jealous frenzy' of Michael's 'passion for Tatyana' and the 'white heat of intensity' it was to reach. While the exact nature and extent of their relationship continue to exercise scholars, Carr held that Michael found in it 'compensation for his immunity from normal sexual love' and Anthony Masters, in a more recent (1979) biography, likewise expressed the opinion that his 'love for Tatyana' provided him with 'a built-in safety device' and that, precisely because she was his sister, 'there could never be any hint of a sexual relationship between them.'[26]

It remains to be added that theirs was a mutual passion, by far exceeding a mere Romantic bond or spiritual affinity of hearts, minds and temperaments. Nor was it short-lived. In a letter to Premukhino written when he was 29, Michael reminded Tatyana: 'You told me last summer that were you not my sister you would have fallen in love with me.' For himself, he referred to their unusual attachment in slightly more explicit, if inconclusive, terms by including a quotation – '"The laws condemn the object of my love"' – pointing to his awareness of a guilty infatuation in the eyes of the world. This quotation, which he addressed specifically 'to you, Tatyana', is the chief documentary evidence for his incestuous love.[27]

But the matter does not end there. Bakunin's later theory of 'direct action', his rebellion against all authority, the fervour of his propaganda that society must be purged by fire and destruction, coupled with his personal exploits, his charm and his spellbinding rhetoric – of which a contemporary said that it had the power to persuade 'his listeners to cut each other's throats cheerfully' – were to make him a hero and cult figure not only to a whole new breed of 19th-century professional revolutionists, but to latter-day groups of the most varied type in revolt against society the world over. The common denominator of the activities of such disparate groups as the Spanish Anarchists, the Latin-American Tupamaros, the IRA in Ireland and the various 'Red Brigades' in Europe and elsewhere is the theory most clearly enunciated by Bakunin and the Russian Narodniks that incendiary acts of terror by small groups, or even individual assassinations – the destruction of a government centre or the 'destruction of the most harmful person in government'[28] – would not fail to rouse the masses (or public opinion) and eventually bring down the most powerful regime.

Besides the attraction of a world without government, without laws, frontiers, landlords and taxes such as he envisioned, there was another reason for the rise of Bakunin's star in Western Europe to the point where he became the towering father-figure of international Anarchism over all other proponents of

violence for violence's sake. He achieved his place in history not only as a dedicated rebel against the state, but also as a champion of social liberation and
equality, of the absolute freedom of the individual from the fetters of all and
any authority, and for his prophetic utterance that the government of the 'scientific Socialists', i.e., Marx and his disciples, would be worse than any tyranny.
Under the pretext of a 'transitional dictatorship', he wrote, it 'will be nothing
else but despotic rule over the toiling masses by a new, numerically small' oli-
garchy.[29]

The powerful figure he became provides a sharp contrast to the sensitive,
gentle, non-violent, butterfly-chasing child of Premukhino as well as to the miserable and forlorn young cadet in St Petersburg, unable to make contact with
others of his age and longing to be back with his family: 'O, dear sisters how I
would like to see you!... How I want to squeeze you in my embrace... I love you
so!' Again, a year later: 'I would give half of my life for the chance of being in
Premukhino if only for a minute... How I envy my brothers for their enjoying all
the time the presence of our parents, and you, dear sisters. What a child I was
when I was happy at the thought of the trip to St Petersburg!' Life in St Petersburg was 'wretched' and filthy. 'There is not a single person', he wrote after 5
years in the city, 'to whom I can open my heart, with whom I could share my
grief, from whom I might expect some small solace... You live together, your
sorrows are not felt so oppressively. You share with each other. But I, here, am
alone, completely alone.'[30] He had just returned from a leave at home and was
now living outside the Artillery School, mostly with an aunt and uncle.

Historians such as Franco Venturi, tracing the development of the Russian
revolutionary movement, have dwelt on the 'weary and difficult road through
philosophy and religion which Bakunin (a man born for spontaneous action)
had to travel in order to reach the world of politics.'[31] His road was indeed long
and tortuous, but while Bakunin was no 'son of the Decembrists' like Herzen, it
has always been known that he was a born rebel. His road led through philosophy; but it has been remarked that 'if all others had been pious sheep, he alone
would have been no pious sheep.'[32] Why? And what motivated his lust to
destroy and his lust for power?

Whereas Bakunin's manifest aversion to physical love has never been contested, the psychological impact of his sexual incapacity, as against the influence of
social and other outside factors, on his bizarre and rebellious personality has
never been seriously studied. In 1934, however, in a brief and neglected mono-
graph published in Belgrade, I. Malinin pointed to an Oedipal factor underlying both Bakunin's incestual problem and his later violent Anarchism.

Then in 1981–82, an American historian, fully cognizant of the scepticism
aroused by the psychoanalytical treatment of historical themes, challenged E.H.

Carr's classic biography on an important point and stood on its head the customary view of the heroic, lion-like Bakunin – the 'cosmic' rebel and 'Grand Inquisitor of total revolution'.[33] Briefly, Arthur P. Mendel's analysis of Bakunin's every step, theory and action showed him to have suffered from a combined narcissistic and Oedipal complex; to have reacted by withdrawing into himself, adopting philosophy as his self-styled 'wife' and turning his pent-up anger into outward aggression; to have concealed his inner weakness and timidity under a variety of masks and public 'power' faces; to have never grown up, and to have been driven by his early evangelical piety and later messianic megalomania to preach 'cataclysmically violent revolutionary strategies' of destruction that are 'barely disguised versions of the Christian Apocalypse'.[34]

Bakunin had already been called a 'big child' and 'a tremendous fraud',[35] but always with a hint of admiration for his fascinating personality and dominating influence. But never before had anyone gone so deeply into his malaise and his contradictory character, or shown 'how much he saw himself walking in the footsteps of Jesus', or attempted to demonstrate that in spite of his championship of 'limitless freedom' he was actually a power-hungry authoritarian and 'a threat to freedom'.[36]

His first rebellion took place during his first home-leave from St Petersburg, when he was 19. It involved his father, his mother, his beloved sisters and broke out over an issue, needless to say, unconnected with politics. Lyubov, Bakunin's eldest sister, was almost 22; Varinka was 21. He regarded them, as well as his two younger sisters, as his 'little flock'. Varinka gushingly assured him that this was so. He had grown up in their feminine company, they all adored him and his sway over their highly emotional natures then and later was extraordinary. No woman would ever be able to give him the admiration he received from his sisters, and this may in fact have been a contributory cause to the sorry condition of a 'eunuch' – a maiden 'Joan of Arc', as Herzen was once to call him – to which he was reduced, a condition whose discovery must have been a shock to this virile-looking overgrown boy on the verge of manhood.

After 4 unhappy years in St Petersburg, Bakunin fell in love with a young woman of 18, Marie Voyekov. She was the same age as Tatyana and provided him with some much-needed social diversion and relief from the discipline of the Artillery School. He had by then been promoted as an ensign to the officer class. They met frequently and flirtatiously, walked, read and went to parties together. At a performance of Beethoven's Ninth Symphony, Marie 'was frightened by the expression on my face,' Michael reported to his sisters that spring. 'It seemed that I was ready to destroy the world.'[37]

Bakunin had as yet entertained no known anarchist thoughts of the kind that would later make him wish to turn the world into a rubbish heap. The wholly platonic romance with the Voyekov girl came to an abrupt end when she left with her mother for a 6-month stay in Moscow. It was a few months later, in August – back at last on home-leave among his sisters and in the cozy bosom of that bee-like family buzzing round his father and each other – that he undertook his first successful conspiracy.

Received at Premukhino with extraordinary jubilation and outpourings of love, happy beyond words after almost 5 years in the Petersburg 'desert', he had hardly settled down when he decided to take Lyubov's future in his hands. Count Bakunin had chosen a certain Baron Renne as the best match for his eldest daughter and Lyubov had dutifully, if not enthusiastically, become engaged to this rich gentleman and officer who had the means to offer her a secure and sheltered life. All three, however, had reckoned without Michael. Upon finding out that Lyubov was about to slip into a loveless marriage, he not only began to incite her to break off the engagement, but organized and led a general revolt of all his siblings against parental oppression and the 'persecution' of Lyubov.

Before Count Bakunin knew what was afoot, the calm of Premukhino was upset by some 'terrible' scenes. Michael's opposition was mounted in the name of the prevalent notion, shared by Ogarev, Herzen and all the incurable Romantics of the age, that 'Love' was the highest fulfilment of man, expressing the ardour, divinity and noblest aspirations of his 'soul' and thus encompassing God, mankind, as well as everything sublime in heaven and on earth. As Ogarev was ecstatically to assure his bride before he was 21:

> To love you means to love everything that is good, to love God and His Universe... The love of mankind for one another, this brotherhood so pure and fair preached by Jesus, is the reflection of the bond which unites us, of the world-soul... The love of man is founded in the love of God.[38]

Bakunin, waging his attack with similar rhetoric, believed or convinced himself – and had no difficulty persuading Lyubov – that to marry without love was both a betrayal of her better self and a 'sin against the Holy Ghost'.

It was not until 4 years later, still raging with fury, that Michael, in a 15-page letter to his parents, was to leave for posterity a telling clue to the reasons why Lyubov's betrothal so deeply affected him. Lyubov, 'a girl brought up in virginal purity', was to be sacrificed to 'the hellish lust' of a man who was going to uncover 'her sacred modesty' and befoul her with 'his vile breath'. How could his parents even have considered abandoning their 'pure' daughter, whom until then 'no unclean attraction had dared touch', to so repulsive and dreadful a fate? 'Better never to have been born...'[39]

Virginal purity, hellish lust, sacred modesty defiled: it is as if Michael Bakunin himself – 'pure and virginal' as he had already styled himself, and now expressing his own aversion to sex while identifying with his sister – was going to be raped. Arthur Mendel, writing in 1981, saw an Oedipal disturbance in Michael further effecting a merger in his mind 'between his sisters and his mother' (whom he was later to accuse of vulgar 'sensuality'), and described it as 'displacing incestual attraction from mother to sisters.'[40]

What is clear is that Bakunin's upbringing in the closed hothouse atmosphere of Premukhino had not prepared him for anything outside that world. When thrown into the harsh male territory of military regimentation and discipline in St Petersburg and frightened of authority, he had felt completely lost. Now, back for a month in the old magic circle of Premukhino, he found it threatened by the intrusion of an outsider.

That magic circle of sisters and brothers at Premukhino was in fact – in the view of one of the early but most thorough historians of Anarchism – 'the most ideal group to which he ever belonged, the model for all his organisations and his conception of a free and happy life for humanity in general.' The close bond between sisters and brothers at Premukhino 'created a microcosm of freedom and solidarity' in which the full expression and 'fulfilment of each one' went hand in hand with 'the best interests of all'. From this soon developed Michael's 'desire to serve all humanity and to give selflessly to others everything he might gain for himself.'[41]

It may be said in a different way that all Bakunin's future work was to dream up fantastic schemes to recreate Premukhino on a universal scale, though at this time the atheism and apocalyptic destruction accompanying them were still distant from him.

The storm over Lyubov's engagement raged throughout Michael's stay in Premukhino. On his return to St Petersburg, carrying on the fight for Lyubov's 'purity' against his parents, he went to his father's sister, Aunt Nilov. He had previously lodged with this stern old lady, but had moved out in a rebellious fit when she tried to control his comings and goings. Now he beguiled even this conservative, old-fashioned lady into championing Lyubov's cause, so that she, too, turned on his father with angry reproaches for denying his daughter's natural right to love.

Michael's campaign, pursued with relentless perseverance, gusto and wile, was so effective that at the end of 4 months the stunned old count, then in his mid-60s, acknowledged defeat and let Lyubov cancel her engagement to Baron Renne. Not content with this, Michael turned the tables upon his parents 4 years later when he accused them of having disrupted 'that marvellous harmony' which hitherto had been the admiration and envy of all who knew

Premukhino. Referring to his own and his sisters' feelings at their parents' readiness to hand over Lyubov to Baron Renne, he wrote to his father: 'You and mother... you, who had hitherto been glad and happy only when they [his sisters] were glad and happy... you suddenly separated yourselves from them... We, who had until that time seen in you the personification of love for your children, did not understand, and still do not understand, what made you persecute Lyubov.'[42]

Nor was that all. Twelve years or so after this summer storm, he was still so affected by it that he was to single out his mother for an attack of extraordinary venom, describing her as 'the source of what is unclean in our family... the source of every sin, and all evil.' In letters to his various siblings he wrote that, but for their father, 'mother would have ruined and corrupted us,' referred to her as 'our enemy – mother, for whom I have no feeling in my soul but damnation,' and declared that 'her presence, her very existence, is an offence to what is sacred.'[43]

By then, Michael Bakunin was 31 and living abroad. He had already achieved some notoriety in Germany, Switzerland and France as a theorist of revolution. At the time when he was rebelling against Lyubov's betrothal, he is not known to have manifested any particular revulsion against his mother of a type traceable to a frustrated sexual impulse. Nor is anything known about his mother's 'despotic' character, to which he later attributed his 'insensate hatred of every restriction on liberty.'[44]

Varvara Bakunin, who seems to have taken some part in the education of her 10 children when they were small, had been a good-looking young socialite and lady of fashion. She may have been a self-centred woman, more preoccupied with her fading beauty and aging husband than with her children. But whether or not she had shown Michael insufficient love, their relationship must have been of a kind which prevented him from forming any stable relations with other women, and in combination with his active-dynamic personality – 'the germ of a colossal activity', as Herzen was to call it, which he bore within him – made him a rebel, whereas none of his siblings became one.

Bakunin, brimming with tremendous energy, was not one to be defeated by his sexual or any other shortcoming. He steeled himself passively. 'Passions... rage within me,' he was to write a year or so after the Lyubov affair, 'emotional forces seethe and demand nourishment, but all this remains inactive... Everything in me demands action, movement, but all my activity is restricted to working for the future.'[45]

Mendel has pointed out that Michael's new aggressive 'rhetoric of power, ambition, anger and defiance' was gained not through opposing 'the blows of fate', but chiefly, in his own words, by suffering them stoically, indeed 'getting pleasure from the blows of fate' without letting them crush him. Mendel sees in this what was to become 'one of Bakunin's characteristic ways' of living with the two opposing poles of his nature: the more he saw himself 'as a long-suffering victim', the greater 'the sense of power' he was to enjoy.[46]

During Michael's visit to Premukhino his father had agreed to pay some of the considerable debts he had run up in excess of his allowance. The turmoil of that summer left Count Bakunin, who loved his children and was trying to do his best for them by his lights, exceedingly perplexed. Henceforth he would be subjected by his son to constant warfare, with hardly a pause and sudden ambushes at every turn. The surrender of his paternal authority was totted up by Michael as a victory of the 'present' over the 'past' – and of the young over the old generation – and further increased his influence over the minds and souls of his sisters.

He was extremely jealous of their suitors and would go to inordinate lengths and do his forceful best to mould, direct and manipulate their feelings at will, trying to run their lives for them, with fatal results for all in the end. None, though, was to be as fatal to himself as his lifelong infatuation with Tatyana.

Michael had not been back long in St Petersburg when he found distraction at the beautiful home of his mother's most distinguished relative, Nicholas Muraviev – a retired senator and former State Secretary – who, moreover, had 7 graceful daughters (besides 10 other children who had left home). Michael, who was not yet 20, found this circle highly stimulating and soon became confusingly enamoured of three or more of these girls. Praising them all for their charm, attractiveness, culture and modesty, 'especially the second daughter', he wrote to his sisters at Premukhino not to be angry or jealous 'if I love them very much (not all the same) since loving them, I love you in them, for they are like you in all the details.'[47] Though nothing much came of this collective romance – except for an erotic novelette written 15 years later, in which he fantasized about his deflowering 'three virgins at the instigation of their father'[48] – it served to exercise the growing powers of seduction which, phenomenally or not, were to make Bakunin no mean lady-killer, adored by women he could not satisfy.

By his own later confession, young Bakunin 'did just about nothing at all' during his military studies, 'working only the last month of each year in order to pass the examination.'[49] And so it happened that within a couple of months of his return from his home-leave at Premukhino, following an insolent reply he gave to a general who criticized his uniform, he found himself dismissed for 'inadequate achievement and inattention throughout the entire course of study.' Just as he had found a second home and charming company in the Muraviev household, he was posted to a lone garrison on the Polish–Lithuanian border. It was a great blow to a young man with a huge ego. He had also run up new debts. A big spender, he had no sense of money and money values – nor the slightest intention of ever working to earn a living – and early developed a life-long habit of borrowing blithely from friends, relatives, acquaintances and even complete strangers without bothering about means and sources of repayment. His was, however, an innocent and generous nature and he would spontaneously give away his last rouble.

At Premukhino, not many months after he had paid up the most pressing of his son's debts, Count Bakunin opened the official gazette and was stupefied to read of Michael's dismissal from the Artillery School. Michael had lacked the moral courage to write home and reveal his humiliation to his family and it was a deflated son who, shortly after his 20th birthday, spent an embarrassing few days at Premukhino on his way to start serving his disciplinary punishment in Poland.

But worse was to follow. 'I am here in an alien land... stuck in a miserable hole... among people who virtually walk on all fours', Michael complained in letters to his family not long afterwards.[50] A tour of duty in Poland, where Russian officers whiled away their spare time gambling, drinking and flirting or having casual love affairs with the local beauties, was a relatively mild punishment. Michael, however, confessing that he was 'quite incapable of finding any charm or satisfaction in the bog of sensual enjoyments' – which he declared 'unworthy' of a human being – found it hard to bear 'the heat, the cold, the fatigue, the hunger, the thirst, and all the other unpleasantness tied to military service.'[51] His fellow-officers were a tiresome lot, and except for attending two balls in the town of Vilna, he was reduced to reading 'the history and statistics of Lithuania' and whatever books he could lay his hands on in a God-forsaken nest.

A garrulous character who was to mesmerize crowds with his speeches, Bakunin needed company to come into his own. Bored to death and complaining that 'eternal silence, eternal sadness, eternal home-sickness are the companions of my solitude', he was now desperately anxious to get out of the army. First, he tried to make himself ill by filling himself up with 'a lot of hot tea' and then lying naked and sweating in the snow. When this proved ineffective – 'Nothing happened. I did not catch even a little cold!'[52] – he seized the first opportunity of getting away that presented itself. Sent on a mission to bring up horses for the brigade from the district of Tver – his native province – he simply went home to Premukhino and never returned to his regiment. Feigning sudden illness he sent in his resignation.

He had spent altogether 7 months in Poland, much of the time sprawled on his bed in a sheepskin coat. But he managed to present himself to his siblings as something of a martyr and a hero, and to half-convince them, by a kind of Hegelian dialectic, that to accept 'voluntary solitude' in a desolate outpost was actually a form of 'egoism', and that it was both vital and more altruistic to cultivate his 'inner being' and an 'instinctive thirst for knowledge' – including a sudden new interest in German philosophy – which he had discovered in himself amidst the routine of barracks life on the Polish border.

Count Bakunin, for all his spluttering consternation at having to shelter a 20-year-old son and officer who was to all intents and purposes a deserter, had no alternative to spending long months exerting every bit of family influence to avert the disgrace of Michael's being arrested and dishonourably discharged. It was the son's second victory over his father. 'Dismissed the service, through illness, at his own request', young Bakunin had consciously, by a deliberate act of will, rid himself of the first social responsibility which did not suit his temperament and taken a step on the road towards becoming the rebellious 'great nomad'. It had been easily, if deviously, accomplished. He had a lively mind and his sturdy body was full of restless energy, but he had no good idea what to do with either or with his new-won freedom. The truth was that an army doctor in Poland had discoursed at some length on German philosophy, but as Alexander Herzen – who had yet to meet him – was to put it in retrospect, Bakunin 'had studied nothing before', could hardly read German, and for him to plunge into philosophy was tantamount to straying 'without map or compass in a world of fantastic projects and efforts at self-education.'

At Premukhino he found that his sister Varinka, now 23, had married a wealthy officer by the name of Dyakov. Michael was soon to become engaged in disrupting her marriage, as he had Lyubov's engagement. For the moment, however, with Lyubov and Tatyana in tow, he departed on a visit to Moscow.

9

Heine Adrift in 1828

At the beginning of June 1829, Tsar Nicholas I – whose wife Charlotte was a daughter of King Friedrich Wilhelm III – arrived on a state visit in Berlin. On 15 June Heinrich Heine, overrating the effect of certain minor setbacks suffered by the Tsar's armies in their ultimately victorious war against Turkey, wrote to Moser: 'I hope that my campaign of this year against clerics and aristocrats will be more successful than the Russian.'

It was 4 years since he had left Göttingen with a doctor's degree in law and a certificate of baptism in his pocket, and he was almost 32 years old. He was 'campaigning', for in the interval he had – in certain sections of *The North Sea* III, and more particularly in *Ideas. The Book of LeGrand* – become a political writer. And in Julius Campe he had found a publisher who, matching his own truculence, was a master of ingenuity in devising ways of circumventing the censorship regulations applying in the various German states, using every trick and loophole to get even daring or questionable material on the market.

The first encounter between the two, marking the birth of one of the most famous and long-lasting author-publisher relationships in literary history, had taken place at the end of January 1826 when Heine walked into the Hamburg bookshop of Hoffmann and Campe in search of a book. Julius Campe, who owned the firm in all but name, took the opportunity of offering his customer a copy of Heine's *Poems*, warmly recommending them. According to Campe's later account, possibly apocryphal, the following conversation ensued:

'"Dear Sir,"' he interrupted me, '"I do not like them; in fact, I despise them."'

'What do you mean?' Campe said indignantly. 'Why Sir, if you despise them you will have to deal with me.'

'My dear Sir, I know them better than you do,' Heine replied. 'It is I who wrote them.' Campe laughed and said jovially: 'Well, well, my dear doctor, if ever you write anything so worthless again, and have no better publisher at hand, I should be honoured to have the name of my firm appear upon the jacket.'

'Don't jest with me,' Heine retorted. 'I may take you at your word.' And he returned the following day with a bundle of manuscripts, saying he had a volume ready for publication. Campe was as good as his word and bought it on the spot. 'From that day on Heine visited me daily in my store and we became close friends.'

It is quite feasible that something like the reported conversation[1] did indeed take place, for the behaviour ascribed to each person was in character. Heine liked disguises, and Julius Campe was an enterprising man with an extraordinary flair for spotting original talent and a willingness to take risks once he found it. He knew the book market inside out and combined a shrewd business sense with an instinct for the type of contemporary, even avant-gardist topics that might stir at least part of the otherwise dull German reading public from its torpor. Thirtyfour years old, the grandson of an eminent philologist, Campe had liberal sympathies and, from Heine's viewpoint, several other advantages besides his savvy in dealing with the censorship. Heine's need to keep in the public eye found in Campe a man who understood the importance of public relations and did not mind a bit of scandal or controversy to help promote his authors and their books. In other ways, too, he was a man who grasped and moved with the Zeitgeist, in the sense of anticipating trends, and sometimes eagerly helping to create them. 'The future belongs to youth', Campe once said, 'and by binding myself to them I feel sure of remaining faithful to the idea of progress.'

On 14 December 1825, a fortnight before his 28th birthday, Heine had confessed to Moser in Berlin that he was in a depressed mood. 'There is civil war again.' He was in 'accursed Hamburg' since November and 'innerly so agitated' and given to 'self-torture' that he could think of nothing to write. 'I very much regret my baptism... if only I could find the peace of mind to finish *The Rabbi*.' Years later he was to accuse Gans – who had been president of the Jewish Verein but converted that very month – of 'abandoning the ship',[2] and the same feeling of moral betrayal engendered by his own baptism the previous summer made it practically impossible for him to resume work on *The Rabbi of Bacherach*. To add to his spiritual crisis, he had yet to find a publisher for his *Harzreise* – Brockhaus had declined and Dümmler had offered a ridiculous sum for it – and Professor Gubitz of Berlin's *Gesellschafter* kept delaying its long-promised serialization. Heine swore never to give a single line of his to that 'scoundrel'.

Campe's purchase of *Die Harzreise* at the end of January 1826 thus came as a Godsend to Heine. Campe also bought, for a sum today equivalent to about $2,000 or $3,000 (there is some disagreement about whether he paid 30 or 50 Louis d'or), 100 of Heine's poems. Heine conceived a title for the volume of mixed prose and poetry: *Travel Pictures* (*Reisebilder*). On 20 January, Gubitz had suddenly started serializing a barbarized version of *Die Harzreise*, its daily instalments corrupted by changes in the text and substitutions of his own, a practice against which Heine had expressly warned him.

A furious Heine now sat down to reinstate the political passages which Gubitz, pleading censorship, had erased or rewritten. Campe produced *Reisebilder* with remarkable speed in mid-May 1826. *Die Harzreise*, written after his expulsion from Göttingen almost two years earlier, was Heine's first prose piece to appear in book form. With its pungent presentation of boisterous aristocratic fops and *Burschenschaft* students roaming the streets of that Hanoverian city famous for its 'university and its sausages' in hordes 'distinguished only by the colour of their caps and pipe tassels' – duelling and forever fighting among each other on its 'bloody battlefields', seemingly carrying on the manners and customs of their 'Vandal, Frisian, Swabian, Teuton' and other tribal ancestors from the time of the great *Völkerwanderung* – it descended on the German public with the effect of a bombshell. *Die Harzreise* made cruel fun of Göttingen's entire academic community, lampooning one of Germany's famous institutions of learning as a pompous citadel through which passed successive generations of students and only the old professors – growing 'little paper slips covered with quotes' in their gardens, which they sometimes 'laboriously transplant into a new bed' – remained fixed, 'immovably firm, like the pyramids of Egypt – except that in these university pyramids no wisdom is hidden.'

The book was indeed banned in Göttingen, but most of Germany's intelligentsia could not fail to be struck by the freshness and effrontery with which Heine unmasked the pretentiousness underlying Göttingen's academic and social life, its 'dissertations and tea-dances', the chattering 'lies of lovelorn woes' of its romantically sighing ladies and the 'bibliomaniac' preoccupations of its portentous baronial professors.

It was not only in the mountains but in the depths of a silver mine that Heine, on his foot journey through the Upper Harz in 1824, had met ordinary Germans at work. His description of his descent into 'the black eternity' of the Klaustal mines, holding on to slippery rungs 'wet as dung' of ladder after ladder, until – guided by a sturdy foreman 'of unquestionable honour and dog-like German loyalty' – he reached the hewn-out galleries where grave-faced men, young and old, spent long days laboriously knocking out pieces of ore, was one of the first pieces of realistic German prose.

Die Harzreise, evoking what became 'the most famous walking tour in the history of German literature,'[3] otherwise brimmed with the youthful exuberance Heine had felt at the time when he made it; with magic landscape descriptions, culminating in the surrealistic scenes of his giddy ascent of the Brocken and the spooky night he spent there; with comic and ironic touches and portraits of the journeymen, peasants, merchants, students and more distinguished 'tourists' and their ladies he had encountered on his hikes or at village inns. It reproduced their talk, affectations, dreams and nightmares, included local myths as well as sentimental Romantic passages, but for all its light, frivolous tone it was so true to life that the Germans could not help recognizing themselves in it.

Reisebilder I – as this first volume of a new genre created by Heine became known – also included Heine's famous 'Lorelei' among the 88 poems of the *Homecoming* cycle, as well as his first 11 *North Sea* poems. These, written in free verse and departing from Heine's lyrical style, were the result of his first adventurous encounter with the elemental power of the ocean, when, sailing for Heligoland in 1823, the boat was caught in a gale and he spent a terrifying night clinging to the railing of the upper deck. 'The sea was like a moving mountainside, the mountains of water crashed against one another and broke over the little boat, tossing it up and down.'

Cowering in 'one of the wildest' North Sea storms, Heine had recorded in a letter written shortly afterwards to Moser (23 August 1823) the 'music' made by the shrieking of the wind, the cries of the sailors, the hissing rain, the moaning of passengers and the hum and roar accompanying the awesome spectacle of the furies of nature which had indeed finally caused the boat to turn about, depositing Heine at Ritzebüttel, to spend his vacation on the coast.

Yet he had come away from that first experience of the ocean with a strange feeling of elation, and had since spent 6 weeks on the island of Nordeney in the summer of 1825. This time he learned to swim and took to the sea like a fish. Christian Sethe and his wife came to spend a couple of days with him and the two friends became reconciled. Besides socializing with a duchess and gambling with some Hanoverian officers, Heine observed the life of the fishermen and boatmen. The sea calmed his nerves. He spent days alone on a fishing barque, and was one of the last visitors to leave at the end of the season.

Loving the sea now 'like my own soul', and having developed a 'harmonious intimacy with this wild element which makes me feel well when it rages most,'[4] he returned to Nordeney in the summer of 1826. By the next spring Campe had rushed through the press and was distributing *Reisebilder* II. It contained another cycle of 11 poems, the *North Sea* II – of a more epic character than the previous year's 11 – as well as a prose section titled *North Sea* III. In the poems Heine relegated the Romantic imagination to secondary place in the face of the cosmic power of nature governing human destiny. 'Who in Germany in those days knew the sea?' Heine was to recall. 'Today everybody knows it.' Indeed, he was the first German writer to discover the majestic beauty of the sea, to celebrate its mystery and magic, and to win lasting acclaim by some as 'the poet of the sea *par excellence.*'

The *North Sea* III prose essay was a different matter. If Heine in his earlier prose writings, from his *Letters from Berlin* to the *Harzreise*, had here and there worked in some suggestive political allusions – such as interrupting his narration of the mining work at Klaustal by remarking, 'I did not go down to the lowest depths where, as some maintain, you can hear the people in America shouting, "Hurrah Lafayette!"' – in *North Sea* III he took a militant political stand. Flitting from the insular character and modest, uniform aspirations of Nordeney's taciturn fishermen to the 'identity of thought and feeling' which the Roman Catholic church for centuries imposed on entire nations, Heine attacked medieval Christianity and its supporting pillar, the aristocracy. True, Renaissance art blossomed even while Rome, like a 'huge spider', held the Latin world enthralled in its 'cross-web'. But the human spirit could not be repressed by statutes, dogma or the pealing of bells. 'The days of spiritual slavery' were over and gone. But then, were people not happier when they lived in ignorance and blind faith before the age of doubt?

At this point Heine's personal *Zerrissenheit*, his famous code-word for the heartbreak and frustrations of unrequited love, underwent one of his deft mutations of meaning to become one with the general *Zerrissenheit*, the malaise and discomfort, of the modern world, a phenomenon particularly affecting the Germans after the post-Napoleonic settlement left them with a patchwork of nearly 40 separate states, condemned to political silence and inactivity under the *Gleichschaltung* of ideas – to use a term, though anachronistic, that was to become notorious in the totalitarian Third Reich – by the reactionary Holy Alliance, and bereft of hope of change.

The great sensation of *Travel Pictures* II, however, was Heine's masterly *Ideas. The Book of LeGrand* – included in the same volume – with its glorification of Napoleon to the drumbeat of the little French tambour evoking the revolutionary libertarian ideas which the martial Emperor had brought to the peoples of Europe pining under its archaic absolutist structure. Heine had already named Napoleon in the same breath with such world-historical figures as Alexander the Great and Caesar, and privately he considered him an epic, tragic hero surpassing those of the *Iliad*. But to sing hosannas to Napoleon, the enemy of the Holy Alliance, as he did in *The Book of LeGrand*, and to compare his recent death on St Helena to the martyrdom of a secular Christ – in a blast at perfidious Albion, Heine wrote that it had shamefully allowed itself to be 'hired by conspiring kings' to serve as the gaolers of 'the secular Saviour who suffered under Sir Hudson Lowe, as it is written in the gospels of Las Casas, O'Meara, and Antommarchi'[5] – was, in the circumstances of 1827, and in view of the religious feelings of the rulers of 'German-Christian' Prussia and their partners in the Holy Alliance, more than a daring act of defiance.

Starting in 1827 – when Russian censors first objected to passages criticizing religious dogma in Heine's writings – and until 1917, all such passages were excised from Russian editions of Heine's work. Closer at home *The Book of LeGrand* bordered on public incitement, since Heine's praise of Napoleon was in fact an attack on the rulers and governments presiding over the repressive-regressive measures instituted by the Holy Alliance in all the states of the German *Bund* in the wake of Napoleon's downfall. On the day before it was published, Heine thought it best to make himself scarce. For all his furious outburst against England, he still thought it the safest refuge, and boarded a boat sailing for London.

Whether Heine's worry that he might be arrested or otherwise harassed by the authorities was justified or not, it is a fact that when later that year he passed through Württemberg, he was expelled from its territory as the author of inflammatory material. With *North Sea* III and *The Book of LeGrand* Heine made his spectacular appearance as a political writer, the lyrical poet suddenly committed to combat in the real world, enlivening Germany's dull public life and eventually to accumulate the influence that, inspiring a progressive literary movement, was to make him something of a force in German politics and a thorn in the flesh of the various bodies, high and low, in charge of thought-control in the countries of the Holy Alliance. For the rest, as a work of art, *The Book of LeGrand* is a brilliant tour de force, loosely stringing together Heine's childhood recollections and his reactions to the tragedy and comedy of historic events and contemporary politics with the most extravagant, absurd, or sublime ideas – '*du sublime au ridicule il n'y a qu'un pas, madame,*' Heine observed – thematically interwoven with a light-handed touch and a kind of Aristophanic humour within a dazzling kaleidoscopic narrative.

Shortly after Heine's return from England in mid-September, Campe published his *Book of Songs*. When he had first started putting together this 'selected' collection of his poems he foolishly expected to get 'not a penny' for it: popularity and the satisfaction of showing his previous publishers, Maurer and Dümmler, that he could 'get along without them' would be his chief rewards.[6] The result was that Campe acquired the volume which, after a slow start, became what Jeffrey Sammons calls 'the most world-famous book of poetry in the German language' for nothing. It was only one day ahead of publication that Heine decided to extract the promise of 'a half-fee' for every new edition – altogether 13 were to appear during his lifetime, and many more afterwards – from Campe, who otherwise fobbed him off with a contract for a third volume in the *Travel Pictures* III series, against a fee of 80 Louis d'ors.

The financial relations between Heine and his publisher have been the subject of controversy ever since that day in 1827. Sammons has calculated that

Campe was to pay Heine during his lifetime the modern equivalent of 'something like 370,000 dollars' and another 225,000 to his widow.[7] But Campe, besides being a better bargainer than the impractical Heine, was not always forthcoming with money when the latter needed it most.

Heine, who suspected Campe of producing unauthorized second printings (which he occasionally did), could surely have found another publisher, but hardly one more intrepid than Campe, or as ready to battle with the censorship and sometimes see his books confiscated. The relationship proved so advantageous mutually that the two were to stick together for 30 years of a stormy 'marriage of convenience', punctuated by much haggling and many crises. While Campe helped to make Heine famous, Heine felt to the end of his life that Campe made a fortune out of him. When told on his deathbed that Düsseldorf was sure to erect a monument to him he reputedly answered, 'I have one already at Hamburg,' and referring to Campe's mansion next to the Börsenplatz, called it 'a magnificent monument erected by my publisher in grateful memory of my Travel Pictures and Book of Songs.' Although Heine exaggerated, he certainly contributed not a little to the reputation and ultimate growth of the firm of Hoffmann & Campe, which exists to this day.

The *Travel Pictures*, Heine wrote to Varnhagen in October 1826, were merely a convenient form for 'saying anything I want... I can now find expression for everything, and care little whether it adds to the number of my enemies.' Indeed, between the summer of 1825 when he obtained his doctor's degree and the consecutive appearance of *LeGrand* and *The Book of Songs* in 1827 his creative powers, the range of his subject-matter, his imagery and his singular talent for pithy, ironic representation rapidly approached their full potential.

Much in his life had changed, but the preoccupations of his essentially self-centred personality continued to revolve around the same old complaints: headaches, moodiness, suspicion, dissatisfaction with the general state of things in Germany, irritation with unfriendly critics and other 'enemies', his up-and-down relations with Uncle Salomon, etc. His 70-odd letters of the period ring with continued echoes of the 'self-torture' and inner 'civil war' of which he wrote to Moser in December 1825. They abound in reports of his literary plans, but also with all sorts of illusory projects and vain hopes of obtaining a professorship – 'I am preparing lectures I hope to deliver at Berlin University,' he wrote in the same 1825 letter to Moser – or some other sinecure, or alternately of establishing himself, with Uncle Salomon's help, as an attorney in Hamburg.

Unless one accepts Heine's statement in his Memoirs that a cussed strain in his character often made him do things contrary to his own nature, his abhorrence of jurisprudence – a subject he found hard to 'get into my head' – makes it difficult to visualize him functioning as a lawyer. All he wanted to do when he left Göttingen was to write. But the law had been forced on him by Uncle Salomon. At Lüneburg Heine had found a friend, the lawyer Rudolf Christiani, who in the autumn of 1825 helped to prepare him for his legal career. Heine began to study court files, but was more interested in Moliere's comedies. When Christiani handed over to him a sure-fire case, Heine – making his first and last appearance in court – promptly lost it.

Next he went to Hamburg. He had not been there long when, on 24 February 1826 – about a month after he had signed his first contract with Campe – he complained to Moser that various people, including his own brother-in-law Maurice Embden, were slandering and maligning him to Uncle Salomon: 'I am sick with indignation and can hardly write.' In two later letters that year, while he was working on *The Book of LeGrand*, he wrote that instead of a hoped-for 'position' in Hamburg he had found only 'enemies', and went on to lament that he was 'living largely in misery.'[8]

More than once he announced that he was going to leave Hamburg, which he described as 'a counting-house by day, and a big brothel at night'. He would go to Berlin, no, he would leave Germany altogether. 'I feel a definite urge to say goodbye to the German fatherland', he wrote to Moser on 8 August 1826, and to Immermann, on 14 October, he declared: 'My nerves are too weak to stand life in Germany.' Yet, except for seeking the restorative calm of another sojourn on Nordeney Island, he stayed in 'accursed' Hamburg for two more years, and in 1828, far from leaving Germany, mobilized two well-wishers to intervene with the King of Bavaria in a hopeless effort to obtain a professorship in Munich.

In view of his misery, frayed nerves, frequent headaches, self-torment and the energy and emotion spent on his constant preoccupation with – and sometimes veritable campaigns against – real or imaginary enemies, one wonders how Heine was able to write and create at all. His personal life between 1825 and his final move to Paris in 1831 have been subsumed by several of his biographers under such headings as 'Drift', 'The Bird of Passage', or Heine's '*Wanderjahre*'.[9]

He was indeed restless, moved from Hamburg to Munich, made a tour of Italy, returned to Hamburg, stayed for a while in Berlin, then in Potsdam, and moved back to Hamburg, with some intervals at Lüneburg. Yet, as Max Brod has pointed out, 'it is wrong to think of the artist as being a perpetually tortured, badgered individual whose nerves are always on edge. Transcending all his limitations and soothing all his irritations is the halcyon tranquillity of the creative process.' Heine himself, in his first Hamburg letter to Rudolf Christiani, indirectly illustrated this at the end of a passage in which – having been the first to inform several people that he might establish himself as an

Advokat, or lawyer, in Hamburg – he nonchalantly reported that 'everybody believes that I will remain here in order to "*advozieren*". I, however, have not the faintest idea what I shall be doing.' Then he added: 'But don't you believe that I am idling away my time here. On the contrary, wherever I sit or stand I am making poetry.'[10]

Heine's attempts to obtain a university post, however unrealistic, were somewhat more serious, for he was desperately grasping for some stability and a secure income to free himself from Uncle Salomon's patronage. At the same time, through all his changes of mood, delusions, depression and fits of ill-temper, his sense of purpose and his awareness of his talent and the uses to which he was determined to put it grew more pronounced and firmer. 'I write little', he declared – indeed, his collected works amount to no more than 7 volumes – 'but what I write is good.' And as early as 1826 something of a new foreknowledge of his destiny and of the political-literary role he meant to fulfil cropped up in his letters.

Three times, in the 4 letters of that year in which he ventilated the idea of leaving Germany forever, Heine specified Paris as his planned destination. And in two of them he mentioned that he wanted to develop a *European* outlook. 'In Paris I will use the libraries, I shall see people and the world, and will collect material for a book that will be European in character,' he wrote to Varnhagen on 24 October. And a few weeks later he observed in a letter to Merckel: 'The task is to touch only upon such topics that are of general European interest.' Heine, in short, wanted to free himself from the straitjacket of conditions in Germany. He was developing a cosmopolitanism, and though he still had doubts and lacked the push to leave Germany, he knew very well what he was doing. He was fully aware of the effect of his current work. 'In The North Sea II I have blazed a completely new trail,' he wrote to Immermann on 14 October. In a letter to Merckel on 10 January 1827, he observed that 'this book [*LeGrand*] will make a great noise... by virtue of its treating of world issues and its life-size representation of Napoleon and the French Revolution.'

The two works mentioned had yet to appear when he wrote. If one adds that almost a year before the publication of his *Book of Songs* he said that 'this will be my *chef d'oeuvre* and will give a psychological portrait of myself', Heine had a keen sense of posterity's judgment.

When he first mentioned his urge to 'say goodbye to the German fatherland' he explained to Moser that 'it is less my Wanderlust than the torment of my personal affairs (for example, the Jew in me who will never be washed away) that drives me hence.' Too proud to take the repudiation of his origin lightly, torn between a feeling of remorse which he tried to make up for by several times declaring that he longed to finish *The Rabbi of Bacherach* – and at one point even that he was going to include it in *Travel Pictures* II – and that attachment which had early made him write, 'My breast is an archive of German feeling, my two books are an archive of German song', his relations with Uncle Salomon during this period reached a state of friction that marked the beginning of the life-long war of attrition between the two of them.

This friction had a much wider background than mere squabbles about financial matters between the money-hungry nephew and the millionaire banker, such as had soured Heine's first seaside holiday at Ritzebüttel in 1823. While there he had been upset by a letter in which his uncle – forgetting that he had promised to give him 800 Thaler for two years – maintained that he had only agreed to give 500. Being an honest man, he added, 'I have kept my word', and took his nephew to task for having drawn the last quarterly 100 Thaler ahead of time. Faced with the end of his stipend or the embarrassing need to renegotiate it, Heine was shocked – 'Isn't this superb?' he vented his feelings to Moser on 23 August 1823 – but did not remind his uncle that the promise had been for 800 Thaler. Instead, he sent him a letter which he described 'as a masterpiece of dignity and persiflage'. He realized that this was an 'unwise' way of dealing with the mighty Salomon Heine, but he could not help himself and this became the tenor of all his reactions whenever he felt shabbily treated by the magnate.

Heine at the time called Hamburg 'my Elysium and my Tartarus, the city which I detest and love most, the place where I am afflicted by the tormented feelings of the damned and for which I pine nevertheless, the city to which I'm sure I will often return in the future.' We know why Heine hated Hamburg and its businessmen and stockbrokers, of whom he had early written that their interest in poetry was confined to 'marriage hymns, funeral dirges or baptismal songs commissioned against hard cash.' Besides being a 'huckster town', it was the scene of his great but one-sided 'love-affair' with his cousin Amalie and other youthful humiliations he had suffered at his 'Castle of Affront'. Less is known about what made Hamburg an 'Elysium' that was to lure him back again and again, unless the fact that Heine coined the double metaphor about the city in the same August 1823 letter in which he mentioned that – succumbing to 'new folly grafted upon old' – he had fallen in love with Amalie's younger sister Therese was not entirely coincidental.

In 1823 Therese was 16 years old, 10 years younger than Heine. According to an artist's portrait of her, she was as beautiful as her cold-hearted sister, but more gentle and sweet-looking; and some biographers, notably Wadepuhl, hold that at 18 or 19, during Heine's 1825–27 stay in Hamburg, she also became more responsive to his attentions. Some of the most beautiful poems of Heine's *Homecoming* cycle are generally believed to have been inspired by Therese. But

269

the evidence for the belief that a romance developed between them during this period when he broke into uncontested fame – let alone Wadepuhl's assertion that Heine even saw himself marrying her – is rather flimsy.

It must be said that Salomon Heine was on occasion generous with his nephew. Immediately after Heine had obtained his doctorate in the summer of 1825, the banker had rewarded him with the princely sum of 50 Louis d'ors. Heine, while enjoying himself on Nordeney Island, socializing with a princess Hohensolm-Lich and other bathing guests, promptly lost most of this money gambling with Hanoverian officers serving in the English 'German Legion'. He abjured gambling for the rest of his life, but found himself in the embarrassing situation of having to write Sethe for a loan of 6 Louis d'ors before he was able to leave the island.

But nothing so much hurt Heine's relations with his uncle as his abuse of the latter's trust on his journey to England in April 1827. For this trip Uncle Salomon had equipped Heine with a letter of credit to the Rothschilds in London in the sum of 200 – according to some sources, 400 – pounds sterling, in either case an extremely generous sum. Salomon had in addition given him cash for his estimated expenses, and the letter of credit was intended merely to show that he was a man of means and high connections. Two days after his arrival in London, Heine rashly went to Nathan Rothschild and cashed the letter of credit. He prudently sent 800 Thaler of it to Varnhagen for safe-keeping against an emergency, and had a high time living on the rest of it during the three and a half months he spent in England. He toured the London docks, visited the Bedlam asylum, attended several House of Commons sessions and observed trials at Old Bailey. In Germany *The Book of LeGrand* was creating a sensation, and on 22 May the London *Morning Herald* saluted the presence in England of 'Doctor H. Heine, the German satirist and poet'.

In a letter from his mother, Heine received the tidings that Uncle Salomon was outraged at his behaviour in cashing a letter of credit expressly given him for 'representational' purposes only. Undeterred, Heine went to the races at Epsom Park and took week-long holidays at Brighton, Margate and Ramsgate. In between, he frequented some of London society, to whom he was introduced by the piano virtuoso Ignaz Moscheles, and saw Kean at the Drury Lane Theatre in *The Merchant of Venice*, *Macbeth*, and possibly some other Shakespeare plays. He complained about the foul English weather but found 'much that is attractive here – Parliament, Westminster Abbey, English tragedy, good-looking women';[11] among the latter may have been the mysterious Mlle Clairmont of Regents Park, celebrated in his love-poems titled 'Kitty' or 'Katherina' (or so it is believed), and otherwise known only from a farewell letter addressed to her before he finally left England in mid-August.

Travelling home in slow stages, he spent a number of days in Holland and a longer spell on Nordeney Island, whence he wrote Merckel that England had 'financially ruined' him. If, as it would seem, he was biding his time before facing the consequences of his actions and confronting Uncle Salomon's wrath in Hamburg, it should be noted that, for all his seemingly disarrayed behaviour, Heine was well organized as a writer. At Nordeney he worked on his *English Fragments*, and from notes apparently made in Holland also began to jot down his *Memoirs of Herr von Schnabelewopsky*, from which Wagner was to take the legend of *The Flying Dutchman*.

It was not before 19 September that he arrived in Hamburg. On the eve of his departure for England he had sent Uncle Salomon the first printed copy of *Travel Pictures* II 'as a token of affection and obedience', and there had otherwise been a noticeable reduction of the strain in their mutually ambivalent relations, as attested by the banker's very gesture in giving him the letter of credit. Heine, for his part, although often fuming against his uncle's 'niggardliness', admired the qualities which made Salomon the richest man in Hamburg, and had privately written that, 'for all our constant differences, I love him very much.'[12] While deploring the self-made tycoon's lack of interest in literary matters, Heine, a *condottiere* of the spirit, felt that he and the *condottiere* of the money world had 'much in common'. He was very keen throughout to have each of his successes and every favourable review and tidbit brought to his uncle's attention through various friends and well-wishers.

Whether this had anything to do with his entertaining hopes of marrying Therese is impossible to say. The slim evidence rests chiefly on two items. One is the letter of congratulations Heine was to write Salomon the following year when, journeying through Italy, he learned that Therese had married a Dr Adolf Halle. The letter expressed 'qualified' joy at the news and contained the sentence: 'Next to myself there is no one to whom I would more gladly grant her than Dr Halle.'[13] And nearly 30 years later Heine's brother Gustav, in reporting to him in 1855 that Dr Halle, Therese's husband, was suffering from an affliction of the bladder which prevented him from urinating, finished his letter with the vulgar comment: 'Let the fact that his instrument doesn't function be your revenge.' In all this it should be remembered that of Therese's own feelings for Heine nothing is known. In 1853 she visited him at his sickbed in Paris – an occasion reported by Heine to his mother with the observation that she was 'accompanied by [her brother] Carl, who was sent as a sentinel to watch that I should say nothing she is not supposed to know'[14] – and afterwards sent him a compassionate letter. Then, as if to add to the mystery, a passage Heine devoted to Therese in his Memoirs was to be excised from the manuscript by his brother Maximilian.

The paucity of evidence does not mean that in 1827, when he was 30, Heine's imagination may not have flown high with hopes or some expectation, founded or unfounded, of marrying Therese. He was returning to Hamburg with two cards up his sleeve. While still in London, he had been pressed by Campe to produce a new volume, *Travel Pictures* III; and he had also (through the instrumentality of Varnhagen) received an offer from Baron Johann F. Cotta – Germany's newspaper magnate and head of its largest publishing firm – to assume the editorship of his prestigious and, within the limits of censorship, liberal Munich periodical, the *New General Political Annals*. But if Heine thought that a solid well-paying position added to his growing literary success made him an eligible suitor for Therese's hand, he was, not for the first time, operating under a delusion.

In 1827 Salomon Heine was well on his way to becoming one of Germany's most important financiers. A substantial part of all municipal and government loans passed through his hands. Early in the century, he had formed a life-long business association with the Paris banker Beer Léon Fould, a granddaughter of whom was later to marry Salomon's young son and heir, Carl Heine. Fould's career strangely paralleled Salomon's own. Both men were born in 1767. Both spent their adolescence as bank apprentices running about town – in Paris and Hamburg, respectively – delivering bills and cashing checks. One day Fould, who had arrived in Paris from Metz with a single pair of socks and no change of clothes, paused at a café and counted a sum of money he had cashed for his employer from the Banque de France. Finding that he had been given 100 Louis d'ors too much, he retraced his steps, only to be told to keep the surplus money because 'the Banque de France never makes a mistake'.

With this for a starting capital, Fould made a fortune which, before the century was out, had enabled him to help finance Bonaparte's Italian campaign. Simultaneously Salomon Heine had worked his way up to manager of the Heckscher Bank, and by the time Napoleon was overrunning Germany he and Fould had cooperated in raising the war contributions imposed by the French on the free city of Hamburg. Illustrating the rise of capitalism through all the *bouleversements* since the French Revolution, both men prospered. Salomon Heine soon bought the Ottensen château near Hamburg where, in 1816, he entertained Fieldmarshal Blücher and later other prominent Germans. By 1828 Fould had acquired the Rocquencourt estate that had once belonged to the wife of Louis XIII.

For a full understanding of Heine's life-long money war with his Uncle Salomon it should be noted that the poet was the poor relation to an immensely wealthy family. Of his father's 5 brothers, two others besides Salomon were rich bankers. In Hamburg lived Salomon's younger brother Henry Heine, who had a highly respected bank of his own. He was the only one of his paternal family who showed some understanding for the poet's troubles and sometimes helped him with money without strings attached. His eldest uncle Isaac Heine died in 1828 at Bordeaux. But two of his sons, Armand and Michel – after accumulating a fortune from the slave-trade in New Orleans – established the Heine & Co. Bank in Paris. (Of Heine's two other paternal uncles, one died as a young bachelor; the other lived in Schwerin, where two of his sons became prominent physicians, but the poet had little contact with them.)

Wherever Heine looked then or later in Hamburg or in Paris he was dazzled by fabulous riches. Only he, the genius of the family, was condemned to permanent money worries. The marriage of Uncle Salomon's son Carl to Fould's granddaughter Cécile united two great fortunes. Cécile, moreover, was a daughter of the Paris banker Elie Furtado. When Carl and Cécile Heine, having no children of their own, adopted the illegitimate daughter of her brother Paul, Cécile became – by a stipulation in her brother's will – the sole heiress of the Furtado fortune as well.

The adopted daughter, Pauline, married the duc d'Elchingen, a descendant of Marshal Ney, and their daughter, marrying into the Napoleon line, became a Princess Murat.[15] Jeffrey Sammons takes this as a sign that 'the ambitious thrust of the Heine wealth was not into middle class assimilation', but into the titled nobility. This is true, but it is pertinent that Cécile's Fould and Furtado families lived in France – as did the owners of the Heine & Co. Bank in Paris, the brothers Armand and Michel Heine. In France the Jews had been emancipated, and Michel – a first cousin of the poet – became a regent of the Banque de France. His daughter Alice was to marry the duc de Richelieu, to divorce him after giving birth to the next duke and then to marry, as mentioned by Sammons, none less than 'Albert I, Prince of Monaco'.

In France, too, starting in the 1830s, Beer Léon Fould's two sons, Benoît and Achille, entered politics and were elected to the Chamber of Deputies. Achille Fould (1800–67) became a leading politician and was to serve three times as France's Minister of Finance under Louis Napoléon.

Salomon Heine's situation in Hamburg was different. Mighty and wealthy as he became, respected for his many charities and public services as well as for his integrity – which made him refrain from engaging in the growing wave of dubious Stock Exchange speculation in industrial and railway shares – he might have aspired to a patent of nobility, but was never even offered citizenship before he died.

The marriages of his 4 daughters, however, were carefully arranged. Only his second-eldest (Fanny), brought, in modern terminology, a member of the free professions into the family: Dr Wilhelm Schröder, a physician. Maurice (Christian) Oppenheimer, the husband of Salomon's eldest daughter Friederike (who died young in 1823), was Salomon's confidential clerk and remained his bank manager, entitled to sign letters in his name. Jonathan (John) Friedländer, who married Amalie, was not only a rich East Prussian landowner but had won the Iron Cross for distinguishing himself as an officer in the 'War of Liberation'. Therese's prospective husband, Dr Adolf (Christian Herman) Halle, was a 33-year-old stockbroker who became president of Hamburg's Commercial Court.

Friedländer lived in Königsberg, but the others were now members of Uncle Salomon's family circle. Heine particularly detested Oppenheimer and the stockjobbing Halle, as he detested all Hamburg with its trading marts, not only because of their constant talk about foreign currency rates, agiotage and buying and selling, but perhaps even more because they were baptized (as was Friedländer; Dr Schröder was a born Christian). They, on the other hand, thought little of him, and treated him with the disparagement of careerists for an idler. To make matters worse, there was his own brother-in-law, the Hamburg merchant Maurice Embden. Heine, out of consideration for his sister Charlotte, tried at first to be on friendly terms with him in spite of their political differences, but in the end they had a mighty row. Heine sometimes had a tendency to blame others for adverse situations of his own causing, but this does not mean that there may not have been some truth to his complaints that Embden, Oppenheimer and Halle spoke badly of him to Uncle Salomon; for they were all, for one reason or another, united against him.

Salomon himself, of course, was nobody's fool, and if Heine, after the Amalie 'affair', had really set his eyes on Therese, the banker must have thought that the nephew whom he was supporting was after his daughters and their money. Curiously enough Uncle Salomon, after strongly insisting that Heine study law, had done nothing to help establish him in the legal profession or some associated career. He had obviously realized that his nephew was an impractical man constitutionally unfit for any of the humdrum occupations that made the world go round. He liked something about the young man, felt a family responsibility for him and sometimes made him unexpected gifts of money. But he was hardly pleased to have his name associated with a dissident writer who, besides annoying the authorities by extolling Napoleon, drew attention (as Heine had done in *Ratcliff*) to the existence of 'two fiercely warring nations, to wit the sated and the hungry', and otherwise reminded Hamburg's several hundred Jewish wealthy inhabitants of the mass of their more 'authentic' co-religionists living in misery in Poland.

In any case, whether Heine's idea of marrying Therese was a phantasm or based on some encouragement, he had ruined his chances, slight as they were, by his breach of faith in cashing Salomon's letter of credit to the London Rothschilds. Salomon was not a man to be trifled with. No sooner had his nephew returned from England at the end of September 1827 than the banker took him to task in a brusque and insulting manner, as is evident from the fragment of a letter Heine wrote to Varnhagen on 12 February (but only sent off on 1 April) 1828: 'Never in my life shall I return to Hamburg; my uncle there, the millionaire, has behaved towards me like the lowest villain. Things of surpassing bitterness have happened to me in Hamburg, things which I should have found impossible to endure had I not been the only person to know about them.' By the time he was writing this, Heine was in Munich, having left Hamburg the previous October, 4 weeks or so after Salomon read him the riot act. What words had passed between them on that occasion remains a mystery. One biographer has written that Heine ended the confrontation by calmly telling Salomon: 'You know, uncle, the best thing about you is that you bear my name.' This makes for a good story, but as far as documentary evidence goes, this remark first appeared in a letter written by Heine 9 years after the event, when it struck deeply enough for Salomon to remember it years later and to keep ironically addressing letters to his nephew with the words, 'Heinrich Heine, Esquire, the founder of the family, after whom all Heines worth mentioning are named', or to sign them 'Salomon Heine, the man who bears your name.'[16]

Heine was in a bitter frame of mind when he set out for Munich on 27 October 1827. On the way he visited his parents at Lüneburg, then went to Göttingen, where he saw Baron Sartorius, his old professor, and his friend Moser, and on to Kassel. There he met the two famous Grimm brothers, and had his portrait done by their younger brother, the painter and copper engraver Ludwig Emil Grimm. Of all the many earlier or later portraits of Heine, Grimm's etching of him in a Romantic, rather Byronesque pose was to become the best-known. Beneath the portrait Heine wrote two lines:

> Cross-tempered, moody, my heart cold,
>> I journey moodily through the cold world.

> (*Verdrossnen Sinn im kalten Herzen hegend*
>> *Reis ich verdriesslich durch die kalte Welt*)

Before leaving Hamburg he had met his cousin Amalie, the haughty, cold adolescent 'queen' and 'madonna' who 11 years earlier had inspired his first tormented love. Now 'a fat lady', he wrote to Varnhagen the morning he visited her on 19 October, 'the good woman arrived yesterday, just on the day when the new edition of my Youthful Sorrows was published.'[17] Of Therese, his supposed new love whom he had just lost, not a word. One of the many places where he broke his slow solitary journey to Munich was at Heidelberg, where his 20-year-old brother Maximilian was studying medicine.

After Heine's death, Maximilian was to write that Heine had purposely and unethically cashed Salomon's letter of credit immediately on arrival in London in order to forestall Salomon's changing his mind and informing Rothschild that the document was only an 'empty form'; Heine authorities, however, doubt this story, and many other episodes in Maximilian's 'Recollections' are considered unreliable.[18]

It is worth noting that before leaving London, Heine had (in the letter of 19 October already quoted) swore Varnhagen to secrecy about the 800 Thaler transferred to him for safekeeping in Berlin: 'No one must know that I have this money.' He added that in view of his rift with his Hamburg family, 'I must at all times have money available for travelling.' From Munich he wrote to Varnhagen on 12 February 1828 that Baron Cotta was paying him 'very generously' for his new editorial job, but stressed that this, too, must remain a secret between them: 'No one must know that I have money... I want to undertake this year something for which I will need money so badly that I would have to steal it from heaven were I not to have it.'

What scheme Heine harboured in his seething mind is an enigma. He had knowingly lived extravagantly in England on Uncle Salomon's letter of credit and had used some of the money cashed from Rothschild to pay off old debts to various friends. From London he had written that he hoped 'to have the strength of mind' not to return to Hamburg, and it is as likely as not that when deciding to put aside 800 Thaler of his uncle's money for future emergencies he already felt at war with Salomon, and was in a momentary mood to break with him. Since early youth Heine had developed an outcast's feeling of standing alone against the world – whether the *Burschenschaften*, the illiberal Prussian regime, the class-conscious rich, whether Christians or Jews, who snubbed him – and while he had friends and acquaintances in various places, he was, both as a poet and as a person, very much a solitary figure. He had no permanent home, no settled position or regular income. His basic insecurity and naiveté in practical matters were, however, counterbalanced by a combination of pride, ambition and imaginative derring-do in his character.

Heine was not simply a non-conformist. Already at 19, speaking in the flush of uncertain first love, he had likened himself to 'a fanatical chess player' who, having 'lost the queen on my first move', goes on playing, 'playing for the queen!' It was not in him to be submissive; his fighting spirit waxed with every obstacle. He played for high stakes, and the peculiar thing about his approach was that he sometimes, with utter unconcern for reality, engaged in risky stratagems while knowing full well that they would ultimately work against him.

Wadepuhl, for one, has claimed that Heine had asked Therese to defy her parents and marry him without their consent. Though a scholar of repute, Wadepuhl unfortunately cited no evidence in support of this assertion.[19] But given Heine's eccentricity and his capacity for self-delusion, it is not inconceivable that he did so and that his appropriation of the letter of credit may have been connected with this or some other quixotic scheme that passed through his mind.

His journey to Munich 'through the cold world' of November 1827 was not all melancholy. At Frankfurt he met and had long talks with Ludwig Börne, whose fame as Germany's sharpest political writer had preceded his own. Börne was later to become the hero of Germany's 'radical' Left, and political as well as personal differences were to drive him and Heine apart in Paris, but for the moment all was friendship between them. On other stops of his journey to Bavaria, Heine was pleased to discover that he was now a celebrity. In Stuttgart he spent several days at the home of Wolfgang Menzel, Germany's foremost literary critic, and it was not until the end of November that he finally reached Munich.

There, a new but short-lived chapter opened in his life. He was most cordially received by Baron Cotta von Cottendorf, who offered him 2,000 Gulden a year to edit the *Political Annals*. It was a comfortable post at a generous salary, seeing that most of the work was to be done by his co-editor, Dr Friedrich Lindner, a well-known liberal journalist and the author of a much-discussed plan to unite Bavaria, Württemberg and Baden into a confederation to counterbalance the reactionary tendencies of Prussia and Austria. Except for a monthly essay, Heine was to be saddled with few responsibilities. He found life among the phlegmatic Bavarians in the 'Athens of beer' – an allusion to the grandiose plans of the new King Ludwig I, an amateur poet and general patron of the arts, to turn Munich into a centre of science, literature and art – tepid and uninspiring, but settled down to live 'like a grandseigneur' in an apartment he rented in a noble mansion.

In Munich, Heine showed the many facets of his complex character. He had found in Cotta, a jovial, cultured, elderly gentleman who, besides being the publisher of Goethe and Schiller, was vice-president of the Württemberg Diet, the nearest thing to an ideal employer. Moreover, Cotta publicly supported the cause of Jewish emancipation, and Heine – 'greatly agitated by the public discussion of the subject' – hailed his speech in the Diet 'a victory for humanity'. Devoting an entire issue of the *Political Annals* to the debate of the bill which in April 1828 granted Württemberg's Jews full civil equality, he privately singled out its importance as 'a first example in a constitutional state' which put 'liberal Prussia' to shame.[20] Cotta, who owned important newspapers in other parts of

Germany, had long-term plans for Heine and had offered him an annual contract. Heine, however, with all his needs 'provided for' to his perfect satisfaction
and security at last in the offing, would not commit himself for more than half a
year.

'I want to be free,' he had written to Campe a few days after his arrival in
Munich. Calming his Hamburg publisher's fears that, tempted by Cotta's
higher fees, he would transfer his works to the latter's publishing firm, he
assured Campe that he would stay with him and promised to devote his 'best
hours' to producing *Travel Pictures* III. Should Munich's 'horrible' climate
prove injurious to his health, he wrote, he would simply pack his bags and go on
a tour of Italy.

At the same time, though ridiculing the King's artistic pretensions by remarking that the painters he patronized looked better than their pictures, he went
out of his way to seek the Royal favour for his appointment to a professorship at
Munich University. For this purpose he cultivated the friendship of Eduard
Schenk, a poet and playwright whom Ludwig I presently chose to be his Minister of the Interior, and of Michael Beer, another of the King's favourite authors
(and a brother of the composer Meyerbeer). In mid-April 1828 Heine published an anonymous review of Beer's tragedy *Struensee* so blatantly designed to
flatter that he wrote Moser: 'And imagine – I, I, I, I wrote it! The gods themselves are dumbfounded. Think what you will.'[21]

On 18 June, Heine asked Cotta to present his books to the King and to say
that he wished to be judged solely by his talent 'and not by the good or bad use
to which it had hitherto been put'; and on 28 July, in a letter to the King
formally proposing Heine for an assistant professorship, Schenk similarly intimated that, like 'several other geniuses in our German fatherland', this particular applicant had committed some youthful transgressions and only needed a
beneficent Royal hand to keep him to the straight path.

Heine's apparent readiness to 'sell his pen to the Bavarian court' for a grace-
and-favour professorship has, to say the least, perplexed some of his modern
biographers.[22] Heine's defenders have argued that, compared to Prussia, 'the
King of Bavaria was at that time a pillar of liberalism, of cultural and political
progress' (as he was indeed until the July Revolution in France); and that even
in his review of *Struensee*, Heine – 'an ebullient genius ruined by his own
naiveté' rather than a coolly calculating opportunist – had highlighted the play's
significance as a cry for freedom and a protest against 'the inequality of the
classes'.[23]

Early during his stay in Munich, Heine had met and struck up a friendship
with Fyodor Ivanovich Tyutchev, a cosmopolitan Russian diplomat married to a
German noblewoman. In their company and that of Schenk and Beer, he began

to frequent the town's aristocratic society and most exclusive circles, thereby incurring criticism from some liberals. Catholic circles influential in the politics of the Bavarian court were likewise annoyed, resenting as they did Heine's ironic treatment of German indifference towards liberty. 'The Englishman loves liberty as he does his lawful spouse,' and will if necessary defend it like a man protecting his 'bed-chamber', they read in Heine's *English Fragments*, which were being serialized in the *Political Annals* and in Cotta's *Morning Chronicle for the Educated Classes*. 'The Frenchman loves liberty as he does his chosen bride,' with the passion of one ready to commit 'any folly for it' and 'to fight for it at the risk of his life. The German loves liberty as he does his old grandmother.' Conservative and Jesuit circles were even more annoyed by what they regarded as irreverent passages about religion in Heine's *Travel Pictures* I.

How Heine meant to continue as a dissident writer in a university post depending on the favour of the King, who was himself a religious mystic, is a mystery. But he has not been widely accused of being ready to betray the cause of liberalism; for Heine might make compromises, but he was to prove a skillful navigator between Scylla and Charybdis. A man of many paradoxes, he soon made his position clear: 'In Munich people think that I shall tone down my attacks on the aristocracy now that I live in the foyer of the *noblesse* and am in love with the most lovable aristocratic ladies – and am loved by them. But they are mistaken. My love of equality, my hatred of the clergy were never stronger than now, it has become practically a bias with me.'[24]

At the beginning of September 1828 Heine was on his way from Leghorn to Lucca. A month before, taking a step he had contemplated from the day of his arrival in Munich, he had packed his bags and left on a tour of Italy. Since crossing the Brenner Pass he had stopped at Trent, inspected the amphitheatre and the palace of the Capuletti at Verona, spent several days sightseeing in both Milan and Genoa, and nearly a week in Leghorn.

By 5 September he had settled down for several weeks in Bagni di Lucca and wrote to Schenk, now Bavaria's Minister of the Interior, that he would next proceed to Florence, and there hoped to get 'the long-expected joyful news' of his nomination to a professorship. He did so in spite of the fact that as early as February he had sensed that there was a whispering campaign against him in Munich and had written, 'I am surrounded by enemies and the intrigues of clerics.'[25] As if to illustrate that his constant talk of being beleaguered by enemies was not based on paranoia, he had hardly departed for Italy when, on 18 August, clerical circles openly attacked the *Political Annals* and Heine personally. In a virulent article in the literary review *Eos*, a leading Jesuit padre, Ignaz Döllinger, besides accusing Heine of blaspheming against the Holy

Virgin in his writings, took issue with his notion that 'all men were born equally noble'. Derisively he wondered aloud what Heine stood to gain 'by the general baronization of the whole human species from Hottentots to Europe's monarchic families', considering that 'his own pedigree goes back straight to Abraham and is understandably much older than that of the first Baron of Christianity.'[26]

From Bagni di Lucca, Heine informed various correspondents that he was 'taking the baths, chatting with pretty women, climbing the Apennines and committing a thousand follies. The mountain air makes one forget one's small worries and sorrows, and the soul expands.' Although he did not speak the language – 'I see Italy, but I cannot hear it' – he observed to Schenk that the country spoke to him through its 'broken Roman columns, crumbling Lombard towers and Gothic pillars.' He knew Latin, and if at night he pretended to converse with the ghosts of the ancients, he found the living Italians with their 'operatic speech' to be most amiable people. 'There is, too, a language which is understood by half of humankind from Lapland to Japan.' The eyes of Italian women, he went on in a high mood, 'speak more eloquently than a Demosthenes or Cicero.'[27]

He planned a longish stay in Italy, but his intention to return to Munich was not affected by the *Eos* attack on him. A letter of 6 September to Moser mentioned his hatred of the clergy and declared the need to be 'one-sided' and partisan. He was the same Heine who had told Varnhagen the previous year that his *Book of LeGrand* had to be written because 'in this servile epoch something had to be done.' In his *English Fragments*, remarking that the printing press and gunpowder had broken the joint 'spiritual and mundane' hegemony of the church and the feudal aristocracy, he had proclaimed 'freedom' to be the 'new religion, the religion of our age'. Now, in the first section of his Italian impressions, *Journey from Munich to Genoa*, written at Bagni di Lucca and throughout the month of October in Florence (to be serialized while he was still in Italy in Cotta's *Morning Chronicle for the Educated Classes* and later to go into *Travel Pictures* III), he was about to announce the age of ideologies and supra-national party strife.

'We are on the battlefield of Marengo.' With this phrase Heine set the stage for his famous series of reflections on the post-Napoleonic era, beginning with the prospect that world history, instead of being moved by the material interests of rapacious princes, might now become 'a history of minds'. He went on: 'Nationalism, with its vanity and its hatred, has become worn and brittle.' Foolish national prejudices and sharp particularities were becoming more and more submerged 'in the universality of European civilization. There are no more nations in Europe, only parties, and it is marvellous to see how well these, despite their great diversity of colours, recognize one another and how well, despite the numerous differences of language, they get on together.'

It was in Italy that Heine, momentarily free of the petty cares and manoeuvres that made up his daily life in Germany, developed the European, indeed, universalist outlook which two years earlier he had mentioned to Varnhagen was his aspiration. The battlefield of Marengo, whether Heine actually visited the scene or invented it, provided him with a suitable setting not only for moderating his previous 'hosannas' to Napoleon and taking a more balanced view of him, but for proclaiming the aims of the new epoch in history.

'What is the great task of our age? It is emancipation. The emancipation... not only of the Irish, the Greeks, the Jews of Frankfurt, the Blacks and the West Indies... but the emancipation of the whole world.' Although Europe had come of age and was 'wrenching itself free from the iron leading-strings of the privileged aristocracy', Heine was under no delusion that it would take a long time 'before the great feast of emancipation can be celebrated' and that meanwhile the age of 'intellectual interests' and conflicting ideologies would be one of struggle.

The dead buried on the battlefield reminded him that 'every inch in the advance of mankind is achieved at the price of rivers of blood... Every human individual is a world that is born and dies with him; beneath each tombstone lies a history of the world. That is what the dead would tell us.' But the 'war for the liberation of mankind' would give life to future generations of 'men born without fetters' and to a world of ideas and feelings 'which we who are slaves cannot even imagine'; and he proclaimed his faith in the ultimate victory of freedom over all world evils. 'Each age has its task, and by accomplishing it advances mankind.' Addressing posterity, he went on:

> Do not laugh when you read this. Each generation believes that its struggle is the most important of all... and we, too, living and dying for the religion of freedom... believe that ours is the most vital struggle ever fought on this earth, even if historic premonition tells us that our grandchildren may look down on it with the same indifference as ours towards the first men who had to fight similarly rapacious aboriginal monsters, flying serpents and giant predators.

On 11 November 1828, together with the manuscript of *Journey from Munich to Genoa*, Heine sent Cotta, at the latter's request, his suggestions for revamping the *Political Annals*, which Cotta had suspended on the termination of Heine's contract in July, but meant to reissue in January. Once again Heine was chiefly to lend his name to the monthly and he suggested Gustav Kolb, one of the most experienced and staunchest liberal journalists working for Cotta's publications,

281

as his preferred co-editor. To Kolb he wrote on the same day that 'at this time of struggle between ideas, journals are our fortresses.' Heine, in short, anticipated the importance of public opinion in Germany, where it had yet to emerge. In the 'rejuvenated' *Political Annals* he intended to give 'the liberal conscience' a suitable organ. He proposed as its motto the phrase from his Italian impressions: 'There are no more nations in Europe, only parties.'

A few days after this, he suffered a series of blows. In mid-November he learned that his long-expected professorship had been rejected by the Bavarian King, Munich's clerical circles having prevailed over Schenk's and Cotta's influence. By 24 November the news that his father's health was rapidly failing put an end to his stay in the beautiful land 'where the lemons blossom' and he set out on his journey home. The historian Ranke, who met Heine during a stopover in Venice at the end of November, wrote to Varnhagen that he looked like a man driven by some strange premonition. Travelling via Verona, Trent and Innsbruck, Heine reached Munich on or about 11 December, only to learn from Cotta that the *Political Annals* would not be resumed.

His parents had recently moved to Hamburg, and he was on his way there when, at Würzburg, the news of his father's death caught up with him. Heine stayed for 6 weeks with his mother and in February 1829 moved to Berlin, where as late as March Rahel Varnhagen noted in a letter that he looked 'completely devastated by his father's death. Not everyone takes it so hard: e.g., his siblings.' Heine loved his father, who 'thought less with his brain than with his heart', and he spoke to Rahel of the 'extraordinary harmony between him and this "splendid" father, who had perfectly understood him.'[28] Rahel, and to some extent Baron Cotta's wife, who happened to be in Berlin and was a great admirer of his, tried to relieve his melancholy. At the princely house of the banker Abraham Mendelssohn he met his 20-year-old son Felix and a few days later, together with Rahel Varnhagen, he attended the historic first performance – a century to the day since the last – of Bach's *St Matthew Passion*, resuscitated and conducted by Felix Mendelssohn.

At the Mendelssohns', Heine met some of Berlin's musical and intellectual personalities and had his portrait done by Felix's brother-in-law, Ludwig Hensel, who painted all the great figures of his time. In Munich, the previous year, Heine had made the rounds of the city's art galleries with Robert Schumann; now he made the acquaintance of Giacomo Meyerbeer, dined occasionally with the Varnhagens, the Cottas, the beautiful Friederike Robert, and Achim and Bettina von Arnim, and met Moser and other old friends.

But his father's death and the blow to his confident hopes of a professorship made him feel out of sorts amid all this socializing. Campe was pressing for more of his Italian impressions to put into *Travel Pictures* III, but Heine's nervous, distracted mood was not conducive to writing. He even quarreled with the Varnhagens – though not for long – but at last, in the third week of April, he took himself in hand. Retreating to Potsdam, to live 'like a lonely Robinson [Crusoe] on his island', he began to write *The Baths of Lucca*. 'Ill and miserable as I feel, I am, as though in self-derision, engaged in describing the happiest time of my life,' he wrote to Friederike Robert on 30 May, referring to the exuberance he had felt in the intoxicating air of the Apennines, which encouraged wild, heroic dreams. 'But how meek and tame I have become since the death of my father! Now I would like to be a little cat cuddling up by some fireplace...' In September 1830 Varnhagen wrote to Heine that Alexander Humboldt, Prussia's enlightened elder statesman and royal adviser, as well as Prince Pückler-Muskau – another liberal who, when not abroad, had access to the court of the reactionary King Friedrich Wilhelm III – thought highly of him. Unknown to Heine, Friedrich von Gentz, Metternich's right-hand man and 'Secretary of Europe' since the Vienna Congress, was about the same time praising him in two letters to his old friend Rahel Varnhagen, which on 5 November led her husband to report to Heine: 'I am able to announce to you a magic and perhaps unprecedented miracle. The famous Herr von Gentz, whose political views you are familiar with but who in spite of these aberrations is our dear friend, always has your songs on his desk, before his eyes, on his lips, in his memory, and is completely under your spell, although he hardly approves any of your political ideas.' All this was most flattering at a time when Heine was under attack from all sides, and indeed he showed Campe one of Gentz's letters to the Varnhagens.[29]

But Gentz was one of the godfathers of the thought-control system that censored his books; Humboldt 'greatly praised' Heine only in the privacy of his circle of intimates; and in the case of Pückler-Muskau, Varnhagen thought it prudent not to mention his name. Instead he identified him as the author of *Letters from a Dead Man* (*Briefe eines Verstorbenen*) and quoted from a letter in which this highly sophisticated and cosmopolitan prince, declaring his great admiration for Heine's talent and wit, acutely observed that 'in spite of his occasional lack of tact... a man capable of writing such moving poetry cannot be all that malicious,' and further stated that he subscribed to Heine's 'political principles and his views on religion.'

Other than such highly placed sympathizers as Humboldt and Pückler-Muskau, not to mention the countless Berlin celebrities with whom he was acquainted, Heine also had closer friends in various places. In Hamburg there was Friedrich Merckel, to whom he had dedicated *Travel Pictures* I. A businessman with a penchant for literature, Merckel regularly smoothed rough edges in Heine's dealings with Campe and also diligently helped to prepare his manuscripts for the press. At Magdeburg there was Immermann, for whom Heine did an unusual service in March 1830. Taking time off from his troubles to revise minutely Immermann's satirical epic *Tulifäntchen*, he spent long hours on a letter of many pages, containing his suggestions for improving its rhythm and metrics, along with the explanatory notes. This 'remarkable and unique' literary document, as Sammons has called it, showing 'the artist Heine still intact and functioning' in the midst of his political writings,[30] also reveals the less-known kindness of his nature, hidden by the foil of his public cynicism. And there were the transitory or enduring friendships he had formed with such radical or moderate liberal writers, publicists and newspaper editors as Börne, Kolb, Johann Detmold (later to become a reactionary Minister of Justice), Wolfgang Menzel, August Lewald and others too numerous to mention.

But politically Heine stood exposed and alone. Of all his potential comrades-in-arms, Varnhagen was practically the only one publicly to extend him support of a sort at a time when he needed it. If, as mentioned before, he sometimes appeared to be an army complete unto himself moving all over the field, it was not only, as he claimed, because of the circumstances forced on him by 'the struggle of the age' – an age presided over with pious mumbo-jumbo by some of undemocratic Europe's mightiest monarchs – but because the pressures of fighting the formidable array of public servants, police apparatus, press, theatre and university supervisors at their disposal brought out a rebellious side of his nature which made him clash and fight on some fronts and issues that a less complicated character would not have wasted his energy and ammunition on

'Can you lend me ten louis d'ors?' Heine asked Merckel on 4 June. His *Travel Pictures* I was about to go into a second edition in July, but although he was constantly writing and publishing, and in addition to his fees from Campe had been allowed by Baron Cotta to draw a certain amount against future work for his newspapers, it was not the first time that he was without money since he had fallen out with Uncle Salomon. Thus, on 18 May 1829, during his retreat to solitude in Potsdam, he had appealed to Moser to send him 40 Thaler immediately, 'otherwise I shall starve to death here.' With the money lent him by Moser he had gone to Helgoland and completed *The Baths of Lucca* there.

Now he was out of pocket again. He promised Merckel to return the money in a fortnight, and at the end of June, feeling the need to restore his nerves by the seaside, left for Helgoland again. 'Where shall I find a resting-place?' he wondered in a letter from the island to his one-time fellow-student, Friedrich Steinmann. Nine years after his ouster from Göttingen University and its *Burschenschaft* – when he had asked Steinmann, 'Where shall I go now?' – he found himself similarly adrift, homeless and disoriented. He wrote to Steinmann that he was 'tired of this guerilla war' with the censorship and the people in power. Reflecting on the irony of the fact that he, who was built for a contemplative life, should have become a political militant breaking his head about 'the problems of the age', he wondered what he had achieved by disturbing the comfort of his countrymen and his vain attempt to arouse that giant 'fool of a German people from his thousand-year-long slumber... He opens his eyes for an instant, but relapses into sleep; he yawns, only to snore all the louder within the minute.' He summed up his personal dilemma: 'In Germany I cannot remain. I have a choice between France, England, Italy and North America.'

10

The July Revolution: Saint-Simon, Fourier and Buonarroti

'We are dancing on a volcano,' remarked Count Achille de Salvandy, a French writer and future Minister of Education, in the course of a grand ball on the night of 31 May 1830. Louis-Philippe, Duke of Orléans, was entertaining the Court of France, led by King Charles X, while allegedly privy, if not actively engaged in, a conspiracy to overthrow him. Charles X, formerly Count of Artois and a brother of the executed Louis XVI, was the second occupant of the throne since its restoration to the Bourbons after Napoleon's fall.

Louis-Philippe's father, 'Philippe Egalité', in committing the 'treachery' of voting for the execution of his cousin Louis XVI, had hardly improved the longexisting strain between the Bourbon family and its younger Orléans branch. Nevertheless, in the midst of the Napoleonic wars, Louis-Philippe, the present Duke, after much diplomacy and a complicated courtship, had managed to marry a Bourbon princess. Marie-Amélie, who became his wife at Palermo in 1809, was a daughter of Ferdinand IV, King of the Two Sicilies, brother to the Bourbon king of Spain and a linear descendant of the 'Sun King'. The match was all the more remarkable at the time as Marie-Amélie's formidable mother happened to be a sister of the executed Marie Antoinette, and had been doubly mistrustful of Louis-Philippe as the son of a 'regicide'.

Louis-Philippe's ball was given in honour of his brother-in-law, Francis II, who had succeeded Ferdinand IV and was on a state visit to Paris. It was a memorable affair not only because of the presence of so many Bourbons, headed by the King of France, but because France was in the throes of a political crisis. The King's chief Minister, Polignac – a so-called Ultra-Royalist whom he had appointed in defiance of the Chamber of Deputies – had been defeated in a vote. Now the victorious opposition was demanding that the King appoint a more representative government, actually petitioning him for it, which was all that the Constitutional Charter granted by the restored Bourbons allowed it to do.

Forty years after the French Revolution had proclaimed the 'sovereignty of the people', the Chamber represented a privileged and exclusive minority of some 100,000 voters in a nation of 25 million. Charles's brother, Louis XVIII, who had originally promulgated the Charter as his 'gift' to the nation in 1814, had left some of the Revolution's achievements untouched. Charles X, who succeeded him in 1824, was a more ingrained absolutist. In the 6 years since he had anointed himself in a medieval ceremony at Reims Cathedral, he had suppressed press freedom and antagonized liberals by a *loi de sacrilège* which imposed the death sentence on the theft of church objects and a whole series of allegedly anti-religious offences. This, protested the duc de Broglie, 'not in 1204, on the eve of the Crusade urged by Pope Innocent III against the Albigensians, or in 1572... but in the 19th century, in a free country where freedom of worship is universally acknowledged.'

The King had further decided to pay an indemnity of a thousand million francs – the so-called *milliard des émigrés* – to returned noblemen for property confiscated during the Revolution. The bourgeoisie, who lost some of the interest on their government bonds – which was reduced in order to raise the funds for the indemnity – were not alone in resenting this bonus to the aristocracy. Except for its beneficiaries, the indemnity and the Law of Sacrilege between them defeated all that had been achieved in 'forty years of hard work and misery' since the Great Revolution; and as though to illustrate that the clock had indeed been turned back to the days of the *ancien régime*, Charles X had reinstated its full protocol and court etiquette.

Marie Antoinette's former dancing master, M. Abraham, who had been out of a job for 25 years, was back on the scene in his jabot with lacy frills, instructing aristocratic young ladies about to be presented at court in the rigorous intricacies of this etiquette. The young comtesse d'Agoult, whose wedding in 1827 was attended by Charles X and the entire Court of France, practised with M. Abraham the three equidistant curtseys she would have to make at court while moving from the gallery towards the King and his gentlemen before he rose and acknowledged her; Madame d'Agoult – whom Karl Marx, by a curious chain of circumstances, was later to meet in Paris – rehearsed for long hours the art of kicking back the long train of the white velvet coat she was to wear over her tulle dress by means of elegant little foot tricks.

Charles X, who was 73 years old in 1830, was a dignified figure. But he was rigid in his views and, making up in obstinacy for what he lacked in sagacity, steadfastly refused to accede to the petition of the parliamentary majority and give up any of his rights under the Charter as he interpreted it. Aloof from his people, he misread their feelings and the signs of the times. Three months before the ball at the Palais Royal, French society had received a cultural shock in the famous 'battle' over Victor Hugo's *Hernani*. Though ostensibly a non-political theatre revolution, it was to have wider consequences and was actually a presage of events in the offing.

The play was written in 28 days and produced in that very fortress of classicism, the Théâtre Français, on 25 February, after 5 months of preparations and newspaper controversy. The interval had permitted Hugo's young friend Théophile Gautier to mobilize a claque of 400 art students from the Quartier Latin. Shaggy-haired, greasy, demonstratively dressed in Spanish cloaks, Robespierre waistcoats and Rubens hats or Henry III caps, and armed with clubs, they had entered the cavernous dark hall early in the afternoon, ready to fight in the cause of youth, Romanticism and 'liberty'.

Strategically disposing themselves about its 1,500 seats, they picnicked while they waited during the long afternoon. As the cloakrooms were locked, some relieved themselves in dark corners, and there was scandal from the moment the lights went on and the stunned bourgeois audience filed in, 'the ladies picking up their satin-shod feet in disgust, their nostrils further offended by the pervasive smell of garlic sausage' and other odours.[1]

Balzac, Dumas, Sainte-Beuve, Stendhal, Prosper Merimée and the entire Romantic young guard were present, Gautier's 'red' (actually rose-coloured) satin doublet, green trousers, black coat and wide hat standing out among all the bohemian garb. Fought amidst uproar, catcalls, jeers and hisses night after night, with the aggressive 'barbarians' and libertarians of *la jeune France* (and the performance by Mademoiselle Mars) finally triumphing over the 'classicists' who had dominated the theatre for two centuries, *Hernani* unleashed passions and emotions which were like a barometric indication that the dynamics of revolution were at work.

'I can understand the furies of 1793', Alfred de Vigny wrote after witnessing the rage provoked by *Hernani*. Charles X, to the extent that he was at all aware of what was happening, was all the more determined to resist the need for change. A fortnight before he was to attend Louis-Philippe's ball, he had peremptorily dissolved the Chamber, fearing that once he yielded to the misguided deputies and the republican newspapers, and gave up his right to choose his ministers, he would lose all. 'When a king is threatened', he told a Court gathering, 'he has no choice but to mount his horse' and fight or else he would 'find himself in a tumbril', transported to the guillotine like his brother Louis XVI.

Ghosts of the French Revolution thus haunted the night of 31 May 1830. Louis-Philippe's receptions and dinners were known for the brilliance and diversity of the company attending them. This time, too, the splendidly illuminated salons of the Palais Royal were filled with politicians of every shade of opinion, along with courtiers, distinguished artists and society leaders with their dressedup ladies. Louis-Philippe was always careful to behave with 'model propriety' towards Charles X but the King, after his formal entry between two lines of Guards, was not too pleased to espy the leaders of the opposition among the company – men like the bankers Jacques Lafitte and Casimir Périer; François Guizot and Royer-Collard, leaders of the so-called 'doctrinaire' partisans of a constitutional monarchy; Adolphe Thiers, who had recently started a radical newspaper, *Le National*, with the express intention of overthrowing Charles; the brothers Bertin, publishers of the *Journal des Débats*, and various deputies who were only moderate royalists or outright republicans.

Adolphe Thiers, a 33-year-old lawyer, journalist and historian, short of stature but not of ambition, is said to have obtained the funds for starting *Le National* from Talleyrand. He and Guizot, a 43-year-old professor of history of Huguenot origin and narrow conservative views, were indeed to become the key figures in French politics in the new 'bourgeois' monarchy of Louis-Philippe of Orléans, which replaced that of Charles.

At a certain point during the ball, Charles walked out onto a terrace. The huge, magnificently festooned and lit-up gardens of the Palais Royal were black with idle Parisians. Sniffing the north wind, Charles remarked, 'Gentlemen, the weather is fine for my fleet at Algiers!' The King, who had set new elections, felt sure that the imminent conquest of Algiers would turn public opinion in his favour and help him to weather the crisis. But when he inclined his head to the crowd below, not a single *Vive le roi* was heard. Instead, there were cries of *Vive le duc d'Orléans!*

Upstairs at 1 a.m., a festive supper was served. Two military bands played, and dancing, gambling and conversation went on till 5 o'clock. Charles, however, though preserving an unruffled countenance, had indicated his displeasure by making his royal exit a full hour before midnight. The comtesse de Boigne found it scandalous on Louis-Philippe's part to have invited 'persons most disagreeable to the King' and, moreover, to have thrown the gardens and courtyard wide open to 'the multitude' at a time when popular discontent 'with the Sovereign was no secret to anyone.'[2]

At such times, or whenever the reigning Bourbons seemed in danger of running out of an heir, the name of the head of the junior Orléans branch always sprang to mind as an 'available' aspirant to the throne. The antagonism between the two branches went back to the days when Louis XIV had suspected his Orléans nephew, Philippe Regent, of plotting to murder the rightful heir; and had more recently been fanned by the behaviour of Louis-Philippe's eccentric father.

Now, on this springtime night in 1830, history seemed to be on the verge of repeating itself. While Louis-Philippe's ball went on upstairs, the ghosts haunting the Palais Royal suddenly ceased to be metaphoric as a swelling mob of unemployed or idle workers and other dissatisfied Parisians began to riot in the gardens below, tore the lanterns from the trees and set fire to chairs and benches amid shouts of 'Down with the king! *Vive le duc d'Orléans.*'

For weeks, Paris had been buzzing with rumours of some conspiracy to dethrone the King. Courtiers and politicians at the ball kept watching each other. Comtesse d'Agoult later recalled that in one of the embrasures of the terrace 'the Duke of Orléans and his sister, Madame Adelaïde, talked at great length' to the men who were to take over power. The duke's Ultra-Royalist enemies suspected that his admitting 'the multitude' into the gardens as well as the troops on hand – who eventually put an end to the rioting – were all part of a deliberate design to show off his popularity and at the same time provide himself with an alibi. They found such scheming at a royal fête vulgar and inexcusable. Even those who ascribed no such evil intention to the Orléanist clique had a feeling of tension and 'Sicilian' knives in the fragrant air.

At the height of the festivities, the duchesse de Berry, the Naples-born daughter of the visiting Francis II of Sicily, joined a circle of 30 high-born ladies in a swirling dance. Watching the lively Duchess leading them in a fast tarantella, the comte de Salvandy was moved to exclaim: 'What a beautiful Neapolitan night!' Then he added the famous comment, almost as an after-thought: 'And just as in Naples, we are dancing on a volcano.' Louis-Philippe's quoted reply was that he had done his best to try and 'open the king's eyes' to the fact that the world had changed and that all the country wanted was a consti-tutional monarchy. But he threw up his hands: 'nobody listens, and God alone knows where all this will lead us in the end.'[3]

Salvandy's *mot* made the rounds of Paris and established the count's reputa-tion as forecaster of the July Revolution, in the final act of which Louis-Philippe was indeed to be installed on the throne of his cousin Charles X.

Many years earlier, when he was about 19, Louis-Philippe, after saving a man from drowning and receiving a public award for it, had written: 'I was born under a lucky star. Opportunities offer and I have only to profit by them.' He was at that time fighting on the side of the Revolution. Shortly afterwards Danton had advised him ito 'preserve' himself for the day when France would come to her senses and might wish to install an Orléans at the head of a reformed type of monarchy.

After that day, soon followed by his father's execution, Louis-Philippe had known 21 years of exile. While France went through the convulsions of the Ter-ror, the Directory, the Consulate and the Napoleonic wars, the new Duke of Orléans had wandered about the face of the world, using altogether 10 different aliases. Faced with critical decisions at every change of regime in France, he had had the good sense to hedge a promise of support for the surviving Bourbons by making it conditional on a constitutional monarchy; at the same time, swallowing his pride, he had united with them when the common menace of Napoleon became overpowering, and had even married a daughter of their Spanish branch.

After Napoleon's fall, and for another 15 years under the Restoration, he had carefully refrained from any public criticism of either Louis XVIII or Charles X. As Chateaubriand contemptuously put it, 'he never said anything significant or worth reporting' at the Tuileries. In fact, he had managed his relations with the Bourbons so carefully that, in addition to the return of the huge Orléans estates, he had received the largest single share of the *milliard des émigrés*. It was with this money that he had restored the Palais Royal to its former splendour, and gradually turned it into a rallying point for the opposition. In short, by steering a prudent course for 40 years and avoiding any commitment to extremes, Louis-Philippe had emerged not only as one of the great 'survival artists' of a tumultuous epoch but also as the richest man in France.

When, at the end of July 1830, two months after the ball in the Palais Royal, the populace of Paris went on a three-day rampage, Charles X chose to abdicate in his own and his son's name. Before leaving for England on 2 August, he appointed Louis-Philippe Lieutenant-General, but expressly charged him to proclaim his 10-year-old grandson and heir 'as King under the name of Henri V', and to act as regent during the boy's minority. Louis-Philippe thereupon crowned 40 years of 'luck' and delicate manoeuvering by announcing the abdication; but he failed to proclaim the succession of Henri V, seizing instead the opportunity of himself occupying the throne left vacant by the abdication.

The new 'bourgeois' king who mounted the throne at the age of 57 was a highly intelligent and courageous man of practical virtues. To mark his accession by 'popular will' and the end of the Bourbon era, Louis-Philippe revised the Constitutional Charter in a sense that no longer made it a royal 'gift' to the people but placed it above the crown; a further revision abolished Roman Catholicism as the state religion and guaranteed freedom of the press. Louis-Philippe also agreed to style himself not King of France, but 'King of the French', and reinstated the tricolour French flag as a symbolic link to the Revolution of 1789.

In 1831 Eugène Delacroix exhibited his painting of a bare-bosomed woman storming the barricades with a rifle in one hand and the tricolour raised aloft in the other. The vitality and élan of this figure of *Liberty Leading the People*, the latter represented by a band of typical Parisians, the strong colours and the sense of drama conveyed by the bodies of the fallen at their feet, caught the poetic symbolism of the July Revolution as the people's victory over absolutism. But the July Revolution, which in three days of popular rioting, street barricades and some rifle fire had installed Louis-Philippe on the French throne, was not only a political one.

Delacroix's canvases, the dramas of Victor Hugo and Alexandre Dumas, Alfred de Musset's and Vigny's poetry, the novels of George Sand, the symphonies of Berlioz and Franz Liszt's and Chopin's music and piano interpretations set the Romantic mood in France from the very start of Louis-Philippe's monarchy. There was a ferment of new ideas, and a change of mores. The old Royalist salons which had been revived under the Restoration continued to function. The chair-ridden and diabetic princesse de la Trémoille, whose library, food, gambling tables and political connections were superior to anyone else's, went on presiding for a time over court-like soirées attended by the prince de Polignac – the fallen Prime Minister – and the Cardinal of Paris, at which aristocratic figures deprived of power and their court positions referred to Louis-Philippe and his new ministers as 'ces gens-là'. Though the salons of some of these entrenched dowagers soon vanished through the death of their hostesses, others, like those of the marquise de Montcalm – sister of the duc de Richelieu – and the comtesses de Castellane and de Chastenais, gradually opened their doors to leading personalities of the new monarchy and to rising intellectuals and artists. Following the success of Hugo's plays, even some ducal hostesses – who had hitherto admitted men of letters only if they were members of the Académie or particularly brilliant conversationalists – began to vie with one another for the company of Hugo, Dumas, the critic Sainte-Beuve, Alfred de Vigny, and Musset. Literary and artistic creators, eccentric, rebellious, bohemian, capable of arousing volcanic passions, stirring theatre audiences or affording vistas of beauty and insights into worlds undreamt-of, suddenly became social lions and practically demi-gods.[4]

The poets, writers and Romantic young artists of that generation, whose revolt against 18th-century formalism gradually turned against the grey dullness of the new bourgeois society, saw themselves as the 'priests', 'apostles' and 'prophets' of a new annunciation. They were, as Victor Hugo unhesitatingly put it, 'the Lord's elect', the bearers of a 'majestic authority no longer dependent on either kings or the great of this earth.'

For a time, the Romantic young artists acted in that rare spirit of comradeship which had united them almost like a band of 'conspirators' in the battle of *Hernani*. Gautier wrote poems addressed to Hugo and helped Balzac write some of his plays; Hugo and Sainte-Beuve, before jealousy over Hugo's wife divided them, wrote poems to each other; Hugo also dedicated verses to Lamartine, Louis Boulanger and the sculptor David d'Angers; Sainte-Beuve corrected George Sand's manuscripts and polished her style; Musset wrote sonnets defending Alfred de Vigny's play *Chatterton* against its conservative critics; Hugo refused a royal invitation to Versailles unless Dumas also was invited; and Delacroix, who was himself musically talented, installed a Pleyel piano in his studio to paint his friend Chopin with George Sand listening spell-bound.

Although this enthusiastic fraternity was not to last, or not among all of them, they all esteemed each other's talents, and there are few instances in literary history comparable to the 72-page article in which Balzac drew attention to the work of Stendhal, paying tribute to a rival genius who was ignored by the critics and had resigned himself to writing for 'the happy few'.

One evening shortly after the July Revolution, while Hugo was writing his *Journal d'un révolutionnaire de 1830*, his confessor, the Abbe Félicité de Lamennais, dropped in on him. An unprepossessing Breton priest, Lamennais that year had started publishing a newpaper *L'Avenir*. The paper's motto was 'God and Liberty', and the radical abbé advocated the separation of church and state. Hugo read him a passage he had just written in his *Journal* forecasting the crumbling of Europe's monarchies and expressing his conviction that 'within a century' they would all be replaced by republics. 'You place the republic into the future', Lamennais objected, 'while we should have it now.' Condemned by Pope Gregory XVI in a special encyclical, Lamennais in 1834 published *Paroles d'un croyant*, a book (soon banned by the Vatican) which shocked public opinion by attacking the Papacy and asserting, in the name of religion, the sovereignty of the people. *Paroles d'un croyant*, stressing the abbé's profession of faith in Christian 'love and brotherhood', gave a religious legitimacy of sorts to early Socialist militancy by calling on 'all sons of the same God' to break the chains of 'slavery' and create a world in which there were neither poor nor rich.

Signalling his break with the Church, the book made Lamennais the bane of the clergy – he was indeed to be excommunicated – but it also made the awkward priest with his struggling conscience an uncomfortable hero of several political salons, lionized by liberals and fashionable hostesses. His book was to run to more than 100 editions and to be translated into practically every European language.

The workers who had taken to the streets in 1830 regarded themselves as the true heroes of the July Revolution, and felt cheated afterwards. France's old-fashioned, derelict factory buildings and small workshops were no more prepared for the industrial boom of the 1830s and '40s than her manufacturers and employers, who reduced wages at the slightest sign of competition or crisis. Men, women and children worked 14 hours a day in appalling conditions and lived in crowded dark cellars, sometimes in a single room. It was calculated that half of the new-born children died before the age of 15 months. There was no social legislation, and the workers in the new industrial centres came to be known as 'white negroes' to denote that they were worse off than the black people in the colonies who could at least breathe fresh air and see the sky, sun and trees.

For a time even Hugo, a liberal in all his majestic bearing but inclined towards religion, saw the only salvation in Socialism – 'Romanticism and Socialism are the same', he declared – though he had in mind a certain type of Christian Socialism.

Two men – Count Henri de Saint-Simon, the prophet of the industrial age, and Charles Fourier, who foresaw the ills that age would breed – were largely responsible for the fact that the July Revolution was not only a political one but a social, intellectual and literary one as well. The 19th century was barely begun, and Hegel had yet to discern in a flash of sunrise 'the form and structure of the new world', when these two so-called 'prophets of Paris' had announced their futurist, though conflicting, visions of a new social order, a new society adapted to the needs and possibilities of the century of industrial and economic progress.

As early as 1803, Saint-Simon, convinced on the basis of certain observations he had made in America that the future belonged to the 'science of production', had come up with a startling plan to place Europe's affairs in the hands of a 'Council of Newton'. More than two-thirds of France's population were still peasants and mostly illiterate when he proposed that 21 leading scientists, captains of industry, bankers and creative artists, to be elected from among the most outstanding in such advanced countries as England, France, Germany and Italy, were to prepare the peaceful exploitation of Europe's 'productive' resources in the age of technology, and to coordinate the rational organization of labour, supplies and distribution in a multi-national effort for the benefit and prosperity of all.

Also in 1803, Charles Fourier had proposed the introduction of a minimum wage in France. By 1815, about the time the great game of history played out between the siege of Moscow and the battle of Waterloo was ending in the Congress of Vienna, Saint-Simon – 130 years before the formation of the European Economic Community – was launching his plan for the unification of Europe into a single political and economic entity. By then, Fourier had for 7 years been propagating his own, different system for establishing 'universal harmony'. Both he and Saint-Simon, raising issues that, together with the struggle between liberalism and reaction, were to divide Europe for the next 50 years, went unheeded, but towards the end of the 1820s their ideas were to inspire not only Heine but early Socialists and Romantic young artists and intellectuals in

France, Belgium, Germany and Russia. Eventually they were to come down to Marx.

A third important figure in the intrigues of this period was Buonarroti – ranked as 'the greatest conspirator of this [19th] century' by no less a master of the art than Bakunin – in whose career, during and since the revolt of 'the Equals', future theorists of subversion, philosophers of social revolution and professional heroes of 'the deed' were to find much to study and emulate. All three men had been born in the Age of Reason, had lived through the French Revolution and the bloodletting of the Napoleonic era. But whereas Saint-Simon and Fourier concluded at an early stage that neither the Revolution nor Napoleon's wars of conquest had solved any of man's real problems – feeling, on the contrary, that all they had produced was one terribly long crisis, a chaotic period of travail towards a new world to be organized on new, sensible and peaceful lines – Buonarroti had come through these upheavals as a living symbol of the spirit that had brought down the Bastille and became the first practical theorist of a Communist society to be established by force.

Few men had led a more extraordinary life than Count Claude-Henri Rouvroy de Saint-Simon, scion of a ducal family claiming descent from Charlemagne and self-styled 'genius'. Born in 1760, a great-nephew of the famous duc de Saint-Simon whose memoirs contain a treasure of information on life at Versailles under Louis XIV, young Henri was a rebellious spirit and at 13 refused his first communion. His wealthy father, a brigadier in the king's army and governor of Senlis, was an enlightened man who saw to it that his bright boy got a wide-ranging education supervised by the philosopher and mathematician d'Alembert, the editor (with Diderot) of the vast *Encyclopédie*, which summarized all human knowledge on the eve of the French Revolution. Before joining the army, as was the tradition of his class, Henri de Saint-Simon also made the acquaintance of Rousseau. In 1777, at the age of 17, he was commissioned a Second Lieutenant.

Two years later he sailed from France to fight under La Fayette and George Washington in the American War of Independence. The enterprising young man – who at home used to have his valet wake him every morning with the words, 'Time to get up, monsieur le comte. Remember, you have great things to accomplish' – distinguished himself in the siege of York and the capture of Brinston Hill, following which Washington made him a member of the Society of Cincinnatus. Transferred as a gunnery captain to the flagship of Admiral de Grasse in the West Indies, he took part in 9 naval engagements before De Grasse surrendered to England's Admiral Rodney in April 1782.

Taken prisoner, interned in Jamaica, and released in the same year, Saint-Simon proposed to the Spanish viceroy of Mexico the construction of a canal to connect the Pacific with the Atlantic through Lake Nicaragua. One thing that had impressed itself on his young mind was that Americans were a nation of *producers*. Everyone in the New World *worked*, there was no leisured class as in static, feudal Europe. This observation led Saint-Simon to the conclusion that the future of European society, if not mankind, lay in the industrial exploitation of nature: 'Industry is the sole guarantee of society's existence, the unique source of its wealth and prosperity.' The idea behind his Pacific-Atlantic canal project was that fast, improved communications would promote industrial expansion. But the Mexican viceroy – like the King of Spain, to whom, after his return to France and resignation from the army in 1788 with the rank of colonel, he submitted plans for linking Madrid to the sea – remained unimpressed.

The fall of the Bastille in 1789 did not surprise Saint-Simon, feeling as he had for some time that the *ancien régime* was doomed. Requesting a 'republican baptism', 'citizen Claude-Henri de Saint-Simon, ex-noble' handed over the parchments and insignia of the Cincinnatus Society, his Cross of Malta and other decorations, and changed his name to Claude-Henri Bonhomme, 'worker'. He became a *sans-culotte* and for a time commanded the National Guard near his estate in Picardy. The Prussian Ambassador to Madrid, Von Redern, had entrusted him with half a million francs to invest in French securities. Saint-Simon used the money to buy, under false names and with small down-payments, a large number of the confiscated estates and church lands which were put up for sale. By December 1793 his extensive real estate speculations – including a bid, in which Talleyrand is said to have been involved, to purchase the lead of the roof structure of Notre Dame – landed him in the Luxembourg prison on orders from Robespierre's Committee of Public Safety.

While in the Luxembourg, that 'antechamber of death', he had a dream in which his ancestor Charlemagne assured him, 'Your success as a philosopher will equal my political and military glory.' The dream spurred his aspiration, of which he had written to his father from America, 'to do scientific work useful to mankind'. First, however, on his release in October 1794, he recovered legal title to the vast properties he had bought in Paris and Neuilly. Making the deferred payments on these holdings in devalued paper money, he became a millionaire, installed himself like a *grand seigneur* near the Palais Royal, and during the Directory entertained bankers and speculators. At the same time he gave stipends to promising scientists, artists and other bright young men. Money was to Saint-Simon only a means. When his business associate, Von Redern, appeared in Paris and asked for an accounting of their affairs, Saint-Simon let him draw up the details dissolving their partnership and left him the major share of the fortune he had made.

Next, he set out to make good his 'passion for science and the public good'. He started methodically to make himself – and was indeed to become – a first-rank philosopher, historian and scientist, a pioneer sociologist and in the end the founder of virtually a new religion. Doing nothing by halves, he gave up his luxurious residence and moved into the vicinity of the new Ecole Polytechnique – in a small street that today bears his name – and there entertained the best-known savants of his time. In 1803, after studying mathematics, physics, biology and psychology, he divorced his wife – a literary lady whom he had married chiefly to increase the éclat of his dinner parties – and went to Switzerland, where he proposed marriage to Madame de Staël, with the idea that the union of their geniuses would produce a child prodigy beyond compare.

'We are likely to think of him as a little mad', Edmund Wilson wrote of him, 'till we observe that the other social idealists of this period were cranks of the same extravagant type.'[5] Yet mad and madder as his life will appear, that same year of 1803 Saint-Simon was making his proposal, in his first published work, *Letter of an Inhabitant of Geneva*, for a 'Council of Newton' to rule Europe and keep the peace. Government by primogeniture, divine right, apostolic succession, military might and political vagaries had failed. The French Revolution and Napoleon's conquests, far from preparing society for the age of technology and mechanical inventions, had between them plunged Europe into chaos. What was needed in the new century was government, or rather 'administration', by competent minds, scientists, mathematicians, manufacturers, capitalists and artists capable of planning, launching and propagating large-scale economic projects and industrial development. No one, needless to say, paid any attention to his bizarre ideas, and by 1805 Saint-Simon, with several careers behind him at 45, was broke.

For a few months the 'French Faust' – as he has been called for his urge to explore every sphere of man and the universe – worked as a poorly paid copyist, studying and writing by night. Then, in 1806, he met Diard – his former valet – who since leaving his service had become rich. Diard paid for the printing of Saint-Simon's *Introduction aux travaux scientifiques du XIX siècle*, in which he laid the foundations of sociology, and supported him for the next 4 years. After Diard's death, Saint-Simon, a peer of France by birth and heir to the title of grandee of Spain, was reduced to living on bread and water. For a short time, in 1813, down with fever and close to dying, he was interned in the madhouse of Charenton, where another inmate was the marquis de Sade. When he recovered, Saint-Simon renounced his inheritance and went on studying and writing on a small pension his family agreed to pay him in exchange.

Within the next two years, with the help of his 17-year-old secretary – Augustin Thierry, the future historian – he produced *De la réorganisation de la société européenne*, in which he outlined his master-plan for a united Europe. Saint-Simon envisaged a European Parliament, and true to his idea that communications were vital to industrial development, he contemplated building a continental network of roads and waterways linking the Rhine, Main and Danube with some of the rivers in Eastern Europe.

For all his utopian faith in reason and scientific progress as a cure-all, Saint-Simon realized that the unification of Europe would not happen overnight. He proposed, in the first instance, an Anglo-French Union, for Britain had a longer parliamentary experience than France, a plan of which at least one scholar has remarked that it anticipated by 125 years Churchill's June 1940 proposal for a Franco-British union which might have changed the course of World War II.[6] In 1815 Saint-Simon thought that the union of France and Britain should be gradually extended to include Germany and the rest of Europe's peoples in 'a single political body', while each was to retain its national independence.

Saint-Simon saw history as a succession of 'organic' epochs of social order and stability alternating with periods of crisis, breakdown and disintegration. He cited the Middle Ages as an example of an 'organic' epoch and held that after the 18th century had done away with all fundamental beliefs, the 19th, if properly organized, promised to be another creative and 'organic' epoch of universal cohesion. For this to happen, men alert to the needs of the age had to take over the role once performed by the clergy and warrior-knights. His reinterpretation of history was the first to stress the paramount importance of the *economic* factor, subordinating even politics. It was to culminate in his vision of a World Parliament, foreshadowing the United Nations.

In the world according to Saint-Simon, the means of production were to be placed in the hands of those capable of running and using them best for the common good. Society was to be reorganized along technocratic yet humanistically inspired lines. It would be technocratic in being run by an élite of scientists, bankers, manufacturers, thinkers and artists, a 'meritocracy of talent' supervising the pooling of all resources in a planned economy. As for the humanist aspect, by absorbing upcoming working-class talent and creating a world of plenty, the technocrats would alleviate the lot and ultimately assure the welfare of the 'most numerous and poorest class', i.e., the proletariat.

With the state actually reduced to a network of banks, and the captains of industry in charge of allocating credits to all forms of production, the new society – whether a republic, a monarchy or whatever – would only need to be administered, not governed. The state would hardly need police or military forces. Saint-Simon believed that all men had equal rights but not that they were equally talented. In his new society all individuals were to be given 'the fullest latitude for the development of their faculties', and to enjoy the 'highest degree of liberty compatible' with the general good. Geared to productivity, providing work for the able and assistance to the infirm, the state would satisfy everyone's needs, eliminating the causes of social unrest.

'To each according to his capacity, to each capacity according to its works' (*A chacun selon sa capacité, à chaque capacité selon ses oeuvres*) was the slogan Saint-Simon bequeathed to posterity. One conclusion of his historical analysis was that Europe had an abundance of unproductive property that fulfilled no social function morally justifying its owners. The French Revolution – catapulting the poorest and most ignorant class into power – had, in the name of democracy, 'legally instituted the most complete anarchy'. The whole political and social system needed to be overhauled and readjusted to the age of industry and technology. He was all for respecting property acquired by merit, but rose against 'the ignorance, superstition, laziness' and extravagance of politicians, ecclesiastics and society leaders, against a world ruled at the top by incompetent 'miscreants', while the great majority of working, productive people who made the wheels of the world go round were miserable have-nots, exploited by a small sector of 'rich idlers', incapable mediocrities and greedy 'general thieves'.

Saint-Simon was actually setting forth the theory of the class struggle. Little did he know, however (to quote Isaiah Berlin), 'to what application this part of his doctrine would one day be put'; indeed, Saint-Simon wanted no class war or revolution that would only result in more crises and anarchy. He put his faith in reason and education. Persuasion and sweet reasonableness were the chief and only weapons he had in mind for achieving a world of brotherhood, social justice and plenty.

'The Golden Age of mankind is not behind us, it is in front of us,' he wrote. 'It is in the perfection of the social order; our fathers have not seen it, our children will arrive there one day; it is for us to pave the way.'

With the collapse of Napoleon's empire, Saint-Simon's insistence that 'the whole of society rests on industry' and the role assigned to capitalist enterprise in his scheme could not but impress the French bourgeoisie, faced as it was with the aristocracy's push to recover vested positions of influence along with its huge estates.

By 1818, the year Marx was born, Saint-Simon was once more a society figure, on intimate terms with the 'textile king' Baron Ternaux, with Lafitte and several regents of the Banque de France, and frequenting the salons of leading industrialists and financiers – men of the very élite he deemed capable of creating a world of plenty based on 'productivity' and 'scientific' distribution in the best interest of mankind. With their help, and assisted by Auguste Comte – the budding 18-yearold philosopher of positivism who in 1817 had succeeded Thierry as his secretary – Saint-Simon was able to elaborate his ideas in a series of periodical publications titled *L'Industrie*, *La Politique* and *L'Organisateur*, extolling the merits of bourgeois enterprise. His rich financial backers, however, hardly subscribed to his notion that such enterprise must serve 'the greatest good of the greatest number' and aim at improving the lot of 'the poorest class'. Saint-Simon predicted that maintaining the old order would lead to civil war, a forecast that was to be fulfilled in the 1848 European free-for-all. He favoured the emancipation of women. They were to be full partners in the new society. By 1817, too, feeling that dogmatic religion had outlived its time – yet aware that man needed spiritual sustenance and a counterweight to the materialism of the industrial age – he was beginning to look for ways of de-theologizing Christianity and transforming it into a socially oriented religion.

Soon the breadth of Saint-Simon's vision became too much for his bourgeois supporters, who began to fear a confrontation with the Catholic Church; and a piece he published in *L'Organisateur* in November 1819 landed him in serious trouble. This was his famous 'Parabole', in which he brazenly proclaimed that if the King of France and all the princes, marshals, cardinals, bishops, priests, judges, government officials and high-born landowners – in short, 30,000 Frenchmen considered most important – were suddenly to perish, France would be aggrieved, but would 'suffer no political harm', because they could be easily replaced by other worthy courtiers, clerics and administrators, without damage to the French genius; whereas, if France suddenly lost 3,000 of her best physicists, mathematicians, physicians, surgeons, pharmacists, architects, shipbuilders, scholars and engineers, or for that matter, her foremost poets, painters, musicians and writers – 'the flower of French society' – then France would lose her prosperity, her place among the nations and her very 'soul' for at least a generation.

'Parabole' was Saint-Simon's way of appealing to King Louis XVIII to become France's 'First Industrialist', that is, to take the lead in creating and promoting the new century's 'Industrial Society'. It was his way of solving 'the frightful crisis involving the whole of Europe', of overhauling its political and social system, and adjusting the Continent to the industrial age without war or revolution and the resulting anarchy. But it was provocatively phrased, and the King was the wrong addressee for such visionary plans.

In February 1820, Louis XVIII's nephew, the duc de Berry – son of the future King Charles X – was assassinated. Saint-Simon, the humanist who envisioned a World Parliament and had spent a lifetime racking his fertile brain to devise a system eliminating national as well as class conflicts and abolishing the causes of violence, was charged with 'morally' instigating the crime. Profoundly humiliated, abandoned during his prosecution by the bourgeoisie and most of his other acquaintances, he emerged from the affair exculpated, but once more, at 60, a pauper. In 1823 he tried to shoot himself, but survived the attempt and spent the last two years of his life adding yet another dimension to his system by putting on paper his concept of a 'New Christianity' reformed and transmuted out of the old into a social religion. Invoking the social vision of the Old Testament prophets and fusing it with the brotherly love preached by the Early Christians, he wrote that – to suit the needs of modern man and the problems of the industrial age – the 'New Christianity' must declare all theology anathema and devote itself instead to the single purpose of improving the 'moral and material welfare of the most numerous and poorest class.'

Saint-Simon died in May 1825, after telling a small group of his disciples, 'My whole life may be summed up in one idea: to guarantee to all men the free development of their faculties.' His last recorded words were: 'The future belongs to us!'

His utopian vista of the development of the industrial world has indeed, at the end of the 20th century, become a reality largely dominated by supra-national scientists, multi-national corporations and technocratic administrators such as he proposed to place in charge of affairs. Artists, too, have largely become the world's trend-setters, opinion-makers and sometimes the directors ot public conscience and emotions; needless to say, though, the state's function has not been reduced to the extent he envisioned, nor does 'brotherly love' prevail.

Saint-Simon died confident of having offered 'enrichment to future generations' and thereby accomplished his life's endeavour. But as with every utopian vision, new philosophy, system or doctrine, let alone a new religion, schisms, deviations, and heresies developed shortly after his death. Already during his lifetime Comte, in his *Système de philosophie positive* (published in 1824), had broken away from the master by proposing an outright industrial dictatorship.

A dismayed Saint-Simon found a more devoted and fervent disciple in Olinde Rodrigues, a Jewish banker with a social conscience. Rodrigues, who had taught mathematics at the Ecole Polytechnique, converted one of his former pupils, Prosper Enfantin, to Saint-Simonism. Enfantin had never finished his studies at the Polytechnique – his father, a banker who had gone bankrupt, became unable to afford the fees – but was to prove a capable engineer, who conceived the Suez Canal project later to be executed by De Lesseps. He had spent most of his twenties in Holland, Switzerland and Russia as the representative of a French wine firm and had only recently returned from St Petersburg. There, for the last two years, he had worked for a French banker and otherwise spent much time in the company of a group of French polytechnicians who were building the first Russian railway.

Rodrigues, impressed by the young man's interest in philosophy, economics and engineering, and by his general verve, had introduced Enfantin to Saint-Simon. He was one of 7 disciples to whom Saint-Simon read his *Nouveau Christianisme*, and who immediately after his funeral met at the offices of Rodrigues's bank to fulfill the master's last wish and launch a journal called *Le Producteur*. While Rodrigues got the banker Lafitte, Ternaux and other manufacturers to finance it, Enfantin spread word at the Polytechnique about the new journal devoted to 'philosophy, science and the arts', and before long Saint-Simonism made a strong impact on students and lecturers.

Soon enough, it engendered a cult, and the original disciples established the so-called Sacred College or 'Church of Saint-Simon'. This was not an unnatural development, given the synthesis Saint-Simon had tried to achieve between religion and the industrial age. A religion practically invites a revelation, and a religious order requires a hierarchy. In the general dissatisfaction with the reign of the restored Bourbons, many young men looked for some new illumination. The next step, not surprisingly, was that Rodrigues, the 'apostle', nominated two men – the charismatic Enfantin and Armand Bazard, a 34-year-old hero of the last stage of the Napoleonic wars – as the two 'fathers' or 'popes' of the Saint-Simonist doctrine. By this time, towards the end of the 1820s, the leading members of the new religious order, reinforced by Michel Chevalier, later to become a foremost economist, and by Hippolyte Carnot – son of the mathematician and famous Minister of War, himself an engineer and future Minister and to become the father of a President of France – began to expound the Saint-Simonist gospel at Carnot's house to audiences of up to 100 brilliant young engineers, economists and medics, students and lecturers, as well as a sprinkling of artists, bankers, professors and magistrates.

In 1829 a committee including Enfantin, Bazard, Carnot, and two others began to collate and prepare for publication an *Exposition of the Doctrine of Saint-Simon*. Following a Christmas convocation of the Sacred College at the Hôtel de Gesvres in the rue Monsigny, a permanent study centre was established on the first floor of the building. The third floor was occupied by the offices of the liberal newspaper *Le Globe*. The next year Henri Fournel – the director-general of the Creusot factories – and a flock of new adherents enabled the College to take over *Le Globe*. At the same time the study centre was dissolved. The two 'popes' and other leaders of the flock, including Fournel, who resigned his job, moved in with their families to live communally, like a sect or monastic order, on the two lower floors and the Hôtel de Gesvres became 'the first temple of Saint-Simonism'.[7]

Before long, proceedings were to take a mystic turn, and Enfantin, claiming that he was a direct descendant of St Paul, proclaimed himself Pope and 'Supreme Father' of the new 'Church of Saint-Simon'. Saint-Simon, proclaiming the equality of women in the new society, had taken the view that a husband-wife couple must be 'capable of working together as full partners in a joint effort.' Enfantin, carrying the master's ideas to unexpected lengths, began to preach a new morality whose laws and full philosophy were to be revealed by a Female Mother Messiah – *la Femme-Mère-Messie* – who was his destined partner at the head of the new church. Pending her appearance, Enfantin moved with several dozen of his male and female devotees to a 'retreat' in the rue Ménilmontant, where members of the sect – for whom he designed a special blue-white costume, including a tunic with *Le Père* printed across the chest – lived communally and extravagantly, singing hymns to him, and otherwise engaging in zany rituals never contemplated by Saint-Simon.

Their antics eventually led to a public trial on charges of their practising free love and the 'emancipation of the flesh'. Saint-Simon's original ideas were momentarily discredited. They remained, however, very much alive. Long before Saint-Simon's slogan 'To each according to his capacity, to each capacity according to its work' was to find its way, after various modifications, into *The Communist Manifesto*, his vision of the new age of planned industrial productivity, with bounty and opportunity for all, made a lasting impression not only on Socialists, early Communists and bourgeois capitalists alike but on avant-garde artists in France and elsewhere.

Heine, Hugo, Lamennais, Sand, Lamartine and de Vigny all found inspiration in his concept of a new and different world. His view that all the upheavals since the storming of the Bastille were merely the prelude to some great step yet to be taken by mankind corresponded to their own convictions. The acquisition of the daily *Le Globe* in the autumn of 1830, shortly after the July Revolution, gave the Saint-Simonists a prestigious organ for the dissemination of their ideas. It catered to intellectual circles both in France and abroad. Young liberals like Hugo and Sainte-Beuve wrote for it, as did the conservative Chateaubriand and a whole galaxy of distinguished academicians. Lamennais was fired by Saint-Simon's message of Christian love and brotherhood; Hugo by the Messianic element, the liberalism and social concern combined in his approach; George Sand by all these, and by his championship of women's equality. The young pianist Franz Liszt was a devoted Saint-Simonist. So were the composer Félicien David, the banker and, later, railway builder Isaac Pereire, and a great number of noted economists, philosophers and historians.

The editorship of the paper was assumed by Pierre Leroux, one of its leading staff-members, who had become an adherent of Saint-Simonism. Leroux was the son of a modest café-owner and one of a new type of self-taught social, actually 'Socialist' philosophers, a term he claimed to have invented. Socialist had, in fact, first appeared as an English noun in 1827 in the magazine of London's Co-operative Society in an article discussing whether it was more beneficial to the economy 'that capital should be individual or common'. The magazine's editor wrote: 'Those who think that capital should be common are the *Communists* and *Socialists*.' The moving spirit behind the Co-operative Society was Robert Owen, the idealistic Welshman and self-made industrialist who in 1800, at the age of 28, had made the New Lanark Mills in Scotland famous by introducing model conditions which stunned his contemporaries: reducing the workday to 10 and a half hours, raising the minimum working age to 10, providing sick pay, retirement pay, infant education and establishing a co-operative store.

While the Nottingham workers in 1811 were smashing the new industrial machines or 'stocking-frames' for producing cheap cotton calicoes which made them jobless, Robert Owen was demonstrating at his mills that England's textile workers could be turned from drunken wretches into orderly men. The revolutionary social amenities established by Owen for his workers and their children had made New Lanark an internationally famous industrial community, a showplace visited by some of Europe's rulers and leading statesmen, including Tsar Alexander's brother and later successor Nicholas.

By 1817, a year before Marx's birth, Owen was on his way to becoming the leading Socialist reformer of the age, the man to whom the Prime Minister, the Earl of Liverpool – as well as the Dukes of York and Kent – looked to rid England of poverty in the economic slump after the Napoleonic wars. His plan was to establish a large number of co-operative villages for up to 2,000 poor each, to be housed in square buildings and engage in mechanized agriculture. The Archbishop of Canterbury had given his blessing to Owen's villages – which Cobbett and other opponents derided as 'parallelograms of paupers' – but the whole project was shot down when Owen incautiously attacked the 'gross errors of every religion' at a public meeting. He was dropped by the establishment about the same time as Saint-Simon was to be dropped by the French bourgeoisie for criticizing Catholic theology and talking about 'terrestrial morality'.

Owen, convinced like Saint-Simon before him that he could solve the problems created by the Industrial Revolution, next took his plans to America. In 1826, after investing £40,000 in a tract of land on the banks of the Wabash in the state of Indiana, he inaugurated the 'New Harmony Community of Equals'. Comprising 30,000 acres of land and an existing village, New Harmony – launched with some fanfare as marking the end of the 'monstrous' evils of 'private or individual property' – was to be a model for the 3,000 or so co-operatives or communes planned by Owen. This first secular experiment in voluntary economic Communism not based on class war collapsed, however, quickly and disastrously within a couple of years, in spite of Owen's economic expertise as a successful manufacturer.

Owen was not only an innovator but a manufacturer devoted to 'the public good' of the type Saint-Simon thought fit to govern the world. Like Saint-Simon himself, Owen sank his money into the realization of an idea that possessed him, and could not understand why, 'in the midst of the most ample means to create wealth', men failed to take the necessary measures, with the result that 'all are in poverty, or in imminent danger from the effects of poverty upon others.' At the same time, Owen's communal venture at New Harmony more closely resembled the social system which Saint-Simon's great rival, Charles Fourier, kept dreaming about all his life.

If Saint-Simon had struck people as a strange genius, none appeared more bizarre than Charles Fourier, the prophet of 'consumerism', who in 1808 – 5 years after Saint-Simon proposed a 'Council of Newton' to govern Europe – had announced his discovery of 'the laws of universal movement missed by Newton'. Like the gravitational movement of matter, he claimed, *social* movement too was ruled by a universal law or code, which mankind, preoccupied with politics, religious dogmas, wars and economic competition, had simply failed to decipher.

Fourier said he had first hit upon the idea while dining in 1798 at a restaurant with Brillat-Savarin, the French gastronomer and author of *Physiologie du goût*. He was charged 14 sous for an apple – more than a hundred times the price, he noted, of similar or even superior apples in the district he came from. The exorbitant price difference shocked him into the realization that there was a fundamental disorder in the 'industrial mechanism'.

Saint-Simon's idea of putting an élite of capitalists in charge of industrializing Europe in the interest of mankind and for 'the perfection of civilization' smacked to Fourier of sheer nonsense – 2,000 years of 'civilization' since Plato, he argued, had brought the world nothing but constant wars, greed, poverty and oppression. Capitalist enterprise would lead only to more cut-throat economic competition, more exploitation of the weak, and more misery. Long before these phenomena were to become conspicuous with the rapid industrialization which marked the 19th century, Fourier warned against the alienation of man in the machine age, and affirmed the needs of the individual.

Unlike Saint-Simon, the *seigneur* who dreamt of Charlemagne and travelled a long way from his noble origins to arrive at a proto-Socialist theory of history, Fourier – as the French historian Michelet put it – found 'Socialism at home in the seething milieu of industrial Lyons.' Born in 1772 at Besançon, Fourier was the son of a well-to-do draper. Realizing at an early age that his father was cheating his clients, and having been taught in the catechism that one must never lie, he told some customers at the store that they were being defrauded, whereupon his father gave him a hiding. 'At the age of seven', Fourier wrote, 'I swore the oath which Hannibal had sworn at nine against Rome: I swore an eternal hatred of commerce.'

Fourier's education was halted when he was 17, for his father – on his death a couple of years earlier – had stipulated that he was not to inherit his large fortune unless he engaged in commerce. Even then, he was to get it only in stages. Over the boy's protests, he was apprenticed to a commercial firm in Lyons. His attempt a couple of years later to set up a business of his own with the first instalment of his inheritance coincided with the 1793 Lyons rebellion against the Convention. During the republican siege of the city, Fourier was arrested as a counter-revolutionary, spent some time in jail and was then drafted into the army. Discharged for ill health in 1796, he started a new business venture which was literally shipwrecked when a consignment of goods ran aground. At the same time, the machinations of an uncle deprived his mother of her own fortune.

Ironically, the young man whose hatred of the social system and of 'the infamy of commerce' was strengthened by watching both the misery of the underpaid textile workers of Lyons and the malpractices of its merchants, was to be forced to spend all his life either as a travelling salesman or as an office clerk in the commercial 'workshops of deceit'.

Once the shocking price charged for an apple had prompted him to start investigating the laws of 'social movement' in the universe, Newton's physical apple became Fourier's social apple. Newton's law of gravitational attraction was fine, but it had not solved poverty or the problems of human unhappiness. For science ignored and philosophy suppressed what Fourier called man's innate 'passions' and that drive for 'passionate attraction that is given to us by nature prior to any reflection and persists despite the opposition of reason, duty or prejudice.' Ten years after making his discovery that 'social movement' followed the same laws as physical motion in a unitary system, Fourier announced that this movement was subject to the gravitational attraction and interplay of 12 fundamental human passions, which were dominant in varying intensity and nuances in different individuals.

The crowning feature of the doctrine of 'Harmony' he expounded in his *Théorie des quatre mouvements et des destinés generals* – published in 1808 at Lyons, though for fear of its being plagiarized he gave Leipzig as the place of publication – was that social progress could be harmoniously achieved on a universal scale by the voluntary association of small groups of suitably matched people living in communes. Fourier ascribed crucial importance to three of the fundamental passions – viz., the 'cabalist' passion for intrigue and combinations, the *papillon* or 'butterfly' desire for variety, and a 'composite' passion for making accords – which animated all social life, movement and association. A thirteenth passion, called 'unityism', combined all the others, and – integrating the happiness of the individual with the happiness of all – made for harmony. With strikingly modern and in his day unprecedented concern for man's emotional and psychological needs, Fourier, a pedantic visionary, spent a good deal of the Napoleonic era working on a mathematically precise calculus of 'attractions' between all types and possible combinations of human character.

Arriving at 'an infinite variety' of types, he finally settled, for practical reasons, on 810 different characters, and stipulated that 1,620 people – or twice 810 – associating in small self-governing communities, or 'phalansteries' as he called them, represented the best chance for every possible character to live and work harmoniously with others most attractive and compatible to him or her. Each would do the work he or she enjoyed best and would be able to pursue individual inclinations in an atmosphere free of social friction and urban pressures, untrammeled by bureaucracy, the impositions of centralized 'authorities' and all the vile results of power politics, mercantile competition and other savage by-products of civilization. In modern terms, Fourier aimed at affording each individual the maximum opportunity for 'self-expression' and 'self-fulfilment'. A multiplicity of such communes would bring about 'universal harmony'.

To enjoy a true sense of well-being, Fourier observed, man had not only to eat and be healthy but to gratify his sensual appetites. Unfortunately, few and often the wrong people were rich. Most others worked at dreary jobs; many gourmets were reduced to eating bread and beans; and music lovers could not afford to attend concerts. In the phalanstery, monotony and drudgery would be eliminated by assigning members to their favourite occupations, or switching them through a diversity of jobs during the day. The communal kitchen would be staffed by those who loved to cook, freeing women of domestic chores and providing rich and varied menus satisfying everybody's 'aromatic' and culinary tastes, according to his purse. There would be no class distinctions and no coercion, but no uniformity or artificial equality either. People who were more talented, more creative or more productive would earn enough to live on a grand scale; others, however, could achieve the same standard if they were ready to do uncongenial labours, for which a higher wage would be paid. All would enjoy the same lavish communal amenities, dining rooms, school, library, 'shops, ballrooms, banquet and assembly halls'.

A life-long bachelor, Fourier loved cats and preferred them to human company. Both as a travelling salesman and in Paris he lived in dingy hotels and boardinghouses. After Heine moved to Paris, he often saw Fourier 'hurrying past under the arcades of the Palais Royal in his shabby old grey redingote.' Yet this reclusive and unsociable character, who kept even his disciples at a distance and had few relations with women (except in brothels), thought of, or fantasized about, gratifying man's so-called 'affective' or spiritual passions – love, parental feelings, friendship, ambition – as well. In a book called *Le Nouveau monde amoureux*, partly suppressed by his disciples and fully published only in 1967, he conjured up a veritable sexual revolution.

Observing the hypocrisy and gloom marking monogamous marriages and family life, he boldly conceived an end to this unnatural state. In the phalanstery, those who wished to could maintain the conventional family unit, but others (such as 'omnigyns', who had a combination of several dominant passions) were to be free to engage in multiple love affairs, 'lesbianism', and 'a host of amorous innovations we cannot yet imagine.'

He cited the example of the Empress Maria Theresa as proof that once women were 'liberated and achieved freedom' they could 'surpass men' intellectually and in every other respect, bar physical force. He called for their admission to academic titles and declared that 'women's emancipation' was not only a basic principle, but a yardstick of social progress. In his compulsive search for perfect solutions, Fourier not only dealt with the problem of 'vocational' suitability in order to fit each individual into the right occupational niche, but thought of providing special love counsellors to advise people on the most suitable partners for a liaison; special consolers of both sexes to soothe the pains of rejected and/or jealous lovers; and young *amours* for the aged. He prescribed free children's education starting from the age of 6; stressed what has become known as the 'leisure principle', and the idea that diversity and pleasure in work increase productivity; and in many other respects, he had notions far ahead of his time.

Fourier's views on love and sex were an integral part of his theory of social harmony. For, underlying his entire system, was the belief that by offering people gratification of their desires and the chance of living 'voluptuously' under optimal conditions of diversity, by rotating work in a manner affording everyone the chance of 'self-fulfilment', he would reduce both poverty and inequality to a minimum, increase productivity and take the sting out of the human passions for intrigue and aggression, turning them into socially useful qualities.

Though there was a streak of the anarchist in Fourier and he raged against poverty, wars, inequality and all the crimes and evils of 'civilization', he was against changing the situation by violence and revolution. Derided as a crackpot when not considered mad, Fourier, like Saint-Simon, believed in the supreme powers of persuasion and education. But these two men, gazing from different standpoints far into the future at two related aspects of the industrial society – mass production and increased consumerism – could not but differ about the way affluence was to be achieved or how its effects were to be handled.

In 1803, the year Saint-Simon published his plan for a 'Council of Newton', Fourier had proposed to Bonaparte the introduction of a 'decent minimum wage' in order to abolish poverty, 'the chief cause of social disorders'. Reignier, Bonaparte's Minister of Justice, was the first of many men who thought Fourier mad when he received his memorandum. Having outlined the quintessence of his system of 'universal harmony' in 1808, Fourier spent the rest of the Napoleonic period elaborating it, and was to give it its final form in *Théorie de l'unité universelle*, published in 1822. The 'frightful' European crisis which Saint-Simon, about the time of the Vienna Congress, meant to solve by proposing the political and economic unification of the Continent made Fourier rage at 'the smarties' who had rejected his discovery of the 'calculus of attractions' in 1808. Accusing them of being responsible 'for all the blood that has been spilled and all the plagues that have been endured since', he pointed out that in the 7 years between 1808 and 1815 France alone had lost 'more than 1,200,000 or 1,300,000 men in battle, apart from the revolutionary plagues.'[8]

With an absolutist, not to say megalomaniac, faith in his own system, Fourier saw in Saint-Simon a false prophet, a 'charlatan' in the line of Plato and Voltaire, whose philosophies – vainly trying to change nature and control 'the springs God put in our souls' – had caused mankind to 'bathe itself in blood for twenty-three scientific centuries.' He, Fourier, had found 'the art of utilizing these springs' for the happiness of the human race and for curing it of the ills and general malaise already produced by 'civilization', which was in itself nothing but mankind's childhood disease.

Fourier foresaw a world inhabited by five billion people – a forecast that was to be fulfilled only in 1987, a century and a half after his death. In a beautiful flight of his utopian imagination, Fourier wrote of 'an immense orchestra arranged for five billion instruments or characters' and promised an age proving 'that God knew how to apply in his theory of the harmony of passions the means through which each one of the five billion individuals will be useful for the happiness of all the others.'

When Saint-Simon, feeling that 'religion will not disappear from the world, it can only be transmuted', eventually launched his idea of a socially oriented 'New Christianity' suiting the industrial age, Fourier would not hear of it, charging rather gratuitously that Saint-Simon's 'Christian industrialism' was another way of imposing a theocratic state on people. Fourier himself, though anti-Royalist, anti-state and anti-church, was not against religion. The Catholic Church – which banned his writings – he detested as a pillar of the established order. Like the state, it oppressed people. But God had His place in Fourier's system of salvation, a God of his own making. Since God had given man social needs or 'passions', he speculated that God must also have devised the ability for man to satisfy them. There must be, he wrote, 'a code guaranteeing justice, truth, and industrial attraction.'[9]

Fourier enjoyed coining new words. *Phalanstère* itself is a neologism, but so, he argued, was *doctrinaire*; and observing that 'John the Baptist was the prophet precursor of Jesus', Fourier styled himself 'the prophet post-cursor' of Jesus, 'announced by Him, and completing His work of the rehabilitation of men, solely in its industrial aspect.' While rejecting Christian piety, meekness and the role of the Church, he often quoted from the Gospels and called himself a 'vice-Messiah', a 'sub-Messiah' and the 'hippo-Messiah' – of Harmony, not Christianity – and would have liked the Church to establish a trial phalanstery. But except for suggesting that the true message of Jesus might find its actual fulfilment in his utopian new world of 'Harmony', he gave no indication of what his religious feelings, if any, were.[10]

Whereas Saint-Simon acknowledged his debt to the social message of the Old Testament prophets and expressed his admiration for the way their people, 'proud of its supra-terrestrial nobility', had since played its role in history throughout its 'universal captivity', Fourier shared the anti-Semitism of Lyons's merchants, who feared the competition of the recently emancipated French Jews. In spite of the great attention he paid to the needs of every conceivable human character, he was in fact one of the first in the line of Socialists whose schemes of universal salvation did not include the Jews, whom he stereotyped and damned under the collective name of Judas Iscariot.

At the same time, he attacked the Christian merchant guilds for their profit greed. By comparison, he wrote, Iscariot was 'an honest man; he is content with a modest profit because he does not maintain such a splendid household as yours.'[11] And his rabid prejudice notwithstanding, Fourier was so sure a single 'trial phalanstery' functioning for 6 months would convince everyone of the universal happiness possible under 'Harmony' that – in his keenness to persuade the Rothschilds to finance one – he promised them 'to reconstitute the Israelite nation, to reestablish in Jerusalem a Jewish monarch, with his own flag, consuls, and diplomatic rank.'

Starting in 1803 and for the next 30 years, Fourier kept bombarding other wealthy individuals, as well as every French government, with his ideas. He offered them to learned societies in France and abroad, and promised the earth to the Tsar if only he would establish a phalanstery in Russia. No individual, institution or any of the French and foreign governments he approached replied to his appeals for a hearing, and he spent most of his life in dire poverty.

From 1826 he worked as a correspondence clerk in the Paris office of Curtis and Lamb, a New York wholesale firm. Punctually at 12 o'clock he would go home to his lodgings to wait for some 'benefactor' to turn his utopia into reality and set up a phalanstery somewhere. He was still alive when the very first, established by Bulgarian villagers at Fâlticeni (now in Rumania), was attacked and destroyed by neighbouring landowners.

Before Fourier died in 1837, Albert Brisbane helped towards his 'voluptuous' living by paying him 5 francs per 'lesson' to be initiated in the principles of 'Harmony'. Brisbane later persuaded Horace Greeley to open the columns of the newly founded *New York Tribune* to Fourier's ideas. These so fired a Russian liberal landowner, Petrashevsky – hero of the famous 'Petrashevsky plot', for his alleged participation in which Dostoyevsky, the writer, was to be sentenced to forced labour – that he built a communal house and started a phalanstery for his peasant-serfs. The peasants promptly burned it down.

Fourier's ideas were to inspire the short-lived American Brook Farm experiment, the Wisconsin Phalanx and the Oneida Community – which combined the Fourierist work ethic with polygamy – and were to crop up periodically all over Europe, to find their way into Latin America, later to percolate into Israel's modern kibbutzim and to be revived in vague form in the 1960s in some 'hippy' communes. Fourier's original concept for communal life, however, has never been fully applied, or not in the manner he prescribed.

André Breton was to hail Fourier as a forerunner of surrealism. But already in the 1840s Heine asked how it was that social reformers like Fourier, 'true benefactors of humanity', were allowed to starve in France. One question that arises in hindsight, especially after the 1989 collapse of Marxism (Leninist-Marxism, to be exact) in the USSR and Eastern Europe is why men like Fourier and, for that matter, Saint-Simon, were so little heeded in their time.

Fourier was a monomaniac who made some aberrant claims for his world of the future, such as that man's life-span in 'universal Harmony' would grow to an average 144 years. For all his extremes, however, he accurately diagnosed the mighty disorders of his age, such as economic inequality, social injustice, hunger and exploitation, state militarism and war, the atomization of urban life (he considered introducing a spell in a big city as a punishment for offenders), male chauvinism and the frustrations and disruption of family life, and some others that are still with us.

Saint-Simon dealt with some of the same problems and many of the features of his industrial (against Fourier's agricultural) vision have come to pass. Did practical success escape these men who dreamed up solutions to real crises because – as Marx and Engels were to claim even while carefully studying their ideas and working them over – they were unscientific 'utopian Socialists' and unable to point a path leading from reality to their vision? Was it, as has been said, because they had learned nothing from the French Revolution? Or, on the contrary, because they deplored its bloodletting and the enormous waste of lives that followed in Napoleon's campaigns, and, having no faith in the people or a new revolutionary upheaval, preferred to put their trust in some enlightened ruler, philanthropist or benefactor who would change society and build their New Jerusalem for them?

What, in short, was the missing element or the weakness that prevented the realization of their scheme? It has been suggested that they did not 'fashion a good war-machine' for their ideas, whereas Marxism was to build several. Yet, as Oscar Wilde was to write in 1890, 'a map of the world that does not include Utopia... leaves out the one country at which Humanity is always landing. And when Humanity lands there, it looks out, and seeing a better country, sets sail. Progress is the realization of Utopia.'

Filippo Michelangelo (or Michèle) Buonarroti, who had joined Babeuf's 'Society of Equals' in 1796 in the first organized attempt in modern times to establish a Communist state and egalitarian society, was as idealistic an aristocrat as Saint-Simon, but a man of different stamp. Steeped in the theories of Rousseau and the French *philosophes*, the suave, highly cultured Italian nobleman shared Robespierre's credo that the founders of the first French republic had every justification to 'crush all the enemies of freedom by means of terror'. Following the apprehension of 'the Equals' on 10 May 1796, Buonarroti was sentenced to 10 years of solitary confinement. After serving the last 6 of them on an isolated island fortress, he turned up in 1806 in Geneva. There, in spite of being under police surveillance, he began to set up a conspiratorial network of secret societies affiliated with the Italian-Spanish-French cloak-and-dagger movement of the famous *Carbonari*. Pledged to 'freedom from tyranny', the *Carbonari* are seen by historians to this day as the prototype of all 'modern revolutionary underground organizations', from Nihilists to Bolsheviks down, some say to the Tupamaros in South America, the IRA in Ireland, and others too numerous to mention.[12]

It was in the mountain regions of Italy that the 'brotherhood', whose origin may or may not go back to the Middle Ages, flourished anew at the time of the Napoleonic occupation. Using terms from the charcoal trade, its secret councils were called *vendite* or 'sales', and its rituals featured woodmen's axes, blocks and/or daggers combined with Christian religious symbols. The *Carbonari* invoked Jesus as their 'honorary Grand Master' and as 'the Lamb' – representing the oppressed – whom each member swore to deliver from 'the Wolf', which stood for the Bourbon tyrants and the Austrian occupants of southern Europe after the Vienna Congress. Their combination of patriotic fervour, 'mutual help' pledges on the Masonic model and various plots and insurrections staged in the cause of liberty during the next decade in Italy and Spain attracted high-minded politicians and officers as well as Romantic intellectuals. In Ravenna in 1820 Lord Byron, a *carbonaro* by temperament as well as formal initiation, amassed an arsenal of guns and bayonets at the Palazzo Guiccioli and dismissed the risk of accidental discovery in the words: 'It is no great matter, supposing Italy could be liberated, who or what is sacrificed. It is a grand object – the very poetry of politics. Only think – a free Italy! Why, there has been nothing like it since the days of Augustus!'

Upon being expelled from Geneva through the intervention of Metternich, Buonarroti moved to Belgium. From Brussels, where this scion of the Florentine nobility set himself up as a music-teacher, he extended the tentacles of his conspiratorial network to similar secret societies that had sprung up in Spain and France. While still in Geneva he had also set up various Masonic lodges, and one feat he seems to have managed was to make important Freemasons, who actually opposed his democratic and republican ideas, work for the cause of Carbonarism, even though it and Freemasonry remained separate movements and were, as Lamartine put it, 'by turns the allies and the enemy' of each other.

Supposedly introduced into France by the Saint-Simonist Bazard, *la Charbonnerie* found such prominent adherents as La Fayette and General Berton. Bazard himself had been initiated into the brotherhood's rites during a stay in Naples. With support from various army elements, the French *Carbonari* staged or attempted during the 1820s some 9 military and popular insurrections against the Bourbons, but these were easily quelled. One that had the most lasting impact, the so-called 'insurrection of La Rochelle', actually never took place – having been discovered before it started – but 4 young non-commissioned officers were caught, brought to trial in Paris and sentenced to death for a plot planned by others which they had not begun to put into effect. Their public execution in 1822 in the place des Grèves – where the guillotine had once functioned – stirred public opinion against the restored Bourbons. Successive generations of Frenchmen would keep the memory of the 'four sergeants of Rochelle' alive every year on All Souls' Day. More immediately, French youths of student age or younger – including some who were to become pioneer Socialists and Communists – joined the ranks of the *Carbonari*.

Auguste Blanqui was still a pupil at a Paris lycée when he saw the troop concentrations in the place des Grèves as the young officers were led to their death, crying 'Vive la liberté' and 'History will judge us!' That night he swore to avenge them. Two years later, at the age of 19, he became a fiery *carbonaro*. Blanqui, whose father had been a member of the 1793 French Convention, came from an educated home. He studied law, then took up journalism and became the parliamentary correspondent of *Le Globe* – shortly before this organ of the liberal opposition was to be taken over by the Saint-Simonists – and the closest friend of Pierre Leroux, its future editor, who was already a *carbonaro*. Although the insurrections of the 1820s were unsuccessful, they had a cumulative effect and *Carbonarism* played a part in keeping up the discontent that led to the replacement of Charles X by Louis-Philippe in the July Revolution of 1830. So did the Saint-Simonist ideas spread by the mixed group of young intellectuals and financiers led by Rodrigues, Enfantin and Bazard.

Enfantin, the most enterprising of the three, had by now realized that 'our power over the people is nil', but that the masses could be stirred by the influence of an élite. In the heat of the July Revolution, however, he departed from Saint-Simon's teaching and on its third day actually sent Bazard to La Fayette, the commander of the National Guard, with a proposal to place himself at the head of a 'provisional dictatorship' that would carry out the Saint-Simonist social programme. La Fayette politely declined. But later that year one of the group's sympathizers, the banker Lafitte, was to head the second ministry formed under the new 'bourgeois' monarchy.

On the eve of the revolution, Blanqui stunned Leroux, the philosopher Théodore Jouffroy and a group of other *Le Globe* editors and contributors by proposing that they set up an insurrectionary committee. 'Before the week is over', he declared, 'it will all be settled by rifle shots.'[13]

Unlike Leroux and other social theorists of change by non-violent persuasion, Blanqui took an active part in the fighting which followed, joining the workers in the streets with his gun. Decorated for directing some of the street battles, Blanqui then and later found inspiration in a book published by Buonarroti in 1828 in Belgium, and soon to be reprinted in Paris. *La Conspiration pour l'Egalité dite de Babeuf* detailed the plot of which Buonarroti had been one of the principal instigators next to Babeuf, and contained a blueprint of the egalitarian Communist republic they had planned to establish by force of arms. The élan with which the uneducated workers of Paris took to the streets in 1830, and the ease with which the Bourbons were toppled in three days – 'les trois glorieuses' – of rioting, barricades and some rifle fire, confirmed Buonarroti's idea that a determined band of men fighting against oppression were capable of seizing power by force and were justified in maintaining it by coercion for the purpose of creating a better society. The result of the uprising also confirmed Blanqui's own conviction that action spoke louder than words, and that deeds were more important than theories.

At the beginning of August, Buonarroti himself arrived in Paris. A venerable figure nearing 70, he had the eminence of a man who had worked with, and was practically heir to, Robespierre, coupled with his leadership of international *Carbonarism*. Living modestly – under the name of M. Raymond – in the rue du Rocher, Buonarroti immediately became active behind the scenes in the proliferating republican societies which, as soon as they were suppressed, kept springing up overnight in the 'bourgeois' monarchy. The most important of them was the Société des Droits de l'Homme, founded by Voyer d'Argenson, a high-born aristocrat and friend of Buonarroti. This organization had subdivisions named after Robespierre, Marat and Babeuf. Among its leaders were Charles Teste, who published a Draft of a Republican Constitution; Albert Laponneraye, author of a Letter to the Proletariat; and Godefroy Cavaignac, leader of the radical democrats, whose younger and conservative brother General Louis-Eugène Cavaignac was to preside over the bloody suppression of the February 1848 revolution. D'Argenson's circle also included a mixed group of veteran *Carbonari* and younger Saint-Simonists.

Blanqui went his own way. Recruiting small clandestine groups of adherents, he was to spend most of the years before and after Buonarroti's death in the mid1830s plotting one insurrection after another, culminating in his armed occupation of the Palais de Justice and the Hôtel de Ville, and his proclamation of a republican government. Although Blanqui was captured, and was to spend almost more years in jail than out, he became France's most outspoken advocate of armed insurrection, the prototype of the dedicated, professional and perennially conspiring revolutionary. The cause to which he was ready to give his life was to complete the unfinished business of the Great Revolution and to pick up, as it were, the thread where Babeuf and Buonarroti had left off in 1796.

Fourier, Saint-Simon and Buonarroti, it will be observed, had developed the fundamentals of their theories practically simultaneously in the first decade of the century, the decade in which Robert Owen was starting his practical social experiments; the decade, too, in which Hegel arrived at his perception of the future of the world in the *Phenomenology of the Spirit*, and towards the end of which Fichte was to develop his philosophy of a German master race, of 'right is might', and to affirm the supremacy of the state by proclaiming that the 'individual must forget himself in the race.'

The germination of most of the issues and ideas that were to divide Europe for the next 150 years was thus completed by the time of Napoleon's apogee. Saint-Simon, Fourier and Buonarroti, although crying in the wilderness during the mad time which saw his rise and fall and the restoration of the old order, went on elaborating their theories, and by the end of the 1820s had each started a different trend in the development of Europe's 19th-century social movements.

Heine, one of the first to discern these trends, was to watch their growing effect at close quarters when he moved to Paris in the wake of the July Revolution. In Moscow, by 1834, Alexander Herzen and other young students were to be questioned by a Tsarist Commission seeking to establish whether their libertarian opinions were not 'imbued with the pernicious doctrines of Saint-Simon'.

Karl Marx and Friedrich Engels, who were only 12 and 10 respectively at the time of the July Revolution – and slightly before them Moses Hess, who was 22 – were in due course to subject the theories of their utopian forerunners to careful study, and to take ideas from each of them.

On the eve of the July Revolution, Heine was on Helgoland Island in dire financial straits and uncertain of his future – asking Merckel for a loan and wondering, on 6 July, where he might find 'a nesting-place'. Ten years later, when he reproduced portions of that letter in his book on Ludwig Börne, Heine interpolated a long passage purporting to represent the reasons which in 1830 made him reject each of the choices open to him. In Italy he would have found 'an Austrian sentry-box in front of every lemon tree'. In England the cost of living was 'twice as high as elsewhere', whereas 'they ought to pay you double for living there.' America? In that land, which he had once thought of as the last resort of freedom, 'several million black- or brown-skinned people are being treated like dogs.' It was a land 'without princes or aristocrats', but material profit was 'the only religion... and money their only omnipotent god', and the brutal treatment of the Blacks and Mulattos subjected Americans of conscience to a 'martyrdom surpassing anything known in Europe'. He mentioned the case of a Protestant preacher in New York who, defying prejudice, had married his daughter off to a Negro, with the result that 'he had to flee for his life, his house was demolished, and his daughter, the poor victim, she was lynched [English in the original].... O Liberty! Thou art an evil dream!'

What about France, then? By antedating to 1830 the so-called 'Helgoland letters', possibly written in whole or in part in 1840, Heine created a problem for scholars trying to establish his actual reaction to the July Revolution. News of it reached him on the island on 1 August. One of the letters in his book on Börne, published in 1840 but datelined 'Helgoland, 6 August [1830]', contains the lines: 'Lafayette, the tricolour flag, the *Marseillaise*... Gone is my longing for tranquillity. Now I know again what I want, what I have, what I must do... I am the son of the revolution. I reach for my consecrated arms again... Give me my lyre, that I may sing a battle song... I am all joy and song, all sword and flame.'

Heine claimed that when he included the 1830 'Helgoland letters' in his book on Börne he was drawing not only on letters but on notes and diary jottings made that year; and it has been established on good authority that his famous metaphor about 'the dog Medor' was culled from a newspaper chroni-

316

cle published shortly after the 1830 revolution.[14] 'This morning another parcel of newspapers reached the island,' he wrote in one of the Helgoland letters dated 10 August [1830]. 'I gulped them up like manna.' Then he went on:

> If only I could see the dog Medor! He interests me far more than the others who quickly jumped to retrieve the crown and offer it up to [Louis] Philippe of Orléans. The dog Medor kept retrieving guns and cartridge-boxes for his master, and when his master fell and was buried together with his fellow heroes in the courtyard of the Louvre, the poor dog sat down on his grave and remained immobile like a statue of loyalty by day and by night, eating little of the food he was offered, shuffling and burying the larger part of it into the ground, perhaps as food for his buried master.

The 'dog Medor' episode, published a decade later in Heine's Börne book, is mentioned here not only as an example of how Heine took a simple newspaper anecdote and artfully turned its canine hero into a symbol of the people who had fought and died at the barricades, enabling others to prance in the role of 'retrievers' of the crown for the 'bourgeois king' in the July Revolution, but because 'the dog Medor' was to reappear in yet another metaphor, in which his fate symbolized how the people were ultimately robbed of their victory by the bourgeoisie.

Letters written by Heine shortly before and immediately after the July Revolution show that since some time in 1828 he had been watching the situation in France by reading *Le Globe*, at the time when it represented the liberal opposition to the policies of Charles X. During his Berlin visit in February 1829, he had sounded out the possibility of obtaining a post as a *Privatdozent* – an unsalaried lecturer living on the fees paid by the students – in the Prussian capital. 'Shall I come to Berlin?' he inquired of Varnhagen on 3 January 1830. Undeterred by the latest rebuff he had suffered in Munich, Heine persisted in his ambition to wrest a post from those who kept denying it to him.

Max Brod, in a sensitive piece, has compared Heine's futile attempts 'to find a post which would enable him to settle down in the Fatherland' to the way K., the hero of Kafka's novel *The Castle*, 'struggles in vain for the right to the normal activity of a citizen, a matter which assumes a life-and-death importance for him as a symbol of integration into society'; and has pointed out that writers such as Novalis, Mörike, Schiller, Goethe, the Schlegel brothers, Uhland, Grimm, Tieck, E.T.A. Hoffmann and Immermann, among others, all held professorships, judgeships or even high state appointments affording them the tranquil security which 'is of great value precisely to those many authors who cannot endure any restrictions on their intellectual freedom.'[15]

317

On 1 August, when Heine was still on Helgoland, Campe drew his attention to a report in Hamburg's *Correspondent* that Charles X had been fired upon during his flight the previous day to Rambouillet: 'The streets [of Paris] bristle with cannon, and there is civil war. The Mayor of Versailles is said to have been hanged [he was in fact only unseated]... The consequences of these terrible measures are incalculable. It all seems to be a repeat performance of the old comedy. Hopefully its duration will not be so protracted as last time.'[16]

Heine later confessed that he was at first 'more interested in the human-interest details' of the July Revolution than in 'the pregnant significance of the whole development', which he did not know what to make of at first. He sensed that it might be an epochal or world-historical event, but behind him lay a personally 'fatal year'.[17] While street-fighting was going on in Paris, Heine, having quarreled with Campe over the paltry fee he had offered for *Travel Pictures* III (and his miserliness in using a cheap quality of paper 'which reminds me of my underpants'), was asking the unimpressed publisher to send him 5 'Friedrich-dor'; and as he wrote to Immermann on 10 August, 'world-history apart, I have had so many private troubles that my brain during these last few months was addled almost into stupidity.' Heine was quite truthful when he wrote, 'In Paris, dear friends, the Gallic cock has crowed, that is all I know.' The telling phrase was published in the 'Helgoland letters' in 1840, but this famous simile for a signal of revolution was actually coined by Heine before the end of 1830.

In April 1830 he had started reading Thiers's multi-volume history of the 1789 French Revolution. He was more impressed by Mignet's account of it, which he read on Helgoland and finished after his return to Hamburg. His later statement to Varnhagen that he was so affected by the coincidental news of the events in Paris that they seemed to him almost a natural 'continuation of my studies', is borne out by Ludolf Wienbarg's finding Heine in a nervous fret one morning, after 'the sharp thump' of the guillotine, the howling mob and the decapitated figures of the Girondists 'rising from Mignet's pages' had caused him a sleepless night. This made Wienbarg – later one of the leaders of the 'Young Germany' group of writers – realize that the 'emotionalism' in some of Heine's poetry was often more sincere than appeared.

Wienbarg's further observation that 'the July Revolution dispelled Heine's morose mood and threw him into a feverish agitation, making him feel that it was about to mark a significant chapter in his own life, too,' dovetails with a diary entry by Varnhagen's sister, Rosa Maria Assing, to the effect that Heine seemed 'very excited by the events in France.'[18] One feature of the toppling of the Bourbons that most impressed him was the fact that after the three-day revolution 'the people themselves' – far from indulging like their fathers in the 'insane atrocities' of the 1793 Terror – 'bound up the wounds of their enemies, and when the deed was done went quietly about their daily business again without asking so much as a tip for the great work they had done!' He was not sure that the same would happen in Germany, and had in fact written to Wienbarg from Helgoland: 'Should the revolution come to Germany, mine will not be the last head to fall.'

He had hardly returned to Hamburg when, on the first day of September, unrest broke out in the city, followed by disturbances in Leipzig, Cassel, Dresden and Berlin. While the disorders were sparked off by a variety of impulses – ranging from demands for a representative constitution in Hesse to manual workers in Berlin clashing with the police following the arrest of several tailors' apprentices – the 1 September riots in Hamburg were a two-day *Hep-Hep* outbreak, with rampaging ruffians attacking Jews in the streets, pillaging their homes and smashing Uncle Salomon's windows before the authorities intervened in force. Witnessing this anti-Semitic outburst perturbed Heine not a little, confirming the apprehensions he felt since his 'proscription' by the *Burschenschaften*. 'The German disturbances threw me into a fit,' he wrote. 'For hours reason left me and my mind was struck dumb.'[19]

Wienbarg, who was one of Heine's boon companions in Hamburg during the autumn of 1830, perceptively noted that 'he was capable of great enthusiasm for great characters and the drama of historic forces unleashed, but an abyss separated him from the commotion of the struggling masses.' Heine himself was aware of this. On 19 November 1830, while preparing the final section of his 'English Fragments' for inclusion in *Travel Pictures* IV, he wrote to Varnhagen that although he knew very well that 'revolution involves all social interests', he was, for the sake of effectiveness, concentrating his fire for the moment against 'the aristocracy and the clergy as its only allied foes.' Admitting that he still felt contempt for 'industrialism', he ascribed it to sheer 'aristocratic pride' which he could not yet eradicate from his heart, and mentioned that he had started work on a new 'political opus'.

This was a short but important essay titled 'Introduction to Kahldorf on the Nobility' ('*Einleitung zu Kahldorf über den Adel*'). The conservative Danish politician Count Magnus von Moltke had argued in a recent pamphlet that the aristocracy, by virtue of its culture, tradition, and experience in running affairs, was best suited to rule a democratic Germany. An author who signed himself 'Kahldorf' (a pseudonym for Robert Wesselhöft) asked Heine to write an introduction to his counter-pamphlet. In his 'Introduction' of some 6,000 words, Heine drew his famous parallel between the history of the French Revolution and the history of German philosophy. Outlining a thesis he was later to elaborate in Paris, he wrote that it was as if the French, too busy to dream while revolutionizing society, 'asked us Germans to do their dreaming for them and

German philosophy has been nothing but the dream of the French Revolution.' He went on: 'Kant, who guillotined everything that resisted his *Critique of Pure Reason*, was our Robespierre. Then came Fichte with his "I", the Napoleon of philosophy.' With his supreme egoism and sovereign will, he quickly, in the name of 'despotic idealism, improvised a universal empire that, collapsing as quickly as it rose', crushed underfoot whatever secret flowers had survived the Kantian Jacobins or had blossomed since. 'The earth trembled; came the counter-revolution'; the Restoration found its symbolic German counterpart in Schelling's philosophy of nature, which glorified 'the past with its mysticism, pietism, Jesuitism, legitimacy, Romanticism, Teutomaniac chauvinism – until Hegel, the Orléans of philosophy, finally founded, or rather systematized, an eclectic form of government' in which he found room for, and assigned a firm constitutional position to, 'the old Kantian Jacobins, the Fichtean Bonapartists, Schelling's aristocratic peers, and his own minions as well.'

Having thus 'happily completed the great philosophical circuit', it was natural that the Germans should now 'switch to politics'. The question which 'makes all hearts tremble' was whether Germany would start its course with the 1793 'system of the Comité du salut publique' or with the new 'bourgeois' monarchy's *Ordre légal*? In short, 'will the German revolution be dry – or red and wet?' Banishing the 'horrible visions' of the 1793 Terror conjured up by the aristocracy and the clergy to 'frighten us', Heine wrote, the priests and nobles of the *ancien régime* had condemned the majority of the French people to utter 'political ignorance' and obscurantism by means of censorship – that 'guillotine of ideas' which may for a time serve despotism, 'but in the end destroys it together with the despot.' In a stab at the conditions under which he was himself writing, he wondered at the complacency of the Germans 'in tolerating for so many years a mind-killing [censorship] law' of the type whose promulgation in France had just cost the last Bourbon his throne.

Heine then made his main point in what he termed a 'moderate' tone: 'Civic equality could now become in Germany, as once in France, the premier slogan of revolution.' Insisting that freedom of the press was essential to a calm discussion of the issues, he warned that otherwise the dispute might degenerate into violent challenges against which 'neither the sharpest arguments of the infantry and cavalry, nor even the cannon which are the *ultima ratio regis* but might easily become *ultimi regis ratio*' (Heine was here performing an inversion of the type which Hegel's 'Young Hegelian' critics were later to apply to their master) – 'would in any way be effective.'

'Kahldorf on the Nobility' was heavily mutilated by the censorship when Campe published it in Nuremberg in April 1831. By that time Heine's *Travel Pictures* IV had been banned and confiscated throughout Prussia.

Although he neither anticipated the July Revolution nor immediately packed his bags to rush off to Paris, it can hardly be said that he was indifferent to it. In the autumn of 1830 he was still clinging to the off-chance of Varnhagen's influence succeeding in getting him a post or some sinecure in Berlin, and more harassed than ever during his long years of drifting and searching in all directions. On 19 November, raging at Uncle Salomon, on whose support he could no longer count, and at Campe's 'knavish tricks', he wrote to Varnhagen that if he was 'not to starve' that winter he must look for 'new resources', and perhaps for a new publisher; in another letter on 30 November he raged at himself, 'at my own incapacity, at my mistakes and my stupidity.' In both letters he sounded a note of alarm at some imminent emergency, and after asking Varnhagen for advice on 'whatever resources might be available to me if the worst should come to the worst,' he concluded the first of them with the equivocal lines: 'You are wrong if you think that because of the contents of my writings the Prussian government might not be interested in me.'

This passage, and his presently approaching Varnhagen with the wild idea to campaign for his obtaining a high municipal post in Hamburg, have caused the statutory controversy between those holding that Heine was ready to compromise his integrity and political ideas for a position ensuring him financial security and those in whose eyes he can do no wrong. The full truth behind each of his zigzagging moves will probably never be known. The September disturbances had forced Brunswick's reactionary Duke Charles II to flee to England and in Hesse, a couple of weeks later, there had been a second popular uprising, amid continued demands for a constitution. In his Introduction to Kahldorf Heine expressed himself in favour of 'the idea of a citizen-king, without court etiquette, without aristocratic hirelings, without courtiers, match-makers, *pourboires* of diamonds and other splendiferous flummeries.' It is doubtful that he believed Prussia would become a constitutional monarchy, but for a while after the July Revolution he seems to have hoped for some liberal relaxations, such as the government's allowing the same press freedom that Charles X had permitted in France until the 'ordinances' that had accelerated his recent downfall.

Some have indeed gone so far as to compare Heine's readiness 'to consider a compromise with the government on condition that his intellectual liberty was guaranteed' with 'the young Marx, whom no one could easily accuse of being indulgent', 12 years later acting against the ultra-radicals and undertaking 'the thankless task of fighting for liberty step by step, while remaining within the bounds of the constitution.'[20]

On 29 November and again on 9 January 1831, Varnhagen brought Heine down to earth, assuring him that he had not the remotest chance of getting a government-approved position in either Berlin or Hamburg. 'In the present

German situation', he wrote, 'there is no room for a Walter Scott, let alone for a Byron.' The soundest advice he had for Heine was to repair his relations with Uncle Salomon: 'He is after all your born mainstay and what better thing for him than to give all his support to a nephew who brings honour to his name.' Heine replied that he had reestablished relations of a sort with Uncle Salomon, but only for the sake of having 'some protection at least against sudden blows, and only in the worst extremity.' Then he made a highly significant declaration: 'My aspiration is to get a steady position at all costs. If I can't get one very soon in Germany I shall go to Paris, where, unfortunately, I should have to assume a role spelling the ruin of all my artistic and poetic talents.' To make things perfectly clear, he added that the move would mean the effective 'consummation of my break with Germany's rulers'.

Was this a kind of ultimatum, as some have said? The idea is not so far-fetched as it sounds if one takes into account that, in the eyes of his contemporaries, Heine was by now 'a literary power in Germany'. Berlin's *Gesellschafter* that autumn called him 'the poet of our age, whose work mirrors the present political ferment in Europe, the political currents and unrest preoccupying all cabinets'.[21] More important, on 19 February 1831, Varnhagen was writing to Heine that his book, *Supplements to Travel Pictures* – which was the title of the first printing of *Travel Pictures* IV – 'is in everybody's hands; the intervention of the authorities has not hurt its distribution, and it is especially being read and recommended – albeit pejoratively – by the upper classes', i.e., by the people who counted in Berlin.

Ultimatum or not, Heine, writing in despair but as one power to another, was indirectly signalling that if all doors to making a living and enjoying a modicum of freedom were closed to him in his homeland, he would have no alternative but to 'break' relations and declare war on Prussia. He was entirely serious, when, in the style of a diplomatic note, he informed Varnhagen: 'Meanwhile, I am not taking any steps until I hear from you whether there isn't a chance of my being able to get something in Berlin – or Vienna(!!!) I shall leave no stone unturned and shall take extreme decisions only if driven to extremity.' Vienna was an idea that had apparently flitted across his mind upon learning that Friedrich von Gentz was an admirer of his poetry, but the three exclamation marks denote that he realized its enormity. At the same time, he must have been aware of the hopelessness of his moves, for his Epilogue to the 'English Fragments' contained a passage expressing his disillusion at the fact that the winds of freedom, wafted into Germany by the July Revolution, had here and there 'overturned the nightlights' and set 'the crimson curtains on some of the thrones on fire, so that the golden crowns grew hot beneath the flaring nightcaps' – but already 'the old myrmidons, with the Imperial police under their command, are dragging along the fire-buckets, sniffing around all the more vigilantly, forging the secret chains all the more firmly, and already I perceive a still more massive prison wall encircling the German people.'

It was not only the anticipation of growing repression that finally prompted Heine's decision to leave Germany. In Paris, at the end of October 1830, *Le Globe* had been taken over by the disciples of Saint-Simon. Since 1828, under the influence of Varnhagen, Heine had shown a growing interest – as did Carlyle and Stuart Mill in England – in Saint-Simon's theories for 'the perfection of society' and the creation of a world of plenty for all. Saint-Simon's idea of putting an end to 'the exploitation of man by man', not to mention the role he ascribed to artists in his vision of society, could not but appeal to Heine, as it did to the avant-garde of France's Romantic artists.

The poet 'consoles, damns, prays, prophesies', wrote Victor Hugo. 'His voice... echoes from one end of the earth to the other. Mankind becomes his flock, hears his works, and ponders them...' Alfred de Vigny, lofty, retiring and less assertive than Hugo, regarded poets as 'the pariahs of society'; but he, too, felt imbued with 'a divine spark... Deep down in my heart I feel a secret strength.' And though given to much introspection, he nevertheless wanted to stretch out his hand to all men, 'comrades in the misery of this world', and saw the poet's task as dictated by his ability to penetrate 'the mysterious causes of the present' and presage the future.

Saint-Simonism solved for Heine not only the 'antithesis' between spirit and the senses, spirit and matter, soul and body, but also helped him with another dichotomy. Fusing Saint-Simonism with elements of Spinoza and pantheism, Heine – notwithstanding Hegel's conservative thesis that God or the 'World Spirit' in history had achieved its end-purpose in his own age – was soon to effect a synthesis of his own between the 'algebra of revolution' that could be read into Hegel's dialectic and Saint-Simon's proclamation that history's task of creating 'the Golden Age of mankind' lay indeed in the future, and not in the past. Under the influence of what he knew of Saint-Simonism in the autumn of 1830, he concluded the book version of the 'English Fragments' with the words: 'The French are the chosen people of the new religion, it is in their language that the first gospels and dogmas have been recorded, Paris is the new Jerusalem, and the Rhine is the Jordan which divides the consecrated land of freedom from the land of the philistines.' Evidently, some time that autumn or at the beginning of the 1830–31 winter of his greatest discontent and uncertain wavering, even as he was thrashing about in all directions without ever ceasing to write – producing his Introduction to Kahldorf and most of the 44 poems to become known as *New Spring* ('*Neuer Frühling*'), besides supervising the publication of *Travel Pictures* III and IV – he discovered in Saint-Simonism a new

323

vision to sustain him. It became, in the words of E.M. Butler's pioneer study, one of the complex forces which drew Heine away from his native land and indirectly 'assumed the proportion of destiny shaping his future.'[22]

If there was more than braggadocio to Heine's threat to 'break with Germany's rulers', it was because Saint-Simonism, compensating in a way for the identity of which he had been robbed, gave him new hope and confidence. At that, he had yet to find the appreciable sum of money required for 'crossing the Jordan' and making the move to France. Lack of funds would have made it impossible for him to move to Paris immediately after the July Revolution even if he had wanted to, a fact, incidentally, hardly ever mentioned either by those who have him going off to Paris in a fit of enthusiasm for the revolution or by those who dwell on his hesitating for 9 months before he departed.

On 10 February, Heine sent a man called Hartwig Hesse, of the Hamburg firm of Hesse, Newmann & Co., a book entitled *Doctrine Saint-Simonienne* that he had read. Referring to his having mentioned it the day before, he wrote that he was attaching an extract 'of the passage in this new gospel of mine which we discussed long ago.' The passage glorified Saint-Simon as one of those 'truly divine' geniuses too absorbed by their 'vast thinking to give a moment's reflection to their personal needs', and extolled his courage – when reduced to living on bread and water – 'to go begging from the rich' for the sake of accomplishing his task on behalf of mankind. In his letter Heine wrote: 'The future will demonstrate to you the great cause which moves me to request your urgent help, and to beg you not for *autant d'argent que vous pouvez*, but for the smallest amount which you may yourself decide on.' He concluded by saying that 'an extraordinary man' like Hesse would understand the 'religious pride' animating him at that moment.

That Heine saw in Saint-Simonism a new vocation is evident from his writing to Varnhagen on 1 April 1831: 'Every night I dream that I am packing my suitcase and travelling to Paris to breathe fresh air, to give myself up entirely to the sacred feelings of my new religion and perhaps to receive the final consecration as one of its priests.'

Of Hartwig Hesse little is known other than that he was a Jew of Danish origin and a philanthropist whom Heine may first have met at his Uncle Salomon's house.[23] Heine had patched up his relations with his millionaire uncle in December 1830, but by March he had another quarrel with him. It was Hesse, believed to have been a supporter of Saint-Simon's ideas, who in the event gave Heine most of the amount required for his move to Paris. The rest was apparently supplied by his more sympathetic Hamburg uncle, Henry Heine.

Heine set out from Hamburg on 1 May 1831. His farewell present to Germany, which he left with 'the soil of the fatherland sticking to the soles of my boots', was the Epilogue to his 'English Fragments', written to bring *Travel Pictures* up to 20 sheets, or 328 pages – which exempted them from pre-censorship on the idea of the authorities that books over this size represented less of a subversive danger because few people read them. It contained his wonderful story of Kunz von der Rosen, the court jester who consoles the imprisoned German people: 'Beneath my cloak I bring you your fine sceptre and your beautiful crown. For you, my people, you are the true emperor, the true master of your land... Your will is sovereign, and the sole legitimate source of all power.'

11

Heine Begins His Life in Paris

On 21 May 1831, two or three days after his arrival in Paris, Heine left the Hôtel du Luxembourg and called at the offices of *Le Globe*. He was received by Michel Chevalier, and their talk led to a lasting friendship. The next morning *Le Globe*, saluting Heine as 'one of the courageous young defenders of the cause of progress', emphasized that he had been fearlessly 'espousing the popular interest in Germany, without falling into narrow-minded nationalism.'[1]

Unlike Chopin, who abhorred the strident aspects of Paris, Heine fell in love with the city at first sight. Sporting a blue jacket and yellow waistcoat, he strolled along the boulevards, studying the architecture, the monuments, the bridges on the Seine and the people about him, whether chic young women or shoe-shine boys at work, with such dreamy-eyed but intent curiosity that Philarète Chasles, a French writer, began to follow, and even to 'walk round him', puzzled by the identity of this 'enigmatic observer'.[2]

Abandoning himself to the rhythm of the city, Heine also made the rounds of the popular dance-halls. For the first time he heard 'loud Gallic laughter', good-tempered, mocking, 'like the delightful French wines or a chapter of Rabelais', and felt so much in his element that a few months later he instructed a friend to tell people in Germany that he was 'like a fish in water; or rather, that if a fish in the sea were asked how it felt, it would answer: "Like Heine in Paris."'[3]

Besides the infectious gaiety, there was the intellectual and political ferment, 'the maelstrom of events' in what seemed to him the continually 'seething revolution', to stimulate Heine in Paris. Five weeks after his arrival he wrote to Varnhagen in Berlin: '*La force des choses* has propelled me to the very top, to Paris, the summit of the world.' Whereas in Germany, as he observed in the same letter, he had known nothing but 'struggle and misery' – his home country had in fact 'poisoned all the springs of life' for him[4] – France received him with open arms, and he quickly rose to literary and social prominence. Remarkably, within 8 months of his arrival he was attending a ball given by the King. To a man long hounded by Prussia's rulers on religious and/or political grounds, it was no mean satisfaction to mix with the *haute volée* at the Tuileries, as he did on 11 January 1832; to be invited two weeks later to a ball at the house of the Prime Minister, Casimir Périer; or to attend the Tuesday evening receptions of General La Fayette. Soon he met François Buloz, the editor of the prestigious *Revue des Deux Mondes*, which, besides serializing French translations of his work, was to carry an article on him by the writer Edgard Quinet, the only one of two portraits (the other was of Carlyle) to appear between its foundation and its temporary suspension during World War II.

During his first two months in Paris, Heine visited the Bibliothèque Royale, the Panthéon and the salon of contemporary painters at the Louvre. He renewed his acquaintance with Ludwig Börne, the sharp-penned critic of Metternich's system. Börne, whose reputation was to be greatly enhanced in the autumn (when 2,000 copies of his *Letters from Paris* (*Briefe aus Paris*) were snapped up in Germany before the book was banned), was now the leader of Germany's so-called 'Jacobin' radicals and of their adherents in Paris. Heine dined and went to the opera with Giacomo Meyerbeer, whose audacious, wildly Romantic *Robert le Diable* was soon to take Paris by storm. Michel Chevalier introduced him to two dignitaries of the Saint-Simonist 'Church' – the dramatist Charles Duveyrier and Hippolyte Carnot, the future statesman – as well as Armand Bazard, one of its two 'Supreme Fathers'. The other was Prosper Enfantin, who had been the moving spirit in investing Saint-Simonism with a dogma, a hierarchy and rites.

On Sundays and Thursdays, he and Bazard, assisted by the 'Sacred College' of 39 members forming its priesthood, presided over soirées attended by Franz Liszt, Berlioz, Sainte-Beuve, Félicien David and a number of lesser-known artists, engineers, medical doctors and army officers. Liszt played the piano and Adolphe Nourrit, the leading tenor of the Paris Opéra, would sing hymns to the new religion and to Enfantin, a spellbinding personality who was gradually emerging as the more dynamic of the two 'popes' and who had composed many of them himself.

Heine spent most of August and September 1831 at Boulogne-sur-Mer, and there is no record of his attending any of these soirées or other functions held at the Saint-Simonist headquarters or 'temple' in the rue Monsigny during those months. Saint-Simonism in 1831 was also being preached at public meetings in the Salle de la rue Taitbout and in 5 halls in the Quartier Latin, at the Polytechnic, the Ecole Normale and some of the lycées. On a tour of the provinces, Enfantin had established 5 district 'churches' at Lyons, Marseilles and other places. Saint-Simonist propaganda – attacking the capitalists, advocating the abolition of class and birth privileges, the limitation of property and of collateral inheritance rights – had gained the movement recruits among the workers of the Faubourg Saint-Antoine in Paris.

327

Heine had gone to Boulogne in the company of the playwright Michel Beer and a German journalist. He found Beer, the author of *Struense*, a great bore – 'He will be immortal as long as he lives,' he quipped – but he enjoyed the sea and made the acquaintance of Odilon-Barrot, the leader of the opposition in the Chamber of Deputies. He was in a relaxed mood, and when there was a sudden downpour on the beach he showed his jocular side by walking up to several Englishwomen who loudly invaded the reading-room, where he was going through some newspapers, and addressing them in hesitant English: 'I hope ladies conversation will not be disturbed by my reading papers.'

Upon his return to Paris on 20 September, he was invited by Börne to join him in a projected new German-French journal. Heine's response was less than enthusiastic, making Börne note in some annoyance that his libertarian comrade-in-arms seemed to prefer to spend his time at the Louvre and to write 'a long report on an exhibition of paintings'.

Gustav Kolb, Baron Cotta's right-hand man, had arrived in Paris, and as soon as he read the manuscript of Heine's report on the exhibition, he wrote to Cotta on 7 October that it belonged with 'the best, most beautiful and most reasoned of Heine's writings'.[5] Serialized from the end of October to the middle of November 1831 in Stuttgart's *Morning Chronicle* (*Morgenblatt*), it was soon to be translated into French and later to be published by Campe in book form under the title *French Painters* (*Französische Maler*).

He was also reviewing musical events for Cotta's paper, though he laughingly confessed to the composer Ferdinand Hiller that he understood 'nothing about music'. Yet Hiller noted that Heine, 'with his imaginative and penetrating mind, heard much more in the music than many so-called musical people. I believe that this is one of the many incomprehensible faculties peculiar to genius.'[6]

Everything seemed to work in Heine's favour in the autumn and winter of 1831. While he was still writing the series on French painters, Kolb invited him to review the French political scene for the *Augsburger Allgemeine Zeitung*, which under his editorship had become Germany's most outspoken daily, uniquely distinguished by its extensive news coverage and its many-faceted treatment of major issues by liberal and conservative writers. Although the paper had to contend with the local Bavarian as well as Metternich's federal censorship, its owner, Baron Cotta – by virtue of his presidency of the Württemberg Diet, his large publishing house and other holdings – was a power in the land, and he steered so carefully and diplomatically between extremes that even Friedrich Gentz, Metternich's chief censor, could not but admire the way the *Allgemeine* dispensed 'the poison together with the antidote' in its pages.[7]

Heine was to work independently of the paper's 8(!) regular Paris correspondents, a number due to the continuing tension between Europe's absolutist rulers and the new 'bourgeois' monarchy in France. Besides, while politically stifled Vienna, Berlin and St Petersburg allowed little but the doings of royalty and official communiques to be reported, France had a Chamber of Deputies, a lively opposition and a relatively free press. Kolb, to whom Heine had once remarked that newspapers 'are our fortresses in the struggle of ideas', wrote to Cotta on 14 December 1831 that with the reactionary system leading to 'nothing good' – i.e., headed for a fall – the issues stirred by the July Revolution were bound 'soon to arise in Germany'; and urged the publisher to engage 'the best political writers' to discuss them before new or upcoming 'young liberal papers' stole the market.[8] Cotta saw the point and Heine, on financial terms laid down by himself, became a premier columnist (in today's parlance) on a highly respected international newpaper. With Europe's eyes fixed on Paris, his articles were sure to attract wide attention.

His very first one not only created a stir but got him into trouble. Published in the *Allgemeine Zeitung* on 11 January 1832, the article contained Heine's statement that the new 'bourgeois' King of the French had forgotten that he owed his crown to 'the sovereign people'. Recent riots at Lyons, where the silk-weavers had struck against their starvation wages, prompted Heine to draw attention to the 'hopeless condition of the lower folk of Paris'. Thousands, he wrote, were dying of misery, and he squarely blamed King Louis-Philippe for the 'gross deceit' of the July Revolution. The Republican *La Tribune* pounced upon the article and suggested that Heine was in the service of France's enemies in the Holy Alliance. By 18 January, *Le Temps* was attacking the German censorship for allowing 'no word to be printed against the Emperors of Russia or Austria or the King of Prussia', but showing 'no similar consideration for the good name of a citizen-king.'

An embarrassed Heine immediately wrote to Cotta that he suspected 'a manoeuvre preconcerted with the German Jacobins, in order to compromise me and to force me to pronounce myself for or against them.'[9] Extracts from his article had in fact been planted in *La Tribune*, in a falsified translation, by Gottlob Franckh, a German bookseller-publisher who, by mass-producing cheaply printed books (he had reputedly sold a million copies of Walter Scott's historic novels in three years), had been Cotta's greatest competitor in Stuttgart. Frankh had recently wound up, some say bankrupted, his business and moved with his money to Paris, where he talked of launching a German-French newspaper that would encourage revolution in Germany.[10]

Börne, although mistrusting Franckh's character – he privately described him as a passionately sincere but hot-headed, 'furious Jacobin' megalomaniac – favoured every project that served 'the good cause' and had placed high hopes in Heine's collaborating with him on it. Börne regarded himself and Heine as 'the two premier writers of the age'. He shared with Franckh a grudge against the *Allgemeine Zeitung*, which had allowed one of its writers to attack his *Letters from Paris* in its columns. Heine sincerely admired Börne's *Letters*. He also shared Kolb's view that Börne had been 'ignobly' treated by the *Allgemeine Zeitung*, which should not have maltreated a work prohibited by the German censorship. But *La Tribune*'s attack on him made Heine wary of Börne and marked the beginning of the antagonism which was to lead to their savaging each other cruelly during Börne's lifetime and beyond.

In his next article in the *Allgemeine Zeitung*, Heine made elegant amends to *Le Temps*. Complimenting it for saying in a hint what others would have tried to achieve by loud polemics, he wrote that henceforth he would refrain from attacking a 'citizen-king' by the licence of a (German) censorship which prohibited any criticism of absolutist monarchs; he only hoped that Louis-Philippe would prove himself to be a true 'citizen-king'. But this was not the end of the affair. *La Tribune*, which itself kept Louis-Philippe under constant fire, had been confiscated. Its editor was to be tried by jury, not for the first time, on charges of *lèse-majesté* and of instigating 'contempt for the government'.

Daumier's celebrated cartoon representing the King's broad-jowled face in the shape of a pear served Heine to give his readers in censorship-ridden Germany an inkling of the unrestrained relish with which the French press made the King the butt of its ridicule. The uproarious aftermath of the affair, which was that Philipon, the editor of *La Caricature*, made the King the laughing-stock of Paris by printing a lithograph of the 4 drawings of 'La Poire' – in which he had shown the court how the King's head could be gradually changed into a pear still faintly resembling his face, but no more than any odd man's face – gave Heine the occasion to illustrate the uses and influence of public opinion. With Philipon facing a new trial, he showed up the futility of the King's attempts to replace the abolished censorship by means of press-trials, each of which only served to compromise him further.

Already in his series *French Painters*, Heine, interlarding his impressions of the 1831 salon with his political views, had used Delacroix's painting of *Liberty Leading the People* to evoke the significance of the July Revolution as a symbol of 'the indestructible spirit of man'. Delacroix struck Heine as the committed artist *par excellence*. The figure of his heroine stepping over corpses to summon the citizenry to the fray with a pain-racked yet defiant expression on her face – 'a strange mixture of Phryne, fishwife and goddess of freedom' in her red Phrygian cap and loose, bare-bosomed dress – suggested to him the wild, elementary 'life-force of the people' throwing off its yoke. At the same time his representing the 'goddess of freedom' as a Phryne, 'a Venus of the streets' of the type he encountered at night in the Passage des Panorames, was in line with Heine's old objection to the repression of sensual enjoyment by religion, reinforced by the new Saint-Simonist call for the emancipation of the flesh.

This was a concept superimposed by Enfantin on Saint-Simon's original advocacy of women's equality, which had led to heated discussions in the 'Sacred College' during Heine's absence at Boulogne the previous summer. Enfantin argued resolutely that the reform of society required not only a new religion but a new morality, not only women's equality but the abolition of all sexual interdicts, including the right – at least for 'mobile' men like himself – to multiple liaisons and 'temporary marriages'. Bazard and others strongly rebelled against this 'legitimization of adultery'. In the atmosphere of exaltation which prevailed at the secret sessions in the inner sanctum of the rue Monsigny, where a dozen or so members of the 'Sacred College' and their families lived together with its two 'popes', Bazard's wife at one moment sided with Enfantin and announced that she was divorcing her husband after 18 years of marriage. Things had come to a head on 25 August, when Bazard had a fit of apoplexy.

Enfantin's mother wrote to her son: 'Are you going to proclaim yourself sole chief of the Saint-Simonist doctrine by taking the wife of the chief you are deposing, and perhaps his children too?'[11] But in a sudden volte-face, Claire Bazard, comparing Enfantin to Satan, packed her things and left the premises. Michel Chevalier worked out a short-lived compromise whereby Rodrigues, the banker who had looked after Saint-Simon during his last years, joined Bazard and Enfantin as a third 'pope'.

In October, Bazard's daughter and another couple were married by the self-appointed Saint-Simonist priests in their specially designed blue-white costumes, not to say vestments, according to a ritual of their own devising. But an adamant Enfantin stuck to his theory, engendering more debates on the paternity of children resulting from 'temporary marriages'. Normally a cool logician, he began to ascribe a mystic role to women and finally announced that all problems would be solved with the advent of a new partner, a Female-Mother-Messiah who alone could help him to formulate the new moral law, and by 9 November 1831 the Saint-Simonist cult had split, with Bazard, Carnot, Pierre Leroux and others leaving the 'Church'.

Heine never mentioned these strange goings-on, which had reached boiling point about the time he was writing *French Painters*, though he must have heard of them from Chevalier, who in December published in *Le Globe* a review of his 'Kahldorf on the Nobility'. On 22 January 1832, following the two marriages performed outside the Catholic Church, the refusal of the remaining Saint-Simonist priests to serve in the National Guard – on the grounds of clerical exemption – and rumours about alleged orgies in the rue Monsigny, the street was cordoned off by a squadron of hussars. Enfantin, Rodrigues and several others were arrested and remanded. Before they were to be tried for illegal association and 'outrage to morality', the single-minded Enfantin ruthlessly removed Rodrigues, Saint-Simon's oldest disciple and heir-apparent, by publicly showing him a letter from his wife lamenting her marital unhappiness. Rodrigues regained his composure sufficiently to say that he was misinterpreting his wife's letter, but left broken-hearted.[12]

On the evening of the arrest, Heine was at a public Saint-Simonist meeting in the rue Taitbout. He was present, as he tersely reported,[13] when 'the Royal Prosecutor' had the hall cleared and sealed. That Heine looked askance at the authoritarian cult, complete with ludicrous rites, into which Enfantin had turned Saint-Simonism is evident from an unpublished note of his. In it he remarked wrily that God must have been desperate 'to save the world' if He had chosen Enfantin for the job; the result was that 'He made Himself ridiculous – and all in vain!'[14] And when, after the second schism, Enfantin moved with a group of his faithful devotees to a hillside 'retreat' at Ménilmontant – there to await the arrival of the mystic Female-Mother-Messiah – Heine thought his retirement from the public scene would turn out 'a good thing' for the Saint-Simonist doctrine.

'It will come into wiser hands,' he wrote to Varnhagen. 'As far as I am concerned, I am only interested in its religious ideas.'[15] What Heine meant by this he was to explain a couple of years later in terms of Saint-Simon's 'Golden Age' of the future – the late count's vision of men of talent in the age of industrial progress transforming the earth into a world of plenty that would assure the material welfare of 'the most numerous and poorest class' as well. 'Now that the dimensions of our planet are known' is how Saint-Simon had started one of the paragraphs in his gospel. Echoing him almost to the word, Heine was to write: 'We have measured the lands, weighed the forces of nature, reckoned the means of industry, and behold, we have found that this earth is large enough; that it... can nourish us all decently if we all work and do not want to live at the cost of another; and that we do not have to refer the larger and poorer class to heaven.'[16]

Heine took from Enfantin the notion of the emancipation of the flesh, which agreed with his own early-expressed pantheist and 'sensualist' approach to life and the social problem. 'God is in our kisses,' he had written in the 1820s in the poem 'Mountain Idyll', foreshadowing a 'Third Testament' that would resolve the conflict between body and spirit. Heine distinguished between 'two social systems which influence all the manifestations of life'. One was based on the 'wanton presumption of the spirit' which sought to subdue, or at least to stigmatize, matter. As against this social attitude – which he called 'Spiritualism' –

Heine defined 'Sensualism' as the attitude which 'aims at the rehabilitation of matter and vindicates the rights of the senses without denying the rights of the spirit, and in fact without denying the supremacy of the spirit.'[17]

In *The Romantic School* Heine was to write: 'We promote the well-being of matter, the material happiness of nations, not because we despise the spirit as do the materialists, but because we know that the divinity of man is manifested also in his visible body, and that misery' – the self-denial imposed by repressive conventional religion – 'destroys and debases the body, the image of God, and ultimately the spirit, too. The great motto of the Revolution, uttered by Saint-Just, "bread is the right of the people", we read as "bread is the divine right of man"', bread in the sense of material well-being and the right to enjoy the pleasures of life.[18]

This facet of his new creed had made Heine, in *French Painters*, describe Leopold Robert's *Reapers* – showing happy young Italian countrywomen gathering up a bountiful harvest while a hefty young labourer jubilantly brandishes his scythe to the sky – as 'an apotheosis of life'. The labourer's gesture and the serenity of the whole scene made him exclaim: '"Heaven is on earth and men carry a divine spark in themselves", that is the great revelation luminously conveyed by this painting.' The Paris public, he added, responded more favourably 'to this painted gospel than to St Luke's', and he noted other signs indicating that Catholicism had lost its hold on French life and art.

From this it was but a short step to his declaring on 10 February – in the third of his political articles for the *Allgemeine Zeitung* – that 'a new art, a new religion, a new life' were being created in Paris. 'Mighty deeds are dawning, and unknown gods are about to reveal themselves.'

The 'new religion' was only in the making, but some of its green ideas visibly influenced Heine's treatment of politics and the social question in the articles he wrote for the *Allgemeine Zeitung*. Altogether 8, some of them longish essays printed in instalments, appeared in the paper between January and July 1832. Then the series was discontinued upon Metternich's intervention. Covering so short a time-span, these articles – better known as 'Conditions in France' (*Französische Zustände*), the title under which (along with an additional piece that did not appear in the paper) they were to appear in book form – hardly offered Heine sufficient scope to encompass 'the whole universal context' of events in France. Nevertheless, before he was interrupted in mid-process he managed to discern and highlight the main issues which were to agitate the 'bourgeois' monarchy for the next 16 years until its fall.

Paris was 'the capital not only of France, but of the civilized world.' Yet, when he looked out from this European 'summit' he could see that Warsaw had

333

fallen, Poland had become a Russian province, and every other patriotic uprising in the wake of the July Revolution – in Italy, Belgium and Spain – had been
suppressed by the reactionary countries of the Holy Alliance. In France itself,
Louis-Philippe appeared to be seeking to attain 'quasi-legitimacy by means of
alliances with the absolutist princes'. In January, besides a number of press
trials, members of the Republican *Amis du peuple* were seized on charges of
alleged 'conspiracy to overthrow the government'; only a few months later a
serious revolutionary flare-up was put down by force of arms. Paris was to be
placed under martial law, seemingly confirming Heine's initial suspicion that
the jovial-looking 'bourgeois' king might carry 'the most absolute sceptre
hidden in his umbrella'.

Besides mining the Paris press for information, Heine – to get to the root of
'the great dispute causing bloody and bitter strife in France' – attended some
of the heated debates in the Chamber of Deputies as well as public party meetings. The King's Orléanist supporters claimed that Louis-Philippe's assumption of the throne in July 1830 had 'saved the peace', for if a republic had been
declared, Europe's monarchs would certainly have invaded France to stamp out
any regime headed by some common *roturier*. To the Bourbon Legitimists,
however, the King remained a usurper. The Bonapartists clung to the glories of
the empire and loved the dead Napoleon more than the living but drab King;
and he faced the fiercest opposition from the Republicans who – as Heine wrote
in his third article (and elaborated in the ninth) – not only held that 'peace
without freedom' was worthless but said more or less openly that the King
deserved a traitor's death for destroying 'the holy liberties obtained by their
fathers in the French Revolution.'

On the evening of 1 February, Heine went to hear Auguste Blanqui address
a meeting of the *Amis du peuple* in a hall packed with 1,500 people. He was
impressed by Blanqui's sincerity and fiery rethoric, but the righteous wrath with
which Blanqui infected the grim-faced audience gave him the feeling of being
transported back to the 'bloody' 1793 phase of the French Revolution. 'Robespierre's last speech of the eighth Thermidor is their gospel,' he wrote of these
radical Republicans. He was appalled by their 'guillotinomania'. They seemed
to be hankering for the days of the Terror, forgetting that this had been instituted by their fathers to save *la patrie* from extreme danger. They forgot, too,
that times had since changed to the point where the sons could now publicly say
things for which – he could not help remarking – 'in North Germany they
would be remanded for life.'

Later the same night, Heine drove to a soirée held by the Legitimists or
Carlists – the followers of the deposed Charles X, of the elder Bourbon line – in
the Faubourg Saint-Germain, only to find that the elegant company there too

were 'plagiarizing' the past, and dreaming of reinstituting the good old days of the *ancien régime*.

At this time Heine shared Blanqui's anger at the bourgeoisie for having installed a 'grocer-king'. As one who felt called to 'decipher the ultimate reason of all phenomena', he meant to discuss the relative merits of republics and monarchies. The cholera which struck Paris in the last week of March forced him to abandon the subject. But he regarded the radical *Amis du peuple* as outright 'retrograde' in their fixation on the past, instead of concentrating on the chances of improving the lot of the masses presented by the 'development of industry and economics'. Unlike the Saint-Simonists, they seemed to 'understand only the externals of the revolution and not its deeper problems. These concern neither forms [of government] nor persons, neither the introduction of a republic nor the limitation of the monarchy; the real problem is the well-being of the people as a whole.'

Heine was writing in veiled terms to a Saint-Simonist sympathizer in Germany, Heinrich Laube – the editor of Leipzig's 'Journal for the Elegant World' (*Zeitung für die Elegante Welt*) – who was indeed soon to be prosecuted and imprisoned. He went on to say that religion had hitherto consoled the majority of mankind for 'living in misery, but now the development of industry and economics' promised to put an end to this state and 'opens the possibility of happiness for all in this world... You know what I mean. The people will understand us when we tell them that they can eat beef instead of potatoes, that they can work less and dance more. Believe me, humans are not asses.'[19]

It was only in *The Romantic School* that Heine was to make public his faith in Saint-Simonism and to define it as a 'passionate belief in progress'. But already in the spring of 1832, he was privately saluting the Varnhagens in Berlin with Saint-Simon's reputed last words on his deathbed: 'The future belongs to us!' Until the police measures against Enfantin and his faithfuls, the French press had treated the goings-on in the 'Sacred College' as a joke. But during the search of its premises in the rue Monsigny the police had raided the offices of *Le Globe* and confiscated three cartfuls of its archives and account books. This had caused a practically unanimous outcry in the Paris papers, giving rise to suspicions that the whole raid had been staged less against Saint-Simonism – which was bad enough, since suppressing a 'doctrine' recalled the practices of the *ancien régime* – than against the influence which *Le Globe*, under the editorship of Chevalier, had achieved by its high standard among intellectuals both in France and abroad. Through it, indeed, Saint-Simonism had found adherents in Italy, Germany, Sweden, the United States and even Brazil. 'All winter these [Saint-Simonist] writings, the Globe especially, have been my nourishment,' Rahel von Varnhagen wrote to Heine in 1832. Saint-Simonism was 'the new

335

instrument, the great discovery which at last touches the old, great wound, the history of mankind on earth. This instrument is working, and sows its seed. It has brought to life indisputable truths.' She summed up its message in one sentence: 'Freedom for the development of human talent.'[20]

The scope offered to talents in the planned Saint-Simonist society of the future – which for all its elitist character would abolish the aristocracy and 'the exploitation of man by man' and promised the betterment of all social classes, including the lowest – was what divided Heine from the 'virtuous Republicans'. Addressing them directly in a piece published in France before it was to appear in German, he specified their different viewpoints:

> We do not want to be sans-culottes, frugal burghers, cheap presidents; we are founding a democracy of gods who shall be equal in splendour, equally holy, equally happy. You demand simple dress, abstemious habits... We demand nectar and ambrosia, purple cloaks, sumptuous aromas, voluptuousness and luxury, laughing nymphdance... To your censorious reproaches we reply in the words of one of Shakespeare's clowns: 'Dost thou think, because thou art virtuous, there shall be no more cakes and ale?'[21]

In May 1832 Bascans, the editor of *La Tribune*, appeared on trial on a variety of charges, including that of having reprinted Heine's sharp criticism of Louis-Philippe in his first article in the *Allgemeine Zeitung*. Uneasy at the thought of having his name dragged through the courts, Heine was pleased when the jury acquitted Bascans, ruling that foreign correspondents could express themselves freely on conditions in France, and French newspapers were free to reproduce their reports.[22] His relief, however, did not last long; for even as the defence attorney for the Republican paper – although not mentioning Heine by name – had called him 'an Austrian-Russian-Prussian agent, and an enemy of France', Metternich in Vienna had had enough of Heine's reports on conditions in France.

In the third of these articles on 1 March, Heine made an allusion to Casimir Périer's powerful physique and his role as the personification of the *juste-milieu* in describing the Prime Minister as 'the Atlas who holds the Stock Exchange, the House of Orléans and the whole edifice of Europe's states on his shoulders.' Périer's early career as an opponent of feudalism and the aristocracy reminded Heine of 'George Canning, the greatest Minister who ever ruled England'. But there the similarity between the two men had ended. Whereas Canning, born in poverty and dependent on the favour of the Tories, had shaken them off and to the horror of his masters had emerged as 'a Spartacus of Downing Street to proclaim the civic and religious freedom of all peoples, thereby winning for

England all liberal hearts', the well-born Périer had become 'petty-minded and grocer-like'. Not only that, but the *juste-milieu*, Heine suggested in his fifth article on 25 March – shortly before Périer succumbed to cholera – had reduced France to a lower state than at the time of Mesdames Pompadour and Dubarry: 'One sees now,' he wrote, 'that there is something worse than the rule of mistresses. There is more honour to be found in the boudoir of a lady of easy virtue than in the counting-house of a banker.' Noting that there had been more gaiety and balls than ever in Paris that winter, he went on to say that 'the supporters of the government, officials, bankers, landed proprietors and boutiquiers', had turned the Stock Exchange into a 'barometer of the people's happiness'. Covering up for the general dissatisfaction, they kept 'dancing *à la hausse*' to give an impression of peace, order and stability and to keep share prices going up.

The last instalment of this article had hardly appeared in the *Allgemeine Zeitung* in April when Gentz, at Metternich's behest, sent Cotta an angry letter:

> Now the cup is full. For a long time the cry has been, 'Away with the clergy and the nobility, they have had their day, requiescant in pace.' But when men like Périer and his supporters, that is to say, officials, bankers, landed proprietors and boutiquiers are attacked in more violent terms than the previous regime of princes, counts and barons, one may well ask, 'Who, then, is to govern the nations?'

To Gentz, the veteran trainbearer of arch-conservative absolutism, Périer and the 'citizen-king' were now the guardians of 'order and peace' against subversive liberalism. He added that he personally respected, even 'loved', Heine as a poet, but it passed his understanding how Cotta could print the scandalous articles of this 'adventurer' in his highly respected paper.[23]

Cotta replied evasively, but continued to publish Heine's articles. Before the end of March, he had actually thanked Heine for the 'life and freshness' his articles brought to the *Allgemeine Zeitung*. He had indeed every reason to be satisfied, for in terms of circulation, too – as Kolb had observed before leaving Paris on 12 February – Heine's articles were 'certainly profitable' to the paper. All, incidentally, appeared unsigned; in order to protect controversial authors against censorship reprisals, the paper identified their contributions by an asterisk, cross, circle or some other mark printed next to the dateline. Heine had chosen a six-pointed star for his personal cipher. What bothered him most was his having to 'pre-censor everything in my own head' while writing it. He frequently voiced complaints that he was being watched by Prussian and Austrian spies – complaints which were long ascribed to his being paranoid, but as Sammons has noted, 'we know today that they were well founded.'[24]

Worse, once Heine had written about the 'guillotinomania characterizing the Republicans', the German 'Jacobins' in Paris and an indignant Börne treated him practically as a traitor to the liberal cause. The scattered 'little revolutions' which had been suppressed in Germany kept the Paris émigrés in a fever. 'Never a day passed', the writer Gutzkow was to note, 'without a manifesto to dethrone this or that prince... Heine was much embarrassed by the countless requests which were made to him as the poet of liberty.'[25] When he finally refused to sign any further proclamations, the rumour spread that he was a hireling. One day he found a dagger wrapped in a Republican leaflet in his post. And now, to cap it all, Gentz in his letter had lumped him together with 'Wirth... and the rest of the revolutionary coterie'.

Johann Wirth was a militant Hamburg newspaper publisher who, forced to flee to Bavaria, had launched a mushrooming movement for 'a democratic German Reich' and a free press. Political meetings being prohibited, he set up a dozen or so 'Press and Fatherland Societies' and staged banquets at which libertarian speeches mixed with patriotic rhetoric were delivered. The societies were soon forbidden, but news of Wirth's 'democratic' struggle caused a frenzy among the 7,000 or so German émigrés in Paris. The majority were humble tailors, shoemakers, carpenters and other artisans or apprentices, but a small number of political refugees, and no one more than Börne – who sometimes treated gatherings of up to 'six hundred journeymen tailors' on Montmartre to fiery republican speeches – made it their job to educate them politically.

Gentz's suspicion that Heine was in league with Wirth was unfounded. Contrary to a tendentious report planted in *Le National* stating that 'Börne and Heine have made common cause with Dr Wirth,' Heine did not react when the latter invited both of them to come and join him 'in the liberation of Germany'. He was in fact as surprised as Gentz himself when Dr Wirth, after a short term in jail, managed on 27 May to stage the greatest political demonstration in Germany between then and the 1848 revolutions: the 'Hambacher Fest', or Festival, in Bavaria. Börne, always expecting revolution 'any day, any hour', had of course left for Hambach Castle in time to see the spectacle of 25,000, some say 30,000, Germans of every political denomination, radical Republicans, liberal monarchists, democrats and Teutomaniacs – including student delegations from several universities as well as some professors – holding a rally in favour of 'German popular sovereignty' and a 'federated, republican Europe'. Between lighting bonfires and joining in patriotic songs, they heard and cheered Wirth and other speakers denouncing the Austrian and Prussian monarchs as 'traitors to humanity'.

Remarkably, too, the rally sent 'brotherly greetings to the enslaved peoples' of Poland, Hungary, Italy and Spain. 'I rubbed my eyes', Heine was to write, 'and asked myself, "Am I dreaming?... Is it possible that Dr Wirth really exists, this brave knight-errant of liberty?"[26] On 1 March he had written to Cotta: 'Sooner or later the revolution will begin in Germany, the *idea* is already there.' But he did not believe that it was imminent, nor had he taken Wirth's 'Press and Fatherland' banquets or his chances of 'liberating Germany' seriously. Indeed, the Hambacher Fest proceeded with great feeling, but ended in chaos, the various opposition leaders being unable to agree on aims and means. Some insisted on an immediate armed revolt; others proposed first to try democratic persuasion; and whereas some raised the question whether the assembly was at all 'competent' (*sic!*) to launch an insurrection, the more chauvinist element made a federated Europe dependent on France's first returning Alsace and Lorraine to Germany and ventilated expansionist plans in the direction of the Balkans.[27] None had a party organization or any political experience.

Field Marshal Wrede with nearly 9,000 troops – half the Bavarian army – marched in to 'pacify the area' and prevent further 'conspiracies'. By 18 June, Wirth and his chief associates had been arrested. 'There was a new wave of persecution in Prussia, Hesse and even in easy-going Bavaria... Hundreds of people were sentenced to death, and although they were reprieved from execution their spirits were broken ...'[28]

On 9 June, Cotta had published the last instalment of Heine's eighth article in the *Allgemeine Zeitung*. Gentz died that day, and it is not known to what extent the publisher's decision, a week later, not to print Heine's ninth article was influenced by Metternich's hint – conveyed through Gentz – that Heine was disturbing the forces of 'order and peace' in Europe, or whether the series on conditions in France was discontinued with Heine's agreement in view of more rigorous censorship instituted after the Hambach Festival. The *Allgemeine Zeitung* was to continue to print his *Tagesberichte* ('Daily Reports') until mid-September, but he sensed that he might soon have his mouth shut altogether; and continually harassed as he was by the radical émigrés in Paris while being defamed by 'the clerical and aristocratic party in Germany as an extremist and *enragé*',[29] he felt caught in the crossfire, even as he had become part of the seething 'maelstrom of events' which was Paris, and of its glittering social life.

It was in all probability at General La Fayette's mansion in the rue d'Anjou-Saint-Honoré that Heine first met with that cross-section of French society that later in 1832 made him declare that in Paris he was 'witnessing world history in the making, and consorting amicably with its greatest heroes.'[30] Heine left no social diary, and not every one of his moves has been documented. But at Boulogne-sur-Mer he made the acquaintance of Camille Odilon-Barrot, one of La Fayette's trusted aides, who after escorting the deposed Charles X to Cherbourg had declined Louis-Philippe's offer of the premiership, preferring the role of leader of the opposition.[31] Heine also knew Baron Ferdinand d'Eckstein, the

Inspecteur-Général of the Paris Police Ministry, who wrote articles on the side for the *Allgemeine Zeitung*.[32] Either Odilon-Barrot or d'Eckstein, or someone Heine met at the house of James de Rothschild, may have introduced him to La Fayette's receptions.

The residence of this venerable symbol of the American and French Revolutions – the 'hero of two worlds', as Heine called him, when not referring to his new role as 'Napoleon of the petite bourgeoisie' – was the most likely place for him to have encountered 'old musketeers who had danced with Marie Antoinette', ex-members of the Directoire, 'high dignitaries of the Empire before whom all Europe had trembled', as well as some of the rising politicians of the day, with whom he soon had more distinctly documented contacts: men like the comte de Salvandy, Adolphe Thiers, François Guizot and Charles-Marie Duchâtel – all of whom were to hold office under Louis-Philippe – or the marquis Edouard de Lagrange, a diplomat and writer. Thiers, the future Prime Minister, was Heine's age, 35; Odilon-Barrot and Guizot were in their early forties; the three others mentioned were a year or two older or younger than Heine. He struck them exactly as *Le Globe* had described him – a man of progressive modern ideas – and not only because he liked to dress in the latest fashion.

Starting in June 1832, François Buloz, the editor of *Revue des Deux Mondes* and a formidable literary arbiter, began to print French translations of Heine's works. Sections of *The Harz Journey*, the *English Fragments*, *The Book of LeGrand* and *The Baths of Lucca* were appearing every other month in this highly respected periodical, and in November *Le Temps* followed suit with Heine's reflections on the battlefield of Marengo. What with these publications and the preparation by marquis de Lagrange of a translation of his *North Sea III*, Heine's *renommé* in France was established.

Victor Bohain, the wooden-legged ex-millionaire and former director of *Le Figaro*, invited him to collaborate on the newly founded *L'Europe Littéraire* – dedicated to the best of French and world literature and to be produced on expensive vellum – and introduced him, over champagne and the delights of French cooking, to a whole galaxy of front-rank writers who were to contribute to the new publication. A high-living and expansive character, Bohain turned the regular dinners of *L'Europe Littéraire* into what one of those invited in 1833 – Hans Christian Andersen – described as 'a kind of Atheneum for the beautiful people of Paris.' Heine was not exaggerating when, within three years of his arrival in France, he wrote to his brother Maximilian that he was 'practically crushed by the extraordinary honours lavished' on him.[33]

At the beginning of 1833, Campe in Hamburg published the German book version of 'Conditions in France'. It contained the ninth article which the *Allge-*

meine Zeitung had not printed. In it, taking up the burning question of republics versus monarchies, Heine professed his unmitigated admiration of the heroes of the French Revolution and their struggle for the first Republic. And yet, he wrote, he would not like to live under the rule of such lofty minds:

> I could not stand being guillotined every day, and nobody was able to stand it, and the French Republic could only win victories and, in winning them, bleed to death. It is not inconsistent of me to love this Republic without in the least desiring to see this form of government reestablished in France – and even less a German version of it.

One could even wish, without being inconsistent, 'that France should again be a republic but that Germany should remain a monarchy.' For the French had the characteristics of a nation tending towards republicanism, characteristics which he summed up as follows: 'Republicans believe in no authority, and respect only laws; they constantly call the upholders of the laws to account, mistrusting them even as they control them; they do not respect individuals, and whenever their representatives rise above the common level of the people, they seek to keep them down by opposition, suspicion, mockery and persecution.'[34] By contrast, the Germans – who still believed 'in individuals, authority, the police, and, above all, in parchment titles' – were by nature royalists.[35]

No wonder that Heine, for all his protestations that he was not inconsistent, aroused the anger of the Börne group in Paris and suspicion among some of the liberals in Germany. The controversy about his ambivalence has flared up over the years again and again until late into the 20th century. He was indeed full of ostensible contradictions. He seemed to agree with Blanqui and the extreme Republicans of the *Amis du Peuple* that the French Revolution had not completed its agenda – 'so long as the Revolution is not finished', he wrote, 'the malaise of the state remains incurable'[36] – and he continued to hack away at the aristocracy and the clergy. Yet practically at the same time he declared in 'Conditions in France': 'A monarchist by inclination, I have become more so in this country by conviction.' Not all his contradictions, however, were what they seemed to be. Heine called the Germans royalists by nature, yet as early as 1 March 1832 he had predicted that revolution would break out in Germany 'sooner or later'. The accent here was on 'later', for Heine knew that Germany was a 'land of thoroughness'.

In the ninth article of 'Conditions in France' he elaborated on this: 'I do not believe in a coming German revolution, and still less in a German republic; the latter I will certainly not see in my lifetime.' But he was 'convinced that long after we have all rotted in our graves they will still be fighting for the republic in Germany, fighting both with words and with swords.' For the Germans had 'never abandoned an idea without fighting for it to the bitter end', no matter how long it might take. In a tribute to the misplaced courage of the organizers of the Hambach Festival he observed: 'Thoughts are free, they glide through the air like birds' and might nest quietly for half a century in Germany's oak trees. 'But what is half a century or even a whole century? The people have time enough ahead of them, they are eternal; only kings are mortal.'[37]

Heine's was not the ordinary journalist's perception of events. Whereas his presentation of them was kaleidoscopic in its range and shifting of subjects, digressions and metaphors, his perception of political developments was telescopic since, like a star-gazer, he was more preoccupied with an attempt to descry their direction, not to say trajectory, than with their immediate effect. He was engaged in this at a time of utter disorientation in Germany, where Metternich, in June 1832, had pushed through the Bundestag Decrees prohibiting all public meetings and empowering the Bundestag to annul the laws of the various member-states of the German Confederation. The hopeless situation there after the Hambach Festival has been described by Golo Mann: 'The Radicals were taken seriously enough to be feared', but they either languished in prisons or met as 'refugees in foreign capitals... Those who thought about these things at all – always a mere minority – did not doubt that there would have to be a change, that the monarchical, bureaucratic, military system was no longer in keeping with the spirit of the age. But who would bring about a change, how and when and what form it would take, nobody really knew.'[38]

This was exactly Heine's predicament in 1832. Revolutions, he observed in 'Conditions in France', occurred when a people's outmoded institutions no longer suited its needs and state of mind. But, immune as he was to the 'foolish illusions' of the German refugees in Paris, he found his pessimistic prognosis confirmed during an August holiday at Le Havre, when the sight of German emigrants about to embark for Algeria, made him exclaim: 'Devil take it! The tenth part of what these people have tolerated would in France have provoked thirty-six revolutions and cost thirty-six kings their crowns with their heads into the bargain!' Heine was neither a political scientist nor a rabble-rousing people's tribune. 'The tribune whose purpose it is to bring about a political revolution', he wrote in his ninth article, 'must not go too far ahead of the masses.' The writer was another matter. He looked at the world from a perspective entirely his own:[39] 'The writer who wants to further social revolution may anticipate his age by a hundred years.' And that is exactly what Heine did. Besides conjuring up the liveliness and drama of French politics, his book portrayed the leading parties and personalities involved and contrasted the beginning domination of French life by the banks and the Bourse with the worsening plight of the lower classes. As one of his most eminent biographers would acknowledge towards the end of the 20th century, 'Heine could see the great social issue of the next hundred years in embryo, and he knew that this was what he saw.'[40]

The German publication of 'Conditions in France' involved Heine in a triple storm. His newspaper articles had been couched in a fairly moderate tone. But for the book version – in reaction to the Bundestag Decrees and the suppression of all liberal hopes in Germany – he had written a Preface attacking its sovereigns in language no one had dared to use before him. He accused them of nothing less than 'high treason against the German nation' and of insulting the intelligence of a people that had 'produced gunpowder, the art of printing and the *Critique of Pure Reason*' and 'imagining that we are more stupid than you are yourselves.' Heine especially castigated 'hypocritical Prussia, this Tartuffe among the states', for basely misusing its philosophers and theologians to impress 'the common people' with the virtues of its absolutist regime. 'Hegel had to justify the existing slavery as [the embodiment of] reason,' he wrote angrily in the Preface.

Hegel had died of cholera in Berlin in 1831, mourned by its intellectual world as second to none but Aristotle and even as a second Christ. His thesis that 'everything actual is rational' ostensibly justified conservatism. The revolutionary antithesis that the future might turn the rational into actuality had yet to be read into Hegel's dialectic.

Hegel's assertion that society, 'the State', was the realization of absolute reason and the only framework assuring individual freedom through the rule of law, served Berlin's state-appointed professors well. Since Hegel also held that the state itself was nothing but the consummation of Divine Providence, or 'the finger of God in history', working to achieve its ends through reason, they were able to present the King – who was the divinely appointed bearer of that reason in 'the state' – as being the subjectified expression of the people's sovereignty. Thus they could glorify the individual's total subservience to Prussia and its feudal monarch not only as a high ideal but as the most advanced philosophy.

The religious side of Hegel's philosophy had yet to be attacked by his so-called 'Young Hegelian' disciples when Heine wrote his Preface to 'Conditions in France'. Shortly afterwards he was to point out that when Hegel spoke of 'the state', he had in mind the *perfect* state. In the Preface he cited Schleiermacher, Moritz Arndt and the historian Ranke among other great minds who had been forced 'to betray God, reason' and their conscience and to justify the Bundestag Decrees in order to keep their posts or stipends. He promised the rulers of the Holy Alliance that he would continue to fight them, as he had in his newspaper articles, by way of helping to form an enlightened public opinion until 'a holy alliance of nations' that would put an end to the war-mongering of the ruling class and devote the moneys spent on armies and horses to the achievement of 'peace, prosperity and liberty' for all. For the book version of the articles he had chosen the motto: '*Vive la France, quand-même*'. He concluded his fulminating Preface with a warning to the German kings and princes not to be so sure that their 'servile' giant clown of a people might not one day, 'from an excess of humour, crack in your skulls with his little finger so that your brains splash up to the stars.'[41]

The German censors not only mutilated the Preface but rewrote and traduced it into an opposite sense. 'I have been made to appear in the eyes of the whole of Germany as a sorry flatterer of the King of Prussia,' Heine thundered at Campe, insisting that 'just because the cause of liberalism is at its lowest ebb the Preface must be published forthwith in its entirety' in spite of the risk that he might be barred from Germany for life.[42]

Shortly afterwards, Ludwig Börne, scandalized by Heine's confession that he was a monarchist, took a blast at 'Conditions in France'. Heine had indeed revised his view of King Louis-Philippe. As he became more familiar with the French scene, he had developed a certain sympathy for the clumsy attempts of the handshaking and much-ridiculed 'bourgeois' king to make himself popular. Although expressly rejecting the 'system' of the *juste-milieu*, Heine had written that Louis-Philippe deserved at least a chance to prove himself as a 'true bourgeois' king. Börne, however, felt that Heine was engaging in Jesuitic casuistry and had hurt the liberal cause.

The July Revolution, which had brought the two foremost critics of absolutism together in Paris, thus also drove them apart. 'Poor Heine', Börne wrote on 25 February 1833 in a new volume of his 'Letters from Paris', was now fearing 'blows from both aristocrats and democrats. To avoid them he must try to go forwards and backwards at the same time.'[43]

To add a tragic irony to Börne's break with Heine, King Friedrich Wilhelm III of Prussia had in January instructed his Ministers to take measures against the works of both of them. 'Conditions in France' was indeed promptly banned in Prussia. Heine, keen to refute the charges of the Radicals that he had sold out to the enemies of liberalism, engaged in long arguments with Campe about how and where to have the Preface printed as a pamphlet. He also wrote a 'Preface to the Preface', but all he managed for the time being was to have a brief repudiation of the fake 'servile' Preface – the only one that had appeared – inserted in the *Allgemeine Zeitung*. He was angry with himself and the world for having to spend energy on these 'trifles, for in less time than this Preface is costing me I wrote half a book.'

The book he referred to, serialized that spring in Bohain's *L'Europe Littéraire*, was to open the two volumes to be published in Paris under the title *De l'Allemagne*; the original German was later issued as *The Romantic School* and 'On the History of Religion and Philosophy in Germany' (*Zur Geschichte der Religion und Philosophie in Deutschland*). True to his promise that he would enlighten public opinion on the evils of nationalism, Heine had resolved to help the French penetrate that mystery of the German mind which made it possible for the advanced philosophies of Kant and Hegel and the works of Goethe and Schiller to co-exist with superstition, religious bigotry, latent Teutomaniac tendencies and the worst possible political reaction. Madame de Staël's famous *De l'Allemagne* had planted in the minds of most French intellectuals an image of Germany as a progressive nation of thinkers and poets, and Heine's very choice of the same title indicated that he meant to debunk that notion. The purpose of his undertaking and the importance he attached to it are evident from a letter he wrote to Merckel in Hamburg at the beginning of April 1833:

> It is perhaps my pacific mission to bring about a rapprochement between peoples, which is what the aristocrats fear most. With the destruction of national prejudices, with the annihilation of patriotic narrow-mindedness, they will lose their best accessories for oppression. I am cosmopolitanism incarnate. I know that this will in the end become the general trend of opinion in Europe; therefore I am convinced that the future is on my side rather than with our Teutomaniacs, these mortal people who belong to the past.

When the full *De l'Allemagne*, bearing the respected imprint of Renduel, appeared in Paris in 1835, Börne returned to the attack on Heine and damned it in a review in *Le Réformateur*. The beginning of the rupture between them, however, coincided with the serialization of sections of the work in *L'Europe Littéraire* and later in *Revue des Deux Mondes*. Heine's name now appeared among those of France's foremost writers. But neither he nor Börne could take their eyes off Germany. There, on 3 April 1833, 50 or so republican students in Frankfurt stormed the chief constabulary post in the mistaken hope that this would become the signal for a popular uprising. The amateurish affair led to the arrest of nearly 2,000 people. Represented as a *putsch*, it gave Metternich the opportunity to form a 'Central Commission' for preventing 'conspiracies' throughout the German states. Prussia, Bavaria and several others joined Austria in additional repressive measures, compared to which the erstwhile Karlsbad Decrees seemed mild.

Börne's agitation for instant revolution was belied, and Heine felt once more confirmed in his views. He refrained from reacting publicly to Börne's attacks on him either in 1833 or in 1835, but the hurt went deep. For the gravamen of Börne's condemnation of him was serious and twofold: Heine, he judged, had 'talent' but lacked 'character' and moral fibre; and as a consequence, he tended to sacrifice truth to 'beauty', or to accept the truth only when it was artistically beautiful.

It was characteristic of Börne to have frowned upon Heine in 1831 for taking time off from the struggle for liberty in order to visit an exhibition of paintings at the Louvre. Similar charges of putting artistic detachment before moral, public or even 'patriotic' considerations had previously been launched against Goethe. Although Börne had joined in the chorus against Goethe, it must be said in fairness to him that he was a keen art-lover himself. In his single-minded political zeal, however, he held then, and even more strongly as his health declined in Paris, that art was a distraction which must be sacrificed to the urgency of the political revolution. Heine, on the other hand, interrupted his work on *De l'Allemagne* to supplement his earlier *French Painters* with a report on the 1833 salon at the Louvre to be published at the end of that year.

When he finally decided, in 1839, two years after Börne's death, to settle accounts with him in his devastating *Ludwig Börne. A Memorial*, he answered the charge that he was less concerned with truth than with beauty and artistic effect by affirming that the artist's sovereign detachment implied neither coldness nor lack of truth. Rather, he compared Börne to a 'child who, without perceiving the meaning glowing from a Greek statue, touches the marble form and complains that it is cold.' But the connection between art, truth, and politics was not the only issue between him and Börne in the dispiriting aftermath of the great Hambach demonstration. Heine could not but support the Hambach demands for the unification of the splintered Germany of his day. But, for one thing, his instincts told him that if ever the common goal of a united Germany was achieved, the rabid nationalists who at Hambach paid lip-service to a cosmopolitan 'federated Europe' but insisted on the return of Alsace would resort to folksy 'Fatherland' slogans to mesmerize the Germans and prevail over the 'democrats'.

For another thing, Heine had come to realize the revolutionary potential hidden in German philosophy. He expected the worst from it, and this lent a far-reaching dimension to his dispute with Börne, which was on the fundamental question of political or social revolution. Börne's Robespierrist turn of mind was immutably fixed on the former. In 1833, the year of their rupture, the French edition of Heine's *The Romantic School* appeared in Paris. He was writing his study 'On the History of Religion and Philosophy in Germany'. In this complementary part of *De l'Allemagne* – published in France in 1834 (though in Germany the two were to appear in reverse order) – Heine prophesied that in a united Germany the explosive potential of German philosophy, in nefarious combination with surviving Nordic myths and primeval folk beliefs, would unleash a violent Teuton rage surpassing anything seen in the world.

346

Heine's assessment that German philosophy was not a local but a world-historical 'affair, affecting the whole human race', and the language in which he conveyed that message to the French in his book, have lent the concluding pages of 'Religion and Philosophy in Germany' particular resonance. After noting that Christianity, to its credit, had to some extent attenuated 'the brutal Germanic joy in battle,'[44] but had not eradicated it, he warned the French:

> When, one day, that taming talisman, the Cross, is broken, the savagery of the old warriors will break forth anew, the frenzied berserk wrath of which the Nordic poets speak so much in song and saga. That talisman has become rotten and brittle, and the day will come when it will pitifully break in pieces. Then the old stone gods will arise from the rubble of the past, and rub the dust of a thousand years from their eyes, and Thor will at last leap forth with his giant hammer, to shatter the Gothic cathedrals. Neighbours! Frenchmen! When you hear the rumble and the rattle of arms, take good care not to interfere with those affairs which we are settling amongst ourselves... Take care neither to fan the fire, nor to quench it. You may easily burn your fingers in the flames.

The German revolution, Heine told the French, would not be milder and gentler because it was preceded by the Kantian critique. On the contrary, Kant having killed God, Kantian disciples 'will emerge who will not act with piety in the world of phenomena either, and will pitilessly devastate the soil of our European life with sword and axe, in order to eradicate the last roots of the past.' Asking the French not to 'sneer at the phantasms of a visionary who foretells the same revolution in the actual world of phenomena which has been accomplished in the world of thought', Heine went on:

> Thought precedes the deed as lightning the thunder. German thunder, of course, is German by nature and not very agile, it comes rolling along rather slowly: but it will come, and when you hear a crashing such as has never been heard in the history of the world, then you will know that the German thunder has at last reached its objective. The eagles will fall from the air at the sound, and the lions in the most distant desert of Africa will nip their tails between their legs and seek refuge in their royal dens. A spectacle will be presented in Germany compared with which the French Revolution might appear as a harmless idyll.

Against this prospect of a world-shattering German 'revolution' of apocalyptic proportions, Heine – animated by his Saint-Simonist faith in the 'progress' of

347

science, industry and human thought – pitted his vision of the '*social* emancipation of man'. This, he affirmed, not only held a better chance of transforming the world than politics alone, but answered the needs of the new age.

In both 'History of Religion and Philosophy in Germany' and *The Romantic School*, Heine upheld his 'sensualist' conception of life, of man's divine right to worldly pleasures and material comfort, as opposed to the conflict between body and soul created in him by the 'spiritualist' or Nazarene approach of self-denial fostered by the Judeo-Christian tradition. Christianity had beneficially restrained the materialist excesses of the Roman world, but by sacrificing reason to blind faith and preaching austerity had caused the great division between spirit and matter (*die grosse Weltzerrissenheit*) and much human suffering, not to mention the Roman Catholic Church's 'throne and altar' partnership in the oppressive policies of absolutist monarchs. Even the watered-down deist form of Christianity, Heine observed in 'Religion and Philosophy', had encouraged despotism.

The French Revolution, as he could see in bourgeois France, had wrought enormous changes, but it had not brought about the absolute equality of men; nor did he believe that any revolution ever would. 'God does not manifest Himself equally in all things,' he observed in a significant passage in 'Religion and Philosophy'. 'But each thing carries in itself the urge to achieve a higher degree of divinity, and that is the great law of progress in Nature', a law whose import the Saint-Simonists had been the first to recognize and proclaim. Heine's pantheism dovetailed both with his 'sensualist' approach to life and the optimistic Saint-Simonist vision of the grand possibilities opened up by the nascent age of technology. Stressing that he was chiefly treating 'those questions of philosophy which we consider socially significant', he summed up the chief features of the emerging new order of things as follows:

> The mind makes inventions that further the welfare of matter; through the progress of industry and through philosophy, Spiritualism is being discredited in public opinion; the third estate is rising; the revolution is growling in the hearts and minds of men; and what the age feels and thinks and needs and wants is enunciated: it is the stuff of modern literature.[45]

In other words, in a world administered by 'talents', with the privileges of birth and inherited property abolished, and equal opportunities of social betterment for all, including the poorest and most numerous class, it should be possible to rescue the majority of people from their material misery; to put an end to the moral suffering involved in the mortification of the flesh and the painful dualism of body and spirit fostered by traditional religion; and to create the conditions for most people to live healthy, happy and free lives right here 'on this earth'.

Heine, the dissident avant-gardist, poet and seer, knew in his bones that change was imperative. The people had the right to free democratic institutions: 'We are free men and want no thundering tyrant, we have come of age and need no paternal care,' he wrote. He did not know how this change would come about. All he felt sure of was that German philosophy from Kant to Hegel led logically and inexorably to political action, i.e., revolution. This was 'the secret' he revealed to the French together with his certainty that another revolution, and more particularly revolution in Germany, would have a devastating effect on Europe. Heine knew that there was a humanist tradition in Germany, that 'the better half' of its people were not necessarily chauvinist Francophobes. But this half were not the ones that bear arms, 'And the hour will come, and like spectators on the steps of an amphitheatre, the nations will crowd round Germany to watch the great tournament.' He warned the French to keep quiet, for 'should the mood seize us to pick a quarrel with you, you may be sure that we shall have no difficulties in devising cogent reasons... If we were formerly, in our servile and sullen condition, able at times to overpower you, all the more should we be able to do so when intoxicated by our new-found liberty... You have more to fear from a liberated Germany than from the combined strength of the Holy Alliance with all its Croats and Cossacks.' Being neither a political tribune nor a party leader, but at best a one-man party, all Heine could do against the stark prospect he conjured up was to plead, polemicize, prophesy, appeal to reason – and warn the French to be on their guard: 'Stay armed, stand quietly at your post with your musket at the ready!'

Simultaneously he proclaimed dialectically that the interaction of religious, philosophical and literary developments of the last few centuries had created a mental climate and brought Europe to the turning-point where, in spite of the reactionary political framework, he could discern a new Europe taking shape. And what he postulated in 1834 as the agenda for the new age of progress, though knowing that it might be achieved only by some future generation, was an approximate vision of those liberal, capitalist-type societies of today in which – with the state assuming a larger or lesser degree of social responsibility for the welfare of its citizens – the individual is free to pursue his physical, material and spiritual happiness as he pleases.

Exile, Heine was later to intimate in his *Ludwig Börne. A Memorial*, greatly exacerbated political tensions among the leaders of the German emigrés in Paris. Their numbers doubled between 1831 and 1836 from about 7,000 to 15,000. Half of them were journeymen tailors, shoemakers and carpenters who had no chance of becoming their own masters in Germany; the rest were masons, tanners, locksmiths, printers and mechanics, besides shop assistants and servants.[46] Only some 200 Germans were political refugees. It was these that Heine had in mind when, in his later memoir of Börne, he echoed the Psalmist's lament, 'By the rivers of Babylon, there we sat, and hung our harps upon the willows',[47] to suggest that in the hothouse atmosphere of emigration, the tiniest difference of opinion which 'in Germany would forever have remained a mere stunted plant of foolishness' quickly assumed manic proportions.

In 1832 the Radicals among the political refugees had set up a *Volksverein* on the model of the 'Fatherland Societies' founded by Dr Wirth on the eve of the Hambach Festival. Out of it in 1834 grew a secret organization, The League of the Outlawed (*Bund der Geächteten*). Börne gave his full support to the Outlawed, which agitated patriotically for a united Germany, but demanded social and political equality. Among its leaders were two intellectuals – Jakob Venedey and Theodor Schuster, who had been tutors at Heidelberg and Göttingen respectively – but its rank and file were uneducated artisans of the type of the 'six hundred journeymen tailors' whom Börne had addressed in Montmartre. Heine had been on the Committee of the original *Volksverein*, but as he fell out with Börne, and the Outlawed soon split into a bourgeois wing and a radical one, he distanced himself from the petty ideological quarrels of various cliques and rival factions trying to sway those of the few ranks of untutored journeymen who were at all politically interested, let alone ready to join clandestine organizations.

Börne's fame as Metternich's foremost critic for 20 years was such that his funeral in 1837 was attended by no fewer than 3,000 mourners. Two years later, when Heine wrote his memoir, he challenged not only Börne's distinction between 'character' and 'talent', truth and beauty, but the growing myth of Börne as the 'holy hero' of German 'ultra-liberalism'. He thought that Börne, in subordinating his talent to the politics of blinkered, fanatical 'Jacobinism', had tragically wasted his genius as an artist. Heine tried to intervene with Thiers to avert Venedey's expulsion in 1835. He helped Venedey and other political refugees with money. But he did so privately. He wondered what virtue the single-minded Börne saw in making a point of eating at the cheap restaurants where the boorish, often illiterate journeymen took their meals. Heine was for the workers and against 'the exploitation of man by man.' But like Marx after him, he was not one to mix 'blissfully' with the unwashed plebs of his day. Moreover, he mistrusted the rule of the masses.

The radicals, he wrote, prescribed a horse-cure which for all its sharpness would only remove 'the scurf' from the face of the old society, 'but not the inner rottenness' at the core of the social body. Even if that radical therapy might 'relieve the most excruciating torments of suffering mankind for a short while', the patient was fated to 'rise from his sickbed and drag himself around for the rest of his life in drab hospital uniform, in the ash-grey garb of equality... Nothing will be left other than Rumford's utility soup' – a cheap army soup made of 'bones, blood, and other nutritious ingredients' devised in the 18th century by Benjamin Thompson, Count of Rumford, when reorganizing the Bavarian soldiery. For Heine's presentiment told him that in radical egalitarian republics, all the world's poetry and beauty would in the end be 'pumped out of life'.[48]

Although later, under the influence of Marx, Heine was to adopt a more radical stand, 'the ash-grey garb of equality' prefigured his fear of the drab totalitarian uniformity which would mark the rule of the proletariat, a fear he expressed by hedging his prediction that 'the future belongs to Communism' with his confessed horror at the thought that its thick-headed iconoclasts would 'mercilessly smash the marble statues of beauty' in their gloomy regimented society.

Whereas Heine's dispute with Börne was on a broad front, touching upon the solution of social issues into the next century, Börne, the moralist, had been prying into Heine's private life. Heine's revenge was to sully the dead man's reputation by working into his memoir some gratuitous insinuations concerning its hero's *ménage à trois* with Jeanette Strauss-Wohl and her husband. As a result the book was received with howls of indignation. Since Heine had alluded in *The Romantic School* to Schlegel's long-standing intimacy with Madame de Staël, it may be noted in passing that each of those whom he attacked – including Schlegel, who in 1832 had taken a stab at him in a derogatory epigram – had first attacked him. Perhaps the best clue to Heine's way of over-reacting to provocation was provided in 1835 by a friend of his – Oskar Wolff, a professor of literature at Jena University – who, after visiting him in Paris, published an article in Leipzig containing the following characterization of him: 'He is a born king of the world, with all the pleasant and unpleasant qualities of such a personage: he thinks royally, loves royally, but also hates and persecutes royally. Unlike a royal despot, he does not condemn his enemies to life-long incarceration; rather, like a royal hero, he slays them.'[49]

Heine told Wolff in 1835 that he hardly expected to return to Germany. Settling into exile had many bitter sides other than feuding with Börne, being calumniated and spied upon. Heine longed for the homeland which responded to his progressive ideas with more hate than understanding and forced him to devise ever new strategies against its censors. The fate of his 'Preface to the Preface', after his original Preface to 'Conditions in France' had been mutilated, may serve as an epitome of the 'strange complications' attending the path of 'an author fighting for Europe's liberty', as Heine saw himself. Campe in Hamburg had reluctantly agreed to issue both the Preface and 'Preface to the Preface' as a separate brochure, to be distributed free of charge to readers who had bought the book before it was banned. By mid–March 1833 the brochure had been printed except for the title sheet. Having, against his own better judgment, given in to Heine's insistence not to submit it to the censorship, Campe meant to mislead the authorities by giving Paris as the place of publication. The new wave of repression after the attack on the Frankfurt Constabulary made him decide without futher ado to destroy the whole edition, except for two copies.

One copy was sent to Campe's nephew in Paris, who published the 'Preface to the Preface' in July 1833 under the bogus imprint of one P. G(au)g(e)r, with Leipzig as the place of publication. The Prussian reaction was a ban on all books by Heideloff und Campe; the unfortunate Gauger, who was a lowly clerk at the firm, was arrested and grilled by the police when he turned up in Germany; and under Prussian pressure the Hamburg Senate ordered Julius Campe too to be interrogated. He denied ever having seen the Paris brochure, and had to swear that he was not the publisher. Nor was this the end of the affair, for in the midst of it occurred the Prussian officers' so-called 'plot' to kill Heine.

He was holidaying at Boulogne in August when he received a letter from one Nolte warning him that a group of incensed Prussian officers had decided to provoke him to a pistol duel and finish him off. Thickening a mystery which has never been entirely cleared up, in October 1833 a Prussian agent in Paris, Klaproth – otherwise an orientalist and occasional journalist – reported that Heine had received 'Herr Nolte's letter' and was now so furious that he planned to launch a dangerous agitation against Prussia. Maximizing the menace represented by Heine, Klaproth suggested that T. (code-word for Berlin's chief of police Tzschoppe) ask the Prussian Ambassador in Paris to have Heine expelled.

The affair became public on 12 November, when the *Leipziger Zeitung* published an anonymous report (believed to have been written by the same Klaproth) claiming that 'Herr Nolte never existed', and that a group of officers in Dresden had simply used his name to drive the fear of God into Heine, who had indeed armed himself with 'double pistols' and scurried for protection to the Paris Chief of Police Gisquet and the Prussian Ambassador Werther.[50] The report said further that Heine, who had allegedly boasted that 'he only had to show himself in Germany in order to produce a revolution', had been exposed as a coward. The punch-line suggested that the reason for any venom he might direct at Prussia should be sought in 'the mythical Herr Nolte'.

Heine felt compelled to publish a 'Statement' (*Erklärung*) denying that he had ever uttered the stupid boast imputed to him, or that he had sought Gisquet's or Werther's protection. Protesting the publication of anonymous insinuations, he wrote that he had taken Nolte's warning seriously after informing himself about the man – who was apparently a merchant by the name of Vincent Otto Nolte (1770–1856).[51] Heine's 'Statement' was duly carried by Baron Cotta and by Heine's Saint-Simonist young friend Laube in their respective newspapers,[52] but the *Leipziger Zeitung*, after creating the public furore, refused to print it, accepting it only as a paid advertisement. The paper's silence made a friend of Heine's – possibly under his inspiration – raise the question why, if 'the fact was no fact', its correspondent so obviously sided with the perpetrators of a plot that never was. And further to mystify posterity, a contemporary Austrian spy soon reported that in November 1833 Werther was in fact instructed from Berlin to obtain Heine's expulsion.[53]

In the end, after all the energy, time and nerves invested by both Heine and Campe, not without some mutual friction, in sundry tactics and stratagems, the 'Preface to the Preface' was not to appear in Germany until after Heine's death. The public, he noted in the 1830s, had 'little idea' of the unusual tribulations besetting the life of a fighting author-in-exile.

Yet, despite the bitterness and complications of exile, Heine lived a full and active life. He had, of course, his eccentricities. Visitors to his rented rooms – first in the out-of-the-way rue de L'Echiquier (where one had to cross two inner courtyards to reach his door), and since February 1833 in the rue des Petits Augustins – noticed that he cared little for elegant furnishings or pleasant surroundings. His chief concern was for quiet locations affording him peace and seclusion for his work. Although he employed a manservant, his household was not particularly orderly. But he was dining regularly with Sainte-Beuve and the writer and historian Jean-Jacques Ampère (son of the physicist) at Bombarda's restaurant in the rue de Rivoli; Balzac had introduced him to the house of the comtesse de Merlin, from which, after dinner, the whole company would sometimes repair to the Opéra or the Théâtre des Italiens; and in the spring of 1833 Franz Liszt was writing to the comtesse d'Agoult, who was of German descent on her mother's side: 'Madame, you asked me the other day to present to you our famous compatriot Heine. He is indeed one of Germany's most distinguished men... May I bring him to you next Tuesday at eight?'

In May, at the monthly dinner of *L'Europe Littéraire*, Heine met and became friends with Hector Berlioz – winner of the 1830 Prix de Rome – and at the next of these gastronomic sprees in June he made the acquaintance of a shy-looking 28-year-old Dane. He was Hans Christian Andersen, who was to confess in his *Memoirs* that the one person in Paris he had been eager to meet was the poet 'who so well expressed all my feelings and moods.' It was reported that Andersen spoke to Heine in halting German, and when he ran out of words he suggested that they switch to French. As he proved not much better at it, Heine asked with a smile: 'What language would you suggest we continue our conversation in?' If his irony hurt Andersen, Heine made up for it when, hearing that the other had been too awkward to call on him, he called on him at his hotel the next day. Andersen wrote to Heine that 'of all modern authors you have had the greatest influence on me and my work.' To prove it, he had some of his own poems specially translated into German, later dedicated others to Heine, and was to visit him again when he was himself famous.[54]

At Boulogne in August, Heine found relief from the vexations of the officers' 'plot' in the company of Sarah Austin – known for her translations from German literature and of Guizot's *Causes of the Success of the English Revolution 1640–1688* – and of her young daughter Lucie. 'He lounged with me on the end of the pier,' Lucie (later Lucie Duff-Gordon) recalled, 'and told me stories in which fish, mermaids, watersprites, and a very funny old fiddler with a poodle, who was taking three sea-baths a day, were mixed up in the most fanciful manner.' The girl in turn taught him an English ballad about the tragic fate of Lady Alice, who took only a spoonful of gruel 'with sugar and spices so rich' that she fell dead, and of the parson who afterwards 'licked up the rest'. The cosmopolitan Austins later lived for a while in Paris, and still later, during the years when Heine lay dying, he could hardly wait for 'the heavenly Lucie', as he called her, to appear in Paris (which she did several times) and reminisce with him about that summer's end at Boulogne. 'The parson drank gruel water,' Heine wrote in a note welcoming the solace her visits brought him.[55]

At the beginning of the winter of 1833–34, he was best man, together with the composer Ferdinand Hiller, at the wedding of Berlioz to the Irish actress Harriet Smithson. During the winter, the *Athenaeum* of London carried Edgard Quinet's profile of him ('German Poets: Heinrich Heine') simultaneously with its publication in the *Revue des Deux Mondes*. In Germany, besides new editions of *Travel Pictures* III and IV, Campe was publishing his report on the 1833 Louvre Salon. Together with his earlier *French Painters*, some poems and his famous fragment of a novel – *The Memoirs of Herr von Schnabelewopski* (from which Richard Wagner was to take the theme of *The Flying Dutchman*) – it appeared in a volume called *Salon* I, which became the omnibus title for a series of three more volumes of his writings on art.

In February 1834, Victor Bohain's *L'Europe Littéraire* ran out of funds. Victor Bouloz of *Revue des Deux Mondes*, however, stepped in and undertook the serialization of Heine's 'Religion and Philosophy in Germany' ahead of its publication in that country. By that time, not only did Heine's acquaintances include France's most prominent writers and artists, but he was himself becoming something of a literary and social lion.

'Heinrich Heine, the famous Heine, came to see me unannounced,' Balzac wrote some time after they had met, 'and although, as you know, I am myself not a nobody, still, when I heard who it was, he took possession of my entire day.' Indeed, the two of them, keen observers of the human comedy, could be seen sauntering for hours on the boulevards, engaged in lively conversation. Heine might fulminate against banks, but at the house of James de Rothschild he met some of the *haute finance* of Paris. The salons had opened their doors to him, and in November 1834 George Sand was intimating to young Franz Lizst that she and Alfred de Musset would be 'happy to make the acquaintance of M. Berlioz and M. Heine.'

Gautier, an early admirer of Heine, wrote that 'He was a fellow like a god, mischievous as a devil, but good-natured with it all, whatever people say to the contrary. I was little concerned whether he regarded me as a friend or supporter, so long as I could listen to his sparkling conversation; for extravagantly as he expended his money and health, his expenditure of *esprit* was more lavish still.'[56]

Heine was by nature and vocation a loner, and not everyone could stand his biting wit or his honesty. Sainte-Beuve, after 7 years of friendship, was most annoyed when Heine published some criticism of him. Berlioz, on the other hand, remained his friend even when, though half-praising him as well as Liszt in a musical review, he singled out Chopin as a genius of a higher order, in a class with Mozart. 'Our friend Heine... has treated us with as much *esprit* as disrespect,' Berlioz informed Liszt, 'but without any malice whatsoever. He has awarded the palm to Chopin, who has long deserved it.'[57]

If one remarkable feature of Heine's rise to prominence in Paris was the readiness of its artistic celebrities to adopt him as one of their own – as Alexandre Dumas was pointedly to inform the German authorities who continued to persecute him even in his exile – another may be seen in the very special relationships he formed with two of the most fascinating women of the age. George Sand and the Princess Cristina di Belgiojoso were as unlike each other as possible. By 1834, in the midst of falling out in Venice with de Musset and then briefly reuniting with 'the golden boy of French poetry', George Sand had caused a furore with her feminist novel *Lélia*. In a diary entry at the end of November ('Saw Heine this morning'), she recorded his view that 'one loves only with the head and the senses, the heart plays no role in love.'[58] Seven years later, in another diary entry, she was to describe him as 'tender, affectionate, devoted, romantic in love.'[59]

Between 1834 and 1836, the year she went to Switzerland and, adopting the sobriquet 'Piffoël', made her famous romp in the company of 'the Fellows' –

Liszt and the comtesse Marie d'Agoult, who had abandoned her husband and eloped with the pianist – Sand changed lovers at least three times. While there is no hard knowledge about Heine's ever joining their number, he and Sand were very soon on terms of endearment and familiarity, calling each other *cousin* and *cousine*; her promptly inviting him to 'come and dine with me today... I have nobody, and you can come *en pantoufles et bonnet de coton*' marked the beginning of what was to be a long-lasting intimacy. Like Gautier, George Sand realized that, far from being spiteful, Heine's 'wit is mordant... but his heart is as kind as his tongue is nasty.' Noting that his cynical, mocking manner frightened and put off those who did not know his 'secret inner life', she characterized him as 'a humorist like [Laurence] Sterne'.

George Sand was spontaneous, warm-hearted and generous, and if her talent, courage and vitality could not but appeal to Heine, her broad humanism and deep-felt sympathy with the oppressed – to be reflected in some of her novels and to culminate in her actively taking up 'la cause du peuple' in the 1848 revolution – made for a further bond between them.

Princess Cristina di Belgiojoso-Trivulzio, too, was a highly idealistic, politically conscious and courageous young woman. While still a girl she had more than once risked her life on hazardous missions for the Italian *Carbonari* against the Austrian occupying authorities in Lombardy. In Paris since 1831, she had refused La Fayette's offer of financial help. In 1834, however, the Austrian Ambassador, Count Apponyi, helped her to get back most of her confiscated Italian possessions. From the garret in which she had painted fans for a living she moved to the elegant rue d'Anjou Saint-Honoré. With statesmen and politicians like Guizot, Molé, Victor Cousin, Thiers, and artists and intellectuals who had previously helped to cook her suppers congregating in her new and unconventional drawing-room she quickly became, at the age of 26, one of the most striking hostesses of the period. Regarding Paris as a 'small hospital' for recuperating political refugees, she not only used her high connections and all her energy and resources to canvass support for her Italian countrymen, but helped prominent as well as lesser exiles from many lands.

It was the age of 'virtuosismo', and deputies, generals, writers, bankers, diplomats, newspaper editors and foreign statesmen flocked to her musical soirées and benefit concerts, at one of which the famous 'piano duel' between Liszt and his chief rival, Thalberg, took place. Together with the duchesse d'Abrantès and Princess Czartoryska she would spend many nights at bazaars to collect money for Poland, with Chopin playing for hours as an attraction. She was a more enigmatic personality than George Sand, and no two people – whether contemporaries or later biographers – agreed either about her character or about her looks. Juliette Adam was to call her 'one of the most beautiful women of the age', and Baudelaire raved about her portrait when it was exhibited in the Salon of 1845; the comtesse de Merlin described her as 'a literary and political lioness, all lazy voluptuousness'; Gautier noted her noble features, but others, including Balzac, dwelt on her pale, 'greenish' complexion. Alfred de Musset lost himself in her sphinx-like eyes, 'so deep, so large... that I can find my way no more,' but when dismissed by her after a short affair he revenged himself in verses, calling her 'a dead woman... who only made pretence of living.'[60]

Heine himself, who visited her twice within one week in January 1834 and saw quite a bit of her during the following months, was stupefied by her presence. In a portrait of her in his 'Florentine Nights' he was to describe the princess's complexion as 'softly Roman, faint shimmer of pearls, noble pallor, morbidezza'; and he caught perhaps that mysterious composite effect of her features that left no one indifferent by comparing her oval, dimpled face with its high forehead, jet-black hair, large burning eyes and pointed chin to the faces of 'great ladies' portrayed in 16th-century Italian masterpieces, a face 'reminiscent of Leonardo da Vinci'.[61] He had every reason to be thankful to her. For it was through her instrumentality that on 27 March 1834 – in the midst of a government crisis – Guizot, the Minister of Education and later Foreign Minister, sent Heine a note saying, 'It will be impossible for me to go with you to the Princess's house at 4 o'clock. Pressing work will keep me at the Cabinet very late. – On Wednesday if that suits you.' Guizot met Heine at the princess's house on 1 April. This and a private meeting with Thiers that she arranged for him the following year may have had something to do with the controversial stipend he was later to receive from the French government.

It was in 1834 that Heine seems to have fallen in love with the eccentric princess. On 18 April, following a particularly stimulating soirée two nights before, he wrote that he was haunted by her dream-like figure, her 'mysterious' lips, etc. However, la princesse malheureuse (as she sometimes called herself) sensibly and tactfully cooled his ardour. Unhappily married to a debauched husband, and already involved in a discreet liaison with the historian Mignet, she wanted no further emotional complications. Heine, too, soon recovered his senses. He admired the Princess's wide-ranging culture, her fine intellect and sensibility and her devotion to the cause of liberty; and once their friendship was freed of the element of desire, it became all the more stable. On 26 June, before leaving for another holiday at Boulogne, he bade a temporary adieu to 'the most beautiful, the kindest, the most admirable person I have met on this earth. The memory of you gives balm to my existence.'

On at least three occasions during Heine's lifetime the Princess showed the remarkable side of her character. One day in October 1834, Heine bought a pair of gloves in the rue Choiseul and fell victim to the provocative charms of the shop assistant who served him. Crescence Eugénie Mirat was a 19-year-old country girl, whose good looks, vivacious temperament and peasant shrewd-ness, combined with a Parisian chic acquired since leaving her village, made up for her lack of education. While consorting with the *beau monde* of Paris, Heine had continued his explorations of the city's bars, bistros and popular *bals dansants*. The group of poems first published in 1833 under the title 'Sundry Women' ('*Verschiedene*') reflected his fleeting adventures with a number of easy young women. Crescence Mirat, however, had Heine hooked. She was young, coquettish, and well aware of the desire she aroused in men. She liked Heine, but was determined to yield her virtue to no man, whether gentleman or peasant, unless it was for a marital or otherwise lasting union.

Needless to say, the resistance of this self-styled 'wild cat' inflamed Heine's urge to possess her. Crescence – or Mathilde, as he renamed her – allowed herself to be taken on Sunday country outings, and she joined him in some of the carnival merriment in February 1835, but otherwise she proved unattain-able. They quarreled, and Heine tried to extricate himself from this 'love affair in which I am up to my neck,' as he wrote to the theatre producer Lewald in Germany on 11 April 1835. 'Since October nothing else has mattered to me... Read King Solomon's Song of Songs: you will find in it all I can tell you today.' And to Campe, a while later: 'Fool that I am, I thought that the time of passion was over for me. I was equal to the eternal gods in calm, composure, and moder-ation – and behold! I raged again like a human being, and indeed like a young human being.'[62]

In a note to Princess Belgiojoso he hinted at 'domestic trouble' as an excuse for not visiting her, and he confided the details to Mignet. The Princess showed her sensitivity by writing:

> Dear friend, M. Mignet has told me about your misadventure and I feel for you with all my heart. I am not laughing at you, and I beg you not to take the matter too seriously or tragically. A spell in the country, the fresh air and smell of grass as you stretch your limbs under a rustling tree, might do you good. Come to lunch in any case on Monday at La Jonchère: leave all your cares behind you in the city and be sure I shall not mock you. A thousand friendships.[63]

And so, in mid-June he went to the princess's château (once inhabited by Madame Pompadour) not far from Paris. He spent 6 'calm and cheerful' weeks there in distinguished and diverting company, and informed Campe that he had regained his peace of mind.[64] But to complete his cure, or to flee farther from Mathilde, he left at the end of July for Boulogne and remained after the end of the season. He was still there in 'voluntary exile' in December, trying to work and to get Mathilde out of his mind. The buxom girl, as he was well aware, lacked all culture, sophistication and manners: 'I am condemned to love only the lowest and the most foolish things,' he remarked in self-disgust in a letter from Boulogne to Heinrich Laube, at the same time confessing that he was 'in the throes of an overpowering passion that often robs us of our clarity of vision and thought, which I personally hate to give up.'[65]

For months he struggled against it, but in vain. Whether it was destiny, as in the case of Goethe and his Christiane, or the mutual attraction between the childwoman Mathilde and the child in Heine – both Ludwig Marcuse and Max Brod, dwelling on Heine's way of saying the most sarcastic things about people and then wondering like an innocent boy why they were offended, have referred to their relationship as the union of 'two children' – some time after his return to Paris at the end of 1835, Heine and Mathilde got together again. The exact circumstances are unknown. According to the traditional account by Alexandre Weill, Heine paid Mathilde's aunt, who owned the shop where she worked, a consideration of 3,000 francs for letting her go and live with him. A well-known journalist, Weill launched this unverifiable story after the death of both protagonists. He further claimed to have heard from Mathilde herself the scene that followed on the night when Heine – while formally keeping his own flat – moved into her lodgings in the rue Cadet and she finally slept with him. Mathilde sat up on the bed and said:

> Henri, I have given you all that an honest girl can give the man she loves and which he can never restore to her. Don't think that I am so foolish not to know that you bought me. If I agreed to be your mistress, it is first of all because I like you best of all the men who ever courted me, and because I am told that Germans are more faithful than Frenchmen. But whether you bought me or not, I did not sell myself! [Moi, je ne me suis pas vendue!] Know then that I'll never leave you. Whether you love me or not, whether you marry me or not, whether you maltreat me or not, I'll never leave you. Do you hear that? Jamais! jamais! jamais!...

'But I don't want you to leave me,' Heine protested. 'I love you, and I shall always love you!' 'And I', Mathilde remonstrated, 'if I didn't love you, should I have done what I have?' 'You're already making a scene,' Heine joked in a mollifying tone. 'I shall never cease loving you.'

But Mathilde was back at him in dead earnest: 'Even if you should, I shall never cease to be your wife.' 'And what would you do if I left you?' Heine asked. 'I should kill myself at your feet!' came her hoarse reply.

Taken aback, Heine, perhaps to distract her, said the first thing that came into his mind: 'Let us have breakfast first.' But Mathilde was not finished with him: 'When my mind is set on something fifty thousand mules will not drag it out of me. I am telling you for the last time, and I won't say it again, I'll never leave you! Wherever you go, I shall go, be it to the end of the world or beyond the gates of hell! I am yours, because you bought me; but you too have been bought, bought by me, you know the price I paid, and you are mine for the rest of your life!'[66]

Authentic or not, the story does convey something of Mathilde's natural pride and assertive character. Although Heine had some idea of what he was letting himself in for, he may well have wondered whether life with this hell-cat would be all bliss or eternal bondage, or heaven and hell combined. Like Tannhäuser he had escaped from the Venusberg and, in Nina Valentin's apt simile, like Tannhäuser he had 'returned once and for all to Madame Venus'. Though Heine certainly enjoyed the company and discourse of intellectual women, the fact is that, oddly or not, the poet of 'the bleeding heart' in his late thirties chose to live with the 21 year-old Mathilde, who never read a page of his poems or his prose; and, curiously, the public in Germany, which had never taken an interest in Goethe's Christiane, soon delighted in a spate of juicy press reports from Paris in which Heine was alternately said to be cavorting in the highest circles with a society beauty, or to be living in promiscuous concubinage with a *grisette*. Mathilde was neither that nor a society lady. She was a vigorous child of nature, young, voluptuous and uninhibited in her lust for the pleasures of life. According to the best account of her, 'to show herself and be seen in public with him was a type of satisfaction to her vanity which she had rarely enjoyed.' She dragged him to the best concerts, causing him 'some droll embarrassment, for he liked to act the bachelor, yet would not deny or abandon her.'[67]

But what Mathilde liked best was vaudeville, restaurants and dancing. She flirted with men for the fun of it, and to drive Heine mad with jealousy. She was no great housekeeper either, being chiefly preoccupied with dresses, hats and finery, on which she spent freely whenever the mood took her. She loved animals, flowers and her pet parrot, but was not one to shine in literary company. For a time, indeed, Heine shunned society. Mathilde took not the slightest interest in his work, his publishing, financial or censorship problems. Heine kept that whole part of his life from her. But if she was not the person with whom he could discuss the conflict between 'spiritualism' and 'sensualism', spirit and matter – or his idea that Shakespeare, whom he called 'a Jew and a Greek', was one of the few who had resolved it – the wholesome, elemental Mathilde suffered from no disharmony between the spirit and the flesh; she sometimes made him feel sexually 'tired as a hunted bull'; and whatever else she lacked, her spontaneity, natural gaiety, laughter, tears, tantrums, and even her rages and the kind of animal quality that required constant taming, proved both a challenge and a foil to his own self-preoccupied genius. Mathilde never gave him a dull moment. 'She constantly cheers me up by the very inconstancy of her caprices,' he wrote humorously.

He became so attached to her that to satisfy her yearning for respectability he visited her family in the village of Vinot, in the Seine-et-Marne département, and for several days – during which the mayor and the priest came to a family lunch in his honour – earnestly went through the comedy of posing as her husband. The comedy grew on him. He was greatly moved to see the happiness in Mathilde's eyes, and felt increasingly responsible for her. Sometimes, of course, it took all his humour to make a virtue of Mathilde's 'delicious ignorance' or to stand her moods and flights of temper; and because Heine sometimes stood back and wondered about the future of their relationship – and at one point wrote Laube of 'the agony to a man of pride and spirit' to yield to a low and foolish passion – literary historians for a long time tended to regard his liaison with her as demeaning. Latter-day biographers, however, incline to the view that any liaison between Heine and some learned, competitive bluestocking would have been short-lived, for they would have made an incompatible couple.

Heine himself early confided in a letter to Mignet that he was perhaps not well suited for 'the brilliant and restless life of the *grand monde*' and its largely artificial preoccupations. Henceforth his life was to move between these two disparate worlds, that of Paris high society with its artists, intellectuals and superior women, and that of anarchic, often uproarious domesticity with the ebullient and earthy Mathilde. For while Heine could not stay away long from society or absent himself from the ball inaugurating James de Rothschild's new Renaissance-style palace – 'the Versailles of absolute money power', as he dubbed it – Mathilde was by convention excluded from some of the salons. He could show himself with her at the Café Montmartre, where his bohemian friends Gautier and Alphonse Royer – a later director of the Théâtre Odéon and the Opéra – would join them with their own mistresses. But he could not easily take her to the cosmopolitan but rather exclusive salon of Alfred de Vigny and his English wife, where in 1837 he engaged a distinguished company in a discussion of Spinoza's philosophy.

That same year, the comtesse d'Agoult, back from her excursion in Switzerland with Liszt and George Sand, took an apartment in the elegant Hôtel de France on the rue Laffitte 'and sent Liszt out to bring in the celebrities'. Heine was thus drawn into the set that formed around the countess and George Sand, two emancipated women who in their different ways defied the conventions of Paris society.

A sneering passage Heine wrote in 1837, in 'On the French Stage' (*Über die französische Bühne*), about the French salons being open to 'the most vicious Messalina so long as her conjugal ram trots patiently by her side', while closing their doors to any girl who may have yielded to a man in an access of innocent young love, is believed to have been his protest against the prevailing mores and *hauteur* of French society.[68]

Mathilde, though proud of Heine, loved him not for his ideas or his fame but as 'her man'. She accepted him as he was without prying into or even bothering to know what went on in his mind; her warmth brought out the gentle side in him as no one else had done before. Plagued as he was by various symptoms of illness, Heine was in two minds about marrying Mathilde or letting her go to make good her chances in life while she was still pretty and young. She, however, had set her mind on him and the security and respectability he afforded her.

During the altogether 7 years of their romance before a pistol duel, like destiny itself, intervened to help him make up his mind, Heine sometimes rebelled against Mathilde's possessiveness. To prove to himself that he might yet escape, he would boast that he was still 'free', and early in 1836 he was indeed discovered disporting himself with two *grisettes* during one of Mathilde's absences from Paris.[69] Two years later Princess Belgiojoso was writing to Liszt: 'I am hardly seeing M. de Musset, who pretends to be working... *En revanche*, I am seeing more of Heine, who says that he has regained his liberty.' (Mathilde, in fact, was merely in hospital with an inflammation.) But it is the rest of the Princess's letter that is significant:

> As you know, I have always maintained that the diabolical Heine is a good devil. I persist in this opinion – and I am grateful to him for his being by and large so constant in his disposition to me in spite of certain petty intrigues to turn him into an enemy. All these attempts have ended in Wasco, and but for a few harmless jokes, I am convinced that nothing in the world could ever persuade Heine to do me the slightest harm.[70]

Liszt had taken offence at a review by Heine, and d'Agoult had taken up the cudgels for her virtuoso by answering Heine in an 'Open Letter' (signed by Liszt) in the *Gazette Musicale*. Nevertheless, she went on cultivating him and he was to see more of her at George Sand's country place at Nohant before the two women broke off their friendship. She proved to be one of the few who – like Berlioz, Gautier and George Sand herself – perceived the hidden kindness in the cynical Heine which Mathilde, in her instinctive way, knew how to bring out in him.

The Italian princess remained steadfast in her friendship with Heine, and their bond was such that she was to be one of the last to visit him before he died. At her frequent soirées, Heine mingled with the other illustrious figures of the musical world, Cherubini, Rossini, Bellini (until his premature death). And besides all the politicians, statesmen and cultural heroes mentioned earlier, Richard Wagner and Karl Marx, Engels, Hess, Bakunin and Lassalle were among the historic figures of a new generation who, growing up on his works, were eventually to seek him out in Paris.

12

Karl Marx in High School and the 'Conversion Conflict'

In the autumn of 1834, when Heine, in spite of the distraction caused by his developing passion for Mathilde, was working on the expanded German original of *Religion and Philosophy in Germany*, Karl Marx was only 16. He was Heine's junior by nearly 21 years, and still had a year to go before graduating from Trier's high school, the Friedrich Wilhelm Gymnasium.

In Trier, 1834 was the year of the 'Casino affair'. It had started in January, when a controversial speech delivered by Karl Marx's father – followed, in short order, by another function at which the *Marseillaise* was sung – so aroused the anger of the Prussian authorities that the Casino Society (*Casinogesellschaft*) was temporarily closed. The Society, founded under the French and meeting in the imposing Casino building, which, besides a library and reading rooms, had a hall where concerts, theatre performances, balls and banquets were held, was supposed to be an non-political social club. Since the 1830 July Revolution in France, however, it had become something of a thorn in the flesh of the Prussian authorities, for its members – among whom were most of the town's leading burghers – had started to give voice to the civic dissatisfaction accumulated in 15 years of Prussian rule. Now several of them were to stand trial on various charges, including treason. The affair kept the whole district abuzz and its repercussions profoundly affected Karl Marx in his last year of high school.

As early as September 1830, two months after the July Revolution, Trier's Prussian Regierungspräsident had complained that the director of the Casino had failed to report a subversive leaflet which had been sent to him. The widely distributed leaflet was one of a series protesting the high taxation and the increasingly heavy 'Prussian yoke', but the latest caused particular worry to the authorities for two reasons. Reminding the King of Prussia that he had broken his 15-year-old promise to grant a Constitution, it demanded an independent legislature for the Rhineland and financial separation from Old Prussia.

'Unless our demands are satisfied', the leaflet threatened, 'we shall heed the call of our [French] neighbours and join their ranks to fight for our welfare.' At the same time, in Coblenz the Oberpräsident of the Rhine Province received, and passed on to Berlin, reports of an inflammatory poster addressed to soldiers of Trier's strong garrison, questioning the validity of their oath to the Prussian monarch. So frightened were the Prussians of the contagious effect of the revolution which had installed a 'citizen-king' on the former Bourbon throne that French travellers coming across the Rhine were not allowed to stay in Trier for more than a night. Even the Bishop of Nancy was ordered to leave town in August 1830.

Karl Marx had begun his high school education at the Friedrich Wilhelm Gymnasium in October of that year. The Gymnasium being considered by the Prussians, in the words of a high official, as another hotbed, like the Casino Society, of liberal ideas and 'francomania', it was placed under discreet police surveillance. Sooner or later it became an open secret that an agent by the name of Nohl was regularly reporting on both teachers and pupils suspected of 'demagogic radical' activities or opinions.

Shortly before Karl entered the Gymnasium, the Prussians had promulgated a decree making anyone smoking a pipe – or even sucking a dead one – when passing a sentry, liable to arrest and prosecution. It was the kind of thing that made Rhinelanders feel worse treated by their arrogant countrymen than they had been by their French 'enemies'. Before Karl Marx had finished his first year at the Gymnasium, economic crisis in the Rhineland added to the continuing political tension between Prussia and the new regime in France. With the Moselle wine trade practically ruined, reports from district after district, transmitted to Berlin via the Oberpräsident, kept signalling increasing poverty and disaffection.

'Because of the dearth of bread and potatoes in the Grand Duchy of Luxembourg', a zealous Prussian sub-prefect in Erfurt reported in April 1831, 'whole gangs of beggars, vagabonds and brigands have started invading the districts of Prum, Bitburg and Saarburg.' The police had 'frequently had to request military reinforcements' in order to stop gangs of marauders.

In Trier itself posters had gone up on public buildings threatening violence unless the flour and meat taxes were abolished. 'A considerable number of the lower class' were reported to be in an ugly mood in pubs and taverns and nearly one-third of Trier's 14,318 inhabitants had to be supplied with free coal, medicine and over 57,000 soup portions to survive the winter. To forestall unrest, the authorities had formed 300 or so members of Trier's riflemen's association into a 'Society for the Maintenance of Public Order'. The burgomaster of Trier, Wilhelm Haw, however, informed the government that they had few weapons, since most of the members had given theirs away to help the Greeks in their recent war of liberation.

Burgomaster Haw had by 1831 become a symbol of the humorous Rhinelanders' passive resistance, which was the only way left to them to express their growing resentment. None of the perpetrators of the seditious leaflets, 'revolutionary' placards and anti-Prussian cartoons which continued to circulate could be apprehended. Burgomaster Haw, pressed by the authorities for an explanation, pointed to the fact that wide searches by the Prussian military had been equally unsuccessful. Haw had often advised the Prussians that they could have a loyal population if they did not rob it of the liberties it had enjoyed under the French.

A subtle and courageous lawyer-politician, the burgomaster steadfastly avoided toasting the Prussian king's health at official functions, but by dint of sheer diplomacy and his placating skills he had managed to keep both the respect of the locals and his office for 12 years. He was, moreover, a member of the Rhenish Provincial Diet, and with a hostile population on its hands, economic crisis and spreading disaffection, the Prussian government, though doubting his loyalty and spying on his every move, considered it wiser not to sack him. While it looked for a pretext to prosecute him even before, it was to find one in the Casino 'affair'.

Assuring the government that only 'the rabble' was restive, Haw kept stressing the role of 'the middle class in maintaining public order'. As early as April 1831, however, Baron Ludwig von Westphalen, the head of the district's police and internal security department, singled out Trier's 'lawyers, bankers, merchants, doctors, notaries', that is, precisely the club's upper-crust membership, as leaders of the pro-French element in town. In case of war with France, wrote the elderly baron in a private letter, 'the Prussian arms' could count on 'no solid, national support on the part of the passive' and 'partly discontented' Rhinelanders. Under the French, he explained, these provinces had simply become 'disaccustomed' to belonging to the German fatherland. His son Ferdinand von Westphalen – who was the sub-prefect reporting from Erfurt on the situation in neighbouring Bitburg – shared the opinion that the Rhineland was as good as lost to Prussia.[1]

Ironically, Baron Ludwig von Westphalen, who included in his letter the high school pupils among those infected 'with this francomania', was the father of the girl Karl Marx, the greatest future rebel attending the Gymnasium, was in due course to court and eventually to marry. The Baron came originally from Brunswick. His father had played an important role in that Duchy's history and his mother was a Scotswoman of noble lineage. No Junker-type aristocrat, he belonged to the more enlightened and progressive wing of Prussian officialdom, and was in fact to take quite a liking to his future son-in-law and to introduce him to Shakespeare, and even to teach him some liberal ideas.

Whereas Karl Marx was only 13 in 1831, Jenny von Westphalen was 17. They hardly played together as children in the garden of the Westphalen house, as was long believed. Rather, it was only some time after he entered the Gymnasium, when his elder sister Sophie and Jenny became friends – and the Westphalens lived for a time in a 'garden house' in the Römerstrasse (today Paulin Strasse), on the other side of the huge Porta Nigra ruin from the Marx home on the Simeongasse – that he and the Baron's daughter became aware of each other.

The wave of political persecution unleashed in the aftermath of the great Hambach demonstration reached the Gymnasium before the end of 1832. Two of Trier's town councillors, and even several young clergymen, had been among the crowds assembled to hear republican slogans and 'the sovereignty of the people' proclaimed at Hambach Castle. While the speakers at the rally and the organizers had been arrested or had fled to France, copies of their addresses and other 'demagogic' literature were found circulating among Trier's high school students.

The headmaster, Hugo Wyttenbach, was placed under surveillance. A brilliant educator, Wyttenbach was one of the founders of the Casino Society. By 1833, a close watch was being kept on the activities of teachers and pupils at the Friedrich Wilhelm Gymnasium. According to official correspondence circulated between Trier, Coblenz and Berlin in the 1833–34 period, two of the Gymnasium teachers, Heinrich Schwendler and Thomas Simon, were suspected of being involved with 'revolutionary circles'; a third, J.G. Schneemann, of being an admirer of French liberalism; a fourth, Johann Steininger, the mathematics and physics teacher, of being 'unpatriotic' and an atheist, overpraising French scientific achievements and undermining the Christian faith of the young by ridiculing the Bible story of the destruction of Sodom and Gomorrah, and attributing it to a volcanic eruption.

Schwendler and Schneemann, like the headmaster Wyttenbach, were doubly suspect, as they too were members of the Casino Society. Schwendler was actually the Society's secretary. One of the things about the Society that incensed the punctilious Royal Prussian bureaucrats, who never referred to the King in Berlin except as 'the All-Highest', was the fact that Burgomaster Haw and other local notables threatened to 'pour their wine under the table' rather than 'drink the health of His [Prussian] Majesty'. The number of times they raised their glasses to toast other people and sentiments was noted and reported back and forth between the Regierungspräsident in Trier, the Oberpräsident in Coblenz and the Minister of the Interior and Police in Berlin. The mayor and several town councillors were said to have variously drunk toasts to 'Freedom', the July Revolution and the downfall of 'absolutism', and Trier's police chief reported that the town's people expected to be 'liberated' by the French.

This was the atmosphere in which Karl Marx's father, towards the end of 1833, prepared for the 'festive banquet' at which the Casino Society was to honour Burgomaster Haw and three other deputies of the Rhenish Provincial Diet. Banquets were politically suspect ever since the 'banqueting societies' which had served Dr Wirth's undercover campaign for a constitution and press freedom. Moreover, the 4 deputies to be feted by the Casino Society (Haw, Valdenaire, Mohr and Kaiser) were to be given a hero's welcome for the way they had represented 'the people' of Trier in the Diet. They were all liberals, while Trier's fifth deputy, a conservative aristocrat, had conspicuously not been invited; and if this was not enough to make it smack of a disguised political demonstration, the juncture was a delicate one, for the King of Prussia was said to be planning to abolish the Rhenish Diet altogether. A preliminary committee of 40 members of the Casino Society, which with a slight stretch of the imagination has been described as Trier's 'country club', had therefore carefully considered all the details.

Justizrat Heinrich Marx was to propose the main toast at the banquet. Whether for his acumen or by virtue of the standing he had achieved among his fellows, he had been chosen to head the actual organizing committee, which included a judge, a notary and two other lawyers. The short 'festive address' he delivered before the 160 leading citizens assembled at the Casino on 13 January 1834 was a masterpiece of diplomatic ambiguity and would have been courageous for anyone in the current circumstances, and not only for a converted Jew who risked a career he had so cautiously built, and at no mean price to himself and his family.

'Gentlemen', he began, 'one sentiment unites us at this celebration.' And launching straight into a tribute to the 4 deputies, he expressed the unanimous gratitude of the gathering for the fight they had put up 'by word and deed, sacrifice and courage, on behalf of truth and justice.' Then he addressed himself to praising Prussia's King Friedrich Wilhelm III for having instituted the Diet, in words which were seen as an indirect protest against any plan to suppress it:

> It is our pleasant, nay holy civic duty to express our deepest thanks and most ardent wishes to our good Monarch, to whose magnanimity we owe the first institution of a popular representation. In the fulness of his absolute power he voluntarily established the provincial Diets, so that the truth should rise and reach the high steps of his throne... with pride we hear even foreign nations praise the justice of our King. But where justice reigns, there truth too must find an open door... His noble heart will always be favourable and open to the just and reasonable demands of his people. Long live His Majesty! Hoch!

The immediate Prussian reaction, uttered by the Minister of Justice Von Kamptz, was one of cold fury: 'The deputies no longer think of themselves as delegates to a German provincial Diet, but as *representatives of the people* and the public in the taverns confirms them in this mania by praising them – *as in England* – for their achievement in averting dangerous plots against the Diet and by making *speeches awarding them the civic crown* [Author's italics].' Burgomaster Haw's attempts to play down the incident and calm the Prussian anger might have had a chance of success, had not the 'Casino affair' had a second instalment.

'Casino affair No. 2' developed less than a fortnight after the first, when – on 25 January – another banquet was held to celebrate the twenty-fifth anniversary of the Society's foundation under the French. On this occasion, some of the assembled elite of Trier, stuffed with food and wine, not only kept singing the *Marseillaise* and the *Parisienne*, but – worst of all – a silken tricolour decorated with symbols of the July Revolution was produced and some of the drunken Casino members kissed and 'even knelt in front of it adoringly'. With Heinrich Marx present, one of his colleagues, Advocate Brixius, rose to declare: 'But for the July Revolution, we would all be eating grass now and be treated like beasts.' Brixius was charged with high treason. Tried in December 1834, he was acquitted, but the state appealed the verdict, and the case was to be heard again in Cologne in 1835.

Although suppressed in Trier's *Zeitung*, news of the Casino incidents was published in Cologne, Coblenz and even Paris. The King of Prussia asked for a report, and the Crown Prince expressed his indignation. Disciplinary proceedings were instituted against Haw for sending the Crown Prince a letter accusing the Regierungspräsident of aggravating tension by his 'unwisdom' and 'tactless' importuning. With the entire town council petitioning the King on behalf of the burgomaster, Haw was let off with a fine of 50 Thaler. Wyttenbach, the headmaster of the Gymnasium, and one of his teachers were placed on a list of political suspects.

The 'Casino affair' is chiefly of interest for its effect on Heinrich Marx's 16-year-old son. Because of an unsubstantiated report that Marx 'at once retracted everything', biographers of Karl Marx have tended to judge him harshly. Thus, Isaiah Berlin, in a cautious but forceful phrase, considered it 'not improbable that... his father's craven and submissive attitude made a definite impression on his eldest son Karl... and left behind it a smouldering sense of resentment, which later events fanned into a flame.' While McLellan described Heinrich Marx's speech as 'characteristically moderate and deferential', Raddatz suggested that, in thanking the anti-Semitic King, Karl's father 'was either seized by *horror vacui* or was mocking him.' The Prussian authorities obviously took the latter view, to judge by the sharp reaction of the Minister of Justice, not to mention the fact that the Paris daily *Le Constitutionnel* saluted 'the liberal speeches' delivered at a 'brilliant banquet' in Trier.

Finally, Padover wrote in 1979 that to the teen-aged Karl Marx 'men like Brixius, Haw, Wyttenbach, and, of course, his father, must have been heroes, symbols of resistance to what was, in some ways, a police state.'

This was most likely the case, with one qualification. Karl's father was involved, together with Haw and Wyttenbach, in efforts to placate the authorities and to have the Casino reopened. He had a prudent, juridical side, which showed when the Prussians foisted a co-headmaster on Wyttenbach in the person of a teacher, Dr Vitus Loers, known for his reactionary views. When Karl Marx later left for the university, he and one other pupil made a point of taking leave of all their teachers except this Loers, whom they obviously regarded as an informer. At the festive installation of this commissar, Heinrich Marx, as he wrote to his son, 'nearly cried over the humiliation of the good Wyttenbach... I told him that you too were greatly devoted to him and that you had meant to write a poem in his honour, but had not done so for lack of time. You have no idea how happy this made him. For my sake, will you please send me a couple of verses for him?'

At the same time he did not fail to mention to his son that 'Loers was most annoyed that you did not pay him a farewell visit. I had to make up an innocent lie and told him... we had called on him during his absence.' The son never answered this letter, or if he did his answer has not been preserved. He admired the bravura of his father's Casino speech, but was less impressed by his apologetic tendency and the little subterfuges dictated by his anxiety not to offend, now that he was politically suspect.

In the autumn of 1834, Karl Marx entered the graduating class of Trier's Gymnasium. The school, adjoining a Jesuit church built in 1563, was situated in a stately late-Renaissance four-storey building, with two towers on the corners and a statue in the front courtyard. In the course of the centuries it had housed an alternating succession of religious and worldly institutions, and under Napoleon the Collège de Trèves. A seminary for Catholic priests in the same complex had been abolished with the Prussian take-over in 1815; a government decree had converted the Jesuit church, over the protests of the Catholic population, into a Protestant-Evangelical place of worship, but the Gymnasium next to it was a secular secondary school.

The 1834–35 school year had hardly started when a ministerial complaint from Berlin drew the attention of the Oberpräsident in Coblenz to the lack of discipline at the Gymnasium. Indeed, most of the teachers, headed by Wyttenbach, not only shared the general Rhenish resentment of the Prussian rule but resisted its attempts to impose any regimentation of the students, physical or mental. Wyttenbach, for instance, had recently rejected a proposal to introduce gymnastic training on the grounds that no teacher was ready to take time off serious educational work and devote it to physical exercises or callisthenics.

Dr Johann Hugo Wyttenbach, whom the Prussians had appointed principal in 1815, had started his teaching career in 1799. He had been raised on the ideas of the Enlightenment, was an admirer of Leibniz, Rousseau and Benjamin Franklin, and the storming of the Bastille, 'for all its cold horror', had kindled in him a 'burning expectation of freedom dawning over all the earth.' The subject he taught was history, but Goethe, on a visit to Trier, was impressed by his understanding of Kant's philosophy. It was largely due to the stewardship of this highly cultured humanist that the Gymnasium had achieved a good scholastic reputation.

Most of the Gymnasium's dedicated teachers had grown to maturity under the liberties granted by the French. A later Prussian report summing up their 'pernicious' influence charged them specifically with passing on their own youthful 'freedom dizziness' to the young generation to which Karl Marx belonged. The composition of his graduating class, however, tells us something else about the school. Of the 32 pupils in the class, the youngest was 16 years old; Marx and two others were 17; most of the others were in the 18 to 22 age group; and two were as old as 24 and 27. This was due to the fact that only 8 pupils, 7 Protestants (including Karl Marx) and one Catholic, were the sons of educated and well-established burghers, such as notaries or officials. They all meant to go on to universities to study law or medicine. The rest, representing the province's vast Catholic majority, were the sons of less affluent artisans, tradesmen, vintners and peasants who mostly sent them to the Gymnasium to take its courses in theology on stipends available to candidates for the priesthood, and sometimes simply to keep them out of the army.

Karl Marx, in a letter to Engels, later referred to the 10 or 11 stipend-holders among his classmates as 'country bumpkins' distinguished by their 'denseness and advanced age'. Due to the economic crisis and other factors, the number of the school's pupils had in the past 10 years fallen from 505 to 320. The Catholics worried that this would lead to a shortage of theologians, but the Gymnasium – having in a sense taken the place of the former French seminary – continued to produce proportionately the largest number of Catholic clerics. As a youth Karl Marx, rather than worrying like his teachers about the adverse effect of this on the school's academic level, was probably more annoyed by the boring company of the 'country bumpkins'. He and a few other classmates belonged to a literary circle that met at a restaurant-bar on Trier's Cattle Market, where they discussed the latest poetry and their latest pranks amid much laughter and raillery.

On the morning of 13 September 1835, Marx set out for the final stage of his school-leaving examinations. The written examinations in religion, Greek,

German composition, Latin, French and mathematics had taken place, in that order, in August. Now, before a 'Royal Examination Committee' headed by Education Commissioner Theodor Brueggemann, and otherwise comprising headmaster Wyttenbach and 6 other teachers, he was to sit for the decisive oral tests in the same subjects (except for German), with the addition of history, geography, natural history and physics. The tests were to last a full week.

Marx was one of 22 pupils sitting for the exams – 10 had dropped out before. Far from being an under-privileged child, he had grown up in comfort, in a family affluent enough to own a house which (as the tax assessors noted when fixing the municipal rates) had 14 windows and doors. The house was full of children, but there were two maids to help his mother. The continuing poverty in the Trier district had in the last two years driven 300 families to emigrate to North America and elsewhere. Karl's father, as an attorney-barrister, dealt with such results of the social situation as theft, prostitution and crime. One of the high school teachers, Thomas Simon, who had been a poor-law guardian, wrote that he made it his job to hold up to the students the 'heart-breaking reality' of poverty. 'What makes a man into a human being', he told them, 'is not the possession of cold, filthy, printed money, but character, principles, reason and sympathy for the weal and woe of one's fellow men.'

At home, at the Gymnasium and in the streets of Trier, Marx certainly saw and heard enough to make him aware not only of the local anti-Prussian feeling but of the prevailing social conditions. There is no shred of information to indicate how this awareness affected him, what sympathy he felt for the woes of suffering humanity, or how early he developed a social conscience. Trier had produced an early Socialist world reformer of some note in the person of Ludwig Gall, a former District Clerk to the Prussian administration in Trier, who – in between establishing a settlement for German emigrants at Harrisburg, Pennsylvania, inventing a 'steam-distillation-apparatus' and eventually developing the world's first washing machine – published several pamphlets graphically describing the poverty and misery of 'the majority of society', day labourers, dirt farmers, manual workers, etc. Gall, however, had left Trier some years before, and the time was yet to come when Baron von Westphalen, who had worked with him in the Trier administration, took a liking to his future son-in-law and acquainted him with Gall's proposals for improving working-class conditions.

If Karl showed any interest in politics or the social question while at the Gymnasium, nothing is known about it. At one point the school was searched, and in 1834 another pupil was jailed for a month for writing a seditious poem. Although Karl's father was now politically suspect, Karl's name never appeared on the police spy's lists of radical students. The future author of *Das Kapital* wrote verse and his aspiration was to become a poet.

Nor was he an outstanding pupil. Only his Latin and German essays earned him the then German equivalent of an 'A' each. His translation from a Greek text by Sophocles was marked 'mediocre', as was his translation of a German text into French. He did slightly better in translating a French passage into German ('fairly satisfactory'); his solution of a mathematical problem was 'satisfactory', but the written test in trigonometry was rated simply 'failure'. Surprisingly, his performance in history was not outstanding. His written essays being the earliest surviving documents in his hand, they have been extensively analyzed, and none more so – in view of his later atheism – than the paper he wrote on 'The Union of the Faithful with Christ according to John 15:1–14, presented in Its Reason and Being, in its Absolute Necessity and Its Effects'.

Young Marx began this essay with some remarks on the pre-Christian era. In a statement almost as categorical as, though more long-winded than, the famous sentence which 13 years later was to open *The Communist Manifesto* – 'The history of all hitherto existing societies is the history of class struggles' – he affirmed that 'History, the great teacher of mankind', had 'engraved with an iron stylus' the fact that even the greatest and most cultured nations in the era before Christ had no morality, and that 'even their virtues were more the product of a raw greatness, of unrestrained egoism, of a passion for fame and heroic deeds than a striving for true perfection... The ancient nations, these savages', were 'inwardly convinced of their worthlessness and they tried to atone for their guilt by sacrificing to their deities. Thus the history of mankind teaches us the necessity of the union with Christ.' Besides history, young Marx invoked 'reason and the word of Christ himself' as 'loud and convincing proof that the union with him is absolutely necessary.' Those who rejected it faced the Lord's judgment, while those who accepted it were purified, since 'God alone can redeem' man from the sinfulness overlaying 'the spark of the divine in his breast, his enthusiasm for the good, his striving after knowledge and desire for truth.'

Embroidering on Christ's parable of the vine and the branch, he filled his long essay (4 pages when printed) with many pious expressions and concluded it by saying:

> Thus the union with Christ affords inner uplift, comfort in suffering, calm confidence and a heart open to love of one's fellows... The union with Christ imparts a joyousness which the Epicurean vainly seeks in his superficial philosophy and the thinker vainly tries to snatch at in the hidden profundities of knowledge, but which the soul can attain only through unrestrained and childlike union with Christ, and through him with God, and which alone makes for a more beautiful and elevated life.

Pastor Johann Abraham Küpper was disappointed both with the contents of this essay and with its florid style. Küpper had baptized Marx as a child. Twice a week in the Gymnasium he had given him and the 6 other Protestant-Evangelical students in the class religious instruction. While in the oral test the examiners declared themselves satisfied with Marx's 'knowledge of the Christian faith and morals' – and, aware of his origin, even remarked that he knew 'a little of the history of the Christian church' – Pastor Küpper had expected his pupil to do better in the essay. Praising its 'vigorous presentation', he noted on the margin that it 'nowhere dealt with the essence' or nature of the union with Christ, that its treatment of the reason for it was 'one-sided', and that Marx had 'demonstrated its necessity only imperfectly.'

Worse, from posterity's viewpoint, the essay tells us little about Marx's religious feelings – so little, in fact, that while Padover thought it 'possible that Karl did not believe the nonsensical pieties' in his essay, 'with their patronizing attitude toward non-Christians past, present and future', Bruce Mazlish has engaged in a lengthy argument to prove the opposite. Although noting that young Marx very soon 'lost his faith' and became a militant atheist, Mazlish held to the position, nevertheless, that Marx was not hypocritical in this particular instance. Rather, 'he accepted the obligatory Christian teachings offered him without undue strain or scepticism', but was caught in a conflict between his ambition and 'his Christian beliefs [which] told him that ambition was sinful.' Mazlish admitted, however, that there is 'no documentation for the cause of his loss of faith, or its vicissitudes.'[2]

Marx's German composition, 'Reflections of a Young Man on the Choice of a Profession', is a different type of document. Unlike anything known or assumed about the environmental and other influences he absorbed during his childhood and youth before he left home to enrol at Bonn University – or even the image we get of him through the prism of his father's letters to him or the tales and reminiscences of his fellow students – in this German essay Marx for the first time speaks to us in his own authentic voice, his 'inner voice', as he called it. Carrying as it does something of the ring of the mighty voice that was to resound around the world, the question as to where it came from, what it represented and how the ideal profession he envisioned at 17 compared with his mature life and work was to cause much discussion in the the last quarter of the 20th century, when 'Marxism' – as Mazlish observed in 1984 – had 'come to hold sway over more hearts and minds, or at least to dominate the ideologies of those in power in proportionately more parts of the world than any one of the major historical religions.'[3]

A mere 7 years after his final high school examinations, Marx began to wield his pen in a manner that was posthumously to assure him a greater influence on

374

history than many an armed conqueror. We know who and what he became, but not who he was as he set out to start life on his own. In his German essay he left posterity a document reflecting a whole range of ideas, problems and 'vicissitudes' agitating his mind – some of them related and others unrelated to the religious conflict troubling his soul – and revealing a number of contradictory influences he experienced at home and at school during the otherwise blank period of his childhood and youth.

It is a document all the more remarkable because, while indirectly lighting up elements that had gone into the making of his personality at 17, it reads almost like a scenario forecasting in outline the course of his own life and his role in history.

> 'He was a terrible tyrant to his sisters, forcing them to play coachman and horses and to drive him down the Markusberg in Trier at a gallop; worse, he insisted that they eat the dirty dough he kneaded into cakes with his dirty hands. But they stood the "driving" and ate the "cakes" without a murmur, for the sake of the stories Karl would tell them as a reward for their compliance.'[4]

This story, which Marx's daughter Eleanor heard a long time later from his two youngest sisters and published after his death, is practically the only extant report of him as a child. Like that other imperious character, Bakunin, though not for the same reasons, the Marx boy lorded it over his 5 sisters and two brothers. Not only was he the brightest and most promising of them, he was also the healthiest and most robust in a brood of 9 sickly children, one of whom had already died while 4 others were to succumb to tuberculosis. He was in every respect his doting parents' favourite, their *Glückskind*, 'Fortune's child'.

The enormous and minute research into his life has established such details as that he was circumcised at birth and taught to write by the bookseller Montigny who lived near the Marx house in the Simeonstrasse. He is believed to have got his elementary education at Trier's Evangelical Volksschule, but there is no record of him before he entered the Gymnasium. As late as 1973, McLellan wrote that 'up to the age of twelve Marx was probably educated at home';[5] and it is not inconceivable that he was prepared for the Gymnasium by his father and some private tutor.

The fact, however, that his father had him and the rest of his children baptized in August 1824, three months after Karl was 6 and had reached school age, would seem to indicate that the timing was connected with his wish to assure his admission to the public Volksschule, which accepted only Christian children. Following complaints that Trier's 50 Jewish children were getting only an 'inadequate' education from private tutors or none at all, the Prussian

375

authorities on 13 September 1824 issued a decree ostensibly putting an end to their exclusion from Christian public schools; in practice, with the inspector of education observing that the textbooks were permeated with references to Christianity and that 'one would have to remove the cross from the school' to make these children welcome, nothing much changed. As late as 1832, according to official figures, 319 Jewish children throughout the Rhineland were getting an elementary education, but none was at a public school, meaning they continued to be relegated to inferior private or Jewish schools (which Christians were forbidden to attend).[6]

Heinrich Marx, who realized at an early stage that Karl had 'splendid natural gifts', did not wait for these developments. Karl and his siblings were baptized in the last week of August 1824, a fortnight ahead of the hypocritical Prussian decree and a year or so before the opening of a Jewish school in Trier, which dispensed only two hours' daily tuition. His father thus made sure that Karl would meet with no hindrance in getting the best available education both at the Volksschule, if he attended it, and certainly at the Gymnasium, which during his 5 years of study there included no Jewish pupils either.

According to Padover, writing in 1979, the baptism of the Marx children – Sophie (8), Karl (6), Hermann (5), Henriette (4), Luise (3), Emilie (2) and Karoline (a three-weeks-old baby) – took place 'in the Trier Evangelical church', that is, in the converted former Jesuit church adjoining the Gymnasium. It was indeed at the altar of this church that Karl Marx was confirmed when he was 14. As far as his baptism is concerned, however, all German authors, Monz, Raddatz, Künzli, maintain that this took place at the Marx home. The baptismal register merely records that it was performed on 26 August 1824. Indeed, although any assumption is as good as the other, Marx's father, always mindful of his steps, probably preferred to avoid the limelight of a church ceremony and the small-town talk likely to be stirred by the public mass baptism of 7 offspring of a well-known rabbinical family, especially as their mother remained Jewish and the father's brother Samuel Marx continued to be the Oberrabbiner of the district.

Marx had chosen Protestantism for himself and his children partly because, even under the proselytizing Prussian regime which had forced him to convert, it was a more enlightened and progressive religion than Roman Catholicism. And it is a little-known footnote to history that this and the baptism of his children in a home ceremony may have saved him and his family the kind of spotlighting that not many years later was to be given to the Catholic baptism of one of its lesser known members – Heinrich Marx's younger brother Cerf (Hirsch) Marx (b. 1790) – and his family of 4 at Aachen (Aix-la-Chapelle). This was made the occasion for a brochure titled 'The Baptism of a Jew-Family on the

Eve of Holy Pentecost 1831, at the Parish Church of St Nicholas in Aachen'. Printed with the sanction of the Cologne archbishopric, with an introduction by the parish priest L.A. Nellessen, this document, recovered and re-published in 1975,[7] emphasized in a rather triumphalist tone that the said Cerf Marx came of an old and 'genuine rabbinical family'. The brochure mentioned his grandfather and great-grandfather; his mother's second marriage to the Chief Rabbi of Amsterdam; the fact that his brother Samuel Marx, the Oberrabbiner, had attended Napoleon's 1806 Great Sanhedrin in Paris; and dwelt at some length not only on the life-story of this Cerf Marx, who was a watchmaker, but on the crowded, three-hour-long church ceremony which his family had undergone and the 'devotion' with which they since attended Holy Mass and marched in processions.

In the case of Karl Marx and his siblings, the 1824 entry in the register contained a note to the effect that the mother, Henriette Marx, while not yet ready to embrace Christianity herself, had agreed to the baptism of her 7 children (the eighth, Eduard, had yet to be born and was baptized a year and a half later). Five respectable burghers and their wives acted as godparents to the children. The men included three of Heinrich Marx's fellow-lawyers and two governnment officials. One of the wives was a daughter of Pastor Küpper, who had prepared Karl for the baptism. More than a century after the event, Künzli's and Hubert Schiel's obliquely ironic assertion that 'the reception of Karl Marx into the fold of Christianity was celebrated by the army of godparents at a great family feast' – for which no evidence has been found – was still drawing debate and denials from others, although the point is immaterial.[8]

The more important facts are, first, that Heinrich Marx allowed 5 years to elapse between his own baptism and that of his children; and secondly, that even then his wife refused to convert on the grounds (stated in the baptismal register) that her parents were still alive. These are the two pillars on which Künzli in 1966 built a whole edifice of references from Marx's personal correspondence and public writings to show the lasting and in many ways nefarious effect on his life, work and whole persona of this 'conversion conflict' and other disjunctive influences he absorbed during his formative years before he left home at the age of 17. Although mostly well-reasoned and documented, Künzli's *Psychographie* raised the hackles of orthodox Marx biographers. Most if not all of them chose to ignore it, and it has never been translated into English.

Künzli proved right in assuming that the reason given by Henriette Marx for delaying her baptism in 1824 was merely a 'pretext', for it has since been established that when she finally accepted baptism in a private, 'almost clandestine' ceremony on 20 November 1825, both her parents were still alive in Holland.

377

Künzli's view that Karl Marx's mother nevertheless remained Jewish at heart to the end of her days is shared by practically all his biographers, on the basis of her oft-quoted letter, written 18 years after her baptism, in which – speaking of the departure of her daughter Luise for distant Capetown – she wrote: 'It seems that the fate of the People of I[srael] is again being realized in me – that my children should be scattered throughout the world...' But Künzli went much further. He claimed that some time before the age of 6 Karl Marx must have noticed his mother's inner conflict in the matter of baptism, and that his parents were divided on the subject; that, whether they argued about it calmly or heatedly before their disagreement became public with his mother's abstention from baptism in 1824, he must have wondered about 'the why and wherefore' of baptism and about the question 'why not mother too'; and that, at the latest in November 1825, when his mother finally gave up her long resistance and Karl was past 7 – 'an age at which even less alert children become conscious of parental dissension' – this conflict decisively and traumatically influenced the images he formed of his parents.[9]

One distinctive feature of Marx's German essay on the choice of a profession is his idealistic approach in proclaiming that 'History calls those the greatest men who ennoble themselves by working for the universal', and in such hyperbolic statements as 'Our happiness belongs to millions'. To man, young Marx wrote at the beginning of his essay, 'the Deity [*Gottheit*] gave a general role, that of ennobling mankind and himself', but man is free to choose 'the most appropriate position in society' from which he can best pursue it. 'This choice is a great privilege of man over the rest of creation, but at the same time it is an act which can destroy his whole life, frustrate all his plans and make him unhappy.' With this note of alarm he introduced a contrasting feature running through the essay, devoting the greater part of it to a catalogue of temptations and delusions – excessive ambition, lust for glory, 'the glitter of great things', inflamed fantasy and 'instincts unrestrained by reason' – that may lure the young to 'plunge headlong towards the goal which we fancy the Deity itself is pointing at', only to come to a fall and find 'our entire existence shattered'.

Fortunately, 'the Deity which never leaves earthlings without some guidance' helps a young man navigate the pitfalls attending the choice of a career. The goal or purpose in life allotted to every man may appear large to him, but is indeed so if it stems from his 'innermost conviction'. This is the supreme test the young man has to apply when carefully weighing all the circumstances. As a last resort, Karl added, when unable to see one's way, 'our heart turns to our parents, who have already encountered the vicissitudes of fate.'

In analyzing this essay, Künzli, a philosopher who also studied Jungian psychiatry, drew attention to the fact that, instead of dealing in concrete terms with the choice of a profession (*Beruf* in German), Marx turned the entire essay into an abstract discussion of the need for a young man to follow his calling or vocation (*Berufung*), to listen to his 'inner voice' and let himself be guided by nothing but his 'innermost conviction'. He further pointed out that in more than one place the young Marx identified this 'innermost conviction', or 'inner voice', or 'the innermost voice of the heart' with the voice of 'the Deity... which speaks softly but firmly'; and that in one place he actually referred to the inner voice as 'the call (*Ruf*) of the Deity'.

Künzli submitted that, far from being metaphorical or reflecting Headmaster Wyttenbach's influence – as the passages about 'ennobling mankind' obviously do – this sprang subconsciously from certain ideas implanted in him by his mother. According to Künzli, the silence later maintained by the adult Marx about his mother induced even sober biographers to follow in his wake and relegate her to a practically insignificant role in his life. Künzli, on the contrary, pointed out that such total repression into the unconscious of the mother and all she represents in most cases 'known to experience' assumes 'a determining compulsive power over the person involved.'

Echoing Horst Wittig's view that 'during his childhood Karl Marx certainly heard from his mother about his ancestors and their religion', Künzli went so far as to declare that, along with some idea of his Jewish heritage, Karl's mother passed on to him nothing less than the ancient notion that as the eldest son he was '"the son of God", that he belonged to God.' In support of this he invoked the Old Testament verse 'Sanctify unto me all the firstborn.'

The *Encyclopaedia Judaica* confirms that 'at one time firstborn sons were devoted to cultic service as temple slaves, Nazarites and the like', but adds: 'Subsequently other arrangements were made for supplying cultic personnel, while the erstwhile sanctity of the firstborn was lifted through redemption.' The Old Testament verse quoted by Künzli actually prescribed the manner in which the Jews, as a reminder of the Lord's sparing them when Egypt's first-born were struck, were to 'redeem every male firstling' for a fee of 'five silver shekels' payable to the tribe of priests. In practice, once a male firstborn has proved himself viable by surviving the first 30 days of life he is, on the 31st day, redeemed in a symbolic ceremony by the father handing the equivalent of 'five silver shekels' (in medieval times, according to the *Encyclopaedia*, 'two Reich-sthaler, today five U.S. dollars') to a descendant of the tribe of Aaron; and since descent from Aaron's tribe is merely presumptive, the *kohen* (priest) often returns the coins to the father.[10]

Künzli, however, attached decisive importance to the Marx family's ancestral heritage. While noting that Karl's father remained unaffected by the potent 'legacy of world-famous scholars who since the fifteenth [*sic*] century distinguished

379

themselves by their sense of justice and social concerns', he wrote that this legacy, like 'a stream temporarily disappearing in a subterranean bed', broke forth again, through the mother's intermediary, in the son. He observed that the father, in trying to guide his son's career after he left home, never once in his letters invoked 'the Deity', but always gave him practical, 'homebaked-opportunist' advice. As for the legacy subconsciously manifesting itself a generation later in the son, Künzli cited more than one instance of such unexpected eruptions, including the case of Karl Marx's own daughter Eleanor, who although half-Jewish and not religious, was to proclaim: 'I am a Jewess.'

Künzli detected in Marx's youthful essay a predisposition, an 'inner preparedness', not only to assume so elevated a role, but to believe in the related idea that he was himself 'god-like' and that – the Deity itself signifying 'perfection' – he must strive to attain similar perfection in fulfilling his universal mission. In support of this, Künzli adduced the fact that Marx was inextricably linking the welfare of mankind and his own perfection in the passage: 'The guiding principle in choosing one's vocation must be the welfare of mankind, our own perfection... The nature of man is so constituted that he can attain his own perfection only when he works for the perfection and welfare of his fellow men. If he works only for himself, he may become a famous scholar, a great sage, an excellent poet, but never a perfect, truly great man.'

Observing that although Karl spoke of men in general terms, 'he would not have been seventeen had it not been first and foremost his own I speaking,' Künzli crowned his probings into the depths of Karl Marx's subconscious as reflected in his graduation essay with the remark that in another of its famous passages – 'Worth is that which most of all elevates a man, which imparts a higher nobility to his actions and all his endeavours, which makes him intangible, admired by the masses and raised high above them' – Marx revealed a subconscious tendency towards 'self-deification'.

There is no evidence that his mother instilled in young Marx anything like 'a preparedness' for a role corresponding to that of a 'son of God'. There is no knowing whether as a child he watched his mother lighting candles on Friday night, or whether the Sabbath and other Jewish holidays, rituals or customs were observed in the Marx home for any length of time. Henriette Marx seems to have received some secular education in Holland, for she could read and write Dutch. But she had grown up in a traditional Jewish home, and unlike her enlightened and assimilated husband it is conceivable that, being proud of her lineage from 'the Exalted' Rabbi Judah Loew of Prague, she inculcated in Karl the idea that he too was one of 'the elect', a special person, destined to be a great rabbi or scholar. One may also accept Stanley Hyman's 'doubt that Marx's childhood was as antiseptic as he would have had it' and subscribe to his view – expressed before the full list of Marx's forefathers was known – that 'one can doubt the inheritance of Jewish thought patterns, but some cultural transmission is certain.'[11]

But this does not mean that his mother passed on to him anything like the erstwhile notion of the 'sanctity of the firstborn', which had lapsed with the destruction of the Jerusalem Temple. It is perhaps fitting to let Karl's mother speak for herself. The personality of this little-known figure best emerges from her long 'Postscript' to one of her husband's first letters to Karl after his departure for Bonn. Written in her ungrammatical German, with hardly a punctuation mark, it is here reproduced with slight abbreviations in the translation by Saul Padover, who has tried to retain the tone and syntax of the original:

> Greatly beloved dear Carl!
>
> with much pleasure I seize the pen to write to you... you can believe me that I greatly yearn for you thank Heaven we are all quite healthy everybody is active and diligent... now you cannot ascribe it to the weakness of my sex if I am curious to know how you arranged your small household, if frugality plays the main role in big as well as in little household expenses which is an indispensable necessity, in addition I permit myself to remark dear Carl that you must never regard cleanliness and orderliness as unimportant because health and cheerfulness depend upon them see to it punctually that your rooms are scrubbed often set a regular time for it – and you scrub my beloved Carl weekly with sponge and soap – how goes it with the coffee Do you fabricate it yourself or what, I beg you to report to me everything about the housekeeping, your amiable Muse will not feel offended by the Prose of your Mother, tell Her that through the inferior the superior and the better are attained, and so keep well if you have a wish for Christmas that I can satisfy I am prepared for it with pleasure so keep well my beloved dear Carl be worthy and good and always keep God and your Parents before your eyes adieu your loving Mother Henriette Marx.
>
> All the children greet you and kiss you and you are as always the most beloved and best.

Vibrant with spontaneity, motherly love and devotion, it is the letter of a practical woman with tubercular children, 4 of whom were fated to die in the next 11 years. A Dutchwoman appalled by the unsanitary conditions in Trier, she is anxious that her son should look after his health and observe elementary hygiene, but hardly sounds like a woman who raised him to some divinely ordained mission.

So much for Karl Marx as 'the son of God'. As for his early tendency to 'selfdeification', it is true that Heine, for all his friendship with and admiration of Marx (whose graduation essay he never read), later referred to him as a 'godless self-god'. But this was because he feared the consequences of his materialistic-atheist conception, and not because he saw any pretence at transcendental inspiration in him, which Marx, incidentally – in spite of the tone of authority of his dogmatic pronouncements – never claimed for them. Marx, who originally repudiated the very term 'Marxism' (which Engels was to launch on its path of ambiguous glory), would have been surprised to hear that in the 1980s he would be called 'the founder of a great, secular' or any 'religion' on a par with Jesus, Buddha and Muhammad.

Yet certain elements forming the gravamen of Künzli's thesis about the traumatic influence of the 'conversion conflict' on the young Marx cannot be dismissed out of hand, and bearing as they do on the high sense of mission conspicuously evident in his essay, they deserve to be briefly summarized.

Marx was by nature a Jungian 'Denktypus', approaching the world via his intellect, rather than with his feelings, intuition or sensations, a view for which Künzli found support in his father's later complaining that the son had more brain than heart. The father, early aware of his son's outstanding faculties, introduced him to the rationalist ideas of his favourite French and German philosophers. Both parents had high expectations for Karl and treated him like a little VIP. But the mother, a homebound woman, busy for years with the birth and raising of children, and a stranger to Trier who never learned to write German grammatically, did not share her husband's interest in the law or in the philosophies of Leibniz or Kant. Thus she had no substitute for the religion she finally gave up, formally at least, for the sake of domestic harmony, her husband's career and her children's future.

This intellectual discrepancy, Künzli affirmed, aggravated the effect of 'the conversion conflict' on the adolescent Marx. The dissension between his parents which he registered as a child was bad enough. To complicate the tensions it created in his young soul, Karl consciously admired his father and largely identified with his Enlightenment ideas of progress; subconsciously, however, the spirited youth who described the ideal career as one 'which offers us the widest scope to work for mankind and the universal goal of perfection for which every position is only a means', was beginning to question his father's petty-bourgeois concerns and his cautious, conciliatory temper, which increasingly made him warn the son to conform and not to overstep the bounds of convention. And to compound matters, buried in the depths of his subconscious lay the notion, implicit in his father's pressing for his mother's and the entire family's conversion, that being Jewish was something to be ashamed of, and the outmoded religion that went with it not worth clinging to or fighting for. 'Contempt for one's own origin', Künzli noted, 'creates a psychological conflict', and Karl's unconscious identification of his mother with 'inferior' Judaism could not but lead to his rejection of both Judaism and his mother. 'One rarely rejects something violently about which one has never had strong feelings,' wrote Bruce Mazlish, invoking Marx's later 'virulent' opposition to Christianity as an indication of his sincere belief in 'the union with Christ' of his religious essay. On the same principle, Künzli suggested that his violent reaction whenever his origin was mentioned and his fierce negation of Judaism were a measure of the potency and force of the subconscious legacy passed on to him by his mother.

This legacy, firing his ambition and imbuing him with the mission to emulate his great forefathers and work for the perfection of the world, placed an enormous responsibility on his shoulders, one, moreover, beset with many problems and at least one insuperable obstacle. According to Künzli, Marx temporarily bridged the conflict between the secularized 'religion of reason' held up to him by his father and the 'voice of the Deity' which he felt was his 'inner voice' by writing in his essay that the Deity gave man a general goal but left him free to make choices. But the gravest and most fundamental problem Karl was unable to solve at 17 was that through his father's conversion and his own baptism he had been brutally cut off from the powerful ancestral tradition legitimizing his sense of being the natural and well-equipped bearer of this special mission.

Adrift in this void, Karl reacted with that anxiety about the fatal consequences of choosing 'a profession for which we do not possess the talent' which runs like a leitmotif through the whole essay. 'Then the most natural consequence is self-contempt... Self-contempt is a serpent that ever gnaws at one's breast, sucking the life-blood from one's heart and mixing it with the poison of misanthropy and despair.' And by way of compensating for this terrible prospect, Marx, listening to his 'inner voice' but alienated from its source, chose the hubris of elevating himself to an 'intangible', invulnerable god-like position high above the crowds.

Thus far Künzli. There were other factors tending to alienate the young Marx. One was his intellectual superiority not only to the 'country bumpkins' at school, but to those of his classmates who (according to his daughter Eleanor) 'loved his pranks' but feared his verbal aggressiveness and 'the biting satiric verses' with which he responded to their raillery, with the result that he made no lasting friendships. He was also affected, of course, by the worry instilled in him by his parents about his weak lungs, which made him mention 'physical constitution' among the obstacles 'often threatening' a young man's career; by his swarthy Semitic complexion and the serious anti-Jewish riots in the Rhineland in 1834 which reminded him of his origin even in relatively tolerant but still deeply bigoted Catholic Trier; and by the fact that, contrary to previous opinions, Pastor Küpper, far from sharing Wyttenbach's and his father's enthusiasm for Kant and Voltaire, taught him that true religiosity implied acceptance of 'the sanctity of the infinite and recognition of man's sinfulness.'[12]

If one adds up all these confusing and contradictory influences on his mind, they form a heavy load for a young man to sort out. It is hardly any wonder that, driven into a dead end, Karl Marx soon turned against both Judaism and Christianity and dedicated himself to the mission of changing and 'perfecting' the world by choosing revolution as his profession.

He concluded his German school-leaving essay with some remarkable lines for a 17-year-old: 'When we have chosen the position in which we can do most for humanity, burdens cannot bow us down, because they are only sacrifices for all. Then we experience no meagre, limited, egoistic joy, but our own happiness belongs to millions, our deeds live on quietly but ever actively, and our ashes will be moistened by the glowing tears of noble men.'

Thus, with high idealistic pathos and enormous ambition, a sense of mission and a rather maudlin final accord asking for nothing but posterity's grateful tears, Karl informed his teachers that he aspired to join the ranks of history's 'greatest men... working for the universal.' As he was soon to begin writing Romantic poetry, and next to try his hand at a novel and a drama, but had accepted his father's practical advice to study law – with a view to his eventually landing a well-paid post at one of the new courts being established in the Trier area – it is all the stranger that he should unconsciously have been prophesying his future life and role in history, the role of the saviour of the oppressed workers of the world, living like a pauper, suffering exile, working year after year at his new gospel in spite of a Job-like affliction of carbuncles and sore boils, not to mention lung and liver ailments, ravaging his body and 'physical constitution'. When he died after a life dedicated to his idea of serving humanity, not many men shed tears on his grave, but his deeds were indeed to survive and give a mighty impetus to history.

One should not imagine Marx leaving the Gymnasium perturbed by the great political questions of the day. Like many of the young in the Romantic 1830s, he had begun to doubt some of the Enlightenment values drummed into him by his elders and teachers. But not for him the trend of those who made a virtue of being misunderstood and paraded their unhappiness with melancholy sighs. He was a high-spirited, ebullient character, rambunctious, self-confident and assertive, and at 17 he was in the throes of first love, having won the heart of one of Trier's most beautiful young ladies.

The beginnings of his romance with the aristocratic Johanne Bertha Julie Jenny von Westphalen are shrouded in some mystery, for after Marx's death his daughter Laura Lafargue was to destroy most of their letters. One of Jenny's, first published in the last quarter of the 20th century, shows that it took her some time to take the young man's courtship seriously. Addressed to Karl in 1838, the letter contains the sentence: 'Do you remember how at the beginning I always said, yes, I love you, how I could never bring myself to say I am in love with you?'[13]

By the time Karl was to leave for university, however, he and Jenny had secretly sworn each other eternal love. Only their respective siblings, Sophie and Edgar, were privy to their hope of formally announcing their engagement the following summer. Jenny, having reason to fear her family's opposition, would neither write to Karl nor answer his letters. This was the start of the young couple's torments, which were to run parallel with, and to last almost as long as, Karl Marx's intellectual travail before he reached the conclusion that society could only be 'emancipated' by Communism.

On 17 October 1835 he embarked on the 'Express Yacht' that would take him down the Moselle and in 16 hours to Coblenz. His parents, his 5 sisters and two brothers and a number of friends were at the pier in the cold to see him off at 4 a.m. At Coblenz he transferred to one of the new Rhine steamers and three days later he registered in the Faculty of Jurisprudence at Bonn University, 'the fortress of Romanticism', which had been Heine's first alma mater 15 years before.

13

The Romantic Russians in Exile and the Coup that Failed in Paris

In October 1835 Alexander Herzen was preparing for his first winter in Siberia. Arrested the previous summer, he had been exiled after being held for 9 months in a Moscow prison. His friend Nick Ogarev had been seized first, on 19 July. Hearing of his arrest, Herzen, who (in the double life he led) happened to be dining with Prince Orlov and other highly placed family friends, made use of these connections to get an interview with Prince Golitsyn, the Governor-General of Moscow. The latter told him that Ogarev had been arrested 'by order of the Tsar' for his part in 'some supper on the 24th of June, at which seditious songs had been sung.'

Two nights later, Herzen himself was pulled out of bed when a police officer came for him. With his father looking on broken-hearted, his mother almost fainting, and maids and manservants rushing after him to kiss his hand, he was led away by a mixed detachment of 8 Cossacks and policemen.

Herzen was 22 years old. What had happened was that on 24 June a stool-pigeon present at a drunken student party had heard a ditty disrespectful to the Tsar. He had thereupon invited the revellers to a champagne party and egged them on to repeat it in time for the police to break in and round up some 20 young men.

Neither Herzen nor Ogarev had been present at either of the 'seditious' parties. Ogarev, however, had been observed singing the *Marseillaise* in front of the Malny Theatre the previous December – a few weeks before the same republican song set off the 'Casino affair' in Trier – together with an older student-poet by the name of Sokolovsky. Although Sokolovsky had not attended the incriminating supper either, he was suspected of being the author of the offensive song. As letters from Herzen were found in Ogarev's room, he was hauled in too. The secret police had long tried to lay their hands on these three for their liberal opinions, but the attempt to implicate them with the group of 20 students arrested at the supper failed, as the investigators found no evidence connecting them with it.

Tsar Nicholas I thereupon appointed another Inquiry Commission. Nothing better illustrates the monstrous workings of his autocracy than some of the things Herzen learned during his long imprisonment. His arrest in July co-incided with the start of a prolonged wave of 'incendiarism' in Moscow. The glare of several fires lit the sky every night. Every morning a magistrate sorted out the people rounded up on the scene of the blazes. About half were released, the others detained, and some were flogged to extract confessions. In his cell, young Herzen could hear the 'wailing screams, entreaties and howls' of the unseen victims. The board appointed to investigate the fires kept 'investigating, that is thrashing, for six months in a row, but had thrashed out nothing in the end.' By then it was winter and Herzen had been transferred to the Krutitsky Barracks. 'The Tsar was annoyed and ordered that the thing was to be finished in three days.' From an old captain of gendarmes who was present at the scene, Herzen heard how the deadline was kept. Culprits were found, including inno-cents who had confessed to arson under the pain of the lashes, and were con-demned to 'punishment by the knout, by branding, and by exile to penal servitude. The porters from all the houses were assembled to watch... A groan of horror ran through the crowd' at the sight of lacerated, wounded backs being beaten with the knout. The rising murmurs made the police hurry, so for efficiency's sake 'the executioners dealt the legal number of blows, while others did the branding and others riveted fetters.'[1]

The new Commission appointed by Tsar Nicholas to investigate Herzen, Ogarev and the others suspected of having taken part in the so-called 'Soko-lovsky supper party affair' was presided over by the Governor-General, Prince Sergei Golitsyn. The Commandant of Moscow, an old general who realized the absurdity of the charges, begged the Tsar to relieve him of membership in it, but Nicholas refused. Another Golitsyn (Prince Alexander) was brought in as chief investigator. Three short scenes recorded by Herzen years later give the spirit, if not the exact letter, in which the investigation which led to his convic-tion, without trial, on charges of *lèse majesté* was conducted:

PRINCE ALEXANDER F. GOLYTSIN: 'My late father's long connection with yours makes me take a special interest in you... You are going straight under the white strap [i.e., into the hands of the political police] or to the fortress... Your father will not survive the day. That you had designs against the government is evident. To merit the mercy of the Monarch you must give proofs of your peni-tence... Write a letter to the Commission, simply, frankly: say that you feel your guilt, that you were led away by your youth, name the unfortunate, misguided men who have led you astray... Are you willing at this easy price to redeem your future and your father's life?'[2]

After 6 months of investigation which had yielded no incriminating evidence, the following exchange took place between Herzen and another member of the Commission, Colonel Shubinsky.

HERZEN: 'I should like to know what charge... what article of the Code are you applying to me?'

SHUBINSKY: 'The Code of laws is drawn up for crimes of a different kind... Do you really imagine that we believed you, that you have not formed a secret society?'

HERZEN: 'Where is the society?'

SHUBINSKY: 'It is your luck that no traces have been found, that you have not succeeded in achieving anything. We stopped you in time, that is, to speak plainly, we have saved you.'[3]

When, after 9 months, the 20 accused were finally assembled before the full Commission and heard the sentences which had been confirmed by the Tsar, Herzen put in a last protest.

HERZEN: 'You told me, Colonel, last time I was before the commission, that no one accused me of being connected with the supper-party affair. Yet in the sentence it is stated that I was one of those guilty in connection with that affair.'

SHUBINSKY: 'Do you wish to object to His Majesty's decision? You had better take care... I shall order your words to be taken down.'

HERZEN: 'I meant to ask you to do so... I am protesting against your report and not against the will of His Majesty.'

SHUBINSKY: 'As though you did not know that you are ten times more guilty than those who were at the supper party.' He pointed at one of the young men who had been pardoned. 'He, now, in a state of intoxication sang some filthy song, but afterwards he begged forgiveness on his knees with tears. But you are still far from any penitence.'

HERZEN: 'Excuse me, [this] is not the point... If I am a murderer, I don't want to be considered a thief...'

SHUBINSKY: 'If I had a son, my own son, who showed such stubbornness, I would myself beg the Tsar to send him to Siberia.'[4]

Sokolovsky the poet and two others were sent to the Schlüsselburg fortress 'for an indefinite period'. One of them, the painter Utin, died in the fortress the following year. Sokolovsky, who was 27 when sentenced, died 4 years later in the Caucasus.

Herzen, Ogarev and 4 others were notified that 'as men convicted of *lèse majesté* by singing seditious songs' they ought 'by law' to be executed or sentenced to penal servitude for life. But the Tsar in his 'infinite mercy' had commanded that they be banished from Moscow to do 'civilian duty for an indefinite period in remote provinces.'

And so Alexander Herzen was taken on 9 April 1835 from the Krutitsky Barracks to Siberia, almost in a wish-fulfilment of his youthful fancies – the dreams of exile, of prisons and deportation he shared with the girl he loved at that time, Ludmilla Passek. The last person to press his hand meaningfully before his departure was, however, another young girl, Natalie Zakharin, who had fainted on the floor of her home upon first hearing the news of his arrest.

'Alexander, don't forget your sister,' she whispered as she turned to leave with his mother. Natalie was actually Herzen's cousin, one of the illegitimate children of his legendary and terrifying uncle, Alexander Yakovlev – the one-time Procurator of the Holy Synod – who had kept a harem of serf-girls in a wing of his large house on Moscow's Tverskoye boulevard. It was the house in which Herzen himself had been born, in the same room where some 5 years later a sturdy concubine-serf of his uncle's, a peasant woman by the name of Ksenia Zakharin, had delivered Natalie.

Herzen might never have seen Natalie again but for several quirks of fate. In 1821, when she was 4, the former Procurator Alexander Yakovlev was allowed to return to St Petersburg and left Moscow together with his retinue, including his whole brood of offspring. Before the dissolute and spiteful old man died, he had – allegedly in order to trick his two brothers, Herzen's father and the Senator, of any prospect of inheriting his vast fortune – married one of his concubines and legitimized this woman's son Alexis, making him his sole heir.

Revolted by the spectacle of his father's debauched home-life to the point where he had once attempted suicide, Alexis had taken refuge in his university studies, and chose to live as a recluse in a room equipped as a laboratory. Disparagingly known as 'The Chemist', he was 30 or so when he inherited, among many other assets, the old man's women and decided to get rid of the whole lot by packing them off – together with his luckless half-sisters and half-brothers, who remained illegitimate – to the remotest of several estates that had fallen to him in the heartland of Russia.

Eight-year-old Natalie might never have been heard of again had not Princess Khovansky – a sister of the deceased ex-Procurator – charitably decided to offer a home to one of his bastard orphans. The elderly widowed princess lived in and ran the large house of her older and frail spinster aunt, the Princess Meshchersky. Natalie, a shy delicate-looking little girl, was separated from her mother and taken to the ancient Meshchersky mansion, where she was given a good education, but grew up waif-like under the strict supervision of the two princesses. There Herzen as a boy first saw her on the rare occasions when his paternal family came to pay their respects to Princess Meshchersky.

Whereas this withered but dignified, waxen-faced lady, born half a century before the French Revolution, was too old and desiccated to offer much love, warmth or inspiration to a child even before she died a year or two later, Princess Khovansky was a heartless termagant. It was only shortly before his arrest in 1834 that Herzen realized how much Natalie suffered under the constant reproofs, taunts and general tyranny of the Khovansky widow. Frequently reminded by others of what she owed her 'benefactress', she bore her fate nobly.

Herzen felt drawn to the intelligent but sad-eyed girl and his visits considerably brightened her lonely adolescence in the gloomy mansion. Natalie struck Herzen as a graceful, gentle 'child on the verge of womanhood' and in an access of sympathy, affection and budding love had lately started calling her 'little sister'.

'A few hours before departure... my last word as I go away shall be for you,' he wrote to Natalie from the Krutitsky Barracks. He had no idea when he would see her again. But 'bright is the thought of your affection,' he scribbled, 'the exile will never forget his charming sister.

'Perhaps... but I cannot finish, for they have come for me...' Then, escorted by a gendarme, he set out on the journey to Perm, on the Siberian border. His stay in prison, the screams that woke him at night and the thought that people who were in all probability quite innocent were lying 'in chains, with lacerated wounds on their backs' only a few paces from him taught Herzen that the true victims of the corruption of justice in Russia were its ordinary, humble people, peasants, house-serfs and workmen, whose 'martyrdom' began before the process of law had taken place. Political prisoners like himself, who were mostly upper-class, were kept 'in close custody and punished savagely, but their fate bears no comparison with the fate of the poor.'

Indeed, Herzen's personal valet accompanied him to Perm, a distance of some 1,300 kilometres from Moscow. They travelled by road from stage post to stage post, a strenuous journey in the rain and sleet of April, and at one point the valet who was to ease Herzen's exile nearly drowned while they were crossing the Volga in a raft.

When they finally reached the Siberian border the Governor of Perm decided that Herzen was to be taken another couple of hundred kilometres further, to live and to work 'under the supervision of the local authorities' in the little town of Vyatka. On his way there, stopping to change horses in a ceaseless downpour, he ran into an elderly officer escorting a crowd of Jewish 'boys of eight or nine years old' who had been impressed for service in the navy or army. 'They stood in thick, clumsy soldiers' overcoats, with stand-up collars, fixing helpless, pitiful eyes on the garrison soldiers who were roughly getting them into ranks.'

The officer commiserated with his charges: 'It's an ugly business... At first the orders were to drive them to Perm; then there was a change and we are driving them to Kazan. I took them over a hundred versts farther back. The officer who handed them over said, "It's dreadful, and that's all about it. A third were left on the way" (and the officer pointed to the cold earth). Not half will reach their destination.' Indeed, looking at their white-lipped faces and blue-ringed eyes 'attesting to fever or chill', Herzen felt that 'exposed to the icy wind blowing from the Arctic Ocean, they were going to their graves... Boys of twelve or thirteen might somehow have survived it, but little fellows of eight or ten... No brush full of black paint could put such horror on canvas.'[5]

But it was only in Vyatka, working in the office of the provincial Governor-General, that Herzen was to realize at first hand the full extent of the brutality and corruption which characterized the misruled and oppressed Russian empire.

He was never to see Ludmilla Passeck again, the girl he had fancied would accompany him to 'the Siberian mines'. Instead, a strange fate was to unite him with his cousin Natalie, the circumstances of whose birth and childhood so much resembled his own.

Nick Ogarev had got off comparatively lightly. He was banished to his father's estate at Ashkeno, in the province of Penza, only some 600 kilometres from Moscow. There he fell for the attractions of a pretty serf-girl and abandoned himself to bouts of sexual gratification alternating with pangs of remorse, feeling as he did that 'a man of pure heart' should eschew loveless sex 'even to the detriment of his physical well-being'. Writing poetry helped him to relieve the conflict between lapses into 'vice' and his conscience, and he sought distraction in Penza's provincial society.

At a ball given by the Governor of the province he met the latter's niece, Maria Roleslav, and was swept off his feet. Two months later, within a year of his arrival, they were married. Maria, the daughter of a dissolute and impoverished landowner, was a vivacious brunette, bright and well-educated, not plain-looking, though of an indifferent type of beauty. Ogarev, who was not yet 22 when he met her, was, if anything, more incurably romantic than Herzen. He had eyes only for Maria's spirituality and her soul. The rapturous moment when 'there broke from our lips the words, "I love you", was recorded', he wrote, 'by the angels in heaven, and it joyfully re-echoed in the great world of the soul.' Nor was that all. 'Am I really an egoist?' he asked himself. No, for God and the universe, too, 'lived' and were comprised in their love, or at least in Ogarev's.

Finding a 'sister soul' and sharing in the Romantic 'world feeling' resolved for Ogarev the conflict between his inner world and bleak reality, and saved him the kind of despair which had driven the ardent young English poet Thomas Chatterton to commit suicide at 17. To be misunderstood and unhappy was the fashion, and poets who did not die young or by their own hand – as did the German Heinrich von Kleist in 1835 – resorted to cultivating their sorrows like Alfred de Musset. In Alfred de Vigny's play *Chatterton*, performed in Paris in

1835, after the eponymous hero has taken his life in a garret, the actress Marie Dorval, impersonating Kitty Bell who secretly loved him, took so convincing a stage fall down a whole flight of stairs to join him in death, that the play – much to its author's consternation – set off a vogue of Romantic suicides.

'You could hear the crack of pistols in the night,' wrote Théophile Gautier. If only Chatterton could have opened his eyes 'on such an abandon of grief, he would have died happy, sure that he was loved and that it would not be long before he met his sister soul.' But Romanticism had other sides than malaise and a morbid preoccupation with death. Women were idealized, ethereal beings. Love, being 'spiritual', had to express not only the depth and ardour of the individual soul, but to embrace the 'world-soul', heaven and earth, and every sublime ideal of truth, beauty, freedom, etc. Byron, the idol of Romantic youth, had fought for the freedom of small nations. The July Revolution in France had raised liberal hopes, but with the suppression of the Polish and Belgian revolts Europe in the mid-1830s abounded with dissatisfied groups and disillusioned nationalities. Everyone invoked God on his side. While the rulers of the Holy Alliance claimed Divine grace, the emergent nations they oppressed from Italy to Poland cried to God and the world that they were being martyred like Christ bearing the Cross.

Ogarev put it all poetically in one ecstatic phrase: 'My soul is strong enough to love you – surely it will be strong enough to follow in the footsteps of Christ for the liberation of mankind!' he wrote to his bride. And 'To love you means to love everything good, to love God and His Universe... The love of mankind for one another, this brotherhood so pure and fair preached by Jesus, is the reflection of the bond which unites us'; and more in that vein.

The Romantic movement had political implications. Sweeping Europe, it was in many countries a reaction to autocracy, and inspired both mystics and atheists, nationalists as well as revolutionaries. 'Our love,' Nick Ogarev wrote to Maria three days before their wedding, 'contains all the germ of the liberties of mankind. Our love is self-abnegation and truth... The tale of our love will be told from age to age, and future generations will preserve our memory as a holy thing.'

In the event, their marriage started off well enough, but Maria was a more level-headed, less mystically inclined and more superficial Romantic than Ogarev, and though their story would indeed come down to future generations in a famous book (E.H. Carr's *The Romantic Exiles)*, it was to be a different tale from the one he imagined.

In Paris, about 9 a.m. on 28 July 1835, King Louis-Philippe mounted his horse, and with three of his 5 sons and a number of military aides spurring theirs to protect him on the flanks and rear – all of them having been warned that there was likely to be an assassination attempt against the King on that day – set out from the Tuileries to review the National Guard and troops of the Paris garrison drawn up on the boulevards.

It was the fifth anniversary of the July Revolution, but early that morning the Minister of Interior, Adolphe Thiers, had 'rushed in like a tornado' to the Tuileries, and motioning the Duke of Orléans (the 25-year-old heir to the throne) and his two younger brothers – who bore the titles of duc de Nemours and prince de Joinville[6] – to an alcove, had informed them in some agitation of reports 'from several sources' that somewhere near the end of the line-up of troops stretching from the Madeleine to the Bastille an 'explosive engine' was waiting to go off. 'Should the King be warned?' Thiers asked the princes. 'Should the review be called off?' According to the prince de Joinville's later account, their unanimous answer was 'that the King should be warned, but that he, well-known for his courage, would never consent to countermanding the review.'

Indeed, Louis-Philippe would not hear of it. At the age of 62 the 'bourgeois King', by dint of prudent sagacity and a knack for doing the right thing, had managed to survive too many turns of fortune not to know that to show cowardice was worse than death. Nor could he disappoint the National Guard or 'the people' on the anniversary of the three-day revolution which had made him King of the French.

Behind the King and his sons rode three Marshals of France, most prominent among them old Marshal Mortier, a hero of many battles; the chief Minister, the duc de Broglie; and Thiers, a small figure precariously balanced on a parade horse. They were followed by the General Staff and by assorted generals and high army brass.

'There is talk of an explosive engine in the neighbourhood of the Ambigu Theatre,' Thiers had warned. Though a house-to-house search of the Ambigu neighbourhood during the early morning hours had yielded nothing suspicious, they were riding 'as into a battle', scanning the faces of the crowd and watching for any movement at the windows on both sides. One of the King's sons and an aide took turns 'keeping immediately behind his horse'. Joinville found that the review was going 'rather well', but noticed many 'individuals with insolent airs, all wearing red flowers in their buttonholes.' The Prefect of the Seine, M. de Rambouteau, was struck by some wearing an outright *mine patibulaire* – that is, the sinister expression of people with the gallows in their faces – such as he felt one saw on 'days of insurrection'.

It was a hot day and the Prefect's imagination may have been over-working, but since the beginning of the month such opposition papers as *La Quotidienne*,

Le Charivari, *Le Corsaire* and *Le National* had been openly forecasting – not to say practically calling for – the assassination of the King 'in the course of the military review on the 28th'. Insurrection, indeed, seemed to hang in the air, some of the lively French press having indulged in such an orgy of reports of plots and conspiracies that on the 26th *Le Charivari* had provocatively noted that 'Yesterday the Citizen-King arrived in Paris with his superb family, without being at all assassinated.'[7] Two days earlier, adding insult to injury, *Le Corsaire* had reported that Louis-Philippe's son-in-law 'Prince Leopold [of the Belgians] has asked his father-in-law for recipes for political assassinations', suggesting that the King himself was a master-plotter. 'Once every year', *La Caricature* had chimed in with a paraphrase of the Ten Commandments, 'thou shalt assassinate!'

The warning which had caused Thiers to rush to the palace was based in the main on a report received during the night by the Paris police prefect, Gisquet, from the commissaires at Montmartre. A certain Boireau, an ironmonger, had been overheard talking of a mysterious 'infernal machine' that would explode and destroy the King the moment he passed a house near the theatre on the boulevard Saint-Martin. He had boasted of it to a young man, whose father had then rushed to the police. A confounding portent to what seemed an ill-starred day was added by that morning's issue of *Le Corsaire* expressing its veiled confidence that 'the Napoleon of Peace' – as the paper dubbed Louis-Philippe in an uncomplimentary comparison with the military Napoleon of old – was not going to survive the next few hours. 'One may bet one's money', it said in an ominous line on the parade about to start, on the King's final eclipse.

In spite of some feverish consultations before he rode out of the Tuileries, there had been little time for any serious precautions other than that none of the usual petitioners was to be allowed to approach his horse, their papers to be collected by the service aides. But the parade passed the Ambigu and reached the end of the boulevard unscathed. Everyone breathed sighs of relief. Close by, however, on the boulevard du Temple, rose an abandoned theatre of the same name. The police – curiously – had somehow neglected to think of this second Ambigu building. Nor had anyone else, and the search had stopped short near the first.

In No. 50 on the boulevard du Temple, a red maisonette which practically touched the last house on the boulevard Saint-Martin, the man named Fieschi stood watching from a fourth-floor window, his 'infernal machine' – 24 gun barrels bound together on an inclined wooden chassis, and pointing at the centre of the roadway – all set and ready. On the opposite side of the boulevard the terraces of the Jardin Turc, a 'pleasure garden' presenting such nightly attractions as 'Egyptian dancing-girls' against a décor of potted palms and cardboard minarets, were crowded with spectators waiting for the Royal procession to ride into view. On that stretch of the boulevard, exactly where the King was now to appear, the ironmonger Boireau a few days earlier had rehearsed parading up and down on horseback, impersonating Louis-Philippe and enabling the plotters to set the exact range. Now, from his vantage point behind a half-closed blind, Joseph Fieschi, a 45-year-old Corsican and hired assassin to whom 'blowing up perfect strangers' was no worse than 'what soldiers do in an ambush', could see the eighth légion of the National Guard, commanded by Lieutenant Colonel de Rieussec, drawn up in front of the Jardin Turc and beyond.

What Fieschi did not know was that the two men who had hired him to design and operate his lethal contraption – seen by some as the ancestor of the modern machine-gun – meant for him to die in the act of executing the King. One of the two, the saddler Morey, a savage old person who had prepared the line of powder charges that was to set all the guns firing simultaneously, had charged 4 of them in a manner that was to make them explode and blow Fieschi to bits at the same time.

As Louis-Philippe with his sons and military retinue rode into the boulevard du Temple at a slow parade pace shortly after noon, a flame suddenly spurted from a window on the left and a fusillade, sounding like that made by a firing squad, was heard.

'Joinville, this is for me!' cried the King to his nearest son. 'I have been hit.' Louis-Philippe had in fact only been grazed by a spent projectile or two, leaving a black smudge on his forehead and a bruise on his left arm. But his horse, wounded in the neck, was floundering. And the venerable Mortier had been shot dead and his crumpled body in its gold-laced and braided uniform of a Marshal of France had landed on the horse of Rambuteau, the Prefect of the Seine. On Prince de Joinville's left Rieussec, the commander of the eighth légion, had been killed, and another officer had had his nose blown off. The young prince, turning his eyes from the 'smoke in front of a window half closed by a blind' to see his father clutching his left arm, failed to notice that his own horse was wounded.

According to Joinville's account, 'Our first thought was that the fusillade would continue. I dug my spurs into the belly of my horse and, seizing my father's horse by the bridle, while my two brothers struck its hind sides with their swords, we dragged him rapidly through the chaotic stampede of riderless horses, horses straddled by swaying wounded, and broken ranks.'[8]

'*Me voilà!*' Louis-Philippe shouted suddenly, feeling miraculously alive and brandishing his bicorned hat. '*Allons!* We must continue. *Marchons!*' Whereupon the National Guardsmen broke ranks and many of the public, including

395

workers recognizable by their blue blouses, rushed forward with spontaneous cries of *Vive le roi*! As they moved away, Joinville 'saw the assault on the house from which the firing had come. The young aides-de-camp had jumped from their horses, and together with the municipal guard and police constables, were scaling the house and its neighbour, the [Café] Mille Colonnes, climbing up the verandas and breaking in windows... The review went on. We ascertained that neither the King nor ourselves had been wounded, but we were still unaware of the large number of victims.'

The 'infernal machine' had instantly killed 14 people. Four others died later. Twenty-two had been wounded. After reaching the end of the line of troops at the Bastille, the royal cortege returned along the same route. Joinville described the roadway as 'nothing but a pool of blood at the spot where the attack had taken place.' The bodies of Marshal Mortier and the other victims had meanwhile been carried across the road to the halls of the Jardin Turc. The old marshal, who, since distinguishing himself in the wars of the Revolution, had survived the great Napoleonic battles of Borodino and Leipzig, had felt ill that July morning. Advised to forgo the review and stay home, he had refused, insisting he must go. 'I am tall, perhaps my body will cover the King.' He was the same Mortier, Duke of Treviso, who in Moscow in 1812 had presented the father of the infant Alexander Herzen to Napoleon and thus been instrumental in helping to get his family out of the burning city, perhaps saving their lives. Besides him and a number of officers and common soldiers, the dead included a 14-year-old girl and an old man. Whatever the ultimate purpose of those who had hired Fieschi, his attempt on the life of the King had failed: it had merely killed or maimed a great number of men and women of all ages and walks of life.

Fieschi himself had escaped being killed by his own weapon. The explosion which was to have executed '*le roi et le régicide*' simultaneously, conveniently and ingeniously shielding the instigators of the plot, had seriously injured his skull. He was bleeding profusely. Nonetheless, by means of a rope, he had managed to let himself down from the fourth-floor apartment he had rented for the crime – under the name Girard – and to land on a lower roof. Surprising a woman who fainted when he suddenly appeared in her kitchen, he had crossed the courtyard of the Mille Colonnes café at a run, reached a cattle farm, and was about to hide in one of the outhouses when he was caught. He admitted that his true name was Giuseppe-Joseph Fieschi, born at Murato, in Corsica; gave vent to his disappointment at having killed none of the royal family; and denied having had any accomplices.

Queen Marie-Amélie had been about to leave the Tuileries palace for the Chancellery in the place Vendôme when a breathless aide-de-camp arrived at a gallop with news of the attempt on the King's life. Before she grasped that he and the princes were safe, the niece of Marie Antoinette burst out hysterically: 'What a horrible people! What a frightful country! They have killed my husband and my sons, the monsters.'[9]

At the Chancellery, Guizot, Admiral Duperre and Persil, the Keeper of the Seals, had been congratulating themselves on the extraordinary 'success of this magnificent review', as Guizot was to recall, 'when the Queen and the Princesses arrived in an agitated state.' This was followed by more hectic scenes and mixed tears when Louis-Philippe and the hale remnant of his blood-spattered retinue finally turned up, several of the generals' wives and other high ladies present rejoicing at finding their men, while others searched frantically for theirs.

Only then, the King having mounted his horse again, did the march-past begin in the sultry afternoon heat, Louis-Philippe sitting through it until the last unit had vanished a couple of hours later. By then the boulevard du Temple was empty of people. The small bands of revolutionaries with red boutonnieres who had mixed with the crowd had run away with everyone else – attempts by some of them later in the day to rally the people 'to the barricades' were easily dispersed – and only the dead horses lying in the mud marked the scene of the hecatomb. Parisians stopped frequenting the Jardin Turc and it soon closed down. Nor did Queen Amélie ever quite recover. From that day onward she felt 'surrounded by assassins'.

The net effect of the Fieschi affair on shocked public opinion was to discredit the opposition. Even republican sympathizers felt that radicalism had gone too far, and that to stage a massacre for the sake of killing one man was too appalling a means to use even for bringing down the monarchy. It meant inviting anarchy and disorder. The popularity of the shaken but unharmed King, on the other hand, rose, momentarily at least, sky-high. His composure and his sense of duty were very much admired. He had all the military and civilian victims ceremoniously entombed, together with his old friend Marshal Mortier, at the Invalides. Entering between the majestic pillars hung with cypress garlands on black drapery, he attended the packed service conducted by the Archbishop of Paris and spent emotionally gruelling hours with the mourners as coffin after coffin – that of the 'young working-girl' leading the procession, flanked by white-dressed maidens – was brought in through the 'sombre avenue' between the pillars to be finally, amid grandiose funereal pomp and incessant mobbing, deposited in the cenotaphs. Then he emerged straight to another review of the army and the National Guard massed around the Invalides.

'I know the French. I know how to manage them,' the King used to say. He had, indeed, managed to move the people, and received a triumphal ovation at the Invalides. Nonetheless, at the Queen's insistence, he soon stopped walking the streets of Paris like a simple bourgeois and henceforth used a heavy armoured coach, a veritable 'rolling fortress', which made a frightful noise. But the massacre of the boulevard du Temple was to have more far-reaching consequences than merely hampering the King's comfort and freedom of movement.

'He was a bravo, a mercenary, nothing else,' Victor Hugo was to write of Fieschi, after attending a session of his trial. He had, indeed, started out by spying on the French for the Austrians while serving as a young man in the Neapolitan army of Marshal Murat. Then, facing imprisonment for theft and fraud in his native Corsica, he had escaped to France and sold his services to the Paris police as an informer. Hugo's impression that Fieschi now 'mixed up his crime with heaven knows what military ideas' seems borne out by the conclusion of modern researchers and historians that he was a mythomaniac and psychopath.

True to his Corsican and apache's code, he staunchly refused to give away the two conspirators – Morey and Pépin – at whose behest he had set up the 'infernal machine' – until he learned from his one-eyed mistress, Nini Lassave, that Morey had said, 'Pity the explosion did not kill him!' Incensed, he became hell-bent on bringing about their ruin, and according to Hugo, 'unmasked everything, concealed nothing, and never told a lie.' A modern version has it that the police 'terrorized' another mistress of Fieschi's, Anna la Borgnese, into divulging the names of the plotters. Anyhow, Fieschi left both police and prosecution open-mouthed by sending them more than once to 'look again' for incriminating evidence they had missed, or gone over but failed to notice. When, after 'triumphing' in a lengthy confrontation with Pépin, and completely crushing him, he was told that he could go and have his dinner, Fieschi replied: 'Dinner? Oh I have dined today. I have cut off Pépin's head!'[10]

Théodore Pépin, who owned a grocery-cum-liquor shop, was a former captain of the National Guard. He had financed the building of Fieschi's machine and the renting of the apartment in the boulevard du Temple. The mastermind who had planned it all was the saddler Morey, whose idea seems to have been that, once the King and his sons were wiped out, the monarchy would be abolished at one blow. Morey was a rabid old man and fanatic republican; Pépin, a bombastic prattler; Fieschi, a desperado and cutthroat; the ironmonger Boireau – whose careless talk had sent the police scurrying to the Théâtre Ambigu – a comic figure. Between them, they were a rather grotesque lot to start a revolution, having not the vaguest plan beyond their murderous action. All of them, however, were members of one secret society or another. Morey was very active in the Société des Droits de l'Homme and Pépin – some say Fieschi – had actually gone to see one of the Society's founders, Godefroy de Cavaignac, at the Sainte-Pélagie prison, where he was held at the time.

Cavaignac, who used to boast that 'the King will not live a day longer than we decide' – adding that the Droits de l'Homme had 'a hundred blindly devoted agents of crime' fretting to shorten his days – seems, however, to have mistrusted these particular conspirators and refused to have any truck with them. If they had any other sponsors or accomplices, none was ever tried, and some points about 'the Fieschi affair' remain a mystery to this day. Besides the fact that the police search had stopped just short of the boulevard du Temple, it turned out that not only Fieschi, but Pépin until 1830, and Morey and Boireau at one time or another, had all been paid *mouchards*, or police informers.

Their trial was to drag on for months. Paradoxically, instead of enhancing the King's newly gained prestige, it combined with other circumstances to help erode it. 'No sovereign in his own capital', Heine had early observed, 'ever suffered so much ridicule as Louis-Philippe.' Since Daumier's famous cartoon representing the King's body in the likeness of a pear, not a day had passed without smeared caricatures of 'La Poire' appearing on the walls of Paris, and there was hardly an insult or cruel mockery he had been spared. He was derided as 'Fip I, the King of Grocers'. His wig, his gestures and his mannerisms were parodied in pamphlets and on the stage. In the opposition press, republican and legitimist satirists vied with one another in depicting the King, in cartoons, words, or both, as a bloody satrap dragging Marianne by her hair; slaying press freedom with a cutlass in his hand; or standing like a giant jailer over both republican detainees and the duchesse de Berry, the mother of the legitimist pretender. The day before the massacre of the boulevard du Temple, *Le Charivari* had outdone itself by printing a list of police measures inspired by the King and a drawing of him made up from head to foot of massacred and contorted bodies – the illustration carrying the obituary title, 'Royal Catacombs, a small mortuary tableau of His Majesty's subjects felled by the servants of Public Order'.[11]

'My sons are my best armour,' Louis-Philippe used to say to console himself when warned of possible assassination attempts. Although feeling for some time that the opposition sheets had declared open season on him, he had managed to take most of the scorn and satire with comparative calm, and sometimes surprising good humour. But he feared that the growing press speculation about his imminent assassination was gradually accustoming the public to the idea that he was doomed, and in fact deserved, to come to a violent and unnatural end. Fieschi's machine – specially designed to kill him together with his sons – convinced him that the opposition organs endangered not only his reign, but the very existence and survival of the Orléans dynasty.

His answer was the draconian 'September Laws' of 1835, three bills openly designed to curb – and in effect to ruin – the opposition press of every republican and legitimist hue. In introducing them in the Chamber on the wave of

399

sympathy for the King immediately after Fieschi's hideous act, the duc de Broglie said that France had to protect 'its king and its institutions' and that, while all parties were 'free within the sphere of the constitutional monarchy', the moment 'they leave that enclosure liberty is no longer their due.' From then on, any 'expressions of the wish or hope' to 'overthrow the government', and not merely the threat or incitement to do so – that is, intent irrespective of effect – were to be treasonable 'acts against the security of the State'. So was 'insulting the King'; arousing 'hatred or scorn of his person or of his constitutional authority'; attributing 'the rights of the French throne... to any other than Louis-Philippe I and his descendants'; or 'taking the title of republican'. Although ostensibly promulgated to prevent newspapers from encouraging more attempts on the monarch's life, the September Laws made it in fact impossible for some of the opposition papers to appear at all.

Already in May, before Fieschi's crime, the *Tribune des Départements*, the most extreme of the republican papers, had been fined out of existence after more than 100 lawsuits. Now the cash 'bond' which every newspaper owner had to deposit was raised fourfold; and maximum fines were doubled to as much as 200,000 francs, while public subscriptions to raise 'the fines, expenses, damages and interest pronounced by judicial sentences' were prohibited. To reduce the chances of acquittal, juries dealing with the lighter offences were to hand down verdicts by simple majority and procedures for speedier sentencing at the assizes were likewise simplified.

In August, while the bills were only being debated, *La Caricature* ceased publication. Its spirited editor, Philipon – who had been the first to print Daumier's cartoon of 'La Poire', and had gone to prison for it – knew that the Press Laws spelled the end of political caricature and witty sarcasm. Indeed, 'No drawing, no engravings, lithographs, medals... of whatever nature and kind' (read one of its provisions) could be printed, exhibited or sold 'without previous authorization'. With a strong current of opinion in favour of curbing the excesses of some of the licentious French press, the new bills were passed in September over the suspicion of many deputies that they meant in effect an end to all freedom of speech and the fear of others that newpapers loyal to the monarchy would also suffer. To allay the latter's concern the Keeper of the Seals told the Chamber: 'Our law would miss its effect if any but the constitutional-monarchic press... were allowed to develop freely after its promulgation.'

By November 1835 the physician and scientist François Raspail, editor of the *Réformateur*, who had already served one sentence for his republicanism, found himself in prison again and his newspaper failing, ruined by three severe fines imposed in the space of a fortnight. More than two dozen republican papers in the provinces had to close down. Daumier applied his mordant pen more and more to social satire. Philipon continued to issue *Charivari*, but had to moderate its tone; and the opposition press as a whole would have to devise ways of writing between the lines to continue its assault on the monarchy.

Fieschi and his fellow-conspirators were tried before the Court of Peers. It was not many months since the mass-trial of the leaders of the 1834 Lyons and Paris insurrections had come to an end. If that trial – marked by tumultuous scenes, shouting matches between the 164 judges and 121 accused, and pitched battles between the latter and the gendarmes – had produced general indignation, Fieschi's trial did not lack for grotesque touches. Whereas the grocer Pépin, ex-captain of the National Guard, frequently broke down, 'wept and talked of his three children', old man Morey, the saddler, sat stony-faced and confessed nothing. He was afflicted with a stomach ailment and had to be artificially fed – which, coupled with his silence, provided the opposition press with an issue, a martyr, and the opportunity to report, first, that Morey had chosen death by starvation, and next, that he had died a heroic protester's death. But it was Fieschi who dominated the proceedings.

'Morey was pale and motionless,' wrote Hugo, who was at the Peers' Court the day before the verdict was to be pronounced. 'Pépin pretended to be reading a newspaper. Fieschi gesticulated, made speeches, laughed.' Since the slaughter in the boulevard du Temple, his one purpose in life was to settle accounts with Pépin and Morey for planning his own death. Having given the Prosecutor and the President of the Court of Peers, Baron Pasquier, precise information as to where, in Pépin's account book, the grocer had entered the money paid to him for the 'infernal machine', he seemed ready to die. Hugo saw him rising to address the Court as follows:

> 'My lords, in a few days my head will be severed from by body. I shall be dead, and I shall rot in the earth... I am going to expiate my crime, and you will gather the fruits of my service. After me, there will be no more riots, no more assassinations, no more disturbances. I tried to kill the King. I shall have succeeded in saving him.'[12]

Fieschi's 'resolute' stance impressed Hugo, but the Corsican's panache did not work on Pasquier. Nor were attempts on the King's life to cease. Fieschi, Morey and Pépin were all sentenced to the guillotine on 15 February 1836 and executed 4 days later. Boireau got away with a mere 20 years of hard labour.

On 19 February, several hours before they were taken to the place of execution, Pasquier came to Pépin's cell at the prisoner's request. Whether in an attempt to buy clemency or for other woolly reasons, Pépin now confessed that he had been a member of a secret society – the Société de Familles, or the 'Familles' for short. Among its leaders he named Auguste Blanqui, the radical journalist who, after walking out on *Le Globe* to join the street-fighting in the July Revolution, had quickly risen to prominence in the ranks of the extremist republican society of the Amis du Peuple.

This group had been forced to dissolve shortly afterwards, only to spawn the formation of the Droits de l'Homme society, with a larger membership on a national scale. When its cells were hit by the prohibition of 'associations of more than 20 persons' even 'divided into smaller sections', Blanqui, a tight-lipped, austere and single-minded character, a vegetarian and teetotaller, had quietly set about organizing the 'Familles', a small, compact society that promised to be a more effective conspiratorial instrument than either the Amis du Peuple or the Droits de l'Homme.

Blanqui, who was of middle-class origin but called himself a proletarian, felt sincerely that in the July Revolution the bourgeoisie – by denying the people political representation and giving the vote to only 200,000 rich Frenchmen – had defrauded and robbed the remaining thirty million of their rights. (The actual figures were 170,000 and twenty-five millions, respectively.)

Pépin had previously claimed that on the morning of Fieschi's *attentat* he personally gave Blanqui and two other men advance notice of the King's imminent assassination. All three publicly denied this, and Pépin admitted that he had in fact never met any of them, but had merely heard of them and of Blanqui's secret 'Familles'. Whatever the truth of Pépin's belated 'confession', on the day of the *attentat* Blanqui had sent his little son with his *bonne* to watch the military review and the King's procession. They were in the café on the boulevard du Temple facing 'Fieschi's house' when the latter had fired. In the ensuing panic, the boy had been pushed to the ground and suffered bruises and contusions. The question whether the presence of Blanqui's son and his nurse at the theatre of the crime was proof of his having had no inkling of the slaughter to come – or whether, on the contrary, Blanqui had cruelly and purposely sent the boy there to provide himself with an alibi and 'escape suspicion as an abettor of the crime' – was to figure prominently in the next conspiracy trial.

This began barely a month after the execution of the three principals of the 'Fieschi affair' when, in March 1836, a quantity of gunpowder and a military training manual were discovered in a small Paris street. Blanqui and some 40 suspected members of the 'Familles' were arrested. Documents were seized showing that the 'Familles' were 6-man cells which were kept in ignorance of each other's existence, and of the identity of the top leaders. The society's purpose was indeed 'the overthrow of the government that has been betraying the nation'. The monarchy was to be toppled by force, though not perhaps by regicide. Members underwent a solemn initiation ritual and were ordered to infiltrate the National Guard, to pinch a quantity of gunpowder, to stand by for orders and never to betray the society under questioning.

The trial which developed out of the 'affaire des poudres', or the 'gunpowder plot', was given additional interest as the prosecution went all out to link the new society to the Fieschi conspiracy. Blanqui, moreover, was a public figure. Together with the Abbé de Lamennais and the barrister Michel de Bourges, he had been one of the members of the National Defence Committee which had monitored, and often protested, the court proceedings in the trial of the Lyons insurrectionists.

Arrested while hiding in the house of one of his lieutenants, Armand Barbès – son of a rich Créole physician – Blanqui had jumped from the bed to wrest some papers from the hands of the police, and managed to swallow them. The police, however, had seized other documents, including the text of a manifesto in Barbès's handwriting calling for armed insurrection. Another of the ringleaders was a printer, Martin Bernard, who had been observed paying regular midnight visits, wrapped in a cloak 'like Mephisto', to the powder factory and 'throwing grains of sand at the window' to gain admission.

The trial took place in August 1836. Blanqui claimed that the powder factory had been set up by a medical student who was a police informer and *agent provocateur*. But Barbès had no good explanation either for the manifesto or for some notes about 'guns' and 'powder' found at his home. The prosecution, armed with the executed Pépin's somewhat dubious last-minute 'confession', submitted that Blanqui had not only had advance notice of the King's assassination but that – while Fieschi was waiting to launch his machine – he had rushed to the home of Barbès and had dictated to him the call for a popular insurrection. Although only an original draft, and no copies for distribution or any other evidence, was ever produced, the court found Blanqui guilty of complicity in the 'Fieschi affair' – and by implication of having ruthlessly sent his son and his nurse to the scene of certain slaughter in the boulevard du Temple in order to divert suspicion from himself. This version has also been taken over by one or two historians – but much of this part of the case remains an unsolved mystery.[13]

Blanqui was sentenced to two years in prison (Barbès to one) and to surveillance for two more. A fierce egalitarian who early called himself a 'Socialist', he was to become France's most tenacious insurrectionist conspirator, so tenacious in fact that he was to spend altogether 33 years – nearly half his life – in various prison cells and dungeons.

The 'September Laws', under which almost any criticism could be construed as a call to insurrection or *lèse-majesté*, and punished accordingly, were so obviously harsh and cut to a purpose that one of the King's own daughters had been appalled by their ill-conceived and repressive character. 'One will not find in them', said Louise d'Orléans, 'that impassive, calm immutability of justice which lends moral force to laws.'[14]

The horror produced by the Fieschi affair had enabled Louis-Philippe to consolidate his position, but the net effect of the 'September Laws' muzzling the press was to deprive all discontented sections of the public of any legal outlet, and to drive the opposition completely underground. Republican deputies now had to call themselves 'democrats' or 'radicals', and with the opposition press masking its criticism in more subtle language than before, the government was faced with the awkward alternative of either prosecuting its innocent-looking innuendo with the full weight of the law – and making itself ridiculous – or being shown up as powerless to deal with it. The worst provisions of the 'September Laws' were therefore not applied, but kept on the statute book, a Damocles sword to be resorted to – as they were in fact some years later – when things deteriorated.

Louis-Philippe seemed to be sitting firmly in the saddle. The majority of the French wanted neither revolution nor upheavals. But military or police measures, or the successive trials or the 'September Laws', did not put an end to the underground ferment. For neither the King nor his successive Chief Ministers ever really dealt with the worsening plight of the workers or stopped to think that one of the underlying causes of the widening discontent might be the fact that France's 'electorate of the rich' comprised less than three per cent of the country's adult males.

'The bank is at the head of the state,' wrote Stendhal. 'The middle class has replaced the aristocracy, and the bank is the nobility of the middle class.' Favouring the big landowners, the 'electorate of the rich' included, in addition, manufacturers, bankers, financiers and those engaged in the insurance, transport and distribution of goods. They and the whole new middle-class 'nobility' of thriving entrepreneurs referred to by Stendhal formed the *haute bourgeoisie* which – with country houses, carriages, liveried footmen, and in every other way – aped the life-style of the old nobility they had ousted from power. But the middle class consisted of many less-propertied sections, professions and trades. The ranks of this lower bourgeoisie, though now sporting top hats and frock coats, continued to be deprived of the vote.

As it happened, on the very morning of Fieschi's *attentat*, Armand Carrel, editor of *Le National* and one of the most serious journalists of his time, had ascribed the discontent in France to the fact that, in spite of the July Revolution, the 'popular mass' of middle-class Frenchmen had been 'denied political participation, first by fine words, promises and exhortations of patience, and then by cannon and cavalry charges.' The discontent of these Frenchmen, who abhorred upheaval and wanted nothing but a peaceful, orderly existence, grew as they saw the Stock Exchange flourishing, and quick fortunes being made all around them. The fact that deputies of the Chamber received no pay or expenses – provincial deputies unable to defray the cost of living in Paris 'could but pray for an administrative sinecure, resign from the Chamber, or starve honourably' – only created an atmosphere of corruption, which in turn resulted in a spreading cynicism.

'Do you know how one gets ahead here? By brilliant genius or through smart corruption,' said the character Rastignac in Balzac's novel *Père Goriot*. 'Honesty leads one nowhere... Talent is rare. So corruption has become the weapon of the all too numerous mediocrities. You will find it everywhere... One must only be careful always to appear outwardly clean: that is the whole morality of our time.'

During the 1830s, too, a new, socially dangerous element was added to the population of Paris – an inchoate, partly illiterate mass of *ouvriers*. Previously they had been migrant, seasonal workers. Now they lived in filth and squalor in crowded, cheaply built industrial quarters. They wore smocks and caps. Often they were unemployed. Their hovels, into which the police did not always dare to venture, swarmed with crime, prostitution and disease-ridden children. The rest of established, frock-coated society regarded – and feared – them as barbarians and savages, or ignored them, until Eugène Sue, in *Les Mystères de Paris*, introduced them into literature and gave his bourgeois readers a thrill and a dread. For the moment, however, they played no role in politics, and not even Blanqui, the self-styled Socialist, included them in his conspiratorial reckonings.

Yet plots and conspiracies continued, and on 25 June 1836 a young commercial traveller by the name of Alibaud fired at the King from a gun disguised as a cane just as Louis-Philippe was driving off from the Louvre in his armoured coach. Queen Amélie and the King's sister, Madame Adelaide, were with him. 'My only regret is to have missed,' Alibaud told his captors. Less than a year after Fieschi's attempt, Alibaud was sentenced to death. Louis-Philippe considered commuting the sentence, but in the end confirmed it.

'Mine is a much sadder task,' the King told a visitor who, finding him one night bent over a copybook, inquired whether he was writing his memoirs. He explained that he was sitting over a list of death sentences which either his own 'conscience or the decision of the Ministry' prevented him from commuting. It bore his notation: 'Alibaud, *à mon grand regret*.'

'I die for liberty!' Alibaud shouted at his execution. It seemed that each trial only led to another, that each forbidden conspiratorial society spawned another. Blanqui was in prison and the 'Familles' were sub-dividing – but Blanqui and another new secret society, Les Saisons, were yet to lead the decade's most serious conspiracy against the monarchy. One phenomenon which Fieschi's bloody deed had in fact pointed up was the element of revolutionary violence which continued to pervade the always passionate play of French politics. Thiers, who had become Prime Minister in February 1836, said resignedly after the butchery in the boulevard du Temple that 'The fecundity of evil is infinite.' He felt that France had become 'a society in disarray' in which lawless bandits, who had neither any programme nor any idea of what their next step would be, were encouraged to start all sorts of conspiracies and to 'set the world on fire', without giving a damn for the consequences.[15]

George Sand related how one moonlit night, while a ball was taking place at the Tuileries, she was standing with the barrister Michel de Bourges on the Pont des Saint-Pères. The palace was splendidly illuminated; its gardens shimmered in a soft radiance; and with a sound of distant music coming across the enchanted scene, she fell into a reverie, only to be brutally wakened by the sepulchral voice of Michel de Bourges launching into a furious tirade on the need for a revolution to regenerate France:

'I tell you', he shouted, 'this corrupt society of yours will never be rejuvenated until this fine river runs red with blood; until that accursed palace is reduced to ashes; until this vast city you are looking at has become a bare waste on which the poor man and his family can drive his plough and build his cottage!'

It is true that Michel de Bourges, whom Lamartine described as a peasant-like 'man cut from a block of granite', had no ready programme for the day after the revolution. The main thing was to change society, and when questioned by George Sand about the next step, he replied: 'How can I know that? The truth doesn't come to thinkers in a mountain fastness. To discover the truths applicable to a society in its birth-pangs, men must unite and act.'

Blanqui, however, giving the matter much thought during his imprisonment after the trial of the 'Familles', reached the conclusion that the overthrow of the old order would have to be followed by a dictatorship until 'the reign of equality' could be established in all fields. It was not only Blanqui and de Bourges who spoke in terms echoing Babeuf and Buonarroti; politicians, journalists and even so melancholy-sweet a poet as Lamartine, who had been elected to the Chamber of Deputies in 1834, vied with one another in the increasing violence of the rhetoric they used against Louis-Philippe.

Already in 1832 Heine, besides referring to the 'guillotinomania' of the republicans, had observed that the legitimists, too, seemed to be fighting the old battles of the French Revolution all over again. To illustrate the point, he had described how – straight from a meeting addressed by Blanqui in language reminiscent of Robespierre – he had hired a cab, and with the cries of *Vive la*

République still ringing in his ears, had driven to a soirée of the legitimists in the elegant Faubourg Saint-Germain. 'Nothing but lights, mirrors, flowers, naked shoulders, glacé gloves and frippery,' was his description of the scene there, 'and a triumphant expression on all faces', as though Henry V, Duke of Bordeaux – the then 11-year-old legitimist pretender – was about to unseat Louis-Philippe any minute and 'the victory of the ancien régime had already been won.'

Revolution, in short, had become something of a cult and continued to exercise a strong hold on the minds of Frenchmen during the course of the 1830s. Well might Louis-Philippe privately protest that he could 'no more have proclaimed Henry V king than I can stop the sun' because 'he and I would have been massacred together before we reached the Hôtel de Ville.' Well might he cry out loud – as he did on one occasion in the hearing of a group of his military aides (much to the embarrassment of the Queen) – that he was not a usurper.

Although the legitimists were divided between the adherents of the boy-pretender and those who wished to see Charles X restored, all of them looked on Louis-Philippe as the man who had taken the throne from its rightful heir. And to republicans of every variety he remained a traitor to the cause of the people, who – even if they had not all rushed to the barricades for him – had toppled the former occupant of the throne by their simple presence in the streets during demonstrations.

This in itself made them a political force, but they remained excluded from the world of politics. Louis-Philippe, elevated by means of a 'popular' revolution, yet refusing to share power, was of course aware that he could be overthrown in the same way. 'I am misunderstood,' he once told Victor Hugo. 'I am said to be proud, I am said to be clever. That means that I am a traitor. It grieves me. I am simply an honest man. I go straight ahead.' With 6 attempts on his life in 8 years during the first decade of his reign – so frequent that they were jokingly seen as 'part of the ceremonial of the opening of Parliament' – Louis-Philippe continued to rule by means of a restricted number of office-holders, and by manipulating the factions in the Chamber. He felt that the Ministers all behaved 'like schoolboys', that they had 'no real appreciation of power, little basic grandeur, no consistency in aim, no persistency of will' – in short, that without him France would be worse off.

He had placed great hopes in Thiers when he appointed him Prime Minister in February 1836. Thiers was supposed to ferret out and put an end to conspiracies against the monarchy and to increase its popularity by arranging a match between the the King's eldest son and a Habsburg princess. He failed on both counts, and instead got France involved in a military adventure in Spain. The King dismissed him after only 6 months in office and later told Hugo: 'Thiers... told me one day when we were in disagreement: "Sire, you are cunning and

407

proud, but I am more cunning than you." "The proof that that is not so," I replied, "is that you tell me so."'[16]

While the highly ambitious Thiers was yet to play a dominant role in French politics, the King appointed the comte Molé in his place in September 1836. It was the tenth government change in 6 years, itself a sign of instability, and the next assassination attempt was only a few months off. Although Louis-Philippe was again to escape unhurt, each try and the trial that followed kept not only his family and the palace nervous, but the whole country in a state of uncertainty.

Something of a panic was caused at the Tuileries on the evening of 31 October, when a garbled message was received that another pretender, Prince Louis Napoleon Bonaparte, a nephew of the 'Emperor of Glory' – and, like the rest of the latter's family, forbidden to enter France – had marched 'through the streets of Strasbourg with a contingent of...' Here the message ended, the semaphore signals having been interrupted by fog.

The future Napoleon III, 28 years old, suppported by a Strasbourg colonel of artillery and others, had indeed appeared in that city the day before with a proclamation beginning: 'From the rock of St. Helena a ray of the dying sun has touched my soul.' He vowed 'to win and to die for the cause of the peoples.' On the strength of the irrepressible saga of Napoleon, reinforced by Romantic enthusiasm and the general dissatisfaction, he had judged the time ripe for a successful coup, but the planned rising was so ineptly organized that, within three hours of his marching off with the colonel's artillery to the sound of music, he was arrested in the barracks of the infantry, who refused to join him. This was not, however, known in Paris and the King and the Ministers spent a sleepless night at the Tuileries. Rather than have another trial, Louis-Philippe wisely let the Bonapartist pretender leave for distant America.

But prince de Joinville was to write: 'The repetition of these conspiracies, these attempts at creating civil war which came from the Republicans, Legitimists, Bonapartists, and the continued need to fight, repress and punish, all weighed heavily upon him [the King], like a detestable burden.'[17] They also did little to convey to Europe's other monarchs and its public opinion the image – for which Louis-Philippe was striving – of his régime as a lasting, and not a shaky, one.

'My daughter cannot bring herself to face the dangers to which the French Royal Family unfortunately remains exposed.' Thus, after Alibaud's shot, had the Archduke Joseph of Habsburg coolly broken off the advanced negotiations for her match with the Duke of Orléans. Internally, however, the King, hoping for better times, continued his policy of the *juste milieu*, or 'golden mean', and managed to hang on. In a speech to the Chamber during the debate on the 'September Laws', Guizot, while still Minister of Education, had denied that the new laws would degenerate into tyranny and the suppression of the constitutional opposition. After declaring that such thoughts could only be ascribed to the King's enemies, 'to the parties who are obedient to absolutist principles' and 'incapable of compromise', he had neatly defined the essence and the merits of the King's middle course:

'Our own policy, gentlemen, the policy of the *juste milieu*, is essentially hostile to absolute principles... It is in the nature of our policy to be an enemy of all excesses, to face about without the least embarrassment, without the least inconsistency, in order to fight now the one, now the other... That', he had added to applause from the centre, 'is what makes our strength.' After Alibaud's and other assassination attempts, the King's politically informed daughter Louise, Queen of the Belgians, summed up the outlook for the family in these cautiously practical terms:

> In the double fear of Henry V and that of a Republic I see two chances for the future of our boutique, which may perhaps save us from succumbing to the same mistakes, and being as easily overthrown, as the Restoration. There is nothing good to come after us and I am confident that we shall maintain ourselves, because we are a necessity.[18]

In 1835, Alexis de Tocqueville, a 30-year-old Norman aristocrat and cousin of Chateaubriand, published the first volume of *De la Démocratie en Amerique*, a work that created an immediate stir by giving Europeans a view of politics and day-to-day life in a free society that differed greatly from their imaginary notion of the United States.

Tocqueville's mission, undertaken as a young magistrate, had been to study the US penal system. Several of his noble relatives having been guillotined during the French Revolution, he expected the worst from elective government by the masses in a republic, but was so fascinated by the functioning of America's institutions that he departed from his itinerary. Rather than confining himself to America's excesses, its prisons and criminal side, so to speak, he set about studying the phenomenon of 'Democracy, in order to learn what we have to fear and to hope' from it. Observing that a democratic system, for all its many ills – which he did not fail to point out – had something to recommend it, he was one of the first to realize that France's privileged 'electorate of the rich' could not be maintained forever against pressure from millions of voteless Frenchmen, and would eventually have to give way to some form of general suffrage.

'You', Guizot promptly wrote to Tocqueville, 'judge Democracy like an aristocrat who has been defeated and who, moreover, is convinced that his victorious opponent is right.' Although Guizot had resigned as Minister of Education, the so-called 'policy of resistance' (to any electoral change) of which he was the foremost exponent continued to carry the day.

Tocqueville, also in 1835, produced his *Journeys to England and Ireland*, in which he described Manchester as a giant industrial sewer. Writing almost a decade before young Friedrich Engels was to publish his *Condition of the Working Class in England*, Tocqueville noted that in Manchester human civilization had attained its highest as well as its 'most brutish' development: 'From this filthy sewer the greatest stream of human industry flows out to fertilize the whole world.' Here civilization worked its miracles and produced 'pure gold' at the price of turning civilized man 'practically into a savage'.

A short, thin, pallid man, Tocqueville was to be elected to the Chamber of Deputies in 1839 and later to serve briefly as Foreign Minister. But moralist, historian and profound analyst that he was, he kept aloof and was too fastidious a personality to exert himself in the political market-place. Though he accepted the need for change and foresaw the spread of parliamentary democracy, he did little to further its progress: he feared, in fact, that governments chosen by, and dependent upon, the politically uneducated, easily swayed and irresponsible masses might interfere with individual liberty and degenerate into new forms of tyranny surpassing all previous 'despotisms' – in ways, he said, that he could neither define nor find a name for, so new was the phenomenon of 'Democracy' in undemocratic Europe. (Totalitarian 'people's democracies' had of course yet to be heard of.)

One prophetic passage included by Tocqueville in the first volume of *De la Démocratie en Amérique* was to come in for particular attention in the second half of the 20th century. Closing that 1835 volume with a comparison between Russia and America, Tocqueville observed that 'the American struggles against the obstacles that Nature opposes to him: the adversaries of the Russian are men. The former combats the wilderness and savage life; the latter civilization with all its arms. The conquests of the American are therefore gained by the ploughshare; those of the Russian by the sword.'

> The Anglo-American relies on personal interest to accomplish his ends and gives free scope to the unguided strength and common sense of the people; the Russian centres all the authority of society in a single arm. The principal instrument of the former is freedom; of the latter, servitude. Their starting-point is different; yet each of them seems marked out by the will of Heaven to sway the destinies of half the globe.

Tocqueville's prediction that the US and Russia would one day emerge as the two dominant superpowers is all the more striking since he had never visited

Russia nor, as far as is known, made any particular study of it; and doubly so if one recalls that only the British Empire, by virtue of its overseas colonies and the global link provided by the Royal Navy, could call itself a world power in 1835. Commenting on this passage nearly a century and a half later, the eminent Russian scholar and long-time US Ambassador to the Soviet Union, George F. Kennan, wrote in 1971 that Tocqueville's remarks concerning Russia 'could not have been better taken and phrased had they been written by a man long familiar with that country.'[19]

Tocqueville also foresaw the grey, atomizing uniformity, the spiritual boredom and loss of individuality that were to accompany the mass age, a point to be taken up before the end of the 1850s by John Stuart Mill in his famous *On Liberty*. Writing of the tyranny of 'public opinion', Mill matched Tocqueville's remarks and observed, long before the electronic mass media were to make the world shrink, that Englishmen, too, 'comparatively speaking, now read the same things, listen to the same things, see the same things, go to the same places, have their hopes and fears directed to the same objects...'

Indeed, Tocqueville had yet to produce the next volume of his work on America when, in the extraordinary financial boom of the mid-1830s – with new industries, banks, entrepreneurs flourishing – Emile de Girardin in 1836 launched France's first low-priced daily, *La Presse*, creating the prototype of a modern mass-circulation newspaper pandering to popular taste, while at the same time shaping it.

La Presse published commercial advertisements and Bourse quotations, and another of its innovations was the serialization of thriller-type novels which left people in suspense from instalment to instalment. It began by supporting the July Monarchy of Louis-Philippe – for which Girardin was said to have received a generous subvention from the court – but as he rose to become a press lord and one of France's leading publicists he developed a brand of varying personal politics, attacking or sparing successive governments according to whether or not they adopted the advice and programmes he offered in his paper.

The July Monarchy had its own mouthpiece in Bertin's *Journal des Débats*, but the opposition was well represented – the republicans by *Le National* and the more radical *La Tribune*; the liberal and anti-clerical party by *Le Courier*; the legitimist but parliamentary royalists by the *Gazette de France*; the dynastic opposition by the *Journal de Commerce*. Thiers had his own platform in *Le Constitutionnel* and after his dismissal in August 1836 he made full use of it to lead the movement for a measure of electoral reform against the 'policy of resistance' of his fellow-historian and former ally, Guizot.

And no sooner had Girardin's low-priced *La Presse* appeared than another intrepid Paris publisher, Dutacq, launched a rival tabloid, *Le Siècle*. In the general press war which developed, Girardin's successful use of cut-up fiction served up in tantalizing daily portions as a circulation booster was to produce a flood of worthless *romans-feuilleton*, but also some enduring and world-wide best-sellers. Balzac's *La Vieille Fille*, for example, first appeared in *La Presse*. George Sand, too, wrote novels for the newspapers. By the next decade, Dumas was to provide *The Three Musketeers* in instalments in *Le Siècle*; *The Count of Monte Cristo* in the *Journal des Débats*; and a number of romances, often from drafts prepared by several hands, for *La Presse*.

Soon Eugène Sue, a former marine surgeon who had previously published a tedious history of the French Navy, was having a huge success with *Les Mystères de Paris*, serialized in the *Journal des Débats* in advance of its book publication in 10 volumes. His equally long *Le Juif errant*, for which he received an 'astronomic' 100,000 francs, was worth every sou to *Le Constitutionnel*, whose circulation it helped to increase sixfold.

Before stepping down as Minister of Education, the conservative Guizot had greatly widened the French school system, providing elementary education for all. Though he had done so for no democratic reasons – rather, all he aimed at was to raise the 'moral' standard of the masses and to give them a chance to improve their souls – the reading public was growing. The simultaneous foundation of the two popular tabloids marked the entrepreneurial spirit of the times, but also answered a need, for the accruing ranks of readers now included artisans and lower middle-class people. If this signalled the beginning of the cultural uniformity described by Tocqueville, the development had political and social implications.

Notwithstanding the increasingly violent political strife, and for all the conspiracies, corruption, and general venality of these years in which almost everything, from votes to newspaper articles, could be bought, the base of French public opinion was broadening. The 'September Laws' were not applied in full, there was an opposition press, and novels like *Les Mystères de Paris* and the serialized works of Balzac and George Sand brought observations and themes taken from reality before a wider readership.

In 1835 a talented young writer, Karl Gutzkow, published in Germany a novel called *Wally, die Zweiflerin* ('Wally, the Sceptic Maiden'), in which, under the influence of George Sand's ideas and others imported from France – partly through the intermediary of Heine – he celebrated the 'emancipation of the flesh', along with a new approach to nature, life and reality. The most objectionable passage in the novel was a scene in which Wally, forced against her will to marry a foreign ambassador, accedes to her lover's request to let him glimpse her nude body as a token of their spiritual bond at the very moment when they are to part forever.

Gutzkow indicated that the scene represented a moment of sheer 'wanton-ness, but a wantonness of innocence and painful eternal renunciation'. The son of a Berlin horse-trainer, Gutzkow had received at the age of 19 the medal of Berlin's faculty of philosophy as Hegel's best student. Since leaving the univer-sity he had edited a literary journal, then had worked for a time as an assistant to Wolfgang Menzel, the editor of the *Stuttgart Literatur blatt* and high panjan-drum among German literary critics. Hegel had warned his pupil against having anything to do with Menzel, and indeed Menzel and Gutzkow soon fell out over the latter's progressive ideas.

Next, Gutzkow joined forces with Ludolf Wienbarg to start a literary review in Frankfurt, the *Deutsche Rundschau*. They made contact with Heinrich Laube, editor of Leipzig's long-established *Journal for the Elegant World* and with other literary editors in Berlin, Frankfurt and Hamburg. Menzel, fearing for his *Literaturblatt* and deciding to quash the rival project in embryo, thereupon launched a public attack on Gutzkow's *Wally*. He wrote that it contained 'ideas of the kind conceived in a brothel', and went on to suggest that Gutzkow had made it his task 'to transplant to Germany the scandalous French licentious-ness, which blasphemes against God in the arms of harlots.'

In September 1835 he denounced Gutzkow to the authorities as the leader of a cosmopolitan, francophile and subversive group which he labelled 'La Jeune Allemagne'. Publicly referring to the yet unborn *Deutsche Rundschau* as presided over 'not by the goddess of justice but by Venus vulgivaga', he called it a 'school of vice' that would extol 'free sensuality' and wage 'war against Chris-tianity, morality and matrimony.'

Menzel was particularly incensed when it was announced that a number of distinguished academics had promised to collaborate on the new journal, which was to be modelled on the *Revue des Deux Mondes*. Perceiving a real threat to his own dominion over contemporary German literature, Menzel warned in a fury that although 'the wild fantasies of a few aberrant youths' might appear harm-less, a spark could ignite 'a conflagration'. Those belonging to the 'Young Germany school' not only wrote obscene books, according to his tirade, but entertained Saint-Simonist ideas and heralded 'an even more dissolute republi-canism, a grandiose harlots' republic ('*Hetaerenrepublik*')...'

In November Menzel named 5 young writers – Gutzkow, Wienbarg, Laube, Mundt and Kühne – as the leaders of this subversive 'school' or movement. Having fabricated it out of Wienbarg's dedication of a book 'to the Young Ger-many', he wrote that it was 'in reality Young Palestine', an obvious stab at Heine, since none of the 5 was Jewish. At the same time he mobilized his reli-gious Prussian patriotism – which had hitherto not interfered with his expressed admiration for Heine, Börne and other liberal authors – to fire a

413

broadside at the university professors who had promised to write for Gutzkow's new review: 'Are not the universities state institutions?' he asked. 'Do Christianity, morality, and marriage no longer count for anything in the State of Prussia?' And how was it that in Prussia, with its vaunted conservative Christian spirit, 'the best-known professors of Berlin, Königsberg and Halle' were queueing up to collaborate with Gutzkow, this 'new and dirty Marat preaching a republic of sans-culottes and sans-chemises?' While 'the Five', as the young writers became known, were indeed pining for some change in Germany's stagnant political and cultural atmosphere, but otherwise held varying views, the 'professors' – including Eduard Gans, Hegel's successor, and other respected figures such as Varnhagen von Ense – had little in common with them other than a generally progressive outlook and a wish for untrammeled discussion of all ideas. Lumping them all together and making them guilty by association, Menzel accused the professors of nothing less than betraying 'the German nationality'.

The upshot was that on 14 November Prussia banned all the works of 'the Five'. Gutzkow was tried on blasphemy charges for *Wally*. He was sentenced to three months' imprisonment, and his fiancée abandoned him. The hardest hit of all was Heinrich Laube. This prolific writer and dramatist – later to be a member of the Frankfurt Assembly and to serve for many years as director of Vienna's Burgtheater – had since the beginning of the 1830s known every kind of political persecution. Originally arrested for his activities in the *Burschenschaften* and for criticizing Prussia's institutions, he had been amnestied, only to be rearrested in 1833 and held for 8 months in solitary confinement in Berlin. In 1834 he had been expelled from Saxony. Under the terms of the amnesty, the old charges could be revived, and his mere designation as one of the 'Young Germany literary school' – which a decree of the Federal Bundestag on 10 December described as 'openly tending to attack the Christian religion in the most insolent way, to denigrate existing social relations, and to destroy all decency and morality' – was enough to inflict on him a sentence of 6 years' imprisonment in a fortress. Laube, who had just been married, was in despair. Only good fortune and the intervention of a liberal prince eventually combined to result in the sentence's being commuted in a way that saved Laube's sanity and enabled him to pull through. But Wienbarg's academic career was finished and, unable to pick up the pieces again, he became an alcoholic. Mundt was dismissed from Berlin University on the day he was to deliver his inaugural lecture. Only Kühne managed to save his skin by denouncing Gutzkow.

In the Federal Bundestag decree of 10 December, Heine's name headed a new list of 'the Five', from which Kühne's had been dropped. The decree banned their works in all the 36 German states, making their governments 'responsible for preventing' not only the printing and publication but even 'the distribution of their writings' through lending libraries.

In Paris, Heine was dumbfounded by the news. He had indeed been invited to write for Gutzkow's stillborn *Deutsche Rundschau*, but had been too preoccupied with other matters to send an answer. He occasionally corresponded with Wienbarg and Laube but did not know any of the others and had no connection with the 'Young Germany' or any other literary school. Yet he was being punished as its progenitor: on 30 November Metternich instructed his henchmen to proceed with special and utmost severity 'against Heine, the spiritual father of the Young Germany.' Nor was that all.

On 11 December, Prussia announced that 'Heine's future literary output, in all languages and wherever published', would come under the previous day's ban. The other proscribed writers (except Wienbarg) had variously dissociated themselves from Gutzkow and all those who had promised to write for his projected review – including 6 of 'the best-known professors' – had bowed to the authorities and hastened to publish denials of any association with him.

It had taken a single influential demagogue, Menzel, to crush the spirit of Germany's young and to quench any stir or questioning by its leading intellectuals – or so it was long believed. But, as Sammons was to note in 1979, 'we know today that... a ban on Young Germany was in preparation before his [Menzel's] articles began to appear, and Heine's own Religion and Philosophy was one of the ban's main motives.'[20]

Another motive in the background was the publication that year of David Friedrich Strauss's *Life of Jesus*. Strauss, a Tübingen theologian and philosopher, did not reject Christianity, but his sensational book questioned the historical authenticity of the Gospels. It could thus be seen as indirectly challenging the notion of the 'divine right of kings' invoked by Europe's monarchs. Once this sanction was taken away, the whole political and social order could be questioned. While the Grand Council of Zürich, which had offered Strauss a professorial chair, promptly offered its resignation, the developing 'Young Hegelian' school found him too moderate. Germany's clerical-feudal governments, on the other hand, feared that the beginning critique of religion would ultimately undermine the whole structure over which they presided, and Menzel's venomous articles served to prepare the public for their harsh measures.

'Curiously', Heine was later to write, 'it is always religion, always morality, always patriotism, which our enemies use to conceal their evil acts,... Never their own miserable interests.' Germany seemed ready not only to silence every free thought but to destroy its only living writer of world significance. Heine himself found it hard to believe at first that Prussia would make itself ridiculous by 'banning books which are not yet written'; but he was to learn to his dismay that the blow was real.

The year 1835 had brought not only tightened censorship, the persecution of David Strauss and the ruthless measures against anyone even remotely connected with the 'Young Germany' affair, but also the hounding of Georg Büchner. In 1835, Büchner was only 23. His play *The Death of Danton* – written before he had left Darmstadt two years earlier to study medicine and philosophy at Strasbourg – had been published by Gutzkow before the 'Young Germany' storm broke out. The year before, Büchner had moved to the university of Giessen, in the Grand Duchy of Hesse, where he organized a 'Society for the Rights of Man' and started a periodical, *Der Hessische Landbote* ('The Hessian Messenger'), which disseminated the ideas of Saint-Simon and Fourier. In 1835, suspected as the author of a leaflet carrying a motto taken from the French Revolution – 'Peace to the cottages, war on the palaces!' – this poet of genius who made himself the spokesman of the mute common people was forced to flee the police, first to Strasbourg, and then to Zürich. There, after completing his doctorate and beginning to lecture at the University, he was to die two years later – but not before having written *Woyzeck*, the forceful Romantic-realistic drama which foreshadowed modern expressionism.

14

Karl Marx's First Student Year in Bonn

Karl Marx was in his first year at Bonn University when the December 1835 Bundestag decree concerning the 'Young Germany' writers was issued. The decree created a general sensation. Marx's reaction to it or to its month-long reverberations is unknown; but that December he joined a literary student circle and had occasion to observe the intensified supervision of all student activities.

On his arrival in Bonn in October, with a comfortable allowance from his father, Karl had installed himself in the best and most expensive rooms directly opposite the university. With its 40,000 inhabitants, Bonn was a free and easy city, three times larger than Trier, and Karl took to it immediately. The university enjoyed the continued prestige of having the great Romantic, August Wilhelm von Schlegel, on its faculty. But it also had a certain reputation for laxness. Indeed, until about the time of Marx's arrival Bonn had escaped the general persecution of both the nationalist and the liberal *Burschenschaft* fraternities. Although proscribed, they functioned more or less openly and the university authorities allowed their 700 students more freedom than any other in Germany.

Lectures had not yet begun when he arrived, and other than studying the scheduled lecture courses – and registering for no fewer than 9 of them – he had time on his hands. Together with 6 other freshmen from Trier, he set about exploring the taverns and wineshops of the friendly city, much of whose student life outside the classroom was spent in drinking, duelling and carousing under the benevolent eyes of Bonn's burghers, who themselves loved a good cup.

He did not think it necessary to notify his parents of his safe arrival. His father wrote him a short letter dated 8 November: 'It is more than three weeks since you left home, and no trace of you! You know your mother and her anxious nature...' Unwilling to admit that he was quite upset himself, he declared, 'I for my part can wait,' but he reproved Karl for his 'negligence surpassing all bounds, which unfortunately confirms my opinion that, in spite of your many good qualities, it is sheer egoism that predominates in your heart.' He found his son irresponsible and asked him to 'calm mother forthwith'.[1]

The letter, however, remained on Heinrich Marx's desk in Trier, as he didn't have Karl's address in Bonn. On 18 November he started another, longer letter to Karl. The two letters were not to be sent off until 29 November, by which time the son had given the first sign of life in the form of a hastily scribbled, barely legible note. It was to the second of his father's delayed letters that his mother added the long Postscript quoted earlier.

It will be noticed that in the first of these letters his father accused Karl of three things: negligence, egoism and 'irresponsible' conduct. 'It is more than curious that we do not even have your exact address yet,' he remarked sarcastically in the second letter. When Karl Marx went to Berlin two years later he neglected again to inform his family of his address. By then his father was to complain: 'Never did we get an answer to our letters; never did any of your answers relate either to your previous letter, or to any of ours.' Nor did Karl ever write to, or inquire about, his sisters and brothers.

There was obviously something missing in Karl's relationship with his parents and his siblings. It was beginning to emerge that he was egocentric, too wrapped up in himself to show or entertain filial or brotherly sentiments or, as his father expressed it two years later, 'So young, you were already alienated from your family.'

Back in 1815, Heinrich Marx had warned one of Prussia's high officials that the discriminatory policy of forced baptisms would alienate and make rebels of the next generation. He may not have remembered this now, 20 years later. Regretting the severity of his first short letter, he declared in his second: 'I am not a pedantic authoritarian. If I have been too harsh with my child, I am ready to admit it... Your letter, though practically illegible, has given me great pleasure.' He observed that 'nine courses seem rather a lot to me, and I don't want you to do more than body and soul can bear. But if you can manage it, very well. The field of knowledge is immense and time is short. You will probably give me a fuller and more detailed report in your next letter, you know how interested I am in everything that concerns you.'

This letter abounds in expressions of confidence in Karl's natural gifts, his 'bright mind', his 'pure' heart, his industry, etc. If his mother in her Postscript seemed concerned about his health and asked that he scrub himself weekly 'with sponge and soap', his father too reminded him that 'on this wretched earth the body is the constant companion of the soul and conditions the well-being of the whole machine. A sick scholar is the most unfortunate being on earth.' This seemingly exaggerated concern with Karl's health was to be justified when it broke down under his tendency to excess.

His mother wrote simply, 'keep well... and always keep God and your parents before your eyes.' His father did not doubt that Karl would always remain 'morally good', but he too found it necessary to add that morality's best buttress is 'a pure belief in God'. Expressing his own shallow deism, he wrote: 'You know that I am not a fanatic. But sooner or later there are moments in life when this belief becomes a true necessity... And what Newton, Locke and Leibniz believed, anyone may submit to.'

In the midst of this loving, semi-moralizing letter, a revealing confession escapes the father: 'I would like to see in you what I might perhaps have become had I been born under equally auspicious circumstances. You can fulfil or destroy my most beautiful hopes.' He was aware that it might be 'unfair and unwise' to place such a burden on his son, 'but who other than nature is responsible for it that men who are otherwise not so weak nevertheless make weak fathers?'

It was only midway through their 30-months-long epistolary dialogue that Heinrich Marx began to realize the extent of his son's 'alienation'; and detecting an unguessed 'demonic' Faustian element in Karl, he was seized with forebodings that his son might in the end realize not his best hopes, but his worst fears.

For the moment, far from giving his father a 'more detailed report', Karl did not answer this letter or his mother's long Postscript. When his parents heard from him again, it was in the form of another hurried note advising them that he had overspent his allowance and was in need of more money.

He had started his studies with great enthusiasm, devouring lecture after lecture – the august Schlegel discoursing on Homer; Friedrich Gottlieb Welcker, an authority in his field, expounding Greek and Roman mythology; G.W.E. d'Alton, on modern art history; and three other professors on Roman law, its history and institutions. With three more courses on Greek literature and aesthetics, Karl was soon overworked to the point of exhaustion and, accepting his father's advice, dropped the last three. After some time, even 6 courses proved too much, and again on his father's advice he was to drop two more. At this point he did not question the authority of his father, who for all his various admonishments kept flattering his ego. Nor did he have any intention of disappointing him.

Professor Welcker found Karl an 'exceptionally industrious and attentive' student, and his other teachers were equally satisfied with his diligence. Karl's interest in jurisprudence, however, petered out towards the end of the first semester, and in the second, although formally continuing courses in German and European law, he was to attend hardly any lectures, preferring to study on his own.

From the beginning, too, he had plunged into Bonn's boisterous extracurricular student life with youthful zest. Besides joining the so-called Treviraner 'Tavern' Club formed by 30 or so students from Trier (hence Treviraner), he had by December 1835 also become a member of the Poetenbund, a Poetry Circle of young writers and literati. By then the renewed crackdown on the *Burschen-schaften*, in progress since the amateurish 1833 student putsch against the Frankfurt Constabulary and the attempt to blow up the Bundestag in Berlin (capped in 1835 by a riot in the capital on the King's birthday), had, upon Metternich's intensified pressure on all German states, reached Bonn's tolerant 'fortress of Romanticism' as well. The process of ferreting out leading *Burschenschaftler* and nationalist or liberal 'subversive' students had started about the time of Marx's arrival, but now it was in full swing. There were daily arrests and expulsions. The only student associations allowed to remain were the Borussia Corps of aristocratic fops – who in the words of one contemporary regarded 'brawling and carousing as the highest aim of the student's life'[2] – and such supposedly non-political *Landsmannschaften* as the Treviraner 'Tavern' Club and other societies based on the regional provenance of their student-members.

Unlike them, the literary Poetenbund was an outright radical group. Founded by two students who had police records, its members included Karl Gruen, one of the early 'true' Socialists whom Marx was later to treat to some of his fiercest invective; and it had connections with a similar literary-political group at Göttingen University, headed by Karl Bernays, the future editor of the Paris *Vorwärts!* ('Forward!'), in which Marx was to publish one of his first Communist articles.

The Poetenbund, in short, was sufficiently suspect for the police agent Nohl, who had spied on Trier's Gymnasium pupils, to be sent over to help the Bonn authorities investigate it. The quarters of the student literati were ransacked and the Poetenbund's rules and minutes confiscated. But as these specified the aim of its gatherings as nothing more incriminating than 'the reciprocal exercise of poetical talents', the matter was passed on to the university court. Although no action followed and Karl's name did not appear in the police report, he and the other would-be poets now had a whiff of the persecution of the 'Young Germany' writers, which continued to be the talk of the day.

Karl had sent a specimen of his poetry to his father, who found it a poor and senseless piece. After reading it 'word for word' he had this to say to his son: 'Frankly, your talents please me greatly and I expect much from them, but I would be grieved to see you make your appearance as a common little poetaster... Only a man of a first-rate talent has the right to claim the attention of a pampered world, which has had a Schiller.' Although delicately counselling Karl not to be misled by enthusiasm and rush into print with his verses, Heinrich Marx was at first pleased with Karl's membership in the Poetenbund, on the assumption – as he wrote him – that a literary circle was 'better than a public house, for young people who enjoy such gatherings must necessarily be educated and better aware of their worth as excellent future citizens than those who assert their worth by excelling in rowdiness.'

He was of course less pleased when he learned at some delay that the Poetenbund was under police suspicion. The fact is that Karl kept his parents somewhat in the dark about his activities. When he was ill his father advised him to exercise regularly, take walks, 'even go riding occasionally', but not to overdo anything; his mother cautioned him not to 'get heated up or drink much wine or coffee' and to refrain from smoking tobacco or 'dancing dear Karl until you are fully recovered.' When Karl, having squandered his allowance, ran out of funds early in 1836, his father sent him extra money. 'Even a scholar', he observed drily, ought to keep some order in his finances, but once Karl had placated him with some lines, all was forgiven; and in an undated letter in May or June – convinced 'by the sincerity and decency of your character' – he wrote that he was sending another 100 Thaler.

By 1 July 1836, however, Heinrich Marx was reduced to pleading with 'dear Karl' to write 'about anything, but write.'[3] The ever-alert father was particularly perturbed for he had somehow got wind of Karl's participating in a certain amount of student rowdiness. His earlier undated letter had included a passage starting with the revealing question: 'And is duelling so interwoven with philosophy?... Don't let this propensity, and if not propensity, then mania, take root.'

Karl had yet to become involved in a duel, but he had been arrested on 13 June for drunkenness and 'noisy revelry' at night. He was sentenced by the proctor to be jailed for 24 hours in the university *Karzer*, where on 16/17 June he had a jolly time entertaining visitors whom the less-than-stringent Bonn authorities allowed in with beer, wine and cards.

The Treviraner Club and the other middle-class student societies meeting at other drinking-houses all resented the snobbish aristocrats of the Borussia Corps, who were (as denoted by the name of the Corps) of Prussian origin and looked down on the rest of the students. The latter made it their sport to ridicule and provoke them, or to respond to their provocations with satire and vituperation, which led to frequent fist-fights, brawls and duels.

Because of Karl's drinking ability, his sarcastic repartee and general assertiveness, he was elected to the 5-member presidium of the Treviraner Club and took an active part both in their carousing and in their verbal and physical duelling with the Borussians. There was a definite element of social animosity between the two camps, but whether or not this affected him in any way, he attended hardly any lectures in the summer semester other than Schlegel's on the elegies of the Roman poet Propertius, and found an outlet for his dynamic temperament and his aggressiveness in the mutual jeering and the regular nightly game of 'chaff' with the Borussia Corps.

Many years later he was to describe this game of 'chaff' which started after the students – 'at about 11 o'clock at night' – were thrown out of the beer-houses and assembled on the market-place, where the members of each society of 'colour' began to insult those of any other colour:

> The aim is to produce one of those frequent and not very dangerous duels which compose one of the chief features of student life. In these preliminary controversies on the market-place, the great art consists in so wording your hits that no actual or formal insult is contained in them, although you vex your opponent as much as possible, and at last make him lose his temper, so that he comes out with that conventional, formal insult which compels you to send him a challenge.[4]

Karl Marx himself fought at least one duel that summer. Although the exact circumstances are unknown, it is believed that it took place at Bonn at the beginning or middle of August 1836. It ended with his being lightly wounded over his right eye.

His father had already decided that Bonn University, with its wild, uncontrolled student life – as a result of which two young people had been killed in duels during the past two years – was too riotous a place for his son. On 1 July he had sent the university authorities a curt note saying: 'I not only grant my son Karl Marx permission but hereby convey to you my express wish that he transfer to the University of Berlin in the next semester. Marx, Justizrat, Advokat-Anvalt.'

According to the school-leaving certificate issued by the university on 22 August 1836, 'Herr Carl [*sic*] Heinrich Marx was sentenced to one day's incarceration' in the university jail for 'disturbing the peace at night, noisy revelry and drunkenness.' Neither his brawls with the young sparks of the Borussia Corps nor the duel, or possibly duels, he had fought were mentioned in the school report. This went on to say, however, that while his conduct had been 'unobjectionable', notice had lately been received of his 'carrying a forbidden weapon in Cologne. An investigation is in progress.' This has led to the conjecture that the duel in which he was involved that August in Bonn may not have been fought with the stiletto he normally carried, but with pistols, which were considered by the students to be a more 'manly' weapon than short daggers or sabres. Carrying them was forbidden.

But apart from the Cologne police report to Bonn University nothing further is known about this, and with his departure from Bonn the progress of the university's investigation into the matter of the 'forbidden weapon' was not heard of again.

On 22 August he left Bonn, not before celebrating the end of the academic year and going on a final spree with the Treviraners. They gathered at the White Horse Inn in nearby Godesberg, drank and smoked from long-stemmed porcelain pipes, paused between roaring songs to relive some famous pranks they had enjoyed, and while thus engaged had themselves lithographed (as those of a later day would have themselves photographed) by David Levy Elkan. This Cologne artist, wellknown for his later being commissioned by the canons of Cologne Cathedral to ornament a historic letter of homage to the Pope (and for some memorable drawings of the cathedral's statuary as well as an illustrated Passover Haggadah he was to leave behind), drew the students in ink on a yellow limestone slate as they sat about or stood posing in the garden of the inn in their coloured vests, narrow pantaloons and short coats, some of them with wine bottles raised high. Karl Marx stood between others in the Treviraner group, his figure half-hidden but his head clearly visible, and as Elkan sketched the crowded scene, catching in a few lines the features of 30-odd identifiable individuals, he was in fact creating the only extant representation of what the future founder of Marxism looked like in his youth.

According to this portrait he was remarkably handsome – not at all 'the ugliest fellow under the sun', as a resident of Trier was to describe him many years later, and a far cry, too, from the shaggy, monumental head known to posterity. He was hairy even then, with a tousled black mane over his high forehead; side whiskers which started as a luxuriant lock covering each temple from eye to ear; a thin moustache; and, shadow-framing his clean-shaven maxillaries, more hair tucked into and chafing the stiff collar of his student jacket in the type of beneath-the-chin beard from ear to ear sported at one time or another by Romantic or simply fashionable non-conformists.

Next thing, during his 7 weeks' vacation at home in Trier, young Marx stupefied his parents with the announcement that he and Jenny, daughter of Baron Ludwig von Westphalen – and a Baroness in her own right – had become engaged. Karl's elder sister Sophie, who was 20 and a friend of Jenny's, had been their confidante and go-between during Karl's year in Bonn. Jenny had refused to correspond with him but would visit the Marx home to get news of him from Sophie. Karl's parents may thus have been aware of their son's romance, but it is not known whether or how seriously they took it until Karl – having lost no time in resuming his wooing of his sweetheart and sealed their secret understanding or 'bond' of the previous year – confided in them that they were engaged and the young Baroness was now his bespoken bride.

The 'betrothal' was, however, highly irregular in one important respect: Jenny, for reasons that will become apparent, hesitated to inform her family. The summer passed. In mid-October Karl left for Berlin University. He finished the first half-year term while Jenny's engagement to him continued to be kept a secret from Baron von Westphalen and his wife. Marx's father was the first to have misgivings about this situation, which placed him in an embarrassing position vis-à-vis the Baron, with whom he had long been on friendly terms.

'Scarcely was the wild rampaging in Bonn over, scarcely were your debts settled... when to our consternation and dismay the sorrows of love began,' Heinrich Marx wrote ruefully to his son in Berlin. But even he could not foresee the prolonged strain and acute conflicts which the proposed match was to produce between – as well as within – the two families, causing the son to complain, 7 years later, of 'the useless and exhausting battles' which 'I and my bride' continued to have to fight 'partly with her pietist-aristocratic relations... and partly with my own family.'[5]

An oil portrait of Jenny, painted when she was 21, shows her in the full bloom of youth: dark auburn hair, a high-browed, oval face, large green eyes, a perfect nose and full lips. It is a soft-looking, extremely well-proportioned face. People were impressed, too, by her agreeable personality; a contemporary who met her a dozen years later was moved to write that he had rarely encountered 'a woman so harmoniously turned out' in everything, heart, spirit and appearance. It is not known which of the Trier schools she had attended, but when she was 16, Baron von Westphalen, true to his half-Scottish descent, had started teaching her English. She was familiar, too, with the works of Heine and the 'Young Germany' literature and, sharing her father's liberal inclinations, is said – in discussions stirred by its recent wholesale prohibition – to have stood up for the writers of this 'modern' progressive trend.

Whether or not she was 'the most beautiful girl in Trier' and the town's 'enchanted princess' (descriptions which Marx recorded when revisiting the scenes of their youth in sentimental middle age 25 years later), she had certainly not lacked for suitors during his absence in Bonn. Few of the Fräulein turned out at the time by the girls' school run by the wife of one of the Trier notaries, or by any of the piously Catholic town's other educational 'establishments for the edification of female youth', were as well-born, well-bred or well-read. Jenny von Westphalen had wit and a sense of humour besides her good looks. Already in 1831 she had been described in a letter as 'much courted' and holding off admirers with great 'sang froid' for a girl of 17. That year she had been fleetingly engaged to Second Lieutenant Karl von Pannewitz, the 28-year-old scion of an old aristocratic family (and very remotely related to her father's first wife).[6]

Other Prussian officers stationed in Trier and some of the district's rich landowners' sons must have found her more attractive company than the average winegrowers' daughters and young matrons whose interests, except for the occasional bluestocking, were confined to *Kaffeeklatsch* and embroidery circles, charity dances and church bazaars.

When Karl returned from Bonn in late August 1836, Jenny was 22 and he 18. But he was a truculent youth, hirsute, dark-complexioned, with black luminous eyes, his look often inward-turned and brooding – yet at other times so penetrating and in argument so piercing that Jenny was to complain only a few months later of his trying to 'obliterate' her with his glance. Of medium height but broad-shouldered, he walked with a lithe gait. Restless, self-preoccupied and dynamic, he combined earnestness with exuberance and an appetite for the roisterous side of student life. He might be boyishly boasting of beer-drinking orgies and duels, but he had been writing poetry since he was 15, he thought of himself as a poet, and he was in love.

It was to be some time before he stopped taking himself seriously as a poet. In the summer and autumn of 1836, he turned out nearly 60 poems, almost a third of them 'Sonnets to Jenny' or otherwise addressed to her, the rest ballads dealing with the more or less obligatory themes of the Romantic fantasy, from stars to graves, ghosts and the nether world, as can be seen from a sampling of their titles: 'Death's Grief', 'The Pallid Maiden', 'Soul Music', 'Song of the Sirens', 'Song of the Elves', 'A Song to the Stars', 'Song of Gnomes', 'The Ghost', 'Romance of the Grave', and the like. Marx made clean copies of them all in his small Gothic handwriting, filling three copybooks with his poetic output – all of it practically worthless and 'built of moonshine', as he eventually realized; and years later he and Jenny would laugh with tears at these youthful follies.

At the time, however, when Jenny received the three collections, the cover of the first bearing the title BOOK OF LOVE and inscribed 'To my dear, eternally loved Jenny von Westphalen. Berlin. 1836. At the end of autumn', and signed K.H.Marx (the other two similarly signed, dedicated and titled, respectively, BOOK OF LOVE. Part Two and BOOK OF SONGS), she shed tears 'of delight and pain'. These three collections, mentioned by Marx's daughter Eleanor and inspected at the beginning of this century by D. Ryazanov and that other early Marx specialist, Gustav Mehring, were to make even this latter hagiographer wonder how such formless 'Romantic harpistry' unrelieved by Romantic magic could have been written nearly a decade after Heine's *Book of Songs*. A few years later the three collections disappeared as though they had never existed – suppressed or mislaid, and seemingly lost to posterity forever.

There was yet more poetry to come from his pen. By 1837 he had produced altogether some 150 assorted sonnets, ballads, romances, epigrams, etc., including 50 which he dedicated to his father in the spring of 1837, about half a year after his engagement. Sophie, his favourite sister, assiduously copied and preserved others in two more collections, making altogether 6. Marx tried to get his literary output published, but no more than two of his poems appeared in print during his lifetime, and for the greater part of the 20th century – while his sister's notebooks remained untraced – they and the 50 ballads, songs and epigrams dedicated to his father were the only available samples of his poetry and poetic imagination. Some of them carried a strange power and showed signs of a demonic streak, if no great literary excellence.

The youthful Marx had a savagely ironic temperament, which – coupled with the intellectual superiority that later enabled him to dominate most arguments and trounce his opponents – made him a forceful and domineering partner in love. When he transferred to Berlin University, his dynamism and slashing wit eventually gained him such a reputation in student circles that Engels, who was two years younger, put him down from hearsay – before ever meeting him – as 'the black fellow from Trier' who 'walks not, hops not, but leaps upon his prey', and otherwise depicted him as being possessed by 'ten thousand devils'.

His wooing of Jenny was characteristically impetuous; in 1836 he pressed his suit, as he later recalled for his daughter Eleanor, like 'a really furious Roland'. Jenny was fascinated by this lusty, swaggering, yet poetic and highly articulate youth whose courtship was both passionate and energetic, couched in terms of lofty visions of bliss, spiritual unity and all the other ecstasies that, like code-words of the exalted Romantic imagination, continued to animate its language. Though irresistibly attracted, she was also perturbed and a prey to conflicting emotions. She was no George Sand prepared to disregard convention. She lived, it must be remembered, in Trier and not in Paris. Embarking on a clandestine engagement and keeping it from her family was for her an adventurous course, tinged with disloyalty. Her conformist views on the role of women were, as it happens, set out in an undated letter written several years after the secret betrothal: 'A maiden's love differs from that of the man; it must be different. She can of course give the man nothing except her love as well as herself and her whole person as she is, undivided and for ever. In normal circumstances the girl must also find her full satisfaction in love of the man, she must forget everything else in that love.' But the circumstances in which Jenny concluded her lovers' pact with young Marx in 1836 were anything but normal.

Although their conversations and her feelings at the time are undocumented, her natural fear that an 18-year-old's amorous enthusiasm might be a quixotic flight of fancy is echoed in the same later letter: 'That I might be unable to retain your youthfully enthusiastic love, I knew from the very beginning', she suddenly blurted out midway through their exceedingly long engagement. But her initial doubts and anxieties, which had only increased with time, were more complex than that:

> O, Karl, my distress lies precisely in the fact that your beautiful, touching, passionate love, your indescribably beautiful expressions of it, the enrapturing images conjured up by your fantasy, all this that would fill any other girl with ineffable delight, only makes me anxious and often plunges me into despair. The more I were to abandon myself to this bliss, the more frightful would be my fate if your fiery love were to die, and you were to become cold and reserved... I am not so thoroughly enchanted with your love because I no longer feel quite sure of it... That is why I frequently remind you of external things, of life and reality, instead of holding fast, as you would prefer, to the world of love, losing myself entirely in it and in a higher, dearer spiritual unity with you that would make me forget all other things...[7]

What 'other things'? When Karl left for Berlin, it was clear that it would take him 6 or 7 years to complete his studies before he could even think of marrying her. She had no idea, we are informed two months after his departure, how her parents would react to her falling in love with a teenager and would-be poet whose chances of being able to support her even then looked nebulous. There was their age difference and 'reality' to consider. But Jenny's problems were complicated by a little-known history of conflict between two sets of Westphalen children sired by her father in two successive marriages, one with a lady of ancient aristocratic stock, and the second with a commoner. As Jenny rightly anticipated, a coalition of her relatives, led by her half-brother Ferdinand, her half-sister Lisette, and her uncle Heinrich von Westphalen, were strongly to oppose and do everything to obstruct her alliance with Karl; and it is chiefly these three that he had in mind when, nearly 8 years later, he testified that 'my fiancée has been involved on my behalf in the toughest of struggles that have ruined her health.'

The long-standing dissension that had divided the Westphalen family since before Jenny's birth exacerbated her struggle with this 'aristocratic' group of her kin to the point where she was made ill. At the same time, the atmosphere of discord and mutual animosities in which she grew up and the hostility shown her since childhood by some of her relatives help to explain why the young Baroness, so 'harmoniously turned out' in everything, was a basically vulnerable person, and why Trier's beautiful 'Queen of the Ball' appeared from the beginning torn and insecure in the face of the advances of an 18-year-old.

Jenny came of an aristocratic family, but one that was neither rich nor of exalted rank. The first Westphalen to bear the title of Baron or Edler or Freiherr, was her paternal grandfather, Christian Heinrich Philipp von Westphalen – the famous factotum of the Duke of Brunswick, who had doubled up as Quarter-master-General and virtually Chief of Staff to his armies in the Seven Years' War – and by the time it was conferred on him in 1764 the title had long lost the one-time power and privileges that went with it.

The fact that Jenny's grandfather had been offered higher ennoblement at the hands of George III of England, together with the post of Army Adjutant-General, spoke of his ability. That he had declined, refusing all 'military honours from both Brunswick and the British Government', throws light on the character of this son of a simple clerk to the exchequer and assistant post-master. Besides engineering most of Brunswick's famous victories, Jenny's grandfather had also left important war papers for a history of the Duke's cam-paigns later published by Jenny's eldest half-brother.

Hailed as 'the Gneisenau of the Seven Years' War', Jenny's grandfather had in the end accepted only the minimum German title enabling him in 1765 to marry the truly aristocratic woman of his choice: Jeanie Wishart, who was of ancient Anglo-Norman stock. Besides being the sister-in-law of the English commander, General Beckwith, she was, on her father's side, a kinswoman of Admiral Sir James Wishart, and descended through her mother, Anne Camp-bell – Jenny's great-grandmother – from the Earls of Argyll. None of this, however, added anything to her grandfather's German rank.

Nor had the Holy Roman Emperor Francis I, when 'graciously permitting Heinrich Philipp von Wesphalen [sic] and his descendants of both sexes... to call and sign themselves henceforth and to all eternity Edle von Westphalen', made him the gift of an estate or bestowed on him some material bounty other than the right to use the modest 'von' before his surname. As a consequence, Jenny's father did not belong to the exclusive caste of the true-blue German aristocracy.

By contrast with those heirs of great estates, Jenny's father, the Baron Johann Ludwig von Westphalen – whose modest title had been confirmed by Prussia in 1834 – owned no property worth mentioning. Worse still, during that same year he had been finally and irrevocably pensioned off after 41 years of government service and several postponements and reprieves. For the last 11 of them he had been the 'highest-paid official' in Trier, but by the time young Marx was pressing his suit in 1836 the Baron was 66 years old. Because of his long and loyal service, he was receiving a charitably increased pension of 1,125 Thaler a year, but his family of 4 now had to count every Groschen – of which there were 30 to the Thaler – and every Pfennig, or penny.

A patrician figure and a highly cultured man who loved to recite passages from Homer – which, as Marx was to be fond of recalling, he knew by heart,

428

along with 'most of Shakespeare's dramas... in both German and English' – the Baron seems also to have been an exceptionally sweet-tempered person whose all-round qualities had earned him uncommonly enthusiastic testimonials of praise from two successive wives.

'English gentleness of character' coupled with 'rare kindness of heart and an always even temper', is how his first wife once summed up his personality. The Baron had married her back in 1798 and she had died in 1807, at the age of 28, leaving him with 4 small children, two boys and two girls. In 1826 and 1827 the Baron's second wife, Caroline von Westphalen, echoed the first in two letters, in one of which she extolled him as 'a splendid character through whom I enjoy paradise on this earth'; in the second, she wrote that after 15 years of matrimony she loved him 'as passionately as the day we first met.' In one of these letters she mentioned the 'storms of life' they had weathered together, for 'fate has frequently treated us unkindly. We have been through manifold stresses in our marriage, but with support such as I get from him my foot never sinks nor falters.'[8]

The two women came from vastly different backgrounds. The first, Elisabeth Albertine von Veltheim, was the daughter of a count and an even higher-ranking aristocratic mother – Friederike Albertine von Pannewitz – whose family could be traced to before 1300, making her a member of Germany's *Uradel*, or genuine ancient nobility. Upon her death, her relatives had taken her two orphaned girls, one of whom was a baby, off the Baron's hands. The two boys stayed with their father. The elder, Ferdinand, was destined to become one of Prussia's most reactionary Police Ministers and to find himself in the unenviable position of having Karl Marx, by then a Communist ringleader, for a brother-in-law.

Caroline Heubel, who became the second Baroness von Westphalen in 1812, was a good-looking woman of 33, but a commoner of relatively humble origin. Her father, Julius Christoph Heubel, was an equerry and horse-trainer, her paternal grandfather had been a bailiff and forest supervisor, and his father (Johann Michael Heubel) the steward, county sheriff and 'regimental quartermaster' of a 17th-century manorial lord. Caroline von Westphalen was in fact the offspring of the union of two nearly synonymous families of riding-masters, formed in 1760, when an earlier Julius Christoph Heubel, an 'outrider and equerry', had married the daughter of Julius Ernst W. Hebel, a horse-trainer who was the son of another 'outrider and equerry' in the same Thuringian area of Rudolstadt.

Little as all this would seem to matter today, it did matter a great deal in the first decades of the 19th century. Combined with other factors, it was in part responsible for the early 'stresses' besetting Caroline's marriage and was to give rise to some of the endless and 'exhausting battles' that characterized Jenny's relationship with young Karl Marx.

'I have four beloved children of my husband's late wife,' Caroline von West-phalen wrote in 1827, boasting that Ferdinand and his younger brother were 'doubly precious' to her because they had been raised from an early age under her 'personal supervision'. Precious they may have been to her, but Ferdinand, for one, hated her intensely. He had in fact left home as soon as he finished school in 1816, 4 years after his father's second marriage. By 1826, when Jenny was 12 and the Baron was transferred to Trier, Ferdinand, having studied at Göttingen and Berlin and entered government service, was heading the Prussian district of Bitburg, which adjoined that of Trier, at the start of a rising career.

Both Ferdinand and Jenny's elder half-sister Louise Friederike, or Lisette for short, had married rich aristocrats. At 20 Lisette had become the wife of Count Adolf von Krosigk. This family was so rich and ranked so high in the stiff hierarchy of the Prussian aristocracy that poor Caroline had shied at the thought of facing them, and absented herself from Lisette's wedding.

Ferdinand, for his part, was promoted in 1830 to head the district adminis-tration of Erfurt with the rank of *Regierungsrat*, or State Councillor, and in the same year he married an extremely wealthy and rather snobbish upper-class woman, Louise Mathilde Chassot von Florencourt. Ferdinand openly snubbed Caroline by inviting his father to join him on a visit to Lisette and the Von Krosigk estate at Rathmannsdorf, but expressly and pointedly telling him in Caroline's presence that neither she nor Jenny could be 'of the party, regret-table as the fact may be'. The family scene ended with the shocked Baron's responding to the insult by giving up the planned trip altogether.

Ferdinand, Lisette, their younger sister Anna Elisabeth as well as Ferdinand's and Lisette's wealthy spouses and their respective Florencourt and Krosigk relatives – all except the younger son, Karl Hans Werner – had nothing but con-descension for the Baron's second wife, notwithstanding the fact that she had seen the two boys of his first marriage through some or all of their adolescent years, besides bearing three children of her own. Of these, only two had sur-vived, Jenny and 17-year-old Edgar, who had finished high school together with Karl Marx only the year before. They were much younger and more open-minded than the other children and the differences in age and outlook between the two sets of Westphalens could not but add to the long-standing tension and accumulated jealousies between them.

These inveterate, snobbish family antagonisms would be of little import but for their troubling Jenny so greatly at the time of her secret 'betrothal'. Long before the start of the actual struggle with these 'pietist and aristocratic rela-tions' which was to impair her health, Jenny – her nerves sensitized by always having been made to feel that she and her mother were somehow inferior – had a strong foreboding that they would haughtily reject the Marx boy as ineligible. She might wish to challenge them, but had to fight down her own awareness of the practical obstacles confronting her union with an ardent but immature suitor. And fascinated as she may have been by him, her dread of a family split added to her own anxiety that, in abandoning herself to his 'indescribably beautiful' effusions, his blissful but impossible and ephemeral 'fantasy' of love, she might be losing her foothold in the world of reality.

But Marx at 18, besides being darkly attractive and full of devilry and wit, bubbled with ideas and was eloquent as they discussed the future and he told Jenny of his plans and aspirations. 'History', this boy had written the year before, 'calls those the greatest men who ennoble themselves by working for the universal.' Whatever the adolescent Marx's sense of mission, there can be little doubt that he half-consciously expected to become one of those rare great men 'admired by the multitude', but 'exalted above it', detached and untouchable, like a saviour or a king. Youths with lesser egos and lesser stuff in them are often animated by vague idealistic or heroic dreams. But when the copy of Marx's early poems made by his sister and the other missing collections finally began to turn up a long time after their mysterious disappearance – some of them to be published for the first time in 1975 – not all his youthful verse turned out to be love lyrics and Romantic moonshine. The poems he wrote between 17 and 19 include previously unknown sonnets on Goethe and Schiller. They reveal his attempts to deal with classical themes and show him preoccupied with the Faust motif; and in one of the earliest, he proclaimed his dynamic, activist attitude to life and the world:

> Never can I quietly pursue
> That which strongly grips my soul.
> Never can I remain at ease
> But must storm without surcease.
> Every beautiful favour divine
> I shall conquer and make mine...

The fact that Jenny requited his love not only satisfied his vanity, but strengthened his confidence in himself – at that time still unremarkable – and supported his ambition. In the same poem he wrote, 'Let us dare everything, never rest, never pause'. All he needed to make these words good was the assurance of her love. If he was romantically exalted, Jenny herself had Romantic inclinations.

Besides, she was in love. Captivated by his appeal, his ardour, his intellect – all so much more exciting than those of the prosaic winegrowers' sons in Trier – she could not but succumb to his many-sided charge. To Jenny, brought up by an enlightened father, Trier with its nearly 14,000 piously devout Catholics was a stuffy and prejudiced 'Popish nest'. She herself belonged to the town's Protestant minority, which that year numbered 828. It was true that she did not lack the courtship of young men, but in her choice of a marriage partner she was rather limited: in 1836, the Rhineland was actually on the eve of the famous Church-State dispute regarding intermarriages which the following year was to lead to the suspension, and soon to the detention in a fortress, of Cologne's Archbishop, Droste zu Vischering, for refusing to abide by an earlier agreement and publicly vowing never to perform a Catholic wedding without the couple's undertaking to raise their children as Catholics.

Karl Marx came from Trier's other minority – its 268 Jews. Jenny knew there would be trouble with all or most of her family. She lived with her parents in a comfortable house with a garden. She had a trousseau, but hardly any dowry, except for some 750 Thaler's worth of bonds. Nor would any inheritance come to her. With a juvenile lover and long uncertain years ahead, she could foresee no end of practical problems. But valiantly she pledged to become Karl's wife: she would faithfully wait for him to complete his law studies in Berlin, or rather – since Marx at the moment had not the vaguest idea even whether the law was really the career he wished to pursue – until he found the right sphere of activity in which he could both serve humanity and support a family.

For there is no mistaking that young Marx's high-minded idealism, his interest in poetry and literature, appealed to Jenny. Herself well-read in both French and German, she was familiar with current literary and literary-political topics, such as the storm caused by David Strauss's *Life of Jesus*, and had quarreled with her half-brother Ferdinand about the persecution of the 'Young Germany' writers. Brought up by an enlightened father, she combined intelligence with humour and a good sense of observation. In one of her few surviving early letters, written from an Alsatian resort, she sarcastically recorded the conversation of several rich French philistines, revolving 'mainly around cherished money, how you make it and how you lose it, around railroad shares, forest sales, mining industry, manufacturing, and the highest compliment these characters can pay one another is "Oh, il sait faire une belle fortune." In this phrase they conceive every perfection...'

She felt uncomfortable about keeping her engagement from her parents and was apprehensive of Karl's intensity in saying they must 'weld' their souls together but making her dimly feel that he would have all of hers or nothing. Yet that is what she did: welded her soul to his, not knowing what she was letting herself in for.

Towards Jenny's father, Karl behaved after his secret engagement as if nothing had happened, and Baron von Westphalen continued to treat him as cordially as before. Now that Karl was on the verge of manhood, the half-German, half-Scottish baron, retired for the last two years – officially on grounds of trembling hands and beginning 'diffuseness' of mind – took, if anything, a greater interest than before in this bright young fellow who on occasional visits to the Westphalen home appreciated his recitations from Homer and Shakespeare.

Karl enjoyed these evenings presided over by the white-haired patrician Baron, who besides being bilingual by birth, had been educated in 7 languages. The Baron was delighted to have Karl sometimes accompany him on his country walks – the celebrated walks through the 'wonderfully picturesque', vine-covered hills along the Moselle River which young Marx was lovingly to recall in later life.

Amazing as it may seem, it was on these autumn walks with the Prussian ex-official that Marx was first introduced to 'Socialist' ideas. By virtue of the post he had held until recently – in charge, among other things, of 'police matters, prisons, gendarmes, hospices for the poor', etc. – Westphalen was acutely aware of the spread of unemployment and delinquency. A vigorous hiker for his age in spite of his slim, almost brittle appearance, he led the way briskly with his cane and talked to Karl not only about Dante, Shakespeare, Goethe and Greek tragedy.

The picturesque landscape through which they walked was one of the wine-growing districts along the Moselle that had been hit to disastrous effect by that year's economic slump in the Rhineland. These districts supplied nearly half of Prussia's total Rhine wine production, and – with hardly a drop of the 1836 vintage sold or saleable, while taxes and interest rates continued high – disaffection in Trier was on the rise. Not only big landowners were affected, but also small farmers who had turned all their arable land into vineyards. And in Trier itself every second citizen owned a little vineyard or two.

The Baron was perhaps all the sadder because shortly after his retirement he had invested 1,000 Thaler – in partnership with Jenny, who contributed 250 Thaler of her bonds – in bottles of a previous vintage whose price had been expected to rise. Now all the cellars were full and his little 'wine speculation' had turned out a dead loss.

Increasing poverty induced Baron von Westphalen to tell Karl about the ideas of Trier's peripatetic inventor and 'Socialist' world reformer, Ludwig Gall, who in 1819 – while serving as District Clerk in the Prussian Administration – had shown great initiative in helping the poor, to the point of chartering a boat and personally accompanying a group of needy emigrants to America, where he established a settlement for them at Harrisburg, Pennsylvania. On his return to his post in Trier in 1822, he had published a book on his American experiences, which elicited high praise from Goethe, and followed it up in 1825 with a pamphlet – 'What Could Help?' (*Was könnte helfen?*) – in which he high-lighted the disparity in bourgeois society between the low value of exploited human labour and the much higher one attached to the money and wealth pro-duced by that very labour. Gall, who had studied chemistry and combined a sci-entific mind with an entrepreneurial bent, depicted the misery of day-labourers in great detail, and emphasized that even the lucky ones who found employment had to support a family and children on less money than the rich spent 'on the upkeep of a single horse'.

The annoyed Prussian authorities transferred Gall to Koblenz and in 1832 – glad to get rid of him after he had patented a 'steam-distillation-apparatus' which doctors thought could help cholera patients by stimulating high perspira-tion – gave him a stipend to sell his patent abroad. In Paris he met Fourier, Robert Owen and the Saint-Simonists, but contrary to some published opinions he did not adopt their theories. His own Fourierist-type commune at Harrisburg had failed, and he felt that by trying to change morality, religion and the political system, these visionaries had all taken on too many tasks for their social ideas to succeed. By 1835, while successfully publicizing his steam-machine abroad, Gall had reached the conclusion that the interests of the moneyed class and the workers were 'diametrically opposed' and that a class struggle was inevitable. Having previously merely appealed to the rich to give an 'infinitessimal' part of their wealth to the poor, he published a more radical pamphlet attacking a system which made the rich get richer and the poor 'more wretched'.

Baron von Westphalen and Ludwig Gall had been colleagues for many years in the Trier administration. In 1836, when the Baron was talking about him to young Marx, Gall was receiving a doctorate *honoris causa* from the University of Liège as well as an offer to become Chief inspector of the Belgian Railways. Finally placed on the retired list by Prussia, Gall moved instead to Hungary. There he eventually ran 10 brandy-distilleries, three breweries and several mills for one of the large landowners. Said to have developed the world's first washing machine,[9] he also installed a steam laundry in the town of Pest, before it was to unite with Buda. Although the Vienna police were aware of his 'politi-cally dangerous' contacts with Kossuth, the future hero of the 1848 Revolution in Hungary, they hesitated to demand the expulsion of a former Prussian *Regierungssekretär*. After the suppression of the revolution, Gall returned to Germany and went on publishing numerous articles on technical as well as social questions. He died in Trier in 1863, not before perfecting a wine distilla-tion process – known in German by his name, *gallisieren* – which much improved the quality of the Moselle wines. Except for having one of Trier's streets named after him, he is today practically forgotten although some of his ideas were to be reflected in Marx's later work.

Not that Karl at 18 was particularly concerned with the lot of the poor and exploited. Nor was Westphalen a Socialist. A liberal-minded aristocrat belonging to the progressive wing of Prussian officialdom, he did not think in terms of Gall's idea that the interests of the workers and the propertied classes could not be reconciled. Rather, he introduced Karl to the social theories of Saint-Simon and his New Christianity. Saint-Simon's proposed solution of the class conflict by enlisting the rich, the capable and the captains of industry to work for the common as well as their own good and not just for private profit, appealed to the Baron – who was a believing Protestant churchgoer – as a way of harmonizing Christian duty with the needs of the new industrial age.

It is not known whether Westphalen ever told Marx of Saint-Simon's slogan, '*A chacun selon sa capacité, a chaque capacité selon ses oeuvres*', or of the book praising Saint-Simonist ideas which a Berlin professor had published that year. Its author was Eduard Gans, Hegel's star pupil – Gans of Ganstown, whom Heine had once ridiculed as a fool if he had himself baptized out of conviction, and if for other reasons a scoundrel – who had since become one of Berlin's most eloquent and admired academics. Referring to factory conditions in England, Gans had spoken of the 'proletariat' and had thrown out a question rarely discussed in Prussia: 'Is it not slavery to exploit human beings like animals, even if they are otherwise free to die of starvation?'

On his walks with Karl in the autumn of 1836, the aging Baron developed quite an affection for the intellectually bright boy – who in turn looked up to him and would eventually come to regard him as a kind of second or 'super-father'. This being the case, it is rather a mystery why Jenny and Karl had to conceal their love from him and could not simply tell so enlightened a parent that they had become engaged. Something of a clue, is, however, provided by an interested and reliable observer in Trier.

Karl would not have been in Berlin long before he heard from this observer that Jenny kept 'tormenting herself' and was 'oppressed' by the fact that 'her parents know nothing, or as I believe, do not want to know anything' about her betrothal. 'Not everything can be reasoned away,' added the informant. 'Nor is the judgment of relatives and the world' – i.e., public opinion – 'to be trifled with...'

The writer was Karl Marx's father.

Before Karl left for Berlin in mid-October 1836, he was provided with bed linen, a travel rug for the 5-day journey by mail coach, shirts and underwear to last him for several months. His sister Sophie had helped his mother go over his wardrobe and sort his things. His 6 other siblings, ranging in age from 10 to 17, added to the general bustle and excitement. The Marx household comprised 12 people, including two maids, and was in something of a 'travel fever'.

435

As the date for Karl's departure approached, one major topic dominated all conversation – between talk about his studies, his plans for the future, what woollens and other essentials he must take along, and which he had better buy in the Prussian capital – whenever the younger children were out of earshot. That was Karl's secret betrothal to Jenny. All communication between her and Karl having to be clandestine, Sophie would go on transmitting messages and letters in both directions. Sophie may have enjoyed her role, but their father was troubled. With his home serving as their post-box, Heinrich Marx, a respected lawyer, wondered how he was to face his ex-colleague Westphalen. Karl had placed him in an embarrassingly false position towards the entire Westphalen family and he wondered, besides, whether Karl had any idea what a serious commitment he had undertaken.

'You know, dear Karl', he wrote, 'only my love for you could have made me let myself in for something that goes against my grain. The role of underhand broker or secret go-between really doesn't suit my character. And do you realize the responsibility you have taken on?' Karl might well protest that he and Jenny were in love. Marx didn't doubt that, but felt that Karl was 'perhaps too young to realize that no duty is more sacred' than a man's towards a woman.

'Dear Karl, at the risk of offending you and hurting your susceptibilities, I will speak my mind prosaically. Let me tell you that all the exaggerations of love, all the exaltations of your poetic temperament, will not bring her one iota of the happiness and peace of mind you wish to give her. On the contrary...'

Marx wasn't sure that Karl fully appreciated what Jenny was giving up for his sake. 'There is, after all, a great imbalance in age and circumstances between her and you.' However, if Karl was serious about Jenny, 'if – after proper self-examination – you persist in your feelings and your purpose, then you must somehow reduce that gap and make up for it through the most exemplary conduct.' Karl must become a man quickly. 'You must somehow demonstrate – I would say you have to radiate the certainty – that in spite of your youth you are a man who deserves the respect of the world. This will raise Jenny in her own and the world's esteem, reassure her and make it easier for her to wait. I know you have it in you. The substance is there, only the form is still rough and needs smoothing and polishing.'

But Heinrich Marx was also hopeful. 'Who knows, perhaps it is a good, salutary thing that your new responsibilities will force you to some mature reflection, caution, even wisdom – not to mention some consideration for human needs – in spite of all the demons driving you...'

Loving his eldest son almost to excess, Heinrich Marx was the first to realize that his exceptional mind, coupled with his dynamism and ambition, might well carry him to greatness. In fact, before Karl was out of his teens his father applied to him the word genius – though not always in a favourable sense – and in one of his letters revealed his innermost feelings: 'Your rise in the world, the flattering hope of some day seeing your name in high renown, are not only, like your earthly welfare, dear to my heart, they are illusions which I have long nursed and which have become part of me...'

But Karl had lately shown more and more of an untractable side. He was self-centred, opinionated, inconsiderate, wild in his enthusiasms and easily hurt when things did not go his way, often moody and evasive. Also, his parents were frightened by his supercilious aloofness and what seemed to them a lack of ordinary human emotions. In a famous passage, Heinrich Marx expressed what really worried him:

> My heart often revels in thoughts of you and your future. And yet, at times, I cannot free myself from gloomy, apprehensive, terrifying ideas, when like a flash the thought strikes me: Is your heart equal to your head, to your abilities? Has it room for those tender, earthly feelings which bring so much consolation in this vale of tears to the man of sensibility? And as it is obviously dominated by no ordinary demon given to all men, is this a celestial or a Faustian demon? Will you ever – and this is not the least painful doubt plaguing my heart – will you ever be receptive to truly human, domestic bliss?...[10]

His mother echoed the thought: '...I let feeling take precedence over reason, and I feel sorry, dear Karl, that you are too rational...'

Heinrich Marx thought highly of Jenny. She was a priceless girl, a noble soul, one in a thousand. 'In the most incomprehensible manner', his son had 'won the heart of a girl that thousands will envy' him for. What's more, Karl had the good luck of enjoying the friendship and benevolent interest of her father. And now Karl had betrayed the Baron's trust by an impetuous, reck-lessly romantic 'betrothal' transacted behind his back. The worldly-wise lawyer knew that Jenny would not marry without her father's consent. Trier was a small town with few secrets. No matter what Karl himself would later say, his father was also well aware that Jenny's step-brother Ferdinand and her step-sister Lisette – like other haughty Prussian aristocrats in 1836 and later – would not easily stomach the idea of her contracting a Jewish alliance, or misalliance.

Nor was it a mystery to Heinrich why Jenny could not disclose her feelings and her engagement even to her father. The amiable old Baron might hold some advanced views for his time, he might be extremely fond of the Marx boy, but that did not necessarily mean that the idea of his daughter marrying Karl – if it occurred to him at all – struck him as less preposterous than it did others in his family, for the same or other reasons.

When Jenny's deep involvement with Karl began to dawn on him, Ludwig von Westphalen apparently preferred to shut his eyes to it and didn't want to know anything, perhaps in the hope that her infatuation would turn out to be a passing fancy. Heinrich Marx, on the other hand, was exceedingly anxious about everything – including Jenny's plight while Karl would be away for many years in Berlin, the much-courted belle having to keep up appearances both at home and in town for an unconscionable time. He was, in fact, caught in a distressing predicament. He was delighted by the unexpected prospect of an alliance with the Westphalens; he was all for it – first and foremost for Karl's sake, but also for the justification, the climax, the mark of full social acceptance it would bring to the tortuous climbing spiral of his life from the ghetto to the rank of *Justizrat*.

But he was sensitive to every side of the situation, aware of every real or imaginary obstacle that might prevent the union. Embarrassed by the clandestine nature of the engagement, he feared the consequences – for his son, who might have botched his chance; for Jenny, and what it might do to her reputation. But most of all, he feared some unbridled, uncontrollable side of his son's promising genius, and was anxious lest Karl's intellectual superiority, conceit and self-absorption ultimately rendered him incapable of making a woman happy.

Besides giving Karl his best paternal advice, the *Justizrat* equipped his son with letters of introduction to several friends or ex-colleagues of his who were justices of the Rhenish High Court of Appeals, which sat in Berlin. Shortly after his arrival in the Prussian capital, Karl registered in the Faculty of Law. He was in a depressed mood. Even the varied landscape and 'broad cities' he saw on his 5-day journey, even Berlin itself, left him cold – or so he was to write home 13 months later – for no marvel of nature nor 'art itself, which [is] not as beautiful as Jenny', could compare to the sensations of his soul or 'the surging' of his blood with longing for her. He might also not be enchanted by the prospect of having of necessity to go on studying jurisprudence, when his chief aspiration remained to become a poet.

But in Berlin, a new world would be opened to him. The drama that now began between father and son, and the separate, otherwise unrecorded torments of Karl and Jenny, would be reflected in some of the moving, increasingly anxious letters – of altogether 17 that survive – that Karl received in Berlin until his father died in May 1838.

15

'The Hand of God' on Bakunin

Karl Marx was not the only 19th-century salvationist who early identified his 'own perfection' with work for the perfection and welfare of mankind. Around the time in 1835 that Marx stressed this idea in his high-school graduation essay, another young man, discovering his calling or vocation in a different climate, was claiming – in clearer terms than Karl's allusion to his 'inner voice' as the voice of 'the Deity' – outright divine inspiration for his 'burning emotion and thirst for action' in the service of 'all humanity'.

Michael Bakunin was not yet 21 when he burst onto the Moscow scene with his eldest sister Lyubov on one arm, so to speak, and his favourite one, Tatyana, on the other. In January 1835, sent by his regiment to buy some horses in Tver, he had absconded without leave to nearby Premukhino. Like his first visit home, during which he had raised a furore over the proposed sacrifice of Lyubov's 'virginal purity' and her marriage to Baron Renne, his latest stay there had been punctuated by quarrels and a running family argument – this time over his refusal to return to his garrison in Poland. Young Bakunin, however, had remained adamant: ignoring his scandalized father's warnings of the risks of desertion and his mother's pleas, he had lied to the Army that he was too ill to continue and sent in his resignation.

His aging father could only splutter. It was to take Count Alexander Bakunin, who was 67 and half-blind, the rest of that year to use high-placed connections and pull every possible string to save his son from disgrace before, on 18 December 1834, he obtained his dismissal from service, 'for reasons of health, at his own request.'

Spending the winter in Moscow when Michael arrived there in March 1835, still in the pose of a smartly uniformed junior officer, were two friends of his sisters, Natalie and Alexandra Beyer. At the apartment of their widowed mother, Bakunin met a high-spirited idealistic youth of noble birth, Nicholas Stankevich, who – though only 22 – was rapidly emerging as the foremost of the Russian Romantics. A self-effacing character, shy, talented and consumptive, Stankevich wore 'the imprint of death' on his pale brow; but the aura of spirituality that sometimes illuminates the faces of TB-sufferers who have not long to live was in his case the outer reflection of a truly contemplative mind and a genuine artistic sensibility.

With his shoulder-long locks and pensive air, his well-cut coat and his silken scarf tied into a huge lavaliere-like knot, the handsome, elegant and soft-mannered Stankevich looked the very image of soulful Russian Romanticism. Although he conveyed the impression of an idle dreamer, he had recently graduated in history, besides studying philosophy and literature. He wrote poetry, played the piano, and also held a sinecure as 'honorary inspector of schools' in a district of his native province of Voronezh. A spellbinding personality, he had a luminous presence that charmed everyone who knew him: he was, in fact, in spite of his youth, the idolized leader and spiritual mentor of a group of Moscow's brightest young people, university graduates and students who were to influence Russian thought across Nicholas I's dark reign and for further bleak decades of Tsarist rule. Among them were 31-year-old historian Timofey Granovsky; the famous Vissarion Belinsky, who was 24 and to become known as 'the father of the Russian intelligentsia', a mighty freedom-fighter in the guise of a literary critic, perhaps the only practitioner of this genre to have a town (Chembar in the province of Penza) re-named in his memory; and others of a small intellectual élite who were to make their impact in other ways. Ivan Turgenev, who at this time was only 17, and only later a member of the circle, was to portray Stankevich as 'Pokorsky' in his novel *Rudin*.

Although Stankevich was to leave a meagre crop of poems and writings, his effect on the Romantic young intellectuals and literati who sat at his feet was such that, by the time he died, his reputation as a sage and practically a saint had spread from them to others of his generation and the next. Tolstoy, for instance, who was barely 13 when Stankevich died, was to declare that he had 'never loved anyone as I loved that man whom I never met. What purity! What tenderness!'[1]

No wonder then that Natalie Beyer was in love with Stankevich. But his exalted idea of love was of a communion of souls touching the stars and enabling a man 'to feel his unity with the world'. More than once, halfway through an affair, he discovered that the woman in question did not come up to his ideal. One married lady had already thrown herself into his arms, but in so doing made him shrink at the intolerable thought that she was out for mere sensual gratification. In Natalie he seemed to have found an intelligent soulmate, but she – like many passionate young women straining to live up to the high-minded notions of their Romantic beaux – had a hard time controlling her instincts. A case of mutually mistaken intentions, this situation had been dragging on for over a year – during which Stankevich had quietly fallen in love with Michael Bakunin's sister Lyubov, whom he had met on one of her previous visits to Moscow. The demure and placid Lyubov, who had cultivated her 'inner life' at Premukhino, appeared to him a heaven-sent personification of his vision of a woman suited for the type of spiritual communion he yearned for. Hesitating, however, to declare his feelings, he had let Lyubov go without telling her how much he felt drawn to her.

By the time Lyubov re-appeared in Moscow together with Michael and Tatyana, Stankevich's romance with Natalie Beyer had reached an impasse as – accused of having trifled with her feelings – he was forced to apologize to her mother. That settled, he and Natalie continued to see each other as part of the 'brotherly' relations prevailing in Stankevich's circle, which often met at the Beyer house. The languorous and frustrated Natalie now transferred her attention to Michael, a tall strapping young fellow, extremely attractive in his uniform. Moreover, whether as a noble gesture of 'renunciation' or from some other feminine calculation, she actually did her best to encourage Stankevich's shy flirtation with Lyubov. Lyubov had fallen in love with him too, but once more Stankevich failed to declare his feelings. Although Lyubov returned to Premukhino, she remained Stankevich's distant inamorata.

Michael Bakunin stayed only a month or so in Moscow, but his visit was a huge success in every way. When he left again at the beginning of April – about the time Herzen and Ogarev were being deported from the Krutitsky Barracks to disappear into exile and limbo – Bakunin, with his 21st birthday still more than a month off, had turned both Natalie Beyer and her sister Alexandra into his fervent devotees, had made his mark in Moscow's most brilliant young circle, and had become Stankevich's best friend, a fact which was to change his life.

Unlike Herzen and Ogarev's other small élite – the coterie of students and 'children' who until their arrest had read Ryleyev's forbidden poems, passed around Saint-Simonist tracts, enthused over Enfantin's 'emancipation of women' and 'the redemption of the flesh', or sung the *Marseillaise* and anti-Tsarist ditties – Stankevich's circle shunned such minor gestures of political defiance, however surreptitious. Rather, their reaction to the Decembrist repression and the appalling new conditions in Russia was to seek refuge in abstract discussions on a high philosophic plane.

At the age of 20 Stankevich, before he ever read of Schelling's theory of 'One Spirit which is the universal creative spirit in everything', had concluded that 'Nature is a single whole.' Though its 'separate things' were unconscious of themselves, the life distributed among them was 'conscious of itself as a whole', since its movements had purpose. Moving upwards on an 'ascending ladder' or pyramid, it reached self-realization in man's individual consciousness. Stankevich was thus innerly prepared for Schelling's idea of the 'Absolute' or the 'World Spirit' finding its apogee in the consciousness of the human 'I' when this and other notions of the early-Romantic German philosopher belatedly became the vogue in Russia.

Considered from a high metaphysical plane, and if one held that all phenomena stemmed from a single underlying and universal purpose, the thing to do in the stifling post-Decembrist atmosphere of general fear and submission was to commune with the 'World Spirit' which immanently governed the course of history. Stankevich had a speculative bent; he had written to his friend Neverov: 'Man is not lost in the infinity of the universe... Conscious of himself as a separate entity', he could establish harmonious contact, as it were, and identify with 'the World Reason. He can penetrate its laws, foresee its purpose and experience the beauty of creation.'

Venturing into the lofty regions explored by the leading, and especially the German, philosophers in their quest for the enigmatic pattern that governed the world, Stankevich's circle tried to discover the eternal verities affording the right perspective for judging ugly and immediate reality and appraising the direction of developments.

But not everything in life was rational, nor was philosophy pure and simple sufficient. Philosophy, Schelling had taught, was 'the universal organum', but 'the keystone of its entire arch' was 'the philosophy of art'. Poets from Shakespeare to Schiller had caught the emotions and other artists had expressed them in enduring masterpieces. Great literature and works of art were not merely the handmaiden of philosophy. Rather, the ideas, observations and reflections sprung from the minds and intuition of artists, and sometimes the visions of mystics, were its apex and its fountainhead – providing better and more valuable insights than scientific facts about coarse 'matter' and precise mathematics, or crass and changing politics, into the play of rational and 'supra-rational' phenomena that moved the world forward by irregular leaps and bounds.

Philosophy and religion, in short, helped man to achieve the self-knowledge necessary for perceiving the 'Absolute'. But only the artist, creating unconsciously, could grasp the mixture of rational, conscious and unconscious phenomena that made the world as a whole, and which in Nature and 'Absolute Reason' were one.

By the time Bakunin appeared in Moscow, Stankevich had studied Schelling and found in him confirmation of his own deduction that man could identify with 'the World Reason... foresee its purposes and experience the beauties of creation.' He had always felt that art alone kept man from 'sinking to the level of the beast.' Poet, music-lover and philosophically inclined aesthete that he was, he required little persuasion to accept Schelling's theory that works of art best captured and reflected the unitary 'essence of Nature'. His whole circle of young men and women were captivated by Schelling's other doctrine – that the world of ideas was more 'real' than the disorderly hubbub and apparent reality of fluctuating external events. These, as one of them remarked, were but a 'shadow show'. But for the refuge offered by Schelling and Plato, Stankevich swore, he would have been 'completely brutalized by the atmosphere that surrounds me...'

'Come on over, please, and we'll chat about the immortality of the soul and all the rest,' read a typical invitation from Stankevich to Neverov. Under an autocracy that allowed the Russian intelligentsia 'to import books from abroad which it forbids us to translate or publish' – as Belinsky was to put it privately two years later – they tried to remain aloof and to ride the surface tide of events while endeavouring to decipher the universal scheme of things by studying literature and the 'philosophy of art'. This made life bearable, and such current miseries as censorship and police surveillance looked paltry by comparison.

At poetry readings in his apartment in the house of Professor Pavlov, and in discussions continued at soirées in the drawing-room of the Beyer sisters and other salons, Stankevich's circle, in short, looked for some transcendental truth. Though consciously or unconsciously indulging in a form of escapism, they nursed some illusory hope that the key to the riddles of history and human existence, once found, would ultimately provide an answer to Russia's manifold problems. Until then, half-insulated from reality and contemplating it with the detachment of Indian yogi as they strove for harmony with the 'World Soul', their chief protest against it took the form of attacking the low level to which Russian literature had sunk.

Stankevich was a protégé of Professor Nicolas Nadezhdin, under whom he had studied at Moscow University. Nadezhdin was the publisher and editor of a review called *The Telescope;* Belinsky was its assistant editor. Besides labouring to put the journal together, Belinsky did double duty as its chief polemicist. His articles, which infuriated the literary establishment, attracted wide attention. *The Telescope*, providing the circle with an outlet for its ideas, added to its importance over that of sundry other young groups then meeting in Moscow.

It was in *The Telescope*, until its suppression a year and a half later, that Belinsky, today considered by one eminent authority as 'the father of the social criticism of literature, not only in Russia but perhaps even in Europe,'[2] first showed the promise of his qualities. Like Stankevich, Belinsky suffered from tuberculosis. But unlike most members of Stankevich's aristocratic set, Belinsky – frail, shy, unprepossessive, clumsy in company but ferocious when provoked – worked hard to support himself. Born in Finland, raised in Chembar, the son of a drunk and embittered ex-Navy physician, he had run away from his poverty-stricken home at the age of 12. At 19 or so he had earned a State scholarship at Moscow

University, including a free bed (with 12 others per room) and beggarly food in a dormitory for needy students. After a year of this, hoping that literary fame would improve his lot, he wrote an heroic peasant drama.

Instead of making his name, the play – *Dmitri Kalinin*, which the University censors found objectionable for questioning serfdom and otherwise criticized as immoral, 'anti-religious' and subversive – directly or indirectly led to his expulsion and the end of his stipend for 'lack of ability' and poor health. He was in fact sick and lax about his studies. At the age of 22, deprived of bed and board, his play banned and unpublished, Belinsky found himself in the street. Professor Nadezhdin saved him from despair by offering him translations for *The Telescope*, and eventually hiring him for a pittance as assistant editor. Saddled with all the drudgery of producing the journal, besides writing his own articles, Belinsky lived and worked in appalling conditions. 'Next to his closet-like room' on a back street 'was a laundry, from which fumes of wet washing and stinking soapsuds invaded his quarters. From the ground floor beneath him came the noise of blacksmiths working.'[3]

To be accepted as an equal in Stankevich's circle was flattering to him: he informed his brother that the stimulating contact with these young people 'distinguished by intelligence, education, talent,' etc., helped him forget his miserable condition as he laboured amidst 'the chatter of the laundresses' outside his door and 'the pounding anvil of the Russian cyclops' below.

'I never felt particularly suited for life in society,' Michael Bakunin had written to his sisters in January 1834, some 13 months before his Moscow visit. After more than 5 years in St Petersburg, the last of them as an ensign at the Artillery School, he felt 'stupid, awkward, inarticulate' and out of place. To overcome this, he had 'immersed' himself in society, had run around 'this way and that', but had found that it offered only trivial pleasures and distractions and 'a terrible emptiness'.[4]

It was some months since his first visit home to Premukhino, and only a couple of weeks since he had prevailed over his father and managed to save his sister Lyubov from the sacrilegious clutches of that abominable Baron Renne. On his return to St Petersburg after this triumph, a minor but fateful incident threw him completely off balance. Until then, the future rebel had taken remarkable care to avoid any serious breach of discipline at the Artillery School, apparently out of a healthy respect for the frightening punishments in force at Tsarist military academies – where cadets risked up to 1,000 lashes even for minor insubordination. On only one occasion had he been confined to quarters for a fortnight, after being caught in a lie. Indolent and self-indulgent, he had managed to scrape through and become an ensign by cramming 'only the last month of the year' before examinations, and otherwise, as he put it, 'doing just about nothing at all.'

In January 1834, however, the general commanding the school had caught him improperly dressed. Reprimanded in humiliating terms, and hurt in his pride, young Bakunin had answered the general with some heat. It is interesting but useless to speculate how his career would have developed had he done otherwise. For the general, angered by the impertinence of a junior officer, had brought about his expulsion from the Artillery School for 'lack of progress and inattention throughout the entire course of studies'. By the time he was 20 in May 1834, Bakunin, disgraced before his family and, as he felt, unjustly punished, found himself transferred to the Polish provinces. There, stuck in a 'miserable hole' in an 'alien land', among uneducated people whom he regarded as no better than animals – 'people virtually walking on all fours', he called them in a letter to his sisters that summer – his animosity against the world increased.

In St Petersburg, where he had been in love with Marie Voyekov's 'fine soul', Bakunin had discovered his impotence. In a curious letter home, he now confessed that any kind of 'sensual thought' caused his 'feelings to dull', plunged his 'soul into black gloom, anguish, suffering, self-laceration'. He went on: 'I collapse into a dreadful, numb despair. All of Nature then seems lifeless to me, dead. Everything appears to me as though through a stifling, bitter fog, gloomy, bent under the heavy hand of a fierce and pitiless fate.'[5]

In all his years in St Petersburg, shrinking from carnal 'vice' and shocked by the depravity of cadets and officers, their amorous 'conquests' and casual affairs, Bakunin had not formed a single lasting relationship with any of the capital's young of either sex.

In Poland, he plumbed the depths of despondency. While his fellow officers fought off the provincial boredom with cards, vodka and any available wench, he declared proudly that he was 'quite incapable of finding any charm or satisfaction in the dirty bog of sensual enjoyments, unworthy of a human being.'[6]

He did attend two balls in the town of Vilna when his brigade went there on parade and a spree, and made a point of noting that the fashionable Polish ladies seemed 'amiable, clever, excellent dancers'. But while his fellow soldiers flirted and made the most of the occasion, such distractions left Bakunin cold.

'Dances, balls, the pinnacle of pleasure for our youth, the highest ideal they can imagine, bored me to death,' he had informed his sisters in January 1834. His laments were to continue throughout the summer and autumn: 'I keep entirely apart from everyone... I live in a desert, there is no one with whom I can share my thoughts, impressions, feelings... I am alone here, entirely alone. Eternal silence, eternal sorrow... darkness reigning in my soul.'[7]

By October, when the brigade moved to winter quarters in the Grodno area, the monotony of military life and its rigours, 'the heat, the cold, the fatigue, the hunger, the thirst', had become too much for him. His alienation from his surroundings was complete; his loneliness, though self-imposed, unbearably oppressive. He was now determined to get out of the Army by any means possible.

One freezing winter night, sweating profusely after purposely having drunk 'a lot of hot tea', he stripped off his clothes and lay down naked in the snow, hoping to fall ill and be sent home. The stratagem was a measure of his despair. 'I lay there for a good half hour, bitterly cold... and what do you think happened? Nothing... I did not catch even a little cold! Nothing at all! And so I had to go right on drudging away as before!'[8]

Yet ever since the summer of 1833, Bakunin had been in the throes of an 'intellectual revolution', and busy building himself an 'inner existence' to insulate him from suffering and the harsh realities of life. 'The vacuum that overwhelmed me had to be filled. I locked myself within myself,' he had confided to his sisters, adding that from that moment he felt 'reborn'. The moment of his rebirth seems to have gone back to a bright June night in 1833 when, being then 10, he had been in a summer training camp with his regiment. Years later, in a letter to his father, he was to describe the unforgettable experience that had come to him that night:

'Everyone around me was asleep, everything was calm. A radiant moon hung over the vast expanse of the camp. With one of my comrades who shared my tent, I began to read the poetry of the dead Venevitinov and his letter to some countess or other. The marvellous night, the star-filled sky, the quivering, mysterious moonlight', he went on – coupled with the verses and the Letter to the Countess N.N. by D.V. Venevitinov, the 'Russian Byron' – had filled him with 'a sense of the infinite and a fiery, mighty love for God's beautiful world, for all mankind, and especially for you, my dear father, and for my mother and my sisters.'[9] He had been altogether overcome by 'a sort of melancholy but blissful languor.' But he had also felt within himself 'omnipotent forces for living, for being worthy to bear the great title of man.'

Venevitinov, before he died at the age of 22, had been the founder, together with Prince Vladimir Odoyevsky, of an earlier Moscow circle, the Society of 'Wisdom Lovers'. In his Letter to the Countess N.N., Venevitinov had explained the notion of the German Idealist philosophers, notably Schelling, that all phenomena – poetry as well as, say, mineralogy – could be neatly arranged and encompassed in a single 'absolute theory' of the universe. A pupil of Professor Pavlov, who taught physics and mineralogy but had been one of Schelling's earliest propagators in Russia, Venevitinov had also forecast the advent of an ideal age: when man reached 'self-knowledge', all sciences would be fused into a single 'science of sciences', and 'Love' and 'Freedom', man's destiny, would prevail.

'All of Nature, all human life', Prince Odoyevsky was to recall of those days, 'seemed very clear to us', that is, predictable. Romantic Idealists perfecting their self-knowledge by cultivating poetry and the arts while waiting for the all-in-one 'science' to arise could leave the study of empirical facts and objective reality to test-tube chemists and others.

For young Bakunin, absorbing them second-hand from Venevitinov, these ideas had been a revelation – at one stroke they offered an avenue of escape from his sexual impotence, the conventional obligations imposed by society and the unpleasant reality of his Army life. Surely, he had written a little earlier, 'we do not exist on earth merely to be deceived and to suffer endlessly?' He, too, could develop his self-knowledge, study, discover the universal scheme of things, find his 'predestined' place in it, and thereby achieve inner peace. Everything in him demanded 'activity, movement', but so far 'the cold, insuperable obstacles of the physical world' had blocked him on all sides.

He was still groping for his destiny, and a prey to Romantic languor. The beginning process of creating a new 'reality' for himself was to be a painful one – 'Where then is reality?' he exclaimed – but suddenly he had felt 'omnipotent forces within myself...'[10]

As his intellectual revolution progressed, what he called 'the whole system of my inner being' was about to be 'overturned'. Impotence could be turned into omnipotence.

In the letter he wrote to his sisters before his departure for Poland, Bakunin had described the start of the process of turning withdrawal and his inner existence into a citadel against the world. 'I studied myself... A warmth so sweet poured through my heart... I feel as though I am being reborn. I feel that I am watching myself being fed and nurtured. Until now I have lived only an external life. I want now to build for myself an inner existence.' And once he had buttressed that internal fortress in his Polish exile, he had proclaimed at the very nadir of his desolation: 'I will stand firm against the persecutions of implacable fate!' He would laugh at its blows. 'Let it beat away.' He was no longer frightened by its attacks. On the contrary, the greater man's struggle against its 'impediments', the greater the chance of 'strengthening his character'.[11]

His withdrawal into himself to be nourished from within, and other symptoms of a so-called pre-oedipal and narcissistic 'child-mother' development, have been comprehensively analyzed – notably by Arthur Mendel in 1981 and Aileen Kelly in 1982 – for their effect not only on Bakunin's contradictory personality, but on his later politics. Mendel, in particular, makes a forceful case for seeing in Bakunin's psycho-sexual disturbance, together with his concomitant

447

need for constant demonstrations of his powers and virility, the ultimate source of his increasingly violent 'millennial aims and destructive means, the roots of his apocalypse.' Even so, the great question to be answered at the end of his life would be the validity of his views and the historical justification invoked by him for his destructive fury.[12]

When Bakunin emerged from his Polish trials and loneliness, he faced the hostile 'external' world with a new, cold cynicism. Henceforth he would treat what he called 'fate' with the defensive-defiant indifference and cunning of a self-styled observer: 'I follow with cold curiosity all the devices it uses to try and crush me. I pity it, because it will not attain its aim. Let it try.'[13]

While in the Polish 'desert' he had studied. His withdrawal from a supposedly inimical world by no means conflicted with the 'love for the whole of mankind' that had flooded his heart that blissful summer night when he had first learned of Schelling's vision of a superior reality. In a camp near Vilna he chanced on a Dr Krasnopolsky, an Army surgeon who had studied the German idealists at Moscow University; from this man, he imbibed more second-hand ideas of their philosophy. He had an ardent 'thirst for knowledge' and 'self-perfection'. Unlike his fellow officers, he would lie on his bed reading, devouring any book he could find, whether of history, mathematics or 'Lithuanian statistics'.

Convinced that he was wasting his life in the Army, and that he was made for better things, he bombarded his family with his pleas for studying and tried to persuade them that to stay on was 'almost identical with egoism', which was a crime. He had been beseeching his father to get him at least a posting close to Premukhino, but would not wait.

In January 1835, having steeled his will, and fancying himself a martyr to boot, he had made straight for home, feigned illness and chosen to become – after 6 years of training for a military career – a deserter. During his furious championship of Lyubov's maiden 'purity' he had been his father's accuser. Now the roles at Premukhino were reversed. But the old count's remonstrations and desperate pleas not to shirk his duties and dishonour the family name hardly made a dent in his son's new stoicism. Young Bakunin's answer was that if Russia was threatened by war he would fulfil his 'sacred duty' to the fatherland and re-enlist.

And now, two months later, he was flourishing in Stankevich's circle of intellectual young men and women. Suddenly, he was no longer awkward and inarticulate, but taking part in drawing-room arguments – about religion, art and literature, the Absolute, the 'World Soul' and what not – with Belinsky and the historian Granovsky; with the poets Koltsov, Klinshnikov and Krasov; the journalist and later publisher Katkov; the philologists Bodyansky and Petrov, not to mention Stankevich himself, and other philosophizing young aesthetes. With

Natalie Beyer's appreciative glance resting on him and Lyubov and Tatyana watching admiringly, Bakunin found his tongue and the voice he seemed to have lost in the Army.

'A pure and noble soul', Stankevich was presently to characterize him. 'So much intelligence, feeling, honesty.' The meditative, somewhat effete Stankevich sometimes suffered from ennui and Michael's (later famous) volubility kept him 'energetic'. Almost from their first conversation, lasting late into the night, they became bosom friends. Stankevich and Efremov, another member of the circle, were to visit Michael and his sisters at Premukhino before summer's end in 1835; Belinsky did so the following year. All went into raptures about Michael, his family and the atmosphere of the place.

'The Bakunin family is an ideal family,' according to Stankevich, who found at Premukhino 'moral happiness' and a hitherto unimaginable 'harmony between the inner and outer worlds.' Belinsky, who was the poorest of them all and troubled by family problems, experienced there a 'harmony and bliss' which refreshed his life. Premukhino was 'paradise'. As a boy Michael had been singing '*Au clair de la lune*' with his adolescent sisters. Now they were all – Lyubov, Varinka, Tatyana and 19-year-old Alexandra – graceful young women. At the sight of them making music with harp and mandolins around the piano, with Michael or one of his younger brothers accompanying on the violin, or all of them singing in chorus, Belinsky felt as if he were 'listening to the rapturous and blissful hymn of perfected humanity.'[14]

Starting with his short Moscow visit in March 1835, Michael, for his part, found in Stankevich's circle perfect soul mates, on whose admiration and understanding he could thrive. In their 'uplifting and ennobling' company he began to 'live a genuine life', to display his mesmerizing charisma and power of rhetoric, and was soon to discover his destiny and vocation. His conquest of Natalie Beyer was extraordinary. Before the end of his Moscow visit she was making it known that 'a woman would want passionately to sacrifice everything' for him. She herself was ready to contemplate 'the most terrible suffering,' even 'self-destruction', if she could thereby generate 'the force needed for his rebirth' or become a 'new woman who could be his guardian angel...'[15]

But Bakunin, as we know, had already been reborn. He had always had an instinct for leadership, lording it over his siblings even as a boy. A rebel by temperament but not yet with a cause, he had a 'thirst for action' and high, though still vague, aspirations. He did not intend to remain a 'meaningless link in the chain of humanity'. Except for Belinsky and the 'peasant poet' Koltsov, most of Stankevich's friends were rich, high-born and idle. All were self-involved Romantic young idealists. They spent almost as much time studying the state of their souls and discussing the fashionable notions of 'self-development' and 'the creative I' as they did on metaphysical speculation and literary arguments. If philosophy and introspection helped to avoid facing Russian reality, Bakunin fitted well into this company. More than any of them, he had been cultivating his 'self' for years, had trained himself to draw strength and defiance from his 'inner existence'. He was quick to realize that Stankevich, Belinsky, Efremov and most of the others were all weak 'Hamlets', sceptics lacking his own energy and 'incapable of great deeds'. The will, he was to inform his new friends, 'is the principal essence of man, when it is illuminated by the holy rays of feeling and thoughts.'[16]

In almost no time he gained a dominant influence over some of them. Bakunin was high-minded, sensitive, impressionable. Ever since his time in Poland, he was, like the others, engaged in a quest for some higher and absolute Truth, some purpose in life, some universal salvation. 'We have the same ideas, the same doubts' – Stankevich was to explain the remarkable affinity that drew them together – 'the same needs'.[17]

Michael's last week in Moscow was a particularly glorious one. Lyubov and Tatyana having returned to Premukhino ahead of him, he basked in the admiration of the two Beyer sisters, saw more of Stankevich, and, never one to be defeated by his sexual or any other inadequacy, responded to Natalie Beyer's obvious infatuation with him by falling in love with her 'soul'. Opening his heart and some of the locks of his secret 'inner existence' to her, he complained of being misunderstood by his family, who thought little of his aspirations or his abilities. Natalie Beyer has left an account of the manner in which he unreeled his frustrations: 'A flood of feelings and ideas' poured from his lips with explosive force. 'It was chaos.' Natalie Beyer was an intelligent, if temperamental young woman. Michael was the new object of her worship. Observing that his mind was like a 'labyrinth' – and that she had had to collect her thoughts 'a thousand times' in order not to be entirely lost in it – she was nevertheless 'shaken to the core' by the eruption of his repressed emotions. In an impetuous fit of protective passion, she wrote a letter to his sisters, suggesting that they did not sufficiently appreciate him.

'We are in a better position to know him as he really is,' she wrote, lecturing them rather high-handedly about Michael's hidden potential. For all her tactless intervention and tone of exaltation, she had sensed the fire in him. Informing Lyubov and Tatyana that Michael's 'heart and mind are filled with flame', she made an astonishingly perceptive observation about this youth who had yet to show any accomplishments:

'His force of character and ardent spirit can achieve great things,' she wrote, 'but these very qualities are all the more dangerous for him because they have been so long repressed.' She added an outright warning: 'You must consider the irreparable harm you may do him, even with all the love you bear him.'[18]

Capping her indiscretion, she entrusted the letter to Michael, who without the slightest embarrassment undertook to deliver it himself, and on arrival at Premukhino proudly presented it to his sisters. He was stunned by their jealous reaction, which went beyond mere resentment of Natalie's strictures and proprietary tone. For weeks they pursued him with their reproaches. The most hurt and incensed was his dear, specially beloved Tatyana, who saw in Natalie Beyer a predatory female and nothing less than a rival out to dislodge her from Michael's heart and alienate his feelings. With all the hurt and heat of her 20 years, she undertook to answer the trespasser's presumption, and sent Natalie a stinging letter.

Poor Michael found himself suddenly impaled on the horns of a real dilemma. All he wished was to 'possess' Natalie Beyer spiritually, yet hers was a pronounced sensual nature, and abhorring as he did all carnal passion, he feared the signs of her long-repressed ardour – a girl 'whose torments I cannot assuage.' At the same time she was the first and only woman not of his family who seemed to understand him, and as such too precious to lose. On the other hand, he could not envisage life without the warming, physically undemanding adoration of his sisters. That alone still kept alive the comforting atmosphere of Premukhino, the lost Eden of his childhood, now that his father had practically given him up as intractable.

No amount of his vaunted force of will, even 'illumined by the holy rays of feeling' and week-long brooding, seemed capable of resolving the imbroglio of his conflicting feminine attachments. What he wanted was to eat his cake and have it too, and this he finally achieved in two bold letters he sent to Natalie – diplomatically addressed to her and her younger sister, Alexandra – between the end of April and the first week of May 1835.

He loved both of them, he assured them, for their 'beautiful souls'. True, he had been carried away by a 'burning, tempestuous passion' for one of them. But such prosaic, selfish love of the flesh, merely 'connected with the senses, and not with the soul', was neither lasting nor worthy of a man. That kind of love was no longer for him. Henceforth he must 'strengthen the love for mankind', show his fellow men 'the way to truth'. But was this not 'really a splendid fate? Is it not really finer than love for a woman?' He was 'a man of the times' with a distinct vocation: 'The hand of God has engraved in my heart the holy words, which suffuse my whole being: "He shall not live for himself."' He was determined to be worthy of, and to sacrifice everything to, 'this holy purpose. It is my one and only ambition... Every other happiness is denied me.'

Claiming divine inspiration for his self-proclaimed calling, Bakunin also sought in these two letters to give a philosophical underpinning to his detestation of the 'animal', that is, sexual side of life and of all things connected with 'matter'. God, he wrote, had 'created animal life and breathed into it the divine spark, a particle of the transcendent idea... What really is humanity? God imprisoned in matter.' The sensual passion in every human being separated him from his 'transcendent origin', and the perfectibility of humanity lay in its striving to 'overthrow the yoke of matter'. His own chosen role was to help in 'the progressive process of God's triumph over matter' by spreading this grand notion. 'To tear from nature its secrets, to reveal them to mankind, to overwhelm matter and habit by the force of one's ideas – is this not really a splendid future?'[19]

Dominating people by means of his will and the force of his ideas was to become Bakunin's ambition and way of life. Natalie Beyer was already under his spell: she had acknowledged his hypnotic eloquence by noting that, for all the 'chaos' of his ideas, his metaphorically flaming mind emitted 'sparks' that 'catch in one's heart and mind without one's noticing.' With a strategy that was to bring him extraordinary successes, Michael now extolled the 'spiritual' union of their souls, and the only kind of love he could offer her, as the purest possible kind of all. At the same time, he appealed for a place in her sister's 'broad and passionate heart' as well.

The two Beyer girls were given the chance of joining him in a sacred and universal cause, becoming the handmaidens, as it were, of its potential leader. For the moment, they went to the country for the summer. But not long after their return Michael – who at the end of May 1835 celebrated his 21st birthday – was to rejoice at being able to 'possess' both their souls .

With Natalie and the temptations of the flesh momentarily out of the way, and his sisters satisfied, Michael was free that summer to begin developing his 'holy' mission. Immediately, with characteristic verve and high-flying imagination, he set about converting his siblings and some of his new Moscow friends. Efremov, one of these new soul mates, came on a visit to Premukhino. Michael made him his first disciple.

Although their talks in the enchanted setting of Premukhino, with its woods, river, wild roses, pond and all, went unrecorded, Michael rejoiced in several letters to Efremov at no longer being 'alone' and exulted with the self-conviction of one chosen for his calling:

'My hopes are not mere smoke, but sacred, inspired dreams... sublime substance given to only a very few on earth, substance that has to be our constant guide in the career of action.' They would not, he proclaimed, 'pass through this temporal world in vain', but strength of will was essential. 'The development of our will is the only solution. When we are able to say *ce que je veux Dieu le veut*, then we shall be happy, then our sufferings will cease. Until then we deserve them.' Later that year he belaboured Efremov again: 'The future is within us... You say that one cannot always do what one chooses to do. Non-sense... Strength of will, my friend, is everything.' [20]

This theme and others now insistently recurring like codewords of a nascent gospel or doctrine he was fumbling to elaborate – the fortifying virtues of the 'inner life', of 'suffering', 'sacrifice' and defiance of 'the outside world' – would not have been so bizarre but for their purpose, which was to bring about 'God's triumph over matter' by fighting sensual passion, the root of all evil.

They must, he was to instruct the younger of the two Beyer sisters, live a 'spiritual life, a life of self-sacrifice' and mobilize 'every possible force of will' to resist 'periods of sensual passion'. Otherwise, they would be sunk 'forever in the mire of animal existence'.

Man's proper tendencies were 'moral and divine', not physical and animal. 'Man himself represents the eternal struggle of the beastly and the divine. The beastly will be destroyed and man will become God. All humanity, all individual beings, will merge into a single person, into love, into God...'[21]

No wonder Herzen was later to describe Bakunin as 'the monk of revolution', or that he has since been called the 'monk of a non-existent church'. From pronouncing his mission to be divinely inspired, it was only a short step to his proclaiming himself to his devotees – as he presently did to the Beyer sisters – a priestly voice speaking in the name of God. And with his veritable phobia of, and virulent campaign against, the fatal, devouring perils of all sensual, 'animal', material life, an aberrant element became definitely manifest in his youthful visionary posture, or posturing. Together with this element – variously described as 'a strain of abnormality' or a 'displaced love of mankind' – went an extraordinary personal magnetism and a spontaneity of action without which Bakunin would never have achieved his heroic stature and later influence.

The latest detailed studies of the dual sides of his bizarre personality have attributed the irreconcilable contradiction between his frightened self and his public marks of power to his psycho-sexual disturbance, leading to his alienation from reality and to a quest for self-fulfilment in utopian-messianic political fantasies, and ultimately to his vision of a world revolution destroying that reality to make room for the healing advent of the millennium. For the moment, the point worth noting is that Bakunin's anomalous attitude towards reality began long before he started his political-social agitation, or even developed any views on the subject.[22]

During the summer of 1835, he was in high spirits. His reconciliation with his sisters had been effected amid mutual protestations of devotion. He had revealed his 'mission' and his message to Natalie Beyer and Efremov, and to climax it all, Stankevich had promised to visit Premukhino. Though his new friends might require firming up, they were kindred spirits sharing not only his ideas and aspirations, but also – though for different, purely Romantic reasons – his abhorrence of gross 'animal' love.

When Belinsky later met Michael's 'little flock' of sisters, as Varinka called them – they struck him as morally 'elevated', angelic beings, immaculate 'strangers to all sins of the body and the flesh!' With Michael's sisters included in this circle, and his parents excluded from it, the platonic loves between some of its members lent it an affectionate intimacy free of 'vice'. It was like a noble brotherhood, recalling the happy family of Michael's childhood, and substituting a new harmony for its broken one.

In July, however, his father recalled him to practical reality. The elder Bakunin, still busy pulling strings to save his son from charges of desertion, had secured a respectable government post for him as special assistant to Count Tolstoy, the Governor of Tver, who happened to be a great-uncle of Michael. It was the kind of government sinecure that suited a gentleman and might also allow him some time for his private pursuits. The very thought of burying himself in an office job, however, was abhorrent to Michael. Later confessing his inability to 'stand firm' against his parent, he ostensibly consented to the post, but for a week afterwards drank himself into a daily stupor 'from morning until night'.

The 'strength of will' he kept expounding having failed him, even 'thoughts of suicide' flashed before his mind, or so he was to claim. By August, having not the slightest intention of keeping his agreement, he was privately confiding to the Beyer sisters and one or two other friends that he might leave home for Moscow or St Petersburg University, perhaps even for Berlin, the Mecca of German metaphysics.

While the issue of the Tver post was not yet acute until his Army discharge would come through towards the end of the year, Michael got busy organizing his 4 sisters, his teen-aged brothers, the two Beyer girls as well as Efremov into a 'holy commune' devoted to his 'divine mission'. The declared purpose of this 'kinship' or 'chorus of souls, fused into one', as he called it – with himself guiding and supervising their spiritual elevation like a benevolent 'father wishing only the inner happiness of his children' – was to make them all 'feel God within ourselves... to be divine beings, free and predestined for the liberation of mankind' from 'the instinctual laws of unconscious', that is, sensual-carnal, 'existence'.

Far from tampering with the innate piety of his sisters, Michael, still deeply religious himself, fed their thirsty souls a new, eye-opening interpretation of the Christian Gospels. To Tatyana it was 'this God whom you are teaching us to understand'; Lyubov felt that he helped them 'to see the purpose of our existence'; swayed by his sermons, Varinka – the only one of his sisters whose marriage to a certain Dyakov he had been unable to prevent – began to feel that she had betrayed her higher 'self' by allowing a 'stranger' – her spouse and the father of her child – 'to profane me with his caresses.' The perfect organization of his commune into 'free' and 'divine beings' was to preoccupy Bakunin well into 1836. By that time, against the self-denial and 'suffering' involved in the renunciation of physical pleasures as 'a necessary condition for happiness', he would offer the rewarding 'bliss' of the spiritual 'inner life', and invoke Jesus: 'Look at Christ, my friends.' He had 'suffered so much', had been misunderstood, 'and yet he was happy.' For the Saviour's life had been one of self-denial and he found all his satisfaction 'in the dissolution of his material I and in the salvation of all mankind.'[23]

Bakunin had yet to reach that high point in October 1835, when Stankevich arrived on his promised visit together with Efremov. Stankevich's stay at Premukhino did little to advance the undeclared romance between him and Lyubov. For the most lackadaisical of Russian Romantics could not work up the courage to pierce the wall of mutual shyness between them. With Stankevich's and Michael's circles now overlapping; with Lyubov, disappointed for the second time after the break-up of her engagement to Baron Renne; with Belinsky becoming hopelessly enamoured of Michael's youngest sister, Alexandra; and the Beyer girls at one point becoming more important 'soul sisters' to Michael than his own sisters, the stage was inevitably set for a complicated cross-current of personal illusions, disillusion and jealousies running beneath their high talk of 'self-perfection', their metaphysical interests and noble and sincere preoccupation with the destinies of mankind.

In the end, all those involved – except for Bakunin himself – were to have their feelings hurt. On the other hand, Stankevich's 10-day visit cemented his friendship with Michael and had the happiest results for both of them. Michael's search for his vocation may have led him onto strange paths, but his intelligence so impressed and stimulated the blasé, ill, often flagging Stankevich that – far from being worn out by Michael's 'torrential eloquence' – he felt revitalized and saved from 'deadly boredom', and undertook to introduce him to Kant's philosophy.

'You are formed for some noble work,' he wrote Michael shortly after his visit. 'You understand things so easily, believe so much in the worth of man that one cannot doubt your destiny.'[24]

If Natalie Beyer had observed the potential hidden in his 'force of character and ardent spirit', these words coming from Stankevich himself – who expressed himself in a similar vein to others, too – could not but confirm the young Bakunin's view of himself as one preternaturally chosen to become a leader or hero of mankind. Indeed, towards the end of 1835 he was inviting Efremov to join him in 'great deeds' and set out with him on 'the lonely trail to our aim'. As soon as his Army discharge came through, he meant to devote himself to it entirely. 'We have the strength... We will not stop.'

By then, however, Bakunin's own strength was being sorely tested. With Stankevich guiding him by correspondence, he had just started studying Kant when the whole Bakunin family moved to Tver for the opening of the winter season. There Michael, rebelling against the 'outside world', obstinately refused to leave his room, let alone to accompany any of his sisters to the balls, receptions and parties they were expected to attend. Let society fall apart – he had not the slightest intention of lifting a finger to help maintain its silly 'proprieties' and hypocritical obligations. And why should he help to throw his pure, virginal sisters into the arms of lovers and beastly men out to corrupt them – he who was destined to stamp out 'sensuality' and the animal lusts of the flesh?

Even Tatyana was now threatened, or so he suspected; a certain Count Sologub was courting her, and she seemed not entirely indifferent to him. Was she perhaps in love with this man? The question nagged at his mind even as New Year's Day 1836 approached, and he fretted over the issue of the government post arranged for him with Count Tolstoy. Michael's official discharge from the Army had come through on 18 December, and as the Bakunins were due to meet the Governor during New Year celebrations in Tver, a decision could no longer be postponed.

Michael's choice was not exactly between a 'hectic, fussy, bureaucratic job', as he called it, and his wish to study, between an office and the university. The job had been specially designed for him. But the practical idea of accepting a comfortable post and pursuing his private study of Kant in his leisure time probably never entered his head. Philosophy had become something of an obsession with him, and Stankevich had written him in praise of 'one-sided intellectual activity.' Besides, his personal freedom to do what he liked was at stake; it was his 'will' against his father's authority. Once again, however, young Bakunin shunned a showdown with his father – this time over his breach of promise, itself only given out of some fear of confronting him – and took wilful but evasive action.

Shortly after the New Year, he packed his bags and ran away to Moscow without a word to anyone, not even his shocked sisters. It was his father, however, who suffered the severest blow. The Count, almost 70, nearly blind and reduced to having the newspaper read to him, worried about the future of his unmarried daughters and that of his estate. Michael, he realized, would never live up to, or even try to assume, the responsibilities of an eldest son. He had personally looked after Michael's first education, and had encouraged him to study. But he felt that Michael, puffing away at his pipe, discussing philosophy at the universe with Stankevich in clouds of smoke, as they had done during the former's visit, was a poor way of acquiring any serious knowledge, as were Michael's ridiculous antics in Tver, locking himself up in his room with a pile of books and 'playing Diogenes' instead of taking his sisters to dancing parties.

Michael's debts, his dismissal from the Artillery School, his desertion – the old man had bailed him out of every kind of increasingly serious trouble. The son never took his advice, and he had lately stopped giving him any. But what angered and grieved him most was Michael's steady drive to 'rule the family' and the way he had gradually deprived him of almost any parental say in the affairs of his 9 children. The old man could see that his daughters were upset by Michael's unseemly flight to Moscow and his egotistical course of action. But as soon as they heard from Michael, they were only too keen to accept his justification of his action. Lyubov, Tatyana and Alexandra had given up all social distractions for the 'bliss' of cultivating their inner lives, and Varinka walked about like 'a fallen woman' expiating the sin of having married Dyakov, a 'stranger' and 'philistine' in Michael's terminology.

Hardly out of his teens, Bakunin had shorn his father of most of his power. Once a wise, undisputed *paterfamilias*, the proud, cultured master of Premukhino was reduced to the pitiful state of pleading to be left the 'moral direction' of at least some of his offspring: 'I am not forbidding you to follow your own path,' he wrote to Michael as soon as the latter had given a sign of life from Moscow. 'But I ardently beseech you at least not to lead Nicholas and the [four other] younger brothers astray.'[25]

Outwardly composed, inwardly boiling, the declining Count clung to his dignity and stately manners. He may not have suspected why Michael could not tolerate the thought of his sisters marrying, and did not know that before leaving he had written to Efremov that the common preoccupations with 'wealth, high society and rank' were not for him. The old Count felt challenged on all sides, threatened by this restive and incomprehensible son who kept subverting his household, upsetting not only his peaceful country retreat but all the standards of civilized behaviour, social norms and responsibilities he had inculcated in his children; in short, his whole world.

It was precisely against this world that Michael had rebelled – against his father's and all parental authority; against the silly 'proprieties observed by well-bred people'; against 'the yoke of hated obligations unillumined by feeling' and 'unworthy of a true man'; against custom, 'cold formulas and rules.'

In Moscow, where he arrived practically penniless, Bakunin gave free rein to his bohemian nature, 'breathed freely' and felt like a new man. In separate as well as joint letters to Varinka and Tatyana he explained his self-styled 'flight from Mecca to Medina' in the terms above quoted and made the further point that he could no longer live with a family that neither understood nor 'respected' him. He did not want to become a prim 'society hero', like Tatyana's Count Sologub, 'the perfect gentleman'. His soul was too big for 'custom, propriety and obligations'. He needed his 'personal freedom', and did not see why he should sacrifice his ideas and 'everything' to the mere 'habit and duties' of family love.

To his father he wrote: 'We have died to each other.' But he begged the Count to believe him, 'now that we are parting forever and are speaking to each other for the last time, that I do not pursue some egoistic goal and that it is not pleasure that I seek on my hard and lonely road.'

Indeed, parting with Premukhino and the privileges of 'wealth, high society and rank' meant having to work for a living. The most comfortable way seemed to give private lessons to a few rich boys. Consequently, on specially printed cards circulated in the houses of his noble acquaintances, M. de Bakunin, Professeur de Mathématiques, offered his services and waited confidently for pupils. None appeared. Bakunin, however, was never one to be long disheartened by financial problems. He lived for a month with Stankevich, then moved in for the next three months with Efremov. Determined never to yield to or be influenced by external circumstances, he lived by his wits, his charm, and his instincts, sponged without compunction on his friends, borrowed from perfunctory acquaintances, then would entertain them lavishly with their money.

'For the world I may be an insignificant creature, nothing, a teacher of mathematics,' he wrote to his sisters on 28 February 1836, 'but for myself, for the friends who understand me, I have risen much higher than before.' Having stifled 'the petty egoism of self-preservation' within himself, and shaken off every yoke, he proclaimed proudly: 'I am a man!'[26]

Indeed, through it all Bakunin had never wavered from the studies he had started the previous November. Shortly after his visit, Stankevich had sent him a copy of Kant's *Critique of Pure Reason* and began helping him through its more abstruse passages. Sometimes they discussed abstract points in daily letters. Stankevich was easily exhausted by Kant's dry style. Wrestling with Kant's 'skullbreaking' metaphysical concepts caused him headaches and insomnia, and afraid that Michael would soon 'throw Kant to the devil' – as he often felt like doing himself – he had warned him to take Kant's indigestible 'mess of boiled kasha' in small portions. But Bakunin's quick mind was as sturdy as his physique, and he had worked his way through the *Critique* with relative ease and remarkable industry even before his departure for Moscow. If his progress amazed Stankevich, it was actually not so surprising.

Since he had turned his back on society and its distractions, German philosophy – the presumed key to the hidden cosmic pattern governing the universe – had become his chief and absorbing interest. Shortly before he deserted from the Army he had wondered aloud what place he was 'predestined to occupy in the universal infinite machine'. Philosophy, helping him to find it, was further to help him in his newly discovered mission – 'to wrest from Nature its secrets, in order to reveal them to mankind, to overwhelm matter,' etc. When the younger of the Beyer girls, Alexandra, following in her sister's footsteps, fell in love with him and, dropping her defences as well as all 'spiritual' pretence, boldly declared that she longed to press herself bodily against him, Bakunin's famous rejoinder – that his love was reserved for his 'jealous wife', philosophy – was not only a facetious epigram covering up for his psychological aversion to all physical-erotic contacts, but contained a grain of figurative truth.

By the time he descended on Moscow at the beginning of 1836, Stankevich's circle had moved on from Kant to Fichte. Plunging with Stankevich into Johann Gottlob Fichte's *Guide to a Blessed Life*, Bakunin fell completely under the spell of this religious philosopher and Romantic moralist whose rousing 'Addresses to the German Nation' were to earn him a lasting and controversial reputation as the 'unarmed phophet' of German nationalism.

'He is the true hero of our time,' Bakunin was to declare some years later. Indeed, Fichte's precept that man 'should be what he is because he wills it'; his sublime 'indifference', as Bakunin duly noted, 'to external circumstances and opinion'; his insistence on 'spontaneity' and his capacity for 'moving directly towards the ends he has set himself' – all this could not but strike a deep chord in the heart of a young man in his early 20s who wished to be no Hamlet and dreamed of a 'career of action'. Long before such directness of aim was to become his own forte, Bakunin noted with pride: 'I possess similar qualities.' Openly expressing his envy of Fichte's 'extraordinary power' while aware that he still had to develop his own, he was all the more attracted to him because Fichte, too, 'had the blessing of God.'

In his youth, Fichte had been dismissed from his Weimar post for proclaiming that through love man was 'immortal as God himself, he is God himself.' Accused of creating or becoming his own god, as it were, Fichte invoked St John: 'He who dwelleth in love dwelleth in God and God in him.' To intellectuals Fichte further offered the challenge and the chance, as Bakunin now discovered, of taking part in the divine plan. For, since God had no existence outside the conscious mind of man, they – as scholars, sages, 'heroes, poets' and members of an élite occupying a superior vantage-paint, and capable of a 'higher morality' – were called upon to serve as 'priests of the truth' chosen by Providence to inspire mankind and make it become what it was meant to be: the image of the divine.

If Bakunin found confirmation in this of his own sacred mission, his sense of predestination as one of the elect, there was more in Fichte that was bound to

459

affect him profoundly. For in the latter's conception, once all men became aware that they were only 'the image, copy and manifestation' of the inward 'Divine Existence', then all conflicts and tension between subject (the individual) and object (the external material world), between the finite and the infinite or 'eternal', would be resolved through man's merger and fusion with the Absolute in a messianic age in which 'love' and 'harmony' would reign universal.

A yearning for love and harmony, for merging his soul with the Absolute – for a 'union with the root of his existence', as it has been called[27] – was perhaps Bakunin's deepest, and psychologically most significant, longing. 'The life of man', he had observed to Natalie Beyer in his May letter of the previous year, 'is an eternal striving of the part towards the whole.' Losing himself in the Absolute, in 'love for humanity and the striving towards the All', was his best hope of resolving the conflict between his strengths and his weaknesses. Nor was he the only one to be captivated by Fichte's vision of a Golden Age. That vision appealed strongly to all the frustrated young idealists of the mid-1830s, holding out as it did the hope and solace of a possible end to their alienation.

None, however, embraced Fichte so fervently as Bakunin. He translated his *Vocation of the Scholar* ('Einige Vorlesungen über die Bestimmung des Gelehrten') and started a veritable Fichtean cult among his friends and disciples. Fichte held that the suffering involved in renunciation of the senses acted as a 'salutary spur', and was a price worth paying in furthering man's striving towards the Absolute. Bakunin had early made a cult of 'suffering' and gloried in the strength he derived from it. From Moscow, in February 1836, not long after he had discovered Fichte, he wrote to his sisters Varinka and Tatyana that 'he who has not suffered cannot love or be happy.' In March he mentioned to them the 'Satanic happiness' of standing alone against the world, and was informing the two Beyer girls that he felt himself a man: 'My purpose is God.' Earth-shaking storms could neither frighten nor deflect him from his path as he advanced, with 'proud and inflexible will', towards his 'high destiny. I am a man. I will be God... I suffer because I am a man and want to be God.' It was at this point that he held up to his followers the figure of

> Christ, who suffered so much, who did not even know the joy of being fully understood by those around him, and yet he was happy, for he was the son of God, for his life was suffused with divinity, filled with self-denial, for he did everything for mankind and found all his satisfaction, his pleasure in the dissolution of his material I and in the salvation of all mankind.'[28]

All that was needed now was for Michael Bakunin to announce that he was himself the son of God and identify his own will with God's will. He came close to it later in 1836 when he wrote to his brothers that Jesus had been 'born man as we were' so that we could 'become God as he did' and that he was living 'directly in Christ and through him in the spiritual world.'[29]

Michael's new Fichtean rhetoric had a dazzling effect not only on his brothers and sisters – who variously declared that he had made them 'really understand man's destiny' and that he was their 'indispensable' teacher – or on such feminine devotees as his Beyer soul-sisters, to whom he became a 'priest of the truth', but also infected even Belinsky, the sharp-minded and visceral critic, who published Michael's translation of the *Vocation of a Scholar* in *The Telescope* without knowing that it represented only one, the chiefly religious, aspect of Fichte's over-all philosophy. Other young Moscow intellectuals, handicapped (as was Belinsky) by their ignorance of German and dependent on Michael's superficial mediation, similarly mistook the part for the whole. Belinsky himself was so captivated by Bakunin's personality that he now began to look up to him as his intellectual superior. Before he was to break free of his influence after several years of hard inner struggle, he kept arguing vehemently with others that Fichte's 'eternal spirit' was the only reality, and all the rest a shadow.[30]

Only Stankevich poured cold water on Bakunin's Fichtean fireworks. Studying the philosopher's system more thoroughly than any of them in a carriage taking him to the Caucasus, he cautioned Michael in a letter in April 1836: 'Out of the laws of mind he [Fichte] constructs a whole world of phantoms, and of the mind itself he makes a phantom. It's all done so neatly! ... but an oppressive sense of complete doubt prevented my enjoying it.'[31]

This surprisingly (for a poet) realistic reservation did little, however, to dampen Michael's enthusiasm for Fichte. The latter's idea that certain men were destined to become 'teachers' and 'guides of humanity' – and that anyone so chosen must always 'act, and therefore be' himself, without yielding to the attractions of the external world – expressed too well what he had long felt about himself. Besides, Bakunin functioned best in an atmosphere of 'exhilarating make-believe', and needed it like air for breathing. Much of his later revolutionary activity was to be a life-long attempt to change the world by imposing 'phantom' ideas and his own fantasies on the 'separate facts' of reality.

Bakunin was too mettlesome a character and too thirsty for action to have the makings of an abstract thinker. In philosophy, he 'sought life,' he was to confess to the Tsar years later, 'I sought deeds.' His delvings into Kant, Fichte and later Hegel were neither systematic nor comprehensive, but he had a knack for quickly seizing on those essentials that suited or reflected – as in the case of Fichte – the needs of his own life, temperament and make-up, or that could be 'dialectically' turned round to serve them. In his own incoherent philosophical writings, modern scholars were to discover 'sparks of truth and astonishing discernment', as

461

well as 'a sense of method in their madness', but that too showed particularly where his thought was 'closely linked with his erratic life.'[32]

With his formidable ego and eloquence, his ambition, intelligence, restless energy and 'the germ of a colossal activity', as Herzen was to call it, he could have become almost anything – 'an agitator, a tribune, a preacher, the head of a party or a sect, a heresiarch or a fighter.' But his philosophical explorations in 1836 were mainly a search for himself. At 22, in spite of his defection from the Army, he was still a Russian patriot and dandyish nobleman with not a care about the Tsar's tyranny or the indignities of serfdom. One of his mother's younger relatives – Sergei N. Muraviev, then in his mid-20s – had actually fired his nationalist feelings beyond anything he experienced in his father's conservative home. During his service in Poland he had also met General Michael Nikolayevich Muraviev, 'the Hangman', who was Governor of Grodno. It was only a year or so since Bakunin, invited by the general to witness his effective methods of interrogation, had written a letter patriotically justifying Muraviev's brutal measures against the Polish rebels on the grounds of inevitable and 'excusable' necessity.

But his personal problems were legion, and torn between the contradictory forces of his character, he strove more than any of his generation for a healing harmony and wholeness. To most of his friends, excepting Belinsky, intellectual speculation was an 'aristocratic urge for self-fulfilment'. To the young Bakunin it was a veritable battle for his identity and his place in life. In his megalomaniac mission, in impersonal love and the welfare of humanity at large, he found a way of relating to a hostile world in which he otherwise felt an alien.

He had yet to find any pupils for private lessons. But there were inspiring evenings in Stankevich's apartment, where his circle met regularly on Fridays and the discussions – about 'God, truth, the future of mankind, and poetry,' as Ivan Turgenev was to write – made the night fly past 'as if on wings'; and the participants would disperse at dawn 'with a kind of pleasant weariness' in their souls. There were also suppers at the house of the Beyer sisters and in other places frequented by Moscow's intellectual young guard and advanced literati.

As depicted by Turgenev, the atmosphere at Stankevich's meetings was one of study, rejoicing and veneration,

> as if I had entered a temple... Imagine, 5 men and 6 boys, one tallow candle burning, tea of the filthiest taste is handed round... But you should have seen our faces... In all eyes there was rapture, and cheeks burned... Pokorsky [Stankevich] would sit with his legs tucked under him, resting his pale cheek in his hand... Rudin [Bakunin] would stand in the middle of the room and talk, talk eloquently, just like a young Demosthenes before a raging sea.

But in 1836 Turgenev had yet to join the circle. Though he met Bakunin only later in Germany, his semi-fictional account of the Romantic atmosphere of the 1830s evoked both the lofty, intoxicating spirit of some of these evenings and the figure of the young Bakunin holding the centre of the stage: imposingly tall and talkative, he was, with his leonine head, impossible to overlook in any company.

But the tea served was hardly of the cheapest kind. The poet Konstantin Aksakov, one of the circle's earliest members, described Stankevich's 'low-ceilinged rooms full of tobacco smoke' as presenting to the visitor 'a lively and variegated', hardly temple-like scene, with Stankevich playing the piano, the sound of voices singing, and 'young and gay faces on all sides.'[33]

'Here [in Moscow] all the capacities of my spirit have unfolded,' Bakunin wrote to his sisters. No longer bound by custom, 'hated obligations' and the family routine of Premukhino, he felt free as a bird. Stankevich's company was so uplifting that 'in his presence, no one could have a cowardly or trivial thought.' He was elated, too, by his new and growing friendship with Belinsky, who in spite of his fierce articles lacked self-assurance in society and was now as impressed as Stankevich had been by Michael's liveliness, energy and aplomb.

Bakunin had been in Moscow barely two months when, in the third week of February 1836, he started a new battle against his father by challenging a certain Vladimir Rzhevsky – who had started courting his elder sister Lyubov – to a pistol duel.

His parents' approval of the match so alarmed Michael (a renewed nuptial threat to Lyubov's 'modesty') that he insisted the duel be fought to the death – at a distance of 'five paces... without seconds who might be able to end it.' The duel ended in fact before it began, for Michael managed to intimidate the poor suitor into signing a promise to sever all contacts with Lyubov. At virtually the same moment, Michael became engaged in a campaign for the 'liberation' of the younger of the two Beyer girls, Alexandra, from the domination of her mother, who was trying to coerce her into a marriage of convenience. Alexandra, who was 20, had taken a fancy to Fedor Rzhevsky – a brother of Vladimir – and was threatening to run away and bury herself for life in a convent.

But Alexandra and Natalie Beyer were now under Bakunin's protection as members of his 'holy commune'. As the benevolent 'father' and spiritual mentor of this self-styled 'kinship', or 'chorus of souls, fused into one' – or 'pseudofamily', as others have called it – he had created for himself, he felt it his duty and only natural to 'deliver' Alexandra from maternal oppression and a forced marriage. He leapt to the task with great relish.

It pitched the domineering young Bakunin, a Fichtean 'priest' of divine 'truth', against the widowed Madame Beyer. He was cool, cynical, impervious to suffering and his weaknesses, which by a mixture of self-deceit and bluff he metamorphosed into a triumph over the flesh, a victory of the 'pure' and God-like over 'beastly' passion, priding himself, moreover, on his 'inflexible will... to achieve my high destiny.' Madame Beyer with her calculating practicality was poorly armed against his combination of evangelism and megalomania. He had made it his mission to lead her daughter back to God and addressed Alexandra in the following terms:

> I speak with you in the name of God, who wants to have you among his children. He will speak to you through my lips... This God, this absolute love, is bliss. Alexandra, I am called to be its priest. Forget that you are speaking to a young man you know... Look on me as the being called upon to deliver you, to open before you the gates of truth.

Alexandra was under no circumstances to throw away her life by hiding in 'passive prayer' in a nunnery. The essence of God was 'freedom', and he, Michael Bakunin, would look after everything.[34]

He did. His 'holy commune' was a paradigm of the many secret societies, brotherhoods, 'alliances, parties and federations' he was to conjure up during his later public career. It was only natural that in running it he showed some of the charisma, commanding authority and capacity for intrigue which were to become his hallmarks. He directed Varinka to help save Alexandra Beyer from her mother's clutches by inviting the girl to stay with her on the pretext that 'she can help you raise your son and ease your suffering'; he instructed Alexandra how to reply; and, by a series of coolly calculated steps mixing courtesy towards her mother with masterful and relentless interference in her household, he soon reduced Madame Beyer, who may or may not have been emotionally out of control, to hysterics. By mid-March he was describing to Varinka how he dealt with one of her tantrums when, arriving at the Beyer house, he heard 'dreadful, piercing shrieks' from the parlour: 'We found the mistress of the house rolling on the floor... Alexandra wanted to run away.'

According to his account, Michael led her and Natalie upstairs and directed them to ignore their mother's carryings-on and her 'terrifying wails'. Madame Beyer, seeing that her daughters 'did not throw themselves at her feet', got up after a while. Pretending that she had fainted, she called for the girls to come downstairs, accused herself of being 'vile, base, loathsome, stupid', and in the midst of this orgy of self-abuse 'suddenly asked if I were there and if I had seen her hysteria.' In the same and other letters he explained with great satisfaction that she couldn't stand him, but was afraid of him; 'We have her firmly in hand... She cannot take a step without our permission,' and 'I will not relax my power.'[35]

Bakunin eventually had his way. He packed Alexandra off to Varinka's estate near Premukhino, saving her both from the iniquity of a forced marriage, as he had saved Lyubov, and from 'the filth' and 'humbug' of life in a nunnery. With that settled, he went on developing his 'holy commune'.

One thing he insisted upon strongly was that both his siblings and his two Beyer soul-sisters fulfil and 'bend to' his will. They must trust him absolutely or 'not believe in me at all.' For his 'I' was of 'divine origin. It commands circumstances. It rules them.' They could hide nothing from him, for he could read their souls, 'foresee your feelings, even your doubts.' And once he had destroyed Madame Beyer's authority, as he had that of his own parents, her daughter Alexandra was told in April 1836 that 'giving yourself in friendship' to him meant giving him 'eternal rights to yourself.' Of Natalie, who stayed on with her mother, he wrote triumphantly the same month that she could do 'nothing against my will.'[36]

His beloved sister Tatyana was so enthusiastic about his teaching and the ideas that drew them 'completely together' in the commune that – having only the previous year raved with jealousy at his interest in the two Beyer girls – she actually urged him to 'resurrect their splendid souls' and help them achieve the 'celestial harmony' of 'the inner life about which you preached to her [Natalie] so much'; and before long the two sets of young ladies vied with one another in their adulation of him. Bakunin preached to them that love was freedom, that convictions – his convictions – came before everything.

To Alexandra Beyer he quoted Jesus: 'Leave everything, father and mother, follow me. For I am the truth...'

Through all this, he continued to translate Fichte's *The Vocation of the Scholar* and to shine in Stankevich's circle. The importance of this circle lay in the fact that it provided young intellectuals – at a time when Russian literature had yet to take off with Turgenev, Dostoyevsky and Tolstoy, and when literary magazines 'reached a reading public of only a few hundred subscribers in all of Russia and died easily of inanition or through government action'[37] – with a forum where they could exchange ideas, read their works and discuss foreign, chiefly German, philosophy and literature. The circle met on Fridays at the house of the Beyer sisters, and it was to Natalie Beyer that Bakunin had first invoked 'the hand of God' for his mission on the basis of the Fichtean notion that man's nature was essentially divine.

In 1836, *The Telescope* was suppressed for publishing an article called 'First Philosophical Letter'. It was written by Peter Chaadayev, the grandson of a well-known historian, Prince Shcherbatov, and a highly educated former Guards officer who had shown a bent for philosophy in his youth. In 1814, at the age of 20, he had entered Paris in Alexander I's honour guard, but in 1821, feeling that only 'he who despises the world doesn't care to reform it', he had resigned from the Army, declining the position of an Imperial adjutant. A close friend of Pushkin, whom he had first met when the poet was 17, Chaadayev associated with the Decembrist officers, but at the time of their abortive insurrection he was abroad as he had been for several years. On his return to Russia he was arrested, but released. An elegant and rather aloof, eccentric figure (*le beau Tchaadaev*, as he was known in society circles), he had studied the philosophy of Schelling, whom he also met in person. He knew some of Hegel's works and had been impressed by his theory of history as a meaningful process. His first 'Philosophical Letter', written in 1829, and the 7 that followed it had been circulating privately in manuscript form among Moscow and St Petersburg intellectuals.

'We are not of the West or of the East, and we have the traditions of neither,' he wrote. 'We take only ready-made ideas... We grow but we do not mature, we advance, but in an oblique line, that is to say one which does not lead to the goal.' An intellectual skeptic, Chaadayev held that Russia's future would be as gloomy as her present. Deploring her lack of roots in the fertile, chiefly Catholic subsoil of European civilization, he attributed her ills and her spiritual barrenness to her Greek-Orthodox religion, which had separated her from the mainstream of European history and any 'progressive movement of ideas'. Without it, Russians with their barbarous past shifted aimlessly and without direction from one theory to another, constantly asking themselves: 'Where are we?... With us, new ideas sweep away the old because they do not spring and grow out of them.'

Whether the publisher of *The Telescope*, Professor Nadezhdin, printed Chaadayev's 'Letter' without his knowledge, or was induced to do so by Chaadayev himself – who is known to have said that he wished to bequeath his ideas 'to the world' – neither of them foresaw its effect, or the personal consequences to themselves.

At a time when Russian officials suspected even the author of the most innocent literary essay of using hidden language – 'by the word Enlightenment he means freedom, the mind's activity is to be read as revolution, and the skilfully contrived middle ground is nothing less than a constitution'[38] – Chaadayev's 'Letter' was like 'a shot that rang out in the dark... It shook all thinking Russia.' Thus wrote Herzen, who read the piece when *The Telescope* reached him in Siberian Vyatka.[39]

The Tsar's angry retaliation magnified its unexpected impact. Acting on his imperial (and presumably psychiatric) authority, Nicholas I ordered Chaadayev to be declared insane. The man of whom Pushkin wrote that in Rome he would have been 'a Brutus, in Athens, Pericles' – and of whom Osip Mandelshtam was to say that he left a mark on the consciousness of Russian society 'as sharp and indelible as that which a diamond cuts into glass' – was forbidden to write, and placed under a doctor's supervision.[40]

The following year, Nicholas I put his seal to a Censorship Law so drastic that Nikitenko, the liberated serf who became a distinguished university professor, resigned his post as a censor. In his diary he observed that when Russia's young found that 'every fresh thought was considered a crime against the social order', that what was expected of them was 'soulless compliance' and that 'educated men in our society were outlaws', the whole young generation 'felt out of gear.'

To this alienated generation, confined to a bookish existence and seeking refuge in the works of Goethe, Schiller and E.T.A. Hoffmann's fantastic tales, Fichte's half-mystic philosophy brought the message that the subjective 'life of thought' actually constituted the true and real life, rather than the 'apparent' or phantom world of external reality. God, in essence, was Knowledge, or Consciousness of Being, 'the true World-Creator', and man's nature was essentially divine: 'Insofar as we are Knowledge, we ourselves, in the deepest root of our being, are the Divine Existence.' While self-cognition and 'pure thought' – rather than the idolatry of ceremonial worship – were the first steps in approaching God, man, according to Fichte, could practically 'will' himself to be God by concentrating on the 'indwelling', 'suprasensual' life of the mind. The more he renounced the external material world, the more he would be 'free to dominate it according to his own will.'

This message not only went directly to Bakunin's heart, but offered to others of his purposeless and 'superfluous generation' the comforting notion that by cultivating their souls and inner lives they were – 'like chess-players who see only their game' (as Bakunin himself was later to put it in his *Confession to the Tsar*) – actually living a higher reality that transcended the grim, repugnant real world around them.

Bakunin had earlier informed Natalie Beyer that 'the separate facts of reality' were less important than the idea they expressed. 'And what is this idea?... Love for humanity, and the striving toward the All, toward perfection.'

No wonder that the gloomy picture of Russia past, present and future presented by Chaadayev shook her progressive young idealists out of their Romantic self-indulgence and escapist preoccupations. Not that they passed immediately from philosophy to political action. Chaadayev's essay was ultimately to lead to the split between the so-called 'Westernizers', keen on adopting the values of Western civilization, and the 'Slavophiles' who, led by Ivan Kireevsky, maintained that Russia would be redeemed not by Western 'logic' but by a combination of reason with intuition and the type of traditional institutions – like the village communes – instinctively developed by the Russian people, and anchored

467

and imbedded in her own history and culture. Alexander Herzen, raised on the best that European civilization had to offer but disillusioned by the materialism of its bourgeoisie as soon as he arrived in Paris on the eve of the 1848 revolution, was to be torn between the two currents. Although he spent the rest of his life in the West, he never lost his respect for the unspoilt Russian peasantry and its communal system. And the dedicated role played by the young intelligentsia of the 1830s, particularly Stankevich's circle, in 'silently undermining the compact crust' of tsarism was to inspire Herzen's life-long belief that 'such fresh young forces', appearing whenever Russia 'had a chance of stretching her limbs', might yet save her and even help to revitalize Western civilization.[41]

But in 1836 Herzen was in Siberia, and in Stankevich's circle hardly anyone thought that the study of philosophy could lead to practical conclusions translatable into action. Stankevich did not think so, nor, as we have seen, did he share Bakunin's enthusiasm for Fichte's 'phantoms'. Stankevich is believed to have influenced Bakunin's refusal to accept the Tver post, but in defending 'one-sided intellectual activity', he made some interesting observations on the mechanics of bureaucratic government and the official Russian idea that 'the State should be a kind of machine.' Remarking that 'a machine is damaged by time' and 'is smashed in order to be repaired', Stankevich wrote that 'the machine is no model for a society.' Men who tried to improve the agriculture of the Russian peasantry were called 'practical... But why not be concerned that the people themselves begin to think and that they themselves find means [for promoting] their own welfare?' In Europe, Stankevich went on, ideas were now abroad to educate the people in science, art and religion. 'These are just dreams, they say; such things have never happened... Every century sees events that never before occurred, and I am convinced that one day things will happen that no one ever dreams of.'[42]

In introducing Bakunin to Kant, Stankevich had warned him not to allow his Romantic, religiously tinged metaphysical speculations and tendency towards abstraction to make him forget reality. He urged him to complement his study of Kant with the study of history. 'Divorced from history, knowledge is dead and dry,' he had written. 'One must join the unity of idea to the variety of concrete facts – such is the ideal of Knowledge.'[43]

But Bakunin, with his mighty ego and capacity for make-believe, was neither mentally nor temperamentally ready to desist from bending the 'separate facts' of reality to his will. His Fichtean metaphysics was merely a phase in his long training for the adventurous role of a revolutionary leader, a hero in the double struggle for 'absolute liberty' and 'love of humanity' in the abstract.

In April 1836, his fourth month in Moscow, Bakunin was engaged by a family called Ponomarev to tutor their son in mathematics and physics. At last he was earning some money. But his mind was on his sister Tatyana at Premukhino and her disturbing 'affair' with Count Sologub. He kept plying her with letters – was she still in love with that prig , or with someone else? 'Answer me quickly, tell me the truth, I beg and beseech you!' At the same time he had to fend off Natalie Beyer, whose long-suppressed 'animal' nature got the better of all his preaching; try as she might to enjoy the bliss of idealized 'spiritual' love, she found no contentment in it. While her sister was away at Varinka's estate, Natalie gave vent to her frustration by letting Michael know that unless they could have a more concrete relationship she was ready to forgo his 'friendship' altogether.

Caught between her intolerable erotic insistence and his conviction that he was the innocent 'cause of the sufferings of a girl I love, but whose torments I cannot assuage,' as he finessed the point to his sisters, Michael fleetingly considered marrying Natalie, but gave up the idea. As E.H. Carr observed, 'the alternative remedy' of leaving the girl alone 'never entered his head.' Instead, he rebuked her for her heresy and for expecting a man like himself, 'capable of ideal love', ever to 'lower himself to the state of being in love.'

As for Tatyana, she sent her brother an intimate letter in which – judging from the fact that she asked him to burn it, and from his ecstatic reply of 15 April – she seems to have done little to discourage his unhealthy infatuation with her. Michael, feeling 'loved again' by his adored Tanichka, confessed that he had not burned her letter. 'I shall keep it for ever, and never part with it for a single moment... Nothing will ever separate us! If you could only know, if you could only feel but half the bliss which your letter has brought me ... How I want to see you again, to press you tightly, tightly to my heart, to tell you things that one cannot say in letters... I feel now that I love you more than anything in the world, you have become my one idol on earth.' Tatyana had made light of her flirtation with Count Sologub, and Michael assured her no other eye had 'profaned' her letter to him.[44]

Eight days later, on 23 April, he could not resist writing to Tanichka again 'how I love you and how I have always loved you, how I suffered at the very thought of your indifference to me and how impossible it would be to replace you in my heart with anyone else.' Tatyana wrote back: 'Thank you, a thousand times thank you! If I had wings I would fly into your arms and press you to my heart.'[45]

Although she assured him again that he had no reason to be jealous of Sologub, and Michael was now calm on this point, he may have begun to be perturbed by the incestuous implications of his jealousy. Before very long he was to discuss his bewildering 'feeling for Tanichka' with the Beyer sisters, and to take his problem to Belinsky as well.

Discussing one another's psyche and love affairs, it should be obvious by now, was natural practice in Stankevich's circle. Moreover, the circle provided each of its members with 'collective support' in 'every department of his life', taking 'an active interest in his moral, physical and financial condition,' often banding together to help him.[46]

Nevertheless, the chief feature of the group remained the free comradely exchange of ideas and 'intellectual stimulation' it offered its members. As against this, the young Bakunin in his 'holy commune' tolerated no dissent among his disciples, but demanded absolute subservience to his ideas. As a self-styled 'priest' and 'servant of God,' he became the 'director of their consciences', as it were, and kept up a ceaseless stream of arguments to brainwash them into submission. It has been rightly observed that Bakunin sought not friends, but 'partisans'.

When his own sisters, exercising the rights of kin, felt free to question his treatment of their father, Michael was hurt. Offended by the suggestion that he was 'tyrannizing' anyone, he took his grievance to the Beyer sisters and assured them that they were 'much more his sisters' than his real but 'involuntary siblings'.

Absorbed with these personal matters and others affecting his commune, he hardly had the mind for coaching young Ponomarev in mathematics and physics. Instead, he gave him a more interesting time by inciting the boy to rebel against his parents, their conventional values and 'moribund' world.

Then, in mid-May, he abruptly packed his bags and left Moscow. Natalie and Alexandra Beyer had each gone away; Stankevich was on a health cure in the Caucasus; and with most of his other friends dispersing for the summer, the city held little attraction for him. Poor Ponomarev, his only pupil, was left in the lurch on the eve of his examinations, and would have to fend for himself. But where was Michael to go? His spirit had 'unfolded' and taken wings, but he was destitute. To his father at Premukhino, which he had stealthily fled only a little over 4 months earlier, he had written breaking off their relations. In his reply, the father had given his rebellious son a piece of his mind:

> True philosophy consists not in visionary theories and empty word-spinning, but in carrying out everyday obligations to family, society and country. You neglect these obligations for the pursuit of chimeras, and chatter about some inner life which compensates you for the loss of everything else... One way is still open to you to prove that your heart is not quite dead... Efface the past by your obedience, and rather believe your blind father than your blind – call it what you will. This is my last word.

Elsewhere in the letter the elder Bakunin ironically suggested that Michael's head was not yet cured of its fever, while 'your heart is silent.' Michael's reaction to his father's lines had been to inform his sisters that he was through with his parents: 'Where love is, there are no obligations,' he had written to them in March. Duty excluded love, and was therefore 'wicked and mean. For me, parents do not exist. I renounce ours. I do not need their love.'[47]

Having burned his bridges to Premukhino, it was nevertheless to Premukhino that he returned in May – not, however, in order to be a 'good and obedient son', but to glory in his new Fichtean role. He confessed that he needed 'people who feel confident under my direction,' and where else was he to find them if not in his devoted 'flock' of 4 sisters at Premukhino?

In that lyrical and romantic setting, with its ivied houses and moonlit grottoes, Michael – idle, unencumbered by responsibilities or economic worry, remote from the sensual allurements of the hated 'external world' – now led them through Fichte's *Blessed Life*, as he had once led them and his younger brothers on their romps through orchards, fields and woods. Instead of singing *Au clair de la lune* on enchanted evenings, they now read and discussed the poetry of Goethe and Schiller. Gone was the awe they had once experienced during Holy Week and other Church rituals – vespers, Gospel readings, confessions, communion, the washing of the icons, Good Friday and Christ's shroud. Now Michael led his intensely pious sisters away from 'that God to whom they pray in churches', hypocritically 'abasing themselves before him', to 'the one who lives in mankind' and 'speaks in the poet.'

Basking in their rapt admiration – while simultaneously guiding the two Beyer girls by correspondence – he began to initiate all of them more fully into his mission of bringing out the divine in man, 'bringing the heaven, the God he bears in himself, down to our earth.'

He had not yet turned atheist. Nor had any of them. On the contrary, as a messianic servant of God, Michael kept invoking Jesus, Calvary and the virtues of Christian (and, in his case, very likely masochistic) suffering required of them in their struggle for inner perfection. Soon enough, however, seeing himself as a second Jesus 'become God as he did', he was to call on his disciples to proselytize for his commune; to remind the Beyer sisters that they had been present at his 'christening into truth, present at the beginning of my eternal life,' and that together they had founded that 'sacred church' which was to be turned into a 'Kingdom of the Holy Spirit' on earth, on the model of the brotherhood that 'He had come among the people' to establish.[48]

When he reached his megalomaniac-militant stage, he would go on invoking the Saviour, but the one who had 'not come to bring peace, but a sword', and would quote St Mark: 'I have come to set a man against his father, and a daughter against her mother', etc.[49] That phase was still a year or so away. For the moment suffering was 'the most sublime manifestation of the divinity of man', as exemplified by his own experience: 'I am a man, and I will be God... I suffer because I am a man and want to be God.'

But the seeds of that combative attitude were already evident in his revolt against his father, against the 'animal' in man (sex) and the material world (society) and its conventional laws and 'cut-price practical morality', in his war for 'the liberation of enslaved mankind', indeed, the whole universe, from its coarse instincts and 'unconscious existence'. This was a war he announced in that summer of 1836 and was to wage at length and relentlessly. It was also a war fought in practice chiefly to undo his sister Varinka's marriage and to save her (as he had saved Lyubov and Alexandra Beyer) from 'the terrifying humiliations' imposed by man's 'beastly passion' upon the modesty and shyness of innocent women. In Varinka's case, he agreed that Dyakov, her husband and the father of her child, was a decent and nice enough fellow. But he had evolved a new argument: whereas Varinka, now one of his most faithful disciples, though a 'fallen woman', was being guided by him towards a celibate state of 'inner perfection'. Dyakov was a coarse sensualist and stood 'outside the Absolute'.[50]

Bakunin's increasing extremism began to manifest itself in his black-and-white division of things into good and evil. 'Either everything is sacred', he instructed the Beyer sisters in August 1836, 'or everything is a wretched farce' and 'putrefaction. Between those poles there is no middle...' There could be no 'golden mean' of the type pursued by ordinary people, only passive retreat or pitiless struggle. From this, it was only a short step to his telling these trusted co-founders of his 'holy commune' – when the time came to raise and transform it into the militant 'Kingdom of the Holy Spirit' – that they must show 'no mercy' to its heartless enemies. 'Our union', he was to remind them, 'was founded on the ruins, on the utter destruction of the laws of the world.'[51]

Only two of Michael's brothers escaped his influence. Nineteen-year-old Nicholas was at the Artillery School in St Petersburg and Ilya, 18, was with an Army regiment elsewhere. But three others – Paul (16), Alexander (15) and Alexis (13) – were at home that summer. Though their father had specifically beseeched Michael to refrain from leading at least his younger children astray, Michael could hardly wait to draw them into the Fichtean orbit and make them full members of his commune. The opportunity came in August, when he escorted the three of them to Tver for the start of the school year, and stayed with them for a fortnight. Impressing upon their young minds his version of Fichte's theory of the 'God in man', of man being what he 'wills' to be, he taught them the virtues of the 'inner life' as a shield against the trivial and boring impositions – such as school – of the external one.

Taking his exhortations about man's 'absolute freedom' and his high destiny seriously, the three youngsters were soon to take theirs into their hands and to run away from school, a result (in this case unintended) proving perhaps better than anything else the spirit of revolt inherent already at this stage in his religious rhetoric.

During his short absence from Premukhino, his sisters joined in an epistolary chorus to sing his praises. Tatyana's heart overflowed with a 'flaming love for this God you are teaching us to know, for you, for all my friends, for all creatures striving towards the same goal as ourselves.' With Alexander, in the name of the three boys in Tver, writing home that he had raised them 'high above our former state' and had become 'indispensable' to them too, Michael returned to Premukhino in an exhilarated mood. Uplifted by the 'identity of our eternal aims', he rejoiced at the new 'divine harmony' he had – now that his father hardly dared, or no longer cared, to interfere in his affairs – found 'in my own family'.

Crowning that glorious summer, Vissarion Belinsky arrived shortly afterwards. It was the end of August, and the extended visit of this consumptive young critic – who by virtue of his tremendous and lasting literary influence would in time come to be regarded as Russia's greatest historian of ideas – Premukhino assumed an importance which would lead, in the 20th century, to its comparison to Madame de Staël's home at Coppet. Belinsky, Stankevich, Botkin, the poet Klinshaikov, and later Turgenev were only some of the intellectuals who at one time or another during the 1830s and '40s came to the patrician Bakunin retreat. There they would be treated by Michael and his sisters to philosophical and Romantic discussions. There too some of them were introduced to the ideas of Fichte, and later Hegel, as well as to the writings of Bettina Brentano von Arnim.

Not many months before Belinsky's visit, von Arnim had created a great stir in Germany by publishing Goethe's *Correspondence with a Child*, three volumes based (with some embellishments) on her own girlishly effusive letters to the Olympian of Weimar. A friend of the Prussian Crown Prince, she was one of the first to grasp and draw attention to the plight of the poor, and to dare to challenge the Prince when he began his absolute rule. Her famous salon in Berlin's Unter den Linden was to become the last refuge of liberalism in the reactionary Berlin of the 1840s. In spite of her flowery style, she is today ranked by some among the great emancipated women of her time – along with George Sand, Marie d'Agoult and George Eliot – and by others as one of the three people, next to Heine and Nietzsche, who embodied 'the spirit of freedom [in Germany] in the nineteenth century.'[52]

In Paris, in 1836, Heine was surprised, in conversation with George Sand about Bettina, to learn that neither she nor other educated French people had ever heard of her. At Premukhino, however, about that time Michael was trans- lating Goethe's *Correspondence with a Child* as a labour of love. His doing so 'at night in the garden, sitting above the grotto, by the light of a lantern,' epito- mized the magic, romantically surreal – though to its denizens entirely natural – atmosphere of that 'nobleman's nest' where, curiously enough, the aristocrati- cally carefree young Bakunin developed into the most violent of revolutionaries.

It was during Belinsky's summer visit to Premukhino, too, that Bakunin's ab- normal infatuation with Tatyana became manifest – with the result that before Belinsky had spent a full month with what Stankevich had described to him as 'the ideal' Bakunin family, he found himself in the centre of one of its periodi- cally raging storms.

Belinsky had arrived in a state of trepidation. He was an ungainly figure worn out by overwork and consumption; he was so poor that some of the money for his visit had been provided by Stankevich and his circle. As diffident as Stankevich himself, but lacking the other's irresistible charm, Belinsky had heard from him so much about this perfect Eden of beauty and cultured leisure that he had anxiously wondered how he – a clumsy, poverty-stricken plebeian – would fit into this refined 'new realm', which at first struck him as breathing 'harmony and bliss'. Like others before and after him, he was entirely and lastingly enchanted by Pre- mukhino's 'flowering oasis' of Nature and 'perfected humanity'. In that country retreat ideally suited for living 'a sublime and transcendent life,' to which he would always dream of retiring to 'cleanse the dust' from his own wretched existence, the unhappy Belinsky – as he later wrote to Michael – found a healing balm that soft- ened his soul, 'its bitterness passed away'. Michael's sisters elicited Belinsky's par- ticular admiration. The contemplative, philosophically minded young ladies struck him not simply as charming paragons of virtue – 'strangers to all sins of the body, free of envy, malice, hatred' – but as the collective 'realization of all my con- ceptions of woman.' They were beyond compare – before them even Stankevich, the most 'elevated' person he knew, was 'a thousand times less than nothing.'[53]

He fell hopelessly in love with Alexandra, the youngest of them. With Michael and his sisters soaking him in Fichtean ideas, he experienced a 'rebirth' and 'resurrection', a second 'christening'. Joining in the enthusiasm of the young Bakunins, he wrote an article for *The Telescope*, extolling Fichte's 'ideal life' as being more real and satisfying than the empty, illusory satisfactions and 'phantoms' of real life.

This article annoyed Michael's father when it came to his attention. Tatyana, on the other hand, greeted it with cries of admiration, which in turn made Michael burn with jealousy – especially when she wrote to her younger brothers in Tver that Belinsky was the true and best interpreter of the new Fichtean 'man-God', better, by implication, than himself. Vissarion Belinsky, who sometimes coughed blood when excited, usually kept his peace in society and spoke little. But when provoked in argument, he became 'Vissariono Furioso', the nickname given him because of his ferocious literary polemics. He had already incurred the displeasure of Michael's father by an aggressive remark at the dinner table which had left the conservative head of the 'ideal' household with the impression that he was a revolutionary hothead. Belinsky's Fichte article did the rest, inadvertently sparking off and bringing down on his head the simmering rages of both Bakunins, father and son.

At the dinner in question, a discussion had developed about the French Revolution. When Count Bakunin expressed his horror at the many heads chopped off by the guillotine during the Terror, Belinsky had been surprised to see Michael taking his father's part. Offended in his sense of history, he not only defended the Terror and the executions but, completely forgetting his host's feelings and impervious to the consternation he was causing, declared that there were many 'heads that still await the guillotine.'

Count Bakunin, retaining his composure as best he could, spared his guest, but when he came upon Lyubov and Tatyana listening starry-eyed to Belinsky expounding the 'transcendent life' – he was reading his Fichte article to them – the old count found it too much to bear. His instinct told him that under the guise of studying philosophy Michael and his friends were not only depriving him of the 'moral direction' of his children, but inciting his daughters to nothing less than revolution, and under his own roof. While he took his anger out on his son, Michael, for his part, could not stand the sight of his beloved Tatyana poring over Belinsky's article, making a copy of it in her delicate hand before he sent it to *The Telescope*. Worse and more galling, she declared that it was an 'inexpressibly' moving revelation of 'the true and holy religion', of which Michael considered himself the chief apostle and head priest.

Michael's savage reaction was to snub, embarrass, provoke and humiliate Belinsky in every possible way. He made crude jokes about him, alluded to his plebeian origin and otherwise did his best to hurt his self-esteem and humble him in front of the family and drawing-room guests. As Alexandra showed little inclination to return Belinsky's feelings of love, he was in the depths of despondency. Yet because of Tatyana's purely intellectual interest in him, Michael chose to scoff at his friend for foolishly imagining that he was a fit object for the attentions, let alone the heart, of a Bakunin girl. In spite of his distress, Belinsky at first made various allowances for Michael's sudden change of attitude. But as his young host's rudeness increased, he began to realize that Michael derived a sadistic pleasure from taunting and maltreating him. He felt, as he put it afterwards, that after stabbing him 'in the heart', Michael followed up 'with a twist of the blade, as though you enjoyed my torment.'[54]

Belinsky's stay at Premukhino thus turned into 'the worst time of my life'. To add to his misery, he received the news that *The Telescope* had been suppressed, his Moscow room searched, and his papers seized by the police. The Tsar's measures against all those involved in the publication of Chaadayev's 'First Philosophical Letter' assumed grotesque and shattering proportions. Professor Nadezhdin was sent to northern Siberia; Chaadayev himself, after being officially declared insane and visited by a doctor for a year, was likewise to be exiled for a time; and the venerable Rector of Moscow University, who doubled as censor, was summarily dismissed from his post. Although Belinsky was to suffer nothing worse than a police interrogation on his return to Moscow, the closure of the review meant the loss of his meagre and only source of income, and threw him back into the bleakest poverty.

As soon as the affair broke in October 1836, Stankevich and his friends began to look for ways of sending Belinsky out of Russia. Waiting for the outcome of their unsuccessful attempts, the unhappy man tarried at Premukhino, returning to Moscow only at the beginning of November. He was thus privy – this time as a bystander – to another emotional tempest that shook the Bakunin household.

Michael's three youngest brothers in Tver, enlightened by him about man's 'great destiny', had found the *gymnasium* routine there so inexpressibly boring by comparison that Alexis threatened to 'cut his throat' unless they were allowed to leave. They developed a single-minded and fervent wish: to continue their schooling in Moscow, under Michael's supervision. Not daring to approach their father themselves, they had, during a short visit to Premukhino in October, persuaded Michael and Tatyana to intercede with him on their behalf. For once, however, Count Bakunin put his foot down.

'Your father would rather die', Tatyana informed them of his reaction, 'than let you go to Moscow with Michael,' who had already had 'such a pernicious influence' on them. For herself, she urged them to be brave and bow to necessity like 'truly great men... Do not fall from the heights to which Michael has already raised you.'[55]

The three boys, finding that her advice hardly tallied with what Michael had previously taught them – namely, that the inner life must be vitalized and 'externalized' by constant 'action' – were disconcerted but undaunted. One midnight in October, having hired a coach, they tried to make a dash for it, but did not get very far because of a disagreement about the fare. Brought back to the house of their maternal grandmother, who raised the alarm at Premukhino, they remained in a rebellious mood, refused to go back to school, and threatened that if they were treated 'like children' they would run away again.

At Premukhino, Count Bakunin saw in their attempted flight further evidence of Michael's corrupting influence on the minds of his children. To Michael's

476

great annoyance he charged Varinka's husband – Dyakov, whom Michael kept denigrating as a simpleton – to deal with the boys, using corporal punishment if necessary to bring them to their senses. In Tver the young rebels prepared to defend themselves, with knives if need be, but Dyakov, approaching them in a friendly and disarming manner, managed to win their confidence; treating them as adults, he invited them to spend some time on his estate and kept them there until they had calmed down.

'I was not in the mood to submit to circumstances,' Paul, the eldest, reported after a while. 'I had just read in Schiller: "All others must, man is a creature who wills..." But I have come to see the necessity of submitting: there are cases in which man must!'[56]

At Premukhino, Michael's discomfiture was complete. The temporary and precarious truce with his father had broken down in a 'host of unpleasantness for Michael', as Tatyana put it. Gone was 'the divine harmony' he had experienced that summer, and with it collapsed the Fichtean philosophy out of which its ecstasies had been spun. It had proved illusory and incapable of bringing him inner peace and keeping out the intrusions of the external world.

Having badly misjudged the effect of his Fichtean rhetoric on tender minds, he was now forced to admonish his junior brothers to return to their studies; to tell them brusquely to stop quoting 'the rights of man' to all and sundry, but to apologize to their parents and 'make up with grandmother'. Half-praising their 'hunger for life' and paying lip-service to the ambition 'to act' which he had himself instilled in them, he was loath openly to recant his teaching, but in a quiet, unblushing *volte-face* now gave them a new moral directive – to the effect that every action must have an 'aim' consistent 'with reason and the conditions around you,' i.e., with the external world. Faced with their admired brother's contradictory homilies, the boys were completely confused. For Michael, the benevolent and influential 'father' of his commune, it was a signal defeat that it was not he, but Dyakov – the detested outsider – who in the end made them see reason and induced them to make up with the family.

And much as he enjoyed torturing Belinsky, he was too intelligent not to be unhappy about the reasons for his jealousy. Bakunin's need for sympathy and his lack of reticence exceeded even the Romantic proclivity for friends to share, bare and mutually dissect their most secret emotions, pains and suffering, and before long he was pouring out his heart to the Beyer sisters: 'I do not know what to call my feeling for Tanichka. I only know that it inflamed me with a jealousy that tormented my whole soul. It led me to almost total degradation.' He, who had 'so sublime a mission' before him, had been overwhelmed by 'base feelings unworthy of me... I became their wretched slave. I lacked the strength to rid myself of them... Ah, this was hell with all its terrors.'[57]

In an access of self-punishment, he was presently to reveal to his own sister too that there was 'much that is vile in me, much that is base.'[58] By that time, April 1837, he was once more in Moscow – having fled Premukhino yet again in November, practically on the heels of his friend and victim, Belinsky. While he was going through the 'hell' made by his tormenting jealousy and his impotence in the face of that autumn's accumulation of crises, Stankevich had beckoned from Moscow. Informing Michael that he was about to receive a complete set – 13 volumes – of Hegel in German, he invited Michael to join him so that they might 'rack' their brains over them together. From Moscow, still in a state of despondency a week before New Year's Day 1837, he had written to Varinka that he meant to 'remake' himself completely. His Fichtean 'inner life' suddenly appeared to him superficial, and the only salvation left to him was 'to destroy my personal "I"... and to find somewhere that harmony outside of oneself that one cannot find within.'[59]

In Moscow, Belinsky had been released by the police; but with *The Telescope* closed and his livelihood gone, he was now on the list of suspects and unable to find other employment. He tried his hand at various occupations, failed, was reduced to living off his friends, and loathed himself for it. Being in desperate straits and in a black mood since his humiliation at Premukhino, he sought refuge from it all in brothels and in a ruinous bout of dissolution that made Stankevich's circle rally to save his fragile health before it was too late. This time it was Bakunin who, borrowing 300 rubles on their behalf, got together the necessary funds to send him away for several months' rest and recuperation in the Caucasus.

From there, in June, Belinsky sent Michael a conciliatory letter. By November, frankly 'confessing' his strange feeling for Tatyana, Michael at last gave Belinsky an intimation of the reason why he had maltreated him at Premukhino. Belinsky's reaction went straight to the point: 'You suspected that T.A. [Tatyana Alexandrovna] was in love with me.' He also delivered a sharp verdict: 'I am not in a position to judge whether your feeling is a natural one. Hegel alone might be able to define and analyze it. Whatever it is, your feeling frightens me: it seems to me abnormal and monstrous.'

Remarkably, they resumed their friendship, being too interested in one another to break it off. But henceforth it was punctuated by increasingly violent philosophic as well as personal disputes – reflecting their different temperaments – alternating with 'ecstatic reconciliations'. Belinsky knew no German and depended on Bakunin to introduce him to Hegel. Regarding himself as the teacher, Bakunin treated Belinsky with infuriating condescension. Admitting that on his part theirs was an intense 'love-hate' relationship, Belinsky came to see Bakunin as a gifted young man with a 'devilish capacity for communicating ideas' and 'an inexhaustible love of God', but accused him of placing 'ideas higher than man... higher than his immediate being', and of sacrificing people like an 'all-gestating and all-devouring Brahma' toying with his victims.[60]

Belinsky was also one of the first to see through Michael's motives in constantly conjuring up and lamenting to his sisters the 'loathsomeness' of marriage and physical love. Himself continuing to yearn for Alexandra, Belinsky was all the more enraged by the way this cold-hearted and 'abstract hero' terrorized them and prevented them from living normal lives. At the same time, with so much unaffected self-revelation and intense philosophic as well as emotional analysis passing between various members of this circle, it was inevitable that Michael Bakunin's unusual 'feeling' for Tatyana did not remain a secret for long. His avoidance of any amorous involvement, his monkish abstinence and horrified reaction to any young man's talk about the pleasures of sex, were all too conspicuous not to be noticed and cause gossip.

At a later date, Bakunin was to suffer an intense humiliation in this most vulnerable point of his manhood, and Belinsky would derive no mean satisfaction from the spectacle of Bakunin's disgrace.

The Engels textile factory in Germany, whose profits once helped to keep Karl Marx in funds, is closing down because of financial difficulties. The last owner, a third-generation nephew of Friedrich Engels – who financed the writing of DAS KAPITAL by Karl Marx – has been forced to sell out after incurring heavy losses in recent years. Situated at Engelskirchen, the factory may be torn down.

(News item, February 1979)

16

Young Engels among the Pietists of the Wupper Valley

One day in 1835, when Friedrich Engels was not yet 15, his father came across a 'dirty book' which the boy had been reading. Young Engels had actually obtained the book, which dealt with the adventures of some 13th-century knights-in-armour, at the lending library in Barmen, the posh part of the twin towns of Barmen-Elberfeld, which faced each other across the Wupper river. It may have been no more or less blood-curdling than the popular English 'penny-dreadfuls' or the gangster stories of a later age. Engels's father, however, was flabbergasted by the nonchalant 'unconcern with which he leaves such books lying about in his escritoires' and so shocked that he reported the find in a letter to his wife while she was at the bedside of her dying father in another town.

'In spite of previous severe punishments', he complained in his letter, 'even fear of chastisement' appeared to have lost its deterrent effect and no longer served 'to make him learn absolute obedience... May God preserve his soul, I often get anxious for the otherwise excellent boy...'[1]

At 39, Friedrich Engels, Sr (father and son bore the same Christian name) was one of the captains of the flourishing textile industry in the Wupper Valley, which already in Napoleon's time had earned the Grand Duchy of Berg the by-name of a 'miniature England'. Now, due to the new cotton-spinning machines, Barmen-Elberfeld was on its way to becoming known as 'the German Manchester'. Engels was the father of 9 children – of whom young Friedrich was the eldest – and otherwise a strict Calvinist and disciplinarian. He permitted few books and none but some edifying 'Christian' novels in his house. Unlike Heine's rationalist mother, who had feared the effect of Romantic fantasies and

Gothic tales on her boy's impressionable mind, Engels regarded all worldly literature as sinful.

In 1835 he was a partner with two brothers in the firm of Caspar Engels & Sons, which manufactured cotton yarn and silk thread. The family had been in this business for generations, ever since a humble Engels ancestor – peddling ribbons and yarn in a 'wicker basket on his back' for years – had saved every Thaler and Pfennig in order to found bleachworks and a small lace-and-ribbon factory in Barmen back in 1770 or thereabouts.

This had grown through the family's industry from father to son, but by 1835 Caspar Engels & Sons had been in trouble for some time due to differences between the three temperamentally incompatible brothers about its management. In due course they resolved to settle their disagreements once and for all. The future ownership of the firm was to be decided by lot. Friedrich Engels lost the draw, but was to prove that he was the most dynamic of the brothers. Within two years, with the money he obtained for his share in the family business, he went into partnership with the British cotton manufacturers Godfrey and Peter Ermen and founded the Ermen & Engels firm in Manchester, which owned the Victoria Mill near Pendleton. This partnership thrived and within another 4 years (1841) Engels would be able to pump money back into Germany and to establish another mill in his native Barmen, and yet a third in Engelskirchen, the one that was to survive until late into the 20th century.

In business he was progressive, believing in modernization and importing some of the first English spinning machines into Germany. In all other things, he was a diehard conservative and staunch believer in the merits of a frugal life and industrious work – not for the sake of enjoying their fruits, but as part of Puritan virtues, the Calvinist doctrine of predestination leaving men little hope of achieving 'particular election' and a state of grace other than by zealous work, preseverance and ascetic religiosity. The strictest, so-called Pietist brand of Calvinism and its sombre life-style had long since gone out of fashion almost everywhere in Germany. But not in the Wupper Valley, where life was more austere and the Pietist view of man's condition and fear of the hereafter continued to exercise the hearts and minds of most of the population.

Recently, the pastor of Elberfeld, F.W. Krummacher – later to become court preacher to the King of Prussia – had created nothing less than a revivalist atmosphere throughout the Valley. Other evangelists in the Barmen-Elberfeld area vied in fervour with Krummacher, but none stirred so much discussion as this fanatical and famous pastor whose sermons Goethe found to have a 'narcotic effect' and who whipped congregations into paroxysms of fear with graphically constructed visions of the horrors of hell in store for sinners.

When abroad, Engels even went to the theatre. At home, however, he was a strict Sabbatarian, a pillar of the community and the church. Pietist Elberfeld had long resisted the opening of a local theatre – as had cosmopolitan Bremen with its ocean-going traffic, another Pietist stronghold. Life in the Engels home in the 1830s was less abstemious than that preached by the thundering Pastor Krummacher, who forbade even so-called 'Christian' novels and prophesied fire and brimstone for those indulging in such frivolous activities as music, dancing, etc. Engels allowed chamber music at home and played the cello himself, but as an employer he could not but agree with Krummacher's condemnation of any leisure, pleasure or artistic pursuit as a form of idleness, and therefore sinful. A self-satisfied bigot, he kept expanding his wealth with a zeal and vigour reinforced by his religious belief that everyone had his predestined place in life.

His wife, Elisabeth, was the daughter of a rather eccentric school principal in the town of Hamm, Bernhard van Haar, who was the author of a pamphlet advocating the destruction of all machines, except for a few specimens to be preserved as museum exhibits. He, too, was a Pietist. But Frau Engels had spent some of her girlhood years in Berlin and was less of a fundamentalist than her husband.

When he informed her in August 1835 of the 'dirty' romance of chivalry which their eldest son had left in a bureau drawer, he was bothered by more than just the nature of the boy's reading. 'Friedrich is such a peculiar, volatile boy,' he wrote. 'May dear God take him under His protection, lest his soul be spoilt. So far he has shown a disturbing thoughtlessness and lack of character, for all his otherwise fine qualities...'[2] And Engels suggested to his wife that a secluded way of life was best for him, as it might help him to develop some independence.

Young Engels had in fact been placed as a boarder with a high school teacher in Elberfeld, as much to save him the walk to and from the Municipal Gymnasium as in the hope that living under the watchful eye and beneficial influence of Dr Hantschke – 'Royal Professor', Latin scholar, author of religious writings, and the school's acting headmaster – would finally instil in him the sense of discipline and 'absolute obedience' which his righteous father had failed to achieve by his own means of correction and 'severe punishment'.

'Money must be no consideration where the welfare of our child is concerned,' he wrote to his wife in this connection. Young Engels was a highly intelligent boy. History and literature were his favourite subjects, and he had an unusual talent for languages. He wrote verses, and wanted to become a poet and writer. For a profession, though, he meant to study law. But his father decreed otherwise. He did not let the boy finish even high school; in 1837 he took him out of the Gymnasium a year before he was to take his final examination.

Higher education was expensive in those days – there was a separate fee for each university lecture – and Heine, Marx, Bakunin, who were large spenders besides, constantly had to wangle and struggle for money during their student days. For reasons known only to himself, though Engels could certainly afford to send his son to the best university, he put him to work in his office before he was 17. It is just possible that he regarded all further study as a waste of time and a college education as positively harmful.

Thus young Engels at 17 met and mixed with the town's mill-owners and clerks. Two years later, in a series of articles titled *Letter from the Wupper Valley* and published under a pseudonym in the *Hamburg Telegraph*, he was to give a damning picture of their world and their values:

> In Elberfeld and Barmen, a person is considered to be educated if he plays whist and billiards, talks a little about politics and has the knack of paying the right compliments... Immersed all day long in their figures and office accounts, they work with a furious zeal and an interest that has to be seen to be believed.

Struck by the way everyone, young and old, clerks and mill-owners, went about their soul-killing drudgery, he observed that 'these people lead an awful life, yet they are quite content with it... In the evening they all troop to their clubs to smoke, play cards and talk politics. At the stroke of nine they all go home. Every day is the same as any other... And woe to anyone who would dare interfere with their ways – he would be irreparably disgraced with all the leading families.'[3] Their conversation, which was mostly about horses, dogs, girls and business, bored him to death. The self-satisfied mill-owners, he noted, were out to stamp their sons into their own likeness: 'The fathers gallantly train the young people, and the latter are only too ready and willing to become their spit'n image.'

It is tempting to imagine Engels as a rebel at 17 during the year he spent working in his father's counting-house, before he was to leave for further commercial training in Bremen. Eight years later, by which time he had become a 'Communist', he was to characterize his father as 'my fanatical and despotic old man'. There would be bitter and protracted rows between father and son over the latter's atheism, his refusal to continue in the family business, and other disagreements, and Engels would accuse his father of subjecting him to 'a wild Christian hunt for my "soul".'[4] But of his boyhood years little is known, except that he grew up comfortably in a large house surrounded by trees and flowers in well-to-do Barmen.

Barmen-Elberfeld had a combined population of some 40,000, about equally divided between the two towns. Engels was to describe Barmen before the end of the 1830s as having a good road as well as 'tastefully modern' red-roofed

483

stone houses rising spaciously between gardens and green bleacheries, woods and meadows. The Engels house was prominent not far from several weavers' cottages where looms clattered late into the night. The household teemed with the noise of Engels's 8 younger siblings – Hermann, Maria, Anna, Emile, Hedwig, Rudolf, Wilhelm and Elise – who in 1837 ranged in age from 3 to 15. With the master of the house and young Friedrich away at the counting house all day, Frau Engels, when unable to control the pandemonium, would put on a nightcap, pince-nez and her husband's 'fur-lined housecoat', and with the whole brood changing costumes, would play masquerades with them. About the courtyard geese fluttered and sometimes there was a flurry of domestics about a pig being slaughtered. Barmen's church was 'the most beautiful edifice in the [Wupper] Valley.'[5]

Elberfeld, on the opposite bank of the river, was a study in contrasts, a dreary industrial slum with smoking chimneys and unpaved or poorly cobbled streets. The tower of its disused, dilapilated old Catholic church served as a prison for delinquents, and its half-finished town hall fronted a narrow, ugly alley. There, on the gloomy streets, loiterers mixed with millworkers and artisans moving about 'in long smocks, with a stooping gait' and a downcast air, 'their hair parted in the middle in Pietist fashion' and their minds filled with the visions of hell to which Pastor Krummacher, 'stomping about the pulpit so that the windows clattered and young girls and old women burst into tears', regularly treated them.

Every night, parties of drunken journeymen trooped about Elberfeld singing bawdy songs. Taverns and pubs were filled to over-crowding, and on Sunday night many slept off their intoxication in ditches, or, if they had neither homes nor employment, 'in haylofts, stables, or on dungheaps...'

Engels was 19 when, contrasting peaceful Barmen with wretched Elberfeld in his articles in the *Telegraph für Deutschland*, to give it its full name, he poured scorn and condemnation on the mill-owners for sanctimoniously tolerating, if not creating, the inhuman condition of their workers. Both sides of the detailed picture he gave were obviously drawn from observations made while he was still at home and working in the factory office.

He was a hot-headed youngster, lanky, blue-eyed, with brownish hair. If he engaged in early disputes with his father before he left for Bremen, it is unlikely that they concerned the obscurantism preached by the fiery Pastor Krummacher. He had been confirmed in the Evangelical church of Lower Barmen, and he was still deeply religious. He had been strictly educated in 'the Wuppertal faith', and at 17 he actually composed a special prayer in verse to Jesus. Shortly afterwards, however, he began to be nagged by doubts and suffered a religious crisis which, 5 months after his 18th birthday, would lead him to write to Friedrich Graeber, a friend and former schoolmate: 'If at 18 one has read

Strauss, the rationalists and the Kirchenzeitung one must either stop thinking for oneself or one must begin to doubt one's Wuppertal faith.' How, he wondered, could one reconcile the two different genealogies of Joseph, the husband of Mary, appearing in the Gospels of Matthew 1:1–17 and Luke 3:23–38. And how, he asked, could one 'make the different statements at the Last Supper (this is my blood, this is the new testament in my blood) or about the lunatics (the one says the devil merely departed out of him, and the other that he entered into the swine), rhyme with one another, or the fact that the mother of Jesus went in search of her son, thinking him mad, although she had received him by immaculate conception... Christ's own words, *ipsissima verba*, which the orthodox keep bragging about, differ in each of the Gospels.'[6]

But while shedding Pietism, he continued to 'love God with all my heart' and confessed his heart-searchings to the same Graeber: 'I am praying daily, nay almost the whole day long, that I will discover the truth. I have done so ever since my doubts began... My eyes are wet with tears as I write this... I feel I shall find my way to God.'[7]

Although soon enough, in Edmund Wilson's phrase, young Engels was 'to find his lost God in the Absolute idea of Hegel', it was to take a while before he attacked Krummacher for turning simple Calvinism into a mystic evangelism rivalling 'Papism and the Inquisition for sheer intolerance'. During his religious crisis he could count on no support or guidance from his unbending father, and it was only when he was 20 – and had been living on his own in Bremen for two years – that he was to ridicule Krummacher as 'the Pope of the Wuppertal Calvinists and the St Michael of the doctrine of predestination', in an article titled 'Rationalism and Pietism' in Stuttgart's *Morgenblatt für gebildete Stände* ('Morning Paper for the Educated Classes').[8]

Before going public, however, he was excoriating predestination in his letters to Graeber: 'What does Krummacher actually say? Many are called but few are chosen, and the rest all suffer damnation. For ever? Yes, he says, for ever and ever into eternity. Even among the Christians', not to mention 'all the heathen peoples who merely exist in order to feed the fires of hell...'[9]

Any such irreverent remarks made at home would of course have struck his father as intolerable blasphemy. Engels professed a sincere belief in orthodox Pietism, whose rigorous and righteous virtues – hard work, frugality, acceptance of one's station in life – happened to be not unfavourable to his business interests. Krummacher was to him an inspired preacher whose evangelizing sermons helped to stem the tide of godlessness threatening to invade the industrial Valley from the non-Pietist Rhineland, and to upset its traditional values.

Rather, any arguments between father and son before young Friedrich left for Bremen in 1838 are likely to have arisen from his shock at the scenes he witnessed during his year at the factory office in Elberfeld. In the pseudonymous 'Letters from the Wupper Valley' – signed S. Oswald and published in the *Telegraph* (whose editor was Karl Gutzkow, of the 'Young Germany') – he was to conjure up the misery and demoralization of the Wuppertal mill hands and home weavers, the child labour, the street fights and the alcoholism, and to write among other things: 'Working in low [factory] rooms, where they breathe more coal smoke and dust than oxygen, for the most part since the age of six, has drained the people of all energy and joy.' And what was left for the home 'weavers who sit bent over their looms from morning to night with the hot stove scorching their spines? Either they become a prey to the existing repulsive form of evangelism, or they fall for the brandy bottle.' When the two combined, the effect was stupefying:

> In Pietist smithies and bootmakers' shops, the master sits with a Bible on his right and most often with a bottle on his left. Hardly any work is being done, the master nearly always reading Bible verses in between gulps of brandy. Every now and then he breaks into a religious hymn to the accompaniment of his choir of apprentices...[10]

Engels's father might have replied that he was not to blame for the Prussians swamping the Rhineland with cheap brandy, nor for some worthless fellows taking the Lord's name in vain and wallowing in sloth and intoxication. He might have pointed out that the weavers' cottages that stood not far from the Engels house in Barmen had been built by the boy's great-grandfather, Johann Caspar, when he had opened the first Engels lace factory. There had been greater misery in the Valley in those days, and only vagrant workers floating from job to job and place to place. Old Johann Caspar had built homes with gardens for them, subtracting the cost from their wages. The sluggards had moved on, the industrious ones had settled down and become the first permanent labour force in the area. Johann Caspar had done his bit to advance the world in a Christian way, through hard work. He had helped to build a flourishing industry where there was none, and he, Friedrich Engels Sr, was helping to modernize it. No lazy drunks were going to stop him or the expansion of trade going on all over the world.

For further grooming as a merchant-manufacturer, Engels's father had arranged for him to work in Heinrich Leupold's Exportfirma in Bremen. Herr Leupold, who was a business friend of his, traded in sugar, exported thousands of bales of linen to America, imported coffee from Haiti, and so forth. He also acted as Consul for the King of Saxony, and was one of Bremen's notables. As Bremen was one of the Hanseatic ports, with huge ships loading and unloading goods to and from all the continents, it was thought that Engels was sure to find life there interesting. He would see how the world of trade functioned and learn everything about marketing, supply and demand, the activities of the Stock Exchange and international commerce.

To make sure, however, that young Friedrich would not stray from the right path in the big city with its port, bars, sailors, bordellos and foreign influences – to cure him, so to speak, of any idea of experimenting with its sinful temptations – his father had arranged for him to lodge with a curate. Pastor Treviranus of the Pietist St Martin's church, of which Herr Leupold happened to be a warden, had agreed to take him in as a boarder and would hopefully keep him out of harm's way.

From his father's reference to the son's disobedience at 15 in spite of 'severe punishment', and from their documented later quarrels, a strong case might be made out for Engels's having been an early rebel. But there is no direct evidence of this, and while he may have wrangled with his parents over various subjects before he left for Bremen, he was later to prove so clever a tactician that he may have kept things to himself and avoided fruitless confrontations.

The merely 'volatile boy' whose lack of independence worried his elders was, however, an extremely bright and alert youth. And when he later verbalized the observations he had stored in his mind, he was to charge the Barmen mill owners, including his father, with ruining something even more important than the environment: 'The very quality of life in this part of the Rhineland, which was once jolly with wine and song', he was to write, 'has been destroyed.' And his vivid description of pollution, mindless mysticism, alcoholism, street brawls, knifing and general misery and dejection added up to a comprehensive and remarkable picture of the ravages wrought by the indiscriminate pace of the industrial revolution not only upon the physical environment and material condition of a population, but upon its very spirit.

Outwardly submitting to paternal authority, Engels dutifully began work as a junior clerk in Leupold's Exportfirma, copying letters, sorting and packing goods, addressing crates and running errands. He was a good mixer, and with his quick grasp of things and enterprising personality he moved about swiftly and easily in Bremen's financial and shipping world, studied it carefully at its vortex, but managed to pursue and considerably widen his own interests at the same time. In Bremen, reading books and newspapers forbidden or unavailable at home, Engels managed by the age of 20 not only to write poetry, compose music and pick up several languages, but to accumulate the rudiments of information that were to make him an all-purpose, if sometimes superficial, 'expert' on an extraordinary range of subjects – economics and military strategy, biology and politics, history ancient and modern, philosophy, even physics – with results totally unforeseen by his father.

487

He was 'volatile' rather in the sense of being versatile than changeable or easy to persuade. If he needed a steadying influence – as his father feared he did and mistakenly sought to give him in the person of headmasters and parsons providing board-and-tutelage – he was to find it before he was 24 in Karl Marx.

Yet it was to take Engels years to escape from Barmen-Elberfeld and the hated family business. In Bremen, beginning to go his own way while ostensibly abiding by the 'old man's' designs for him, Engels became increasingly cynical and flippant, and early developed a knack, as well as the technique, of moving adroitly in two distinct worlds and making the best of both – a faculty he was to carry to the perfection of an art in later life. While becoming a 'bourgeois manufacturer' outwardly carrying on the 'filthy trade' of three Engels generations before him, he was to exact a terrible revenge on his father and all he stood for.

*'I, too, like (St) John in his time, have been called upon to bear witness of the Light.
I am not that Light, but only its herald.'*

Moses Hess, Diary, 7 January 1836.

'I am more of an apostle than a philosopher...'

Letter to Alexander Herzen, 1850.

17

Moses Hess and 'The New Philosophy'

In Cologne, on 16 September 1836, a young man confided in his diary with underlining that from the time when he was 11 and into his 'fifteenth or sixteenth year' he had masturbated almost every day. The young man was Moses Hess. The diary he kept, as far as is known, off and on for only a little over two years, has never been published in its entirety. He was nearly 25 when, recalling the early physical and mental stress which by 16 or so had nearly reduced him to a wreck, he wrote the entry which 130 years later would remind the author of his first biography of Rousseau's *Confessions*.[1]

When he was a little over 19, Moses Hess had written to a friend of his – one M. Levy, of whom little but the name is known – that some three years or so earlier, after he had 'read and studied an unconscionable lot', he had gone through a 'gigantic inner revolution', a raging adolescent turmoil lasting perhaps two years. 'I could have become its victim. It was a stiff struggle. Always new dangers, new resources. At long last – freedom won.'[2]

It was only in his 1836 diary that he amplified this in a somewhat florid period style:

> I doubt that anyone ever knew a harder inner struggle than I... The flowering of my body was actually over when my soul began to blossom. If that can be called flowering of the body which otherwise goes by the name of physical debauch. I can hardly grasp even now how anyone who indulged in such excesses at so tender an age as I did managed to stay so healthy in body and mind, though both –

body and mind – were, to be sure, much weakened. It is perhaps remarkable that as soon as my spiritual crisis began, my physical one ceased. At the time I am speaking of I was as chaste as Joseph. I had, in fact, not one obscene fantasy left, certainly a rare phenomenon in a youngster who from his eleventh into his fifteenth or sixteenth year kept masturbating almost every day! But enough, now: when I began to study, I stopped being unclean. My chief problem, of course, was religion, from which I later moved on to the principles of ethics...[3]

It was not without great agony, Hess went on, that he saw his Jewish religion collapse before his eyes.

Nothing remained. I was the most miserable person in the world. I became an atheist. The world became a burden and a curse to me... I could not stand the situation. I worked without rest to rediscover my God... I had to have a God – and I did find him, after a long search, after a terrible fight – in my own heart. This heart, with its love and kindness, inspired the world with an ethical order, created unity within diversity. I did not possess a personal God any more, but I had a moral world order.

Born in 1812, Moses Hess was 6 years older than Karl Marx. The religious crisis which kept him in the throes of a 'terrible' struggle in his late teens reached its culmination around 1829, although he describes it in 1836. In 1837 Marx was going through a similar or worse inner crisis in search of 'new gods' at the age of 18 and falling ill from stress. But Marx at that age was wrestling with Hegel's philosophy; it was philosophy that led Marx to atheism. Moses Hess, in the retrospective of his struggle, writes in his diary that at the time he did 'not yet know any German philosophy – nor did I know any philosophy at all.' He had in fact received hardly any secular education.

Hess was almost 9 years older than Engels, and his religious crisis preceded the latter's by the same number of years. Whereas young Engels could not stand his Pietist father's bigotry and the oppressive, ultra-Calvinist atmosphere in Barmen-Elberfeld, Hess rebelled early against an overdose of Talmud and the strict Jewish orthodoxy of his father.

The idea of a moral world order, of reason and a moral principle ultimately governing history and world events in spite of all man-made conflicts and evils – an idea conceived early on by Hess and to guide his attitude to the social and political issues of his day and their solution – was to earn him a special place in the gallery of strong egos represented by such ruthless and doctrinaire 'doctors of revolution' as Marx, Engels and Bakunin, or even Lassalle.

To become the first Communist in Germany, Hess was to convert young Engels to his social vision. He was to exert a strong influence on Marx, who – as has only recently been recognized – took more than one of his ideas from him. By the time he died Hess would also be acknowledged as 'the father of German Social Democracy',[4] and posthumously as the prophet of a third Jewish Commonwealth before the term Zionism had even been coined, let alone made its political appearance on the world stage. Less aggressive and morally more sensitive than either Marx or Engels, Moses Hess was to have the unique distinction of standing in one lifetime at the cradle of the three most successful 19th-century redemptionist creeds whose separate triumphs and mutual clashes were to lead to the ideology-ridden world of the 20th – even though Marx and Engels, in the 1848 *Communist Manifesto*, for reasons of their own, dismissed his pioneering role. Later, they privately heaped invective on Hess, deriding him as a woolly-headed 'enthusiast and a fantast'. But while Marx and Engels themselves continued to have a healthy respect for him and refrained from further attacks on him in public, they set the tone for Hess's stature and significance to be minimized or obliterated in most Marxist literature.

Unlike Marx, Hess – in the words of Isaiah Berlin – believed that 'social equality was desirable because it was just, not because it was inevitable.' Speaking at Cambridge in 1959, after more than a century of intense depreciation of Hess during his lifetime and after, Berlin called him 'an exceptionally penetrating and independent thinker who understood and formulated the problems with which he was dealing more clearly than the majority of his critics.' Observing that the rival diagnoses of 'the more celebrated founders of "scientific" Socialism... have stood up badly to the test of time,' he stressed that the questions raised by Hess were not only 'exceedingly live issues today', but had, if anything, become 'more critical than they were in his own lifetime.'[5]

Thirty years after Berlin spoke, the turn of events in the USSR was to provide an illustration of Hess's foresight on just one of these 'live issues'. Hess was the only one of the 19th-century Socialist prophets who fully and openly supported the struggle for independence of Europe's small nations. Realistically assessing a phenomenon which Marx missed, he realized that the tide of nationalism which increasingly swept Europe throughout that century was part of an historic process and represented a force that would contend with Socialism for the hearts and minds of men.

Edmund Silberner, in his 1966 biography of Hess, including sections of his diary and other new material, saved him from the long oblivion to which not only Marx and Engels, but Kautsky – by the suppression of his works – had long condemned him. In 1926 Georg Lukàcs, a 20th-century Marxist trend-setter, presented Hess as an 'honest revolutionary' who had come closer than anyone to

Marx's concept of materialist dialectic, only 'tragically' to fail to master it in the end. Forty years later Silberner pointed out that this was irrelevant, as Hess never wanted to be a dialectician. Having assembled the complete 'Hess file', he concluded that this 'dreamer' derided as an utopian had 'in some respects proved a greater realist' than the 'practical' Marxists.[6]

Finally, by 1985 S. Avineri, no mean authority on Marx, put the shoe on the other foot. On the question of nationalism, he wrote, 'traditional Marxism committed one of its most tragic mistakes in misreading the hieroglyph of history.' Marx, he suggested, had ignored the stirrings of nationalism because they did not fit the neat architectonic categories of the great system he was building. Hess, not having a system to defend, had been 'more attuned to the *Zeitgeist* of the nineteenth and twentieth century.'[7]

Karl Marx was 'Fortune's child' and spoilt by his parents in Trier. Engels came from the security of one of the wealthiest new manufacturers' homes in Barmen-Elberfeld. Moses Hess, born at no great distance from either of them in Bonn on the Rhine, grew up as a deprived child in that city's former ghetto. He came, however, from a well-known family. His great-grandfather, David Tebli Hess, had been chief rabbi of the town of Mannheim. In 1762, when Engels's great-grandfather Johann Caspar was still peddling yarn and ribbons, Hess's great-grandfather was adjudicating divorce cases brought before him from the Principality of Cleve. Little is known of Hess's grandfather, Nathan, except that he had moved to Bonn, where he established a grocery and general store. Hess was later to portray the piety, scholarliness and loving kindness of this grandfather in glowing, possibly embellished terms: 'He was one of those sages or scribes who, without making a métier of it, had the title and knowledge of a rabbi' and spent his time after the affairs of the day 'studying the Talmud and its many commentaries till late after midnight.'

Born in Bonn in 1790, David Hess, Moses's father, was 4 when the gates of its old ghetto were smashed with axes upon the entry of French troops. He later moved with his wife Helena to Cologne. In that city, which for more than 300 years before its occupation by the French had admitted no Jews at all within its gates, David Hess opened a store, worked hard and made good. Within two decades, he was to become a partner of the Hess & Horst sugar refinery, and later its sole owner. The refinery was to survive until close to the 20th century.

Moses Hess was 4 or 5 years old when his parents departed for Cologne in 1816 or early 1817. Only 30 or so Jewish families had by then come to live in Cologne, too few to establish a school of their own, and under the discriminatory restrictions reimposed by Prussia in the annexed Rhineland, the child Moses would have had to be baptized before being admitted to one of Cologne's elementary *Volksschulen*. Confronted by the same dilemma which Karl Marx's father in Trier solved by baptizing first himself and then his children, the parents of little Moses left the boy with his grandfather in Bonn, which had a traditional Talmud school.

Thus Moses Hess grew up without his parents. His mother sometimes came to visit him in Bonn, but at the end of November 1825, shortly before his 14th birthday, she died of pneumonia at the age of 38. It was only some time later, when the boy was nearer 15, that his father arranged for him to join him in Cologne.

In one of his moving, if slender accounts of his childhood, Moses Hess – in *Rome and Jerusalem*, published in 1862, when he was 50 – wrote that 'until recently' his mother appeared to him in dreams almost every night. Of her physical presence he recalled chiefly something she had said to him at bedtime one night, during one of her visits to Bonn. Mentioning that one of her remote (and to date unidentified) ancestors had been a great rabbinical scholar, she had told him that he was lucky to live with his learned grandfather. For, she quoted, 'It is said that where grandfather and grandson study the Torah together, there God's teaching lives forever.' Hess added that his mother's words 'must have made a deep impression on me. For I remember them to this day, although I have never again come across this legend [*sic!*] about grandfathers and grandsons.'[8]

A couple of pages later Hess corrected himself and inserted a note to the effect that his mother's words were not a 'legend' but a saying inspired by the Bible verse 'a threefold cord is not quickly broken.' (*Ecclesiastes*, 4:12.)

Unaware that his *lapsus* would one day be held against him, Hess in *Rome and Jerusalem* lovingly conjured up the figure of his studious and saintly, 'snow-white-bearded' grandfather, who looked after him benevolently, along with the flavour of Jewish holidays celebrated at his home and the moving stories he heard from him at other times about the destruction of the Temple and 'the expulsion of the Jews from Jerusalem'. Yet in his diary entry of 16 September 1836, written before he was 25, he summed up the central experience of his childhood between the ages of 5 and 15 in a few stark sentences: 'What education did I get? Born and raised in [Bonn's] Jews' Street; beaten black and blue over the Talmud until I was fifteen; inhuman teachers, corrupt friends for company, led astray and seduced into secret sinfulness, my body enfeebled and my spirit vulgar and crude, this is how I entered upon adolescence.'

This is an intriguing passage, conflicting as it does with the idyllic scenes of 'life with grandfather' to be evoked in *Rome and Jerusalem*. Coupled with the fact that Hess at 50 apparently did not know that his mother's 'legend' was actually an exegetic commentary on a Bible verse, it has lately been used to discredit the sincerity of Hess's biographical statements.

493

In 1862, impressed by the struggle of Greeks, Poles and Hungarians to re-enter history and more particularly by the Italian Risorgimento – as evident from the very title *Rome and Jerusalem*, linking together the two 'eternal' cities – Hess stated that the 'resurrection' of 'nations believed to be dead' was becoming 'a natural phenomenon'. His prophecy that the Jews, too, would 'struggle for their national rights' came after he had been preaching Communism for some 25 years. Although, true to his egalitarian faith, he envisioned the future Israel as a democratic, Socialist-type state, 'nationality' was anathema to Socialists, and the idea of a revived Jewish nation was utterly ridiculous in the eyes of his own liberal friends.

In 1992, more than a century later, S. Na'aman, a noted Marxist scholar, suggested nothing less than that in *Rome and Jerusalem* Hess built himself a sort of fictitious biography. He supposedly did so to show that both his Communism and his new 'illumination' went back to his childhood roots in traditional Judaism. Na'aman submitted that Hess had neither a good knowledge of Judaism nor any great attachment to it. All his latter-day professions of Jewish feelings were simply designed to make him momentarily appear as a prodigal son returned to the fold.

S. Avineri, taking a fresh look at Hess in 1985, wrote that 'the combination of nation-building and social reconstruction suggests that *Rome and Jerusalem*, rather than the Communist Manifesto, did correctly divine the spirit of the age: a universal quest for redemption, yet anchored in a concrete historical culture.'[9]

Na'aman, besides depriving Hess of his credibility, interpreted his confession that he had been 'beaten black and blue over the Talmud' as yet another proof of his lacking 'dialectical sharpness, as proved by all his philosophical writings'. Na'aman's 'historical-critical study of Hess's life and work from a post-Marxist perspective' thus revived the old Lukacz theory of 1926 with a new twist: Hess, a bungler and 'dabbler, which he always remained', could never really become a philosopher. His Talmud teachers, who were most likely private tutors, vainly tried to drub some analytical power into him, but all they accomplished was to cause him a mental 'blockage'.[10]

Hess himself forestalled this argument by describing himself not as a philosopher but 'more of an apostle', a herald and a prophet. 'Prophecy means, among other things, perceiving the true drift of history, hearing the challenge of history and articulating the response.' This appears in the work of a third scholar, Harold Fisch, a study written in 1978 from a Zionist viewpoint,[11] which adds yet another dimension to the continuing controversy about Hess.

Nothing is known about his teachers. Their brutishness does not particularly attest to their being fit to impart the dialectical subtleties of the Aramaic Talmud to a child. But his idea of a 'moral world order' – first mentioned in a letter he wrote when he was 17 – was directly inspired by the ancient Talmudic precept that virtue carries its own reward, and that one 'transgression' leads to another. As in other instances, Hess quoted it chapter and verse;[12] and whatever the trouble with his early education, one may certainly agree with Isaiah Berlin that Hess was 'indelibly' affected by it: 'Images and symbols drawn from the history of the Jews remained with him to the end of his life,'[13] and no wonder.

All the world reformers were social messianists. Saint-Simon, the 'Napoleon of industry', went back to the spirit of brotherhood of the early Christians, Moses Hess to the Old Testament prophets. Amid the increasing tension between philosophy and theology, the raging conflicts between the bourgeoisie, the aristocracy, the workers and other forces in the age marked by the overlapping Industrial and French Revolutions, he always sided with the underdogs and to each of the salvationist movements he pioneered or fructified he brought – quite apart from abstract thought – a sense of morality and justice, and an instinct for history.

It is generally agreed that Hess's evocation of his childhood in *Rome and Jerusalem* is sentimentally coloured. Young Engels passed almost daily by the two-storey house in Barmen where his great-grandfather had lived after founding the family fortune in the previous century. Hess lacked the security of such firm roots. There was only the idealized memory of his grandfather to cling to – and some image he must have built in his mind of his mother, whose regular appearance in his dreams until late into his mature years itself indicated the extent to which he missed her. Helena Hess, née Flöhrsheim, was the daughter of the rabbi of Bockenheim, near Frankfurt. Moses Hess may or may not have known the source of the exegetic commentary on 'the threefold cord' she was quoting when she urged him to study, but this does not mean that he was insincere or moved by political opportunism when he recalled it.

Hess was a youth who distinctly created his own future. Reunited at 15 with his father in Cologne, he still felt, according to his diary, like 'a very pious Jewboy'. He could hardly read German, felt only 'loathing for the Talmud' and lusted for a sampling of life and extramural activities. But his father – a dry, unimaginative, rather gruff, unresponsive man who had little understanding of the boy's needs – allowed him none and treated him distantly.

Coming from the 'prison house' of Bonn, Moses found himself caged again. The boy probably bore his father a grudge for taking his mother away from him in childhood. The father, however, gave him more reasons for resentment. A strictly orthodox believer, David Hess was a respected merchant and pillar of Cologne's small Jewish community and its synagogue – as Engels's father was of his church – and either because of that or to compensate for the scholarly education he had missed while making his way, he wanted young Moses to go on studying. But he insisted on his studying the hated Talmud and nothing else.

Like Engels at 15, Moses Hess had found an outlet for his mundane fantasies in cheap novels and romances of 'banditry' read on the sly. And he, too, aspired to become a writer. But he had hardly any experience of life, his father for a time refusing even his pleas to let him work in a grocery he owned.

They seem to have worked out some compromise, for in 1831, when he was 19, Hess wrote to a friend that he was 'helping Father' in the grocery store, adding that he went 'rarely to the theatre... because Father frowns upon it' and it was, after all, one's duty to respect 'even parental prejudices...'[14] His father, on the other hand, had agreed to pay for his private tuition in French, and he was taking lessons to improve his faulty German as well. But the precarious truce and *modus vivendi* they had reached was not to last. Moses 'reluctantly dragged' himself for some time to more enforced Talmud studies, then suddenly balked and abandoned them completely.

By the time he was 21, Moses Hess in fact fled his father's home and absconded to Holland, not before having secretly sold – while his father was busy establishing the Hess & Horst sugar refinery – a large coffee consignment to be paid upon delivery and arranging with his cousin Leopold Zuntz in Bonn and another accomplice to collect the payment and send it after him. Also to follow him in due course was a girl called Lena, with whom he had fallen in love. All searches for him proved fruitless. Hess's father and his two teen-aged sisters and two brothers – Lazarus, who later became a banker, and Samuel, who at that time worked with him in the grocery store – were greatly upset by his disappearance.

What made Moses Hess, who had switched from religion to the 'principles of morality', conceive at 21 of so frantic a scheme and go to the length of defrauding his father? For one thing, driven by a huge curiosity about what lay beyond the confined Jewish world in which he lived, he had started to read Rousseau, Spinoza, Goethe, Madame de Staël. 'I was to devote myself entirely to the business', he wrote to a friend, 'but already my interests and activity lay in different directions and my father was not the man to attract me back to himself.' The father kept him on a tight purse-string, but Moses, hungry for experience, had been borrowing money in order to go out with friends at carnival time and otherwise keep up with artistic and theatrical events. His letters between the ages of 17 and 19 show him arguing – with cousin Zuntz and others – about man's combining a 'rational' nature with a 'moral instinct'; besides profuse quotations from Rousseau, they display a beginning familiarity, if no more, with Epicurus, Helvetius and Holbach's *Système de la Nature*.

Horst, his father's partner in the new sugar refinery, was not a Jew. But except in some highly intellectual circles – and not in all of them – Germans and Jews did not mix socially. And David Hess was the last man to welcome or to understand his son's interest in the wide Gentile world and its secular culture. The fact that the father, who was in his forties, suffered from asthma and a touch of tuberculosis added to the mutual tension at home.

For another thing, since his 'inner revolution' young Moses Hess had been toying with atheism. By the time he was 20 he was communicating to a friend notions which could not but vex his father. He genuinely believed, he wrote, in 'the absolute divinity of our commandments'; so long as the Jews had been dispersed and were now denizens and 'brethren of manifold nations' these commandments could no longer be held sacred. Emphasizing certain words, he went on to declare: 'It is both *contemptible* and *ridiculous*... to worship the obsolete laws of a State that fell to pieces so long ago,' let alone to worship them 'with *idolatrous* awe'. And he compared the existing form of orthodox Judaism, with its hallowed rituals and ancient observances, to a worm-eaten tree.[15]

This was open rebellion against his whole upbringing and all that his father held sacred. In whatever way the son manifested his opinion of these observances at home, David Hess – who felt that they and nothing else had saved the Jews from extinction, against all odds – must have been continually stung by his views. The father was later to become president of Cologne's Jewish community. His son's questioning of the tenets by which it lived may have struck him as almost worse than atheism.

It was in the spring of 1833 that Moses bolted and arrived in Holland. He waited for cousin Zuntz to collect the money from the underhand coffee transaction and for his pretty Lena to arrive. Her education had been 'neglected', which meant that it was nil; she came of a boorish family and worked as a servant-girl in Bonn. It is not known what qualities of heart or character she possessed that kindled the young man's feelings for her to the point of wishing to marry her. Hess had a self-confessed inability to 'resist the inner goodness' of anyone. He may well have seen in Lena, raised in misery, a flower he was picking from the mud. And it is a fact, whatever its significance, that years later his *grande passion* would be for another beautiful girl reduced by hard luck to even worse distress. His infatuation with red-haired Lena was such that at one point he declared: 'I shall hardly ever find a woman who suits my individuality better than L.'

Lena was Jewish, but Moses feared or was sure that hardly anyone in the Hess family, least of all his father, would lightly accept his marrying a girl who did menial work in a household of their acquaintance. And without his father's financial support he and his love faced the prospect of being destitute together. Lena was thus very likely the prime motivation, among several, for his scheme to elope, if not its instigator. The first part of the 'coffee coup', so to speak, had gone off well. No one but Zuntz and one of Moses Hess's friends – Hermann Levié – knew of the sale; only they and Lena knew that he was in Holland. Once he got the money and Lena joined him there, nothing would stand in the way of their secret romance.

Things continued without a hitch. The coffee was duly delivered and paid for, and Zuntz sent Moses a money-order as arranged. As time passed, Moses waited in Holland, but the money never arrived. As was learned later, the money-order had been deficiently addressed and the whole scheme collapsed over this snag. The Dutch postal authorities, unable to locate young Hess, eventually returned the letter containing the money to Cologne – where it was promptly delivered to his surprised father. David Hess thus learned of the connection between the son's disappearance, the coffee sale and Lena.

Moses was stranded without a penny in Holland, or so it is believed, for, according to his biographer, his travels are shrouded in complete mystery. Whereas McLellan in his biography of Marx held that Hess picked up 'Communist ideas after running away to Paris', Isaiah Berlin, in a 1959 lecture reprinted in 1979, stated that 'he went to England, where he starved miserably, then to Holland and France', and that 'it was perhaps among the poor German émigrés – mostly left-wing exiles – that he imbibed the radical ideas then in vogue.' Edmund Silberner, however, who did comprehensive research for his biography, writes that there is no evidence whatsoever that Hess met the leaders of the Socialist movement in Paris during the 1830s.

What is known is that he first turned up in Frankfurt some time in the spring of 1834, roughly a year after he had absconded, and sought refuge with his late mother's relatives there. According to Silberner, he arrived looking 'completely shabby and worn, like a beggar.' The Frankfurt relatives received him well, fed him, set to work on his father to make him agree to a reconciliation, then returned the prodigal son – attired in a new set of clothes – to the latter's house and a 'most cordial welcome'.

And so Moses Hess was back at his father's table, and back in groceries. Having 5 years earlier quoted the Talmudic admonition to flee from transgression, and added his view that what distinguishes man from all other creatures is reason and a mighty 'moral instinct' so 'contrary to nature' that 'the slightest deviation from it induces "pangs of conscience"', he felt all the more contrite about his fraudulent adventure in the coffee trade and its consequences.

Oppressed by a sense of sin, he thanked God like a penitent for having saved him at the last moment from the brink of 'the yawning abyss of hell before me.' By February 1835, feeling cured of passion, immorality and its dangers, he was writing in his diary: 'I have won...'

498

That summer Lena, disappointed by the failure of his hoax, married another man. Hess sent her a wedding present, and partially consoled himself with the thought that because of her lack of education she would probably never have satisfied him.

The sugar refinery was making money and his father was becoming a man of substance – before long, David Hess would be regarded as a man worth 100,000 guilders – but Moses complained that he never had a penny of his own. 'I must become independent of my father,' he wrote in his diary in May 1835. This sentiment – to be echoed 10 years later by Engels's 'I must get away' – marked the failure of his reconciliation with his parent a year or so after his return from his abortive bid for freedom. During the summer of 1835 he toyed with new schemes to make himself free of, or at least to reduce contact and recurring friction with, his miserly and 'peculiar' father. But all his plans came to nought and at one point he saw no way to escape other than to start hunting for a rich but 'infinitely loving' bride. But how to find her? 'Per introduction into respected families', he noted in his diary. It was a fantasy he was to chase for years.

He was back in the grocery business, but teaching himself 'Latin in the morning, arithmetic in the evening after supper, then English, then history, then reading, etc.' His copious book list shows that he read, or planned to read, a diversity of works on world history, Napoleon, physics and physiology; it also included such authors as the comte de Ségur, Benjamin Constant, Victor Hugo, Chateaubriand, Goethe, Schiller, Heine, Fichte, Moses Mendelssohn and Spinoza.

Hess, who had never finished high school, had so far managed to acquire a wide-ranging, if uneven and self-taught base of knowledge. He hoped some day to obtain a special dispensation, and his father's financial agreement, to supplement it with academic studies, and was indeed eventually to enroll at Bonn University under a provision allowing him to attend lectures, but not to sit for a degree. But this was still two years ahead in 1835 when his autodidactic labours produced an amazing result. One evening early in June of that year, he was walking with his friend Hermann Levié when he began to talk about ways of building 'a better social order'. His idea, he explained, was to abolish property inheritance rights. And before long he was to enter in his diary a significant phrase: 'The privileged and the under-privileged will always face each other with mutual hostility.' The French Revolution was not yet over, he noted, and a greater drama was in the offing.

Karl Marx was preparing for his high school matriculation in Trier, and Engels was only 14 when Hess addressed the conflict between the 'haves' and the 'have-nots', i.e., the class-struggle. And by November and December 1835 he was not only attacking the aristocracy of birth as well as the aristocracy of

499

money – 'every rule not based on personal merit' – but also, in short order, proclaiming that 'one morning, before anyone has time to notice, the whole arrogant species that prides itself on its primogeniture, the whole aristocracy with all its wealth and inheritance rights will find itself flat and annihilated on the floor.' For 'the time of liberation', he wrote in his diary on 13 December 1835, was at hand and 'approaching with mighty steps'.

What was more, in what might seem a sudden fit of megalomania, he declared that he was himself the herald of a new divine teaching that would liberate mankind. In November he had started writing a book, which he meant to preface with a 'Call to the German People', and by 7 January 1836 he was confiding to his diary, which was neatly arranged and obviously meant for publication, that he was the terrestrial but God-inspired messenger called upon to show men a light they had failed to see: 'The Son of Man, when he came down on earth to deliver mankind of sin', had not been comprehended. He, Moses, had been chosen to announce a different – or, rather, an additional and complementary – salvation. 'It is written: "And the light shineth in darkness, and the darkness comprehended it not."' With the Gospel of St John for his text, he went on: 'I, too, like John in his time, have been called upon to bear witness of the Light. I am not that Light, but only its herald. I am pursuing my calling, for the world shall be set free so that through freedom it can reach the truth and achieve perfect cognition of God.' For the spirit had to be free before it could seize and grasp the truth. This could not happen so long as the aristocracy held sway and mismanaged things. His message, the new gospel, was likewise spelled out in his diary:

'Therefore I announce to you in the name of the Holy Spirit, of Truth: Break ye the fetters, tear up the chains with which ye have been bound in order to degrade ye to the beasts of burden that can be yoked and driven to work. Arise ye, have confidence and courage.'

He meant to call his book 'The Annunciation of Liberty in the Name of the Holy Spirit'. It was to appear in October of the following year under a less pretentious title: *The Holy History of Mankind*. While the book bore the imprint of one of Germany's most important publishing firms, its author remained anonymous, having – for fear of his father's disapproval no less than that of the censorship – chosen to identify himself merely as 'A Young Disciple of Spinoza'.[16]

This book, dedicated to 'all God-fearing Governments', was not only the first Socialist book to appear in Germany but one that dealt presciently with some of the main problems and developments that were to preoccupy Europe for a century and more. Adopting the apostolic tone of one who felt bound both to warn the world of impending disaster and to point the way to salvation, Hess – for all his writing in the convoluted, quasi-religious style that characterized much of contemporary political-social and metaphysical literature – stated with great clarity that 'the growing wealth of one section of society and the increasing poverty of the rest of the population' created a 'social illness' and a gap which was ultimately bound to assume 'terrifying' proportions. This was a topic which had not yet come up for public discussion in Germany. So far, only Ludwig Gall had tried to draw attention to it in a few confiscated leaflets and tracts. The writings of Saint-Simon and his followers circulated among intellectuals and were discussed in private talks and correspondence, but the programme they offered to adapt society to the age of technology had yet to be brought before the public.

'The new mechanical inventions and the daily expansion of trade and industry', Hess noted, seemed potentially to be of the greatest benefit to mankind. Yet, paradoxically, they only served to widen the inequality, and 'the way our laws and institutions are made' favoured this process: the rich would become richer, the masses poorer, and the exploitation of the many by the few – besides representing an intolerable injustice – would in the end create an explosive state of 'social misery' and moral stress leading to revolution.

Hess wrote most of *The Holy History of Mankind* in something of a trance in 1836. He could not foresee huge multi-national and supra-national corporations. But he predicted that 'in our time' share companies, industry and big business would 'eventually swallow up all individual activity in one enormous universal throat...' And when he wrote that 'Mammon is the only power in society since free trade and industry became predominant, and as they expand the mightier will become the power of money... More and more will man be enslaved to that Satan of Mammon, and human beings will remain without any holy bond, without a country, without a family,'[17] he anticipated by some 8 years Marx's famous thesis, in the *Economic and Philosophic Manuscripts* of 1844 (which, at that, were to be published only in the 20th century), on the alienating power of money, which estranges man from the product of his labour, from society, his fellow-men, etc.

But it is not for its social message alone that *The Holy History of Mankind* has today gained recognition as being in many respects an extraordinary work. Rather, what makes it extraordinary is the manner in which the young Hess fused religion and politics, state and church, reason and feeling, man's social needs and his emotional requirements in order to integrate that message with an optimistic vision of the perfect society. This lay necessarily in the future but was on its way towards realization in a well-ordered cosmos in which nature and the historic process moved dialectically forward under the impulse of a set of eternal principles.

Hess declared history to be 'holy' because he held that God played an active part in its movement towards a meaningful purpose – a role not unlike that ascribed by Hegel to the Absolute Spirit, or the Absolute, or the secularized absolute, though Hess had yet to study Hegel. To suit his purpose, Hess divided the history of mankind into three main eras:

1) The first, or Biblical period, ruled by God the Father, began with the election of Abraham 'from a mass of idol-worshippers to found a nation through which the knowledge of God would spread all over the earth.' It lasted until Judaism, losing the original unity between God and people and its internal cohesion in sectarian strife, went into decline.

2) The Christian period, ruled by God the Son, began with the advent of Jesus. His *sui generis* mediation between God and man helped to make Christianity universal. But the God in Jesus was a revelation of the soul, and with Christianity divorcing religion and morality from politics and human relations by placing salvation in the other world, it gradually degenerated as Catholicism, with its emperors, prelates and institutions, forsook love and mercy in favour of temporal power struggles and idolatrous ceremonial. Protestantism intervened as a corrective, but the strident inequality between men in the feudal Middle Ages and the stirrings of rationalism heralded the inevitable decline of Christianity.

3) Finally, Spinoza inaugurated the third and on-going main period, to be ruled by the Holy Spirit. This era – which Hess divided into a sub-period titled 'The [French] Revolution' – is the age of modernity and the future. Spinoza had perceived God not only in his soul but had apprehended him with his whole being, feeling and reason combined, as a universal presence manifest in all creation. To Spinoza, therefore, 'knowledge of God' was also 'knowledge of life'.

It was Hess's thesis that the divine principles governing world history ultimately unite 'superior reason' with 'supreme justice'. Knowledge of God being 'knowledge of life' meant that the same principles could harmoniously regulate the whole reality of human life. He wrote that 'Our Master', Spinoza, had taught that 'in all of nature man has nothing which draws him nearer to his human calling, to the knowledge of God, than his brethren, his fellow men. Hence man should associate with his fellow men, live in society.' Once man, like Spinoza, reached rational cognition of God he did not have to trouble his soul and labour his mind in search of his 'calling' or existential purpose in life. In directing attention to man's needs as a social being, Spinoza had reunited what Christianity – 'relating solely to the inner man' – had separated: he had joined and blended together again human political and social problems with the underlying religious ethics which had suffused them in antiquity, when religion and political life, ruled by the same divine order, had been one in the Jewish State before the destruction of Jerusalem.

The Christians, according to Hess, 'never possessed a social order based on God; they never had a holy state or a divine law.' Mosaic law, on the other hand, dealt with the needs of the inner as well as the outer man: religion and politics, church and state were intimately fused, had one root, bore one fruit. The Jews saw no difference between religious and political commands, between the duty to God and the duty to Caesar. These and other dichotomies disappeared in the face of a Law that was not intended for the body or the spirit alone but for both.

At the same time, as we know from his diary, Hess had ceased to believe in Judaism and its outmoded practices and customs. He had actually pronounced its obituary in the very first entry opening his diary on New Year's Day 1835: 'The Mosaic religion is dead and defunct.' In years to come he would recall his late grandfather's white beard glistening with tears while he read to him stories of the destruction of Jerusalem; but in the summer of 1835, shortly before starting *The Holy History of Mankind*, he had chosen the mourning day commemorating the fall of the First as well as the Second Temple in Jerusalem – in 586 BC and AD 70, respectively, both reputedly destroyed on the 9th of Av by the Jewish calendar month – to travel for his pleasure to Bonn over the protests of his orthodox father, who – though wearing a top hat and no beard – spent the day praying and fasting.

The main thrust of *The Holy History of Mankind* was against property and inheritance rights, including the 'inheritance of merits'. Thus, in Hess's book the Jews were the people 'in whom knowledge of God had become hereditary', but who had forfeited that spiritual legacy when they had ceased to toil for it and proved themselves unworthy of being its latter-day heirs. In primeval times, when the goods and 'treasures of society' had been open to all, there had been true and full equality. In the course of centuries of historic development, however, egoism, greed, historic rights, the inheritance of property and spiritual possessions had piled up an accumulation of inequalities generating such extreme forms of exploitation of the majority of society by a minority that the situation was moving towards an explosion.

The French Revolution had failed to solve this problem. The new enemy was not the old nobility but the aristocracy of money. Like every aristocracy, that of the rich concentrates in its own hands all the powers of society while misery and serfdom arise. The rich have become the enemies of progress and they will be its enemies in the future.

It would take time before men reached the rational as well as all-round 'knowledge of God' which had come to Spinoza. But Spinoza, the prototype of modern man who had healed the schism created by Christianity, and after him the ideas released by the American and French Revolutions, marked the start of a new historic process enabling man to turn the ideal into reality. Salvation lay neither in Schelling's 'philosophy of nature' nor in Hegel's 'philosophy of the mind'. Each expressed an incontestable side of the truth, but neither a divine cosmic order nor life itself could be conceived 'exclusively as either nature or mind'. Salvation could come only from a fusion of feeling and reason, calm and movement, past and future, just as these elements are fused in real life.

The salvation offered by Hess in his concluding chapter, which bore the rather sensational title 'The New Jerusalem and the Latter Days', was to be accomplished in two stages. The title was sensational in view of the fact that 'the New Jerusalem' was not in Palestine, but to be established 'in the heart of Europe'; but it was wholly in tune with Hess's messianist message and tone.

The ultimate redemption would come not only out of the fusion of past and present, but out of the 'union' of two European nations of contradictory character – France, the country of political struggles, 'of world-historical political revolutions', and Germany, the country of great spiritual controversy and religious preoccupations. 'Out of a union of these two, the New Jerusalem will be established.'

To avert the clash of colliding interests and passions that was bound to lead to revolution, Hess proposed to start tackling the root problem of economic inequality – the right of inheritance – without delay but in a gradualist manner. Natural and historic rights could not be abolished at one go. 'Nature knows no standstill, but also no leaps.' But just as man, after his temporary sojourn on earth, returned his soul to the Creator, so the state had the right to claim as its own and to 'inherit' the capital and property he had accumulated – on condition that the state look after the welfare of its citizens by apportioning to each an equal share of its resources. As the state developed and prospered, this initial reform would eventually, in the second stage, make possible the smooth achievement of complete equality.

For what Moses Hess was envisioning at 25 was actually 'the Kingdom of Truth' on earth. The thrust of his metaphysical-eschatological concept of the progress of world history led to his statement that collective ownership – ensuring the just distribution of the resources of society to all – 'is the final aim of social life'. His vision included modern and advanced versions of

- the welfare state, with free education for children and a national health service or 'medicare' system;
- women's liberation, with full equal rights and freedom from domestic and sexual subjugation;
- the elimination of poverty and crime;

- representative government;
- a League of Nations and, at a more distant stage in the consummation of his vision, the dissolution of all national frontiers.

In the state of the future, ruled by 'intelligence' and representative government, religion and politics would again be one, as they had been before Christianity introduced a cleavage between spirit and matter, church and state.
Politics, expressing the spirit of the people, would no longer divide rulers and
the ruled. As society, moving towards perfection, would gradually act more and
more in conformity with the eternal principles of a moral world order, mankind
would reach a stage of awareness enabling it to regain the original innocence
that had been its own during its infancy at the beginning of history.

'Man will no longer eat his bread in the sweat of his brow, but in free enjoyment of the pleasures of life'; and woman, likewise recovering innocence, will
share it with him to the full. Women will be given the same humanist education
as men, and marriage – freed of prevailing coercive arrangements – will be
based on 'free love', and no longer on chains of bondage. Writing in 1836, Hess
observed that the idea of free love was not new, but following the loss of 'blind
faith in authority' marital laws had to be abolished. 'Before Christ woman was a
nonentity; in the Orient woman is a slave to this day.' In the New Society her
emancipation 'will be complete'.[18] With the present family structure subject to
conventions and external laws, the state will take over the education of children, for true political freedom cannot be reconciled with the values imposed
on them by arbitary parental authority. Ultimately, however, when 'everyone
will carry the law in his breast', the ideal, 'patriarchal, pure family life' will
again come into its own. The state will be wise and prosperous enough to look
after the aged and infirm, and will not spare the means to establish the best
institutions for the rehabilitation of 'sinners' and the retarded.

Moved by the same aspiration for unity and equality, men in a society in
which the welfare of each depends on the welfare of all and 'the riches of the
whole' are shared, will act in unison and harmony. With the elimination of class
differences and competition, the benefits derived from the identity of interests
between the high and the lowly, between bureaucrats and citizens, will be so
manifest that 'no patriotism known in any of the old states will compare with
that of the new League of Nations.' Instead of hatching wars of conquest, all
will aspire to advance the progress of humanity. Where the conflict between
patricians and plebeians, the poor and the rich, caused 'disturbances, injustices
and horrors', peace will reign.[19]

The League of Nations will be composed of states and communities professing a diversity of 'external' faiths. Each will live like a world of its own, but all,

including the sincerest believers in Christ, will live on a higher level of consciousness in the Spinozist 'knowledge of God' which comes through reason and feeling. Theirs will be the 'Kingdom of Truth', in which man – true to the moral nature which is in him, and made whole again by the union of spirit and matter, ethics and politics – will be at peace with God and the world and find his calling and his greatest satisfaction as a social being in joining his fellow-men to work for 'the highest good of mankind'.[20]

Hess's statement that at one point in the final stage of perfection the restored patriarchal family 'will form a state of its own' has given rise to the interpretation that the state will eventually become superfluous, or lose its current meaning.[21]

Moses Hess wrote *The Holy History of Mankind* behind his father's back, as it were, while continuing to mind the grocery store for him, but amidst increasing friction at home. Though aware of his son's gradual estrangement from Judaism, David Hess would have been appalled to know that Moses, besides being about to pose as the bearer of a new annunciation *à la* St John, was preparing to raise Spinoza to the stature of a prophet of the New Age and some final redemption. For although Spinoza had never accepted baptism, and his *Tractatus Theologico-Politicus* – in which he developed his rationalist metaphysics, denying the possibility of supernatural phenomena or miracles – was in fact denounced by Christian theologians, orthodox Jewry continued to regard him as a renegade.

In January 1836, while secretly working on his book, Moses, driven to despair by his inability to buy the latest literature on his father's short allowance, had actually turned for help to Wolfgang Menzel, the prominent German critic and editor of the *Literaturblatt*. Describing himself as a young 'Israelite of well-to-do family, though never disposing of a penny', he wondered whether Menzel, who did not know him from Adam, could help him to get books cheaply; he confessed that he had never finished even secondary school but, fishing for a job on the *Literaturblatt*, he declared that he would 'gladly leave house and home... if I could but live by your side'.[22]

Both this and another letter to Menzel shortly afterwards exist only in draft and no reply from Menzel has ever been found. Nevertheless, Hess's very idea of appealing to Menzel has puzzled biographers, and the question whether he was naive or simply did not know that the editor of the *Literaturblatt* was the notorious informer who had instigated the ban on Heine and the Young Germany writers, and a known anti-'Israelite' into the bargain, has never been settled.

Hess's reading so far had been chiefly in French; he lived, worked and wrote in total isolation and his ignorance of the cultural scene in Germany was such that he actually sat down to translate Rousseau's *Emile* without knowing that the German translation had been available for several decades. Of the genesis of the futurist social vision he unfolded in *The Holy History of Mankind*, Hess himself was later to say: 'When I began to write my first book... I knew nothing about Saint-Simon... nothing about Hegel, nothing about Heine, nothing about the so-called Young Germany.'

Yet this 'sincere and enthusiastic radical' was soon – in the words of Isaiah Berlin – to be 'far in advance of even the Hegelian Left'[23] and its discovery of the revolutionary kernel in Hegel's dialectic. Not only that, but already in 1836 when Hess, in the course of working on his manuscript, read Heine's *History of Religion and Philosophy in Germany* – and all he knew of Hegel was from this and other second-hand gleanings, while the beginning clamour of the master's left-wing critics had yet to reach his ears – he dared to question Hegel's system on two points. Hegel's philosophy of history, like Schelling's philosophy of nature, Hess wrote in *The Holy History of Mankind*, were 'each in its field incontestably meritorious, but must be rejected when and insofar either of them lays claim to be absolute science, or a theory of salvation.'[24]

How to explain this? A note written by Hess as early as 1830 shows that as a youth he had a certain mistrust of systems. Rather than attacking systems 'and building new ones in their place', he had written, 'one should fight their errors and do justice to their other sides... then shall we come upon the pure unadulterated truth.'[25]

It was perhaps his very unworldliness, his being unacquainted with the dominant 'scientific' doctrines and unencumbered by the ideas of fashionable authorities, that gave free reign to his intuition and the independence of mind he was to show throughout his life. Wittingly or not, he challenged the arbitrary verdict in which Hegel had confined Judaism to the 'dunghill' of history.

In what S. Avineri was to call 'a programmatic revolution in modern European historiography', which had 'conventionally viewed the progression of world history as involving Greece-Rome-Christianity', Hess's treatment of 'the Jewish people and its heritage, which includes both Jesus and Spinoza, as the holy history of mankind' was one of the 'first revolts' by a secular, non-orthodox Jew against 'most of the European philosophers of history, who, following Christian theological preferences, found it difficult to grant Judaism a significant role in history... Hess turned what was viewed as a marginal element in history – Judaism – into its core.'[26]

To make no mistake about it, young Hess's own division of world history into three main stages – each transformed through crisis, decline and collision with new forces as it passed into the next – fitted remarkably well Hegel's dynamic of history and his triadic dialectic of thesis, anti-thesis and synthesis.

Hess had read Herder, and like him compared his three stages to the childhood, adolescence and maturity of mankind respectively. They also, for a third and ingenious thing – and disregarding such lacunae as his leaving out the Byzantine Empire – corresponded to the Christian Trinity. Christ, Hess wrote, had made God accessible to all and 'faith in him will never die'. And Hess expressly placed 'the period of the future', inaugurated by Spinoza, under the sign of 'the Holy Spirit'. Christianity, he noted in the margin of his manuscript, represented 'a transitional stage from the old social order to the new: it lived in hope of the future Kingdom of Resurrection.'[27]

Christianity had thus abandoned mundane reality and the social world for the world of the spirit. But as a universal religion it was best fitted to bring about the new age of 'unity and equality' through a synthesis with Spinoza's world-view, which reconciled spirit with matter, reason with feeling, God with man as a conscious, rational, social and moral being living in harmony with himself and nature.

As for Judaism's role, Hess himself had pronounced the Mosaic religion to be dead. But like most of the secular Jews living in the Prussian state, which placed the accent on Christian triumphalism and had yet to grant them civic rights – and especially as a Rhenish Jew born to enjoy freedom and these rights under the French, only to have them snatched away – he was bound to struggle for his identity, buffeted in all directions as he was caught in the same predicament as Heine and in a sense Marx himself, and ultimately solving it in a way entirely his own.

But what was the source of his early preoccupation with the social question, where had this self-taught, 24-year-old 'Israelite of well-to-do family' seen the plight of the masses exploited by the new machines? Though many of his pronouncements on the misery caused by egoism, greed and cut-throat competition seem to have been inspired by Charles Fourier, Hess's idea of men uniting in a 'great League to support each other like brethren' for the highest good of mankind as well as their own echoed Saint-Simon's cherished ideals of bringing about the 'association of all men on the globe'. Unlike Saint-Simon's disciples, however, Hess did not believe that 'supreme equality' could be magically conjured up out of Christianity, without any mediation. For Christianity, he declared in *The Holy History of Mankind*, was itself 'the apex of inequality' and had yet to heal 'the cleavage which occurred in humanity after the decline of the Jewish state' and to restore the unity of religion and politics, state and church and social life before it could assume the leading role in establishing 'the New Society'.

Like Marx, like Bakunin, Moses Hess had a sense of vocation and mission. In writing his first book he felt, as he confided to his diary in January 1836, that he was pursuing his 'calling'. But where did his evangelizing zeal come from, his eagerness to 'bear witness of the Light', to go into metaphysics and help mankind with its social problems by helping it 'to achieve perfect cognition of God' so soon after he had buried his own religion? Was he out to establish a new religion, a synthesis of Judaism and Christianity?

'I wrote *The Holy History of Mankind* with the Bible in one hand and with the *Ethics* [of Spinoza] in the other,' was all he volunteered a couple of years later in an unpublished manuscript.[28]

In the book itself, Spinoza figured very little, and Hess invoked him only as having proved that, just as theology and philosophy, faith and science, can peacefully co-exist, so 'Jews and Christians, being both of divine nature, can live side by side in peace.' But how to square Hess's assuming the role of divine oracle and his apostolic ardour, not to say bravado – which by the time he was 25 and finishing the manuscript made him write in his diary, 'Napoleon rejuvenated the world politically, if I succeed in my task they will call me the Napoleon of religion' – with his apparent loss of faith?

'I have always had only one passion, namely, to spread happiness and joy' – these words which Moses was to address 10 years later to his mistress and eventual wife, albeit in a private and intimate connection, reveal a clue to one of the mainsprings of his personality. They show a motivation fundamentally different from the anarchist or purely materialist conception that was to mark Bakunin's and Marx's programmes of salvation; and it is no wonder that Hess's close collaboration with Marx during most of the crucial next decade was to end in a bitter split.

Tall, thin, wearing a moustache and a frock-coat, Moses Hess at 25 was not merely a highly sensitive and intelligent young idealist, but a perennial seeker after truth and justice. His diary abounds with self-proddings to study 'the newer philosophy and theology', to devote himself to science, etc. In a significant entry in May 1837 he noted that when he told his friends he had reached his goal 'because I can now devote myself entirely to studying' – he was indeed that year to enroll at Bonn University, which the much younger Marx had already left for Berlin – 'they all wanted to know the end-purpose of my studies. They believe one can only study to achieve something else. I, however, love studying for its own sake.' Although Hess sat in as a listener on some curiously assorted courses – history, medicine, magnetism, electricity, philosophy – and only for three semesters, the base of his self-taught and uneven knowledge on a variety of subjects was broadened. As he never ceased studying on his own, he reached a point of erudition which made it natural for contemporaries to refer to him as 'Dr Hess'.

It was probably because his father agreed to pay for his university tuition that Moses Hess stayed on with him. In his single-minded devotion to study for its own sake he never bothered about money: 'For the life I want I need no more than the means I already have – sufficiency, industry, and a little wisdom of life.' At the same time, he was possessed of great energy and dynamism. It was through his own efforts and constant struggle that he became a writer. 'A writer?' he had asked himself a year or so before starting his first university semester. 'What education did I have? None. Where did I study? Nowhere. What? Nothing.' Hess had a missionary streak. His appetite for learning also represented an urge to teach others. He had strong ethical feelings and a 'conciliatory' temperament – as he was on one occasion to tell Marx – yet he had no lack of aggressiveness. His was a strong super-ego; when moved by injustice he felt deeply committed to repairing it and would attack it with vehemence.

A thoughtful, soft-looking young do-gooder, Hess was nevertheless to become not merely a writer and thinker, but a militant agitator and active fighter. The coming upheaval would be bloodier than the American and French Revolutions – he had privately noted before he was 24 – and both the old feudal and the new moneyed oppressors would be knocked out to lie, in boxing terms, 'flat and annihilated on the floor'; and in an unpublished segment of *The Holy History of Mankind* he compared the aristocracy and its influence to a 'poison infesting the veins of society'. Ministries and dynasties would change, but unless inherited privilege was abolished 'the heart of society will be lacerated and torn to pieces by a ceaseless war' between the haves and the have-nots until either the present order or those enslaved by it won. 'Woe, if it remains! Woe, if it is defeated!'

Adding that he knew that kings, statesmen and diplomats would not heed his message but that he felt impelled to warn the world in time of the coming chaos, Hess gave a clue to his burning need to hold up a light – like St John – to humanity struggling in darkness, when he wrote: 'We feel like the Hebrew prophet who is called to account by the Lord whether he has fulfilled his mission – our conscience never for a moment stops raising its voice and asking: Hast thou carried out thy task?'[29]

Hess's messianic streak would persist through his later militant atheism, for he was at heart deeply religious. For the full sources that inspired his highly original, if idiosyncratic, world-view in *The Holy History of Mankind*, we must go back to some of his earliest extant letters reflecting the polarity of conflicting tendencies and emotions struggling in his soul. On the subject of atheism, he wrote when he was 17 to his cousin Leopold Zuntz: 'Entirely pure conceptions of God and atheist conceptions are so closely interwoven that it is almost impossible to reach the former without first getting over the latter.'[30] It was a concept that the future 'bellwether' of German Communism and co-founder of its rival Social-Democratic Workers Movement, as well as prophet of Zionism, was to experience in his own person and to exemplify throughout his restless life.

On the subject of the moral world order, he wrote in the same letter, 'Everything in the world, in the whole of nature, is arranged with supreme reason' and with 'such perfection in all its causes and effects' that to speak of 'supernatural' miracles was a contradiction in terms and set limits to divine reason. He also submitted that Providence's greatest gifts to man were reason and his moral instinct.

In February 1830, shortly after his 18th birthday – writing to an unknown correspondent (identified only as 'I... cK...se'), with whom he carried on a philosophical argument that year – he developed the proposition that 'Nature, the physical course of the world, is as far as can be ascertained conspicuously governed by the highest reason – I say conspicuously, because here and there some things in the course of the world must appear unjust to our limited reason. To explain them to myself I would have to be all-knowing and possessed of the highest reason.' However, since even limited knowledge of the universe convincingly showed that it is founded on the highest reason, he went on, 'then I have to conclude that the thing whose full justice I could not see for the reason stated must in reality possess the highest degree of perfection.' In the course of this demonstration to the unknown correspondent, Hess inserted the observation: 'A society made up exclusively of pure unmixed evil-doers and scoundrels has no chance of lasting because they will tear each other out of existence.'[31]

On the subject of Spinoza, he quoted (again in the same letter) a Socratic passage from Moses Mendelssohn's *Phaedon*, stating that 'the human species is made for sociability', and he commented exultantly, 'Spoken straight out of my heart! What a divine idea!' If, as it seems, he had not yet read Spinoza, it must have given him great satisfaction eventually, in writing his book, to be able to quote the passage from 'the Master' dwelling on man's need to 'associate with his fellow men, live in society', as a way both of satisfying his natural urge for 'sociability' and of contributing to the harmony of the universe.

On the subject of Judaism and history, he had written to a friend in 1831: 'I daresay I am a genuinely pious Jew, but only insofar as I am a pious man. When the former conflicts with the latter, I am a human being at the expense of the Jew.' The 19-year-old humanist, while declaring his belief in 'the absolute divinity of our commandments in the Land of our Fathers', then put in a strong reservation: 'Precisely because of the genuineness of our faith I also believe that they [the Commandments] lost this absolute divinity when we ceased to be one nation... What is it that attests to the divine origin of our ancient laws? The fact that they are founded on eternal truths, wisely modified according to time and place... We worship the ancient oak, but neglect the root – ha! the root has long since been eaten up by worms, the tree has ceased bearing fruit. It merely stands there out of ancient habit. Soon, soon, it will collapse in a rotten heap ...'[32]

Hess's aim was thus not to effect a synthesis between Judaism and Christianity. In the New Society of the future, Jews and Christians would be able to co-exist without friction. But Hess's diary shows that the predicament of the German Jews in his own day presented him with no mean quandary. On the one hand, he was estranged from the orthodox form of Judaism, and actually felt that 'Christianity is the religion perfectly suiting the present'; on the other, the assimilationist trend, which led some Jews to the baptismal font for solely opportunistic reasons, seemed to him unworthy and cheapening. He saw in fact no reason why even 'enlightened' secular Jews should embrace Christianity so long as it neither granted them emancipation nor lived up to its role as a true world religion and devoted itself to 'the salvation of man in the widest humanist sense'. Christianity, in short, instead of trying to convert the Jews by means of 'exhortation, temptation and threats' (as in Prussia), had to improve its social ethics to convince them that it was a better faith than their own.

The social and universalist vision that made Moses Hess transport the New Jerusalem to the heart of Europe was thus animated by his express recognition, in *The Holy History of Mankind*, that Christianity had reached a higher stage, and had a greater potential for uniting men, than Judaism, rather than being a mere attempt to escape the horns of his personal dilemma. The Jews had always been few. Long suffering had by now reduced them to an 'airy nebulum... a spirit without a body.' For all their glorious ancient history, they hardly had a chance of ever being resurrected as a people – or so he felt in the mid-1830s.

Like William Blake, who had proposed to build Jerusalem 'in England's green and pleasant land' – an England freed of aristocracy, inequality and other evils – the young Hess took his original inspiration from the Old Testament vision of 'The City of God' in Ezekiel. But he fused it with Spinoza's rationalist reconciliation of the spiritual and the material into a Socialist programme, the first of its kind in Germany publicly to deal with ways of averting the competitive excesses of industrial society and its accompanying chaos and miseries.

What constitution best fitted the New Society, 'the future empire (or league of nations) in which intelligence predominates and all are free and equal?'

The question brought Hess back to the synthesis of politics and religion, the unity 'between rulers and the ruled', which had originally characterized Judaism, and which Spinoza had universalized. 'The history of mankind provides us with one example of a constitution which did not fail to impress itself on a people,' Hess wrote in the last climactic pages of *The Holy History of Mankind*.

> We mean that ancient, holy people's state which was destroyed long ago, but continues to live until this very day in the feelings of its scattered members. In the Jews, in this despised people, which has remained loyal to its old customs and which reawakens now, after a long sleep, to a higher consciousness and is about to end its wanderings, to which God condemned it until it would see His visage again – in the Jews, we say, their old Law revives again.

Calling this a more vivid and eloquent 'testimony to its holiness than any other historical monument' and 'all the salvaged documents of its ancient time,' Hess rose to a final peroration:

> This people was destined from the beginning of time to conquer the world – not like pagan Rome by the strength of its arms, but by the inner virtue of its spirit. Like a haunted spirit it wandered through the world which it conquered, and its enemies did not succeed in vanquishing it, because the spirit is indomitable. This spirit now permeates the world; the world yearns for a new constitution worthy of the Old Mother. It will appear, this new holy constitution, the old Law will rise again, transfigured. Out of the old world condemned to chaos, the genius of humanity will rise.

The Holy History of Mankind, with its message that, by the dialectics of history, worn-out Judaism still had a universal mission to fulfil before the Jews themselves disappeared as a people, attracted little attention in 1837. The luxuriously printed but anonymous volume received in fact only two reviews. But if not in the eyes of the world, it established the young Moses in his own mind as a writer.

It was, however, to take him two years to produce his next work, *The European Triarchy*. In 1838 he spent a fortnight in Frankfurt in the company of Berthold Auerbach, with whom he shared a common interest in Spinoza. Unlike Hess, Auerbach, a former rabbinical candidate, had studied law and philosophy at three universities, including Heidelberg. In 1837 he had published a novel, *Spinoza, Ein Denkerleben* (A Thinker's Life). Before becoming widely popular with his 'Black Forest Village Stories' (*Schwarzwälder Dorfgeschichten*) – for the English edition of which Gladstone was to write a foreword – Auerbach also translated Spinoza's *Collected Works*.

Aside from being introduced by Auerbach to some of Frankfurt's literati, and occasional visits to Bonn, Hess continued at the end of the 1830s to live a rather lonely life in Cologne. 'Sequestered with my books and ideas', he was to write to Auerbach on 15 March 1840, 'I am out of touch with literature and have little opportunity for contact with literary people.'

And yet there he was, intervening in the increasingly heated debate between Hegel's disciples of the Right and Left. His new work, *The European Triarchy* – in which he developed a 'philosophy of action' and otherwise proved himself an original and far-sighted political and social thinker – was to earn him the respect of advanced intellectual circles.

While acknowledging Hegel's greatness, Hess declares in his second book that 'a philosophy of history which, like Hegel's, recognized as rational only the past and the present "what is" has accomplished only half its task.' Although the revolutionary kernel is inherent in the Hegelian dialectic, Hegel himself, for reasons dictated by time, circumstance and his own temperament, shied away from predicting the future. Yet, Hess submitted, it is the task of a philosophy of history to examine the past and the present, and out of these two known dimensions – what has been and what is – to deduce a third and unknown dimension, *that of the future that is in the process of taking shape*. By solving this task, the philosophy of history becomes a philosophy of action,[33] and it is this added new dimension that places the whole of world history in a new light.

So far only a Polish student of Hegel, August von Cieszkowski, had spoken in a study published in 1838 of the need for a 'philosophy of action' which, instead of presenting man as the unconscious tool of 'the World Spirit', ought in future to turn to 'praxis' and enable man to shape his own life and social condition.[34] The philosophy of action, however, had been independently foreshadowed by Hess in 1837 in his first book, in his future-oriented view of history moving towards the New Age. In *The European Triarchy* he went much further. First, he made the social problem his paramount consideration; and secondly, he took the Young Hegelian Left to task for going overboard in their abstract speculations on the future, dismissing all past history without realizing or caring that, in the process, they were discarding the ethical values accumulated in the course of it. He pointed out to them that Hegel's philosophy had remained in the abstract realm of the 'pure *Idea*': it could not create any new historic reality. What could do that was the blend of speculative philosophy and philosophy of action whereby Spinoza in his *Ethics* had bridged the gulf between past and future.

Hegel had acknowledged Spinoza's role 'in the emergence of the knowledge of God which he himself, Hegel, continued and developed.' But Hegel's philosophy was unable 'to transcend itself' and advance to Spinoza's synthesis of speculative thought and philosophy of action which, putting an end to the Christian separation of spirit and matter, had reconciled body and soul, politics and religion, morality and social concerns under a single set of principles governing both nature and the reality of human life.

In a veiled reference to the need for 'political freedom', Hess wrote that the Reformation in Germany had 'emancipated the human spirit. But if you are against full *realization* of the freedom of the spirit, why emancipate it? You would have done better to leave it shackled in paganism, Judaism or the Catholic Church... *If political freedom without freedom of the mind is a monstrosity*, then the latter without the former [i.e., without political freedom] is a no lesser monstrosity.'[35]

Hess's philosophy of action was in fact part of a wider programme for the social and political reorganization of Europe. What he was telling the Young Hegelian Left was that 'the philosophy of action is the viable germ of the future', and that Hegel had done only half the job. But in his revolutionary potential he had left behind a veritable treasure which they, as his heirs, must further develop by nursing this germ and working *actively* to change the present, instead of indulging in violent but passive *theoretical* criticism and 'sterile metaphysics'.

It was not only by propounding a philosophy of action that Hess was in advance of the radical Young Hegelian Left. *The European Triarchy* – as Hess himself, in a first reference to it, described it to Auerbach on 15 March 1840 – dealt with 'the social problem, which, as you can see from the newspapers, is now on the agenda in England. It is becoming clear, as I suggested in my *Holy History of Mankind*, that our century is the staging-period for a revolution whose consequences will be more far-reaching and profound than the one produced by the last.'[36]

Except for a section produced in 1839, Hess wrote most of *The European Triarchy* in 1840, during the feverish year in which a new king came to the throne of Prussia, sounds of war could be heard between Prussia and France, and there was a general war scare in Europe as a result of the 'Oriental crisis' and the sequence of events which led to the formation of the Quadruple Alliance, the British bombardment of Beirut and the fall of the Thiers government in Paris.

In the midst of this military and diplomatic crisis, Hess was actually forecasting the ultimate emergence of a united Europe and, at the same time, laying the foundation of Marxism ahead of Marx himself. Then, when he met that 'young man' in the flesh and instantly recognized in him 'the greatest, perhaps the *only* living *genuine* philosopher', he began a close collaboration that lasted nearly 10 years until he was displaced by the young Engels.

Hess's relationship with the historic Marx-Engels duo was to be marked by an up-and-down struggle to maintain his independence of mind and his view of a fundamentally ethical world order against their dogmatic economic determinism. 'Not the needs of the stomach' alone prompt social reform or revolution, he was to argue, but also 'the needs of the heart' and ideas springing from a sense of justice.

18

Marx the Student in Berlin

Karl Marx arrived in Berlin in October 1836, the year the first train steamed into London and elegant hansom cabs for two, recently patented by a Mr Hansom, began to appear in its streets. Victoria, the future Queen of Great Britain, was 17 and Marx was one year older almost to the day.

For public transport, steam-driven trams had been plying the streets of London for some years now. Berlin had only horse-drawn omnibuses and some sections of the city could be reached only across open fields. Some of the original defence walls ringing the medieval city had been torn down, but, except at the spacious and relatively new Brandenburg Gate (built in the 1790s), access to the centre was still via the old toll-gates – the Potsdamer Tor, Frankfurter Tor, etc. – flanked by disused little gatehouses.

With some 300,000 inhabitants, Berlin – capital of 15 million Prussians – was the second largest German city after Vienna. But it was a city barely beginning to emerge into modernity, and as Prussia itself was a young and upstart country, it lacked the character, tradition and civic spirit of a capital, as Madame de Staël had already noted.

'Berlin is not a city at all,' Heine wrote some 8 years before Marx's arrival there. A Cologne art connoisseur had described it as a conglomerate rather than a city – parts of it looking like 'a larger (provincial) Mannheim', the river boats on the Spree like a Dutch scene, while the 'enormously tall' Old Castle and the statues at the start of the famous Unter den Linden promenade evoked something of Paris. A remarkable number of people also noted Russian influences and certain features reminiscent of St Petersburg. 'Much of St Petersburg has stuck here,' a Berlin poet and journalist wrote in 1841; and almost 30 years later Dostoyevsky, arriving 'tired, livid and stiff', after a 48-hour train journey through rain and fog, was horror-struck when he 'suddenly perceived at first glance only this: that Berlin was incredibly reminiscent of Petersburg. The same straight, ruler-drawn streets, the same smells...'[1]

In Marx's youth, Berlin housed military-minded Prussia's largest garrison. As a royal residence and government centre, it teemed not only with army men and Junkers in uniform, but with court officials and the whole hierarchy of

517

office-holders – who in those days were mostly titled aristocrats – running the various Ministries that controlled Prussia's centralist bureaucracy. The city had hardly any industrial plants and not much of a financial *haute volée*, though not a few of its residents were wealthy noblemen.

It was, in short, a staid, placid and – according to some contemporaries – 'dead' but strictly regulated city in which a 'churchyard stillness and barrack-room atmosphere' prevailed. Yet it was young Marx's first big city, and though lacking the bustle, spirit and charm of Paris, it was a far cry from God-forsaken Trier and the quiet little academe of Bonn.

And this city of soldiers, shopkeepers and 'royal' civil servants was also a city of scholars. 'Look! The University next to the Arsenal!' Professor Eduard Gans once instructed a French visitor. 'That is the symbol of Prussia.' Characteristically, the imposing Arsenal on Unter den Linden was the first great 'modern' building put up in Berlin at the end of the 17th century. It may have been characteristic, too, that the many war symbols and victory trophies decorating its walls and portals – eagles, escutcheons, palm and laurel leaves, as well as Medusa heads – included 22 statuary representations not of its fallen heroes, but of the impaled figures of its enemies.

Along Unter den Linden, besides the Arsenal and the University, rose the Opera House with its 'Corinthian Temple' architecture, as well as some rich private mansions. Berlin had a famous Singakademie, plenty of concert music, and a Komödiehaus with more than 600 seats. There was the Tiergarten and there were coffee-houses and taverns; gardens and tall-spired churches as well as monumental buildings.

That first year at the University, Marx chiefly studied law under two of Berlin's most influential professors: jurisprudence under Baron Friedrich Karl von Savigny and criminal law under Eduard Gans. Between these two men a quiet battle had been going on ever since 1822 when Hegel obtained the appointment of Gans, his 25-year-old disciple, to an assistant professorship, only to see it quashed after most of the faculty, led by Savigny – the veteran and distinguished but dryasdust jurist dubbed by Heine 'the Troubadour of Pandects' – objected on the grounds of the candidate's religion.

Hegel continued to favour Gans and was merely biding his time for another opportunity. When the French philosopher Victor Cousin was arrested as a 'subversive' in Dresden, Hegel – obtaining his transfer to Berlin under conditions of house arrest – directed Gans, who spoke French, to keep him company. This was a mutually profitable move, for Gans privately initiated Cousin into the substance of Hegel's Philosophy of Right, and, when he followed Cousin to Paris on his return, was introduced to his colleagues at the Sorbonne. Gans acquainted other leading French intellectuals with Hegel's ideas and made valuable contacts for himself.

But it was only on his return from Paris towards the end of 1825, by which time he was ready to change his religion, that Gans obtained an assistant professorship, and finally in 1828 a full one. Between then and 1836, he had emerged as a radical humanist academic. He had made more visits to Paris, and had not only adopted Saint-Simon's programme for the social transformation of society, but become its spokesman in Germany. Since Savigny and Gans offered different interpretations of Hegel (who had died in 1831), the battle between them in the Law Faculty had shifted to philosophical ground.

> Today Gans concluded his lecture on the philosophy of history. So many had come to listen that the large hall with its gilt decorations was filled to overflowing. The eloquent professor lifted the curtain for a glimpse of the future... The lower classes will catch up with the higher ones, just as the middle class has caught up with the nobility. History, ceasing to be inaccessible to the lower classes... will then comprise all classes equally, all will become active members of history... Tears came into my eyes. The large audience sat in solemn silence, as though taking leave of the Past and hearkening in awe to the giant steps of the approaching Future, which seemed to knock on the doors of the great old hall.[2]

This was the effect on V.S. Pecherin, a 27-year-old Russian who was in Berlin on a scholarship, of a lecture delivered by Eduard Gans in 1834. Pecherin, who returned to Russia with a Berlin degree and taught for some years in St Petersburg, but was to take the first occasion to flee Russia 'as one flees the plague', acccurately noted that the future revealed by Gans corresponded to the Saint-Simonist vision. Savigny, the leader of the so-called 'historical' school of jurisprudence – treating law as an organic development of the nation's past, customs and institutions – stressed the conservative side of Hegel's philosophy as justifying Prussian absolutism. Aristocratic, nearly 60 and more or less a reactionary, he was to become Prussia's Minister of Justice within 5 years of Marx's arrival.

Gans, the baptized Jew, was a different sort of scholar altogether: 40 years old in 1836, with round face and side whiskers, his head decked by a thick crown of curly hair, he was restless, apoplectic and a lively speaker who now had 'the whole of Berlin' sitting up and listening to his daring opinions on suppressed topics of the day.

Gans stressed the modern aspect of flux, change and movement dialectically implicit in Hegel's view of history. In a book published in 1836 he had the temerity to speak of 'hundreds of emaciated and miserable men and women' in factories slaving for a single master for a pittance, and to ask: 'Do you not call it slavery when a man is exploited like an animal, even if he is otherwise free to die of starvation?... That the state must care for the poorest and most numerous class... is a deep view into our times, and the pages of history will one day be filled to overflowing with the struggle of the proletarians against the middle class...'[3]

Hegel seemed to have answered all the questions, solved all the problems of a baffled world and left nothing for his disciples to do but sit back and enjoy their bliss. But the world continued out of sorts, and intellectual unrest had set in. Berlin University, unlike others in Germany, admitted the general public to the lectures of its professors. Gans's ideas were like a breath of fresh air in those 'fusty times' and his eloquence attracted not only students, but capacity audiences – including clerics as well as officers, officials and artists. They were widely talked about, for the subjects he discussed – such as the lot of 'the poorest and most numerous class', in the Saint-Simonist formulation – were almost unthinkable at the time as a public topic in Berlin.

Prussia's old King Friedrich Wilhelm III, the last European monarch to hold his throne since the time of the French Revolution, was allied both to Tsar Nicholas I (besides being his father-in-law) and to Metternich, and remained a dyed-in-the-wool reactionary. In New York, by 1836, James Gordon Bennett had founded the cheap mass-circulation *Daily Herald*. In Paris, too, where the Arc de Triomphe had just been completed, two popular newspapers, *La Presse* and *Le Siècle*, made their first appearance that year. Other papers, in spite of the 'September Laws', continued to criticize and battle with the government. In Prussia there was no such thing: no free newspapers or uncensored books, no public meetings, performances or academic institutions which were not supervised by Metternich's central commission, which continued to keep an eye on 'subversion' in all 36 German *Länder*. In short, there was no platform where political or social ideas could be openly aired.

Of course, censorship varied according to time, place and the whims and watchfulness of individual officials. In the Prussian capital it was, if anything, stricter than in most other places in Germany. There was a measure of academic freedom at some of the universities, partly because they were state-controlled, and partly because of the great respect in which scholars were held in Germany. Indeed, when the new King of Hanover abolished its Constitution in 1837 and peremptorily dismissed 7 Göttingen professors for daring to protest his suppression of it, there was an outcry all over Germany.

Besides counteracting Savigny's reactionary conception of law, Gans also taught modern history in a cycle of lectures titled 'The Last Fifty Years'. This gave him a chance to discuss the French Revolution; he presented it as a forward movement and dwelt freely on its ineffaceable political consequences. For a time he was tolerated, the King and his advisers relying on the preponderant old guard of conservative professors to combat his influence and uphold the hallowed values of the absolutist 'German-Christian' state. A year or so later, however, his lectures were to grow so 'free' that they were repeatedly banned. Even Heine, who never forgave Gans his baptism – in spite, or because, of his own apostasy – could not help admiring the courageous stand of his one-time friend. In his book on Ludwig Marcus, Heine was to go on castigating Gans, the president of Berlin's erstwhile Jewish *Verein*, as 'the captain who... saved himself first' from the foundering ship. But, recognizing the Gans-Savigny conflict for what it was – the new fighting the old, liberal ideas trying to break to the surface through the crust of reaction that enveloped politically muzzled Berlin – he could not forgo singling out Gans as 'the most energetic apostle of Hegelian philosophy', the man who 'savagely fought the lackeys of antique Roman Law ... Poor Herr von Savigny! How his soul whimpers and whines under his [Gans's] kicks...'

Gans was dead when Heine wrote this (in 1844) and otherwise paid him tribute as a fiery spirit who unmasked the 'servility' inherent in Savigny's effort to dress up Roman law in modern garb and thus 'furthered the development of the idea of liberty in Germany.' But in 1836 the brilliant Gans, who was very popular with his students, still had three years to shine.

Although Karl Marx did not take to Hegel immediately, and in Berlin continued to write poetry as a sideline, he followed the philosophical dispute between the Law Faculty's two rival luminaries with great interest. At the end of the first semester, Savigny's report stated that Karl Marx was an 'industrious' student, but from the fact that Gans gave him a higher mark – 'exceptionally industrious' – it seems that he made the greater impression on Gans.

On one of his first walks in Berlin, Marx had noticed a plaque on a building in the Leipziger Strasse – LESSING LIVED HERE – and, deciding that what was good for Germany's great classicist was good for himself, promptly rented lodgings there. In this respectable and rather expensive neighbourhood he was centrally located, close to the heart of the capital, and only a short way from the University. The University overlooked the approach to Berlin's Opera House, but the new arrival from Trier, at least by his own account, had no eyes for the gay scene of 'smart coaches, marching soldiers and sporting nymphs' which had kept Heine's eyes glued to the classroom windows 15 years earlier. Having dutifully delivered his father's letters of introduction to Justice Jaeningen, Justice Esser and Privy Councillor Meurin – all members of the Rhenish High Court of Appeals – Marx had been well received and invited to their homes, but he never bothered to call again. His father was appalled by his son's 'impolitic and rude neglect' of these gentlemen and their kindness.

521

'Frequenting society', Heinrich reminded him on 3 February 1837, more than three months after his departure, could be 'diverting, recreational and instructive' for a young man. Besides, now that Karl was 'no longer alone', but had his fiancée to consider, these contacts might be important for his future. Karl must cultivate them, but must do so, 'it goes without saying, in an honourable and worthy manner.'[4]

Karl Marx, not yet 19, thought little of this worthy advice, and even less of spending his time in the company of dignified judges. In fact, having come to Berlin 'to study jurisprudence', driven by an irresistible 'urge to grapple with philosophy' and to combine it with law and art into a single grand system, he soon dropped out of society altogether. Deserting the world in order to 'immerse myself in scholarship and art', he shut himself in and spent practically the whole of his first year in Berlin on his self-imposed task, wrestling on his own with philosophy and aesthetics, reading law and writing poetry in between.

The extraordinary story of his disorganized life and activities during his first year in Berlin was unreeled backwards in a famous letter he wrote to his father on the night of 10/11 November 1837, 13 months after his arrival there, the only letter of any he wrote in nearly 4 years to have been preserved:

> When I left you a new world had just opened before me, the world of love, at first a love drunk with longing and hopeless desire... Arrived in Berlin, I broke all existing ties, made only few and reluctant visits... In my then state of mind, lyric poetry inevitably became my first interest, at any rate the most agreeable... But my whole previous development made this poetry purely idealistic. My heaven, my art, became a distant Beyond, as distant as my love... Everything real grew misty... Feeling was expressed without moderation or form, nothing was natural ... everything built of moonshine... rhetorical reflections... perhaps also a certain warmth of emotion and youthful exuberance. These are the characteristics of all the poems of the three volumes that Jenny received from me.[5]

He had sent the first of these volumes, *The Book of Love*, to Jenny for Christmas 1836. When she picked it up at the Marx home on 27 December, she was moved to tears, but Marx's father was horrified that his son – far from taking his responsibilities seriously – was again wasting his time on bad poetry and fruitless philosophic speculations. The next day Sophie wrote to assure her brother that 'Jenny loves you; if the difference in age worries her it is only because of her parents. She will now try to prepare them little by little... Jenny visits us often... She is never allowed to leave us before ten o'clock, how do you like that?'[6]

But on the same day that Sophie sent this hopeful intelligence their father began his series of alarmed letters:

> 28 December 1836: I have spoken to Jy [Jenny]. I wish I could have entirely reassured her. I did my best, but not everything can be reasoned away. She has no ideas as yet how her parents will react to the relationship... I leave it to you to appreciate [her] situation... She is making an immeasurable sacrifice for you – she shows a self-abnegation which reason alone can fully value. Woe betide you if ever in your life you should forget that!...

Again the lawyer was appealing to his son, who would have to work many years before he could offer Jenny anything like security, to show his mettle and prove that he merited the world's respect, could earn and 'win it at the double-quick, proving your steadfastness and future earnest striving, and imposing silence on evil tongues. How best to make a start is something you alone can decide...'[7]

Karl, who had been impressed by Professor Gans's criticism of existing legal institutions, apparently gave his father some idea of the faults he found with them, for in the same letter of 28 December, Heinrich Marx reacted to his son's ambitious scheme to devise a grand new legal-philosophical system with the following dry, diplomatic lines: 'Your views on law are not without truth, but if welded into a system they are apt to produce storms [of controversy], and you have no idea how violent scholarly disputes can become.' He advised Karl to moderate 'offensive' passages and express them in more acceptable form 'if they cannot be completely removed.'[8]

Five weeks later, having become, against his will, his son's confidential love-courier and go-between, he communicated to Karl the impression – his own, or gained from Jenny – that her parents didn't want to know anything about the engagement. He had other joyless news for him, along with advice:

> 3 February 1837:... I have gained the unlimited confidence of your Jy. But the good, lovable girl is ceaselessly tormenting herself, she is afraid of harming you by causing you to overstrain yourself... A letter from you – which you may enclose – could comfort her, but it must not be one dictated by the fantasies of a poet. It should be full of tender, devoted feelings of pure love, as I have no doubt yours is, but it must clarify your relationship and set out your specific hopes clearly and with firmness, so that they carry conviction...
>
> What do you think of your father? Don't you find that I am amazingly well qualified for the role of broker? How badly I might be

judged were my intervention known! What impure motives could
not be imputed to me! But I have nothing to reproach myself with.

Young Marx's enormous labours on the 'system' would eventually turn out to
have been futile. But only his long letter of 10/11 November 1837 afforded his
father (and us) a retrospective glimpse of some of his life at the beginning of
that year, and some idea of the tremendous energies applied to his self-imposed
task by a youth not yet 19:

> ... I had to study jurisprudence and felt above all an urge to wrestle
> with philosophy. Both became so intertwined that I went through
> Heineccius, Thibaut and the sources like a schoolboy, completely
> uncritically; for instance, I translated the first two books of Pandects
> into German and also tried to elaborate a philosophy that would
> cover the whole field of law. As introduction I prefixed a few meta-
> physical propositions and carried on this ill-starred opus as far as
> public law...[9]

In short, he was engaged in a growing 'work of almost three hundred pages'. It
continued to grow, and while writing it he not only translated the two books of
Pandects – the 50-book collection of Roman Law codified by Justinian in the
6th century – but got into the habit of scribbling down whole passages from all
the books he read. Working day and night, engrossed in philosophical speculations or copying long excerpts from Lessing's *Laokoon*, Solger's *Erwin*, Winck-
elmann's *History of Art*, Luden's *German History*, and other works, he was
developing the life-long habit that, on any question that interested him, would
make him devour everything ever written about it and fill copious notebooks
with his comments and ideas. At the moment, in Berlin, he was of course too
busy and absorbed to write home frequently, but translated Tacitus's *Germania*
and Ovid's *Tristia* – and, given to excess in everything – also began 'to learn
English and Italian on my own, i.e. out of grammars, though I have not yet got
anywhere with them...'

This part of Marx's letter, which was to become known in time as his letter
of confession, describes only the first of his eventually fruitless labours that
year. In February, Jenny suddenly sulked and obstinately refused to write him a
word before and unless their betrothal was made public. At the same time his
father, misled by the number of courses for which his son had registered – and
having no precise idea of his activities until Karl unreeled the whole story
retroactively that November – was under the false impression, and 'overjoyed',
that Karl was energetically 'striving to consolidate your future vigorously and
with dignity. Only, dear Karl, do not fall into the opposite, and don't overdo

anything,' he warned him – in vain, but with good reason, in his letter of 3 February. Before the New Year, Karl had mentioned that he would aim at an academic career. His father found that an excellent plan, and the idea of his son's eventually achieving a professorship in spite of his youth cropped up before he had completed his first winter at university.

The winter term was to end around Easter time. Now, at the start of February 1837, Heinrich Marx, having already once assured the boy who was the apple of his eye that he had many years to live to his and his family's benefit – 'and if my pre-sentiment is not wrong, to the benefit of mankind' – reassured him that one more semester wouldn't matter. Confident that 'with your natural gifts and present industry you will achieve your aim,' but knowing his tendency to excess and mental overwork, he cautioned him 'not to neglect the body'. Health was 'the most precious asset' of all, and scholars needed it more than anyone. To keep him healthy and in good cheer, Marx sent a consignment of wine to Karl. And before he realized that Karl was going to run up living expenses that year approaching the annual salary on which a Berlin City Councillor had to maintain a family, he also sent him 'a letter of credit [for a sum] higher than you asked for... since I now have confidence that you will not spend more than is necessary.'[10]

By March, however, Heinrich Marx sounded a double alarm bell. Not only was he worried by his son's character – 'is your heart equal to your head, to your abilities? Has it room for... tender, earthly feelings? Will you ever be receptive to truly human, domestic bliss?' etc. – but there was a new anxiety about Jenny, whom he had come 'to love like my own child'.

> 2 March 1837:... I have noticed a disquieting phenomenon in Jy. She shows at times, against her will, a kind of fear, a fear heavy with foreboding, which does not escape me.
>
> What does, what could it mean? I am unable to explain it, but unfortunately my experience is not easily deceived.
>
> Your rise in the world, the flattering hope of some day seeing your name in high renown... [these] are illusions which I have long nursed... But I can assure you that the realization of these illusions [alone] will not make me happy. Only if your heart remains pure and purely human and no demonic genius is ever capable of alienating your heart and estranging it from its better feelings – only then will I find the happiness that, through you, I have been dreaming of for years. Otherwise, the most beautiful purpose of my life will be destroyed....[11]

In Berlin young Marx, grappling with the philosophy and 'the metaphysics of law, as I gratuitously christened it – i.e., first principles, reflections, definitions' – had been spending sleepless nights dividing 'the whole field of law' before he realized that the 'ill-starred' long opus resulting from his cerebrations was 'written with boring prolixity', 'full of hair-splitting', and suffered from the same flaw as his poetry. Just as in the latter 'the conflict between what "is" and what "ought" to be' had led to 'rhetorical reflections taking the place of poetic thoughts', so in his philosophy of the law, 'the same opposition of "is" and "ought", which is the peculiar hallmark of idealism, proved a disturbing hindrance and engendered [a] hopelessly mistaken division' between form and content.

Come November, in the famous letter of confession, he would go on explaining at great length to his father how this erroneous division had fouled up his philosophy of the law, making him 'barbarously misuse' Roman conceptions 'in order to force them into my system'; and how abstract 'definitions divorced from all actual law and every form of law, just as they are in Fichte', led him from the start into 'mathematical dogmatism', and 'obstructed any grasp of the truth' in his metaphysics as well: 'The nature of the triangle permits the mathematician to construct and demonstrate it, but it remains a pure abstraction in space and does not develop any further.'

Some time before the end of February, he gave up, after almost 300 pages and a vast effort, convinced that his legal-philosophical system would get nowhere because in the 'living world of ideas' it was not enough to 'circle round a subject, reasoning back and forth...' Rather, 'when we give concrete expression to the living world of thought, that of Law, the State, Nature and the whole of philosophy, the object itself must be studied in its own development, arbitrary divisions must not be intruded and the rationale of the Thing itself must evolve out of its inner contradictions and find unity within itself.'[12]

The historian Arnold Künzli has commented that young Marx, in his philosophical speculations, was unconsciously grappling with his own basic existential problem: his search for the reality of 'the Thing' (or object) itself was a desperate attempt to end his alienation from the world at large and to make contact – on an abstract intellectual level – with reality. Marx himself referred to this alienation in his letter when describing his state towards the end of the winter semester: 'My manifold occupations kept me awake many a night during the first term. I fought many battles, struggled with much inner turmoil and external proddings – and yet in the end I found myself not richer than before, while I had deserted nature, art and the world, and had alienated friends.'

In March he found himself at a dead end, with his father's 'external proddings' and reproaches hanging over him, and worried by Jenny's refusal to write.

The only clue to her 'fears' and to what was going on at the time in her home is a sentence of Heinrich Marx's informing Karl in February, 'Jenny I see seldom. She is not free to do what she wishes.' In his letter of 2 March, also, he impressed upon his 'man-boy' of a son that only a lifetime of tender love could compensate for what she had already suffered, let alone the suffering still in store for her; but in the same letter it was father, again, who guided him through his first-known crisis with his sweetheart. Karl had apparently offered to write to Baron Ludwig von Westphalen formally asking for his daughter's hand. Heinrich Marx reported that Jenny was pleased, but feared so direct an approach. He therefore counselled Karl, 'for her peace of mind, give us eight days' notice before mailing your letter,'[13] and he, Heinrich Marx, would prepare the ground for the Baron to give his consent. He was the all-round conciliator, the Nestor, mentor and tactful negotiator. Indeed, by the end of March, Jenny's parents are known finally to have given the couple their blessing.

But this was not the end of the imbroglio. Before long, Jenny succumbed to some mysterious illness or depression. Heinrich Marx kept assuring his son that 'even a prince could not seduce her away from you. She cleaves to you body and soul.' But months were to pass without her writing him a word.

In Berlin, Karl was about to complete his first semester. Spring was in the air and narrow-waisted young ladies escorted by swaggering Junker officers were beginning to parade the new 1837 fashion – puffed-out sleeves and cloche skirts showing the ankle – up and down Unter den Linden. Marx, to go by his telescoped November account, hardly noticed them. Unable 'to get by without philosophy', and undaunted by defeat, he reacted to the trouble with Jenny by throwing himself once again into philosophy's embrace and seeking solace there in vain: 'I wrote a new basic system of metaphysics, but when it was finished I was again forced to realize its futility, and the perverse topsy-turviness of it and of all my previous endeavours.'[14]

Reverting to his first love, he had also taken up poetry again. 'At the end of the term once more I sought the dance of the Muses and the music of the Satyrs...' He wrote ballads and sonnets, began a comic novel, *Scorpion and Felix*, and tried his hand at writing a 'fantastic drama' to be called *Oulanem*. Later he was to find that the one was 'forced' and the other uninspired, but all the same in April he prepared clean copies of the play and several chapters of the novel, and also gathered 40 of his ballads and assorted poems into a neatly handwritten volume, bearing the dedication 'TO MY DEAR FATHER ON HIS BIRTHDAY, 1837: A WEAK MARK OF ETERNAL LOVE', and sent the whole parcel to Trier.

He would be 19 in May. With prospects a long way off of a 'professorship', or even a lower-rung academic post, and his father during the summer constantly badgering him with his 'responsibility' towards Jenny, he aired a variety of schemes: he would make a name for himself by emulating Lessing and becoming a playwright; or distinguish himself as a poet, or as a drama critic; he might even launch a theatre journal.

By August he heard from his father that Jenny had been ill for a long time; and a few months later he received the following cryptic information: 'That she loves you with the most selfless love is beyond a doubt, and she was not far from sealing it with her death.'

Jenny's trouble was not the only one that summer. By August, Heinrich Marx too was ill, beginning slowly to succumb to the two hereditary Marx maladies: tuberculosis and liver disease. But by that time Karl was no longer in Berlin. At the end of April or the beginning of May, collapsing from half a year's overwork and emotional tension, he suffered what would nowadays be termed a physical and mental breakdown. When a physician sent him to the country to rest for a while from his legal and philosophic-cum-literary exertions, he traversed 'the whole of the long' Prussian capital and left it by 'the gate to Stralau'.

Having made his way on foot to this hamlet of fewer than two dozen houses nestling on a narrow land arm between the river Spree and the lakes of the Havel, he allowed his 'languishing body' to 'mature and acquire a robust strength'. A natural (now largely built-up) beauty-spot within short hiking-distance of the capital, Stralau had an inn kept by a fisherman which served as a favourite rendezvous for some of Berlin's educated, better-off youths who – after a day's swimming and picnicking – congregated for drinking parties in the garden of the inn. There, under the garden trees, young Marx was to relax and recuperate from his excess of cerebration and inner travail. But he could not rest without philosophy. In November, taking up the tale of his failed attempts to build 'a new metaphysical system', he described the extraordinary transformation that came over him at Stralau, though not before more stormy wrestling and arguments – with himself, with Hegel's ideas and with some of Hegel's young disciples, such as a Dr Rutenberg, whom he met at Stralau:

> A curtain had fallen, my holy of holies had been shattered and new gods had to be found.... Setting out from idealism – which, by the way, I compared and nourished with that of Kant and Fichte – I came to the point of seeking the Idea in the real itself. If the gods had formerly dwelt above the world, they had now become its centre.[15]

Künzli, who sees in young Marx an 'obstructed rabbi', is not surprised that his 'psychological conflict' in Berlin should have led to his physical collapse or that he should desperately have searched for 'the Thing', the 'idea in the real'. In his view, the 19-year-old's attempted 'philosophical reconstruction of the God from whom he had been alienated, the God who to his forefathers represented reality pure and simple', was a bold leap forward. It shows Marx's creative side, but it operated only on the intellectual plane. Marx's 'inner conflict' and his alienation from society would remain unresolved, for, while his intellectual forefathers acted within 'the pre-established harmony' of their religion and their people and were able to unite 'the transcendental with the living reality of a human community', Marx had been estranged from both.[16]

Even if an element of genetic culture had been transmitted to the young Marx, he was of course completely unconscious of it. But as for the way the unconscious acted to heighten his creative power and his intellectualism at the expense of his emotional faculties, we have only his own story of his travail and precoccupations at Stralau to go on: 'I had read fragments of Hegel's philosophy, but disliked its grotesque, craggy melody. Once again I wanted to dive off into the sea, but this time with the firm intention of finding our intellectual nature to be just as necessary, concrete, and firmly established as our physical one. I wanted to stop fencing and bring the pure pearls up into the sunlight.'

With renewed vigour he set about the task of writing 'a philosophic–dialectical discussion of the godhead as it manifests itself per se, as religion, as nature, as history.' Intent on 'reuniting art and science, which had wholly diverged', he plunged into new studies, natural science, Schelling and history. The result was a 24-page essay in dialogue form. And what happened was that 'this work... this dearest child of mine, reared by moonlight' and titled *Cleanthes, or the Starting Point and Necessary Progress of Philosophy*, caused him 'endless headaches and is so confusedly written – for it had actually to be a new logic – that even I can now hardly make head or tail of it...' and it delivered him, 'like a false siren', straight into the hands of the enemy – Hegel.

Marx was so annoyed, so stunned, at his forced surrender that, 'unable to think for several days, I ran like a lunatic around the garden by the dirty waters of the Spree... I even went on a hunting party with my landlord, ran to Berlin and wanted to embrace every street loafer I met.'

Next, in the summer semester which would end in August, he studied – 'industriously', according to Professor Helffter's mark in the University record – Ecclesiastical Law, Common German Civil Procedure and Prussian Civic Law. But the dry record gives no idea of his labours or his continued struggle with Hegel. Straining to find the Absolute, the universal 'Idea', he devoured more heavy books, which he listed in the November letter to his father – among them Savigny's *Law of Property*, Feuerbach and Grohlmann's *Criminal Law*, Kramer's *De Verborum Significatione*, Wanning-Lagenheim's *System of Pandects*, and Mühlenbruch's *Doctrina Pandectarum*, individual works by Lauterbach, Civil Trials and above all Canon Law. The first part of Canon Law alone (Gratian's *Concordia discortantum Canonum*) contains several thousand ecclesiastical documents, but he also translated part of Aristotle's *Rhetoric*, read Francis Bacon's *De Argumentis Scientiarum*, studied Reimarus's *On the Instincts of Animals* 'with great delight', besides working his way 'through the capitularies of the Frankish kings [i.e., their collection of ordinances] and the letters that the Popes addressed to them.' The result was that his health gave way again to the strain of inner and outer pressures.

'Upset by Jenny's illness and the futility of my fruitless and shipwrecked intellectual endeavours, I fell sick, as I have already written to you, dear father.' The letter mentioned has not survived, but to judge from his father's reply of 12 August, it was a letter full of laments, written in a 'black' mood. Reminding Karl that 'you must and will soon become the father of a family,' he appealed to him not to 'tear your heart and that of your dearest at the slightest storm', but to face upsets 'with manly courage, composure, resignation and good cheer.' Karl had many excellent qualities, but in view of Jenny and 'your coming alliance', his father called on him to curb 'your raging passions, violent outbursts and sickly susceptibility.'

Indeed, whatever the unconscious, irrational element at work in the dynamic young Marx, his anger at his inability to vanquish Hegel was such that – as he recapitulated events in the November letter – 'when I recovered, my consuming vexation at having to make an idol of a view I hated made me burn all my poems and sketches for novels.'[17]

Jenny's mysterious illness, coupled with Heinrich Marx's remark that she was not far from 'sealing' her love with her death – and the occurrence of the word 'suicide' in a letter of hers to Karl – for a time raised the supposition that she might have contemplated ending her life. Karl's letters to Jenny were eventually to be destroyed by their daughter Laura. Jenny's letters to him, or those that escaped the 'sifting' and suppression of many of his papers by successive executors (his daughters, Engels, and various Communist Party organs) and some others discovered only later, were to end up in Moscow. Of these, as late as 1975, only poor, practically illegible photostats were available to Western scholars at Amsterdam's International Institute for Social History. In an undated fragment of a letter of hers to Marx, one historian at the beginning of the 1970s detected 'a shrill, almost hysterical tone' as well as signs that 'the relationship between Karl and Jenny was not only a highly complex one', but early marked by serious quarrels.

From the little that could be deciphered, Professor F.J. Raddatz quoted such remarks as 'base' or 'vulgar girl' which he assumed Karl had called Jenny in a letter – as well as the following charge by Jenny:

It was not just a stabbing glance; you wanted to crush me... If you could do that at a moment of highest love transport, what can I expect when it has cooled? One... would be suicide, but things must be still worse for that... Another time it would be the death of me...[18]

The original of this damaged letter, its beginning and end missing but the handwriting restored, has since been published as part of the mammoth 100-volume *Marx-Engels Gesamtausgabe* launched in 1975 by Moscow's Marx-Lenin Institute. The fuller text shows that it was written some time in May 1838, after Karl had been on a short visit to Trier and he and Jenny had a violent verbal altercation in the course of which he called her names. The letter, which will be discussed in its proper context, does not enlighten us about the nature of Jenny's condition or the state of affairs between the couple in the summer of 1837.

Nor can one say conclusively whether her continued 'fears', 'torment' and 'suffering' were early symptoms of the nervous depression to which years of financial misery with Marx in London would later reduce her, or whether she was merely sick to death of waiting, or dying romantically of loneliness, frustration and possible recriminations she faced at home. On 16 September 1837, half a year after Baron von Westphalen's reluctant approval of the betrothal, the older Marx hinted in a letter to Karl at some ambivalence on the part of Jenny's parents when he informed his son: 'I have not shown your letter to [Baron] Westphalen. These very good people are of a peculiar sort. They discuss and belabour everything ceaselessly and from so many sides that... since you are not going to change your studies this year, I see no reason why I should provide them with the stuff for new fantasies...'[19]

The Westphalens' fear, not unreasonable from their viewpoint, was that Jenny would end up a wilted old maid before Karl, who might have stolen her heart like a furious Roland but was still boyishly uncertain of his vocation, could ever offer her a reasonably secure life. To become a teacher, to start a law or medical practice – even more, to obtain any kind of professorship – Marx, after many years of studying for a degree, would have to pass further examinations by a State Commission. Jenny's parents might have rich relatives, but they themselves lived in genteel poverty and would be unable to contribute to the couple's support. If they ceaselessly discussed and belaboured Karl's chances of a career – or entertained any 'fantasies' about making him change his studies – it was not only because they believed his prospects to be poor and remote. Social prejudice also played a part, and they could not but share the view his father impressed on him in December, namely, that with her excellent merits and social standing, she was making a great sacrifice by giving up her brilliant position as well as her prospects, tying her destiny to the shaky and bleak future of a younger man.[20]

The undisguised antagonism of Jenny's half-brother Ferdinand, who about this time in his career became head of 'internal affairs' in the Trier district, with the title of *Oberregierungsrat*, exacerbated these discussions and her parents' misgivings. Between the constant talk at home and the wagging tongues of what Jenny herself calls that 'tiniest, most miserable gossip-nest' which was Trier, she – refusing to see other young men and unable to attend dances unchaperoned – found the atmosphere increasingly unbearable. Against it, now and for years to come, she had only Karl's romantic and 'indescribably beautiful expressions of passionate love' – to use her own words – to cling to. She was 'mindful of external things, of life and reality.' All he could offer was a 'higher, dearer spiritual unity' with him. She wanted to believe in it, but sounded almost like his father warning him against his 'exaggerations of love' when, more than two years later, she wrote: 'O, Karl, my distress lies precisely in the fact that... the enrapturing images conjured up by your imagination, which would fill any other girl with ineffable delight, only serve to make me anxious and uncertain...'[21]

And yet, sick, depressed, or romantically indisposed, she held out and cleaved to him, would remain true to and hold on to him, year after year. But some time during that summer of 1837, she temporarily left, perhaps fled, dreary, gossip-hungry little Trier without a word to dear Karl in Berlin.

'Jenny is not yet back,' his father informed the complaining young fiancé in a letter of 16 September. 'She has the idea that it is unnecessary to write to you...' And his mother added, 'I believe that Jenny's silence stems from a virginal shyness', commenting that this 'only enhances her other charms and good qualities.'[22]

Heinrich Marx himself had spent part of August trying to cure a worsening cough at Ems spa. From there, on the 12th, he had informed Karl in Berlin that his elder sister Sophie was not well either, constantly and 'unsuccessfully medicinating'. And his sickly 11-year-old brother Eduard had only some months to live. Eduard, Heinrich wrote pathetically in the same letter, had become 'thin and emaciated... a prey to that darkest dejection – actually fear of dying – so rare and so heart-rending in children. You know Mother. She does not leave his bedside, harassed day and night, and I in constant fear that she will collapse under the strain...'

He pled with Karl to write to the boy, 'but make it sound as if he were completely well again.' And his mother, too, was in want of encouragement. A letter from Karl would 'do wonders for her mood.'

How did Karl react to the crisis at home? According to his father, hardly at all. Sometimes he did not write home for months on end, and then only in 'meaningless', fragmentary notes unrelated to previous correspondence. He had a way of glossing over inconvenient questions, jumping to new subjects and dropping old ones like 'still-born children' never to be heard of again. And some of his rare, no longer existing letters consisted of no more than a few hastily scribbled lines.

'Yes', his father noted with bitter sarcasm several months later, 'your letter did contain something: complaints about Jenny not writing... That was all Mister Son had to tell his parents...' Before that, when writing from Ems, he had put his finger on what he deemed a specific flaw in Karl's character:

> Though I love you more than anyone in the world – your mother excepted – I am not blind, and still less do I mean to be blind. I make every just allowance for you, but I cannot altogether help thinking that you are rather more of an egotist than is necessary for self-preservation... To abandon one's self to sorrow at the slightest contrary wind, to bare a wounded heart at every grief and to tear the hearts of the loved ones as well – is that what goes by the name of Poetry?... No, only weakness, pampering, self-love and arrogance reduce everything to one's self...

Always gentle when rebuking his son, Heinrich Marx regretted his harsh new tone. Admitting that his own temper had been affected by his failing health, the accumulation of sick cases in the family, and further by Jenny's long illness, 'the ambiguity of my position vis-à-vis the W[estphalen]s – I, who never deviated from the straight path', he reminded Karl that 'neither honours, nor riches nor fame will make your wife and children happy. You alone can do that, your better self, your love, your tenderness...'[23]

With its advice to him to curb his 'violent outbursts and sickly susceptibility', the letter of 12 August was one of 4 increasingly reproachful ones in which Heinrich Marx – torn between admiration for his son's intellect and apprehensions about what he perceived to be his anti-social character – revealed a little-known image of young Marx as a weak, self-centred, conceited, hyper-sensitive, highly vulnerable young man whose 'dear ego' required constant caressing, who stamped his foot with rage over Jenny's silence, or submitted to 'phantasmally black thoughts'. The gravamen of the father's various accusations was that Karl lacked feeling, that he did not relate to other people's needs and emotions and took only a spurious or feigned interest in their troubles while constantly bewailing his own.

None of the future 'doctors of revolution' had a more understanding parent than Karl Marx's – not bigoted like Engels's father, not narrow-minded like Bakunin's, nor doting like Lassalle's. Anxious and concerned – perhaps over-concerned – to bring out the best in his son, Heinrich Marx throughout treated Karl with an 'instinctive delicacy' which would be remarked upon a century later. Karl had been wavering between poetry, philosophy, law and drama, between a 'professorship' and a theatre journal? His father went along with every one of his projects, but tried to save him from pitfalls. The theatre, he pointed out early in March, was a world unto itself fraught with no end of 'intrigues, cabals and jealousies'. Nevertheless, if Karl wished to write for the stage, his father was ready to bear the financial cost of the experiment. He only suggested that Karl choose a modest subject to try his hand on for a start.

As we know, Karl never wrote any play other than *Oulanem*, which by August and the end of the summer semester he had burned together with his novels and poetry: 'The Kingdom of True Poetry glittered before my eyes like a distant fairy palace', but distant it remained, 'and all my creations dissolved into nothingness.'

While still taking law courses during the summer and reading to exhaustion as he struggled with Hegel, he had ventilated various other projects, either seriously or to fob off his father. By mid-September his father's nerves snapped. With infinite patience he had followed Karl's staggering activities, manifold ambitions and changing schemes for nearly a year. Having impressed upon him back in February that he must come to a firm decision – 'if not this second, then this year, and once made, you must keep it firmly in mind and pursue it unswervingly' – he had a sinking feeling that Karl had been frittering away another university year and that, far from sticking to a purpose, he had done nothing to live up to his responsibilities to Jenny.

'Whether you choose this or that for a career is, at bottom, the same to me,' Heinrich wrote with feigned indifference on 16 September 1837. His innermost wish had been, of course, for Karl to follow in his footsteps and become a lawyer or jurist, but he made only a curt reference to his disappointment: 'The obvious course seemed repugnant to you, and I must confess that I, seduced by your precocious opinions, came round to applauding your opting for the goal of a teaching position, whether in jurisprudence or philosophy, and ultimately I even found the latter preferable.' Still, he took up every proposal for a 'practical' career which Karl sent up like so many trial balloons. The career of a drama critic was a meritorious one but took a long time to build. Nor, Heinrich remarked, was it a path always strewn with roses – the great Lessing himself, for all his fame, 'lived and died as a poor librarian.' As for Karl's suggestion of a government post as Assessor in the judiciary, this, with some patronage, was occasionally a stepping-stone to better things, but – Heinrich pointed out – an Assessor received no salary for several years, and without patronage Karl might in the end find himself stuck indefinitely in the lowly position of an assistant judge.

'What shall I advise you?' Since Karl was not keen on practicing law, a 'teaching position' must remain his 'end goal... A person could play a great role in Bonn as a professor of jurisprudence.' Literary pursuits – 'a few distinctive works, a great poem or a sterling tragedy or comedy' – could be reconciled with, and might even help towards, an academic career. Failing that, Heinrich did not exclude the idea of his son's becoming an Assessor, not in the judiciary, but in the public administration, for – considering Karl's poetic inclinations – 'it is easier to imagine a singing government councillor than a singing judge.' Karl must decide for himself, so long as 'you choose what best suits your talents... You have been paving your own way, and may henceforth do so.'

But he could not forbear reminding him that 'at her age' Jenny was making a sacrifice such as no ordinary girl in her right mind would think of; that circumstances of Karl's own making were such as to force upon him a 'vital decision' of the type which would not normally bother a youth of his age for a long time yet; and that he had 'to make haste' with whatever he did. And having, in the same letter of 16 September, assured him of Jenny's love, he expressed his confidence that Karl would act as 'sagacity and duty – towards oneself, and even more so towards persons to whose welfare one has committed one's self – imperatively command. It is demanding much of a nineteen-year-old to be worldly-wise, but he who at nineteen...'[24]

That was the nub of the problem, in that broken-off sentence. It is not unlikely that had Karl not got himself secretly engaged to the Westphalen daughter, Heinrich Marx would still have expected great things of his son, but would 'not normally' be so pressing with his constant attempts to recall him to reality and his obligations. As it was, 'the main effect of Heinrich's admonishments', it has been rightly remarked by one Marx biographer, was 'to unsettle his son's already troubled spirit still further.'[25]

What is more, their hitherto intimate relationship was shattered. Though constantly ignoring his father's advice and pursuing his own ends, the touchy young man was hurt and shaken by Heinrich's criticism and strong disapproval. Heinrich, on the other hand, found it increasingly hard to understand this beloved, exceptional son over whom he had taken so much trouble, who embodied his highest hopes, yet was as good as estranged from him.

But there was more than the common 'generation gap' to their conflict, which had yet to reach its dramatic climax. Before it did, still in September, Heinrich Marx, with his income now reduced by illness, and his hair 'standing on end at the thought' of 5 daughters to marry off, offered to support Karl for another three years rather than let him do anything that would interfere with his academic prospects.

As for the missing Jenny, the whole family seemed involved in Karl's 'affair' with the pining Westphalen daughter and the tidings of her return. In August, Heinrich reported that she had been seen by a mutual acquaintance on a Rhine steamer. At last Karl's mother, Henriette, in a hasty Postscript to the letter of 16 September just quoted, informed him that Jenny's mother 'today spoke to our children.' Jenny, she announced, 'is expected back today or tomorrow... She could hardly wait to return to Trier and is longing to hear from you... May the Almighty show you the right way to whatever you prize most, and for this we pray and beg you: Be of good courage and overcome, the crown goes to him who perseveres... For the autumn I'm having wool jackets made to protect you from catching colds. Write real soon dear Carl your eternally loving Mother.'[26]

Jenny herself, however, maintained her obstinate, mysterious silence and wrote not a word to Karl.

At some unknown date before 10 November – when he was to recapitulate the events of his first year in Berlin in the long letter of confession to his father – Karl Marx apparently sent home a short fragmentary one, to which Heinrich Marx reacted with some caustic lines:

> 17 November, 1837
> Dear Karl! Is your general headquarters still at Stralau? At this time of the year...? Where else, then? That is the question. The first practical requirement of correspondence is: to know a forwarding address – I must rely on the kindness of other persons.

Heinrich Marx, little improved since his cure at Ems, was nettled at Karl's neither taking the slightest interest in his dying brother – little Eduard was to die in December – nor really answering his August or September letters. Among other things, Heinrich had asked to hear about his 'positive studies'. Instead, all he got from Karl was some disjointed lines (no longer extant and apparently self-pitying) complaining about Jenny's silence. Heinrich described them as 'an empty, formless, meaningless fragment... bearing no relation to what went on beforehand... an *abzerrissener* [torn-off], worse still, a *zerrissener* [pessimistic] letter'. *Zerrissen* can mean anything from 'melancholy' to 'torn, tattered, dismembered', but in the 1830s *Zerrissenheit* was practically a code-word standing for the alienated Romantic generation's moody world-weariness. Heinrich hated this fashionable 'modern word', in which all idle weaklings 'muffle themselves when quarrelling with the world for not rewarding their lack of effort with palaces, millions and carriages. This *Zerrissenheit* disgusts me, and I least expected it from you.' He then upbraided Karl for giving in to dejection, for throwing up his hands in a fit of despondency at 'the first difficulty, the first miscarried desire! Is that strength? Is that a manly character?' Heinrich reminded him that he was Fortune's favourite:

> Has not everything smiled upon you since you were in the cradle? Has not Nature most splendidly endowed you? Have not your parents wrapped you in the most lavish and profuse love? Have you ever gone without your reasonable wishes being satisfied? And have you not also, in the most incomprehensible manner, won the heart of a girl that thousands will envy you?

As though to prove his point, he had good news – Jenny had broken her silence. The circumstances are unknown, but Henriette Marx seems to have played some part in them, for her husband wrote:

> Your good mother, who is softer than I and frequently still remembers that we, too, were once little Cupid's plaything, raised the alarm and the all-too-good parents of your Jy could hardly wait to comfort the poor injured heart...

Jenny's letter to Karl, Heinrich concluded, was undoubtedly already in his hands, 'unless the lack of a proper address led her epistle astray...'[27]

In Berlin, some time during the evening of 10 November, Karl had started his long letter of confession to his father. Sitting up till 4 a.m., he filled 4 folio sheets – folded into 16 pages – more than 3,000 words altogether. This first and most revealing of young Marx's surviving letters – long believed to have crossed his father's of the 17th – is now known to have been in the latter's hands by that date.[28]

If Heinrich refers on the 17th chiefly to the son's earlier *zerrissener* scrap of a letter, and not to his long confession of 10/11 November 1837, it may be because this had only just reached him in Trier and he was too overwhelmed by his son's outpourings. Young Marx's letter – which would take up 10 large-size book pages when printed in modern type – is in every respect an extraordinary document. To the father it was so stunning that it would take him three weeks to digest and consider before he reacted to it. The letter starts with a grand sweep:

> Dear Father: There are moments in life which stand as landmarks, delimiting the close of a period, but at the same time pointing firmly in a new direction. At such a point of transition, we feel compelled to survey the past and the present with the eagle eye of thought in order

537

to arrive at a true conscious realization of our actual position. Yes, world history itself loves such a retrospect, loves to look at itself, which often makes it appear to be moving backwards or standing still, whereas it is simply leaning back in an armchair to understand itself...

From this unusual simile of world history in an armchair trying 'intellectually to comprehend its own action, the action of the mind', Karl passed suddenly to nothing less than a veritable paean to his parents. To the individual, he wrote, 'every change is partly swan song, partly overture to a great new poem' gestating 'in brilliant but still hazy colours; and yet we want to erect a monument to what we have already experienced, so that it should regain in sensibility what it has lost in action'; and where could we find a more sacred abode than in the hearts of our parents, 'the most indulgent judges, the most intimate participants, the sun of love whose fire warms the innermost centre of our endeavours! How better could much that is disgraceful and blameworthy receive forgiveness...? How else could the frequently hostile turn of fortune and the errors of the mind escape the reproach of being due to a twisted heart?'

Here was young Marx not only answering his father's 'most precious' – actually reproachful – August 'letter from Ems', but 'casting an eye back' over his agitated first year in Berlin and actually half-admitting to some weaknesses in his character. But besides invoking hostile fortune he asked for his 'errors of the mind' to be seen as the inevitable 'result of an essentially necessary state of affairs... Allow me to view my situation (as I do life in general) as the expression of an intellectual activity roving in all directions, in science, art and private endeavours.'

Here he gave his account of his thrashing about in all these directions – the poetry he wrote, abandoned and resumed until it 'dissolved into nothingness'; the opposition between 'is' and 'ought' that obstructed his 'ill-starred' 300-page opus on 'the metaphysics of the law'; his search for 'the idea in the real' and for 'new gods' which he hoped to find in book after book read, excerpted or translated; his first collapse, and his renewed efforts at Stralau to discover the 'philosophical-dialectical development of the divinity in religion, nature and history', only to find himself driven against his will into the arms of Hegel; his running 'like a lunatic around the garden'; his second illness, and his burning of all his 'poems, sketches for novels' and other papers in a cool 'consuming' rage at Hegel, at Jenny's silence, at himself and his own 'shipwrecked' labours when he recovered.

Writing late into the night, he brought his father up to date on the latest events in his life – his conversion to the new 'world philosophy' and his admission to a Berlin Doctors Club of avant-garde intellectuals and so-called 'Young Hegelian' philosophers:

During my [second] illness I had got to know Hegel from beginning
to end, as well as most of his disciples. Through several gatherings
with friends at Stralau I got into a Doctors Club, comprising several
university tutors and the most intimate of my Berlin friends, Dr.
Rutenberg. In our arguments many conflicting viewpoints emerged
and I attached myself ever more firmly to the currently prevailing
world philosophy which I had thought to escape... To this was added
Jenny's silence and I could not rest until, through several bad pieces
like The Visit, I had acquired modernity and the viewpoint of contemporary scholarship.

At this point, as he wove back and forth through time, he admitted to his father
that he had 'not gone into all the details', had 'slurred the nuances', and
'perhaps not described clearly to you the whole of this last semester.' When
reading German Law in the summer semester, he had studied 'the capitularies
of the Frankish kings' and 'the letters of the Popes to them', chiefly because of
his interest in the metaphysics of law and in a general metaphysical system.
Now, fascinated by Hegel's subtle dialectic which preserved the 'is' even while
changing it into the 'ought', he was actually about to make philosophy his chief
and almost exclusive concern. But to his father he broached the old-new plan of
preparing for government service as an Assessor. He had met a man called
Schmidthänner, who told him that if, after his third law examination, he went
to Münster in Westphalia, he would become an assistant judge in a matter of
three years, for 'there the stages are not rigidly fixed as in Berlin and elsewhere.
If later one obtains a doctorate, then there is also a much better chance to get an
immediate appointment as a supplementary professor.'

No one knows whether all this – including his sudden declaration that he
really preferred jurisprudence to public administration – was an earnest or wild
plan, or some kind of sop to his father to show that he was not neglecting 'practical' considerations and might still land a professorship of a kind; at the same
time he had 'by no means abandoned' the plan to start a theatre and art journal,
particularly now that all the aesthetic celebrities of the Hegelian school had
promised to contribute.

Towards morning on 11 November, he concluded his letter with the following paragraphs:

However, my dear Father, best of fathers, would it not be possible to
talk all this over with you personally? Eduard's condition, my darling
Mummy's afflictions, your own illness – although I hope it is not too
serious – all this makes me wish, nay, makes it almost a necessity that
I fly to you...

But he doubted that his father would give his 'permission and consent', and pleaded with him:

> Believe me, my dear, beloved Father, it is no selfish purpose that drives me – though it would be bliss to see Jenny again – but rather a compelling thought which I cannot put into words... I beg you, dear Father, whatever you may decide, not to show this letter, or at any rate this page of it, to my angelic mother. My unexpected arrival will perhaps cheer up that great, splendid woman. In the hope that the clouds hanging over our family will gradually disperse; that I may be allowed to suffer and weep with you and perhaps, being near you, to give tangible proof of the deep, heartfelt sympathy, the immeasurable love, that I can often only express so badly; in the hope that you too, dear, eternally loved Father, mindful of the agitated state of my storm-tossed soul, will forgive where the heart – overpowered by the fighting spirit – has often seemed to err, and that you will soon be fully restored to health so that I may myself press you to my heart and tell you all,
>
> Your ever-loving son (Karl M.)
>
> Forgive, dear Father, the illegible handwriting and the bad style; it is almost four o'clock, the candle is burnt out and my eyes are sore; a real anxiety has come over me and I will not be able to calm the ghosts I have roused until I am in your dear presence.
>
> Please give my love to my sweet, wonderful Jenny. I have already read her letter twelve times, discovering new delights in it each time. It is in every respect, including style, the most beautiful letter that I can imagine written by a woman.[29]

It is in many ways a curiously contrite letter, at the end of which the prodigal seemed to be pleading, practically begging, to be reinstated in his father's love. His frankly 'slurred', possibly dissembling, yet fervid, confession of the adventures and misadventures he had met in his colossal, boundless quest for knowledge and self-expression might have been his sincerest attempt yet to reach out to his parent. When this particular letter – found among his mother's papers in 1863 and preserved by his sister Sophie – eventually reached his daughter Eleanor in 1895, 12 years after Karl Marx's death, she was justifiably excited, recognizing in her father's youthful confession an 'invaluable' biographical document. Two years later, when preparing its first publication, she more specifically defined its importance as a perfectly unconscious picture of the young Marx drawn by himself.[30]

For the first time, perhaps, Karl revealed himself to his father as he really was at that stage of youthful exuberance, uncertainty and bottomless ambition to tackle questions above his strength. He dramatized his struggle with Hegel, but in Trier, in November 1837, Heinrich Marx was stupefied. Karl's jumbled account of a year's chaotic nights of study, re-study and discarded or burnt writings, rather than conveying to the father the image of a youth searching his way through trial and error and attempts in all directions, confirmed his fear of Karl's excessive self-preoccupation. After his beer-swilling two semesters in Bonn, instead of pulling himself together in Berlin and developing from a wild, unruly youth into an orderly person, from a negating genius into a genuine thinker, from a dissolute ringleader of profligate youths into a sociable human being, Karl seemed to have gone from bad to worse, to have spent his second year of study cultivating his ego, engaging in vain, weird, purposeless mental acrobatics, assuming a scholarly pose and aimlessly, anarchically 'flitting and floating about in all the fields of knowledge...'[31]

Heinrich Marx's reply arrived on 9 December 1837, and this was only one of the accusations he flung in Karl's face.

19

Marx and the Influence of Hegel

In July 1897, shortly before she decided (feeling 'half a traitor') to give his youthful letter 'to the world', Eleanor Marx wrote that her father hated to have his private life 'dragged into public'. In an introduction to its publication, 60 years after it was written, she observed that Marx was in Trier in 1863 when, on his mother's death, his older sister Sophie found and took possession of his letter among other papers, and added: 'He surely did not know of [its] existence ... fortunately so, or he undoubtedly would have destroyed it.'[1]

It was in this introduction that Eleanor dwelt on Marx's deep attachment to his father and related that 'he never tired of talking about him' and always carried an old daguerrotype photograph of him.

There is no reason to doubt this statement, or that during Karl Marx's childhood and adolescence an unusually strong relationship developed between father and son. But to judge by their 1837 correspondence, the bond seems chiefly to have been based on the former's grasp and early appreciation of the son's exceptional mind and potential, and on the latter's basking in his adulation. And it is a curious fact that Heinrich Marx in 1837 – long before Eleanor was born – was not at all impressed by Karl's protestations of 'immeasurable' filial love and his readiness to 'suffer and weep' with his family. Young Marx probably loved and respected his father in his own way. In later years, as so often happens, he would even greatly revere his memory. But at that time the father felt distinctly that his superintellectual son tended to mistake sentimentality and the mawkish display of emotions for the real thing.

Heinrich Marx's reply to his son's confession is unusually, deliberately – one might say, desperately – harsh. 'Never did we get an answer to our letters,' he lashed out at Karl on 9 December 1837; never a coherent picture 'of our beloved son's actions, what he was actually doing and thinking ... Months would go by without a letter.' Worse still,

> when you knew that Eduard was sick, Mother suffering, I ailing – and not only that, but cholera raging in Berlin – your next letter mentioned not a word about any of this. Instead, it barely contained a

few badly scrawled lines and an extract from [your] diary, entitled
The Visit, which, frankly, I would rather not have received, a crazy
concoction which only goes to show how you have been squandering
your talents and staying up nights to give birth to monstrosities...

Yes, your letter did contain something: complaints about Jenny not
writing...[2]

Writing a few days before the death of his 11-year-old son Eduard, Heinrich
Marx was bitter. But he pointed an early and unerring finger at certain traits –
such as a lack of feeling – that would later strike others in the adult Karl Marx.
His ignoring the fate of his little brother while bemoaning his own was, in a
way, an early paradigm of the shocking letter of condolence he was to address
one day to Engels on the death of the latter's beloved mistress, Mary Burns: a
letter which, chiefly devoted to listing and bewailing his debts, bills due and
every other financial woe of his own, nearly put an end to their friendship.

Reading and re-reading Karl's long, effusive letter of confession, the father
found it devoid of any real sympathy. Looking in vain for some warmth or
comfort in it, he did not count its words; that was left for modern scholars to do
and to determine that of the letter's 3,000 to 4,000 words fewer than 100 'refer
to family. The rest was entirely Karl.'[3]

Heinrich also made it clear in his letter that he was not favourably impressed
by Karl's new friends in the Doctors Club. This was a group led by Dr Bruno
Bauer, a 28-year-old philosopher and 'theoretician of religion' who, for the past
three years, had been lecturing in theology at Berlin University. Of medium
height, fair-haired, sharp-eyed, with a pointed nose and a high, domed forehead,
Bauer looked scholarly, but his compact presence, finely chiselled features and
calm, confident air made more than one of his contemporaries – including Varnhagen von Ense, the diplomat-writer – refer to him as 'practically a Napoleonic
figure'. Bauer's brilliant philosophic mind combined with critical sharpness and
the biting wit of a first-class polemicist, his high self-esteem and intangible conviction that whatever principle he adopted must be true, were to move Heine to
call him a 'godless self-god'. Varnhagen, too, in his Diaries, refers to this opinionated streak: 'Under a cold exterior he burns with an inner fire. He will brook
no opposition and will sooner be a martyr to his own convictions.'[4]

In short, Bauer was the type of man who both invites and thrives on antagonism. Whether because of this or other affinities, young Marx quickly became
Bauer's closest associate, comrade-in-arms and boon companion. Bauer's criticism of the Bible had already got him into some hot water with Hengstenberg,
the Dean of Berlin's Theological Faculty, but at this time (in 1837) it had yet to
reach the radicalism that in a couple of years would cost him his academic career.

Other leading members of the Doctors Club with whom Marx developed close ties included Karl Friedrich Köppen and Dr Adolf Rutenberg. Köppen was a 29-year-old former history teacher, who was to dedicate his *Frederick the Great and His Opponents* to his 'friend Karl Marx of Trier'.[5] He also produced an expert – and lasting – work on Tibetan Lamaism and the origins of Buddhism. Rutenberg, a former *Burschenschaftler* several times imprisoned for radical student agitation, and recently dismissed from a post as a geography-and-history teacher at the Cadet School, was now making a name for himself as a journalist in Berlin writing for provincial newspapers.

With these new friends and others of the Doctors Club, such as Max Stirner – another young philosopher, who became famous as the proponent of bourgeois 'ultra-individualism' and a theorist of anarchism – Karl Marx now spent a good deal of his time in a coffee-house in the Französische Strasse, and in taverns and beer-cellars. In a bohemian atmosphere, they kept track of foreign newspapers, read and criticized each other's articles and poems, but also traded jokes, epigrams and doggerels deriding the 'philistines' of Berlin's staid, self-satisfied middle class. The voluble Bruno Bauer emitted barbed witticisms between clouds of smoke 'that could drive a locomotive'. Uncommonly zestful, prankish and fun-loving for a serious New Testament scholar, Bauer was a heavy drinker. Marx, coming from the Moselle wine region, could hold his own; so could Bauer's younger brother Edgar, a theology student about to turn atheist, with whom Marx in middle age was to throw stones at London street lamps; and so, too, could Köppen, whose pub-crawling with Marx on another occasion was recalled by the latter as 'a real joy'.

They drank, smoked and joked, but most of their coffee-house time was spent in hair-splitting philosophic arguments. Some 60 years later, Max Ring was to recall those days: 'In this circle of aspiring young men... our special interest was the philosophy of Hegel, which was then in its primal bloom and more or less dominated the educated world. Individual voices, however, were occasionally raised against the Hegelian system and a split between the Right and Left among the Hegelians was already beginning to become noticeable.'[6]

It was the theologian Bauer who stood for a good while at the forefront of the battle between the factions. For it was in the field of religion that the conflict was first joined. Heine, even while saluting Hegel's masterly philosophical achievement in providing an 'accomplished' system scientifically embracing 'the entire world of phenomena', had already noted in *Religion and Philosophy in Germany* that some of Hegel's ambiguous, cryptic phrases could be read as a 'dubious' philosophical justification of 'the existing State and Church'. The Right Hegelians viewed the implicit legitimacy conferred on Prussia's clerical-autocratic regime merely as a necessary feature of the whole rational 'system'. The nascent Left Hegelian school, on the other hand, had begun to feel that 'man makes religion'. Man invents gods, saviours, myths, rituals and whole philosophic systems, all in order to help him understand a seemingly incomprehensible world. Yet religious dogma, divine revelation and these very myths stand in the way of his seeing, and dealing with, the world as it is.

'Religion is only the illusory sun which revolves round man as long as he does not revolve round himself,' Karl Marx proclaimed some years later. The task of history, he postulated at that time, was 'to establish the truth of this world', and the final task of philosophy was to turn 'the criticism of theology into the criticism of politics.'[7] But that time had not yet arrived.

In 1837, with pious Prussia and Christians all over Germany not yet recovered from the consternation caused by David Strauss's *Life of Jesus* – the second volume of which appeared in 1836 – Bauer paradoxically started out as a conservative Right-wing Hegelian and defender of Christianity against the claims of the new Left of Young Hegelians. He was one of those faithful Hegel disciples of whom he later wrote: 'Like blissful gods they dwelt in patriarchal tranquillity in the realm of the Idea which the Master had bequeathed to their understanding. The dream of a time of perfection entertained by the chiliasts [i.e., the believers in the millennium] seemed to have been fulfilled, when it was upset by the lightning of reflection striking the empire of blissfulness.'

The 'lightning' was Strauss's book: Bauer observed that it had illumined in a flash 'the crisis' of theology and 'the malady of our times'. Forcefully as Strauss argued that the Gospels were myths grown out of some communal imagination, he allowed that this collective fantasy might have been woven around some kernel of fact, though he had found no evidence for the historicity of Jesus. Nor did he attack Christianity as such, or question its superiority as a religion, a sacrosant notion officially vented in the 'German-Christian' State of Prussia on every suitable and unsuitable occasion.

Nevertheless, Bauer, intent on healing the breach or 'crisis' between religion and philosophy revealed by Strauss, set out to refute what Engels later called 'Strauss's vague myth theory, according to which anyone can hold for historical as much as he likes in the Gospel narrations.'[8] But intense critical scrutiny of the Gospels over several years led Bauer against his will in the opposite direction – to start claiming around 1840 that Jesus might have existed, but that everything recorded of him was the invention of Mark. And then he proceeded to stun clerics, academics, the Prussian establishment as well as the educated German public by declaring, in his bold three-volume *Criticism of the Synoptic Gospels (Matthew, Mark and Luke)* – published in 1841–42 – that Jesus never existed but was entirely a product of the combined imagination of the Jewish philosopher Philo (who lived in Alexandria, not Palestine) and the Roman Seneca, coupled with Greek influences.

Bauer was the son of modest and devout parents who owned a small china-shop and who were never able to understand why or how their son had made it his task to undermine Christian tenets by affirming that, on strict theological examination, the Gospels were the conscious creation, that is, fabrication, of writers and poets who – rather like Homer creating Greek gods in the *Iliad* – simply invented a religion.

During the various stages of his move towards extreme radicalism, Bauer not only aroused the wrath of his fellow-theologians and other anti-Hegelian academics, but also found himself in the crossfire between the conservative Right and the new Left of the two diverging camps among the Hegelians themselves. Besides doubting the Gospel record, he kept steadily advancing towards the conclusion that 'the further development of theology leads to its dissolution... the progress of philosophy' means its divorce and 'liberation' from any association with 'its religious antagonists'.

Nor did Bauer hesitate to criticize the Dean of the Theological Faculty. Ernst Walter Hengstenberg, having got off to an even more brilliant academic start than Bauer with a professorship at the age of 24, was by 1837 the author of a highly praised three-volume 'Christology' of the Old Testament, besides other Bible commentaries. He was also the founder of the *Evangelische Kirchenzeitung*, a clerical journal that lasted for a hundred years and has been called an organ of 'the most ruthless intolerance'. In openly attacking Hengstenberg's pietist views, the bellicose Bauer was actually challenging the man who was to become the century's staunchest champion of 'neo-Lutheran orthodoxy' in Germany.[9] But at the end of 1837, when young Marx joined the Doctors Club, the storms around Bauer were only brewing and not yet boiling.

The interpretation of some of Hegel's abstruse pronouncements – what they signified, or the extent to which they could be turned to mean their exact opposite – proceeded amid heated debate among the club's members. This introduced a healthy ferment into Berlin's conservative university establishment and placid intellectual life, but at this juncture the Doctors Club was far from being a political or revolutionary group.

At one point Bauer instructed Karl Marx that 'philosophy will lead the battle... never in any state has there been so much to be done' as in Prussia. But as late as March 1841, he held the view that 'theory is today the strongest practice', and politics remained far from their minds. In fact a contemporary lampoon satirized the endless philosophizing in the Doctors Club with the words,'Our deeds are *words*', flaying its aloofness from the practical affairs of life, as though 'mental abstractions are bound to come true of themselves.'[10]

It took several outsiders not connected with the club, notably Moses Hess, to advocate a 'philosophy of action'. But before Hess, Marx, Engels and several radicals of the bourgeois intelligentsia, turning from religious-philosophic rumination to the reality of everyday politics, realized that philosophy had the potential to become 'the mother of revolution', Bauer's *Criticism* would have united Prussia's entire clerical-political establishment, from the King down, to press for and obtain his removal from any teaching post.

Called in 1842 'the Robespierre of theology', Bauer was eventually to go the whole circle and become an atheist. But as much as he was to condemn Christian theology and its practitioners – comparing the former to a mental prison in which 'the detainee may walk round, but never leave,' and saying of theologians that 'in the panic of their souls no lie is evil enough not to appear justified' to them – he never opted out of the Church, on the principle that salvation must come to 'the prison' (i.e., the human mind) from within.

As Bauer's philosophy did not embrace the transformation of society and he refused to follow his young disciple – that is, to become a Marxist – Marx was eventually to turn against his spiritual mentor and best friend, and to ridicule him and his brother, Edgar Bauer, as 'The Holy Family'. Conceited to a degree, contemptuous even of his peers, Bauer was too proud and principled to use 'philosophy as a meagre cloak merely to deceive the censorship' – the method of which Engels would one day boast[11] – and other than treating him as a catalyst, Marxist history later tended to consign his theories to oblivion and to write him off as an ineffectual 'critic for criticism's sake', a nihilist spinning destructive chimeras in his mind but unable or unwilling to descend from his nebulous tower to the dull middle class, or the witless masses.

Following his repudiation by both reactionary Prussia and the Marxists, Bauer became for a time the proud 'hermit of Rixdorf', a forsaken village where he carted his own vegetables to the market for a living. He turned out more books on Jesus, Bismarck and Disraeli, and helped Richard Wagner to edit the chauvinist, anti-Semitic *Bayreuther Blätter* before he died in 1882, a bank clerk. It was only after his death that one or two historians, examining the early work of this uncompromising 'pure critic' on its own merits, rated him as one of the first German philosophers of revolution.

Back in 1837, however, Dr Bruno Bauer, 28 and full of life, was only debunking Strauss to save 'the honour of Jesus' and protect the Saviour from 'unscientific' misrepresentation. He befriended the second-year student Marx, another budding 'self-god', but not yet godless. Bubbling with high spirits and beer, the two of them kept 'Hegelizing' in taverns along with Köppen (who, before proving his erudition in his work on Buddhism, was chiefly conspicuous for wearing a coat with epaulettes and sporting a rapier) and Rutenberg (a hot-tempered fellow, occasionally involved in street brawls).

'Your Irreverence', they greeted each other ceremoniously at their gatherings. Their uninhibited talk and bohemian ways attracted public attention, but for the moment the club's speculative discussions and ebullient antics were tolerated as a combination of academic expansiveness and student mischief. Altenberg, Prussia's veteran Minister of Education and Public Worship, was a Hegelian sympathizer, and it would be another year, another two or three semesters, before the authorities, realizing where their questioning of Gospel truths and established religion might lead, started to watch and worry over the Young Hegelians.

In his so-called confession letter of 10–11 November 1837 to his father, young Marx, after describing with marvellous brevity – in the words 'these thoughts were registered by my body' – how a year's mental overwork had caused the physical and nervous breakdown that had sent him to recover at Stralau, added a significant sentence: 'I did not suspect that there my anaemic and languishing body would mature and acquire a robust strength.' A 'curtain had fallen', Karl explained, 'my holy of holies was rent asunder and new gods had to be installed.' He had read Hegel, but did not care for him. At Stralau, diving into the sea of Hegel's philosophy, he had struggled to escape its 'grotesque, crazy' siren song, only to be seduced by it and to be saved from despair by Bauer and company's converting him to 'the viewpoint of contemporary scholarship'. It was as though his exciting discovery of Hegel had more to do with his recovery and maturing than the prescribed rest he did not take. If Bakunin referred to philosophy as his 'wife', young Marx in his letter spoke, lover-like, of throwing himself 'into her arms'.

It is doubtful that his ailing father in Trier would have approved if he had known that before long Karl would not only challenge Hegel and stand Germany's 'intellectual titan' on his head, but atheistically challenge God as well and install Man in His place. But his son's emotional account of his herculean studies, endless headaches, inner storms and mad antics and rages during and since his stay at Stralau filled Heinrich Marx with horror at the thought that Karl was now under the influence of harebrained new friends who believed that a 'deluge' of senseless and disordered ideas was automatically a sign of genius. Having had more than one example of Karl's excessive bookishness, he feared that his son was in danger of becoming a brooding, distracted, morose type of scholar:

> God help us! Disorderliness, stupefying dabbling in all the sciences...
> Unruly barbarism, running wild with unkempt hair in a learned

548

dressing-gown... Shirking all social contacts, disregarding all conventions... your intercourse with the world limited to your sordid
room, where perhaps lie strewn in classical disorder the love letters
of a Jy [Jenny] and the well-meant, tear-stained exhortations of your
father...

was it in that 'workshop of senseless scholarliness' that Karl expected to 'grow
the fruits' and 'gather the harvest' that 'will delight you and your loved one'
and make a well-born lady like the Baroness Jenny happy? True, Karl was only
19, but if he was old enough to make his loved one give up her prospects for
him, then it behooved him at least to do something 'to create for her a future...
worthy of her, in the real world and not in a smoky room with a smelly oil lamp
and a crazy scholar.'

This added a double and tragic misunderstanding to the hitherto simmering,
now openly seething and perhaps inevitable conflict bedevilling the remaining
relations between father and son. Just as Karl Marx had embraced 'modernity'
and Hegel's 'currently prevailing world philosophy' at the beginning of the
path that would lead to his sensational reinterpretation of it in a manner and
with a force that was to leave a permanent mark on the world, his otherwise
astute, understanding father had no way of making head or tail of what his son
was about or what he was after.

Karl Marx himself had at this point no idea what his next step would be. In
the same month when he gave his father an account of his vast labours, troubles
and mixed plans to become a judicial Assessor or start a theatre journal, he registered for a course in criminal law, but attended no other lectures in the
1837–38 winter semester. In the summer he heard Eduard Gans, Hegel's heir,
expounding Prussian common law, but thereafter he lost interest in jurisprudence and pursued such mixed studies as logic, geography, the drama of
Euripides and a course on Isaiah by his friend Bruno Bauer.

Early on, through the spirited Bauer, Karl was introduced to that great Romantic and libertarian lady, Bettina Brentano von Arnim, whose salon on Unter den
Linden was 'the last refuge of freedom' in Berlin. Clemens Brentano and Achim
von Arnim – Bettina's brother and husband, respectively – were the compilers of
the famous Romantic anthology, *Des Knaben Wunderhorn* ('The Boy's Magic
Horn'). Bettina's salon was frequented by socially prominent Berliners of every
class and denomination, young and old, conservatives and liberals. There Marx
met such well-to-do people as Heinrich Beer, who had the distinction of having
studied philosophy under Hegel himself, and the banker Wilhelm Beer. The two
were brothers of the composer Giacomo Meyerbeer, and their mother, Amalie
Beer, was hostess to Berlin's aristocratic-enlightened and intellectual élite.

In these salons, and in certain other houses which opened their doors to private Doctors Club sessions, Marx attended Shakespeare recitals, mixed with the famous Devrient and other actors, with his own professor – the celebrated Gans – and with established or aspiring philosophers, journalists and others sympathizing with, or interested in, the club's 'modern' ideas.

In short, by the time he was 20, Karl Marx obtained entry into some of Berlin's fashionable intellectual-artistic circles. At that, his father was not far wrong in fearing that Karl was becoming an unsociable character. For in truth he did not really join Berlin's social circuit. He was a bit young to be interested in Bettina Brentano, who could have been his mother, or impressed by the plaster head of Jupiter or the representation of Goethe with Lyre and Psyche decorating her salon. Heinrich Beer – whom Heine ridiculed in a spoof saying that Hegel liked him because he preferred the company of persons 'of whom he knew that they did not understand him' – was an eccentric who spent a fortune collecting theatre posters and thousands of walking sticks. Although his brother Wilhelm was a more serious character – a banker and amateur astronomer, he studied the planets from an observatory in his garden, and was to be co-author of a standard work on the subject, containing the exact measurements of the visible surface of the moon – Karl shared neither of his interests.

He had a much more lively and exciting time in the company of his Doctors Club cronies. And, for another thing, he showed early on his bookish estrangement from the world by concluding that he did not need the university at all; during three of his remaining 6 semesters in Berlin, he attended no lectures whatever, preferring to plumb philosophy by himself in his room.

Knowing none of this, his father pointed out to him on 9 December 1837 where his duties as a human and social being lay. Unwittingly identifying Karl's tendency towards extremism, he reminded him that 'as a man one is a spiritual being as well as a member of society, a citizen', and suggested that Karl's duty was to put his 'unusual talent' and 'splendid gifts' to the best use in a harmonious way 'physically, morally, intellectually and politically.'

Exaggerating in one direction merely bred caricatures: 'Morally it breeds exalté dreamers; politically – intriguers; and spiritually – scholarly bears.'

For once, Heinrich Marx was determined to be 'merciless' with his idol. And he lashed out at Karl all the more bitterly because he had allowed himself, against his better judgment, to become so deeply involved in the affair with Jenny.

'Scarcely was the wild rampaging in Bonn over, scarcely were your debts paid', he wrote, 'when to our consternation the sorrows of love began. Like truly good-natured parents in novels we became its heralds and its cross-bearers... even played perhaps unbecoming roles,' all for the sake of the son's happiness. But the son, 'so young, yet already estranged', has caused them 'much grief, and little or no joy.' And what about Jenny?

Yes, he had a great debt to pay off, for a noble family renouncing its just expectations of so 'admirable' a daughter had a claim to 'great requittal'. After thus alluding to the attitude of some or all the Westphalens, Heinrich Marx gave full vent to his own mortification in the matter: 'Truly, thousands of parents would have refused [her] their consent. And in moments of gloom your own father almost wishes they had done so – for in my heart I care too much for the well-being of this angel of a girl, whom I love like a daughter, and for whose happiness I am all the more apprehensive...'

A letter written by Jenny to Karl Marx the following year (but first published only after 1975) makes evident how she responded to the affection and solicitousness shown her by his father during what was for her the miserable summer of 1837. Writing on 24 June 1838, she recalled that it was a year to the day since she walked with Heinrich Marx to his vineyard at Kurenz:

> The day brings back to me his dear, splendid image... We were alone and spent two or three hours conversing about life and such serious matters as religion and love. He spoke precious words, golden words that went straight to my heart, spoke to me with a love, kind-heartedness and devotion such as only a soulful man as he could have shown. My heart returned him this love and will for ever preserve it.

He was, she went on, very sad that day, racked by coughs and weighed down by his awareness that little Eduard had not long to live. Jenny picked strawberries for him,

> and you should have seen... the heavenly, unforgettable smile he gave me! Later he cheered up, even became jocular and teasing to the point where he kept calling me Frau Präsidentin... Your little father proposed that I take him for an interim-husband, since with you it will take so unconscionably long... Whenever I looked up to him, he would ask roguishly, 'And how is my gracious Chief Lady?'[12]

It is evident, too, even from this flirtatious little scene, that if Heinrich Marx originally favoured Karl's betrothal to Jenny as the high mark, among other things, of his family's total assimilation and social merger with its German surroundings, his heart was even more set on the match now that he had got to know, and become very fond of, her as a person. That she was a priceless girl, a noble soul, one in a thousand, had been a recurring theme in his letters to Karl in Berlin. By now he had resigned himself to certain things about Karl, such as his turning a deaf ear to the simplest requests. One of them was to 'please go and see Herr Justizrat Reinhard'. Privy Councillor Reinhard represented Heinrich Marx before the Rhenish High Court of Appeals in Berlin in a case which the latter originally won in Trier, but lost before a superior court in Cologne. As the case was dragging on for years, all Marx wanted to know (before he finally won) was whether the Berlin hearing had at last been set.

A veteran barrister, Heinrich Marx had seen several of his friends and colleagues, such as Justices Jaeningen, Esser, and others promoted from Trier to this Rhenish High Court in Berlin. For himself, he had secretly hoped to land a seat on the magistrate's bench. Meaning to consult Jaeningen about his chances – besides establishing possibly valuable connections for his son – he had more than once practically begged Karl to 'please do me a favour' and visit him. But with age and illness creeping up on him since August, when he wrote to Karl ruefully that he had meant to ask nothing of him that went against his 'dignity' or his 'grain', he had given up hope of the Bench. The ebbing of his life brought on a quickened concentration of the uncommonly strong wish he communicated to his son when he was only 17: 'to see in you what I might perhaps have become had I come into the world under similarly favourable suspices.'[13] This, and his declaring him to be 'the sole purpose of my life', naturally placed a terrible load on Karl.

In Trier, Jenny found in Karl's father a more understanding and trusted confidant than her own, one who – more sensitive than anyone to her predicament – provided her with a substitute paternal shoulder to lean on. It is likely that her beauty and very presence brought forth in the older man something of his youthful dash, the faintest suggestion that he – the worldly-wise, practical conformist and doer – would know how to appreciate her and respond to her needs better than his immature and wild Lothario of a son who spent all his time and energy philosophizing and had yet to learn the art of making a woman happy. Considering how faithfully, from the moment Karl fell in love with Jenny, Heinrich Marx had deployed all his tact to keep their vulnerable romance going, his almost wishing that her parents had refused their consent to the match was perhaps his most grievous cry, giving the full measure of his disappointment in Karl.

He was appalled, too, by the fact that Karl, besides wasting his talents and his time, had also let a lot of money run through his fingers: 'As though we were made of gold, our Mister Son gets through almost 700 Thalers in a single year, against all [our] agreements, against all custom, whereas the very richest do not spend 500...' Indeed, the poet Freiligrath in 1837 lived 'most comfortably on 180 to 200 Thaler per annum.' A Berlin City Councillor at the time drew a salary of no more than 800 Thaler a year.[14] Heine, as we know, had attended Berlin University and lived like 'the richest student of the aristocracy' on 400 to

500 Thaler a year. And in 1842, Richard Wagner was to inform Brockhaus, the publisher, that for his and his wife's maintenance for the next half year he would need 200 Thaler.[15]

By every comparison, the 700 consumed by young Marx in 1837 was an exorbitant sum. Revealing as his fascinating letter of confession may otherwise be, it actually leaves a good deal of his life and activities in Berlin shrouded in obscurity. Thus Heinrich Marx had no good idea (nor have we) what he spent the money on. His other letters, since destroyed, cannot have been more enlightening, for Heinrich Marx complained of rarely being informed 'of our son's actions, what he is actually doing...' Nevertheless, he paid an additional debt of 160 Thaler that Karl had incurred, and so informed him in his stern diatribe of 9 December 1837.

Not to be unfair to Karl, his father took part of the blame upon himself. It pained him to hurt his son. But neither, for once, did he want to yield to sentiment, 'for I feel that I have been too permissive... and therefore that I have in a sense become your accomplice.' He would do the son justice: Karl was no waster, no spendthrift. But how, he asked, 'can a man who feels compelled to invent a new system every 8 or 14 days and has to tear up all his previous painful labours each time, how can he, I ask, be bothered with trifles? How can he submit to petty orderliness... [when] it takes no time to write another cheque?'

In Karl's lack of moderation and any kind of self-discipline Heinrich Marx saw part of the cause for the utter nonchalance with which Karl seemed to treat his 'sacred duty' towards Jenny. His apparent failure to honour the obligations of his betrothal, his apparent lack of concern, offended Heinrich's sense of honourable conduct, his sense of values, ethics, proprieties and convention. It was by his strict adherence to all these that he had gained acceptance in society in his time. This conforming rationalist, who believed in the inherent goodness of man, wrote to his son on 2 March: 'Only if your heart remains pure and purely human, if no demonic genius is ever capable of alienating and estranging your heart from its better feelings – only then will I find the happiness that, through you, I have been dreaming of for many years. Otherwise the most beautiful purpose of my life will be destroyed.'

And now, aging and sick, with a dying child and his dreams shattered, he realized that he had failed, that young Marx was ungovernable and would not change. It is a tragic letter, tragic for both father and son, but more for the former. For Heinrich Marx, having come to regard his son as the cynosure of his existence and his own life's greatest 'purpose' and achievement – 'I, too, have achieved something, enough to have you, not enough to satisfy me' – now actually knew that he was defeated. But with his remaining strength, he made 'a last desperate effort' – as Edmund Wilson described it – 'to save his son from turning into something which the father dreads.'

And what he seems to have dreaded most was some unfeeling, almost inhuman – or not ordinary human – streak in Karl's character. It was the 'demonic genius' to which he had referred in his letter of 2 March, wondering whether it was 'a celestial or a Faustian demon'. Eight months later, in his reply to Karl's letter of confession, he felt confirmed in his worst fear – which was that Karl might grow not simply into a brainy, self-absorbed, hyper-erudite, remote or wool-gathering scholar, but into a negative genius, one who surveys the universe with a cold, abstract eye while taking little notice of the needs of the individual or those nearest to him.

The effect of the letter on Karl may be presumed to have been all the more shattering as his father had tirelessly nursed and encouraged his self-image as a boy of genius blessed by Nature with unusual gifts and extraordinary faculties. All his devoted counsels and remonstrances were pragmatically aimed at guiding Karl towards a 'professorship' or any bourgeois career that would bring him distinction, financial security and 'domestic bliss' with Jenny. Karl, however, was trying to find his vocation in life, rather than a profession. His whole search for some absolute 'truth' governing the world, perhaps for his own identity and his place in relation to it, appears in hindsight a preparation for some calling or mission he felt destined to fulfill in life. Whether or not Karl got that sense of vocation by cultural transmission from his ancestors, his father – while constantly trying to recall him to earth – had by his frequent insistence on his high potential unwittingly confirmed him in this mysterious feeling of being made for great things and some special destiny.

But now his father had abruptly withdrawn his seeming approval of it and presented Karl with a charge-sheet accusing him of failing to live up to practically every one of his responsibilities – to his parents, to his brothers and sisters, to his admirable and noble fiancée, and ultimately to himself, to his talents and his duties as a social being.

Unfortunately, Karl's account of his tempestuous quest for 'new gods' to be installed in his 'holy of holies' took his father into abstract spheres remote from his lawyerly mind, and both its substance and its language grated on his nerves. Karl wrote excitedly about his new friends in the Doctors Club, whose night-long arguments helped to hone his perception of the possibilities latent in Hegel's dialectics. But to his father the Doctors Club was a bunch of 'new fiends' using 'a deluge of words' to hide the emptiness of their confused minds, showing that the father – though familiar with Enlightenment philosophy and possibly even knowing some Hegel – had no idea of the intellectual ferment going on among the 'Young Hegelians'; and eventually, in one of his last few letters, he admits that the very terminology or jargon employed by these philo-sophic celebrities of 'modernity' struck him as both foreign and distasteful.

For his part, Karl Marx may have been so deeply hurt by his father's rebuff that, having for once trustingly opened up and bared his soul to his parent, he would henceforth vehemently protect it by suppressing all references to his per-sonal life. No wonder his daughter Eleanor, knowing how he hated to have it exposed, hesitated long before publishing his youthful letter of confession towards the end of the century.

Karl in 1837 had of course the advantage of youth over his father. In his maturity he was to sow 'fruits' and prepare a 'harvest' of a type and magnitude beyond anything his father could have fathomed. Even so, Heinrich Marx's insight into his son's make-up is striking, and more than one future historian would note that in later life 'Marx would often get to hear the same or similar reproaches' and accusations as those hurled at him by his father.

In his irritable mood, Heinrich Marx finished his letter with the words: 'To come here at this moment would be sheer nonsense.' He knew that Karl didn't mind missing lectures – 'though you have probably paid for them' – but in gos-sipy Trier a mid-term visit would apparently have caused raised eyebrows and tittle-tattle to the effect that he had been sent down for some misdemeanour. Though 'no slave to [public] opinion', his father wanted 'at least to maintain das decorum' (in the original). Possibly, too, he suspected that Karl's sudden wish to see the family was inspired by some selfish purpose. 'Except when you need her', he grumbled, 'you do not remember even Sophie, who has done so much for you and Jy... come home for the Easter vacation,' he suggested, 'or 14 days earlier, so pedantic I am not, and rest assured that I will receive you with open arms and there will beat for you a father's heart.'

They were never to meet again, or so it was thought until the last quarter of the 20th century. On 10 February 1838 Heinrich Marx, bedridden by then for a month, wrote again to Karl. In a letter that has not survived, Karl had answered his father's severe charges with some reproaches of his own, as is evident from the father's reply: 'To go into dissertations on each and every one of your com-plaints', Heinrich wrote in a trembling hand but with undiminished sarcasm, 'is above my present strength, and when it comes to the art of abstract reasoning I am altogether no match for you, especially as I would have to master the termi-nology to have a chance of ever penetrating the holy of holies, and for that I am too old.'

He was also too weak to rein Karl in any longer and was resigned to the idea that Karl would never pursue a practical career enabling him to look after his family, but would go wherever his intellectual 'demon' drove him. He added only one comment on the subject: 'If you can square your conscience with your philosophy and modestly unite them, well and good.'

But he could not help remarking that all Karl's 'transcendentalism cannot do away with one point on which you have cleverly chosen to maintain an aristocratic silence: I mean the paltry matter of money... We are now in the fourth month of the judicial year, and already you have drawn 280 Thaler. I have not earned that much this winter.'

Indeed, Heinrich Marx's practice had been at a standstill for two months, ever since – about the time in mid-December when he buried his son Eduard – he was confined to his bed.

But he strongly denied Karl's imputation that 'I misjudge you or fail to appreciate you. Neither the one nor the other. I do full justice to your heart and your morality, as witness the incontrovertible proof I gave you... when I did not insist on an explanation and let you off in a very dark matter' – apparently referring to the pistol duel fought by Karl during his first college year. 'Only true faith in your high morality could impel me to do that, and thank God I have never abandoned it...

'For all that, I am not blind,' he insisted, even as he gave up the struggle. 'It is only out of sheer fatigue that I lay down my arms. Yet believe always and never doubt that I carry you in my innermost heart and that you are one of the strongest levers of my life.'

Sophie Marx reported on the same day that their sister Louise, 17, was down with scarlet fever, Caroline, 14, 'unwell', and the consumptive Henriette, 18, 'not in the most amiable humour'. Only Emily, 15, was 'lively and in a good mood.

'I am now singing daily for Daddy,' Sophie added, 'and also read for him... Poor Daddy is very restless, and no wonder, his practice dead all winter, while expenses are now four times what they were, and he made a special effort today to write you a few lines.'

And in the last of these lines Heinrich Marx was suddenly full of praise for Karl, who had evidently made certain promises since December. His father was cautiously enthusiastic: 'Your last resolve is highly laudable, well-calculated, wise and praiseworthy and if you carry out your promise it is likely to bear the best fruits. Rest assured, you are not the only one to make a big sacrifice. We are all in the same boat, but reason must prevail.'

He concluded, 'I am exhausted, dear Karl. I am sorry I cannot write more. I would have liked to embrace you with all my heart.' It is almost as if some sort of reconciliation were in the offing. But Karl had already announced that he would not take up his father's suggestion to come home for Easter, as is evident from his mother's writing – on the same day, 10 February 1838 – in her poor German, without punctuation:

... Your dear father is very weak may dear God soon restore him to strength I am still healthy dear Carl and resigned to my situation and composed... I am most unhappy that you will not come home for Easter I let feeling take precedence over reason and I regret dear Carl that you are too rational you must not measure my deep love by the length of my letter there are times when one feels much but is able to say little so fare you well dear Carl write your good father soon which will certainly contribute to his speedy recovery.

Your eternally loving Mother, Henriette Marx.[16]

Five days later, she asked Karl to write 'loving' letters, for 'then father reads them several times over'; and then she remarked:

My good Carl so much is being asked of you the human heart cannot contain it all a propos heart, you call your illness dilatation of the heart this worries me exceedingly write me dear Carl are you completely well or still suffering, do not over-exert yourself... not to consume your time I relieve you of writing to me directly for knowing your loving heart I know you will not forget me...

Before sending this letter off on the 16th, she added that his father's cough 'is significantly better'. But he had strong pains and 'the doctors say he has the creeping gout.' Father was in fact too weak to add more than two sentences in his own hand: 'Dear Karl, I greet you with sparse words, more I cannot yet manage. Your father, Marx.'[17]

The next document is a letter in Jenny's hand. It is the fragmentary, undated letter, from a poor photostat of which Professor F.J. Raddatz – as mentioned before – published in 1975 a passage in which Jenny accused Karl of having called her a base, 'vulgar girl', and used the word 'suicide' in describing her shock. Raddatz assumed that Marx's fiancée was reacting to an offensive letter written by him. The restored text of Jenny von Westphalen's original letter – as subsequently published in Section III of the *Marx-Engels Gesamtausgabe* – shows not only that the name-calling occurred during a person-to-person quarrel, but has cleared up several other mysteries as well.

For one thing, we learn from it for the first time that Karl Marx arrived on a visit to his parents in Trier at the beginning of May 1838. Jenny, not surprisingly in view of her affection for his father, had been a frequent visitor to the Marx house: 'She takes a personal interest in everything and often cheers us up,' Karl's mother took care to inform him on 10 February. The incident referred to in Jenny's letter now appears to have taken place during his brief stay in Trier. With the beginning of the letter missing, the published text opens in mid-sentence:

... 'to be a vulgar girl', that is the only thing I said. O Karl, Karl, the look you gave me, even now it sends a shiver through my being. I felt as if my heart must break. I still feel the pain, only more fully, no longer so stabbing, but still deep enough. But you were not satisfied with your glance, you wanted to crush me... My heart stopped its beat; you realized what you had done, and asked to be forgiven.

Elsewhere in the letter she writes: 'Karl, that you called me a vulgar girl, that you were capable of saying such a thing to me, particularly at that time, was unfair.' The time-frame is important for more than one reason. The incident occurred at 'a moment of highest love', making Jenny wonder: 'What may I expect once it has cooled? The very thought of it is hell itself. To nourish it would be suicide, but for that things must get still worse. Forgive me for writing this, but occasionally I'm still convulsed by a stab of pain.' Jenny next provides a valuable set of dates: 'The day was the 3rd May; on the 7th you left; on the 10th he was no more.'

'He' who is no more was Karl's father, who had died on 10 May 1838. Jenny, writing some time after that date, had more to say about the atmosphere on the 3rd, when her quarrel with Karl took place, and the reasons why his insult was 'too much. There was a premonition of death, but more terrible, for the end was not yet. Every day brought more worries, more pain, more fear. What I felt that day has not yet recurred. Another time it would be the death of me!'

It is in this letter, incidentally, that Jenny recalled how 'at the beginning' she shied away from pronouncing the words 'I am in love with you'. It throws some light on the personalities of the young couple and their relationship that Jenny at 24 finds it necessary to instruct Karl Marx on the difference between 'to love' and 'to be in love'. She loves, she writes, her brother Edgar. 'With you I am in love. Do you understand what I mean? You're not offended?' Fearful of losing this imperious youngster who could 'crush' her with his transfixing glance, she swore to God that 'this was never the intention, but I was so hurt, so irritated, and you know how vain I am – Karl, please forgive me just this once, burn this letter and forget it'.[18]

Heinrich Marx was buried in Trier on 13 May. His epitaph might well have been the words he had written to Karl: 'I, too, have achieved something, enough to have you, not enough to satisfy me.'

Karl, who had just turned 20, did not attend the funeral. Whatever the reasons that made him decamp for Berlin a couple of days before his father's death, the itemized list of accusations with which the latter had presented him – deliberately, 'to have you swallow them like pills' – in his letter of 9 December

1837 must have hurt him to the quick. The bitterest to swallow, besides the charges of egoism, of 'aristocratically' wasting money he had not earned, of being 'estranged' from his family, etc., must have been his father's expressed foreboding that he was on his way to becoming a 'demonic' or 'Faustian' genius. For the last two years Heinrich had been dimly aware that Karl was aiming at some lofty purpose in life. At one point, he had even declared him capable of accomplishments that might 'benefit mankind'. At the same time he had given his son mixed signals and contradictory admonitions, culminating in his final charge-sheet.

On Karl's side we have only his letter of confession to go on and it is impossible to say at what point he began to feel in open conflict with his father. By the time of the death, his alienation from the only person he respected seems to have been complete. More than one historian has in fact observed that Karl was to spend the rest of his life trying to disprove his father's accusations. The reactionary conditions in Prussia which, in another context, had made the lawyer clairvoyantly predict in 1815 the alienation of the next generation, instead of getting better, got worse after his death. When they presently hit the son full face, Karl Marx, like Börne and Heine before him, would choose to exile himself from his native country, marking his double alienation, not to mention that created by his having been cut off at the age of 6 from his ancestral roots in the past.

Before that, in a supremely ironic twist, Karl found a kind of ideal substitute or super-father in the person of Baron von Westphalen – Jenny's father – to whom he was to dedicate his doctoral dissertation. But angst-ridden Jenny, having preserved a lock of his own father's hair, sent it to Karl on 24 June 1838, along with a long, effusive, but sincere letter evoking the virtues of the 'splendid' man who had understood her delicate situation better than her own parents did and had stood by her at a melancholy time in his cheerfully adopted role of 'interim-husband'. Jenny, in short, provided the kind of eulogy which Karl Marx, carrying an old daguerreotype photograph of his father but 'never willing to show it to strangers', would never write.

20

Heine and His Tycoon Uncle Salomon

'For the last three months', Heinrich Heine wrote to his publisher on 30 March 1838, 'I have felt an inner desolation such as I've never known before.' In mid-May, about the time Karl Marx's father was dying in Trier, Heine's physician, Dr Sichel, forbade him to read and write. It was not the first time Heine had trouble with his eyesight, but he had suddenly started seeing everything double and was in danger of going blind.

It was a little over two years since a brash Heine, at the first indistinct news that Prussia was about to crown the Federal proscription of the Young Germany writers with a decree banning 'Heine's future literary output in all languages', had informed Campe: 'I am healthier and more cheerful than ever and am fully enjoying all the delights of the season... Prussia will never dare to commit the unheard-of and prohibit books which have not yet been written.' Such an act was sure to expose it to 'ridicule on top of public indignation', and if Prussia really resorted to such 'proscriptive folly', the intention could merely be to humiliate him.

'Some démarches from my side', he felt, would put an end to the whole 'hue and cry'. And while Campe, stupefied by Prussia's step and losing his usual acumen for once, kept giving him contradictory advice – urging him on 12 January to undertake something against the ban, and on the 18th to do nothing that might offend the German governments – Heine had promptly made his 'démarche' by drafting a Statement to the German Federal Diet. Published on 30 January 1836 in the *Journal des Débats*, and subsequently in the *Allgemeine Zeitung* and two other German newspapers, Heine's declaration to the Hohe Bundesversammlung said in part:

> Gentlemen, you have accused, judged, and sentenced me without
> giving me either a verbal or written hearing, without charging anyone
> with my defence, or even sendinme a summons. This is not the way
> the Holy Roman Empire, whose place has been taken by the German
> Bund, acted in similar cases.

'Doctor Martin Luther of glorious memory', he reminded them, 'was provided with a safe-conduct and permitted to appear before the Reichstag to defend himself publicly against all accusations.' For himself, he asked merely to be given 'the freedom of the printed word'. He would use it to prove that his writings – far from being 'irreligious or immoral' – stemmed from a 'genuine religious and moral synthesis' long adhered to by 'our most celebrated writers, poets and philosophers, and not only by the so-called Young Germany literary school'; and he would use it also to dispel any public misconception that he was denying his writings, as might be inferred from his 'enforced silence'.

Eating humble pie without abjuring his convictions – which is what some of the Young Germany writers were doing to theirs at the time – Heine had assured the deputies of the Bundesversammlung that his letter was not a protest, but 'a plea to lift the interdict you have pronounced against whatever I write'; and that he held them in the respect becoming 'the highest authorities of a beloved homeland', whose laws he would always obey.[1]

'My childish syrupy submissive letter', he had written Campe on 4 February, 'is sure to have a good effect.' Was Heine naive? He had a childish streak in him, and sometimes enjoyed exploiting it, but his speaking of 'démarches' reminds one that, using the diplomatic journalese of one power to another, he had once before threatened to break relations with Germany's rulers. He was sure that his name would live long after most contemporary monarchs were forgotten, and his self-estimate was that of the literary genius, as which indeed he was ultimately, if posthumously, to be recognized. His naiveté lay in his expecting despotic Prussia to treat him accordingly. If his self-image often blinded him to the prevailing reality – so that Campe had to disabuse him of any illusion that the German 'governments have a good opinion of you. The devil they do' – it also helped him to hold his head above water while swimming against the current.

Besides, within days of addressing the Bundesversammlung by way of sounding the enemy, he was making a move – in the same letter of 4 February – to show up the ludicrous, nonsensical character of the ban by suggesting that Campe publish a book of his without submitting it to censorship. In January, Heine had been flitting about between the rue Cadet, where Mathilde lived, the Hôtel d'Espagne (where he was staying temporarily) and the Cité Bergère, where a new apartment was being readied for him. Nevertheless, in between discussing an English edition of his works with Hayward, the translator of Goethe's *Faust*, having his portrait taken by Johannot, frequenting the salon of Princess Belgiojoso, striking up a new friendship with the marquis de Custine – a *grand seigneur* with literary aspirations at whose soirées Chateaubriand read from his works and Chopin would play – and otherwise 'enjoying the delights of the season', Heine had put the finishing touches to his 'Florentine Nights'. He now proposed that Campe publish this belletristic work, 'touching on neither politics nor religion', together with an equally 'harmless' essay on Elemental Spirits, under the title of *Salon III*.

Would Campe be ready to defy the ban by printing *Salon III* uncensored? The book could hardly be accused of containing seditious material. 'Or', enquired Heine on 4 February, 'do you consider it too daring to put my name on the title page?'

By 8 March he was sending Campe the manuscript of *Salon III*, emphasizing that if he was unable to print the book uncensored, he had 'better not print it at all'. He made this a 'point of honour', declaring that 'I represent at this moment the last shred of German intellectual freedom'; and to show how serious he was, he hastened to follow up with another letter, saying that if there was no way of eluding Prussian censorship, Campe was not to honour a cheque he, Heine, had drawn on his account with the firm.[2]

On the night of 29 February, joining *le tout Paris* at a rare double event, Heine had been to the Grand Opéra for the premiere of Giacomo Meyerbeer's *Les Huguenots*, and then repaired to the inaugural ball given by the Rothschilds at their renovated palais in the rue Laffitte. Leaving it at 4 a.m., he went more or less directly to his desk without having had any sleep. 'Giddy with ideas and images' picked up during the night, he set them down in somewhat pell-mell fashion, but felt too exhausted to write a full review of the opera which, with its dramatic conflict between Catholics and Protestants, its spectacular *mise en scène* and its musically superb fourth act, confirmed Meyerbeer as the uncontested king or 'pope' of European opera.

Observing that a masterpiece requires several hearings to be appreciated, Heine declared in his short report that Meyerbeer was 'the greatest living master of counterpoint' and otherwise quoted the opinion of experts that in inventiveness and perfection of form *Les Huguenots* surpassed even Meyerbeer's phenomenal *Robert le Diable*, never dreaming that for a hundred years or more his detractors would seize on this to claim that he had not attended the premiere at all.[3]

After the Rothschild ball, Heine dined on two separate evenings in the first week of March 1836 with Meyerbeer's mother Amalia Beer, the wealthy Berlin hostess whose charitable works had elicited a singular gesture from Prussia's anti-Semitic Friedrich Wilhelm III – the award of the Order of Queen Luise in the form of a special medal substituted for the usual cross – and with the composer himself, besides attending another performance of *Les Huguenots*. Dining with the rich and famous was all very well; but within days, Heine learned that Campe, acting against all instructions, had submitted the manuscript of *Salon III* to the Berlin Censorship.

'Sick with annoyance' at having his plan spoiled, Heine was all the more furious when he learned that Campe had acted in compliance with a new Prussian regulation, which – ostensibly easing the ban – allowed the prohibited 'Young Germany' writers to publish future works so long as they obtained the imprimatur of the 'Supreme Censorship Commission' in Berlin. As this had hitherto not been required for works published in any of the German states other than Prussia, Heine felt that by conforming to the new regulation Campe had walked into a trap and had created a dangerous precedent.

'Prussia wants to buy me for my own money!' he exclaimed. 'For a book of mine to pass its censorship I would have to avoid anything derogatory to it; I could heckle foreign states so long as I lovingly stroke Prussia's pelt – and all this in return for being allowed to pocket a royalty of a few Thaler which actually represents my own-well-earned money.'[4]

He not only forced Campe to withdraw the manuscript from Berlin's 'Supreme Commission', but sent a 4-page-long statement to the *Allgemeine Zeitung*. Besides protesting Prussia's censorship manipulations, he produced a series of arguments challenging the constitutional legality of the Bundestag decree summarily 'banning even my harmless poems everywhere'.

Most of it being struck by the censor, the *Allgemeine Zeitung* printed a note saying that the full text had met with 'hindrances', but quoted the fact that Heine, rather than accept a 'Prussian imprimatur', had 'ordered his publisher to withdraw his manuscript from Berlin.' Now Campe, whose printers had refused to set up Heine's work, spluttered with anger, and as so often happens between coalition partners, the two quarrelled over which of them was causing the other the greater trouble. Once Heine realized that the Prussians were out 'either to ruin me or to turn me into a villain' – 'they will not succeed in the latter purpose', he declared to Campe on 14 March – he was full of fight. The unequal battle was accompanied by a good deal of 'disinformation' – such as Heine's allegation that Prussia had threatened to stop circulation of the *Revue des Deux Mondes* in Germany if it published anything by Heine, and from the other side an officialsounding claim that Heine, the great fighter against the reactionary *status quo*, had offered his 'complete submission' to none but Metternich himself.

No evidence, at least no written evidence, has been found to indicate that Prussia at this time was threatening any Paris newspaper for which Heine wrote. At the beginning of March 1836, Heine drew Campe's attention to an article on his *De l'Allemagne* which had appeared in the London *Quarterly Review*. After blandly, if inaccurately, informing its readers 'without breach of delicacy that his mother was a Prussian lady of good family', but that his father was one of those de-judaized Jews 'whom Sheridan wittily likened to the blank leaf between the Old and New Testaments', this piece contained a passage saying that Heine had 'transplanted himself to Paris, and there associated himself in an intimate league, offensive and defensive, with the most violent section of the Jacobin Propagandist – whose plans embrace the entire extirpation of the Christian faith... and the total abolition of monarchy and aristocracy in Europe.'[5]

Published about the time when the Bundestag had issued its ban, this made Heine – who kept affirming his 'monarchic principles' and had come under fire from Börne, the chief of the German Jacobins in Paris, precisely for keeping his distance from the radicals – feel that there was an 'orchestrated' smear campaign against him, especially as a German newspaper in March dug up another unfriendly piece about him which had appeared in the *Quarterly Review*. Heine, the *enfant terrible* who had lately toned down his aggressiveness, saw himself as a moderate. He never understood, or refused to accept the fact, that Europe's conservatives, let alone the German governments, regarded him as a thorn in their flesh or simply hated him. His anger at his maltreatment by these governments was mixed with consternation, for convinced as he was that he could read 'the tendency' of society, and that what he wrote about its future must be of interest to their statesmen, he clung – like a man who is the victim of some terrible misunderstanding – to the illusion that these statesmen must by now have realized that he was not writing for the 'vulgar' masses in order to stir political revolution. Rather, his revolutionary spirit was of a more philosophical kind, and aimed – in the best Saint-Simonist fashion, one might say – 'at the conversion of the most highly placed persons.'[6]

It was in a message sent by the Prussian ambassador to Vienna, Count Maltzan, to King Friedrich Wilhelm III, that Metternich was reported to have told him in great confidence about receiving a letter from the '*fameux Heine, renfermant la soumission la plus complète de ce détestable écrivain.*' Maltzan, writing in July 1836, saw this as one of the 'beneficial effects of the wise Federal resolutions' against the Young Germany writers. The original of Heine's supposed letter to Metternich has never been found, and the unsettled matter of his 'submission' to Metternich remains one of those battlefield mysteries baffling historians long after the combatants are dead. Complicated by two letters in which Heine claimed that 'in Austria Prince Metternich is, I hear, uncommonly sympathetic to me', it has led to the assumption, among other theories, that Heine's 'intransitive mind' made him the prisoner of some *idée fixe* remote from reality.

In March 1836, Heine received the welcome news that the new Baron Cotta – who had succeeded his father as head of his publishing empire – wished him to resume writing for the *Allgemeine Zeitung*. The news was brought to him by August Lewald, an actor-playwright of many talents who edited Cotta's *Allge-*

meine Theater-Revue as well as the *Europa* magazine. Lewald was much younger than Heine, but a lasting friendship developed between the two men and in the first week of April Heine took Lewald round to Meyerbeer, to the historian Mignet, to Janin, Sainte-Beuve and George Sand.

Towards the end of April, the eminent Viennese playright Franz Grillparzer arrived in Paris. As Heine kept his address at No. 3 Cité Bergère secret, it took Grillparzer two days of inquiries before he was able to call on him. The short-sighted Heine, who had never met him, opened the door and took him at first for the marquis de Custine. Grillparzer found Heine 'in the best of health... We had an hour's excellent conversation,... I have hardly ever heard a German writer talk better sense.' On 6 May the two of them dined at the Rothschilds in the company of Rossini and others. Grillparzer noted in his diary that Baroness Betty was 'amiable, educated, eloquent' and practically like a 'goddess' compared to Baron James's 'common' appearance and manners.[7]

Heine was much feted, he observed, but left early. He had come in from Le Coudray, a village within 10 hours' drive from Paris, where he stayed from the beginning of May to the end of July seeking (as he wrote to Campe) 'undisturbed solitude and fruitful peace of mind.' His 'Florentine Nights' had been serialized in Cotta's *Morgenblatt* as well as in *Revue des Deux Mondes*, and in June an excerpt had been published in Moscow. At the beginning of July the *North American Monthly* magazine devoted two articles to him. Both Grillparzer and Lewald noted that he had put on some weight. But there was to be no peace for Heine that summer, and the next couple of years were to be one of the most harassed and unfruitful periods in his life.

First, if he was determined not to let Prussia succeed in turning him into 'a villain', it succeeded in ruining him financially. Ever since March, he had been complaining about money problems. Grillparzer described his apartment – which Heine had described to Campe as 'splendid and voluptuous' – as consisting of 'two small rooms... the second of which, Heine's study, was even tinier but looked almost spacious because of the practically total absence of furniture. His whole ostensible library consisted of a single book which he said himself was a borrowed one.' Heine, in short, seemed to him to live in straitened circumstances. In July, indeed, during one of his brief forays to Paris, flashily dressed as usual, he was borrowing 600 francs for a month from the publisher Renduel.

But money was not Heine's only problem. He was infatuated with Mathilde, but still resisting her attraction. For well over a year – until he was finally to succumb and move in with her at her flat in the rue Cadet – No. 3 Cité Bergère served as a convenient *pied-à-terre* where he could assert his 'freedom' by indulging in erotic adventures. Grillparzer, who besides writing successful plays enjoyed a government sinecure, bequeathed to the world his shock at the way Heine, receiving him in a morning robe, had without further ado led him into his 'disorderly household' of two rooms, 'in the first of which two grisettes were fooling about...'[8] Living even then part of the time at Mathilde's, Heine in a sense had not been entirely bluffing when describing his own bohemian apartment as a 'voluptuous' one; and it was no wonder that he kept its address secret, although he did so chiefly in order to keep out both nosy importuners trying to pry into his private life and visiting German well-wishers eager to write home that they had seen him.

After 'a very pleasant time in Paris', within a week of Grillparzer's unannounced visit, he was writing to Lewald from the village of Le Coudray: 'Now my M[athilde] is sitting next to me in front of a large fireplace and is sewing new shirts for me... She cheers up my life through the very constant inconstancy of her caprices.' Lewald, perhaps the only one of his intimates to whom Heine had so far introduced Mathilde, described her as 'a pretty brunette with fiery eyes'. Heine now half-cynically and half-humourously boasted to Lewald that Mathilde – having taken the trouble to read the French translation of his *Travel Pictures* – had been seized with a deathly pallor when coming upon an erotic scene. 'She is so jealous... that I had to promise her in future to address any words of love in my books exclusively to invented, idealized figures.'[9]

Nevertheless, at the beginning of August, hardly returned to Paris – while Mathilde had gone to another place in the country – Heine was discovered by a man called Steege in the company of two grisettes, Céleste and Augustine. Steege, of whom nothing but his address in the Place Sorbonne is known, seems to have had some claim to Augustine. He made a scene, and wrote a letter demanding satisfaction. Heine arranged to meet him at a café. Steege did not turn up, Augustine was in hysterics, and a complicated correspondence took place before the affair was settled without a duel.

Heine and Campe had by now grudgingly settled their differences. Heine's libertine affairs would have been less relevant had they not embroiled him in what – on 1 September, in separate letters to Mignet and Campe – he described as '*embarras domestiques*', probably with the jealous Mathilde, which interfered with his work just as the war against the ban moved towards new developments: 'I feel at this moment like a harassed dog, assailed by unforeseen and most embarrassing events which necessarily have an adverse effect on my literary activities.'

At Le Coudray, he had been working on his 'Elemental Spirits', the essay which – together with 'Florentine Nights' – was to go into *Salon III*. But it turned out that the two works together were not enough to bring the volume up to 21 sheets, or 320 pages, the peculiar watershed fixed by the Prussian authorities, though the book could still be suppressed.

Choosing a new tactic, Heine decided to augment the volume with a *Vorrede* (Preface), and since he could not write anything blatantly political, he would turn it into a violent broadside against Wolfgang Menzel – the nationalist literary critic who was held largely responsible for instigating the Bundestag ban – exposing his role as 'the Informer' in terms so offensive as to provoke him to a duel, or show him up as a coward. But Prefaces spelled trouble for Heine, as when he had been forced to write his 'Preface to the Preface', and the same thing happened again. In his letter of 1 September to Campe, written from Amiens – where he had developed symptoms of some mysterious, 'cholera-like' disease – Heine for the first time confessed to the unnerving effect the constant thought of censorship, 'now that the most innocent thing is suspect', was having on his writing: 'Three times I wrote the Preface to the Salon up to the middle', he wrote bitterly, 'and three times I destroyed it. What use is it to write, if it is not printed?' His mood may have been influenced by his coming down with jaundice, which within a day or two forced him to return to Paris, where he was bedridden for the rest of the month. On 5 October he left for Marseilles, and on the 7th he described to Campe the horrible 8 days he had spent 'neither eating nor sleeping, only vomiting and cramps.' He intended to spend the winter in Italy, and promised soon to supply the 'few sheets required to complete Salon III.' But he was not completely cured and got only as far as Aix-en-Provence, where he learned of an outbreak of cholera in Naples and gave up the idea of travelling to Italy.

From Aix another cry of despair emerged in a letter to Princess Belgiojoso: 'Madame', he wrote on 30 October 'should I not make an ignoble peace with the authorities across the Rhine in order to escape all these worries of exile and this fastidious want which is worse than utter poverty?... I am more sick in soul than in body; the jaundice is now in my heart.'

It was in this state of mind, some time in October, with his nerves 'racked by the commercial noise' of Marseilles and perhaps remembering that he had once nursed Uncle Salomon's son through the cholera in Paris, that Heine turned for help to his Hamburg relative. Doing so in ill-conceived reproachful terms in a letter which has not survived, he could not resist coining the phrase which Uncle Salomon never forgave him: 'The best thing about you is that you bear my name.'

The result was that by November he was broke. 'Only a fool or a friend will now lend me money,' he candidly informed Moses Moser, the Berlin friend of his youth. 'I have recently had the bitterest quarrel with my uncle, the millionaire; I could not stand his base meanness any longer.' Moser never replied to his plea for a loan of 400 Thaler in the name of their old but now lapsed friendship.

In April, Lewald had offered to interest a publisher in Stuttgart, where his

Theater-Revue appeared, in the production of a Collected Edition of Heine's works. From time to time Heine inquired, but although Lewald sounded encouraging, the matter dragged on through all the long months when money worries, sexual dissipation, domestic troubles, illness, and 'the sheer insanity' of having to write like 'a stammerer with half a tongue' because of 'the censorship sword over my head', conspired to stall his pen. On 20 December, restored to health in Paris, he promised Campe to send the long-delayed Preface to *Salon III* within 8 days. He was finally to post it on 23 January, but by then catastrophe had struck.

Heine informed Campe that – as the result of what he vaguely called 'a series of the most incomprehensible events' – he was '20,000 francs in debt', a not inconsiderable sum equal to George Sand's total income that year. Already in November Heine had hinted to Moser that some 'amiable but frivolous' French friends had taken advantage of him and caused him 'great financial damage'. Months later, he amplified somewhat in a letter to his brother Maximilian: 'Through the most abject villainy of a friend for whom I stood guaranty and with whom I deposited money, I was placed in a disastrous situation.' Writing after the event, he added that it took the greatest efforts 'to satisfy every demand', to avert the prospect of being taken to the Saint-Pélagie debtors prison and 'avoid laying myself bare to my enemies. That was the principal thing.'[10]

Always suspicious and circumspect, he was keen to protect himself against his enemies' sniping and gave no further details, thereby laying himself open for more than a century to the guesses and speculations of legions of students about how he had got into this disastrous situation in the first place. Had he gambled? Had he lost money in an unsuccessful speculation in railway shares and were his creditors insisting on immediate payment? Had he lightly undertaken an obligation for a friend, or was it some piece of blackmail resulting from the dubious company he kept? Was he really facing debtors prison? Or had he perhaps just made up the whole story 'to gain sympathy and account for the hole in his pocket'? All these theories have been put forward by biographers and literary historians.[11]

The fact is that nobody knows, and this remains yet another Heine mystery. To compound matters, in his 23 January letter to Campe, Heine mentioned Metternich's being 'sympathetic' to him; and in his letter to Lewald two days later he repeated this claim but added that 'even in Prussia the highest and most influential statesmen have made utterances in my favour... Without my having to utter a single word against my convictions, people are giving up their misgivings. They are of course aware of my bad standing with the Jacobins.'[12]

That he had a secret admirer in Metternich's chancellery – in the person of Gentz, Metternich's right-hand man and former 'Secretary of Europe' – Heine knew from their mutual friend Varnhagen. According to the latter, Gentz had made Metternich see 'the indescribable magic' of Heine's poetry and wit. Gentz was now dead, but a letter of his is cited describing Metternich's delight at some barbed remarks about Talleyrand in the *Allgemeine Zeitung*, only to be told by Gentz that they were from the pen of 'the devil himself [Heine], the man whom no censorship can beat.'[13]

Heine must have known, however, that Metternich had hardly become his well-wisher, and it is not surprising that the two letters in which he tried to make him out as one have been cited as an example of his 'pathological' inability 'to apprehend accurately the objective reality of his life.'[14] It is just as plausible, however, that in both letters Heine was simply bluffing in order to allay the censorship fears of two different German publishers.

In the Preface he finally sent to Campe he attacked German nationalism as a tool of the darkest reaction. Knowing that Campe had been badly hit by the ban and was otherwise in a gloomy mood – 'There is now in Germany no struggle with the despots... we are all the anvil on which they are hammering with raw brutality,' the publisher complained[15] – Heine assured him that he had taken every trouble 'to treat the most delicate subjects in a manner that disarms the governments.' At the same time he insisted that the Preface must be printed without 'one iota being omitted... our whole relationship depends on it.' Emphasizing that his moderation was gaining him the goodwill of Germany's statesmen was his way of persuading Campe not to 'sacrifice' him in the jittery manner which had made him – unnecessarily, in Heine's view – submit the material of *Salon III* to Berlin.

The same type of objective was even more transparent in his letter to Lewald, which was written in an analogous context. Lewald had recently come up with two Stuttgart publishers vying to produce a *Gesamtausgabe*, or Collected Edition, of Heine's works. One of them, headed by Johannes Scheible, was actually offering 20,000 francs, payable in two instalments, for his Collected Work plus his Memoirs, which he had started writing. The extent to which Heine represented a censorship risk to publishers is evident from the fact that when Scheible submitted his formal offer to undertake the *Gesamtausgabe* he demanded that 'in deference to Prussia' they should be 'softened down', i.e., cleared of some of the radical things Heine had written at one time or another. Scheible had yet to raise this point when Heine, correctly assessing the problem, anticipated him by conveying to him through the intermediary of Lewald that the German governments knew that he had distanced himself from the Jacobins.

After he received Scheible's formal offer, Heine informed him that 'should the present censorship rigours against me remain in effect' and create a situation where he would have to choose between jeopardizing the *Gesamtausgabe* or 'having to humiliate myself before the authorities and incur the suspicion of betraying my own opinions', he was ready instead to waive 5,000 francs of his fee by way of compensating the publisher. He was sure that he ran no risk in doing so, for within a year he would, 'as far as my honour permits, satisfy Pr[ussia]' with his moderation.[16]

If there was something of an *idée fixe* about this, it stemmed from his illusion that his moderation was of greater worth to the German governments 'than the servility of our Teutomaniacs' and from his now regarding himself as more of a 'philosophical' than a political revolutionary, a man, that is – as he suggested to Lewald – standing above the petty daily fray of society and chiefly concerned to 'illuminate its tendency' and future. He was, after all, the poet-prophet who knew 'the watchword of the future'. In the Preface he had just sent to Campe, berating Germany's nationalists for stirring up the old bogey of Francophobia, he declared that 'in the kingdom of the mind they [the French] are our brothers' and once again foretold that a day would come when their material interests would bring the two peoples together as allies within a federated Europe.

Heine's *Salon III*, to be published later in 1837, included his Tannhäuser ballad, which was to inspire Wagner's opera. Even before that happened, Heine was fully conscious that in his poetry and prose, his satires and polemics, he was making a first-rank contribution not only to the literature of Germany but to its political culture. If his attempts to reconcile the opposites sometimes made him look as if he were charging windmills, this, given his nature as a lone knight-in-armour – and the absence at the time of the international support which dissidents and political exiles nowadays receive from far-flung countries – was part of his way of fighting reality.

Scheible's offer happened to coincide with the arrival in Paris of a Mr Hvas, who invited Heine to write an introduction to a German edition of *Don Quixote*. Since Hvas, who represented Brodag's 'Classical' Library – the second Stuttgart firm which had approached Heine to stipulate his terms for a *Gesamtausgabe* – was offering 1,000 francs, Heine was doubly pleased to accept. *Don Quixote* was one of the first books he had ever read; and the 500 francs he got as a down-payment was the first money received in his hour of financial distress.

All the solace Campe had been able to offer him on 28 January 1837 was to advise him to repair his relations with his Uncle Salomon. Nevertheless, on 17 February Heine notified Campe that Scheible was ready to sign a 10-year contract for a *Gesamtausgabe* of 12 volumes. Although down for weeks with a persistent 'flu – 'a juste-milieu illness which allows you neither to live nor to die' – Heine was now as busy as a man keeping three balls in the air. While waiting for

Campe's reaction, he had to keep Scheible's interest alive, but on 24 February he informed him that before signing their contract he felt in decency bound to offer the *Gesamtausgabe* to his long-time publisher 'on the same terms as proposed by others'. Although he frankly thought that Campe would not take up the offer, the opposite happened. An acrimonious bit of haggling ensued – with Campe claiming that the rights to a Collected Edition were his in the first place, Heine insisting that he had never sold him anything but individual books, and Campe accusing him of disloyalty and claiming that he had to mortgage his house to match Scheible's terms.

The upshot was that Heine sold Campe his Collected Works for 20,000 francs, of which he was to get 5,000 on signature and the rest in instalments over the next 30 months. He and Campe knew each other well enough to be familiar with their individual wiles, but as they tried to make the most of their cards, there was more bargaining on specific paragraphs, publication dates, etc. Heine accused Campe of dragging his feet, causing him the embarrassment of making Scheible think that he was 'leading him by the nose'; and letters kept shuttling back and forth before the final contract was hammered out at the beginning of April.

Campe turned out to be the tougher businessman, for Heine, in a hurry to get the first down-payment and to be freed of his creditors, gave him as a bonus the right to reprint any number of new editions of his single volumes already published without further payment.

But what use was a contract so long as Heine's writings were banned? At Campe's insistence, Heine, who only 8 months earlier had bitterly asked what use it was to write if it was not printed, agreed to publish a notice saying that the *Gesamtausgabe* of his works to be issued by Hoffmann and Campe 'will not be printed before both the author and the publisher may count on the non-partisan good will of the various German censorship authorities.'

With the censorship wall blocking him in all directions, and the fate of the *Gesamtausgabe* now at stake, everything depended on his vaunted ability to obtain the good will which would make Prussia lift or at least relax the ban on him. On 13 April, he confidentially disclosed to Campe that he planned to ask his old Berlin friend Varnhagen von Ense to write the prospectus for the *Gesamtausgabe*. The quiet-spoken Varnhagen, though a liberal and on the retired list, continued to be well-regarded at the Prussian Court, and sometimes had the King's ear. Heine observed to Campe that Varnhagen's name on the prospectus would be 'doubly advantageous. I intend to make my peace with Prussia insofar as my honour permits.'[17]

During the third week of May, Heine went with Mathilde to Granville in Brittany. During this holiday, he was working on his controversial *Ludwig Börne,*

571

A Memorial, which he had started towards the end of January, three weeks before the death of his great Jacobin antagonist. He also made a start on 'the proposed novel of my life', which he thought at the time would fill three volumes. Before leaving Paris he had driven, at 6 a.m. on 1 May, to the Bois de Saint-Cloud to fight a duel with a young Frenchman.

Heine was very jealous of the coquettish Mathilde. They had been dining together with J.H. Detmold, a liberal lawyer and old friend of Heine's, at the popular Boeuf à la Mode restaurant when a group of aristocratic students drinking at a nearby table began to flirt rather ostentatiously with Mathilde. Upon overhearing one of them make a suggestive remark, Heine got up and hit him. The ensuing fracas ended with cards being exchanged, and Detmold's consoling the agitated owner with the remark that he could now enrich the soufflés on his menu with a *soufflet* [slap in the face] *à la Heine*. The student involved chose a baron and a cavalry captain for his seconds. Heine, not to be outdone, enlisted as his second Count Ignace de Gurowski, a dashing young Polish socialite-in-exile. The result was that Heine, accompanied by Gurowski and his other second – a doctor by the name of Massarellos – drew up at the appointed place in grand style, in an equipage with 4 thoroughbreds, liveried attendant and all.

The duel was to be fought with cavalry pistols at 15 paces. According to contemporary newspaper reports – in *Le Courier Français* of 4 May and in Augsburg's *Allgemeine Zeitung* of the 11th – each of the two principals 'fired and missed', after which they exchanged expressions of mutual esteem and left the park. The *Allgemeine*'s informant, however, claimed that the duel was provoked by a Frenchman at the café who had loudly criticized German manners; and by the 24th the *Abendzeitung* of Dresden was declaring that 'Heine duelled for the honour of the fatherland.' To cap it all, Dr Massarellos, writing more than 40 years after the event, claimed that the affair was settled without a single shot, the Frenchman's seconds accepting his assurance that Heine, the great poet, regretted the incident, whereupon one of them had actually joined Heine's party for breakfast at a restaurant in the park. Since Heine was involved in quite a few duels in Paris, the assumption is that Massarellos may have mixed up two different encounters, and that on this particular occasion both principals simply fired in the air.[18]

Heine enjoyed his stay in Brittany. He visited Chateaubriand's birthplace at Saint-Malo and Mont Saint-Michel, explored the Breton coastline, talked to fishermen and studied the scene of the Vendée wars. Mathilde was with him, and but for mentioning that her 'wildcat' temperament still frightened him sometimes, he sounded happy. He had about finished *On The French Stage*, and was playing with the idea of visiting London for the purpose of comparing

English stage and musical life with those of France and Germany. In mid-July, however, Mathilde was taken ill and the couple, finding no good doctors in Granville, set out on the return journey to Paris, travelling three days and two nights before reaching there on the 18th.

Barely arrived, Heine met with Balzac on the same day. The novelist confided in him that he meant to rest from his gargantuan labours on the *Comédie humaine* and switch to writing for the stage, because in the theatre one could make a fortune more quickly and with less effort. Heine dampened his enthusiasm and gave him a piece of advice which Balzac promptly reported to Madame Hanska: 'I mentioned to Heine my idea of writing a play [*faire du théâtre*]. He said to me: "Beware! A man who is used to serving time at Brest cannot get accustomed to Toulon. Stick to the jail you know."' Balzac found the allegory apt enough to add: 'It is true that I now work like a man sentenced to penal servitude.' He was to realize that there was wisdom, too, in Heine's impromptu witticism when his play *Vautrin* – based on the eponymous and enormously popular figure he had created in *Père Goriot* and *Les Illusions perdues* – proved a dismal failure in 1840.

On the same day of his return to Paris, though exhausted from his long journey, Heine dashed off a letter to Campe pressing him – not for the first time – for news of his *Salon III*. The fate of this 'tame', non-political book, coupled with that of the Preface blasting the chauvinism of Wolfgang Menzel, would show whether and to what extent he could go on publicizing his ideas in Germany in spite of the ban. On 29 July, with no word from Campe yet, Heine asked the lawyer Detmold, who had returned to Germany, to find out anything he could about *Salon III*. His letter to Detmold contained, among other things, the ominous news that Heine's left arm was semi-paralyzed and 'withering daily'. Two days later, having spent only a fortnight in Paris, he and Mathilde departed for Boulogne. As she disliked the place, they left on 3 August and spent the rest of the month at Le Havre. Heine loved swimming in the sea and hoped that it would improve his blood circulation and the condition of his left arm.

Unknown to him, *Salon III* had in fact appeared in Germany in mid-July. Besides 'Florentine Nights', a fragmentary novel stringing together a series of 'fairy tale-like' episodes – and memorable chiefly for a passage on the violinist Paganini and a word-portrait of Princess Belgiojoso – the book contained Heine's 'Elemental Spirits'. In this essay Heine transported his readers to the ancient oak forests of Westphalia, where 'the voices of primeval time' echoed more truths of life than some of Germany's modern literature.

An omnivorous reader in spite of Grillparzer's remark about the absence of books in his study, Heine quoted Charlemagne's capitularies to prove the persistence of pagan beliefs in Germany. He used old ballads and plays to conjure up the whole spirit world – elves materializing out of trees, dwarfs mining the earth beneath stones, nixies in white dresses wet at the hemline emerging from watery abodes – that continued to inhabit the German imagination. Adding a fourth element, he remarked that the devil, besides being the 'great logician' depicted in Dante's *Inferno*, was the only 'fire spirit' cool enough by nature to bear and even enjoy the flames of hell.

'Not everything that is buried is dead', was Heine's refrain as he tried, not for the first time, to penetrate the deepest layers of the German soul. Rehashing one of his favourite themes, he observed that the early Christians had destroyed the Greek temples and marble statues not so much because these were dedicated to pagan deities, but because they believed them to be 'strongholds of real demons... The first Christians would rather be martyred than worship the devil Jupiter or the she-devil Diana, let alone the arch-she-devil Venus.'

This view is demonstrated in Heine's Tannhäuser ballad, the main and explicit purpose of which was to allegorize the hold which the pagan past still exercised on the German subconscious. 'The past is the actual homeland of man's soul and he is seized by a longing for feelings he once experienced, be they ever so woeful. That is what happened to Tannhäuser, whose song is one of the strangest linguistic monuments preserved by the German people.' At the same time as the eroticism pervading it fitted Heine's philosophy of 'sensualism', the Tannhäuser legend spoke to his heart all the more because he could identify with its hero. When he wrote the ballad in October 1836, Heine, like Tannhäuser, had been struggling to escape the temptations of Mathilde. The Tannhäuser who in the last stanzas of the poem takes a dig at Hamburg – the city of Heine's own unhappy youth – and then declares that, rather than ever live in that 'rascally' mercantile town, he prefers to settle down to domestic bliss in the Venusberg with the she-devil and her household of 'fair women', spoke for a Heine who already inwardly knew that he was to end up with Mathilde in the Venusberg of her rooms in the rue Cadet.

Since writing that finish to Tannhäuser, he had discovered that life with Mathilde – as he had confided, not without some irony, in his letter to Detmold of 29 July 1837, shortly before leaving Paris for the seaside – involved being dragged to the vaudeville theatre and sitting through 4 shows in one evening in a suffocating hall steaming with the summer heat. In that letter, besides mentioning the trouble with his left arm, Heine hinted cryptically at some new financial catastrophe that had befallen him: 'It is truly strange how misfortune lately pursues me. Hardly did I start introducing the strictest order into my affairs when the most unforeseen disaster upsets everything.' Coincidentally, on the same 29th of July, Campe had posted a letter to Boulogne informing Heine of the publication of *Salon III*, but as he was in Le Havre the news took a long time reaching him.

Though Heine considered the two works making up *Salon III* harmless enough, he was most anxious to know what had happened to the provocative Preface in which – besides accusing Germany's Francophobic nationalists of poisoning the minds of the mob by equating xenophobia with patriotism – he had attacked Wolfgang Menzel, the panjandrum of German literary critics, as a dishonourable man of small talent who had exploited 'the frightened silence' prevailing in the fatherland to incite its ministers against Germany's progressive young writers, whose books these ministers never read.

Heine's self-styled 'bomb of a Preface' had in fact been censored out of *Salon III*. With the foresight of a strategist, however, Heine had persuaded Campe to issue the lengthy Preface as a separate pamphlet under the title *Über den Denunziaten* ('On the Denunciator'). 'You owe it to the young writers', he had exhorted the publisher, informing him as early as January that he was ready to waive any royalty for this separate publication. For once, Campe had immediately agreed and – since the main purpose of the exercise was to provoke Menzel to a duel – had even gallantly offered to fight him in Heine's place. For the Preface to achieve its aim, Heine, doing his aggressive best, had accused Menzel of cowardice and hurled every other possible insult at him. In a stinging passage applying to him the racist standards prevalent in Menzel's own Teutomaniac circles, he wrote: 'This hero of *Deutschtum* and champion of German nationalism does not look at all like a German; rather, his features are those of a Mongol... every cheekbone a Kalmuck!... If the Mongol hordes ever come to Stuttgart, the Bashkiris will immediately hail him as their long-lost brother.' Rubbing it in, Heine went on to say that this was 'of course very grievous for a man who constantly beats the drum of nationalism and inveighs against everything foreign.' After noting that, contrary to 'the old-German race-brokers, we regard the whole of mankind as one large family whose members prove their worth not by the colour of their skin or their bone structure but by the impulses of their souls and their deeds,' Heine, from his bitter exile, concluded his polemic with the words: 'Greetings to those who suffer in the fatherland.'

'On the Denunciator' had now appeared as a separate brochure simultaneously with *Salon III*. At Le Havre, however, Heine was completely cut off from the world. Mathilde behaved very well, he was to report, but he himself fretted over the fate of his Preface, and even more over his new and otherwise mysterious financial disaster, which may have been connected with a good part of his previous debt of 20,000 francs that was still owing.

On 5 August and again on the 29th, he dispatched two significant letters to his younger brother Maximilian. Addressing him as 'the only one in our family who silently understands me', he poured out his heart. Since Max, who was now a successful physician in St Petersburg, was vacationing at Uncle Salomon's château in Hamburg, Heine – besides discussing his medical problems with him – informed him of the insulting manner in which the banker had answered his plea for help the previous October. And for the first time he hinted that he might revenge himself in his Memoirs. Much as he wished to have them 'published only after my death, I need money, and impecuniousness might force me to treat the world to a great [family] scandal.' The veiled threat was out.

Heine had by now lost the use of his left forearm, and suffered from three-day migraines. Added to his vexation at the German censorship and his financial worries, these infirmities did much to spoil (as he himself realized) the effect of the 15 sea-baths he managed to take. And he was feverishly turning over in his mind how best to put into practice a piece of advice given him by his brother Max on 12 August – to the effect that Uncle Salomon was after all a noble-hearted and generous man, and that the best way to regain his favour and financial help was to send him a 'gemütliche' letter free of sarcasm and demands for money.

On 1 September, through the intermediary of Max, he sent Uncle Salomon a letter in which he humbly declared that his soul 'painfully' yearned to remove 'the misunderstanding' between them and to be reinstated in the place he had once held in his affection. Insisting that 'only once in my life did I offend you, and that at a time when I was down with jaundice... and only with words,' he reminded Salomon that 'ours is a family of frank and quickly raging characters, whose harsh words are as quickly forgotten, and certainly regretted within the hour. Who knows this better than you, dear uncle, whose harsh words could kill a man if he did not know that your heart is full of goodness, loving kindness and generosity.'

So far, Heine was acting on Max's advice, which corresponded to the course repeatedly urged on him by Campe, Baron Cotta, Varnhagen, Kolb and other well-wishers. But he was acting against his own nature. And for all the apologies and submissive expressions of devotion he worked into his letter, his pride rebelled and his hand, as though working against his own strategy, guided his pen to inform his uncle, at the very beginning of the letter: 'My conscience is clear, and I have besides seen to it that, when we are all long since in our graves, my whole pure, spotless though unhappy life will find its just recognition.' Briefly mentioning his political and personal troubles, he implored his uncle to understand his difficult situation. But at the end of the letter he again asserted

the pride of intellectual superiority born to me and the consciousness that no one in the world can, with fewer strokes of the pen, more
powerfully revenge himself than I for all the injuries openly or
secretly inflicted on me. But tell me, what is the final reason for the
curse that lies upon all men of great genius; why does the lightning
of misfortune strike the superior minds, the towers of humanity,

most often, while it so lovingly spares the low thatched skulls of mediocrity? Tell me why the man who is so soft, so compassionate, so merciful to strangers shows himself so hard now to his poor nephew?

Max rightly judged that Uncle Salomon would be furious at being treated to thinly disguised threats. Nor would he appreciate the last lines, in which Heine personalized the ancient question: 'Why do the righteous suffer, while the wicked prosper?'[19] He therefore decided not to deliver the letter to their uncle.

Why Heine, seeking to ingratiate himself with his uncle, should have chosen to do so in a counterproductive manner raises the whole question of his relationship with Uncle Salomon, the man whose fortune he regarded as if he was entitled to a share of it. An auxiliary question that has exercised his biographers almost as much is the mystery of what Heine did with all the money he earned. Sammons, writing in 1979, estimated that Heine's total income was 'probably larger than that of most civil servants and professional people.' Wadepuhl, totting up Heine's income for the 1831–39 period, arrived at a figure of 116,300 French francs, equivalent in 1970 purchasing power to DM 580,000 in Western Germany. He ascribed Heine's recurring money problems to 'Stock Exchange speculations – which, however, only started later and sometimes brought him a profit' – and to Mathilde, in her 'insatiable lust for finery and ostentatious clothes, literally throwing money out of the window.' Indeed, Heine often called Mathilde a *Verschwenderin* (spendthrift). Sammons, doubting that she was as careless with money as he made her out, and noting that Heine never acquired any property or lived luxuriously, was led to suspect that his poverty was perhaps 'partly subjective... He may have been a little galled at the size of some huge literary fortunes being made in France,' *e.g.*, Balzac's obtaining in 1835 'a 50,000-franc advance plus 1,500 francs a month or half the profits for works as yet unwritten.'[20]

Balzac himself, however, spent such vast sums on all sorts of extravagant or illusory projects that he was often forced to flee his creditors, illustrating the curious phenomenon that certain imaginative artists may be perfectly capable of depicting in detail the operation of the money world but far less expert at handling their own finances.

In Heine's case, there were two decisive factors at play in 1837. He was not only a free-lance writer-in-exile without any regular or steady source of income, but also a prohibited one. Secondly, he was beginning to show increasing symptoms of the illness that was eventually to confine him for years to a 'mattress grave'. Headaches had troubled him since his youth; now his left forearm was impaired; and on or about the last day of August he developed an 'hourly worsening eye trouble'. But even before this added predicament was to force him to hasten his return to Paris, Heine's seaside letters to Max included some gloomy reflections: 'When I sometimes look at myself in the mirror I am terrified: I'm beginning to look exactly as my father did after his handsomeness went out of his face... What with the harassed life I've been leading, and the mental and physical toll of the last years, the advance guard of decrepitude has caught up with me.'[21]

He was 40, growing fat, and his nerves were on edge. Financially insecure, worrying that he might become an invalid just as he had assumed responsibility for Mathilde's upkeep too, he made Max privy to more sombre thoughts on 29 August: 'How shall I fare in old age? Honestly speaking, I do not dare think of it! I shall probably join those of Germany's noblest and greatest men who went to their graves broken-hearted, and in a torn jacket.'

Some of this lament may have been meant for Max to repeat to their uncle, but within a day or two of dispatching it on 1 September, together with the letter to Uncle Salomon, he was struck by the eye-affliction which was to render him 'unable either to read or to write' for weeks, and meanwhile filled him with `terror at the feeling of going blind'.

Significantly, Heine's thoughts at Le Havre turned more than once to his father. 'My late father used to say, I am not a false man, I can only utter and speak what I truly feel.' And what Heine truly felt was that it was not he who owed the Hamburg magnate an apology, but the other way round: 'It is not Uncle who has reason to complain, but *I*.' From Heine's viewpoint, the only crime he had committed the previous October was to have sent his uncle a letter which should have moved him to pity rather than anger; instead, Salomon had responded in a nasty manner, 'flaying me with the most cutting insults.' Heine raged all the more at the situation which forced him to make amends to his uncle for another reason. 'You know', he had remarked to Max, 'I always loved this man as though he were my father.' That was the crux of Heine's ambivalence towards Uncle Salomon, the man whom – following his own father's business fiasco – he had come to regard since adolescence as a second father. Uncle Salomon had become the protector and provider who looked after Heine's parents and paid for his higher education and that of his two brothers. But it was Uncle Salomon who, without hesitation, had bankrupted his father the moment he thought it necessary, had declared him mentally unfit and sent him off to wilt away at Oldensloe, disrupting Heine's parental home in a manner which cannot but have had a lingering traumatic effect on him.

At 16, in his uncle's château at Ottensen, Heine had dined with the likes of Fieldmarshal Blücher. But even while bedazzled by Salomon's diamond-bedecked daughters, he had early come to detest the atmosphere at the 'Castle of Affront', feeling that Salomon's snooty business associates and hangers-on were no friends of his, but mocked and maligned him behind his back. Now, from Le Havre, so many years later, he warned Max not to heed 'the scandalous rumours' spread about him by their uncle's toadies and sycophants. What galled him most, to judge by this letter, was that, while he was making their name famous 'in the world at large', the family seemed not to care a hoot about him or his reputation. On the contrary, 'my own uncle', the substitute father, while turning his back on him, played host to his most notorious detractors, who were sure to be 'royally received' at the château in Ottensen. Thus 'a miserable worm, the doctor' – apparently a pun on Professor Dr Wurm, who had published an article against Heine – 'recently, I am told, dined at my uncle's table, although he insulted me by grossly referring to the circumstances of my birth; and my own uncle provided the old maid Speckter, whom he [Wurm] wished to marry, with a trousseau. This vermin [Heine went on with his word-play] is well matched, for nowhere have my writings been more nastily attacked than in the house of this Speckter.' Heine cited Campe as one of his informants.

In the last analysis, Heine's interlarding his apology to Uncle Salomon with reminders that he wielded a mighty pen may have stemmed simply from his being a polemicist. Anyhow, so convinced was he that Uncle Salomon's mal-treatment of him was not only unjust but the result of some 'whispering cam-paign' against him, that he did not hesitate to communicate to the banker his suspicion that his cousin – Salomon's son Karl – might have been influenced by all the hostile 'hissing' to the point of suppressing a loving letter he, Heine, had sent him in June from Granville.

Although Heine suspected plots everywhere and tended to dramatize the wrongs and injustices done to him – rarely admitting that some of them might be self-provoked – he was a man hounded not only by the official apparatus of the German states, but by various conservative writers in them as well as by the German radicals in Paris. Both parties often denigrated him in the press, and his complaints were seldom without some foundation. From Le Havre he strongly denied to Max rumours circulating in Germany that he was in the pay of the French government. But the story of the 'French pension' he supposedly received since 1836 was to appear for a century and more in all Heine literature before its partial unravelling showed that he did not lie at the time. In fact, he obtained a French stipend in other circumstances several years later.

Heine's claim that he was being 'calumniated by both Christians and Jews'[22] might sound like so much hyperbole were it not known that, besides Menzel, Heine had also been attacked in the *Evangelische Kirchen-Zeitung* by Hengsten-berg – the dean of Berlin's theological faculty – as well as by Börne, Berthold Auerbach, J. Weil and other German-Jewish intellectuals.[23] And whatever the truth about Dr Wurm and the Speckter spinster, Salomon Heine was a promi-nent public figure and along with his entourage certainly felt uncomfortable about being associated with Europe's stormy petrel.

579

Heine was all the more hurt as he inwardly admired the financial acumen, the energy and daring by which Uncle Salomon, without studying anything, had become 'the greatest millionaire in Hamburg' – to end up, in fact, as the greatest on the continent – and for all 'the mighty divergence' of their opinions, he even felt a certain affinity with him. 'We are essentially much alike in our nature and our character,' he had written years earlier. 'The same headstrong boldness, coupled with an unfathomable softness of sentiment and incalculable caprice.' Salomon had struck him at the time as 'a remarkable man who unites great faults with the greatest merits',[24] a description in some respects fitting Heine's own character.

Heine had a strong sense of family; but the fact that Salomon, by dint of both his money and his dominant personality, was its head only complicated their relations. Salomon was widely respected as a great philanthropist, and Heine himself in a well-known poem and elsewhere was to praise his public spirit and the generosity of his charitable work and donations to various Hamburg institutions. But he could not for the life of him understand that the man who, among other things, founded 'institutions to help petty dealers' should 'inexplicably' leave his own nephew to founder in undeserved misery.[25]

The threat to use his Memoirs as a weapon against his uncle did him a great disservice. For while the major part of the Memoirs, and with it his full case against Salomon's behaviour in this family squabble, was to be suppressed, Heine's own letters were to be combed by posterity for every foible or nastiness that could be held against him.

By mid-September 1837, after daily bloodlettings in Paris and other treatment by Dr Sichel, Heine's eyesight was restored to the point where he could make out the blurred form of letters; but more weeks were to pass before he could take to his pen and resume work. Before that happened, he felt well enough at the end of September to accompany Mathilde on a visit to her native village of Vinot in the Seine-et-Marne département. It was 'an incredibly idyllic experience', he wrote to Campe on 3 October, after their return to Paris. It was during this visit that Heine, for the sake of Mathilde's parents, went through the comedy of posing as her husband.

Now he remarked to Campe that his passion for Mathilde was becoming more 'chronic' by the day. He was nearing the end of his convalescence and feeling tolerably well, except for worrying about the future. As things turned out, he had good reason to worry.

Still waiting for the effect of his 'Menzeliade' – the brochure 'On the Denunciator', containing the otherwise censored text of his Preface – Heine was even more anxious about the result of the gamble he had undertaken in his half-pleading, half-threatening letter to Uncle Salomon. To make sure that Menzel would not miss reading 'On the Denunciator', Campe, at Heine's behest, had arranged for a copy of it to be delivered to him in person by a trusted friend in Stuttgart, together with a note giving Heine's address. Author and publisher had planned and co-ordinated every detail of this move, but Menzel gathered his bespattered dignity about him and pretended that it was beneath him to duel Heine, or anyone else for that matter, such as Gutzkow, the author of *Wally*, who had likewise challenged him to fight.

'If ropes could be written, he would long have been hanged,' may stand as Heine's disgusted epitaph of the once-liberal critic who had become the literary prosecutor of the Young Germany writers. But after all the labour, planning and tactics he and Campe had invested in putting together and launching 'the bomb of a Preface', the bomb had proved a dud. Shortly after this became clear, on 22 October Campe sent Heine the news that his harmless *Salon III* – which had appeared with censorship approval, but without the Preface – was being confiscated all over Prussia and Bavaria. *Salon III*, with 'On the Denunciator' reinstated in its rightful place as a preface, was not to be published until a year after Heine's death.

October 1837 was a month of bad tidings. Close on the heels of Campe's letter, Max Heine – who had 'confiscated' Heine's questionable appeal to Uncle Salomon – on the point of returning home to St Petersburg, informed him that all his efforts to soften the heart of their mighty relative had failed. If Heine had left Le Havre 'shuddering' at the consequences of his letter to the magnate perhaps misfiring, the consequences were now upon him.

With publication of his *Gesamtausgabe* blocked by censorship, he was reduced to racking his brain to devise some form of truce with the Prussian administration. As for Uncle Salomon, Heine was not finished with him either. On the contrary, the greater his setback on one front, the more pressed and determined he felt to advance on the other, even though dealing with Salomon meant riding a lion.

'Uncle Salomon [is] the lion of our [family] menagerie,' he had written some 4 years earlier. But soon he was approaching him again, and for years to come in their up-and-down relationship he would employ one manoeuvre after another to ride 'the great despot before whom everyone trembles', hanging on to his quarry with the righteous obstinacy of a dispossessed son and the persistence of one who was by nature and habit wont to pursue every challenge with all the more gusto the greater the odds against him.

On New Year's Day, 1838, Heine's head was brimming with new ideas. Some time had passed since he had conceived the project of founding a German-language newspaper in Paris. With himself as chief editor, it was to be no ordinary newspaper, but one that – besides easily surpassing Germany's dull press in quality – would beat all foreign competition as well. For the *Pariser Zeitung* was to be written in Paris, but 'to be printed at a place just across the border in Germany', whence it could be speedily distributed, beating the mails on which the French newspapers imported into Germany depended.

In the course of the autumn, with his eyes much improved, he had resumed his social life, seeing more of George Sand and her new friends, Franz Liszt and the comtesse d'Agoult, at the latter's well-attended receptions in the Hôtel de France, before she was to depart to Italy for the accouchement of Liszt's daughter, Cosima. In December, Heine had another long conversation with Balzac. And on some unknown date that December his *souper de noces* with Mathilde had taken place, following which he had moved in with her 'for life', on the terms allegedly demanded by her. On New Year's Day, however, Heine was writing to Lewald that Mathilde had developed an intestinal inflammation and was at a *maison de santé*, where he was visiting her daily. In a subsequent letter he confidentially described to Lewald some details of his planned newspaper.

It was an old-new project. His declared objective was twofold, 'to make a lot of money in order to carry on my wars, and to build a formidable bastion from which I can keep up my cannon barrage to best effect.'[26] But supposing he managed to establish such a platform for the artillery of his ideas, what use could it be, seeing that the whole venture depended on the paper's circulation in Austria and the German states not being obstructed by Prussia, which had recently shown Heine its intolerant face? He had long vacillated for fear of undertaking anything that might smack of buying peace from Prussia on terms of 'servility'. But now that he could print nothing political, he thought he had found a way of getting round the ban. The *Pariser Zeitung*'s stand on political matters would be non-partisan. Prussia could hardly object to a neutral newspaper, while he would simply transfer his battle and 'swing my oriflamme on the literary field'.

By 12 February 1838 – having apparently 'through superhuman eloquence found an ass of an entrepreneur ready to risk 150,000 francs on the paper'[27] – he was asking Varnhagen von Ense in Berlin to convey to the Prussian court his adherence to the monarchic system and his readiness to offer any other guarantees 'reconcilable with my honour'. He enclosed a memorandum to Baron Wilhelm von Werther, making the same points and merely insisting that the *Pariser Zeitung* be granted 'freedom of expression with regard to events in the Rhine provinces'. Varnhagen duly went to see Werther and on 23 February reported back to Heine that the outlook seemed favourable.

Heine exulted. He paid little attention to Varnhagen's addendum that a formal licence for the newspaper depended on Rochow, Prussia's Minister of the Interior. Mathilde was still in hospital at the other end of Paris and in between travelling for hours to visit her and starting an affair with a variety actress – '*je jouis de ma pleine liberté, et j'en abuse même*', he wrote to Detmold on 16 February – his imagination worked feverishly. He could see his newspaper taking shape. All news material and articles on and from France, England and western Europe would be posted at 6 in the afternoon to Strasbourg, then taken across the Rhine to a printing press in Kehl; there the German news and other 'fillers' would be inserted and special couriers would take the ready paper further to distribution centres. In this way they would beat not only the French newspapers, but also the reports which the leisurely and mostly unreliable German correspondents in Paris (at least two of whom were in the pay of the French police) sent home by mail.

Although the project hung on a slim chance and looked like another of his phantasms – almost a replay of his 1828 attempt in Munich to wangle a professorship if only he were allowed a modicum of freedom to speak his dissident mind unhindered – it was based on a remarkably modern approach. Heine had watched Emile de Girardin's mass-circulation *La Presse* revolutionize journalism. People in Germany, he wrote, had no idea of the 'upswing taken by the advertising business' in France in the last two years. In Paris, newspapers were being 'founded in the full knowledge that due to the high cost of production losses will rise at the same rate as circulation increases – but the profit from advertising makes up for that. *La Presse*, for example, rakes in 100,000 francs a year from advertisements alone.'[28]

Balzac comes to mind again. In 1836, with great fanfare, Balzac had launched the *Chronique de Paris*, on the idea that a newspaper bearing his name was sure to be a huge success, only to see months of labour and 40,000 francs quickly go down the drain. Heine's position was infinitely more precarious. He might feel 'like a fish in the water' in Paris, but his chief audience was in the German lands subject to Austrian and Prussian thought-control. But like Balzac he, too, counted on his name – 'now that I am so popular in England and France, Russia and America' – to work miracles and overcome all obstacles.

On 2 March 1837, however, Varnhagen conveyed to him Baron von Werther's reply, to the effect that because of the Bundestag ban the *Pariser Zeitung* would, 'for the time being', not be allowed into Germany. Varnhagen's personal advice to Heine – interspersed with his usual counsel to observe political moderation – was that he should nevertheless dare and proceed with the foundation of the newspaper.

The news reached Heine shortly after he had taken a recovered Mathilde out for the first time to the Opéra Comique. It was carnival week, and they continued on to a masked ball. Heine had just completed a prospectus for the *Pariser*

Zeitung. Contrary to Varnhagen's advice, he had sense enough to realize that 'l'affaire est tombée dans l'eau' and to set the project aside. He seems to have done his homework, for he wrote Varnhagen that even if Prussia had given its consent the paper would have lost 80,000 francs during its first year alone – and more before it stood a chance of making a huge profit some time in the third year; and he could not risk other people's capital on a shaky basis. But he was bitter: 'Is it not horrible', he wrote to Meyerbeer on 24 March, 'that a government without law or justice robs me of my fortune and prohibits me *a priori* to exploit my name, acting in the pettiest fashion to ruin my miserable finances.'

He added that the Bundestag ban alone had cost him 60,000 francs. Before the ban, he could have obtained 80,000 francs for a *Gesamtausgabe* of his works, while the *Verbot* had forced him to sell the rights to Campe 'for a miserable 20,000, just to have bread, medicine and firewood for the winter.'[29] The figures might have been exaggerated, but the damage was true.

Once before, when he felt abandoned by Uncle Salomon, Heine had resorted to diplomacy – not his own, for he was too righteous and hot-tempered for diplomatic niceties – to regain his favour. In the spring of 1822 the Berlin publisher F.W. Gübitz and the banker Liepke had arranged to see Salomon Heine and put in a good word for his nephew. Disarming his complaint that Harry was a wastrel who had yet to learn the value of money, they had got him to agree to grant the young 'genius' a three-year annuity for his university studies.

Now, as then, Heine turned to a mediator who could talk to Uncle Salomon on his own terms. Giacomo Meyerbeer, himself the scion of a banker's family, was not only famous and a millionaire, but also a man of artistic sensibility. He was at that point in Germany. 'So you, too,' Heine wrote to him on 24 March, 'have heard these stories that I have nastily offended this man [Uncle Salomon], repaying his generosity with the blackest ingratitude.' He then proceeded to solve the 'riddle' of his relationship with Uncle Salomon from an entirely new angle, one that is particularly interesting because Heine – as he explained in a separate note – wanted Meyerbeer to show this letter to Uncle Salomon. 'You know the tenacity of my feelings,' he wrote. 'They are engraved in my heart like a plate of steel, and much though I may beat my chest, I cannot destroy that limitless respect and affection which from earliest childhood I have felt for my uncle – and that is what annoys me, vexes me and eats me up!'

What vexed him most was that Salomon had never done anything out of the ordinary for him, such as 'securing my existence'. The public imagined that 'the great millionaire who freely gives away money to strangers must be generosity itself towards his nephew, the poet.' In fact, however, all the 'generosities, benefactions, support and other signs of largesse' ever bestowed on him by Uncle Salomon added up to a 'trifling sum – (as you will one day be able to see when I tot them up to the last penny in my Memoirs).' Because he loved him, he had never asked his uncle for any 'great sums' comparable to those of which he was being 'ravaged' by others. True, Salomon was a man of 'wise heart and deep feelings', but he had never done anything 'genuinely proper [*ordentlich*] and really decent' for him. What was more, deep down in his soul Salomon knew it. 'The rift between Heinrich Heine and Salomon Heine', Heine declared, was too deep to be healed by soothing words:

> Just as I am annoyed with myself for being unable to stop loving my uncle, in spite of all the irritations I have suffered through him, so my uncle is annoyed with himself for never, in spite of my merits and just claim, having done the right thing by me, he, the famous million-aire whom the world regards as my patron... Against this self-accusa-tion of his better feelings he seeks all sort of excuses and finds them in faults and offences allegedly committed by me... Even if you were to refute each of his complaints against me down to the minutest detail, you will have achieved nothing.

To leave no doubt about it, Heine explained in his note that what he was after was for Uncle Salomon to grant him 'a fixed annuity, small as it might be', to give him stability against the depredations of misfortune. That was 'the special, proper thing' he expected of his mighty relative. In the letter itself, he detailed his latest troubles, the 'killing' of his newspaper and Mathilde's relapse into illness – she was now 'spitting blood... and is to be sent to her mother's village, the doctor wants her to drink milk and sleep in a cowshed.' Heine admitted no more than that Uncle Salomon had 'sometimes been very fair' to him. But he called him 'a high and noble soul' and – playing on the traditional Jewish respect for learning and learned men, of which he was the only one in the family – he subtly bolstered his appeal by saying: 'He respects the poor and needy scholar far more than rich hucksters.'[30]

Heine was not exaggerating his woes. Within a week or so of posting this letter to Meyerbeer, leaving it to the maestro's 'ingenuity' how to go about getting him the pension he was angling for, Mathilde had to be rushed back to the clinic from which she had recently been released. Heine himself was again troubled by his eyes, and Dr Sichel warned him that he was still in danger of going blind. This is when he wrote to Campe of his 'inner desolation' , and no wonder. Having spent the whole winter on the 'damned' newspaper, he was still desperately grasping for financial security.

To Laube, whose confinement to a fortress had been commuted to house-arrest at Muskau, he wrote confidently that 'Menzel, Tieck and their consorts will rot one after the other... We have to defend ourselves, and I, too, will soon again intone some critical dance-music.' But he felt exhausted from the turmoil in which he lived; and in a possible reference to Mathilde's sexual demands before her second hospitalization, he added: 'I am as tired as a hunted bull... How I would like to be in some peaceful German fortress, with a sentry in front of the door to keep out my mistress and my other worries. I thirst passionately for silence!'[31]

At the beginning of May, he moved provisionally to the Barrière Saint-Jacques, to be close to the clinic where Mathilde was interned. Shortly afterwards his eye-trouble got worse. 'Suddenly I could not see anything, or rather I saw everything double and blurred,' he wrote to Campe on 18 June. For 4 weeks he had been unable to read or write, and even now he could only scrawl. The only ray of light came in the form of an offer from the French publisher Henri-Louis Delloye, to write – against a fee of 4,000 francs – the accompanying text to a volume of copper engravings depicting Shakespeare's female characters as seen by various artists. The result was 'Shakespeare's Maidens and Ladies' (*Shakespeares Mädchen und Frauen*), an essay which he uncomfortably began to dictate on 7 July, feeling that dictation cramped his style. But after filling 10 octavo pages and finishing it in one flow in a little over a fortnight, he judged that although it was 'no great masterpiece', it had turned out 'a solid and beautifully homogeneous piece, which is sure to be well received by the public.' And so it was when Delloye published the volume in a de luxe edition in the autumn.

Back in April, Prussia had formally lifted the ban on Heine's *Book of Songs* (a second edition of which had been published in 1837). This seemed to him an opportune moment to follow up with a second volume of the book which had made him famous. He had been planning it for some time, and in spite of his eye-trouble, by June 1838 he had put together a large collection of poems to go into this sequel (*Nachtrag*) to the *Book of Songs*. For an Epilogue to this new volume, he sent Campe a polemical essay titled 'Swabian Mirror' (*Schwabenspiegel*). For a long time he had wanted to settle accounts with the so-called 'Swabian school' of poets which, led by the evangelical pastor Gustav Schwab – ironically, an admirer of Heine's *Book of Songs*, but morally scandalized by his erotic bent – had pressured the editors of a literary Almanac to abandon their plan to feature Heine's portrait on the frontispiece of the 1837 volume. And early in 1838 a minor Swabian poet, Gustav Pfizer, had published a lengthy and devastating critique of Heine's writings, dismissing his treatment of German philosophy ('which profound and precise thinkers spent their lives cogitating about') as being on the level of a 'nursemaid's tales', and otherwise accusing him of self-gloriously 'obtruding... his not exactly charming personality' on every subject-matter.

Heine's 'Swabian Mirror' began humorously enough with his inquiring who were the representatives of the Swabian School – were they Schiller, Schelling, Hegel and other native sons of their calibre? – only to be told that these cosmopolitan European celebrities were disdained in Swabia as unpatriotic. Heine was on solid ground both in suspecting that Menzel was behind Pfizer's attack on him (Pfizer's article had indeed appeared in a journal co-edited by him and Menzel) and in cutting Pfizer down to size. For Pfizer's poetry had already been compared by Goethe to a moral-religious-poetical beggar's coat 'so adroitly cut and buttoned that, even if an elbow shows, this blemish appears to be sheer poetic inspiration.' Remarkably, Heine refrained from crossing swords with Pastor Schwab, whom he had previously praised in *The Romantic School*. Now he again singled him out as the leader of the Swabian School, 'no whale' like Schiller, but certainly 'a herring among saltless sardines'. To lend further irony to their relations, Pastor Schwab was one day to dedicate a poem to Heine in which he asked to be received in his 'castle of poesy', eliciting Heine's remark: 'How terrible... in this rotten world one cannot even rely on one's enemies!' But this was years later, and long before then the second volume of the *Book of Songs* – including its 'Swabian Mirror' epilogue – was to lead to two separate, though connected imbroglios, that were to sour his life during the remainder of 1838.

In mid-August, having finally dared to leave his eye doctor and the whirl of Paris behind him, he had hardly settled down for a holiday at Granville when he received a letter from Karl Gutzkow – who since his prosecution as one of the Young Germany writers had become the editor of Campe's *Telegraph für Deutschland* and his literary adviser – warning him that some of the poems planned for the second volume of the *Book of Songs* were too frivolous for the German public. This, coming from the author of *Wally*, who had himself been sent to jail for obscenity, struck Heine as sheer hypocrisy, and doubly so, seeing that some of the poems concerned had already appeared in *Salon I*.

In a short but acerbic reply on 23 August, he informed Gutzkow that, although his enemies might use some of these poems against him, he would 'print them with a good conscience, as I would the Satyricon of Petronius and Goethe's Roman Elegies had I written those masterpieces.' Stressing that the issue was 'not the moral requirements of some married bourgeois in a corner of Germany, but the autonomy of art', Heine wrote, 'My slogan remains: art is the purpose of art, as love is the purpose of love and even life itself is the purpose of life.' These lines launched a notion which may or may not have inspired, but was certainly akin to, Théophile Gautier's *l'art pour l'art* (a term said to have been originally coined by Victor Cousin). In Heine's case, however, the 'autonomy of art' had to be stretched to include the prerogative of writing poetry not exclusively for its own sake, but for the sake of making a better world. Though he was of course an aesthete, he was also a poet-prophet, who informed Gutzkow in the same letter: 'I am fertilizing my mind for the future; having not long ago read the whole of Shakespeare, I am now, here by the sea, reading the Bible – and what public opinion thinks of my previous writings will depend very much on the course and turn of events.'[32]

It is doubtful that Heine had read the whole of Shakespeare while writing about his heroines when he was half-blind, especially as in July he had also moved to a new apartment at 23 rue des Martyrs. But what he was telling Gutzkow in essence was that posterity's judgment of his works might be different from that of some of his contemporaries, including Gutzkow himself. In *On the French Stage* he had expressed his confidence that 'the Lord... without Whose providence no sparrow falls from the roof' and Who moved the flux and turns of history, 'will surely not allow whole nations to become the victim of miserable, shortsighted, arbitrary government.' He would 'show His signs and His wonders to the Pharaohs of modern time,' as he had once to those of ancient Egypt, 'the land of rigid castes and deified oxen.' Heine thus drew solace for the future from the Bible, and in an obvious reference to his own fate wrote that 'those whom the prophet warns are angry at his doom-laden message and stone him. Sometimes the prophet is cast into a dungeon until his prophecy comes true... [but] the Lord always performs what seems best to Him and what He has determined, though He takes his time over it.'

And it was in *Shakespeare's Maidens and Ladies* that Heine had recently expressed himself on the poet-prophet relationship, stating that the poet – 'like the mathematician, who can immediately specify the whole of a circle and its midpoint if one gives him only the smallest segment of it' – is instantly able, when shown 'only the smallest fraction of the phenomenal world', to perceive its 'whole universal connection... he knows, as it were, the circumference and centre of all things.'

Gutzkow had been an early admirer of Heine, although he was later to gloss over the fact that he had actually invited him to be the presiding genius of the Young Germany group and to maintain that he had always found his writings 'distasteful' and 'fit for commercial travellers'.[33] In 1838, Heine still respected Gutzkow's talent. He sensed the weathervane in him, but also a potential rival. Gutzkow was as cocky as he was himself, and the fact that he had taken the liberty of warning him that the second volume of the *Book of Songs* would only further damage his 'sinking reputation in Germany' hurt Heine to the quick.

To compound matters, Campe informed him on 26 August that Gutzkow was about to write a biography of Börne, thus preempting his own *Ludwig Börne. A Memorial*, which he had started but laid aside because of the newspaper project and his eye trouble. And to cap it all, while he was at Granville he learned that Ludwig Wihl – a would-be journalist and nincompoop whom he had befriended in Paris – had on his return to Germany published, in Campe's own *Telegraph* of all places, an article full of 'perfidious insinuations' about his private life. Indeed, Wihl demolished the picture – publicized by Lewald in Germany – of Mathilde as a 'theatre princess' and presented her instead as a 'modest, childishly endearing' but uneducated Frenchwoman who had reduced Heine, the supposed party-goer 'flying from one salon to the other', to such undignified domestic tasks, for a German writer, as 'buying a turkey in my presence'. In one indiscretion after another, Wihl hinted, without naming Uncle Salomon, that the latter's withdrawal of his support had robbed Heine of his 'inner freedom', to the detriment of his creative power; and that though Heine was superficially known in Paris as an *homme d'esprit*, not a few Frenchmen regarded him as a *farceur*. The article was particularly infuriating to Heine when he saw it because it affected a tone of deep concern for him. But since he considered Wihl a fool 'with an honest sheep's face', who was not even worth taking public issue with, he could only rage.

Gutzkow, however, posed a real dilemma. Heine did not hesitate to describe him to Campe as a 'quarrelsome, provocative caviller' – Gutzkow had indeed fallen out with several of his former Young Germany associates – but he was in a quandary how to neutralize the man's influence on Campe. Heine's reputation in Germany may have been sinking, but he continued to be newsworthy and the constant butt of malicious gossip. To this he was inured. But the fact that Campe and Gutzkow, instead of defending him in the *Telegraph* against the Swabian Pfizer's attack, had allowed Wihl to malign him in a manner which supplied ammunition to the 'foxes' – i.e., the conservative writers who kept defaming him – seemed to him as incomprehensible as it was embarrassing.[34]

Yet, in the matter of the *Book of Songs*, Heine beat a curious retreat. He fully expected his 'Swabian Mirror' to create a literary scandal. Whether he thought it impolitic to start a row with Gutzkow at the same time, or for other reasons, he suddenly declared that the second volume of the *Book of Songs* – which Campe had decided to issue in spite of Gutzkow's reservations, though it was running into trouble with the censorship – mattered little to him and that he was ready to wait until it could be printed in the *Gesamtausgabe*. As things turned out, the second volume of the *Book of Songs* was not to appear until 1844. By then Heine had entered upon his radical phase, and the volume, titled *New Poems* (*Neue Gedichte*), included – besides the lyrical ones objected to by Gutzkow as immoral – his long 'Germany. A Winter's Tale' (*Deutschland. Ein Wintermärchen*). Sold out and going into a second printing within two months, the book was to be confiscated and banned in all the German states; but Karl

Marx arranged for the 'Deutschland' poem to be serialized in the radical Paris *Vorwärts!*.

As for the 'Swabian Mirror', which in 1838 was an Epilogue to a book whose publication was delayed, Campe issued it in the autumn in a new periodical of his, Yearbook of Literature (*Jahrbuch der Literatur*). When Heine saw the published version, he was shocked to find that it had been tampered with and 'mutilated' out of recognition – whether by Campe or the Saxon censor is unclear as the original manuscript no longer exists. Cut off as he was from conditions in Germany and the pressures under which Campe worked, Heine had as usual forbidden him to submit the 'Swabian Mirror' to the censor.

As he was privately accusing Campe of complicity in the mutilation of his piece and publicly denying authorship of the form in which it had appeared, an open dispute with his publisher was in the offing.

It will be noticed that throughout all the turmoil of 1838 Heine was engaged in fending off criticism or the denigration of his person or his writings, as in his 1837 attack on Menzel in 'On the Denunciator'. But it was also evident that since the Bundestag ban he had produced no real major work. The little that he did publish contained his usual pearls of wit and linguistic gems as well as passages of rare perception – such as his portrait, in *Shakespeare's Maidens and Ladies*, of Edmund Kean impersonating Shylock at the Drury Lane Theatre, where he had seen him 11 years earlier. But if in 1826, a year before that London visit, Heine had first ventilated the idea of going to Paris, feeling that in Germany he was increasingly fenced in by the 'wall' of Prussian restrictions, he was now, if anything, in a worse position, still beating his head against that wall or spending most of his time between his ailments on stratagems to circumvent it or find a crack in it.

In many ways he had been through it all before, even before he left Germany. Now, as then, what energy he had left went into defending his name and honour in literary and personal polemics, refutations, bickerings, complaints and squabbles, not to mention his side-campaign for Uncle Salomon's financial support.

The fact that he was in free Paris made it the most frustrating and fruitless period in his life so far. For what he wanted to write he could not print, and he felt he was becoming a 'hack writer', a role for which, as he wrote Campe, 'I am damned little fit for.'[35] He was at a dead end, and one might well have wondered whether he would ever recover his creative powers.

Shortly before Heine's departure for Granville, Chopin had sent on to him a *billet* from George Sand, informing him that she might soon go abroad. Writing from her country seat at Nohant, she regretted not having seen him lately in Paris and inquired about his well-being. In reply he sent her a sad, beautiful and loving letter which has intrigued biographers ever since. Written from Granville on 17 August 1838, it read in part:

> ... A thousand thanks! I would like very much to have seen you! The beams from your eyes would have done me good. I am very sad. You don't know about all my misfortunes. At this point I am suffering from a physical blindness which is just as distressing as the moral blindness that has afflicted me for four years and which you know about.
>
> ... I love you very much, with all my heart, with every bit of my heart. If you are free, enjoy your freedom! As for me, I am still in terrible irons. And it is because I am chained up every evening with particular care that I have not succeeded in seeing you in Paris. But when I have served my time, I shall join you, even if it is at the end of the world...[36]

It has been suggested that Heine's phrase about 'the moral blindness that has afflicted me for four years' alluded to Mathilde; and his reference to his being 'chained up every evening with particular care', supposedly by Mathilde, would seem to support this view. On the other hand, Hirth, the editor of Heine's letters, has read into Heine's readiness to follow George Sand to the end of the world nothing less than a cry of love: 'The two lines he expected from her were: "Come to me! I am yours."'[37] But there is no evidence for this or the story of the great amour between them propagated by others, though Sammons has observed that, 'given Sand's habits, it is not impossible' that they may have engaged in episodic love-making.[38]

What is certain in all this is, first, that in 1838 Heine was having an affair with a variety actress, Mlle Olivier, for whom, through Meyerbeer, he arranged an audition with the director of the Opéra Comique; and secondly, that he had yet to become reconciled to the idea of being tied for life to Mathilde, a point he seems to have reached when he took the practical step of sending her in due course to a boarding-school for girls to pick up a modicum of education and social manners.

As for George Sand, all Heine expected of her was to see her in Paris in October. His rhetorical phrase about following her to the end of the world was accompanied by the qualification 'provided that in the meantime you will not have been caught and carried off to a penal colony again, my beautiful, liberated convict of love.' He knew that she had set her eyes on Chopin and he obviously regarded her as much a prisoner of her passions as he was of his own. Finally, there is every indication that in speaking of his moral blindness he included not only Mathilde but that 'inner desolation' which stemmed from his recognizing that for the past few years he had not been living up to either his talent, his high self-image or the commensurately worthy task he felt cut out for.

In his letter to Gutzkow of 23 August 1838, written shortly after he had informed Campe that the second volume of the *Book of Songs* meant little to him, he had included the following sentence: 'Honestly speaking, the great issues of European life continue to interest me much more than my books – *que Dieu les prenne en sa sainté et digne garde!*' This looks at first sight like an inflated excuse for giving up his volume of poems, until one remembers that 12 years previously, 4 years before he left Germany, Heine had written to Varnhagen and to others that if he went to Paris it was for the sake of his aspiration to develop a cosmopolitan European outlook and to devote himself to topics that were of general European interest'.

The Prussian administration might have reduced Heine to the position of a hack writer, but his spirit was not quite broken. If his character and temperament had not changed, neither had his goal.

The best-laid plans may come to naught, but even a desperate one may succeed when favoured by circumstance.

It happened that Uncle Salomon's son and heir Carl was to marry the pretty, 17-year-old Cécile Furtado-Fould, one of the richest heiresses in Paris. Carl was the cousin whom Heine had nursed and pulled through the 1832 cholera epidemic in Paris. Carl had returned to Hamburg but, having early set his eyes on Cécile, had periodically asked Heine – who was well acquainted with the girl's family – for news of her. It was in fact Heine who had mediated the match; and it was he who, in July 1838, 7 or 8 weeks before the wedding, accompanied Carl on a visit to his fiancée at her family's castle at Rocquencourt in Provence. Before returning to Hamburg again, Carl sent Heine a gift of 2,000 francs to cover his moving expenses to the rue des Martyrs.

In September, Carl, Uncle Salomon and other relations descended on Paris, and Heine, back from Granville and his annoyances there, took part in a round of receptions and dinners given by his uncle and the Furtado and Fould millionaires to celebrate the couple's nuptials. Shortly afterwards, on 3 October, Uncle Salomon was making Heine a gift of 2,000 francs and asking him to show him around Paris.

On 7 October, referring to Heine as 'Harry', Uncle Salomon summed up his impressions in a letter to his daughter Therese: '...What a talent, the more's the pity. But I am beginning to believe that he is better than I thought. He has promised to improve his ways and to make better use of his money' – Salomon's old complaint – 'only I am afraid that he will not keep his word. He has a sincere attachment to Carl.'

It was in this auspicious atmosphere of family feasting and jollity that Meyerbeer, a week or so before the marriage of money to money, had put in a word for Heine with Uncle Salomon. Already on 23 September, the maestro had conveyed to Heine the news that Uncle Salomon had agreed to grant him an allowance of 4,000 francs annually, to be paid in quarterly instalments, starting in January 1839.

What Heine had secretly wished for years but failed to achieve with his abrasive manner, Meyerbeer accomplished for him in less than an hour. As related by Varnhagen von Ense, Heine is supposed to have written into Salomon's autograph book as early as 1831: 'Dear Uncle, lend me a hundred thousand Thaler and forget forever your loving nephew H. Heine.'[39] Whatever the truth of that anecdote, Uncle Salomon, who even now did not quite believe that Heine would mend his ways, had never forgotten that he had once cashed in London a substantial letter of credit entrusted to him not for use but merely as a token of his financial standing. It had never occurred to the Hamburg magnate that, rather than obdurately trying to teach his talented nephew the value of money, he might have eased his lot and saved him much distraction by setting up a trust fund for him.

Such an arrangement would not have made Heine less aggressive on issues that really mattered to him. Indeed, although immediately after New Year's Day 1839 Salomon transferred the first instalment of 1,000 francs, Heine – following a press notice by Campe disclaiming that he was in any way responsible for the mutilation of the 'Swabian Mirror' – engaged in a public quarrel with him and, in his righteous pursuit of what he saw as the truth, indiscreetly quoted from the publisher's letters to him. Nor can it be said for certain that a trust fund would have averted the bitter 'inheritance war' that Heine, after Salomon's death, would have to wage against Cousin Carl, who was if anything to prove more tight-fisted than his father, while lacking his stature and his qualities.

As it was, the winter of 1838–39 marked the end of the mutual acrimony between Heine and his uncle. The first thing he did after hearing that Salomon's cheque was waiting for him at the Fould Bank was to take Mathilde to the boarding-school in the rue Chaillot. As she was absent except for weekends, he resumed his social life. Before the year's end he had dined at Meyerbeer's with Alexander von Humboldt and other distinguished company. Now he was often at Cécile's parents. Her father, the banker Elie Furtado, was to take his corrections to the Book of Songs – the first volume – to Hamburg, where Campe was preparing to issue its third edition even as he and the author were washing their dirty linen in the press. Cécile's mother, Rose Furtado, kept inviting him to her Paris salon. She and everyone else, including Uncle Salomon, praised the tactful way in which he had exerted his influence on Cécile, his young admirer, to bring about the match. Soon Cécile herself was asking him from Hamburg to send her his autograph for her album, and all was harmony in the family. On 7 January 1839 he wrote to Laube that he was 'well and hearty... living intensely, writing little and publishing nothing.' His eyes were still troubling him intermittently, and he seems to have been in the throes of some lassitude. His fingers were itching to write something new but it took him some time to become his own self again. By 4 March, at last – before attending a literary party at the marquis de Custine's, where Balzac read his comedy *A l'Ecole des Ménages* – he announced to Cécile in Hamburg: 'I am doing a lot of work...'

He had resumed writing *Ludwig Börne. A Memorial*, the work he was to proclaim 'the best I have written' – an opinion largely shared by Thomas Mann and others in posterity – but which immediately caused a scandalous furore culminating in a pistol duel, whose most serious consequence was that the thought of Mathilde's uncertain future if he died without providing for her was to precipitate him into marrying her.

21

On the Threshold of the 'Extraordinary Decade'

On the evening of 1 January 1838, after nearly three years of exile spent working in the office of the Governor of Vyatka, Alexander Herzen, accompanied by his valet, arrived in Vladimir, where he was to spend what became 'the best and brightest year' of his life.

During his term in Vyatka, the Governor, Tyufayev, was dismissed for having the brother of his mistress, who interfered with their affair, locked up in a madhouse (where he died) and then trying to dispose in the same way of a merchant about to lodge a complaint against him. By the time of his dismissal, however, Tyufayev, who had started life as a circus acrobat, had misgoverned several provinces and terrorized merchants, contractors, government clerks and whole populations. As in the rest of the vast regions beyond the Ural, villages would be uprooted and their land given away as 'uncultivated' to senior officials, who in turn sold it to merchants.

In one such case, when several villages suddenly found their land 'cut away right up to their woodyards and houses and given as private property to merchants', several years of litigation led to their being assigned an equivalent but swampy tract of land instead – and then, after more petitions, being given 'another half swamp in addition to the swamp they already had', together with a demand for rent. When the peasants refused to pay, Tyufayev sent in a police detachment which 'seized a few persons, flogged them, restored order... took the money, handed over the "guilty parties" to the Criminal Court... Several men were punished with the lash and sent into exile.'[1]

When Herzen was ordered to write a report on the affair, pending a reinvestigation, it was two years after the events. By the time he left Vyatka, the case was not yet resolved, and he never knew whether the land was returned to the villagers. In the Governor's office, and sometimes in his dining-room, he heard from Tyufayev, his successor and their clerks and guests, so many horrifying stories that he 'could' – and later did – 'fill volumes' with details of the 'abuses of power and the roguery of officials.'

It was in 1852 that Herzen wrote down his recollections of his youth as a political prisoner, to be published in part after his move abroad in two Russian-language journals in London. His extraordinarily detailed account illustrated the ease with which Western Siberia had been plundered by Pestel – the father of the executed leader of the Decembrists – while he actually lived most of the time in St Petersburg. With a network of henchmen opening every letter that left the province, and friends in high places in the capital, he had been able to rule, or misrule, his fief so effectively from a distance that it was said of him he could see from Petersburg 'what is being done in Siberia'.

Herzen's Memoirs, a monumental work to be published in full (first in Russian and then in English) only in the 20th century, was to become not just a literary classic, but to provide a compendium of the arbitrariness, the corruption, cruelty and oppressiveness of life – as well as the sheer insanity of public affairs – in Tsarist Russia. Though he was celebrated in the West for his championship of human rights and freedom of thought, his writings – in spite of his opposition to Marx – were to be printed by the Soviet authorities with 'corrective' ideological comments.

At that, the picture he gave in *My Past and Thoughts* of the chronic, apparently paranoid inability of Russian governments over a long period of time to trust their own people, drew attention to one of the factors helping to explain how a Soviet system that abolished tsarism was able to spawn – and to maintain for 70 years – a new monstrous bureaucracy spying on its own citizens, complete with Siberian gulags.

On a personal plane, Herzen indulged in a month-long 'orgy of love' in Vyatka with an attractive young woman who was married to an elderly invalid. When his ardour cooled, he was afraid of her tears, and after her husband died he fretted for months with remorse. During this unhappy period, there rose before his eyes the luminous, virginally pure image of his 17-year-old Moscow cousin Natalie, whom he had taken to calling his 'little sister'. Increasingly longing for the girl who had pressed his hand with 'unexpected strength' when seeing him off before he was transported to Siberia, yet hesitating to declare himself, Herzen sounded Natalie out in a letter hinting that he felt more than affection for her.

'You seem somewhat agitated... your letter frightened you more than it frightened me,' the young girl replied with the sudden composure of a woman aware of her feelings. 'I worship, I pray, I love,' she wrote in another letter. She was a sad-eyed, serious, solitary girl, raised under the heel of a mean-spirited, capricious old widow, who had constantly made her feel that the amenities and education she enjoyed were more than she deserved.

As soon as Princess Khovansky discovered Natalie's romantic correspondence with her nephew – whom she considered a dangerous 'political criminal' – she ordered her servants to intercept their letters. When not confining Natalie to her room, she obliged her to sit knitting by her side while she defamed the 'unfortunate' and godless young Herzen to her eye-rolling lady-companions. Natalie often dreamt of going home – 'but where was my home?' She had always found solace in the Gospels. Love heightened her romantic-religious fervour to fever pitch.

'You will present me to God as He desires me to be,' she wrote to Herzen in one of her clandestine letters. 'If I had not this faith, however great my love I would not give myself to you.' Herzen, too, affected by 'Socialist' ideas 'drawn from the Gospels', went through a mystic phase in Siberia, which lasted for several years. Like his boyhood friend Ogarev, he was capable of invoking romantic love, humanity at large and the sufferings of Christ in one breath. But he was far more sanguine: 'In my embrace your separate existence will disappear,' he informed Natalie. 'Love was destined to bring you to me, and love will bring you to God.' Feeling alone would not satisfy him – for over and above his private life was his special obligation to work 'for the good of mankind' – but his soul was big enough to absorb hers: 'You are I: Alexander and Natalie do not form We but only my own I. My I is full, for you have been completely swallowed up; and you no longer exist.'[2]

For her 19th birthday, he sent Natalie a portrait of himself by the Swedish-Russian artist A.L. Vitberg, who was a fellow exile in Vyatka. Natalie sent him a bracelet and a medallion. With the Princess Khovansky now dragging her, more dead than alive, to stuffy drawing-rooms in an attempt to marry her off, and her lady-companions and hangers-on treating her like a 'slave', Natalie spent listless months feeling 'all alone on the edge of a precipice and a whole crowd of them doing everything they can to push me over.' Gazing at Herzen's portrait, or contemplating a star in the sky over Moscow 'at the same moment' as the prisoner in Vyatka, so that 'we can both be sure that nothing separates us but distance', helped Natalie to keep her sanity in a hostile and oppressive environment.

At one point, she wondered whether Herzen's portrait and her bracelet would, after 'a hundred years... warm some other heart' and tell 'the story of our sufferings, of our love.' She knew that Herzen had loved before. 'For me, however,' she wrote, 'this is the first time that the light illumines my soul.'[3] But she was ready to lose herself in him 'as a star in the sun', and waited to meet God through him.

Herzen's arrival at Vladimir – where, though still an exile, he exulted at being so much nearer 'to Moscow, to my home, to my friends' – was alarming to Princess Khovansky. Determined to keep her niece out of her nephew's reach, the old lady intensified her matchmaking efforts to the point where she promised prospective candidates for Natalie's hand a dowry of 100,000 roubles; next, she threw in an estate as well; and to remove objections to marrying her off by force, and perhaps to salve her own conscience, she had a priest confirm that doing so would be no sin in Natalie's case, since she was an orphan.

Natalie reacted to 'the awful, loathsome scenes' of introduction to which she was being hauled 'on a chain' by pretending to one suitor, a colonel, that she was 'a complete imbecile', and informing another that she was in love with someone else and appealing to his honour to withdraw. While she was near her wit's end, Princess Khovansky was so enraged by Natalie's passive resistance that she had the girl locked up in her room, with two maids on guard. She then summoned a family council.

Herzen's father, Ivan Yakovlev, declared that he was 'a poor judge in affairs of the heart' and refused to attend. But her other brother – the Senator – and 'His Excellency' D.P. Golokhvastov (a cousin of Herzen's) arrived the next evening. The conference took place in the presence of the Princess's nurse and chief companion, while Natalie was still under lock and key upstairs. After much futile talk, 'the accused' was brought in. Asked for the reason why she refused an excellent match offered to her, Natalie replied: 'You know it.' The men frowned at her, and mentioning that it was a long time since she had seen 'our unfortunate Alexander', asked how she could be certain of him. Natalie said that she was, and anyway, 'whatever his intentions may be, I cannot change mine.' Having surprised everyone by standing her ground, she launched into an account of the slights and humiliations to which she was being subjected. Turning to the Senator, she appealed to him to 'do what you like, but take me out of this life,' and burst into tears.

'So that's our nice, modest girl,' the companion said to the Princess. 'There's gratitude for you.' At this, the Senator lost his temper and a grotesque scene ensued. 'Of whom is she speaking?' he shouted. 'Why is this creature here at all?' The companion ran out of the room in tears. The Princess, berated by the Senator for allowing a stranger to mix in family affairs, sniffed her salts and told Natalie to go upstairs and stay there.

'It is time to be done with all this Bastille business,' the Senator rebuked the Princess. He took his hat, but before driving away, this uncle of Herzen's – the assiduous party-goer and man-about-town, who for all his artificial life was less stony-hearted than the rest of the Yakovlevs – went up to Natalie's room and promised her that she would not be married against her will. The Princess, to go by the account left by Herzen – who was at the time editing the *Vladimir Provincial News* – was devastated. As the Senator left, she lay on her bed 'while four maids rubbed her hands and feet, moistened her temples with vinegar, and poured Hoffman's drops on lumps of sugar... So ended the family council.'[4]

The upshot of the affair was that on 3 March, Herzen, having provided himself with false papers, paid the first of two secret visits to Moscow. Natalie's position in the Princess's house had, needless to say, become untenable and Herzen's father would do nothing for her, on the evasive pretext that what the Princess did 'in her own house was not his business'. With the help of a friend and some trusted servants, Herzen set in motion certain clandestine arrangements – including a rendezvous in a graveyard – and managed to elope with Natalie to Vladimir, where, on a bright May day in 1838, they immediately got married.

After Herzen's disapproving father refused to 'add one kopeck' to his son's bachelor allowance, the aristocratic young couple brought up in homes where 'half a dozen flunkeys ran about with bowls and dishes' at dinner, began their domestic life in unfurnished quarters with no linen, no crockery, etc., living on whatever spartan meals Matvei, the valet doubling as cook, was able to concoct. Natalie, however, shy of people and in Herzen's eyes 'unique' and superlative in everything – 'noble and delicate... gentle, mild, gracious... a young girl with all the poetry of a loving woman'[5] – was ready to live with him, as she put it, like 'hermits in a forest'.

After a year of their lyrical 'struggle with poverty', Herzen's father's resistance broke down and he and Natalie's half-brother, the 'Chemist', helped them with substantial money gifts. They paid off their debts and were able to rent a large empty flat in a manor house, and to engage a young Greek maidservant. But in all his writings, then and later, about their continued hardship, Herzen referred to this period as one of happy, carefree bliss. 'All was kinship and harmony' between them as they shut out the world and played like children, raced each other about the 'big, scarcely furnished salon... jumped over the chairs', read poetry or engaged in earnest discussion.

In the spring of 1839, Ogarev, still living in exile at Penza but sometimes permitted to travel, came on a visit to the Herzens at Vladimir. It was nearly 5 years since he and Herzen – daily companions since boyhood, who had shared 'cigars on the sly', sworn their soul to the anti-Tsarist struggle, and otherwise 'entered deeply into each other's lives' – had been arrested and separated. They now fell into each other's arms.

Ogarev had brought his wife, Marya Lvovna, the 'quick-witted' and 'piquant' niece of the Governor of Penza, whom he had married in a state of high ecstasy, finding that their love contained 'all the germs of the liberties of mankind' and much else besides. Herzen later claimed that there was something about her that disturbed him from the first. At the time, however, he found her 'above all praise' and exclaimed in a letter: 'What a woman Marya Lvovna is!... Nick is happy indeed to have found such a companion.' For himself, he felt that with Natalie he had reached 'the highest limit' of personal happiness. His bond of friendship with Ogarev was a true compact of their romantic souls. The joy of the two men at their reunion was intensified by the thought that both of them had found spouses worthy of admission into their spiritual alliance.

Herzen was not yet out of his mystical phase. (He had in fact recently written two verse-dramas in a self-styled 'religious Socialist spirit'.) On a table in his room in Vladimir was a small iron crucifix which Ogarev had given him at their parting. The rite of initiation that followed has been described by Herzen both in a letter written at the time and – with an extraordinary emotion still felt years later – in his Memoirs:

> 'On your knees!' said Ogarev, 'and let us give thanks that we are all four here together.' We four sank on our knees before the Divine Martyr, prayed, and thanked Him for the happiness He had vouch-safed to us after so many years of suffering and separation. We kissed His pierced feet, and kissed one another exclaiming: 'Christ is risen!'[6]

Not unnaturally, Marya Lvovna found the whole scene 'childish and affected'. She was a more level-headed and down-to-earth character than Ogarev, her mystic-poetic 'do-gooder' of a husband, whose guilt-ridden conscience presently – when he inherited three estates upon his father's death – made him decide to give away the largest of them to his peasants. Marya Lvovna, sharing neither his hatred of servitude nor his social concern (certainly not to the point of self-abnegation), saw no practical reason why they should lose an estate worked by nearly 2,000 hands.

To appease her, Ogarev liberated the serfs but sold them the estate on a 'hire-purchase' basis, to be paid off over 10 years. He regretted that this transaction, for which he had to seek, and eventually received, the Tsar's approval, robbed one of his good actions of perfection, 'since I stand in fact to lose nothing.'

The Ogarevs stayed only a couple of days in Vladimir. Though Herzen was later to claim that he noticed Marya Lvovna's aloofness during the scene with the crucifix, marking her from the beginning as an outsider, he wrote her an enthusiastic letter celebrating the solemn moment of their prayer: 'Hosanna! Hosanna!... At that moment was completed the mystery of Natalie's union with you and of yours with us. At that moment we four became one.'

Except for the unintoxicated Marya Lvovna, they were living in a dream which could hardly last. Whether Herzen noticed her reserve then or only later, it certainly cast a tiny shadow over his and Ogarev's high-flown antics. It was in fact an omen of the way these four were destined to 'get into each other's lives' in unfortunate ways: a long drawn-out drama spanning Herzen's and Ogarev's remaining years in Russia and the later decades of their revolutionary activities abroad.

First, Marya Lvovna turned her marriage to the soft-souled Ogarev into a triangular relation with a friend of his. Then Natalie, in one of the strangest 'dual' loves in a world full of strange loves, tried to create a 'triangle' of 'love and friendship' with her beloved Herzen and one of his best friends – the radical German poet Georg Herwegh – and in the end, after Natalie's death, Herzen himself formed another 'triangle' with Ogarev's second wife, who bore him three children to add to the three orphaned by Natalie's death. Ogarev assumed formal paternity for the three born out of wedlock.

These domestic tangles, with their resultant emotional crises and cross-complications between friends and lovers, were to be played out across half of Europe, as Herzen moved from one Western capital to another. Since he, Ogarev and Herwegh were by then public figures, as was Bakunin – the equally famous friend of all three of them, whose actions more than once bore upon their affairs – their scandals reverberated throughout Europe's politically oriented intelligentsia. Besides the excruciating agony caused to the protagonists, the two successive triangles, geometrically cool as they sound, further affected Herzen's two sets of children. Those of the first set, raised by Malvida von Meysenbug (later to become a friend of Nietzsche), developed a conflict of loyalties between her and the mistress their father borrowed from Ogarev, who wished to act as their substitute-mother. Of the second set, one was to end her life at 17.

Herzen left an emotionally harrowing account of his and Natalie's tragedy in a section of his Memoirs – 'A Family Drama' – first published shortly after World War I, 50 years after his death.[7] And in 1934, almost a century to the day after Natalie as a young girl wondered whether 100 years hence anyone would remember their sufferings and their love – while Ogarev was assuring Marya Lvovna that theirs would be 'told from generation to generation' – the interconnected dramas of their lives would be conjured up in a more detached way in E.H. Carr's classic study *The Romantic Exiles*, along with the ill-fated involvement of Bakunin with one of Herzen's daughters in the so-called 'Nechaev affair'.

This was Herzen's eldest daughter, Tata (Natalie), born in Vladimir in June 1839 shortly after the scene with the crucifix. Taken abroad at the age of 8 and never to see her homeland again, she grew up struggling for her identity in the strained 'hexagon' of her father's relations with Malvida von Meysenbug and Ogarev's second wife. After her father's death in 1870, Tata became a wealthy young heiress, and felt bound, along with Ogarev, to support Bakunin's anarchist conspiracies. She fell under the spell of his demonic pupil Serge Nechaev – who, outdoing his master, was to perfect the modern terrorist technique of 'violence for violence's sake' – and was drawn into the horrendous conflict between this outright assassin and Bakunin. The dark genius of Serge Nechaev was in due course explored by Dostoyevsky in his novel *The Possessed*, and the famous 'Nechaev affair' would be used by Marx to oust Bakunin from the First International on gratuitous charges.

In 1931 Tata Herzen published her *Reminiscences*, giving the world a somewhat coloured picture, possibly distorted by her great age at the time of writing, of her relations with Nechaev. But only in 1974, with the first publication of her private diaries and letters in Michael Confino's *Daughter of a Revolutionary*, was her story fully revealed. That publication also cleared up several mysteries concerning Bakunin and Nechaev – such as the question of the true authorship of the famous anarchist handbook, *Catechism of a Revolutionist*.

It all started when the first-generation heroes and heroines of these extraordinary events met again in the winter of 1839–40, this time in Moscow. There they ran into Bakunin, Belinsky and that other group of emotionally entangled but intensely philosophizing young men and women, 'truth-seekers' all, who had originally gravitated around Stankevich but had since come under Bakunin's domination.

Released from confinement to Penza, Ogarev was the first to arrive with Marya Lvovna in the autumn of 1839. As he resumed contact with his former student friends, Marya Lvovna – now rich but bored and seeking stimulation – began to give parties for them and other members of Moscow's avant-garde intellectual élite. They included the historian Timofei Granovsky, recently returned from three years in Berlin to take up a professorship; M.N. Katkov, who was likewise to teach at Moscow University before becoming an influential journalist; the translator Nicholas Ketcher; Vasily Botkin, a widely travelled and polyglot tea-merchant's son of refined tastes and philosophic inclinations; and finally Paul Annenkov, a literary critic. Later to be known as 'the aesthetic tourist' because of his insatiable interest in seeking out the writers and thinkers who shaped Europe's ideas – Heine, Marx, Proudhon, George Sand, among others – Annenkov was to produce a biography of Stankevich as well as a memorable study of the decisive change in Russian intellectual currents set in motion by Herzen, Bakunin and Belinsky during 'The Extraordinary Decade', as he called it, beginning in 1839.

Herzen, released from exile soon after Ogarev, arrived in Moscow in the course of the 1839–40 winter and was one of the first to witness the change. Happy to be back in his old home and to renew the friendships of his student days, he found that few of those flocking to the Ogarevs belonged to his and Nick's old politically minded circle. Rather, they were friends or members of Stankevich's 'speculative' circle and he could not fail to notice two young men who had risen to prominence in it: Michael Bakunin, with his imposing stature, and Belinsky – 'each with a volume of Hegel's philosophy in his hand' – who were cutting a swathe in Moscow's young literary, fashionable salons where, between champagne dinners and dancing, 'desperate disputes' raged night after night on every insignificant pamphlet ordered from Berlin 'and read to tatters and smudges... so long as Hegel was mentioned in it.'[8]

Although Herzen in his Memoirs, written 15 years after the event, telescoped things somewhat (and he actually saw more of Belinsky in St Petersburg than in Moscow), he successfully evoked the preponderance which abstract German thought and its veritable 'Mahabharata' of heavy and often indigestible philosophy had gained in Moscow's intellectual circles during his absence. To this he opposed his own view that the Russian spirit, which preferred life to abstraction, was to assert its vitality by 'transforming even Hegel's philosophy'. A tribute to the personality of Stankevich included in his Memoirs further gave the impression that it was the latter who had initiated the desperate disputes about the definition of Hegel's 'all-embracing spirit'.

Actually, Stankevich had left Russia in 1837, more than two years before Herzen's arrival in Moscow. During this interval the mesh of romantic relationships that had entwined more than one member of Stankevich's circle all ended in ruin, none more tragically than the Stankevich-Lyubov affair. A tenuous romance at best, begun when the young leader of the Russian Romantics saw in the demure, introspective Lyubov Bakunin the luminous image of the ideal woman, it had foundered the moment he realized that she did not come up to his idea of love as a sublime experience enabling a man 'to feel his unity with the universe'. Unwilling to hurt her, the high-minded, tubercular and lackadaisical Stankevich temporized; but he felt bound by the proprieties to encourage her hopes, and kept her and her parents on tenterhooks for a year before going through the motions of a formal betrothal in April 1837.

Bakunin had played his usual meddlesome role in the crazy-quilt of romances around him, but this time with a difference. For once, the self-appointed guardian of Lyubov's 'purity', who had done his utmost to drive off her earlier suitors – and was, besides, campaigning for the 'liberation' of his sister Varvara from the 'animal' lust of her own husband and the father of her child – kept encouraging Lyubov and his parents to believe in Stankevich's 'holy, superhuman' love. At the same time, ignoring Stankevich's protests, he read and discussed his letters to Lyubov with the Beyer girls and others before transmitting them to Premukhino. So did his three sisters at the other end before passing them on to Lyubov.

This, of course, put pressure on Stankevich, who had started studying Hegel and, under the influence of Hegel's cryptogram 'all that is real is rational', was trying to reconcile his idealism with reality. In May 1837, realizing that his reluctant betrothal to Lyubov placed him in an untenable situation, he had written to Michael: 'This horrible catastrophe was no doubt necessary to save my soul from otherworldliness, from softness – to destroy that inner world of fantasy, to set me down in the real world.' But he kept putting off the marriage on the pretext that he was waiting for his father's consent – all the while calming Lyubov by extolling love in abstract terms as 'the highest of feelings, the crown of creation... For love one forgets all other ties, all relationships, all obligations, love shatters all bonds.'9

The upshot, briefly, was that Stankevich, racked by tuberculosis and some-times feverish to the point of delirium from the added torment of his false posi-tion, soberly decided that the only honourable course for him was to sever the 'bond' with Lyubov. To prepare her for the *coup de grâce* he hinted to her alle-gorically – à propos a performance he had seen of *Hamlet* – that he perceived in her the character of Ophelia, and worked in Hamlet's 'I never loved you' in a passage reading:

> Ophelia is pure, tender and innocent... She has a child-like attach-ment to her father and brother... when she becomes dimly conscious of a new feeling, she is ready to lock [it] up inside herself so as not to overstep the bounds of obedience to her father. The counsel of her brother (those stupid people always interfere) [an allusion to Michael Bakunin] strengthens her decision... At her father's command she returns to Hamlet his gifts and his letter, and in great grief hears his mad words: 'I never loved you.' These words were capable of wound-ing her deeply but could not drive her mad. Only the sudden and violent death of her father could do that...10

Whether Stankevich really believed this or was only trying to ease his con-science, he did apparently fear for Lyubov's delicate constitution. She was a sickly person of extreme sensitivity, and rather than tell her that he had no intention of marrying her, he resolved to leave Russia, hoping that time and a long separation would do their work and let her down gently. His father had just given his consent to the marriage, and hers his formal acceptance, when Stankevich informed Luybov that the doctors were sending him off to cure his lungs at Carlsbad.

'You remain for me just as sacred as you ever were,' he wrote before taking flight without so much as a farewell visit to her. Significantly, Michael Bakunin was one of two friends he consulted before his departure. Sister Varvara was the only one to take up the cudgels on behalf of Lyubov, protesting: 'Why does he leave her for a whole year?... In the eyes of heaven he and Lyubov are husband and wife even if his health forbids marriage in its earthly sense... Let them go to Carlsbad together. Lyubov too is weakly and could benefit from the waters. Lyubov will be his friend, his sister'[11] – which may help to explain why Michael Bakunin had encouraged the idea of her marrying Stankevich. It was the only kind of marriage he really approved of.

Stankevich left Moscow in August 1837. He went on corresponding sporadically with Lyubov about her health and well-being, but carefully and cruelly never mentioned marriage again, although they remained engaged in the eyes of the world. Lyubov, longing to hear at least that he loved her from a distance, expired slowly of consumption and heartache and was buried a year after his departure.

In between curing himself at various health resorts, Stankevich spent most of the next two years in Berlin studying philosophy 'at source' under Professor Werder, a pupil of Hegel. He was never to return to Russia. Taken ill while travelling in Italy, he died in 1840, during the summer after Herzen's arrival in Moscow.

Thus Herzen could not have met Stankevich at the start of 'the extraordinary decade'. But Stankevich's influence was evident from the sense of loss at his death experienced by all who knew him (it affected Belinsky like 'the deaths of Pushkin and Lermontov... after such blows life has lost much of its meaning') and by the way they continued to revere him. In his Memoirs, Herzen was to call Stankevich 'one of those idle people who accomplish nothing', but whose extraordinary gifts, profound thought and magnetic personality had reared 'a regular legion of savants, writers, and professors, among them Belinsky, Bakunin and Granovsky.' Considering that these were men of different temperaments – Granovsky a 'conciliatory' character, Belinsky shy and frail but famous for his vehemence in argument, not to mention Bakunin's huge ego and grandiloquent way of dominating discussions – it was indeed remarkable that they all accepted Stankevich's intellectual superiority as this soft-spoken, contemplative but disciplined young thinker guided their first steps in the exploration of German philosophy from Kant to Schelling and Fichte.

But when it came to Hegel, Stankevich had no more than initiated Bakunin into his philosophy, leaving him to sort out its mysteries for himself. After he went to Berlin and studied Hegel under Werder, Stankevich's 'reconciliation with reality' progressed as far as his accepting the idea 'that life, when comprehended by mind', was not a series of accidental or coarse phenomena, but governed by the universal 'Spirit' or Absolute. Although he was attracted by the rational in Hegel – and converted both Granovsky and Konstantin S. Aksakov, an earlier member of his circle who happened to be in Berlin, into devotees of

Hegel – Stankevich himself never became either an orthodox or a dialectical Hegelian, perhaps because 'his fastidious intellect and refined and poetic nature rendered him incapable of crude generalizations',[12] or he shrank from absolute theories.

He remained the idol of his circle long after Herzen's friend Ogarev reformed its ranks and provided it with a new intellectual and social centre. The following lines written by Herzen about Ogarev – another soft-souled man whom he defended against philistine charges of idleness, and whom he found so akin to Stankevich that in his *éloge* of the latter he even mixed up their names – fit Stankevich's personality and role just as well, and may stand as their joint epitaph: 'To serve as the link, the centre of a whole circle of people, is a very great work, especially in a society both disunited and fettered.'[13]

And disunited it was, the 'legion of savants, writers and professors' who, since Stankevich's departure, had come to be dominated by Bakunin and Belinsky. And the bone of contention in the debates which by the time of Herzen's arrival on the scene had split it into two camps – debates in which he took an active part as they moved to their climax – was precisely the concept of 'reconciliation with reality'.

Bakunin had a talent for drawing. One day in 1838 he did a likeness of himself and sent it to the Beyer sisters with the following inscription: 'I find in it... a sort of diffuseness and lack of definition: it is unfinished, as I myself am unfinished.'

He was unfinished but in the midst of a painful process of 'remaking' himself. This had started with his excruciating self-discovery, late in 1836, of the implications of the jealous fury that had raged in him for weeks at the mere false suspicion that his younger sister Tatyana was falling in love with Belinsky. His realization that there was 'much that is vile in me', coupled with his inability to rid himself of it, had made him unburden his soul to the Beyer sisters: 'I do not know what to call my feeling for Tanichka', he had written to them in an undated letter, except that it had inflamed him with a 'tormenting jealousy... Base emotions overwhelmed my entire being. I became their wretched slave... Ah, this was hell, hell with all its terrors.'

To his own sisters he had merely confessed the collapse of his belief in Fichte. His personal Fichtean 'I' and 'will' had proved of no avail in his emotional crisis. In this hour of his dark distress and moral degradation when he 'craved death', Stankevich had offered him a new lease on life by inviting him to join him in the study of Hegel in Moscow.

'The work went swiftly', Annenkov was to write 40 years later, dwelling on Bakunin's 'superlative' facility for dialectic; and in the 20th century Isaiah Berlin would observe that Hegel's '"dialectical" struggle of "opposites" which (somewhat, it seems, like a diesel engine) moved by a series of sharp explo-sions... suited Bakunin's temperament well since, as he himself was fond of saying, he detested nothing more than peace, order, bourgeois contentment.'[14]

Bakunin's agile mind indeed quickly took to Hegel's quizzical but stimulat-ing paradoxes as one takes to a challenge. Stankevich had in fact invited him to 'rack' their brains together over Hegel, not only because Bakunin knew German but because he could think of no one better suited as a partner for dis-cussing such abstract notions as Hegel's concept of the 'Absolute'. That had been in November 1836.

Bakunin had hardly studied Hegel more than a month or so when the 10 core members of his 'holy commune' – his 4 sisters, 4 brothers, and two Beyer 'soul' sisters – began to hear in individual and collective reports of his revival through Hegel. Henceforth he would do nothing but study, concern himself with nothing 'other than what is tightly bound with universal life'. His subjective Fichtean 'personal "I" must be destroyed', his futile 'inner life' deracinated to make room for 'that harmony outside of oneself that one cannot find within.' On 10 January 1837 he was still explaining to his sister Varvara that his Fich-tean 'I' had to go because 'I have a fiery nature, my feelings seethe... I am pas-sionate, egotistical, jealous and, finally, there is not within me those qualities that fit others for life in society', and candidly telling her that 'only absolute life can bring me happiness and preserve my dignity. Departing from it, I am capable of any crime.'[15]

A little over three weeks later, on 4 February, he was victoriously announcing to his entire sister- and brotherhood that 'my *personal I* has been forever des-troyed... my individuality entirely dissolved in the Absolute.'[16]

He had a phenomenally quick grasp, but one should not be misled into thinking that he immediately mastered the intricacies of Hegel's system. It was to take him a couple of years to acquire enough of its scholastic and convoluted historicophilosophical jargon to be able to strut about Moscow's intellectual salons as the foremost, if not undisputed, authority on Hegel. For one thing, Bakunin was an irregular student in spite of his various declarations; for another, his study was often superficial, for rather than probing methodically and deeply, his mind quickly spotted and roved to and from those ideas which suited – or could be turned to serve – his emotional needs.

By the spring of 1837 Hegel (via Stankevich) had brought Bakunin his first salvation. In Hegel's equation of the 'real' with the 'rational' he found that abs-tract 'harmony outside oneself' which helped to still 'the indescribable torment' of his inner life. In the light of Absolute Reason and the manifestations of exter-nal reality, all those 'dreadful humiliations' of which he had been the victim now appeared to be the trivial result of 'futile, egotistical introspection', subjective fantasies and contemplative self-absorption à la Kant and Fichte. Having reached a truce of sorts with his turbulent inner self, Bakunin admonished his brothers and sisters to 'stop talking about external and inner life. There is no such division.' And to his other neophytes, the Beyer sisters, went the instruction: 'None of us should think about how things might be better with us; instead one should regard the external world as something *given*, in which he must find himself and thereby transform the *external into the internal*.'[17]

In April 1837, just as he was achieving 'reconciliation with reality' in a narrow personal sense, Bakunin's first spurt of Hegel studies came to an abrupt end. Stankevich, faced with the self-inflicted 'catastrophe' of his betrothal to Lyubov, left Moscow to sort out his feelings and ponder his next step on his father's estate. In June Bakunin returned to Premukhino to find his family of 10 in alarm over Stankevich's ominous postponement of the marriage. Michael was quick to offer his siblings the balsam of 'life in the Absolute' and his new perception that suffering was the wail of romantic illusions and tormenting self-analysis.

Each of the 'doctors of revolution' expressed his persona in the ideas and theories he launched upon the world. The preaching of none, however, so obviously and transparently reflected the ups and downs of his personal life and fluctuating moods as did Bakunin's. He meant to take a second and more serious plunge into Hegel's philosophy in the calm of Premukhino. But that summer, consternation reigned among the Bakunin clan at Stankevich's written *adieu* and departure abroad. Even if the disappointed Lyubov knew that her brother had condoned his friend's action, she expected little consolation from Michael as she was – by her own confession – normally afraid to talk to him and used to avoid him because 'everything about him was so tempestuous and had a terrible effect on me.'[18]

Indeed, Bakunin's stay at Premukhino was marked by a series of family storms in which he embroiled himself and others. Although he was in the process of 'remaking' himself, he was the same old Michael. Even before the tragic turn taken by the Lyubov-Stankevich affair, he resumed his struggle for the 'liberation' of Varvara from her husband. In the spring of 1837, the deeply religious and devout Varvara, who in a moment of 'weakness' had married the landowner Dyakov – but had since left him, together with their child, feeling sinful for having allowed a man she did not love to 'profane' her – came under increasing pressure from her parents to return to him. At the same time Michael, who was still in Moscow, kept warning her that resuming a loveless life with her husband would be nothing less than a crime. In her dilemma Varvara, recognizing that the otherwise decent Dyakov was not to blame for her sin – and feeling, moreover, that she was still bound by church vows to the father of her child – conceived the idea of inviting him to come and live with her for a while 'as brother and sister' at Premukhino. Dyakov agreed, and did his best to keep his word; but by the time Michael returned to Premukhino in June, Dyakov was gone, the experiment having failed for various emotional reasons, and Varvara was all the worse for it. Michael, who had promised that he would 'shrink from nothing' to save her, thereupon launched a complex campaign to do so. He began by persuading his parents that Varvara was in urgent need of a health-cure at Carlsbad. Without mentioning that the plan was for Varvara to remain abroad together with her two-year-old son and a nurse – or that he meant to hitch on to them and leave as well – he wangled a half-promise from his father to contribute 1,000 roubles towards Varvara's health-cure.

In November, Michael departed for Moscow, his head swarming with ideas for raising the considerable finances required for the execution of the whole plan. Stankevich, who was in on it, had promised to pay off Michael's debts and to support him at the rate of 1,500 roubles a year if he joined him abroad. For the rest, Michael planned to sell Varvara's jewelry, and reckoned he could get even the weak-willed Dyakov to pitch in with some money for his wife's defection.

The plan might have succeeded had not Count Alexander Bakunin discovered that Varvara was to be separated from her husband for an indefinite length of time and that Michael intended to escort her to Carlsbad and then proceed to Berlin, the fountainhead of Hegelian wisdom. The old man was furious with his son, and at his behest Dyakov presented Varvara with an ultimatum: she could either go abroad with him, or he would force her to leave their son behind. At the same time, Count Bakunin wrote to Michael that his cup was full. With three unmarried daughters on his hands, he accused his eldest son of trying to crown his constant incitement of his siblings against their parents by destroying the marriage of Varvara, their only wedded child. As Michael reported to all and sundry, his father in this letter 'declared war' on him and told him in so many words 'either to become once and for all a truly Christian son' or to end his 'philosophical visits to Premukhino'.[19]

On Michael's side, the 'war' for Varvara's deliverance from a loveless marriage was supported by all the young members of Stankevich's former circle, including Belinsky and Stankevich himself, who encouraged it from abroad and even offered the money for Varvara's journey. The 'war' – which some students have seen in essence as 'the struggle to save a single human being, incidentally a woman, from heavy bondage to social forms' imposed by family, church and state[20] – was to be a protracted one. While in the midst of it Bakunin was to attract the attention of Moscow's intellectual world by publishing an article on Hegel's philosophy, the highly sensitive, musically and intellectually gifted

Varvara – an ardent votary whose letters on religion and love have been cited as providing 'important evidence of the spirit of the age'[21] – was both the chief instigator of the struggle and its victim.

Emotionally exhausted by inner conflict and the friction with her parents, she found comfort from despair in Michael's persuasive new teaching of universal 'reality' superseding individual joys and suffering. Addressing him in his own Hegelian lingo as one 'enlightened by eternal reason, for whom nothing is dark', she appealed to him to act as if he were father to her son, and to save her: 'Oh, Misha, enlighten us by the light of reason and truth, give us immortal, conscious life... Misha, you were sent to us by God... I would perish without you.'[22]

Michael did not disappoint her. He had made legal inquiries how to stop Dyakov from vetoing Varvara's trip abroad. 'God and the law are on our side,' he assured her, guessing that Dyakov would anyway not go to court for fear of a scandal. Barred from Premukhino, Michael was going to spend New Year's Eve 1838 at the Kazitsino estate of two maiden aunts. To lure Varvara away from their father's influence he instructed her, if there were more arguments with their parents, to 'ask for horses and come to Kazitsino with your son and Taniusha. Be calm and steadfast.'[23]

On 15 December he had written to his father that famous long litany of a letter – more than 20 printed pages in the existing draft – in which he had evoked his happy childhood ('the best period' of his life) at Premukhino. But he also countered his father's charges with some of his own. 'Over the last year', he wrote, just when he needed 'the love and advice of a father, especially a father like you', he had discovered that he had no father to whom he could bare his soul with 'all its wounds'. In a mixed tone of supplication and rebellion, he begged his parents 'to restore their love to their children' and to save Varvara, but did not hesitate to harangue them with militant quotations from the Scriptures and Jesus: 'I have come not to bring peace, but the sword. For I have come to divide son from father, and daughter from mother and bride from bridegroom.' He seems not to have remembered, or relied on his parents not to remember, that the verses he was misquoting from Matthew end with the sentence: 'And man's foes will be those of his own household.'[24]

Already during his Fichtean period, Michael had told the members of his 'holy commune' that he was preaching to them 'in the name of God speaking to you through my lips'. Hegel's Absolute, too, stood for God in his mind. Because his parents, instead of love, had imposed 'slavish submission' on their children, Jesus approved of his war against them.

In February 1838 he went to Tver, where he stirred up another revolt at the home of the Beyer sisters. Yet, remarkably, in the midst of his continuing manoeuvres on behalf of Varvara and while on the move during the winter from Premukhino to Moscow to Kazitsino and Tver, he read and made notes on parts of Hegel's *Phenomenology of the Spirit*, his *Encyclopaedia* and *The Philosophy of Religion*, in preparation for the article he was to publish. And in a singular feat accomplished during this period of his 'reconciliation' with Hegel's reality – at the very time he ostensibly destroyed his Fichtean 'I' and was telling his adherents to forget their romantic illusions and petty soul-searching and to 'live every hour in the Absolute tightly bound up with the universal' – he quickly and characteristically found a way of reinserting his subjective personal 'I' into Hegel's objective reality. He did so simply, one might say, by universalizing his 'I'. He was in transition to Hegel but, retaining Fichte's view that every man possessed 'the universal within himself', he comfortably concluded that he could attain the universal without giving up his own individuality. His reasoning about Hegelian reality and external 'circumstances' went something like this:

'Circumstances do not depend on us', but 'we can change them. We can give to them the divine character that lives within us... The main thing is to be prepared for anything and never act contrary to our beliefs.' By infusing reality with the universal or 'divine character' that lived within him, Bakunin, as he informed the members of his 'commune of the Holy Spirit', became 'the ruler of all external circumstances. They must take that *form, that direction, which I give them.*'[25]

More than 100 years after Bakunin's death, Arthur Mendel was to demonstrate through many examples that the young Bakunin divided Hegel's 'objective' world into two parts – one comprising the 'really' Real, that is (in Bakunin's words), 'everything that exists and acts' and is therefore necessary and must be accepted; the other was 'that dead and soulless necessity to which those submit who are crushed by fate' and whose undeveloped consciousness succumbs to 'a multiplicity of illusions – terrible, frigid, meaningless illusions that we think are real.' Bakunin, in short, remodelled 'external, objective Reality in his own image.'[26]

At the same time, the complex facets of his personality and his charisma should not be ignored. In the autumn of 1837, when he had first felt 'that harmony outside oneself' offered by Hegel, Lyubov – previously afraid to talk to him because of his domineering manner – had found him the soul of gentleness. His conversation suddenly proved a great balm and consolation to her. 'We have got to know and love each other still better,' she wrote shortly after he had left Premukhino in November.[27]

Not only Varvara placed her life in the hands of her God-sent saviour; after his February 1838 visit to the Beyer sisters in Tver, Alexandra, the younger of the two, wrote to him in a different kind of exaltation: 'I stood before you silently as before God. He was ready to receive me... but you were looking at me sadly and saying: I cannot receive you. I read my sentence and went away – I did not want you to see my tears flow.' Michael's famous reply was that philosophy, 'my jealous wife... bids me say that you are rather bold to forget that she alone has the right to my love.'[28]

He had developed a new cynical imperviousness, and throughout that 1837-38 period of his supposed surrender of his 'will' to external Hegelian reality, he kept imposing it on his devotees. 'All wills must give way before the one that appears before them as God's interpreter', he had informed them on the commune's foundation in the summer of 1837. And now, in February 1838, even as he was writing his article on Hegel – his first original work, to be published in the *Moscow Observer* – he was tightening his hold on them and reminding them that 'all who have once entered into this commune will never leave it.'[29]

In March, Belinsky was offered the editorship of the *Moscow Observer* and the challenge of putting this bankrupt journal back on its feet again. After fleeing to the Caucasus to escape arrest, he had returned to Moscow in September 1837. When Bakunin arrived in November, the two had a 'reconciliation' of sorts. In fact, Bakunin, when not away from Moscow on his intrigues at Kazitsino or on the Beyer estate at Tver, was staying with Belinsky.

It was in the revamped April 1838 issue of the *Moscow Observer* that Bakunin's article on Hegel appeared, in the form of an introduction to three of his 'Lectures to High School Students' (*Gymnasium Vorträge*). In Bakunin's translation, these were the first of Hegel's works to be published in Russia. In his signed article, Bakunin showed himself to be an outright conservative Hegelian of the 'Right'. It could not be otherwise, for he had yet to hear of the existence of the Young Hegelian 'Left' which had begun its agitation in Germany.

In a more learned tone than in his private letters, he argued that Kant and Fichte had destroyed 'any kind of objectivity and reality' in favour of an 'abstract, empty "I" absorbed in futile, egotistical self-contemplation.' He blamed the Enlightenment for having caused man's 'sickly alienation from any kind of natural and spiritual reality', leading to the triumph of materialism and 'soulless flesh'; and went on to say that the result was 'the bloody' French Revolution which had destroyed religion and the state.

Hegel's 'what is real is rational, and what is rational is real' had done much to redress the balance, but more remained to be done:

> The guillotine applied its bloody standard, punishing everyone who
> had even slightly risen above the mindless crowd. Napoleon stopped
> the revolution and restored social order, but he could not cure the

main sickness of France: he could not restore religion, and religion is
the substance, the essence of any state.

Finally, Bakunin's praise of Hegel turned into a veritable paean of Russian
reality. He deplored the fact that Russian education, instead of developing the
religious feelings and aesthetic sense of the young to preserve them 'from all
the dirty unenlightened side of life', filled them 'with empty, meaningless
French phrases'. Like Hegel, the 'grace-and-favour' professor construed or
misconstrued by his orthodox Right-wing disciples as a supporter of the
'divine' right of Prussia's monarchy, Bakunin wanted to see a strong and active
Russia devoted to Tsar and fatherland. He crowned his presentation of Hegel
with the observation that 'happiness lies not in fancy, not in abstract reading
but in living reality', and the following exhortation:

> To revolt against reality is to destroy in oneself the vital source of
> life. To reconcile with reality in all aspects and all spheres of life is
> the great task of our time... Knowledge requires rigorous discipline,
> and without it there is no knowledge... Let us hope that our new gen-
> eration will also abandon its illusions and cease its empty and sense-
> less chatter... will reconcile itself with our beautiful Russian reality...
> and feel at last the legitimate need to become real Russians.[30]

This mélange of Hegel and young Bakunin's personal feelings jolted his friends
out of their complacency. For just as the realization of his own problem with his
sister 'Tanichka' had forced him to reach outside himself, so the inconclusive
emotional involvements cutting across the circle – Stankevich's 'betrothal' to
Lyubov, Belinsky's hapless infatuation with Alexandra, not to mention the two
cultured Beyer sisters entertaining the circle for years while repressing their passions first for Stankevich and then for Bakunin himself – made them and all the
young Russian 'truth-seekers' privy to their affairs dimly feel that for all their
high-flown talk they were living in a world of fantasy divorced from the claims of
life. Although Bakunin, in Annenkov's phrase, initiated 'a new phase of philo-
sophism on Russian soil with his proclamation of the doctrine that "all that *really*
exists is sacred",' his rise in Moscow's intellectual circles was not immediate.

The first to challenge him was in fact his editor and roommate, Belinsky, the
most upright and conscientious representative of the Russian intelligentsia. For
months, Bakunin had been drumming Hegel into Belinsky, who was sincerely
keen to penetrate the ultimate mystery of German metaphysics in the hope of
finding peace of mind at last. But he found it hard to repress his feelings and
surrender his conscience and moral instinct to an abstract theory of reality
which Bakunin presented to him as nothing less than 'a universal revelation...

a compulsory law of human mentality... without any possibility of correction, addition or change.'[31]

Disadvantaged by the fact that he knew no German, Belinsky protested and asked questions to which Bakunin, who took a 'voluptuous' pleasure in philosophical argument and exposition, responded with the 'infallible truth' of Hegel's ideas, or his own quickly improvised ones. He was a hard taskmaster. When Belinsky at one point flatly told him that he wanted to live his '*own* life, according to my own mind', and not according to half-understood scientific axioms and metaphysical deductions, Bakunin reacted with an undisguised disdain which Belinsky never forgot.[32]

Still, he went on labouring for months, imposing on himself a 'cruel intellectual discipline' and a voluntary but 'excruciating ordeal' that drained his strength. The upshot was that the effort to turn the *Moscow Observer* into a pseudo-philosophical journal soon 'wore out its editor' as well as its readers.[33]

These two, Bakunin with his leonine air and superior eloquence, and Belinsky – shy, hard-working, poverty-stricken and feeling inadequate because of his unfinished university education – were in fact destined to go through all the points between 'love which is near to hatred, and hatred which is near to love', as Belinsky later put it. Already in mid-March 1838 Bakunin had moved to the apartment of Botkin, preferring to lodge with this rich philosophizer who could always be touched for a loan; and soon enough he and Belinsky were blaming each other for damaging the reputation of the *Observer* and bringing it to ruin.

With their first major dispute to come only in the autumn, Bakunin's so-called 'second Hegelian summer' started auspiciously enough. In May 1838 he went home to Premukhino to celebrate the success of his war for the 'liberation' of Varvara from her husband. Under Michael's relentless pressure, his father and Dyakov had got tired of the fight and, after complicated negotiations, Varvara was finally to leave for the Carlsbad waters with her son and a servant. There was a sad side to Michael's victory, for in the end Stankevich, while contributing towards the expenses of Varvara's journey, had declared himself unable to finance Michael's stay abroad as well. But Varvara was to spend 4 years in Europe on money raised by Michael in selling her jewelry and silver, and more funds provided by her father, by Stankevich and even, as Michael had foreseen, by her husband.

As for Stankevich's role in the 'emancipation' of Varvara, some time or other after his betrothal to Lyubov he had in fact transferred his airy *amour* to her sister. His correspondence with Lyubov contains hints that in Varvara's 'verses, her music [and] her letters' he detected an ability 'to seek everything within herself', which seemed to him to offer 'the ideal existence for a man, and is an even greater ideal for the woman who is capable of it.'[34] Varvara, the first to realize that if Stankevich truly loved Lyubov he would not have left Russia without her, had always adored him. On her own in Europe, though not yet divorced, she was eventually – more than a year after Lyubov's death – to follow his call and the dictates of her heart, and join him in Italy, from where they openly declared their love in letters to Premukhino shortly before Stankevich's lungs gave out and he died.

Before Varvara set out for Carlsbad in June 1838, Bakunin at Premukhino, 'happy as it is only given children to be happy', sent his mother – who had gone to Moscow to equip her daughter for the journey – the first of the only two affectionate letters he was ever to write her. In July, making notes on Hegel and variously guiding Lyubov, Tatyana, Alexandra and his brother Nicholas to read the works of Goethe, Schiller and Pushkin, he wrote that at last he felt a 'real harmony... based on the rational freedom of each member of the family.'[35]

While in Moscow, Countess Bakunin had invited Belinsky and Botkin to visit Premukhino. When they arrived, Michael's friendship with Belinsky flared up again. By that time, however, a melancholy pall was descending on Premukhino, for Lyubov was dying. Nor was Belinsky fooled by the 'harmony' and peace of mind Michael seemed to have achieved since his 'reconciliation with reality'. Belinsky still burned with resentment at Michael's insufferably patronizing and authoritarian manner; but he agreed to come because he felt that he had sufficiently freed himself of Michael's dominance to accept him 'as he was', provided Michael did the same with regard to him.

'There was no peace', Belinsky summed up his visit, 'only a patched-up armistice.'[36] At the beginning of August, a few days after he and Botkin departed, Lyubov died. This 'dreadful negation... the monstrous nakedness of pan-destructive, omnipresent, and omnipotent death' – painfully affected Michael. Mobilizing against it every philosophical-religious consolation he knew, the heroic 'suffering' of his Fichtean period, Christ's crucifixion, resurrection and redemption, his new Hegelian dialectic of the world progressing through crises to renewal, and even, curiously enough for Bakunin, the suffering experienced by a mother in giving birth, he wrote to Varvara in September: 'Human life in general is a life of struggle, dissension, and suffering, for the grandeur and the strength of reality can be known only by the grandeur and the intensity of the contradiction from which the spirit makes its way towards self-concentration.'

At the same time, he mentioned his renewed 'doubts, weakness, spiritual blindness'. He was still in this sombre pensive mood, and trying to concentrate on his studies, when Belinsky suddenly broke the 'armistice'. In September and October he sent Michael three long letters – veritable 'dissertations', as they became known between the two of them – in which, striking at the heart of

Michael's self-deceptive 'reconciliation with reality', he told him point-blank that for all his ability 'to *think* wonderfully well about reality', to 'chatter and make a lot of noise... and sound terribly wise' about it, he knew reality in theory, but actually lived outside it.

What did Michael know about real life? 'You can explain reality to others', Belinsky wrote, 'but you yourself let it pass you by... In fact you have not lived at all.' Because he always determined by thought what others understood directly, naturally, spontaneously, 'even without going to school', Michael was incapable of establishing any authentic emotional relationships and did not know the simple 'act of life... Ideas are dearer to you than man.'

It was in this letter that Belinsky, preferring the truth to a 'false' relationship, accused Bakunin – even while acknowledging his 'powerful spirit', superior intellect and 'devilish capacity for communicating ideas' – of 'monstrous pride... a desire to subjugate' and insincerity towards friends, and compared him to 'an all-gestating and all-devouring Brahma' to whom friends and lovers were mere 'victims and toys'. Holding up a ruthless mirror to Michael, he described him more specifically as a man driven by his excessive 'strength, elemental power and spiritual restlessness to strive incessantly for some goal in the distant beyond, dissatisfied with the present, even hating the present and himself in the present... that is your character,'[37] and rounded out the portrait by dwelling on his heartless cynicism. 'You crushed everyone with your weight, and made it difficult for any ordinary person to love you.'

Nor was that all. Mercilessly attacking Bakunin at his most vulnerable point – his attachment to his sisters and the suffocating mind-control he had established over them – Belinsky ridiculed the artificial 'doctor's robe' of philosophy he had forced on them. This, he suggested, ruined their natural lives, and they might be better off without it:

> You led them into the realm of thought, and gave them a new life. But I have strong reasons for thinking that they would very, very much like to escape. Before they learned the importance of abstract thought, they were saved from this desire by the simple feeling of submission to providence... The corner-stone of their knowledge is the two magic words: 'Michael says'...[38]

Belinsky correctly foresaw, as he wrote to Stankevich, that Bakunin was not made for a life of abstract thought and quiet contemplation: 'He craves movement, turbulence and battle', and his lack of 'any sense of reality' would always lead him towards extremism. His struggle to 'liberate' his sisters, he observed to Stankevich, was inspired less by 'love for them and their happiness' than by a thirst for action, a proclivity for heroics, 'bravado and bombast'.[39]

In his 'dissertations' to Bakunin, Belinsky not only stripped him naked to his soul and innermost motivations, but set out to teach him a lesson in 'reconciliation with reality'. It was not the abstract contemplation of one's navel and the world practised by Bakunin: it meant coming to grips with living society and the world. Reduced by penury as he was to teaching young clerks at Moscow's Mining Institute how to write clear office letters, Belinsky looked at them as they were, 'not through a preconceived theory', and was beginning 'to find common interests in talking with the kind of people with whom I thought I could never have anything in common.' This was an authentic relationship, not like some circle of idle world-remote theorizers who could afford to play about with abstract concepts and criticize everything without any responsibility or obligation on their part.

Though reeling under this general assault, Bakunin took the high ground and wrote Stankevich that Belinsky had gone to the extreme of idealizing 'any ordinary, commonplace, existing being'. But there was more from Belinsky. 'The drama of life', he advised Bakunin, 'is so arranged that people of all roles are needed.' If things depended on him, he would have asked for another role, 'but, you see, they do not like these requests, they insist that I be not what I would like to be, but what they want. So I will play the role that was given me.' And he announced that, having joined 'society', he enjoyed the strength and fascination of real life: 'I am no longer a candidate for membership in society, but a member of it. I feel it in me and myself in it, attached to it, grafted onto its interests, poured into its life, fusing my life in its own.'

Once an idea had got hold of him, Belinsky was not afraid to pursue it to its conclusion. Having embraced Hegel's 'reconciliation with reality' in the travestied form taught him by Michael, he now threw the grim implications of Hegelian 'necessity' back in his face in a famous passage:

> Reality is a monster, armed with iron claws and iron jaws: whoever does not voluntarily surrender to it will be seized and devoured by it... We constantly meet victims of its vengeance. Free individual actions, unreconciled with external necessity, deviating from the life of society, produce collisions... Yes, live not as you like, not as you think you should, but as the ruler decrees, and that ruler is – civic society.[40]

Bakunin climbed on his high horse again and wrote Belinsky that he could easily draw from his own 'store of *transcendental* and *logical* tricks all the proof needed to amaze even your terrible reality with its iron jaws and claws.' Accusing Belinsky of capitulating to the opinion of the crowd and simply adopting its 'stupid voice' as 'your new philosophy', he recalled him to the 'sacred voice of truth' and 'independent thought'.[41]

Belinsky, however, took a different view of things: 'I recognize personal, autonomous freedom, but I also recognize a higher will. *Collision* is the result of a hostile conflict between these two wills. So – everything is and will be as it is and will be. If I stand, fine. If I fall, there is nothing to be done about it. I am God's soldier: he commands, I march ...'[42]

In their religiously coloured Hegelian parlance, God stood for the Absolute, the divine 'Reason' governing universal reality – as in Belinsky's later phrase: 'The word *reality* has become for me equal in meaning to the word *God*.' By the time Belinsky wrote this he had travelled a further stage in his 'reconciliation with reality' to the point of upholding the principle that 'might is right' and accepting – though not for long – the idea that the reality of the Tsar's autocracy in the 'holy' Russian fatherland was part of a divine scheme.

The epistolary Belinsky-Bakunin duel in the autumn of 1838 was not the end of their tortuous 'love-hate' relationship. A year later the two of them were living together again in Moscow, but their final break was imminent when Herzen arrived to assist in the great Hegelian debates. He was unknowingly to help set these two vehement protagonists on their different paths to glory.

Whether the combined impact of the monstrous 'negation' of Lyubov's death and Belinsky's assault made Bakunin realize that his only alternative to assuming some of the obligations of 'civic' life was either 'to escape it or destroy it' – justifying Mendel's view that he had 'parts of his apocalyptic vision ready in hand' at this early stage, only waiting to be translated from 'abstract fantasy into the language of politics' – the fact is that already in July 1838, before Lyubov's death and the clash with Belinsky, he had passed the word to the founder-members of his commune: 'Everything that is only external must be destroyed', and only that which was 'both external and internal' – that is, whatever he could accept and internalize, as it were – allowed to remain.[43] The conflict between his subjective Fichtean militancy and his acceptance of objective Hegelian reality defied the cleverest 'transcendental tricks' of his mind.

But just as Stankevich's call at the end of 1836 to come to Moscow and study Hegel had saved him from an earlier crisis, so now, in the winter of 1838–39 – in the midst of his first long sojourn at Premukhino in years, playing the devoted son, 'affectionate and respectful but firm' towards his father, even taking a passing interest in the affairs of the family estate – destiny itself seemed to reach out for him.

Contrary to his custom, Bakunin had not gone to Moscow for the winter because, other than Botkin and Efremov of Stankevich's former circle, he had hardly any friends left there. Both of them, at his request, kept sending him a large variety of religious, philosophical and historical works to keep his mind busy with. According to his notebooks, during the winter and spring of 1839 he read a mixed batch of literature, from Gibbon's *Decline and Fall of the Roman Empire* to the *Koran*, and from Guizot's *History of French Civilization* to a book on differential calculus, besides helping one of his younger brothers with Greek and English grammar.

In the midst of these random studies, a parcel from Botkin arrived, containing a copy of, as well as summaries from, a philosophical journal, the *Hallische Jahrbücher*, recently founded by Arnold Ruge at Halle in Prussia as the organ of the new Hegelian 'Left'. This journal, which in spite of its title was a monthly, came to Bakunin as a great find. From its pages and abstracts of its articles he learned for the first time of the stormy controversy which, since David Strauss's *Life of Jesus*, had split Hegel's German disciples into a 'Left' and a 'Right' camp.

Scenting action and resuscitated by his old dream of going to Berlin, Bakunin became increasingly restless. He presumably intended to throw in his weight with the conservative 'Right', for he warned his sisters not to be misled by Strauss, whom he called a Mephistopheles doomed to defeat. By 13 May he was writing to Stankevich that the time had come to tear himself away from 'the narrow sphere of individuality, to enter into a living relationship with universal life'; and that he was ready to live in a garret on bread and water, go around in old clothes, to satisfy his 'boundless thirst for knowledge'. Their common friend Efremov was about to depart for Berlin, and Bakunin added (probably giving vent to his own feelings) that Efremov had 'to tear himself away from vile family life, from old habits, senseless depressions and vacuous, useless probing into himself.'[44]

With Berlin now 'a matter of life and death' to him, as he announced to Stankevich, it was obvious that Bakunin would leave no stone unturned to get there. Indeed, he was to spend the year to May 1840 on various attempts, most of them futile, to raise the money necessary for his stay abroad. It was a restless year of changing moods, as his hopes rose and fell, but interspersed with travel and other activities, including his publishing a second article on Hegel, making the acquaintance of Herzen and Ogarev and becoming the leading light in the philosophical discussions among the intellectuals who began to gather regularly at Ogarev's Moscow receptions.

In the year or so since Stankevich had gone back on his promise to provide him with the wherewithal for leaving Russia together with Varvara, Bakunin had found no other benefactor to finance his scheme. His chief hope of getting any of the money needed in 1839 thus remained focused on his father. But Bakunin would not have been Bakunin had he not clashed with his father that summer over an impossible scheme he conceived to complete Varvara's 'liberation' by obtaining her final divorce from Dyakov. What he later called the ensuing 'battle' with his parents was accompanied by 'ignoble manoeuvres, tricks, accusations and attacks' on their part. Nonetheless, in mid-July, having – but for two short visits to Moscow with Tatyana – spent a relatively peaceful year at Premukhino trying to be a model son, he set out for St Petersburg to take the matter of the divorce personally in hand. As he did not dare confide his intention to his parents before he left, his father was furious when he learned of his undertaking after the event.

'Your efforts and petitions stand no chance of success', Count Bakunin wrote to Michael in St Petersburg. Indeed, although an undismayed Michael sought intervention in high quarters and eventually obtained an audience with L.V. Dubbelt – the feared assistant head of the notorious 'Third Department' of the Imperial Chancellery, in charge of spying on all the Tsar's subjects – the latter refused to bend the strict Russian divorce law. As his father continued to reproach him for having acted behind his back, Bakunin sulked and did not write home for two months. Nor was he in the mood to visit his bedridden mother in Moscow when he learned that she had been taken ill during a visit there. In the end he was to spend an 'oppressive' 4 months in St Petersburg.

He had not planned a long stay and had no money, but this was never a problem for Michael Bakunin. He went at first to lodge with one of his Muraviev cousins. Then, having outstayed his welcome, he moved at midnight, without a kopeck in his pocket, to Demutov's Inn – one of the most expensive in the city – and in the middle of the night sent back to the Muravievs for his luggage. Belinsky was later to portray Bakunin's way of sponging on people: 'One day he meets Z[aikin], and the next he asks him for money, takes it, and then again a second time, a third, and so on. Then what does he do with the money? Drinks Rhine wine, which Z[aikin] denies himself, even though he makes some 15,000 a year... [Michael] was always going to the theatre, with Z[aikin] always getting him tickets...'[45] In the end, Bakunin moved in with a former Artillery School comrade.

In September, having met A.A. Kraevsky, the editor of the *Notes of the Fatherland*, Bakunin began to write his second essay on Hegel for this prominent St Petersburg journal. He was still penniless and in a mood of despondency and inner 'chaos'; but he had learned to fight and suffer and had written to his sisters that one had to drink 'the whole, bitter cup of unhappiness' to know what happiness was. For the first time, too, he recognized that he could not continue to reject every kind of obligation or responsibility. He had been right to do so hitherto, for 'there is no truth in obligations that have no other basis than cold duty, for such obligations are the compulsion of slavery, the negation of the infinity of the inner spirit. Love is the essence, the beginning and end of life.

'But', he went on, love 'must also be actual', like truth. If it did not go 'beyond possibility to actuality', then there was no truth in it either. 'From this point of view, I was completely wrong. I sinned against truth when I rejected responsibility.'[46]

While pursuing his Hegel studies, Bakunin read a Life of Fichte, and again extolled him as a 'true hero of our age' for his utter disregard of 'external circumstance' and public opinion in his unwearying move to an 'appointed goal'. Having privately suggested that not every love is true love, he now postulated philosophically in his essay that 'usually, everything existing, every finite thing is called real, and in this lies the error. Only those things are real in which reason, idea, and truth are present in their entirety. All the rest are illusions and lies.'

Thus he suggested that not everything that appears to exist is rational and therefore 'real', effecting what Arthur Mendel, with historic hindsight, called 'a very successful and fateful merger' of Fichte and Hegel. Mobilizing Fichte's ardent zeal, but transforming his 'one-sided' subjective 'I' into an objective 'I', he allied his militancy with Hegel's reason in history and 'the indomitable power' of the Absolute itself.

In this often mentioned but little discussed essay, Mendel detected signs of Bakunin's imperceptibly and perhaps unwittingly moving towards a 'Left' Hegelian orientation. Indeed, the essay contained a hint that the world could be made 'rational' and 'real' through the destruction of those 'external' circumstances that he, Bakunin, had already classified as 'vile, meaningless' and illusory, and of which he wrote (to his sisters) that they represented 'the negation of the infinity' of man's 'inner spirit' and (in his essay) that they contradicted, and were incompatible with, the 'boundlessness of his inner ideal essence.'[47] It was a far cry from his earlier acceptance of Hegel's objective 'external world as something given', but not an unnatural development considering that, dividing the world of reality, he had since decided to submit only to that part of it which represented 'real' necessity, but to resist what he described as the 'dead and soulless' type of necessity.

Otherwise, however, the essay presented the same conservative Hegel of the 'Right' whom he had introduced to the Russian public in his earlier article in the *Moscow Observer*. The first part of his new essay was not to appear before the following spring, when it created something of an intellectual stir. But in October 1839, his guardianship of his sisters, as so often before, cut across his intellectual endeavours. Botkin had fallen hopelessly in love with Michael's 23-year-old sister Alexandra – hopelessly, because as soon as Count Bakunin learned from an uncle of hers that the two of them were carrying on a hectic secret correspondence, he wrote politely to Botkin to say that he could not accept him as a socially eligible suitor for his daughter's hand. Poor Botkin, the tea-merchant's son, who by the prevailing standards ranked inferior even to Belinsky (who was a doctor's son), sent Michael 400 roubles and appealed to him to rush and 'defend' Alexandra from her parents and 'her aunts and uncles', for he was the only one capable of protecting her: 'Go to her, go to her, you will resurrect her – for God's sake, I implore you. Drop everything. I have sent 400 roubles... But move, move, time is precious. She may be dangerously ill.'[48]

Botkin's roubles providentially saved Michael from his melancholy existence in St Petersburg. Instead of rushing to Premukhino, however, he left in October for Moscow and established himself there for the winter. With both his parents variously accusing him of having advised Alexandra to marry Botkin if she loved him, and of having otherwise begun the whole affair by failing to warn them in time – and on top of it borrowing money from the rejected suitor – the epistolary fire from Premukhino was such that he hesitated to go there; and when he finally went he was so disgusted by the lack of 'humanity, religion, or love' in the cherished paradise of his childhood that after a few days he hastened back to Moscow. With ricochets from Botkin, and Alexandra in the end falling ill, the affair was to drag on for months.

In the midst of it all, Belinsky – a year after having vehemently assailed Michael Bakunin in his 'dissertations' – sought his company. The short, tongue-tied and stoop-shouldered Belinsky with his sunken chest, and the huge-proportioned 'thunder-hurling' Bakunin could apparently neither part nor live together. Their new reconciliation was not to endure, but while it lasted Belinsky – in spite of his reservations about the other's 'unscrupulous, disingenuous' character – once more succumbed to his charisma and rhetoric, to the point of writing Stankevich in the autumn of 1839: 'I came to Moscow from the Caucasus, and Bakunin was here too – now we are living together. During the summer he studied Hegel's philosophy of religion and of law. A new world opened out before us. "Might is right and right is might." I can't describe to you with what feelings I heard these words. To me it was a liberation.' He went on:

> I grasped the meaning of the fall of kingdoms, the righteousness of conquerors. I understood that there is no such thing as savage material force, no domination of the bayonet and the sword, no arbitrary power. Nothing happens by accident. And at last there came to an end my weary guardianship of the human race, and the significance of my fatherland appeared to me in a new light. The word reality has become for me equal in meaning to the word God.[49]

This passage from a lengthy letter, begun in September 1839 and finished in October, shows how far Bakunin, and with him Belinsky, had travelled from Stankevich, the quondam leader of the Moscow circle, who studied philosophy for the intellectual pleasure of it. Belinsky, dazzled by the simplicity of 'might is right', was, as usual, to go the whole hog and develop a fatalistic belief in the rationality of the tsarist autocracy and to submit to it – all in the name of 'reconciliation with reality' – with a self-styled mystic joy that not only stupefied his friends but in the end was to make him feel disgust with himself. As for Bakunin, when he made up with Belinsky in the autumn of 1839 he was only halfway through the painful process of adjusting to reality; shifting positions every so often, he was groping for the right philosophical path 'to enter into a living relationship with universal life', and he was continually so bewildered by a maze of contradictions that by February 1840, giving up the posture of the divine messenger through whom 'God speaks to you', he was to write his sisters: 'I am no longer fit to preach to others. I myself need to be instructed. While I was preaching to others, a host of insidious foes crept into my soul, which I must now expel.'[50]

Belinsky's report on how Bakunin converted him to 'might is right' is of added interest because, posted in October 1839, it reflects the confusion and beginning divisions among Moscow's young intellectuals as they tried to digest German metaphysics, and Hegel in particular, at the moment when the former 'circle' was revived with Ogarev's arrival in October and the soirées began at which Bakunin – introduced by Botkin – met Granovsky, Katkov and others, including Herzen towards the end of the winter.

Botkin vied with Ogarev's wife, Marya Lvovna, in giving receptions, dinner-dances and musical parties. On New Year's Eve 1840 they dined on sturgeon, woodcock and champagne. Bakunin, who is said to have drunk 9 glasses and to have danced 'very gracefully', began that January to feel in himself 'something of the same sort' of strength and imperviousness to public opinion that distinguished Fichte, though he still needed – as he declared to his sisters – to develop his ability to rely calmly and exclusively on himself 'and to act independently of and in opposition to everything external'. His mind was now so firmly set on Berlin that in two letters written in February he declared, first, that he simply could not 'stay here for another minute... I must study... Learning is my entire life', and secondly, that he expected nothing less than a 'baptism, a transformation' and the start of a 'golden period' once he managed to immerse himself 'in the vital atmosphere of European life, where divine thought breathes in science, religion, art, nature, people, everything.'[51]

In April, the first part of his essay on Hegel finally appeared in the first issue of *Notes of the Fatherland* and his short 'reign over the circle of philosophizers' in Moscow – as Annenkov was to call it – began. Kraevsky, the editor, congratulated Bakunin on his splendid 'model of a philosophical article in Russian.' Granovsky, who had spent two years in Berlin, most of the time studying Hegel in company with Stankevich, wrote to Bakunin that 'in these things' he had advanced much further than they had; and having read the manuscript of the second part of Bakunin's essay – which was meant for the July issue but was never published – he declared it to be 'intelligent, simple and to the point'. Even Belinsky, who had by now quarrelled with him again, admitted that 'this man can and must write, he will do much to advance the thought of his father-land.'

In short, Bakunin became the Hegel expert 'consulted whenever any obscure or difficult point in the Master's system required elucidation', as Annenkov was to put it. Both Annenkov and Herzen were to evoke the phenomenal hold which Hegel's all-embracing philosophy had taken on the minds of the 'truth-seekers' gathering at Ogarev's house. In Annenkov's words:

> A person unacquainted with Hegel was considered by the circle vir-
> tually a nonentity, a fact which gave rise to desperate efforts on the
> part of the many whose mental resources were scant to become fully-
> fledged human beings at the price of gruelling and brainracking
> work which stripped them of the last vestiges of any natural, simple,
> spontaneous feeling and understanding about things.

According to Herzen, 'People who loved each other avoided each other for weeks at a time because they disagreed about the definition of "all-embracing Spirit", or had taken as a personal insult an opinion on "the absolute personality and its existence in itself"'.[52] Herzen immediately registered that the circle now dominated by Bakunin – preoccupied exclusively by 'speculative' questions, and totally uninterested in political affairs and the social hubbub – treated him and Ogarev's French-inspired activist ideas with the 'respectful indulgence' due to returned exiles, but looked down on them as figures of the past, while Hegel and their own interpretation of his works represented modernity.

The fundamental division, however, as Herzen recognized, was another. The greatest harm, he wrote, was done by Hegel's phrase 'all that is real is rational' and the issue that split the circle into two camps was the conflict between Bakunin and Belinsky over 'reconciliation' with that rational reality. Herzen met Belinsky in Moscow only briefly, if at all, for Belinsky was summoned to St Petersburg to help to edit and lend his prestige to the *Notes of the Fatherland*. He had finally thrown off the tutelage of Bakunin, of whom he later said to Annenkov that he had 'snatched' his soul by 'devious means'. At the beginning of 1840 he accused Bakunin directly: 'You cannot stand it when anyone does not think or do as you do.' To Botkin, he wrote that he 'hated' Bakunin, hated the way the indolent swashbuckler, while engaged in no activity other than rhetoric, managed by sheer high phrases not only to make 'a lot of noise about philosophy and himself' but to 'lord it over others', while he, Belinsky – confined in St Petersburg to a small over-heated study adjoining a 'damp and frigid' living-room – was reduced to reading mediocre works and forced to write reviews of them for the use and pleasure of the esteemed public of imperial Russia, and, moreover, to do this reading and writing without knowing German. 'And then there are the hemorrhoids, headaches, cramps, nausea, trembling hands and feet.'[53]

Faced with this grim reality, Belinsky published in the winter of 1839–40 a series of articles in which, with his usual violence, he attacked all his former idols, including Schiller, the poet of liberty, whom he accused of having presented him with 'an abstract ideal of society, cut off from the geographical and historical conditions, built in mid-air'. Belinsky's articles led to more strife and controversy in Moscow. Herzen, by his account, was so stunned by Belinsky's invoking Hegelian 'reason' to justify the tsarist 'reality' that he broke with him. As for Bakunin, Herzen had the impression that he was 'being driven by his revolutionary instinct' in the other direction, away from the conservative Hegel of the Right he had taught Belinsky and whom the latter was now glorifying. Not that Bakunin had become a Left Hegelian, but he had begun to realize that by Hegel's logic one had to travel, in order to reach one's goal, in the other direction.

With everyone, including Belinsky, praising his essay on Hegel in *Notes on the Fatherland*, Bakunin was all the more keen to set off for Berlin, so keen in fact that, although Alexandra had been taken ill with grief over her unhappy romance with his friend Botkin, he refused appeals to deal any further with the matter, declaring that he was now concerned only with a way of getting to Berlin: 'I have to get out of all the trivial life of family and friends.' Botkin, who had housed and fed him for nearly a year, was furious at his sudden indifference. He claimed that Michael had actually advised Alexandra that she had to choose between 'husband and brother', or Botkin and himself. All their friends in Moscow thought Michael's attitude scandalous, and Belinsky chimed in to express his rage at 'this abstract hero born to bring ruin on himself and others, a man with a fine mind… but the blood of a rotting salt cod.'

In his despair at failing to find the funds for his journey, Bakunin turned for help to Stankevich. But Stankevich let him down again, disappointingly advising him not to give up Berlin, but to find some 'work in the meantime'. Belinsky ridiculed the Berlin plan as so much self-deceit. 'Is he going to fly there through the air and live on air?' he asked sarcastically, adding that if Michael was really serious he would 'give lessons, take the candidate's examination and then live, as Granovsky did, on a government stipend.'[54]

But Bakunin had his own way of going about things. On 24 March he composed a long letter to his father which E.H. Carr has justly called 'a cunningly woven tissue of humility and independence, of sincerity and ingenuity.' Confessing his past mistakes, but affirming that he had come to realize that he could no longer 'shirk all social conditions with impunity' but must earn his bread and become 'an active member of the state', he nevertheless declined his father's wish that he take over the running of the family estate. He was simply not made for it, nor for a military or government career of 'low rank without a university degree.'

Like the young Marx in his famous 1837 'letter of confession' to his father, Bakunin dangled before his father the happy possibility of his attaining a professorship. And almost in a replica of the shortcut proposed by Marx when he had told his father about obtaining fast promotions in Westphalia, Bakunin tried to convince his father that the quickest and easiest way to obtain a university chair in Moscow was to study in Berlin. In Moscow, he argued, the candidate's examination alone (before the master's degree) took 4 years and was 'most difficult and uncertain'. In Berlin, he had learned from 'some young professors', he could obtain a doctor's degree in three years, after which the Russian doctorate would be a simple matter and his way smoothed to a professorial chair. He clinched the argument by pointing out that the Russian government itself, 'dissatisfied with our universities, sends professors abroad for their education; not one of the Russian universities can provide a classical, scientific education, for the attainment of which there remains to me only one single means – Berlin.'[55]

Count Bakunin's expectations of, and relations with, his son were of course different from those between the Marx father and son. But Michael's tactics succeeded. What the two parents had in common was being resigned to the fact that they had lost control over their sons' lives. Although Count Bakunin compared Michael to 'another Don Quixote, in love with a new Dulcinea' and forgetful of his 'obligations' as the eldest son, he was sufficiently mollified by his promise to reform his ways – to live frugally and avoid student 'orgies' and 'the filthy swamp of sensual pleasure' – to promise him part of the three-year annuity of 2,000 roubles which Michael had asked for, as long as the income from the estate permitted.

Now that his dream was almost within reach, but his maintenance not yet fully assured, Bakunin the gambler and perennial borrower boldly approached Herzen on 20 April 1840 – less than three weeks after their first meeting – with a request for a loan of 5,000 roubles to help him attain 'the human and only aim of my life'.

Herzen, impressed by Bakunin's personality, his arguments against the new reactionary stance adopted by Belinsky, and his dedicated quest for knowledge and self-perfection, not only advanced him 1,000 roubles but, enlisting Ogarev into the scheme, undertook to supplement Count Bakunin's annuity with any sums required to cover the financial cost of his planned three-year stay in Berlin.

In a state of exaltation, Michael left Moscow before the end of May on a month's farewell visit to his family at Premukhino. The 'nobleman's nest' of his childhood was in full bloom. Everything was once again peace and family harmony. 'It was a sad parting with father, sisters and even with dear mother, who has recently shown me in her own way that she loves me,' he was to recall. 'God, how my heart was breaking when I said good-bye to Papa...' Now that he was leaving, he strongly urged his brothers and sisters not to 'forsake father, we are all obliged to repay him for all the suffering he has borne.'[56]

In the last week of June, he set out from Premukhino on the first stage of his journey. Tatyana, Alexandra and his 5 brothers drove with him as far as Kasitzino. There he parted from most of them, but Paul and Alexis continued with him to Torzhok. 'The three of us', he wrote later, 'drove and cried as we went, and the thrush was singing in the bushes.' After this emotional farewell, Michael rode on alone to St Petersburg, where he arrived on 26 June. He was in high spirits, and meant to visit Belinsky and make his peace with him before catching a steamer for Lübeck and Hamburg three days later.

Yet on the night of 28–29 June, his last on Russian soil, he was to address a pathetic farewell to his siblings – 'Do not forget me, love me, dear friends. I have no one else besides your little world' – and to exhort brother Nicholas to 'cling closely and firmly to our little circle, and remember that no Belinskys or Botkins can ever replace it.'[57]

Michael was leaving Russia under a cloud of scandal, with his whole world reduced to his original devotees, his siblings; none of his many friends and acquaintances, 'savants, professors' and would-be intellectuals who had flocked around him, bothered to see him off. One by one, he had antagonized them all – Belinsky, by his arrogance and superior air; Botkin, by his disloyalty to an old friend and benefactor; Granovsky, by opening his letters to Efremov; the Beyer sisters, by forgetting to invite them to Premukhino for goodbyes before they had left for their remote summer estate. And in the end, he managed to alienate even the good-natured 'Nick' Ogarev, by blurting out that at one of the soirées hosted by Ogarev he had surprised his wife, Marya Lvovna, in a compromising situation with Katkov. Ogarev was deeply hurt and all the more bitter as he had just contributed a sum to Herzen's fund for Bakunin's trip to Berlin. He not only refused any further support but called Bakunin a 'reptile'. Ogarev was of course angry with Katkov, but wrote Herzen that Katkov, compared to Bakunin, 'is what nobility is to baseness'.

No wonder that on his last night before embarking, Michael wrote that during his brief stay in St Petersburg he had 'realized at last that the former circle of my supposed friends no longer exists'. The only people who took an interest in his departure and kept him company on his third and last day in St Petersburg were, curiously enough, his new acquaintances, Herzen and his wife Natalie. Whether Herzen's financial generosity and friendliness towards Bakunin were due to his not knowing him well enough or to finding in him an ally in his own quarrel with Belinsky, the fact that his friend Granovsky had a high opinion of Bakunin – calling him 'a real talent for speculation... capable of achieving a great deal in science' – may provide a further clue to Herzen's trusting in what he later called Bakunin's 'revolutionary instinct'.

It may have been instinct, but – unlike Herzen and Ogarev, who had been active young rebels and had suffered for it – Bakunin had yet to develop an interest in political and social questions, which he regarded as beneath his dignity. It is true that towards the end of 1839 he had written to his sisters that 'action, *die Tat*, is life's only fulfilment', and that Stankevich had drawn his attention from Berlin to the Polish Hegel student August von Cieszkowski, who in a radical interpretation of the master's dialectic, had recently proclaimed[58] that it was time for his disciples to move from aloof contemplative theory to an interventionist philosophy of action and 'praxis', i.e., to apply their knowledge of Reason and the Absolute in history to shaping the future reality of 'life and social conditions'.

But Bakunin was far from having become a Left Hegelian. He was a man in transition, caught up in inner conflicts and quarrels with the outside world. He had heard of Cieszkowski and Ludwig Feuerbach, but was totally unaware of the intellectual ferment in Germany as the increasingly radical Hegelian Left either sought to demolish Hegel as impossibly conservative for having concentrated on past history and ignored the future, or subtly argued (as did Bruno Bauer, of the Berlin Doctors Club) that Hegel's dialectic itself ultimately led to 'atheism, revolution, and republicanism'.

Bakunin lusted desperately for action, so desperately that he had told his sisters that unless he went to Berlin he would go to seek 'vital action and a vital dynamic existence' with the military in the Caucasus. But this stemmed less from any idea of applying philosophy to life than from his feeling that he must get away from 'debasement into philistinism' and from such 'vile trivia' as 'the vacuous strife with family and friends'. These, he had written Stankevich, had broken 'the kind of abstract spiritual strength which is my only strength'. This self-assessment, borne out by all who knew him personally or by reputation – *e.g.*, Belinsky, who called him 'this abstract hero', or Granovsky, who wrote that 'in the sphere of active life, he can do nothing at all', or Annenkov, who was to remark, 'The whole of life presented itself to him through the prism of abstraction' – may help to explain why Bakunin could not immediately pass from purely speculative thought to a philosophy of action.

Herzen had yet to immerse himself in Hegel and to arrive at the discovery that his formula about the rational being real and all that is real is rational contained 'the algebra of revolution'. All the 'Hegelizing' Moscow intellectuals had a problem in reconciling the working of the Absolute in history with the tsarist reality around them. While Belinsky temporarily accepted it (as he accepted his hemorrhoids) as part of the grit of existence and simply because he wanted 'to live like everyone else', Bakunin on the eve of his departure from Prussia had reached a dead end.

On 18 June, 12 days before his departure, he had actually written to Stankevich – who was critically ill in Rome, where he had recently been joined by Bakunin's sister Varvara and her son – to report that his soul was so ill 'that not a single healthy spot remains in it'. But he had boundless energy. With his emotional needs and the conflict between his impotence and his wish to dominate temporarily sheltered in his inner bunker, Bakunin – his optimism bolstered by the success of his plan to put Russia and his past behind him – not only hoped to regain his 'abstract spiritual strength' but confidently expected to be reborn in Berlin.[59]

He spent the night of 28–29 June writing farewell letters to Premukhino. He asked his 'dear, fine, wise Tatyana' never to 'take away your love from me; it is more than necessary to me. Everything that in any way enters your life must be known to me.' He wrote words of advice to each of his sisters and brothers, but was further to single out Tatyana by including in his first letter from German soil the following tell-tale quotation: '"The laws condemn the object of my love." Taniusha, this refers to you. Dear, good girl, write me soon and love me as you have.'[60]

He finished writing at 6 a.m. on the morning of the 29th. Addressing his final letter to the Beyer sisters, he apologized for not seeing them before leaving Russia and soothed their ruffled feelings by assuring them that 'everything that enters into my life shall be known to you', an inversion of the phrase he had just written to Tatyana.[61]

Later in the morning Herzen came to fetch him. They sailed together along the Neva to the port of Kronstadt. Michael embarked, but then a sudden gale forced the steamer back to shore. He refused to disembark, and the last Herzen saw of him was standing on deck, 'his tall, strong figure wrapped in a black cloak and drenched by the rain.'

The steamer finally sailed out into the Baltic on 30 June 1840. Bakunin spent most of the stormy 5-day voyage 'on deck... not taking my eyes off the grandiose new vista.' It brought back to his mind, he wrote, 'Heine's poems that so well express this stark yet profound northern beauty, and also Walter Scott's Pirate. Everything is somehow sad, mournful, yet also grand, boundless, powerful'[62] – enough to lift his spirits and fill him with new faith in himself.

After landing at Lübeck, he spent three days in Hamburg. Then, together with an army colonel he had met on the boat, he set out by coach on the 4-day journey to Berlin, where he arrived on 13 July, though by Prussia's Western calendar the date was 25 July.

Berlin, the fountainhead of Hegelian wisdom (which, until the new university year began, he was to study for a start in private lessons with Professor Karl Werder), was indeed to cure the illness in his soul, which reflected nothing but the philosophical dead end he had reached with his speculative mental acrobatics. He was fed up with the futile polemics and theorizing in Russia, and 'on closer acquaintance with metaphysics' he became – as he was later to write when describing his initial period in Germany in his famous *Confession to the Tsar* – convinced of the triviality of all metaphysics. 'I sought life in them, but found merely death and boredom; I sought deeds, but found absolute inaction.'[63]

Indeed, his first impression of the Germans was that they were philistines and that their hair-splitting intellectuals all suffered from 'the prevailing philosophy disease'. Nor was his cure quick. But once he discovered the Hegelian Left's application of Hegel's dialectics to politics and its increasingly radical talk of the World Spirit and History relentlessly, mercilessly and inevitably moving to tear down and sweep away the old world – its social order, dogmas, institutions and whole 'system' – in order to create a new one of increasingly rational men controlling their own destinies, he had an illumination. In the Young Hegelian talk of crises, catastrophes and cataclysms being merely stepping-stones in the progress of humanity, he found a power and an inspiration that perfectly clicked with his own credo that 'everything that is only external must be destroyed'.

He was 26 when he arrived in the Prussian capital in 1840 and, as it had done for Marx in 1836, Berlin opened up a new world to him. He was soon to overtake not only his former friends stuck in the mire of Russian reality but also the radical Hegelian Left in Germany, and to announce publicly a theory of action all his own – 'revolution, our common bride'.

And so he was at last to find his vocation, his 'holy mission'. Transferring his self-centred fantasies, his self-confessed love for the fantastic, for unusual, unheard-of adventures, for undertakings that open up a boundless horizon and whose end no one can foresee to the field of 'political and social action', helped him to sublimate and overcome his emotional problem and the resulting inner coldness which set him apart, making Belinsky, Granovsky and many others after them remark that he loved ideas, but not people. In the common cause of revolution to demolish the existing order and make room for a better society, he was ultimately to find an outlet for his passion to destroy, fulfilment for his abstract love of humanity as well as the long-sought 'living link with the universal'. Instead of his becoming a great philosopher, his leonine temper and personal magnetism, his intellect, eloquence and capacity for intrigue, would all be devoted to his career as an all-European rebel and conspirator, the incendiary prophet of world-wide Anarchism in its many forms and Marx's future opponent in the First International.

Nicholas Stankevich never lived to see the letter of 18 June 1840 in which Bakunin announced his imminent arrival in Berlin. On his way from Rome to Como in the company of Varvara Bakunin and her little son, Stankevich had died in her arms on the 12th at Novi Ligure, a village on the road between Genoa and Milan.

Shortly before he succumbed to tuberculosis at 27, mourned by all the young Russian intelligentsia whom he had introduced to Goethe, Schiller and the wonders of German philosophy from Schelling and Kant to Fichte and Hegel – and to be particularly revered by both Bakunin and Belinsky for his 'saintliness' and superior moral character – Stankevich had likewise been about to make the transition to 'real life'. In his last letter to Bakunin, written in May, he had remarked, à propos the radical interpretation of Hegel in Germany, that 'the Idea is the life of the Absolute; as soon as we have reached the Idea, we no longer need science.' But 'from the Idea we can build life, and there the Idea inevitably becomes action.'[64]

Alexander Herzen, having watched the Moscow 'circle' split over Hegel, began to study him in earnest and reached the conclusion that 'if the existing social order is justified by reason, the struggle against it, if only it exists, is also justified.'[65] At summer's end in 1840, at his father's insistence, Herzen took a job in one of the ministries and moved to St Petersburg. Belinsky was there, but Herzen was in no mood to see the man who, instead of preaching 'conflict', argued in favour of a contemplative, Buddhist-type reconciliation with the authoritarian reality. In the end, however, the two were persuaded to meet.

'Do you know', Herzen recalled telling him, 'that from your point of view you can prove that the monstrous tyranny under which we live is rational and ought to exist?'[66]

Belinsky, who had recently realized that he had fallen into one of Hegel's logical traps and suffered great moral pangs over it, thanked him for bringing up the subject, 'otherwise I should not have known how to begin.' By October he was writing to Botkin: 'May my putrid urge towards reconciliation with reality be damned! Long live the poet Schiller, noble advocate of humanity.' Courageously denouncing his own recent writings as 'revolting nonsense', he declared to Botkin in the same and subsequent letters that he would never make his peace with the 'vile' reality prevailing in Russia. As for Hegel's World Spirit and the historic process, he wrote that even if he attained to the highest rung of human development envisaged by Hegel,

> I should still have to ask him to account for all the victims of life and history, all the victims of accident and superstition, of the Inquisition and Philip II, and so on and so forth... Reality is an executioner... All Hegel's talk about morality is utter nonsense, since in the objective realm of thought there is no morality... The fate of the individual, of the personality, is more important than the fate of the whole universe and the health of the Chinese emperor, the Hegelian Allgemeinheit.[67]

Once Belinsky had reached this turning-point, he never looked back. He began to read histories of the French Revolution. Without moving from St Petersburg, he discovered 'a new world' in the speeches of Robespierre and Saint-Just – what was needed, he wrote, was their 'two-edged sword of word and deed'. Attacking the horrible spectacle presented by Russia under Nicholas I,

> of a land where men buy and sell other men without even the cant of the Americans, who say that Blacks are not men... a country where there are no guarantees of personal liberty, honour, or property, but where... the government is well aware of what the landlords do to their peasants and how many landlords have their throats cut by their serfs every year, [68]

he became the sharpest critic of the tsarist tyranny.

In 1848, a few months before the workers' rising in Paris, Belinsky, in search of treatment for his advanced tuberculosis, was for a short while reunited in that city with Herzen and Bakunin. But he returned to St Petersburg, where he died soon afterwards at the age of 27.

22

Heine's Warning about Communism and the Struggle against the King of Prussia

In France the 'extraordinary decade' may be said to have started in May 1839 with the insurrection of the Société des Saisons, led by Auguste Blanqui. Sentenced to two years in prison in August 1836 for the conspiracy of the Society of Families and the 'gunpowder plot', Blanqui had been released 14 months later under a general amnesty of political prisoners.

The Society of 'the Seasons', like that of the 'Families' before it, was a clandestine offshoot of the original Société des Droits de l'Homme, whose broken-up remnants had gone underground after the prohibition of unauthorized associations of more than 20 people. The pyramidal structure of the Society of the Seasons, starting at the base formed by small cells of 7 members – each known as the Week, while its head was identified as Sunday – has been described as follows:

> A Month had four Weeks or twenty-eight members, twenty-nine with the leader, July. Three Months made up a Season, which, with the top man, Spring, added up to eighty-eight members. The highest division, a Year, had four Seasons totalling three hundred and fifty-three men, including a responsible revolutionary agent. The blueprint called for three Years, or more than a thousand members. At the summit was a triumvirate, consisting of Blanqui, Barbès and Bernard. The first of the three was commander in chief... The arrest of a Week, even a Month, would not disable the entire organization. Only those at the top knew what went on below them.[1]

Blanqui, the former parliamentary correspondent of *Le Globe*, was one of the few educated young men who sought contact with 'the people', believing in its ability, if guided by an élite, to take its fate in its hands. Although Paris was out of bounds to Blanqui under the terms of the amnesty, he had secretly entered the capital and explored several strategic objectives to be attacked by the insurrection. But he had hardly had time to organize mass support. Still, with France in the throes of a seemingly endless government crisis since January 1839 – when her political parties, though divided between themselves, had formed a coalition to bring down the 'personal government' exercised by King Louis-Philippe through his chief Minister, Molé – he persuaded his two lieutenants, Armand Barbès and Martin Bernard, that the time was ripe for action. Elections held in March had failed to give Molé a majority, and 6 attempts to form a government had since come to nothing, chiefly because Thiers and Guizot refused to serve under one another. By May, the political haggling and uncertainty had caused an economic slump. Blanqui, counting on the growing ranks of the unemployed, decided to strike.

On 12 May 1839 some 600 of the altogether 900-strong 'Seasons', reinforced by a number of German and other foreign workers, barricaded several streets and bridges, and not only seized the Palais de Justice and the Hôtel de Ville, but proclaimed a provisional revolutionary government. With Blanqui at its head, it was to include the two other members of his troika; but the list read out from the balcony of the Hôtel de Ville also included the names of Voyer d'Argenson and Laponneraye, the founders of the Société des Droits de l'Homme, as well as the Abbé de Lamennais. Both the abbé and d'Argenson denied any involvement or connection, while Laponneraye was actually in prison at the time.

The insurrection was put down by the National Guard on the afternoon of the following day – not before 100 people, including 30 soldiers, had been killed – but the occupation of the Hôtel de Ville and the very thought that, had Blanqui's men seized the Préfecture de Police and the area of Les Halles (as he seems to have planned), they would have cut off the capital's food supply, was enough to make the King exclaim: 'We are in troubled waters.'

Even so, the insurgents had proclaimed a republic from the balcony of the Hôtel de Ville, and the King feared the psychological effect both at home and abroad. Metternich, watching the manoeuvres of France's bourgeois politicians to wrest some of the power from the King in the name of representative government, had indeed remarked with no little *Schadenfreude*: 'France is back in 1830' (the year of the July Revolution). At home, discontent was such that Alphonse de Lamartine reminded the Chamber of Deputies that Louis-Philippe's government, 'born of the people, should belong to the people', and accused it of ignoring the masses. Paris had indeed begun to bulge at the seams with industrial slums, where low-paid or unemployed *ouvriers* and journeymen – who earned on average 1 franc and 38 centimes a day when they worked – lived in rat-infested alleys swarming with drunken men and sluttish women, criminals and diseased or errant children.

Blanqui's insurrection had failed because these depressed people were apathetic, but Lamartine, remarking (albeit in a different context) that France was 'bored' with a government that lacked any central or directing idea, warned that 'the boredom of people finally leads to upheaval and ruin'. The immediate upshot of the insurrection of the 'Seasons' was that the frightened coalition of political factions, which had seen victory within reach, stopped their bickering and helplessly watched Louis-Philippe appoint another 'personal' government under Marshal Soult. Both Thiers and Guizot were excluded, and the King seemed once more in full control.

Blanqui had managed to escape but was captured in October. On 31 January 1840 he was sentenced to death by the Court of Peers. The following day Louis-Philippe commuted the sentence to life imprisonment, as he had the death sentence pronounced on Barbès in a separate trial. On 4 February, Blanqui was transferred to a dungeon in Mont Saint-Michel, which was then and for many years later inaccessible except at low tide.

That February Heine resumed writing articles on a regular basis for the prestigious *Augsburger Allgemeine Zeitung* on his favourite subject, 'the great issues of European life'. Relieved of financial worries by the annuity he had obtained from his uncle, and with the newspaper paying him the highest fee it had ever offered to a columnist, he emerged from his last two frustrating years of self-styled 'inner desolation'. There was a concomitant improvement in his health and at the age of 42 he felt rejuvenated.

By now he had achieved a European reputation. He was read in Germany and France; various of his ballads, poems and songs were appearing in English in London; in Moscow, 'Nick' Ogarev, having already published translations of Heine in Belinsky's now defunct Observer, was issuing a volume of his 'Songs and Poems'. Since January, in addition to his usual social activity among the rich and famous, he was seeing from time to time a starving young composer, Richard Wagner, who, having recently arrived in Paris, had set a French translation of Heine's 'Die Grenadiere' to music and paid 50 francs to have it printed, in the hope of earning a fortune with it.

More important, Robert Schumann was sending Heine his music to the original German 'Die Grenadiere' and a whole cycle of his poems, Romances and Ballads. And Charles Hallé, the German-born British conductor and pianist, had recently brought him Felix Mendelssohn's book of songs, opening with the setting of Heine's 'On Wings of Song' (Auf Flügeln des Gesanges). Mendelssohn and Schumann thus joined Schubert, Liszt and Brahms, to mention only a few of the great composers inspired by Heine's poems.

Heine appeared never to have been in such 'robust health', to look so 'handsome and winning... with no indication of the sufferings that were to be his later on' – as recorded, respectively, by Lord Houghton (R. Monckton Milnes) and Charles Hallé – or to shine so brilliantly in society as at the beginning of the

1840s. His unruly dark-blond locks, roguish expression, blinking short-sighted eyes and 'tight lips à la Voltaire' struck some as giving him a 'satyr-like' appearance, while the British theatrical agent John Mitchell, meeting him in 1840, described him simply as 'round, ruddy, smiling sardonically' and ready at any moment to say 'something very wicked or very witty, or both.'[2]

Indeed, his every quip, *joli mot*, flash of irony or sarcastic sally was reported, passed on and immortalized in diaries, letters or memoirs – whether George Sand recording his 'devilish clever hit' in calling Alfred de Musset 'a young man with a great past' or Varnhagen von Ense the epigram in which he polished off both the composer Jacques Halévy and his brother Léon by saying of this professor of French literature: 'He's as dull as if his brother had composed him.'

When Balzac's drama *Vautrin* closed in March 1840 after the first night, Heine, who had warned his friend against his venture into playwriting, vented his anger at the newspaper critics – who, 'often echoing the claque, turned worse plays into a success' – for savaging a genius like Balzac. 'They remind me of a pack of eunuchs', was his sardonic comment, 'laughing at the father of a hunchbacked child.'[3]

In his *Fantaisies de Claudine*, Balzac was to quote Heine's 'superb definition of love as perhaps the "secret malady of the heart"', and later to dedicate to him his story 'Un Prince de la Bohême', so that future readers 'should by the union of our names know of the intellectual sympathies uniting us.'[4]

In January 1840 Heine, deciding that Mathilde, though 25 years old, was still as deficient in matters of social etiquette as she was in geography, history and literature, had once again placed her *en pension* at Mme Darte's finishing school for girls. This freed him to put the finishing touches to his *Ludwig Börne. A Memorial*, little dreaming that his ferocious assault on the late 'ultra'-radical hero of the German Jacobins in Paris would be greeted with cries of 'sacrilege' not only by his followers but by most liberal opinion in Germany.

Heine had written most of the book during the second half of 1839. Laube, who read the manuscript before Heine sent it off in February 1840 for publication in Germany, did his best to persuade him to tone down the virulence of his attack on Börne. Heine, however, fended off Laube's arguments for moderation with the remark, 'But isn't it beautifully written?' and throughout the storm that followed he was to stand by his right to affirm the superiority of his world-view over that of his late adversary.

Ludwig Börne, among its many gems and riches, contained a couple of pages in which Heine – challenging Börne's venomous treatment of the House of Rothschild, which he had attacked as 'bankers of kings' and upholders of the Holy Alliance – portrayed 'these Rothschilds' to the contrary as the great democratic 'levellers' of the age. The head of the Paris house, especially, Baron James de Rothschild, 'this Nero of finance, who from his golden palace in the rue Laffitte reigns as absolute emperor over the Stock Exchanges of the world, is, like his predecessor the Roman Nero, ultimately a powerful destroyer of patrician privileges and the founder of a new democracy.'[5]

One of the issues between Börne and Heine had been the question of political or social revolution. Contrary to Börne, who thought the situation in Germany so inflammable that he expected 'the smoke of indignation' to burst into the flames of revolution any moment, Heine did not believe that Germany was at all ripe for revolution. At best, if it happened at all, it might end in the same kind of dull bourgeois philistinism now prevailing in France under Louis-Philippe. With his Saint-Simonist faith in reason and progress, he held on to the more far-reaching vision of the total social emancipation of man from poverty, religious doctrine and every kind of oppression, believing it had a better chance of achieving political changes as well.

Heine pointed out that if Richelieu had abolished the sovereignty of the feudal nobility, and Robespierre had simply cut off its heads, the land remained. It fell into the hands of new estate-owners who had continued the aristocratic pretensions of their predecessors under a different name until Rothschild arrived on the scene and 'destroyed the supremacy of landed property', converting it and its income into money which carried 'the privileges previously attached to land.' Rothschild had, of course, in this way created a new aristocracy of money, but money – 'more liquid than water, airier than air' – was transitory: 'Soon got, soon gone.' The money aristocracy, in short, could never do such 'lasting harm as that which had been rooted in the soil.'[6]

Heine not only managed to present James de Rothschild 'from three converging points of view', including 'Rothschild's alleged self-estimate as a man who has advanced civilization', and his own perspective of him as against Börne's;[7] he did something more. Within a year of his move from stagnant Prussia to the bustling political, social and artistic scene in Paris, Heine had observed in 1832 that 'the creators of a new world' were 'merrily busy' conceiving a new society and a new life. When propounding now in 1840 through the mouth of Rothschild the requirements for outstanding men in a 'new order', he may not have had in mind the alliance between German philosophy and French politics that Moses Hess and Karl Marx would be seeking in a few years in Paris.

Hess had sent him his *Holy History of Mankind* together with an adulatory letter,[8] which Heine never bothered to answer. As for Engels, Bakunin and Ferdinand Lassalle, budding 'social authorities' who were later to converge on Paris, he had not even heard of them. Yet he was setting the agenda for the new decade – unwittingly because all prophecy is necessarily vague; and wittingly because he kept his ear to the ground. Within weeks of finishing *Ludwig Börne*, he was exploring the industrial plants and ateliers of the Faubourg Saint-Marceau, where he discovered rumblings of 'Communism' among the workers of Paris at a time when Marx was still studying at Berlin University.

Heinrich Laube had personally experienced Prussia's treatment of dissidents, both during the persecution of the *Burschenschaft* students in the early 1830s – when he had been held in solitary confinement, without being charged, for the better part of 9 months – and as one of the Young Germany writers arrested and prosecuted at the end of 1835. Sentenced in 1837 to 6 years in a fortress, he had been saved from this fate by Prince Pückler-Muskau's using his influence to have the sentence commuted to 18 months' 'house arrest', which Laube spent in the greatest comfort on the estate of this liberal and eccentric prince.

A talented and prolific writer and dramatist, Laube – who was later to serve for many years with distinction as the director of Vienna's Burgtheater – shared Heine's Saint-Simonist ideas from the 1830s. The Heine-Laube friendship was one of the most enduring. Surviving occasional disagreements, it lasted for altogether more than 20 years until Heine's death. Laube, who had arrived in Paris with his wife in May 1839, was eager to meet and gather material on France's literary celebrities for the benefit of the readers of the *Journal for the Elegant World* in Germany. Heine, however, who for all his lofty poet's detachment loved to explore the soul of a people through its folklore, advised him first to tour the French provinces and to talk with fishermen, tradesmen and *midinettes*. But Laube saw much of Heine on his return to Paris in the autumn, and in his letters and later memoirs he left – besides many insights into Heine's personality – a record of his intense social life in the winter of 1839–40.

In a matter of 6 weeks or so, Heine took Laube to visit Victor Hugo at the Port-Royal; to make a surprise call in the afternoon on George Sand, who received them informally in a brown peignoir, patted Heine familiarly and conversed with them in her coffee-coloured boudoir or 'little salon' in the rue Pigalle, rolling small cigarettes which she offered round on the flat of her palm while Chopin prepared coffee; to a soirée, for which Heine dressed up in a red-brown velvet jacket with white tie, at the house of the marquis de Custine in the rue de la Rochefoucauld. There Laube listened to Heine bantering with Balzac, and made the acquaintance, among others, of Alfred de Lamartine. There followed several evenings at the theatre, a dinner with Meyerbeer, and a visit to the house of Alfred de Vigny, the retiring philosopher-poet who, since his rupture with the actress Marie Dorval – and in spite of the success of his *Servitude et grandeur militaires* – lived in even greater solitude than that 'to which genius condemns one'. During the same 6 weeks, Heine also introduced Laube to the Abbé de Lamennais, the defrocked priest and social philosopher whose latest book, *De l'esclavage moderne*, had been written in prison; to Emile de Girardin, the rising newspaper baron and founder of *La Presse*, whose wife Delphine now eclipsed her mother (Sophie Gay) as a hostess, besides being the pseudonymous author of a widely read series of *Lettres parisiennes*; to Jules Janin, the famous *feuilletoniste*; to the critic Henri Blaise de Bury, and to other literary lions and artistic celebrities.

France's intellectual leaders, Laube noted, normally gave little time and attention to foreigners. By contrast, 'the most secluded doors' opened to Heine and 'George Sand, Balzac, de Vigny, Victor Hugo, Janin and all the rest of the literary notables treated him as their peer.'[9]

Laube left Paris on 4 February. Heine had mailed the manuscript of *Ludwig Börne* to Campe in Germany on the 1st. To his dismay Campe was not enthusiastic. It was only after Heine engaged in a prolonged campaign of salesmanship and on 18 April sent Campe a new manuscript of the book – including the section titled 'Letters from Helgoland' that the publisher agreed to produce the volume that was to become famous not only in the field of literary polemics but in the history of German political literature in general.

On the 1st of March, a new government crisis in France had ended with the appointment of Thiers as Prime Minister. As Mathilde was still *en pension* at Mme Darte's school, Heine continued to visit her on Sundays. But he was also, as he wrote on 24 March, now seeing George Sand every day, reporting to the *Allgemeine Zeitung* on the chances of the new government, working on the new section of his Börne book, asking Campe for a 2,500 francs advance, selling him a fourth sequel to his *Salon*, and making an indirect approach to Uncle Salomon to pay him his quarterly annuity in a lump sum for several years in advance.

It was in the midst of these activities, between attending the tumultuous premiere of Balzac's *Vautrin* and then joining 'everyone distinguished by rank, birth, talent, vice or riches' at the opening night of George Sand's *Cosima*, that Heine took time off in mid-April to visit the workers of the Faubourg Saint-Marceau. On 30 April – having in an earlier article described Thiers as a statesman whose 'understanding of material interests exceeds that which he brings to social institutions' – he was sending to the *Allgemeine Zeitung* his report on the angry mood and the inflammatory literature he found in the industrial workshops of Paris: 'I found there the speeches of old Robespierre, also the pamphlets of Marat, circulating in several new editions, at two sous a copy; Cabet's

History of the Revolution; Cormenin's poisonous leaflets; Buonarroti on the doctrine of Babeuf and his conspiracy, all writings smelling of blood...'[10]

His visit to the workers' quarter left an indelible impression on him:

> The songs I heard there seemed to have been composed in hell and the refrains rang with furious anger. The demonic tones making up those songs can hardly be imagined in our delicate spheres, until heard with one's own ears in the huge metal workshops where half-naked figures illumined by angry sparks from the forge sing them with a sulky, defiant air, beating the time with their iron hammers: the boom of the anvil makes for a most effective accompaniment to the scene of passion and flames.[11]

'Dying of hunger, dying of cold, the people robbed of rights' and 'eating iron' while idle profiteers 'glut themselves with gold', was the burden of a song made popular by the followers of Babeuf in the days of privation and political disappointment during the last gasps of the Revolution. It is not known what songs Heine heard in 1840, but with corruption rampant under Louis-Philippe and gold once again the dominant society value, the workers in their smocks and caps and the frock-coated, top-hatted gentlemen of the bourgeoisie faced each other like two hostile camps.

While the workers were angry and resentful, the bourgeoisie – which included middle-class elements, and not only Stock Exchange speculators collecting treasures and country houses and otherwise trying to ape the life, leisure and material luxuries of the aristocracy they had replaced – lived in growing fear of 'the barbarians' crowding the industrial suburbs of Saint-Marceau and the Faubourg Saint-Antoine. These filthy, unruly, and often lawless quarters, where even the police did not always dare show their faces, teemed with hordes of lost or abandoned children. In 1840, 130,000 errant children were reportedly 'found' in Paris, more than 10 percent of a total population which was slightly less than one million.

Blanqui, who, after his release from Mont Saint-Michel upon the fall of Louis-Philippe, was to stage more conspiracies – and to spend altogether 34 years, or half his life, in prison, besides 10 years in exile – had been fortified by his *carbonaro* experiences in the belief that violent revolution alone could effectively change the situation. Nothing is known of any direct contact between him and the ageing Buonarroti, who had died in 1837. But he knew Voyer d'Argenson, the founder of the neo-Babouvist Société des Droits de l'Homme, of which Buonarroti had been the grey eminence. Blanqui himself, during the 1839 investigation of 'the Seasons' and later, denied ever taking his inspiration from Babouvism.

Though he claimed originality for his philosophy of 'action, not thought', his career in and out of jail made him appear in the eyes of many as the practical, if not nominal, inheritor of the conspiratorial tradition personified by Buonarroti to the end of his life and transmitted in his writings. Involuntarily, Blanqui came to be seen as a link with the 'neo-Babouvist' idea of armed revolution by a minority, on the lines, if not on the model, attempted by Babeuf and Buonarroti in 1796.

Alexander Herzen, reading the draft laws and police decrees prepared by Babeuf, was to be shocked into remarking that they seemed to have been conceived by a despotic tsar of Russia and 'not by the first French Socialist'. For these decrees – believed to have been written wholly or in part by Buonarroti – showed that the republic they contemplated was not only to be a dictatorship, temporary or otherwise, but that they had plans ready to 'relocate' part of the population in communal villages. In addition they meant to classify citizens according to their 'usefulness to the fatherland', with those not fitting certain fixed criteria to be stripped of political rights and liable to be sent to 'correction' camps.

Herzen's horror notwithstanding, Babeuf's plan for a proletarian *coup d'état* and the tenets of the Babouvist doctrine for establishing an egalitarian society, as expounded by Buonarroti along with the strategy of minority rule imposed by force, were to provide an object-lesson that later social thinkers had to relate to in one way or another, and that was not lost on the doctors of revolution from Marx to Lenin. Thus the 1796 'Conspiracy of the Equals' was to achieve a significance far beyond its import at the time when Babeuf and Buonarroti plotted and staged the last episode of the French Revolution.

In 1840 Europe had gone through the war fever of the 'Oriental crisis', which was precipitated by the threat – for the second time in 10 years – of Mehmet Ali, the rebellious Viceroy and Pasha of Egypt, to overrun Constantinople and seize control of the Dardanelles. His first threat had been averted by the landing of 15,000 Russian troops on the shores of the Bosphorus. For that service rendered to Sultan Mahmud II at his request, Tsar Nicholas I had in 1833 obtained a 'friendship treaty' which opened the Dardanelles to his warships in times of crisis, while closing them to his enemies. By the spring of 1840, when Mehmet Ali held Syria and was poised to march again – and France under the bellicose Thiers was only too willing to back him and to extend its influence in the Orient – British statesmen were horrified at the prospect of this adventurer splitting the Turkish empire and severing the route to India. To make matters worse, Mahmud II had died and been succeeded by the 17-year-old Abdul Medjid. The very thought of this boy-Sultan's being tempted to invite the Russians back again to Constantinople – enabling them to pluck the 'stone in the Turkish diamond ring' without much effort – was enough to alarm most of Europe, though not the French.

This crisis had just come on the boil in February 1840 when the notorious Damascus Affair occurred. Following the disappearance of a Capuchin friar and his Moslem servant, the Capuchins charged the Jewish community of Damascus with ritual murder. Two of its notables were tortured to death, a third converted to Islam; a barber signed a false confession, but as the Chief Rabbi and others neither broke down nor admitted to having bottled and distributed the friar's blood for Passover, some 60 Jewish children were seized in order to extract confessions from their mothers. It was some time before the scandalous news reached Europe that the French Consul in Damascus, Count Ratti-Menton, abusing his formal status as protector of the 'Latin' Christians, had not only actively helped to foment the charges but had personally, together with the local Turkish governor, supervised the inquisitorial investigation.

In the face of British protests, the French government, eager to maintain its interests in the Near East, stood by its Consul. Ironically, it was the Consul of reactionary Austria in Alexandria, Von Laurin, who produced evidence exposing Ratti-Menton's shocking role before world opinion; after that the increasingly revolting revelations were to occupy Europe's press and parliaments – where they existed – all through the summer of 1840.

In Paris, Heine, the 'subliminal' Jew and champion of human rights, who, when asked by Laube in a different connection why he always seemed to bristle with suspicion of some evil plot in the air, had answered him in a half-jesting but grim tone, 'My skin comes from Palestine and has been tanned by Christians for 1800 years! The baptismal water has done nothing to improve it',[12] felt personally affected by the issues raised by the 'affair'. On 7 May, having obtained the Austrian Consul's full report – of which the French papers had so far given only a partial account – he sent it to the Augsburg *Allgemeine Zeitung*, together with an article in which he accused Count Ratti-Menton of having 'distributed to the mob in Damascus' a paper recalling the type of medieval horror story that 'witches, werewolves and Jews need the blood of pious Christian children for their Satan worship', which in Europe had become the stuff of legend and fiction. Drawing attention to the nefarious consequences of infecting the naive but fanatical population of the Orient – who anyway regarded both Christians and Jews as no better than dogs – with the bacillus of old superstitions, Heine warned that 'Today they are killing Jews. Tomorrow the mob, drunk with blood, will attack Christians',[13] a prophecy which was to be fulfilled in 1860, when the Druses staged a massacre of Christians in Syria.

By May, Von Laurin had managed to persuade Mehmet Ali in Alexandria to stop the torture of the imprisoned Damascus Jews. At the same time Britain,

Austria herself and Prussia – acting behind France's back – were secretly trying to bring the Tsar into a 'Quadruple Alliance' aimed at putting an end to Mehmet's designs on Constantinople by forcing him out of Syria. In London, Lord Palmerston, who was the chief architect of this coalition, condemned the Damascus 'blood libel' and the Lord Mayor voiced a Christian gathering's shock at the ignorance and hypocrisy still prevailing 'in our enlightened age'.

In Paris, however, Thiers – having sent a vice-consul to Damascus to conduct a mock investigation of the Consul – continued to protect Count Ratti-Menton. The French Premier thought that an Anglo-Russian alliance was something not only unlikely but 'unnatural'. Convinced that Mehmet Ali, who now commanded the Turkish fleet – which had long since surrendered to him in Alexandria – was too strong to be dislodged from Syria, and bedazzled by the idea that this powerful ally would help to restore France to her one-time position as the main Christian power in the Levant, Thiers was ready to risk war for this chance, against the alternative of abandoning an important client. This led him, in answer to questions in the Chamber of Deputies, to dismiss the Damascus affair by suggesting that the Oriental Jews were religious fanatics, implying that Ratti-Menton's actions were possibly not entirely unjustified. In spite of Heine's friendly relations with Thiers, this was too much for him to swallow.

'The answer of Monsieur Thiers was a masterpiece of perfidy,' he wrote in the 3 June issue of the *Allgemeine Zeitung*. 'To hear him talk, one might have thought that the Jews' favourite dish is Capuchin meat.' Heine was capable of caricaturing Jews, especially baptized ones, as mercilessly as bigoted Christians. His *Ludwig Börne*, which was now in the press in Germany, contained a fictional scene in which he and Börne, walking through Frankfurt's ghetto, had once discussed the question whether one could 'turn lice into fleas' by pouring baptismal water on them. As if forgetful of the fact that they were themselves both baptized, he had Börne expatiate on the ridiculous sight of 'old lice originating in Egypt in one of the plagues that visited Pharaoh suddenly imagining they have become fleas and starting to jump about in Christian fashion', only to catch himself suddenly and interrupt Börne with great humour by remarking: 'In the house of the hanged man one should not speak of the rope.'[14]

But the Damascus blood libel reawakened in him 'the great Jewish sorrow' (*der grosse Judenschmerz*) which in 1824, the year before his own baptism, had made him start writing *The Rabbi of Bacherach*. That historical novel, of which Heine had never finished more than a couple of chapters, opened with the 15th-century rabbi and his family assembled on Passover in the festively decorated hall of his house. As he breaks the unleavened bread and begins to recite the Haggadah tale of the Exodus – 'This is the bread of affliction which our ancestors ate in the land of Egypt; let all who are hungry enter and eat' – two tall, muffled strangers posing as Jewish travellers are admitted and welcomed. In the midst of the joyful recital of the miracles of the Exodus the rabbi's face pales with horror as he notices the dead body of an infant – smuggled in by one of the two strangers in the folds of his wide robe – lying under the table. Recovering, he goes on singing and pouring out wine as if nothing had happened. But when a silver basin is brought in for the guests to wash their hands before the meal is to begin, he takes advantage of the interruption to motion his wife to the door and flees with her through the night all the way to a rock overlooking the Rhine. There he explains to the beautiful Sarah that his happening to look beneath the table-cloth had saved them from an attempt to charge him with ritual murder.

Heine had done a fair amount of research before beginning *The Rabbi of Bacherach*. A massacre of Jews had taken place in the town of Bacharach – its real name – in 1283, but Heine's story, although set in the 15th century, was based on a blood libel followed by a pogrom which had occurred in 1287 in the neighbouring town of Oberwesel.

Heine's reaction to the new 'blood libel' in Damascus was twofold. Although he had lost some of the original notes for *The Rabbi of Bacherach*, he now resumed work on it and informed Campe that he would soon have a 'topical' if fragmentary novel ready for him. At the same time, with the passionate pamphleteering zeal of a Zola, he continued his campaign in the *Allgemeine Zeitung*. In article after article,[15] dealing with every side of the issue, he made it clear that what was at stake concerned not this or that people but mankind – an end to 'the use of torture once and for all' in the Orient as in the West – and went on citing the strict dietary laws of the 'priestly folk of Israel', unmasking more of Ratti-Menton's machinations, and denouncing the indifference of the French press ('Is this France, home of enlightenment, of Voltaire and Rousseau?'), as well as the cowardice of some of France's leading assimilated Jews, who remained conspicuously silent to avoid any suspicion of double loyalty.

Among the few he singled out for praise was Adolphe Crèmieux, a French Jewish lawyer and future Minister of Justice, who had the temerity to state that 'France has betrayed us'. Indeed, in July 1840, even as Tsar Nicholas I was publicly joining the Quadruple Alliance – to cries of 'perfidious Albion' in Paris and war preparations on all sides – Crèmieux and Sir Moses Montefiore were rushing to Alexandria to ask the Pasha of Egypt to have the Damascus Jews tried by a court of Europeans. Mehmet Ali refused, but was ultimately to release the surviving prisoners without any judicial proceedings, as 'an act of justice'.

In two articles written on 27 and 29 July, Heine proved his power as a political analyst by indirectly forecasting the outcome of the 'Oriental crisis'.

Observing that Thiers, the historian, seemed to think that he had missed his true vocation as a 'supreme field-commander', Heine depicted the diminutive Prime Minister 'lying on his stomach over maps covering the floor of his study, sticking black and green pins into the paper, just like Napoleon.' Referring to Thiers's work on his multi-volume *Histoire du Consulat et de l'Empire*, he commented, 'Pity, he has not yet reached [Napoleon's] Russian campaign and the great retreat. Had Monsieur Thiers progressed as far as Waterloo, his enthusiasm for the martial arts might have cooled down somewhat.'

As against this, he wrote that the 'arch-prosaic' English were excellent at politics because they never allowed their imagination to run away with them. 'Keeping their eyes focused on the naked facts, they exactly assess the exigencies of time and place, and pursue their calculations undisturbed either by their heart-beat or by the flapping of wings of grand ideas.' On a caricatural note, he ascribed their success in politics as in industry and 'all realistic' endeavours to their cool temper: 'The perfume of the lotus intoxicates them as little as the flames of Vesuvius warm them up. They carry their tea-kettles up to the brink of the volcano, and there they drink tea spiced with *cant*.' (Heine used the English word.)[16]

The 'Oriental crisis' was to reach its climax and resolution on 11 September, when a British fleet bombarded Beirut and then sailed straight to Alexandria. An ultimatum brought Mehmet Ali, who had started his phenomenal career as a tobacco-merchant, to his senses and he was satisfied to keep Egypt as its recognized hereditary ruler.

On 7 October, amid rumours in Paris that Thiers was about to declare a state of war, Heine praised the restraining hand of Louis-Philippe, whose throne was now 'in greater danger from wounded national feelings than from all the dangers of the [Quadruple] Alliance.' Indeed, Thiers had decided to restore French pride by dispatching a fleet to the Mediterranean. 'But that means war!' Louis-Philippe exclaimed when he heard of it. Thiers said that the alternative was the humiliation of France. 'You talk like a journalist,' the King replied. He disliked Thiers intensely and had had about enough of his reckless policy, which had landed him, the 'King of Peace', in a confrontation with the same coalition which had defeated Napoleon. Determined now to get rid of this vainglorious little man, he was all the happier when Thiers himself presented the opportunity.

On 28 October the King was to deliver the speech from the throne in the reconvened Chamber of Deputies. When he found that Thiers had inserted into the speech a bellicose phrase – to the effect that France had not been the first 'to deliver the peace of the world to the fortunes of war' but was ready to act the moment 'the global balance was upset' – Louis-Philippe put his foot down. 'I want peace, and not war,' he told Thiers bluntly. 'We have armed ourselves to the teeth out of prudence, and not for military adventures.'[17]

The next day, Thiers was forced to resign and yield his place to the prudent Guizot, who was recalled from his ambassadorship in London.

The Tsar, content to have driven a wedge between France and England – and believing that he only had to bide his time as the Turkish empire was either 'dying or dead already' – presently gave up the trump of his Dardanelles treaty and signed the 'Straits convention' which closed them to the warships of all nations.

Heine's 1840 strictures on the 'war lust' of the 'imperialist' Thiers, not to mention his 'perfidy' in the matter of the Damascus blood libel, naturally raised the matter of the state pension of 4,800 francs a year paid to him by the French Foreign Ministry – as was to be revealed by a Paris periodical during the 1848 Revolution. The *Revue rétrospective*[18] at that time obtained secret Foreign Ministry documents showing that Heine had been receiving this stipend from the 'bourgeois monarchy' since the autumn of 1840, when Guizot took over the Foreign Ministry from Thiers. A greatly embarrassed Heine, reacting with a public statement on 15 May, and again in a Retrospective Statement inserted in 1854, two years before his death (when his collected articles in the *Allgemeine Zeitung* were reprinted practically without change in book form), vehemently denied that Guizot had ever asked him for the slightest service in return, or that he had ever performed one. The gist of Heine's explanations in both Statements was that the stipend was one of the gratuities given by the French government to thousands of exiles persecuted in their homelands. He himself had accepted it after the infamous Bundestag decrees of 1835 had sought to ruin him by banning all his extant as well as future writings:

> That this financial assistance was paid to me from the pension funds of the Foreign Ministry, which are not subject to public control, was due to the fact that the other treasury departments had exhausted their budgets... When I thanked him [Guizot] for continuing my pension in spite of my radical views, he said to me: 'I am not the man to refuse a German poet in exile a loaf of bread.' These were Monsieur Guizot's words to me in November 1840. It was the first and also the last time in my life that I had the honour to speak to him.[19]

By linking the pension to the 1835 Bundestag ban on his books and writing that Guizot continued it, Heine did himself a great disservice. For this immediately led to the assumption that he had obtained it from Thiers, and not necessarily during his 8 months in office in 1840 but during his earlier short tenure as

Prime Minister in 1836. It was not only during his lifetime that Heine was forced to defend his integrity as an independent writer. The matter was not cleared up until 120 years after his death, and during that time the French state pension inspired generations of writers on Heine either gleefully to malign or unwittingly to question the character of the man, who – engaging more violent sympathies or antipathies than almost any other writer – was by the last quarter of the 20th century to be regarded as 'one of the most controversial in Western literature.'[20]

One notable exception was Max Brod, who maintained that Heine never betrayed the libertarian causes he stood for. But as late as 1974 a serious scholar like Wilhelm Wadepuhl was to claim that Heine had started receiving the stipend as early as 1833.[21] It was only in 1977 that the discovery in Guizot's own files of a document relating to Heine's pension made it possible to reconstruct the chronology, circumstances and political implications of the matter in a manner coming as close to the truth as may ever be ascertained. First, the theses antedating the start of the stipend to 1833 or 1836 were both proved groundless, for the document in the Archives Nationales explicitly mentions that it began in 1840.[22]

Since the document described it as an '*allocation établie par Mr Thiers et confirmée par Mr Guizot (pas de decision écrite) 4,800*', it must originally have been granted some time after Thiers began his second premiership on 1 March 1840. That date happened to coincide with the end of the advances Heine had been regularly drawing from Campe on account of the *Gesamtausgabe* he had sold to him in 1837. A source which had so far provided him with some 6,000 francs annually, or half his and Mathilde's yearly outlay, had dried up. It was in this situation that he had made his unsuccessful approach to his Uncle Salomon for an advance payment on his quarterly annuity.

Noting these circumstances, Michael Werner – who in 1977 analyzed the whole subject in the light of the new find – was led to conclude that it was in March or April 1840 that Heine turned for help to Thiers. As for the crux of the matter, the question whether Heine 'sold out' and became Thiers's hired mouthpiece, Werner, on the basis of a detailed scrutiny of his utterances at the time,[23] stressed that Heine, on the contrary, showed 'a remarkable independence of mind in judging his policies'. With regard to Guizot's continuing the pension, Werner found that in his case the 'humanitarian' reasons invoked by Heine prevailed and 'we must by and large admit that Heine could with justice say that all he ever wrote about Guizot in the *Allgemeine Zeitung* was always dictated by an independent view and strict truthfulness.'[24]

Anonymous reports insinuating that Heine was writing 'in the pay of the French government' – and others accusing the *Allgemeine Zeitung* of pursuing a 'fifty-year-old policy of sowing discontent in France' ever since the French Revolution – had appeared in a Leipzig newspaper as early as the spring of 1840. The source of both stories was O.R. Spazier, a German journalist in Paris inimical to Heine. When he planted these reports in the French opposition press, the *Allgemeine Zeitung* responded with a long statement proving that Spazier was a shady character whose articles the *A.Z.* had been rejecting for years, and who had in fact threatened to bring it into disrepute.

On 7 June, Heine followed suit with a notice of his own denying that he was 'Thiers's apologist'. Since his discovery of the 'Communist' rumblings among the hungry workers of the Faubourg Saint-Marceau he had indeed steadily criticized Thiers's neglect of social institutions, his dissembling behaviour in the Damascus affair and his combative, quasi-Napoleonic stance in the Near East crisis.

In two batches dispatched on 17 and 24 July 1840, Heine sent Campe the manuscript of *The Rabbi of Bacherach*. Together with some 20 poems and his collected articles 'On the French Stage' – earlier serialized in Lewald's *Theater-Revue* – it was to make up the *Salon IV* volume in the series of that name. With a third new chapter added to the two originally written nearly 16 years earlier, *The Rabbi of Bacherach* was now 'a fragment' of a novel. Heine was aware that the new chapter did not quite come up to the gripping evocation of 'the great Jewish sorrow' he had achieved in the first part by mingling stories of the ancient Exodus with blood libel in the setting of a Passover feast. His mind was on his *Ludwig Börne*, which was about to appear. By comparison to that, the *Salon IV* was a tame book, so tame that Heine in fact urged his publisher to issue it simultaneously with *Börne*, 'so that this scandal-book, this roaring lion, may drag the innocent lamb which is Salon IV along behind him.'

Heine was obviously aware of the provocative character of his *Börne* book and fully prepared for its stirring up a hue and cry. About to leave for his annual holiday at Granville, he wrote Campe with affected calm: 'I leave that book to its fate. Let it bite its way forward in the world. It was born with teeth.' The book, however, was fated to bite back. *Ludwig Börne* was to unleash a controversy that continued into the 20th century, with two such figures as Thomas Mann and Karl Kraus taking opposite sides.

The *Börne* book and its stormy aftermath did not, however, deflect Heine's attention from the French scene, and throughout this period he continued his regular correspondence for the *Allgemeine Zeitung*. The articles he wrote for this paper for altogether three and a half years between 1840 and 1844 – later collected in two volumes under the title *Lutezia* (the German spelling of the ancient Latin name of Paris) – reflected the political-social problems and intellectual currents that were increasingly agitating France at the beginning of the second decade of Louis-Philippe's reign. Heine was to claim for *Lutezia* the merit of 'an historical document in my pithiest style' on the developments that set the stage for the fall of the 'bourgeois' monarchy, and it has indeed been hailed as one of his most important books.

As early as December 1841, almost two years after his visit to the angry workers of the Faubourg Saint-Marceau, Heine was informing the readers of the *Allgemeine Zeitung* that 'the propaganda of Communism speaks a universal language as simple and elementary as hunger, as envy, as death. It is a language that can be quickly learnt by every people.' In the same article, noting the 'colourful bounty' of New Year's gifts beckoning from shop-windows in the rue Vivienne and elsewhere – 'luxury articles and objets d'art... gold, silver, bronze, precious stones... in the imitation Renaissance style which is the ruling fashion of the moment' – he remarked with mock modesty that even a casual boulevard *flaneur* like him and 'no great politician' could descry an impending cataclysm in the sullen, menacing mien of the people walking the streets. 'The cult of materialism, of self-seeking, of money', he wrote, was leading to the moral and political disintegration of French society, causing 'the dissolution of all bonds of ideas and the extinction of the last bit of communal spirit.' The result was that 'the Chamber of Deputies, like the whole of French society, has become fragmented into so many factions and splinters that no two people any longer agree on any issue... so that there is never a vote expressing anything like a general will without which no representative system can function.'[25]

While pointing at the same vices and corruption which Balzac was unmasking in novel after novel, Heine informed the German public on 11 December 1841 of his 'firm conviction' – well before the February revolution which was to topple Louis-Philippe, and to pit brother against brother in the all-European civil wars of 1848–49 – that 'sooner or later the whole bourgeois comedy in France, together with its parliamentary superstars and its whole cast of extras, will come to a horrendous bad end.' Deliberately using stage terms, he added: 'Then an Epilogue will be played, its name: The Communist Regimen!' Although at the time he expected it to be of short duration, he foresaw that it would 'mightily shake and purify all souls. It will be a genuine tragedy.'[26]

Heine was, of course, not the only one to see the demoralizing, not to say soul-destroying effect which a decade of bourgeois rule was having on France, its people and institutions. In May 1840 Victor Hugo published *Les Rayons et les ombres*, a collection of poems in which he dwelt, among other themes, on the dry, drab cynical materialism that seemed to have done away with all faith and every value and ideal once held by Frenchmen. Mechanically they continued to go to church, but they had lost faith in religion. Caught in their material pursuits, not only piety but any feeling for beauty and the sublime seemed to have gone out of their lives. In one poem Hugo complained that men's hearts were no longer moved by 'the dawn, or the lily; neither angel nor child' evoked any shining response in them. Calling on God to contemplate 'the blind', lustreless 'men of this age',[27] he apostrophized the deity: 'Extinguish your suns, or rekindle their flame! Take back your world, or give them back a soul!'

It was Heine who pointed out the political and social implications of Hugo's remarks: 'The French ship of state has had too many holes bored into its bottom by the silently gnawing teeth of mice', he observed in December 1841. Speaking of 'the destructive doctrines rampant among the lower classes', he warned that it was 'no longer a matter of equal rights, but of equality of enjoyment on this earth. Some 400,000 raw fists in Paris are only waiting for the slogan to turn the idea of absolute equality into reality.' The idea that men were no longer ready to wait for the Kingdom of Heaven, but were claiming the good things in life in the here and now, was something that neither the King who thought he knew 'how to manage' the French nor his Ministers took into account. In 1840 the first newspaper written 'by workers for workers', *L'Atelier*, made its appearance for the avowed purpose of exposing in 'detail the vices of our social organization and the reasons why the workers die of hunger by the side of immense fortunes.' About the same time, the lawyer and journalist Louis Blanc came up with the novel postulate – in an essay titled *Organisation du travail* ('The Organization of Labour') – that everyone's 'right to work' was a basic right.

It followed that society not only had to provide its members with the necessary education to develop useful skills, but that the state actually bore some responsibility for the material welfare of its citizens, a pre-Marxian notion that was to become part of subsequent Socialist theory and to be 'accepted in some degree by all democratic industrial societies.'[28] For a start, Louis Blanc proposed the immediate establishment of state-subsidized 'social workshops', or industrial co-operatives, to inaugurate a type of 'revolution by consent' which he hoped would in time lead to a full-blown co-operative society, eliminating capitalism without bloodshed or pains in a democratic republic.

Organisation du Travail was confiscated by the police on suspicion that its 'revolutionary' contents threatened public order. Heine, the great debunker, ran into Louis Blanc and was quick to light up the moral absurdity of the situation in an apt phrase, congratulating him on becoming 'the most guillotinable man in France.'[29] Once the authorities realized that the book was actually meant to avert revolution, *Organisation du Travail* with its message that everyone had 'the right to work' was reprinted many times.

While Louis Blanc's advocacy of universal suffrage and social and political reforms won him increasing popularity among the workers, his *Histoire de dix ans*, a remarkably well-written critique of the first decade of the July monarchy, published in 1840, earned him the respect of political and intellectual circles. But his plan for establishing 'social workshops' was to be put to a severe test in 1848, when he became a member of the French Provisional Government.

It was also in 1840 that Pierre-Joseph Proudhon, a 31-year-old printer, published a book-length memorandum, dedicated to the Academy of Besançon, whose rhetorical title, *Qu'est ce que la propriété?* (What is Property?), he answered with the resounding proposition: 'Property is theft!'"

Becoming known simply as *What is Property? Theft!*, Proudhon's book was promptly disowned by the Besançon Academy, which only the year before had awarded him a three-year scholarship of 1,500 francs a year to enable him to study in Paris. The embarrassed Academy asked him to delete his dedication in any further editions and announced that he would be summoned to Besançon to explain his 'anti-social doctrines' at a public hearing. As the provincial scandal spread to Paris, the Minister of Justice, Monsieur Vivien – pressed by demands to have Proudhon prosecuted – took the unusual course of reading the book himself. He was sufficiently impressed by its quality to request the Paris Académie des sciences morales et politiques to help him decide whether it had any scholarly value or was a seditious political tract. Proudhon's public appearance before the Academy of Besançon was to take place only in January 1841 and the question of his prosecution – not to mention the continuation of his scholarship grant – remained in abeyance until the following spring.

In the same year, Etienne Cabet published his *Voyage en Icarie* – written in London and first issued in 1839 under a different title[30] – and placed before the French public his vision of an ideal Communist republic in which all means of production were owned by the state, and everyone, physicians and cobblers, received an equal wage. And again in the same year, George Sand, moved by the suffering of the poverty-stricken workers, published – much to the horror of her friends and the delight of her critics and jealous rivals – the first of several 'Communist' or 'Socialist' novels, the two terms being at the time so vague and undefined as to be interchangeable.

For all the inflammatory ring of *What is Property? Theft!*, Proudhon did not attack all forms of private property. He was in favour of people owning their homes, gardens and small plots – 'three acres and a cow' – but against excessive property acquired without effort through title or inheritance. This he considered property which encouraged idleness and/or exploitation and became a source of multiplying wealth, and through it, of socially immoral power and privilege. Property, however, was an absolute right anchored – along with liberty, equality and security – in the 1793 Charter of the French Revolution and the Code Napoléon. Proudhon could argue that the property system created an inherent inequality, but all legal and economic philosophy at the time was against him; property, moreover, had become (as it still is) an integral part of the social order. Proudhon also attacked the wage system, pointing out that workers were being paid individually but not for the 'surplus value' of the 'simultaneous convergence of their efforts': 'Two hundred grenadiers raised the obelisk of Luxor on its plinth. Could a single man working for two hundred days have accomplished that? Yet by the capitalist's accounting, the sum of wages would be the same.'

An autodidact, Proudhon had taught himself Latin, Greek and Hebrew, and later cited as his chief sources of inspiration 'the Bible first, Adam Smith next, and eventually Hegel'. To achieve prominence as a self-styled 'anarchist' fiercely opposed to institutions and all authority, whether by the state, by capitalism or by centralized Communism, Proudhon thought little of science and regarded industrial progress and the advance of technology as an evil. He placed individual liberty and equality above everything and proposed a federalist system of workers' and producers' associations that would fight the encroachments of 'the tyrant state', abolish the wage system, prevent the excesses of capitalism and its accumulation of political power, and otherwise protect the interests of middle- and lower-class professionals, artisans, farmers and small proprietors.

Combative to a degree, he argued volubly during his appearance before the Academy of Besançon on 15 January 1841 that the views expressed in *What is Property? Theft!* represented the inchoate feelings of millions. The members of the Academy present were divided among themselves, and intimidated by his fierce rhetoric – he threatened, among other things, to take the case to the newspapers and make them all look ridiculous – formally voted 16 to 14 to annul his scholarship; since discontinuing it required a two-thirds majority, this meant in fact that he was to go on receiving it for the period stipulated. A couple of months later, Professor Adolphe Blanqui, a distinguished political economist, submitted to the Minister of Justice his report on Proudhon's book on behalf of the Paris Académie des sciences morales et politiques.

Professor Blanqui – a brother of Auguste, the leader of 'the Seasons' whose death sentence had been commuted to life imprisonment – was a staunch upholder of the property system, but a fair-minded man. After an inner debate which gave him two sleepless and 'terrible' nights he declared that, for all its crude approach and aggressive tone, *What is Property? Theft!* was a scholarly *dissertation d'académie*, 'and not at all an incendiary pamphlet'. With the King's Prosecutor thus staved off, the Professor sent a long letter to Proudhon in which he paid him an unexpected compliment: 'You have done for property what Rousseau did eighty years ago for literature.' While vindicating the principle of property, Blanqui admitted that many abuses committed in its name required correction, but cautioned Proudhon to beware lest his vigorous social 'metaphysics' be misused by street-corner demagogues to incite the starving to pillage and pilfering.

Far from moderating his convictions or his tone, Proudhon not only published Blanqui's letter but by the end of the year followed it up with a pamphlet – *Warning to Proprietors* – threatening them and the governing bodies that unless they introduced social equality and stopped 'levying tribute' from the workers 'on the plea of functional inferiority' the consequences would be so terrible that assassination, pillage, insurrection, general strike, arson and even regicide would pale by comparison.

This time his printing shop, which was nearly bankrupt, was promptly raided by the police, and the pamphlet confiscated. Hauled before the Assize Court on charges of inciting against the government and the constitutional right of property, Proudhon resorted to self-styled 'judicial mystification', couching his defence in language so abstruse that it all became 'a paté of indigestible political economy'. The upshot was that the prosecutor, the judge and the jury – and to add a farcical element, his own lawyer – all declared that the arguments were above their heads, and the text of the pamphlet itself was hardly looked into.

Left to decide 'whether there was a philosophic bottom to my doctrine', as Proudhon triumphantly reported the success of his tactic, the jury found it impossible to be sure that 'this man working in a field of ideas inaccessible to ordinary people' was guilty, and acquitted him.

Proudhon's opposition to the concentration of all means of production in the hands of the proletariat, or any single class, for fear that it would produce a dictatorship, was later to be savagely attacked by Karl Marx. Nonetheless, Proudhon was to achieve considerable influence as the father of the so-called Syndicalist movement, which persists to this day in France and some of the Latin countries.

Etienne Cabet, born at Dijon in 1788, was – like Proudhon – a cooper's son. But he belonged to an older generation, and after studying law on a scholarship, he had reached Paris as a young barrister after Napoleon's fall. Although, like most of the other early Socialists, he had been a member of the secret Carbonari – rising in fact to a high position in the Supreme Vente, Council or Lodge (from the Italian *vendita*) of the French Charbonnerie – he had turned away from its violent methods. The Charbonnerie's insurrections had played a part in the ousting of Charles X, and under Louis-Philippe Cabet had become

Secretary General of the Ministry of Justice. Subsequently elected to the Chamber of Deputies, he had by 1834 become so disenchanted with the July monarchy and started to attack it so violently in his newspaper *Le Populaire* that, to escape imprisonment, he had been forced to flee to Belgium, was expelled from there, but then found asylum in England.

Cabet spent most of the years 1834–39 closeted in the Reading Room of the British Museum, writing *Voyage to Icaria*, about an imaginary island whose inhabitants lived in bliss and prosperity in a 'Communist' republic. He knew Thomas More's *Utopia*, but whereas More in 1516 had conjured up an imaginary republic in order to satirize government malpractice, religious intolerance and general human folly, the purpose of Cabet's work was to demonstrate that his particular vision of a society based on 'a community of goods' was a practical proposition. The mythical Communist state of Icaria owned all the means of production and used them according to a planned economic schedule to create a world of plenty. In line with Saint-Simon's ideas of industrial mass-production, Cabet wrote that if a certain article was needed, 100,000 workers detached from the labour force produced it simply by increasing 'the daily period of general work by a mere five minutes'. He objected, however, to the inequality created by Saint-Simon's meritocracy of talent. In Icaria everyone received an equal wage: 'Not everyone can be a doctor, and since some want to be cobblers' and the world needs them, 'it follows that cobblers deserve to be as happy and satisfied as doctors.'

In his obsession with egalitarianism, Cabet carried it to the point of absolute uniformity – to follow the example of Icaria, everybody would live in the same type of houses, use the same furniture, the same curtains and carpets, wear the same clothes, eat, work and sleep at the same time. Although the citizens of Icaria elected a National Assembly whose laws and decisions had to be approved every 4 months by democratic committees – thus ostensibly enabling citizens to exercise their 'share of sovereignty' – these committees did not really amount to representative government. In practice, the National Assembly, acting in the name of 'popular judgment', decided what made the people happy, and Cabet proposed 'the absolute necessity that society concentrate, direct and dispose of everything and that it submit all wills and action to its rule, its order and its discipline.'

Whether, as has been said, this was an early omen of Communist totalitarianism, or merely the fantasy of an authoritarian temperament and 'literary dictator' ruminating alone in a library in a foreign country, Cabet, who had fought hard in France for freedom of the press and other libertarian causes, now veered towards curtailing the freedom of the individual for the sake of a higher cause.

At the same time it must be remembered that to unemployed workers in 'the hungry forties' the prospect of equal housing, furniture, food, however uniform – and to their wives the promise of 'hats, berets, turbans, bonnets', feathers and artificial jewelry, mass-produced but designed by fashion experts and competing in elegance with those worn by the rich – represented not only an upward step, but luxury and dreamland with all its attractions. Indeed, starting in 1840, Cabet's 600-page *Voyage en Icarie* ran to 6 editions. Next to Louis Blanc's *Organisation du travail*, it became one of the most popular Socialist books of the decade in France, and was translated into English, German and Spanish.

Icaria was built out of a strange mélange of ideas and influences, including Rousseau's belief that man's nature was intrinsically good and perfectible, Saint-Simon's faith in the blessings of mass production, and Robert Owen's determination to change the prevailing conditions and revolutionize society at one blow, not by arms but by 'practical example and persuasion'.

In later developments, Robert Owen was to go over to Paris to help raise funds and supporters for Cabet to set up his dreamt-of Icaria on actual soil – not in France, but (like most of these experiments) across the Atlantic. By the end of the 1840s, Cabet was buying the Mormon town of Nauvoo on the Mississippi, where Joseph Smith, the founder of the Church of Latter-Day Saints, had recently been killed. Cabet was there with a large group of Frenchmen, making a start to implement his ideas, only to find that his authoritarian temperament worked against him.

In *Voyage to Icaria* he had written that in that ideal republic 'everyone goes to bed at ten and from ten to five o'clock in the morning the streets are deserted', adding significantly: 'Such a curfew imposed by a tyrant would be an intolerable vexation, but adopted by an entire people in the interests of its health and of good order in work, it is the most reasonable and useful of our laws.'

Whereas it had been pardonable for a man fantasizing in the British Museum to regulate life in his fictional Icaria and to prescribe that 'in the interests of the people' everyone there 'eats from two to three', etc., at Nauvoo Cabet's prohibition of alcohol and tobacco and his attempts to regiment food habits and sexual mores were to lead to his being expelled from his own Icarian community shortly before his death at the age of 68.

In 1840 George Sand was a European cult figure, having already produced some 20 of the nearly 100 novels – not counting the 20 volumes of her *Histoire de ma vie* – that she was to publish during her lifetime. Although not many of them compared with *Lélia*, her early and much-discussed masterpiece, they dealt not only with love and human passions, but echoed, in Ernest Renan's later phrase, all that the age 'hoped for, thought, felt and suffered'. At that, her adoption of the supposedly male pseudonym of 'G Sand', her unconventional ideas, striking, sometimes masculine dress and emancipated 'feminist' notions – coupled, needless to say, with stories of her love-affairs with a string of such public figures as Alfred de Musset, Michel de Bourges, Mallefille, Chopin – not only fed Paris gossip but added to the curiosity and conversation of intellectuals, social reformers and socialites in drawing-rooms all over Europe.

Heine in 1840 called George Sand a 'champion of social revolution'. Indeed, in view of the glaring misery of the unemployed, it was almost inevitable that after her boldly frank discussion of the inferior social status of that other 'half of humanity' – the women – George Sand, whose 'great-hearted, generous nature' impressed even Balzac, would sooner rather than later take up the cause of the oppressed common people. Balzac, incidentally, after visiting her at Nohant, stuck to his notion that 'to emancipate women means their ruin', and concluded that Sand 'has the characteristics of a man, ergo she is not a woman.' Heine, for his part, maintaining the mystery of her identity to the uninitiated among his readers in Germany, referred to her in his articles in the third person masculine.

'The novels of this daring author have displeased both the aristocracy and the bourgeoisie,' he wrote à propos the premiere of her play *Cosima* at the Théâtre Français in April 1840, in which she was expected to announce her new social views. The aristocracy, he explained, feared that 'with his "irreligious" views' Sand was going to attack the Church, its bulwark against republicanism, while the bourgeoisie felt threatened by 'his immoral principles' and feared an attack on matrimony.[31] *Cosima*, however, left both institutions alone and contained no social message. This was to come a few months after the insipid play flopped disastrously, causing George Sand the loss of a considerable sum she had invested in its production.

'Madame Sand is going over to Communism, and is undertaking to preach to the workers,' Sainte-Beuve wrote sarcastically that August, shortly after she published *Le Compagnon du Tour de France*. This was the first of three novels – the others were to be *Horace* (1842) and *Le Meunier d'Angibault* (1845) – in which she depicted a journeyman-carpenter, a miller, a mason and other hard-working proletarian heroes as paragons of virtue, kindness and manly fortitude, and contrasted their well-spent lives with the selfishness and hypocrisy of contemporary French society. Dwelling on the justifiable rage of the worker with his 'hideous sores, his horrible illnesses and his vermin', she reminded the bourgeois who washed their hands of 'the terrible fact of poverty' that once the grime was removed from these dregs of society they would discover that 'there are not two peoples, there is only one!'

Idealizing 'the people', she was to encourage a dozen manual workers – including a cobbler, a locksmith, a barber and a baker – to write verse, and to proclaim that a mason by the name of Poncy had it in him to be the greatest poet in France. Her aspiration, she told the realistic Balzac, was 'to depict man as I wish he should be, as I think he ought to be,' an aspiration matching Saint-Simon's formula that all men must be given 'the fullest latitude for the development of their faculties.' Saint-Simon's criticism of the institution of marriage, except as a voluntary union between two compatible characters, coupled with the demand of his followers for universal suffrage, including that of women – who were not to get the vote in France until a century later, in 1945 – could not but touch a deep chord in George Sand. As early as 1832, in *Indiana*, she had first raised the flag of revolt against 'the injustice and barbarity of those laws which still govern women in marriage, in the family, and in society.'

During her infatuation with the lawyer Michel de Bourges, she had fought hard to resist the inflammatory ideas of this hotheaded republican advocate of violent revolution. For a time, she had embraced the pure-hearted but simplistic gospel of the Abbé de Lamennais. In the end, earnestly looking for a solution to the social problem in the welter of confusing and confused panaceas being offered on all sides, she had turned for enlightenment – much to the Abbé's annoyance – to that early apostle of Socialism, Pierre Leroux.

The founder and former editor of *Le Globe*, Leroux had by 1840 achieved the reputation of a philosopher. A stout widower with a 'big, knobbly head, a lopsided face' and a brood of children, he had edited several encyclopaedias and was working on a 'system' – on which he published two volumes in 1841[32] – romantically combining elements of Christian brotherhood with such secular ideas as democracy, social equality, the redistribution of wealth, and the civic as well as sexual equality of women. This system or 'new religion', which he called Communism, and sometimes Communionism, was bound to appeal to the great emancipator that George Sand was; and indeed, some 10 years later, Leroux introduced the first bill to give women the right to vote at least in municipal elections.

'Very dirty' and 'dingy-looking', according to most accounts, Leroux was charitably described by Heine as an unrefined 'angular figure which never acquired any grace', but an excellent man withal. George Sand kept assuring her wagging friends that her relations with the ungainly Leroux were 'not the sort of equivocal infatuation which frivolous women feel for their doctors or spiritual directors', nor of the type akin to her love-affair with Chopin, but perhaps the most serious act of faith in all her life. Captivated by his gospel and 'the bright glow of his mind', she claimed that theirs was a miracle of 'spiritual

657

love', called Leroux 'a new Plato, a new Christ', and became his devoted hand-maiden, propagating his ideas with all the energy and passion of which she was capable.

The Abbé de Lamennais, during his 4-months stint as editor of *Le Monde* in 1837, had refused to publish an article by George Sand on 'The Role of Passion in a Woman's Life' and would not hear of opening the paper's columns to Leroux's purported new 'religion... especially since his well-known views include the opinion that Jesus Christ sanctioned adultery.' Nor would Buloz, the editor of the *Revue des Deux Mondes*, who had done much to help George Sand's literary career, have anything to do with him or his writings. Calling a plague on both their houses, she impulsively decided to undertake the financial risk of founding a periodical to provide her grimy philosopher-friend with an independent platform of his own.

The *Revue indépendante* was founded in the summer of 1841 at her beloved country estate in Nohant, where first Leroux and next Louis Viardot arrived for longer or shorter vacations. Viardot, long-time manager of the Théâtre Italien, had recently resigned to become the impresario of his newly wedded wife, the rising 21-year-old opera star Pauline Viardot-Garcia. Twice Pauline's age, Viardot dabbled in Left-wing politics. While she made music or played billiards with Chopin, Sand, Viardot and Leroux made detailed plans for the establishment of the new periodical, complete with a press of its own.

Lamennais greeted the appearance of the *Revue indépendante* in November 1841 with the remark: 'Madame Sand... faithful to her new prophet, is busy preaching Communism.' The serialization of her proletarian novel *Horace* before its publication in book form assured the new revue a certain interest in literary circles, but not for long. Her 'Communist' novels, too, were to cost George Sand a temporary decline in popularity.

Although Lamartine declared that 'Pierre Leroux will one day be read as Rousseau's Contrat Social is read today', Sainte-Beuve cynically observed that 'he flounders about in philosophy like a buffalo in a bog'. Leroux was fated to be similarly treated by posterity, which at times has overrated his importance as a social thinker and philosopher of history, and at others underplayed it. As for the element that attracted George Sand to him, Heine left perhaps the best clue when he described Leroux as an authentic 'son of the people... not merely a thinking but a feeling philosopher', one combining a mind capable of rising to 'the highest speculation' with a heart that had 'plumbed to the full' the depths of the people's woes, and in a sense personified them. Leroux was very poor and made a virtue of austerity. George Sand was moved by the proud stoicism with which he bore his lot, though he accepted money from her to help support his family. Admiring his ascetic self-denial while exerting himself on behalf of mankind, and enthralled by his humanist, Christian-Socialist brand of Communism, she saw in him nothing less than a saint.

Heine, though he praised Leroux's selfless efforts on behalf of the lower classes, was only too well aware that he lacked method. So far, he wrote, Leroux had only assembled the material and 'scattered building blocks for a Communist or any system or religion.' Leroux was to play a role during the 1848 revolution in Paris, as were Louis Blanc, Proudhon, Barbès and Martin Bernard – the two former associates of Blanqui's – while George Sand was to become virtual Minister of Propaganda of the provisional republican government.

Even before that, Leroux, among his 'building blocks', launched a new Socialist slogan which was to prove of more worth than a brick of gold. He adapted Saint-Simon's original formula – 'To each according to his capacity', placing the accent on merit – to read: 'From each according to his ability, to each according to his work.'

Louis Blanc, retaining the first part, was to give the second its final egalitarian stamp – 'To each according to his needs' – the two parts together making up the slogan which Marxism was to emblazon on the future edifice of Socialism.

While the best minds in France were preoccupied with these problems, in censorship-ridden Prussia even the word 'social' was forbidden in the press. No event could more suitably have inaugurated 'the extraordinary decade' in Germany than the death in June 1840 of Prussia's King Friedrich Wilhelm III and the ascension to the throne of his son, 45-year-old Friedrich Wilhelm IV. Unlike his father, who had started his rule in 1797 and was thus a vestige of the age of absolutism and old-world reaction, the new King had often, during his long years as Crown Prince, spoken of the need for national unity, of liberty, democratic principles and freedom of speech. In 1840 Prussia had none of these – no national parliament, no free newspapers or uncensored books, no public meetings, performances or academic institutions which were not supervised; no platform, in short, where political or social issues could be openly aired.

Instead, she had 8 provincial Diets packed with noblemen and big landowners, including – besides certain princes who had hereditary seats – dukes, knights and wealthy Junkers with huge estates. Legislation being entirely the King's prerogative, the Diets had only advisory powers. The King, anyway, convened them irregularly at his pleasure; and as details of their proceedings were not communicated to the press, all but their decisions remained hidden from the public.

The new King was known to be intellectually gifted, eloquent and witty, interested in science, art, architecture, antiquities, music and poetry. Expectations therefore ran high that, being so much more susceptible than his father to new ideas and the needs of the age, he would at last make good his father's promise – solemnly given in 1815, after Waterloo, and several times repeated before his death, but never kept – to grant his subjects a representative constitution. With the beginnings of industrialization, especially in the annexed Rhineland, a wealthy new middle class as well as the free professions resented their exclusion even from the sham 'Diets', while the liberal intelligentsia fretted at the amount of censorship and official thought-control. Although this varied in the rest of the three dozen German states, the situation in some of them was not much better. Their burghers looked for leadership to Prussia, which claimed to be the most advanced and enlightened of them all.

All accounts of Friedrich Wilhelm IV present him as a well-meaning, personally 'brilliant' autocrat, but wayward, erratic and attracted by an idealized, incurably romantic vision of Prussia as a glorious medieval Christian State. 'The Romantic at odds with his age', in Golo Mann's phrase, 'he wanted to rule with the consent of the people', but according to his own notion of it as a feudally hierarchic 'society... of happy peasants, honest townsmen, pious clergy, faithful nobles, the prince among his vassals.'[33]

Nothing, however, completely explains or so well illustrates his peculiar and frequently wrong-headed way of responding to the new realities of his time than the view he took of his position as 'King by the Grace of God'. Pious by nature, raised in his father's mystic conceptions, he took this formula to mean, first, that his responsibilities, though heavy, were to God alone, and secondly, that his very office endowed him with exalted faculties and God-given wisdom. God, he once candidly remarked to one of his intimates, 'has endowed the King with supernatural powers, which miraculously elevate him high above anyone else, be he ever so high-placed or the most trusted confidant',[34] making it clear that this superiority of monarchs applied to both their intellectual powers and their emotional make-up. And to his friend Carl von Bunsen, the Prussian Ambassador to London, he intimated that 'there are things which one only gets to know as king'. His personal aide-de-camp, Von Gerlach, noted that the King regarded him as well as his Ministers as so many 'dunces, because in transacting practical current affairs with him', none of them was able to rise to 'his sublime train of thought' or to follow its byways.[35]

Friedrich Wilhelm IV had been 11 years old at the time of the Prussian defeat at Jena, when Napoleon's entry into Berlin had forced his parents and the entire royal household to flee in haste to the far end of East Prussia. A highly impressionable child, he had early imbibed the notion that the French Revolution and all that Napoleon represented were evil, and he developed an unshakable faith in the old order and the sanctity of the royal office. His reliance on divine inspiration and the patronizing, patriarchal attitude towards his people that he brought to the throne were compounded by the impulses of an unsteady character whose moods changed from periods of indecision to misplaced obstinacy.

The extent to which the King's make-up rebelled against the very notion of granting a constitution was to become evident during the events of the 1848–49 revolution. Unable to stomach the idea of 'a piece of paper with lots of paragraphs being inserted like a second Providence' between him, the ruler by God's grace, and his people,[36] he dallied and dithered so long before, under the pressure of those 'horrible' events, he could bring himself to permit the discussion of a constitution that by the time he did so the first all-German parliament was assembling at Frankfurt.

When this so-called National Assembly, after protracted discussions, voted to offer him the crown of emperor of a reorganized and united Germany, Friedrich Wilhelm IV – not many years before he would have to abdicate because of mental derangement and *Gehirnschwäche* ('weakness of the brain') – rejected the dream of a united Germany because accepting the crown from a 'gaggle' of professors and democratic politicians, and not from the hands of princes equal to him in rank, would have meant abdicating the divine right of kings and recognizing the sovereignty of the people.

While this was in the future, the King from the beginning pursued such a zigzag course that it was to take his subjects and the rest of Germany a year or two to make out what he wanted or stood for. Indeed, Metternich was soon to remark that there 'is a distinction between what the King wants today and what he will do tomorrow.'

The King's first step – an amnesty he granted to all political offenders – seemed, however, to justify the hope that he was inaugurating a new era of liberalism. A speech he made shortly after his coronation to the provincial Diet of East Prussia was greeted with jubilation. The deputies assembled at the castle in Königsberg having submitted to him a carefully phrased petition for a constitution, the new monarch rose from his throne, advanced to the edge of the balcony overlooking the throng that packed the courtyard below, and raising his right arm as if taking an oath, swore to be a just and merciful Christian king. He spoke and spoke, and finally rose to a peroration in which he called on God, 'for the benefit of Germany and the world, to preserve our Prussian fatherland, manifold and yet one, like that precious metal, which, made by the fusion of many, is but one and all the more precious – subject to no other rust than that of the centuries which renders it fairer still!'[37]

Although there was no mention of a constitution in these bombastic phrases, they had an intoxicating effect and electrified the country. In the general excitement, the lack of substance in the King's rhetoric passed unnoticed. All he had in fact told, or meant to tell, the deputies was that, on the subject of making the Diet more representative, they could have full confidence in his intentions. Burghers throughout the German lands, however, moved by the royal eloquence, construed the King's words to imply the promise of a constitution. Although his inclinations were literary and artistic rather than military, his impulsiveness was such that once – while taking part as Crown Prince in some army manoeuvres – he had been so carried away by the military music and the clang of arms that he continued the exercise into the outskirts of Berlin, oblivious to the panic and hundreds of shattered windows caused by the blast of his cannon.

Similarly, he had been carried away at Königsberg by his bent for elocution. The spectacle of an absolutist ruler making public speeches to his subjects was so unusual, and so elated the Germans, that the Court chancellery was forced to issue a communiqué dispelling any misconception that 'His All-Highest Majesty' had promised to grant anything like a representative constitution.

But the King went on speechifying. On one solemn occasion, to please his hankering for all things medieval, an army parade was followed by a march-past of the guilds with their old flags and traditional symbols. It began to rain, and while inside Berlin's castle Prussia's princes, dukes and high clergy were swearing loyalty to the King, the city and provincial representatives waiting to take the oath in the Lustgarten Square outside were being soaked in the downpour together with a huge crowd of spectators.

A grotesque scene ensued. The King finally appeared on a balcony and began to harangue the people who had been waiting for two hours in the whipping rain with a long address. The crowd saw him gesticulating, but could not hear his words in the pelting rain. Whenever he seemed to pause, the multitude, hoping that he had finished, burst into loud cheers. Four times they shouted their hurrahs, but each time the King motioned that he had more to say. He did not finish before he had raised his right arm and called in a crescendo voice: 'I shall keep my vow uttered here and in Königsberg, so help me God! In witness whereof I raise my right arm to the heaven!... and may the fructifying rain of God bless this hour!'[38]

The impromptu allusion to the weather did nothing to reduce the bathos of the occasion or the uncertainty about whether the King had promised anything – and if so, what. If anything, Berliners began to suspect that meaningless declamations passed with their new monarch for deeds.

Karl Marx was in Berlin at the time, and working on his doctoral dissertation on a subject which we may for the moment short-title as 'Epicurean Philosophy'. He was 22, and had 5 years of university studies behind him, one at Bonn and 4 in Berlin. By way of preliminary research he was as usual filling 7 copybooks with notes on, and lengthy excerpts in Greek and Latin from, the works of some 60 authors: starting with Aeschylus, Anaxagoras, Aristotle, their long list ranged through every letter of the alphabet to Cicero, Democritus, Epicurus, Hesiod, Heraclitus, on to Plutarch, Pythagoras, Seneca, Socrates, Tacitus, Thales, Xenophanes and Zeno.

Dr Bruno Bauer, the moving spirit of the Berlin Doctors Club, which Marx had joined a couple of years earlier, had been urging him on for months to take his final examination in Berlin and to proceed with the dissertation.

Bauer himself was no longer in Berlin. This principled theologian and philosopher, whose book on the Gospel of St John, published in 1840, was soon to be confiscated, had been penalized for his increasingly outspoken criticism of religion and his quarrels with Hengstenberg, the powerful Dean of Berlin's Theological Faculty. A sympathetic Minister, Altenstein, who had more than once bailed him out of trouble with his superior, had in 1839 considered promoting him to a professorship. Bauer's bellicosity, however, had antagonized most or all of his faculty colleagues, and by autumn 1839 Altenstein had decided to transfer him to a lectureship at Bonn to keep him out of harm's way. Bauer now hoped to be able to install the young Marx in a lecturer's chair in Bonn, and had plans and expectations for the two of them to do 'great things' together, though he was also advising the young doctorant that 'it would be foolish of you to devote yourself to a practical career. Theory is now the strongest practice'.[39] Bauer kept bombarding Marx with the idea that the growing collision between state and science had now reached the point where a catastrophe was in the offing. He was referring to the so-called *Kirchenstreit*, or 'Church dispute', which had been agitating Germany since the 1837 arrest by the Prussian authorities of Cologne's Archbishop Droste zu Vischering. The archbishop's transfer to a Prussian fortress – the most sensational event of its kind since Napoleon had kidnapped the Pope – and his continued detention for insisting that the children of mixed Protestant-Catholic marriages must be raised in the latter faith had naturally become a source of festering conflict with the Vatican, and thus had a political side to it. But it was not that side that Bauer had in mind when he spoke of a catastrophe.

Bauer called the clash of problems faced by Prussia a battle between state and science because one of the Prussian demands made to Droste before he was charged with high treason had been that the training of priests be transferred from his seminaries to the largely Catholic but state-controlled theological faculty at Bonn. Georg Hermes, the head of that ostensibly more enlightened and 'scientific' faculty, had been enlisted to help the prolonged diplomatic effort to settle the conflict between Prussia and Pope Gregory XVI.

663

Hermes had done his bit by proclaiming that Catholic dogma, far from being in disaccord with Kant's philosophy, actually conformed to it. To Bauer, needless to say, this was neither philosophy nor science, but a perversion of both. It triggered a peculiar phenomenon. The chief issue that was to preoccupy Prussia's new King and his subjects between 1840 and 1843, besides the vexing problem of the constitution, concerned neither any direct criticism of the King's policies nor, for that matter, a temporary flare-up of border tension with France during the 'Oriental crisis'. Rather, and significantly, what developed was a veritable battle over questions pertaining to the sphere of philosophy and metaphysics.

Bauer was in the forefront of this battle. Its eruption was not so surprising in view of the fact that it was in philosophy that Prussia, more than any other country, had found the strongest support for its absolutism. The battle was between the upholders of Hegel's 'royal state philosophy' – claiming to represent the apex of human thought and the ultimate in 'science' – and various groups of the 'Left' or Young Hegelian critics of the master.

Hegel had made his pronouncement that society, as expressed in the state, was the embodiment of Absolute Reason, to which the individual must necessarily submit as 'the only framework' assuring his 'freedom through the rule of law' in the years after the Congress of Vienna had restored the old reactionary order in Europe. By comparison, Prussia might at the time have appeared to him a progressive state. Hegel had also legitimized the king as the personification both of the state's 'reason' and of the people's sovereignty, and had made yet a third relevant pronouncement – to the effect that world-history had reached its highest stage in Western civilization, or, as he called it, 'the Germanic world'. Although Hegel had said before his death that he had in mind 'the perfect state', all universities had gone on invoking this 'royal state philosophy' as the ultimate proof that Prussia remained both the most rational and the most liberal of European nations.

The situation in 1840 was that the academic old guard of orthodox Hegelians of the Right continued to maintain that Hegel had reconciled all contradictions between religion, history, philosophy and the state, and that his all-embracing 'world-historical system' was final; whereas the young Left guard argued that precisely because it had achieved all that was possible in theory, 'philosophy must now descend into the battlefield of practice and deal concretely with life and social conditions.' This was the cry, launched in 1838 by August von Cieszkowski, which Moses Hess in 1840 was busy developing into a 'philosophy of action'.

Bauer, for his part, was ridiculing the orthodox Hegelian academics for dwelling like 'blissful gods in patriarchal tranquillity in the realm of the Idea' bequeathed to them by Hegel. Bauer not only felt that they were living in a fool's paradise; he knew that Germany was entering upon a period of extraordinary intellectual ferment. For one thing, working as he was on his Criticism of the Synoptic Gospels, he was himself preparing to raise a storm by presenting Jesus as the fictional creation of writers in Alexandria and Rome. Bauer was well aware that to do so in the 'Christian-German' state of Prussia, where the Established Church and the state were closely intertwined, was tantamount to attacking the state itself. The storm might cost him his last academic post. But Bauer, whom Bonn's small, largely Catholic theological faculty treated with the mistrust due to one of the new-fangled Young Hegelian 'heretics' and troublemakers, was prepared to face the consequences.

For another thing, he was at this point convinced that philosophy had a topical message to offer, carrying a mighty revolutionary power and unique appeal. A brilliant philosopher, proud but humiliated, he was forced at Bonn to conceal the revolution he was preparing by dismissing Jesus as a fictional figure.

Marx was the only one to whom Bauer dared confide that he was about to demolish Hegel's famous 'reconciliation' of philosophy with religion, and he did not mince words about the explosive, world-transforming effect he expected: 'The catastrophe will be terrible and far-reaching. I would almost say it will be greater and more terrible than that which heralded the advent of Christianity.'[40] 'The [Prussian] state in its blindness', Bauer argued, was vainly trying to hush up the issues facing it by means of 'a Chinese police system'. But the more oppressive the state's police system became, the sharper the clash of opposites tearing at its fabric. No one enjoyed the dialectics of this situation more than Bauer. Indeed, the *Kirchenstreit*, though originally sparked off by the question of mixed marriages, had thrown open not only the issue of relations between church and state, between Catholicism and officially Protestant Prussia, but a wide range of related ones, such as freedom of conscience, rationalism versus atheism, etc. With a large Catholic population in the Prussian-annexed Rhineland and other parts of Germany, even such questions as the state's right to scrutinize university lectures and theatre performances which – in the absence of a parliament – could not be normally discussed, had suddenly become the subject of a heated national debate, and the censors had their hands full.

The dialectical thesis Bauer kept putting to the young Marx was that Prussia – reduced to fighting back with nothing better than stupid 'apologetics' and a repressive police system – was losing control of the situation. This was philosophy's great opportunity: 'Philosophy, at last coming of age under this very repression', Bauer had advised Marx in March and April 1840, was now in the best position to lead the battle and win it too. 'Our epoch becomes *more and more*

terrible and beautiful, he wrote. It was beautiful because the people who identified the state with their own interests 'have prepared their final fall, for which
they deserve our thanks... The future is too certain to entertain even a moment's
doubt.' Philosophy would 'triumph... A single blow will be decisive.'[41]

It was for this 'blow' that Bauer wanted to have Marx by his side in Bonn.
His bellicose talk was on a strictly philosophical plane, though bound to have
political implications. He kept stressing to Marx that his Bonn faculty colleagues – 'poor blockheads', as he referred to them, when not calling them
worse names – had not the faintest idea of 'philosophy and its present-day significance', and did not hide from him the fact that Bonn was 'the university
which produces the least for science'.

He felt sure that by a joint and resolute effort, with philosophy for their weapon, the two of them would determine the outcome of the battle between
'science' and the absolute state.

At this time, Karl Marx did nothing without consulting Bruno Bauer, who
was 10 years his senior and guiding his career. Besides, he respected Bauer for
his sharp wit and polemical bent, second to none but his own. Bauer remained
the spiritual head of the Doctors Club and Marx shared his belief that philosophy had reached a major turning point. As Marx was to put it in his notes for
the dissertation: 'Like Prometheus who stole fire from heaven and began to
build houses and settled on the earth, so philosophy, evolved to impinge on the
world, *turns itself against the* [phenomenal] *world that it finds*. So it is now with
the Hegelian philosophy.'[42]

Marx's dissertation, whose full title was to be 'On The Difference Between
Democritus' and Epicurus' Philosophy of Nature', has not survived in its entirety.[43] But his very choice of subject and his description of Epicurus (341–270
B.C.) as the 'true radical enlightener of antiquity' – greater than his forerunner,
Democritus (460–370 B.C.), whom C.M. Bowra was to describe as the ancestor,
however remote, of modern atomic physics, while Marx himself called him the
'foremost encyclopaedic intellect among the Greeks' – represented the beginning of the young doctoral candidate's departure from Hegel.

For, contrary to Hegel's elevation of the state and its monarch as guarantors
of true freedom embodying the highest universal reason, Epicurus' evaluation
of the state was simply a function of its usefulness to its citizens. Marx treated
Democritus' and Epicurus' theories of the universe from the viewpoint of their
relation to philosophy. While Democritus' theory that the atoms fell vertically
subjected all phenomena, including the heavenly bodies, the gods and even the
human mind, to immutable laws of cosmic necessity, Marx highlighted the
innovation introduced by Epicurus' assertion that the atoms swerved irregularly. This meant that nothing was fixed and immutable and freed the human

'mind' and 'will' from the inexorable laws of Democritus' 'total philosophy'.

Besides stressing that Epicurus 'openly attacked the ancient religion' and describing him as the father of 'Roman atheism, insofar as it existed', Marx quoted with approval from Lucretius' *De Rerum Natura* the lines in which this Roman poet eulogized Epicurus as the 'Greek who first ventured to raise his mortal eye' to heaven and resist 'the monster... of oppressive religion' threatening mankind.

Marx shared Bauer's idea that a great 'total philosophy' such as Hegel's was inevitably followed by a period of catastrophic upheaval. His interest in the speculative philosophic systems of the Epicureans, Stoics and Sceptics was all the greater as the problems faced by these late or post-Aristotelian philosophers seemed to him and the other Young Hegelians to bear a striking resemblance to their own situation after Hegel. There was a faint basis to this analogy in the sense that the Greeks had discussed the relations between man, reason and their gods engaged in lusty antics and vengeful plots and wondered whether the gods themselves were not subject to some higher cosmic principle or 'necessity' governing the world. Hegel had enthroned the absolute as governing the world order, and the kings as its bearers, and now his disciples faced the consequences. In drawing a parallel with the Greeks in his notes for the dissertation, Marx alluded to its bearing on the contemporary situation in Germany in veiled but unmistakable terms: '[In] the storm that follows a great, a world-philosophy', he wrote, 'someone who does not appreciate this historical necessity must consequently deny that man could continue to live at all after a total philosophy'; or else – he went on in a stab at the old guard of the Hegelian 'Right' – he could only claim 'with some of our misguided Hegelians that mediocrity is the usual form in which absolute mind appears; but a mediocrity that gives itself out to be the normal appearance of the absolute has itself degenerated into a boundless pretension.' As against this, defining the more courageous course available to the inheritors of a total philosophy, he held up the example of Themistocles, who

> when Athens was threatened with destruction, persuaded the Athenians to quit their city completely and found a new Athens on another element, the sea. Nor should we forget that the period that follows such catastrophes is an iron one, happy if it is marked by titanic struggles, lamentable if it is like the centuries that limp behind the great periods of art and busy themselves with imitating in wax, plaster and copper what sprang from Carrara marble like Pallas Athene from the head of Zeus, father of the gods.[44]

Instead, the Epicurean, Stoic and Sceptic philosophers had gone on to found a 'new Athens' which, becoming the model for Rome, shaped the rationalist philosophy of a new empire. Theirs had been one of those 'unhappy and iron' periods following upon a total philosophy, when the 'gods are dead and the new goddess has as yet only the obscure form of fate, of pure light or of pure darkness.' Marx suggested, however, that the unhappiness is due to the fact that the 'soul of the period shapes itself on all sides in isolation'. The new goddess of thought 'still lacks the colours of the day' – until she happily finds the 'subjective consciousness' of the philosopher who will objectify thought's relation to reality: 'Thus, the Stoic and Epicurean philosophies were the happiness of their time. Thus, the nightbutterfly, when the universal sun has sunk, seeks the lamplight of a private person.'[45] The new generation of Hegelians could either limp behind the past or make a clean break like their Greek precursors, and look to the future.

Marx, who had started making notes for his doctoral thesis at the end of 1839, left the main work on it for the second half of 1840. He spent the early months of that year on a book debunking the travestied philosophy of Hermes, the former Bonn faculty head, who had meanwhile become the editor of Cologne's clerical *Kölnische Zeitung*. He sent the manuscript to Bauer together with a letter to the publisher Marcus. The letter no longer exists, but it says something of the young author's unworldliness and crude arrogance that Bauer decided not to deliver it, and wrote: 'Perhaps you might write in such terms to your washerwoman, but not to a publisher whose good will you want to win.'[46]

As for Marx's manuscript, Bauer took it personally to Marcus, who rejected it out of hand. The anti-Hermes book, which was in fact never published, was only one of several inconclusive projects – another was a book on Hegel's religious philosophy – which Marx toyed with or made a start on while preparing his dissertation. Bauer, living like a recluse at Bonn, had urged him in the spring of 1840 to stop 'dithering' and go through with the 'farce' of his final examination in Berlin. He had also advised him how to apply for a lecturer's licence and did not hide from his young confidant his loneliness among his bigoted faculty colleagues, or his impatience to see him by his side in Bonn.

In the autumn, however, Marx was making such extensive notes for the dissertation that they far surpassed its central theme. He saw the dissertation – as he was to explain in a Preface he prefixed to it upon its completion – merely as 'the preliminary to a larger work' he meant to produce on 'the cycle of Epicurean, Stoic and Sceptic philosophies'. Their speculative systems, he declared, were the key to the 'true history of Greek philosophy and the Greek mind in general.'[47] And, with all due respect to Hegel, he chided this 'giant thinker' for having failed to recognize their prime importance. In quoting

668

David Hume on the 'sovereign views of philosophy' being demeaned 'when she is compelled on every occasion to defend herself... and justify herself in the eyes of every art and science... One is put in mind of a king who is accused of high treason against his own subjects',[48] Marx seemed to be echoing Bauer's 'Philosophy has come of age'. But his conception and approach were as original and challenging as his admiration of 'the Greeks [who] will always remain our teachers' was genuine. He presented Epicurus as the ethical and wise philosopher who accepted no outside 'knowledge' or doctrine, refused to submit to Democritus' materialist 'necessity', and scrutinized everything with a calm and independent mind. Making Epicurus the spokesman of his own credo, Marx wrote in the Preface: 'Philosophy, so long as a drop of blood still pulses in her world-conquering, absolutely free heart, will always cry out to her opponents, with Epicurus: "Godless is not he who destroys the gods of the multitude, but he who foists the conceptions of the multitude onto the gods."'

But of all things in Greek antiquity it was the mythological hero of Aeschylus' *Prometheus Bound* that caught Marx's imagination and impressed itself for life on his rebellious mind. In the notes for his dissertation he spoke of the 'titanic struggle' of the philosophers under review. But already before he was 20 Marx's own titanic 'I' had sounded a note of Promethean defiance in a poem in which a kind of superman or demiurge scornfully promised to fling his gauntlet 'full in the face of the world'. By the time Marx wrote the Preface to his dissertation, the disdainful attitude towards God and the existing world reflected in his earlier poem appeared to have been no mere tempestuous expression of a youthful Romantic mood. Now he not only openly identified with Prometheus but adopted him as the all-time standard-bearer of philosophy from antiquity to modernity. Quoting the confession which Aeschylus had put into the mouth of Prometheus, Marx wrote: 'Philosophy makes no secret of it. The confession of Prometheus: "In a word, I detest all the gods" is her own confession, her own slogan against all the gods of heaven and earth who do not recognize man's self-consciousness as the highest divinity. There shall be none other beside it.'[49]

'Self-consciousness as the highest divinity' was of course a notion that would have perplexed Aeschylus himself when he wrote his Prometheus trilogy, in the two lost plays of which he had 'the heartless' Zeus in the end release the rebel from the mountain rock in the Caucasus, as though to show that 'the fulfilment of power is in reason and justice'.[50]

Marx did not mention this. In the Preface he transformed the myth of Prometheus into a vehicle serviceable across the ages for his own philosophy, and taking Prometheus' defiance for his motto, flung it in the face of the academic establishment – which was full of Hegel's old faithfuls and other supporters of a quietist *status quo* – by concluding with the words:

669

To the pitiful March hares who rejoice at the apparently worsened civil position of philosophy, she repeats the answer given by Prometheus to Hermes, the servant of the gods: 'Be sure of this. I would not change my evil plight for your servility. I would rather be chained to this rock than spend my life as Father Zeus's faithful messenger.' Prometheus is the foremost saint and martyr in the philosopher's calendar.[51]

Marx was now a confirmed atheist. In an Appendix to the dissertation he disparaged Schelling's, Kant's and even Hegel's conceptions of God. Schelling having lately broached a mystic 'philosophy of revelation' which belied his younger days, Marx reminded him that in 1795 he had written, 'The time has come to proclaim to the better part of humanity the freedom of minds' and asked sarcastically: 'If the time had already come in 1795, what about the year 1841?' Of Kant, who had summed up the ontological proofs of the existence of God under the heading of speculative reason, Marx wrote that this means nothing because imagination could be as powerful as reality: 'Has a real Thaler any existence except in the imagination?... Bring paper money into a country where its usage is unknown, and everyone will laugh at your subjective imagination. Come with your gods into a country where other gods are worshipped and you will be shown to suffer from fantasies and abstractions.'

As for Hegel, Marx observed that he had 'turned all the theological proofs of the existence of God upside down, that is, he rejected them in order to justify them.' Marx then asked: 'What kind of clients are those whom the defending lawyer can only save from conviction by killing them himself? For instance, Hegel interpreted the conclusion from the world to God as meaning: "Since the accidental does not exist, God or Absolute exists." However, the theological demonstration is the opposite: "Since the accidental has true being, God exists." God is the guarantee for the world of the accidental. It is obvious that the reverse can also be said.'

Summing up this part of the Appendix, Marx wrote that 'all proofs of the existence of God are proof of his non-existence. They are refutations of all concepts of a God.' The true proofs would sound the reverse of this:

'Because nature is poorly contrived, God is.' 'Because the world is irrational, therefore God exists.' 'Because there is no thought, there is God.' But what does all this say, except that, 'to him to whom the world is irrational, and who is himself irrational, God is? Or irrationality is the existence of God.'[52]

23

Georg Herwegh, 'The Iron Lark of Revolution'; Heine on Ludwig Börne

Though Karl Marx was hoping to publish his dissertation, developed into a larger work, it was not at all clear which way the new King of Prussia would go. Friedrich Wilhelm IV showed his nation a double face. Having inaugurated his reign with an amnesty of political prisoners, he relaxed the censorship regulations. The Grimm brothers – who had been sacked from Göttingen University for their political views – were appointed to the Berlin Academy of Sciences and the nationalist Ernst Moritz Arndt was restored to the Bonn University chair from which he had been dismissed 20 years earlier. Even the normally bitter Dr Bauer was momentarily moved, after taking part at a festive dinner in honour of Arndt's return, to write to his brother Edgar on 25 July 1840: 'My name was called; I had to rise; the enthusiasm with which I joined the celebration was boundless. I embraced Arndt; hurray, I am to be allowed to be part of the faculty! I was supremely happy.'[1]

His euphoria was short-lived. After a brief intermezzo or 'honeymoon', during which the King toyed with various reforms, he began to go the other way. He adorned his court with such cosmopolitan and liberal-minded figures as Prince Pückler-Muskau and Alexander von Humboldt, but also packed the court and his Cabinet with so many conservative Junkers and orthodox Pietists that the role of Humboldt – the world-famous natural scientist – was eventually reduced to reading aloud from the *Journal des Débats*, while the King indulged in his favourite pastime and drew landscapes or made architectural sketches. When the post of Minister of Education and Public Worship became vacant on the death of the liberal Altenstein – Bauer's protector – the King appointed the reactionary Eichhorn, who was sure to tighten control over Prussia's universities.

Worse things were to follow by the time Marx had everything ready to apply for his PhD diploma. At the end of February 1841, three or four weeks before he wrote the Preface to his dissertation, a sensational pamphlet titled 'Four Questions by an East Prussian' was distributed all over Berlin and in other cities. The anonymous pamphlet, which was promptly confiscated, created a great stir because its author had sent a copy of it to the King and had signed his name to it: Dr Johann Jacoby of Königsberg. In his 'Four Questions', Jacoby, a 'bour-geois-democrat' member of the East Prussian Diet, and otherwise a well-known physician, went straight to the heart of the issue of the promised constitution which Friedrich Wilhelm IV had been trying to bury under a mountain of sten-torian but evasive rhetoric. In clear and reasoned arguments, Jacoby pointed out that the people were entitled to a parliament not as an act of mercy but 'as of right', and not only because they had reached maturity but because the constitu-tion solemnly promised by the previous King his father was anchored in legisla-tion promulgated on 22 May 1815 as part of the Federal Act of the German Bund.

The King's response was swift and brutal. Although Jacoby's sole crime was no more than an infringement of censorship regulations, he was subjected to a month-long interrogation. He was then charged, first, with rebellious incite-ment; next, with *lèse majesté*, punishable with 4 years' incarceration in a fortress; and finally with high treason, punishable with death. There followed a judicial rigmarole as the case wandered from lower to higher courts at the same rate as the charges preferred became ever more grave. The Supreme Court in Königsberg, doubting that there was a case for high treason, declared itself incompetent and sent the case back to Berlin. The King thereupon issued a *Kabinettsordre* instructing it to continue the proceedings. Paul Jacoby in his turn insisted that he wanted a fair trial, not in Königsberg, where his fellow-burghers might be prejudiced in his favour, but in Berlin. He got his way, and the Berlin Supreme Court eventually sentenced him to two and a half years of hard labour in a fortress and the loss of his civic honour.

The protracted Jacoby affair, which was to last for three years and to end with his complete rehabilitation by the Supreme Court, kept the issue of the constitution alive. While Jacoby himself, though defamed by the East Prussian Junkers for being 'of the accursed seed of Jacob who denied Jesus', became a national hero for his courageous stand, the absurdity of the situation in abso-lutist Prussia was to be shown up in August 1842 when the state declared that any mention of one of its own laws – that of 22 May 1815, invoked by Jacoby – constituted incitement and its appearance in print was forbidden.[2]

The cogency of Jacoby's arguments in 'Four Questions', however, could not be spirited away and from the moment of its publication his pamphlet had a lightning effect which has been compared to that of the Abbé Sieyès's mani-festo 'Qu'est-ce que le Tiers Etat?' defining the Third Estate's aspiration to be recognized as a parliament on the eve of the French Revolution.[3]

In Prussia there was no revolution, but the high expectations placed by Ger-many's freedom-hungry democrats in Friedrich Wilhelm IV were severely sha-ken, even as the King's honeymoon with liberalism seemed to continue. For while pamphlets had been excluded from the censorship relaxation, cartoons were permitted. The King himself, who in his adolescent days had been warned by his tutor – J.P.F. Ancillon, a Huguenot theologian and historian – that doodling away his time drawing pencil sketches 'may be a very useful occupation for a good-for-nothing, but the state is not a Gothic temple and no people have ever been ruled by means of Romantic drawings,'[4] continued to spend much of his time drawing sketches of medieval castles. Although his favourite play was Ludwig Tieck's outmoded 'Puss in Boots' (*Der gestiefelte Kater*), he also conceived and personally supervised great schemes for turning Berlin into a cultural centre rivalling Paris. He staged poetry readings and musical fêtes at Sans-Souci and went to great lengths to entice the celebrated Meyerbeer away from his successes at the Paris Grand' Opéra in favour of a post as General-Musikdirektor in the Prussian capital. But he remained intent on pressing Prussia into what a contemporary soon called a glorified medieval mould, 'full of priests, knights and serfs'.[5] An illustrious scholar like Alexander von Humboldt was increasingly disturbed – as were the few other liberals and free-thinkers at court, such as Pückler-Muskau and Heine's friend Varnhagen von Ense – by His All-Highest Majesty's all-knowing tone and by his pietist endeavour to 'christianize' science.

This endeavour, which Dr Bauer was girding himself to fight from his chair in Bonn, was soon to be felt at the universities as the King's new Minister of Education began sedulously to scrutinize lists of their academic staffs with a view to removing those suspected as 'radical' Hegelians.

No wonder then that Bauer, in the spring of 1841, after the start of the Jacoby affair, felt that he must hang on to his lectureship at Bonn and tread a cautious path lest anyone get wind of 'the blow' he was preparing. At the same time he kept a sober watch over the progress of Marx's dissertation. On 12 April, he warned him to cut out the confession of Prometheus – 'I detest all the Gods' – and under no circumstances to write anything that might give premature offence 'and furnish the blockheads with a convenient scandal and a weapon to exclude you for a long time from a university chair... Once you are in the chair you can say anything you like.'[6]

Marx, however, had already sent off the dissertation to Jena University. He had chosen Jena on Bauer's advice, because its small university – at which Fichte and Hegel had once taught – required no public examination such as he would have been obliged to undergo in Berlin, where he also faced some risk of being blackballed because of his friendship with Bauer. At Jena, on the other hand, he could count on the support of a liberal professor of literature, Oskar Ludwig Wolff, whom he approached with a request to 'expedite the sending over of the diploma'.

673

Indeed, on 15 April, a week after he submitted his dissertation, Jena University granted him – with despatch and in his absence – the degree of 'Doctoris Philosophiae Honores'. Shortly afterwards he left Berlin and returned to his native Trier, where both his mother and his fiancée were anxiously waiting for him. He had dedicated the dissertation to Jenny's father 'Privy Councillor Herr Ludwig von Westphalen' as 'a mark of filial love'. In a rare emotional outpouring Marx turned his dedication into a veritable hymn to his future father-in-law. Holding him up to 'all those who doubt the power of the Idea' as a man who welcomed 'every progress of the time with enthusiasm', he extolled the 71-year-old baron as an idealist who

> recognizes the Truth before which all the intellects of the world appear, not recoiling from the shadow of retrograde ghosts in the oft-darkened skies of the age – and, with divine energy and assured, manly look, sees through all the masquerades into the Empyrean, which burns in the heart of the world,[7]

a paean which sounds almost as if Marx was settling accounts with his own late father. But his father had shown little enthusiasm for the Hegelian 'Idea' and no understanding for Karl's irresistible philosophic drive to penetrate to the heavenly fire 'which burns in the heart of the world'; on the contrary, in his practical concern for Karl and the family he meant to found with Jenny, Heinrich Marx had tried to keep his eyes to the ground and urged him to apply his talents to a socially acceptable career.

'You, Fatherly Friend', Marx went on in his dedication to Westphalen, 'have always been a living proof that Idealism is not merely a fancy but a reality. Physical well-being, I do not have to entreat for you. The mind is a great magical physician to whom you have entrusted yourself.' As Künzli, analyzing these things in depth, was to remark, neither 'the great magical physician' – the mind – nor the supportive friendship of the Baron were to have it in their power to cure Marx's inner alienation or the unresolved conflict with his father, whose heritage 'he denied, but who remained a piece of himself'.[8]

As for his mother, nothing is known of what went on between her and Karl during his stay in Trier, where the new doctor of philosophy celebrated his 23rd birthday in May, except that – as part of the liquidation of his father's estate – they signed an official *Erbvertrag* (inheritance settlement) before a notary.

The document was signed on 23 June 1841.[9] Henriette Marx gave Karl 750 Thaler as an advance against his share in her future estate. But these financial matters apart, and notwithstanding the fulsome dedication to Jenny's father, there was a cloud over his visit. For according to a surviving, if badly preserved, letter written by Henriette Marx in May 1840, none of the Westphalens, except for Jenny, had so much as paid her a condolence visit in the two years which had by then elapsed since her husband's death. 'The girl one is in love with may possess the most beautiful and sublime virtues', Karl's mother remarked to him in this letter, 'yet every family has a fundamental characteristic... That of the W.[Westphalen] family is that they either exalt you to heaven or tread you underfoot, they know no proper *juste milieu* relationship.'

As far as can be made out from the partly torn letter, the rift had been triggered by Marx's making an unfortunate remark about Jenny and/or members of her family. The Westphalens, hearing about it from a third party, took offence. What pained Karl's mother was that, although the third party – a Herr Schlink – later apologized, Jenny's parents continued to ignore her 'as though they had never known me'. But there was a wider background to these hurt feelings. It appears from the letter that the 'good Councillor' (Jenny's father) had come under pressure from the bigoted and uppity children of his '*uradelig*' (genuinely aristocratic) first wife not to go through with Jenny's marriage to her 'Jewish-born fiancé'. Jenny's half-sister Lisette and her reactionary half-brother Ferdinand, together with their snobbish, pietist, anti-Semitic von Krosigk and Florencourt spouses are presumed to have been the unnamed branch of the Westphalens whom Karl's mother had in mind when she wrote that 'They wanted to break off the relationship [i.e., Jenny's betrothal], which would have caused you the greatest unhappiness.'[10]

Henriette Marx added that only 'exaggerated maternal love' had made her bear this humiliating treatment: 'They would have shown me greater respect if I had told them, Do as you like, I do not care.' She had indeed suffered in silence without mentioning anything to Karl for two years. In her 1840 letter she made a point of noting that 'the good Councillor' himself had not been among the 'active' instigators of the boycott against her. But, for all 'the manly look' Karl admired in him, he had apparently kowtowed to his relatives, for, as she put it, 'he was not allowed to visit us any longer.' Ironically, Karl's angst-ridden father had warned him early on that there was an 'imbalance' in the social circumstances of the two families and that 'the judgment of relatives... is not to be trifled with.'

In any case, the rift marked the beginning of what Karl Marx two years later was to call 'the most violent battles' Jenny had to fight, 'partly against her pietistic aristocratic relatives' and 'partly against my own family'.[11] It cannot have made his visit to Trier a happy one.

As for Jenny, who was 27 and engaged to him for 5 years now, she was soon to miss his presence again but to go on loving him by correspondence. For he was to leave at the beginning of July. Philosophy and Bauer's promise of a lectureship were calling him to Bonn. But he was still in Trier when the next public storm to agitate Germany simultaneously with the Jacoby affair broke in May. The protagonist in this case was Prince Pückler-Muskau. This widely travelled, eccentric aristocrat had an estate which was famous both for its gardens – which were a European showpiece – and for his exotic concubine, Machbuba, a slave-girl he had acquired on his travels. It was on this estate that Laube had spent 18 months of house-arrest until 1839. Married to a daughter of Hardenberg, Prussia's late Chancellor, Pückler-Muskau enjoyed the King's friendship. But he was an admirer of Heine, who was later to dedicate one of his works to him, and also a great ladies' man. Adored by hostesses in Berlin, Paris and other European capitals for his combination of charm and wit, he was too worldly-wise and sophisticated to share Friedrich Wilhelm's pietism. Varnhagen was later to record in his diary that, after a formal evening at court, Pückler-Muskau would come to his house for some refreshing free conversation.

In 1841 they had much to say about the furore aroused by the publication in May of a volume of verse called 'Poems of a Living Man' (*Gedichte eines Lebendigen*), which was a mocking attack on a book Pückler-Muskau had published anonymously during the 1830s. The author of the offending book was a young poet, Georg Herwegh, who had also created a tempest by attacking Germany's most popular poet at the time, Ferdinand Freiligrath, who in the name of 'pure art' and his belief that poets had better things to do than mix in political party strife, had written:

> The poet stands on a loftier watch-tower
> Than on the party battlements.[12]

In the name of 'engaged literature', young Herwegh replied:

> Be a man: For or against?
> And your slogan: Slave or free?
> The gods themselves stepped down from Olympus
> And fought on the party battlements.[13]

Not that Germany's so-called 'democrats' had any party programme or other battlements to fight on. In the absence of a parliament, they had no practical experience of politics or party organization. Nor did Herwegh live in Germany. A spoiled mother's son who had abandoned his theology studies and then deserted the Prussian army, running away to Switzerland, he was 24 when he published his 'Poems of a Living Man' in Zurich. In the general frustration created by the Prussian King's unwillingness to grant any political reforms, he expressed the yearnings of German youth for a literature reflecting their interests and the spirit of the age. His attack on Pückler-Muskau's book made him the instant hero of Germany's young radical and 'democratic' intellectuals even before he challenged Freiligrath's position.

The genesis of 'Letters of a Deceased Man' was as piquant as the circumstances of Pückler-Muskau's marriage to his wife Lucie. This daughter of Prince Hardenberg was 40 years old when she abandoned her previous husband in order to marry the suave Pückler, who was 9 years her junior and had been courting one of her young daughters. The couple lived happily for some 10 years or so. When his fortune began to dwindle disastrously, they decided by common consent on a divorce, with the express idea that he should marry some rich heiress to save his estate. The prince thereupon set out on a leisurely tour of Western Europe, interrupted by occasional visits to his divorced Lucie, and the first two volumes of 'Letters of a Deceased Man', subtitled 'A Fragmentary Diary from England, Wales, Ireland and France', were followed during the 1830s by more volumes of 'Letters from Germany, Holland and England'. These consisted of practically daily letters he sent her from those countries, reporting on his adventures and experiences in the course of his quest for a wealthy bride.

His anonymous collection, publicly praised by Goethe, was at first attributed to Heine, for Pückler's cosmopolitan outlook and his casual tone of a man-of-the-world observing society gave the books a 'modern' ring rare in Germany at the time. His travels spanned a full decade, at the end of which he returned home with the exotic Machbuba but without a wealthy bride. Princess Lucie, whatever her feelings, never wavered in her love for Pückler; they resumed their life together and he is said to have been extremely devoted to her. Their harmonious relationship was in fact to continue into old age.[14]

In 1840, Georg Herwegh, barely arrived in Switzerland, had made a name for himself by publishing a number of rousing poems. In June of that year he recited one of them at Strasbourg at the unveiling of David d'Angers's bronze statue of Gutenberg, commemorating 400 years since the invention of printing. In this poem Herwegh called on all people to awake and stand up like a single army: 'Forward to battle!/Gutenberg carries our banner'.

Although the reason why people should stand up and fight was not made clear, Herwegh's stanzas had a libertarian ring with their references to Gutenberg, the printed word, press freedom. He was an extremely handsome young man and quickly became the darling of the German colony in Zurich.

Some 10 scholars hounded as radicals in Germany had found a haven at the University of Zurich since its foundation in 1834. The case of Georg Büchner, who had been forced to flee Giessen in the Grand Duchy of Hesse and completed his play *Woyzeck* while lecturing on medicine in Zurich, has been mentioned before. Büchner had died at the beginning of 1837, but his flatmate,

677

Wilhelm Schulz – another runaway from Giessen – taught political science in Zurich, and by 1840 more German émigré lecturers and professors were employed there.

The Nestor of Zurich's otherwise mixed German colony was an earlier student leader from Giessen, Adolph August Follen, a domineering and eccentric person. In the years after the Congress of Vienna, Follen had attracted immense notoriety in Germany as the head of the so-called 'Blacks' of Giessen, the patriotic student fraternity which had been most violent in the *Burschenschaft* demonstrations against the continuing political division of Germany. Before making a sensational escape to Switzerland from prison in 1821, he had called for 'daggers, rifles and axes' against Metternich and the Holy Alliance, and dreamt of establishing a German empire oddly combining Teutomaniac and democratic features.

Follen, who had married a rich Swiss miller's daughter, lived in an imposing house waggishly called the Kaiserburg. The ceiling of its main hall was decorated with the imperial double eagle holding in its claws the sceptre and the imperial orb, while a portrait on the wall showed Follen dressed in the full regalia of a German emperor. For 'he could never forget' – wrote a member of his circle – that Germany's befuddled and intoxicated *Burschenschaftler* had once seen in him the man destined to be Germany's new Kaiser.

By the time Herwegh arrived in Zurich, Follen had become an influential member of the Grand Council ruling the canton of Zurich. In the young poet's bombast and revolutionary fervour, Follen may have seen the image of his own youthful self. He invited Herwegh to live in his house and it was in the bizarre atmosphere of the Kaiserburg that Herwegh wrote his 'Poems of a Living Man'.

Julius Fröbel, a younger German professor of mineralogy at Zurich University – who since his arrival had likewise married a rich local girl and acquired Swiss citizenship – heard Herwegh's provocative poems at a reading arranged by Follen. A practical-minded idealist, Fröbel had long realized that Switzerland was an excellent location for printing and distributing into nearby Germany 'democratic' literature not subject to mutilation by censorship. With his wife's money and more capital from his father-in-law, he founded a publishing firm in Zurich, the Literary Comptoir, which began its existence by launching Herwegh's poems into the world.

Although the book was promptly banned in Prussia, copies were smuggled into the country, and the success of the volume lampooning Pückler's collection of letters exceeded all expectations. The mocking arrows Herwegh directed at the prince's hedonism, his weary distractions and the aristocratic world he stood for, coupled with his ringing calls for 'action' and his catchy rhymes, went straight to the hearts of the young, who took up his cry to 'Tear the crosses out of the earth!/Turn them all into swords!'[15] and sang the verses while brandishing their beer jugs. Herwegh's message, however, was not at all clear. But for the revolutionary sound of 'swords', his political ideas remained vague and undefined. Nevertheless his fiery stanzas gave the drinking, singing students a hazy, satisfying feeling that they were striking a blow against tyranny.

Later in 1841 Ferdinand Freiligrath, a talented 31-year-old former commercial clerk, published a poem, '*Aus Spanien*' ('From Spain'). An earlier volume of wildly passionate poems had won him acclaim as Germany's leading lyrical poet. Steering clear of the topics of the day and evoking outlandish scenes in the style of Victor Hugo's *Les Orientales*, his early poems had a success which enabled Freiligrath to leave his job and retire to Weimar. Now, in '*Aus Spanien*', written in the ferment created by Herwegh, Freiligrath affirmed the poet's aloofness from the political market-place and held up the artist's vocation as affording him a loftier vantage point than that possible 'on the party battlements'. His conservative stand won Freiligrath an annual pension of 300 Thaler from the approving King, and together with another recipient of the royal favour he moved to a small resort on the Rhine, to be away from the fray and write poetry.

Although this gave Herwegh the occasion to ridicule the two of them for their 'servility' in a poem titled 'Duet of the Pensioners', it was Freiligrath who was ultimately to emerge as the true revolutionary poet. But at the time, Herwegh's 'battle' with Freiligrath and his attack on Pückler (which was indirectly aimed at the King) combined to gain him an extraordinary reputation. As his 'Poems of a Living Man' went into edition after edition, his rise marked the beginning of a new trend in Germany, the so-called *Tendenzdichtung*, 'engaged' or committed literature. The lyrical poets had stepped into the political vacuum, and Fröbel's Literary Comptoir, which he had founded to 'promote the awakening political spirit in Germany', was to become a centre for the dissemination of some of the first 'Communist' literature across the border into Germany.

Before the end of 1841, Franz Liszt was setting two of Herwegh's poems, including the popular '*Rheinweinlied*', to music. Herwegh himself, catapulted to fame as the most daring of all 'political lyricists' of the German tongue – of whom altogether 4 were to achieve some note – was visiting Paris. Dingelstedt, another of the 4, was already there, and together they paid homage to George Sand's championship of the oppressed, informing her that 'Germany's youth loves you and deifies you'. They announced at large the imminent springtime of German revolution.

'Books', Herwegh declared, 'have lost their intrisic value – they count only if they instigate to action.' Young, handsome and romantic, cocky and eloquent,

Herwegh with his radical talk – deprecating the Muses and his own poetry, extolling Proudhon and calling for deeds like some angry young Robespierre – made an impression in some of the most elegant Paris salons.

'Give me action!' he would cry. Starting in 1841, he was to make one splash after another. A tragi-comic audience he later had with King Friedrich Wilhelm IV was to have unexpected consequences directly affecting Karl Marx's future. Bakunin was so captivated by his dash and luxurious lifestyle that had Herwegh 'gone to America', he wrote, 'I would have followed him even there.' For a time, Herwegh was to be the lover of the comtesse d'Agoult and, before making a final splash of notoriety by destroying Herzen's marriage, the flamboyant poet was to stage in 1848 a march-past through the streets of Paris in 1848 of 'the Herwegh Legion' on its way 'to liberate Germany'.

The aftermath of that march, however, was to show him up as a political nonentity. Vainglorious to a degree, lacking character and judgment, he was easily intoxicated by his own fiery lyrics. A lascivious playboy, he was as spoilt and self-indulgent as the blasé Pückler-Muskau, though lacking his wit.

Only Heine saw through Herwegh from the very beginning and recognized his verbal fireworks for what they were. Herwegh's notoriety and the feverish enthusiasm he stirred in Germany's youth and her democrats in general had yet to reach their peak when Herwegh arrived to be fêted in Paris in December 1841. That same month, after meeting him, Heine wrote his poem, 'To Georg Herwegh', in which he pricked him for announcing a false spring. Heine doubted that Germany was ready for revolution.

Although much of the new *Tendenzdichtung* produced by Herwegh and a couple of other political lyricists was to turn out to be mere noise and bravado, the hugely successful 'Poems of a Living Man' gave voice to a beginning German opposition of sorts, however amorphous. In other ways, too, the 1840–41 period was one of great ferment. It was against the background of the illusory hope of imminent revolution stirred by Herwegh in the breasts of Germany's beer-swilling youth and its frustrated intellectuals that Heine's *Ludwig Börne. A Memorial* caused a double outrage lasting from the summer of 1840 on through most of 1841. During the same period Moses Hess wrote and published *The European Triarchy*, the book in which Marx was to find the synthesis of German philosophy, French revolutionary practice and English economic experience that eventually became the theoretical foundation of Marxism. Bakunin, newly arrived in Germany, went through long months of acclimatization in 1840 and 1841 before he began to feel the pangs of that hoped-for rebirth which was to lead him to the proclamation of a philosophy of revolution of his own.

Marx, having obtained his doctorate and moved to Bonn, was to remain there until the end of 1841. While Dr Bruno Bauer was honing philosophy into the ultimate weapon for the destruction of Prussia's police system and clerical tendencies, Marx kept expanding his dissertation into the larger work of the cycle of Epicurean, Stoic and Sceptic philosophies. As late as the winter of 1841 he was still hoping to publish its 'preliminary', the dissertation, which was in fact not to appear in print during his lifetime.

Nor was his larger work ever completed. There were 'political and philosophical affairs of quite another kind', as he called them, which brought all these plans to nought. At the same time they blocked his path to a lectureship and the distinguished career for which he seemed virtually predestined.

Heine had originally called his polemic against Börne simply *The Life of Ludwig Börne* (*Leben Ludwig Börnes* in German), but had then decided on a more effective title: *Ludwig Börne. A Memorial* (*Eine Denkschrift*). He was still in Paris on 23 July 1840 when he received the galley proofs and saw to his 'horror' that Campe had high-handedly changed this to *Heinrich Heine über Ludwig Börne* ('Heinrich Heine on Ludwig Börne'). As the German word 'über' can be taken to mean either 'on' or 'about', Heine felt this unfortunate world-play was sure to cause affront as an example of his sheer presumption. He promptly asked Campe to change the new 'abominable' title 'without fail'. Ignoring this protest, Campe published the book under the unauthorized title of his own devising. He claimed that it was too late to change it and gave other lame excuses. If, as it seems, he wished to add outrage to Heine's most provocative book, he succeeded.

Börne, who had died in 1837, had been Metternich's foremost critic for 20 years. No fewer than 3,000 of the then 15,000-strong German colony in Paris had attended his funeral. In Germany, too, Börne's high principles and exemplary life had earned him the respect of friends, followers and opponents alike, including liberal-minded circles who did not share his radical views. Death had added a halo to his name. In his book, Heine was not only attacking a dead man, but one in whom Germany's democratic elements had come to see, in contemporary language, 'the holy hero' of 'ultra-liberalism'. It was this growing myth that Heine set out to destroy and he did so in a manner which produced howls of 'sacrilege'.

But *Ludwig Börne. A Memorial* was more than a savage polemic; otherwise it would hardly have become the subject of a controversy that was to flare up again and again in the 20th century. The conflict between the two men had started in the passionate days following the July Revolution in Paris, when Heine – who did not share Börne's soaring hopes in the possibility of an imminent upheaval in Germany – had refused to join forces with him at the great 1832 Hambach Rally. Börne had thereupon compared Heine to 'a boy chasing butterflies on the battlefield' or 'flirting with the girls' in church while everybody prayed for the victory of the fighters. With Börne spying on Heine, subjecting him to a self-confessed 'chemical analysis' and conducting first an underground and then a public campaign against him, their animosity had been further nurtured by a clash of temperaments. Heine had soon introduced, in his *History of Religion and Philosophy in Germany*, his theory that divided all people into two personality types – Judeo-Christian 'Nazarenes' tending to 'spiritualize' matter versus sensualist 'Hellenes who vindicate the rights of matter and save it from the usurpations of the spirit'.

In *Ludwig Börne* he took up this theme again and made it clear that by 'Jews' and 'Christians' he did not mean a certain people, but was referring to 'an innate as well as acquired' outlook and orientation of the mind. 'All people', he wrote, 'are either Jews or Hellenes', the former lean and ascetic, the latter realistic, life-affirming and life-enjoying. This theme was later to find its counterpart in Nietzsche's contrasting 'Dionysian' with 'Apollonian' types and in Thomas Mann's reflections on the antithesis between spirit and art. In Börne, Heine obviously saw an abstemious, self-mortifying 'Nazarene', and in himself a joyous, sensuous 'Hellene'.

He did not hesitate to reproduce the full text of an article in which Börne had publicly condemned his tendency to sacrifice truth to beauty, or to accept the truth only when it was artistically beautiful. Challenging Börne's distinction between 'character' and 'talent', Heine – recalling that Börne had often expressed his contempt for Goethe's aesthetic detachment and had described his indifference to politics as 'servility' – in his turn compared Börne to a child touching a statue and complaining that it feels cold. Börne's 'subjective' obsession with the politics of blinkered, fanatical 'Jacobinism', Heine suggested, had rendered him incapable of appreciating 'the objective freedom, the Goethean manner' of the artistic creator who is 'the master of his subject, no matter what it is, and knows how to knead it to give plastic expression to his thoughts, feelings and views.'[16]

'What is character?' Heine asked. The stupid mass, he answered, celebrates as a man of character the one whose 'superficial and narrow-minded view of life' expresses its own 'in popular language in the market place'. This banal standard, however, can only be applied to those authors whose pen is inspired by expediency and the public mood. Börne had struck a sensitive point when, ridiculing Heine's refusal to commit himself totally to any political dogma, he had written that while every ordinary mortal had to fear 'the blows of fortune' raining down on his back from one direction only, poor Heine had two backs: fearing blows from both aristocrats 'and the democrats, he must, in order to avoid them, crawl forward and backward at the same time'.[17]

Heine pointed out that it was precisely the type of author, who, lacking the creative patience required by art, panders to the public and is admired as a character – and not the man of talent – who keeps shifting positions. Since a writer's deeds are his 'words', the works of this type of author will remain ephemeral. The implication was that Börne, whose rousing revolutionary oratory appealed to the half-educated, partly illiterate artisans, apprentices and journeymen making up most of the German colony in Paris, belonged to this class of rabble-rousers. By contrast, Heine affirmed the sovereignty of the true creative artists who are not 'slaves of the word', but command it at will. Unaffected by flights of enthusiasm, 'they write objectively and their character does not show in their style'.[18]

Heinrich Laube, after reading the first version of the book, had warned Heine that it smacked of an 'impious' personal vendetta against a dead popular hero. 'But he was my enemy,' Heine exclaimed, 'the enemy of my superior *Weltanschauung*!' If so, Laube suggested, 'you must contrast Börne's exclusively political thought with your superior *Weltanschauung*'. Laube's idea was that Heine should include a statement on his attitude to the July Revolution, thus 'erecting a mountain' whose shade would soften the effect of 'the personal feud' and all glaring and offensive passages and 'make the climax of your book'.[19]

Heine had indeed been playing with the idea of writing a book on the July Revolution. But in the end he decided that this would make a 'mountain' requiring a separate book. Instead, he inserted into the final version of his polemic against Börne the section comprising his so-called Helgoland Letters, dated from that island during the 6 weeks of the July Revolution of 1830.[20] Though no 'mountain', these Helgoland Letters enabled Heine to set his conflict with Börne against the emotional background of the July Revolution and to highlight his identification with the cause of the people. News of the events in Paris had reached him on the island while he was reading Thiers's and Mignet's accounts of the French Revolution, so 'they seemed to me the most natural thing in the world, like the continuation of my studies.' Fired by the idea that the storming of the Bastille had been no vagary of history and that 'the French cock has crowed again', he, 'the son of the revolution', had reached for his lyre 'to sing a battle song: I am all joy and song, all sword and flame!'[21]

In the 4 other sections of his book, Heine depicted Börne as an austere, puritan, rigid moralizer, petulant and dogmatic, watching like a political commissar lest anyone, especially Heine, should depart from republican 'virtue' or betray 'the party line'. At the same time, he was eaten by

> the petty jealousy of the little drum-master toward the big drum-major: he envied me the big plume that so boldly exults into the air... the skill with which I balanced the big baton, the loving glances thrown to me by the young girls and which I returned perhaps with some coquetry...[22]

In short, Börne the ascetic Nazarene was opposed to Heine the sensualist Hellene who looked at the world with the self-assurance of one who has 'the gods of the future' on his side.

The Börne-Heine dispute was on a broad front, for the conflict between the spiritualist/Nazarene and sensualist/Hellene outlooks concerned not only the relation between art and politics but touched upon the great soup question – *'die grosse Suppenfrage'*, as Heine called it – and more specifically upon the question of political versus social revolution as the best solution of the plight of the hungry masses. Börne's Robespierre type of mind was immutably fixed on political revolution. To Heine, who had come to Paris to develop a cosmopolitan European outlook, the question whether people lived in republics or monarchies seemed less important than the question of how they lived. Captivated by Saint-Simon's idea of industrial 'progress' and of a 'golden age' in which writers and artists would play a leading role in bringing about the material as well as spiritual improvement of 'the poorest and most numerous class', he had early in the 1830s communicated his conclusions to Laube in the words: 'People are not asses'; they no longer looked to heaven, but demanded gratification of their practical as well as sensual needs on earth. He could foresee a time when 'they shall eat beef every day instead of potatoes, and work less and dance more.'[23]

In his Börne book Heine singled out Shakespeare as a genius who, being both 'Jew and Greek', had reconciled repressive antimaterialist 'spiritualism with art', i.e., with what Heine regarded as the more wholesome Greek 'sensualist' approach. Heine believed that these two elements struggled in the Western mind, as they did in his own. In the passage about Shakespeare he suggested that their synthesis was 'the task of European civilization as a whole.'[24]

Heine himself had tried to establish such a synthesis in *The Romantic School* and in *History of Religion and Philosophy in Germany*. There, in the mid-1830s, he had prophesied a changed Germany in which artists and intellectuals, 'the party of the flowers and nightingales, will be intimately connected with the revolution. Ours is the future,' were his words. While this last had been the slogan of Saint-Simon, Heine had made it his job in the two works mentioned to survey the history of the political, religious and intellectual developments which had led to the French Enlightenment and the parallel achievements of German philosophy, culminating in Hegel's concept of the Idea as a force immanent in history. Besides observing that this force seizes man, especially the writer, whether he wants it or not, 'and whips him into the arena, like a gladiator forced to fight for it',[25] Heine had anticipated the activist interpretation of the Young Hegelian Left in such phrases as 'Thought precedes action as lightning precedes thunder', or the meaningful statement,

Thought yearns to become deed, the word wants to become flesh. And miraculously! man, like the God of the Bible, only has to utter his thought and a new world is born, there is light or there is darkness, the waters separate from the mainland, and even wild beasts may appear. The world is the signatura of the word.[26]

Heine's vision of revolution, for all its utopian element, was thus philosophically grounded. Countless studies have been devoted both to the interpretation of Heine's futurist vision and to the tracing of its roots and stages of development. In *Ludwig Börne. A Memorial*, he allegorically compared his and Börne's arrival in Paris in the immediate turmoil after the July Revolution to the encounter of two ships on the high seas during a furious storm. Börne is seen 'standing at the helm of his ship defying the monstrous waves... Poor man! his ship was without anchor and his heart without hope... I saw the mast breaking, the winds tearing the rigging apart.'

Börne is the old sea captain sailing with outdated charts and otherwise unequipped to ride the storms of the new age. In France, revolution had led to the July Monarchy, which only made the rich richer and increased the ranks of the poor. Börne with his entire crew and all the various factions of his radical partisans who spent the 1830s in fruitless agitation for a Jacobin revolution looking back to 1789, were thus from the beginning condemned to perish. At the same time, there was more than that to the allegory of the two ships. For as Börne is about to go under with his vessel, Heine – who in other places let on that he and Börne saw eye to eye on many issues, and should in fact have been comrades-in-arms in the struggle against the reaction – concluded the scene with these words: 'I saw him stretching out his arm to me... I dared not seize it, I dared not jeopardize the precious cargo, the sacred treasures which had been entrusted to my safekeeping... I carried on board my ship the gods of the future.'[27]

But who are these mysterious gods of the future? They have in the main been connected with Heine's early adoption of the millenary belief in a new revelation or 'third testament' religion that would succeed Christianity. He had alluded to it in a poem in his *Harz Journey* a year before Saint-Simon – described by his disciples as 'the third prophet' after Moses and Jesus – had published his *New Christianity*. Lessing had spoken of a coming age of perfection and Heine, in *The Romantic School*, had praised him for expressing in all his works this healing 'religion of reason', 'this great social idea, this progressive humanism, this religion of reason whose St John he was, and whose Messiah we are still waiting for.'[28]

Heine wrote in the same passage that Lessing also had 'political tendencies, something uncommon among his contemporaries'. And he hinted at the correlation between Lessing and Saint-Simonism by noting that the former's *Education of the Human Race* (*Die Erziehung des Menschengeschlechts*) had been translated into French by Rodrigues, Saint-Simon's oldest disciple.

The idea of a coming age of perfection through a universal messianic redemption is deeply rooted in the literature of the Jewish prophets. In his Börne book, Heine remarks that 'the Jews are made of the dough out of which gods are kneaded', and suddenly launches into the tale of the 'Captive Messiah', which he had ostensibly heard from the mouth of 'the great Rabbi Manasse ben Naphtali of Cracow' during his youthful visit to Poland in 1822: 'The Messiah, he said, was born on the day Titus the villain destroyed Jerusalem. Since then, he has been living in splendour and joy in the most beautiful palace of heaven. He wears a crown on his head, too, like a true king... but his hands are fettered with golden chains!'

To Heine's astonished question about the meaning of the golden chains, the rabbi replies that the Messiah is a handsome, exceedingly dynamic and powerful young man. Whenever he hears the cries of anguish of his people, he would fain 'rush down to earth to start the work of redemption prematurely'. Four hefty 'state councillors' disguised as angels would not be able to hold him back if his hands were not fettered. Gently reminded by them that the 'time is not yet ripe', he covers his face and cries.[29]

Thus the inspiration of Heine's vision of the future came from several sources. Without excluding one another, sometimes the one prevailed, sometimes the other. In the tale of the 'Captive Messiah', he was probably unwittingly expressing that school of Messianism, notably represented by the Golem-maker of Prague, the 'Exalted' Rabbi Judah Loew, which – contrary to others who saw the birth pangs of the Messiah in every crisis – was against 'calculating the end', on the idea that man himself must improve his ways to be ready for the era of final redemption.[30]

Heine's vision combined reason with the irrational, philosophy with messianic hope, political freedom with social justice, spiritual and intellectual satisfaction through poetry and art with 'the natural rights of matter' and the Saint-Simonist rehabilitation of the flesh. He had not studied Saint-Simon's detailed economic theory. He accepted the premise that modern technology rationally applied and a society throwing off national divisions, racial prejudice and the chains of religious orthodoxy in favour of a more enlightened and humanist faith could make a world enabling all men, rich and poor, not only to work but to dance, to feast on 'cake and ale' and to enjoy the pleasures of life.

Marxists and non-Marxists in the 20th century were to engage in a veritable 'war of quotations' from Heine in their attempts to define the exact future envisioned by him. No one has convincingly done so, nor is it possible to separate

Heine the aesthete from Heine the revolutionary, the lyrical poet from the serious thinker and cruel satirist, for they were all one man. Perhaps the shortest definition of his vision of society is that it aimed at the total social emancipation of man, assuring the individual's liberty of conscience and his right to pursue his happiness as he pleases to a degree that would only be achieved in some parts of the Western world in the 20th century. It was a modernist vision far ahead of his time, and differed entirely from Börne's Jacobin conception of revolution, which struck Heine as 'a horse-cure'.

To lift the morale of Germany's liberals, Heine concluded the tale of the 'Captive Messiah' with the remark that he had often thought of it: 'In evil days it seems to me that I even heard with my own ears a rattling as of golden chains and then a desperate sobbing'. And addressing his conflict with Börne more directly, he wrote: 'It will take a goodish while before we find the great healing salvation for the painful sickness of mankind. Until then all sorts of quack doctors will appear with domestic cures which will only aggravate the illness.' He had already written elsewhere that revolution would come to Germany one day, for the idea of it was there, sleeping in the German forests. But that time was not yet. As for Börne's revolutionary agitation, Heine made no secret of the fact that the idea of a proletarian regime filled him with the worst forebodings. Continuing his train of thought about the 'quack doctors' with their instant solutions, he brought his self-styled defence of his superior *Weltanschauung*[31] in his Börne book to a climax by writing:

> Here come the radicals and prescribe a horse-cure which for all its sharpness will at best only remove the scurf from the face of the old society, but not the inner rottenness at the core of the social body. Even if that radical therapy succeeds in bringing temporary relief to the most excruciating torments of suffering mankind... the patient is fated to rise from his sickbed and drag himself around for the rest of his life in drab hospital uniform, in the ash-grey garb of equality... Nothing will be left other than Rumford's utility soup,[32]

a cheap army soup made of 'bones, blood, and other nutritious ingredients' devised by the 18th-century Benjamin Thompson, Count of Rumford, when reorganizing the Bavarian soldiery.

There was some contradiction in Heine's stand, for while he saw himself as a leading warrior in the struggle against 'the exploitation of man by man' and every kind of oppression, he insisted on maintaining his sovereign independence as an artist. Börne had no room for art, having sacrificed his own considerable artistic inclinations to his chosen role as a political tribune. To Heine, however, the artist was king, 'for beauty and genius are also a kind of monarchy'. Besides, he had learned that even Saint-Simon's vision of a golden age of progress had elements that could be turned into totalitarian dogma.

In 1835 Heine had dedicated his *De l'Allemagne* – containing his excursus combining Saint-Simonist ideas with remarks on the revolutionary potential of Hegel's philosophy – to Prosper Enfantin, the self-styled 'Pope' of Saint-Simonism. Enfantin, who was using his forced stay in Egypt and his engineering skill to sketch plans for digging the Suez Canal, replied with a long 'apostolic' letter. He lectured Heine on industrial development's requiring a hierarchy and order, and not the chaos of revolution. Showing little interest in German philosophy, he had praised the Catholic Church and the repressive policies of Metternich and the Holy Alliance.[33]

Ironically, at the very time that Enfantin had criticized Heine's individualism in the name of the interests of industry and the reactionary *status quo*, Börne had castigated it in the name of republican virtue and the cause of revolution. Heine called a plague on both their houses. In *Ludwig Börne* he gave vent to his strong presentiment that any egalitarian republic founded by fanatical, dogmatic ideologists would end up in a drab, spartan regime as oppressive as the clerical-aristocratic one. There would be no room for nightingales or genius 'in the commonwealth of our new puritans'. Mediocrity would rule, and 'all traditional gaiety, all that is sweet and fragrant, all poetry will be pumped out of life.'

Ludwig Börne. A Memorial ended on a suitably nightmarish note, Heine dreaming of the Muses fleeing into the forest and dissolving in a spectral fog before he woke up to 'the roar of the mob approaching in the distance.'[34]

His book consisted of many strands. Authentic quotations from Börne's writings were accompanied by Heine's personal recollections of him. Imaginary conversations between the two of them, in some of which Heine, to deflect the censorship, put some of his own ideas into the dead man's mouth, were interlaced with observations on a host of subjects and people – Moses the Lawgiver and the Bible as 'the portable homeland' of the Jews; the great drama of the Passion of Christ the Redeemer, and mankind still divided and suffering and awaiting some new annunciation; Homer and the old Greeks, the Renaissance, Shakespeare, Napoleon and the Rothschilds, besides Goethe; politics, the July Revolution, journalism, art, and what not. Yet for all this diversity, Heine – giving free rein to what he had once called 'the association of ideas' – wove all the strands thematically together into a fabulous fabric without ever losing control of the main threads or blurring the two figures of Börne and himself, clearly outlined in the foreground. As clever and witty as it was ferocious, and not a little conceited, there was magic in Heine's treatment of the subject, though in the view of his detractors it was black magic.

At the beginning of the 20th century, Thomas Mann declared his admiration for Heine's *Ludwig Börne*, calling it a work of art: 'Only he who understands the blissfully detached smile with which he fended off friends who warned him of the human, personal, political offensiveness of the book by answering: "But isn't it beautifully written?" – only he can appreciate the memorable phenomenon represented by this Jew-artist among the Germans!'[35]

Shortly afterwards, the Viennese critic Karl Kraus, in an essay included in *Downfall of the World through Black Magic* (*Untergang der Welt durch schwarze Magie*),[36] attacked Heine's pose as a sovereign artist, and, taking up the cudgels on behalf of Börne, accused Heine of being an unprincipled *feuilletonist*. During the 70 years since the publication of Heine's Börne book, the nationalist German Reich – with the notable exception of Nietzsche – had marginalized Heine as un-German, whereas H.G. Atkins was to write: 'Whatever the Germans may think, for the rest of the world Heine is the representative German poet after Goethe.'[37] The controversy about *Börne* was resumed with greater vigour after World War II, generating a host of studies, especially in Germany, as part of the general debate on Heine's *oeuvre* in a conscience-stricken country which in the Nazi period had made public bonfires of his books. The effort to reinstate Heine into German literature and to ascertain his significance in it became all the more intense as, during the Cold War, East- and West-Germany, each maintaining separate Heine Institutes, practically vied with one another in the research, publication and interpretation of his work. East Germany claimed Heine as a herald of Marxism. In the West, too, as Sammons was to remark in 1979, the revival of Heine studies came to ride on the wave of student radicalization and the recrudescence of Marxism among young scholars; although independent studies were not lacking, the result, as Sammons observed, was that Heine's *Ludwig Börne* was 'defended as a statement of higher revolutionary vision ideologically superior to Börne's sentimental moralism and archaic, petty-bourgeois neo-Jacobinism, and as an insight into Germany's unreadiness for revolution' at the time.

It is worth noting in this connection that Friedrich Engels, who in 1840 was 20 years old, joined in the chorus of disapproval which greeted the publication of *Ludwig Börne*, calling Heine a pessimistic, exhausted Tannhäuser, and his book one of the most 'inane' ever written in the German language.[38] Paradoxically, it was Karl Marx who, in a little-known letter written in 1846, was to vindicate Heine, the champion of liberty and human rights who sometimes called himself a monarchist, against Börne, the intransigent revolutionary.

On 5 April 1846, living by then in Brussels, Marx sent Heine a letter saying that he had by chance come across a 'slanderous libel against you: Börne's posthumous letters.' These so-called letters were actually a collection of remarks by Börne denigrating Heine, which had previously been omitted from Börne's printed *Letters*, and were now published in answer to Heine's book. Marx's comment was that he was surprised to find that Börne could be 'so boring, petty and insipid'. As for the harsh contemporary criticism meted out to Heine's Börne book, Marx wrote: 'A more doltish reception than this book has received at the hands of the Christian-German donkeys will hardly be found in any period of literature, although no German period has been lacking in doltishness.'[39]

Marx's defence of Heine was influenced by two factors. First, since writing his book on Börne, Heine had adopted a more radical political stand; secondly, Marx had in the meantime spent 15 months in Paris, and he and Heine had seen quite a bit of each other. Drawing attention to Marx's letter at an International Heine Congress in 1972, Hans Kaufmann was to suggest that Marx's interest in Heine's *Börne* was aroused by two fundamentally different conceptions of revolution presented in the book: a specifically 'petty-bourgeois-democratic one [Börne's], and another pushing beyond that limited horizon [Heine's]' to the all-encompassing, logically interconnected 'religious, philosophical, political and social emancipation' of man foreshadowed and held up by Heine in all his works since the mid-1830s.[40]

Whether it was this or simply the element of 'Young Hegelian' philosophy in Heine's *Weltanschauung* which made Karl Marx rank Heine over Börne, the joke was ultimately to be on Marx. For 'the ash-grey garb of equality' in Heine's *Börne* prefigured his fear of the drab totalitarian uniformity which would mark the rule of the proletariat, a fear Heine was to express by hedging his later prediction that 'the future belongs to Communism' with his confessed horror at the thought that its thick-headed iconoclasts would 'mercilessly smash the marble statues of beauty' in their gloomy regimented society.

Besides his urge to demonstrate his superior *Weltanschauung*, Heine had been unable in his Börne book to resist the temptation of settling accounts with his antagonist on a matter over which he would have been better advised to remain silent. As a moralist, Börne had systematically pried into Heine's private life, and persistently flayed his frivolous and 'lewd' womanizing. Heine's revenge was to sully the dead man's memory by working into his book some gratuitous insinuations concerning Börne's moral hypocrisy in presiding over a dubious *ménage à trois* with his friend Jeanette Strauss-Wohl (the former Jeanette Wohl) and her husband.

It was a recidivist trait in Heine which led him to make these insinuations which, needless to say, were to draw the greatest fire and cries of scandal when his book appeared. In 1832, after Heine's former professor, the great Schlegel, had taken a stab at him in a derogatory epigram, Heine alluded in *The Romantic*

School to Schlegel's long-standing intimacy with Madame de Staël. Heine's derogatory passages in *Ludwig Börne* were another instance of this technique of petty reprisal, but it cannot be denied that in both cases the victim had attacked Heine first. Perhaps the best clue to Heine's over-reacting to provocation with the 'hysteria' of the sensitive and arrogant artist 'maximizing precisely that with which he was reproached'[41] was provided as early as 1835 by a friend who knew him from his youthful days in Hamburg. He was the Jena University professor Wolff who later helped to expedite Marx's doctorate. After visiting Heine in Paris, Wolff characterized him in an article as 'a born king of the world, with all the pleasant and unpleasant qualities of such a personage', and added: 'He thinks royally, loves royally, but also hates and persecutes royally. Unlike a royal despot, he does not condemn his enemies to life-long incarceration; rather, like a royal hero, he slays them dead.'[42]

This came so close to Heine's view of himself that the words may even have come from his own mouth.

On 11 August 1840, a few days after Campe had placed *Ludwig Börne. A Memorial* on sale in Germany's chief cities, Heine left Paris with Mathilde for their annual holiday at Granville. On the 28th he wrote that he was bathing in 'idyllic peace' in the Channel, completely indifferent to the 'imprecations' and 'shouting' he expected the book to receive. What mattered to him was the verdict of the future, and of that he felt sure.[43]

For all his inner turmoil, Heine bravely held on to this posture throughout the storm of protests and outright maledictions that followed. To give but a few examples of the general condemnation, by friends and foes alike, that blew into his face, Karl Goedeke, the premier literary historian at the time, described Heine's book as a 'colourful harlequinade made up of witticisms, jokes, moodishness, humour, cynicism, calumny and lies', and compared Heine himself to 'a poisoner who relied on the stupidity of the Germans not to see through his gross tricks in serving them up a deadly fruit.'[44]

Gutzkow wrote an indignant Preface to his own biography of Börne – which had been held up by Campe – and to Heine's great annoyance it was given an advance printing in article form in Campe's own *Telegraph für Deutschland*. In October 1840 Jeanette Strauss-Wohl published *Börne's Verdict on Heine*, the collection of Börne's previously unpublished aspersions on Heine which were later seen by Marx. The press continued to condemn Heine's book in no uncertain terms; even *The Journal for the Elegant World*, which was friendly to him, had nothing better to say for it in two articles in the autumn of 1840 than that 'in executing Börne Heine has rendered a great service to Austria [and that] no one has the right to play Aristophanes when writing the obituary of a dead man.'[45]

Heine had indeed executed Börne, but when Campe bluntly summed up the situation for him in two sentences – 'Do you fully realize the extent of your mistake? There are people who commit suicide, who give up their life of their own free will, but a literary suicide is something new.' – he continued to put up a cool front, declaring: 'Used as I am to imprecations, I remain innerly calm, knowing that the future belongs to me.'

The only mistake he would ever admit to was his having cast doubts on Börne's sexual mores, and several years later he was to apologize publicly to Strauss-Wohl for having misrepresented her character and questioned her honour.

24

Founding the *Rheinische Zeitung*

At the end of January 1841, the Leipzig firm of Otto Wigand announced the publication of Moses Hess's second book, *The European Triarchy*. Like his first, this appeared anonymously, the publisher counting on the effect of 'curiosity which makes people guess, talk about and buy' books. While anonymity had brought Hess's earlier *Holy History of Mankind* no more than two insignificant press notices, the contents of the new book caused a stir in the circles of 'educated Germany'. The *Athenäum* was in fact the first to review it, and no wonder. For one thing, here was an outsider, a non-Hegelian, proclaiming that Hegel's 'philosophy of the objective spirit' was incapable of creating and giving birth to 'a single historical action'. Hess informed the radical Young Hegelians that Napoleon had been right to dismiss the Germans as 'a nation of ideologues'.

As mentioned earlier, Hess postulated in *The European Triarchy* that a philosophy of history which – like Hegel's – dealt only with the rational development of past and present history had performed only half its task: the full task was to extrapolate 'from these two known dimensions – what has been and what is – the third and unknown dimension of the future which is in *the process of becoming*. By accomplishing this task, the only one worthy of it, the philosophy of history becomes *a philosophy of action*.'[1]

Although Hess gave credit to Cieszkowski's 1838 study proposing a 'philosophy of action', he also took him – along with the other Young Hegelian radicals – to task for missing an element 'essential to rounding off the totality of history'. Whereas Hegel had been a prisoner of the past, Cieszkowski and the Hegelian Left – amazingly, in Hess's view – went overboard in the other direction, being so single-mindedly preoccupied with the future as to ignore or completely write off the past, thereby 'missing the sense, significance and unfolding of the historical process in which that future is rooted and out of which it is to grow.' For another thing, *The European Triarchy* was by its very title an indirect answer to the anonymous author of a recent work advocating a European 'pentarchy' composed of Europe's 'Big Five', in which reactionary Russia and Austria would be predominant. The author of that plan, as it turned out, was a Saxon-born German in the Russian State service. Hess, who was also soon

identified as the author of *The European Triarchy*, foresaw a united Europe arising in time out of an initial league – and under the leadership – of France, Germany and England. Continuing the futurist vision outlined in his first book, he
wrote: 'One is not yet used to the idea of treating Europe as one single organism. Yet nothing is more important than this idea.'[2]

Hess observed that the population of Europe was divided at the top by the
various states and churches representing it. But these basically superficial
'superior' power structures with their external political and religious trappings
were bound to change and disintegrate one day, and when that happened 'the
inner unity of the peoples of Europe will manifest itself in all its vitality.
Roman-Germanic Europe has one history, one culture, inter-related customs
and linguistic and tribal affinities.'[3]

Although Europe had fortunately not grown into a 'uniform' monolith, 'this
large and diversified mass of land and nations constitutes a single organism
jointed and articulated into a multiplicity of limbs – German, French, English,
Protestant, Catholic, Anglican', etc. But for all this pluralism Europe did not
need 'to have one law imposed upon it, nor one form of government, one belief
or any other coercive measure in order to feel united and strong.' In language
that might sound apposite if delivered at the Brussels headquarters of the new
Europe emerging at the beginning of the 1990s, he reminded his readers that
any injury to the smallest part of this (European) organism is painfully registered by the whole of it; but as he had written most of the *Triarchy* in 1840 he
gave as an example the trans-national effect of such tremendous events as the
French Revolutions of 1789 and 1830.[4]

As for the vaunted 'equilibrium' maintained by the 'unholy Holy Alliance',
Hess observed that this rested on standing armies and intimidation, and could
neither guarantee peace nor solve the most pressing of all contemporary problems, which was 'the glaring antagonism between poverty and the aristocracy of
money, between burgeoning wealth on the one hand, and misery consuming
itself in perpetual sweat and blood.'

Although Hess was only at the beginning of his life-long career as a Socialist,
he saw in this antagonism a 'great, world-historical struggle', moreover one
which 'had not yet even reached its apex.' But so convinced was he that world
history was not haphazard but 'essentially free, ethical and providential' (it was
of course beset with contradictions and degenerations, 'but the World Spirit is
not so stupid as to give in to evil out of simple inaction or sheer fear') and so
sure that rational man, becoming conscious of his social nature, would ultimately realize his own need for association and co-operation with his fellows,
that he ventured to predict that 'A general European war will indubitably lead
to a general European alliance', a united Europe in which truth, justice and the

ethical imperative would prevail and peace, order and freedom would no longer be a pious dream.

But why a Franco-German-English league at the helm of the new Europe? For one thing, to keep the Russian Empire out of the European concert. Hess regarded Tsarist Russia, which had inspired the Holy Alliance, with deep suspicion. True, it had helped to overthrow Napoleon and the upper levels of Russian society were European-educated, but by and large semi-Asiatic Russia remained alien to the spiritual values and the pursuit of 'freedom, civilization and progress' common to the European nations. It might take centuries before Slavic Russia – which had never experienced anything like the German Reformation or the French Enlightenment and Revolution, and whose church always slavishly bent to the Tsar's will – really became saturated with European culture. Hess feared Russia for another reason: 'It might intervene to crush any future revolution in Europe', as it was indeed to do in 1848.

For another thing, both Germany and France, the former by means of the Reformation and the latter through the Revolution, had already given a great impetus to the building of the New Age. They had to learn from each other, but – and this was a point Hess kept stressing – 'both of them should go to school and learn from the English.' This was a novel idea, for the conventional wisdom among intellectuals on the Continent around 1840 was to disparage the English as a nation of shopkeepers, regardless of the fact that there was more freedom in England than in any of their own countries.

'The English are the most practical nation in the world,' wrote Hess. Although there was no separation of church and state in England, he remarked that there was more religious tolerance there than in most places. What the Germans and French had to learn was that English institutions, precisely because they were practical, promoted progress. Hess explained this paradox by pointing out that the 'inner and external resistance' provoked by these institutions, far from signifying weakness, had in practice positive results, just as the tensions within the Catholic Church, and between it and its emperors, had sparked libertarian ideas. In industrial England the social gap was most sharply evident. But that pragmatic country, which was already busy reforming some of its medieval institutions, could be expected to play a paramount role in solving the social problem – either peacefully or by means of revolution.

Hess's visionary scheme for a united Europe under the aegis of France, Germany and England was based not only on geopolitical considerations – 'France has the Mediterranean, and the Romance nations grouped around it; England looks out on the world's oceans; Germany has links with Scandinavia, and Central and Southern Europe' – but on others as well: the 1789 Revolution had shown that the French had both the will and the aptitude for political action.

'The French Revolution was an ethical revolution, related to the material as well as the spiritual interests of society.' But it was in the character of the French to be 'swept from earth to heaven, and from heaven to earth, without conquering either' – with the result that they had remained stuck midway between materialism and idealism. The German, on the other hand, 'is an idealist', strong in abstract philosophy. 'The English are the nation of praxis more than any other nation. England is to our century what France was to the previous one.' It would take the cooperation of these three psychologically different nations to bring about the New Europe, and the English were best suited to provide its laws. In Hamburg the *Telegraph für Deutschland* greeted the appearance of *The European Triarchy* with a rave review. Brockhaus's *Literary Sheets* thought well of it too and other reviews were generally favourable. Only one periodical branded the author as an exponent of 'extreme revolutionarism'. The critic of Berlin's learned *Athenäum*, while recognizing the book's topical significance, had other reservations. The organ of the Doctors Club could not but take exception to Hess's way of depriving Hegel, with all due respect to his achievements, of the crown of the philosopher who had developed a universally valid world-historical system.

In line with his thesis that the French and the Germans had to learn from each other, Hess presented Saint-Simon in *The European Triarchy* as a man who descried the future and its problems. While he combined a drive to action with the fiery eloquence of a passionate heart, Hegel, tending to contemplation, perceived the past with the abstract eye of 'a calm, cool, logical mind'. In Hess's view, however, Saint-Simon and Hegel each held only part of the truth. It was Spinoza who was the first to proclaim 'the absolute unity of all life... perceived the totality [of phenomena] in his time, at the end of an eventful period, and the beginning of a new age.'[5]

Whereas Spinoza reconciled spirit and nature, Hegel, in Hess's view, had been one-sided. 'The apex of German philosophy', Hess wrote, 'is a reflection of our idealistic past – the nature of action which takes in the future as well as the past has not yet dawned in German philosophy.' Cieszkowski and the Left-Hegelian school had begun the transition from theory to action, but German philosophy still had to catch up with practical life.

These points, and Hess's proposed synthesis of German theory, French political practice and English economics, were to be echoed in Karl Marx's first formulations of his Communist conception:

> In Germany one is now beginning where France and England left off... Hitherto philosophers have left the keys to all riddles lying in their desk... Now philosophy has become worldly-secular [and] has

joined battle not only outwardly, but inwardly too. If we have no business with the construction of the future or with organizing it for all time there can still be no doubt about the task confronting us at present: the ruthless criticism of the existing order, ruthless in that it will shrink neither from its own discoveries nor from conflict with the powers that be.

That philosophy must turn its attention to the great problem of the age – the social problem – was another point made by Hess in *The European Triarchy* which Marx was to adopt, as is evident in the following passage:

> The existence of a suffering mankind which thinks and of a thinking mankind which is suppressed must inevitably become unpalatable and indigestible... It is our task to drag the old world into the full light of day and to give positive shape to the new one. The more time history allows thinking mankind to reflect and suffering mankind to collect its strength the more perfect will be the fruit which the present now bears within its womb.

But these reflections were to be put on paper by Marx more than two years after Hess's book appeared at the beginning of 1841. It immediately established Hess's reputation among Germany's radical intelligentsia to the point where the reviewer of the *Athenäum* – in spite of Hess's 'Spinozism' and his express statement that he did not belong to 'the Hegelian school' – practically adopted him as a Young Hegelian.

Hess now frequented a circle of progressive young 'democrats' which had formed in Cologne. Among them were several of the founders of the future *Rheinische Zeitung*, including Georg Jung, a well-to-do assistant judge who, taking an interest in Young Hegelian ideas, was impressed by Hess's radical approach; Jung's friend Dagobert Oppenheim; Rudolf Schramm, a liberal lawyer and future politician, who had read *The European Triarchy* in manuscript; Ludwig Braunfels, a lawyer who doubled as a journalist; and several other lawyers and members of the free professions. Although Hess's circle of friends and acquaintances had considerably widened, he was not a happy person.

At 29, he continued to live in Cologne with his gruff father, who remained unsympathetic to his impractical interests. Wilting for years under his father's unfeeling manner and the coldness he seemed to exude, Hess kept commuting to Bonn to attend university lectures, but chafed at his continued dependence on his parent. For the past two years he had been trying unsuccessfully to enter the bookselling and publishing trade, 'the only business' he could think of that offered a chance of escaping his father's tutelage while suiting his inclinations. The obstacle was that for capital he had to apply to his father, who would only grant him funds if and when he married. The orthodox father's stipulation, needless to say, was that the bride had to be a Jewish girl of good family, but Moses had so far failed to find one.

On 10 March 1841, three days before *The European Triarchy* was to be reviewed in the *Athenäum*, a feeling of spring in the air stirred in Hess so acute a yearning for love and companionship that he actually appealed to the writer Berthold Auerbach in Mainz to help him find a suitable girl to marry: 'How can I rejoice with the new season, lonesome and alone as I am?' he wrote. 'The earth is waking from its long winter slumber, but I feel sad and out of sorts.' The friendship he had struck up with Georg Jung and some of Cologne's politically minded young intellectuals – who all had rich families and money to throw about, while Hess's father kept him on a short string – did not, apparently, compensate for the affection he had missed since childhood; it was 8 years now since his abortive elopement attempt with the red-haired Lena, who had failed to turn up at their rendezvous in Holland.

Before writing to Auerbach, Hess had confided his genuine 'need of love' to Ludwig Braunfels, who replied that he was a fool and gave him a piece of worldly advice which he reproduced in his letter of 10 March 1841 to Auerbach: 'Your father is said to be worth 100,000 guilders. You are considered a man of letters who will presently rise to fame. Stipulate the claims one is entitled to make in these circumstances and before you know it you will have a beautiful woman to call your own and a handsome fortune into the bargain.'

To Auerbach Hess observed that, though his father was not quite so rich as Braunfels thought, 'he will be so within a couple of years... and since he is known to be a miser people believe him to be even richer than he really is'; moreover, a professional bookseller with more 'experience' than capital happened to be ready to take him in as a partner.

No marriage, no bookshop, Hess explained to Auerbach, adding that he could not resist finding some logic in 'the project' outlined by Braunfels. It was true too that he had made something of a name for himself in Cologne and once he got the money for the bookshop he was assured of a social position 'which should, I believe, satisfy even the richest Jewish girl...'

Fearing that if he did not seize this opportunity life would pass him by, Hess convinced himself that marriage was the only 'plausible' solution for him and concluded this part of his letter by giving Auerbach 'full authority to initiate a match for me...'[6] He then passed on to other matters, including 'the Prussian constitutional issue' raised in Jacoby's *Four Questions* and the philosophies of Fichte and Hegel which he was re-studying in preparation for an essay on 'The

Philosophy of Action'. Later that spring, Hess paid a personal visit to Auerbach in Mainz. Auerbach, who was to write the highly popular *Village Stories from the Black Forest*, introduced him to the town's notables. If this was a bride-hunting visit, nothing came of it. He enjoyed the social side of the visit and in fact was eventually to contract a mixed marriage – though not exactly of the type he advocated in *The European Triarchy*. But he was in any case spared from spending more time looking for ways to make himself independent from his father by the financial collapse of a new-born Cologne daily, the *Rheinische All-gemeine Zeitung*, which spurred a group of influential citizens – in quest of a voice in public affairs – to take over its licence and launch a more powerful and better-funded paper on its ruins.

The *Rheinische Zeitung*, which became famous in its time for its daring political verve and historically by virtue of young Marx's association with it, was about to be born. Hess played a leading part in its foundation. The moving spirit behind the project was his rich friend and radical convert, Georg Jung, who immediately offered him the editorship. By 23 June 1841, Hess was informing Auerbach that he had been invited 'to head a new newspaper... a solid, very solid enterprise.' To give him a modicum of journalistic experience – of which he had none – Hess was placed for a short time in charge of the bankrupt daily's literary supplement; thus 'initiated in 8–9 days in the myster-ies of editing a newspaper, albeit an insignificant and non-political one', he threw himself into the preparations for the new one with all the pent-up energy and zeal of a man long idle.[7]

By mid-August the formerly lonesome Hess was having talks with several deputies of the Rhenish Diet and busy canvassing shareholders and prospective contributors for the new paper. In July or August he received a visit from Pro-fessor Julius Fröbel, the Zurich millionaire who in May had published Her-wegh's *Poems of a Living Man* and now planned to exploit that success and start a radical German review in Switzerland to be edited by Herwegh.

By the time the issue of shares for the *Rheinische Zeitung* began, Hess had raised part of the capital and was exerting himself for the balance among his acquaintances. Four 'lawyer-friends' of his were almost sure to become future board directors, and counting on his confirmation as editor-in-chief, he promised Braunfels – who had run a Coblenz newspaper for 4 years until its suppression – to engage him as assistant editor.

'The undertaking', he wrote, seemed assured of a splendid future – which was no wonder, seeing that Jung was allied by marriage to a banking house, and another of the group, Rudolf Schramm, was the son of a wealthy manufacturer, while a third, Dagobert Oppenheim, was a co-founder and co-owner of Col-ogne's Oppenheim Bank. And these were only three of the so-called Cologne circle of affluent liberal-bourgeois democrats – bankers, industrialists, lawyers, doctors, etc. – who were to back the new venture.

The *Rheinische Zeitung* came into being with an impressive share capital exceeding 30,000 Thaler. The Rhineland was in many ways Prussia's most modern and best-developed province. Its industrialists had continued to do well for themselves under the new rulers. But they and Cologne's rich, cultured élite resented not only the mindless Prussian laws after the French liberties, but the whole idea of being governed by a feudal caste of aristocratic paper-pushers who often referred the slightest matter back for decision to 'His All-Highest Majesty' in Berlin. They found it ridiculous that in the Rhenish Diet, which the King convened irregularly at his pleasure – and which, anyway, had no power to resolve anything, only to make recommendations – issues of wider than local concern could only be discussed when the 'All-Highest' so moved. At that, the growing bourgeoisie was under-represented in the Diet and the intelligentsia and middle class remained entirely excluded from it.

The sponsors of the *Rheinische Zeitung*, in short, wanted democratic representation and a greater say in provincial as well as national affairs. They favoured a constitutional monarchy and were ready to compaign for equitable laws, freedom of thought and religion, and against censorship of ideas. Theirs was to be an outspoken newspaper standing for progress, though hardly a radical one.

Things, however, were to turn out differently. The bourgeois merchants and lawyer-politicians among the shareholders represented a wide diversity of interests. While all wished to see the restoration of civic rights they had enjoyed under Napoleon, some were were chiefly interested in railway expansion and the extension of customs unions to the advantage of the textile industry; others attached greater importance to pressing the political issue of the constitution; and the paper's editorial staff was to be composed largely of academics with philosophical ideas who meant to fight Prussia's feudal-clerical policies. Jung, who had frequented the Doctors Club in Berlin, may have promised the editorship to Hess, but he was interested in staffing the paper with Young Hegelians, and he and Oppenheim were eventually to bring Karl Marx onto the scene.

Marx had moved to Bonn at the end of July 1841, but on his way there he had spent some time being dined and wined in Cologne by Jung, Oppenheim and their circle. On or about 10 August, Jenny, addressing Marx as her darling *Schwarzwildchen* – literally, 'little wild boar' – wrote at the start of one of her more ecstatic letters: 'how glad I am that you are in good spirits and that my letter cheered you, and that you long for me; that you live in tapestried rooms and have drunk champagne in Cologne and that there are Hegel clubs there, and that you dreamt [of me] and that, in short, you are mine, my own darling little wild boar...'[8]

Whether Hess met Marx, who was 6 years his junior, at one of the Cologne champagne parties or at Bonn University, their encounter was to have far-reaching consequences for both. On 2 September, in a letter to Auerbach, Hess described the 'overwhelming' impression made on him by 'a man who is now one of our friends, though he lives in Bonn, where he will soon be lecturing.' In this justly famous letter, Hess called Marx 'a phenomenon' and prophesied:

> Be prepared to meet the greatest, perhaps the only genuine philosopher now alive, who will soon... attract the eyes of all Germany... Dr Marx, as is the name of my idol, is still a very young man (about 24 at most) who will give medieval religion and politics their *coup de grâce*. He combines the deepest philosophic seriousness with the most biting wit. Imagine Rousseau, Voltaire, Holbach, Lessing, Heine and Hegel united in one person – *I say united, not lumped together* – and you have Dr Marx.[9]

Marx was never to be so succinctly summed up as in these lines written before he had conceived any theory of note or published anything except two insignificant poems. Elsewhere in his panegyric, Hess added that he had always wished 'to have a man like him as my teacher in philosophy... Patience! now I, too, may yet learn something!'

This may explain the paradoxical fact that it was Hess himself who was ultimately to 'persuade the financiers' of the *Rheinische Zeitung* to offer Marx its editorship.[10] As it turned out, however, Marx was to learn quite a few things from Hess.

'All who knew him were convinced of the great future awaiting 26-year-old Doctor Marx... and his beautiful young wife,' Heinrich Böll was to observe in a little-known essay published 120 years after Marx's first contact with the founders of the *Rheinische Zeitung*. Böll, winner of a Nobel Prize for Literature – and himself a Rhinelander, born and bred in Cologne – conjured up a vivid picture of the career Marx might have made, but sacrificed: 'It is not difficult to imagine Marx as a young, celebrated professor' commanding a large following and much sought-after, or 'being elevated to Prussian Cabinet rank as a progressive young Minister, to be immortalized in a Biedermeyer painting with a couple of medals decorating his expensively clothed chest, surrounded by his wife and children, a picture of German bliss...'[11]

Indeed, Marx was barely 23 years old that summer of 1841, and the most brilliant career seemed to be his for the asking. Others besides Moses Hess expected young Marx to become Germany's foremost philosopher, equal to – and in time perhaps surpassing – Kant, Fichte and Hegel. Admired by all in the

Doctors Club, second to none but that searing wit and erudite critic, Dr Bauer, he had taken little time to make manifest the promise of genius his father had perceived in him. His head was like a power-house or 'a factory of ideas', as his Berlin friend and sometime drinking companion, the historian Karl Köppen, had commented in a letter in June 1841. If Köppen was one of what might be called Marx's own clique in the Doctors Club, the awe-struck Hess was not. Yet three months later he, too, was proclaiming him his idol. By October, Jung was pronouncing Marx 'one of the most incisive minds I know', and before many months Arnold Ruge, editor of the German Yearbooks (*Deutsche Jahrbücher*), was adding his testimony and declaring Marx 'a perfectly excellent head'.

Nor was it by intellect alone that he had made his mark. 'Domineering, impetuous, passionate, full of boundless self-confidence, at the same time deeply earnest and erudite,' thus Gustav von Mevissen, one of the shareholders of the *Rheinische Zeitung*, was to recall him. Young Marx's sinewy, hirsute appearance made Mevissen describe him as 'a powerful man... with thick black hair springing from his cheeks, arms, nose and ears...' Engels, who was to arrive in Berlin in the autumn, had yet to meet Marx when he wrote a long satire in verse on the members of the Doctors Club, containing his famous doggerel about 'the black fellow from Trier, a savage monster', pounding the ground with his heels and advancing with clenched fist, 'raving and raging mad, as if a thousand devils had him by the hair.'

Written from hearsay, on the basis of Marx's Berlin reputation, the exaggerated portrayal conveys nothing so much as a sense of restless vigour and aggressive dynamism. There is, in short, little doubt that everything about young Marx, his mental powers and range, his ebullience, his pugnacious spirit and his very bearing, marked him as an extraordinary personality in the eyes of those who knew him. Together with his dark, not to say demonic, attraction, it was a combination that also held Jenny in thrall, and never more so than by the end of that summer of 1841, when – still clinging to their youthful and tenuous bond of love for 5 tense long years – she was approaching the old-maid age of 28.

Karl had done nothing by way of hurrying his studies in order to speed up the day of their marriage. Even now, more than a year since he had obtained his doctorate in Berlin, he was living in Bonn. Jenny remained a prey to loneliness in Trier, bravely bearing the commiserating glances which the denizens of that 'Popish old nest' had for advanced spinsterhood, while struggling with her own doubts, frustrations and anxieties. Indeed, her letter to her 'little wild boar' shows her living vicariously through his champagne bouts, his Hegel discussions, his plans and frolics with the famous and to her unknown Bruno Bauer. Written from her 'little bed' during a sick spell, it is an effusive, somewhat *exalté* and unreal letter, abounding in endearments and diminutives, but its feverish tone is less the result of running a temperature than of something else. She is alarmed at the prospect of his starting

> to meddle with politics. That is dangerously perilous. Karlchen, always remember that your darling is waiting for you at home, is hopeful and miserable and entirely dependent on your fate. You dear, dear little heart, if only I could see you again. You asked for only 2 lines, and now this little page is almost full... But you, Herzchen, won't be angry with your little Jenny, will you...

Her head is 'pitiably empty, and whirring and humming with a rattle and clatter' as of wheels and mills, but her

> little heart overflows with longing, love and ardent desire for you, my endlessly beloved... O Liebchen, how much I think of you and your love through the sleepless nights, how oft have I not prayed for you [and] blessed you... A kiss on every finger... Fly, fly to my Karl and press yourselves hot on his lips... Whisper to him all the small charming secret sweetnesses that love inspires... I must stop, my hand is a complete hubbub.

At the very end comes the question: 'Is it not true that I can marry you after all?'[12]

She sounds overwrought, insecure and affected by that 'continuing sexual repression' which in the mid-1970s was to make one scholarly author ponder the likelihood that Jenny 'remained a virgin throughout her long engagement'. Yet her next letter – written only 5 weeks after the other, but first published in 1975 – reveals a new and different Jenny. It contains hints of some sexual rapport that strengthened her attachment to Karl and of her mother's anxiety that they respect the proprieties incumbent on engaged couples in 1841. 'Mother', she wrote on 13 September, 'is again after me with all her old reproaches.' Jenny had been spending some time at Neuss, on the Rhine north of Bonn, and her mother was sending Edgar to pick her up at Cologne – midway between the two towns – and insisting that they must 'absolutely observe all inner as well as external decencies, otherwise I shall not be allowed to visit you in Bonn,' apparently on the way back to Trier. 'All this dropped like a ton on my soul. Inner as well as external decencies!! – o my Karl, my sweet only Karl!'

> And yet, Karl, I cannot, do not, feel any remorse. When I shut my eyes firmly and conjure up the vision of your smiling face I am filled with bliss at the thought that I have been everything to you... O Karl, I fully realize what I have done and how the world would outlaw me,

I know all that, yet nevertheless I am happy and cheerful and would not trade even the memory of those hours for any treasure in the world.

She only trembles at the thought that 'I shall have to go on living apart from you for so long, surrounded by woes and misery...' She details some of her younger brother Edgar's debts and his 'deranged financial situation', and mentions two sums of 40 and 30 Thaler she received from home – but they melted so quickly that 'I hardly have enough left for the return journey...'

In her August letter, Jenny had coquettishly complained to her *Schwarzwildchen*: 'You might have praised me a little for my Greek and my scholarliness' and had gone on to observe, rightly and in some resignation, that 'you Hegelizing gentlemen are never ready to acknowledge anything, be it ever so superlative, if it does not exactly conform to your ideas – so I must modestly rest on my own laurels.' Now she wrote: 'What a beloved sweet, unique heart's darling you are!... Imagine me, Herzchen, still lying in my little bed dreaming and lost in (morning) reverie when Thekla brought me your small, crumpled little letter... How I rejoiced, thankful and brimming with love! Do you really enjoy my letters? I can never quite believe it. And how proud and vain my little flatterer makes me!' Karl had apparently praised her 'humour, wit and vivacity' and her 4-page reply to his 'crumpled little' one was as packed as ever with endearing diminutives – the 'little wild boar' had now become her 'beloved little angel' – and with signs of some basic insecurity: 'Isn't it true, Karl, that you will now remain faithful to me for ever and ever and work it out that I can become your wife?' But for all this lingering, long-nursed anxiety, it was a much more confident, calm and less prudish Jenny who now addressed him: 'Actually, you had better not fetch me from Cologne', for it might 'raise scruples at home, but you will come, won't you, please, please.' And: 'Karl, how angelically good you are... and Karlchen, I am not angry with you for kissing that woman, I am even a little glad if you enjoyed it, that is how I love you, but...' And she warned him that as for 'allowing another to enjoy that highest bliss which I can hardly fathom for myself – no, Karl, that I cannot.'

This time Jenny sounds more like the adult woman she was, but after humorously describing Neuss and a visit to Düsseldorf, her mind turned back to the treasured memory which was the true *Leitmotif* of this letter: 'Once more I lived through every blissful hour. Again I lay against your bosom, happy in the ecstasy of love! And how you smiled at me, shining with joy. Karl, Karl, how I love you!' She struggled for words, and the sum of all that her 'heart, senses, thoughts, everything, past, present, future' was capable of inscribing was: 'I love you inexpressibly, limitlessly, timelessly, immeasurably...'[13]

Virgin or not, she was obviously consumed by a strong attraction to Marx and there was now a new element of erotic intimacy that could not but cement her faithfulness to their bond and his hold on her. She remained not only or simply true to him and their youthful vow, but entirely at his beck and call, completely amenable, not to say subservient to his will, his needs, impatient but resigned and waiting for him to settle their future throughout his year-long commutings from Trier to Berlin, from Berlin to Bonn, and between Bonn and Cologne.

His alliance with a titled nobleman, whether of 'ancient or exalted' stock or not, certainly did not diminish his chances of landing a lectureship in Bonn and distinguishing himself in a university career. Sooner or later he might be called to join Prussia's ruling hierarchy in some high office. And the likeliest juncture when a great future could indeed have been his was now, between the ages of 23 and 24 (and not when he was 26 and had left Germany for self-chosen exile in Paris).

But it was not to be. At that time Marx had tied his fate to Bruno Bauer's, and by September 1841 the extraordinary Dr Bauer was already in hot water with both Protestant and Catholic professors at Bonn, with his students, and with the authorities in Berlin. Bauer, the 'pure critic' and theologian who had lost his faith, has in recent times been described as an 'intellectual rapist'. He was indeed, in describing his own method of Gospel criticism, to resort to aggressive sexual symbols: 'He combats theology, even in the Gospels, and in the course of this combat forces his way into the sanctum of religion, and when he has penetrated its theological forecourts [*propylaea*] he profanes it with relish.'[14]

In April 1841 Bauer had published the first volume of his *Criticism of the Synoptic Gospels*. He relished the furore it caused in the theological world and most of the academic establishment. In March, before the book was even out, he had declared to Marx that the second volume was going to add another 'hefty blow'. This indeed landed to effect when it was published in September. Bauer had hoped to exploit the rivalry between Bonn's two theology schools – one Protestant, the other Catholic – but his undisguised contempt for his colleagues of both denominations united them all against him. In August, during the interval between the appearance of the two volumes, his lectures were disrupted by pious or incited theology students, and the new reactionary Minister of Education, Eichhorn, had discreetly begun to ventilate the possibility of sacking Bauer.

It was a characteristic of this brilliant radical scholar that, having practically annihilated the basis of Christianity in his two volumes by declaring that the Gospels were non-historical myths created by writers and poets, he seemed to think that his total rejection of all theology and theologians was no obstacle to his continued presence in a theological faculty,[15] and he had since launched another attack on 'the Government tendencies' in a provocative article titled 'The Christian State and Our Time'.

In May, at the beginning of the whole hullabaloo, a semi-official suggestion had been put to him from the Ministry of Education in Berlin that he shift from theology to teaching church-history and formally apply for that chair. The fanatically principled Bauer, however, was not going to give up the battle between 'science and the state' or the formidable weapon represented by his method of 'pure criticism'.

'I cannot apply, I must keep myself pure,' was his reply, transmitted through his brother Edgar in Berlin, to the Ministry's offer.[16]

With Marx in Bonn since July, Bauer hoped at last to produce the world-historical crisis about which he had written to him in confidence. For a start, the two of them planned to launch a periodical – to be titled *Archives of Atheism* – meant to discredit Prussia's clericalism on theological as well as philosophical grounds. Before long, Jung described Marx in a private letter as 'quite a desperate revolutionary'. He added that Marx, Bauer and Feuerbach were 'getting together to found a theological-philosophical review, so the old Lord God had better surround Himself with all His angels and have mercy on Himself, for these three are sure to drive Him out of His heaven.'[17]

It is apparent that Marx had moved to Bonn not only to make good the chance of obtaining a lectureship, but to help Bauer raise Cain, intellectually speaking. To collaborate with Bauer on a provocative anti-religious periodical was not the ideal recipe for obtaining a chair. Nevertheless, in September 1841 the *Archives of Atheism* had not yet appeared – the periodical was in fact never to materialize – and for the moment Marx's prospects remained open. Dr Bauer had not yet been suspended, and in spite of the forces allied against him, the Ministry, while considering ways of getting rid of him, was intent on avoiding a scandal.

Next, Bauer committed a careless mistake. In Berlin on 28 September, he rose to speak at a soirée in honour of Karl Th. Welcker, a distinguished professor and well-known liberal who had taught law at Freiburg and Karlsruhe universities. Welcker, who had already lost one chair because of his outspoken views, had just been dismissed for the second time. On his way to Berlin, liberal groups in several towns had feted him at dinners and other protest-and-sympathy demonstrations which caused a great stir. The crowning affair was a 'serenade' to him organized by Bauer and his friends of the Doctors Club in Berlin, after which Welcker was escorted in festive procession to be dined and wined at a tavern.

There Bauer proposed a toast in the spirit of the Left Hegelians. But it was a veiled allusion he made to the absence of a constitution in Prussia that most annoyed the King. 'To root out the dragon-seed of Hegelianism', as the King put it to his friend Carl von Bunsen,[18] had long seemed to him imperative in view of the increasingly radical doctrines spread by the new 'leftist' philosophers. Friedrich Wilhelm IV had already summoned Hegel's inveterate adversary – the venerable Schelling himself – from Munich to Berlin to deliver a course of lectures expressly designed to denounce and demolish the atheistic neo-Hegelian trend-setters. Schelling's course, which was widely publicized and awaited with great interest, was scheduled for the winter term. Before it was to start in mid-November Dr Bauer was suspended. Disciplinary proceedings were instituted against him, but as these promised to be protracted, his lecturing post was to hang in the balance for some time. The outcome was far from certain, as the theological faculties of all the universities would have to be consulted before any drastic measures could be taken against him.

In Paris, on 14 June 1841, Heine was walking in the rue Richelieu when he was rudely accosted by a stranger. It took the short-sighted writer some seconds to recognize that the gentleman abusing him in German was the husband of Jeanette Strauss-Wohl. It was nearly a year since the publication of his book, in which – questioning the late Börne's reputation as a high priest of morality – he had referred to the Strauss-Wohl ménage à trois. Whereas Madame Strauss-Wohl had reacted promptly and with aplomb to Heine's attack on her worshipped hero, her husband had been seething for months over Heine's innuendo. In a couple of merciless lines about the trio, Heine had suggested that Strauss was not the sort of frivolous husband whose 'marital tolerance disarms ridicule'. Rather, he reminded one of that species of 'cuckolded asses full of gall' mentioned in Indian lore.[19]

Strauss thus had good reason to be bitter when he ran into Heine in the street. There were no witnesses to the verbal altercation which took place. On 23 June, having handed Strauss his card, Heine left with Mathilde for a planned holiday at Cauterets in the Pyrenees. They had not been there long when he received the news that Strauss claimed to have publicly boxed his ears. By July, Strauss and his friends were planting paid items camouflaged as news reports to this effect in the German newspapers. As headlines such as 'Heine Slapped in the Face' and others promising juicy details spread all over Germany, Heine assured his friends that the whole incident had consisted of 'a few stammering words babbled out by this trembling individual. I gave him my address, saying that I was about to leave for the Pyrenees and if he wished to discuss anything with me it could certainly wait a couple of weeks until my return, seeing that he had already waited for twelve [*sic*] months.'[20]

He mounted a counter-campaign in the press. Whereupon Strauss named three honourable gentlemen, Koloff, Dr Schuster and Hamberg – all friends of the late Börne and leaders of the German radicals in Paris – who claimed to have witnessed the incident. Heine was eventually to prove that they had not been present, and the affair took a new turn when the three admitted that in their fury at Heine's *Börne* they had been ready to bear false witness against him on the basis of mere hearsay. On his return to Paris, Heine charged his friends Théophile Gautier and Alphonse Royer to call on Strauss and demand a formal apology. Strauss refused and in his turn appointed two seconds. He chose swords. Heine insisted on pistols. Strauss switched to sabres. Heine stuck to 'pistols, the distance twenty steps, the first shot to be decided by lot.'

While the two parties hassled about rules and weapons, news of the imminent duel added to the general brouhaha. Richard Wagner published an article taking Heine's side against Strauss; Gabriel Riesser, a leading Hamburg Jew who knew and trusted Strauss, publicly declared himself so indignant that he challenged Heine to a duel and offered to come to Paris for the purpose; some of the German press speculated that Heine was probably too cowardly to fight at all and Campe, not without some malice, egged him on to disprove this 'legend'.

Heine, however, needed no prodding: 'I am not a man who allows himself to be publicly insulted in the heart of Paris.'[21] He was burning with anger, not so much at Strauss, 'the poor devil', as at 'the calumnies and defamation' that filled the German press. His insistence on pistols has been seen by some as a sign that he was wearily abandoning his life to chance, but to go by his own testimony he was keen to prove his honour once and for all by 'a deed' that would give the lie to all his detractors.

It is true that he was frustrated. On New Year's Day 1841 he had received the news that Uncle Salomon, in a fit of displeasure, had cut his annuity from 4,000 to 2,500 francs and in a turn of the screw had ordered it to be meted out to him in weekly instalments of 50 francs. Heine had hoped that his 'roaring lion' of a Börne book would drag the 'lamb' of the *Salon IV* in its trail of success, but in March 1841 Campe had reported that 'the lion' was hardly selling and 'the lamb' was limping behind. Campe had offered, however, to issue the fourth edition of the *Book of Songs*, and during the spring, in spite of headaches and eye-trouble, Heine had known hours of pleasure going over his own verses to emend previous misprints.

Nor had he allowed his social life to suffer. Before leaving for the Pyrenees, he had attended lectures at the French Academy and 6 of the musical season's highlights – including two piano recitals by Liszt, another by Chopin and a benefit concert to which both Liszt and Berlioz lent their talents to collect funds for a Beethoven monument in Bonn. Robert Schumann was setting some of Heine's folk songs to music (Opus 64), and Liszt his *Loreley*. And on 28 July, the opening night of the ballet *Giselle* – inspired by Heine's folk tale – had taken place at the Paris Grand' Opéra with the famous Carlotta Grisi in the title role. The triumph of this ballet was the brightest news Heine received while he was at Cauterets.

But none of this compensated for the loss of his reputation in Germany. His holiday having been spoilt by the Strauss scandal, Heine, who always thrived when the whole world was against him, recovered from his recent lethargy by the spectacle of Germany's literary critics and its democratic trendsetters – Goedeke, Gutzkow, Arnold Ruge, and the now famous Georg Herwegh, too – all making common cause with the likes of Koloff, Dr Schuster and Hamberg, the three false witnesses, to drag his name through the mud. Embittered and engaged for weeks on several fronts, pressing Strauss to agree to pistols, unmasking his lying supporters in Paris, bombarding the German press with rebuttals of each abusive item that kept popping up – and simultaneously rebuffing Riesser and others who had offered to fight him in Strauss's place with the advice 'to go and hang' themselves if they were tired of life – Heine conducted himself with the mixed courage of a desperado and the cool-headed implacability of the convinced fighter for truth, which was his favourite stance.

The duel was by way of a daring gambit to regain the respect of the German public, or at least that section of it which he trusted to see through 'intrigues' and to have remained loyal to him in spite of the hullabaloo. The duel, as he put it, was not for the sake of obtaining satisfaction; it was a 'manifestation'.

It finally took place early on the morning of 7 September in the valley of Saint-Germain. Strauss, winning the throw of dice, was the first to fire. His bullet grazed Heine's hip without injuring the bone. Heine fired into the air. According to an apocryphal story he is supposed to have said that 'the sky was so clear and blue' and the air so filled with the fragrance of the fields that God did not wish him to die on a morning when nature's 'most beautiful things' were on display. What Heine actually wrote to Campe while he was laid up for a few days with a swollen and black hip was that, for all the slight physical damage he had incurred, he saw himself as the moral victor.[22]

A fortnight before the duel, he woke up to the fact that Mathilde's life and future were as much at stake as the honour for which he was ready to risk his own. They had been living together as husband and wife in what he called a 'wild' conjugality. To her he was *mon homme*, while he, though increasingly attached to her, preserved a sense of liberty, however illusory. He had always felt responsible for her, but never to the point of legitimizing their relationship. The prospect of the duel made up his mind for him.

And so it was that on 31 August he married Mathilde at the Catholic church of Saint Sulpice and the following day in a civil ceremony at the Préfecture. To pre-empt criticism that he, who so often ridiculed the church, its institutions and the hypocrisy of bourgeois marriages, had 'submitted to a religious ceremony', he wrote that he did so because Mathilde, 'who comes of a strict Catholic family, would not have considered herself married without this ceremony'.

From that day to this, it has puzzled historians that a brilliant man who was on intimate terms with George Sand, the Princess Belgiojoso and some of the most brilliant women of the age should have married Mathilde, who was chiefly interested in frippery and fashions and often exasperated him with her mindless chatter and childish tantrums. It seems, however, that what Heine found in society was the stimulation which satisfied his intellectual needs; otherwise he was a world unto himself and shared his genius with no one. And for all the *grand amour* of his youth, his subsequent short affairs and the lyrical and other songs in which he, 'the poet of the bleeding heart', dealt with every aspect of love, Mathilde was the only one who aroused and maintained his passion for any length of time. It has been suggested on the basis of certain verses that his passion was in fact spent and that at the time of the duel 'he felt himself liberated from Mathilde as never before'.[23] This may have been so, but the question is what he should have done when the problem of their relationship became acute. He could not in good conscience consider sending Mathilde back to her mother or leave her alone and helpless in the world.

Announcing his marriage to Campe on 5 September, he wrote that he had felt in duty bound to confer on his 'beautiful and pure-hearted' mistress the honourable status of a legally wedded spouse. He informed his sister Charlotte briefly and humorously on 13 September that he had married 'the good-looking young woman with whom I have been quarreling daily for more than six years.' But it was in a letter he wrote on 13 October to August Lewald that he alluded to the exigency which had prompted him to act:

> You will have learned that a few days before the duel I was faced with the *necessity*, in order to secure Mathilde's position in the world, to turn my wild marriage into a tame one. This marital duel, which will not cease before one of us is dead, is certainly more dangerous than my short duel with Salomon Strauss.[24]

Thus Heine knew what he was doing. He made it no secret that Mathilde had grown on him. He was 44, had mellowed, and his days as an amoral young Hellene were over. Mathilde had tamed him, not vice-versa, and he was settling down – as he actually intimated in another letter written 4 days before he took her to church – to the comforts and 'respectability of petty-bourgeois domesticity, which will remain the same after the marriage as it was before it.'[25]

One unexpected and happy result of Heine's marriage was that Uncle Salomon, who at the beginning of the year had cut his annuity, promptly raised it from the original 4,000 to 4,800 francs a year. The capricious but not ungenerous millionaire was apparently pleased that his nephew seemed at last to have settled down.

In August, while Heine was marrying Mathilde and Hess and Marx were busy with their respective newspaper projects, Michael Bakunin set out from Berlin on a holiday jaunt in western Germany. With him were his sister Varvara and her 5-year-old son. They planned to spend several weeks at Ems spa, and then to visit Frankfurt and Dresden.

It was a little over a year since Michael had arrived in Berlin. He was no sooner there than he received the shocking news of Stankevich's death in Italy. Shortly afterwards Varvara, who had been with Stankevich during his last moments, had arrived from Italy with her son. Though grief-stricken by the death of the young man she had worshipped, she was composed – consoling herself by the religious-philosophical reflection that 'death, the disappearance of an individuality', was merely its return to and 'immersion once more in the general, in God', in nature[26] – and Michael Bakunin was relieved when the sister he had 'liberated' from her husband set up house for the three of them.

But his first year in Berlin, the city where he had hoped to be united with the universal, had not been an altogether happy one. Professor Karl Werder – who, since introducing Stankevich and Granovsky into the mysteries of Hegelian philosophy, had become a kind of guru to all Russian students seeking illumination in Berlin – had given him a few private lessons, but had soon left on his summer vacation. Left to his own devices in alien Berlin, Michael felt rather lost and homesick. And the news he received from Premukhino was that beloved Tatyana had never been 'so deeply, hopelessly depressed' and that she and his other siblings felt 'like a flock without its shepherd... Without you nothing is right.' Michael himself was so despondent that he wrote to them: 'We have remained alone. Around us stretches nothing but a vast wasteland on which we come upon caricatured shadows of our own life.' It was all very well to bolster his 'flock' and his own spirits by adding that 'in this isolation we are not alone' and referring them to the 'spiritual and blessed life' that would sustain them all with its eternal truth.[27] But the truth was that the Germans struck him as 'terrible philistines', and that most of his time during his first three months in Berlin was – as he confessed in a letter to Herzen – 'given over to worries'. When not reading Pushkin, Gogol and Lermontov, he whiled away his time by going over all the newspapers in the coffee shops one after another.[28]

Providentially, before the end of that summer Ivan Turgenev turned up in Berlin. The 22-year-old son of an idle Russian aristocrat and a tyrannical mother who ran the 5,000 serfs of the estate she had brought into the family with a ruthless fist, Turgenev claimed to have 'democratic views and enthusiasm for the U.S.A.' – first displayed, by his own account, at the age of 15 when his fellow-students at Moscow University nicknamed him 'the American'. These had germinated early and grown, together with his life-long aversion to violence, as he observed the outright sadistic brutality with which his mother punished her subjects for the slightest misdemeanour. His father, before he died when the boy was 16, had transferred him to St Petersburg, where he had obtained a university degree in 1837. Then Turgenev had spent the next two years studying history, Latin and Greek, as well as Hegelian philosophy, in Berlin. There he had inevitably fallen under the spell of Stankevich, although the latter had taken no great interest in him. Nevertheless, young Turgenev's feelings, as he admitted at the time, were 'like great waves... On the title-page of my [copy of Hegel's] Encyclopaedia is written: Stankevich died... I met Bakunin... From all the rest of my past life I do not want to carry away another memory.'[29]

In short, Turgenev transferred his admiration to the leonine Bakunin, who was 5 years his senior and accepted it as his due, besides its being a boon. For one thing, Turgenev knew his way about Berlin geographically and socially; for another, he had plenty of money and was always good for a loan. Besides, Bakunin could not but relish the role of playing mentor to this gentlemanly youth and eager would-be disciple who declared himself 'happy to be able to address you as "thou"'. And to cap the auguries for a felicitous relationship, Turgenev not only shared his own interest in art, music and literature but meant to resume his studies in the autumn under his former teacher, Professor Werder, for whose courses Bakunin had already registered. Turgenev's infectious optimism and the youthful exuberance with which he dwelt on the coming university year – 'Let's count the months of pleasure, from 1 October to 1 May, seven months, 210 days... It will go splendidly for us, the university, study, and evenings we will gather at your sister's, go to listen to good music, organize readings. Werder will visit us'[30] – not only delivered Bakunin from his loneliness and gloom but rekindled the vision he had entertained in Russia of a 'golden' future in store for him in scholarly Berlin.

In October he had in fact moved into Turgenev's apartment. Free of the domestic chores and responsibilities of living with the frequently ill Varvara and her child, he let his sisters at Premukhino know that after them, the Beyers, and Stankevich, Turgenev now ranked fourth in his affection. In his new mood that autumn he also found a way of reconciling himself to Stankevich's death by adopting the theory of personal immortality. The paradox inherent in it presented no great trouble to Bakunin, who was presently to proclaim 'contradictions' to be 'the basic law' and very spice of life, and eventually to come up with a philosophy of 'creative destruction'. Dialectically disposing of any mystery or confutation about personal immortality, he gave his sisters a metaphysical explanation of it based on the concepts of 'suffering' and 'negation' taken from his old Fichtean store of arguments: 'In contrast to material life, which possesses only what it appropriates, Spirit possesses only what it surrenders. And death, that total destruction of individuality, is the supreme fulfilment of this mystery and is therefore the supreme fulfilment of the personality... a blessed revelation of immortality.'[31]

The winter of 1840–41 proved as exciting as Turgenev had promised. 'The static freeze that had begun to threaten the flow of my inner being has gradually disappeared,' Bakunin reported shortly after embarking with great zeal on a programme of studies which included logic and the history of philosophy under Werder, as well as courses on phenomenology, physics and theology. 'I feel alive and free.'[32]

He was enthusiastic about Werder, who exuded an air of *Gemütlichkeit*, took a friendly interest in his Russian students, wrote poetry and, besides a book on Hegelian logic, was engaged in a stage play, *Christopher Columbus*. 'What a wonderful man,' Michael wrote to Herzen. Werder, who was only 31, seemed to him the personification of that admirable 'living, free union of knowledge and life' to which he himself aspired and had vainly been striving for.

For Bakunin, at last able to satisfy his declared thirst for knowledge, it was a great thing to earn Werder's friendship and to have the informal professor read the first act of his play to a gathering at Varvara's. Further marking his re-entry into society after the cloud of scandal he had left behind in Moscow and St Petersburg, Bakunin became a habitué of the Russian salon maintained in Berlin by Madame Frolov. He also took up riding and fencing, and together with Turgenev he regularly attended weekly performances of the Beethoven Symphonies. But on most evenings during that winter a small circle of their friends would come up to Varvara's apartment to drink tea from a samovar. Werder sometimes brought a lady-friend, and they discussed philosophy and art, read poetry, joked and laughed and occasionally broke into song. 'We have scarcely a moment's peace,' Varvara wrote to her sisters.

One evening, among the Berlin celebrities who frequented Madame Frolov's salon, Bakunin found himself in the presence of Bettina Brentano von Arnim, the legendary Romantic, friend of Beethoven and Goethe, and author of the three-volume *Goethe's Correspondence with a Child*, a fragment of which Bakunin had, some years before, spent nights translating by lantern light in the garden of Premukhino. The petite, elf-like, 52-year-old widow of Achim von Arnim – the poet and compiler, together with her brother Clemens Brentano, of the famous *Des Knaben Wunderhorn* – was to enter German political and cultural history for her indefatigable championship since the 1830s of a constitutional regime and freedom of the press in Prussia; for speaking up against nationalism and the clerical establishment; and for drawing attention to the social problem of the starving Silesian workers long before it was to explode. In 1840 she used her influence with the new King – whom she had known since his brighter days as a 'progressive' Crown Prince – to appoint the brothers Grimm to Berlin University after their dismissal on political grounds from Göttingen.

By 1841, Bettina's famous salon on Unter den Linden, which Bakunin had been frequenting since the previous autumn, was the rallying point of Berlin's leading liberals. Marx would presently make his appearance in her drawing-room; and among its older habitués was Varnhagen von Ense, the ex-diplomat and friend of Heine. Although Varnhagen, both by nature and because of his Court connections, tended to be cautious about his liberal opinions, the King's policies were so freely criticized at Bettina's that her own brother-in-law, the arch-conservative Professor von Savigny, refused on one occasion to enter the house when coming to fetch her daughters to a ball, preferring to wait outside and walk around in the dark.

But of the political opinions Bakunin heard there, of the constitutional issue raised by Jacoby's *Four Questions*, or the intellectual ferment and the revolution in thought created by the writings of Strauss, Feuerbach and Bruno Bauer and their attacks on religion – which in Prussia was tantamount to attacking the State – there is, strangely, not the slightest mention in his correspondence from Berlin.

This is all the more surprising as he also had long private talks with Varnhagen, who on one occasion recorded in his diary that Bakunin gave him 'some noteworthy reports about Russia'. Bakunin impressed Varnhagen, who knew that he had published a fragment of Bettina's Goethe correspondence in Russian, and thought him a solid young man of 'independent mind' and 'noble spirit'. Bakunin permitted Varnhagen to believe that he had translated the whole work, but that the rest of the manuscript was lost.[33]

Varnhagen had not only known Hegel, but was the co-founder, together with the late Eduard Gans, of the Hegelian *Yearbooks of Scholarly Criticism*. He could give Bakunin any illumination he needed on the political issues agitating Germany and on the battle between the conservative Hegelians of the 'Right' and the increasingly vociferous ones of the 'Left' with their philosophy of action. Since the beginning of 1841, Bakunin was also consorting with a genuine revolutionary, H. Müller-Strübing, a journalist whose opinions had earned him a death-sentence. His sentence was twice commuted, and in 1840, having emerged from 5 years in prison, he spent his time hobnobbing with Russian students at the coffee shops and wine bars they frequented.

The almost total absence in Bakunin's correspondence of any sign of the impact made on him by the Young Hegelian Left's novel attempt – such as he had certainly not seen in Russia – to apply philosophy to politics thickens the mystery of how he was able, by the end of 1841, within 18 months of his arrival, to put on paper a sensational philosophical theory that beat even the most radical of them at their theoretical game of dialectically deducing from Hegel's rational philosophy the justification for action to destroy 'what is' – i.e., the existing order and its mouldy institutions – in order to speed the movement of history which would inevitably displace the old for the new in a series of cat- aclysms and explosions. While they were still arguing how to pass from philoso- phy to 'praxis', Bakunin was to come up with a programme for 'the complete annihilation of the present political and social world', and the establishment on its ruins of that world of freedom, harmony and reason predicated by Hegel as the highest stage of human development.

Bakunin did report home that Werder's *Columbus* was 'a marvellous, pro- found work'. But except for occasionally including such tidbits as that he and Turgenev had dressed up flashily for a soirée at Mlle Solmar's – Turgenev 'in a green velvet Don Juan styled coat, and I in a violet velvet jacket'[34] – his letters reveal little of his actual life and activities in Berlin. What they show is Bakunin chiefly preoccupied and busying himself, as before, with the affairs of his 'holy commune of the Spirit' at Premukhino, trying to run the lives of his siblings by remote control.

For the better part of 1841 he was actually engaged in a new campaign on the old 'home front', as he referred to it. His beloved Tatyana continued to feel depressed and his favourite brother Paul, who was 21 and studying law at Moscow University and had become a fervent Hegelian under Michael's guid- ance, was having trouble working out his 'reconciliation with reality'. Michael decided to rescue them from the 'philistinism' and 'customary conventions' of their parents and to arrange for both of them to join him in Berlin. Money was no problem, for Turgenev would advance it.

But there were other obstacles, and Bakunin's method of dealing with them shows him at his plotting best. Since his father regarded him as a corrupting influence and 'the enemy of his peace', it would be useless and counterproduc- tive to approach the old man – on whose financial support he depended, Herzen and Ogarev having withdrawn theirs – and strain his relations with him. The whole thing must be handled delicately through an agent. And he chose his brother Nicholas for the job. Nicholas, however, who had been away for years at the Artillery School in St Petersburg, was the one brother who had remained immune to Michael's charisma and to his sway over their 8 siblings. Michael regarded Nicholas as a 'phlegmatic lazy-bones', but to assuage Varvara's doubts about his own desertion of Premukhino, leaving their aged father to cope with the affairs of the estate, he had told her that Nicholas would be a strong support for the old man and the rest of the family. And yet in March 1841 he started coaxing and inciting Nicholas to take up arms against their father: 'So now, dear Nicholas... aren't you pleased with this easy opportunity to distinguish yourself on the home front of our own family?... Rise up, arm yourself and act.'

Nicholas was not to mention anything about Tatyana. It was only after his parents agreed to send Paul to Berlin that he was to bring up the matter of Tatyana's going with him. Michael's brief to Nicholas was that he 'must act, quickly and powerfully', and send dear Tatyana and Paul 'off to us as soon as possible. We are waiting for them in Berlin.'[35]

Simultaneously, Michael had to deal with a crisis which had developed on his flank, at the Berlin end of the family 'home front'. Varvara, who lived with her little son in a third-floor apartment not far from the one he shared with Turgenev, was about to yield to parental appeals to return to Russia and make her peace with her husband Dyakov. Michael, who had moved heaven and earth to 'liberate' her from a loveless marriage, would not hear of it. He had to promise her, however, that if she insisted on returning to Russia he would negotiate an arrangement ensuring that the 'animal' Dyakov would never molest her physically.

In view of his preoccupation with these various affairs, it is no wonder – given the lack of documentation about the way in which he arrived at it – that some scholars should have concluded that he performed the move from speculation to action by a spontaneous 'leap' involving a complete break with his past. Thus Franco Venturi, in his classic *Roots of Revolution*, wrote that there was 'no gradual progress from his [Hegelian] political orthodoxy to his revolutionary ideas... All the concentrated inner life of his preceding years had prepared him for a leap', and suggested that 'direct contact with the discussions of the Hegelian Left' transformed Bakunin 'in one bound' into a man of action.[36]

More recently, Bakunin biographers have taken pains to demonstrate that there was no break and no such 'transformation'. Besides the conspicuous absence of any reference in Bakunin's correspondence to the ideas of the Hegelian Left, they cite his continuing fixation in Berlin on the affairs of his sister and the brotherhood at Premukhino. More than one passage in his letters shows how the unchanged duality of his nature and his emotional needs – swinging from affirmations of a desire to throw himself 'into the real world in order to live and act' to bouts of inner weakness, solitude and dejection – continued to dictate his views. 'We remain here as orphans': nothing illustrates better than this sentence written at the end of spring 1841 Bakunin's estrangement from 'the real world' and his inner isolation. His feeling of being orphaned may have been influenced by Turgenev's imminent departure on a prolonged visit to Russia, but the desolation he expressed was to recur even after his advance to a philosophy of action and revolution.

His 1841–42 correspondence abounds in passages marking a renewed withdrawal behind 'the sturdy gates and locks' of his monastic inner self. In that 'forbidden temple' he could, as before, lick his wounds and comfort himself with the Fichtean virtues of 'negation' and suffering, virtues which he went on extolling to others by writing, for instance, 'Suffering is the animating, the vitalizing principle of existence, illuminating ordinary experience, elevating it to the spiritual. Without suffering, without negation, everything would be dead and motionless'. In the 'splendid mansion' of his inner self he could also, as he wrote to the same correspondent, gather his strength and 'rather rejoice in our being chosen to bear truly human suffering'.[37]

As he was not at all the spontaneous man of action, his rejoicing came from that obverse element in Fichte's philosophy, the concept of the suffering man who – realizing his divine nature, and pitting the 'force of faith and the force of will' against external obstacles in his way – rises to the heights of God, in the sense of 'God become man'. It was to these Fichtean 'forces' that Michael Bakunin, upon hearing that his brother Paul, in the attempt to effect a Hegelian 'reconciliation with reality', had reached the impasse of confessing to Alexandra Beyer that he felt lost like 'a phantom' and 'my knowledge gives me no reality', resorted when instructing him not to leave everything to 'the destructive movement of everyday life':

> It is only when our thoughts, feelings, and aims clash with ordinary life that they appear to be so many illusions, phantoms, empty fantasies. But they rise out of the depths of our souls [and] it is not they, but ordinary, everyday life that is the most dreadful phantom, which shackles us invisibly with paltry but strong fetters. Through force of faith and force of will, its eternal companion, we must cast these fetters off.[38]

All this was a very un-Hegelian way of coming to terms with 'reality', reminiscent of the transmogrified Hegel whom Bakunin had been invoking years before in Russia when declaring that reality could be bent to his will 'and must take the form and direction which I give them'.

Paul Bakunin arrived unannounced in Berlin in August 1841, to find both Michael and Varvara gone. They had left no address, and Paul had a hard time tracing them. He finally discovered them vacationing at Ems spa. The arrival of his favourite brother for an indefinite stay in Germany pleased Michael Bakunin, but from his point of view it was only a partial victory, for the chief object of his campaign by proxy had been to get his 'fine, wise', spiritually languishing Tatyana over to Berlin. Brother Nicholas had managed to persuade their parents of the wisdom of letting Paul air his mind abroad before the fancy he had conceived for Alexandra Beyer developed into a serious romance. But they would under no circumstances agree to expose Tatyana, the demure 26-year-old jewel of their household, to Michael's corrupting influence.

With Varvara, her son and Paul – 'the whole family on my hands', as he wrote home to Premukhino – Michael travelled in September from Ems to Frankfurt and then to Dresden. There they were to split up. Varvara, liking the city and irritated as much by Michael's high-handed intervention in her marital affairs as by her failure to stand up to him, decided to spend the winter in Dresden; and so, curiously enough, did Paul, Michael's initially eager but befuddled disciple, whom he had hoped to teach more about knowledge and life.

Michael himself spent about 6 weeks in Dresden, where, towards the end of September, he made the acquaintance of Dr Arnold Ruge. A prominent figure, Ruge was the editor of the *Hallische Jahrbücher* (or Yearbooks), which had been known since its foundation in 1838 as 'a citadel of free philosophy'. Upon its suppression in Prussian Halle, Ruge had transferred its publication in March 1841 to the Saxon capital under the changed title of *Deutsche Jahrbücher*,[39] and it had been moving steadily to the Left, into the arms of Dr Bauer and his cronies in the Doctors Club.

Ruge, who was well-to-do, also had publishing connections in Zurich, enabling him to have material that was sure to be prohibited in Dresden printed in Switzerland and smuggled into Germany. In this manner he was soon to publish Karl Marx's first and still famous political essay on the Prussian Censorship Law, and for the next few years he was to be one of the prime animators of the German radical movement.

Dr Ruge has also long been credited with effecting 'Bakunin's first introduction to neo-Hegelianism'. E.H. Carr described it that way in his *Michael Bakunin*, which was the first comprehensive biography of the anarchist hero when it was published in 1935, and the only one, as it turned out, to be available in English for the next 40 years or so. Yet, for all the mystery surrounding the exact stages of the psychological drama of Bakunin's conversion to revolution (as Aileen Kelly was to call it in 1982), Bakunin's own correspondence contains some hints that this might actually have started within half a year of his arrival in Berlin, about 8 or 9 months before he met Ruge. Thus in a letter advising

Paul to rebel against 'destructive' everyday reality, he sought to explain a fairly long interval of silence in the following terms: 'I have not written to anyone because a new revolution is occurring within me. I am passing through a transformation... This winter I lived a remarkable life.' He gave no details, but wrote enthusiastically that his former faith and strength were gathering 'as though for a resurrection' and even spoke of the long-expected 'rebirth' in Berlin as something that 'has already begun in my soul.'[40]

In May, similarly hinting to the Beyer sisters that he was going through 'new, splendid, and difficult' experiences, he added – and for once one may believe him – 'I am still not able to give a clear account of it all, either to you or to myself.'[41]

Confused as he was, he longed all the more for his devoted 'little flock' at Premukhino, and had waited anxiously through the summer for the arrival of Tatyana and Paul. It had taken Karl Marx in 1837 the better part of a year's mental struggle to work his way from orthodox Hegelian philosophy to the radical theses extracted from it by Bruno Bauer and the Doctors Club. Bakunin obviously had a harder time adjusting the second-hand or self-developed philosophic ideas he brought with him from Russia to the higher 'science' prevailing in Berlin, not to mention the energy consumed by his secret struggle with a tormenting sexual deficiency that set him apart and which, in ways he could not help, made him both cynical and the narcissistic prisoner of his emotions.

It was from this disjointed emotional side of his nature that Bakunin saw in Professor Werder, who was the first to introduce him to Hegelian 'science', the figure of a whole, integrated man. In his early letter to Herzen, Bakunin had made the point that Werder's wholeness was not the result of 'the dead letter, but the fruit of a religious, inner striving'.[42]

Now, Bakunin's own inner striving was nothing if not religious; for years he had been preaching to the saintly 'commune' of his sisters, brothers and 'soul'-sisters that God spoke to them through him. Hegel, shortly after seeing Napoleon ride to the historic battle of Jena, had observed that philosophy 'does not belong on the streets and in the market place, yet it is not alien to man's actions.' Taking this point a stage further, Werder taught that philosophy was in no way 'a cowardly nostalgia, a commodious cloak to cover hypocrisy. Just the opposite – we want to elevate ourselves through it towards a humanity blessed with divine force, but also blessed with the strength of heart and the courage of liberty.' And just as Hegel had seen in Napoleon 'the World Spirit... concentrated in one point' in a single personality 'dominating the entire world from horseback', so Werder in his *Christopher Columbus* dramatized the life of the hero who, reaching beyond 'the frontier' of his own being, realizes his divine potential against all obstacles and becomes the instrument through whom 'Spirit moves forward in a leap' to inaugurate a new epoch.

A tendency to 'go beyond', coupled with a 'religious striving' to realize his divine potential, a craving for absolute liberty and heroic struggle were all in Michael Bakunin's character or pervaded his fantasies. Add to this Werder's view of history's hero being, as in his play, harassed – as Bakunin felt he was – by a pack of petty philistines, and you have not only the reasons for Bakunin's adulation of Werder but 'just the kind of Fichte-Hegel blend' which, as Arthur Mendel wrote in 1981, provided Bakunin with the new philosophical rhetoric he had been looking for 'to express his own merger of Fichtean subjective voluntarism and the Hegelian objective Absolute.'[43]

Mendel, in short, turned Werder – dismissed by both Carr in 1935 and Aileen Kelly in 1982 as a minor figure,[44] which he was – into 'the most powerful influence on Bakunin' during his first semester in Berlin, the man who had caused him to write home in January 1841 that he felt the first uncertain stirrings of a 'rebirth' and of a 'new revolution occurring within me.'

As for his Dresden encounter in the autumn with Ruge, whom he saw more than once before he returned to Berlin at the end of October, Bakunin was disturbed by the way he and the Left Hegelians on the *Deutsche Jahrbücher* based their assault on the existing order and institutions chiefly on an all-out critique of religion as the source of all evils pervading 'the system'. He wrote to Premukhino from Dresden that Ruge erred 'in being one-sided in everything that concerns religion, art and philosophy.' On the other hand, he noted, in Germany one-sidedness might be just the thing to shake the people 'out of that rotten, stagnant golden mean in which they have been wallowing for so long.'[45]

By his own admission just before he reached Dresden, Bakunin had changed a great deal but not 'with respect to the inner necessity of my life'.[46] Following his contact with Ruge, he decided to learn more about the Left Hegelian philosophy. In this sense, their encounter was to mark a turning-point on his road from abstract speculation to militant action. But as he left Dresden to return to Berlin for the start of the winter semester, he was aware that his problem would be to find a way of reconciling the atheism of the Hegelian Left with his own emotional and mystic-religious needs.

Providentially, on the train taking him back to Berlin he read a book by the Abbé de Lamennais, the defrocked Breton priest who already in 1834, in *Les Paroles d'un croyant*, had attacked the Established Church for supporting all the tyrants who subjugated their peoples. Lamennais's view that the Church must yield its material interests to morality and justice was part of his conviction that society as constituted was heading for disaster and civil wars, as 'the multitude of peoples and nations' – realizing their 'divine strength' as 'sons of the same God and brothers of the same Christ' – were bound to rise in rebellion against the 'slavery' imposed on them by human masters. Although his ultimate vision was of a world of brotherly love and social equality in which all were able 'to eat of the fruit of the earth and come and go without anyone saying to them: Where are you going? No one can pass this way,'[47] Lamennais's zeal led him to such radical proclamations as that 'liberty does not offer itself, it has to be seized' and the whole social organism reformed even at the cost of 'purification in the fire of a fearful war'. Indeed, Harold Laski was to call *Les Paroles d'un croyant* 'a lyrical version of the Communist Manifesto.'[48]

The book Bakunin read on the train was *Politique à l'usage du peuple*, containing the articles published by Lamennais in 1837 during his short stint as editor of *Le Monde*. Bakunin learned from it not only that religion could be reconciled with 'liberty' – the abbé's motto 'Dieu et la Liberté' included freedom of the press and self-determination for Europe's small nations – but that in alliance with politics it provided the very answer to the 'contradictions' responsible for all the ills of the age. The fighting abbé's frequent invocations of Christ could not but appeal to Bakunin, who had taught initiates into his spiritual 'commune' that 'the moral will of man is the will of God, and nothing can stop its plans from being carried out.' His letters to Premukhino in the autumn of 1841 show that Lamennais's book came to him as a revelation, for now he could see the future shaping up and becoming 'living' reality. The coming age, he wrote in his letters, was one of 'bloody contradictions'. Not only were contradictions 'the most profound basic law of all life and all reality', they were a manifestation of the eternal living God, lending life its 'mystical, sacred meaning' and fascination; they were there to be surmounted by 'manliness, reality, deeds', otherwise life would be reduced to baneful 'philistinism' and that ordinary, everyday existence which he could not endure.[49]

The 'bloodiest' and most glaring of all contradictions, he learned from Lamennais's book, was the gulf between the feasting rich and the wretched poor who, according to the abbé, constituted five-sixths of the human race. Perhaps the most important thing Lamennais's book taught Bakunin was that divine strength was achieved not by the individual but by the collective. Although he had hitherto hardly given a thought to the poor, he was to couple the plight of the 'disinherited class' with the militant activism of the radical Hegelian Left.

Thus armed, and with 'the eternal, living God' still on his side, Bakunin was to divert Hegelian philosophy from its rationalist approach, which led to atheism, and to substitute for it the formula 'politics is religion and religion politics'. It was, however, to cost the high priest of the little 'commune' of

Premukhino a year-long struggle – with German philosophy and himself – before he found the right way of expanding it to embrace the rest of suffering humanity and the right philosophical language in which to phrase a powerful call for a revolution aiming at nothing less than 'the complete annihilation of the existing political and social world'.

25

Cultural Divisions in Berlin and Paris

On 15 November 1841, Schelling gave the inaugural lecture at Berlin University of a course on his new Philosophy of Revelation. This positive system, he had confidently informed the Minister of Education, would not only put Hegel's 'negative', rationalist system in its proper place but would leave his atheist 'leftist' disciples agape, bereft of ammunition and arguments for debate.

'You have no idea with what impatience I await Schelling's lectures,' Bakunin wrote home. He was not the only one to be excited. It was 40 years since Schelling, as a young professor at Jena, had proclaimed the concept of the Absolute. With philosophy now making such inroads in German politics as to force the King to mobilize one philosopher against the teaching of another, Dr Bruno Bauer, Marx and their consorts and the whole of intellectual Berlin held their breath for what promised to be a battle royal of wider than academic import.

A young man recently arrived in Berlin went so far as to declare that anyone who had 'the slightest inkling of the power of the spirit over the world' could tell that the battlefield 'where the mastery over German public opinion on issues of politics and religion – that is, over Germany itself – will be decided is at the University, in Hall Nr. 6, where Schelling is delivering his lectures.' The young man was 21-year-old Engels, who was to be mentioned by future historians as having attended the inaugural lecture, along with Kierkegaard and Bakunin. Engels was doing a year's service as a volunteer in a Guards regiment stationed in Berlin. Not being required to live in barracks, he had rented private lodgings not far from the university and started attending lectures – as a temporary auditor – in his spare time. He described the memorable occasion as packed to capacity by 'men of all nations'. With the university's 'own notables and coryphees of learning in reserved seats next to the rostrum', students and young soldiers rubbed elbows with 'grey-bearded staff officers' and with Jews and Moslems; there was a babel of 'German, French, English, Hungarian, Polish, Russian, Greek and Turkish' tongues, then a hushed silence as Schelling made his way to the platform.[1]

'The philosophic system which I established was only one side of the whole, namely its negative side': thus the white-haired, 67-year-old Schelling announced his theme. Hegel, he went on, had presented that 'negative philosophy as the absolute one.' Hegel scholars, critics and faithfuls in the audience gritted their teeth as the respected philosopher of Romantic Idealism declared that if Hegel nevertheless deserved a place 'among the great thinkers', it was because he had done his best to prove the existence of the Absolute through the logic of history. But the Absolute was unknowable; it could be 'attained only by exercising one's reason', yet must include 'something more than reason'.

Schelling's patronizing and transparent attempt to discredit Hegel from the first as a man who had appropriated his ideas but had only half-understood them boded ill for the King's intentions. It was almost inevitable that this would provoke a violent counter-barrage, and indeed over the next two years poor old Schelling found himself refuted, vilified, rarely defended and often ridiculed in a flood of scholarly, polemical and satirical pamphlets.

Engels was the first to enter the fray. Schelling had promised to unveil the complete edifice of the 'philosophy of revelation' towards the end of his course in the spring. Engels did not wait for him to do so. In an article he wrote at the end of November and published in mid-December, he attacked Schelling for desecrating the grave of the 'great master', and declared merciless war on him. Schelling was eventually to announce a 'divine principle in history', explaining it as an evolutionary, God-creating process in which myths, societies, peoples, art forms and in the second stage 'revealed religion independent of reason... arise in lawful order.' His own vision was of a third, 'philosophical religion.'

But in trying to describe it, Schelling stumbled. For all he was able to reveal of the new 'God-creating process' was couched in vague, mystical terms. In the end he defined his philosophical religion as 'a final goal' and had to admit that it did not yet exist. The anti-climax was all the greater as Schelling, besides boasting that he would beat 'the unvanquished' Hegel and pull the bottom out of his system, had promised that he would build a new fortress in which 'henceforth philosophy shall be able to rest securely.' 'Schelling's God', Heine was to remark with his usual sarcasm, shared the fate of other 'great German works': like the mighty Cologne Cathedral or the Prussian Constitution, 'it was never finished.'

Ludwig Feuerbach's *Essence of Christianity* – published shortly before Schelling's inaugural – had convinced the last doubting Young Hegelian that nothing, no revealed religion, 'exists outside Nature and Man'. Nevertheless, Berlin's leading rationalist theologians, Professors Marheineke and Paulus, held their fire until Schelling had delivered the last of his lectures, and opened up with scholarly broadsides and considered criticism only in the summer of 1842 or as late as 1843. Young Engels brooked no such delay. He boasted in his article that 'Never has youth flocked to our ranks in such numbers.' Speaking of and for the Young

Hegelians he met at the university, he was cocksure in predicting their ultimate victory; and during the winter, between exercising with the 12th Guards Foot-Artillery company in the snow and mud of the Grützmacher Platz parade ground, he wrote an anonymous 55-page pamphlet, 'Schelling and the Revelation',[2] which was published even before Schelling had delivered his last lecture.

The spunk and expeditiousness shown by Engels in launching the first broadside against Hegel's conservative detractors – before Marx had published anything other than two poems – was of course to elicit the admiration of generations of Marxist writers. Although Engels defended Hegel with more enthusiasm than academic authority, his mettlesome approach and unrestrained polemical gusto achieved their purpose, which was to 'provoke the enemy' and spark off the controversy that was soon to develop in force. It was Arnold Ruge's opinion that the author of 'Schelling and the Revelation' (who he assumed was Bakunin) had 'outstripped all of Berlin's [orthodox] old donkeys' and left them far behind.

Engels announced in his pamphlet that 'The day of the great decision, the battle of nations, is drawing near.' In spite of the bluster in his words, the merchant's son who had never completed high school did not fail to grasp the political significance of the philosophical-religious war of ideas which was now out in the open and moving towards a climax.

The campaign against Bruno Bauer was part of the same battle. On 14 October – two months before Bauer was scheduled to explain his provocative remarks at the Welcker party to a hearing before Bonn's University Judge – the King was personally instructing his Minister that Bauer's teaching career must be brought to an end one way or another. For his part, Bauer 'burned with an inner fire' and – in Varnhagen's later appraisal – 'would sooner be a martyr to his convictions' than compromise one iota. A proud man and not a little arrogant, he felt surrounded by pygmies on all sides and over the years had come to identify his fight with the cause of science itself: 'In me they want to quash science,' he had declared early on to his brother Edgar.[3] In October 1841, unruffled by the proceedings against him, and determined on the contrary to 'push matters to the ultimate test whether what I am teaching is not the correct theological development', he was calmly sending to the printers an anonymous pamphlet titled 'The Trumpet of the Last Judgment on Hegel the Atheist and Anti-Christ'. Pretending to be a 'denunciation' of Hegel ostensibly written by a strict Christian fundamentalist, this was an artful piece in which Bauer made a parody of the rightist interpretation of Hegel's philosophy of religion and re-interpreted it as a form of atheism.

In a more serious vein, Bauer and Marx in that same month were rumoured to be going ahead at last with their plan to start the *Archives of Atheism* in Bonn.

725

Marx, except for those occasions when he had been entertained by Georg Jung and others of the Cologne circle, had by now spent some three months in the little university town. His association with Bauer had become so close that he was thought at the time – and for more than a century afterwards – to have collaborated with Bauer on 'The Trumpet of the Last Judgment'. This was not the case; but the pamphlet had hardly made its appearance in November when Bauer, who was intent on exacerbating the situation, invited Marx to join forces with him on a sequel whose content was expressed in its very title: 'Hegel's Hatred of All Religious Art and His Destruction of All the Laws of the State'.

While Bauer was writing one section of it, Marx undertook to provide several chapters demonstrating the revolutionary side of Hegel through his attitude to religious art. For this purpose he began extensive research on the subject. The combined polemic was to be signed with the lower case initials b.m. (Bauer, Marx).

In Berlin, Friedrich Wilhelm IV, the monarch who believed that God endowed kings with supernatural powers and greater wisdom than ordinary mortals, did not worry much about Dr Bauer's or Marx's plans and pamphlets. The only Marx the art-patronizing King had likely heard of was not Karl, but A.B. Marx, the music professor who had once helped 17-year-old Felix Mendelssohn to perfect his *Midsummer Night's Dream* overture, and more recently had applied through Meyerbeer for royal funding of an oratorio. As for Bauer, the King, having indicated his wish to see him punished for his part in the 'scandalous' Welcker affair, had turned his attention to artistic matters. On 28 October at his private theatre in the so-called 'new palais' at Potsdam, he had presided over a grandiose staging of Sophocles's *Antigone*, performed by actors, orchestra and a Greek chorus made up of seven choirs. Mendelssohn, summoned to Berlin during the summer, conducted the incidental music he had been specially commissioned to write. The rising young Paris opera star, Pauline Viardot-Garcia, had recently appeared in recitals both at Court and at the Royal Berlin Opera; and throughout the autumn and winter the King, between affairs of state, spent much time planning, approving, or discussing with Count von Redern, the 'General Superintendent of Royal Spectacles', the details of a succession of increasingly brilliant Court fêtes, balls, pageants and musical and theatrical events.

As Mendelssohn found, the King fancied himself as 'the rediscoverer of Greek tragedy'. Meyerbeer, who was among the select audience invited to Potsdam for the 28 October performance, noted in his diary that every word spoken by the chorus had been set to music and the stage 'entirely rebuilt like that of a Greek theatre'. Mendelssohn's sister, Fanny, found the resulting effect much nobler... than our stupid changes of scene and absurd foot-lights. Who ever saw light coming from below? Then the curtain sinking instead of rising, so that the heads of the actors are seen first, is much more sensible than our fashion of making acquaintance with them feet foremost, as it were.[4]

Mendelssohn treated his one-year Berlin stint as Kappelmeister as one treats 'a sour apple which must be eaten'. This was not Meyerbeer's reaction. His presence in the Prussian capital since May had generated a spate of rumours that Europe's most celebrated living composer was at last willing to replace the veteran Spontini in the post of General Musikdirektor. Courted and shown the highest honours in Berlin, Meyerbeer had dined in July with 'His All-Highest' Prussian Majesty himself and the French statesman Thiers. The cultured Princess of Prussia, wife of the heir-apparent (to become Kaiser Wilhelm I) and herself an amateur composer, had asked to see him 4 times. Scholars, stage personalities and music-loving celebrities showered him with invitations, artists submitted their works to him, and the sophisticated Humboldt, who occasionally undertook missions for the King without damage to his liberal reputation – on one occasion he apologized to Meyerbeer for 'the barbarity still prevailing in our [Prussian] institutions' – engaged in a patient and subtle campaign to lure him to Berlin.

Although Meyerbeer, frequenting the city's élite, was sufficiently taken in by the cultured ambience he found in these circles to write to Heine on 28 September 1841 of 'the new social and intellectual conditions prevailing here since the ascension of this spiritual, genuinely human monarch',[5] his heart remained in the scene of his triumphs, Paris, where the 130th performance of *Les Huguenots* was taking place. But his wife and his aged mother lived in Berlin. *Les Huguenots* and his earlier work *Robert le Diable* were being premiered or repeated that year in London, Stockholm, Vienna, Dresden and other places, yet in Berlin it had not yet been produced and he was being publicly needled to give up Paris 'for the honour of being a wholly German composer'. At the same time Paris was waiting for him and his long-promised new opera, *Le Prophète*.

While Meyerbeer was to hesitate for nearly a year between Paris and Berlin, Richard Wagner, the future revolutionary, was making an outright bid for the 'mighty patronage' of Prussia's art-loving King. On 20 November, from his cheap lodgings in a run-down building in Paris, he was informing Meyerbeer that he had appealed directly to the King and was about to send the score of *The Flying Dutchman* 'to Count von Redern with the request to permit its performance in Berlin in the course of this winter... All this, however – I know – will unfortunately help me very little.' Thanking Meyerbeer for the good word he had put in for *Rienzi* in Dresden, and fawningly addressing him as 'my patron, without whom I shall not achieve anything', Wagner went on: 'I implore and beseech you from my innermost heart perhaps to drop a line in my behalf to Count von Redern.' Redern had in fact sent the score of *The Flying Dutchman* to Meyerbeer, after Baron von Lichtenstein, the stage director, had turned it down on the basis of the text, declaring it was 'too hazardous'.[6]

On 7 December, between receiving Humboldt and visiting the new British ambassador Lord Westmorland, a music-lover and amateur composer who perpetrated no fewer than 7 operas, Meyerbeer took time off from his sundry affairs to pay a call recorded in his diary: 'Visit to Redern in order to recommend to him the score of The Flying Dutchman by Richard Wagner.' On 9 December he wrote to Redern that in view of Wagner's 'talent and his extremely reduced circumstances', he doubly deserved to have the stage doors of 'the Court theatres which officially patronize German art' thrown open to him.

Dr Bauer appeared before the University Judge in Bonn on 9 December 1841, and was subjected to what he described as a 'vulgar farce' and ridiculous 'inquisition' concerning his part in the serenading and banqueting of the dismissed Professor Welcker at the end of September. By Bauer's own account, he was asked three questions, in answer to which he admitted that he had been one of the organizers who had planned the whole programme of the demonstration. As for the incriminating toast proposed on the occasion, he told the academic judge:

> Besides finding myself in general agreement with the speeches and toasts delivered on this occasion, my part... was limited to toasting Hegel and more specifically his conception of the (reasonable) state in order to point out how much it surpasses – in daring, liberality and decisiveness – the state conceptions prevailing in South Germany.

What particularly incensed the King about Bauer's toast was that it went against the official Prussian line, which extolled Baden and South Germany as models of constitutional 'parliamentary liberalism'. Welcker was not only a distinguished academic, but the leader of the opposition in Baden, which lent the soirée a political character. A further sting in Bauer's toast was its implicit allusion to Prussia's lack of a constitution.

Bauer wrote to his brother,'To think that all this nonsense will be put on paper and sent to Berlin!' As indeed it was, generating a flurry of official reports and endless deliberations. The theological faculties of all the universities had been invited to submit opinions on the two volumes so far published of Bauer's *Criticism of the Synoptic Gospels*. Unfortunately for him, Bauer's tactics were not as good as his principles. At an earlier stage he had confided to his brother that he was 'too involved in the battle' to give it up: 'it has too corrosively, too deeply eaten into my soul... it will not end for me before I have gone through all the turns and twists.'[7] This may explain why he – who had cautioned Marx not to give premature offence to 'the blockheads' who could reject his lectureship – had thrown caution to the winds with his impulsive remarks at the trivial Welcker demonstration, thus delivering himself into the hands of the King.

Bauer was not a man to leave well enough alone. In the first week of December, having created a new stir with his 'Trumpet of the Last Judgment on Hegel the Atheist and Anti-Christ' – and with the procedural machinery for sacking him already set in motion – he was writing to his brother that he hoped the sequel to 'The Trumpet' would help to convince his enemies that he was not joking.

A little later, when he learned that 'The Trumpet' had been prohibited as well as confiscated, he reacted by turning his Bonn rooms into a 'pop'-style exhibit on the subject of the French Revolution. He had a carpenter mount on cardboard 'sixty pictures, portraits and scenes' from those glorious and bloody days, making a large tableau on one wall, and the floor was strewn with revolutionary posters, cartoons and books and newspapers of the period, which he had his maid haul in heavy baskets from the university library.

'It is the talk of the town,' he reported gleefully to Edgar.

From Berlin, his 21-year-old brother, quoting circles in the Ministry of Public Worship, Education and Medical Affairs, had written that 'the gentlemen here', far from appreciating the seriousness of Bruno's stand, regarded his action as outright madness. Bauer, however, went on working defiantly on the third volume of *The Synoptic Gospels* and otherwise approached his partly self-invited martyrdom fortified by that mocking spirit which revelled in intellectual jokes and hoaxes. His latest, the Bauer-Marx sequel to 'The Trumpet', was to be another denunciation of Hegel, pretending to come from a right-thinking and pious Christian. Under this guise, 'Hegel's Hatred of All Religious and Christian Art and His Destruction of All the Laws of the State' was designed to show that, if rightly interpreted, the philosopher whom authority invoked as a spiritual pillar of the Prussian state had provided a revolutionary thesis going against the whole ideological structure on which the 'Christian Prussian' state and its institutions were based. When 'The Trumpet' was confiscated Bauer had to think of a less incendiary title and proposed to Marx that they call the joint polemical treatise 'Hegel's Doctrine of Religion and Art as Seen from a Pietist Viewpoint'.

But whereas Bauer soon finished the part he had undertaken to write, Marx's research into religious art dragged on from November through December, and on into the spring. Months after he had obtained his PhD degree he was still busy adding certain, only partly preserved, notes to his doctoral dissertation, such as the note – obviously written in reaction to Schelling's November lectures – quoting the early Schelling's refutation of the existence of God against the latter-day Schelling's 'philosophy of revelation'. At the end of 1841 and early in 1842, he wrote and re-wrote a new Preface to the dissertation. Stating that 'The treatise that I herewith submit to the public is an old piece of work and was originally intended as part of a comprehensive exposition of Epicurean, Stoic and Sceptic philosophy', which 'political and philosophical' circumstances prevented him from completing, he went on to say that the systems of these 'philosophers of self-consciousness' had been 'underestimated up to now by the philosophers', let alone by lesser 'schoolmasters'. In the final text he toned this down, but – not to minimize the importance of his dissertation – wrote that it would 'at any rate show how little' the Greek speculative philosophers had so far been understood.[8]

He was obviously still expecting to have the dissertation printed, just as he still hoped to get the coveted lecturer's position in Bonn. Otherwise, all that is known of his life at the time is that at the end of December he packed up his writings and left Bonn abruptly for Trier. Jenny's father had fallen desperately, mortally ill. Marx, too, came down with some illness and was bedridden in Trier even as the *Rheinische Zeitung* – the newspaper which decades later would earn Lenin's accolade as the platform on which Marx made his first steps 'from revolutionary democratism to Communism' – was coming into the world in Cologne.

Almost nothing in life came easily or without pain to Moses Hess.

In Cologne, throughout December 1841, the bankers, manufacturers and leaders of the liberal professions who had founded the company that was to launch the *Rheinische Zeitung* on 1 January held frequent board meetings. Jung and Oppenheim had between them put up 20,000 Thaler to see the paper through its first year and were elected general managers with joint responsibility. Among the other shareholders who became members of the board of the paper were such bourgeois captains of industry and prominent Rhineland financiers as the bankers Ludolph Camphausen and D.J. Hansemann, later to serve briefly as Prime Minister and Finance Minister of Prussia respectively; Merkens, longtime president of Cologne's Chamber of Commerce and a member of the Rhenish Diet; Gustav von Mevissen, chairman of the Rhine Railroad Association, a future Under-Secretary of State for Commerce and founder of industrial companies and of several of Cologne's banks, including the large Schaffhausenscher Bankverein; and Rudolf Schramm, a well-to-do lawyer and politician.

The rest of the board of 31 included more lawyers, doctors and citizens of substance.

As if to compound the irony, the Prussian government actually supported the creation of the *Rheinische Zeitung*, a fact which could not but exacerbate the unprecedented sparring with the Prussian authorities that was to land the new paper into some famous hot water. According to a secret report in the Austrian State Archives, the government hoped that the *Rheinische Zeitung* would act as a 'counterweight to Catholicism' and its widely read mouthpiece, the *Kölnische Zeitung*, which had taken an anti-Protestant stand in the dispute over mixed marriages. The Rhine industrialists, for their part, were keen to have a daily of their own better equipped to give forceful expression to their secular modern interests – railroads and rapid industrialization, protectionist tariffs, etc. – than the Church-oriented *Kölnische* whose interests, for all the circulation it had built up over the marriage issue, remained chiefly parochial. Jung and Oppenheim, on the other hand, were Young Hegelians and keen to have the *Rheinische Zeitung* join in the battle of ideas against Prussian absolutism. And Moses Hess, alone among the founders, had Socialist notions.

At a shareholders' meeting on 8 December, Schramm, later elected to Prussia's Constituent Assembly, referred to Hess as 'the founder of the under-taking'. Others saw in him its 'chief editor and soul'.[9] Indeed, Jung had promised him the editorship and Hess had spent half a year working assidu-ously to put the new venture on its feet, marshalling shareholders, capital and contributors, besides running the company's previous newspaper (the *Rheinis-che Allgemeine*) until its scheduled closure on 7 December, a day before the meeting.

Yet when the board was constituted on 10 December, he was given no seat on it – on the pretext, as he claimed, that his 'financial circumstances' were not of a type to 'inspire confidence' – and all he was offered for his services was a posi-tion on the staff. Enraged, Hess told the board that he had 'not founded this enterprise in order to be placed in a subordinate position' nor would he 'accept as mercy what I can claim by right.'[10]

He wrote to Berthold Auerbach in Cologne on 13 December:

> Damn these dogs! They ought to be hanged, all of them. All they
> have is money and arrogance... Jung would be all right if he wasn't so
> rich. These people believe that wealth gives them a prerogative... I
> have now consorted with the best among the aristocrats of money.
> They are the last with whom I will have any friendly truck.[11]

Two days later Ludwig Braunfels, editor of the *Rhein- und Moselzeitung* before its suppression, wrote that 'Jung and Oppenheim, treating Hess with the greatest ingratitude and perfidy, want him to be an editorial slave,' though he was 'the man who brought it all about.'

His side-tracking was only one outward manifestation of a tug-of-war which had been quietly raging for months among the sponsors and backers of the new paper. Jung and Oppenheim wanted it to be a polemical paper that would open its columns to Bauer, Marx and their friends for the type of slashing, all-out campaign against Prussia's excesses that the sharp-minded Young Hegelian critics seemed best fitted to wage, striking at the ideological basis and the very philosophy which enabled an autocratic monarchy to practise thought-control, inequality and the suppression of every freedom while posing as liberal. The other wealthy sponsors, wishing merely to achieve a greater say for themselves in political and economic matters, would have none of the neo-Hegelian hot-heads. As for Hess, a budding Socialist at 29, the manufacturers and business-men among the shareholders found him, not unnaturally from their viewpoint, too much of a 'radical' for their taste and hardly the person to be entrusted with the task of setting the paper's editorial tone.

On 24 October they had in fact invited the respected economist and prophet of industrialization, Friedrich List, to assume the post of editor-in-chief. List, who had spent years building railways in North America, had, since his return, done much to promote German rail construction. His recently published, and to this day well-known treatise, *A National System of Political Economy* – challenging the theories of Adam Smith – advocated protectionist tariffs to facili-tate the rapid development of Germany's young but ambitious industry, along the lines favoured by the business interests behind the *Rheinische Zeitung*.

List, however, had declined the post, pleading a broken leg and suggesting to the embarrassed founders that in Hess the *Rheinische Zeitung* had 'so important a talent' among its assets that they need not fear for its success.

With money interests, politics, Young Hegelian philosophy and an element of racial prejudice, too, mingling like strange bedfellows in the making of the paper, Hess's troubles had actually started early in October, when he still believed himself to be the editor-designate. Braunfels claimed that Hess had promised him an editorial job. Hess, besides protesting that he lacked the authority to do so, had on 10 October, in a letter mentioning rumours that the new paper might get 'too much of a Jewish tinge', summed up for Braunfels the hints he had received from several shareholders in these words: 'For all your baptism, you are still a baptized Jew – and one Jew on the newspaper is enough if it is to avoid that tinge. Jung... is too sensitive to say such a thing straight to my face, but to others he expressed the same view.'[12]

Braunfels protested that he was being sacrificed to 'plebeian prejudice' and pointed an accusing finger in an unexpected direction. In a letter to Berthold

Auerbach written in mid-October, he asked: 'How can this rumour have started at all, seeing that hardly anyone in Cologne knows me, with the exception of Jung and his crowd. That these very people oppose me is due to their Hegelizing: at bottom it is Bruno Bauer and Dr Marx who – despising me as a non-Hegelian – are manipulating Jung like a puppet on a string.'[13]

Whatever the truth of this, the upshot was that by the beginning of December, with less than a month to go before the scheduled start, the *Rheinische Zeitung* had found itself in the peculiar position of having a lavish share capital of 33,000 Thaler, but no editor. Between 8 and 14 December, hectic board meetings succeeded one another, marked by upset after upset. Thus, on the 12th, Oppenheim was informing Heine in Paris that another economic theorist, Gustav Höfken – a protectionist like List – was to edit the paper jointly with Hess; but by the 14th Höfken had emerged as chief editor and Hess was being asked to stay on merely as a contributor. Fuming, he refused.

Finally, on 23 December, with only a week to go, Jung gave him 'practically a free hand' to do what he liked 'on the editorial side' as well as a respectable salary 'and 5% of the net profit.' The paper, however, had barely published its first issue when, on 2 January, Hess quarreled with Oppenheim, refused to work under Höfken and resigned in a huff. Next, Jung quarreled with Höfken over an article dealing with Schelling's philosophy, and Höfken resigned.

According to a report by an agent of Metternich's, the bone of contention was 'an article written in Bonn, but pretending to come from Berlin', which debunked Schelling's 'revealed religion' and his attack on Hegel. 'The managers, Jung and Oppenheim', the agent went on, 'insisted on its publication', but Höfken was so disgusted by 'this ironical article' – apparently a parody written by Bauer or one of his friends – 'that he refused to accept it' and preferred to take his hat and leave.

Whether or not this was the true and only reason, the Young Hegelians were indeed waiting in the wings. But by 16 January, with Höfken resigning while Hess was preparing to bring suit, the two-weeks-old *Rheinische Zeitung* was like a ship without a captain, a clear course or an agreed destination. Born amid policy dissensions and editorial squabbles, it seemed to be heading for nowhere, and destined to founder.

In December, Franz Liszt had arrived in Berlin, and the simultaneous presence of him, Meyerbeer and Mendelssohn occasioned a series of memorable concerts and musical Court and society events. The Prussian capital's winter season could not have been more glittering or exciting even as Schelling in his lectures went on exorcising Hegel's ghost and Bruno Bauer and young Marx were busy thinking up cutting arguments and philosophical puns for their pamphlet war.

733

Berlin's *News of State and Learned Affairs*, reporting on a 'dazzling soirée' held on 4 January at the palace of the Crown Prince of Prussia in the presence of 'the musical celebrities currently in town', wrote that the 'climax came when, with Meyerbeer conducting, Mme Ungher and several singers, accompanied by Herr Liszt, rendered the fourth act of *Huguenotten* in its entirety with all the choirs. The extraordinary musical creation made a great impression on the august gathering.'[14]

Meyerbeer noted in his diary for 19 January: 'For twelve o'clock I had been invited to a musical dejeuner by the Princess of Prussia. Liszt played. This was my third dejeuner at the Princess's since Liszt's arrival. Recently the King and Queen were also there. Today only the Queen was present, the King having already left for London.'

For the flashy, vainglorious Liszt these were heady occasions. In his ardent desire to get himself a patent of nobility by any possible means, the onetime 'piano huszar' was soon asking Marie d'Agoult in Paris to design a coat of arms for him. Friedrich Engels reported to his sister Marie that the charismatic Liszt made 'the ladies fall so madly in love with him' that they fought at his concerts and 'came to real blows' over a glove dropped by him. Chiding the 18-year-old Marie, who was at a boarding school in Mannheim, for her innocent interest in the activities of the Royal Family, Engels informed her on 5–6 January that 'the All-Highest is leaving on the 16th of this month for London in order to hold His Royal Highness, the little English prince [Edward, Prince of Wales, later Edward VII] over the baptismal font.'

The tone of his letter, including his sarcastic remark that after a visit to Russia the King was sure to 'spend the summer amusing himself at Potsdam, the autumn on the Rhine, and then move to Charlottenburg for the winter and more amusement',[15] suggests that his radical Berlin student friends thought little of Friedrich Wilhelm IV and his Court's cultural diversions.

Engels himself, a lanky figure in the blue uniform with yellow-striped facings, red shoulder-straps and red flaps of the Guards Foot Artillery, lived privately, and in his own words, 'very pleasantly', in an elegantly furnished room in the Dorotheenstrasse. An early *débrouillard*, he sometimes feigned toothache to skip a night march or avoid freezing during Sunday church parade, and when down with cold and 'cannon fever' from cleaning six-pounders in the rain or snow on the Grützmacher parade ground, would cure himself with punch and rum. Soon promoted to the non-commissioned rank of 'bombardier', Engels took his military duties in his stride, managed to attend university lectures as well as quite a bit of theatre and opera, and generally enjoyed life.

At a Rhenish restaurant where he liked to dine on his favourite dishes, or at one of the coffee houses along the Dorotheenstrasse, he met Edgar Bauer,

734

Bruno's younger brother. The two were about the same age, and Engels with his irreverent streak and Edgar, the disillusioned theology student, quickly became companions. Soon they rose to prominence among a group of Berlin students and Young Hegelian intellectuals who made it their practice to scoff demonstratively at religion and the monarchy in public places. Mouthing libertarian and revolutionary slogans in the coffee houses and wine shops where they met, *Die Freien*, or 'The Free Ones', as they called themselves, gradually took the place of the Doctors Club, which had been slowly falling apart ever since the elder Bauer brother had been transferred to Bonn.

It was over the noisy but purposeless exhibitionist antics of the *Freien* that the two great friends, Marx and Bruno Bauer, were to have their first quarrel.

In the first half of January 1842 the Berlin public and the rest of Germany learned that King Friedrich Wilhelm IV had issued a decree ostensibly liberalizing the Censorship Law, originally promulgated in 1819 for 5 years but enforced since then with varying severity for 22. According to the decree, 'in order now to free the Press of any unsuitable fetters which are not part of his All-Highest's intention', the King had issued 'a direct highest order to the Royal State Ministry expressly disapproving of any coercion of literary activities.' Prefaced by these reassuring terms, the new so-called Censorship Instruction prepared by the Ministers of Education, Foreign Affairs and Police – who were to be in charge of its implementation – was widely and mistakenly acclaimed as the beginning of press freedom.

The King still enjoyed something of a liberal reputation, and with the arts flourishing under his personal and attentive patronage, many were misled into thinking, like Meyerbeer before them, that their hopes in a new era might still be fulfilled.

On 26 January, Bruno Bauer sounded the alarm to Marx, who had left for Trier shortly before the New Year: 'In Berlin they are now in dead earnest, the affair is becoming serious, they are issuing prohibition after prohibition.'[16] Indeed, the hand of censorship which had earlier forced Arnold Ruge to move the *German Yearbooks* to Dresden now reached out to his journal there and suppressed several articles by Bauer, another by Feuerbach, and one written by Ruge himself; and at the same time that Bauer's provocative 'Trumpet of the Last Judgment' was being confiscated, sales of his earlier book, *The Evangelical Church in Prussia and Science*, published in 1840, were prohibited.

In Leipzig the censors mutilated several poems by Heine scheduled to appear on 27 January in the *Journal of the Elegant World*, and suppressed his salute to Dingelstedt – 'On the Night Watchman's Arrival in Paris' – altogether. The forbidden poem was printed and distributed as a handbill. Pro-Heine petitions were circulated in Leipzig, but in Paris Heine had more reasons to fume: Hofmann & Campe had been placed under a wholesale ban and barred from selling his – or any – books anywhere in Prussia!

Forty newspapers refused to print a statement by Julius Campe. The astute publisher, who by a combination of defiance and compromise had so far managed to get the works of more than one 'undesirable' author past the shoals of censorship in the various German states, vowed that he would no longer bow or make concessions to Prussia's 'infamous despotism'. Heine, indirectly hit by the fourteenth or fifteenth proscription in a German land of some or all his works, declared 'open war with Prussia', and abandoning his 'moderation', was ready to offer his hand to the shabbiest radical 'demagogues' whose untimely activities he had hitherto scorned.

When Bauer's news reached Trier, Marx was seriously ill. His address for post was 'care of Government Councillor von Westphalen', who was slowly dying, and whom he had come to support during his ordeal. If Jenny had to nurse both patients she at least, in the sixth year of her engagement, now had her fiancé to herself for an extended time. When Marx recovered he promised to let the printer have his section of the tract he had undertaken to write jointly with Bauer 'within a few days'. But he never despatched the manuscript. Instead, on the same day – 10 February 1842 – he sent off to Arnold Ruge in Dresden an urgent article titled 'Remarks on the Latest Prussian Censorship Instruction'. Showing up the new regulations for what they were – 'new fetters for the press' – Marx's first political article, designed for Ruge's *Deutsche Jahrbücher*, is to this day considered a polemical masterpiece. Ruge, who had met Marx in Berlin, was impressed by it, but felt that it would never pass the Saxon censorship. He decided to hold it for a volume he planned to produce in Switzerland.

The new press regulations, purporting to liberalize the old Censorship Law, actually tightened it by empowering every censor to prohibit at his discretion any material which he felt or fancied had been written in a spirit of 'vehemence, over-intensity', or 'arrogance'. The censors were thus set up as arbiters privileged to judge not only the content, but the intent, tone, form, tendency and style of any article or piece of literature. Taking up this particular aspect, Marx wrote in the article he sent to Ruge:

> We now depend on the temperament of the censor... You may write freely, but every word must be a curtsey to the liberal censorship. The law permits me to write, but I am to write in a style that is not mine! I may show my mental visage, but first I must arrange it in the prescribed expression...

Attacking the whole censorship system as 'terroristic' – because it exposed the writer 'to the most dreadful terrorism, the jurisdiction of suspicion' and penalized 'not action as such, but the state of mind of the actor' – he asked a fundamental question: 'Is truth then to be understood simply in the sense that truth is what the government deems fit to order...?'[17]

Marx's manuscript contained many other pungent sallies and ended with a quotation from Tacitus: 'Rare is the good fortune of those times in which one may think what one wishes and say what one thinks.'

The piece had yet to appear in print when the absurd situation created by sometimes dull-witted bureaucrats blue-pencilling the works of great writers was well illustrated by the censor Dolleschall's famous verdict on Dante's *Divine Comedy*. A veteran Cologne police chief, Johann Dolleschall had been a censor for 10 years when he was presented with a proposed newspaper advertisement for a German translation of *The Divine Comedy* and promptly struck it out with the remark: 'Divine things should not be made a comedy of.'

'Fie upon this Germany!' Moses Hess was to exclaim. 'Censorship has completely demoralized it.' Hess's fortunes had changed within a fortnight of his resignation from the *Rheinische Zeitung* on 2 January. No sooner had Höfken tendered his on the 16th than George Jung had come running to Hess. 'Suddenly, the day before yesterday', Hess wrote to Auerbach on 19 January,

> the word was out that Höfken had left and that they were prepared to sign a contract with me and by last night everything had been settled entirely to my satisfaction – Höfken gone, he was really not up to the position of chief editor, and today I was back editing the paper together with Dr Rave in quite gemütlich fashion... Jung is again fast friends with me... I am glad I did not compromise on any point... I am being treated so lovingly, so humbly, that it is a joy.[18]

Reinstated as acting chief editor at 600 Thaler a year – the same salary Marx was to get when he eventually took over – Hess, backed by Jung and Oppenheim, set the tone which turned the *Rheinische Zeitung* into a fighting newspaper. In two letters to Auerbach, who had become a contributor, he urged him to be 'more incisive, more oppositional', and in what may be seen as a policy statement stressed 'the radical spirit' which was to distinguish the *Rheinische Zeitung* from any other paper then appearing in Germany: 'What we print is not an echo of hypocritical Germany as it is at present,' he wrote. The *Rheinische Zeitung* was not afraid of the censorship. It wanted neither articles 'smelling of cotton and customs union' nor the type of sweet, idyllic stories which filled the pages of most German newspapers. It preferred to have columns 'struck out' by the cen-

737

sorship rather than 'make concessions, and if we cannot write the way we want, we would rather not write at all.'

Newspapers from France, Britain, Italy, Spain and one from Russia reached the offices of the *Rheinische Zeitung* in Cologne's Schildergasse. Compared to developments abroad, the absence of any political life or liberties in Prussia stood out crassly and the stark contrast fired the zealous reformer in Hess to a ringing indictment:

> In the whole German fatherland no healthy limb has been left alive, everything is rotten, nerveless, degenerate – I mean, as far as politi-cal-social life is concerned – and but for a little surviving private virtue and German philosophy, Germany would be lost forever... Why does Germany not rise to express its revulsion at the despicable reaction now rearing its brutal head in Prussia? Because the Ger-mans are philistines and lack any political sense and any sense of freedom.[19]

The *Rheinische Zeitung* would not dish out mere honeyed 'flatteries to Ger-many', Hess concluded, and the future would prove 'who does better by the fatherland', those who criticize or those who praise, 'the censorious preachers, or the apologists.'[20]

By the time he wrote this in May 1842, Hess was no longer alone in setting the trend of the *Rheinische Zeitung*. Adolf Rutenberg, the radical Young Hegel-ian journalist who had once introduced Marx to the Doctors Club, had been brought in from Berlin and formally appointed chief editor. Hess remained as co-editor and the two worked together without any conspicuous friction. Under Rutenberg, though, a host of his Berlin friends and former cronies of the Doc-tors Club, led by Bruno Bauer and his younger brother (who happened to be Rutenberg's brothers-in-law), began to contribute to the paper even as Bruno Bauer's fate as a lecturer was about to be settled.

Dr Rutenberg's appointment had been engineered by Jung and Oppenheim. It signalled the victory of the paper's two chief financiers and of their intellec-tual interests over the rest of the board of merchants and industrialists, who were already dismayed by Hess's disapproval of articles on 'cotton and customs', which was precisely the kind of material many of them favoured.

Rutenberg was to prove an unfortunate choice. He was Bruno Bauer's peer in wine-bibbing capacity and buffoonery, if not in ideas; he had taken a prominent part in organizing the Welcker soirée and otherwise attracted the attention of the authorities by taking part in the activities of Bauer's supporters among the Berlin *Freien*, who created disturbances in cafés and restaurants by various pranks. Engels, for instance, had taught his dog to growl at the word 'aristocrat', and was therefore under police surveillance from the moment of his arrival in Cologne.

Worse, Rutenberg – who had been recommended to Jung by Marx – was a loud-mouthed character but a superficial, happy-go-lucky journalist, so little capable of directing a newspaper and its policy that Marx himself was eventually to declare him 'impotent' and unfit for the job. However, he and the two Bauer brothers, Dr Ruge, the writer Max Stirner, Gutzkow, Köppen – and, as of April, young Engels, the newly promoted 'bombardier' – and other Young Hegelians filled the columns of the *Rheinische Zeitung* with philosophical articles directed against religion and Prussia's attempt to 'christianize science'.

Though Jung and Oppenheim believed that these sharp young academics would help to reform Prussia, their abstract cerebrations – along the lines of Bauer's thesis that 'pure criticism' was the ultimate weapon in the battle against the state – were unrelated to any practical social or political ends. Hess, on the other hand, felt that Germany needed something else 'besides a little private virtue and German philosophy:... what it primarily needs is education, genuine, practical, political education.'

By April 1842 he became the first man in Germany to draw public attention – in an article titled 'The Communists in France' – to the ideas of the latter as a social message worth studying. In Paris, Girardin's *La Presse* had recently received a copy of a 'manifesto' – sent by mail and signed by a group calling itself 'the true Communists' – attacking social injustice and the unfairness of the system of popular representation by 'the electorate of the rich'. Girardin had printed it as an example of dangerous aberrations worth combatting. Hess, who in his *Holy History of Mankind* had already warned of an impending cataclysm between 'the aristocracy of money' and the dispossessed, got round the censorship by quoting the manifesto and commenting that the 'historical phenomenon' of Communism, developing out of the ideas of Saint-Simon and Fourier, deserved serious consideration on its merits as a movement whose adherents could no longer be ignored or rhetorically 'dismissed as lunatics belonging in an asylum...'[21]

This was more than the Prussian authorities had bargained for. They had licensed the *Rheinische Zeitung* partly as a token demonstration of the ostensible new 'press freedom' and censorship relaxations, and also in the hope that 'this newspaper of philosophical and enlightened principles' would serve as a counterweight to Catholicism. But 'the Prussian Government had hardly expected' – as Metternich's agent chose to express it in his confidential report – 'that this bunch of Hegelians and baptized Jews could so pervert things.' The Oberpräsident of the Rhine Province had, however, prudently given the *Rheinische Zeitung* only a temporary licence. Pending final approval by the three Ministers in overall charge of censorship in Berlin, the licence was revocable at any time. By 11 March, when the paper was not yet three months old, its 'spiteful tendency' and atheistic articles had so aroused the wrath of the three 'Censorship Ministers' that they were actually instructing the Oberpräsident in Coblenz, Bodelschwingh, to stop its publication as of April the first.

They were, however, in something of a quandary when Bodelschwingh pointed out that the paper was backed by some prominent and 'highly respected' shareholders – the Prussian governor in Cologne himself, Regierungspräsident Von Gerlach, happened to be one of them – and that its suppression would not only cause these well-meaning and influential citizens undeserved financial loss, but was bound to turn public opinion against the government. In the face of these arguments the three Ministers postponed their decision and the *Rheinische Zeitung* was reprieved until the summer.

On 28 February, in another 'liberal' gesture, the King had with a stroke of his sanctimonious pen and some fanfare lifted the 7-year-old *Verbot* banning all works, past and future, of the 'Young Germany' group of writers – on condition that they sign an undertaking henceforth 'conscientiously' to abstain from writing 'anything that offends religion, the fabric of the state, or morality'. Three of the 5 writers involved, Laube, Mundt and Gutzkow – Heine's 'radical' opponent, who by a special dispensation had been allowed to become the editor of the *Hamburg Telegraph* – signed this loyalty pledge.

The fourth, Wienbarg, refused to comply. The fifth was Heine. The King had pointedly excluded him from this optional amnesty by expressly limiting it to those of 'the Five' who resided in Germany. In view of the embargo on all Hofmann & Campe books, he was in fact under a double curse in Prussia.

In Paris, that February, people were fighting for tickets to one of Chopin's rare concerts, at which Pauline Viardot was also scheduled to sing to his accompaniment. The concert took place on the 21st and was, as George Sand noted, brilliant and lucrative as well, bringing in more than 5,000 francs – a record profit which inspired the *Revue Musicale* to describe it as a 'magnificent occasion where simplicity was married to grace and elegance, and where good taste served as a pedestal to riches.'[22]

George Sand's 'Communist' novel, *Horace*, continued to be serialized in advance of publication in the *Revue Indépendante*. It contained a malicious portrayal of the comtesse d'Agoult. The long-drawn-out public battle between the two women – in which Balzac was preparing to intervene with his novel, *Béatrice*, on the d'Agoult-Liszt affair – was now on and, with no war more serious to disturb the carnival atmosphere of Paris, Heine was one of the few who saw through appearances and continued to send out warning signals.

On 7 February he had sent to the *Augsburg Allgemeine Zeitung* the article beginning with the words '"We are dancing here on a volcano" – but we are dancing.' The article, built around his famous interpretation of the new high-kicking dance which was to become known far and wide as the (French) cancan, gave a disturbing picture of the background to the February debates in the Chamber of Deputies, which in historic hindsight would be ranked among the most important in the life of the July Monarchy.

In his sparkling, ostensibly flitting style, Heine passed from the dancing of Carlotta Grisi in *Giselle* to the lusty roundelays of the nymphs of pagan times. He mentioned Salome's dance before Herodias and his rewarding her with the head of John the Baptist as the reason why the Church, which otherwise 'embraced all the arts and used them to its advantage', condemned dancing. Then, after describing the 'courtly coolness' and graceful but punctiliously chaste manner adopted by the French ballet in the age of Louis XIV as an attempt to neutralize the 'archpagan' voluptuousness of this art, he wondered how to define the cancan for the German public. 'Well, then: the cancan is a dance which is never performed in decent society.'

With a garish, lusty, vulgar energy, the common people of Paris whirled and swirled about at carnival time. By comparison, the boredom, indifference and blasé atmosphere at upper-class balls and dancing soirées, at which dress, appearance and decorum counted for everything and black-tailed men and coquettish women shuffled about with a tired air – 'the prevalent fashion being only to pretend to be dancing' – struck him as another symptom of the corruption, greed and self-seeking which had come to mark the French bourgoisie: 'No one has the slightest desire to entertain the other person and this egotism manifests itself even in the dancing of today's society.'

On the other hand, 'The dancing of the lower classes, much as they try to ape the genteel world', still had some reality to it, albeit a regrettable one. Juxtaposing the goings-on in the popular amusement places with 'the mannered rigidity' of the classical ballerinas whose eyes and 'lewd smiles constantly contradict their legs', belying their prim air and sexless movements, Heine conjured up not only the strident, shrill music accompanying the cancan, but the display of 'demonic lust' he had recently witnessed at a grand but spooky revelry at the Opéra Comique. There, in the atmosphere of a veritable *Walpurgisnacht* (witches' night), 'the Devil himself played with full orchestra' and the 'satanic spectacle' reached its climax 'when the gallopade resounded with a crash... It seemed that the ceiling must soon burst and the whole crowd and crew would suddenly soar up on broomsticks.'

In the midst of this outpouring, Heine worked in a rapier-like thrust at the methods to which Louis-Philippe's administration had sunk: 'In the public dance halls every quadrille is watched by several policemen or communal guards who darkly supervise the dancing morality... This surveillance of popular entertainment, incidentally, illustrates the state of affairs here and the measure of freedom the French have to date achieved.'

But the tighter the straitjackets, he observed, the more daringly and inventively did the Gallic spirit express its opinion of the world in the insolent movements and provocative, 'ironic entrechats' of the cancan and similar 'unspeakable dances' – mocking, as he saw it, the hypocrisy of society's sexual mores and its bourgeois values as well as every touted notion of 'patriotism, loyalty, faith, family values, heroism, God...'[23] All the things, in short, which had been turned into a sham.

The February 1842 debates in the Chamber dwelt on the issue of the 'electorate of the rich' – which restricted the number of Frenchmen entitled to vote to those 170,000 able to pay a certain statutory amount of taxes – and opposition demands for some parliamentary reforms. They were held some 16 months after Guizot had replaced Thiers as the dominant figure in the Soult-Guizot Ministry. King Louis-Philippe, happy to have got rid of the bellicose Thiers, whose self-confessed interest in 'politics on the grand scale' had nearly involved him in war with England and the other powers, was even happier with his choice of Guizot. In this diplomat he had found a man who – paradoxically or not for a brilliant historian and former liberal who in 1830 had actually drafted the protest which had sparked off the July Revolution – not only agreed with his favoured policy of 'peace, prosperity and stability' but, being on principle opposed to any kind of change, raised resistance to it to the level of a doctrine. 'Resistance' became in fact the by-name of his Ministry which, composed of enemies of any reform from the centre and right of the Chamber, was to stay in power during the critical 1840–48 period.

François Guizot, whose dogmatic, schoolmasterly manner prompted Heine to refer to him as 'the poor *rector magnificus* of France', believed in 'the sovereignty of reason', and not in the sovereignty of the people. Not everyone was fit to govern, but it stood to reason that the rich, the talented and the educated were better qualified than others.

His famous advice to the millions of unenfranchised Frenchmen was '*Enrichissez-vous par le travail et l'épargne*' (Get rich by working and saving). Guizot felt justified in making this statement by the fact that France was indeed moving towards prosperity. In 1842 the government initiated a plan for a national railroad system. With subsidies offered to private constructors, more and more locomotives, tracks and tunnels were about to be built; with new machines, the textile industry was expanding; and 6 years hence Paris would be the world's greatest manufacturing city. Guizot's formula was in line with his policy of the *juste milieu*, 'the golden mean hostile to any excess' – either of revolution or reaction – which he had enunciated as early as 1835; by his lights, it was a reasonable and equitable way of both satisfying demands for representation and ensuring good government. Under the French representative system there was rarely a homogeneous majority in the Chamber of Deputies – rather, majorities 'were made up of groups which might vote together one day and then might never vote together again'.[24]

The King normally chose his premier from among the most influential deputies, with the result that the talk and betting in the salons was always between Thiers and Guizot, Guizot and Thiers. Guizot was a master at manoeuvring between the shortcomings of this fluid system and the latitude it gave him to distribute patronage in the form of government jobs to deputies ready to be bought. The fact that salaried government officials were eligible to double up as deputies – as did 80 in 1842, besides 69 servants of the crown whose posts did not depend on the government – helped him to secure conservative majorities.

It was precisely this practice which the opposition attacked in the February 1842 debates and which were to be the major issue in the elections that were held several months later. Besides proposing a modest increase of the electorate by including anyone eligible to sit on a jury, the opposition demanded that deputies should no longer be allowed to hold salaried government posts until a year after their mandates expired. Leading the opposition was Thiers, the head of the Left-Centre 'Party of Movement'. Thiers had often spoken of the need for these reforms but, when in power, had always found some pretext for deferring debates on the subject.

The clamour for reform was general. It came not only from outlawed secret societies and outright republican or legitimist opponents of the monarchy but from many of the younger generation who were hungry for new ideas and disgusted by the spreading corruption and nepotism. The King's own heir, the duc d'Orléans, had in 1840 written to the painter Ary Scheffer: 'The present epoch is prosperous and peaceful, but it is too dull not to become soon stagnant and consequently corrupt; innumerable vulgar and mean little interests seethe under an apparently united surface which can perhaps only be disturbed by the most violent upheavals.'[25]

Guizot, however, whom Heine compared to the Obelisk of Luxor both for his *immobilisme* and for being out of tune with his time, held on firmly to his view that 'universal suffrage' was the ruin of democracy and liberty. He was highly unpopular, and had been hung in effigy during prolonged riots the previous summer, when peasants and townsmen in several provinces had got wind of a planned tax rise. But this was not the kind of thing to ruffle Guizot: 'A good minister must be unpopular,' he rationalized. Convinced that France's institutions were perfect, he argued in a professorial tone that the task of those at the helm was to keep her citizens in place and to educate them – or as he put it, to 'call them to the duties' which they were properly 'fit to carry out'. He expected the cream of the nation, the deputies and peers, to support the monarchy with a view to assuring law and order, and preventing anarchy.

The ageing Louis-Philippe, who had survived 10 assassination attempts in as many years, was now chiefly concerned to consolidate the legitimacy and continuity of his monarchy. Neither he nor Guizot realized that, by obstructing even the slightest reform or any new idea, they were actually undermining its stability. Blocked in the Chamber, some of the more extreme deputies took their grievances to the licentious French press, with the result that there was an unprecedented wave of censorship trials. A.A. Ledru-Rollin, the new leader of the radical 'Democrats' – who were actually the former Republicans, forced to use a new name to avoid prosecution under the notorious 'September Laws' of 1835 – was sentenced to 4 months in prison for a political speech. This caused a public outcry and led to a new trial, which ended with his acquittal. But another tribunal had jailed the publisher of the daily *Le Siècle* for 6 months on another debatable charge. Nothing, however, equalled the trial and sentencing early in 1842 of Dupoty, the editor of the republican monthly *Le Journal du Peuple*, on charges of complicity in the attempted assassination of one of the King's sons, the duc d'Aumale. The young duke, returning from the Algerian campaign, had entered Paris the previous autumn at the head of his regiment when, in the midst of a hero's reception, an impetuous member of one of the secret societies fired a pistol at him, killing an officer's horse without injury to the rider. The culprit, a self-confessed 'Communist' by the name of Quénisset, who was described as a halfwit, said that he sometimes read *Le Journal du Peuple*.

Under the September Laws, Dupoty had therefore been arraigned before the Chamber of Peers. The chief evidence introduced by the prosecution, other than the argument that the would-be assassin had been influenced by reading his paper, was an article in which Dupoty had remarked on the fuss made by the government about a horse, when it had viewed with complacency the 1834 'massacre of the people in the Rue Transnonain' depicted in Daumier's famous drawing. Although no proof was offered that Dupoty had known of the attempted assassination or had any connection with those who had plotted it, he was found guilty of 'moral complicity' and jailed for 5 years. Quénisset was condemned to death, but reprieved by the King. Dupoty's conviction caused such wide misgivings and protests that the relevant article of the September Laws was never again applied. But the *Journal du Peuple* never recovered after Dupoty's imprisonment.[26]

As for the low-paid or unemployed and voteless *ouvriers* swarming in filth and squalor in the rapidly growing industrial slums, they lived on the periphery of society and figured as little in the King's or Guizot's political calculations as the young girls, earning 6 sous a day and reduced to seeking through a cold and systematic prostitution the sustenance which they lacked,[27] of whose plight Ledru-Rollin kept reminding them. Guizot was of course aware of the writings of Pierre Leroux, George Sand, Louis Blanc, Proudhon and Cabet, not to mention lesser authors of violently republican and outright revolutionary tracts, but he regarded most advocates of political and social reform as frustrated utopian dreamers who, yearning for tumultuous events, busied themselves with making and unmaking governments, nations, religions, society, Europe, the world.[28]

'I am suspended!' wrote Bauer from Bonn to his brother in Berlin on 3 March 1842. He had been told nothing officially, except that an 'investigation' was in progress. 'But which kind? Could it be that the pitiable Welcker affair is also being dragged in?' He was suspended, but pending the outcome of the proceedings, continued to lecture. He gave a histrionic account of how he first 'coolly' ignored the murmuring protests of his audience of theological students, and then built his demonstration of Gospel contradictions to a powerful climax until he had them 'all shaken and listening as if chained to their seats.'

Marx and Hess, he added, had both witnessed his performance. Then the hounded critic of Scripture went on relating with relish that during carnival week in Cologne he had indulged in some 'terrible nonsense. I performed the third part of The Trumpet of the Last Judgment in the street and had some delicious fun' until a pious and shocked Catholic had recognized 'the Trumpet-player... By the time I was back [in Bonn] the faculty already knew everything.'

It was also on 3 March that Jenny's father, Baron Ludwig von Westphalen, died in Trier. On the 5th, Marx learned that Bauer had been suspended *per lit de justice* (by Order of the King). On the same day he offered Ruge, among several manuscripts, his section of the jointly planned Bauer-Marx manuscript of *Hegel's Doctrine of Religion and Art as Seen from a Pietist Viewpoint by b.m.* – which he had long promised to send to Bauer's printer in Leipzig. Whether his object was to dissociate himself from Bauer, having perhaps had enough of Bauer's oddities and his way of mixing scholarliness with pranks and theatricals, is not known. In any case, when the Hegel book finally appeared anonymously in May, under a new title, it comprised only the sections written by Bauer. It was there that Bauer described his own method of criticism as forcing 'his way into the sanctum of religion' to 'profane it with relish'.

Curiously, Marx too resorted to sexual symbolism when he later attacked Bauer. Savagely mocking 'St Bruno' and his self-styled 'irresistible personality', he wrote that he 'would undoubtedly be a danger to the feminine sex' but alluded to his inward-turned character: 'He will hardly pick any flowers but rather allow them to wither in infinite longing and hysterical yearning for the irresistible personality who possesses this unique sex and these unique, distinct sex organs.' This passage, rightly or wrongly, has been adduced as evidence that Marx too may have seen Bauer as something of an 'intellectual rapist'.[29]

But his break with 'St Bruno' was still a couple of years off and in the spring of 1842 they were together again in Bonn. Before that, on 29 March, Bauer was informed that his teaching licence had been withdrawn. Bonn's Evangelical-Theological Faculty, supported by the unanimous vote of all such faculties at other universities, had ruled that his attitude towards the Evangelical Church and theology as expressed in vols. I and II of his *Criticism of the Synoptic Gospels* was irreconcilable with the post of a theology teacher. As for his part in the Welcker soirée, Eichhorn, the Minister, had decided to overlook his 'unsuitable' behaviour, since he was anyway being dismissed.

Thus ended the career of this savagely 'pure critic' and self-lacerating theologian. 'The last radical academic to leave the stage,' his dismissal spelled the end of Marx's chances of an academic career. If he could have made them good at all, it was before his 24th birthday in May 1842 – and not when he was 26 and living in self-chosen exile in Paris; but that does not seem to have been his main purpose, or not at any price. His very association with Bauer defeated the prospect of his obtaining the Bonn lectureship – in the pursuit of which he had invested altogether a year's time – and so did everything he wrote in the winter of 1841–42. He started a new preface to his doctoral thesis, apparently still toying with the idea of applying for a university post, but at the same time wrote his slashing attack – albeit not under his own name – on the King's censorship measures. Together with it he offered Ruge on 5 March both his atheistic observations on Christian art and another piece in which he promised to 'combat the *self-contradictory, self-cancelling hybrid of constitutional monarchy*', italicizing the words. None of this appears as if he was in earnest about making a state-sponsored career, the only kind available in Prussia at the time.

Compromise was not in his character. He would be a lecturer, but only on his own terms. Like Bauer, Marx had hoped to force his way into the 'sanctum' of Bonn's conservative academic establishment and to ravage it with his machine – philosophy – from within. It had taken him a long time to realize that such tactics were no longer possible, but once he did, he turned from atheist polemics to the current issue of the censorship, marking his entry into politics, though not in today's sense of the word. Unlike Bauer, he would not be a martyr.

In February, Jenny had turned 28. His presence by her side during her father's illness no doubt drew the two of them together, but the old man's prolonged death-struggle and the comings and goings of relatives made this a trying period not conducive to work. And the death of Westphalen reduced Jenny and her mother to living in genteel poverty. Once, during Westphalen's lifetime, there had been talk of his Scottish inheritance – as mentioned in a preserved family letter – but nothing more is known about it except that years later Jenny's uncle, Heinrich Georg von Westphalen, was to leave over '1,500 Pounds sterling'. Jenny's father, at any rate, left his family little besides a small pension and an honourable name.

Her mother, Caroline von Westphalen, had also once hoped to get a share of the estate – said to be worth £50,000 – left by an uncle of hers, Wilhelm Storch, described in letters as an 'American Croesus'. The Prussian Embassy in London had been enlisted to help; but nothing ever came of these efforts, and according to one source the Storch estate in 1973 continued to be administered in London.

Young Marx, for his part, had no income whatever. He was now almost completely alienated from his mother, who refused to advance him any more money, unable to see why he should do nothing to help support her and his 5 sisters and one younger brother. Their quarrel was further fed by the mutual distaste which Jenny and his mother had developed for one another. The addition of the lifelong antagonism between Jenny and her haughty half-brother, Ferdinand von Westphalen – to whom Marx may have referred as 'an aristocrat *comme il faut*' but who, together with her uncle, Heinrich Georg, vociferously opposed the idea of her marrying him – made for multiple domestic tensions, with Marx very much in the centre.

These various strains, which were to come to a head during the summer, hardly made his stay in Trier a pleasant one. More immediately, the death of Westphalen, who had been like a second father to him, could not but affect him profoundly. Yet the fact that Jenny now depended on him more than ever does not seem to have changed Marx's plans any more than the loss of his prospective post in Bonn did; he went on working, as if nothing had happened, on the 4 articles he had promised Ruge.

But he was very restless. Trier was dreary and depressing. He wrote to Ruge on 20 March that he planned to leave shortly 'for Cologne, where I shall set up my new residence', for the very idea of returning to Bonn and suffering the proximity of its theology professors seemed too terrible to contemplate. 'Who would want to have to talk always with intellectual skunks, with people who study only for the purpose of finding new dead ends in every corner of the world.'[30]

But he stayed only a short time in Cologne, deciding on second thoughts that life there was 'too noisy'. He had asked Ruge to send his mail to Cologne 'care of Jung', but seems to have feared that Jung and the wealthy, champagne-drinking Cologne set would distract him from work; and so it was to Bonn with its 'insufferable' professors that he went after all. 'Marx has come back here,' Bauer rejoiced in mid-April. The two intellectual companions had some high old times celebrating their reunion with a springtime outing. Bauer boasted of their antics: 'In Godesberg we hired a couple of donkeys and galloped like madmen around the hill and through the village. Bonn society stared at us more amazed than ever. We were jubilant and shouted, the donkeys brayed.'[31]

Having finished writing the third volume of the controversial *Synoptic Gospels*, Bauer was full of fight and planning a campaign to force the Minister of Education, Eichhorn, to rescind his dismissal. Marx thought this a foolish idea which would get Bauer nowhere, but felt that it was 'good Bauer doesn't let the matter rest.' The 4 articles Marx had several times promised Ruge were long overdue; in a letter written to Ruge on 27 April 1842, he referred cryptically to the troubled time he had been through.

> You must not become impatient if my contributions are delayed for a few days more – but only for a few days. Bauer will probably inform you orally that this month, owing to all kinds of external muddles, it has been almost impossible for me to work. Nevertheless, I have almost finished. I will send you four articles 1) 'on Religious Art', 2) 'on the Romantics', 3) 'The Philosophical Manifesto of the Historical School of Law', 4) 'The Positive Philosophers'... I have abandoned my plan to settle in Cologne... Bonn remains my residence for the time being.[32]

Only the third of the 4 articles and essays supposedly requiring 'only a few days' to finish was ever completed. The one on religious art, already promised 'within a few days' in February, had by now grown 'almost to book size'. But by October, Ruge was still waiting for it and he never received it or any of the others.

In the same letter of 27 April, however, Marx had a piece of news: he informed Ruge that he had 'sent the Rheinische Zeitung a long article on our last Rhenish Diet, with a frivolous introduction concerning the Prussian State Gazette.'

For the first time ever, King Friedrich Wilhelm IV had allowed newspapers to publish the debates – albeit in summarized form and without mention of the names of speakers – of the 6th Rhenish Provincial Diet, which had sat in Düsseldorf throughout June and July of the previous year. Now, three-quarters of a year later, the public learned that several deputies had presented petitions from liberal citizens demanding something new: freedom for the press to discuss

political matters. The semi-official General Prussian State Gazette had thereupon, in March 1842, run three articles built on the proposition that legislative
matters, the functioning of the 'state-machine' and politics *per se*, were of little
interest to the public, and had better be left alone by the newspapers. The
Gazette's unabashed argument ran succinctly as follows:

> In England and France everything – the question of the poor, the
> sugar problem, the Negro question – is inextricably mixed up with
> political interests. If the public there pays any attention to parlia-
> mentary debates, it is only because these problems can affect the
> preservation or fall of the political system.

> Not so in Prussia: here the Government never misuses administra-
> tive and legislative measures for purposes of political manoeuvering,
> never foists upon them an artificial interest which they intrinsically
> lack. Here, when one speaks of Corn Laws, one thinks strictly of
> corn and bread...

> Our press will therefore hardly be able, even under the mildest cen-
> sorship, to turn such matters into a political lever.[33]

'The Prussian State Gazette has reminded us', Marx observed wrily in the
article he had sent to the *Rheinische Zeitung*, 'that we in Prussia have representative local government and that the daily press is permitted to discuss the proceedings of these Provincial Diets if it can. The State Gazette, in its classic
self-confidence, thinks that what the Prussian newspapers lack is not permission, but ability...' But disposing of the Gazette's pharisaic cant and 'lullabies'
was only part of Marx's long article, which carried the title 'Debates on the
Freedom of the Press and the Publication of Parliamentary Proceedings' and
was to be published in 6 instalments. If in his first, as yet unpublished,
'Remarks on Censorship' he had called censorship 'terroristic' because it
attacked the state of mind of the writer, he now took up the wider issue of
freedom of thought. Attacking the Diet's majority decision to reject demands
for a Press Law guaranteeing freedom of thought, Marx pointed out that a
Press Law was not

> a repressive measure directed against the freedom of the press...
> Laws are not meant to repress freedom any more than the law of
> gravity which keeps the heavenly bodies in perpetual motion
> represses movement just because I would be killed if, in violation of
> it, I were to try to dance in the air... Rather, the absence of a Press
> Law should be seen as an exclusion of freedom of the press from the

> sphere of legal freedom, for legally recognized freedom exists in the state as law... A people's statute book is its Bible of freedom.
>
> A Press Law treats freedom as the normal condition of the press... It must always be present, even when never applied, as in North America, while censorship, like slavery, can never become legal, even if anchored in a thousand laws.

Ridiculing the muddled thinking, inverted logic and obfuscating oratory which had marked most of the press debate in the Diet, leading various speakers to argue that censorship actually made for better newspapers – or alternatively that man and society were imperfect or not mature enough to be handed perfect freedom of the press – Marx wrote in another place: 'The greatest orator of the French Revolution, whose ever thundering voice sounds yet into our time... Mirabeau, in short, trained himself in prisons. Does that mean that prisons are colleges of oratory?... The reasoning of our speaker is imperfect, governments are imperfect, the Diets are imperfect, freedom of the Press is imperfect, every sphere of human activity is imperfect – but then nobody has the right to exist, and man altogether has no right to exist.'

Attacking the censorship from a different angle, Marx declared that two decades of it had corrupted and impoverished the German mind and language. Even informed philosophy 'ceased speaking German, because the German language had ceased to be the language of thought. The spirit spoke in incomprehensible, mysterious words, because comprehensible words were no longer allowed to be reasonable.' The effect had been to plunge German literature into what he called 'its Evening-News period' of philistinism and obscurity, providing him with 'self-evident historical proof of the contention' – which expressed his own trenchant indictment – that 'censorship has irresponsibly retarded the development of the German mind and spirit in a disastrous way.'[34]

With this article, Marx made his prose debut in print at the age of 24, its first instalment actually appearing on his birthday, 5 May. The whole series was published anonymously 'by a Rhinelander'. For all his little-documented, erraticseeming activities in the winter and spring of 1842, he had obviously kept an eye on the *Rheinische Zeitung* and remained in close touch with its two influential directors, Jung and Oppenheim. Starting with his previous year's champagne bouts and 'Hegel club' discussions with them in Cologne, these contacts had sufficiently blossomed for Marx to be able to influence the appointment of Adolf Rutenberg as the paper's editor-in-chief.

The last instalment of 'Debates' had yet to appear when Prussia's Minister of Interior and Police, Rochus von Rochow, angrily referred to it on 19 May as another of the 'ceaseless attacks' which lent the *Rheinische Zeitung* 'the character of a party and opposition paper'. But Ludolf Camphausen, the future Prime Minister, received an inquiry from his brother: 'Who is the author of the excellent article in the Rheinische Zeitung?' Jung and Ruge vied in their praise of it – the former calling it 'beautiful', and the latter 'superb, the best thing written on the subject' – and Oppenheim invited Marx to spend Whitsun in Cologne.

The polemical gusto, pungent style and ironic panache he brought to his espousal of a free press could not but thrill Cologne's liberals. In describing the 'Evening-News period' of German literature under censorship, Marx had made merciless fun of the editor of Dresden's *Evening News*, whose name was Winkler, proclaiming him a *Krähwinkler*, or petty philistine; but as Winkler wrote under the pseudonym Theodor Hell – meaning 'Bright' – he added that 'it would be difficult to ascribe to him even such brightness as can be found in the marshes at midnight.'

In his next published piece – a sharp attack on the political editor of the rival *Kölnische Zeitung*, Karl Hermes – Marx again played on the name of his antagonist. Reminding his readers that 'the Greek Hermes was the god of eloquence and logic', he threw in blandly: 'Whether it was Hermes or his son, the goat-god Pan, who wrote the ailing article in No. 179 [of the *Kölnische Zeitung*], let the reader decide for himself.' Such puns and double puns, coupled with copious literary references and allusions – to Shakespeare, Goethe, Schiller, Aristotle, Epicurus, Socrates, Spinoza, Hegel, Voltaire, Newton, Rousseau and many others – were something the intelligentsia, or its non-conservative section, could wholeheartedly savour.

One other group in Berlin took an enthusiastic delight in Marx's articles. Friedrich Engels and his new friends among Berlin's *Die Freien* had called Bauer's dismissal and the government's gross intervention in academic freedom 'the event of the century'. *Die Freien* included not only ebullient students but quite a few known Young Hegelians and former members of the Doctors Club, such as Max Stirner and Köppen, the expert on Tibetan Lamaism. Like the Doctors Club before them, *Die Freien* had no practical aims or programme, but flaunted their bohemian life-style and talked loudly against the clerical character of the Prussian state. The nearest thing to an active step they ever considered during their noisy beer sessions at Stehely's and other cafés and taverns, was to secede from the church in a collective demonstration.

Engels's army drill left him sufficient time for pub-crawling and he felt very exuberant among *Die Freien*. He had a quick pen and a lively style. Following up his 55-page polemic, 'Schelling and the Revelation', which had appeared in March, he continued to fan 'the great controversies of our time' and had since produced 'Schelling, the Philosopher in Christo' (sgd. Fr. Oswald),[35] another cruel parody of the distinguished philosopher's new mystic 'system' published

751

in Berlin in May. By June Engels set about immortalizing *Die Freien* in a mock heroic poem written in defence of Bauer.

The tone and style of this 47-page spoof satirizing the establishment may be guessed from its title, which reads in full: *The insolently threatened, yet wonderfully redeemed Bible, or THE TRIUMPH OF FAITH. Being the terrible, yet true and profitable HISTORY of the quondam Licentiate, BRUNO BAUER. How the same, tempted by the Devil to leave the Pure Faith, became the Supreme Devil, and how he was finally shaken and kicked out. A CHRISTIAN EPIC in Four Songs.* It depicts a huge battle swaying and shifting from Heaven to Hell to Earth and back again as a riding column of theologians and pious Bonn professors – determined to destroy 'the great whore of Babylon, the Goddess of Reason' – set out in hot pursuit of the blasphemous *Freien*. Incited by the Devil and led by Bruno Bauer, they barricade themselves in a 'book fortress' made up of radical publications, but the forces of piety break in and give them bloody noses. As the Devil takes flight and vanishes into the depths, Bauer, 'the son of hell' and Super-Devil, rises above the clouds to lead the final assault on Heaven. The anxious Virgin Mary and fluttering angels support the godly ranks, while Hegel, Voltaire, Robespierre, etc., help the attackers. Bauer, armed with his trumpet, slays the Archangel Michael and is about to storm God's dwelling, when a celestial breeze wafts before his nose a parchment carrying an inscription. Pale and trembling, he reads it – 'DISMISSED!' – and with the Bible saved by this 'heavenly word', the host of angels break into hosannas while the horrified troop of godless *Freien* flee back to earth.[36]

The Triumph of Love is less memorable nowadays for its tumultuous, interplanetary plot or its ironies than for the little portraits, like verbal cartoons, which Engels drew in a few lines of Ruge, Rutenberg, Köppen, Stirner and the other more conspicuous neo-Hegelians and *Freien*. It is also valuable for the way Engels saw in his mind's eye an impetuous Marx – whom he had yet to meet – arriving full of fight to join the fray on the side of the atheists:

> Who rushes behind in a blustering storm?
> A black fellow from Trier, a savage monster.
> He walks not, hops not, but leaps on his heels,
> Pounding the ground in a fury, he stretches his arms wide,
> As though ready to seize the whole canopy of Heaven and tear it down,
> And clenches his angry fist, raving and raging mad,
> As if ten thousand devils had him by the hair.

26

Problems for Marx and the 'Bourgeois King' of France

Die Freien, or 'Berlin's beer-literati' – as Dr Bruno Bauer himself, while still in Bonn, had derisively referred to them – represented no serious threat to the Prussian government. Their pranks and verbal heroics annoyed some of the public, but what worried the authorities was that these Young Hegelian lecturers and students wrote learned and clever articles criticizing the clerical character of the 'Christian-German' State of Prussia in the columns of the *Rheinische Zeitung*, which was rapidly becoming a 'philosophical' newspaper.

Then in June 1842, Cologne's rival *Kölnische Zeitung* carried a report concerning the intention of *Die Freien*, as a first practical step, 'to proclaim their recession from the Church publicly and by signature of its members.' This had prompted the paper's political editor, Karl Hermes, who had Catholic leanings, on 27 June to write a leading article – to become known as 'The Leading Article in No. 179 of the Kölnische Zeitung' (which was actually the title of Marx's riposte to it), strongly condemning the spate of atheist philosophy which had lately found its way into the press. Hermes, without naming the *Rheinische Zeitung*, demanded that the censorship put an end to it. His line of argument was briefly that newspapers were no place for the 'dissemination of philosophical and religious views', which, 'by their very nature exceed the power of comprehension of the masses.' Christianity, the only true religion confirmed by 'the highest results of scientific research', was the foundation of all European states. In discussing religion, the daily press had to stay within the boundaries of Christian dogma; and 'the state must strictly prevent teachings contradicting, mocking or otherwise hostile to the fundamental truths of Christianity' from appearing in the columns of 'publications addressed to the masses'.

In his polemical reply, Marx pointed out that 'Philosophy has done with regard to politics what physics, mathematics, medicine and each science has done in its respective sphere.' Just as Francis Bacon 'emancipated physics from theology', and just as Copernicus's discovery of the true solar system had been made in disregard of the Biblical sun standing still over Gibeon, so philosophers from Hobbes to Hegel – looking at 'the state through human eyes' – had begun to 'deduce its natural laws from reason and not from theology... No more than you ask the doctor whether he is a believer should you put this question to the politician.'

As for Hermes's 'scientific research', it was like 'the Indian Brahmin who proves the sanctity of the Vedas by reserving for himself alone the right to read them!' In other passages, Marx showed up the 'mindlessness' of the demand that newspapers must not be allowed to discuss religious or philosophical questions, particularly in a 'so-called Christian state' where religion itself had become an object of politics:

> If such questions already interest the public as news, they have become questions and topics of the day, and then the question is not whether they should be discussed... [If] newspapers not only should but must discuss political questions, [then] as a matter of course, philosophy, the wisdom of the world, seems to have more right to concern itself with this world, politics, than does the wisdom of the other world, religion.

Marx did not attack the state as such. He described it as 'the great organism in which juridical, moral and political liberties must be realized' on the basis of human reason for all law-abiding citizens. But he questioned its presumption to make their 'human rights' dependent on their subscribing to a particular religious faith and dogma. He reminded Hermes that the Catholics of 'poor green Eire' did not appeal to a state religion which was not theirs, but to the 'rights of humanity'.[1]

When Dagobert Oppenheim at the *Rheinische Zeitung* received Marx's reply to Hermes he feared that 'the beastly censor' Dolleschal would cut it to shreds. Informing Marx on 4 July that the *Rheinische Zeitung* was being mercilessly censored, and that Hermes might insist in any case on obtaining the name of the author – as he had done with regard to one of Hess's articles – he asked whether it would not 'create quite a furor if you were to put your name to the article?'

Although Marx did not sign it – this and all his future articles in the paper appeared anonymously – his article, published in three instalments on 10, 12 and 14 July 1842, attracted a fair bit of attention. For here was an upstart paper challenging the respected bourgeois *Kölnische Zeitung*, and through it Prussia's religious state philosophy. But he was still far from achieving anything like a national reputation. The *Rheinische Zeitung* was only a regional newspaper, and between 10 May and mid-July – spanning the weeks during which the altogether 9 instalments of Marx's first and second article appeared in its columns – the interest of Berlin society, its officialdom and cultural élite was focused on Meyerbeer's *Huguenotten*, which was finally being publicly performed in Germany in an unprecedented series of 5 premieres within 8 days, at one of which the great singer Schröder-Devrient placed a garland of flowers on the composer's head. This had been followed on 31 May by the ceremony in which the King awarded Prussia's merit award to him and the other new 'knights of the German nation'. Because of an eye inflammation, Meyerbeer was excused from the supper at which the King entertained the new 'knights' at Sans-Souci. But 8 days later, His Majesty received him in a specially blue-curtained room 'to soften the sunlight, with blue glass to dim the light of the lamps in the evening.'

At the same time the King, before departing for St Petersburg to attend the silver wedding of the Tsar and the Tsarina – his sister Charlotte, rebaptized Alexandra Feodorovna – reshuffled his whole music-and-spectacles establishment. Amid great suspense before each announcement, Von Küstner replaced Count von Redern as 'General Superintendent of Royal Spectacles' and Redern became the same for 'Court Music', with the title of Excellency. Richard Wagner, having left Paris with his wife Minna and crossed the Rhine in an access of maudlin patriotism ('I, a poor artist, with bright tears in my eyes, swore eternal loyalty to my German fatherland'), arrived in Berlin to get wind of these changes. No wonder he found the city 'utterly depressing', for the new appointments dashed his hopes of an early production of *The Flying Dutchman* in that city.

While Wagner left for Dresden and soon raged at the clumsiness shown by his 'plump, lazy, vulgar' and 'accursed' Saxon compatriots in staging the 6-hour version of *Rienzi*, the cultural flurry in Berlin moved towards it climax in mid-June. Even as Marx's article for the *Rheinische Zeitung* on the church-state dispute was being suppressed, the King, Alexander von Humboldt and other officials were putting the finishing touches to a coup which they hoped would put Berlin on an artistic par with Paris. On the 16th, the King, the Queen, and the Court attended another festive performance of *Die Huguenotten*, at which the appointment of Meyerbeer – the pillar of the Paris Grand'Opéra – as General Musikdirektor of Prussia was at last an-nounced to the distinguished audience. Spontini, whom he was replacing, had a 'tearful audience' with the King. A few days later the new appointment was posted on the doors of the Berlin Opera.

Meyerbeer, having ended 'the war between the two capitals' over his person by obtaining the King's agreement that for the next two years he would spend only 4 (and thereafter no more than 6) months in Berlin annually, had already left for Paris when the news was published in the press on the 23d. Reports of his engagement and reviews of *Die Huguenotten* continued to fill the columns of German journals and periodicals, and by 4 July, when Marx's polemic against

Hermes reached the *Rheinische Zeitung*, the French press was reporting that Meyerbeer had declined the King's offer of a salary in favour of getting a decent prima donna for the Berlin Opera. On that day, the *Rheinische Zeitung* had exactly 841 postal subscribers.

'Do you know anything about Die Freien?' Marx inquired of Ruge in Dresden on 9 July. He was afraid that they were engaged in sheer braggadocio 'to annoy the philistines' and that Hermes and the *Kölnische Zeitung* might use any 'stupidities' they committed as a stick against the *Rheinische*. 'It is fortunate', he added, 'that Bauer is in Berlin.' Marx thought, erroneously, that Bauer at least would rein in *Die Freien* and keep them from making themselves and a good cause ridiculous.

But Bauer had no sooner arrived in Berlin in April than he was drawn by his brother Edgar into the circle of these 'beer-literati' whom he had previously deprecated. He was their hero and unable to resist their enthusiastic bear-hug. He found that, besides writing articles protesting his dismissal, they were ready to stage demonstrations and otherwise take part in his campaign against the Ministry of Education. Marx, for his part, felt sure that Hermes was out to draw him into more polemics. He was determined to dispose in his own way of Hermes's 'babblings' – 'mediocrity shall no longer enjoy the privilege of immunity', he told Ruge in his letter of 9 July – but he now had a stake in the *Rheinische Zeitung* and feared that the radical rhetoric and reckless antics of the swaggering *Freien* would both alienate the paper's wealthy sponsors and jeopardize whatever liberalization it might achieve as an organ of the Rhenish opposition.

Bauer had no such restraints and nothing to lose. Now that he was cast out of academe, his negativist-nihilistic streak led him to proclaim that every new world-historic principle, when carried to its extreme consequences, must of necessity express itself in 'vandalism' and a merciless 'destruction'. Hegel's notion of self-consciousness, he wrote that year, pointed the same way: 'Only a battle of annihilation can carry *die Sache* [the matter] to its conclusion.' For thus deducing revolution from philosophy, Bauer – whom Marx and Engels, and their followers after them, managed for a long time to confine to oblivion – is nowadays seen by some scholars as a link in the chain leading from Heine's 'Thought precedes action as lightning precedes thunder' – through Moses Hess's call for a 'philosophy of action' – to Marx's later formulation that 'it is the philosopher in whose brain the revolution starts.'

Marx himself was back in Trier, having been alerted there from Bonn at the end of April by the impending death of an aunt of Jenny's. It was from Trier, in the midst of a money quarrel with his family and other troubles, that he had written the masterly polemic against Hermes. In his letter of 9 July he complained to Ruge:

> I had to spend six weeks in Trier in connection with another death. The rest of the time was split up and poisoned by the most unpleasant family controversy. My family laid obstacles in my way, which, despite the prosperity of the family, put me for the moment in very serious straits. I cannot possibly burden you with the story of these private scandals; it is truly fortunate that scandals of a public nature make it impossible for a man of character to be irritated over private ones.[2]

With this noble statement he passed on to other matters, leaving a permanent stain on his family, chiefly his mother. Poor Henriette Marx! On the basis of this letter and some cynical or jocular sallies by the disgruntled son, practically all but the most recent of his biographers were to put her down for posterity as a wealthy but miserly, unfeeling woman who abandoned Marx to life-long penury. Modern investigation shows the truth to have been somewhat different. Actually, his mother had financed his quite expensive university education to the tune of 1,111 Thaler. When her husband's total estate of 22,110 Thaler had been settled in June 1841, assets to the value of 11,136 – representing her dowry and other monies she had brought into the marriage – had gone to Henriette Marx in accordance with a contract of partition signed during her husband's lifetime. Of the remaining estate, she had received half – to the value of 4,501 Thaler – her portion of the estate amounting, in round figures, to 16,750 Thaler, chiefly in property, as Karl's father had left very little ready cash.

One thing about the settlement that seems to have embittered Karl from the beginning was that it gave his mother the usufruct for life of a quarter of the 4,501 Thaler to be divided among the 7 Marx children. The share immediately due to each of them had thus been reduced from 482 to 361 Thaler. This meant that Karl had drawn not only his share but some 750 Thaler as an 'advance' on his future inheritance.

Since then his mother had sent him more money, while he did not even bother to inform her that he had taken his degree. At the beginning of 1841, when she left Trier for a short while, she instructed Marx's sister Sophie to inform him that if he needed money for any purpose he had only to write.[3]

Yet, whenever in the future Marx refers to his mother at all it is in connection with money matters; and whereas several classical and some of the best biographers of Marx describe her as a self-absorbed woman 'given to laments and humourless moralizing', more recent researchers have been forced to the conclusion that 'the portrait of the hard-hearted, stingy mother who abandoned the son in the hour of need is a legend which Marx himself did his best to promote. In reality he was repeatedly assisted by her, even with large sums.'[4]

Indeed, 6 years later, when he was 30, a married man and the father of three children, she was to send him another, quite considerable 'advance' (6,000 francs), only to be shocked by the Trier police's coming to question her, as Marx had just been expelled from Paris. He, on the other hand, was continually devising schemes to make his mother 'shell out her money'; at the age of 40 he expressed to Engels the possibility of making 'the old woman... believe that my inheritance is threatened by the [Prussian] authorities...' And yet the following year she wrote off the original 1,111 Thaler as a 'gift' and the year after that he reported from a two-day visit to Trier that she had 'destroyed several previous promissory notes which I once gave her.' This unexpected and 'pleasant result' of the visit – after an estrangement of two decades – prompted him to declare (to Lassalle) that he was suddenly 'interested in the old woman because of her very fine esprit,' while at the same time informing Engels in a different vein that she was 'rapidly going towards her dissolution...'

When she finally died two years later, it turned out that he had drawn another sizable advance of some 5,000 Dutch florins. At that, thanks to his mother's economic management, he was to inherit quite a substantial sum in cash and securities.

At the time of the 'unpleasant family controversy' in July 1842, Frau Marx was 54 years old. Widowed at 50, with 6 children besides Karl to support – including his retarded brother Hermann, then 23 years old (and to die later that year), and his sisters Sophie (26), Henriette (22), Louise (21), Emilie (20), and Caroline (18) – she managed her resources with the foresight and prudence of an experienced housewife. Unable to count on any help either then or in future from Karl, she had to think of making provision for 5 dowries and trousseaux for her daughters and of her own advancing years at a time when social insurance and old-age pensions were unknown. She therefore invested some of her capital in loans and securities and ran a 7-person household on the income it brought her, which, at the 4 per cent bank rate current in Trier, at first amounted to some 700 Thaler a year, a little less than Karl at 19 had spent on himself alone during his first 12 months in Berlin.

Later, when Marx's uncle, the Dutch banker Lion Philips, began to look after her savings, her income may have doubled. But this had not yet happened and meanwhile hers was a life filled with frequent sorrows – in the 5 years between 1837 and 1842 she lost her husband and two boys, and in the next 5 she was to bury two daughters in a row. Although the last 10 years of her life were to be materially comfortable, she had some reason for being 'given to laments'.

Raised in Holland, she had neither roots nor any real friends in Trier. Nor, to judge from a remark by one of her daughters, did she find much spiritual comfort in the religion to which she had reluctantly converted for her husband's and convenience's sake: 'To see the place to which the Children of Israel have been banished!' one of Karl's sisters, who had been baptized together with him, was to write of the bigoted town in which their mother was to live out the rest of her life. To these various problems was added Karl's total rebuff of her maternal love.

'He wanted nothing from her but money,' is the verdict of one modern historian. Practical, down-to-earth and very circumspect with her money Henriette Marx may have been, but nothing shows her to have been callous towards her eldest and favourite son. While his father had castigated him for being 'rather more of an egoist than is necessary for self-preservation', his mother felt that 'too much is being asked of you, my good Karl, the human heart cannot comprise and bear it all.' Only once did this woman who took her personal tragedies with great composure, and whose 'unflappable' spirit Marx himself was later to extol, complain with 'bitter tears' of her son's growing alienation. In 1840 she had written to him: 'Never will you make the moral sacrifices for your family which all of us made for you.'

By the time of the quarrel he mentioned to Ruge in 1842 she knew that, other than making constant demands, this learned doctor-son of hers – the family's pride, its *Glückskind* and admired intellect – had no further use for her or any of his siblings. One has to remember his mother's early solicitousness to appreciate the hurt to a woman with an archetypal family sense.

To Karl, on the other hand, it was a galling fact that his mother had retained control of the major portion of the total Marx estate, and no matter how many 'advances' he got on his future inheritance, he kept a jaundiced eye fixed on her prosperity and her purse; and occasionally he was to wish her dead.

His troubles during his 1842 visit to Trier were certainly real, but there was one side to them which he suppressed for the time being and did not mention to Ruge in his letter of 9 July. Significantly, he stayed at a Trier hostelry called Zu Venedig, or the Venice Inn, and not at Jenny's house. For within her aristocratic family the inveterate tension between the two sets of the late Baron's children had by now led to an equally bitter, and if anything, more cold-blooded rupture. Upon Westphalen's death in March, those of his first marriage had lost all reticence in their hostile attitude towards Jenny's mother, the Baroness Caroline. Led by the late Baron's brother, Heinrich Georg von Westphalen, now the doyen of the family, and by Jenny's half-brother Ferdinand, they had closed ranks against her and Jenny. Caroline and Jenny had meanwhile been reduced to living on the late Baron's modest pension, a large part of which had been consumed by the medical expenses of his year-long illness.

759

Living with them for the last 25 years had been Caroline's sister Christiane Heubel, whose very presence in the house was a constant reminder to Jenny's half-siblings Ferdinand and Lisette that the Baroness Caroline herself had been born a commoner. They could never forget that their mother – née von Veltheim and now dead and buried for 35 years – had been a noblewoman of ancient stock, while the Baroness Caroline was the product of several generations of Heubel equerries, bailiffs and stewards who had looked after the horses, or the houses and domains, of their lords and betters.

In short, while Karl Marx, emotionally speaking, boycotted his mother, he and Jenny and her mother Caroline – the family into which he hoped to marry – were now themselves boycotted by the older and nobler branch of the Westphalens.

Jenny's aunt Christiane, whose illness had brought Karl Marx to Trier, died on 12 June 1842. Some time later that summer, the widowed Baroness Caroline, twice bereaved in the space of three months, left Trier together with Jenny. For the next year or so they lived in great penury at Kreuznach, a small spa some 50 miles from the woods and vineyards where Jenny and Marx had walked and become secretly, romantically engaged 6 long years before. The career-conscious and reactionary half-brother Ferdinand is known to have hated the idea of Jenny's marrying a baptized Jew and resented having his name associated with Marx. But racial-religious prejudice and the fanatical opposition of Jenny's 'pietist-aristocratic' relatives to her marrying young Marx were only two of the elements that fanned long-nursed, smouldering antagonism and led to the final rupture between the two branches of Westphalens.

Neither Ferdinand nor Jenny's half-sister, the wealthy Lisette von Krosigk, lifted a finger to help her or their stepmother Caroline throughout the misfortunes which befell them in 1842. Jenny's less arrogant half-brother, Karl Hans Werner, had died young in 1840. Significantly, the Baroness Caroline, having dissolved her household in Trier, was to return there only after Ferdinand was transferred in 1843 to the post of Regierungspräsident of the Liegnitz district. She was to live there for another 14 years in utmost privation, her household effects when she died amounting to a little over 100 Thaler. Jenny alone would attend her mother's funeral and pointedly sign the obituary notice 'in the name also of my absent siblings'.

By that time, Ferdinand von Westphalen had served for 6 years as Prussia's Minister of the Interior and Police and was hardly anxious to have any connection with Jenny and thereby draw public attention to his being the stepbrother-in-law of Karl Marx, by then a notorious Communist liable to be imprisoned if he showed his face in Prussia. And three years later (1859), when Ferdinand published a *History of the Campaigns of Duke Ferdinand of Brunswick-Lüneburg* (being the war notes left by his grandfather, Heinrich Philipp, who as the famous Duke's factotum had devised most of them) and prefaced it with a history of the Westphalen family, he eliminated all mention of his stepmother Caroline from his father's biography, glossing over his second marriage altogether, as though it had never taken place or lasted a full 30 years. Thus he also expunged Jenny and her younger brother Edgar from the family record and, needless to say, saved himself the embarrassment of being connected in the public mind with Karl Marx.

On 23 or 24 December 1859, Jenny's anger at Ferdinand's suppression of her mother and herself would explode in a letter to Friedrich Engels. 'Our humane, truly noble and generous father', it said in part, had been 'Shakespeare-oriented and not Bible-minded – a crime for which the pietist son could not forgive him even in his grave.' Her mother, she protested furiously, had looked after her stepchildren 'with a devotion and a self-sacrificing love such as even a mother's own children are seldom lucky enough to enjoy.'[5]

Ferdinand, however, was not the only one to blot out unpleasant facts from the public record. In this one respect the aristocratic Prussian Police Minister and the prophet of the proletariat were to act curiously alike, for Marx, too, for different reasons, was to do his best to prevent any public mention of his own family antecedents. After Jenny's death in 1881, when her French son-in-law, the journalist Charles Longuet, mentioned in an obituary that her marriage to Karl Marx had met with 'trouble' because, among other things, 'there were many prejudices to overcome, the strongest of which was racial prejudice: it is known that the illustrious Socialist is of Jewish origin', Marx hotly contested this, called it 'simple invention', and wrote to his daughter Jennychen: 'There was no prejudice to overcome... Longuet will greatly oblige me by never mentioning my name in his writings.' But Longuet, a serious journalist on Clemenceau's *La Justice*, had heard the story from Jenny herself or from his wife.

On 14 June 1842, Marx attended the funeral of Jenny's aunt. He remained in Trier till mid-July. Besides his attack on Hermes he wrote while he was there another essay in his series on the Debates of the 6th Rhenish Diet. This dealt with the 7-year-long 'Church-State dispute' between the Vatican and Prussia, originally ignited by the Cologne Archbishop's refusal to transact mixed Catholic-Protestant marriages unless their progeny were committed to the Catholic faith. The issue had finally been settled in May by King Friedrich Wilhelm IV and his government giving in to the Pope. Marx had sent his article, which was to have been his second in the *Rheinische Zeitung*, to the paper but it was twice suppressed by the censorship, on submission and on appeal. Although the article has not survived, Marx's opinion of the settlement is evident from a passage in his letter to Ruge of 9 July: 'Before the entire world, Prussia has kissed the Pope's mule, and our government automatons walk the streets without blushing.'[6]

On 12 July, a couple of days after his letter to Ruge, Marx and his mother and the rest of his Trier family attended the wedding of his sister Sophie to the Dutch lawyer Wilhelm Schmalhausen. As Sophie and her husband settled in Holland, Marx was later to pay fairly frequent visits to that country, where his Philips relatives also lived. During his London miseries, Marx never hesitated to apply for help to his uncle Lion Philips, most often managing to 'lure some dough' – and sometimes, as he reported, to 'squeeze' considerable sums – out of him.

Before leaving Trier, Marx wrote to Ruge in Dresden, 'Do not imagine that here in the Rhineland we live in a political Eldorado. It takes the most unswerving persistence to push through a paper like the Rheinische Zeitung.'[7]

There was a new spirit and determination, a new purposefulness, to his writing. He now looked to the *Rheinische Zeitung* for a living; and whether or not he was already thinking of taking over from Adolf Rutenberg, whom he had helped into the editor's seat, he now had enough influence on the paper to declare to Ruge that 'sooner or later he will be shown the door', since he had proved a disappointment and 'absolutely incapable'.

Marx returned to Bonn on 15 July, not before remarking presciently to Ruge that the fight for the *Rheinische Zeitung* was only beginning.

In France the political struggle between the reformist partisans of 'movement' and Guizot's party of 'resistance' had just reached a dramatic climax in elections held on 9–12 July. Guizot, having defeated the opposition in the first session of the Chamber, had availed himself of his right to dissolve it at what seemed a propitious moment. The outcry over the press trials had died down; the country was quiet; and Guizot hoped to exploit the disunity in the Chamber, of which Heine had remarked the previous autumn that no two deputies agreed on any subject. King Louis-Philippe, too, was confident of Guizot's victory, for the general atmosphere was one of apathy and the two chief opposition parties – the Left-Centre led by Thiers and Odilon Barrot's Dynastic Left – could find no electoral issue to stir up the electorate. The two were flanked on the left by Ledru-Rollin's weak 'Democrats' and on the right by an equally weak splinter group of Legitimists.

At the last moment, however, the opposition found an issue in the 'Right of Search' treaty which the government had signed with England, allowing British warships to inspect French vessels suspected of plying the African slave trade. This was the kind of topic that played on national feelings and Guizot was sufficiently worried to hold up ratification of the treaty. For the first time, he was not sure of a conservative majority.

Indeed, in Paris the opposition won 10 of the district's 12 seats. Although the government claimed victory in the provinces and an overall majority of 70, the results were still being calculated when tragedy struck the House of Orléans.

On 13 July the King's eldest son, Ferdinand Philippe, duc d'Orléans, was on his way from the Tuileries to Neuilly in a phaeton four-wheeler drawn by two horses when the postillion's horse took fright and galloped. With the vehicle flying out of control towards the Chemin de la Révolte, the 32-year-old duke – after checking with the postillion that he could not hold back the runaway horses – stood up and jumped out of the low open carriage. He fell with his head against the pavement and fractured his skull. Taken to a nearby grocer's home, he died without regaining consciousness at 4 in the afternoon, surrounded by the King, Queen and other members of the royal family and state dignitaries who crowded the modest premises.

Rumours of his death were disbelieved until 6 p.m., when the Paris theatres cancelled their performances. The new heir to the throne was Louis-Philippe's grandson, the 4-year-old comte de Paris, about whom the liberal-minded duke now lying dead had wondered only two years earlier whether he would in time become 'one of the artisans of that social regeneration which can at the moment only be glimpsed across the barrier of great obstacles and perhaps torrents of blood'.[8]

Although Louis-Philippe had never allowed himself to be guided by his son's progressive views, his loss was a severe blow to him. Aside from his personal grief, his grandson's age meant that a Regent would have to be provided for him. Whether the reins should be placed in the hands of the boy's widowed mother or given to the duc de Nemours – Louis-Philippe's second son – was a question not covered in the 1830 Charter. Guizot wanted to pass a regency law favouring Nemours, but with some of the opposition claiming that this was an issue for another general election, a whole new political game was about to start even as the King stood hollow-faced and tearful during the crowded funeral service at Notre Dame.

'What projects vanished, what calculations deceived!' the Austrian ambassador, Count Apponyi, observed in his journal. Indeed, the septuagenarian King suddenly realized, as did many Frenchmen mourning in sympathy with him, how shaky was the basis of the July Monarchy and how uncertain its future, vulnerable to such unpredictable accidents as a horse run wild. Guizot had reason to fear that he would lose the vote in the Chambers, for Nemours was almost as unpopular as he was himself. As Heine put it, Nemours, by contrast with his late 'noble-looking' brother, had the haughty look of an 'aristocrat'.

But the King wanted the Regency for his son and not for his widowed daughter-in-law, the Duchess Hélène, who had been a Mecklenburg princess. He had reportedly told Thiers in private that he would never entrust the throne of France to a woman, and least of all 'to a foreigner, and a German to boot'.

Everything now depended on Thiers. The duchess was an intelligent woman with a liberal reputation, and all branches of the opposition expected his lead to overthrow the government on the regency question. The King, having recovered some of his composure, opened the new session with a short speech from the throne in which he declared that the Regency properly belonged to the prince closest to the throne in the order of succession established in the 1830 Charter, that is, Nemours.

Ledru-Rollin for the 'Democrats' asked that the nation should be consulted. Guizot replied that the King and the two Chambers were 'the sole legitimate and regular organs' expressing the national sovereignty. Lamartine, who represented no party except his admirers among the intelligentsia, the women and the young, delivered one of his winged speeches in which he claimed that 'awarding the Regency to a woman' would only 'restore the government to parliament and replace the royal dictatorship with that of the nation... The law you are making is neither conservative nor dynastic. It is pregnant with revolutions and usurpations.'[9]

Odilon Barrot, in the name of the Dynastic Left, likewise attacked the proposed law. Then Thiers rose and to everyone's surprise – including that of Guizot – announced that, in order to save the monarchy and the parliamentary system, he would vote for the government's law. He appealed to everyone to follow suit, for 'behind the government lurks the counter-revolution, and in front of it I see an abyss; the only safe ground to stand on is that of the Charter.'

Thiers's change of front threw the opposition into disarray. Whether he believed that Guizot would not last long and wished to win the good will of the King and signal to him that he was 'available', or, on the contrary, wished to write his history of Napoleon – considering that a grander task than 'small-scale' day-to-day politics – the net result was that Guizot, who had nearly lost the recent elections with all his candidates 'deserting like rats', won the parliamentary battle with a majority beyond his dreams. With many now defecting in the opposite direction, the vote in favour was 310 to 94.

But the victory of the policy of 'resistance' set France on a fatal course. With the opposition finally split by Thiers's *volte-face*, frustrated radical deputies and diehard republicans, seeing no hope of even modest reforms, turned more and more to extra-parliamentary circles and methods. Nor, after Thiers's withdrawal, was there anyone in sight to threaten Guizot's ability to maintain his majority by ever more venal methods. With his conservative creed buttressed by the loftiest intellectual and sincere moral arguments, Guizot kept the lid on a country simmering with the disaffection of voteless masses, liberal writers, underpaid workers, licentious newspapers and secret societies plotting revolution.

In general, 1842 is regarded as the watershed year when the July Monarchy, which the King and Guizot exerted themselves to consolidate, began to speed headlong towards disaster. According to one of his biographers, the Swiss-born Guizot was 'often unable to understand what was happening in France', and it was no wonder that he has been blamed for preventing the King and the government 'from discovering the true sentiments of the French people.'[10]

The King, who knew 'how to manage the French', showed the same lack of vision. Blind to everything that cried for that social regeneration which his own forward-looking son had considered imperative, he allowed the opinionated and doctrinaire Guizot to ride roughshod over the human needs, the new trends, ideas and under-currents of his time.

'The French ship of state has had too many holes bored into it by the gnawing teeth of mice,' Heine had written on 11 December 1841, 7 months before the summer elections and subsequent regency debate. Observing in the same article that Guizot was powerless against this internal danger, he had predicted that 'the whole bourgeois comedy in France, together with its parliamentary superstars and extras' would come to a bad end.

The principled Guizot, who in the aftermath of the regency vote presided undisturbed over some incredible abuses, is seen in modern times as the man who turned the comedy of representative government into a farce, and ultimately precipitated the collapse of the July Monarchy.

'Violent upheavals' and 'torrents of blood', 'revolutions and usurpations', 'counter-revolution' and 'an abyss in front' – the terms used respectively by the duc d'Orléans, Lamartine and Thiers between 1840 and 1842 – all denoted fear and an awareness that France was moving towards some unnamed catastrophe. It was Heine who, in his articles of the period, gave a name to this fear and designated its source. In his article of 11 December, he had pointed to the 'destructive doctrines' which had taken hold of the lower classes and singled out the elementary and universal appeal of the propaganda of Communism. Referring to the growing number of industrial workers who demanded not only 'equality of rights, but equality of enjoyment on this earth', he had warned that 'in Paris 400,000 raw fists are only awaiting the slogan to translate the idea of absolute equality into reality.'[11]

Reading the Paris newspapers and otherwise keeping his finger on the pulse of the French people, he had a better, and certainly a more far-sighted, awareness of its mood than its rulers had. But it was in two pieces written in June and July

1842 that Heine showed that intuitive grasp of things which justified his claim that the articles he sent to Augsburg's *Allgemeine Zeitung*, later to be collected in *Lutezia*, had the merit of 'an historical document'. In the first of these, datelined 20 June 1842, less than three weeks before the elections, Heine noted that none of the reformers who hoped to replace Guizot wanted the violent overthrow of the existing order, but he pointed to the 'dark forces lurking in secret' who might misread the government crisis and parliamentary machinations as a signal for revolution:

> The terrible wheel would then begin to turn again and we would see an antagonist arise who may prove the most formidable of all who ever attacked existing society. At present this dreadful antagonist still lives incognito, like some poverty-stricken Pretender, in the basement of official society, in those catacombs where, between death and mildew, the new life is germinating.
>
> Communism is the secret name of this terrible antagonist, which offers the rule of the proletariat with all its consequences in place of the rule of the present bourgeois regime. The duel will be breathless! How will it end? Only the gods and goddesses who know the future can predict that. We know only one thing: Communism, although little spoken of today and still lying dormant on its miserable bed of straw in the recesses of garrets, is none the less the sombre hero destined to a great role in the modern tragedy.[12]

Before publishing the article, Kolb, the editor of the *Allgemeine Zeitung*, changed the last sentence to read 'great, if only temporary, role in the modern tragedy.' Heine promised to watch the 'secret rehearsals' of Communism, which was only waiting for its cue to make its stage entrance. The Communists' activities seemed to him 'more important than all the election bustle, party squabbling and Cabinet intrigues.'

When Heine wrote this in June, Thiers was still expected to ride the wave of Anglophobia caused by the 'Right of Search' treaty. There were voices calling for war. Recalling this in his next article – written on 12 July, the day after the elections but before the results were in – Heine predicted that a war engulfing Europe would end with 'the ruin on the battlefield' of Germany and France:

> But that would have been but the first act of the great drama, a prelude, as it were.
>
> The second act is European, the world revolution, the great duel between the have-nots and the privileged haves of the aristocracy of property. And when that comes, neither nationality nor religion will

> make any difference: there will be only one fatherland embracing the earth, and only one faith... Will the religious doctrines of the past in all countries put up a desperate resistance, and will this attempt perhaps constitute the third act? Or will the old absolute tradition take the stage again, this time in some new costume and with new cues and slogans?

> How will this drama end? I do not know, but perhaps there will be a single shepherd and one herd, a shepherd driving a uniformly shorn, one-voiced bleating human herd before him with an iron staff!

> Wild, dark times are coming. Their boom can already be heard...

The term 'world revolution', which Heine pronounced in this visionary article, antedated by 75 years the use the Bolsheviks were to make of it after the 1917 October Revolution in Russia, but no one can say exactly what Heine was prophesying. The 'Communist' doctrine against which he was warning – and news of which, ironically, Hess was just about then smuggling past the censorship into the *Rheinische Zeitung* in Germany – was still vague and undefined at the time. It harked back to Buonarroti's book on the 1796 'Conspiracy of the Equals', which Heine had seen circulating among the Paris workers. The term 'Communist' meant different things to different people. It was loosely and indiscriminately used by the collectivist Colins, by George Sand in her innocent novels glorifying the proletariat, and by sundry clandestine groups in subversive tracts and pamphlets. But Heine knew Jacob Vennedey, a former Heidelberg lecturer closely connected with the one group from whose ranks the first Communists with anything like a nascent doctrine for the violent overthrow of society were to emerge before Marx ever dreamed of it.

This was the small but tightly organized League of the Just (*Bund der Gerechten*) of German artisans, journeymen and apprentices in Paris, whose underground cells had been 'rehearsing' for years to make their debut some day, when the public limelight was suddenly to fall on their plans in the sensational trial of their leader, Wilhelm Weitling, the Communist 'King of Tailors'.

But Heine was looking far beyond his time, as is evident from his addressing the last line of his article to 'our grandchildren'. He was actually writing about a 'new apocalypse' so terrible that

> the prophet who will want to write it will have to invent new monstrous beasts by the side of which the older animal symbols in Saint John will appear like softly cooing doves and little cupids.

> The gods will hide their faces out of pity for humankind, their long-time foster-child, and perhaps also out of worry for their own fate.

> The future smells of Russian leather, of blood, of godlessness, of lashes and much hard whipping.
>
> My advice to our grandchildren is that they had better come into the world with very thick hides on their backs.[13]

As no revolution took place in 1842, Heine's warning against the indistinct dangers of Communism fell on deaf ears. In the European mind, as Heine was to recall, May of that year became a 'month of disaster'. On the 5th, the day Marx's first contribution to the *Rheinische Zeitung* was published in Cologne, some old houses in Hamburg caught fire, causing a three-day blaze which, fuelled by winds and jets of blue flames from exploding alcohol vats, devastated half the city. On 8 May, a train accident on the Paris-Versailles railway line caused 150 deaths and hundreds of casualties; and the same month an earthquake in Haiti took another great toll of human lives. Heine spent anxious days before he received the news that his mother, who lived in Hamburg, had escaped to her daughter's house before the fire reached her own. He was moved to learn that the 71-year-old woman had insisted on going back to the house in order to save some manuscripts and papers of his. His sister Lottchen, offering to go in her place, arrived at the abandoned house to find two looters ransacking it amidst flying sparks and gusts of smoke. She grabbed the box with Heine's papers and ran out of the door, but her clothes caught fire and she fainted. When she recovered, the house was a smoking ruin and the box was gone.

It was during the 'great fire' that Heine's Uncle Salomon – whose own town house was blown up by Prussian army sappers in an attempt to contain the fire – showed his public spirit. With more than one insurance company going bankrupt and Hamburg's banks refusing to discount bills of exchange, he not only waived his insurance claims but was the only banker to discount bills at an uninflated rate, thus maintaining the city's credit and preventing speculators from exploiting the disaster. Further, he organized a low-interest loan of 32 million marks – subscribing a quarter of it himself – and in other ways helped uninsured small businessmen and the homeless.

In Paris Heine would later joke about Hamburg's firemen and write that when the souls of the victims arrived in heaven and were asked about the fate of the city's famous fire brigade they replied: 'It survived intact, minus its glory.' The premises of his Hamburg publisher, Julius Campe, had been destroyed, whereupon Prussia, to show its concern for the stricken city to which it had sent military and other relief, lifted the ban imposed on the firm's books. Heine's works, however, did not benefit from the relaxation, and he could only fume at their remaining *verboten* in Prussia and most other German states.

But life for him, too, went on and he continued to watch the 'destructive' course of events in France. On 29 July, shortly before Guizot was to scatter the opposition in the Regency vote, he informed the Augsburg *Allgemeine Zeitung* that what kept the July Monarchy alive was not so much fear of a republic as the 'instinctive fear of Communism... of the rule of His Majesty King Rat, the thousand-headed hydra who would soon come to power... instituting a new, unheard-of proletarian regime, complete with all the tenets of collective ownership.'[14]

Besides his articles for the Augsburg paper, he was supplying Laube's *Journal for the Elegant World* with some of his *Neue Gedichte* and working on what he described as 'a little humorous epic', *Atta Troll, A Midsummer Night's Dream*. Conceived during his month-long vacation in the autumn of 1841 at Cauterets, *Atta Troll* – to become his longest poem so far, running to some 2,000 lines – has for its eponymous hero a performing bear such as Heine might have seen dancing in the piazza of that town in the Pyrenees on the French-Spanish border. Breaking loose from his chains, Atta Troll flees across the mountains to the valley of Roncesvalles in Navarre, the valley where Roland, the legendary hero of the medieval *Chanson de Roland*, blew his horn and with his mighty sword Durandal tried to stop the Saracen onslaught on Charlemagne's Frankish troops.

There, united with his cubs in the hidden mountain cavern where he was born, Atta Troll, no ordinary bear, but a politically committed 'bear with a cause', serves Heine to poke fun at Germany's political poets, or *Tendenzdichter* – all 4 of them, Herwegh, Dingelstedt, Freiligrath and Hoffmann von Fallersleben – who, taking up the pose of tribunes in the radical fashion of the day, turned serious political issues into 'rhymed newspaper articles'.

In June Heine had addressed an ironic salute to one of the four *Tendenzdichter*. His poem 'On Dingelstedt's Arrival in Paris' – first suppressed in Leipzig under another title – was published by the *Rheinische Zeitung*. It was Heine's first contribution to that paper. As he suspected, Dingelstedt was indeed a shallow radical who later became a conservative Court councillor. He also rightly detected the nationalist streak in Hoffmann von Fallersleben, one of whose songs, beginning with the line 'Deutschland, Deutschland über Alles' – banned in 1841, and partly responsible for Hoffmann's dismissal from Breslau University in the same purge which removed Bruno Bauer – was eventually to be adopted as the German national anthem, ironically enough during the Weimar Republic.

Heine was not against writing political verse; he only ridiculed poets who lacked talent and that grasp of 'the great progressive ideas of mankind' instinctive to the true poet. *Atta Troll* was in fact a political work, in the sense that

Heine satirized every grotesque aspect of what passed for politics in Germany from the superior vantage point of the 'independent' sovereign artist he claimed for himself. Through the voice of Atta Troll, he declared that he would 'Always fight with loyal ardour / For Mankind and for the sacred / Rights of Man that we are born to'. But Atta Troll, the bear who belongs to 'the upper class of beastdom', also informs his cubs that below them, 'In the darkling social spheres of woe and anguish / In the beast world's lower strata / Want and pride and hate are breeding' anger and dangerous doctrines.

Next, standing with his son beside him on his favoured cliff – the Blood Stone where the Druids 'in the age of superstition slaughtered human sacrifices' – the bear howls down into the gully words that reflect Heine's increasing preoccupation with the social problem. His message is that the 'more enlightened' men of his day no longer killed each other out of religious zeal, but out of sheer self-seeking egoism.

Through the figure of Atta Troll, Heine could attack not only 'the plebiscitary decrees of the orators of the day', but everything he detested in Germany: philistinism, national prejudice, the preponderant role of religion ('In the starry tent above us / Ruling all the world, majestic / Sits a polar bear, a titan') as well as its opposite pole, atheism. If there was some ambiguity about his stance between these and other extremes he dealt with, the reason was, first, that he was a contradictory character; secondly, *Atta Troll* was written at a time when, as Heine put it, 'the big riot whipped up by my enemies of every complexion' against his book on Ludwig Börne had not yet died down. Indeed, at the beginning of July 1842, young Engels, in an article published in Arnold Ruge's *German Yearbooks*, was accusing him of nothing less than apostasy. Engels did not know that Heine was about to adopt a more radical course. By November, shortly after Marx took over the *Rheinische Zeitung*, Heine was to write to his friend Laube that they 'must not hide our political sympathies and social antipathies... We must harmonize our efforts with those of the [aforenamed] Yearbooks and the Rheinische Zeitung.'[5]

Atta Troll not only marked Heine's return to political writing but also, as he was later to comment in a Preface, the end of 'the thousand-year sway of Romanticism. I myself was its last abdicated King of Fable.' Completed in October 1842, the first version of his self-styled 'swan-song of the dying age' was to be serialized in 10 installments at the beginning of 1843 in Laube's *Journal for the Elegant World* in Leipzig. In its final Canto (27), addressed to Varnhagen, Heine refers to the 'wild din of battle' raised by the *Tendenzdichter*, and observes that Romanticism no longer suits the realities, the mood or the problems of the strident modern world: 'Other times, and other birds! / Other birds, and other songs.'

It now remained to be seen how far Heine would go in his new radical phase while maintaining both the sovereign 'rights of the spirit' – i.e., of poetry and, it goes without saying, of genius – and what was sure to be an individual stand. Published in book form in 1847, *Atta Troll*, with its mix of legend, fact and invention, was to become one of Heine's best-known works. While his supple verse forms made his best American biographer in 1979 think of Longfellow's *Hiawatha*, a more recent British biographer has found 'the nearest equivalent (apart from rhymelessness) in Byron's Don Juan.'[16]

For the Christmas break of 1841, after registering for the university winter semester, Michael Bakunin had returned to Dresden to be with his elder sister Varvara and his brother Paul, who had chosen to stay on in the Saxon capital. There was some tension among them, for Varvara seemed to be giving in to her parents' pressure to return to her husband in Russia. Tearing up a letter she meant to send him and drafting another for her to sign, Michael had boasted of his power to change Varvara's mind in this terse report to sister Tatyana at Premukhino: 'You remember how she would rebel and listen to nobody and do everything on her own – and then give way. So it was now.'[17]

But Varvara had only reluctantly given in. Dyakov had been quite decent in letting her stay abroad with his son for more than three years, and Varvara felt guilty for depriving the boy of his father and vice-versa. Besides, she had had about enough of Michael's continual harping on her 'crime' in having married the 'animal' Dyakov in the first place. But Michael would not let her go home before he negotiated an arrangement ensuring that Dyakov would keep his hands off her. As Turgenev was about to leave for Russia – and ready to visit Premukhino – Michael had given him 'full powers' to set these negotiations going through his brother Nicholas Bakunin.

And so, shortly before the Christmas which Michael spent with 'half my family' in Dresden, Turgenev was meeting his sister Tatyana at Torzhok. It was not their first meeting, for earlier in December Turgenev had spent a week at Premukhino. And there Michael's 'dear, wise, beautiful' Tatyana – object of his forbidden love and inordinate jealousy – had desperately, hopelessly fallen in love with him. By the end of that December week, the budding writer had become the focus of all the emotions previously absorbed by her precious, idealized Michael.

Turgenev, however, did not return Tatyana's feelings. Living in fear of his cold, vindictive mother, he had always sought and found affection among her house-serfs. Tatyana's very intensity may have frightened him, and although he remained in Russia – and was to see her again in Moscow in the spring of 1842 – he preferred to have a non-committal affair with a seamstress. Tatyana, who worshipped Turgenev as she had once worshipped Michael's other friend, Belinsky, withdrew within herself and never recovered from this second rebuff.

As for Varvara, who had agreed to postpone her return to Russia, she was impatient at Michael's negotiations, which were sure to be long-drawn-out. Although Dyakov had soon agreed to renounce all physical contact with his wife, demanding only 'rare' visiting rights to their son, the difficulties of winter travel were to keep Varvara marooned in Dresden until the summer.

After Bakunin returned to the bachelor flat he had rented close to Berlin University, he may not have devoted some of the spring, as he had announced he would, to boning up on Schelling, on Fichte and Hegel's logic. Unlike Turgenev, who was later to say that after thrashing about in the 'German ocean' of philosophy he 'emerged from its waves' more of a Russian 'Westernizer' than a real philosopher, Bakunin at the time seriously meant to explore that 'ocean' further. Although he had been disappointed by Schelling's inaugural lecture, finding it 'insignificant', he is known to have met the 'philosopher of revelation' in person. But without Russian company to stimulate him, and further plagued at intervals by an abscess and toothache which robbed him of sleep, he missed his sisters and in letters to Premukhino expatiated on his solitude, as he had done while a soldier in an isolated garrison 6 or 7 years earlier. He seems to have distracted himself as best he could by reading Shakespeare, but little is known of the courses he actually took before he obtained his diploma.

Some time during the spring, he became acquainted with the Left-Hegelian literature whose impact on him is reflected in the clever rhetorical use to which he put it in the essay that was to make his fame. This essay, titled *The Reaction in Germany* and to be published in the autumn of 1842, was directed, as implied by its title, against what he called 'the Reactionary party... now ruling everywhere'. Whereas much of the text was devoted to the conflict between the 'Positivist' upholders of the existing order and the Democratic 'Negativists' who professed the principle of revolution, Bakunin distinguished between two major divisions within the Reactionary party:

> To the one belong the pure consistent Reactionaries, and to the other the inconsistent, compromising Reactionaries. The first... feel that the positive and the negative get along no more than fire and water... [They] have the practical energy of their convictions and speak in clear words... With the Compromisers, however, it is a curious matter. They are wily; oh, they are clever and wise!... The Compromisers want nothing else but to stifle the only vital principle of our age... They say to the Positivists: 'Hang on to the old, but permit the Negativists at the same time to resolve it gradually.' And to the Nega-

tivists: 'Destroy the old, but not all at once and completely, so that you will always have something to do... Leave us, the elect, the pleasure of completing totality for ourselves.'[18]

It was against these hypocritical, 'immoral' Compromisers that Bakunin directed his sharpest barbs and chief assault. Declaring that the spirit of revolution which had 'convulsed the whole world to its foundations' in 1789 was not dead, he informed them that 'right now it is burrowing – if I may avail myself of this expression of Hegel's – like a mole under the earth.' It was in this passage that Bakunin expressly referred, italicizing the names, to the works of Strauss, Feuerbach and Bruno Bauer. In a reference to the Left-Hegelian literature flooding Germany, he upbraided the Compromisers:

> Are you blind and deaf and have you no eyes nor ears for what goes on around you?... You speak of resolution, of reconciliation! Just look around you and tell me what has remained alive of the old Catholic and Protestant world. You speak of the subjugation of the Negative principle! Have you read nothing of Strauss, Feuerbach and Bruno Bauer, and do you not know that their works are in everyone's hands? Do you not see that the whole of German literature, books, brochures, newspapers, indeed, the works of the Positivists themselves, are unwittingly and unwillingly permeated by this negative Spirit? And you call this reconciliation and peace![19]

The overall theme of Bakunin's essay was that the struggle for 'the realization of freedom' had become the foremost issue of the age, heading 'the agenda of history'. And the quintessence of his thesis was that the 'contradiction' and unremitting conflict between reaction and democracy could only be solved by the revolutionary application of the principle of 'negation', leading in practice to the total destruction of everything positive. There could be no compromise between the forces of the past and those of the future. Although the essay was couched in the jargon of Hegelian dialectics, Bakunin achieved a shortcut to revolution by simply leaving out Hegel's 'reconciliation' between thesis and anti-thesis.

Not only that, but in the revolutionary process of destroying everything positive the 'party of negation' – that is, democracy itself – must be destroyed. For at this stage 'Democracy does not yet exist independently' and lacks 'an affirmative consciousness' of its true historic role as the instrument of an unprecedented universal transformation. Only when it has ceased to be a mere negation and completed 'the annihilation of the present political and social world' will democracy be reborn as 'a life-giving revelation', capable of starting a new phase of history and building a new world on the ruins of the old.

'Contradictions, bloody contradictions', the basic law governing all reality and lending 'meaning' to life, first appeared in Bakunin's correspondence in late autumn 1841, after he had read the abbé de Lamennais's *Politique à l'usage du peuple*. In Lamennais, too, he had discovered that religion represented a more powerful political weapon than abstract philosophical 'criticism'. Abstract thought, he had written in a letter before the end of 1841, could negate the past, but it could not build a new reality. It will be remembered that in 1841 Moses Hess had stated in *The European Triarchy* that just as our concept of a tree does not enable us to create a tree, so Hegelian philosophy is incapable of producing a single historic deed.[20]

Whether or not Bakunin had already read Hess's book, he wrote to Varvara and Paul on 27 October that a new world could be built only by someone expressing a simple 'universal, practical and vital principle of a new religion, a new life, a new reality.'[21] As Hess's approach was Spinozist and ethical, it was most likely that Bakunin's model at this stage was Lamennais, whom he described as an example of 'authentic apostolicism' animated by 'simple love and profound unwavering faith in the future of humanity',[22] and whose religious inspiration spoke to the heart of the founder and 'high priest' of the 'holy commune' at Premukhino.

The difference between then and now was that Bakunin's new religion would be 'political and social struggle' on a universal scale. In his essay he would present freedom as 'the one true expression of justice and love' and call for combined political and religious action. His own tone was nothing if not apostolic: 'For us alone, who are called the enemies of the Christian religion, for us alone is it reserved, and even made the highest duty even in the most ardent of fights, really to exercise love, this highest commandment of Christ and this only way of true Christianity.'[23]

At the end of the winter semester 1842, Bakunin left Berlin again and moved to Dresden. Whatever Young Hegelian 'books, brochures, newspapers' he had read in Berlin during the spring, it was in Dresden, with Arnold Ruge for his guide, that he became more closely acquainted with the discussions going on among the radical Hegelian Left. The universal 'catastrophe' which Bauer kept predicting, far from frightening Bakunin, was grist to his mill. But whereas Bauer's apocalypse was the result of an extremist interpretation of Hegel – he claimed that Hegel's teaching ultimately and logically led to 'atheism, revolution, and republicanism' – Bakunin was to undo the rational foundation of Hegel's philosophy, and ultimately to do away with philosophy altogether, all by means of dialectically applying Hegel's concept of negation to philosophy itself.

Bakunin called Hegel 'unconditionally the greatest philosopher' of the age for having made 'contradiction' the keynote of existence. Hegel had reached the 'highest summit of modern, theoretical' thinking. In the process he had 'already gone above theory – granted that at the same time he still remained within theory – and postulated the new practical world.' But this new world, Bakunin went on, would by no means be completed 'through theories already worked out, but only through an original act of the autonomous spirit.'

Bakunin's autonomous act was to take Hegel's concept that every organism 'carries negation within itself as an immanent condition necessary to its vitality' – but only until 'the Negative is transformed into an independent principle' – and to hang on it the conclusion that, from that moment on, the original organism is dead and ceases to exist. Arguing 'logically' that the Positive plays a paradoxical double role – combining restful, apathetic self-sufficiency with simultaneous exclusion of the Negative – he wrote that 'this activity of exclusion is a motion and so the Positive, just because of its positivity, is in itself no longer the Positive, but the Negative; in that it excludes the Negative from itself, it excludes itself from itself and drives itself to destruction.'[24]

If there was a hint in this that 'real philosophy ought to negate philosophy,'[25] Bakunin did not express that in so many words. Rather, for 'historical corroboration' of his theory, he cited Protestantism as one of the negations long inherent in the Catholic world, which had considered it a 'heresy' until Luther, rejecting all advice for moderation, nailed his theses to the door of his church. And with the mystic-religious element still strong in him, Bakunin went back to *Revelation* and quoted 'what the author of the Apocalypse said to the Compromisers' of his own day: 'I know thy works, that thou art neither cold nor hot: I would thou wert cold or hot. But because thou art lukewarm, and neither cold nor hot, I will begin to spue thee out of my mouth.'[26]

Bakunin did not vent his fury either at the 'weak' party of 'democrats' or at the out-and-out reactionaries in power, but at that section of the latter whom he called Compromisers, who were holding up his own apocalypse because they sought moderate reforms where only total destruction would do.

In August, some weeks before his *Reaction in Germany* was to appear in print, Bakunin was reunited in Dresden with Turgenev, back from his prolonged stay in Russia. It was a joyful reunion, but also a parting of the ways. Both of them had changed. If they had something in common it was that each, for different reasons, was about to give up philosophy – Turgenev, after meeting Belinsky in St Petersburg in 1843, in order to begin writing poetry and prose and to devote himself entirely to literature; and Bakunin, because by August he had reached the conclusion that philosophy and theoretical speculation were a German 'disease' which led politically nowhere.

In 1843, Turgenev was to meet and fall in love with the singer Pauline Viardot-Garcia during her debut in St Petersburg. Although he had a daughter by his mother's seamstress-serf, he was to follow Pauline and her husband like a slave wherever they went during her international operatic career. Whether or not they had a sexual relationship has not been established. He and the husband were good friends, and he appears to have been devoted to the Viardots as a kind of surrogate family.

As for Bakunin, he had long maintained in Russia that studying philosophy and getting a degree in Berlin would open the way to a professorship at Moscow University and enable him to settle down to a respectable career. He had once called philosophy his 'wife', but had now reached the point of abandoning her in favour of a new mistress, revolution and 'deeds'.

In his famous 'Confession to Tsar Nicholas I', sent from prison in 1851, Bakunin was to explain why, after filling his head with the most empty abstractions, he became convinced in 1842 of

> the triviality of all metaphysical writings. I sought life in them, but found merely death and boredom; I sought deeds, but found absolute inaction... I understood at last that life, love and action can be grasped only through plunging into life, love and action. I finally renounced transcendental science – for all theory is grey – and threw myself headlong into practical affairs.[27]

Bakunin could change theories, but he could not, as Belinsky observed, change his nature. Philosophy and Hegel had served their purpose, and could be discarded in favour of what Bakunin was to call his

> love for the fantastic, for unusual, unheard-of adventures, for undertakings that open up a boundless horizon and whose end no one can foresee... I should have been born somewhere in a forest in America, among the western colonists... where all life is a ceaseless struggle against wild men, against wild nature, and not in an ordered civil society. Also, had fate wished to make me a sailor from my youth, I would even now probably be a very respectable man... But fate did not will either the one or the other...[28]

The 'Confession' is a long document, mixing possibly sincere sentiments whose truth cannot be verified with passages written in a tone of obeisance and contrition which is jarring when coming from so determined a rebel, even if the tone were feigned. The self-styled adventurer with 'a love for the fantastic' and a ceaseless 'need for movement and activity' fits the public image of Bakunin, but there is no way of telling how much of the 'Confession' represents the real man. Arthur Mendel devoted much of his 1981 biography to demonstrating that throughout his life Bakunin turned the world into a stage on which he acted out his fantasies of power in order to disguise his most intimate problem and to make it possible for him to live with his sexual inadequacy. In 'The Reaction in Germany', in Mendel's view, he assumed 'a new, violently activist posture to hide his essential fear and passivity.' Referring to Bakunin's use of such expressions as 'loving surrender', not to mention the ambivalent 'ruthless surrender', Mendel observed that

> it is at least highly unusual for an heroic, 'violent' revolutionary out to destroy the existing order of things to speak repeatedly of 'loving surrender' to the Spirit 'in order to consume it,' being 'permeated by it' in order to reveal the revolution's 'pregnant nature' and be 'born anew'.[29]

As mentioned earlier, Bakunin abolished the phase of 'reconciliation' in Hegel's dialectic of thesis, antithesis and synthesis. By having the 'antithesis' simply destroy the 'thesis', he was able to maintain that withdrawal and detachment from society which, in Mendel's view, had always been 'the ground of his being'; but whereas they had previously been a source of shame, they now became – thanks to 'the gift of the dialectic' – one of pride. 'By allying himself with the revolutionized Absolute as it prepared the cataclysmic birthpangs of the new world... and by adopting a rhetoric of boundless violence appropriate to this imminent apocalyptic transmutation', Bakunin not only gained 'an invaluable illusion of promethean virility', but could feel himself 'virtually' omnipotent. There was no change from the earlier Bakunin, who at Premukhino had tried to prove to himself and others 'how powerfully he could suffer and passively, masochistically endure... With the help of "left" Hegelian dialectics [he] constructed a world view that adequately met his need to be violently passive.'[30]

Aileen Kelly in 1982, likewise stressing that there was 'no break, no decisive turn from the inner to the outer world, or from philosophy to action,' has called Bakunin's embarking on a revolutionary career in *The Reaction in Germany* a *coup de théâtre* 'which continues to mystify his biographers', but chiefly, in her view, because of its seeming unexpectedness. 'After 1842 as before', Bakunin sought to achieve wholeness through a mystically conceived mission, 'a sublimation at one and the same time of his need for self-assertion and of his longing to identify with a meaningful collective entity... The difference was that henceforth he would seek to realize his fantasy through the transformation of the external world.'[31]

Bakunin's move from the Hegelian 'Right' to its 'Left' and beyond – begun in the winter of 1841–42, when 'bloody contradictions' had first entered the vocabulary of his letters to Premukhino, along with talk of his beginning 'rebirth' and advice to members of his original 'commune' to abandon the 'theoretical pseudo-wisdom' which he had himself preached to them – was completed by the time *The Reaction in Germany* appeared. Shortly afterwards he wrote to his siblings: 'I do not want happiness – nor do I think of happiness. Deeds, deeds – expansive sacred deeds – this is what I want. A broad field stands before me. Mine will not be a trivial destiny.'[32]

Throughout this period, Bakunin went through a substantial crisis. It was as if the old, emotionally weak Bakunin in him was ceaselessly rising to interfere with his striving to tear himself away from the 'world of illusions', to confront 'reality in all its wretched nakedness' and to develop an image and a theory centred on 'manliness and deeds'. At the beginning of this process, in January 1842, he remarked to Tatyana that an ordinary life was not worth living: 'Better one moment of real life than a series of years lived in moribund illusion.' Yet the Bakunin who left Berlin University at 28 and settled down in Dresden to embrace the world and work in earnest on the revolutionary plan of salvation he was to offer it in the closely printed pages of his *Reaction in Germany* was well aware of his fundamental coldness and alienation from the world. He wrote to Alexandra Beyer on 7 April,

> My heart, in spite of the passion languishing within it, is surrounded
> by a thick husk of ice that repels even those who may wish to become
> close to me, and very few people are able to break through it... I know
> that there is in me something repulsive and that it is very difficult to
> love me.[33]

In June, as though to confirm his words, his elder sister Varvara caused him a discomfiture which, if not the worst of his life, took him by surprise. She who 'would rebel... and then give way' – had at last freed herself of his tutelage and slipped away with her son to Russia and her husband without so much as a goodbye. A contrite Bakunin wrote her a letter half-apologizing for having been 'sharp' with her and hurt her feelings: 'But, believe me, Varvara, it hurt me so much too, and I repented every time so sincerely and so bitterly, that you ought to forgive me... I tried to do by force things which cannot be done by force. It was childish, I admit, and I swear to you that I will never do it again.'[34]

That Turgenev or anyone had replaced him in Tatyana's heart, whose love was his life-line to Premukhino, Bakunin did not know even after Turgenev's return in August. Curiously, however, before the end of the summer he felt a compelling need to remind Tatyana of their special bond:

> Yes, Tatyana, you are mine, and I am yours, before all the others. I
> have long known this, but it has been a long time, a very long time

since I have felt it as keenly as I do now... Continue to write to me,
friend, help me to come out of myself and to speak with you, and you
will then see how strong, how constant, and how impassioned is my
love for you.[35]

But Tatyana now worshipped Turgenev from afar and did not reply to
Michael's effusion or to another impassioned letter he sent her. Nor were his
relations with Turgenev what they had been before. During the months he
spent in Moscow, Turgenev had taken a low-ranking post in the Ministry of
Internal Affairs, only to quit it as soon as he became fed up with the bureaucracy. This, and his decision to go abroad again, so infuriated his tyrannical
mother that she cut off his allowance. Turgenev was thus no longer in a position
to lend Bakunin money and bail him out of debt, as he had often done before.
Bakunin still had his younger brother Paul for company in Dresden, but Paul,
too, having lost interest in German philosophy and politics, ceased to be his
eager disciple.

Even as he worked through the summer at the heroic revolutionary persona
which was to appear in his essay, Bakunin all the more acutely felt the disintegration of his devoted 'commune' at Premukhino and the loss of that mutual
bond of love with his flock of siblings which was to him 'not a shadow, not a
dream', but 'our guardian angel', the sole source and sustenance of 'our faith...
of all that is holy and vital in us.'[36] And the same Bakunin who, after the publication of his essay, boasted of 'a broad field' of action and deeds opening before
him, subsequently filled his letters to Premukhino with a crescendo of gloomy
passages denoting his terrible old feelings of loneliness, isolation and stoic
suffering upon his entry into a new 'wasteland'.

Mendel has quoted all his expressions of anguish and fear in support of his
thesis. But as in the case of Marx, it is important to remember that no one in
1842 and for decades later read Bakunin's private correspondence except for its
addressees, and sometimes the censors who intercepted it.[37] His unheroic
moments and the whole psychodrama which led him to reach out through his
'husk of ice' to the rest of the world – if only to transform it according to his
fantasy and inner needs – were largely unknown in the 19th century and did not
diminish the effect of his essay when it appeared, with its author posing as 'a
Frenchman' by the name of Jules Elysard.

The Reaction in Germany, with its thrilling phrases, gave a foretaste of the
later Bakunin, the spellbinding orator whose rhetoric, according to a contemporary, would mesmerize listeners to the point where, no matter what he said,
they would have 'cheerfully cut each other's throats if he had asked them.' Published anonymously in Ruge's learned *German Yearbooks for Science and Art*,

779

Bakunin's essay came at a time when the Hegelian Left, endlessly discussing the explosive force in Hegel, spoke in a dozen voices of a 'philosophy of action', but even its best minds had no idea how to launch one in practice. Bakunin, dialectically proclaiming the destructive urge to be a creative one, showed them how to start Hegel's 'diesel engine' going as though by magic.

Still, this alone, sensational as it was, would not have done the trick had he not coupled the mystic fervour which he substituted for Hegel's reason with a message touching upon the rapidly developing 19th-century social problem. Taking up the cause of the disinherited, 'the poor class' constituting the majority of human beings, Bakunin wrote in his peroration:

> This class whose rights have already been recognized in theory... is everywhere assuming a menacing attitude and is beginning to count the ranks of its enemy... and to demand the actualization of the rights already conceded to it by everyone.

> All peoples and all men are filled with a kind of premonition, and everyone... faces with shuddering expectation the approaching future which will speak out the redeeming word. Even in Russia, in this endless and snow-covered kingdom which we know so little and which perhaps a great future awaits, even in Russia dark clouds are gathering, heralding storm. Oh, the air is sultry and filled with lightning.

> Therefore we call to our deluded brothers, repent, repent, the kingdom of God is at hand!

After invoking the 'eternal Spirit, this old mole' which had completed 'its underground work' – especially in England and France, where societies 'wholly alien to the present political world' were arising from 'new sources quite unknown to us' – the essay ended with a sentence, 'The passion for destruction is also a creative passion',[38] which summarized the pent-up, now released motive force animating the old/new Bakunin in his future career as an international rebel.

27

A Red October Scatters the Budding Doctors of Revolution

As though guided by a secret hand, developments both expected and unforeseen came to a head in October 1842. On the 8th, Friedrich Engels was discharged from his military service as a 'one-year-volunteer'. A few days later, the 22-year-old youth left for Cologne and walked into the offices of the *Rheinische Zeitung* in the Schildergasse, where he was received by Moses Hess.

Engels, who had already contributed several articles to the paper, was to leave the following month for Manchester, and Hess invited him to send reports on the social conditions in England. The British Parliament's rejection of the Chartist Petition and the ensuing workers' riots had convinced Hess – as he had stated during the summer in an article on 'The Approaching Catastrophe in England' – that revolution there was more imminent than expected, for the simple reason that there was no political solution to the problem of social misery. Young Engels fully shared this view and the two parted on friendly terms, not before Hess convinced Engels that Left-Hegelianism, pursued to its logical conclusion, led to Communism.

'We discussed the burning topics of the day,' Hess wrote about this talk with Engels, 'and he, a first-year revolutionary, left me as a zealous Communist.'[1]

On 15 October Karl Marx arrived in Cologne and moved into the editor's chair of the *Rheinische Zeitung*. Engels had missed him by a few days, but was to see him on a return visit before his departure for England. Oddly enough, the two young men whose historic partnership was to influence the world for the next century and a half did not hit it off at their first meeting. Marx had heard that Engels belonged to the rowdy *Die Freien* in Berlin, and therefore coolly dismissed him.

Ironically, the Prussian authorities had indirectly helped Marx into the editor's seat by pressing the owners to fire the incumbent Rutenberg because of his connections with *Die Freien* and his past record as a *Burschenschaft* student agitator. But it was most likely the letter sent by Marx on 25 August, while he was still in Bonn, to Dagobert Oppenheim which secured him the editor's post. He suggested that under Rutenberg the paper was being run by its contributors rather than by its editor. Referring to an article submitted by Bruno Bauer's brother Edgar, the leader of *Die Freien*, Marx warned that so outspoken a tirade 'against the foundations of the present state system' might lead to harsher censorship measures 'and even the suppression of the newspaper'. Such 'comfortable armchair abstractions', he noted, were already arousing the resentment of most liberals engaged in 'the laborious task of winning freedom step by step, within the constitutional framework.' In a brief editorial policy statement that could not but please the board, he then wrote:

> I consider it essential that the Rheinische Zeitung should not be guided by its contributors, but that on the contrary it should guide them. [Edgar Bauer's article] affords the best opportunity for indicating a definite plan of operations to the contributors. A single author cannot have a view of the whole in the way the newspaper can.[2]

Besides his incisive intellect, his polemical bent and philosopher's reasoning faculties, this is indeed what Marx brought to the *Rheinische Zeitung*: leadership, a firm hand, a radical but circumspect editorial policy and an extraordinary ability to see 'the whole' of a situation. Social or indeed any kind of revolution was far from his mind, and not for a moment did he at the time contemplate anything in any way subversive against the 'great organism' of the state within which political freedom was to be achieved.

Sooner or later he would inevitably have had to confront the idea of 'Communism', a loose term to whose increasing circulation among the workers of Paris Heine kept drawing attention. In June 1842 Wilhelm Weitling had published an anonymous tract in Switzerland addressed to and titled *The Young Generation*. In it the runaway leader of the banned Paris League of the Just presented Communism as a 'scientific form of government' and called for the overthrow of the representative system. More recently, Fourier's disciples had held a congress at Strasbourg to discuss the master's ideas. In October, while Bakunin's *Reaction in Germany, A Fragment by a Frenchman* (to give it its full title) was making a splash in intellectual circles, the attention of these circles was caught by a volume published in Leipzig, *Socialism and Communism in Present-Day France*.[3]

Its author was Lorenz von Stein, a Silesian-born student who had been sent to Paris on a Prussian government stipend to investigate the extent to which the German workers there had been infected by subversive French ideas. Dutifully fulfilling his role as a stool-pigeon, Stein sent his report to Prussia's Minister of Police, Rochus von Rochow. But, having academic ambitions, he expanded it into a thorough study of the various social theories and revolutionary movements in France.

In another ironic touch, although Stein condemned both the Socialist and Communist philosophies current in France, his volume had the effect of acquainting the German public with ideas of which, as Karl Grün, the editor of Mannheim's radical *Abendzeitung*, was to observe, 'hardly ten people in Germany had heard or thought of' at the time.[4]

During the same month the poet Georg Herwegh, coming from Switzerland, capped his meteoric rise as the idol of Germany's radical youth with a triumphal tour of Germany. The author of *Poems of a Living Man* and an army deserter, he was feted by Germany's 'democratic' circles not merely like a prodigal son or homecoming hero, but a long-expected saviour. Banquets were to be staged in his honour in Leipzig; students serenaded him in Jena; in Dresden there was Arnold Ruge's circle, including Bakunin, to pay homage to him; in Berlin *Die Freien* were eager to acclaim him; and in Königsberg, Jacoby of the famous *Four Questions* and his friends were waiting for him.

The practical purpose of Herwegh's triumphal tour was to turn *Der deutsche Bote aus der Schweiz* ('The German Messenger from Switzerland') – a small review published by his patron in Zurich, Julius Fröbel – into a political monthly to be circulated in Germany, and to enlist prominent contributors to it. The excitement of Germany's assorted liberals, democrats and radicals was heightened by the fact that Herwegh's itinerary seemed designed to unite the liberal groups in the Rhineland, in Berlin and in East Prussia for the first time into something like a national opposition.

Midway through Herwegh's three-months tour, the King of Prussia himself, as though to crown the extraordinary public homage to him, made known his wish to meet 'the iron lark of revolution' in person.

It was against the background of these developments and the ultimately disastrous consequences of Herwegh's 'audience' with the erratic King that Marx began in mid-October what he had presciently called 'the fight for the Rheinische Zeitung'.

The only hint that Marx would one day make the 'Communist' idea his own was perhaps Hess's early observation that this young man had it in him to administer 'the death-blow to medieval religion and politics.' And ironically, in his very first editorial, which appeared on 16 October 1842, the day after he took over, he had to rebut charges that the *Rheinische Zeitung* had Communist tendencies.

On 29 September Hess had published an article, 'Government According to the Communist Principle', which dealt with Weitling's claim that Communism was a scientific form of government under which the leaders of every branch of life would be chosen according to their ability. Weitling's call for the abolition of the representative system did not shock Hess because that system favoured the bourgeois section of society and was otherwise a sham: without bread and education, Hess had remarked in April, the common people were in no position to discuss state affairs and take part in public life. And some of Weitling's ideas struck him as original because prevailing social disorganization cried out for reform.

In addition to that, on 30 September Hess had reproduced a report on housing conditions in Berlin which had appeared in Weitling's *Young Generation*. The report described a block of 5 tenement buildings in which some 3,000 people lived in crowded misery in 400 units, with more than one family squeezed in what were mostly one-room flats.

These items, and another report on the lectures delivered at the Fourierist congress in Strasbourg, had prompted the Augsburg *Allgemeine Zeitung* to charge the *Rheinische Zeitung* with entertaining Communist sympathies. In his rebuttal, 'Communism and the Augsburger Allgemeine Zeitung', Marx ridiculed the rival paper for concentrating on 'the meals of the Strasbourg scholars' while ignoring the substance of the proceedings at their congress. He then wrote:

> The passage under attack runs as follows: 'Today the middle class is in the same position as the nobility in 1789; then the middle class laid claim to the privileges of the nobility and obtained them, today the class that possesses nothing desires to share the wealth of the middle classes who are now in power,... the fact that the class which today possesses nothing desires to share the riches of the middle classes is plain to anyone who goes around the streets of Manchester, Paris and Lyons.

Did the *Allgemeine Zeitung*, he asked sarcastically, believe that its 'displeasure and silence can alter the facts of the age?' As for his own newpaper's attitude towards Communism, Marx stated truthfully and emphatically in this famous article that it did not concede even 'theoretical validity to Communist ideas in their present form, let alone desiring their practical realization, which it anyway finds impossible, but it will subject these ideas to a fundamental criticism.'

The danger of Communism, he observed, lay not in attempts at its practical realization. Any such attempt, even a revolt by the masses, could always be put down with cannon. But 'ideas that have overcome our intellect and conquered our conviction, ideas to which reason has riveted our conscience, are chains from which one cannot break loose without breaking one's heart; they are demons that one can only overcome by submitting to them.'[5]

Marx had no intention of submitting to Communism. All he intended was to undertake a critical examination of the subject. The point that the 'new teaching' of Communism was worth studying on its merits had first been made in the *Rheinische Zeitung* by Hess in April of that year, on three grounds. First, the Communists were a secret party about whose plans and activities 'the wildest notions' circulated in Germany. Abroad, however, the Communists were taken seriously not only by the popular masses but by the educated. Finally, a 'new teaching' should not be judged by the number of its professed adherents, for ideas had a force of their own.

While the honour, dubious or otherwise, of converting Engels to Communism incontestably belongs to Hess,[6] his relations with Marx were to become so complex over the years that they have been the subject of much controversy. At the stage under review, 6 years after Hess, curiously enough, had cast himself in the role of the apostle of a new annunciation (he confided feverishly to his diary, 'I, too, like John in his time, have been called upon to bear witness of the Light'), Engels certainly played a decisive role in stimulating Marx's interest in Communism.

Already in *The European Triarchy*, and then in the columns of the *Rheinische Zeitung* for months before Marx assumed its editorship, Hess had been drawing attention to the social question which other German papers largely ignored or shunned for fear of the censorship. Thus, in two articles titled 'The Riddle of the 19th Century' and 'The Political Parties in Germany' – published in April and September respectively – Hess had informed his readers of the 'sudden discovery' that a large part of humanity lived in poverty and slave-like misery, alienated and excluded from civilization and its benefits. The task of the 19th century was to remove this blight and to solve the conflict between pauperism and the aristocracy of money.

Developments in France and England at the beginning of the 'hungry forties' had led Hess to the thesis – which Marx defended in his first editorial – that while the French Revolution had helped the bourgeois Third Estate to take over the privileges of the nobility, no one had foreseen that the original idea of 'liberty and equality' for all would be jeopardized by the economic deprivation of the major part of society. Hess neither called himself a Hegelian nor went to the destructive extremes of the Left-Hegelian radicals. Like Marx at this stage, he was not against the state. He thought that if not in France, the revolution would come to industrialized England. Germany, which had yet to develop a modern industry, still had some time to solve the social problem peacefully if she wanted to avoid the inevitable class conflict and to 'preserve the unity of the state.'[7]

Besides his linking the struggle for political liberty with the social issue, one major step which made Hess the bellwether of Communism in Germany was his initiative in getting the editorial committee of the *Rheinische Zeitung* to form a discussion group which met once a week in the evening at Cologne's Laacher

Hof to debate political and social questions. Among those who attended regularly were at least two board members: Georg Jung and Gustav von Mevissen. Mevissen, who had lived for a time in Paris, lectured on the theories of Saint-Simon or on the condition of England's low-paid industrial workers which he had observed at first hand during a visit. Papers on other subjects were examined and thrashed out from several viewpoints. Marx joined the circle at the end of October 1842.

For a newspaper to run an internal 'debating society' whose discussions sometimes developed into seminars on political and social questions was, and still is, a rare phenomenon. But then the *Rheinische Zeitung* was an unusual paper. Several members of this circle, such as Dr Karl d'Ester and Friedrich Anneke, were later to become Communist activists. Whether this was due to Hess's influence is not known. In his biography of Hess, Edmund Silberner declared that Hess's articles, the ideas he brought to the circle's debates and his daily contacts with the new editor helped to convince Marx of 'the necessity' to undertake the theoretical study of Communism which was to lead to his adoption of it, and that 'Hess thus had a fateful influence on Marx.'[8]

While Silberner submitted this as a 'not too risky assumption', Marx's biographers, and Marxologists in general (with some notable exceptions) continued to treat Hess's influence on Marx, then and later, as marginal; and in the post-World War II period the literature produced by the European Marx 'industry', especially in East Germany, called Hess every name from 'utopian' to 'reactionary', when not disqualifying him as an 'inefficient' thinker and complete 'wash-out'. The exceptions were David McLellan, Robert Tucker and a few others who, to one degree or another, acknowledged Hess's role in the development of Marxism.[9]

Yet the rehabilitation of Hess continued to meet with opposition. For example, in 1982 a Marxist biographer of Hess, scrutinizing his 'dossier' in commissar-like fashion, described the discussion group of the *Rheinische Zeitung* as a 'party club' and dwelt on its importance as the nucleus out of which grew 'the party of the Rheinische Zeitung' – as the eponymous periodical Marx established in 1848 to fan the flames of revolution would become known among some of its contemporaries – without bothering to mention that it was Hess who organized that nucleus.

In 1985, however, the noted Marx scholar S. Avineri restored the balance by summing up the relations between Hess and Marx as a complex 'symbiosis of ideas' which, for all their quarrels on political issues, bound them together 'despite all the differences in stature and in philosophical approach.'[10]

On 30 September, a fortnight before Marx's arrival in Cologne, Hess and the rest of the editorial committee or 'party club' of the *Rheinische Zeitung* had hosted a festive dinner in honour of Herwegh. A month later, after having being widely entertained by 'democratic' groups at various stops on his triumphal journey, Herwegh arrived in Dresden. There Arnold Ruge, who was in charge of the 8-day-long festivities in his honour, had arranged for him to stay with Michael Bakunin in the apartment he shared with his brother Paul and Turgenev.

The hugely built Bakunin and the delicate-looking Herwegh, who was the younger, took to each other immediately. Both were self-indulgent, narcissistic characters. Herwegh, with his poetic gift, was as brilliant and eloquent in conversation as Bakunin himself. His flamboyance went well with his good looks and romantic air, and his charming manner won him many hearts. Selfish to a degree, he cared as little for others as did the cynical Bakunin. Moreover, Herwegh had for the past year or so been proclaiming that 'action' spoke louder than theories, and Bakunin – who had just thrown philosophy to the winds and in *The Reaction in Germany* advocated nothing if not the most drastic action to build a new world on the ruins of the old – could not but exult at finding in the celebrated young poet not only a man after his own heart but one who understood his vigorous new political credo.

The two, in short, made fast friends, and before Herwegh, accompanied by Ruge, left Dresden for Berlin at the beginning of November he directed Bakunin's attention to the works of George Sand. Soon the Russian, who had spent so many years grappling with Hegel and German philosophic abstractions, was reading her latest novel, *Consuelo*, and developing a veritable cult-worship for its author. Bakunin was later to enter into correspondence with Sand, and just before the 1848 revolution the anarchist-in-exile would write to her: 'Please think occasionally of a man who venerated you even before he met you, for often in the saddest days of his life, you were a consolation and a light.'[11]

Within 10 days of his arrival in Berlin, the dashing Herwegh met and became engaged to one of his young admirers, Emma Siegmund, the daughter of a well-to-do silk merchant and court purveyor. Her dowry, in the form of an allowance of 6,000 Thaler per annum (10 times the salaries of Hess and Marx), assured Germany's leading radical *Tendenzdichter* – the 'poet with a cause' who was to turn out to be a luxury-loving sybarite – of a pleasurable life for the rest of his days.

And to climax all his easy triumphs there came the unexpected news that the King wished to meet the rebellious idol of Germany's youth. Besides his inflammatory poems, Herwegh had addressed an ode to His Prussian Majesty, appealing to him in flattering terms to end the clerical stranglehold on the state and suggesting that by instituting a constitutional monarchy he had it in his power to stem the menacing tide of the age.

Herwegh's audience with the King created a sensation in Germany even before it took place on 19 November. Friedrich Wilhelm IV was his usual voluble self. Whether it was his wish to take up Herwegh's challenge or sheer curiosity or caprice that had prompted his invitation, Prussia's 'All-Highest Majesty' tried to be gracious and remarked to the poet that he had already received one of his 'adversaries', Thiers, 'and I am very glad to meet you. We must each remain true to his reputation, I as king, you as poet.'

Herwegh, aware of the fact that Germany's radicals were in two minds about his exchanging pleasantries or engaging in any sort of parley with Prussia's hypocritical absolutist ruler, behaved rather awkwardly. Before dismissing him, the King remarked that he despised lack of character but respected honourable enemies and 'forthright opposition'.

While the radical Left declared Herwegh to be a renegade, some of the King's chief courtiers and close advisers were annoyed by his receiving a deserter from the Prussian army. In St Petersburg Tsar Nicholas I was baffled by his quixotic Prussian brother-in-law's folly in helping the international fame of a rebel and subversive poet. A few days after the audience, Herwegh's planned monthly, the 'German Messenger from Switzerland', was banned in Prussia before it had even started publication. The measure could have been expected, for German reviews printed by expatriates abroad were forbidden in Prussia as a matter of routine, but its timing seemed revengeful, and not accidental.

Herwegh learned of the ban while being feted in Königsberg. Pricked by accusations from the Left, he sent the King an undignified, partly plaintive and partly irate, letter in which, losing all sense of proportion, convention and protocol, he accused the King of breaking his promise to respect forthright opposition and boasted that the ban on the monthly would have as little effect as that previously imposed on his *Poems of a Living Man*, which was now in its fifth edition.

To compound matters, a couple of weeks later Herwegh, or one of his friends, committed the indiscretion of having his bristling but 'confidential' letter published in the *Leipziger Allgemeine Zeitung*.

Retaliation, when it came, was severe. Herwegh was to be seized by gendarmes and escorted to the stagecoach in Stettin. Forbidden to leave the coach and exercise his legs in Prussian Halle, he was then refused permission by the Saxon authorities to stop in Leipzig; and so the Romantic young political lyricist was forced to make his way back to Switzerland ignominiously.

Before the end of October, while Herwegh was still in Dresden, Marx had published in Cologne the third article in his series on the 'Debates of the 6th Rhenish Diet'. This time, out of more than 100 or so bills and motions which had come before the Diet, Marx picked an economic topic. His new essay, 'Debates on the Wood-Theft Law', dealt ostensibly with an innocuous matter – a government proposal to stiffen the punishment of wood-theft and the felling of trees by impoverished small farmers, vintners and day-labourers, which had recently become widespread.

Marx's essay, published in 5 issues between 26 October and 3 November, contained his first utterance on a problem which had social and political implications. The gathering of dead wood by the poor had always been a recognized custom in the Rhineland. Before the new law was debated in the Rhenish Diet, however, the Prussian State Gazette had advised its deputies that when considering the new law they were 'to think only of wood' and timber, and were 'not to try to solve each material problem in a political way – that is, in connection with the whole complex of 'civic reasoning and civic morality.'[12]

Thus encouraged, the Diet, consisting exclusively of representatives of the 4 estates – princes, knights, large landowners and land-owning city magistrates – introduced even harsher sentences into the law in order to protect the forests they owned, at a time when industrial progress in the Rhineland was causing a rising demand for timber. Marx, on the other hand, treating the Wood-Theft Law precisely from that aspect of civic reasoning which the Prussian State Gazette had recommended to the deputies to forget, condemned the rapacious feudal spirit of the whole legislation: 'On behalf of the masses of the poor who have no political or social possessions... we reclaim for poverty the right of custom, and moreover a right of custom which is not a local one but which is that of poverty in all lands.

Although this right was reserved only to the 'lowest and elementary mass of propertyless people', Marx argued that in an age of general law 'rationally customary rights' were nothing but 'the custom of legal rights... because custom has become the custom of the state.' Having by now read Proudhon, Marx wrote: 'If every violation of property without differentiation or further definition is theft, would not private property be theft? Through my private property do I not exclude a third party from the property?'

He then berated the members of the Diet for putting their own interests above those of the province which they had been charged to represent. 'The feeling for right and law is the most important provincial characteristic of the Rhinelander,' he wrote. 'But it is self-evident that particular interests know no fatherland and no province either...'[13]

Marx's article – especially a passage in it saying that the Diet was 'treading the law underfoot', so infuriated the Prussian *Oberpräsident* of the Rhine Province, Von Schaper, that on 10 November he informed the Minister of the Interior in Berlin that he was going to prosecute the author of the article for his

789

'insolent criticism of the existing state institutions'. On the 12th, on orders from the three 'censorship ministers', Cologne's Governor, Von Gerlach, confronted the *Rheinische Zeitung* with the alternative of changing its 'hostile' tone or having its licence revoked.

In its reply, the *Rheinische Zeitung* assured the Governor that, far from wishing to introduce 'superficial' French ideas into the Rhineland, it supported Prussia's 'progressive' policies. Marx, who had actually drafted the carefully considered letter signed by the publisher, mentioned that the paper had given in to the government's wishes by firing Rutenberg and expressed his confidence that its encouragement of German liberalism was not unwelcome to King Friedrich Wilhelm IV. But in response to the Governor's demand to have the new editor presented to him for approval, he coolly remarked that he knew of 'no legal provision' justifying this and asked Governor Von Gerlach to name that (non-existent) paragraph in the 1819 Censorship Law.[14]

Marx was caught in a crossfire. Pressed by the paper's shareholders to moderate his editorial policy, he was at the same time at the centre of a conflict which had erupted in Berlin between Herwegh and Bruno Bauer's 'ultra-Left' Young Hegelian *Freien*, who condemned the vainglorious poet for having foolishly allowed the King to use him to make a show of pretended liberalism.

Herwegh in his turn, on 22 November, 5 days after his audience with the King, sent Marx for publication a letter denouncing the empty 'revolutionary' swagger of *Die Freien* and their aping of Jacobin and *sans-culotte* behaviour. At the same time Meyen, a leader of *Die Freien*, challenged Marx to justify his slashing their articles of late. On the 25th, Marx, having for some time felt that the paper's identification with the anarchic group did it more harm than good, featured the main points of Herwegh's condemnation of their antics on the front page of the *Rheinische Zeitung*.

This act signified his open break with Bruno Bauer, his former friend and mentor, and what he called the whole clique of Berlin 'windbags'. A few days later, venting both his motives and his irritation in a long letter to Ruge, Marx admitted that he had himself 'thrown out' as many articles by *Die Freien* as the censor, 'for Meyen and Co. sent us heaps of scribblings, pregnant with revolutionising the world and empty of ideas, written in a slovenly style and seasoned with a little atheism and Communism (which these gentlemen have never studied).'

Marx had now started reading the works of Saint-Simon and Fourier and the Socialist or Communist writings (as they were interchangeably called) of Pierre Leroux and Eugène Cabet. But that he was still far from embracing the new Communist 'world outlook' is evident from his informing Ruge of the categorical answer with which he had brushed off Meyen's protest on behalf of *Die Freien*:

> I declared that I regard it as inappropriate, indeed even immoral, to smuggle Communist and Socialist doctrines, hence a new world outlook, into incidental theatrical criticisms, etc., and that I demand a quite different and more thorough discussion of Communism, if it should be discussed at all.

Marx had turned the *Rheinische Zeitung* into one of Germany's most interesting and outspoken newspapers. With 400 subscribers at the beginning, its circulation had trebled from about 1,000 when he took over to 3,400. But there were days when its appearance was in question because of savage censorship mutilation. Trying to pilot it safely through increasingly stormy waters, a hard-pressed Marx concluded his letter to Ruge in a somewhat nervous state:

> We now have to put up from morning to night with the most horrible torments of the censorship, ministerial communications, complaints of the Oberpräsident, accusations in the Provincial Assembly, howls from shareholders, etc., etc. Since I remain at my post only because I consider it my duty to prevent, to the best of my ability, those in power from carrying out their plans, you can imagine that I am somewhat irritated...[15]

With Marx in this mood, it is no wonder that he was rather curt with the boyish-looking Engels when the latter – stopping in Cologne in November on his way to England – paid his second visit to the offices of the *Rheinische Zeitung*.

Engels had spent the weeks since his first visit in October with his family at Barmen. It was not an entirely happy farewell visit, seeing that his Calvinist father, finding it a heavy cross to bear to have a son 'who is like a scabby sheep in a flock and openly opposes the belief of his forefathers', had at the time written to his brother-in-law that he had stopped quarreling with his son because disputes only made him 'more obstinate'. Recalling that as a boy Friedrich had shown 'genuine religious feelings', Engels hoped that his son would eventually realize the hard way 'that he must bow his head humbly before the hand of the Almighty.'

Young Engels thought that he knew the whole 'filthy' cotton business from his father's factories at home in Barmen and Engelskirchen. But under threat of having his allowance cut off, he had agreed to go to Manchester all the more readily as he too was tired of quarreling with his father. His mother grieved herself sick every time they had a row; and in Manchester he would be at the very centre of the social tremor he expected to sweep England before long.

He had barely arrived in England and had yet to see the Victoria Mills at Pendleton operated by Ermen & Engels or any other cotton manufacturory when the *Rheinische Zeitung* carried an article of his with the dateline 'London, November 30' [1842]. In spite of the failure of the Plug Plot riots – following which Ermen & Engels had in August thanked the police in the *Manchester Guardian* for protecting their property – Engels affirmed that revolution in England was imminent.

He was to cling to this mistaken belief for a long time, even as he settled down to work in the Ermen & Engels counting-house at 2 Southgate, St Mary's, off Deansgate, in Manchester, and gradually became an experienced businessman. An easy mixer, he frequented the Cotton Exchange and consorted with the aristocracy and rich merchants. Soon he also found himself a girl friend, a red-haired Irish working-girl, Mary Burns, who operated a new machine, a 'self-actor', at the Ermen & Engels mills.

Manchester was then the capital of the industrial world, but visiting the slums with Mary Burns after a cotton slump was like a guided tour through Dante's *Inferno*. It was on these tours that Engels observed the utter wretchedness prevailing in the city's poverty-stricken quarters which he was later to describe in his book *The Condition of the Working Class in England*, in scenes conjuring up

> the quarters without sewage milling with unemployed, with scavengers and beggars; the dilapidated cottages with broken windows patched with oilskin and the cellars and damp holes swarming with destitute families living in filth and foul air, in streets infested with herds of little pigs; the children playing among piles of garbage and excrement when not fed into factories; the teenaged girls and pregnant women replacing the men as cheap labour in the mills, or plying prostitution,

and other scenes of poverty and degradation on a mass scale.

But Engels's book, incorporating his first-hand observations of conditions in industrial England both at the Pendleton Mills and on extensive tours of Lancashire, was not to be written for a couple of years.

In mid-December the *Rheinische Zeitung* dispatched Hess to Paris, to act as its French correspondent. During the next 15 months that he was to spend there, he lived with a pretty blonde German milliner whom he had met either before he left Cologne or on a visit to that city the following summer. Sibyl Pesch, who was 22, was the uneducated daughter of a Catholic day-labourer. For more than a century thereafter, most Marxist-Socialist literature has presented her as a promiscuous girl driven by poverty to supplement her meagre wages with hours put in at a bordello. According to some accounts, however, she had been at it only for 5 days before the Hess allegedly picked her up in a tavern, and – falling for her attractions and moved by her heartbreak story – decided to save her, installed her for a while in a rented apartment, and then took her to Paris.

It was only in the second half of the 20th century that Hess's modern biographer, after a thorough investigation, traced the various strands from which 'this web of lies and evil slander' may have been fabricated. Even so, the fact that Hess, instead of marrying *une femme et une fortune*, started in 1842 or 1843 to live with this proletarian Catholic woman certainly completed his break with his family, his religion and his bourgeois background. In order not to aggrieve his orthodox Jewish father publicly, though, he did not marry her until after his father's death at the end of 1851. Although barely literate, the future Frau Hess was a bright, quick-witted person whose charm and vivacity brought a ray of sunshine into Hess's hitherto lonely life. A more amiable and even-tempered nature than Heine's 'wildcat' Mathilde, she never embarrassed him in the company of his friends; on the contrary, according to a Paris police report, 'with her bright mind, she quickly, in his circle, became a fervent Socialist.'[16]

Their stay in Paris proved a happy and fruitful period for Hess. Besides being cordially received by Heine, who praised him to Campe as 'an excellent political writer', Hess was the first of the politico-philosophical group of German intellectuals connected with the *Rheinische Zeitung* to establish personal contact with French Socialist thinkers. One of the German radicals in Paris introduced him to Etienne Cabet, the author of *Voyage en Icarie* and editor of the Communist *Le Populaire*; in March 1843 he was attending one of the weekly gatherings of Fourier's disciples at the home of their leader, Victor Considérant; and he gradually made the acquaintance of Louis Blanc, Pierre Leroux and others.

Between December 1842 and the beginning of 1944, now that he was able closely to observe the working of French social currents, Hess wrote a series of articles and essays – for the *Rheinische Zeitung*, the *Kölner Allgemeine Zeitung* and a volume to be published by Herwegh in Zurich – in which he developed his own particular brand of Communism as the 'ethical' movement of the future.

On 24 December, the *Leipziger Allgemeine Zeitung* had published the text of Herwegh's abrasive letter to the King of Prussia. The King was furious. Within 24 hours the Leipzig paper was suppressed. The order for Herwegh's expulsion followed 4 days later. Nor was that all. On 3 January, at Prussia's behest, the Saxon government ordered the closure of Ruge's *German Yearbooks*, which had published Bakunin's essay. It was the second suppression of this philosophical journal since its suspension had forced it to change its name and move to Dresden.

793

Prussia now seemed bent on muzzling any free opinion, and Marx's *Rheinische Zeitung* was likely to be next in line. Already in December the Berlin authorities – fearing a public outcry in the Rhineland if the paper were closed – had dispatched a special envoy to the province to assess the strength of the reaction to that eventuality. Towards the end of December, Marx had further incurred the wrath of the authorities by a three-part article attacking Prussia's sham 'parliamentary' system of provincial Diets based on fixed classes or 'estates'.

While the liberal financiers of the *Rheinische Zeitung* supported the Diets and only opposed the preponderance of aristocrats in them, Marx was against the very system of representation by sectarian estates. The provincial Diets were, in his view,

> nothing more than a society of special interests privileged to encroach their delimiting particularism on the state... They are self-constituted anti-state elements within the state. They are by nature inimical to the state, for in its isolated activity any special element is always an enemy to the whole. It is precisely this whole which conveys to the particular a feeling of its nothingness by giving it an awareness of its limits.[17]

Besides thus questioning Prussia's vaunted 'representative' system, Marx also engaged in January in a polemic with Oberpräsident Von Schaper. A lengthy series published earlier by the *Rheinische Zeitung* on the economic distress of the Mosel wine-growing peasants – whom the Customs Union had gradually reduced to ruin and utter poverty – had been publicly contested by Von Schaper, who hotly denied the accuracy of the data contained in the series.

With the sword of Damocles already hanging over the paper, Marx set out to reply in a 5-part series – 'Justification of the Mosel Correspondent' – of which one part was suppressed and only two others appeared before the *Rheinische Zeitung* was to be banned. Having learned something about the working of economic processes, Marx demonstrated at length in these two articles that it was measures dictated by the Prussian administration, and not any failure of the small vintners, which had created the objective conditions for their impoverishment.

The fact that 'very highly placed statesmen were thoroughly exposed' in these articles was the last straw that brought about the suppression of the paper, or so Marx believed at the time. Actually, it was the personal intervention of Tsar Nicholas I which ultimately decided the King of Prussia to shrink no longer and administer the death-blow to the newspaper.

On 4 January the paper had published an article violently attacking Russia and the Tsar's military despotism in particular. On 8 January, at a ball at the Winter Palace in St Petersburg, the Tsar gave the Prussian ambassador a piece of his mind in language so sharp as to render the diplomat speechless. King Friedrich Wilhelm IV himself was not a little intimidated when he received a personal letter of protest from Nicholas, his brother-in-law and most powerful ally.

On 21 January, less than a month after the suppression of the *Leipziger Allgemeine Zeitung*, the three Prussian Ministers in charge of censorship decided – in the presence of the King – to suppress 'its whorish sister on the Rhine'. A mounted courier was dispatched to Cologne with the royal edict interdicting the *Rheinische Zeitung* on the grounds that it had lately 'surpassed itself in insolent language and in pursuing a tendency... to undermine state and church, stir up discontent, slander the government... ridicule the censorship in Prussia and Germany, and to insult friendly powers.'

As a sop to the paper's shareholders and subscribers, the edict gave them 9 weeks to recoup what they could of their losses by allowing its publication until 31 March 1843. During this reprieve it was submitted to double and treble censorship. The dull-witted Dolleschall had been replaced in December – not before he had suppressed 140 articles in the *Rheinische Zeitung* – by a more cultured censor. Every evening he submitted the entire blue-pencilled newspaper for further vetting to Cologne's Regierungspräsident, who in his turn had to send all the sheets to the Oberpräsident of the Rhine Province. The new censor was soon replaced by a third and more sophisticated one sent from Berlin, Wilhelm Saint-Paul.

On 12 February, the board of the *Rheinische Zeitung* held an extraordinary general meeting of shareholders to consider the situation. Marx was disgusted to find that not a few of those present were in favour of saving the newspaper at the price of toning down or even entirely abandoning its opposition to the government. He had prepared a lengthy refutation of the government's charges and after much discussion the shareholders agreed to incorporate it in a memorandum to be submitted to the government. Leading burghers in Cologne and the chief Rhenish cities had meanwhile started flooding the government with petitions to revoke the ban on the paper. Marx, however, realistically assessed that the chances of the paper's survival under the existing political circumstances were practically nil.

He decided to go public. So far only a number of initiates but not the general public knew that he was the editor of the pugnacious *Rheinische Zeitung*. But on 28 February, Karl Grün, the editor of Mannheim's *Abendzeitung* (Evening News), published an article in which he not only named 'Dr Marx the editor who set the tone' of the proscribed paper but singled out his

> incisive mind, the truly admirable dialectics with which he bit and
> gnashed his way into the hollow utterances of deputies to destroy

795

them from within; rarely has one seen such critical-destructive virtuosity, so brilliant a display of hatred of the so-called positive, such an ability to catch it in his nets and strangle it... a peculiar gift and rare manifoldness of talent.[18]

Although signed by Grün, the article had been written by Marx himself. He had earlier asked one of his colleagues and comrades-in-arms, Karl Heinzen, to place the article in the press so as to 'lay the blame for everything pernicious that appeared in the *Rheinische Zeitung* exclusively at my door', but Heinzen had refused. Grün, who had been one of Marx's fellow-students at Bonn University, agreed to sign his peculiar self-eulogy, not knowing that before long Marx, turning against him, would maliciously denounce him to Proudhon as a 'charlatan'.[19]

Marx had been toying with the idea of resigning since the end of January. He was – as the censor Saint-Paul, after several conversations with him, put it in his reports to Berlin – 'the spiritus rector, the guiding spirit' of the *Rheinische Zeitung*, 'a man who would die for his views, of whose truth he is absolutely convinced.' In his planted article, Marx, of course, made himself out to be the paper's evil spirit, and though it has been said that in that article he wished to appear as 'the captain standing upright at the mast' of the sinking ship, there is some evidence that he hoped by his tactic to save the newspaper if he resigned. According to Heinzen it was Marx himself who suggested to Saint-Paul the idea – which the latter twice passed on to Berlin as his own – that once he was removed the paper would be harmless enough to be allowed to continue.[20]

But with Count Nesselrode in St Petersburg continually reminding their ambassador of the Tsar's displeasure, the Prussian authorities ignored this suggestion, turned a deaf ear to all petitions from the Rhineland and even refused to receive a deputation of the newspaper's shareholders.

After riding the seas for altogether 15 months, the paper came to a halt, as decreed, on 31 March 1843, its staff saluting its readers in a farewell poem (not by Marx), calling on the figure of Columbus who 'was at first despised' but nevertheless found the new world, and wishing its friends *Auf Wiedersehen* on a new shore.

Marx had left the paper a fortnight before its sails collapsed. On 18 March it carried a short notice, inserted the day before, to the effect that, 'due to the present censorship conditions, the undersigned has resigned from the editorship. Dr Marx.' As early as 25 January, when the censor had been subordinated to Regierungspräsident Von Gerlach and 'our paper had to be presented to the police to be sniffed at' every night, often preventing its appearance next morning, he had written to Ruge: 'It is bad to perform menial services even for the sake of freedom and to fight with pinpricks instead of clubs.' He felt sick and

tired of 'hypocrisy, stupidity, raw authority and our [German] cringing, bowing, back-turning and word-picking.' He felt in fact relieved that 'the government has given me back my freedom.'

He was 25 and jobless, and thought of emigrating, for 'I can do nothing more
in Germany. Here one is forced to live a counterfeit existence.'[21]

He had not seen Jenny in all the months since the previous summer, when she
had moved with her mother to Bad Kreuznach. 'I cannot, must not, and will not',
Marx wrote in the same letter of 25 January, 'leave Germany without my fiancée.'

But where was he to go? And what were they to live on? His first idea was to
go to Switzerland, to colloborate with Herwegh on the revamping of the
Deutsche Bote, and he asked Ruge what he thought of this plan. He was clutching at a straw, for all attempts to relaunch the *Deutsche Bote* – which had actually
ceased publication the previous October – in a larger format failed after Prussia
had banned its import. Still, Zurich with its millionaire Professor Fröbel and
his Literary Comptoir, which, since successfully launching Herwegh's poems,
had greatly expanded its publishing activities, was the closest German cultural
centre where an émigré writer might continue his political struggle without
starving; and he consulted Ruge because he, too, though not so rich, was a man
of substance, and a talented editor whose *German Yearbooks*, now suppressed,
had achieved an influence out of all proportion to the number of its subscribers,
which was never higher than 600.

Moreover, Ruge had a business arrangement with Fröbel, whereby the latter
had just published in Zurich on his behalf a volume containing material he had
expected to be censored in Germany even before the suppression of his periodical. It was in this volume, 'Anecdotes of the Most Recent German Philosophy
and Journalism',[22] that Marx's later famous 'Remarks on the Latest Prussian
Censorship Instruction' appeared a year or so after it was written.

Next, in several letters to Marx between 1 February and 8 March, Ruge had
come up with a new plan. He invited Marx to become his co-editor if he
managed to resume publication of the *German Yearbooks* either in Dresden or
abroad, and offered him a fixed salary amounting – together with extra fees for
articles – to 850 Thaler, more than he had earned on the *Rheinische Zeitung*.
Replying on 13 March – 4 days before his resignation – Marx was only too glad
to accept. But he thought that Dresden as the venue for producing 'a poor copy
of the deceased' journal, even if the authorities were to permit it, would not do.
Something new and fresh was needed. And he invoked Talleyrand's reply to the
allies who had toppled Napoleon: 'When Paris was taken, some people proposed
Napoleon's son with a regency, others Bernadotte, while yet others suggested
that Louis Philippe should rule. But Talleyrand replied: "Louis XVIII or
Napoleon. That is a principle, anything else is intrigue."'

In the same way, he suggested, the best venue for producing the new, monthly Yearbooks was either Zurich or Strasbourg. He saw it as combining the German philosophical-theoretical approach of Ruge's former Yearbooks with the militant political line of the *Rheinische Zeitung* and his own new interest in French political and social ideas, and proposed that it be called 'German-French Yearbooks' (*Deutsch-Französische Jahrbücher*) – 'that would be a principle,... an event of consequence.'[23]

In a burst of plans and activity, Marx had taken time off in the first week of March to spend 8 days with Jenny at Kreuznach. Although the projected new periodical would take months to materialize, he brought her the tidings that at long last their marriage was in the offing; and shortly after writing his last articles for the *Rheinische Zeitung* and submitting his resignation on the 17th, he left on an unexplained trip to Holland, possibly to visit his relatives there and to see whether he could get another advance on his inheritance – or 'my property', as he put it – while his mother was still alive.

At Kreuznach, Marx ran into the famous Bettina Brentano von Arnim, who was about to publish her allegorical story, *This Book Is the King's*, in which she was going to surprise her one-time friend Friedrich Wilhelm IV with prison records, statistics and a general survey of all that was wrong, false and oppressive in his Christian-Prussian realm and among his 'deformed' and 'bilious, befogged' counsellors, one of whom was her arch-conservative brother-in-law, Von Savigny, Prussia's new Minister of Justice. As Marx had published an article attacking his 'Historical School of Law', which justified Prussia's reactionary legal system, he and Bettina had much to talk about. According to a contemporary, Jenny complained that her young fiancé 'spent much of his week in Kreuznach walking and talking late into the night with this spirited but dowdy-looking elderly lady.' But Karl had hardly left when Jenny, having waited since her early twenties to be married, wrote to her future husband:

> I did not know how dear you were to me in my deepest heart until I
> no longer saw you in the flesh; I have only the one faithful portrait of
> you standing so full of life before my soul in all its angelic mildness
> and goodness, heightened love and spiritual lustre. If you were back
> here again, my dear little Karl, what a capacity for happiness you
> would find in your brave little girl... Do you still remember our twi-
> light conversation, our beckoning games, our hours of slumber. Dear
> heart, how good, how loving, how attentive, how joyful you were.

She asked Marx to buy her 'new laces if you can get them cheaply', and suggested that a garland of roses 'would best suit my green dress', but being practical, and lately reduced together with her mother to saving every household

Groschen, she suggested in the same letter that he leave the shopping to her, for fear that he would overspend. With a kind of arch humour that was to stand her in good stead in dealing with the intellectually superior and domineering Marx, she remarked that, although beyond knitting socks women were condemned to 'wait, hope, suffer' passively, she wished to put in a strong veto against establishing the German-French Yearbooks at Strasbourg: she feared that, once he emigrated, Germany might never allow him to return.[24]

In Marx's mind too, the projected new periodical and his marriage were so closely related that in his letter of 13 March he informed Ruge of his proposed marriage in what was for him almost an effusive tone:

> I can assure you, without the slightest romanticism, that I am head over heels in love, and indeed in the most serious way. I have been engaged for more than seven years and my fiancée has been involved on my behalf in the toughest of struggles that have ruined her health. These have been in part against her pietist and aristocratic relations, for whom 'the Lord in Heaven' and the 'lord in Berlin' are equally objects of religious cult, and in part against my own family, in which certain clerics and other sworn enemies have ensconced themselves. For years, my fiancée and I have been fighting more useless and exhausting battles than many other persons three times our age.

Ruge had enlisted the interest of Otto Wigand, a radical publisher who normally printed and distributed the *German Yearbooks* for him, in the projected new monthly. In view of the restrictions in Germany – and spurred by Fröbel's success in Zurich – Wigand was keen to establish a business foothold in Switzerland or France. Ruge proposed to Marx that the three of them meet to finalize the project before the summer. Marx replied that since 'all the preliminaries, the announcement of the marriage, etc., take considerable time I could, if necessary, spend a few weeks in Dresden... As soon as we have concluded the contract, I would travel to Kreuznach and get married.'[25]

In the end, the contract was to be signed not with Wigand, but with Professor Fröbel.

In the second half of March, Marx sent Ruge a letter from Holland, in which, comparing the German 'despotism' to a ship of fools, he spoke for the first time of revolution: 'A Ship of Fools can perhaps be allowed to drift before the wind for a good while; but it will still drift to its doom precisely because the fools refuse to believe it possible. This doom is the approaching revolution.'[26]

Marx returned to Cologne before the end of March, and while Dagobert Oppenheim was seeing the last few issues of the *Rheinische Zeitung* through the

799

press, he set to work on the first of two articles which, together with two sent from Manchester by Engels, and letters, poems or other contributions by Heine, Herwegh and Bakunin, were eventually to go into the inaugural issue of the *German-French Yearbooks*.

In Switzerland, on 8 March 1843, Georg Herwegh, with Michael Bakunin acting as best man, had married Emma Siegmund, the heiress he had acquired in Berlin shortly before his misbegotten audience with the King of Prussia.

It is more than likely that the wave of repression in Germany sparked off by that audience – and more particularly by the lack of political sense of this conceited young 'poet with a cause' in allowing his 'confidential' protest to the King to be published – would have come sooner or later in other circumstances. As it was, the closure of the *Leipziger Allgemeine Zeitung* and Herwegh's expulsion marked the end of the year-long 'Young Hegelian' agitation in Germany, of which Engels in England was to write (in Robert Owen's *New Moral World*) that under the nose of the censor things had been published 'which even in France would have been punished as high treason, and, if uttered in England, would have led without fail to a trial for blasphemy.[27]

The consequences for German liberalism were disastrous. During Herwegh's 1841 visit to him in Paris, Heine had given him the verses warning him that the revolutionary 'spring of which you sing is only in your song', but ridiculed him in another poem for trying to assume the role of the Marquis Posa, the Spanish King's counsellor (in Schiller's play *Don Carlos*), who hopes that words will persuade the ruler to reform himself and his regime. The poet Freiligrath, whose refusal to take a political stand on the 'party battlements' had been publicly criticized by Herwegh, remarked with a certain *Schadenfreude* that if Herwegh had been expelled for his poems he would have been a hero, but to incur this punishment for his sheer arrogance and stupidity, and in the process to compromise a good cause, showed that beneath his laurel leaves he was nothing but a conceited Swabian fool.

None, however, made Herwegh out so mercilessly as a political somnambulist as did Heine in a poem titled 'The Audience'. Notwithstanding, it was only in 1849, when Herwegh theatrically marched off from Paris at the head of a 'German Legion' to help liberate the fatherland during that year's uprisings, that the inglorious end of the expedition was to expose the otherwise talented poet for the amateur strategist without sense or foresight that he was.

Until then, Herwegh maintained his European reputation as Germany's premier revolutionary poet. For a year or two after his expulsion from Prussia, he even played a significant role in making Zurich the second most important radical centre of German expatriates after Paris. It was also the second largest, for besides the German colony in Zurich many Germans worked as day-labour-ers in several areas of Switzerland, and among them the fugitive leader of the Paris League of the Just, Wilhelm Weitling, was propagating his new brand of 'scientific' Communism.

Herwegh had brought with him from Germany another new-fangled propo-nent of violent action for the overthrow of the old order. Michael Bakunin had just abandoned his old wife, philosophy. Switzerland was the beginning of his quest for the new fiancée on whom he had fixed his mind. He was to be on the lookout for her for 4 years until, sensing her approach, he would exultantly write to Georg and Emma Herwegh: 'I await my, or, if you will, our communal bride – the revolution.'[28]

28

Bakunin Falls in Love with 'the People' and Marx Gets Married

Bakunin had turned his back on Germany immediately after New Year's Day 1843. Upon hearing of Herwegh's expulsion he fled from Dresden, with 250 Thaler borrowed from Ruge, 'like a partridge before the hawk'. He had a sudden attack of *Angst* – as he explained on 8 January to the publisher Wigand – that the Saxon authorities, who, under pressure from Prussia, had refused Herwegh permission to stop in Leipzig, might hand him over to Russia, which was tantamount to death.[1]

At Karlsruhe he caught up with Herwegh, and together they travelled via Strasbourg to Zurich. In his *Confession to the Tsar* Bakunin later admitted that he acted over-hastily, but his flight was only part of the psychodrama which had accompanied his labours on *The Reaction in Germany*. His revolutionary call for 'the complete destruction of the present political and social world' had brought him both acclaim and notoriety. Arnold Ruge, who had published it in October 1842 in his respected *Yearbooks*, expressed the opinion that Bakunin had 'outstripped all the old donkeys' of Young Hegelianism; and to this day it is considered one of the best articles Bakunin ever wrote.[2]

At the end of that month, Bakunin had known a glorious week in the company of his new friend Herwegh. But October also brought about a conjunction of circumstances which plunged him into a morbid mood of increasing desolation. First, his public advocacy of revolution to destroy the existing world order meant that there was no future for him in Tsarist Russia. He had dimly realized this ever since – abandoning his touted plan to obtain a Berlin doctorate which would get him a quick professorship in Moscow – he had moved to Dresden. But now that he was grappling with 'reality' by choosing to become a revolutionary dedicated to heroic-destructive deeds, he decided it was time to inform the family at Premukhino and on 9 October had coolly written to his brother Nicholas that he would never return home to 'ruin the only career remaining to me.'[3]

Secondly, on 3 November – the day after Herwegh left Dresden for Berlin – his younger brother Paul likewise departed for the Prussian capital, to travel from there a couple of weeks later, together with Turgenev, to Russia and home. Seeing Paul off at the Dresden railway station, Bakunin was overcome by the thought that he was parting not only from his brother but 'from Premukhino, from Russia, from all my past' and foresaw a dismal future in which he would 'be alone, without love, perhaps even without human sympathy... Loneliness has always been there ahead of me, and sooner or later I had to enter this wasteland.' But he was so depressed that several times he wished for death. On the 4th he wrote to Premukhino: 'Only alien faces surround me. I hear only alien sounds... As I write to you I am crying, weeping like a child, Paul's departure tore off the husk which encased my heart.' In another passage he appealed especially to his sisters to 'give Paul back' to him:

> Let him come back next spring. There are so many of you together, but I am – alone. I need Paul, and I know that he needs me... Alone I will grow completely hard. Do you see how weak I am? I ask this of you as a woman, since I am at this moment as weak as a woman. This will pass, I know, and soon. But only its expression will pass; as the innermost essence of my heart, it will never pass.

Tatyana, to whom he said, 'You are mine, and I am yours, before all the others,' did not reply to his letter, and aware that he had by now become a stranger and a 'ghost' to his brothers and sisters, he sent her a portrait he had drawn of himself, and shared with the others his nostalgia for their childhood romps and other scenes whose memory he hoped would bring him to life in their minds. Beginning with an autumn evening in the woods near Premukhino, he wrote:

> Do you remember how a flock of cranes flew over? Now I am in the country to which the cranes fly from you. Do you remember our walks in Mytnits wood? Have you been along my favourite path this summer? What has happened to my trees in the little wood? We lighted a fire there one spring, in Holy Week. Lyubov was ill then and near to death, and she came in a carriage to join us... Then I went away... We drove all together to Kositzino [on his final departure from Russia]; and then do you remember, sisters, how we said goodbye in the evening? Did you feel then that we should never see one another again?

Towards the end of his pathetic letter, Bakunin sounded a brave note:

> A great future awaits me yet. My presentiments cannot deceive me. If I can achieve only a tiny fraction of all that is in my heart, I ask nothing more. I do not ask for happiness... Deeds, deeds – expansive, sacred deeds – this is what I want... I am once more strong, fear nothing and am ready to go forward, head erect.

Before saying goodbye to his siblings – 'and yet again good-bye. A wave of the hand and we will live on without looking back' – Bakunin, truthfully and with self-knowledge, described his situation in words sketching his destiny for many years ahead: 'Know, my friends, that beyond the seas there lives one who will never cease to be your friend, who thirsts for your love because, apart from you, he has no home of his own in the world...'[4]

Between this letter of 4 November and Herwegh's expulsion just before the new year, Bakunin felt increasingly isolated and insecure. In earlier periods of depression he had, by his own account, known more than one moment of apprehension, fantasizing about being imprisoned. During the summer, while working on his incendiary essay, he had even written to the Beyer sisters in Russia that he faced with equanimity the possibility of being killed. But now that the prospect seemed real, he was seized by fear of the Saxon authorities, the Prussian government and the dreaded Tsarist 'hawk'.

For the rest, there was nothing but debts to hold him in Germany – debts left behind in Berlin, and debts contracted in Dresden. In October he had asked his brother Nicholas to sell his portion of his father's estate and send him the money, since he would never return to Russia. On the basis of this expectation he had wangled a sizable 2,000 Thaler in loans from Arnold Ruge alone, promising him that if everything failed Turgenev would repay him. So far, however, neither his family nor Turgenev had been forthcoming.

And so Bakunin had attached himself to Herwegh and set out for Switzerland and new horizons. His hyperbolic later statement that he would have followed Herwegh anywhere, even if he had gone to America, contained a grain of truth in the sense that the two were a well-matched pair. To Heine, Herwegh might be a political sleepwalker excited by his own fiery verse-slogans and living in a world of revolutionary phantasms. But Bakunin himself, asexual as he was, unable to make contact with the world by means of the senses and emotionally cut off from it by the 'thick husk of ice' covering his heart 'in spite of the passion languishing within it', lived in a world of abstract ideas and fantasies which he projected on reality. Herwegh was to him the ideal man of action he himself had chosen to become. Vainly imploring his sister 'to help me come out of myself', his only way of reaching out through the 'impenetrable, cold crust that often repelled people from me' was to embark on the career of a revolutionary who would solve the bloody conflicts and 'contradictions of the age' in a manner resolving his own inner drama, the conflict between the impotence that made him 'weak as a woman' and his frustrated need to prove his virility by setting the world on fire: 'The passion for destruction is also a creative passion.'

Bakunin doted on Herwegh. Shortly after their arrival in Switzerland in the second week of January, the Russian installed himself in a bachelor apartment affording a magnificent view of Lake Zurich, stretching away 'mirror-clear' in the sun just steps away beneath his windows, and snow-capped mountains gleaming beyond. Bakunin was thrilled by the beauty of the Swiss landscape, but it also induced in him a feeling of indolence which made him forget all his plans for action and deeds. On 10 and 20 February he wrote to Premukhino that when not reading George Sand, who appeared to him a much greater 'prophetess' than Bettina von Arnim, he spent his time in day-dreaming and contemplation:

> Sometimes I lie for hours on end on the couch, gazing at the lake and the mountains, which are especially beautiful at sunset, watching the tiniest changes in the incessantly changing panorama; and I think, think of everything, and feel sad and cheerful... and everything in front of me is hidden in a mist.[5]

He had rowed with Herwegh on the lake, and they 'dreamed and laughed and were merry together.' But even as he was informing Premukhino that he loved Herwegh as 'brother loves sister', Herwegh – on 12 February – had been ordered by the ultra-conservative Grand Council governing the Zurich canton to leave its confines.

Herwegh's expulsion came a month after he had returned to the warm fold of Zurich's group of expatriate German academics. This included such distinguished figures as Lorenz Oken, the first rector of Zurich University on its foundation in 1833, previously dismissed from Jena for his 'radical democratic' views. The most active leaders of the group were Herwegh's two special patrons, the wealthy publisher Fröbel and A.A. Follen, the legendary *Burschenschaft* leader whom his Romantic fellow-students had wished to proclaim German emperor and whose Zurich house was known as the Kaiserburg for the portrait of him in imperial regalia that dominated its main hall. Until the so-called *Züriputsch* of 1839, the Zurich Grand Council had been in the hands of liberals and 'democrats' of various denominations, and Follen had been one of its most influential members.

In 1839 the offer of a chair at Zurich University to the theologian David Strauss – who had been dismissed from Tübingen for his daring, scholarly but allegedly 'unChristian' *Life of Jesus* – scandalized Zurich's conservative and orthodox Lutheran circles. In the storm caused by the ensuing *Züriputsch*, in which some 40 people were killed in clashes between religious peasants from the provinces and Zurich's democrats, the Grand Council was forced to resign. Control of the cantonal government passed to the conservatives, and the appointment of Strauss – whom Albert Schweitzer was later to call 'the most truthful of all theologians' – was promptly revoked.

It was in the aftermath of the *Züriputsch* that Professor Fröbel had given up his chair and founded the *Literary Comptoir* for the dual purpose of 'combating the reaction in Switzerland' and promoting the awakening political spirit in Germany. Herwegh had made the success of the new firm with his 1841 *Poems of a Living Man*. Between then and 1843, Berlin's *Athenäum* had called it a day and the 'Young Hegelian' movement was disintegrating. The serial suppression of even mildly liberal papers, not to mention that of Ruge's *Yearbooks* and the *Rheinische Zeitung*, had silenced all criticism. During the same period Fröbel published, or was in the process of producing, the political songs of Hofmann von Fallersleben and the works of such radical philosophical and/or politico-philosophical writers as Bruno Bauer, Arnold Ruge, Moses Hess, Karl Marx, Ludwig Feurbach, Karl Grün, Johann Jacoby and many others. This, together with Fröbel's recent acquisition of the bi-weekly *Schweizer Republikaner*, which he turned into the chief Swiss democratic newspaper, made his *Literary Comptoir* the paramount centre of opposition to the establishment in Germany.

Although Herwegh's tour of Germany had ended in ignominy, he was an international celebrity, the star of Fröbel's firm and the adored glamour-boy of the dozen or so active or retired professors and lecturers who formed the core of Zurich's liberal movement. His was a name to exploit and a volume he was about to edit out of the articles he had collected for the aborted *Deutsche Bote* – containing some of the most virulent material criticizing the Prussian autocracy ever to appear in print – was to cause a sensation when it appeared.

Herwegh's fame made him a thorn in the flesh of Zurich's conservative Grand Council. An offensive article against the Council which he had published before his tour of Germany, and for which he had been fined, served as the formal pretext for his expulsion in February 1843; and on 3 March, in spite of protests by Professor Oken and other liberals, Herwegh had to move to the neighbouring canton of Aargau.

It was there, in the little resort town of Baden, that his wedding to Emma Siegmund took place. Bakunin, making the most of his role as best man, acted as if he were master of ceremonies and moved about with the avuncular delight and pride of a man marrying off two bright and beloved young members of his family. He met several of Herwegh's friends, including Follen, who remained the leader of the German colony in Zurich.

But Herwegh himself soon left for the canton of Bâle, which had offered to grant him citizenship. From there he took his wife on an extended honeymoon trip to Italy. Then the couple moved for the duration to Paris, where Herwegh, installed in carefree and comfortable luxury on the money provided by his cultivated and adoring Emma, resumed his acquaintance with Heine, Hess and George Sand. He became the special darling of the comtesse d'Agoult and otherwise a sought-after celebrity in French literary salons and in the cirles of prominent German and Russian exiles or tourists. He was befriended by Marx and Ruge when they arrived, and eventually by Herzen, whose life he was to ruin by seducing his wife.

No one was more disconsolate to see Herwegh leave Switzerland than Bakunin. Herwegh's wedding had been an enjoyable diversion, but starting in February 1843, at the first notice that Herwegh might be expelled, and throughout the spring, he was once again a prey to a wretched feeling of loneliness and isolation, and gave vent to his black mood in a flurry of letters to Premukhino, imploring Paul

> to come back quickly and bring Tatyana to me... I am waiting for you,
> Paul, and, if possible, bring Taniusha to me. Your obligation, friends,
> is to use all available means to see to it that Taniusha comes abroad.
> This is a sacred obligation.

Again and again he harped on the same theme, sometimes pleading with Tatyana directly: 'Is it really true that there is no way for you to come abroad, so that you could teach me to live economically? You could be my housekeeper, Taniusha, and how tranquilly and well we would live. Paul, bring Taniusha.' And in another letter: 'Dear sister! Taniusha, Sasha, don't forget me, I am depressed, deeply depressed.'[6]

But none of his family replied. Although Michael claimed to possess the singular faculty of 'fusing the personality of those I love with my own so that... I see with their eyes and feel with their feelings', and assured his sisters that 'When I say I, I say We, I do not exist apart from you,' this was pure fantasy. His bond with the world of Premukhino, 'the source of my life, the origin of all that is living and best in me,' had in fact become one-sided. The hold he used to exercise over his flock of devotees had been broken by Varvara's slipping away to be reunited with her husband. Paul, in whom he had seen his brightest disciple, was to settle into the modest position of a provincial high school teacher. And even his beloved Tatyana wrapped herself in silence.

'What a vendetta with philosophy!' Herzen had exclaimed in Moscow upon reading Bakunin's *The Reaction in Germany*. 'He is wiping out all his former sins.' Even Belinsky, Bakunin's strongest critic, was impressed by his clarion call for revolution to the point of declaring that Michael and he 'had sought God by different paths, but met at last in the same temple.' Bakunin had published his essay at a time when Herzen had formed a new Moscow circle. Over supper at his house, Granovsky, Chaadaev, Belinsky (whenever he came over from St Petersburg) and others, 'Westerners' and so-called Slavophiles, argued out their differences. But while they idly chattered about anything 'of significance in any sphere of knowledge, in any literature or in any art', Bakunin had taken a step which left them far behind. As Aileen Kelly was to write in 1982, Belinsky – who had told Bakunin in 1838 that the striving of his ego to develop was 'fated to do so on an enormous scale' – could not have predicted 'the grandeur of the scale' on which Bakunin would resolve his 'inner chaos' or the way he would invest 'the drama of his inner life' and divided self 'with apocalyptic significance'. Bakunin's struggle to resolve his inner contradictions could now be seen as 'part of a cosmic process of unceasing revolution.'[7]

But to Bakunin in the spring of 1843 the admiration of Herzen, a congratulatory letter from Belinsky or Botkin's readiness to be reconciled with him brought little relief from his depression. These former friends of his represented Russia, with which he had broken, and both it and they were now 'beyond my memory'. The only Russia he cared for and that remained alive in his fantasy was confined to Premukhino. He lusted for 'deeds' and had assured his siblings that he feared nothing and was ready to meet the great future awaiting him. But he felt stranded and as desolate in Switzerland as he had as a young artillery ensign in the Polish 'desert'. To this was added his fear of going to prison, for he was overwhelmed by debts.

Like Marx, who sometimes wished his mother were dead so that he might obtain what he considered his inheritance, Bakunin was haunted for decades by the idea that if only his portion of the Premukhino estate was sold, all his troubles would be over. But whereas Marx periodically wangled advances from his mother or his relatives, all that Bakunin ever managed was to offer the imminent prospect of his inheritance as security to gullible creditors, such as Ruge.

In April, however, he decided to take a holiday. He knew an Italian singer by the name of Pescantini, from whom he had borrowed money in Dresden. Pescantini and his Russian-born wife owned a house on the island of St Pierre in Lake Bienne. Putting aside all his cares, Bakunin spent 10 happy days there: 'I strolled, sang, climbed mountains, enjoyed nature, translated Schelling, read some Italian, fantasized, built castles in the air and waited for you, Paul.'[8]

Bakunin's method of handling his creditors was unique. In March, before departing for Lake Bienne, he had written Ruge a letter to keep him at bay. Mentioning that Follen had suggested he write a book about Russia, he informed Ruge that this was absolutely out of the question. The book would take a year to write: 'During all that time I would have to live at someone else's expense', and pride forbade him to do that for he had 'firmly resolved never again to be financially obligated to anyone.' The way he put it, his pride in 'unlimited independence' was the only possession he still had, and he must keep his honour unstained. In case this logic failed to convince Ruge, he added: 'I must tell you, dear Ruge, that I feel a kind of revulsion at the idea of writing as the only source of income.'

Next he sent Ruge a promissory note drawn on Turgenev's bankers in St Petersburg. The note was for 2,500 Thaler instead of the 2,000 he owed. He asked Ruge to send him the balance which would keep him until summer.[9]

On his return to Zurich at the beginning of May, Bakunin found himself in a situation which would have driven another man to despair. The St Petersburg bankers had refused to honour the note drawn on Turgenev's account; Ruge was indignant and insisted on repayment; and Bakunin had other debts, amounting – as he now confessed to Premukhino – to some 10,000 roubles altogether. '*Adieu mon honneur et ma liberté car on me mettra en prison*', he wrote to his siblings, declaring that he would 'not evade the unpleasantness' of jail, but would seek it out to prove to his creditors that 'I had no intention of deceiving them… Had I less faith,' he wrote, 'I would really shoot myself', but that would leave a stain on his honour without solving his debts. Besides begging that his father should sell his share of the estate, that his aunt should mortgage her land, that money should be borrowed from Turgenev or from Madame Yazikov,[10] Bakunin made clear several points about his attitude towards debts. First, he broke them down into different classes. The most serious ones were those threatening imprisonment or dishonour. Other kinds could be disregarded. Secondly, as he instructed his brother Paul, one must do one's honourable utmost to pay 'our debts', but this didn't mean 'that we must fall into despair if our efforts fail. Believe me, nothing will force me to lose my belief in my worth and my future.'

Thirdly, and most significantly – as he put it to Ruge when explaining why he would not alleviate his financial situation by writing a book on Russia – absolute independence was for him the *sine qua non* of his existence. What he was doing or not doing was dictated by 'the inner necessity of my being'.

The same applied to his new revolutionary confrontation with the world. For years he had preached to his small commune that his was a divine voice; not so long ago he had instructed Paul that, contrary to the philistine belief that one's cherished fantasies were vacuous illusions, it was the reality of 'ordinary life that is the most dreadful phantom', shackling man by wretched little chains to be 'thrown off by the force of faith and the force of will'. Bakunin neither shot himself nor went to work 'in the sweat of my brow' as a common labourer, as he kept assuring everyone he would if everything else failed.

Having exploded in *The Reaction in Germany* all the theories of the 'castrated philosophers', he was himself reduced for the moment to theorizing about 'the dawn of the new world', a world 'that we sense within us', yet predicated to arise on the rubble of the existing one. But where was he to take the army of followers needed to destroy it? In the midst of his indolent days in Switzerland he found the answer in Weitling's *Guarantees of Harmony and Freedom*.

'Only the people', Weitling had written, 'have the audacity to put the arm of destruction to work.' The phrase came to Bakunin like a revelation. Weitling's Communism appealed so little to him that in an article in Fröbel's *Schweizer Republikaner* he described it as 'a form of unbearable oppression imposed on a herd in pursuit of exclusively material aims.' Suddenly, however, he realized that the proletarian 'herd' was 'the people – and by the people I understand the majority, the broadest masses, of the poor and oppressed.' Communism, he went on, was still crude and too materialist, but – like 'all the great acts of history, all liberating revolutions, it has issued from the people,' and the people with their 'creative fire' were destined to bring about 'the society of brotherhood and freedom, the Kingdom of God on earth... a new religion, a religion of democracy.' For in line with his concept of 'creative' destruction,

> it is only possible to create, really create, through a truly electrifying contact with the people. Christ and Luther came out of the simple people, and if the heroes of the French Revolution set with a mighty hand the first foundation of the future temple of freedom and equality, they were able to do so only because they were reborn in the tempestuous sea of the people's life.[11]

In the people with their destructive-creative 'fire' Bakunin found not only the chief agent in history, not only the bearer of that 'holy spirit of freedom and equality' which became the secular substitute for God and the Absolute in his new 'religion' – a religion which had revealed itself to the people 'in thunder and lightning' in the French Revolution – but also his future international rebel army. As Richard Hare observed, if Bakunin had decided to become a man of action earlier, he might have risen to glory as a Russian Governor or Field Marshal. As it was, exiled and penniless, he had no alternative but to 'recruit his own private army and general staff from the crowd of international malcontents and riff-raff.'[12]

Hare did not mention who this 'riff-raff' were, but it will be shown how Bakunin might have come to the idea of recruiting them. For the moment, after returning to Zurich from his vacation with the Pescantinis, he found that his load of debts had been taken care of during his absence. His long-time friend and devotee, Natalie Beyer, had dramatically urged his siblings at Premukhino to tell their parents that, unless they redeemed their eldest son immediately, the day might come when no amount of 'gold or remorse' would appease 'the awful knowledge that they have lost him, perhaps caused his death.' As a result, the feeble old Count Alexander Bakunin had scratched together 1,800 roubles, which were on their way to Michael. Tatyana, for her part, had appealed to Turgenev to pay the 2,000 Thaler Michael owed to Ruge, eliciting from Turgenev the icy letter which hurt her for the rest of her life. Turgenev, however, who had been separately approached by Ruge, sent Michael 2,200 roubles in two instalments.

With his mind thus eased, Michael was ready for the major event of his life so far – his meeting with the tailor Wilhelm Weitling. The latter arrived in Zurich in May 1843 with a letter of introduction from Herwegh. So impressed was Bakunin by Weitling's proud and dignified bearing, not to mention the revolutionary 'passion and fire' he descried in this manual worker – the first 'proletarian' he had ever spoken to – that in answer to Ruge's pessimism about the prospects of revolution he held up the tailor's 'faith in the liberation and the future of the enslaved majority'. He extolled the 'creative fire... the warmth and flame' burning in the common workers Weitling represented. 'Communism does not spring from theory but from the people's instinct, and this is never mistaken.' Referring to Weitling's own revolutionary passion, Bakunin, who for psychosexual reasons had no outlet for the turbulent passions that agitated his own being, remarked to Ruge with obvious envy: 'What indefinable bliss such striving and such power give a person.'[13]

The idea of putting the people's 'arm of destruction' to work, of leading it 'to construct among the ruins and the putrefaction that surround us a new world of freedom and beauty', gave Bakunin the sense of limitless power he lusted for all his life. The people with their simple practical 'instinct' became the instrument for achieving the creative and 'liberating' task which only a few thinkers and poets were 'noble enough to surrender themselves' to totally and irrevocably, a task for which he was ready 'to give all my life and blood'. And, given the fact that he knew no other reality than that shaped by his fantasy and satisfying his 'inner needs', it should come as no surprise that he would begin to see in the people his partner in nothing less than an Idealist-Romantic 'love'-affair, as is evident from his alternate use of 'they' and 'she' in the following passage of a letter he was to send to Premukhino two years later:

> I am passionately in love. I do not know if I am able to be loved as I
> would like, but... I know that they [sic!] do care for me a great deal. I
> want to, I must deserve the love of the one I love religiously, actively.
> She is now enslaved by the most terrible, the most shameful slavery,
> and I must liberate her by struggling against her oppressors...[14]

From this it would be only a short step to Bakunin's writing to the Herweghs, another two years later: 'I await my... bride – the revolution. We will be truly happy, that is, begin to be our true selves only then, when the whole world is engulfed in flame.' The political element in Bakunin's philosophy of violent revolution was always bound up with the personal. But it was not before 1981

811

that Arthur Mendel made the first attempt to work out in detail the connection between 'his impotence, his incestual attraction to his sister Tatyana, his marriage in which the children were fathered by a close friend and follower' and his theories and actions.

In Bakunin's falling 'passionately in love' with the 'people' and his whole ecstatic rhetoric about the people's 'electric contact', their 'passion and fire', their 'warmth and flame', Mendel has seen not only his way of releasing pent-up 'animal passions, but also a way of maternal reunion that was both narcissistic and... incestual.'[15]

'A vain, egotistical woman. None of her children loved her', was to be one of Bakunin's milder judgments of his mother. As he had written to his brother Nicholas in 1842 while he was still in Germany, he saw in his mother a woman of 'vulgar nature and unclean tendencies'. He not only accused her, in another letter written the same year, of having 'ruined all our lives. Oh, how much harm mother did to [Tatyana]! How many crimes she has piled up behind herself',[16] but three years later, unable to forgive her, he was to condemn her to utter damnation. Urging his siblings to stand together against all 'enemies', he directed his special venom against 'our enemy – mother, for whom I have no feeling in my soul but damnation and the most profound disdain. She is the source of what is unclean in our family. Her presence, even her existence, is an offence to what is sacred.'[17]

And the same year, in a letter to his brother Paul – the one in which he declared his passionate love for the people – his fury with his mother reached such a level that he wished on her the same merciless retribution as on his political enemies.

> As for our mother, I damn her. In my soul there is no room for any other feeling but hatred for her... Don't call me cruel-hearted. It's time for us to leave the world of fanciful and powerless sentimentality... Not forgiveness, but implacable war on our enemies, because they are the enemies of all that is human in us, enemies of our dignity, of our freedom... Yes, the capacity to hate is inseparable from the capacity to love. We must forgive our enemies only after we have thrown them down and utterly triumphed. But as long as they remain on their feet, no mercy and no respite![18]

As early as 1937, E.H. Carr cited a contemporary witness to the effect that in his old age Bakunin 'attributed his passion for destruction to the influence of his mother, whose despotic character inspired him with an insensate hatred of every restriction on liberty.'[19]

Carr left it at that, but Mendel's 'psychobiographical' approach and his analysis of every scrap of Bakunin's letters and writings led him in 1981 to the startling conclusion that 'it was his own oedipal dread' of being drawn into the world of his 'vulgar' mother that 'inspired such otherwise inexplicable outrage, strong enough to assault "even her existence".'

Tracing Bakunin's birth and oral imagery from the time when, at 20, he locked out the outer world to experience 'a warmth so sweet' and to be 'fed and nurtured' from within to his later talk of being 'reborn in the tempestuous sea of the people's life', his constant 'hunger' and 'thirst for revolution', Mendel wrote:

> Bakunin is passionately in love with the 'people' as both nurturing mother (birth, hunger, thirst) and electrifying, intoxicating, sensual wife, able to provide the long-desired 'paroxysm', the 'passion and the fire'. Both 'warmth and flame' are needed, the narcissistic 'warmth so sweet' and the sexual-incestual 'passion and fire'.[20]

No less revealing, in Mendel's view, was the love-hate dualism evident in Bakunin's associating – in one and the same letter – 'mother' and 'enemies', and 'love' and the 'people'. Mendel has cited chapter and verse to demonstrate Bakunin's 'sublimation of blocked sexual passion' into apocalyptic revolutionary fervour; but needless to say, it was his concomitant cynicism and lust for power, coupled with his striving to 'go beyond' and that spellbinding, charismatic quality which enabled him to persuade people to risk their lives in the execution of the wildest plots, while himself going from strength to strength and achieving heroic fame through real or imaginary 'suffering', that were to make him a figure larger than life.

Bakunin did not engage in any revolutionary activity in 1843. He spent most of the summer and autumn disporting himself with the Pescantinis at a villa they had bought near Nyon overlooking Lake Geneva, where – true to form – he created mischief between the couple by trying to 'liberate' Johanna Pescantini from her husband. Nevertheless, through his meeting with Wilhelm Weitling and his discovery of the 'people', Switzerland was an important station in the development of the social message that was to become part and parcel of his total war for the overthrow of 'existing reality'.

Weitling was by all accounts an extraordinary personality. Bakunin did not bother to study his plans for organizing the perfect society. He was impressed by Weitling's messianic fervour and his readiness to use the most violent means against the establishment and the rich. Indirect evidence to be published in Switzerland within weeks of the Weitling-Bakunin meeting showed that one of the means considered by the tailor was to unleash the 'thieving proletariat' – that is, to hasten the revolution and give it a violent push once it started by liberating 20,000 thieves, murderers and other criminals.

813

Although this idea was shot down by the Central Authority of the League of the Just and never appeared in the publications for which Weitling was to stand trial in the autumn of 1843, it is a reasonable assumption that the fanatical tailor discussed it with Bakunin. The latter, of course, knew that in Russia, too, as Richard Hare has put it,

> Pestels failed without Pugachovs. The former must enlist the brigand rank and file, and make their pent-up passions flow like molten lava... Lenin was at one with Bakunin when he exclaimed that he would rather employ a professional safe-breaker in the revolution than the philosopher Plekhanov.[21]

For the rest, Weitling's statement in *Guarantees of Harmony and Freedom* that 'the perfect society has no government, only an administration; no laws, only obligations; no punishments, only corrections,' suited Bakunin's own temperament and life-long opposition to all laws, 'political, criminal or civil', in any way restraining his liberty. He quoted it in his May 1843 letter to Ruge, adding: 'We begin decisively, more and more resolutely to get rid of the old rubble.' They must waste no time in starting to effect the apocalyptic 'break between good and evil by catastrophic means.'

Karl Marx, reacting at the beginning of May to Ruge's despair of ever seeing a revolution in Germany, bolstered his spirit with entirely different arguments. The contrast between his rational approach and Bakunin's temperamental and 'instinctive' one forecast that these two protagonists – who were to meet a year or so later – would never be able to get along and were ultimately destined to clash like two gladiators in the Socialist arena.

Already in March, writing from Holland, Marx had observed to Ruge that, 'in comparison with the greatest Germans, even the least Dutchman is still a citizen.' Abroad, the despotism and 'the perverted nature of our [Prussian] state' stood revealed for all the world to see, making one hide one's face in shame. 'Revolutions', he went on, 'are not made by shame', but 'shame is a revolution in itself... Shame is a kind of anger turned in on itself. And if a whole nation were to feel ashamed it would be like a lion recoiling in order to spring.'

Marx was aware that 'even this shame' was not yet to be found in philistine Germany. But it was precisely its 'desperate situation', he told Ruge in his May letter, that filled him with hope: 'Let the dead bury the dead and mourn them. In contrast, it is enviable to be the first to enter upon a new life; this shall be our lot. True, the old world belongs to the philistines. But we must not treat them as bogeymen and shrink from them in terror.' On closer inspection these lords of the world

are lords of the world only in the sense that they fill it with their
presence, as worms fill a corpse. They require nothing more than a
number of servants. Their ownership of land and people... does not
make them any less philistine than their servants, [who] accumulate
for their masters like a breed of slaves or a stud of horses.

'This whole society', Marx went on, 'is geared to the hereditary masters.' All
the latter wished was 'to live and procreate. In this they are like animals.'

Politically, the whole of Prussia struck him as an *'animal kingdom'* (emphasis
in the original), in which the King was 'the only political person'. While his
caprices constituted 'the thought and action of the Prussian state, the masters
accept themselves as they are and place their feet where they naturally belong:
on the necks of the political animals who have no other vocation than to be their
"loyal, obedient subjects".'

Against this stark picture of a 'dehumanized' society produced by centuries
of barbarism, Marx posited the notion that by re-awakening 'man's self-esteem
and sense of freedom' a community of men would ultimately be achieved that
'can fulfil their highest need, a democratic state'.

Among the reasons he cited for his confidence was the prospect of an alliance
between 'the thinking people' and 'the suffering people', i.e., between the intelligentsia and the proletariat, although Marx did not use these terms. In an accurate prognosis of the historic process he further forecast that

> the system of industry and commerce, of property and the exploita-
> tion of man, will lead much faster than the increase of population to
> a rupture within existing society which the old system cannot heal
> because, far from healing and creating, it knows only to exist and
> enjoy.

'The more time history allows thinking mankind to reflect and suffering mankind to collect its strength', Marx assured Ruge, 'the more perfect will be the
fruit which the present now bears in its womb.'[22]

Although Lenin was to detect indications of Marx's transition 'from revolutionary democratism to Communism' in his early articles in the *Rheinische
Zeitung*, it will be noticed that in the letter of May 1843 to Ruge – written from
Cologne – Marx did not name 'the fruit' gestating in the womb. Communism
preoccupied him; one might say it was gestating in his mind, as is evident in his
discussing the 'existing' forms of it in a third letter to Ruge later in the year. But
more time was to pass before he devised his own version of it.

On 10 May, he left for Dresden to meet Ruge in person and discuss the state
of the projected *German-French Yearbooks* with him and his new partner,

Fröbel, who was ready to co-finance the new venture and had promised to come to Dresden. Marx was still there on the 21st when his marriage banns were published at the civil registry office in Kreuznach. Some trouble in Switzerland forced Fröbel to postpone his visit. On the 26th, his post as co-editor of the future monthly having been assured by Ruge, Marx hastened to Jenny in Kreuznach to complete the preparations for their wedding.

On 8 June, a few days before they were to sign a marriage contract at her mother's house, Switzerland was rocked by a series of sensational developments. First, Weitling was arrested in Zurich; and shortly after that the police raided Professor Fröbel's publishing house and confiscated an inflammatory volume edited by Herwegh. Then the authorities published an official report – 'The Communists in Switzerland, According to Weitling's Papers' – which alarmed the chancelleries of Europe, warning as it did that Weitling and his clandestine League of the Just had established 'a spider's web' of international connections and were conspiring to undermine the established order of the church and the monarchies.

At Kreuznach, Marx and Jenny went about their business undisturbed. The marriage contract, signed on 12 June and witnessed by a notary, established a community of goods between the couple, but exempted each of the partners from liability for any premarital debts contracted or inherited by the other. Seven days later they were married at Kreuznach's civil registry office and – on the same day – married again in a religious ceremony in the town's Protestant-Evangelical Pauluskirche. Four local residents, including a doctor of medicine and an innkeeper, acted as witnesses at the first function, and two others at the religious ceremony.

Few people attended either event. Of the Westphalen family, none but Jenny's mother and her younger brother Edgar were present. Marx's mother had given her agreement to his marriage in writing in January, but neither she nor any of his 5 sisters – including Sophie, who had been his faithful go-between with Jenny during the secret phase of their engagement – came to celebrate the occasion with him.

The double boycott seems to have disturbed the alienated Marx less than it did his bride. The newly-weds, having waited for 7 years for this consummation, were presumably happy as they departed on their honeymoon to Schaffhausen and the Rhine Falls in Switzerland. Their love had triumphed, thanks chiefly to Jenny's having withstood a long endurance test. Almost as soon as they were back in Kreuznach and under her mother's roof, waiting to hear from Ruge and Fröbel whether they were to emigrate to Brussels or Paris – depending on the choice of venue for the *German-French Yearbooks* – she got a foretaste of what their married life would be like.

Marx, withdrawing 'from the public stage' into his study, was to spend the rest of the summer and the beginning of autumn immersed in an 'ocean of books'. Besides Montesquieu's *L'Esprit des Lois*, Machiavelli's *Il Principe*, Rousseau's *Contrat Social* and works on the French Revolution, he read some 20 history books – histories of France, Venice, Poland, Germany, Sweden, the United States, and a 7-volume history of England. Several others of those mentioned being multi-volume editions, it has been calculated that he went through, digested or consulted about 30 volumes altogether, comprising more than 10,000 pages.

He was at last setting to work on a two-part essay, 'Critique of Hegel's Philosophy of Right', in which, with all due respect to his admired master, he was going to repudiate, paragraph by paragraph, Hegel's doctrine of the state and his glorification of its monarch. For historical background he copied and incorporated into it extensive, sometimes 50-pages-long, excerpts as well as notes from the sources mentioned. This essay, running to 130 pages in print – of which he had actually written to Ruge more than a year earlier that it was finished – was to take him quite a while to complete.

Wilhelm Weitling was to be tried on a variety of charges, including instigation to crimes against property, incitement to rebellion, and also blasphemy, for having sent to the printer a book – *The Gospel of a Poor Sinner (Das Evangelium des armen Sünders)* – depicting Jesus as a Communist and the illegitimate child of 'a poor girl', Mary. His arrest and the official report accusing the Paris-based League of the Just of an international conspiracy are reminders that Heine, in the early 1830s, for all his conflict with Ludwig Börne, had expressed his envious admiration for the ability of that sophisticated writer and aesthete to speak in the tones of a 'people's tribune' when addressing 600 semi-literate German tailor's apprentices in a hall on Montmartre on the need for revolution.

Those tailor's apprentices tell us something about the composition of the German colony in Paris. When Weitling arrived there in 1836, he found that half of the 15,000 Germans there were journeymen tailors, cobblers and carpenters. The colony grew at a staggering rate – within the next 10 or 11 years it swelled to 70,000 (some say 80,000) souls. But the ratio of journeymen tailors, cobblers and carpenters remained steady: by 1847, according to the best statistics, 34,000 plied these three trades. The rest were artisans – blacksmiths, tanners, masons, locksmiths, printers, mechanics and assorted manual workers – or shop assistants and servants.

Less than 1,000 were described as merchants, diplomats, journalists, artists or simply 'adventurers'. The number of political refugees, however, at no time exceeded several hundred. In 1832 several of them, encouraged by Börne, had formed the League of the Outlawed (*Bund der Geächteten*), which called for political freedom in Prussia and the other German states. In 1834 its radical wing split away to form the secret League of the Just *(Bund der Gerechten)*. Consisting mostly of artisans and apprentices, it added social agitation to the earlier platform and demanded 'bread and education for the masses'. Weitling, who was 27 when he reached Paris in 1836, quickly rose in its ranks and by 1837 had become a member of its presiding Central Authority.

The League of the Just was involved in Blanqui's 1839 insurrection (or so Engels was to claim half a century later). Although the extent of its participation has never been ascertained, one of its leaders, Karl Schapper – a seasoned revolutionary who had taken part in Mazzini's expedition to Savoy in 1834 – was caught at one of Blanqui's barricades; and a number of German artisans were among those arrested or dispersed during the abortive putsch.[23]

Whether they were out in the street by accident or on the League's orders, it is known that, while for many years the French workers resented the growing number of Germans who undercut their wages – leading to fierce clashes in the proletarian Faubourg St Antoine – the League of the Just had by now established contact with Blanqui's Société des Saisons and other French secret societies.

In the searches which followed the unsuccessful insurrection, some of the League's papers were seized. Schapper, after spending 6 months in jail, was expelled to England. For a time, nothing more was heard of the League of the Just, and it was thought that it had been smashed for good together with Blanqui's organization. It had, however, only gone underground under Weitling's leadership.

Born in October 1808 in Prussian Magdeburg on the Elbe, a town ravaged in the fighting of the Napoleonic wars, Weitling was the product of a chance encounter between a French officer, Guillaume Terijon, and a German housemaid. Terijon spoke of having him legitimized and educated in France, but in 1812 he marched off with the Grande Armée for Moscow, never to return.

During the subsequent Prussian siege of Magdeburg, the boy was placed out of town in the care of his grandmother, who survived the privations of the time by selling 'matches, lampwicks, tobacco and chicory'. Early apprenticed to a master tailor who worked him hard in exchange for lodging and providing him with his daily black bread and sauerkraut, he came out of his adolescence a handsome, blond, blue-eyed six-footer.

At 18 or so he left Magdeburg, and for the next 10 years – without a passport or other papers, as he had never served in the army – he tramped his way back and forth across the German states and Austria, equipped only with a *Wanderbuch*, the certified journeyman's book in which every future employer would record his name and his remarks on him. But for shorter or longer intervals during which he found employment as a ladies' tailor in Hamburg, Leipzig, Dresden, Vienna, Paris and Vienna again, Weitling had spent most of his time on the road, walking from village to village, and often playing hide-and-seek with the Prussian police, to whom he was a fugitive army shirker.

Although Weitling had barely finished elementary school, he had managed, during his wanderings, to teach himself Greek and Latin and to acquire a kind of education. When he settled in Paris and joined the League of the Just, he impressed its leaders with his eloquence. They quickly realized that in this young proletarian autodidact, who combined an ascetic way of life with the zeal of a Christian evangelist – and who besides knowing the Bible by heart was capable of quoting or referring to Aristotle and Pythagoras, Socrates and Homer – they had found a man who might be most effective at propagating their ideas among the workers. By 1838 the Central Authority had indeed charged Weitling with the task of formulating the League's aims and programme.

He carried this out in two successive volumes. Whereas the first, *Mankind As It Is and As It Ought To Be* (1838), harked back to the spirit of brotherly love which had characterized the early Christian communes and called for application of various Socialist-Communist ideas borrowed from Saint-Simon, Fourier and Robert Owen, the second – *Guarantees of Harmony and Freedom*,[24] published in Switzerland in December 1842 – was a fervent and militant appeal to the masses of the oppressed to take their fate in their hands, to abolish the rule of money and overthrow the existing order by means of revolution, 'not necessarily a bloody one, though twenty years of chaos wouldn't be too great a price for the new social order', for the purpose of establishing a 'scientific form of Communist government'. Weitling contemplated three means for achieving social reform. First, propaganda, persuasion and enlightenment, all of which required 'a free press and public trials'; second, 'escalation of the existing disorder' to the point where 'the people's endurance will snap, this is the surest means.' Thirdly, if all else failed, there was the lesson of history to be applied, which taught that 'the religions spread by means of wars and revolution served to topple or to maintain dynasties and through wars and revolution the Reformation of the Church obtained recognition.'[25]

As a last resort Weitling thus advocated 'a war without mercy', a social revolution which would be the 'last theft'. The rich were to be disarmed; the proletariat would be given arms and form a people's militia. Once power was seized, there must be no armistice and no truck with the enemy. 'The head of the snake must be crushed at one blow.' But he stressed several times that this did not mean staging 'a bloodbath among the enemy or robbing him of his freedom, only depriving him of the means to hurt us.'

Weitling was an internationalist. Not only was all private property to be abolished – though he offered state pensions to those willingly giving up theirs at the start of the age of universal brotherhood – but, he proclaimed, 'the concept of different languages, of frontiers and fatherland, are of no more use to mankind than all existing religious dogmas. All these concepts are absolute traditions whose damage becomes ever more palpable the longer they last.'[26]

The League of the Just had two features which distinguished it from other early Communist or 'proto-Communist' groups and were to lend it an importance quite beyond its numbers. For one thing, it had a tightly knit clandestine structure which was not only to survive its transmutation, before the end of the decade, into the Communist League, but to serve as a model – as Marx was to admit in 1860 in *Herr Vogt* – for the organization of the First International in 1864.

For another thing, the League of the Just had by 1843 established secret branches in England and Switzerland, which took their guidance and instructions from the Central Authority in Paris. When Karl Schapper arrived in London as an exile in November 1840, he founded an Education Society (*Bildungsverein*) of German artisans which met regularly in Great Windmill Street. In 1842, he was joined by Heinrich Bauer, another member of the League's Central Authority expelled from Paris. Bauer was a shoemaker. Schapper had a university education but made his living as a printer. The two had no difficulty establishing a branch of the League among the German workers in London, to which the Education Society with its wide variety of activities – lectures on history, geography, labour relations, politics, astronomy, etc., besides language and singing lessons, dance evenings and other entertainments – served as a convenient front. Unmolested by the police, who did not feel that any radical opinions entertained by these aliens threatened Britain, the English branch of the League of the Just, starting with about 100 members, was eventually to absorb several other existing German associations in London.

A year earlier, in May 1841, the Central Authority had sent Weitling to Switzerland, to spread the League's message there. Although the Swiss police kept an eye on him, and he was often forced to move from canton to canton, he managed, in an extraordinary spurt of activity in the two years before his arrest, to organize or infiltrate a variety of workers' educational clubs, singing societies, communal dining halls and cooperative taverns, and to turn them into branches or recruitment centres of the League in Lausanne, Vevey, Neuchâtel, Geneva, Zurich, Aarau, Winterthur, St Gallen, Bern and other places. At the same time, while living frugally by his needle and subsisting on a pittance, he maintained a vast correspondence, wrote and singlehandedly produced a monthly, *The Young Generation*, and while his major work, *Guarantees of Har-*

mony and Freedom, was still in the press, he set to work on *The Gospel of a Poor Sinner*.

The Central Authority in Paris, which continued to function clandestinely under the leadership of a Danzig-born physician, Dr August Hermann Ewerbeck, and a former Berlin philologist and poet, Germain Mäurer, wanted this volume to 'shake the Germans to the root of their soul'; and at the beginning of 1843 it had pressed the tailor to have it ready in time for the Leipzig Fair. Weitling received mail under several aliases and his May visit to Zurich, where he was to land in the arms of the police, had been prompted by Dr Ewerbeck's directing him to establish 'close and intimate contacts with *Bakunin* and *Fröbel*: this will profit you (and our cause)'.

He had earlier been sent 75 francs 'for clothes, so that you should no longer appear as a ragged beggar.'[27]

The investigation of Weitling was conducted by Johann Caspar Bluntschli, the most powerful figure on (and later president of) Zurich's conservative Grand Council. A good deal of the post received by Weitling for over a year had been seized on his arrest during the night of 7–8 June 1843, and within a month or so Bluntschli was able to submit his report, *The Communists in Switzerland, According to Weitling's Papers*, to the Zurich Council. This document exposed almost in full the Paris League of the Just's Swiss connection, but it contained some other interesting revelations. The name of Weitling's successor at the helm of the League, Dr Ewerbeck, hardly rings a bell today, but in the 1840s it was 'marked in red ink' (in the language of a contemporary account) and kept on file in the chancelleries of various European governments, including those of all the German states. Dr Ewerbeck's subversive non-medical activities were closely watched by the French police, the Prussian Embassy in Paris, and by authorities as far as St Petersburg, who kept track of him through 'Russian spies masquerading as democrats in France and Germany'.

Interest in the Weitling case thus exceeded both the scope of the charges against him and the borders of Switzerland. The sensation caused by Bluntschli's report, which was widely sold and distributed, had hardly died down when, on 19 July, the Zurich police raided Professor Fröbel's *Literary Comptoir*. The success of this radical publishing house had long been an irritant to Bluntschli and the canton's Grand Council. Bluntschli's men confiscated copies of a German volume which bore the title, *Twenty-one Sheets from Switzerland (Einundzwanzig Bogen aus der Schweiz)*. Edited by Herwegh, it contained articles and essays from the pens of, among others, Dr Bruno Bauer, Arnold Ruge, Moses Hess, David Strauss and young Engels. Most of these articles – in some of which the church and the monarchies were savaged in

821

unprecedented terms – had been collected or commissioned by Herwegh for the *Deutsche Bote*, the projected monthly which Prussia had banned in advance of its publication. The volume with its ironic title – volumes of more than 20 printed sheets were formally exempt from Prussian censorship, though they could always be suppressed – thus represented the poet's revenge for the humiliating 'finis' which the Prussian King had written to his triumphal tour of Germany.

Herwegh's revenge was all the sweeter as copies of *Twenty-one Sheets* had already been shipped into Germany before Fröbel's premises were ransacked. But the embarrassment this caused the Swiss as well as the German authorities was a laughing-matter compared to the shocking contents of the publication. One article, entitled 'The Philosophy of Action' (*Die Philosophie der Tat*), contained the following: 'Gods and monarchs are sanctified persons raised above reality, and thus *no persons* at all; the monarch, like God, is incomprehensible *majesty* – to be adored without further thought by falling on our knees.'

In other passages religion and politics, i.e., the church and the state, were described as twin molochs. 'The state is a facsimile copy of the Christian God, who allows His first-born Son to be crucified, and looking with pleasure on the sacrifice, builds His Church "on this rock" of martyrdom.' The Christian God in his turn, the writer went on, had copied this from the Jewish 'Moloch-Jehovah' who demanded the sacrifice of the firstborn. Admittedly, the Jews had substituted animals for sacrifice, but originally and fundamentally it was human sacrifice on which both church service and state service were built, and in the 19th century priests and kings continued to feed 'on the sweat and blood of their subjects.'[28]

Coming on top of Bluntschli's report and the revelation of Weitling's blasphemous treatment of Christ, this could not but raise the blood-pressure of conservative or simply church-going, law-abiding citizens. The fact that a well-known poet like Georg Herwegh had lent his name to a collection of such revolting material added to the scandal in both Switzerland and Germany.

In Cologne, Moses Hess, who was on a summer visit to his home town from Paris, feared imminent arrest. He was the author of the violent diatribe against the church and the state, as well as two other articles in *Twenty-one Sheets* which – besides setting the tone of the whole publication – were to have no small influence on Marx. Attacked on 18 July in a Swiss newspaper, Hess at the same time found himself named in Bluntschli's report, which quoted letters from Dr Ewerbeck to Weitling describing Hess as a man who was excellent at converting 'the highly educated' to Communism. Expecting to be detained for questioning by the Prussian police, Hess considered hastening his return to Paris, but in the end thought better of it. He stayed on in Cologne long enough to meet Ruge, who came to see him at the end of July, in company with Fröbel himself.

In the midst of the uproar involving his firm in Zurich, Fröbel had come over to help Ruge with the starting capital for the foundation of the *German-French Yearbooks*. Ruge had just been to see Marx at Kreuznach, to inform him that, once the place of publication was decided upon, their long-planned monthly could be launched in a matter of months. In Cologne, Ruge and Fröbel secured Hess's participation in the project.

At the beginning of August, Hess departed with Ruge for Brussels. It took them only a few days to decide that the Belgian capital with its small and politically disinterested German colony was no suitable location for a radical monthly, and they went on to Paris. Arriving there on the 9th, Hess – who had already met most of the leading French Socialist and Communist thinkers – began to take Ruge round to such figures as Cabet, Considérant, Blanc and Leroux, with a view to enlisting their collaboration on the new Franco-German periodical.

Fröbel continued for a while to travel about Germany, making various business arrangements. In Zurich, Councillor Bluntschli fumed. Weitling's mail showed that Fröbel had refused to meet him in Zurich, warning him – in a communication made on 5 March 1843, through the Swiss Communist August Becker – not to risk showing his face in Zurich at all, and that after reading Weitling's incriminating *Gospel of a Poor Sinner* he had refused to publish it, letting him know, again through Becker, that 'at this moment the fate of Zurich's whole radical party is on his [Fröbel's] conscience [i.e., at stake] and to preach Communism now may well trigger a second Straussiade',[29] leading to untoward political consequences, as had the *Züriputsch* provoked by the offer of a professorship to the controversial theologian David Strauss.

Although very cautious in his contacts with Weitling, Fröbel had sent him, through another intermediary, lists of radical booksellers in Germany to help distribute *The Gospel of a Poor Sinner* there. Fröbel, however, was far from being a convinced Communist. Rather, he was a bourgeois idealist and radical 'democrat'. He abhorred the idea of abolishing private property, but realizing that 'the down-trodden and oppressed people' might one day discover that they were the huge majority of mankind, he had opened the pages of the bi-weekly *Schweizer Republikaner* to every social theorist and agitator, including Becker, Weitling and Bakunin.

In an ambiguous message to Weitling, he had asked Becker to convey that only the future would show how far he could agree 'with the various ideas of Communism, but meanwhile my heart belongs to the cause. I divide people into either egotists or Communists, and in that sense I belong to the latter.' He was,

823

in short, a sympathizer, or to use an anachronistic term, a 'fellow-traveller' of early Communism.

Regardless of Fröbel's sentiments, Bluntschli saw in him nothing less than a public danger. He had been seeking the opportunity to smash Fröbel's political publishing house ever since May, even before Weitling's arrest. The professor's indirect support of Weitling, coupled with the fact that his *Literary Comptoir* had published Herwegh's *Twenty-One Sheets*, gave him his pretext.

Fröbel was to be prosecuted for an 'offence against religion'. More immediately, and even worse, Bluntschli's report discredited Fröbel's publishing house politically and was to ruin it financially. Fröbel was forced to give up control of the *Schweizer Republikaner*; and although Arnold Ruge and August Follen joined that summer in pouring money into the *Literary Comptoir*, the publishing house which had become the main centre of politico-philosophical and literary opposition to the reactionary regimes in Germany was forced to retrench – and to close down a couple of years later.

Bluntschli regarded Fröbel as a seditious publisher around whom Hess, the poet Herwegh, Dr Bruno Bauer, David Strauss and the other writers of *Twenty-One Sheets* had formed a Communist 'ring' operating parallel, or in some form of association, with Weitling's secret League of the Just to undermine the established order of society. Bluntschli was firmly convinced that they were engaged – as he wrote later – in an

> undisguised attempt to recommend Christianity and the monarchy to the hatred of the peoples as 'heavenly and earthly tyrannies' to be overthrown, their expectation being that an alliance between German philosophy, which extirpates religion, and the French political spirit, which takes equality seriously and breeds Communism, will improve the world.

Bluntschli wrote this when describing *Twenty-One Sheets* in his reminiscences, published some 40 years after the event.[30] But as Hess had openly declared both these tendencies – down to the use of the term 'heavenly and earthly tyrants' – Bluntschli hardly needed that much time to reach his conclusion, and acted on it in 1843.

As for Weitling, he was brought to trial in the autumn of that year for blasphemy and the other charges mentioned. The prosecution did not fail to bring up the hope expressed by Weitling that by 1844 he would have 40,000 followers, enough to start 'the revolution', especially if half this force were to consist of professional criminals somehow to be taken out of jail.

The fact that this 'apparent plan' was inferred from the letters addressed to him by Dr Ewerbeck and others – for Weitling's own letters had escaped confiscation – had forced Bluntschli to admit that, even if executed, this 'impractical' plan would at worst have caused public disorder, without 'breaking up the state'. Actually, from Paris a shocked Dr Ewerbeck had reacted to Weitling's fantasy by writing him that to let 20,000 rascals loose on society was 'like trying to found the kingdom of heaven by unleashing the furies of hell'; and Becker, as well as the Communist journalist Sebastian Seiler and other correspondents, had all joined in bringing Weitling to his senses by variously reminding him that 'we cannot kill the world with raw iron, we must first kill it morally, only then can we bury it', or that to use criminals would not only pervert all the noble reformist ideas of Communism but went against his own morality.[31]

Indeed, the whole idea contrasted so strongly with Weitling's religious and moral inspiration – and with his efforts to raise the self-esteem of the manual workers of his day, to teach them dignity, honour and respect for others – that it has been rightly dismissed as the 'temporary aberration of a highly overworked and unusually excitable individual'.

Weitling seems to have written *The Gospel of a Poor Sinner* during the spring of 1843 in a state of growing emotional and nervous tension. Although warned of the danger of showing himself in Zurich, he had decided he must

> plant our flag in the enemy camp... Persecution will promote our cause. I must go to Zurich, where the people are being misused by a hypocritical priest-ridden party,... Let me be the persecuted. Yea, I will take my cross to Zurich; if it becomes too heavy to carry, some Simon will surely turn up there.[32]

He was driven by a sense of urgency, and during the months he was to spend in jail his main fear was that he might be killed before accomplishing his mission. He suspected the Chief Warden of having hired a murderer, or charged the prison doctor, to do him in quickly. At his trial the tall, blue-eyed 34-year-old tailor, who normally cut a handsome figure with his neatly trimmed beard, looked gaunt and haggard. Speaking in his own defence, he said rather blandly that beyond wishing 'to wipe out property' he had never preached armed revolt. Eloquently and with great vigour he refuted the charge of having blasphemed Jesus. He admitted that in the *Gospel of a Poor Sinner* he had written that over the centuries love had gone out of religion until it became a slavery 'and the God of Christianity was turned into a monster, a God with human features, yet without human weaknesses'; but, while regretting the use of so crass a word as monster, he submitted that his criticism was directed against the notion of the *supernatural* Jesus and not against the person of Christ. To drive home his point, he argued that on the same basis as he was being charged even 'the New Testament itself, if it were to be printed for the first time in Zurich, is not sure to escape confiscation.' And he quoted the verses – in Epistle to the Romans 8:3, II Corinthians 5:21 and Galatians 3:13 – in which Paul variously called Jesus a sin, a curse and cursed.

Jesus himself, he remarked, never called himself 'God', only 'the Son' or 'Son of man'. And reciting more New Testament verses, he declared that but for Jesus's being 'set on the right side of the throne of the Majesty in heavens (Epistle to the Hebrews, 3:1) we can be one with him... be resurrected and glorified with him and yea, according to Matthew 5:48 we can be perfect even as God Himself.' His argument was that it was Paul who had made Jesus 'spiritually more perfect' than ordinary mortals. To Weitling, Jesus was 'a prophet of freedom and love, and if, according to John, God is the word and love, Jesus is also God.'[33]

Weitling was sentenced to 6 months in prison. Professor Fröbel got off with a lighter sentence: two months for his 'offence against religion'. Altogether Weitling spent nearly a whole year in a Swiss jail before he was expelled to his native Prussia. During the last three months of his incarceration he lived, by his own account, in a state of nightmarish anxiety, fearing a plot to kill him or declare him insane. Every rattle at his door made him wince. 'The unexpected appearance of the Chief Warden would freeze my tongue with fear,' he noted in his journal. 'At night I barricaded my door in order not to be taken unawares. I feel that one can go berserk here.' At times, when he felt his head throb and feared that he was really going mad, he would collect himself and overcome his terror by starting to sing or count numbers.

Yet, after every bout of dread and despair, Weitling – who before leaving for Zurich had assessed the promotional value of persecution – pulled himself up with the thought that his very suffering would hasten his eventual triumph. He concluded his second defence speech with a peroration thanking his judges for having lit

> a magic fire in my breast: on my resurrection it will light up your shame, and to my friends it will be an incendiary torch, a firebrand... I am happy and proud to be the accused and not the accuser... I have celebrated my resurrection, proceed ye now with the Last Judgment.[34]

This and his copious use of biblical imagery when speaking of himself, sometimes in words alluding directly to the Passion of Christ, have led to the suggestion that the mystically inclined tailor had come to see himself not simply as a crusader but as a 'second Jesus' and the Messiah of Communism who would redeem the world of the evils of Mammon.

After Weitling's extradition the following year, Heine was to run into him at Campe's bookshop in Hamburg. He recorded 'the famous tailor's' habit of lifting his right knee to his chin with one hand and rubbing his ankle with the other. When Heine inquired what itched him, Weitling replied that it was the scars left by the manacles with which he had been chained to the walls of the prison.

His sensational trial made Weitling internationally known. Heine may have been repelled by the tone of feigned indifference with which, hiding his conceit, Weitling drew attention to the signs of his 'martyrdom'; yet to the discontented riff-raff of his day these were the stigmata marking the true revolutionary believer, and the sincerity and fervour Weitling brought to the recital of the woes of the poor, in terms taken from his own experience, spoke directly to the hearts of the manual craftsmen, journeymen and apprentices whom industrialization had pushed to the margin of society. So did the prospect he held out to them of a world without privileged princes and priests, 'without frontiers and fatherlands' and generals who marched off cohorts of men 'like marionettes' to be killed in senseless wars, a world in which the money of the rich would be replaced by new currency notes bearing the imprint 'worth one hour (or fifteen minutes, or whatever time length) of real labour' instead of the face of some autocratic ruler, and everyone would have access to free education, old-age relief and to the possibilities offered by science in an age of universal equality and social justice.

To the extent that Germany's workers were at all socially conscious, Weitling was their hero. His *Guarantees of Harmony and Freedom* went into three printings and was translated into French, Swedish and Norwegian. He also made an impression in progressive intellectual circles. Ludwig Feuerbach, the materialist philosopher and theologian, who in his *Essence of Christianity* had declared God to be merely a projection of man's mind, called Weitling 'the prophet' of the working class; Gottfried Keller, the Swiss novelist and poet, applauded 'the spirit and fire' of Weitling's writings; Karl Marx was to acclaim his *Guarantees of Harmony and Freedom* as 'the brilliant literary debut of the German workers' and to hail Weitling as a 'theorist of genius'.

And Heine, for all his reservations about the tailor and his ideas, called his *Guarantees* 'the catechism of the German Communists'. Weitling's League of the Just, with its several hundred tailors, cobblers, carpenters and other artisans and apprentices in Paris, and another couple hundred in London, was indeed unexpectedly to open the annals of Communist history.

In September 1843, three months or so into the Weitling affair and before the prison sentence, Marx, writing from Bad Kreuznach, congratulated Arnold Ruge in Paris on the choice of that ancient French 'bastion of philosophy... and capital of the modern world' as the location of their new venture, the *German-French Yearbooks*. Charting the programme for the new journal, Marx for the first time declared that philosophy must pass from theory to practice. Their

827

task was to apply it to 'the ruthless criticism of the existing order, ruthless in that it will shrink neither from its own discoveries nor from conflict with the powers that be.'[35]

As for the best way for philosophy to join the battle to influence opinions and events in Germany, he thought that since religion and politics dominated public life there, 'our task must be to latch on to these subjects in whatever state they are.'[36]

Marx had in fact 'latched' onto them almost immediately upon his and Jenny's return from their honeymoon, when he had sat down at her mother's house in Kreuznach to spend arduous days and nights on the completion of his long-planned 'Critique of Hegel's Philosophy of Right'. In one of his convoluted paragraphs Hegel had written:

> In contrast with the sphere of private rights and private welfare (the family and civil society), the state is on the one hand an external necessity and their higher authority; its nature is such that their laws and interests are subordinate to it and dependent on it. On the other hand, however, it is the end immanent within them, and its strength lies in the unity of its own universal end and aim with the particular interest of individuals.[37]

Hegel, Marx submitted, had got it all wrong. Pointing to the unresolved antinomy between external necessity and immanent ends, he wrote that in the name of his preconceived 'universal Idea', Hegel had inverted the true relationship of the family and civil society to the state.

> The family and civil society are the preconditions of the state; they are the true agents... [they] make themselves into the state... the political state cannot exist without them... And yet [in Hegel's speculative philosophy] the condition is posited as the conditioned, the determinator as the determined, the producer as the product...[38]

In short, Hegel had turned the mass of 'human beings out of which the state is formed' into something both unreal and 'subordinate' to the abstract state. Quoting and extensively analyzing over 50 paragraphs of Hegel's doctrine of the state, Marx demonstrated in page after page the 'mystification' created by Hegel's claim that the Prussian state, its bureaucracy and its legislature represented high 'universal' principles and worked 'impartially and in perfect harmony' under the guidance of an all-wise monarch embodying the 'personality of the state' and its 'sovereignty in human form'. In sharp sarcastic passages, Marx pointed out that Hegel had turned the whole of civil society into an 'artificial person...' In the monarch, on the other hand, the person contains the state within himself... The bureaucracy sees itself as the final aim of the state... The aims of the state are transformed into the aims of the bureaux and vice-versa. The bureaucracy is a magic circle which no one can escape. Its hierarchy is a hierarchy of knowledge. The apex entrusts insight into particulars to the lower echelons while the lower echelons credit the apex with insight into the universal, and so each deceives the other...

Just as religion does not make man, but man makes religion, so the constitution does not make the people, but the people make the constitution. Man is not there for the benefit of the law, but the law for the benefit of man... That is the fundamental character of democracy.[39]

The method followed by Marx in his 'Critique' was largely inspired by Ludwig Feuerbach. It was Feuerbach who had declared in *The Essence of Christianity* that, contrary to Hegel's view of God as the 'Absolute Idea', it was not God who created man in His image: rather man had created God in *his* image as a reflection of his own 'inner nature'. In a more recent work, *Provisional Theses for the Reformation of Philosophy* (which Marx had read early in 1843), Feuerbach demonstrated that by proceeding from the Absolute Spirit to man, Hegel had inverted the true relation between thinking and reality, had placed 'man's essence outside man', or – as Marx was later to put it – Hegel had turned the process of thinking into 'an independent subject, the demiurge of the real world, and the real world is merely the external, phenomenal form of "the Idea".'

When Marx wrote that family and civil society were not 'products' of the state, he was protesting Hegel's idea of the monarch as the personification of reason, and his overlooking the fact that office-holders were individuals chosen according to birth, while the rest of society was treated like 'a stepmother' and denied participation in political life.

Marx applied what S. Avineri has called 'Feuerbach's transformative method' to Hegel's philosophy. Describing his own way with dialectics as the exact opposite of Hegel's, Marx was later to write that the 'mystification' created by Hegel stood everything on its head. 'To discover the rational kernel within the shell, it had to be turned right side up again.'[40]

In the late autumn of 1843, by the time Marx emerged from his months of seclusion at Kreuznach, he had also completed the greater part of his acerbic, not to say vitriolic, essay 'On the Jewish Question'.

In a glaring example of the hypocrisy which characterized Prussia's ruling establishment, King Friedrich Wilhelm IV had in 1841 issued the text of a draft law which proclaimed sanctimoniously that 'the Government recognizes a miraculous essence in the extraordinary historical development of the Jews, the causes for which have not been established', but went on to offer them – 50 years after their emancipation by the French Revolution – 'an adequate field of action which would not impinge on the Christian state' in the form of state-controlled medieval-type corporations 'on the model of Posen'. At the same time, the draft law stipulated that Jews would be 'excluded from military service, and self-evidently from offices and positions of honour for ever.'[41]

The proposed law came as a blow to the Jews, many of whom had fought as volunteers in Prussia's 'War of Liberation' against Napoleon, only to be debarred in the aftermath from academic, teaching and elective or government posts and from the magistracy. As late as 1842 the county of Wittgenstein, annexed by Prussia after the Vienna Congress, boasted a police ordinance outlawing 'heathens, Gypsies and Jews'. Although this was an extreme case, the position of the Jewish intelligentsia in Germany, who were denied civic equality unless they converted, was particularly tragic. Even Giacomo Meyerbeer, on whom the King of Prussia showered every favour though he refused to be baptized, lamented in 1840 in a letter to Heine:

> No *pommade Lyons* and no *griffe d'ours*, not even the bath of baptism
> can restore the tiny piece of foreskin that we were robbed of on the
> eighth day of our life; and he who does not bleed to death on the
> ninth day will bleed for it his whole life unto his death.[42]

Unexpectedly, the Rhenish Diet – itself clamouring for greater representation in the affairs of the Province – acceded in 1843 to insistent petitions by the Jews and granted them 'complete equality in civil and political matters'. One of the petitions had actually been forwarded to the Diet by Marx while he was still editor of the *Rheinische Zeitung*. He had done so in the expectation that it would be rejected, and not before explaining to Ruge that 'revolting though the Israelite religion is to me, embitterment against the government grows with every petition that is thrown out.'[43]

The King, whose undisguised intention – expressed in the very text of the proposed law – was 'to keep Jews and Judaism totally outside the state', overrode the vote of the Rhenish Diet simply by declaring that it had no competence in the matter. The struggle for the emancipation of the German Jews was to go on until 1869.

The 1842–43 debates in the Rhenish Diet had spilled over into the press. A couple of liberal newspapers favoured Jewish emancipation. Two prominent writers, however – Karl Hermes, the editor of the clerical *Kölnische Zeitung*, and Marx's former friend Dr Bauer – dismissed the very idea of it. Hermes argued that to grant unbaptized Jews equality offended the very nature of the Christian-Germanic state. In 1843 Bauer published a book, *Die Judenfrage*, in which he postulated in essence that Christianity could not give the Jews emancipation, nor did they deserve it, so long as both religions clung to their respective prejudices.

Marx's essay 'On the Jewish Question', written in the form of a review of Bauer's book, contained extensive quotations from it, which – as in the case of Hegel – he critized one by one in the polemical vein for which he was to become famous:

> The German Jews want emancipation. What sort of emancipation
> do they want? Civil, political emancipation.

> Bruno Bauer answers them: No one in Germany is politically emancipated. We ourselves are not free. How are we to liberate you?... If
> the Jew wants to be emancipated from the Christian state then he is
> demanding that the Christian state give up its religious prejudice.
> But does the Jew give up his religious prejudice?

Marx proposed to turn the question round: 'Does political emancipation have the right', he asked, 'to demand from the Jews the abolition of Judaism and from man the abolition of religion?' Having excerpted 50 pages of notes from a German translation of Thomas Hamilton's *Men and Manners in America*, and more pages from a book on the United States by Gustave de Beaumont, Marx used both of them to switch the debate from the theological aspect to the relation between religion and the state. In Prussia, he wrote,

> the Jew is in religious opposition to the state which acknowledges
> Christianity as its foundation. This state is a theologian ex professo...
> In the United States there is neither a state religion nor an officially
> proclaimed religion of the majority, nor the predominance of one
> faith over another. The state is foreign to all faiths... Nevertheless,
> North America is preeminently a land of religiosity as Beaumont,
> Tocqueville and Hamilton all assure us.[44]

But Marx distinguished between *political* and *human* emancipation. The separation of church and state, as in America, did not free man from religion. On the contrary, man was caught in a conflict between his double role as a *citoyen* (citizen) and as a *bourgeois* member of civil society.
As Marx put it,

> Man emancipates himself politically from religion by banishing it
> from the province of public law to that of private law. It [religion] is

831

no longer the spirit of the state where man behaves... as a species-being, in community with other men. It has become the spirit of civil society. And civil society, based on private property and revolving around commerce, saleable goods and the profit-motive, is 'the sphere of egoism' and makes for 'bellum omnium contra omnes, the war of all against all'. Political emancipation was thus not enough, for even the perfected political state is by its nature the species-life of man in opposition to his material life... Man leads a double life, a life in heaven and a life on earth... in the political community he regards himself as a communal being, and in civil society he is active as a private individual, regards other men as means, debases himself to a means and becomes a plaything of alien powers.[45]

The concept of man as a species-being (*Gattungswesen*) had been launched by Feuerbach. Unlike the brute animal, man is not only 'conscious of himself as an individual', but 'is in fact at once I and Thou: he can put himself in the place of another, for this reason, that to him his species, his essential nature, and not merely his individuality, is an object of thought.' Feuerbach, as mentioned, had taken the myth out of Hegel's 'Absolute Idea' by postulating that 'man created God in his own image'; paradoxically, however, man, miserable earthling that he was, had then fitted him out with transcendent attributes such as universal love, justice, eternity, and made God the object of his worship. Showing that Hegel had inverted subject and predicate, substituting illusion for the real world, Feuerbach's thesis was that all the learned Hegelian mumbo-jumbo about God and the Absolute Spirit 'alienated the essence of man from himself'.

Feuerbach's 'transformative method' offered Marx a whole new perspective, an optical revolution in which the world suddenly appeared to be standing upside down. Years later, recalling the 'liberating effect' of Feuerbach's *Essence of Christianity* on Germany's young intellectuals, Engels was to write that 'in one blow it... placed materialism back upon the throne... The spell was broken.'[46] For Marx, too, it was as if the mists had lifted. For the first time he beheld the world as it really was: a world, as he wrote in 'On The Jewish Question', in which 'man makes religion'.

Marx had yet to reach the conclusion that 'men make their history'. But in this essay he was on his way to adopting the materialist conception of history. Pointing out that the relation between man's particular religion and his citizenship was 'only one aspect of the universal secular contradiction between the political state and civil society', he wrote that 'man was not freed from religion – he received the freedom of religion. He was not freed from property – he received the freedom of property. He was not freed from the egoism of trade –

he received the freedom to engage in trade', in an atomized society in which 'private interests set every man against his fellow-man'.[47]

'On the Jewish Question' was written in two parts. Bauer had followed up his book (*Die Judenfrage*) with an article on 'The Capacity of Present-Day Jews and Christians to Become Free'.[48] This time he affirmed that, as between the Jewish and Christian religions, the latter was the superior one. For while 'the Christians' were essentially human and had only one step to make to 'dispense with religion altogether', the Jew – restricted by God's commandments and his way of life – was 'by his very essence not a human being, but a Jew.' The solution offered by Bauer to the Jews ran as follows: 'If they wish to become free the Jews should not embrace Christianity as such, but Christianity in dissolution, religion in dissolution, that is to say the Enlightenment, criticism, and its outcome – free humanity, or, in other words, atheism.'

At this point Marx gave the whole discussion a new turn by taking up 'the special position of Judaism in the enslaved world of today' and its relation to 'the emancipation of the world'. Suddenly he asked: 'What specific social element must be overcome in order to abolish Judaism?'

There, it was out. The 'revulsion' he felt for 'the Israelite religion', which he had recently mentioned to Ruge, must have burned in him for a long time, for it burst forth now in rapid-fire sentences:

> Let us consider the real secular Jew – not the Sabbath Jews, as Bauer does, but the everyday Jew. Let us not look for the Jew's secret in his religion: rather let us look for the secret of religion in the real Jew.
>
> What is the secular basis of Judaism? Practical need, self-interest.
>
> What is the secular cult of the Jew? Haggling. What is his secular God? Money.

Having looked for the 'specific *social* element' necessary to overcome 'in order to abolish Judaism', Marx had his pat answer ready. If the social basis which made huckstering, haggling and bargaining (Marx used the German word *Schacher*) possible were abolished, the Jew and 'his religious consciousness would vanish as an insipid haze in the vital air of society...'

> ... we recognize in Judaism the presence of a universal and contemporary anti-social element whose historical evolution – eagerly nurtured by the Jews in its harmful aspects – has arrived at its present peak, a peak at which it will inevitably disintegrate.
>
> The emancipation of the Jews is, in the last analysis, the emancipation of mankind from Judaism.

833

'Money', Marx wrote elsewhere in his essay,

> is the jealous god of Israel before whom no other god may stand... The Jew has emancipated himself in a Jewish way not only by acquiring financial power but also because through him and apart from him money has become a world power and the practical Jewish spirit has become the practical spirit of the Christian peoples... Judaism has managed to survive in Christian society and has even reached its highest level of development there. The Jew, who is a particular member of civil society, is only the particular manifestation of the Judaism of civil society.

In other words, Christians too practised haggling and hucksterism. Marx's attack was thus directed against capitalism and the hypocrisy of Christian civil society which had allowed itself to be corrupted and Judaized, as it were, by money-worship:

> Only under the rule of Christianity, which makes all national, natural, moral and theoretical relationships external to man, could civil society separate itself completely from political life, tear apart all the species-bonds of man, substitute egoism and selfish need for those bonds and dissolve the human world into a world of atomistic individuals confronting each other in enmity... Money debases all the gods of mankind and turns them into commodities... The view of nature which has grown up under the regime of private property and of money is an actual contempt for and practical degradation of nature... The species-relation itself, the relation between man and woman, etc., becomes a commercial object. Woman is put on the market.

For all this, and for 'the purely *formal* rites with which the world of self-interest surrounds itself', Marx blamed and condemned the Jews in a series of staccato pronouncements hurled at the world like truths that needed no proof:

> Civil society ceaselessly begets the Jew from its own entrails.

> What was the essential basis of the Jewish religion? Practical need, egoism.

> The chimerical nationality of the Jew is the nationality of the merchant, of the man in general.

> Christianity sprang from Judaism. It has now dissolved back into Judaism.

The Christian was from the very beginning the theorizing Jew…
Christianity is the sublime thought of Judaism and Judaism is the
vulgar application of Christianity. But this application could not
become universal until Christianity as perfected religion had theoretically completed the self-estrangement of man from himself and
from nature.

Only then could Judaism attain universal domination and turn alienated man and alienated nature into alienable, saleable objects subject
to the slavery of egoistic need and to the market.

Marx's essay concluded with the words: 'The social emancipation of the Jew is
the emancipation of society from Judaism.'[49]

In 1966, Arnold Künzli, a philosopher and Jungian psychologist teaching 'the
philosophy of politics' at Basle University, introduced an interesting theory
about the reasons which prompted Marx to launch his extraordinarily violent
diatribe against the Jews and Judaism. In Künzli's estimation, Marx wrote this
particular essay because Bauer's *Die Judenfrage* and his subsequent article on
the same subject offered Marx 'an excellent opportunity to dissociate himself
publicly from the Jews and Judaism'. Moreover, Künzli suggested, he solved
the problem of lending conviction to this proclamation by a stroke of genius
and a *coup de main* that 'integrated the Jewish Question in his new philosophical
system, the system whereby vanquishing Hegel, he would destroy the existing
world and create a new one in its place.'[50]

Indeed, 'On the Jewish Question', written after he had completed his book-
length 'Critique' of Hegel's doctrine of the state, represented a stage in Marx's
intellectual development and his progress towards Communism. Following this
essay, in which he embraced the notion that civil society means the alienation of
man from society and his 'species-being', Marx was to take up the cause of the
proletariat in his next essay, written after he left Germany.

It is as if he had to purge and exorcise his Jewishness and to flee that 'civil
society based on alienable private property, commerce, trade, profits' to which
his father, being a lawyer, also belonged before he could find shelter in a doctrine opposed to economic individualism.

29

Marx, Prometheus and 'Moses in Search of a People' (An Excursus)

Author's Note: An Excursus is usually printed at the end of a book. If I have departed from convention it is because Marx's angry, wholesale condemnation of the Jews and Judaism is so emotionally charged as to tell us little about the subject – or not much that would stand up in an objective court – but all the more revealing about Marx's personality at the point when he was about to discover the proletariat and to become the Marx of history. S.B.

Marx is believed to have finished his essay 'On the Jewish Question' in December 1843, after he had left Germany. It was to appear in February 1844, but was read by few people and evoked hardly any reactions. In the aftermath of Hitler and Stalin, however, it became the subject of a vast literature by Marxists and Marxian scholars, Jews and non-Jews, who had to decide the delicate and embarrassing question whether Marx was or was not an anti-Semite.

Towards the end of the 20th century Bruce Mazlish, in *The Meaning of Karl Marx*, took Marx's 'emancipation' from Judaism to mean 'eradification' and suggested that though Marx 'was not – repeat, not' – anything like 'a Nazi, or even an anti-Semite as such' and would probably have recoiled violently from the 'practice' of his thought, nevertheless his thought 'brought him close to the ravings of an Adolf Hitler' and did 'lend itself to misuse by later doers of deeds.'[1]

In November 1844, in a new polemic against Bauer titled *The Holy Family*, Marx repeated essentially the same views about Judaism in somewhat attenuated form. In this work, explicitly claiming to have solved the Jewish question, Marx used the German term *auflösen*, literally 'to dissolve'. It was in the Moscow version of this book, published in 1956, that this was translated as 'to abolish'. As Julius Carlebach pointed out in 1978, in one of the most comprehensive analyses of Marx's essay, Marx did not mean to provide 'a warrant for genocide'.[2]

Perhaps the most balanced view of the solution Marx may have entertained is that offered earlier by Edmund Silberner in his statement that what Marx had in mind was 'a painless liquidation of the Jews' in a 'humanely' emancipated society. 'Whether this utopian-millennial society is likely to be realized in the near future or in the more distant one... Whether the Jews themselves are inclined to be satisfied with this solution – or rather shall we say: dissolution – is of no importance at all: the verdict of history is unconditional and irrevocable.'[3]

That the 25-year-old Marx's essay on the Jews and Judaism was to an unusual degree emotionally coloured is evident from his resorting to such low imagery as suggesting that 'the monotheism of the Jew is in reality... a polytheism that makes even the lavatory an object of divine law.'[4] That he was inspired by a strong personal animus is further shown by his unusuallnegligent, theologically, historically and sociologically unfounded treatment of the subject.

In identifying egoistic, huckstering Jews and Judaism with bourgeois capitalism, Marx not only passed over the fact that the Jews had existed long before capitalism but carelessly, to put it mildly, falsified reality by omitting the fact that in his own day the majority of the Jews in Germany and the rest of Europe east of the Rhine, far from being Rothschilds or even traders, were engaged in lower-middle-class occupations or belonged to the poor. The greatest mass of them lived in abject misery in Tsarist Russia and Poland. The image of the Jews conveyed by Marx, however, was that all of them belonged to a single class – the 'exploiting' bourgeoisie.

Silberner has shown that 'Marx strongly objected when others used improper synonyms, and persisted in uncovering their "tricks".'[5] Most recently, in his book-length Hegel critique, he had in fact berated the master for deducing reality from abstract ideas.

Nowhere did Marx mention 'the Jewish people' or their history, or bother to explain their survival since antiquity until the day when he discussed 'the Jewish Question'. He accepted Hegel's description of the Jews as a once-glorious but particularist and redundant people made passive by their 'slavish' obedience to God. At the same time he accused them of seeking to dominate the world. Denying them any nationality, he gave them *grosso modo* a vague artificial identity, declaring 'the chimerical nationality of the Jew' to be 'the nationality of the merchant'.

Mazlish, noting in 1984 that 'between 1.5 and 2 billion people' in Russia, China and elsewhere – more than the number of those professing Christianity, Buddhism, and Islam – were at the time being dominated by regimes claiming their inspiration in one form or another from Marx, brought in the figure of Jesus and wrote: 'Like another Jew before him, who converted to a faith of his own making, Marx became the founder of a new, world-wide religion, named after him: Marxism, instead of Christianity (Jesus' name becoming Jesus Christ.)'[6]

In order to evaluate Marx's secular religion, Mazlish observed, it is not enough to read his texts: 'We have to comprehend his psychological commitments... which is why we must know the text of his life; and why it matters who Karl Marx was.' He went on to stress that any text by Marx discovered a long time after his death – such as his *Paris Manuscripts* – 'helps us to understand [him] in a new way... The same is true of his life... It was a real person Karl Marx, and not some spectre, who wrote Marx's works.'[7]

Marx not only publicly denounced Judaism but practically damned it to perdition. It is therefore all the more remarkable that so many writers should have seen in his moral fervour the spirit of the ancient Jewish prophets and the influence of 'an unbroken succession of rabbis'. But who were they? By the 1970s only a couple of his early ancestors, including two rabbis of Padua – Judah ben Eliezer Halevi Minz (1408–1506) and his successor, Meir Katzenellenbogen (1473–1565) – had been identified. Both were indeed great scholars, and the University of Padua counted Katzenellenbogen 'as one of the most illustrious minds of his age.'[8]

In 1988 the Karl Marx Study Centre in Trier cryptically named a certain 'Eliezer, born c. 1370' in Mainz as Marx's earliest hitherto known ancestor. But other than designating him as the father of the above-named Rabbi Minz (a name derived from Mainz), it shed little light on who Marx's forefathers were or what they represented.

As mentioned earlier, Karl Marx's paternal ancestry has recently been traced back to the 11th-century RASHI – an acronym for Rabbi Shlomo Itzhaki (c. 1040–1105) – one of the greatest rabbinical scholars and Bible exegetes of all time. This has been established after more than 200 years of research into a pedigree compiled in the 15th century by an ancestor of the distinguished Katzenellenbogen of Padua. From the time of the First Crusade and for nearly 800 years, Marx's forefathers laid down the law on issues affecting the religious as well as the worldly conduct and practices of many of Europe's Jewish communities, which, though segregated, enjoyed a fairly large degree of internal autonomy. A few of them achieved such influence with the Christian rulers of the day that they were granted the authority to impose capital punishment.

In short, Marx was the scion of a continuous line of scholars, philosophers, metaphysicians and spiritual rulers older than some of Europe's ruling dynasties – the Hohenzollerns, for example. And on his mother's side Marx was descended from the 16th-century Rabbi Judah Loew ('the Lion'), the legendary creator of the Golem of Prague, a homunculus or manikin he is said to have made out of clay and to have infused by a secret formula with a certain amount of intelligence.

It may be asked how this matters. Marx was cut off from his extraordinary intellectual heritage by his father's conversion and his own baptism at the age of 6. That might be the rub: Marx has been called 'the alienated man par excellence'.

To list 28 generations of Marx's ancestors from the 11th century on would take too much space. The following short summary, focusing on the most prominent figures among his previously unknown forebears, will complement the hitherto known 'text' of Marx's life and may shed new light on the real and conflicted person who wrote his works, including the rabid essay 'On the Jewish Question'.

- RASHI, born about the time Macbeth became king of Scotland, left his native Troyes, capital of the Champagne province of eastern France, before he was 20 for the Rhineland. After studying at the chief centres of Jewish learning at Worms – which to this day has a Raschistrasse – and at Mainz, he returned to Troyes when he was about 25.

  Around 1070, under Count Theobald I, one of the more benevolent rulers of the Champagne, he started a Talmudic yeshivah academy of his own. As his fame spread, gifted young men from among the altogether 7,000 Jews then living in the Franco-German lands came to study with him. Like many of the inhabitants of the Champagne province, RASHI owned a vineyard and lived off its produce; but besides running his academy, he made it his life-task to edit and elucidate the Old Testament and the Babylonian Talmud.

  The latter, especially, was a formidable task, for since its completion in Babylon about 500 C.E. the errors of copyists and a welter of juridical, ambivalent or mystical interpretations had – as described in the most recent study of RASHI[9] – rendered the authentic text of this huge collection of legal case-histories practically 'incomprehensible' to students.

  RASHI 'broke the code' of the Talmud text and cleared it of the accumulated chaff of centuries. To this day, all editions of the Old Testament and the Babylonian Talmud carry RASHI's lucid exposition and running commentary (which influenced subsequent rabbis and Bible exegetes, including not a few Christian scholars) in special type on the margin of the text.

  The monumental scale of his work, written by candlelight or dictated in his old age to one of his sons-in-law, may be gauged from the fact that re-editing the same Babylonian Talmud and updating it, with the help of computers, with the latest data on the culture of

Babylon at the time of its conception, took Adin Steinsalz, the first to attack the task since RASHI, more than 20 years.

• RASHI had no sons, but his three daughters were all learned women – a phenomenon perhaps not so remarkable, for between the 9th and 13th centuries Jewish women enjoyed a high social status,[10] and indeed there was a 15th-century female ancestor of Karl Marx who enjoyed a high scholarly reputation.

• In the second half of the 11th century RASHI's eldest daughter Jochebed married Meir ben Samuel of Ramerupt, so named after the hamlet north of Troyes, close by the Aube river, where he was born about 1060. A scholar known from contemporary literature as 'the Venerable', he gave the Kol Nidrei prayer recited on the eve of Yom Kippur its present-day form and died in 1135.

RASHI's second daughter, Miriam, married one of her father's most outstanding pupils, Rabbi Judah ben Nathan. A native of Falaise in Normandy, Judah spent the rest of his life at RASHI's academy at Troyes. When RASHI died in 1105, Judah completed his monumental Talmud commentary, but punctiliously marked the exact spot where RASHI had finished writing by inserting a note: 'Here our master ceased commenting. From here on it is the language of his pupil Judah ben Nathan.'[11]

• RASHI had 5 grandsons, whose additions and elaborations to his commentaries, known as *Tosaphot* (supplements), appear in all standard editions of the Talmud. Four of them were the offspring of Jochebed and Meir of Ramerupt. Their task and the one performed by subsequent Tosaphists in elucidating difficult Talmud passages has been compared to the work of the *glossatori* of Bologna who prepared the commentaries to the Roman *corpus juris* and to that of the Christian scholars who wrote the apparatus of *glossae* which became part of the standard version of the vulgate Bible throughout the medieval Christian-Latin world. While the line leading to Marx continued via a daughter of Jochebed's named Hannele, it is her better-known brothers – especially Samuel (1085–1158) and Jacob (1096–1171) – who furnish some picture of the 12th-century life and the background against which the third generation of RASHI's family pursued its scholastic activities.

Christian scholars at the time sometimes quoted opinions obtained from learned Jews – *ab erudissimis Hebreorum* – on matters of Old

Testament interpretation. In another form of intercourse, RASHI's grandson Samuel, acronymically known in literature as the RASHBaM (for Rabbi Shmuel bar Meir), took part in 12th-century disputations with Christian theologians. The RASHBaM, after studying under RASHI at Troyes, returned to his native Ramerupt, and he and his brother Jacob – popularly known as RABBENU TAM after the verse in Genesis describing Jacob the patriarch as *tam*, a man of integrity – turned that rural place into a Talmudic centre where gifted students of all classes, rich or poor, lived together. None of the rabbis then or for the next few centuries received any salary for acting as spiritual shepherds to their communities.

RASHI's fifth grandson, Rabbi Yom Tov of Falaise, another great Tosaphist who moved to Paris some time before he died in 1140, was a son of Miriam and Judah ben Nathan.

- In the 12th century a great-granddaughter of RASHI via Jochebed married Jehiel ben Matityahu, or Mattathias (Trèves) a surname here bracketed because the family had yet to adopt it. The RASHBaM and RABBENU TAM referred to this Jehiel, who lived in Paris and died there in 1189, as 'our close relative', and in one place as 'the bridegroom.'[12] The Trèves family was to provide 8 successive rabbis in various parts of France, including

- Mattathias V TRÈVES (c. 1335–87), Chief Rabbi of France. In the two centuries since the death of RASHI in 1105 the Talmud had been burned in Paris and the Jews had been several times expelled, readmitted, and expelled again. Thus it was that Mattathias was taken as a child to Spain. Raised and educated in Barcelona, he was in his late twenties when the Jews were recalled to France. The new king Charles IV, shortly after his accession in 1364, appointed him Chief Rabbi of Paris and eventually of all France. Mattathias Trèves founded a Talmudic yeshivah academy in Paris and the King exempted him and his family from wearing the Jew-badge. Upon his death, his son

- Johanan TRÈVES (born c. 1360) succeeded him as Chief Rabbi under Charles VI. Johanan, some of whose writings, *responsa* and rulings have survived, was married to a daughter of Manessier de Vessoul, the wealthy *procureur-général* and *commissaire* responsible for the taxes of the Jews of central and northern France. A sister of Johanan married one of their father's pupils,

- Samuel SPIRA, a name denoting that he originated from the German town of Speyer, which for some time after Charlemagne was known by the Roman name Spira. Indeed, this couple moved to Germany and settled not far from Speyer, at Heilbronn, where in the 15th century

- the 'Rabbiness' Miriam SPIRA (c. 1403–50), a great-granddaughter of the French Chief Rabbi Mattathias V Trèves and a highly educated woman, was recognized as an authority on Jewish law and achieved the singular distinction of being allowed to dispense it ('from behind a curtain') to advanced students at the Talmud academy of Heilbronn, headed by her father, R. Shlomo Spira, and after his death by Miriam's husband,

- R. Aaron I ben Nethanel LURIA (1400–60), who, though born in Italy, was the fourth descendant of a family whose founder – known for a long time only by the name of Samson (Shimshon) of Erfurt – had been Chief Rabbi of Thuringia. During one of the waves of persecutions, his grandson Nethanel had fled to Italy. Before settling in Mantua, he lived for a time in Loria, a small town west of Bassano in the Vicenza district. Nethanel's son Aaron, who was to become known in the *responsa* literature by the name of Luria (or Loria), went back to Germany, married the learned Miriam Spiro, and became Rabbi of Heilbronn (in succession to his father-in-law) and of Würzburg. The increasingly renowned Luria family kept records of its antecedents. It was in fact one of Aaron Luria's and his wife Miriam's sons,

- R. Johanan LURIA, the head of another academy in Alsace and author, among other homiletic works and some poetry, of a Kabbalistic commentary on the Old Testament – *Meshivat Nefesh*, now in the manuscript collection of Bodleian Library, Oxford University – who compiled a comprehensive, as well as a short, pedigree of his family, only to lose them, along with his fortune, either in the Burgundian War (1474–77) or in the Emperor Maximilian's 1499 war against the expanding Swiss Confederation, in both of which its victorious troops trampled and pillaged their way across Alsace.
In his old age Johanan Luria retired to ancient Worms. To his dying day in 1512 he is said to have mourned the loss of his two pedigrees, his grief over their disappearance 'exceeding that which he felt at the loss of his worldly possessions.'

He had, however, shown his 'short' pedigree to Joseph of Rosheim (1478–1554), well-known as the 'commander of all Jewry in the Holy Roman Empire' – an originally self-styled title later recognized by the Emperor Charles V – who reproduced its text in a short *pour-mémoire* of his meeting with R. Johanan.

In due course that *pour-mémoire* found its way to the Bodleian Library and in the 18th and 19th centuries three copies of that 'short' Luria pedigree actually appeared in print. They caused a spate of research into the Luria connection with RASHI which was beset from the beginning by the difficulty of identifying those of Johanan's forefathers who, living before the family adopted the surname Luria, were mentioned merely by their first names – *e.g.*, 'Samson of Erfurt'. Worse, by referring to this Samson as 'son of the Rabbiness Miriam' – while he was actually the paternal great-great-grand-father of her son Johanan – the pedigree created an insoluble riddle.

The documented story of how this and other conundrums that bedevilled research into the Luria family's descent from RASHI – research begun before Karl Marx was born and conducted without any reference to him – were only solved and its pedigree deciphered in 1988, will be found in the Appendix.

The direct line from RASHI to Karl Marx continued through a brother of the pedigree's author. This second son of the 'Rabbiness Miriam',

- R. Jehiel II ben Aaron I LURIA, was born in 1430 in Heilbronn. In the three centuries between 1350 and 1650, 90 German cities one after another expelled their Jews. Their expulsion from Mainz had driven Judah Halevi Minz at the age of 53 south to Italy, where by the time he died at 98 he had turned Padua into the chief centre of Jewish learning in Western Europe. In 1467, when the wave of persecutions hit Heilbronn, Jehiel Luria migrated east to become the first rabbi of Brisk (nowadays Brest-Litovsk) and its district in dynastically united Poland and Lithuania, whose Jagiellon rulers offered the newcomers not only asylum but autonomy, and invited the most capable of their leaders to improve the economy of their vast but undeveloped territories.

  By the time Jehiel Luria arrived there, an earlier arrival was serving as financial adviser to King Sigismund I. Jehiel married his daughter and, in the process of founding the Polish branch of the Lurias, fathered or became otherwise related to 5 of the most eminent Jewish scholars of the 15th and 16th centuries, three of whom were Marx's direct ancestors. The first was Jehiel's grandson, the previously identified

- R. Meir KATZENELLENBOGEN (1473–1565). Born in Prague, but taking his name from that of his father's small town of origin in Hesse, he went to complete his studies at the ageing Minz's Talmud academy in Padua. There, after adding Minz to Marx's family tree by marrying his granddaughter, he became the academy's rector in 1525. For the next 40 years he also headed the rabbinical court of the Republic of Venice. Honoured by non-Jews and Jews alike, his portrait hung in the Great Hall of Padua University and the synagogue reverently left his seat vacant for a century after his death.

The two others were Jehiel Luria's great-grandsons:

- R. Joseph ben Mordecai Gershon HACOHEN (1510–91), who, besides presiding for 50 years over a similar academy in the Polish capital of Cracow, achieved lasting fame with a volume of his collected *responsa* on economic and financial matters; and

- R. Moses ISSERLESS (1525–72), head of Cracow's rabbinical court, whose wide-ranging erudition and interest in such varied fields as Greek philosophy, Kabbalah and astronomy, were to earn him the soubriquet of 'the Maimonides of Polish Jewry'. The magnificent synagogue he built – one of the few in Poland to escape destruction by the Nazis in World War II – has been renovated by the Polish government, complete with the ancient plaque inscribed, 'Here Rabbi Moses Isserless conversed with God.'

- A third great-grandson of Jehiel, indirectly related to Marx, was R. Shlomo LURIA (1510–73). After heading the Talmud academy of Lublin, founded in 1451 by the mighty R. Shlomo SHAKHNA (who as Chief Rabbi of Lesser Poland had been given the right of capital punishment), he established his own academy in the same city. A stringent and dogmatic personality, to become renowned under an acronym as the MaHarSHaL of Lublin, he reproved Isserless for devoting time to philosophy and otherwise grazing in foreign fields. Isserless, however, compared his excursions into philosophy to refreshing walks in an 'orchard of wisdom' and would not give them up.

These 4 Luria forefathers of Karl Marx were no mere interpreters, but so-called 'decisors' – men who had a huge body of Talmudic jurisprudence and precedent before them and ruled like Chief Justices on questions and appeals on a wide variety of actual cases and practical matters submitted to them by rabbis from many parts of Europe. They were among the greatest codifiers of Jewish law. But as some of this was 1,700 years old even before their time – roughly, the age which saw the voyage of Columbus, the advent of Luther, the massacre of the Huguenots, the destruction of the Spanish Armada – the 'decisors' had to adapt it to new customs which had developed among a widely scattered people to devise creative solutions to new problems and situations facing them at every turn in a Christian world which was itself changing.

By their writ, millions of their people regulated their lives, their social conduct and group habits. While some rabbis in Europe's crowded ghettos withdrew into dry bookishness and Talmudic casuistry, Marx's ancestors, through centuries of continuous expulsions from Germany, rode the waves of forced migrations – of which their own lives afford a graphic picture, and during which countless other thousands perished or were reduced to beggary – with the resilience and resourcefulness of an intellectual elite. The *responsa* and legal opinions of these 4 Luria offspring, printed and reprinted with commentaries, additions, and local adaptations in a proliferating literature, have by now probably been more widely quoted than those of the great American jurist Oliver Wendell Holmes.

Finally, while the Polish branch of the Lurias started the spectacular efflorescence of Talmudic scholarship in Poland, the star of the most famous of all the Lurias was rising elsewhere: Isaac ben Solomon Luria, a great-grandson of Johanan (the author of the pedigree), was the legendary 16th-century mystic and Kabbalist whose theory of the creation of the universe in a cosmological drama of divine 'implosion' and explosion has lately aroused interest as a *sui generis* prefiguration of the big-bang theory of modern physics.

- A later ancestor of Karl Marx via the Luria line was Saul WAHL-KATZENELLENBOGEN (1541–1617), who, after studying languages and secular sciences at the University of Padua, went to Brest-Litovsk in Lithuania to complete his parallel rabbinical education there. Prince Mikolaj Kraysztof Radziwill, impressed by the young man's culture and his knowledge of worldly affairs, is said to have introduced him at court. In 1578 Poland's King Stephen Bathory leased him some sugar refineries as well as the salt pans in the Grand Duchy of Lithuania. Later he was appointed to farm the king's taxes and bridge tolls in the Brest-Litovsk region.

Saul Wahl-Katzenellenbogen appears in some sources as titular 'King of Poland' during the constitutional deadlock following Stephen Bathory's death in 1587, when the council of nobles was unable to decide between the two candidates to the succession – Sigismund III and Prince Maximilian of Prussia – and the Polish crown remained vacant. On Prince Radziwill's suggestion, the council is said to have unanimously voted to bestow it temporarily on Saul Wahl-Katzenellenbogen, as a trustworthy man who could be relied upon not to usurp the throne. Saul's interregnum, however, is said to have lasted only until the next day, when his recommendation that the Swedish-born Sigismund III be elected swayed the vote in the latter's favour.

Be that as it may, on 7 June 1589 King Sigismund raised him to the rank of a *servus regis*, exempting him and his lands and property from the jurisdiction of the courts and any other authority, and making him accountable to no one but his royal self. His name was to appear on all state papers signed by subsequent Polish kings confirming the wide autonomy granted the Jewish communities in the administration of their internal affairs.

- The marriage of Saul's granddaughter Nessla WAHL-KATZENELLEN-BOGEN with a great-grandson of the late scholar Joseph ben Mordecai Gershon Hacohen of Cracow brought together two branches of RASHI's Luria offspring.

- The grandson of this couple was Rabbi Aaron LVOV. While Marx's other ancestors had migrated from Germany to Poland or reached it via Padua, Aaron Lvov – named after the Polish city of his birth – moved in the other direction and settled temporarily in Trier. When its rabbi, Joseph Israel of Worms, died in 1682, Aaron Lvov succeeded him. Before moving on from Trier to Westhofen in Alsace in 1692, he married a daughter of the head of the famous rabbinical court of Frankfurt – Isaiah Chaim Ben Zwi Spira, a scion of the 15th-century 'Rabbiness Miriam' Spira descended from RASHI. Most subsequent rabbis of Trier were either of the Worms or the Lvov line, as the two families intermarried.

- The most prominent of them was Joshua Heschel Lvov. Born at Westhofen in 1692 and a scholar of European renown, he held the post in Trier for only 10 years (1723–33) before leaving it to serve for the next 40 as Chief Rabbi of the Duchy of Brandenburg-Ansbach. Finally, on the death in 1788 of the incumbent Moses Lvov, his son-in-law Mordecai Halevi Marx succeeded him as rabbi of Trier. He and his wife Hayya or Eva Lvov – a woman descended in two converging direct lines from RASHI – were the paternal grandparents of Karl Marx.

As for Karl Marx's maternal ancestors, the mystery surrounding them – which in 1893 elicited his daughter Eleanor's remark, 'Strange that my father's semi-Dutch parentage should be so little known' – has since been solved, but not entirely. For while late in the 20th century Heinz Monz, after yeoman research, established that Henrietta Pressburg's father, Isaac – who in 1785, at Nijmegen in Holland, married Nanette Cohen – was an offspring of Michael Simon Pressburg, the one-time Purveyor of Mint to three Habsburg emperors, little attention was paid to Nanette Cohen's ancestry.

Yet this grandmother of Karl Marx came of a well-known and distinguished family, and through her Marx was a direct descendant of the 'Exalted Rabbi' Judah Loew ('the Lion') of Prague – the legendary 16th-century creator of the Golem. This adds a couple of centuries as well as quite a bit of significance to the maternal lineage, besides more lustre to the otherwise fabulous family-tree of the founder of Marxism; yet to this day it is strangely overlooked. The Golem legend, which existed long before Judah Loew was born in 1525, has given this ancestor of Marx – sometimes called 'the miracle rabbi of Prague' and otherwise known as the MaHaRaL, a Hebrew acronym which in transposition would read OTRal, for 'Our Teacher Rabbi Loew' – a world-wide reputation associated with Kabbalism and magic, obscuring his importance as a scholar, moralist and philosopher of history.

But one more short round of genealogical tree-climbing is needed to connect the originally Hungarian Pressburg family with Nanette Cohen in Holland. Simon Pressburg, the Imperial Purveyor to the Habsburgs, had 6 sons and two daughters. One of the daughters married Lazarus van Geldern and was the great-grandmother of Heinrich Heine. The second son, Michael Lazarus Pressburg (1687–1756), lived intermittently in Vienna and Pressburg and was recognized by the Habsburg authorities as 'leader of the Trans-Danubian Jews', meaning those of Hungary, of which Pressburg (today's Bratislava) was the capital until 1784. A son of his, Hirsch 'Hijman' Pressburg, figures in the latest official genealogy of Karl Marx issued by the Marx

Study Centre in Trier as the putative father of Isaac Pressburg, Karl Marx's grandfather.

Dr Paul Jacobi of Jerusalem, however, noting that this otherwise well-known Hirsch 'Hijman'[13] never had a son by the name of Isaac Pressburg,[14] has identified Isaac's father as the son, not of Michael Lazarus Pressburg but of his youngest and more famous brother, Samuel Pressburg (1696–1762), the financial agent for the Russian Empress Anne, who for a time figured among Vienna's 10 richest Jews. Samuel Pressburg and his wife, Fraedchen, had 8 children. One of them was called Chaim, and sometimes Chaim-Hirsch, which – rendered as Hyman-Hirsch – may have caused his being confused with his cousin Hirsch 'Hijman'.

If this identification of Samuel and Fraedchen Pressburg as the grandparents of Isaac Pressburg is correct, then Karl Marx was the great-great-grandson of another early but well-known capitalist. For Fraedchen Pressburg was a granddaughter of Jost Liebman (c. 1640–1702), court jeweler to two Hohenzollern rulers, the Elector Frederick William of Brandenburg and Prussia's King Frederick I. He was, besides, one of the founders of Berlin's Jewish community.

The new identification also helps to explain what brought Marx's grandfather Isaac to Nijmegen in the Netherlands in 1775. He had an aunt (a daughter of Samuel and Fraedchen Pressburg) living in that town. Her husband, a former Chief Rabbi of Ansbach, was Meir Nymwegen (Nijmegen) Gomperz of Cleves, of that remarkable old family whose widespread branches, under such variant spellings as Gumpert, Gompers, Gompertz and Gomperz, were to produce Samuel Gompers (1850–1924), one of the founders of the American Federation of Labor and its president in 1886, besides a number of British mathematicians and inventors, Prussian bankers, physicians and rabbis and Austro-Hungarian industrialists, politicians and philosophers.

On 8 April 1785 Isaac Pressburg, 38, had married Nanette Cohen, the 21-year-old daughter of a distinguished Amsterdam rabbi. Nanette and Isaac had two sons and two daughters. While the eldest of them, Henriette Pressburg, born in September 1788, was to become the mother of Karl Marx, her sister Sophie was to marry the banker Lion Philips, one of the forefathers of the Philips electronics corporation. Marx's grandmother Nanette, to move to that branch of his family tree, was the daughter of Solomon David and Sarah Cohen, née Brandeis; and this Sarah came of a line of rabbis going back 7 generations to the 'Exalted' Rabbi Judah Loew, the MaHaRaL of Prague.

This line started when Loew's daughter Gittel married Simon Halevi Brandeis, head of Prague's rabbinical court until his death in 1635, and continued in the following uninterrupted order of male succession: Rabbi

Samuel Brandeis, who died prematurely in 1628; Simon Brandeis, head of Prague's Jewish community until his death in 1664; Jacob Halevi Brandeis, who moved from Prague to act as rabbi and judge to the communities of Koretz and Sorek in Byelorussia; Moses Halevi Brandeis, born at Sorek in 1685, who moved back to Fuerth in Germany and in 1733 became Chief Rabbi of Mainz, where he died in 1767; and Jacob II Halevi Brandeis, born at Fuerth and later Chief Rabbi of Darmstadt as well as Düsseldorf and its district. Before he died in 1774 he lived for a time at Ems in Holland. He was the father of Sarah Brandeis who married Amsterdam's Rabbi David Solomon Cohen. This couple's daughter Nanette was the grandmother of Karl Marx.

In short, 'the Exalted Rabbi' Judah Loew, the MaHaRaL of Prague, was Karl Marx's forefather 10 generations removed. And while some of Marx's maternal ancestors had been court purveyors and financiers, others in unbroken succession were well-known rabbis in several parts of Europe.

To this day a statue of the MaHaRaL of Prague, erected by the city fathers in 1917, can be seen at the entrance to the town hall of the Czech capital, the only statue of a rabbi in any capital. Stories of Rabbi Judah Loew's Golem haunting the rafters of Prague's medieval Altneuschul synagogue – often intervening to save not only the Jews, but the city itself from sundry catastrophes – so caught the popular imagination in Bohemia and Moravia that during World War II the Czech underground hid the statue from the Nazis and put it back in place after the war. The line where the statue was cut from its plinth remains visible to the naked eye.[15]

The MaHaRaL is said to have created a homunculus out of the common clay silicate covering the earth (*adamah*, in Hebrew) out of which Adam was made, and to have infused it with a rudimentary intelligence by putting the forbidden Name of God in its mouth. The mythical Golem has inspired novels, plays, poems and films.[16]

The Golem came to haunt Norbert Wiener, the father of modern cybernetics, when – declaring that 'the machine... is the modern counterpart of the Golem of the Rabbi of Prague' – he weighed the moral problems involved in man's ability to play God and design an electronic 'creature' or artifact.[17]

In 1988 a New York exhibition on the theme of the Golem occasioned such descriptions of the 'creature' fashioned by the MaHaRaL as 'a Frankenstein monster, a robot, a Caliban... an ur-version of artificial intelligence machines and computers.' The allegory of the MaHaRaL destroying his own Golem after it had served its purpose or run amok has been interpreted – by Gershom Scholem, among others – as a cautionary tale on man having to retain control of the powerful mechanical toys he creates.

Judah ben Bezalel Chaim Loew was the scion of a family as old as RASHI's, or older. A child prodigy, he studied Latin, read Plato and Aristotle, and besides running the affairs of the Jews of Moravia – of which he was Chief Rabbi from 1553 to 1573 – and later presiding over Prague's Talmudic academy, he became an outstanding mathematician. He was in touch with Tycho Brahe, the Danish astronomer (and discoverer of the 'Nova' planet), whom the Habsburg Emperor Rudolph II invited to Prague after clerical and other persecution forced him to abandon his famous Oranienborg observatory. In the event, the Emperor himself desired to meet the 'Exalted Rabbi'. It was a time of change. The Jews of Prague, enjoying a respite from expulsions and persecutions, took part in the general intellectual ferment.

'They say that recently a certain place' – America – 'has been found, called by them a New World, previously undiscovered,' Rabbi Judah Loew noted. With his blessing one of his disciples, David Gans, who had first studied in Poland under the great Isserless but had since become an astronomer, mathematician and historian, prepared certain charts for Tycho Brahe and worked with his young assistant, Johannes Kepler, the other genius who was to revolutionize the conception of the planetary system.

In February 1592 the Emperor invited Judah Loew to a private audience. The subject of their conversation has remained a mystery to this day,[18] unless it had something to do with the Emperor's interest in alchemy and Kabbalism and his known attempt in 1600 to obtain a copy of the Hebrew 'Book of Creation' (written some time between the 2nd and 6th centuries) dealing with the mysteries of the creation of the cosmos, from which so-called 'practical Kabbalists' later derived the secret formulae giving them the presumed ability to create an artificial man or woman, a Golem, robot or automaton.

As Byron Sherwin has noted in one of the latest studies of Judah Loew, the MaHaRaL never engaged in this type of Kabbalism. Rather, he was well-versed in theoretical Kabbalism, which seeks 'to reveal the concealed', that is, to penetrate the mysteries of the nature of God and the creation of the universe. His many works on ethics and social questions are strewn with 'anticipations' of a variety of later concepts, ranging from Kant's theory of the method of knowledge, through Hegel's dialectics, to 'Bergson's metaphysics and Einstein's physics.'[19]

While this is a large subject, it is the MaHaRaL's modernist philosophy of history and his concept of Messianic redemption that may be of interest and significance in relation to the theory of salvation his descendant Karl Marx was to proclaim 10 generations after him.

In 1599, long before Giambattista Vico, in his *Scienza Nuova* (1725), assigned to man any role in creating social or general history, Rabbi Judah

Loew – in a remarkably early affirmation of the principle of national self-determination – wrote that each nation has the right 'to be free' and that 'the subjection and oppression of one nation by another is against the proper order of reality.'[20]

As Martin Buber has pointed out, 'this short clear-cut statement of the basic rights of nations' – made two centuries before the French Revolution, and remarkable for its inclusive universality – 'has never been surpassed in power and clarity of expression.'[21]

Like Vico, the MaHaRaL of Prague in 1599 presupposed a divine world-order. But whereas Vico was unable to provide a cogent conception of history because nature remained the mystery of the Creator and man's actions had 'unintended consequences', the MaHaRaL's historical analysis logically connected all phenomena in a universal scheme subject to rational and unifying laws, as did the analyses to be undertaken more than two centuries later by Hegel and Marx. Unlike their absolute schemes, however, the MaHaRaL postulated that room must be allowed for the possibility of supra-rational laws intervening, causing what might appear to man as 'deviations'.

History was purposeful but timeless. Redemption was certain and predictable, but the MaHaRaL carefully kept the idea of the Messiah as impersonal as possible, defining it as 'a potentiality existing in the world.' Man, he wrote, 'was not created in his final perfection... He is born and exists in order to toil towards the actualization of his perfection... the realization of his potential.'

Messianic redemption, in short, awaited consummation in the dialectical process of history, but man could and must hasten its advent – speed up what Hegel, writing in a different context, was later to call 'God's work in history' – by striving for perfection and preparing the conditions for the new age, which would be 'of this world', but a world transformed into a new creation.

When postulating in 1599 that every nation was unique and entitled to its 'appropriate' territory, its language and freedom of worship, the MaHaRaL declared that any denial of these basic rights was 'a distortion' of the natural order of things. The Jews' exile from the land of Israel – the only land ever promised to a people and specifically designated as 'the place appropriate' to it – was certainly an anomalous disturbance of the world reality of a plurality of nations, and would not last forever. Exile itself, he argued dialectically, was thus 'the best proof and clear evidence' of Messianic redemption, when the disturbed world order would be repaired.

Was Karl Marx using a strikingly similar dialectic when he proclaimed that the proletariat, precisely because it was a totally 'dehumanized' class outside the sphere of civil society, was destined to bring about the universal and 'total redemption of humanity'? But how was it that this heir to an established Messianic tradition without compare turned so violently against his origins as to suppress all traces of it and to strike the people endowed from birth with a universalist outlook and a sense of history from his book of history? And with George Steiner suggesting that Marx might be called 'a false or parodistic Messiah',[22] and Bruce Mazlish in 1984 arguing that the baptized Marx received his Messianic urge in its Christian form, where does all this lead us?

It leads us to the inner drama of Marx's life. Mazlish called it his 'demonic-god-like [Promethean] struggle.' He quoted the following lines from a famous pamphlet published by Marx in 1852: 'Men make their own history, but they do not make it just as they please... but under circumstances directly found, given and transmitted from the past. The tradition of all the dead generations weighs like a heavy alp on the brain on the living.'

Commenting on these lines, Mazlish called Marx a man who made a historical revolution 'out of his personal nightmare'. But this alp or nightmare has been little explored because Marx himself imposed a complete taboo on it. Significantly, however, he concluded the passage from which Mazlish quoted the above lines with these words:

> The beginner who has learnt a new language always translates it back
> into his mother tongue, but having assimilated the spirit of the new
> language, he can produce freely in it only when he moves in it with-
> out remembering the old and forgets in it his ancestral tongue.[23]

Could it be that Karl Marx left a clue here to his own personality, the conflicted man and genius who thundered like Moses, prophesied like Isaiah, suffered like Job (or if you will, like Jesus), but who chose Prometheus for his role model?

Prometheus, Marx wrote, 'is the foremost saint and martyr in the philosopher's calendar,' and it is generally believed that he identified with him because Prometheus, whose name means 'Foresight', had the gift of prophecy, and because he defied the gods and brought light to the abodes of men. But there may be another reason as well. Marx, a scion of the legendary creator of the Golem, saw himself not only as the creator of a new world, but of a new type of man. 'The entire so-called history of the world is nothing but the begetting of man through labour,' he wrote, and 'Self-generation... is the only practical refutation of the theory of creation.' The world-redeeming role he assigned to the proletariat certainly depended for its fulfilment on the masses of the future, after a prolonged and bloody fight for power, undergoing a change of nature, abandoning all strife and switching to a peaceful life of collective bliss, like newly created men.

Prometheus, according to one tradition, not only stole fire from heaven, but also 'created the first men, fashioning them from potter's clay.'[24] He was thus, in one respect, a mythological counterpart of Marx's ancestor. Adopting him may have been one of Marx's ways of ridding himself of the 'tradition of all the dead generations' weighing like a heavy incubus on his brain. But this nightmare never left him even after he silenced, not to say cut out, his 'ancestral tongue' in order to prophesy the great collective society of the future in the 'new language' of philosophy, under the symbol of its 'saint and martyr,' Prometheus.

To crack his taboo and unravel his inner drama we must turn first to the sources and evidence adduced by Marx for his characterization of the Jews.

In Marx's characterization of the Jews, the catchword was 'egoism'. He took the cue for this from Feuerbach who, in *The Essence of Christianity*, had declared that – contrary to German Protestantism, in which 'Love makes man God', so that once man realizes that God is only a reflection of his inner nature he can embrace his fellow-men in universal love – 'the Israelite religion is the most narrow-hearted egoism... The Israelites opened to Nature only the gastric sense; their taste for Nature lay only in the palate; their consciousness of God in eating manna... The Israelites did not rise above the alimentary view of theology.'

In further passages, Feuerbach quoted Old Testament verses dealing with food, such as, 'When the seventy elders ascended the mountain with Moses, they saw God, and when they had seen God, they ate and drank.' Feuerbach's comment was, 'with them what the sight of the Supreme Being heightened was the appetite for food.'[25] In short, the gluttonous Jews were averse to the Greek cultivation of the arts and science.

When Marx wrote that the essential basis of the Jewish religion was 'practical need, egoism', or that the Jewish religion had only 'contempt for theory, for art, for history, for man as an end in himself', he was rehashing Feuerbach's thesis. Feuerbach in his turn had been influenced by his friend Friedrich Daumer, the renegade theologian who, even as the 'Damascus blood libel' was being exposed as a fabrication, was researching medieval legends for his book *Secrets of Christian Antiquity*, in which he claimed that not only the Jews but Christians too had practised human sacrifices as well as cannibalism.

Easter, Daumer wrote, 'was the solemn feast when the Semites sacrificed children'. But whereas the Hebrews early purified their cult by substituting animal sacrifices, 'one sect continued to perpetuate the ancient cannibalistic horrors.' Naming Jesus as the leader of this clandestine sect, Daumer claimed that at the Last Supper he became suspicious of Judas by the latter's disgust when offered a piece of human flesh. Proceeding to reveal the secret mystery of Christianity, Daumer stated that it was fundamentally based on 'human sacrifice to God, beginning with the immolation of the body of its own God on Golgotha, and infinitely continued by imitation in the holy communion.' In proof of Christian ritual murders, Daumer cited 'the innumerable child abductions in the Middle Ages... the mortification of the soul, the flesh, and the inquisitions imposed by orthodox faith, the gallows, auto-da-fés, Saint Bartholomew's Night, the witch-trials, the massacres of Jews, etc.'[26]

It is worth noting that by 1844 Feuerbach himself broke with Daumer, realizing that he was 'unreliable and the slave of a sick imagination'.[27] Marx, however, was presently to be carried away to the point of irrationality in accepting Daumer's pseudo-scientific scandal-book as incontestable truth. In 1847 in London he was to declare, in an address to the German Workers' Educational Society, 'that the supreme thing in Christianity is human sacrifice.' According to the minutes first published in English in 1976 in the *Collected Works of Marx and Engels*, he said:

> Daumer now proves in a recently published work that Christians really slaughtered men and at the Holy Supper ate human flesh and drank human blood. He finds here the explanation why the Romans, who tolerated all religious sects, persecuted the Christians, and why the Christians later destroyed the entire pagan literature directed against Christianity. Paul himself zealously argued against the admission to the Holy Supper of people who were not completely initiated into the mysteries. It is then also easy to explain where, for example, the relics of the 11,000 virgins came from.

Quoting further medieval 'documents' from Daumer's book, Marx, having earlier finished off the Jews and Judaism, hoped that Daumer's 'exposure' would administer the *coup de grâce* to Christianity and all religion:

> Human sacrifice was sacred and has really existed. Protestantism merely transferred it to the spiritual man and mitigated the thing a little. Hence there are more madmen among Protestants than in any other sect. This story, as presented in Daumer's work, deals Christianity the last blow; the question now is, what significance this has for us.[28]

But when he had published 'On The Jewish Question' three years before the London address, Marx still agreed with Bauer's view that Christianity was superior to Judaism. His assertion that the Jews had infested Christian society with the spirit of money-worship might have come from the mouth of his detested enemy, the anti-Semitic King Friedrich Wilhelm IV, who wrote that the Jews were 'soiling' the whole hierarchic order of the classes 'which alone constitutes the German nation'.

The most striking thing about Marx's 1844 essay is that neither then nor later, when he was to repeat its gist in *Das Kapital*, did he – the 'man of science' and 'infallible' prophet who tirelessly researched every subject on which he wrote – undertake an independent study of the Jews or their history past and present. In 1861, years after he wrote his essay, he was (in a letter to Engels) to call Ferdinand Lassalle 'the Jewish nigger' and to cap this crude epithet by quoting a dubious work on Egypt as proof that the biblical 'Exodus is nothing but the story told by Manetho about the expulsion from Egypt of "the people of lepers" headed by an Egyptian priest named Moses. Lazarus, the leper, is thus a prototype of the Jew and of Lazarus-Lassalle.'[29]

While uncritically accepting every anti-Jewish stereotype down the ages, Marx never bothered to adduce the slightest evidence to substantiate the charges be made in 'On The Jewish Question'. Rather, as Julius Carlebach observed, he took the description of the German philosophers 'from Kant to Bauer as absolutely authentic images of Jews and Judaism' and established 'the continuity of Jewish self-imposed slavery first to the law (Kant), then to God (Hegel), to egoism (Feuerbach) and money (Marx)'.

> The method by which Marx achieved the final reduction of the Jew... is the same he had employed so effectively... to turn Hegelianism, which was standing on its head, back on its feet. This was accomplished by reversing subject and predicate... If for Bruno Bauer the secret of the Jew is in his religion, then for Marx, the secret of the religion is in the Jew... If for Kant (and indeed for most of Christian Western Europe) the Jew is a trader, then for Marx *the trader is a Jew*.[30]

In his classic *Karl Marx*, first published in 1939, Isaiah Berlin wrote that the budding prophet of the proletariat – being determined to spare himself 'the sarcasms and insults, to which some of the notable Jews of his generation, Heine, Lassalle, Disraeli, were all their life a target' – simply 'decided to kill the Jewish problem once and for all so far as he was concerned.'[31]

If this, or the wish to declare 'himself before all the world not to be a Jew' – as Otto Rühle put it[32] – was his intention, it was to prove singularly unsuccessful. Most of his latter-day biographers, noting that 'egoism' is a leitmotif that pervades Marx's raillery against the Jews and Judaism, and recalling that he had himself been accused by his father of being 'more than an ordinary egoist', have traced his anti-Jewish outburst at the age of 25 to the fear of 'self-contempt' which, unusually for a 17-year-old, he had expressed in his high-school essay on choosing a vocation. Contrary to some early Marx biographers who focused on his transition to materialism in 'On the Jewish Question' and (in the words of Mazlish) dismissed his farrago of anti-Jewish 'nonsense and bad reasoning' as a regrettable 'lapse of sorts', the philosopher Nathan Rotenstreich, in 1959, was appalled by the striking 'infiltration of irrational, mythological elements into so rational a system as that of Marx when the subject was the problem of the Jews and their history'.[33] And an historian and Marx scholar like Mazlish, writing in 1984, stressed that – other influences aside – 'words such as "egoism" and "money" in Marx's writings' always had profound 'personal meanings for him'.[34]

Besides self-contempt, self-hate has been suggested as a prime source of the otherwise inexplicable intensity of Marx's Jew-hatred, which S.K. Padover described in his 1978 Marx biography as 'a canker which neither time nor experience ever eradicated from his soul'.[35] Murray Wolfson, too, called Marx's essay a 'catharsis of self-hate';[36] and Werner Blumenberg wrote that the gratuitous, often 'witless' aspersions cast by Marx on the Jews in his letters to Engels were 'first and foremost a typical example of "self-hate"'.[37]

The phenomenon of self-hate prevalent among some of Germany's baptized Jews in Marx's time has been the subject of a well-known clinical study by the philosopher Theodor Lessing.[38] Born in 1872 and baptized a Lutheran during his student days, Lessing himself experienced the mental torment of this peculiar malady of the spirit and traced it to the fundamental theme of sin and punishment running through the record of the Jews' historic experience in the Old Testament, in which great glories are regularly succeeded by dire disasters. The Jews, unable to live up to the high mission for which they were chosen, are always sinful, and always punished by the Lord. Unlike other peoples, the conscience-striken Jews often blamed themselves for their misfortunes and tended to see their tormentors as instruments of the Lord, a circumstance which their oppressors turned against them in order to absolve themselves of their own guilt in maltreating them.

On the heels of Voltaire's declaring the Jews to be 'contemptible', and Hegel's describing them as a 'reprobate' people, a new phenomenon began to affect those baptized Jews in Germany who, in their effort to enter society and become 'more German' than the Germans, adopted the negative image of Judaism of their cultural environment. The famous Rahel Levin wrote in 1795 that to be Jewish was 'one long bleeding'. Marx was not the only one to repeat Manetho's ancient fib about the Exodus of the 'Jewish lepers' from Pharaonic Egypt. Theodor Lessing cited a highly placed lady who confessed that 'no self-deception helps to wipe out the disgrace of my origin: it sticks to me like leprosy.'

Though Marx was baptized at the age of 6, he was a Jew by both 'descent and common consent', which meant that, try as he might to hide his Jewish origin or to suppress any reference to it, his friends and foes alike were to keep reminding him of it throughout his life. Shortly after his essay appeared in February 1844, Marx's friend Arnold Ruge was to call him 'an insolent Jew'; the Catholic party of the Rhineland regarded him as nothing else; Bakunin was to write, 'Herr Marx is a Hebrew... intolerant and absolutist like Jehovah, the Lord God of his ancestors.' And starting in 1850, with Richard Wagner, racial anti-Semitism began to appear in Germany. In an analogy to the Nibelungs, who, 'restlessly busy, like worms in a dead body, ransack the innards of the earth [for] the hard metals out of which the fateful ring that is to give them control of the world is to be fashioned', Wagner described the Jews both as 'worms swarming and crawling' over the decomposing body of German music and as the spooky, 'ghostly rulers of the world', controlling gold and the money markets. Violently opposed to their civic emancipation, he was eventually to warn his patron, Ludwig II of Bavaria, that they would cause the downfall (*Untergang*) of mankind.

Now that racism was added to religious prejudice and social ostracism, the German Jews were under attack from all sides. Some sensitive natures were driven to commit suicide. Marx, needless to say, was not one to seek that way out. He veiled himself in silence. In 1875, when Dr Eugen Dühring, undeterred by his awareness of Marx's own 'mockery' of Jews and Judaism, proceeded to assail both 'Jew Marx' and the 'Jewish Socialism' of 'Marx and Company' in a book on political economy,[39] Marx did not respond. Whether his own Jew-hatred rendered him defenceless against anti-Semitism and he was hoist with his own petard, he let Engels undertake the job of replying in his famous book known as *Anti-Dühring*; though Engels, reluctant to step into a minefield, shied away from any reference to the specific attack on Marx's Jewishness.

Marx himself never publicly returned to the Jewish problem, but was to rave all the more violently against Jews and Judaism in his private utterances. One of the many pejorative terms he applied to them – 'lice' – sounds as bad as 'worms'. Nonetheless, it should be stressed that, for all the outward similarity between Marx's 'The emancipation of the Jews is the emancipation of the world from Judaism' and Wagner's 'redemption by downfall', there is a world of difference between them, as there was between the two men.

Marx, raging against all religion, wanted primarily to see the social conditions which made men reach for the consolations of religion abolished. Once that happened, he speculated, the Jews would disappear. Wagner wanted the perdition of a race. On 12 November 1880, according to Cosima Wagner's Diaries, a 'highly agitated' Wagner told Hermann Levi – who at the command of Ludwig II of Bavaria, and over Wagner's objections, was to conduct the first performance of *Parsifal* – that 'as a Jew he has only to learn to die.' Wagner kept tormenting Levi, but Levi survived.

Not so Joseph Rubinstein, Wagner's court pianist. In 1872, Rubinstein, a highly impressionable and divided soul who was 23 years old, had read Wagner's *Jewry in Music*, and asked the composer in a pathetic letter to 'save' him from the 'curse' weighing upon his race. A pupil of Liszt, Rubinstein was allowed to join the so-called 'Nibelung Chancellery', which included more than a handful of talented Jewish musicians who worked indefatigably to help establish Wagner's fame. A year after Wagner's death in 1883, Rubinstein took the only course of redemption from the 'curse of Ahasuerus', the Eternal Wanderer, which Wagner left open to the Jews and killed himself.

Finally, the most famous case of self-hate (documented by the victim himself) was that of the young Austrian psychologist and philosopher Otto Weininger. In 1902, under the influence of Wagner and others, he converted to Christianity. The following year he caused a stir by publishing *Sex and Character*,[40] an anti-Semitic and anti-feminist book (it went into 18 editions within the next 15 years), in which he declared that the Jew was even worse than Woman, who was interested only in sexual pleasure, in procreation or prostitution, weakly depending on man for the definition of her identity. That same year, being caught in the double trap of his own philosophy of male superiority and the realization that there was no escape from his inferior Jewish being, Weininger killed himself at the age of 23.

Theodor Lessing had meanwhile returned to Judaism. His study of Jewish self-hate was published in 1930. In 1933, having been ousted from the university at which he had been lecturing, he was living at Marienbad in Czechoslovakia when he was assassinated by Nazis dispatched there for that purpose.[41]

'Hate, like love', Weininger had written in *Sex and Character*, 'is a phenomenon of projection: man only hates him who disturbingly reminds him of himself.' With that confession before him, Arnold Künzli in 1966 devoted much of his massive 800-page psychological analysis of Marx to a Jungian probe for the roots of his self-hate. The unusual thing about Künzli's undertaking is that he subjected to detailed investigation not only everything known about Marx's personality from his own or other utterances, but also the way it came to be reflected in his theories and works.

Noting that the 'inner hell' of Jewish self-hate could be both destructive and creative, Künzli concluded 'beyond any doubt' that both these forces burned like a 'mighty fire' in Marx. Besides the anti-Semitic climate of the age, he traced its roots primarily to Marx's hatred of his mother. It was she whose reluctance to be baptized caused the 'conversion conflict' that marred his childhood, and she who clung to her Jewish ways even after her formal conversion. It was with her that he quarreled over money, and whereas his siblings described her as the 'woeful mother' who, after his father's death and other misfortunes, devotedly looked after her family, to Marx she was the tight-fisted termagant who withheld what he regarded as his rightful inheritance. But for this abysmal alienation from his mother, Künzli argued, Marx's Jew-hatred would hardly have taken the extreme form it did, leading this 'born analyst and philosopher of history' high-handedly, crudely and in a non-empirical, superficially generalizing way to brand the Jews and Judaism as a sect whose 'jealous god is money' and whose cult is 'huckstering, practical need, self-interest'.

After Marx embraced Communism, capitalist 'oppressors' and 'exploiters' became his fair game, and by the mid-1850s, a decade or so after his essay 'On the Jewish Question', he was to indulge in the most vicious Jew-baiting in three articles about Europe's financial system published anonymously in the *New York Daily Tribune*. In the first two, he launched a concentrated attack on the wealth and power of the Rothschilds and the handful of Europe's other prominent Jewish bankers, at the same time questioning their stability. Insinuating that because of 'the Jewish aversion to land', the Rothschilds owned no great estates to fall back on in a crisis, and predicted that the Crimean War would lead to a financial crash caused by 'the representatives of this particular race'.

In the third article, under the title 'The Russian Loan' – concerning 50 million roubles floated by the House of Stieglitz in St Petersburg – he commented:

> Stieglitz is to [Tsar] Alexander what Rothschild is to [Austria's Emperor] Franz Joseph, what Fould is to [Emperor] Louis Napoleon. Thus we find every tyrant backed by a Jew, as is every pope by a Jesuit. In truth, the cravings of oppressors would be hopeless, and the practicability of war out of the question, if there were not an army of Jesuits to smother thought and a handful of Jews to ransack pockets.[42]

To hold 'a handful of Jews' responsible or co-responsible for making wars and tyranny possible might pass as a rhetorical hyperbole. But in Marx's description,

859

Stieglitz was the prototype 'of the freemasonry of Jews, which has existed in all ages.' His chief partner in negotiating the Russian loan, on the other hand (the Amsterdam banking house of the Hope family, who happened to be Gentiles), 'enjoy great prestige in Europe from their connections with the Dutch government and their reputation for great integrity and immense wealth.' But they lent to the Russian loan 'only the prestige of their name', Marx wrote, while 'the real work is done by the Jews and can only be done by them as they monopolize the machinery of the loan-mongering mysteries... In Amsterdam they number not fewer than 35,000, many of whom are engaged in this gambling and jobbing of securities.'

Ironically, Marx's own Van Geldern and Pressburg forefathers had once been 'Court Purveyors' and financiers to princes, kings and emperors. But compared to the wealth of Gentile bankers and captains of industry, the role of the 'handful' of prominent Jewish bankers in the development of modern capitalism was marginal. Even so, Marx had every right to attack them, were it not for the fact that – as Edmund Silberner has pointed out – he did not attack capitalists in general but chose to concentrate his assault on '"exploiters" who happen to be Jewish'.[43]

In writing of Amsterdam's 35,000 Jews, Marx, virtually condoning the Inquisition, went on to say that they included many of the worst descendants of the Jews whom Ferdinand and Isabella drove out of Spain, and who, after lingering a while in Portugal, were driven from there as well; not only that, but these men had 'their agents at Rotterdam, the Hague, Leyden, Harlem... and various other places in the Netherlands and surrounding German and French territories'. These agents, in their turn, were better informed than 'the smartest highwayman in the Abruzzi' about to rob 'a traveller's valise or pocket' about where to find 'loose capital'. They would create a market for the loan and at the same time pocket 17 million roubles of it. By writing in this vein and concluding 'Thus do these loans, which are a curse to the people, a ruin to the holders and a danger to the government, become a blessing to the houses of the children of Judah',[44] Marx, the historian of capitalism and otherwise a well-informed man, who cannot have been unaware of the poverty of the Jews in large parts of the Continent and of their pariah status in some, was carried away to the point of creating the impression that all the Jews were stock-jobbers and profiteers engaged in the 'loan-mongering' machinery which was ruining Europe.

But how could Marx identify 'the Jew' with the capitalist overlords, he who is supposed to have substituted the plight of the enslaved proletariat for that of the Jews? Künzli has offered the explanation that, to Marx, 'masters and slaves were but two forms of one and the same self-interest, one and the same alienation. The submissiveness of the slave is a symptom of the same evil as the lust for exploitation of the master. Seen in this light, the slave represents the capitalist system with its alienation just as well as the master.'

Künzli's analysis went on:

> The Jews could therefore be seen by Marx both as slaves and as masters. His hatred was directed at the slavishness in Judaism because it had done nothing to put an end to the egoism of bourgeois society and the bourgeois state; the masters he hated for doing everything to exploit the latter in their own interest.[45]

Baptized in childhood and uprooted from the 1,000-year-old tradition of his forefathers, Marx, according to Künzli, was practically 'born into a world of alienation'. Although his father Herschel-Heinrich had entered a protest against Prussia for forcing him to choose between conversion and his family's livelihood, he had ultimately given in. This may have unconsciously generated in the son when young a feeling of contempt both for the submissive of his Jewish father and for the religion he so easily discarded, along with an equally unconscious tendency towards revolutionary radicalism. The result was his ambition – corresponding to his own high valuation of himself – to assert 'to himself and the world' that he was 'a non-Jew and would not tread the path of submissiveness.' His mother, on the other hand, appeared to him as both 'slavish' and 'masterful' – the former because of her somewhat lacrimose religious devotion, and the latter because of her firm and prudent management of her household budget and financial resources. Künzli held that 'if Marx in public identified Judaism only with the masters, he did so precisely in order to appear in the eyes of the world as the no-longer-Jewish prophet of revolution',[46] while in his private anti-Semitic utterances he identified Judaism predominantly with the supposedly 'slavish-feminine' element in the Jewish soul, which represented everything that Marx rejected in his life.

In short, in Künzli's Jungian interpretation Judaism became Marx's 'shadow', the 'personal darkness' which, on the one hand, represents the 'rejected, repressed element of our psyche', and on the other, the 'general-human dark side in us... the structural readiness for the inferior and the dark in every man.'[46] To Künzli, Marx's anti-Semitic utterances were thus 'a mirror revealing the dark side of his soul.'[47] And since Marx's negative 'shadow' – self-hate – was a 'projective' phenomenon, Künzli used the simile of the cinema projector. Just as the latter magnifies a hundredfold the image appearing on the screen, so Marx's subconscious, maximizing the negative image of the 'egoistic, money-worshipping' Jews, demonized them as capitalist 'loanmongers' engaged practically in a world conspiracy which, as he wrote in the *New York Tribune*, had to be 'exposed and stigmatized'.

In the revised third edition of his Marx biography (1963), Isaiah Berlin wrote that 'his origin was a personal stigma which he was unable to avoid pointing out in others.'[49] If for the last few words one substitutes 'projecting on others', this is an anticipation of the theory Künzli was to amplify in 1966. And the longer he looked at the dark unconscious side of his subject, the more convinced he became that Marx himself 'essentially saw the world through the distorting mirror of his negative relation to his mother, his unconscious contempt for his father and his Jewish self-hate.'[50]

Many have felt that Marx loved humanity in the abstract or were struck by the contradiction between the rational thinker and the vehemence bordering on the irrational with which he attacked not only his rivals but even insignificant foes and former friends. But none has shown, as Künzli has don, quoting example after example, that the Marx who spent hours playing with his children and stopped to pat the head of every urchin he met on his London walks was the same Marx who, in his demonic youthful poems, had displayed a curious mixture of self-deification and self-hate:

> So a god has snatched from me my all
> In the curse and rack of Destiny.
> All his worlds are gone beyond recall!
> Nothing but revenge is left to me!
>
> On myself revenge I'll proudly wreak,
> On that being that enthroned Lord,
> Make my strength a patchwork of what's weak
> Leave my better self without reward!...

In other verses written at 19, he had looked down with disdain upon the world and mocked 'the stormy pilgrimage' of humankind, its 'frenzied race that never ceases towards the Indeterminate'. No, he would not join these 'wretched pigmy giants' who would all go down together with the rubble of a world condemned to destruction.[51]

By the time he was 25, he expressed his contempt – in 'On the Jewish Question' – for the 'human rubbish' ('*Menschenkehricht*') on which the Christian-German state was based. Marx may have loved the proletariat, but he despised people. 'Human rubbish' was not a one-time definition. In 1862, when he was 44, Marx began to describe people as 'rabble', as in a letter to Engels referring to his isolation and saying 'the portion of humanity which is here can kiss me... what rabble!' He went on using this term, but in his old age he returned to 'human rubbish', writing from his convalescence at St Aubins: 'The steamers with their cargo of fresh human rubbish have not yet arrived.'[52]

The contempt for humanity at large that Marx expressed when young could not but grow after the failure of the 1848 revolutions and the bitterness of life in exile. In a letter to Lassalle written in 1858 he confessed that, after the events of the past 10 years, 'contempt for the masses as for individuals has become the common wisdom of every rational being [English in original]... If I were to follow my inclination, I would wish that the superficial calm continue for some years as this is the best time for scientific projects.' But, he added, 'stormy times are imminent, and any such philistine thoughts will be swept away by the first storm.'[53] Künzli has seen this as an indication that Marx was conscious of the conflict between his 'contempt for the masses as for individuals' and his chosen vocation as the saviour of the masses. As a scholar, Marx would gladly retire to his study and his books and let mankind look after itself. But history with its 'storms' intervened every so often to remind him that the birth pangs of 'the new Communist man' were approaching and that it was his task to help history deliver it.

In Künzli's words, it is for the sake of and to the cause of this 'future man' that Marx sacrificed his private inclinations and overcame his contempt for the masses. Far from being animated by 'love thy neighbour' or interested in 'men in the here and now' – that is, in the human rubbish that he all too often 'despises, mocks and hates' – his concern and his love were for 'the great collective We of the future'.

To Marx, in Künzli's view, 'man was an eschatological concept', a concept which came to him unconsciously by way of his Jewish heritage. Künzli called Marx 'a rabbi, albeit a renegade rabbi, estranged from his God, his community and his people. He lived solipsistically only for his vocation.'[54]

For the other side of his demonic, demigod-like 'contempt for mankind' was a salvationist tendency. Both had appeared in Marx's school-leaving essay at 17 – the first in the curious observation that 'self-contempt is a serpent' that 'sucks out the heart's lifeblood and mixes it with the venom of hatred for humanity'; the second in his uncannily prefiguring his own life by opting for a martyr's crown and a vocation 'in which we can do most for humanity... then we experience no meagre, narrow, egoistic joy, but our own happiness belongs to millions... and our ashes will be moistened by the glowing tears of noble men.'

The turning point was the year 1843. In September, having begun the essay 'On the Jewish Question', he wrote a letter to Ruge setting out the guide-lines for the projected *German-French Yearbooks*, declaring that it must not 'hoist a

863

dogmatic banner', and least of all a Communist one. He ended the letter with several cryptic sentences showing a definite salvationist-apocalyptic tendency:

> The world has long entertained a dream of something which it only needs to become conscious of in order for it to possess it in reality.

> Our task is not to draw a sharp mental line between past and future but to complete the thought of the past...

> What is needed above all is a confession, and nothing more. To obtain forgiveness for its sins mankind needs only to declare them for what they are.[55]

Künzli has taken these lines as a strong indication that, from the beginning, Marx approached the social question as a 'salvationist problem of history'. He compares the Marx of 1843, locked up in his study at Kreuznach, to Moses, but 'a Moses in search of a people'. He was out to 'emancipate', i.e., to save mankind from the alienation caused by self-interest and egoism.

Robert Tucker, in a penetrating study,[56] seems to have been the first to point out that 'alienation' is a concept of modern psychiatry, denoting a loss of identity. Künzli went further. Arguing that both the curious 'confession' required by Marx of mankind for its sins to be forgiven and his seeking the answer to the social problem in history before he ever studied Socialist literature in earnest were essentially, if unconsciously, Jewish. Künzli summed up Marx's acute problem at this stage as follows: 'Marx was not only a German philosopher. He was also a Jew.' But as a Jew cut off from his people and community he was a stranger to himself, 'uncomfortable in his own skin... If he wanted to live on as a philosopher he had to overcome Hegel' – a 'titanic', Promethean task which he had forecast in his doctoral dissertation when writing that there was life 'after a total philosophy', but only for the man who, not content to spend his whole life lolling blissfully 'in his own skin', was bold enough to 'build a new world, become a world-creator by his own efforts.' But, as Künzli pointed out, Marx was facing 'the second great task of his life: If he wanted to live as a Jew and fulfil his vocation, he had to find his people...'[57]

But what were the 'sins' that mankind had to confess and atone for? Künzli went by the thesis that the Jews, as the 'chosen people' charged from the beginning of their nationhood with a transcendental mission of redemption, have an in-built collective sense of guilt for falling short of fulfilling it in the imperfect here and now; and that even Jewish 'self-hate' is, metaphysically speaking, nothing but a desperate 'wrangling with God' (as in the case of the innocent Job), or a rebellious refusal to share in the burden of the Jews' alone having to atone through age-long suffering and dispersal for the general sins of mankind.

Marx repressed this guilt and was eventually to project it on capitalism and its 'modes of production', magnifying its objective evils by piling on it all those with which he charged the Jews and 'Judaized' Christian civil society. Nowhere in his profuse public and private writings did Künzli find any sign of Marx's being aware that his own fateful alienation – from his family, his forefathers, his people and their collective destiny, and soon from his native Prussia – might be related to the theory of alienation which was to become a fundamental theme of his whole work.

The more stringent the taboo, however, which his Jewish self-hate imposed on the subject, the stronger became his unconscious tendency to conceive of alienation as a general human problem. His vocation was to redeem mankind from it, but as the Jewish way of redemption – through the intermediary of a people allied to God – was no longer his, he had to find another way to 'complete the task of the past' and to build a bridge to the future.

Giving an additional dimension to the basic question of the motive power that ultimately drove Marx (and, more specifically, why him of all the bourgeois Young Hegelians) to become the prophet of the proletariat at a time when few German philosophers had anything but contempt for 'the people', Künzli asked:

> How did the German philosopher Karl Marx, estranged from the German people by the anti-Semitism of the age and – by his introjection of this anti-Semitism – estranged from his own Jewish people as well, find his way back to a people? How did this Moses-Marx, who only lived in his books and had lost almost all contact with reality, find his Israel, or a substitute for it?

For an answer, Künzli went back to the three articles on 'The Prussian Wood-Theft Law' published by Marx in the late autumn of 1842. It will be remembered that in those articles the young editor of the *Rheinische Zeitung*, condemning the landowners who were trying to protect their rich forests and the timber industry, had protested, on behalf of the masses of the poor who had no political or social possessions, that the gathering of dead wood was a 'universal right of custom', the right of the poor in all lands.

Künzli focused on a passage in these articles in which Marx allegorically compared the poor to 'the dry thin branches' of cracked wood they were collecting. Just as in the forest 'firmly rooted' trees with mighty trunks absorbed all the air, sun and water, so society was divided into a privileged class of masters and a still raw one of dispossessed slaves who, like the dead wood in the

865

forest, were 'dissevered from organic life'. Nature, Marx wrote, treated the poor more humanely than the human lords and masters who denied them the right to dead wood.

Marx called the poor 'the elementary class of society'. In Künzli's view, this unusual characterization marked the discovery by the deracinated, fundamentally alienated Marx of 'a group of people entrapped in a "Jewish fate" without being Jews, and with whom he could identify without being a Jew. The discovery of poverty enabled Marx to fulfil his profoundly Jewish mission – the redemption of mankind – while remaining a non-Jew or even an anti-Jew.'[58]

Significantly, Marx had referred to Prussia's 'infamous materialism' in advising the Rhenish Diet to disregard 'civic reasoning and civic morality' when considering the Wood-Theft Law, and had called this 'a sin against the Holy Spirit of the nations and of mankind.' Just as universal poverty knew 'no fatherland', he had observed, 'so forest owners are the same in Kamchatka as in the Rhine province and particular interests know no fatherland and no province either'; and seeing the masters as both perpetrators of the sin of alienation and its victims, he blamed the state which sanctioned their privileges and set people against each other for presiding over a system that dehumanized man. Künzli deduced from this that Marx's primary social concern at this early stage on his road towards 'historic materialism' was not the material plight of 'the elementary class', the poor, but a redemptionist urge to abolish its alienation and the alienation of man in general. Marx had indeed concluded his third article on the Wood-Theft Law in November 1842 by stressing that what was at stake was 'the very salvation of mankind' (*'um die Menschen zu retten...'*).

In further support of his thesis, Künzli quoted the letter written by Marx in May 1843, in which – describing to Ruge 'the animal kingdom of politics' produced in Germany by 'centuries of barbarism... now standing before us as a complete system based on the principle of the dehumanized world' – he had observed on the theme of masters and slaves:

> The hereditary masters are the aim and goal of the entire [Prussian and German] society... They accept themselves as they are and place their feet... on the necks of the political animals who have no other vocation than to be their loyal attentive subjects [i.e., their slaves].

If one considers that the central historic experience of the Jews, told and retold in every generation, is the Exodus story of Moses revolting against the yoke of the Egyptian pharaohs and leading the Israelites 'from slavery to freedom', what is more natural than Künzli's suggestion that Marx – after accomplishing his task as a German philosopher by demonstrating that Prussia, far from being

866

the rational state glorified by Hegel, was actually the modern counterpart of Pharaonic Egypt, the land of servitude – turned to 'the second great task of his life... to find the people whom he would lead out of Hegel's Egypt-Prussia',[59] and upon discovering 'the elementary class of the poor', adopted it as the 'chosen class' to substitute for the 'chosen people'. In what other group of people, Künzli asked, 'could he find his personal experience of alienation so incarnated as to enable him... to speak, revolt, destroy, achieve power and announce salvation in its and his own name?'

While not diminishing Hegel's influence on him, Künzli submitted that when Marx, straight from his honeymoon, buried himself in his study with a mountain of history books, he did so primarily in order to find out to what extent the sufferings of the poor were historically relevant, and whether they had 'the salvationist potential' to serve as his medium for changing the world by translating philosophical theory into practice. His chosen vocation was to bring 'happiness to the millions' by putting an end to the alienation of man, but Marx, the 'new Moses', had to find out

> the transcendental meaning of the people of the poor. The questions which Marx addressed to history... were the same which his great rabbinical ancestors had addressed to the Talmud in their intense search for the transcendental meaning of the people of Israel.[60]

There have, of course, been dissenting voices, and at least one scholar has firmly stated that 'the eschatological element in Marx's thought... is a direct consequence of his Hegelian antecedents' and 'cannot be traced to any direct influence of the Judeo-Christian tradition as such, nor did it originate in Marx's ancestral background... Künzli begs the question by wholly disregarding the problem of the extent of Marx's own awareness of those specific Jewish traditions held responsible for his views.'[61]

This assertion ignores the fact that, however much or little Marx knew of his illustrious rabbinical forefathers, Künzli's theory was based on his conscious repression of it. To suggest that Marx had not the faintest idea of his ancestry shuns the question of how his youngest daughter Eleanor – who was born in London and never knew her grandparents – came to know of her paternal descent from 'an old Hungarian Jewish family driven by persecution to Holland... [they] became known by the name of Pressburg, really the name of the town from which they came', unless she had heard it from Marx himself. And Marx himself in 1850, Künzli pointed out, 6 years after publication of his essay damning the Jews, drew an astonishing parallel between 'the proletariat' and 'the people of Israel' when he wrote, in *The Class Struggles in France*: 'The present generation is like the Jews whom Moses led through the desert. Not only will it have to conquer a new world, it must also perish to make room for those men who will be fitted for a new world.'[62]

Künzli is not the only one who has dealt with Marx's total silence on the emergence of a Socialist Jewish proletariat under his very nose. The foundation in 1876 of a 'Social Revolutionary Association of Jewish Workers' in London, and its resolutions making 'a dramatic and clear distinction between the few exploiters and the many exploited among the Jews', were extensively reported in two consecutive issues of *Vpered*, a Russian-language periodical edited in London by the revolutionary Peter Lavrov. Marx, who took a keen interest in Russia at the time and had taught himself the language, kept 'an almost complete file' of this journal in his library.[63] He referred Engels to an item about Bakunin in the first of the two issues in question, and to a forthcoming article in the second. But he never wrote a word about either the nascent Jewish Socialism in London or about the revolutionary stirrings among the Jews in Russia reported in *Vpered*, just as he was to keep silent about the 1881–82 wave of anti-Jewish pogroms in Russia.

These events, as Julius Carlebach has observed, were 'relevant to the history of European society'. The fact that none of them drew a single comment from Marx, 'the man whose great interest and concern was to analyse and interpret the world in which he lived and the events that changed it', struck Carlebach as an odd and grave omission. Having some reservations about Künzli's posthumous Jungian analysis of Marx's self-hate, Carlebach preferred to speak of Marx's 'blockage' in matters concerning Jews and Judaism.[64]

But Carlebach had no explanation for Marx's 'irrational response' on the death of his wife to an obituary published by his son-in-law Charles Longuet in the Paris daily *La Justice*, of which he was the editor. On the basis of information he can have heard only from his wife or his mother-in-law, Longuet wrote that Jenny's marriage to Karl Marx had met with many prejudices, 'the strongest of which was race prejudice. It is known that the illustrious Socialist is of Jewish origin.' Whereupon a fuming Marx wrote Longuet a letter in which he called him a liar, a 'genius at invention', and asked him never to mention his name again.

To Künzli, the reason for Marx's disingenuous behaviour – forgetting in his rage that shortly before his marriage he had himself complained that the violent opposition of Jenny's 'pietist and aristocratic' relatives had nearly ruined her health – was obvious. So long as the Jew was a capitalist and nothing else, Künzli wrote, 'Marx could not possibly be a Jew.' This was his alibi in the eyes of the world, and any mention of his origin or of Jewish proletarians would have shaken his alibi as well as the system he built on the theory of Christian bourgeois society's being 'Judaized to the core'.

868

Significantly, it was left to Marx's own daughter Eleanor and to his closest, life-long associate – Engels – to correct, not to say disavow, Marx by acknowledging the existence of a Jewish proletariat. Engels did so in a letter published on 9 May 1890 in the Social-Democratic *Arbeiter-Zeitung*, in which he called it 'the most exploited and the most miserable' group on earth. Marx had been dead for 7 years when Engels stressed that, compared to the wealth of American Gentile millionaires, or that of England's landed gentry or even of the great Rhineland industrialists, Jewish wealth was negligible – a far cry from the 'universal domination' of which Marx had accused it, first in 'On the Jewish Question', and later in his articles in the *New York Daily Tribune*.

Later that year, on 21 October, Marx's daughter Eleanor ('Tussy'), in accepting an invitation to address a protest meeting in London's East End against the latest pogrom of Jews in Russia, wrote to the organizers that she would be very glad to speak 'at the meeting of Novbr. 1st, the more glad, that my Father was a Jew.'[65]

In the midst of the great 1888–89 wave of 'Match Girl' strikes, 10,000 tailoring workers in the East End had put down their needles for 6 weeks in a demand for a 72-hour week; and in January 1890, 4,000 Jewish workers belonging to 8 unions, including 'the Hebrew Cabinetmakers' Society; Stick and Cane Dressers' Union; International Furriers' Society... Tailors and Pressers' Union... United Cap-Makers' Society and International Journeymen Boot-finishers' Society',[66] had met to found the Federation of East London Labour Unions. Against this background, Engels's public letter is believed to have been written in an attempt to disabuse some of Germany's leading Socialists at the time of the idea that anti-Semitism, although reactionary, might be helpful in ultimately inciting the workers and groups of *petit bourgeois* against capitalists in general.

But what induced Eleanor Marx, who since the age of 17 had acted as her father's secretary, was present at his political discussions with his chief lieutenants, supervised the first English edition of *Das Kapital* and was a passionate believer in his ideas, to emphasize that her father was a Jew, thus not only undoing in 4 words – as her biographer Yvonne Kapp put it – 'the baptism of her paternal grandfather' but drawing the attention of the world to what her father tried all his life to conceal?

'Tussy' Marx was not only the most intellectually gifted of Marx's three daughters, but facially his very image and possessed by the same fiery temperament. Marx himself is reported to have said that his eldest daughter Jenny (called 'Jennychen' to distinguish her from her mother) 'is most like me, but Tussy... is me.' Her whole life revolved around him, and on his death, when she was 28, she became his literary executor (together with Engels), which provided her with the extraordinary activity of sorting and helping to publish his manu-scripts and spread his message of social revolution. She also became a political writer in her own right, an acclaimed public speaker and trade-union organizer, a co-founder with Engels of the Second International.

The daughters of forceful fathers often have serious problems. By her own confession, Marx caused Eleanor 'long miserable years' by stubbornly opposing her marriage to a French radical ex-count disowned by his family. 'Yet in spite of everything', she wrote, she and her father's 'love and trust in each other' remained the same. It was only 12 years after Marx's death, when Engels in turn was dying, that she learned to her shock and disbelief that Freddy Demuth, an uneducated working man, was not Engels's bastard son, but her own half-brother, the offspring of Marx and their maid-of-all-work.

No one can say for certain what made Eleanor – who on her mother's side was of Scottish-Prussian descent – declare that she felt 'drawn to the Jewish people', or what led her to seek her Jewish roots among the workers in White-chapel; or, for that matter, what prompted her, while doing her utmost to fulfil her father's legacy, proudly and more than once to assert, 'I am a Jewess' or invoke his rabbinical ancestry and reveal the highly vulnerable spot he tried to cover up by a self-imposed taboo on his origin.

In her biography of Tussy, Kapp wrote of 'the conflict that must have tor-mented Eleanor' as she tried to reconcile 'her father's anti-Semitic fleers with her own awakening pride in her Jewish antecedents, roused... by the poverty-stricken and persecuted working-class Jews – from all lands – to whom Marx had never given much thought.'[67]

Shortly after her father's death, Eleanor, in defiance of convention, had established a 'free love' ménage with the controversial Dr Edward Aveling, a married man of many parts – scientist, popular lecturer on Darwinism, radical Socialist and notorious libertine and philanderer – whom George Bernard Shaw was to feature in *The Doctor's Dilemma* as a 'scoundrel' and 'blackguard' in the character of Dubedat. She lived with Aveling for 14 years, but in 1898, stunned by a cruel act of deceit on his part, she committed suicide. In the opinion of Kapp, 'Aveling alone could not have destroyed Eleanor', and she counts her disappointment at the fact that 'the mainstream of the British working-class movement' of the time turned its back on Marxism among the complex factors and 'final despairs' that made her choose suicide.

But the life and death of the spirited and gifted Eleanor, who poured all the boundless energy and love previously reserved for her father into the fight for the exploited workers of every nationality and other humanitarian causes, raises the question whether Marx's personal alienation did not repeat itself with destructive effect in his daughter – or daughters (her sister Laura was to commit suicide 13 years after she did) – who lacked his ability to shape reality to his will.

As for Künzli's thesis that Marx, shortly after writing 'On the Jewish Question' in a paroxysm of self-hate, paradoxically and unconsciously substituted the suffering but 'chosen class' of the proletariat for the persecuted 'chosen people', Edmund Wilson had made the same analogy when he wrote that Marx transferred his righteous anger at 'the social disabilities of the Jew as well as the moral insight and the world vision derived from his religious tradition in all their formidable power to an imaginary proletariat';[68] and many others have seen in Marx a universal Jewish prophet in the tradition of Isaiah and Amos. It is, however, one thing to compare Marx metaphorically with Moses by writing, as Friedrich Heer did, that 'there blazed forth from this wanderer between two worlds, between mankind's farthest past and farthest future, such fires as accompanied the passage of Moses's people,'[69] and another to prove Marx's own self-identification with Moses by means of a Jungian analysis of his writings. And Carlebach has rightly warned against the dangers iin attempts 'to deduce a person's feelings, attitudes and expressions from such... uncorroborated evidence.'

To note that Künzli has given a fascinating portrait of Marx as the alienated man *par excellence*, a Faustian genius often driven by uncontrollable, intuitive or noumenal forces, is not to endorse his theory that Marx saw himself as a 'new Moses' or to accept his conclusion that the prophet of Communism – in spite of his life-long struggle to cancel the transcendental element connected with his origin and his salvationist vocation – was, dialectically speaking and against his will, a 'modern prophet of Israel'.

It was actually a time-bomb that Marx manufactured in 'On the Jewish Question'. Like many of his works, this essay was largely ignored during his lifetime. This changed early in the 20th century. Starting in 1920, Hitler began to refer approvingly to Marx's 'solution' to the Jewish question. The theme was taken up by other Nazi propagandists, not before Hitler had noted with delight that the 'scientific' demonstration of 'the danger of Judaism originates from none other than a Jew.'[70]

Shortly after the end of World War II, Edmund Silberner, examining the effect of Marx's anti-Jewish essay on modern Socialism in 'Was Marx an Anti-Semite?', observed that

> Hundreds of thousands, if not millions, of [Marx's] adepts read Zur Judenfrage with the same zeal and ardour as they read The Communist Manifesto. Those who accepted his views were much more

871

numerous than those who ventured to formulate objections or qualifications.

Challenging all theories that Marx was, unknowingly, 'a product of Judaism, a
continuator of its prophetic traditions, "the Isaiah of the capitalist society",' on
the grounds that they transgressed 'the limits of rigorous thinking', Silberner
pointed out that neither Marx's fanaticism nor his self-styled singleness of
purpose are exclusively Jewish attributes. 'Prophets of any nationality' must
possess these characteristics, 'or else there would be no prophets at all. Were
Fourier, Owen, or Lenin less imbued with [them] than Marx?'

Silbener's scholarly study, originally published in 1949, was later incorporated into his expanded work on *Socialists and the Jewish Question*. By then
(1962), with a new generation of Marxists, 'the Left', 'the new Left', etc., by
and large imbibing Marx's idea of the Jews as an 'anti-social element', he saw no
reason to change one of his original conclusions – which was that

> Willingly or not, Karl Marx contributed powerfully to provoke or
> to strengthen anti-Jewish prejudice among his Christian followers,
> and to estrange from their own people a good number of his Jew-
> ish admirers. He thus unquestionably holds one of the key posi-
> tions in what may, or rather must, be designated by a new but
> appropriate term as the anti-Semitic tradition of modern Social-
> ism.[71]

Of course Marx cannot be blamed for the crimes committed by Hitler or Stalin.
Words were his chief weapon. Wherever he took his inspiration, his anti-Jewish
essay is the most conspicuous, if not the only example, of his capacity to use
and misuse language, and at the same time a flagrant illustration of the ancient
adage of his forefathers that 'death and life are in the power of the tongue', i.e.,
the word.[72]

Künzli's wide-ranging study of Marx's inner character, which S.K. Padover
described as a 'solidly and meticulously documented account with a special
slant' (whereas Bruce Mazlish in 1984 regretted that it had not been translated
into English[73]), has not received the attention it deserves. Yet in the flood of
20th-century literature on Marx, it is precisely the special angle chosen by
Künzli that makes his book so interesting. After a century which has seen both
the apogee of Marxism and the end of the myth that all Marx's theses and theories were pure science, it was high time for an exploration of the extent to which
Marx's character and subjective being, or what Robert Tucker called his 'inner
drama', affected and was projected into the mighty social drama he conjured up
in his works.

This is precisely what Künzli has done in his 'slanted' but well-researched psychological study. Not all his findings are convincing, but he has illuminated much of the dark enigmatic side of Marx's contradictory personality, and we may refer to him again briefly whenever he has something plausible or relevant to say as we follow Marx's road from 'On the Jewish Question' to the discovery of the 'proletariat' and *The Communist Manifesto.*

30

The 'Doctors' Gather in Paris and Marx Discovers the 'Proletariat'

In 1843 and 1844 a group of extraordinary characters converged on Paris, City of Light and 'Mother of Revolutions', bustling with the creators of a new world and with 'men of gifts more varied, more striking and more articulate than at any time since the Renaissance.' The new arrivals, in non-chronological order, were Karl Marx, Moses Hess, Michael Bakunin, Friedrich Engels and Ferdinand Lassalle. Atheists, non-conformists and dissenters – each eager and burning to remake the world in his own image – they were all young.

Dr Karl Marx, slim, broad-shouldered and darkly handsome, was 25 when he arrived at the end of October 1843 with his wife Jenny, a stately beauty of 29 with an elaborate coiffure falling in curls and ringlets about her shoulders, who was 4 months pregnant. They made an attractive couple and were happy to have left the stale air of Germany behind them. 'The very air here breathes servitude,' Marx had written to Arnold Ruge in Paris, several weeks before his departure. Although he was about to become a man without a country, he had congratulated Ruge on the choice of Paris as the venue for the publication of the *German-French Yearbooks* and looked forward to the combined challenge of co-editing a periodical in the 'capital of the modern world' and the chance of having a platform for the dissemination of his ideas, not to mention the financial security that went with it.

It seemed an auspicious time to be launching the bilingual Yearbooks and effecting the planned fusion between advanced German philosophy and the political experience of the French Socialists. The curtain was about to rise on what Heine, in one of his 1842 articles in the Augsburg *Allgemeine Zeitung*, had called the great unpredictable 'duel' between the haves and the have-nots. Since then, in another article for that paper titled 'Communism, Philosophy and Clerisy' and datelined 15 June 1843, he had remarked that, though the disciples of Saint-Simon and Fourier kept raising the social question, they were 'not driven by any demoniac necessity'. They were not, he went on to predict,

> the predestined instruments whereby the supreme Will of Mankind
> will realize its mighty intentions. Sooner or later the scattered family

of Saint-Simon and the whole general staff of the Fourierists will join the growing army of Communists, lending their formulae to the brute force of necessity, and playing a role similar to that of the Fathers of the Church.[1]

Heine was far from enchanted by this prospect. As for Marx, he had only begun to study Communism. In his September letter he had advised Ruge that philosophy must join the practical 'battle' by engaging in 'the ruthless criticism of the existing order' without flinching from 'conflict with the powers that be'. This was the sole conclusion he had reached so far. But how to translate philosophical theory into practical politics and action?

'The question "where from?"' – he observed to Ruge – 'presents no problems, the question "where to" is a rich source of confusion.' In Paris, within two months of his arrival, Marx was to find the agent and the weapon with which to render philosophy capable of changing the reality of the world.

He had brought with him to Paris his essay 'On the Jewish Question' and the book-length manuscript of his earlier *Critique of Hegel's Philosophy of Right*. Though the *Critique* itself was not to be printed until long after his death, he began in December 1843, in Paris, to write an Introduction to it. It was in this Introduction, which came to only 14 pages and was published in the first issue of the *German-French Yearbooks*,[2] that Marx for the first time proclaimed the proletariat to be not only the 'universal class' but the class that would dissolve the existing world with all its forms of 'self-alienation'.

Having in the two earlier manuscripts challenged Hegel's view that the Prussian bureaucracy constituted a universal class, and repudiated the faith of his ancestors and all religion, the young Marx began his short Introduction to his Hegel Critique with the statement that in Germany 'the criticism of religion' – which was the premise of all criticism – had been 'essentially completed': 'Man, who looked for a superman in the fantastic reality of heaven and found nothing there but the reflection of himself, will no longer feel disposed to find the mere appearance of himself, the non-man [*Unmensch*]', and will turn away from this illusion to seek his true reality. Religion, Marx wrote, 'is only the illusory sun which revolves around man as long as he does not revolve around himself.' What he meant by this has been the subject of much interpretation, although he himself explained it quite well: 'He will think, act and fashion his reality like a man who has discarded his illusions and regained his senses' – that is, the present *Unmensch*, the non-man or non-being, living only a shadowy existence in the illusory consolation of religion, will assume his true human 'reality' as a man in the real world.

Continuing Feuerbach's idea that 'man makes religion, religion does not make man', Marx 'humanized' man, as it were, in this key passage. Before long he was to criticize history as well by writing that 'History does nothing... rather it is real living man who accomplishes all that... History is nothing but the activity of man pursuing his own goal.'[3]

Before that, in the Introduction to his Hegel Critique, he coined the famous phrase about religion being 'the opium of the people'. In a noteworthy passage he acknowledged that religion was both 'the expression of real suffering' and 'a protest' against it: 'Religion is the sigh of the oppressed creature, the heart of a heartless world and the soul of soulless conditions. It is the opium of the people.' His point was that to call on the people 'to give up their illusions about their condition is to call on them to give up a condition that requires illusions.'[4]

From religion Marx passed to history and philosophy. Postulating that once the other-worldly religious form of 'human self-alienation' had been unmasked, the task of history is to establish the 'truth of this world', he declared that

> the immediate *task of philosophy*, which is at the service of history...
> is to unmask self-alienation in its *unholy forms*. Thus the criticism of
> heaven turns into the criticism of earth, the *criticism of religion* into
> the *criticism of law* and the *criticism of theology* into the *criticism of politics*.[5]

Unlike Hegel's bureaucracy with its sectarian interests, the proletariat – according to Marx – had a truly universal character because its suffering was universal. But in investing the German proletariat with an historic role that would revolutionize not only their own country but change the world, Marx came up against a double problem. Politically, stagnant Germany had remained at the anachronistic level of absolutist France before the storming of the Bastille. 'According to the French calendar', Marx sadly observed, Germany had 'barely reached 1789, much less the vital centre of our present age... Fortunately, we Germans are not Scythians... We have lived our future history in thought, in *philosophy*. We are the *philosophical* contemporaries of the present.'[6]

The whole purpose of the *German-French Yearbooks* was to fuse philosophy, in which Germany was in advance of its time, with the French revolutionary spirit and political practice. But Germany's proletariat had yet to be born – hardly 4 per cent of its labour force were industrial workers – as Marx himself realized when he stated that 'the conditions and breeding ground' for a radical revolution 'appear to be lacking.' Young Marx, however, as Bruce Mazlish has observed, had his scenario for his world drama ready and was eager 'for a revolution now... A new actor – or hero – must be found.'[7]

That Marx was speaking of an 'imaginary proletariat' which in Germany had yet to be called into existence; that this new protagonist, besides possessing certain attributes, must be coached and rehearsed for the historic role assigned to him; and that at the same time the capitalist bourgeoisie must be painted in the worst colours to play its part as the villain of the piece – this is all evident from two passages in Marx's 'proletarian manifesto', as his Introduction has been called. In the first he wrote:

> If one class is to stand for the whole of society, then all the deficiencies of society must be concentrated in another class [*Stand*], one particular class must be the class which gives universal offence... one particular sphere of society must appear as the notorious crime of the whole of society, so that the liberation of this sphere appears as universal self-liberation.

To make things crystal clear, he added: 'If one class is to be the class of liberation *par excellence*, then another class must be the class of overt oppression.' The problem was that no class in Germany possessed 'the consistency, acuteness, courage and ruthlessness which would stamp it as the negative representative of society.' Bourgeois capitalism must therefore be cast – or 'demonized', as Künzli would say – into that role. But compounding the situation was another 'limitation' which Marx highlighted: all classes in Germany lacked both 'that breadth of spirit which identifies itself, if only for a moment, with the spirit of the people' and 'that genius which can raise material force to the level of political power, that revolutionary boldness which flings into the face of its adversary the defiant words: I am nothing and *I should be everything*.'[8]

This last dialectical phrase contains in a nutshell the solution whereby Marx – 'in one *salto mortale*', as he himself called it – proposed to override the 'limitations' standing in the way of a radical revolution in Germany for which the preconditions were lacking, and created, not to say invented, the 'proletariat' as a world-historic force. But what were the attributes of this 'class', born in his mind and yet to be formed, and why was it destined to emancipate the 'existing world' from all forms of 'self-alienation'? Marx put it all in question-and-answer form in the second relevant passage of the Introduction to his Critique of Hegel:

> So where is the positive possibility of a German emancipation?

> Our answer: In the formation of a class with radical chains, a class of civil society which is not a class of civil society, a class which is the dissolution of all classes, a sphere which has a universal character because of its universal suffering, and which lays claim to no *particular right*

877

because the wrong it suffers is not a *particular wrong* but *wrong in general*;... a sphere of society which cannot emancipate itself without emancipating itself from – and thereby emancipating – all the other spheres of society... and which can therefore redeem itself only through the total *redemption of humanity*.

This dissolution of society as a particular class is the *proletariat*.[9]

In a masterly application of the Hegelian process of thesis, negation (*Aufhebung*) and synthesis, Marx wrote that just as philosophy with its universal truth 'finds its *material* weapons in the proletariat', so the 'universal class' of the proletariat 'finds its intellectual weapons in philosophy... Philosophy cannot realize itself without transcending [*Aufhebung*] the proletariat, and the proletariat cannot transcend itself without the realization [*Verwirklichung*] of philosophy.'[10] The social group which stood in opposition to 'all the other spheres of society' and by its very 'universal' nature could not liberate itself from them except by their total dissolution and the liberation of the whole of mankind, would build a new society. In the final synthesis, philosophy itself would be absorbed in this process of its realization.

Marx concluded his Introduction with a series of apodictive sentences sounding like self-evident truths:

In Germany no form of bondage can be broken without breaking *all* forms of bondage. Germany, which is renowned for its *thoroughness*, cannot make a revolution unless it is a *thorough* one. *The emancipation of the German is the emancipation of mankind.*

The *head* of this emancipation is *philosophy*, its *heart* the proletariat...

When all the inner conditions are met, the *day of the German resurrection* will be heralded by the crowing of the Gallic cock.[11]

Needless to say, Germany was never to be 'emancipated' by its proletariat. The image of the 'Gallic cock' crowing revolution had first been used by Heine, who in his book on Ludwig Börne had also ironically hailed religion for sweetening 'the bitter cup of suffering mankind with a few drops of sleep-inducing spiritual opium.' Moses Hess, in an article published the previous summer in *Twenty-One Sheets from Switzerland*, had mentioned religion in a social context as helping to alleviate the despair of the dispossessed just as 'opium helps with painful illnesses'.[12]

But Marx's formulation was the more memorable one, and the spread of Marxist literature was to lend wings to his religion/opium equation. Neither the

German bourgeoisie nor Western capitalism were to be 'dissolved' or brought down by the working class, and where it nominally rose to power in Marxist disguise it was imposed from above – by Bolshevik putsch in Russia or elitist vanguards and military conquest elsewhere – and ended in the dictatorship of power groups. A time would come when Marx's speculative conception of the proletariat as the 'universal class' would appear to be inherently flawed, and its revolutionary potential, too, would prove a myth: 'Even the most committed Marxists' were ultimately to admit that 'the proletariat had not fulfilled Marx's expectations.'[13]

But that would be written in 1988, and no such doubts entered the mind of the young Marx who arrived in Paris at the end of October 1843. He was not yet a Communist. As recently as September, in his last letter from Germany to Ruge in Paris, he had advised his future co-editor that the *German-French Yearbooks* 'must not raise a dogmatic flag, quite the contrary. We should try to help the dogmatists to clarify their ideas. Communism, in particular, is a dogmatic abstraction.'[14]

In Paris that winter he made the first move from theory to practice. Whether he found in the proletariat a 'new actor' best suited to play the role of social catalyst in the fray of practical political action or was nouminously inspired by the example of Moses – who, as Künzli would insist, likewise had to 'form' a people out of a rabble demoralized by 'cruel bondage'[15] – his theoretical *salto mortale* was yet, in ways unforeseen by him, to have major consequences on the future of the world.

Waiting for Marx in Paris were Moses Hess, at 32 the eldest of the chief protagonists of the drama now beginning, and Arnold Ruge, who since his arrival in August 1843 had brought over his family from Dresden in a large omnibus packed 'with his wife, a brood of children and a huge calf's leg'.[16]

Hess, sent to Paris by the now defunct *Rheinische Zeitung* in December 1842, had been living there with his young mistress for nearly a year before Marx's arrival. Early initiated in the Marx-Ruge project and long acquainted with some of the leading Paris Socialists, Hess used his contacts to help Ruge enlist their collaboration on the *German-French Yearbooks*.

Their joint effort, however, had met with little success. The French had only a confused notion of the advances made by German philosophy and were in no hurry to enter into 'a scientific alliance' with it, as Marx called it. The social philosopher Leroux appalled Hess and Ruge by talking of the mystical Schelling as a 'rational realist'. Informed of this shortly before he was to leave Germany, Marx had turned to Feuerbach and asked the philosopher he admired to do 'a great service to our enterprise' by contributing an article that would 'expose' Schelling, who had cunningly enticed 'even a genius like Leroux' to believe that he was the author of a universal philosophy. Marx's idea was that, since Schelling provided Prussia with a philosophic justification for its policy, an attack on him would 'wound the Prussian Government to the quick.'

'The best Paris writers', Marx assured Feuerbach, had agreed to help forge the new 'Franco–German scientific alliance'.[17] But this was at best wishful thinking. For one by one, Leroux, Cabet, Blanc, Considérant and other advanced intellectuals declined to write for the *German–French Yearbooks*. Leroux was amiable, but regretted being busy with the invention of a simplified printing machine designed to enable anyone to produce illegal literature without risk of being traced by the police. Cabet, the utopian Communist, could not understand how philosophy had driven the Germans into atheism. The French radicals were anti-clerical, but atheism in France was a thing of the past. The Socialist Blanc raised the same point as Cabet; a disciple of Robespierre and the Jacobins, he was a deist. Considérant, the leader of the Fourierists and editor of *La Démocratie pacifique*, opposed violence and political agitation on principle, clinging to Fourier's idea that universal harmony would spread once the first phalansteries were established no matter where, in France, Russia or America. In short, the upshot of the discussions between Hess and Ruge and their French interlocutors was that the two parties realized with a shock how little they knew about each other's ideas and the trends in their respective countries.

Lamartine, the poet and Republican deputy, was the only one to promise to contribute to the Yearbooks. But to compound matters, it looked for a time as if the periodical would be short of German contributors as well. Herwegh had extended his prolonged Italian honeymoon and gone on to Ostend; Bakunin was somewhere in Switzerland, but could not be located; and Feuerbach, whom Marx had counted on to help to bring about the Franco-German alliance (Feuerbach having been the first to suggest the need for one), declined to provide the requested attack on Schelling, on the grounds that Marx's whole journalistic project was misconceived, a premature attempt to move from theory to practice 'before the theory has been perfected'. And this was indeed to prove the case.

Karl and Jenny Marx had some housing problems during their first two months in Paris. Ruge had proposed to them while they were still in Germany that they and his family and the two Herweghs – who finally turned up in November – should live in a communal household, a sort of Fourierist phalanstery, with the women sharing domestic duties. For this purpose he had actually rented two floors at 23 rue Vaneau, in a part of the Faubourg St Germain largely inhabited by Germans. But Herwegh's bride Emma would not hear of it. Born into a wealthy family, she had no wish to start her marital life by cooking, dish-washing, sewing and wiping the noses of Ruge's brood of children. She also wondered how a nice little Saxon woman like Frau Ruge could possibly get on with the highly intelligent and even more ambitious Madame Marx, who was far more knowledgeable than she.[18]

Herwegh needed little persuasion from his wife to take an elegant apartment in the rue Babt. Karl and Jenny moved in with the Ruges, but after a fortnight Jenny had had enough of the communal experiment and they moved from No. 23 to No. 31 rue Vaneau, only to move again in December to No. 38 in the same street, where they finally settled down.

Among other Germans living in the building was Germain Mäurer, a leader of the League of the Just. It was in that third household, where Jenny was in the spring to be delivered of their first daughter, that Marx wrote throughout January 1844 the Introduction in which, by what Robert Tucker has called a 'momentous metamorphosis', he turned the proletariat into 'the living, breathing, suffering expression of self-alienated humanity, and also its rebellious expression – alienated man in revolt against his condition.'[19]

The offices of the *German-French Yearbooks* were close by at 22 rue Vaneau where, in November and December 1843, even while moving house, Marx had been busy together with Ruge preparing their new journal. The first deadline set for its appearance was November 1843. But in November, Ruge went to Germany, and Marx felt he could not very well begin with the printing until his return. And there were other difficulties, as evident from a typically pugnacious letter Marx sent on 21 November to Fröbel, whose Zurich printshop served as a forwarding address for some of the manuscripts.

> Dear Friend, Your letter has just arrived, but with some very strange symptoms.
>
> 1) *Everything* which you say you enclosed is missing with the exception of *Engels's article*. This, however, is all in pieces and is therefore useless. It begins with No. 5.
> 2) The letters for Mäurer and myself were wrapped up in the enclosed envelope which is post-marked St. Louis. The few pages of Engels's article were in the same wrapper.
> 3) Mäurer's letter, which, like mine, I found open in the enclosed envelope, is also superscribed in a strange hand. I enclose the page with the writing.
>
> Hence there are only two possibilities. Either the *French* Government opened and seized your letters and your packet... However, we do not believe that the French Government has perpetrated the kind of infamy which so far only the Austrian Government has permitted itself...

If your Swiss people have perpetrated the infamy I will not only attack them in the *Réforme*, the *National*, the *Démocratie pacifique*, the *Siècle*, *Courrier*, *La Presse*, *Charivari*, *Commerce* and the *Revue indépendante*, but in the *Times* as well, and, if you wish, in a pamphlet written in French.

These pseudo-Republicans will have to learn that they are not dealing with young cowhands, or tailors' apprentices....

Please excuse this scraggy letter. I can't write for indignation.

Yours Marx.[20]

As if that and Ruge's tarrying in Germany were not enough, Lamartine had reneged on his promise to write for the Yearbooks, on the pretext that he did not wish to 'interfere' in German affairs; and from Frankfurt a discouraged Ruge, who had yet to return to Paris, had at the beginning of December advised Marx to write to Proudhon, 'otherwise we shall have to start without Frenchmen. Or, we should alert the women, [George] Sand and [Flora] Tristan. They are more radical than Louis Blanc and Lamartine.'[21]

Flora Tristan was the first writer to unite the struggle for women's emancipation with the class struggle. Daughter of a wealthy Peruvian landowner and a Frenchwoman, she lost her father when she was 6, and had thereafter led a strange, restless life, mostly destitute, brutalized when young by a French husband and bearing three children. In 1838, at the age of 35, she began her career as a writer on social questions with the publication of her *Travels of a Pariah*.

Marx was on his honeymoon when she declared in *Union Ouvrière* that now that the bourgeoisie had made itself 'both judge and party' over the rest of the nation, the task of the toiling masses was to unite and 'form the working class'. Whereas Marx was to arrive at Communism by way of abstract, *a priori* thinking, Flora Tristan was the first of the early Socialists to set the proletariat a common and clear objective developed from her own personal experience of its woes. Urging France's 7,000,000 factory hands to organize themselves both as a political party and as a trade union, she reckoned that if they collected voluntary membership dues of 2, 4 or 8 francs they would in one year raise a capital of up to 56 million francs and start acquiring 'real power'. She was also the first to postulate that the proletariat everywhere were bound by the same universal interests, and to proclaim the 'universal union of working men and women', without distinction of nationality, sex or other differences.

The Communist Manifesto was to define 'the immediate aim of the Communists' in terms not merely echoing but virtually identical with hers: 'Formation of the proletariat into a class, overthrow of the bourgeois supremacy, conquest of political power by the proletariat', and again: 'Organization of the proletarians into a class, and consequently into a political party.' And, needless to say, Marx and Engels were to inscribe on their banner the universality of the workers' movement and 'the common interests of the entire proletariat, independently of all nationality.'

Though there is no evidence that Marx acted on Ruge's advice and contacted Tristan, it is known that he was familiar with her writings. This raises the question why Marx and Engels were to mention her only once in all their writings, and then only briefly.

Long before Marx's arrival in Paris, Hess had made the acquaintance of Heine, who regarded him as an 'excellent political writer',[22] and of Dr Ewerbeck and Germain Mäurer, the two leaders of the League of the Just in the absence of Weitling. Although, as far as is known, Hess never joined the League, the Prussian Ambassador in Paris, von Arnim-Suckow, reported to Berlin in September 1843 that Hess was 'one of the chiefs of the Paris Communists and the ablest head among them.' Ever since his name had appeared in Bluntschli's alarming report in Switzerland, Hess had become the subject of increasing attention from the Prussian authorities. In October the Prussian Minister of the Interior had in fact suggested to Foreign Minister Von Bülow that he intervene with the French government with a view to arranging 'the expulsion of Hess from France so that – if he cannot be legally prosecuted and punished – he should at least be removed from the centre of the most subversive activities.'

Von Bülow replied that the French authorities would intervene only if they regarded Hess's activities as dangerous to themselves. Ambassador von Armin-Suckow had reported that an untroubled Hess had openly thanked Bluntschli for the popularity he had brought the German Communists in Paris, whose numbers – according to the ambassador – had indeed swelled by several hundred 'tailors, saddlers, cabinet-makers and mechanics' as well as the former *Republikanische deutsche Assoziation* joining their ranks en bloc.[23]

In his book *The European Triarchy*, Hess had pointed out that Hegel's abstract philosophy was 'incapable of producing a single historical deed', and had proposed a 'philosophy of action' differing from all previous philosophies of history in that 'from the two known dimensions of past and present it deduces a third unknown one, which is the future in the making... This changes the whole physiognomy of history.'[24]

This antedated by two years Marx's 1843 statement that it was philosophy's 'task to drag the old world into the full light of day and to give positive shape to the new one', as well as his decision later the same year to 'attempt to discover the new world through the critique of the old,'[25] which led by the end of

January 1844, when he completed the Introduction to his Critique of Hegel, to his annunciation of the proletariat as the emancipator of mankind.

When Marx observed in this revolutionary Introduction that the reactionary *status quo* in Germany was an anachronism corresponding to 1789 'by the French calendar', and that in Germany 'we are about to begin at the point where France and England are about to finish,' he was echoing the call for a synthesis of advanced German philosophy with French political practice and English economic experience which Hess had already advocated: 'The Germans must learn from the French, and the latter from the former, and both must learn from the English [for] England's institutions, being practical, generate progress.' If England figured little in Marx's Introduction that was because he did not know much about English conditions and institutions at the time.

Whereas Marx never mentioned 'Communism' in the Introduction and was not to adopt the term until the summer of 1844, Hess had devoted most of his time in 1843 – as he wrote in a letter to a friend – 'exclusively to the philosophical development of Communism'.[26] He had done so in numerous articles on the railway scandals, political corruption and growing social agitation in France published in the *Rheinische Zeitung* before its closure and later in other German newspapers and more especially in the notorious *Twenty-One Sheets from Switzerland*.

In November 1843, in a two-part article in Glasgow's *New Moral World*, Engels had informed its readers that, besides the 'popular' Communist movement led by Wilhelm Weitling, there was another 'philosophical party' in Germany which advocated Communism. Engels named Hess 'the first Communist of this party'. Explaining to his English readers that Hegel's masterly and 'unassailable' system could only be 'overthrown from within' by his own Young Hegelian disciples, Engels wrote that all that remained to be done was to prove to the German people 'that either all the philosophical efforts of the German nation, from Kant to Hegel, have been useless – worse than useless; or that they must end in Communism.'[27]

Having acknowledged Hess as the leader of German 'philosophical' Communism, Engels did not find it necessary to mention that Hess had been the first to assail the seemingly impregnable Hegelian system by writing as early as 1841 (in *The European Triarchy*) that Hegel's philosophy of history, limiting itself 'merely to presenting the past and the existing present as rational, has only accomplished half its task.'

Engels was more negligent when he wrote that Hegel's system could only be toppled 'from within'. For Hess, who expressly refused to join the Hegelian school, had shaken that system to its foundations from without. He had actually converted Engels to Communism by convincingly arguing that the Young

Hegelian movement, relying on purely *theoretical* criticism, faced the alternative of disintegrating or embracing Communism.

Without going into these subtleties in his article, Engels laid particular stress on the fact that German philosophical Communism was not inspired by 'either French or English' Communist ideas but stemmed 'from that philosophy which, in the last fifty years, Germany has been so proud of.'

As it happened, in the same month of 1843 when Engels's article was published in Glasgow, Marx in Paris had a brush with Hess, who had given Marx two essays for the first issue of the *Geman-French Yearbooks*. Marx accepted one for publication, but rejected the other – 'not without great *embarras des débats*', as he wrote to Fröbel on the 21st. Curiously, however, Hess was to be paid for this unpublished essay, which was titled 'On the Essence of Money'. It is hardly likely that Marx meant to hold it over for the second issue, for then there would have been little reason for an 'embarrassing' argument.

'On The Essence of Money' was to be published the following year in Darmstadt's *Rheinische Zeitung*. Although it was one of Hess's most important essays so far, Marx's decision not to include it in the first issue of his journal would not be worth mentioning were the essay not to become part of a protracted 20th-century debate about the 'philosophic' stage in Marx's move towards Communism, with some scholars arguing that in the famous *Economic and Philosophic Manuscripts* which Marx wrote in the second half of 1844 he borrowed heavily from Hess's essay.

Hess belonged to the small company of Marx's intimate friends during his first months in Paris. Jenny Marx was later to write that 'Hess and his wife' (actually his young mistress Sibyl Pesch, whom he was not to marry until 20 years later) belonged to their first social circle, which otherwise comprised 'principally Heine and Herwegh' and only two others: Dr Ewerbeck of the League of the Just and Adolphe de Ribbentrop, an aristocratic gentleman of whom little is known.[28]

Thus Hess and Marx saw a fair amount of each other during Marx's first winter in Paris. Hess was to leave the city in March 1844, but later rejoined Marx in Brussels, and for all their later discord the two men were to remain bound together in a mutually stimulating intellectual relationship which has been called nothing less than 'symbiotic'.

The first issue of the *German-French Yearbooks*, a double number in book-size format, finally came off the press at the end of February 1844. On his return from Germany, Ruge had fallen ill, leaving Marx to edit and produce the 237-page volume single-handed. This introduced a first strain in the relations between the two co-editors, but was nothing compared to Ruge's shock when he read Marx's Introduction to his Critique of Hegel. Ruge could not for the life of him see how the tiny, still invertebrate German proletariat was to become the 'emancipator' of mankind.

Ruge lacked Marx's revolutionary temperament. It was in fact hardly a year since Ruge, despairing of ever seeing a political change in Germany, had asserted that the docile German 'nation has no future, so what is the point of appealing to it?' It had taken three letters from Marx between March and September 1843, as well as a letter each from Bakunin and Feuerbach, for Ruge finally to announce his support of the 'new philosophers'.

Their whole correspondence with Ruge was reproduced in the first issue of the Yearbooks. The volume featured not a single French contributor, and the German ones were mostly émigrés, except for Feuerbach who – though he had actually refused to write anything for the new journal – was represented by his 1843 letter to Ruge, as was Bakunin, who had yet to turn up in Paris. Besides Marx's Introduction to his Hegel Critique and his virulent essay 'On the Jewish Question', the only noteworthy items were a 10-page article by Hess titled 'Letters from Paris' and two articles sent from Manchester by Engels. Other contributors were Dr Johann Jacoby, who recapitulated his trials and tribulations since he had dared to send his *Four Questions* to the King of Prussia; and Ferdinand C. Bernays, a talented journalist who had been expelled from Bavaria and had just been appointed one of the two editors of the German-language *Vorwärts!* founded in January in Paris.

The only internationally known contributors were Herwegh and Heine, each of whom was represented by a poem. Heine had volunteered his satirical and derisive 'Hymn of Praise' to King Ludwig, the art-loving, initially liberal but increasingly reactionary ruler of Bavaria who was later to be forced to abdicate in the wake of his affair with the notorious Lola Montez. Heine called the 'Hymn' 'the bloodiest thing I ever wrote', and the Bavarian customs officials are said to have 'doubled up with laughter' upon reading it. But Ruge was not amused to learn that the same officials had confiscated more than 200 copies of the *German-French Yearbooks* and that another 100 had been seized by police on a Rhine steamer. It is not known how many copies of the 1,000 printed were smuggled into Germany. Whereas the French press and public totally ignored the new publication, Metternich threatened booksellers handling it with severe punishment and Prussia issued warrants for the immediate arrest of Ruge, Marx, Heine and Bernays, to face charges of high treason and *lèse-majesté*, if they set foot on its soil.

In short, the *German-French Yearbooks* failed disastrously. Marx, having nothing to lose but his salary, was keen to continue publication. Ruge had his reservations about the first issue, feeling that 'Marx's epigrams' were simplistic and that 'but for my illness, I would have corrected some of his crudities.' But Ruge admired Marx's 'scholarly capacity' and the 'extraordinary intensity' he brought to his work. Having recently made a small fortune in railway shares, Ruge was considering ways of reviving the journal and moderating its tone, when Marx began to talk openly about Communism in March 1844. This was too much for Ruge. In coming round to the views of 'the new philosophers', Ruge had embraced only Marx's and Feuerbach's atheism, but not the proletariat. As for the Communists, they were to him a small sect of German manual workers who wished to repartition private property and whose ideas, as he wrote to Ludwig Feuerbach, 'lead to a police state and slavery.'

Once he had reached this conclusion, the hitherto hidden differences in character, outlook and temperament between the placid, merely reformist Ruge and the impetuous, revolutionary Marx suddenly came to the fore. Ruge discovered that Marx was righteous, cynical and arrogant. Marx, for his part, began to see in Ruge a narrow-minded 'bourgeois' publisher and 'bookseller'.

Financial quarrels aggravated what began as a seeming conflict of ideas. Marx kept pressing for his salary. Ruge claimed that whatever money had come in had gone 'in the first instance to Marx whose needs were the most urgent', and only then to the rest of the staff and contributors. Refusing to throw good money after bad, he further infuriated his former co-editor by giving him a quantity of unsold copies of the first issue of the *German-French Yearbook*, which was also the last, in repayment for anything he might still owe him.

Jenny was now pregnant, and she and Marx might have starved had not his wealthy Cologne friend Georg Jung sent him in mid-March 1,000 Thaler collected among former shareholders of the *Rheinische Zeitung*.

On 1 May 1844, Jenny gave birth to their first child. Jennychen, or 'Cleverface', as they soon nicknamed her, was a lovely but sickly infant, whose restlessness and frequent fevers gave her parents hardly a quiet moment.

In other respects, too, the spring of 1844 marked the beginning of a new phase in Marx's life and work during his stay in Paris. The first phase, during which he had been writing the Introduction, as well as editing and supervising the publication of the *German-French Yearbook*, was about to come to an end with his final break with Ruge one evening in late March.

In April he began to work on his *Economic and Philosophic Manuscripts*, which were to become famous a long time after his death as the *Paris Manuscripts*. A third phase was to begin in July, when Marx and his radical friends were to gain control of, and to obtain a new mouthpiece in, the Paris German-language *Vorwärts!* (Forward!).

887

This does not mean that the three periods, each marking in retrospect a stage in the development of Marx's ideas as reflected in his writings, did not overlap with one another or with personal events in his life, such as his attending an 'international democratic banquet' or his staying behind in Paris when Jenny was to depart on a summer-long visit to her mother in Germany together with their baby.

The 'international democratic' event, which opened on 23 March, had been organized by Ruge while he and Marx were still on speaking terms. One of the participants was Bakunin, who when last heard of in 1843 had been electrified by Weitling's notion of changing the world by apocalyptic means. Before turning up in Paris in March, Bakunin had spent the previous summer and autumn – a period that coincided with Weitling's trial and imprisonment – in quiet leisure as a guest of the singer Pescantini on the shore of Lake Geneva. From there he had moved on to Berne, only to flee Switzerland in February 1844, as he had earlier fled Dresden, for fear of the tsarist 'hawk'.

The fact that Bakunin's name had been linked in an official Swiss report with that of Weitling and the activities of the Paris-based Communist League of the Just had not escaped the notice of the authorities in St Petersburg. While Bakunin was enjoying his long Swiss holiday, they had approached his old father at Premukhino, notifying him of his son's activities and demanding that he order him to return to Russia. A pained Count Bakunin replied truthfully that he had no control over his intractable eldest son's actions.

At Berne the unsuspecting son had meanwhile run into another musical acquaintance from his days in Dresden. Adolph Reichel, a young pianist and composer, took not the slightest interest in politics. Bakunin's love of music had drawn them together. The two were still celebrating their reunion in Switzerland when, on 6 February 1844, the Russian Legation in Berne served Michael with an official summons to return home forthwith. He left Berne 24 hours later, departing for Brussels together with Reichel and his sister Mathilda, who had taken what turned out to be a lasting – if, needless to say, unrequited – fancy to Michael.

Bakunin had not been long in Brussels when he received an invitation from Vasily Botkin – his former pupil and the one-time rejected suitor for the hand of Michael's sister Alexandra – to visit Paris in March. On arrival, he was delighted to meet such old friends as Herwegh, who was now a rich member of Paris society; Count Grigori Tolstoy, a Russian landowner whom he had earlier met in Dresden; Ruge, the man who – besides keeping Bakunin out of debtor's prison by advancing him money against unauthorized bills drawn on Turgenev's bank account – had helped to make his international reputation by publishing his 1842 essay on *The Reaction in Germany*; and, naturally, Botkin.

Bakunin was surprised to learn that a letter he had addressed to Ruge, in which he had castigated Germany's 'castrated' intellectuals for living in the clouds and forgetting that revolution requires 'the force of the whole people', had appeared in the now defunct *German-French Yearbooks*; but not at all surprised that Botkin should have invited him to be a member of the Russian delegation at the international round table called by the ambitious Ruge for the purpose of co-ordinating and expanding 'democratic' propaganda.

And so it was that Bakunin, the rebel who had just defied Tsar Nicholas I by refusing an order to return to Russia, together with Botkin, the wealthy Moscow tea-merchant's son and literary critic, and Count Tolstoy – who employed serfs on his trans-Volga estates but spent much of his time abroad consorting with leading European liberals and maintained a large establishment in the elegant rue Mathurins – represented 'revolutionary' Russia at this unusual gathering of European thinkers and world reformers. Ruge, Marx and Ferdinand Bernays, the editor of *Vorwärts!*, made up the German delegation; and the French contingent, led by Pierre Leroux, included Félix Pyat and Louis Blanc, the future proponent of 'the state as an instrument for the liberation of the proletariat'.

Although nothing came of their confabulations, it was at this conference that Marx and Bakunin, the two great future antagonists, had the first occasion to study each other. Both were disappointed by the gradualist approach and limited aims of the French. Marx had read *The Reaction in Germany*, in which the Russian had stated that 'the passion for destruction is also a creative passion' and spoken of the complete annihilation of the present political and social world. And Bakunin, who stayed only a few days before going back to Brussels, was sufficiently impressed by Marx's erudition and the spirited atmosphere around him (not to mention the excitement of life in Paris) to return there within three months. By then, Marx made his headquarters at the editorial offices of *Vorwärts!* and Bakunin moved with his few possessions into an adjoining room; and the two were for months to rub shoulders almost daily in an amicable but argumentative and uneasy relationship.

On or about the evening of 26 March, a couple of days after the 'international' conference, Ruge paid a visit to Marx at his home. It was there that the tension between the two men came to a head when Ruge brought up certain rumours circulating about Herwegh. The dandyish poet, who only three months earlier had been presented by his young wife with a 'genuine boy' – as he proudly announced in a short bulletin-style note to his friends – was said to have started an affair with the comtesse Marie d'Agoult. Ruge, offended in his puritan feelings and indignant at the poet's self-indulgent and ostentatious way of life, was later to write to his mother that Herwegh was spending 'a fortune' on every kind of extravagance. According to the account Ruge gave his mother of the conversation with Marx,

> I expressed my outrage at Herwegh's way of life and his laziness. Carried away by my anger I several times called him a rascal and I said that when a man is married he ought to know what he is doing...

> Marx said nothing and took friendly leave of me. But the next day he wrote to me to say that 'Herwegh is a genius who has a great future before him'; he, Marx, was indignant that I called him a rascal, and that, on the contrary, my views about marriage were narrow-minded, philistine and lacking in humanity... He could no longer work with me as I was only interested in politics, whereas he was a Communist. We have not seen each other since.[29]

Herwegh was indeed a sybarite whose character and life-style, in the words of a contemporary, 'would have better fitted a Marquis of the Regency' than a revolutionary poet.[30] Marx was eventually to come round to Ruge's view of him. But until that happened Marx not only befriended him – even intervening with Heine to stop lampooning the vain poet – but also joined Herwegh on his social gallivantings with the rich and the famous in some of the foremost Paris salons.

In the spring of 1844, in letters to Feuerbach, Fröbel and others, Ruge launched the characterization of Marx as a fanatical, egomaniac, hate-filled genius, who called anyone daring to disagree with him by such pejorative terms as heretic, brute, bookseller, merchant, capitalist or bourgeois, and would not hesitate 'to flash his teeth and slaughter anyone standing in his way or obstructing him, the new Babeuf.' Perplexed by Marx's theoretical leap to Communism – which he had earlier declared to be one-sided and 'dogmatic' – Ruge called him a 'tricky Eulenspiegel of dialectics' who reserved to the last moment the privilege of declaring that 'black might as well be white', or vice-versa.[31]

Writing to Feuerbach on 15 May, Ruge acknowledged that Marx 'has by nature the aptitude of a scholar and writer,' but added that 'his critical talent sometimes degenerates into extravagant dialectic... When he has worked himself sick without going to bed for three or four nights he is at his most irritable and violent.'[32] Marx, for his part, was not one to forget or forgive. A 'great savant' with a big ego 'fully conscious of his own value', he treated his adversaries – as Herwegh was ultimately to find out – with a pitiless sarcasm, 'cold and cutting as the executioner's axe'.[33] Marx reserved for them every kind of vituperation in his linguistic arsenal, but he also had other weapons. Within months of his break with Ruge he published a sharp polemical article against him and 8 years later was to dip his pen in low ridicule and write of him: 'Ruge stands in the same relation to the German revolution as does a placard on certain street-corners: Here it is permitted to piss.'[34]

Professor Fröbel, the co-publisher of the *German-French Yearbooks*, was facing financial ruin in Switzerland and had been the first to withdraw his support from the journal. Neither he nor Ruge, nor even Herwegh with his radical rhetoric and poetic revolutionary flights, ever became Communists. Variously calling themselves 'democrats', liberals, or 'humanists', they were merely the stage-hands – some would say history's handmaidens – setting the props and pulpits for the main prophets of the ideological struggles that were to dominate much of the world in the 20th century.

31

The Relationship between the Prophet of Communism and the Poet who Foresaw its Horrors

When Karl and Jenny Marx arrived in Paris at the end of October 1843, Heine was on a visit to Germany. He returned on 16 December, and a few days later – perhaps as early as the 20th, and certainly before New Year's Day 1844 – he met Marx through the intermediary of Arnold Ruge, though some say it was Dr Ewerbeck who effected the introduction. Marx had been understandably eager to meet Heine, having grown up on his writings and modelled his own youthful poetry on Heine's *Book of Songs*.

Heine, for his part, was familiar with Marx's handling of the *Rheinische Zeitung*. He had praised its radical line to Laube in November 1842 and was curious to meet its fighting editor, now a refugee like himself. 'A young Titan with tousled hair', is how Marx in the flesh impressed Heine. In spite of the age difference between them – Marx was not yet 26, and Heine was almost 21 years older – the two had much in common and took to each other instantly. Both came from the same Rhineland which had had an unforgettable taste of the French liberties under Napoleon. Both had received a humanist education and hated Prussian clericalism and German nationalism. Both had a mordant wit. Heine, the elusive poet and rebel of all causes who moved lightly on 'all the dancing floors of philosophy', expressed his views in elegant, ironic verse and prose on all the 'battlefields' where freedom and justice were under attack. The scholarly Marx was more single-minded and purposive, but excelled in razor-sharp polemics.

For the next 6 months or so, and again in the autumn of 1844, the two saw each other frequently. There is no first-hand record of their conversations, but Marx's daughter Eleanor later heard from her parents that 'there was a time when Heine came to see them daily' to 'read them his verse', and that Marx often even helped him to 'correct and polish it to perfection'. But they obviously had much else to talk about – whether French politics and personalities, Heine's recent visit to Germany, or Bonn University, where each had spent part of his student days.

According to an unverifiable story, whenever Marx came to Heine's place the frivolous Mathilde, unable to follow their German jokes or their talk about philosophy and literature, would set out with a friend of hers for the boulevards.

But, these second-hand reports aside, there is every evidence that theirs was a genuine friendship based on respect for each other's genius.

Heine was already a European *éminence*. Marx in Paris was at the juncture of becoming the Marx of history. It was a crucial time 'in the lives of both men, one with common determinants in the rising level of German repression.' Their relationship thus had 'an inescapable epochal dimension.'[1] So epochal, one may add, that more than a hundred years later it was to generate a trend to maximize Marx's influence on Heine. In the Preface to the French version of his *Confessions* (*Geständnisse*) – published ahead of the German edition – Heine, speaking of Marx and the other Communist agitators, was to write:

> The more or less recondite leaders of the German Communists are great logicians... They are undoubtedly the most capable heads and the most energetic characters in Germany. These doctors of revolution and their ruthlessly determined disciples are the only men in Germany who are truly alive, and it is to them, I fear, that the future belongs.[2]

That last sentence appeared in the German original of the *Confessions* without the words 'I fear' (*je crains*). On the basis of this and other utterances, including some of his radical poems, a flood of literature in the 1960s and '70s in Germany (and more especially in the then Soviet-allied East German Republic) but also elsewhere, sought to demonstrate that, under the force of Marx's iron logic, Heine embraced Communism.

Although Heine was eventually to refer to 'my thick-headed friend Marx' as a 'godless self-god', some 20th-century authors were to go so far as to declare that what Marx 'loved' in Heine was the forerunner 'who, like some John the Baptist, had announced the new Saviour, the Proletariat.'[3] The truth is that Heine was indeed a forerunner, but not in the sense of the literature mentioned. As early as 1823, in his *William Ratcliff: A Tragedy*, he had forecast the class-struggle by writing of two fiercely warring nations – 'the sated and the hungry'. In 1828, on the battlefield of Marengo, he had predicted the brewing social storms and clash of ideologies in the famous phrase: 'There are no more nations in Europe – only parties!' Karl Marx was only 10 at the time. He was still in his teens when Heine had proclaimed the people's 'divine right to bread'.

Heine had also been the first to detect the revolutionary kernel in Hegel's dialectic, which Marx had recently made it his job to uncover in detail by standing Hegel upside down. Marx not only adopted Heine's opium/religion equation or his 'Gallic cock' as a symbol of revolution, but the seeds for some of the ideas he launched in his new 'proletarian manifesto' – the Introduction to his Hegel Critique – had been sown by Heine years earlier.

When Marx wrote in the Introduction that Germany, politically backward, had 'barely reached 1789' and that its advanced philosophy had lived 'in thought' developments which its history had missed since the fall of the Bastille, he was echoing an idea Heine had put on paper as far back as 1831. That year, Heine had written in his Introduction to *Kahldorf on the Aristocracy* that German philosophy – with Kant as its Robespierre, Fichte its Napoleon and Hegel its duc d'Orléans – had 'dreamed' its way through all the phases of the French Revolution. He had further developed this parallel in the mid-1830s in his *History of Religion and Philosophy in Germany*.

As Nigel Reeves has observed, 'Heine's despair at modern man's *Zerrissenheit* (alienation) fully anticipated Marx's anger at industrial man's alienation.'[4] Heine's epigram, 'Thought precedes action, as lightning precedes thunder', encapsulating the idea of an explosive revolutionary potential hidden in philosophy, antedated by some 10 years Marx's dictum: 'Revolution has its start in the philosopher's brain.'

All things considered, one may justifiably say that over a long period Heine provided Marx with more intellectual stimulation and direct or indirect inspiration than the other way round. In fact, as early as 1956, even as the hullabaloo about Heine's having succumbed to Marx's superior and overpowering logic was beginning to build up, William Rose pointed out that 'Marx's doctrine, which was still in process of formulation' during their association in 1844, 'had no influence whatsoever on Heine's thought either then or later.' Nor have more recent authorities on Heine been able 'to detect any new ideas or perspectives that [he] might have obtained from Marx.'[5]

Within less than a year of the publication of his *Confessions* Heine, in the French Preface to *Lutèce* (*Lutezia*), stressed once again that his earlier 'admission that the future belongs to Communism' had been made 'in an agony of dread and fear... I think with horror of the time when these gloomy iconoclasts will come to power',[6] and went on to conjure up a prophetic picture of how the horny hands of 'the victorious proletariat' would 'smash the marble statues of beauty' and, caring little for poetry and the works of genius (including his own verses), would reduce society to a bleating herd living on the same 'Spartan black soup'.

Still, there is no gainsaying the fact that in the same Preface to *Lutèce* he also wrote:

> Yet I admit openly that this same Communism, so hostile to all my interests and inclinations, exercises an irresistible fascination on my soul that leaves me defenceless...
>
> A terrible syllogism holds me in its grip, and if I am unable to refute the premise 'that every man has the right to eat', then I am forced to

submit to all its consequences... I see all the demons of truth dancing triumphantly around me, and at length the generosity of despair takes possession of my heart and I cry out:

'For long this old society has been judged and condemned, let justice be done! Let this old world be smashed in which innocence is long since dead, where egoism prospers and man battens upon man! Let these whited sepulchres be destroyed from top to bottom, these caverns of falsehood and iniquity. And blessed be the grocer who shall one day use the pages of my poems as paper-bags for the coffee and snuff of poor old women, who, in this present world of injustice, too often have to go without that solace! Fiat justitia, pereat mundus!'[7]

Nevertheless, the striking thing about the friendship formed by Marx and Heine in 1844 is that it lasted so well, not because but in spite of the fact that Heine never accepted Marx's nascent Communist doctrine. Their lively intercourse did lead to Heine's tone becoming more militant than ever. But he had been on the move towards a more radical stance for quite a while, as is evident from his having advised Laube in November 1842 that they must 'harmonize' their political efforts with the radical line pursued at the time by Ruge's Yearbooks and Marx's *Rheinische Zeitung*.

According to Ruge, Marx advised Heine to sharpen his satire, and on one occasion told him: 'Go about it with a whip!'[8] But Heine's cruel 'Hymn of Praise' to King Ludwig of Bavaria, lampooning the hitherto inviolate person of a crowned head, had been written before he met Marx and so had his *Atta Troll*, the epic story of a rebellious bear, which ended with the lines, 'Other times, and other birds/Other birds, and other songs', clearly indicating Heine's realization that with the death of Romanticism the problems of the 'hungry forties', which accompanied the modern industrial and railway age, required a blunter and more realistic approach.

That meeting shortly before New Year's Day 1844 marked the beginning of one of the most creative and fruitful years in the life of each of them. During 1844 Marx continued his polemic against Bruno Bauer, his erstwhile bosom friend and mentor, and quarreled with Ruge. Sooner or later he was to turn against Weitling, Kriege, Hess, Proudhon, Bakunin and every other friend, associate and comrade-in-arms who dared to disagree with him. How was it, then, that he maintained a mutually stimulating friendship with Heine without Heine's slavishly subscribing to his view of the world?

The answer may well begin with Heine's *Germany, A Winter's Tale*. This masterly sequel and counterpart, not only in its title, to his *Atta Troll, A Midsummer Night's Dream*, was begun by Heine immediately on his return from

Germany in December. Although it matched *Atta Troll* in length, Heine wrote its 27 cantos and 510 stanzas in one spurt of 4 or 5 weeks and finished the first draft of it by the end of January 1844, about the same time that Marx was completing the Introduction to his Hegel Critique.

As suggested by its German title, *Deutschland, ein Wintermärchen*, Heine's poem is a fairy tale. Like *Atta Troll*, it has its portion of dreams and hallucinations, but this time Heine dealt with the political situation in Germany – which after an absence of nearly 13 years he had found more depressing than he had expected it to be – in a direct style which has been compared to 'body-blows straight from the shoulder'.

This epic poem was most often cited in Socialist circles after World War II in support of the thesis that under Marx's influence Heine became a convert to Communism. Yet the poem itself, disproving that myth, helps towards a better understanding of what drew the poet and the philosopher together to the point where the young Marx, packing his bags upon his expulsion from Paris, would dash off to the middle-aged Heine a note saying, 'Of all the people I am leaving behind here, those I leave with most regret are the Heines. I would gladly include you in my luggage! Best regards to your wife from mine and myself. Yours K.Marx.'[9]

Heine had set out for Germany on 21 October 1843. Though he had been living in Paris for more than a dozen years now and was married to a Frenchwoman, he thought and wrote in German. His major audience, too, was in Germany and the old home country, with all its problems, was always on his mind. 'Thinking of Germany at night', he had written in a poem, 'robs me of my sleep.' He mistrusted the bombast of the slovenly political *Tendenzdichter* with their 'egalitarian twaddle', but realized that his friend Laube and his publisher Campe – who separately kept telling him that he was out of touch with developments in Germany – might have a point and that a new generation with new ideas might have grown up in the fatherland during his absence.

Besides, the years abroad had made him homesick for Germany. But most of all, he felt a pressing need to see his 72-year-old mother, who had been burned out of her house during the great Hamburg fire. As he reasoned in the poem *Night Thoughts*, 'The fatherland will live forever/But that dear old woman may die'.

The Prussian ambassador having refused him a visa, Heine departed quietly for Brussels and, travelling via Osnabrück and Bremen, reached Hamburg before the end of October, about the time Karl and Jenny Marx were landing in Paris. At 46, Heine no longer looked like a 'German Apollo with his high forehead, clear as a piece of marble'. His once sparkling blue eyes were half-blind –

'I can hardly read my own scribble,' he was to write before long – and with his face partly distorted by numbness on one side, he had warned his mother not to be frightened by his changed appearance. He himself, however, was shocked to see that age and worries had shrunk his mother, who had lost everything in the fire and got nothing from an insurance company bankrupted by the mass of claims. 'It is a shame,' he wrote. 'She now lives in two small rooms... and is too proud to go out as she doesn't have the means to entertain visitors herself.'[10]

Heine's family in Hamburg – the city of bankers, shippers, stockbrokers, 'whores and no muses', where he had spent some of his unhappy youth – went out of its way to entertain its famous prodigal son. His sister Charlotte, his two wealthy uncles, Henry and Salomon Heine, Madame de Voss (Charlotte's eldest daughter) and others vied to fete him at a succession of suppers, receptions and dinner dances. These family reunions lifted his mother's spirits (the frail old lady was in fact to live to the age of 88 and to survive Heine by three years), and another effect, as Heine reported to Mathilde in Paris, was that his usually gruff Uncle Salomon, softened by age and the fact that 'I did not ask him for money', was pleasant to him.

'I now stand high in his favour', Heine wrote. Indeed, before the end of the year Salomon Heine, who had saved the city of Hamburg from financial insolvency in the wake of the great fire, was to send the Catholic Mathilde a Christmas gift of 400 francs. Heine, of course, also hoped that Uncle Salomon would remember him in his will.

More immediately, a relaxed Heine used his time in Hamburg for frequent talks with his publisher Julius Campe and managed to renegotiate their contract, which had 4 more years to run. The new contract, to go into force in 1848, was one of the most satisfactory achievements of his Hamburg visit. As he explained its advantages to Mathilde on 25 November,

> in return for ceding him the right to exploit my works in perpetuity, he will pay me an annuity of 1,200 marks (or approximately 2,400 francs). Should I die before you at any date from 1848 onward, this annuity will be paid to you; but should I die before that date, my publisher undertakes to begin paying you 2,400 francs per annum at once.[11]

In addition to admonishing Mathilde, in the tone of a jealous lover, not to be frivolous ('Remember, my eye is always on you, I know everything you do, and what I don't know now I will learn later'), complimenting her on her improved spelling, and informing her that his entire family had the highest opinion of her, Heine stressed to Mathilde that 'as of now, your future is assured, as the above-mentioned sum will be paid to you for life. That is the basis of our contract.'

897

The question of Mathilde's future after he was gone had recently been preying on his mind. She had been 19 when he first picked her up in a shop; now she was double that age. The letters he wrote to her every three or four days show that, for all his treating her like the flighty, untutored child-woman she was, he missed her, and loved her enough to feel responsible for her fate. In order not to abandon her to the lot of an impecunious widow, he sold the whole of his future literary output, thus ensuring that Mathilde – who was to survive him by 35 years – would live in comfort on the annuity stipulated, and regularly paid to her, by Hoffmann und Campe to the end of her days. For the rest, Germany's foremost but financially harassed poet and prose writer – who had always yearned for a professorship or some sinecure to enable him to write without worry and humiliations – had at last obtained the security of a fixed, if modest, income from his publisher, which, together with Uncle Salomon's annual stipend of 4,800 francs, not to mention the 'French pension', would enable him to maintain a decent living standard.

For his journey to Hamburg, Heine had chosen an itinerary that crossed as little Prussian territory as possible for fear of being arrested. For the same reason, which was not wholly imaginary – the following September Prussia was to issue an order for his arrest, to be renewed every year – he declined Vanhagen's invitation to visit him in Berlin. But the new contract aside, any risk he had taken also paid off handsomely in the great stimulus which 'breathing the very air of Germany' gave to the poet in him, as is evident from the verve and sustained vigour with which, on his return to Paris, he produced so lengthy a poem as *Germany, A Winter's Tale* in little over a month.

In the second half of the 20th century, this poem was to achieve 'the highest canonical standing. In East German schools', as Jeffrey Sammons observed in 1979, 'it occupies a position second only to Goethe's *Faust*.'[12] There are passages of unprecedented violence in it, such as Heine's reaction to the Prussian eagle staring at him from the top of the post office in Aachen:

> If you fall in my hands, you ugly bird,
> I'll pluck out every feather,
> And chop the claws off both your feet
> And tie them up together,

and then he will put it up on an airy perch and award a prize to the first marksman who'll shoot it. He declares to Barbarossa that he has come to hate the black-red-gold German colours. His conversation with the Rhine river god who prays for the return of the French is equally provocative. Campe feared that *Germany, A Winter's Tale* would be forbidden and Heine – to forestall 'the higher criticism' of censorship and accusations that he was a Francophile ready

to 'slander' the German colours and to surrender the Rhine to the French –
wrote in September 1844 in a Preface to the book version:

> Calm yourselves, I shall respect and honour your colours when they
> deserve it... Plant the black-red-gold flag on the heights of German
> thought, make it the banner of a free humanity, and I will give my heart's
> blood for it... I love the fatherland just as much as you do. Because of this
> love I have lived in exile for thirteen years... I am a friend of the French
> as I am a friend of all people when they are rational and good. I will
> never surrender the Rhine to the French, for a very simple reason –
> because the Rhine belongs to me... My cradle stood on its shores, and I
> do not see why the Rhine should belong to anyone other than its native
> children. I do not find it as easy as you do to annex Alsace and Lorraine
> to Germany, for the people of these lands hold fast to France on account
> of the rights they won through the French Revolution...
>
> However, the people of Alsace and Lorraine will rejoin Germany if we
> complete what the French have begun; if we surpass them in deeds as we
> have already done in the realm of thought; if we rise to the heights required
> by the farthest consequences of that thought; if we destroy servitude... if we
> redeem the god who dwells within people on earth... if we restore to their
> proper dignity the poor people disinherited of happiness... all Europe, the
> whole world will become German!
>
> Of this mission of Germany and its universal role I often dream when I
> walk under the oaks. This is my patriotism.[13]

The cosmopolitan Heine, who even before first leaving Germany had adopted a
supra-national outlook and announced that in Paris he would devote himself to
'topics of general European interest', was now proclaiming what some 10 years
earlier he had only hinted at – namely, that the Germans must live up to their
own philosophy. Marx had just reached the same conclusion. In January 1844,
when Heine was writing his poem, Marx asked in the Introduction to his Critique of Hegel:

> Can Germany attain a practice *à la hauteur des principes*, that is to say,
> a revolution that raises it not only to the official level of modern
> nations but to the human level these nations are about to achieve in
> the immediate future?

Having hit on the proletariat as the 'material weapon' for translating philosophy
into action, Marx openly speaks of revolution. The skeptical Heine in his poem
presumably also speaks of revolution, but in fact, nowhere in *Germany, A Winter's Tale* is there any definite commitment.[14] Once before, in his memoir of

Ludwig Börne, Heine had spoken of radical extremists advocating an egalitarian 'horse cure' that might be worse than the social disease they meant to heal. The fact that the first association that came into Heine's mind when overwhelmed in his poem by chamber pot smells was Saint-Just's remark that the sickness of society requires a stronger cure than 'attar of roses' or other palliatives, would seem to indicate that by January 1844, when he expressed that thought, he had not changed his mind and continued to be impaled on the horns of the same dilemma between the pros and cons of proletarian revolution which in 1855 – 10 years after Marx left Paris – he was poignantly to describe in the French Preface to *Lutèce*.

The articles assembled in that collection had, however, all been written at the beginning of the 1840s. It was in one of them that Heine described Communism in 1841 as the 'terrible antagonist' waiting to assume its 'great role in the modern tragedy' – or its 'great, if only temporary, role in the modern tragedy', as the sentence had been amended by the *Allgemeine Zeitung*. And in another, originally published in mid-summer 1843, less than half a year before he was to meet Marx, he had written of the 'growing army of Communism'. The 'dangerous' doctrines against which Heine kept warning in these articles were those of the early French Communists Cabet and Dézamy; of the Paris workmen who sang the songs of Babeuf; and of the German artisans belonging to Weitling's League of the Just. Marx at that time shared the same low opinion of Cabet, Dézamy and Weitling; a month before his arrival in Paris he had mentioned them by name when describing the existing forms of Communism to Ruge as 'a dogmatic abstraction'. It was only in the summer of 1844 that he was to produce the first elaboration of his own Communist theories. There was thus no disagreement to cloud the first half-year of the Heine-Marx relationship.

On the contrary, Heine's *Germany, A Winter's Tale*, with its violent diatribe against Prussia, 'this bastard state' of 'Gothic fancies and modern lies', fortress of medievalism, social injustice and nationalism, satirized the very things – 'hypocrisy, stupidity, gross arbitrariness', etc. – which Marx had cited as his reasons for leaving Germany. Besides the common ground provided by this, Marx could not but appreciate the qualities that were to make posterity judge *Atta Troll* and *Germany, A Winter's Tale* as 'masterpieces of wit, packed with topical allusions yet suffused with Romantic images for which there is no parallel in German literature.'[15]

Other than contributing suggestions about this or that rhyme, Marx had nothing to do with the original draft which Heine completed at the end of January. In February, while Marx was busy seeing the *German-French Yearbooks* through the press, and for a time thereafter with its liquidation, Heine – a great perfectionist and re-writer – started polishing his 2,000-line poem. He did this between attendances at a soirée of the comtesse Merlin, a performance of Mendelssohn's Scottish Symphony, a concert by Berlioz, a new opera by Auber, another by Monsigny, and two concerts by Liszt, with whom he also had several talks in connection with the series on the Paris musical season he was writing for the *Allgemeine Zeitung*. At the same time he was working on his long essay on Ludwig Markus for the same paper, preparing a new edition of *The Book of Songs*; and producing some of the radical verses to become known as *Poems for the Time* (*Zeitgedichte*).

It was in mid-April when, working in this off-and-on fashion, he put the finishing touches to *Germany, A Winter's Tale*. It was to go through 4 printings in the autumn, three in Germany, before it was *verboten*, and one in Paris. Eleanor Marx wrote later that her father and Heine daily spent hours 'endlessly revising a little ten-line poem'. But this piece of family lore, if not entirely untrustworthy (Eleanor was not yet born), most likely referred to the beginning of the summer, when Marx's influence on Heine began to be felt in the above-named political *Poems for the Time* and most notably in his treatment of the first German workers' revolt in his famous *The Silesian Weavers*.

On 17 April, shortly before he was to send Campe the manuscript of *Germany, A Winter's Tale*, he described it to his publisher as 'the most impudent, personal view of the whole ferment agitating present-day Germany.' As part of that ferment Heine included in the poem a couple of optimistic stanzas about 'a new generation' in Germany preparing to replace the 'old hypocrites'. Indeed, liberal circles, whose hopes in Friedrich Wilhelm IV had been disappointed, talked more openly than ever about democracy, and cosmopolitanism and international ideas were in fashion. But Heine was not fooled by this. As William Rose has observed, 'the German character had not changed' so much that abstract liberal internationalism could influence 'the collective national attitude' and deter it from swinging to a narrower national objective. Heine did understand the German character and the German mind, and the tumult which was disturbing the 'graveyard stillness' of the German scene did not seem to him to be an indication that his compatriots had reached political maturity.[16]

In short, Heine did not believe that Germany was ripe for revolution. Revolution, he had written, would come to Germany one day, for once these thorough people got hold of an idea they never let go of it. But he did not think that the proletarian mob was its chosen instrument.

In one of the oddest scenes in *Germany, A Winter's Tale*, Heine encounters a pack of wolves in the forest. With eyes gleaming in the dark, they represent the political *Tendenzdichter* whom he detested, but it seems that they have only come to honour him 'in their savage way/With a light-show and a chorus./It's a serenade, I see it now.' In a feigned gesture of solidarity and reconciliation,

Heine assures his 'fellow-wolves' that they can count on his support and that – although he sometimes wears a sheepskin because of the censorship – he will always 'howl with the wolves'.

This ironically grotesque scene has been cited as an example of Heine's insincerity, and no wonder. For he had hardly finished the long poem when he wrote to Campe: 'I hope it will administer the death-blow to the prosaic-bombastic tendency of our political poets'. And about the same time, reacting to the refusal of the *Allgemeine Zeitung* to publish one of his articles on the musical season, he wrote to Kolb:

> Is it no longer permitted in Germany to write freely about virtuosi?...
> Or are you frightened by my suddenly refurbished reputation as a
> tribune (I have acquired it in the same way as the servant-girl got the
> baby) – from a denounced renegade I have suddenly again become a
> saviour of the fatherland.[17]

To Campe again, after sending him the manuscript of *Germany, A Winter's Tale*, Heine stressed that he had gone over it repeatedly, had emended the most offensive passages, 'and the poem is now so tame that you have nothing to fear from above [i.e., from the authorities], while I risk being misinterpreted again from below' [i.e., by the radicals]. In a letter to his friend Detmold, on the other hand, he wrote, 'since this opus is not only radical-revolutionary, but also anti-national I shall naturally have the entire press against me, either under the influence of the authorities or that of the nationalists, not to mention non-political enemies and pure literary scoundrels.'[18]

What is one to make of all these ambiguities? They can only be explained by Heine's intention to depict 'the whole ferment in present-day Germany', which implied giving a multiplicity of perspectives on the situation, as reflected through the prism of his own contradictory pulls and inner conflict. In his own mind, the various characterizations he gave in the poem to different people were not so contradictory as they appear. If there is one thing that emerges clearly from his ironic remark to Kolb about his 'suddenly refurbished reputation' as a tribune, it is that he did not want to be associated with the *Tendenzdichter* beyond a certain point. He saw a need for an alliance with the radical opposition, but it was at best to be a temporary alliance.

There was in fact not a single party in Germany with whom Heine could or wished to be identified. Steering his own political course between reactionary conservatism and the extreme radicals, he was navigating between Scylla and Charybdis. Another factor that has to be taken into account is that he was always writing with the censor's scissors at the back of his mind, and in the particular case of *Germany, A Winter's Tale* he used his great ingenuity to get by not only the 'higher criticism' of the censorship (as he called it), but to get over the usually fearless Campe's hesitations to print the work in the first place.

He was satisfied that his poem was as 'radical-revolutionary and anti-nationalist' as he could afford to make it in the circumstances. It was to be published first in September 1844 in a mixed volume under the innocuous title *New Poems*. At the same time Campe was preparing to publish it in book form. For this separate edition, Heine wrote a preface in which, anticipating 'the hue and cry' it was sure to raise, he took the occasion to attack

> these pharisees of nationalism whose antipathies coincide with those of the governments, who fully enjoy the love and esteem of the censorship, and who can set the tone for the daily press when it is a question of attacking those opponents of theirs who are also the opponents of their anointed rulers.

From Hamburg, Heine wrote to Marx in Paris that in this preface, of which he sent him the galley proofs, 'I have openly and decisively thrown down the gauntlet to the nationalists.'[19] But only 11 years later, in the 1855 French Preface to *Lutèce*, did he reveal that his hatred of German nationalism was actually the prime force which moved him towards that radicalism that reached its high point in 1844, the year of his personal contacts with Marx.

Heine rightly foresaw that the collected articles in *Lutèce* would one day be regarded as historical documents providing a host of information in 'daguerreotype' style on the July Monarchy, the political situation in Germany and the contemporary cultural scene populated by such figures as Delacroix, Balzac, George Sand, Chopin, Liszt, Meyerbeer, Mendelssohn, Berlioz and countless others.

'The hero' of the collection, however, he identified as 'the social movement'. In the French Preface, he disclosed that the *Allgemeine Zeitung* had often mutilated, distorted or suppressed his political articles, especially those dealing with 'Socialism, or to call the monster by its name, Communism'. He had put up with this because of his awareness of the brutal constraints to which his friend Kolb, the editor of the paper, was subjected. Nonetheless, Heine emphasized, he had managed 'to paint the devil on the wall' of this widely read newspaper. Through his articles, he went on, Communist groups dispersed in many lands learned to their great surprise of the constant progress of their cause. At a time when that cause was little known, they learned that they were not the least of forces in the world, but the strongest party of all; and that, though their day had not yet come, patient waiting was not a waste of time for the men to whom the future belongs.[20]

Heine's view of the eventual advent of Communism in the future was a deeply gloomy one. Not only did he feel 'an agony of dread and fear', but he anticipated the destruction of his own world. 'I foresee all this and I'm filled with immeasurable sadness when I think of the ruin with which the victorious proletariat threatens my verses, that will sink into the grave with the whole of the old Romantic world.' Finally, about 'to lose my mind as I see all the demons of truth dancing in triumph around me', and unable to refute the premise 'that every man has the right to eat', he gives in to the commanding voice of logic and cries out: 'Let justice be done! Let this old world be smashed in which innocence is long since dead, where egoism prospers and man battens upon man!...'

But logic is only one of two voices that wrest this cry from Heine's breast.

> The second of the two imperious voices that possess me, and which is even more powerful and infernal than the first, is that of the hatred I feel for that party of which Communism is the chief antagonist, and which is therefore our common enemy.
>
> I speak of the German nationalists, that party of false patriots whose love of the fatherland consists only of an idiotic aversion to strangers and the neighbouring peoples... I have always detested these remnants or descendants of the Teutomaniacs who have only modernized their ancient ultra-Teuton costumes – I have fought them all my life, and now that the sword falls from my dying hand I am consoled by the conviction that Communism, which will be the first to encounter them on its path, will crush them to death, not with a mallet, but with a giant coup de pied.[21]

What emerges clearly from the Preface to *Lutèce* is, first, Heine's intention to let the world know that he had realized the historic potential of Communism long before it became an actual force. This book contained the 1841 article in which he had declared that 'Communism speaks a universal language as simple and elementary as hunger, as envy, as death.'

Secondly, the 'terrible syllogism' which nearly drove him crazy was the dilemma of a man who not only realized that the rotten old society, of which he had written in June 1843 that it had, for all its might, lost its moral fibre and was defending itself out of sheer inert necessity, without any self-respect or faith in its cause,[22] was condemned to die, but who also foresaw that Communism and the particular type of German nationalism spearheaded by Prussia would step into the void as the two forces whose clash would decide the future of the world.

The 1855 Preface has to be read in conjunction with Heine's writings over a period of time. It then becomes evident that his fear of what a proletarian regime might do to modern civilization, 'the achievement of so many centuries', went hand in hand with his presentiments, expressed in 1843, that 'the growing army of Communists, lending their formulae to brute force', would at the end of a fanatical class-struggle arrogate to itself the role and infallible authority 'of the Fathers of the Church.'

But what he dreaded even more was an outbreak of that elemental Teuton 'berserk fury' which he had foreseen and warned against in his *History of Religion and Philosophy in Germany* as early as the mid-1830s. In the 1855 Preface he once more warned the French that German nationalism was lusting for a war against France, such as Bismarck was indeed to instigate and win in 1870–71. The bloody suppression of the 1848–49 revolutions all over Europe, Heine wrote in the 1855 Preface, had brought a resurgence of the Teutomaniacs in Germany 'and today they are again howling invective [at France] with the permission of the highest authorities in the land.'

Heine actually concluded the Preface with the words: 'Go on howling! The day will come when you will be crushed by the fatal coup de pied. With this conviction I can quietly quit this world.'

Significantly, he twice repeated that Communism was 'the chief antagonist of that [German nationalist] party, which is therefore our common enemy and which I hate from the bottom of my heart... Because of that hatred I could almost fall in love with the Communists',[23] thus clearly indicating that, faced as he was with a choice between two evils, Communism, for all his reservations about it, appeared to him as the lesser, principally because he saw in it the chief bulwark capable of stemming some future tide of German nationalism. The 1855 Preface actually provides post-hoc confirmation that this was the main reason for his seeking a temporary alliance with Germany's radicals at the beginning of the 1840s. Besides being consonant with what he had written to Detmold in September 1844 about *Germany, A Winter's Tale* ('not only radical-revolutionary, but also anti-national'), it reveals that it was the latter feeling which inspired the former.

Heine's alliance with Marx was, politically speaking, likewise temporary. Already in 1856, less than two months after Heine's death, the journalist Theodor Creizenach observed in an article published in Frankfurt that Heine's association with Ruge and those of Hegel's radical disciples who became Communists 'went no deeper than the surface'. Noting that 'a gulf' separated Heine from the blinkered dogmatists 'who make a virtue of one-sidedness', Creizenach quoted an anonymous radical author who, having, like Heine, contributed to the *German-French Yearbooks*, asked him whether he was satisfied with the line (*Richtung*) taken by the journal. Heine had replied: 'I would be more satisfied by the execution [*Hinrichtung*] of their enemies.'[24] The story may be apocryphal, but the pun sounds authentic.

In the second half of 1844, when he was to collaborate with Marx on the outspokenly Communist German-language journal *Vorwärts!*, Heine did not hesitate to tell him that he felt uncomfortable at being identified with its provocative line; and eventually – in the 1852 Preface to a new edition of his *History of Religion and Philosophy in Germany* – he was to remind Ruge, Feuerbach, Bruno Bauer as well as Marx and the rest of that group, of the fate of 'the Babylonian king who thought that he was God but fell from the height of his self-conceit and ended up crawling on the ground and eating grass.'[25]

This hardly points to his having been converted by Marx to his new doctrine. On a personal plane, however, their relation was such that in 1852 Heine asked his secretary to draw the attention of Marx, who had by then started his exile in London, to the Preface in which he called him a thick-headed 'self-god'.

Marxist writers have tended to explain away Heine's patent unease about Communism by attributing it to his knowing only Babeuf's form of Communist dictatorship. He had indeed got his first idea of Communism from the Babouvist songs and slogans he heard in 1840 in Paris. Heine's close contacts with Marx continued after the latter's expulsion from that city. Between 1846 and 1848 Heine was more than once visited by Engels, at the time when he and Marx were elaborating the ideas they were to pack into *The Communist Manifesto*. This appeared on the eve of the February 1848 revolution. Shortly after its outbreak, Marx, during a short stay in Paris, went to see Heine a couple of times. He did so again in 1849, and they kept track of each other through common friends well into the 1850s, after Marx's peregrinations had taken him to exile in London.

In short, Heine may be credited with the ability to distinguish between Marx's new Communist doctrine and Babouvism. It has been said that Marx was Heine's intellectual superior. This is to introduce an element of competition where none existed. Heine was a poet, a satirist and visionary, a champion of freedom, justice and human rights. He was, by his own admission, 'not an abstract thinker'. He was a social critic but not a practical revolutionary, and he certainly did not aspire to be another rabble-rousing 'political tribune' or *Tendenzdichter*. 'In the breast of the writers of a people lies the image of its future,' Heine had written in the mid-1830s in *The Romantic School*. Then in 1838 – in *Shakespeare's Maidens and Ladies* – he had declared that the poet shared with the mathematician, who can immediately specify the whole of a circle and its midpoint if one gives him only the smallest segment of it, the faculty of perceiving at once 'the circumference and centre of all things' when 'only the smallest fraction of the world of phenomena is offered to his view... He comprehends things in their broadest compass and deepest midpoint.'[26]

From this followed the role he chose for himself as suiting him best. Hinted at and occasionally made explicit in more than one passage of his writings, it was that of a herald of change, anxious to impart to the educated public the auguries and omens he perceived from his superior vantage point, along with his view of a better world.

For instance, the 'Hymn', found among his papers and published posthumously, was written according to some in 1840, and according to others, as early as 1830; he wrote in it:

> 'I am the sword, I am the flame.
>
> 'I illumined your way in the darkness, andwhen the battle began I fought in the vanguard, in the front ranks.
>
> 'Round about me here lie the corpses of my friends, but we have won. We have won, but amid the jubilant songs of triumph we hear the chants of the funeral rites. We, however, have time neither for joy nor for sorrow. Once again the trumpets ring out, new fighting is ahead.-
>
> 'I am the sword, I am the flame.'[27]

The tone of this piece of 'poetic prose', in which Heine appears as a torch-bearer pointing the way to, if not actually ushering in, a new age, is one of mixed triumph and sorrow. Unlike the propagandistic *Tendenzdichter* with their exalted phrases, he was aware that the new age would be born out of blood, sweat and tears. He himself paid a heavy price for constantly flaying the absolutist monarchs and ruling classes of his day who denied freedom and human rights to all but themselves.

Nowhere, however, did he more explicitly define his self-chosen role than in the short poem 'Doctrine', in which he called himself simply a 'drummer boy'.

> Go drum the people up from sleep,
> Drum reveille with youthful fire,
> March onward drumming, on and on –
> That's all the knowledge you require...

Written in 1842, but published in *Vorwärts!* only two years later at the height of his intimacy with Marx, this poem with its artfully naive simplicity is another expression of Heine's radical phase: for a moment the champion of art for art's sake seems ready to let poetry serve as a political vehicle for applying advanced German thought to reality. But while we know that this phase was not to last, 'Doctrine' reminds us that, since his early portrait of the little French drum-major in *The Book of Legrand*, Heine never strayed from his path as a committed artist, committed to nothing more, but also nothing less, than rousing the people, especially the German people, from their sleep.

But this was only one side of him. For all his frequent changes of masks and postures, his anxieties and his basic insecurity, his self-esteem was no less than Marx's. But it was as a shining literary star, second to none but Goethe, that he wished to be seen by posterity, and not as an ideologue; and if he succeeded in making 'poetry out of politics' it was as much due to his talent as to his penetrating and many-faceted perspective and the inner conflicts of his often divided self.

His adoption by Marxism notwithstanding, Heine, in the 'terrible syllogism' which held him in its grip to the last, put before the world the possibilities of perversion inherent in any absolute doctrine; with his uncanny intuitive faculty he was pointing at, even if not exactly anticipating, the kind of dilemma which liberal intellectuals in the 20th century were to confront when they discovered with a shock the crimes committed by Stalin in the name of 'orthodox' Marxism.

As for Marx, a puissant character if anyone ever deserved that archaic term, he was in 1844 bursting with youthful confidence and possessed for the next few years by a double purpose – that of proving that historically, socially and economically the proletariat was 'the universal class' and finding ways of teaching that class how to change the world by means of its own emancipation. He would fight any of his friends and cronies who gave signs of being an actual or potential rival with the same fierceness with which he sought to destroy opponents; and it was precisely because he and Heine did not compete in the same field that they could enjoy each other's intelligence and wit.

Although there is no record of their conversations and only three of Marx's letters to Heine have survived, their relationship was actually summed up by Heine in a passage of his single extant letter to Marx: 'Dear friend,...Forgive my confused scribbling. I can hardly read what I wrote – but after all, we need few words in order to understand each other! Heartily, H. Heine.'[28]

Throughout his life, Marx liked to quote Heine in his writings and did so almost as frequently as he quoted Shakespeare, borrowing striking definitions, scintillating word constructions and sometimes whole lines. The fact that Marx realized the importance of Heine and treated him with respect, affection and an indulgence which he did not show to others – even after Heine recanted his atheism on his deathbed and opted for a personal God – is evident from the way he spoke about him to his family. According to Eleanor Marx, he would say of the only friend he made during his stay in Paris, 'Poets are strange fellows. They are made that way, and one must let them follow their own bent. One cannot judge them by the standards that apply to ordinary or even outstanding people.'[29]

32

Marx's Work in Paris

The summer of 1844 came to Paris in June with a sweet smell of lilac and a riot of white and red chestnut blossoms. But Karl and Jenny Marx were housebound and far too busy looking after Jennychen, their sickly new-born baby, to stroll about the boulevards or join the crowds filling the sidewalk cafés. They were inexperienced parents. They had no wet-nurse and by mid-June the 6-weeks-old Jennychen was or appeared to them so close to death that the desperate mother bundled her up and took her by mail coach to her own mother in Trier, to which city Caroline von Westphalen had recently moved back from Bad Kreuznach. The baby arrived there 'miserable and in pain' from a swollen underbelly, but Jenny was soon able to inform Marx that the family doctor had worked a miracle and that

> the dear little Cleverface suckles splendidly at the breast of a healthy young wet-nurse, a girl from Barbeln, the daughter of a boatman with whom my dear father had often sailed... Despite her suffering, the child looks marvellously lively... In Paris, we certainly would not have managed to save her.[1]

As Jenny was to spend three months with her mother, Marx had their apartment in the rue Vaneau to himself throughout the summer of 1844. Relieved of financial worries by the 1,000 Thaler Georg Jung had providentially sent him in March, he had the quiet and leisure to concentrate on his *Economic and Philosophic Manuscripts*.

Having started on this project in April, he had since characteristically and methodically excerpted 24 pages from Etienne Buret's *Misère des classes laborieuses en Angleterre et en France*, another 19 from John Mill's *Elements of Political Economy*, and filled altogether 9 copybooks with 200 or so pages of notes and excerpts on and from some 30 works on political economy, including those of Adam Smith, J.B. Say, David Ricardo and the Swiss Sismondi, besides Michel Chevalier on the French economy and Coffinières on the Bourse and the effect of stock exchange speculations.

As Engels was later to testify, Marx at the time 'knew absolutely nothing about economics' – to the point of being unfamiliar with some of its elementary terminology. Yet in a Preface to the *Economic and Philosophic Manuscripts* he wrote: 'It is hardly necessary to assure the reader who is familiar with political economy that I arrived at my conclusions through an entirely empirical analysis based on an exhaustive critical study of political economy.'[2]

Was Marx being disingenuous? Not necessarily, and not consciously. As usual, he took his first inspiration from Hegel, who had compared civil society to a battlefield where everybody's egoistic private interest clashes with everybody else's. Adam Smith had postulated that it is self-interest, and not benevolence, that makes 'the butcher, the brewer, or the baker' feed society and produce its wealth to the ultimate benefit of all its members. Hegel accepted the Scottish philosopher's dictum, with one reservation: 'The concentration of disproportionate wealth in a few hands', he observed, led to 'the creation of a rabble of paupers' at the other end of the scale. It was the only problem to which Hegel found no solution in his otherwise integrative system.[3]

He saw in man's labour, which satisfies his own needs while serving those of others, his way of projecting himself into the social stream. Marginally, Hegel noted that the modern division of labour had an alienating effect on the individual 'whose work becomes machine-like', but he regarded this as the inevitable compromise built into the structure of society.

Marx, however, was set on the 'emancipation' (i.e., the salvation) of man from his alienation by abolishing the conditions that created it. Nor was Hegel Marx's only inspiration. Feuerbach and Hess both played a role in leading him to political economy. But it was the 24-year-old Engels – whom Marx had brushed off during their first and only meeting so far – who from Manchester guided him to the real thing.

One of the two articles which Engels had contributed to the German French Yearbooks – 'Outlines of a Critique of Political Economy' – struck Marx as a brilliant piece of writing. In March, shortly after the collapse of the journal, he had written a letter to Engels, which was to lead to the latter's visit to Paris in August 1844 and the beginning of their historic partnership.

But whereas Engels in his article had given a factual review of English factory conditions, commerce, capital and labour based on first-hand observation or referenced studies, Marx had a more grandiose plan. He meant to publish a series of separate booklets on economic subjects, in which, as he wrote in the Preface, he would only touch on the interconnection of political economy and the state, law, morals, civil life, etc., and finally he would 'attempt, in a special work, to present them once again as a connected whole.'[4]

This endeavour has been rightly described as a project for a lifetime. Having in his previous essays stood Hegel's philosophic notions of religion and the political state on their head, Marx was logically turning to political economy.

But hurrying as he was to encompass its influence on all spheres of life, he plunged into it before he had really mastered the subject, driven apparently by the same irresistible urge to find some absolute universal 'system' which during his *Sturm und Drang* period as a freshman student in Berlin, had fired him with the ambition to 'elaborate a philosophy covering the whole field of law', only to abandon the attempt after 300 pages. Although Marx never finished the *Economic and Philosophic Manuscripts* either, theirs was to be a different fate of lasting importance.

Marx thought he was writing 'empirically', but used the word in a sense all his own. The first of the 4 Manuscripts, for instance – on 'Wages, Profit of Capital, Ground Rents, Alienation of Labour' – consisted mostly of long excerpts from Adam Smith's *On the Wealth of Nations*,[5] in which the Scotsman who is to this day regarded as 'the father of all economics' argued that individuals pursuing their self-interest in a free market 'invisibly, without knowing it, advance the interest of society.' For this thesis, Smith, nowadays seen by some historians, philosophers and economists as a champion of democratic capitalism who did not mean that greed rules the world, was long stamped as a diehard conservative advocate of laissez-faire, and so he naturally appeared to Marx too. But his way of refuting Smith was to quote some 10 pages of text and statistics on the exploitation of women and child-labour in England, from a study published by Wilhelm Schulz, one of the expatriate German lecturers in Zurich.[6] Then, as though to beat Smith at his own game, Marx wrote forcefully:

> From political economy itself, using its own words, we have shown that the worker sinks to the level of a commodity;... that the misery of the worker is in inverse proportion to the power and volume of his production; that the necessary consequence of competition is the accumulation of capital in a few hands... and that finally... the whole of society must split into two classes of property owners and propertyless workers.

Marx's empiricism consisted of pitting one economist's study against another's, and adding his own pithy comments. In the process he announced the class-struggle. What made the *Economic and Philosophic Manuscripts* of 1844 a landmark on his road to Communism was his original development of the concept of man's 'self-alienation' in the labour process under capitalist conditions.

With moral indignation and a good deal of psychological insight, Marx observed that, while 'the savage and the animal at least have a need to hunt, to move about', wage-labour 'emasculates' the worker of his elementary human needs

and 'mortifies his flesh and ruins his mind.' Reducing him to a sub-human, actually sub-animal existence, the new machinery and the division of labour force
him

> to revert once more to living in a cave, but the cave is now polluted by
> the mephitic and pestilential breath of civilization. Moreover, the
> worker has no more than a precarious right to live in it, for... should
> he fail to pay, he can be evicted at any time. He actually has to pay
> for his mortuary... Light, air, etc., – the simplest *animal* cleanliness –
> ceases to be a need for man. *Dirt* – this pollution and putrefaction of
> man, literally the sewage of civilization – becomes an *element of life*
> for him.[7]

'*Political economy*', Marx charged, '*conceals the estrangement in the nature of labour by ignoring the direct relationship between the worker (labour) and production.*'
It was true, he wrote, that 'labour produces marvels for the rich, but it produces
privation for the worker. It produces palaces, but hovels for the worker. It produces beauty, but deformity for the worker... It produces intelligence, but
idiocy and cretinism for the worker.'

Marx distinguished 4 forms of man's resulting alienation – first, from the
product of his labour, which belongs to the capitalist; secondly, from his productive work itself, which gives him no creative joy but turns him into the slave
of a machine; thirdly, from his essential nature as a species-being, that is, from
the advantage he holds over animals of being able 'actively and actually to contemplate himself in a world he himself has created'; and fourthly and finally
from his fellow-men, i.e., from the community and his own humanity.

Marx thus greatly elaborated Hegel's original concept of alienation, which
centred chiefly on man's unique faculty to be both subject and object and to
observe his own actions as if he were a spectator. The paradox that 'the worker
becomes all the poorer the more wealth he produces,' was noted by Marx, who
further observed that, just as religion robs the individual of the spontaneous
activity of the human imagination, of the human brain and the human heart, and
reappears as the alien activity of a god or of a devil, so the activity of the worker
is not his own spontaneous activity. It belongs to another; it is a loss of his self.[8]

This 'loss of himself' is the dehumanization of man. In the *Economic and
Philosophic Manuscripts* Marx announced for the first time that Communism
aimed at the abolition of private property, for the capitalist system based on it
not only reduced the alienated worker to acting freely only in 'his animal functions – eating, drinking, procreating', but deprived him of the chance of 'creating' his own life as a man through his labour and degraded him to the dependent
status of one 'living by the grace' of another:

> A *being* sees himself as independent only when he stands on his own feet, and he only stands on his own feet when he owes his *existence* to himself... But I live completely by the grace of another if I owe him not only the maintenance of my life but also its *creation*, if he is the *source* of my life. My life is necessarily grounded outside itself if it is not my own creation...[9]

The idea that man creates himself through his own labour was Hegel's. In the last of his *Economic and Philosophic Manuscripts* Marx subjected Hegel's 'dialectic and general philosophy', with special reference to his *Phenomenology of the Spirit*, to a new scrutiny. Clarifying his own ideas, as he had done in his book-length Kreuznach Critique of Hegel, by matching them against those of the master, he challenged him with the observation: 'For Hegel human nature, *man*, is equivalent to *self-consciousness*. All estrangement of human nature is therefore *nothing* but *estrangement of self-consciousness*.'

Hegel's battlefield, Marx submitted, is all in the mind. 'The only labour Hegel knows and recognizes is *abstract mental* labour.' Hegel's self-conscious man has to supersede or 'transcend' his alienation, but this whole process takes place in thought and the imagination, as part of Hegel's all-encompassing universal 'Idea'. This enables Hegel to 'bring together the separate elements of previous philosophies and present his philosophy as *the* philosophy' and as absolute science.

For Marx this is not enough. His 'corporeal man' is a species-being in relation with other men. He has passions, instincts as well as sensual needs and has to assert his productive force, and to overcome his alienation in the real world. The consequence of Hegel's philosophy – and this was Marx's harshest criticism of it – reduces the historical process to an eternal 'shuttling back and forth of thoughts'.

In a short section of the *Manuscripts*, Marx dealt with Money. Calling it the 'omnipotent' power which, like a 'pimp between need and object', enables man to gratify his sensual and other requirements, he quoted Mephistopheles in Goethe's *Faust* (Part I, Scene 4),

> If I can pay for six stallions,
> Are not their powers mine?
> I speed along, a proper man,
> As though I had four and twenty legs,

in order to exemplify the power of money to change even man's individuality.

> That which I can pay for, *i.e.* which money can buy, that am I, the possessor of the money... The properties of money are my properties

and essential powers... I am *ugly*, but I can buy the *most beautiful* woman... The effect of *ugliness*, its repelling power, is destroyed by money. As an individual, I am *lame*, but money procures me twenty-four legs. Hence, I am not lame... I am *mindless*, but if money is the *true mind* of all things, how can its owner be *mindless*?...

Describing money as 'the bond of all bonds', the 'chemical power' cementing society, Marx pointed out that to the same extent it was also the chief universal '*agent of separation*' between men. Money 'transforms loyalty into treason, love into hate, hate into love, virtue into vice, vice into virtue, servant into master, master into servant, nonsense into reason and reason into nonsense... As the existing and active concept of value, it is the universal *confusion* and *exchange* of all things.'[10]

And, widely versed in world literature as he was, he turned to Shakespeare's *Timon of Athens*. In one of the speeches in which its embittered outcast hero curses gold and the corruption of the world, he found Shakespeare's endorsement of his own view of money as 'the common universal whore, the universal pimp of men and nations,'[11] and praised Shakespeare for 'bringing out' so well the point that money 'is the *visible god-head* transforming all human and natural qualities into their opposite.' Whatever Shakespeare had meant in his time in the phrase, 'Come, damned earth,/Thou common whore of mankind', Marx himself attributed to money nothing less than a supernatural, 'divine', though evil power and the property of making man worship it while it appropriates his labour and robs him of his soul.[12]

'*Communism* is the solution of the riddle of history', he stated in the *Manuscripts*. Claiming that it was 'a genuine, comprehensive and real science,' he wrote: '*Communism* as the positive supersession of *private property* and *human self-estrangement*... is the complete return of man to himself as a *social*, i.e. human, being – a return become conscious, and accomplished within the entire wealth of previous development.'

In other ways, in his first venture into economics, Marx anticipated many of the theories he was to spend a lifetime elaborating, and none more than those concerning money and the concept of alienation. Ironically, in 1844 Marx had no money worries. On 31 July, Jung followed up the 1,000 Thaler (or 4,400 francs) he had collected for him in mid-March with another handout of 800 francs. Marx, who had expected to live in Paris on an annual salary of 1,800 francs, had thus by the end of July received more than 5,000 francs from his bourgeois well-wishers, a sum which should have allowed him a couple of years of undisturbed work on his first Communist writings. But this was not to be the case.

For the supremely intelligent Marx, who all his life wrote like a man possessed about money, was totally impractical when it came to handling it. His was a legendary 'inability to husband his financial resources'.[13] Even during his gloomiest years in London he was incapable of managing the large sums he received from friends and followers. The pattern of a small band of wealthy devotees intervening every so often to keep Marx and his wife from the poorhouse while he racked his brain in the service of humanity was set early on by Dr H.J. Claessen of Cologne, a contributor to Georg Jung's first fund collection, who wrote to Marx that he felt it a privilege 'to compensate you for the sacrifices you have made for the common cause.'[14]

In 1844, however, only his practical-minded wife worried about their future. To judge from her letters from Trier, everyone wanted to know whether he had a steady income. Although Jenny put a brave face on it, reporting that she was showing off her best Parisian dresses and successfully making the locals believe that her husband supported her in opulent style ('For one thing', she wrote, 'I am more elegant than all or any of them, and for another, I have never in my life looked better and more glowing than now'), she brought up the matter of a 'steady income' twice in one letter of 21 June:

> Dear heart, I have too great an anxiety about our future, both in the
> long and the short term, and I think that I shall be punished for my
> present high spirits and exuberance. If you can, please allay my fears
> on this point. People talk far too much about a steady income. I then
> answer simply with my red cheeks, my white flesh, my velvet cloak,
> my feathered hat and my fine ribbons.[15]

Even after she learned of the new windfall of 800 francs from Jung, she continued to be anxious. 'How good that you now again have some cash', she wrote, but cautioned him: 'Although the exchequer may be full at the moment, remember how quickly it empties and how difficult it is to fill it again!' Dominated by her 'dark master', whom she also endearingly called the 'High Priest and Bishop' of her heart, she did not press him to do anything in particular, apparently knowing that the idea of taking up any kind of 'steady' occupation for the simple purpose of supporting himself and his family was foreign to his mind.

Rather, she wrote that they were probably going to have a second baby soon after her return to Paris. 'People with the smallest means have the most children,' she added ruefully, showing her familiarity with the idea then current among Marx's Socialist friends that the poor multiplied at a faster rate than the means of production.[16] But for all her loving devotion to him and her shared faith in his cause, an undertone of financial anxiety runs through most of her letters from Trier, almost as if she had a premonition that summer of the horrendous years of privation in London during which she and Marx, having already lost a little boy, would have to postpone the burial of an infant daughter because they did not have the money for the funeral expenses. 'The lifeless body' of one-year-old Franziska, Jenny was to write in her Reminiscences, was left overnight 'in the back room,' while she and Marx 'went into the front room and and made our beds on the floor. Our three living children lay down by us and we all wept... She [Franziska] had no cradle when she came into the world, and for a long time was denied a last resting place,' until she ran in desperation to the house of a French refugee who lent her two pounds for a coffin.[17]

As money during those wretched years became for Marx an existential problem with which he had to struggle most of his life, the fierceness of his attack on it grew. Ultimately, when dealing with the power of capital, which is accumulated money, Marx was to describe it in *Das Kapital* as 'dead labour which, like a vampire, is resuscitated only by sucking the labour of the living, and the more it sucks in, the longer it lives.'

Observing in 1984 that 'Marx's own humanity and psychology speak through some of his seemingly "objective", philosophical, critical statements', Bruce Mazlich asked: When Marx excoriates money as the universal 'whore' and 'the pimp' of men and nations 'is he merely gilding his economic analysis or encrusting it as well with feelings derived from his youthful relations to his father?' Similarly, when Marx writes that man 'only stands on his own feet when he owes his existence to himself' and not to another who provides him with sustenance and thus 'creates' his life, 'and when he then adds "Self-generation... is the only practical refutation of the theory of creation", is he achieving a sense of total personal independence by claiming to have created himself?'[18]

Dealing with both these questions 20 years before Mazlich, Arnold Künzli answered them by quoting a passage in *Das Kapital* in which Marx described the birth of capital in the following words: 'If money, according to Augier, "comes into the world with natural blood stains on one cheek", then capital is born like a baby dripping blood from head to toe, and from every pore.'

Künzli calls that 'as remote from scientific analysis as can be.... This is no longer economics, but sheer demonology.' In analyzing Marx's psyche, Künzli did not hesitate to declare that, though he stamped capitalism as 'sucking' the blood and sweat of the workers, Marx himself took money all his life from Engels and others like an unconcerned suckling expecting nourishment from its mother until it is sated. This resulted in an inner conflict between, on the one hand, his superior intellect and his high 'vocation' or hubris to create a new man, one who, in Marx's phrase, 'owes his existence to himself [and] stands on his own feet', and, on the other, his own dependence on others to supply him and his family with their daily bread.

So sharp was this conflict that, in Künzli's view, Marx's only way of solving it was subconsciously to transfer the guilt for his inability to achieve financial autonomy on to 'money' itself, which had to be denied any positive quality and to be painted in the blackest colours as a satanic force; and so vexing and existential that it became the motive power which drove him to keep 'dissecting this demon from head to toe to get to the bottom of its secret.'[19]

In short, according to Künzli, the dragon had to be killed and money had to be abolished for Marx to regain his absolute autonomy and lead mankind to salvation. Whatever the merits of Künzli's psychological analysis, Marx would not have been Marx had he chosen a practical career with a steady income to support his family. As an idealistic 17-year-old, he had written: 'Our happiness belongs to millions.' In his maturity, shortly after he had finished the first part of *Das Kapital*, he explained to a friend why he had not answered his letters: 'Hovering at the edge of the grave as I was, I had to use every moment when I was able to work to finish my book, to which I have sacrificed health, happiness and family.'

With only a slight stretch of the imagination one can guess from Marx's next few lines what his answer to Künzli might have been:

> I must laugh at the so-called 'practical' men and their wisdom. If one chose to be an ox, one could of course turn one's back to the sufferings of mankind and look after one's own skin. But I should really have considered myself impractical if I had checked out without completely finishing my book, at least in manuscript form;[20]

and even Künzli was to admit that in the process of ruthlessly demonizing and 'dissecting' money every which way, Marx reached a number of insights into the nature of a capitalist society based on money which 'decisively deepened the knowledge of men about their socio-economic conditions.'[21]

There was a humanist side to Marx's *Economic and Philosophic Manuscripts* that was not to be discovered until almost a century after he wrote them. On 15 May 1844 Ruge, in a letter to Feuerbach giving his version of his conflict with Marx and their final break, included the following observation about his former co-editor: 'He reads enormously, works with uncommon intensity... but never finishes anything, and always breaks off to plunge anew into an ocean of books.'[22]

Ruge may have been the philistine that Marx made him out to be, but he was no fool. He perceived the oddity of genius when he saw it, recognized that Marx was by nature an 'eternal student' and accurately foresaw that when driven by some new idea he would abandon work in progress in order to explore it. Marx had important things to say in the *Manuscripts*, but in July he interrupted work on them. He resumed it briefly in August but then gave it up altogether.

The first of the 4 *Manuscripts* broke off after 36 pages; of the second, dealing with 'Private Property,' only 4 pages were ever found; the third, containing sections on 'Needs, Production and Division of Labour', on 'Communism' and on 'Money', ran to 68 pages, of which the last 23 were blank; the fourth consisted of only 4 pages. The result was thus an unfinished and disorganized work with many gaps. Not published until 1932, the *Manuscripts* caused an enormous stir among both Soviet ideologues and Marxist and non-Marxist writers everywhere. And no wonder – for, in spite of their fragmentary character, they showed that it was philosophy and psychology – rather than the concrete economic determinants he was later to invoke – that moved Marx in 1844 towards Communism. Quite apart from his dubious claim that he was founding a new and 'real science' and that 'the *whole of what is called world history* is nothing more than the creation of man through human labour', the *Manuscripts* bore the imprint of a philosophical and idealistic young Marx who, in the midst of discussing political economy and condemning money as 'the universal whore', could use lyrical language:

> Assume man to be man and his relation to the world to be a human one, then love can be exchanged only for love, trust for trust... If your love as love does not call forth love in return, if through the *vital expression* of yourself as a loving person you fail to become a *loved person*, then your love is impotent, it is a misfortune.[23]

This passage, envisioning a system in which man, instead of material counters, will exchange 'love for love and trust for trust', was eventually to elicit George Steiner's comment that Marx 'is all but paraphrasing Isaiah.' Marx went on: 'Communism equals humanism, and as fully-developed humanism equals naturalism; it is the genuine resolution of the conflict between man and nature, and between man and man, the true resolution of the conflict between existence and being... between freedom and necessity, between individual and species.'[24]

In March 1844 Marx became acquainted with the first real proletarians he had ever met in the flesh. Mäurer and Dr Ewerbeck, the two intellectuals who had assumed the leadership of the Communist League of the Just in the absence of Weitling, took him to the gatherings of the German artisans and apprentices in a hall at the Barrière du Trone, in the rue de Vincennes, where – according to a Prussian police spy – 'thirty, or often one hundred or two hundred German Communists met on Sundays' and 'talked of regicide, the abolition of property, war with the rich, etc.'

Dr Ewerbeck had also initiated him into some of the secret French workers' societies. Marx was impressed by the earnestness and revolutionary zeal he found at their meetings. In the *Manuscripts* he was enthusiastic about the fact that the workers taking part did not confine themselves to 'smoking, eating and drinking', but sought education, 'company, association, conversation.' He wrote that 'The brotherhood of man is not a hollow phrase, it is a reality.' He could see 'the nobility of man shining forth from the work-worn figures' of the French Socialist workers.

The Economic and Philosophic Manuscripts present us with a 'humanist' Marx who – having already proclaimed the proletariat to be the 'universal class' before he ventured into political economy – now went so far as to promise that out of the 'sewage' of civilization he would create a new autonomous man. He, Marx, only had to make him conscious of his degradation for this man to raise himself to his innate human dignity and nobility. Marx could do so because he believed, as he was to write in *The Holy Family*, that 'the propertied class and the class of the proletariat present the same human self-estrangement. But the former class feels at ease... recognizing estrangement as *its own power*, and finding in it the *semblance* of a human existence.' The proletariat, on the other hand, 'feels annihilated in estrangement; it sees in it its own powerlessness and the reality of an inhuman existence'; this makes it attain consciousness of its alienation and through urgent need it 'is driven directly to revolt against this inhumanity.'[25]

In other words, what he, the abstract philosopher, knew theoretically, the proletariat would be compelled by historic necessity to do in practice. Its revolt would translate the vision of earlier 'utopians' of what society *ought* to be into reality and in the process would save all men, including the capitalist, from 'the same human self-estrangement'.

The new man, Marx stated in the *Manuscripts*, would then be able not only to stand on his own feet but to partake of 'the entire wealth of previous development' – that is, of all the advantages of civilization – and to enjoy a life enriched by education, intellectual interests and 'sensuous' pleasures like music and art now denied to him.

This is a far cry from the simplified terms in which Engels was to salute him at his graveside in 1883 when he said:

> Just as Charles Darwin discovered the law of evolution in organic nature on our planet, so Marx discovered the fundamental law of evolution in human history; he discovered the simple fact... that mankind must first of all eat and drink, have shelter and clothing, before it can pursue politics, science, religion, art, etc.[26]

It was a long time before anyone made the point that, while human beings obviously 'cannot engage in politics and cultural pursuits without eating and sleeping, it does not follow that eating and sleeping explain the form politics and intellectual activity take'; and that while a people's politics and culture may be causally affected by the level of its economic development, the materialist conception of history is flawed by taking it as a 'foregone conclusion that everything that happens in a society that is of any importance must have an economic explanation.'[27]

But how is one to square the young idealistic Marx of 1844 with the mature, determinist Marx whom Engels was to canonize in his funeral oration as the founder of historic or 'Marxist materialism' and as the prophet who laid down the 'scientific' iron laws of the movement of history and society? In November 1843 Engels himself had described his and Marx's Communism as being inspired by neither 'French nor English Communist ideas' but by the German 'philosophical' school led by Hess. Marx's *Manuscripts* do indeed show that influence. Sixteen years later, however, Marx himself omitted this 'philosophical' stage from a brief retrospective account he gave of the development of his opinions.

With the *Manuscripts* remaining unpublished for nearly a century, he created something of a riddle whose solution was to divide generations of Marx interpreters into two camps. Lenin, not knowing of the existence of the *Manuscripts* or their humanist, 'philosophical' inspiration, compounded the problem by declaring that Marx passed directly from the Introduction in which he first spoke of the proletariat to his full-blown economic interpretation of history.

The rise of Hitler in the 1930s, shortly after the publication of the *Manuscripts*, delayed the intense debate that was to erupt with all the greater force after World War II on the question whether there was or was not a radical break between the 'humanist', idealistic young Marx and the mature founder of 'scientific Marxism' and the materialist conception of history.

During the next few decades, the debate reached its height with the birth of Eurocommunism. As the Communist Parties of Italy and Spain and sections of the French Communists not only repudiated the horrors of Stalinism but dissociated themselves from their Leninist heritage as well – to proclaim themselves 'parliamentary' Socialist democrats with 'full respect for human liberties' – it assumed wide-ranging political and social implications and until late into the 20th century engaged not only Marxist ideologists and sympathizers but students and intellectuals worldwide.

Was Lenin's brutal dictatorship inherent in Marxism or based on 'a perversion or misunderstanding' of it? This was only one of the questions that became the subject of heated dispute. But Marx in the 1840s did not dream of this hornet's nest of controversy, and it is mentioned here chiefly to underline the importance his *Economic and Philosophic Manuscripts* and other 'early writings' were to play in posterity's assessment of how his ideas kept developing and sometimes changed in the process, or were changed by others.

In July 1844, Marx and his friends gained control of *Vorwärts!* ('Forward!'), a semi-weekly German-language review which originally avoided politics and dealt chiefly with the theatre, opera and artistic gossip and tittle-tattle. Its publisher, Heinrich Börnstein, a former actor and enterprising journalist, had launched the journal with the help of a loan obtained from Meyerbeer, on the promise that Heine would be one of the contributors.[28]

When Heine started in May to contribute some of his most radical political poems, the paper changed in tone. By mid-June *Vorwärts!* was carrying Heine's 'The New Alexander', in which he brazenly had the Prussian King confess that, brought up as he had been by his Huguenot tutor Ancillon in the spirit of his published theory *On the Reconciliation of Extreme Opinions*, he had grown up 'A hybrid, neither fish nor flesh./... A mixed-up tangle/Blending all our time's extremes.' No paper in Germany would have dared to publish such verses. Heine crowned their insolence by alluding to the King's weakness for alcohol: 'I find my faith in Jesus Christ,/ In Bacchus my consolation.'[29]

In Germany, at the beginning of that June, several hundred Silesian handloom weavers had attacked a couple of cotton mills and smashed the weaving machines which – coupled with the competition of cheap British cotton goods – were reducing them to starvation. It was the first workers' revolt in Germany. Although hardly on the scale of the 1834 Lyons weavers' strike – which had brought 50,000 workers to the streets and had taken the use of artillery fire and a toll of over 1,000 casualties to put down – the rising of the hungry Silesian weavers caused extraordinary excitement among the Germans living in Paris, whose number had swelled since 1836 at a staggering rate from 15,000 to 70,000, some say 80,000.

Marx had yet to start writing for *Vorwärts!* when, on 10 July, the paper carried Heine's 'The Silesian Weavers' ('*Die schlesischen Weber*'). In this most militant of his poems, Heine showed the strikers working on Germany's shroud and 'weaving a threefold curse in it'. Stanza after stanza, to the refrain of 'We're weaving, we're weaving!', they curse first God, then the King and finally the 'false' German fatherland.

The poem created a sensation among the German colony in Paris and beyond, but Arnold Ruge belittled the significance of the event which had inspired it. While Heine left Paris for Hamburg on 20 July to settle a serious dispute which had arisen between him and his publisher Campe, Ruge, in an article on the Silesian weavers' strike in *Vorwärts!*, was putting forward the argument that 'in an unpolitical country' like Germany the sporadic misery of the factory districts was not seen as a matter of universal concern, let alone as a disaster to the whole civilized world.

In Germany, he went on, the Silesian events belonged 'in the same category as any local shortage of food or water.' The Prussian King therefore viewed them as a simple 'failure of the administration or of charitable institutions'; and because only 'few troops were needed to deal with the feeble weavers', the King had not been reduced to panic, as reported in a French newspaper.

Marx was incensed. He was not only irritated by Ruge's remarks about '*unpolitical Germany*' and 'feeble weavers', but outraged that Ruge, who was a Saxon, had signed the article 'A Prussian', allowing for the impression that Marx was the author. Marx promptly wrote a two-part reply in *Vorwärts!* in which he accused the anonymous 'Prussian' of 'literary swindle', and otherwise subjected him to a drubbing in his best polemical style. Ruge, who favoured political reform in Germany within the existing system over social revolution, had concluded his article with the statement that '*A social revolution without a political soul... is impossible.*'[30] Marx's riposte was: 'A "*social*" revolution *with a political soul* is either a composite piece of nonsense... or nothing but a paraphrase.' To the extent that 'every revolution dissolves the *old order of society* it is *social*,' he remarked, and to the extent that it 'brings down the *old ruling power* it is *political*.'

> All revolution – the *overthrow* of the existing ruling power and the *dissolution* of the old order – is a *political act*. But without revolution *Socialism* cannot come about. It stands in need of this political act just as it stands in need of *destruction* and *dissolution*. But as soon as its *organizing functions* begin and its *goal* as well as its soul emerge, Socialism throws its *political* mask aside.[31]

In this circuitous way, Marx announced that Socialism aimed at revolution. In one of two curious passages of his polemic – titled *Critical Notes on the Article 'The King of Prussia and Social Reform'* – Marx referred Ruge to the 'Weavers' Song' (a misnomer for Heine's 'The Silesian Weavers'). A poem can, of course, be a potent political weapon, and Heine's stanzas with their rhythmic resonance and stark revolutionary message would in the fulness of time be sung by generations of German workers. The striking thing, however, is that Marx used the words which Heine put into the mouths of the Silesian weavers as *empirical* evidence against Ruge.[32]

Ruge was to 'think of the Weavers' Song, that intrepid battle-cry in which the proletariat at once proclaims its antagonism to the society of private property in

the most decisive, aggressive, ruthless and forceful manner.' Not only that, but
Marx invoked Heine's poem as proof of the superiority of the Silesian rebellion
over those staged by French and English workers, none of which had shown
'the same understanding' of the nature of the proletariat:

> This *superiority* stamps the whole episode. Not only were machines
> destroyed... but also the *account books*, the titles of ownership... The
> Silesian workers turned also against the hidden enemy, the bankers.
> Finally, not one English workers' uprising was carried out with such
> courage, foresight and endurance.[33]

Marx next launched into a veritable panegyric of 'Weitling's brilliant writings
which surpass Proudhon's from a theoretical point of view'. He further placed
the Communist tailor's *Guarantees of Harmony and Freedom* above anything
that the German bourgeoisie, with all its 'philosophers and scholars', had ever
produced on its political emancipation, and he extolled the level of education
and capacity for revolution of 'the German Cinderella', the fairy-tale name he
applied to the 'new-born' German proletariat.

Who was this collective Cinderella? Of the 34,000 journeymen tailors, shoemakers and carpenters who had emigrated from Germany to Paris,[34] several
hundred formed the rank and file of Weitling's clandestine Communist League
of the Just. There were also the small secret Communist cells he had established
in Switzerland before his imprisonment and those that had been set up in
London. Behind them stretched the larger unorganized mass of the poor and
dispossessed. Marx had written of them in his Wood-Theft articles; and now
that a small group of them had risen in protest in Silesia, he declared that the
German proletariat was the *theoretical* component of the European proletariat
just as the English proletariat was its *economist* and the French its *politician*. The
vocation of Germany for social revolution was as classical as its incapacity for
political revolution.[35]

Whether by hailing Weitling's writings as the 'titanic and brilliant literary
debut of the German working class' and contrasting 'these gigantic children's
shoes of the proletariat with the dwarf-like proportions of the worn-out political shoes of the German bourgeoisie', Marx was simply predicting 'a vigorous
future for this German Cinderella', or was carried away by his hubris to blow up
the small group of Paris Communists and the Silesian strikers into the standard-
bearers of European Socialism, the result of his polemic against Ruge was twofold. On the one hand, it was to lead to Prussia's instigating the eventual
suppression of *Vorwärts!* and Marx's expulsion from Paris. On the other, in
publicizing the short-lived weavers' revolt, it did much – next to Heine's poem –
to focus the *Zeitgeist* on the problem of poverty and starvation, with the result

that within two years J.M. Radowitz, one of the Prussian King's counsellors, would advise him that 'the proletariat like some giant monster lies there, and with it the bleeding wound of our age, pauperism, is laid bare.'[36]

Marx's fragmentary *Economic and Philosophic Manuscripts* had been laid aside. None of the separate booklets on economic subjects he had planned to publish ever appeared. Of his great scheme to write a 'special work' on 'the interconnection of political economy and the state, law, morals, civil society, etc.', only the first stage was to be realized 20 years later in *Das Kapital*. Flush with money in the summer of 1844, he was under no financial pressure to finish the *Manuscripts* and have them printed. No one knows what Marx spent his money on, but the fact is that by the end of the year he had run out of it and had to rely on 50 Thaler his friends were to collect for him in February 1845, to be followed by 122 francs in March.

In the letter Ruge sent his mother shortly after Marx's break with him, he had written that Marx was 'spending more time than ever' with the profligate Herwegh, who had succumbed to 'all the seductions' of Paris, 'its luxurious mansions, its flower shops, its women', and further hinted that Marx took part in Herwegh's gallivantings, 'not without youthful adventures'.[37]

Curiously, a letter from Jenny sent from Trier in mid-August included a cryptic passage in which, besides expressing her longing soon to be in his arms again in Paris, she wrote of being a prey to a 'dark feeling of anxiety, the fear, the real threats [?] of infidelity, the seductions and temptations of the world metropolis.'[38]

Herwegh did, indeed, introduce Marx to some of the society of Paris, and Marx may have joined the frivolous poet in exploring its low life, too. But there is no evidence that he engaged in any kind of frolics that interfered with his work. Rather, and ironically, it was Ruge, who, by minimizing the Silesian weavers' revolt as a 'local' event, seems to have deflected Marx from ever finishing the *Manuscripts*.

Although Marx's response to Ruge did not appear until August, he had been in touch with the journal's publisher Börnstein since mid-July. By then, Meyerbeer was refusing to grant Börnstein any further loans, and Heine, before leaving for Hamburg on 20 July, had tried to enlist Ruge's financial support in an attempt to save the publication. Heine may also have been instrumental in helping Marx and his friends to take over the paper, with the result that Börnstein, instead of fresh funds, obtained a stable of talented intellectual writers. He appointed his sharp-witted friend Ferdinand Bernays – who had contributed to Marx's *German-French Yearbooks* – as his co-editor.

In July, too, Michael Bakunin, having found that Brussels was too placid a place for one whom Belinsky a few years earlier had described as 'a prophet and thunder-hurler',[39] moved permanently to Paris. Arriving in the company of his pianist friend Reichel – whom he had persuaded to give up a post as a teacher at the Brussels Conservatoire – Bakunin resumed his friendship with the poet Herwegh and Count Grigory Tolstoy. He also, as he wrote later, met 'fairly often' with Marx.

Starting in August, when Marx began to have a say on the policies of *Vorwärts!*, he and Bakunin actually saw each other regularly once or twice a week. For Bakunin, after living for a while with and at the expense of Reichel, moved with his possessions into a large vacant room belonging to the journal's editorial offices, which occupied the first floor of a building in the rue des Moulins. Börnstein, who offered him the room, was surprised to find that the worldly belongings and 'entire ameublement' of the towering Russian consisted of no more than 'a folding bed, a trunk and a zinc wash-basin'.

In his memoirs, published 40 years later, Börnstein was to describe the transformation his paper underwent in the hands of its new staff and contributors:

> There soon gathered round *Vorwärts!* a group of writers such as no other paper anywhere could boast, certainly not in Germany... Besides *Bernays* and myself, who were the editors, there wrote for the paper *Arnold Ruge, Karl Marx, Heinrich Heine, Georg Herwegh, Bakunin, Georg Weerth, G. Weber, Fr. Engels, Dr Ewerbeck* and *H. Bürgers.* These men wrote not only very brilliantly but very radically. *Vorwärts*, as the only uncensored radical paper in the German language anywhere in Europe, soon had a new appeal and the number of its subscribers multiplied accordingly.[40]

At the weekly editorial conferences in Börnstein's office, 'twelve to fourteen men, all smoking heavily, argued with great passion and excitement' and so loudly that 'the windows could not be opened, because a crowd would immediately have gathered in the street to find out the cause of the violent uproar, and very soon the room was concealed in such a thick cloud of tobacco smoke that it was impossible for a newcomer to recognize anybody present.'[41]

It was at these editorial conferences, and often in Bakunin's room with its folding-bed and wash-basin, that Marx and Bakunin took each other's measure. Börnstein may have embroidered the grotesque editorial scene, but not the heat of the debates. Marx and Bakunin were two of the century's most opinionated men. A third was the stocky, bespectacled Proudhon, the only French Socialist who took an interest in the activities of the Germans and joined their discussions. Each was fanatically set on imposing his views on the world. Before they could do so each applied all the force of his convictions and argumentative powers to prevailing over the two others, hoping thereby to convince the small band of intellectuals around them of his ideas, his vision of the future and his strategy for remaking society. Marx, by his own account, often engaged the self-taught Proudhon in 'night-long discussions' on social and philosophical questions: 'I infected him to his great injury with large doses of Hegelianism, which, owing to his ignorance of the German language he could not study properly.'[42]

As for Marx and Bakunin, the rivalry between these two great antagonists would one day break up the First International. But at the beginning of their relationship, Bakunin was obviously impressed by Marx's scholarship and wit. A quarter of a century later, after some mighty ideological clashes with him, he evoked their first meetings in Paris in 1844 in the following terms:

> My understanding of political economy at the time was nil, and my Socialism was purely instinctive. He, though younger [by four years] than I, was already an atheist, an instructed materialist, and a conscious Socialist... I very much respected him for his knowledge and his earnest and passionate devotion to the cause of the proletariat, although there was always an admixture of personal vanity to it; I eagerly sought his conversation which was always instructive and witty when it was not inspired by petty spite, which unfortunately happened very often.

Bakunin shared Marx's low opinion of the priggish Ruge. Like Marx, he much preferred the company of Herwegh, the impetuous and extravagant poet. Bakunin's view of Germany's backwardness was as contemptuous as that of Marx. But, although they had some things in common, there was no 'real intimacy' between these two, as Bakunin was the first to admit: 'Our temperaments did not allow it. He called me a sentimental idealist, and he was right. I called him morose, vain and treacherous, and I too was right.'[43]

The truth is that in 1844 Bakunin was more jealous of Marx than Marx of him, and with good reason. Marx's articles in the *Rheinische Zeitung* and the *German-French Yearbooks* had by now won him not only a name but friends and a group of devoted followers, including some who were wealthy enough to send him money to ease his exile. By contrast, Bakunin in all his years abroad had published nothing other than *The Reaction in Germany* and a letter printed in the *German-French Yearbooks*. In that letter, addressed to Ruge in 1843, he had asserted that revolution required 'the force of the whole people'. But Bakunin had no contact with the 'people'. Whereas Marx was introduced by Dr Ewerbeck to the inner councils of the Paris League of the Just and occasionally took time off to attend the meetings of Weitling's tailors, cobblers, and carpenters, Bakunin was too much of an aristocrat and a Romantic to believe that these simple manual workers and apprentices were the ideal material for a liberating revolution.

Like Marx, Bakunin spared no effort to convert Proudhon to his version of the revolutionary potential in Hegel's philosophy. He was still at it two years after Marx had left Paris, and the intensity of his protracted night-long arguments with the Frenchman may be gauged from the fact that Professor Karl Vogt, after listening one evening to their endless talk about Hegel's *Phenomenology*, became so bored that he went home to bed. When he returned next morning he found them 'sitting in the same places before the burnt-out embers in the fireplace, summing up the argument they had started the evening before.'[44]

By the time this episode occurred, Bakunin was once again living with Reichel at the pianist's modest apartment in the rue de Bourgogne. Proudhon often went there to listen to Reichel's Beethoven, but, as Herzen put it, 'the philosophical discussions lasted longer than the symphonies.' Although Bakunin treated Proudhon without Marx's condescension, he was no more successful in making a Hegelian out of him. Rather, the mild-mannered but feisty Proudhon's fierce stand against all institutions and any authority, coupled with his insistence that society as constituted was condemned to death, could not but have a fruitful effect on the Russian's own 'passion for destruction'. In the end it was Proudhon who would convert Bakunin and finally set him on the road to anarchism.

At the height of his later conflict with Marx, Bakunin was to publish a spiteful profile of him, but to pay him the tribute of writing 'Marx as a thinker is on the right path. He has established the principle that juridical evolution in history is not the cause but the effect of economic development, and this is a great and fruitful concept.' But, he added,

> Proudhon understood and felt liberty much better than he. Proudhon, when not obsessed with metaphysical doctrine, was a revolutionary by instinct... Quite possibly Marx could construct a still more rational system of liberty, but he lacked the instinct of liberty – he remains from head to foot an authoritarian[45]

and he was ultimately to challenge Marx's whole doctrine by declaring that a state ruled by the proletariat would be as evil as any other state. Whereas Bakunin, three years before his death, was again to give Marx the credit of having proved 'that economic conditions always precede (and fashion) the political and legal situation,'[46] Marx was less generous in his appreciation of Bakunin. From the beginning he regarded him as a muddle-headed 'Cossack'. Marx's correspondence with Engels does contain a favourable, if qualified reference to Bakunin – 'I liked him very much, better than last time' – but how little he changed his original appraisal may be judged from the name-calling he and Engels applied to the Russian over the years: 'Monster. Perfect blockhead. Stupid. Aspiring dictator of Europe's workers. Insolent. Flatterer. Ambitious, vain impotence. Quack. Charlatan. Ignoramus. Miserable liar. Prussian spy. Austrian government agent.'[47]

That Bakunin was to see in Marx 'an authoritarian', while Marx was to call him a would-be 'dictator', is not surprising. From the beginning of their acquaintance in Paris, each of them sensed the lust for power in the other. In 1844 Marx was a young man engaged in that process of 'self-clarification' which, originally announced in his programme for the *German-French Yearbooks*, was meant to help him decipher the direction of history and the hidden aim 'of the struggles and wishes of the age'. This, he had declared to Ruge at the time with a world-embracing ambition, 'is a task for the world and for us.'[48] Bakunin's ambition and lust for power were no less than Marx's. Two months on the Paris boulevards, he once remarked, 'was enough to turn a liberal into a Socialist,' but he was beginning to doubt whether all the French and German Socialist talk and theorizing would ever lead to anything. He sat in on the discussions at *Vorwärts!* but nothing of his appeared either in that newspaper or in those of the French opposition, like Girardin's *La Presse* or the republican-democratic *La Réforme*, though he met the editors of both.

Bakunin thirsted for action. The last days of civilization, he was to recall, seemed near when he arrived in Paris, but it was to take him a little longer to find an outlet for his revolutionary energy. He and Marx, each realizing the other's potential, respected, feared and mistrusted each other, quite apart from the unruly Russian's dislike of German discipline and Marx's well-known Russophobia. Outwardly, however, their relations in Paris were friendly, and Jenny Marx confirmed in her *Reminiscences* that Bakunin – together with 'Heine, Herwegh, Mäurer, Tolstoy, Annenkov, Bernays and tutti quanti' belonged to the Marxes' social circle during the second half of 1844 and until the end of their stay in Paris.

Although Paris was a great social observatory and 'capital of revolution', it was not all deadly seriousness. Mecca of freedom, the Paris where Marx argued into the small hours with Bakunin, Proudhon and the editors of *Vorwärts!* was not only the Paris of class frictions, of great luxury and vice clashing with poverty, of secret societies and Communist agitators. It was the constantly exciting centre of art and artists, the Paris of Victor Hugo, Balzac and George Sand, of Delacroix and Daumier, of Meyerbeer, Liszt and Chopin, of great hostesses, romances, literary feuds and petty intrigues.

In 1843, George Sand, having earlier accused Victor Hugo of not being 'sufficiently interested in humanity... it is because his heart lacks fire that his Muse lacks taste,' was calling him 'a man of genius who has been lost by praise and is going straight to the lunatic asylum.' Hugo, already elected to the Academy, was in fact heading straight for a peerage. At that, in his *Journal d'un révolutionnaire de 1831*, he had early forecast the crumbling of Europe's monarchies and expressed his confidence that within a century they would all be replaced by republics. By the 1840s, he was actually beginning to write that powerful masterwork of compassion for suffering humanity, *Les Misérables*, and he apparently had enough fire, spark and genius left in him to become the most eloquent spokesman for liberty against the ambitions of Louis Napoleon.

Marx admired Victor Hugo's works. He read them, as he did those of Balzac and George Sand, with gusto, and later would quote from them all in various contexts. There was good reason for his interest, for the novels of Balzac, George Sand and, for that matter, those of Eugène Sue, were paradoxically to prove more effective in undermining the social order and sowing mistrust in the July Monarchy than the multitude of contemporary Socialist-Communist tracts and pamphlets offering various solutions to the growing social problem. In exposing the passions, vices, manners and morals of the bourgeoisie, Balzac, like most of his fellow-writers, was seeking less to help the downtrodden proletariat than to present French society, in all its aspects, virtues and deficiencies, in a comprehensive picture for the general improvement of mankind.

Eugène Sue's scandalous novel *Les Mystères de Paris* was serialized in daily instalments in the *Journal des Débats* before it was published in 10 volumes and became a world success. Sue was a former navy surgeon, and no Socialist. He had started his writing career with a sea-romance, *Kernock le pirate*. In his *Mystères de Paris* he was primarily concerned to produce a sensational *roman-feuilleton*; yet the novel, with its scenes of glaring corruption, struck Marx as such 'a slap in the face of bourgeois prejudices', that he was prepared to exploit it in a lengthy analysis.

Everything, including fictional reality or the kernel of reality reflected in fiction, was grist to his mill. At the same time he was having a taste of *la vie mondaine* in the brilliant social circle of the comtesse Marie d'Agoult. This noblewoman, who had defied all the conventions of her class in 1835 by eloping with Franz Liszt when he was still a lowly 'piano huszar' – and then had borne him three children, one of whom (Cosima) was to marry Richard Wagner – had money, elegance, rank as well as an independent mind that keenly absorbed new trends and ideas in politics as in fashion. She also had literary ambitions, and after various efforts was to write what some modern scholars consider 'one of the best contemporary histories' of the 1848 revolution; others have ranked her with George Sand as one of the great 19th-century emancipators.[49]

Her sumptuous Renaissance-style drawing-room in the rue Neuve des Mathurins was thronged with French literary and artistic celebrities and foreign diplomats, but was also open to such political exiles as Adam Mickiewicz, the national poet of oppressed Poland, and Georg Herwegh. It was most likely Herwegh who, after succeeding Liszt as the countess's lover in the spring of 1844, first took his friend Marx along to one of her soirées. Herwegh's freebooting Russian friend, Bakunin, was also delighted to come along on occasion, if only to refresh 'the habit of French politesse and French mendacity' in the d'Agoult salon. It is not known whom the two met there, but among the countess's habitués were the poets Lamartine, Alfred de Vigny and Alfred de Musset; Sainte-Beuve, the literary critic; Emile de Girardin, the 'Bonaparte of the press'; the architect Felix-Louis-Jacques Duban, in charge of the restoration of the Louvre, who had designed the countess's drawing-room; Louis de Ronchaud, the Conservateur des Musées, who lived in the Louvre; the painter Henri Lehmann, and the more famous Ingres; the novelist Sue; the playwright Ponsard; the composer Meyerbeer; Edward Bulwer-Lytton, during his service at the British Embassy and whenever he passed through Paris later; and various other diplomats and distinguished foreigners.

At that time Mme d'Agoult was one of the most talked-about people in Paris, because she and George Sand – who once travelled as a group with Liszt and Chopin, socialized and enjoyed themselves together – had fallen out and were engaged in a literary guerrilla war. This had begun with George Sand's denigrating the countess in *Horace* and then inspiring Balzac's unfriendly novel on the d'Agoult-Liszt affair (*Béatrix, ou les amours forcés*). The countess prepared a novel of her own on the George Sand-Chopin affair. The mutual 'slaughter of pianists' was in full swing, and contrary to the suggestion in some accounts that Marx is likely to have met Chopin at Mme d'Agoult's, this was hardly the case. But with Jenny away in Germany for the better part of the summer and Heine too out of town, Marx enjoyed mingling in the d'Agoult salon with some of the *beau monde* of Paris in a luxurious setting of crystal chandeliers, Persian carpets, satin-upholstered settees, little tables *en laque de Chine*, and exquisite porcelain – at the very time when he was becoming the theoretician of Communism.

Marx also attended several of Grigory Tolstoy's receptions at his splendid *hôtel de ville* in the rue Mathurins where the Russian count entertained a cosmopolitan crowd of diplomats. Marx's friendship with the count is evident from the fact that, when Engels arrived for a short visit to Paris, Tolstoy was one of the first and few people to whom Marx took him. A frequent visitor there was, of course, Bakunin, who wrote that the ambience at his Russian friend's house warmed his 'petrified soul'. But because of Ruge's allegation that Marx spent much of the summer of 1844 in 'youthful adventures' with the playboy and sybarite Herwegh, his presence in Mme d'Agoult's salon has attracted more attention.

With its boulevard cafés, its bohemians and *demi-mondaines*, Paris was an intoxicating city, with temptation at every corner. Heine's Mathilde was a former shop-girl, and before her he had often had *grisettes* staying with him. Moses Hess, on his return to Paris a couple of years later, went hunting for them, or so Engels was to claim. Engels himself, though, was to write Marx that 'if there were no Frenchwomen, life would not be worth living. But so long as there are grisettes, well and good.'[50]

Engels came to Paris on 28 August 1844 for a short visit. He was on his way home to Germany from England, but the week and a half during which he stopped in Paris would be described a century later as 'one of the most decisive ten days in history'.[51] He later wrote that he and Marx took to each other immediately: 'We found ourselves in complete agreement on all questions of theory and our collaboration began there and then.' The tall, blond and 'Teuton-looking' Engels and the swarthy Marx proved to be ideal partners in more than one way. Engels was a cheerful, outgoing young man, brash and practical-minded. Marx was reticent and serious. Engels was quick-witted and combined an easy-going approach to life with a good business sense and a grasp of philosophical questions with a talent for simplifying complicated ideas. He loved riding, swimming, wine and women. He enjoyed life and was in many aspects the obverse and foil of the brooding abstract thinker Marx.

In one of his first letters to Marx after his arrival home in Barmen (informing him with glee that in his book on the condition of the English workers he was going to 'charge the English middle classes at the bar of world opinion with mass murder, wholesale robbery and all the crimes in the calendar'), Engels wrote that he was glad to take time off from dealing with abstract philosophical problems and to be 'actively concerned with real live issues'.[52] In short, he lived in the real world. Marx, as Herwegh said of him, 'knew the world more in theory than in practice'. By henceforth bringing the 'live issues' preoccupying men in the real world into Marx's secluded world of books, Engels was to become Marx's chief link with the life beyond his study, besides supplying him with the economic facts and empirical foundation he badly needed for his theories.

They shared an interest in historical developments, a love of literature and a bent for sharp, polemical thrusts. The legend of Engels's linguistic faculties, partly fostered by himself – he once boasted that he learned Persian in three weeks and found it 'mere child's play' – was not entirely a myth. For he did in time learn to read and write more than 20 languages, including Old Nordic as well as Arabic. Engels was not entirely cool and unemotional, as he has sometimes been depicted. When excited he stammered, with the result that he was said by some to stammer 'in twenty languages'.

Just as in Bremen he had made the best of his stint as a junior clerk in an export firm, Engels in his middle age organized his days as a prosperous industrialist so well that he found time not only for business, politics and writing, but also for studying biology, chemistry, botany and physics. On the basis of the year he had spent in the Berlin Guards Foot Artillery and copious reading, he also became – in his own eyes and those of some others – a military expert, eventually to be nicknamed in Marx's circle as 'the General'.

From Marx's viewpoint, Engels's 1844 Paris visit proved a blessing. It was as if he had been sent by the goddess Fortuna herself. How and where else would Marx, 'Fortune's child', have found a clever, educated and worldly-wise young man who, besides seeing eye to eye with him on all theoretical issues, was ready not only to serve as his disciple, friend, companion, amanuensis and collaborator for life, but from the very beginning, without a second thought, saw it as his natural duty to look after his financial needs? Starting with the modest sum of 50 Thaler which Engels collected for him at a time when he was still far from being the independent gentleman of means he was eventually to become, Engels soon offered Marx his fee for his *Condition of the Working Class in England*, so that 'the curs shan't have the satisfaction of seeing their infamy cause you pecuniary embarrassment.'[53]

In the aftermath, when he became a capitalist gentleman in Manchester, and later in London, he was to supply Marx and his family with all their material needs until Marx's death 39 years after their Paris meeting.

Just as remarkable, if not more so, is the otherwise assertive Engels's unconditional acceptance of Marx's intellectual superiority, an attitude which enabled him to work in close harmony with him for nearly 40 years, never once questioning his leadership, or ever, as far as is known, expressing any criticism or dissent such as may be common even among friends.

Engels was aware of Marx's domineering personality even before they met. Both Edmund Wilson and Künzli have cited his hatred of his pietist father – whom he variously described to Marx as a 'fanatical old despot' and a 'filthy *Schweinehund*' – as responsible for his apparent predisposition to 'live in the shadow' of a stronger personality, and to see in Marx something of 'the parental authority [he] had rejected in his father.'[54]

Be that as it may, Engels went through his early lean years as a journalist and Communist agitator in Brussels and Paris with the same unflappable buoyancy and suppleness he was later to show during his Jekyll-and-Hyde existence as a partner in his father's Ermen & Engels mills in Manchester – commuting between the respectable house he maintained in town and the cozy one in Salford where he lived with his Irish mistress Mary Burns. He frequented the Cotton Exchange and rode to hounds with the gentry, nonchalantly squaring his conscience and his 'horrible' fate as a 'money-grubbing' manufacturer living off the sweat of the workers, by providing Marx with funds and tirelessly assisting him to advance the cause of the 'downtrodden' proletariat.

The historic relationship was largely based on that devotion, bordering on self-effacement, which was to make Engels declare 5 years after Marx's death:

> What Marx achieved, I could not have achieved. Marx stood higher, saw further and surveyed more ground more quickly than we others. Marx was a genius, the rest of us were talented at best. Without him the theory would not, by a long way, be what it is today. It therefore rightly bears his name.[55]

There were two sides to Engels. He had a flair for the dramatic, and his quick pen and lively style made him an effective propagandist; but in his ardour he sometimes presented his over-confident hopes as facts. Twenty-one months spent in England had strengthened his imported idea that Britain was rife for revolution to the point of declaring – in an article written before he came to Paris – that if only the anti-unionist Daniel O'Connell would show more good judgment and resolve he could easily make himself master of Ireland. Falling into sheer bombast, he went on: 'What men! Genuine proletarians and Irishmen to boot, wild, fanatical, unbridled. Give me 2,000 Irishmen and I will topple the whole British Monarchy.'[56] Years later, referring to his unfulfilled prophecies, he was to say with some justice: 'The wonder is not that a good many of them proved wrong, but that so many of them have proved right.'

Other than meeting Bakunin, Tolstoy, Ewerbeck and Bernays, Engels spent most of his 1844 Paris visit in intensive discussions with Marx. Their talks have not been recorded, but a 20th-century biographer has written:

> With all the enthusiasm of young messiahs they proposed to overthrow the existing political and social order. Capitalism was to be replaced by a new kind of socialism. Established religions and philosophies were to be swept aside in favour of a new materialist ideology. The boldness of their plans was matched only by the astonishing successes that they eventually achieved.[57]

Stripped of hyperbole, this is what may have swum before their minds. But for the moment what Marx proposed was that they settle accounts with their old mentor, Dr Bruno Bauer. The Young Hegelians had by now been reduced to

933

political insignificance but published a little-read literary review upholding Bauer's theory of 'critical criticism'. Engels thought it would be fun to have a last stab at Bauer and wrote some 20 pages – his contribution to their planned pamphlet, which was to be titled *The Holy Family* (Bruno Bauer and his two brothers) – before he left Paris in September. He had no idea that Marx, irked by Bauer's elevating himself to the position of a super-critic looking down on 'the sufferings and joys of society' and laughing 'like the Olympian gods over the perversity of the world', would spend the coming months writing 300 pages for what had been intended as a spoof.

Marx had evidently discussed his unfinished *Manuscripts* with Engels, for the latter had not been back in Germany long before he urged his new friend to use his accumulated notes for a book on economics. 'Forge the iron while it is hot,' he kept admonishing Marx, stressing that there was a demand for such a book. 'Do as I do,' he advised, 'get yourself a date by which you definitely want to be finished... Down to work, then, and quickly into print!'[58] Engels was yet to learn that dates and deadlines meant nothing to Marx.

Engels had hardly left Paris when, on 12 September, King Friedrich Wilhelm IV in Berlin ordered that the publisher of *Vorwärts!*, Börnstein, as well as Heine, Marx and Ruge, should be arrested the moment they tried to cross the border into Prussia. Already at the end of July, the Prussian ambassador to Paris had made representations to the French government requesting the suppression of *Vorwärts!*. This followed an attempt on the life of Friedrich Wilhelm on 26 July. On that day, Heinrich Ludwig Tschech, a frustrated former burgomaster dismissed from his post at Storkow, had fired two shots at the King. He missed both times, but while the controlled Prussian press was at pains to stress the personal, non-political motive of the attempt, *Vorwärts!* took the opportunity to point out that the hitherto sacrosant person of the Prussian King was no longer inviolate, and that as an absolute ruler who had failed to learn the lessons of Charles I and Louis XVI, he was now free game.

Friedrich Wilhelm and his ministers felt that they had had enough. They had tolerated Heine's ridiculing the King in his poem 'The New Alexander', published in *Vorwärts!*; and now this 'garbage' of a German newspaper in Paris was justifying regicide as the only means left against German absolutism. At the beginning of August, it followed up with Marx's article against Ruge, in which he openly declared that Socialism could not come about 'without revolution... overthrow and dissolution'. Upon a further protest by the Prussian Ambassador von Arnim, France's chief minister, Guizot, promised to have Bernays, the co-editor of *Vorwärts!*, prosecuted. He was eventually to be sentenced to two months in the Sainte-Pélagie prison and made to pay a fine of 641 francs, including costs, on the charge that the paper had failed to pay its licence fee.

934

But as for prosecuting *Vorwärts!* for opinions expressed in its articles, this, Guizot pointed out, was a charge which had to go before a jury. Ambassador von Arnim, rightly fearing that the defendants, as often in jury trials, would use the stage for long political speeches and turn the tables upon his country, politely hinted that Prussia regarded this as an unsatisfactory solution.

An impasse of several months followed while Prussia, other than saving face by the ineffective order of 12 September for the arrest of Börnstein and the others, sought alternate means of silencing *Vorwärts!* and its writers.

From Trier, Jenny Marx informed her husband not only that their little Jennychen had so well recovered that he would hardly recognize her when they returned, but also that the ex-burgomaster Tschech had been reduced to begging and starvation in Berlin before he tried to shoot the King. Referring to his deed as a 'socially motivated assassination attempt', she added a phrase which might have come from Marx's own mouth: 'This is yet another proof that Germany is not ready for a political revolution, but for a social one all the more so.'[59]

Also preparing to return to Paris was Heine. On 21 September, 9 days after the Prussian order for his arrest at the border, Heine – who had actually been in Hamburg since the last week of July, having arrived there together with Mathilde by boat from Le Havre in order to avoid Prussian soil – wrote to Marx that he had received a 'hint from higher up' to leave, and planned to be back in Paris within a fortnight or so.

His business in Hamburg was the difficulties Campe was making over publishing *Germany, A Winter's Tale*. He travelled with Mathilde (who would not go without her parrot) out of a natural wish to introduce her to his mother and those of his family who – with the exception of his Uncle Salomon and a few others – had never met her. Uncle Salomon was now 77 and not in the best of health. His fortune, estimated at 41 million francs, made him one of the richest men (if not the richest) in Europe. On a visit to Paris a couple of years back Salomon had complimented his nephew on his 'well-behaved wife', and on his return home had thoughtfully sent her a Christmas present. But if Heine hoped that Mathilde's presence by his side would improve his chances of Salomon's remembering him with a tidy sum in his will, he was to be disappointed.

Heine's family gave Mathilde a friendly reception and feted her in style. But Mathilde soon felt out of sorts in the opulent environment of the old nabob, whose idea of the good life was to dine with his family and various rich, self-satisfied guests – on crab soup with raisins, smoked ox meat, pheasants, hares and English pudding washed down with champagne and choice wines – and then repair to the theatre. The fact that she hardly spoke a word of German did not help. Salomon's two sons-in-law admired her well-developed figure and found her charmingly naive and vivacious, but the women thought her loud and temperamental, and there was no rapport between the two parties. On 9 August, after only a fortnight or so in Hamburg, Mathilde chose to return to Paris by herself, on the pretext that her mother had been taken ill.

To make matters worse, Heine soon got into one of his usual arguments with Uncle Salomon. The failing and irritable banker was annoyed by the way his nephew kept insulting royal personages and exposing their vices; and asked who he thought he was to have written the insolent 'Hymn' to King Ludwig of Bavaria. Heine replied that the King of Bavaria 'writes verse, and he spoils my trade.' At one point – as Heine later reported to his sister – their uncle 'got so agitated that he even hit me with his stick.'[60] A couple of days later, however, Salomon was apologizing to his nephew and by 11 August Heine was dining with his uncle at Ottensen.

With Mathilde gone, Heine was free for his negotiations with Campe. The two always got on better face to face in Campe's office behind his bookshop or in the literary cafés they frequented in the evening. Heine's eyes were deteriorating – 'I am ¾ blind... the left eye is completely shut, the other is blurred,' he wrote to Detmold in mid-September[61] – but in between attending a theatre and an opera performance and another dinner at Ottensen castle, he spent most of his time supervising the publication of the fifth edition of his *Book of Songs*, the 'Buch der Lieder' which had made him famous when he was young.

While this appeared at the beginning of September, Heine went on correcting the proofs of his volume of *New Poems*. He had won his battle with Campe: *Germany, A Winter's Tale*, of which he sent Marx the advance proofs on 21 September, was to be included – together with his *Tannhäuser*, his topical *Zeitgedichte* and a number of ballads – in *New Poems*, making a volume of over 20 sheets and thus exempting it from pre-censorship, just as he had wanted. To be on the safe side, Campe issued it under a Paris imprint, Dubochet et Cie, on 25 September. At the same time, in his letter to Marx, Heine asked him to print the section containing *Germany, A Winter's Tale* in *Vorwärts!* and to enlist Moses Hess and other of their friends to drum up favourable reviews of it. He knew what he was doing, for the onslaught he expected was not long in coming.

In the first week of October, Campe brought out the inflammatory poem in a separate edition in Hamburg, which contained Heine's famous Preface. At the same time the Paris edition of *New Poems* was being confiscated in Prussia, which also requested all the states of the German Bund to prohibit it. In mid-October Campe published a second printing of *Germany, A Winter's Tale* in Hamburg, but on the 17th *New Poems* was prohibited in Hessen. On the 18th, the same prohibition was announced in Hessen-Nassau; on the 20th in Brunswick; on the 21st in Lübeck; on the 23rd in Frankfurt. Both *New Poems* and the separate *Germany, A Winter's Tale* had also been prohibited in Denmark. But starting on 23 October and throughout November, *Vorwärts!* kept serializing *Germany, A Winter's Tale* even as more prohibition orders were issued in Mecklenburg, Württemberg and Bavaria.

Heine left Hamburg on 9 October. It had been a productive but also hectic and enervating summer. His eyes had improved somewhat, but his headaches had returned. His *Silesian Weavers* was being distributed as a clandestine leaflet in Prussia as he set out for Paris via Amsterdam, The Hague and Brussels. He was tired, as he had written to Marx on 21 September in a scribble he could hardly read himself, of being spied upon: 'my legs are not made for wearing iron manacles such as those to which Weitling was chained.'

Heine did not mention his running into Weitling in Campe's bookshop, but he may have told Marx after his return to Paris what he was later to write about the ex-tailor in his *Confessions*: namely, that Weitling was a talented man but a dangerous rabble-rouser. Heine never hid from Marx his opinion that once the proletarian 'rats' and 'cohorts of destruction' were unleashed, they would bring down the 'entire social edifice' in their levelling zeal. Nor did he hesitate to tell Marx, this time in his letter of September 1844, that *Vorwärts!* had lately exceeded the most extreme radical bounds. He had a feeling that the paper's days were numbered.

As it happened, shortly after Heine returned to Paris in mid-October, Marx received a letter from Weitling. Expelled from Hamburg, the martyred leader of the League of the Just had transferred his activities to London, where some of his former Paris associates had established a secret branch of the League. He offered Marx his friendship and invited him to write to him. Ironically, Marx was presently to confine Weitling to that oblivion which was to make Heine refer to him in the *Confessions* as the 'forgotten' author of 'the first catechism of the German Communists'.[62]

Jenny Marx had returned to Paris with the recovered Jennychen in September. Shortly afterwards, as she had foreseen, she became pregnant with her second child. Jenny had brought with her the 'healthy young wet-nurse', Gretchen, who had helped to nurse Jennychen back to health in Trier. Jennychen, however, remained a sickly infant, and her parents often feared she might not survive.

This led to the memorable occasion when Heine, dropping in on them one day in the autumn, found the baby having a fit of violent convulsions. Karl and Jenny Marx and the wet-nurse, fearing for her life, stood about half-paralyzed, at a loss what to do. Heine took one look at the situation and said: 'The baby must have a hot bath.' He prepared the bath himself, placed the baby in it, and as Marx would often say, saved Jennychen's life. Marx said it so often in the hearing of his children that after his death his youngest, Eleanor, communicated the episode to the Socialist leader Kautsky, who published it in 1895.[63]

Marx spent most of the autumn of 1844 writing his part of *The Holy Family*. What infuriated Marx about Bauer and his monthly, *Allgemeine Literatur-Zeitung*, was its elitist view that Hegel's 'World Spirit' moved the process of history, and that the proletarian masses were merely one element of society. In Bauer's view the self-interest or 'enthusiasm' of these masses sometimes even hampered the progress of history, of which the philosophers with their 'pure thought' were the true wardens.

In *The Holy Family* Marx retorted that the toiling workers could not rid themselves of their industrial masters by 'reasoning them away through pure thought'. Summarizing some of the ideas he had put on paper in the *Manuscripts*, he stated again that not history, but man, had to change the industrial conditions which degraded him – 'History is nothing but the activity of man pursuing his aims.' Stressing the relation between 'the mode of production' of any given period and mankind's historical progress, he declared that 'together with the thoroughness of the historical action, the size of the mass whose action it is will increase.'[64]

But these politico-economic statements were largely wasted because *The Holy Family* – in most of which he satirically reviewed reviews of books which had appeared in Bauer's periodical – was hardly the kind of material that would appeal to any but a very limited public. Engels was surprised to learn that the contemplated brochure had grown into a book of almost 300 pages. He thought that 'the sovereign derision that we accord to the Allgemeine Literatur-Zeitung is in stark contrast to the considerable number of pages we devote to its criticism.'[65]

Marx finished *The Holy Family* some time in November 1844. At the end of the month, after trying in vain to have it printed in Paris, he sent the manuscript to the Frankfurt publisher Zacharias Löwenthal, who accepted it with the realization that this book about another publication had no great chance of success unless he managed to drum up some accompanying sensation.

In mid-December, a couple of months before it was to be published, Marx received his author's fee of 1,000 francs. Shortly afterwards, the proddings of Engels, Georg Jung and a couple of other Communists in Germany that Marx should write a book on economics seemed to bear fruit when another radical publisher, Karl W. Leske of Darmstadt, offered him a contract for a two-volume work, to be entitled *A Critique of Politics and National Economy*, and proposed coming to Paris early in the new year for the purpose of negotiating the contract and a suitable advance.

33

The 'Doctors' Take up Their Positions for the Coming Revolution

Though 1845 started off with good auguries for Marx, he soon received bad tidings. The Prussian King and his advisers had at last found a way of putting an end to *Vorwärts!*. The sophisticated Alexander von Humboldt was sent to Paris as a special envoy of Friedrich Wilhelm IV to King Louis-Philippe. On 7 January he presented the King with a lengthy letter and a special gift – a splendid porcelain vase – from Friedrich Wilhelm. Two years earlier the latter, under pressure from the Tsar, had suppressed the *Rheinische Zeitung*. Now he invoked the solidarity of kings against a journal which encouraged regicide, calculating that Louis-Philippe, who had so often been a target of attempts on his life, could hardly turn a deaf ear to such an appeal.

On 11 January the French Minister of the Interior ordered the expulsion of 8 foreigners associated with *Vorwärts!*, including Marx, Heine, Ruge, Börnstein and Bernays. The order was to go into effect within 24 hours of its delivery, but after protests in the French press its execution was postponed. Heine, however, had been born in the Rhineland under French occupation; this gave him the right of residence in France and he was exempted from the order. Börnstein closed down *Vorwärts!* and used the reprieve to enter the service of the French police and to have his expulsion rescinded. Ruge protested his innocence and, being a Saxon citizen, not a Prussian, he was allowed to stay.

Bernays was in jail, not to be released before the end of February. From Sainte-Pélagie he complained that his trial and imprisonment had consumed all his means, 'and if friends do not help me, I must leave here as a beggar.' This was indeed to be his lot before he eventually emigrated to the USA.

Marx was given a hint that he could stay if he would stop writing against friendly powers. He refused, and he and Heinrich Bürgers, a young journalist who had worked on *Vorwärts!*, were the only ones to go. As Jenny was to write in her Reminiscences: 'Suddenly, at the beginning of 1845 [actually on 25 January], the police commissioner came to our house and showed us an expulsion order made out by Guizot at the request of the Prussian Government. "Karl Marx must leave Paris within 24 hours," the order ran.' Marx, however, was granted a week's delay. This was lucky for him, for the Darmstadt publisher Leske was in town. On 1 February 1845 he signed a contract with Marx for the two-volume *Critique of Politics and National Economy* and gave him an advance of 1,500 francs.

The same day, several hours after dashing off the note to Heine saying, 'Of all the people I am leaving behind here... I would gladly include you in my luggage!', Marx took the stage-coach to Belgium together with Leske and Bürgers. They arrived in Brussels on 3 February and spent the night in a hotel. The following evening Marx went to visit Ferdinand Freiligrath, the poet who, during the 1842 furore created by Herwegh's revolutionary verses, had attacked him in the name of 'pure art' by reminding him that 'The poet stands on a loftier watch-tower/Than on the party battlements.'

In those days, when Herwegh eclipsed his own fame, Freiligrath had calmly accepted a royal Prussian pension. For this he had been attacked in Marx's *Rheinische Zeitung*, and Marx himself had privately called him an enemy not only of Herwegh but of freedom. Since then, however, Freiligrath, drawing his own conclusions from the serial closure of Ruge's Yearbooks and the *Rheinische Zeitung*, Herwegh's expulsion and the general wave of repression in Prussia, had climbed down from his 'lofty watch-tower'. After renouncing his royal state pension, publishing an uncensored book, and declaring in a Confession of Faith ('*Glaubenbekenntnis*') that he was joining the freedom fighters who were 'bravely trying to stem the reaction,' he had, to escape arrest, fled with his wife to Brussels.

Marx's visit, by way of making amends to him, gained him a life-long friend in Freiligrath. Although too independent-minded to become a 'toe-the-line' Communist, Freiligrath, closely collaborating with Marx in 1848–49, was to become the poet of those revolutionary years, acclaimed for his articles and poems distributed as leaflets.

At his apartment in February 1845 Marx met the radical journalist Karl Heinzen. These two and a couple of other German intellectuals, such as the young but rising poet and satirist Georg Weerth, helped him to overcome the not-too-friendly reception given him by the Brussels authorities.

On 7 February, a couple of days after his arrival, Marx addressed a petition to King Leopold I 'humbly' requesting permission to take up residence in Belgium. Brussels had once offered asylum to Buonarroti, the hounded last hero of the French Revolution, and he had there written his famous book on The Conspiracy of the Equals. Now it had only a small colony of political refugees and other émigrés from France, Poland and Germany. The Belgians tolerated them as long as they did not engage in political propaganda. Marx, however, had no sooner arrived than the Prussian Ambassador demanded his expulsion. There followed a 6-weeks-long flurry of Belgian inter-office correspondence – the suspicion being that Marx planned to start publishing *Vorwärts!* in Brussels, while the German police sought to make sure that he did not mean to return to Prussia.

Marx was eventually permitted to stay, but not before he signed a pledge in the office of the Sûreté Publique, consenting 'on my honour not to publish any work on the politics of the day.' Later, when he began to feel harassed by Prussian police spies and feared that at the slightest breach of his pledge the Belgians, like the French, would expel him without further ado, he wrote to the Mayor of Trier and asked for an 'emigration permit' to the USA. Whether he was serious or not, he received no answer, and became so furious that he wrote a second letter renouncing his Prussian citizenship. The two letters were passed on to the authorities in Berlin, who felt that it would be no loss to denaturalize and get rid of him. Before the end of his first year in Brussels, Marx thus ceased to be a Prussian citizen and became a man without a country.

When he left Paris, Jenny had remained behind in order, as she was to recall in her *Reminiscences*, 'to sell my furniture and some of my linen. I got ridiculously little for it, but I had to find money for our journey. The Herweghs gave me hospitality for two days. Ill and in bitter cold weather', she and her 8-months-old child followed Marx to Brussels in mid-February. 'There we put up at Bois Sauvage Hotel, and I met Heinzen and Freiligrath for the first time.'

The 'Bois Sauvage Hotel' was actually a tavern which Georg Weerth, who lived there for a time, described as cheap but run by 'honest, somewhat stupid people', who spared no effort to please their guests. The Marxes stayed there for only a month before moving temporarily into Freiligrath's vicinity. According to Jenny, 'In May we moved [again] into a small house... in the Rue de l'Alliance, outside Porte du Louvain', a slum quarter. She was pregnant again, and they had no money at all.

In January, Engels had allowed himself to be persuaded by 'the doleful expression' on his parents' faces 'to give huckstering another trial' and work for a while in the office of his father's textile factory. But within a fortnight he was writing to Marx in Brussels:

> Another motive was the course my love affair was taking. But I was sick of it all even before I began work; huckstering is too beastly, Barmen is too beastly, the waste of time is too beastly and most beastly of all is the fact of being, not only a bourgeois, but actually a manufacturer, a bourgeois who actively takes sides against the proletariat.[1]

He had not yet developed the cynicism and savoir-faire which in his maturity were to enable him to play a double role, and added in the same letter, 'A few days in my old man's factory have sufficed to bring me face to face with this beastliness, which I had rather overlooked.' Always a gay blade, the versatile Engels worked off his 'simmering rage' by putting the last jolly accords to a love affair with a girl to whom he had made certain promises before going to Manchester and by 'recording daily the most horrifying tales about English society' for the book he was writing. From the beginning, Engels stressed to Marx the impressive change he had found in the Wuppertal Valley on his return after less than two years' absence: 'The Wuppertal has made more progress than in the last 50 years, it has become more civilized; everyone is interested in politics and in resisting authority.' Before the end of January, he had this to say about the growing interest in Communism: 'The Wuppertal Communism is a reality [une vérité], indeed almost a force. You have no idea how favourable the soil is here. The most stupid, insolent, philistine people, hitherto without any interest in anything in the world, are beginning almost to rave about Communism.'[2]

Engels may be pardoned for giving Marx so optimistic a picture. Moses Hess, who had returned to Cologne in the spring of 1844, had shortly afterwards likewise remarked to Marx on the 'spread of Socialism' in the Rhineland. Writing in the wake of the stir made by the Silesian weavers' strike, he had forecast, 'before long the whole of educated Germany will become Socialist, radically Socialist, I mean Communist.'[3]

Hess, together with Georg Jung and a few other intellectuals, had since then founded a Communist Club in Cologne. Engels had no sooner returned to Germany than he visited Cologne and resumed contact with Hess. Among the club's prominent members were three medical doctors – Andreas Gottschalk, Karl D'Ester and Robert Daniels – who were later to play a role in Communist history. The club's other leaders included the poet H. Püttmann, Karl Grün, the editor of a Mannheim newspaper whose expulsion from Baden had given him national prominence, and the painter G.K. Köttgen. It was through Hess and his club that Engels, after Marx's expulsion from Paris, launched the subscription in Cologne, Düsseldorf and Westphalia that collected 750 francs for him. At the beginning of 1845 Engels and Hess also frequently met at Bonn and in Barmen-Elberfeld.

Near the end of February, Engels was reporting to Marx: 'Here in Elberfeld wondrous things are afoot.' He and Hess had started staging public debates on Communism before the manufacturers, judges, lawyers and notables dining out on Saturday nights at the largest inn in Engels's home town, which was becoming a major centre of the cotton, silk and textile-dying industry. The first of the debates had taken place on 8 February. To disguise what may have been the first public Communist propaganda meeting in Germany, the evening opened with an artistic programme – complete with harp-playing girls, a poetry reading by

Püttmann and excerpts from Shelley – after which Hess delivered a lecture on 'The Ills of the Industrial Age'.

Dwelling on the abysmal gap between rich and poor threatening to 'destroy our civilization', he demanded the abolishment of the old system of competition, which was 'downright robbery', and argued that only the peaceful adoption of Communism would forestall an eventual revolution dictated by misery. Engels, who spoke after him, tried to demonstrate to the factory owners present that abolishing social differences would abolish 'not only crimes against property, and the need for police forces, but standing armies as well, since aggressive wars would cease', while defensive wars would be won by people fighting for their hearths with a devotion before which 'modern armies with their machine-like training would disperse like chaff before the wind.' Engels wrote to Marx that the discussion which followed lasted until 1 a.m. and that, while this 'first meeting was forty strong, the second drew 130 and the third at least 200' people.

The second and third meetings took place on 15 and 22 February. According to Hess's biographer, some of the factory owners at first refused to be convinced by what they heard and responded with grunts, but the debates grew ever more lively. A lawyer from Cologne and the painter Köttgen joined Hess and Engels in expounding Communism, while the director of Elberfeld's theatre was most eloquent in opposing it.[4]

The curious Communist debates to an audience washing down their beefsteaks with wine came to an end when Hess and Engels ventured to announce that their next topic would be 'Ways of Introducing Communism under Present Circumstances'. This was accepted after some discussion. Applause at the first debate had gone mostly to those who opposed or ridiculed Communism. But gradually it became equally divided, and the meetings had aroused great interest. The local manufacturers, aware by now that poverty breeds unrest, were ready to listen, having no idea how to go about reforms or what 'Communism' meant. But the fourth meeting never took place. A deputation of Elberfeld workers – who so far had not dared attend, but now wanted to sit in on the debate – found the inn patrolled by gendarmes brought in from Düsseldorf.

Hess's protest to the mayor was of no avail, but his and Engels's speeches were to be printed in the *Rheinische Jahrbücher*, a quarterly dedicated on its masthead to social reform which was to be launched in September by Leske.

At the beginning of March, Hess moved to Elberfeld and took a room at the City of London inn. He and Marx had for some time prepared to co-edit a monthly to be called *Gesellschaftsspiegel* ('Society Mirror'). A local 'Communist bookseller' undertook to publish it. When Engels wrote to Marx that even if the Communist debates would ultimately be banned 'we have stirred things up so mightily that every publication representing our interest will be voraciously read here,'[5] he had these two periodicals in mind. With a third, the *Westfälische Dampfboot*, edited by the Socialist Dr Lüning in Bielefeld, sympathetic to their cause, both Hess and Engels felt that the year-long agitation conducted by Hess in the Rhineland and Westphalia, and intensified since Engels's arrival, had led to Communism's making 'enormous strides' in the area.

To keep things in proportion, it needs to be noted that the first issue of the *Gesellschaftsspiegel* – the only one whose production Engels took a hand in before he left his home-town – sold 330 copies in Elberfeld, mostly to workers. Copies passed from hand to hand and it was also distributed at inns. Subsequent issues were also read by German workers in Paris and London as well. All things considered, it may, at a guess, have reached an audience of one or two thousand at most.

Nonetheless, just as Marx had found in the 100 or 200 Communist tailors, tanners, and carpenters meeting at the Barrière du Trone – 'half a dozen journeymen', as Ruge contemptuously dismissed them – confirmation for his view of the German proletariat as a rising 'Cinderella', so the altogether 12 issues that appeared of the *Gesellschaftsspiegel* were seen by some contemporaries as constituting the chief Socialist organ in Germany.

On 17 March, Engels wrote to Marx that he had finished his book, *The Condition of the Working Class in England in 1844*, and sent the manuscript to the publisher Wigand in Leipzig. Engels had by then received a copy of *The Holy Family*. Having contributed so little to this book, he was surprised to see its authors named as 'Friedrich Engels and Karl Marx', in that order, and feared that the very title would 'lead to family upsets with my pious father.' The sanctimonious senior Engels could not bear the idea of his son's conducting Communist debates with the likes of Hess, becoming a police suspect and disgracing him in the community. Engels junior faced such shocked 'long faces' and family interrogation about his activities that the atmosphere at home was 'enough to drive one bananas'. Referring to 'the sheer malice' behind his father's 'wild Christian hunt' for his soul, Engels poured out his heart to Marx:

> The old man's wrath has been further exacerbated by my declared intention of giving up the huckstering trade... If I get a letter it's sniffed all over before it reaches me... I go out – the same expression. If I sit in my room and work – Communism, of course, as they know – the same expression. I can't eat, drink, sleep, let out a fart, without being confronted by this same accursed lamb-of-God expression...

> Were it not for my mother, who has a rare fund of humanity – only towards my father does she show no independence whatever – and whom I really love, it would not occur to me for a moment to make even the most paltry concession to my bigoted and despotic old man.

But as it is, my mother is making herself ill with her constant fretting, and every time she gets particularly upset about me, she is
afflicted with headaches for a week. It's more than I can bear, I must
get away, and hardly know how I shall be able to stand the few
remaining weeks here.[6]

He finally left at the beginning of April. A passage in an earlier letter, saying that
perhaps 'the police wouldn't like' his propaganda 'so that I could with good grace
make off across the border', suggests that he had been rather hoping to be forced
to leave, probably also as a way of extricating himself from his local love affair.

He went straight to Brussels and moved into a house adjoining the one in
which Karl and Jenny Marx lived in the shabby rue d'Alliance. Not only Marx
but Jenny too welcomed this new friend of his whom in time she was to come to
resent for sharing her husband with her for the next 37 years, until her death.

In September, Hess, having been made to feel unwelcome by the authorities
in Elberfeld, arrived in Brussels with his mistress. He rented an apartment at 3
rue d'Alliance. Marx lived at No. 5, Engels at No. 7.

In the course of the three years Marx was to spend in Brussels, there formed
around him a group of some 20 German Communists and other radicals who
admired him. Some lived there more or less permanently and some – like the
poets Freiligrath and Weerth – only for a couple of months, but would return
on visits. The most notable of them was Weitling, who, since meeting Heine in
Hamburg, had been given a hero's welcome by the German workers in London.
One of the most memorable figures to join Marx's circle was Wilhelm Wolff,
also known as Lupus or 'Kasemattenwolff' for having escaped from a Silesian
fortress after 4 years' incarceration for a violation of the press law, a man whose
friendship with Jenny and Marx was, as she wrote, 'dissolved only by his death
in 1864', when he left them his entire estate of £825.

Others were Joseph Weydemeyer, a former Prussian artillery officer who had
become a radical journalist in Westphalia and spent 4 months in Brussels as a
guest of the Marxes; Sebastian Seiler, a German registrar who had helped Weitling in Switzerland and since arriving in Brussels ran a press agency; Jenny's
younger brother, Edgar von Westphalen, whom both she and Marx were very
fond of, and who lived with them for a year or more until the end of 1847; and
two typesetters, Karl Wallau and Stephan Born.

Marx's friends in Cologne, Georg Jung and Dr Roland Daniels, also came on
visits. Except for the two typesetters, Marx's circle consisted chiefly of German
professionals or intellectuals. 'Among them were three physicians, nine journalists and writers, including two poets. In 1845, their average age was twenty-
eight.'[7]

There was at this time complete harmony between Marx, Hess and Engels. Not only were they next-door neighbours, but with Marx now flanked by Engels, his new young lieutenant, and Hess – Germany's first Communist and one of the first to have recognized in Marx the young man 'who will give medieval religion and politics their coup de grace' – this triumvirate was at the core of the circle that planned to revolutionize the world.

Marx and Hess were chronically poor. Engels too, though born into a rich family, was momentarily out of pocket, his father having cut off his allowance – or so Georg Weerth wrote at the time. Marx's financial affairs are so difficult to unravel that, contrary to Padover's statement that when Jenny joined him in Brussels in mid-February 1845 'there was no money', David McLellan has written that the Marxes at this time had 'a comfortable source of income from the sale of the furniture and linen in Paris and the 1,500 francs advance that Marx had received [from Leske] for his forthcoming book,' not to mention the 1,000 francs he had earlier got for *The Holy Family*. or the nearly 1,000 francs Engels and Hess had collected for him about the very time of Jenny's arrival.[8] Indeed, adding up all the sums Marx had received since the previous summer, one can suggest that he should have been in funds for a couple of years.

And yet, whether his difficulties began in February 1845 or only in May 1846, when he wrote to Weydemeyer in Germany, 'I am in a serious financial predicament. In order to make ends meet for the time being, I recently pawned the last gold and silver things and a large part of the linen', until the eve of his expulsion from Brussels at the beginning of 1848, when his mother sent him about 6,000 francs as an advance on his inheritance, Marx constantly had to appeal to friends and supporters to bail him out of debt and chronic insolvency.

The contract Marx had signed with Leske provided for the manuscript of the two-volume *Critique of Politics and National Economy* to be delivered in the summer of 1845. But Marx felt, after devouring more quantities of books on economics in the Brussels Municipal Library, that he still needed more research on the subject. Besides, he and Hess might be poor and Engels financially insecure, but their heads teemed with many new projects. One of them was sparked off by a book published in Germany by Max Stirner, a friend of Bruno Bauer from the days of the Doctors Club in Berlin. In *Der Einzelne und Sein Eigentum* ('The Individual and His Property'), Stirner claimed that man had to free himself from the delusions and humbug inculcated in his mind over thousands of years by the tenets of Christianity, the principles of the French Revolution, the clamour of the bourgeoisie and now by the Communist preachers. Communism, he wrote, rightly attacked the injustice of private property, 'but the power which Communism wishes to vest in the collective is a more frightening prospect than the pressure I suffer from individual property-owners.'

Stirner's general thesis was that only man's 'individuality' could save him from the oppressive 'religious, political, philosophical figments of the imagination'. 'I as an ego,' he wrote, 'set myself against the chimeras with which man in our time besets himself... They must be scattered by the will and the penetrative clarity of the ego which knows I am alone in the world, dependent on myself alone and the creative powers that are within me.'[9]

As early as January 1845, before leaving Barmen-Elberfeld, Engels had – in answer to a letter from Marx concerning Stirner's book – written to him that Hess 'read me an article, which he is shortly to publish, about [Stirner's] book. In it he says the same as you, although he hasn't read your letter.'[10]

Hess's article, 'The Last Philosophers', was published a couple of months later by Leske in Darmstadt, by which time Marx was beginning to feel that attacking Bruno Bauer in *The Holy Family* had not been enough and that he must wage 'a last battle' to demolish Bauer, Stirner, Feuerbach and other speculative idealists. He and Engels planned to do so, with Hess's participation, in a polemical work to be titled *The German Ideology*. This seemed to Marx more important than writing the book contracted by Leske; for, as he was later to explain to the baffled publisher, to 'prepare the public for the point of view of my Economics', he first had to dispose of 'previous German intellectual thought' which was diametrically opposed to his own.

Another project conceived by Hess and Engels, and in which Marx was involved, was to produce a 'library' of German translations of the works of foreign Socialists, such as Buonarroti, Fourier, Dézamy, and Robert Owen. And there were other distractions. In April, Jenny's mother sent the Marxes a precious 'gift' in the person of Lenchen (Helene) Demuth, the trusted maid who had served in the Westphalen household since before she was 12. In June, when Jenny left together with the 14-months old Jennychen to spend the last months of her second pregnancy with her mother in Trier, she took Lenchen along and then brought her back to Brussels. Lenchen, who was 21, turned out to be indispensable: her skill in running the house, raising the children and managing all things ultimately impressed even Marx to the point of declaring that she 'could have managed the universe'. She became, in fact, a member of the Marx family, firm and and stable as she went with them through all their domestic crises until Marx's death, following which she was to look after Engels in his old age.

In July, while Jenny was away, Engels took Marx on a visit to England, for which, according to Engels's biographer, his father paid.[11] Indeed, the elder Engels is known to have later sent his rebellious son monthly remittances to Paris to keep him away from Barmen-Elberfeld and out of harm's way. Marx and Engels spent several weeks in Manchester, where Engels was glad to see his

Irish girl friend Mary Burns again. He took Marx to Chetham's Library, where they sat together in Engels's favourite alcove where (in Engels's words) the stained glass window ensured 'that the weather is always fine,' and Marx took the opportunity of studying and making excerpts from the works of William Cobbett, William Thompson and other English economists.

They then spent some time in London. Engels introduced Marx to the Chartist leader George Julian Harney, who, as editor of the Socialist *Northern Star*, appointed Engels as its European correspondent. They also met the leaders of the German Workers' Educational Society, a legally constituted Society which functioned at the Red Lion public house near Piccadilly. While justifying its name by running a well-organized programme of educational and artistic activities, including 'lectures on history, geography, astronomy or labour conditions (every Sunday); discussions with French members (every Monday); contemporary politics (every Tuesday); singing lessons, language and drawing classes, dance evenings and literary recitals (on the four remaining days in the week)', it was actually a front organization for the London branch of Weitling's League of the Just. From its leaders – Karl Schapper, Joseph Moll and Heinrich Bauer – Marx and Engels learned much about the structure and the overt and covert activities of both organizations. It is not known whether they also met Weitling himself while they were there, but they heard with interest that, since the enthusiastic reception the martyred 'King of Tailors' had been given on his arrival in London, ideological differences had arisen between him and the local leadership.

At a meeting held in London in June 1845, shortly before the visit of Marx and Engels, he pressed for an early revolution. Everybody, he claimed, was

> ripe for Communism, even the criminals. Criminals are a product of the present order of society and under Communism they would cease to be criminals. Humanity is of necessity always ripe for revolution, or it never will be. The latter is said by our opponents. If we follow them we shall have no choice but to fold our hands on our knees and pray till roasted pigeons fly into our mouths.[12]

To Weitling's surprise, the leaders of the London branch, all former associates of his, disagreed with him. Schapper, himself a veteran revolutionary who had known Georg Büchner and Mazzini, said that 'the truth could not be knocked into people's heads with rifle butts', and the majority voted with Schapper. Bitter experience and the moderating influence of British politics – and perhaps most of all the recruiting success of the Chartists – had taught Schapper and his friends that there could be no instant revolution by a conspiratorial minority, but that the masses had to be educated for it.

In September, some time after their return to Brussels, Marx interrupted work on his *Politics and National Economy*. His mind was set on *The German Ideology*, and Leske would have to wait for his book until Marx and Engels had disposed of Stirner's anti-social 'ego' theory and all 'previous German intellectual thought'. On 26 September, shortly after returning from the visit to her mother, Jenny gave birth to their second daughter, Laura. And in London, that month, about 1,000 people attended a 'Festival of Nations' to celebrate 'the establishment of the French Republic on 22 September 1792.' The organizers were the international society of Fraternal Democrats, born a year earlier at a celebration in honour of Weitling. As befitted its name, the society's slogan was 'All Men Are Brethren'. 'Love' and 'brotherhood' had indeed figured widely in Weitling's early writings.

London, of course, had a larger colony of foreign radicals from many lands than Brussels had. Half of the 250-strong German Workers' Educational Society were in fact Poles, Russians, Italians, Swiss, Scandinavians, Belgians and French. The main speakers at the ''Festival of Nations' were Harney for the Left Chartists; Dr Berrier-Fontaine, a French Republican and disciple of the Communist Cabet; and Weitling for the German Workers' Society and the League of the Just. Prison may or may not have upset Weitling's 'already precarious mental balance', as has been claimed, but it was his speech that galvanized the crowd and was constantly interrupted by applause. Attacking repacious 'national rulers' who broke the international solidarity of the working class by leading its members to war against each other, he asked rhetorically:

> Is it the interest of sheep to be led by wolves to fight against sheep likewise led by wolves? (Loud cheers). Is it possible that the people can be more murdered than we are by our cruel money-men, who rob us by their stock-jobbing, money dealing and speculating; by their currency and by their bankruptcy, by their monopolies, church and land rents, who by all those means rob us of the necessities of life, and cause the death of millions of our working brethren to whom they leave not even potatoes enough to live upon. (Great cheering)... Is it possible then that we could be more stolen from, and murdered in a time of political war, than we are now, in a so-called state of peace?

He finished by extolling 'the feeling of universal brotherhood... whose fire will soon melt away the ice-mountains of prejudice which have too long kept brethren asunder. (Long continued cheering).'[13]

The *Marseillaise* was sung and toasts proposed to Thomas Paine and 'the fallen Democrats of all countries'. Although Marx and Engels had been invited, they did not attend the Festival. But Engels, in a long report on it written shortly before New Year's Eve 1846 for the *Rheinische Jahrbücher* (newly launched in Darmstadt), highlighted the significance of 'the alliance of democrats of all nations living in London.' Noting that even Hungary and Turkey had been represented by one-man contingents, he stretched a point and – seeking to appeal to all groups who variously and interchangeably called themselves 'Socialists', 'Communists' or 'Democrats' – wrote, 'Democracy nowadays is Communism... If the proletarian parties of the different nations unite they will be quite right to inscribe the word "Democracy" on their banners, since except for those who do not count, all European democrats in 1846 are more or less Communists at heart.'[14]

Engels was very good at this type of hyperbole and simplification, and propaganda was now one of his and Marx's new objectives. The very confusion which permitted Engels to equate 'Democracy' with 'Communism' indicated a pressing need to define the latter. For this purpose Marx had begun to plan the establishment in Brussels of a Communist Correspondence Committee. Its chief aim, as he described it in a letter to Proudhon inviting him to join it from Paris, was to exchange information and air possible 'differences of opinion' by way of 'exchanging ideas and impartial criticism' between the Socialist movements in Germany, France and England.[15]

There was, however, to be more than this to the Brussels Correspondence Committee. In the same letter to Proudhon, Marx revealed that he had made arrangements with the German Communists and Socialists for a regular correspondence, 'which will be devoted to discussing scientific questions, and to keeping an eye on popular writings, and the Socialist propaganda that can be carried out in Germany.'[16] This meant that he was out to screen, sift and supervise the exposition of Communist theory all over Western Europe.

'Screening' was to become the Marxist code-word for dismissing anyone whose works and opinions differed from those of Marx and Engels, just as 'self-clarification' was to become the heading under which they were eventually to sum up the purpose of their all-out attack on post-Hegelian philosophy in *The German Ideology*. By way of attaining 'self-clarification', they were to launch a new polemic against Bruno Bauer, but to devote most of the first volume of *The German Ideology* to heaping scorn, ridicule and every kind of invective and vituperation on Max Stirner and his Ego. In the second volume they planned to aim their fire at the 'true Socialists' – a collective pejorative they applied to those idealistic intellectuals who, ignoring both reality and historic conditions, philosophically proclaimed the absolute 'truth' of Communism and the 'brotherhood of man', instead of firing the proletariat to revolution.

Marx and Engels had high hopes of publishing *The German Ideology* in a new quarterly to be financed by two Westphalian businessmen, Julius Meyer and Rudolph Rempel. In November, Moses Hess, in discussions with Meyer and subsequently at a conference with Meyer, Rempel, an accountant and a printer, had obtained a firm promise that the two businessmen would advance the capital for the first two book-size volumes of the quarterly. Hess, Marx and Engels were to figure as the publishers but would also be paid handsomely for their editorial work, and would be further entitled to a third of any net profit; the second third would go to the two financiers, and the remainder into a fund for further expansion.

Besides providing a vehicle for the publication of *The German Ideology*, the project would give the Marx-Engels-Hess triumvirate what practically amounted to a publishing house of their own. In addition, Meyer had promised Hess that he might finance the 'library' series of important Socialist works in German translations which Hess and Engels had conceived some two years earlier. Marx was to write the introduction for the French authors and Engels for the English.

Some time during the winter of 1845–46, Hess began to translate Buonarroti's *Conspiration pour l'Egalité dite de Babeuf* for this series. At the same time he continued to edit, from Brussels, the monthly issues of the *Gesellschaftsspiegel*, which appeared in Elberfeld. He also acted as the editor in all but name of the quarterly *Rheinische Jahrbücher*, of which the poet Püttmann was only nominally the editor.

In March 1846, Hess moved to Verviers, a depressing little industrial town which was closer to Elberfeld, where he hoped to be less exposed to police supervision. But, as he wrote to Marx, he found it 'a barbarous place devoid of anything to refresh the soul; bad beer, expensive meat, dirty bourgeois, crawling proletarians', and grocers who sold nothing on credit.[17]

In Brussels, Marx and Engels were engaged in setting up the Correspondence Committee and working on *The German Ideology*. They wrote most of it late at night at Marx's home, cracking jokes and roaring with laughter into the small hours, often disturbing Jenny, Lenchen and the two babies in their sleep.

In spite of their perennial money problems, Karl and Jenny Marx kept open house for Communist friends and visitors. At the beginning of 1846, Weitling and Weydemeyer each spent several months in Brussels. In February the poet Freiligrath arrived. The small German colony, Jenny was to write in her Reminiscences, 'lived pleasantly together. Then we were joined by some Belgians, among them Gigot, and several Poles. In one of the attractive cafés that we went to in the evenings I made the acquaintance of old Lelevel in his blue blouse.' Philippe Gigot was a young Belgian Communist who worked as an archivist in one of the Belgian Ministries; Joachim Lelevel, a revolutionary who had taken part in the 1830–31 Polish insurrection, was a distinguished historian. They and a few others were the only non-Germans admitted to the circle of refugee Communist thinkers.

Hess was to return for another stay in Brussels and Jenny Marx spent some time with his mistress (and later wife) Sibyl, who often acted as an 'auntie' to her children. Some 30 years later, in a letter to Marx, Sibyl was to evoke 'the happiness of those years in the 'forties when we lived next door to one another in Brussels.' But this nostalgically recollected harmony did not last long.

Marx and Engels had yet to finish the first volume of *The German Ideology* when the newly founded Brussels Correspondence Committee, headed by themselves and Gigot, met on 30 March 1846 to stage the first Marxist purge in history.

The meeting took place at Marx's home. Engels, Gigot, Weitling, and 4 other Communists – Joseph Weydemeyer, Sebastian Seiler, Edgar von Westphalen (Marx's brother-in-law) and Louis Heilberg – had been invited to discuss a simple and effective definition of Communism acceptable to its followers everywhere. But Marx turned the evening into a showdown with Weitling and launched a ferocious attack on the tailor's brand of 'artisan Communism'.

In addition to the Committee members, Marx had invited a guest, Paul Annenkov. This Russian landowner and 'aesthetic tourist' was fascinated by art and artists as well as the 'game of politics', and on his constant travels he sought the acquaintance of Europe's prominent writers and radicals. Marx, Heine, George Sand, Proudhon, Herwegh and Leroux were only some of those he added to the list of such Russian artists and thinkers as Gogol, Turgenev, Tolstoy, Belinsky, Herzen and Bakunin, whose circles he had frequented in Moscow and St Petersburg. In a section of *The Extraordinary Decade*, published 34 years after the event, Annenkov – of whom it has been said that 'he had so few axes of his own to grind, he could freely indulge his pleasure in watching his more impassioned friends grind theirs, usually on each other'[18] – has left an account of the axing of Weitling by Marx on 30 March.

On the following day, Weitling wrote a different account, but Annenkov's has justly entered most literature on the birth of Communism, because of the sharply etched profiles he drew of the dramatis personae, especially Marx. Although Annenkov was not a Communist and remained to the end of his days a prudent liberal aristocrat, Marx had taken a liking to him and corresponded with him for years. To Annenkov, the detached spectator who never uttered a word during the proceedings and went through life unperturbed by the ideas of the various radicals he met, Marx was a flamboyant personality emphatically different 'from the types of people I had left behind in Russia.' Recalling in

1880 the 'heated debate' he had witnessed in Brussels he was to evoke him in the following words: 'Before me stood the figure of the democratic dictator incarnate, just as it might be pictured in one's imagination in moments of fantasy.'

As for Weitling, the rift between him and the leaders of the London branch of the League of the Just had widened since the London Festival of Nations. Schapper, Moll and Bauer, not without pain, were increasingly disillusioned by their former leader's mixture of evangelical zeal and revolutionary fervour. Moreover, while frequently invoking Christ as 'the prophet of Communism', he had developed dictatorial tendencies à la Babeuf. Schapper had been shocked to hear him declare at one of their sessions that 'revolutionary Communism must have a dictator who rules over everything. The dictator should not have more than anyone else and be allowed his position only so long as he works for the general good.' Transcripts of the London League's discussions show that Schapper found – as Bakunin had a couple of years earlier – that Weitling's Communism 'would be just like soldiers in a barracks... In Weitling's system there is no freedom.'[19]

Weitling was increasingly isolated and embittered when he arrived in Brussels, hoping to work for the newly established German Correspondence Committee. He could count on a minority of followers in London and influential friends at the Central Committee of the League of the Just in Paris. Although shorn of his wings, he still considered himself its leader and, having hardly any funds, he had, before his arrival in Brussels, informed Marx, Engels and Hess in a joint letter that he counted on their hospitality and looked forward to 'drinking your beer, tasting your grub, and smoking your cigars.' Since January, he had in fact been having his daily meals at Marx's house.

In a letter sent to Moses Hess at Verviers on 31 March, Weitling wrote: 'We met again in pleno yesterday evening. Seiler brought up the question "How best to carry on propaganda in Germany", but said that he would not go into it because it might touch off some sensitive issues. Marx insisted that he elaborate. Seiler refused. Both became irritated.' According to this report, a 'vehement' Marx then summarized the problem in the following terms:

1) A screening of the Communist Party must be undertaken.
2) This can be achieved by criticizing the incompetent and separating them from the sources of money.
3) This screening is now the most important thing that can be done in the interest of Communism.
4) Whoever has the power to get money from the money-men also has the means to oust the others and it would be well to do so.

5) 'Artisan communism', 'philosophical communism', must be fought, and the feeling that it is all merely a day-dream must be ridiculed: word-of-mouth propaganda, secret propaganda, the word propaganda in general, must not be used in the future.

6) The early realization of Communism is out of the question; the bourgeoisie must first come to the helm.

Weitling further remarked to Hess that Weydemeyer too had said a few things against him, though in a less violent tone than Marx and Engels.

> Gigot and Edgar [von Westphalen] said not a word. Heilberg [spoke] against Marx from a non-partisan viewpoint. So, in the end, did Seiler, with admirable composure and bitterness. I myself became violent. Marx surpassed me. It all ended in an uproar, with him jumping around. He was especially provoked when I said: 'All I understand from our discussion is that he who can find the money may write what he wants.'

Weitling rightly suspected that Marx meant to exclude him from 'the publishing house enterprise' and would further attack him in print. He did not know if he would be able to defend himself, he told Hess, since he had not a penny to his name. He added: 'I see in Marx's head nothing more than a good encyclopaedia, but no genius. His influence is through personalities. Rich people have made him an editor, voilà tout.'[20]

Weitling might, of course, have asked what had changed since Marx had praised his *Guarantees of Harmony and Freedom* so fulsomely as 'the brilliant literary debut of the German working class'. Not that this would have helped him. Marx, who had little patience with self-taught preachers, would have made short shrift of him by telling him that it was time to pass from 'primitive' Communism to the 'scientific' understanding of the economic structure of bourgeois society and that, as he was later to put it in his *Herr Vogt*, 'our task was not the fulfillment of some utopian system but the conscious participation in the historical process of social revolution that was taking place before our eyes'[21] and the education of the working class towards that purpose.

In the 20th century, some argued that to call the showdown with Weitling a 'purge' was an inappropriate reading of pre-1917 events, and that in any case there was no 'party' in the true sense of the word.[22] This is true, but disregards two facts. By the mid-1840s, long before anyone dreamt of Lenin, Marx, Hess, Engels, Weydemeyer, Schapper and others loosely used the term 'our party' in the sense of 'our camp'. Moreover, in the spring of 1846, Engels made a point in *The German Ideology* of stressing that 'since the actual birth of a Communist party in Germany' – by which he meant Marx's nuclear group of supporters in Brussels – the philosophical 'true Socialists' had become obsolete and could at most influence the petty bourgeoisie and the bunch of impotent literati whom they regarded as its representatives.

And if the axing of Weitling was not a purge, what was it? It was followed on 11 May by the Brussels Correspondence Committee's resolutions against Hermann Kriege, a Westphalian journalist and follower of Weitling who had been sent to New York by the League of the Just and had there launched a weekly entitled *Der Volks-Tribun*. Affiliated to the recently founded National Reform Association, Kriege's weekly advocated a shortened 10-hour working day and the abolition of slavery. It also supported the Reform Association's demands that 1,400,000 acres of public land that had not yet 'fallen into the hands of thieving speculators' should be divided up into homesteads for America's farmers.

This way of adapting Socialism to the American dream of private property was anathema to Marx. The series of resolutions adopted by the Brussels Correspondence Committee proclaimed that Kriege's journal did 'not represent Communism', but on the contrary compromised the Communist party in Europe as well as in America and demoralized the workers. Together with a 14-page 'Circular against Kriege', the resolutions were sent to all the Communists in Germany, France and England and followed by a campaign deriding Kriege's plan to provide every farmer with his own 'pile of manure'.

That Marx's Brussels Committee had embarked on a policy of purges was recognized by Proudhon as soon as he received Marx's letter – written on 5 May, a week before the resolutions against Kriege – inviting him to join it. In his reply, Proudhon scathingly reminded Marx of the case of Luther, who overthrew Catholic dogma only to establish his own 'apparatus of excommunication and anathemas... For God's sake,' he wrote, 'let us not – simply because we are at the head of a new movement – make ourselves the leaders of a new intolerance, let us not pose as the apostles of a new religion, even if it be the religion of logic, the religion of reason.'

Whether the showdown with Weitling was 'the first Marxist party purge', as Edmund Wilson called it, or the 'political excommunication' of Kriege set 'a historic precedent for future Communist party purges', as Padover claimed, Proudhon, sensing Marx's authoritarian tendency, wrote to him:

> Let us give the world the example of an informed and farsighted tolerance... Let us gather together and encourage all dissent... Let us never regard a question as exhausted, and when we have used our last argument, let us if necessary begin again – with eloquence and irony.

On these conditions, I will gladly enter into your association. Otherwise – no![23]

Besides being no partisan of violent revolution, Proudhon – who warned Marx
that the French proletariat would give him 'short shrift if you offered them only
bloodshed' – may have been shocked by a postscript in which Marx wrote: 'I
must denounce to you M Grün of Paris',

> The man is nothing more than a literary swindler, a species of charla-
> tan, who seeks to traffic in modern ideas. He tries to conceal his igno-
> rance with pompous and arrogant phrases but all he does is make
> himself ridiculous with his gibberish. Moreover this man is danger-
> ous.

Karl Grün, whom Marx and Engels were attacking in *The German Ideology* as
a 'true Socialist', was the former editor of the banned *Mannheim Abendzeitung*. Expelled from Baden, he had moved first to Cologne, where he was one
of the leading members of its Communist Club, and later to Paris. A former
fellow-student of Marx at Bonn, he had been a contributor to the *Rheinische
Zeitung*, and it was him that Marx chose to sign and publish the valedictory
lines Marx wrote in praise of himself after that paper's closure. Not in his
wildest dreams would Grün have imagined that Marx would one day call him
a charlatan. In fact, Marx insinuated to Proudhon that Grün, in a recent book
on *The Social Movement in France and Belgium*, 'has the audacity to describe
himself as tutor to Proudhon, claims to have revealed to him the important
axioms of German science and makes fun of his writings. Beware of this para-
site.'[24]

The truth was that, after Marx's departure from Paris, Grün had taken over
the job of helping to keep Proudhon, who understood no German, abreast of
German philosophical writings. But Marx's virulent denunciation of Grün was
as unwarranted as the relentless campaign in which he attacked him for his supposed disregard of historical and class distinctions. For Grün, in a lecture
delivered in 1844, had actually stipulated the class struggle in terms not unlike
those which were to appear in *The Communist Manifesto*:

> History so far has been a single relentless struggle between the fortu-
> nate haves and the miserable have-nots and oppressed. In Greece
> they were called helots, in Rome slaves, in the Middle Ages they were
> known as serfs; in Russia they call them peasants, in North America
> blacks; in civilized England, France and Germany we call them pro-
> letarians... History can be summed up as social slavery, serfdom and
> dependence on property![25]

Marx's merciless campaign against Grün, attributed by some to 'fierce personal jealousy, fed by hatred and malice', may also have been fuelled by the fact that Grün wielded a certain influence with the German Communist workers in Paris. Dr Ewerbeck was one of the first to write to Marx, on 15 May 1846, that he could 'in no way agree with your grudge against and hatred of Grün.' He added that he did not know 'what exists personally between you', but noted that Grün was liked by the artisans of Paris and did very good work among them. Ewerbeck did not know that to win over those artisans and remove Grün from the scene was Marx's next target.

As for Proudhon, his urbane reaction to Marx's insinuations against Grün was to write: 'My dear Monsieur Marx, I appeal to your calmer judgment.' Grün was a political refugee living in exile and penury, with a wife and two children to support. He had only his pen to make a living by, and live he must. What, Proudhon asked, did Marx expect him to write about 'if not modern ideas?' Together with Proudhon's 'No' to the Correspondence Committee unless it guaranteed freedom of opinion, this rebuke infuriated Marx all the more as he had attached great value to the membership of France's most important Socialist at the time. Engels, in a postscript to the invitation Marx sent Proudhon, had expressed the hope that he would 'not deny us your cooperation' and assured him of his 'deep respect' for his writings. But later in 1846, when Proudhon's *Philosophie de la Misère* appeared in Paris, Engels was the first to write to Marx in Brussels that this two-volume work 'is bad... and not worth the 15 francs it costs.' Marx, however, eager to settle accounts with Proudhon, took the trouble to read it and before another year had gone by he was publishing his polemical *Misère de la Philosophie*. The book, printed at his own expense, was to sell only 800 copies, but it gave Marx the satisfaction of lashing Proudhon as a 'petty bourgeois' and a 'bad economist' who 'passes in France for a good German philosopher, [whereas] in Germany he passes for one of the strongest French economists.' As Marx himself was later to write, this ended his friendship with Proudhon 'for ever'.

The attempts of Marx and Engels in the spring of 1846 to enlist first George Harney and then Karl Schapper as London correspondents of the Brussels Committee likewise failed. The Londoners mistrusted the two of them. They disliked their 'intellectual arrogance', and Karl Schapper protested at their treatment of Kriege. But Marx and Engels had effectively destroyed Weitling's influence and thought they only had to bide their time before the London branch of the League would fall into their hands.

Nor had they been impressed on 11 May, when they passed the resolutions condemning Kriege, with the argument put forward by Weitling – who was the only one to vote against them – that the Communists had powerful enemies enough in Europe to turn their weapons against their supporters in America.

On 20 May, Hess wrote to Marx that he had received a rather desperate and confused letter from Weitling, and expressed strong feelings about the treatment Weitling had received: 'You two have driven him crazy and now you wonder that he is mad. I do not wish to have anything more to do with this whole affair; it makes me want to vomit. Shit in all dimensions.'[26]

The penniless Weitling, ostracized but reduced for a time to continue to take his meals at Marx's table, was indeed in a pitiful state, but he was far from crazy. On 16 May, 5 days after being outvoted in the matter of the the resolutions against Kriege, he had written to Kriege: 'The Brussels intriguers regarded me as their worst enemy. My head was therefore the first that had to be felled. Those of the others will follow next and in the end it will be the turn of their friends' heads.'

Shortly afterwards he left Brussels for Luxembourg. There he hired himself out as an assistant tailor and worked until he raised the fare to go to America. He left later in 1846, having realized too late, as he put it, that he had been 'a donkey to believe that what we had to do was to direct our talents against our enemies.'

In the same month when the 'Weitling affair' was ostensibly ended, the first signs appeared of a crack in the harmony which had hitherto prevailed among the Marx-Engels-Hess triumvirate. Hess was not a supporter of Weitling. On the contrary, he called Weitling a 'revolting character... and a dirty fellow in money matters'. But he thought that Marx had conducted himself in a manner which fostered 'party strife', instead of preventing it. And he ended the letter in which he expressed these opinions with the words: 'Good bye to the party!'

He then received an annoyed letter from Marx, who tried to persuade him not to leave the party and stressed that private miseries had nothing to do with party strife. Hess replied on 29 May: 'The irritation in your letter is pardonable, because I wrote to you in the same tone... You are also right in separating private misery from party strife, but both of them are enough to spoil my pleasure in our joint work for this party.' He added the observation that Marx was 'a dissolving element', whereas his own nature was 'conciliatory'. 'Fare thee well! With you personally I want to have many more contacts. With your party I will have nothing more to do.'[27]

Although his personal contacts with Marx were indeed to continue, and before long he even became reconciled with 'the party',' Hess learned from the Weitling affair that independent-minded Communists, 'abandoned' by the party, must rely on their own means to make their voices heard. He was fed up with the 'dog's life' he was leading in uncivilized Verviers, and informed Marx that he planned to leave for Cologne, where he hoped to find a material basis for his existence that would allow him to continue his Communist writings undisturbed. The man who had been the first to recognize Marx's genius had now discovered the negative 'dissolving' drive in him.

This unforeseen epilogue to the Weitling affair took place against a wider background, and was not unconnected with the sudden collapse of the 'Westphalian publishing house' project in which both Marx and Hess had placed high hopes of improving their financial situation. The 'private misery' mentioned in their letters referred to the fact that both of them were deeply in debt; Hess had just enough money left to cover the fare to Cologne.

Marx learned of the failure of the project on the very day he was announcing in a letter to Weydemeyer that he and Engels had practically finished the two volumes of *The German Ideology*. Although the publishing house project had been initiated by Hess in discussions with the two Westphalian businessmen, Marx and Engels – on behalf of the newly formed Brussels Correspondence Committee – had dispatched Weydemeyer to Westphalia to make the final arrangements for the publication of the new quarterly in which *The German Ideology* was to appear. On 30 April, Weydemeyer reported back that he had made little progress and proposed that Meyer should form a joint-stock company at Limburg in Holland, since in Germany manuscripts of less than 20 sheets were subject to preliminary censorship. Marx's reply of 14–16 May is of interest because he displayed in it an unusual practical sense. He wrote that the Limburg idea might be all right for pamphlets, 'but books of more than 20 sheets are best printed in Germany proper.' He then expounded a plan of his own

> which (1) will nominally leave Meyer out of it altogether, (2) will make things very difficult for the governments and (3) strongly commends itself insofar as the dispatch arrangements would be placed in very efficient hands.

> Vogler, who resides here and has a commission agent in Leipzig, a man chiefly engaged in the dissemination of books liable to confiscation, would, you see, take over the whole bookselling side. The books themselves would be printed in Germany. In each case the editor would appear as publisher, i.e. 'Printed by the Author.'

How much Marx relished the idea of the new quarterly and the prospect of the imminent publication of *The German Ideology* is evident from two passages in this letter. In one, he informed Weydemeyer that the manuscripts of the work would be sent shortly. 'The second volume is almost ready. As soon as the manuscripts for the first volume arrive (in two consignments) it would be most desirable that printing should begin.' In the second he wrote: 'if Meyer agrees to Vogler's proposal we could start at once...'[28]

He had reached this point in his letter when he received a disturbing one from Weydemeyer. Meyer was hedging and would only guarantee the publication of one volume. With Engels sitting beside him, Marx wrote to Weydemeyer that he desperately needed 1,200 francs to cover his debts. He concluded with the words: 'As you can see, misère on all sides! At this moment I'm at a loss what to do... All this financial stress has come on top of much work, domestic duties, etc. Yours M.'

That Marx and Engels expected Meyer and Rempel to publish *The German Ideology* at all was rather curious in itself. Meyer was the owner of an ironworks, but wrote libertarian poems and articles on the side. Both he and Rempel were ready to back a Communist publication, but they were not Communists of Marx's denomination. Rather, they were supporters of a group of intellectuals associated with the *Westphalian Dampfboot* and the *Trier Zeitung*, whom Marx and Engels derided in the second volume of *The German Ideology* as 'true Socialists' and accused of writing about Communism in a manner palatable to the petty bourgeoisie, but neglecting the masses. Yet there was method in the Marx-Engels game-plan. They were out to split the 'true Socialists', to win over some of them to their own camp and to discredit the others. As early as 30 April, Weydemeyer had written to Marx in Brussels: 'We must absolutely gain control of the Westphalian Dampfboot.'

The upshot was that by July, Meyer and Rempel, invoking financial difficulties, withdrew their offer altogether. Quite apart from disagreeing with the authors in principle, the two financiers had other good reasons for their decision. Several chapters in the manuscripts referred to by Marx were not in a finished state. The very first and major chapter of the whole work, entitled 'Feuerbach', remained to be written and was in fact never completed. Even in their unfinished state, the two volumes would take up a costly 596 pages to print and Meyer and Rempel felt that the nearly 400 pages devoted to caricaturing the figure of Stirner alone would, for all the clever mockery and persiflage, hardly hold the interest of more than a few readers – a verdict supported by pro-Marxist authors in the 20th century. Besides, the two entrepreneurs feared that a book which, between much trivia and such gems as 'Philosophy is to the study of reality what masturbation is to sexual love', contained passages on the class struggle and the revolutionary mission of the proletariat would bring the authorities down on them.

Marx and Engels, however, remained confident that another radical publisher would soon undertake the risk of publishing their book. When all their efforts failed, Marx even planned to launch a publishing company of his own in

Germany. He offered shares at 25 Thaler each, but this dream came to nothing when he found only 12 takers in Cologne.

In 1847 Marx and Engels finally abandoned *The German Ideology* to 'the gnawing criticism of the mice'. As Marx was later to put it, they did so 'all the more willingly as we had attained our chief purpose – self-clarification.'[29] The unfinished book was only to be published in Moscow in 1932, nearly 50 years after Marx's death and almost 90 after it was written. It was then discovered that, buried among all the witticisms, the puns and the pithy argument with all the philosophers of 'pure thought' from Hegel to Feuerbach and Stirner, were passages in which Marx and Engels formulated the essentials of a new theory of history.

Communism, they wrote, differed from all previous movements in history. In the clash of interests between the individual and the community, the state, which supposedly represented the latter, was divorced from the real interests of the individual. Community life is always based on the classes and determined by the division of labour which separates men and causes one group to dominate all the others: 'The struggle within the state, the struggle between democracy, aristocracy, and monarchy, the struggle for the franchise, etc., are merely the illusory forms in which the real struggles of the different classes are fought out among one another.'

Postulating that economics and the mode of production at a given historical stage determine the social consciousness of man, they claimed that revolution is the driving force in history. It was bound to erupt the moment the dispossessed and exploited labour force ceased to put up with the concentration of the technological means of production and all ownership in the hands of a single dominating class, enabling it to dictate the lives of everyone. Anticipating *The Communist Manifesto*, they stressed the historical necessity of a revolution in which the proletariat must overthrow the state in order to assert their own personality; 'For the practical materialist, i.e., the Communist, it is a question of revolutionizing the existing world, of coming to grips with and changing the things found in existence.'[30]

The most recent English translation of *The German Ideology* (1976) opens with Marx's Theses on Feuerbach. These were 11 short notes he jotted down in April 1845. They contained the gist of the defects, limitations and inconsistencies in the secular but still speculative-idealistic philosophy of Feuerbach, which Marx enlarged upon in the uncompleted first chapter – but the last to be written – on the man whose work he had previously admired.

The final and most famous Thesis summed up the whole argument in a single phrase: 'The philosophers have only interpreted the world in various ways; the point, however, is to change it.'[31] That is what Marx meant by 'practical-critical', i.e., revolutionary, activity. Had he written nothing else, he would have deserved a place in the history of ideas. Engels, who after Marx's death published the 'Theses' found in one of his notebooks, described them as 'the first document revealing the brilliant kernel of the new world outlook.' He further wrote that when he, Engels, joined Marx in April 1845 the latter had already worked out his theory and 'put it before me' in practically complete form, suggesting that most of the theoretical passages in *The German Ideology* were written by Marx, rather than his new young disciple.

Engels also recalled how much the two of them, 'bold devils then', had enjoyed making impudent fun of Stirner and the 'true Socialists'. In 1846, however, when the prospect of getting the work published had faded, Marx was at his wits' end. An appeal to Herwegh for a loan had remained fruitless, and so had attempts to get money from his mother and from one of her acquaintances in Cologne. Even his former bourgeois admirers in that city – such as Georg Jung – had become disenchanted with his new radical ideas, and Marx wrote that he did not care 'to be beholden to them'.

The fact that Marx, rather than systematically finishing any of the works he had so far started, clarified his thought by way of engaging in one polemic after another with thinkers dead or alive, kept him in constant penury, with consequent stress and untold embarrassments along the way. To help him out, in the summer of 1846 Weydemeyer organized a money collection in Westphalia, and wrote that a couple of hundred francs would soon reach Marx through Rempel. Hurt in his pride and feeling that he was made to appear 'beggarly' in the eyes of 'the party', Marx promptly returned the money to the sender. Weydemeyer, unable to see why his money collection was more 'beggarly' than the one made for Marx at the time of his expulsion from Paris, accused him of rudeness to his sympathizers and wrote that if Marx wanted to split 'the party' he, Weydemeyer, would in justice be bound to choose the other side.[32]

Marx and Jenny had by then been forced to give up their household in the rue d'Alliance and to move with their two babies and Lenchen back to the cheap Bois Sauvage tavern. In October they moved to a modest apartment in the Ixelles surburb of Brussels, where Jenny gave birth to their first son, the ill-fated Edgar. Some 6 months later, Marx was reduced to such financial straits that, without any qualms about 'the party', he resorted to drawing bills on Hess and Bernays, indirectly threatening them with debtor's prison unless they paid him some money he claimed they owed him. He charged Engels to deal with the matter: 'Since it is very pressing, I expect you not to let a day go by before settling everything and informing me.'[33] And before the end of their stay in Brussels, the Marx family moved back to the Bois Sauvage tavern for the third time in three years.

Hurt as badly or worse by the collapse of the Westphalian publishing house project in the summer of 1846 was Moses Hess. The news that it was dead before it was born had been conveyed to him by Meyer, one of the two financiers, shortly before Marx learned of it from Weydemeyer. Hess, who had made the original arrangements with Meyer, had been looking forward, as had Marx, to getting 3 Louis d'or per edited sheet from the projected quarterly. He had further spent months translating Buonarroti into German, but the planned 'library' series of Socialist writings was now likewise stillborn.

Meyer offered him 30 Thaler for his troubles. Hess wrote on 17 May that he was in 'too deep a money jam' not to accept that as a loan until his situation improved. But worse than his financial distress was something else. On 6 May, addressing Marx as 'Dear Marco', Hess asked whether he had received any news from Weydemeyer about the state of the publishing house project. Countless letters of his own to Meyer, he explained, had remained unanswered. He did not know at the time, but learned soon enough, that Weydemeyer – as he confessed to Marx on the 13th – had expressly instructed Meyer not to answer Hess's letters but to hand them to him. By the 20th, when he reproved Marx for having ousted Weitling in a manner which made him want to 'vomit' and said farewell to the party, Hess might have guessed that Weydemeyer's intrigue against him in Westphalia had not been conducted on his own authority.

The Westphalian setback coincided with several others that Hess had suffered by the summer of 1846. The Elberfeld *Gesellschaftsspiegel* he had been editing from Brussels and Verviers was about to fold up, its printer bowing to police harassment and intimidation. And the quarterly *Rheinische Jahrbücher*, for whose material Hess was largely responsible, suffered an even worse fate. Although published in a format of more than 21 sheets, and thus exempt from censorship, its first issue had been confiscated in the Rhineland because of its 'extreme radical Communist' tendency, and its generally 'criminal contents'; and in March all copies of it that reached Prussia had been seized and destroyed.

For publishing it, the unfortunate Leske was charged by the government of Hesse with high treason and blasphemy. Püttmann, the nominal editor, fled with the material for the second issue to Switzerland. He eventually managed to publish it there in December, with the result, among others, that Engels's long account of the London 'Festival of Nations' only appeared a year after it was written.

On 29 May, Hess responded to Marx's attempt to persuade him not to leave the party. 'You have every right to be irritated,' he wrote, and added significantly: 'Not so Engels; my letter was not addressed to him at all, and as for the "kissing", I leave that to his Mary.'[34] He rightly suspected that Engels had started manoeuvering to push him to the sidelines. Marx, too, did not mind seeing the influence of the leader of 'philosophical Communism' reduced. Indeed, the short section in *The German Ideology* which the two of them devoted to attacking Karl Grün's book on *The Social Movements in Belgium and France* contained a veiled criticism of Hess:

> The outline and general ideas... of Grün's book are copied from Hess, whom Herr Grün paraphrases indeed in the most lordly fashion. Matters which are quite vague and mystical even in Hess, but which were originally – in the Einundzwanzig Bogen – worthy of recognition, and have only become tiresome and reactionary as a result of their perpetual reappearance in the Bürgerbuch, the Neue Anekdota and the Rheinische Jahrbücher at a time when they were already out of date, become complete nonsense in Herr Grün's hands.[35]

Thus the word was out: Hess's ideas were obsolete and their repetition in such periodicals as the *Rheinische Jahrbücher* even gave them a reactionary tint. The irony of it all was that Hess himself had not only dissociated himself from Grün and the 'true Socialists' but had contributed two essays to *The German Ideology*, one of which Marx edited and included in chapter V of the second volume, some 80 pages after the attack on him in chapter IV.[36] Only the fact that *The German Ideology* was never printed during their lifetimes saved Hess from the embarrassment of being publicly branded in this fashion.

After briefly toying with the idea of emigrating to the USA, as Marx in Brussels was to do shortly afterwards, Hess left Verviers for Cologne in July. There, after assuring himself of some financial help from his father, he resumed contact with his friends of the local Communist club, Daniels and D'Ester – the two physicians who were also friends of Marx – and by 21 July he was informing Marx that he had set in motion the establishment of a publishing company that was to replace the stillborn Westphalian project. D'Ester was helping him to raise 6,000 to 10,000 Thaler for the company, to be obtained by selling shares at 100 Thaler each to subscribers in 'Elberfeld, Westphalia, Berlin, Silesia and well-off Communists and democrats everywhere.'

There now began an ambiguous period, as for the next two years Marx and Hess remained in close touch, and Hess even rejoined 'the party', while behind the scenes Engels engaged in every trick he could think of to ruin Hess's reputation and discredit him both personally and politically. Circumstances connected with the irregular civil status of Hess's mistress Sibyl Pesch played into Engels's hands. The couple had no sooner arrived in Cologne than it turned out that Sibyl – whom Hess had falsely registered as his wife – would have to leave town. Hess dispatched her to Brussels and wrote to Marx that he was placing her under his protection, and hoped that Frau Marx would show her the same friendship as hitherto. Knowing that Engels was at Ostend and planning to go to Paris, he iasked whether he would be prepared to smuggle Sibyl across the frontier to France.

At Ostend, Engels was holidaying with his parents and sister. He, too, had apparently reached a reconciliation with his 'despotic' father. On 27 July, referring to the 'Frau Hess affair', he wrote to Marx:

> It's bad, but one cannot possibly let her suffer for the stupidities of Hess; I shall therefore try to smuggle her across the border if, that is, I get enough money from my old man for the journey to Paris, which is still not sure. Send the enclosed scribble to the beloved man of God in Cologne to cheer him up. So the woman is in Brussels already?

On 29 July, Marx forwarded Engels's 'scribble' to Hess. In it Engels informed Hess that he would do 'my utmost to smuggle your wife [sic!] across the border, but all the same it's unfortunate that she should not have a passport.' In a note of his own, Marx informed Hess that his wife was unwell and bedridden, but 'Sibyl is quite cheerful. Seiler is her cavalier servente.'[37]

In August, Engels left for France and duly smuggled 'Father Hess's spouse' across the frontier. On the 19th, shortly after having consigned her 'to oblivion, i.e., to the furthest end of the Faubourg St Antoine' working-class quarter, he reported to Marx: '*Madame Hess cherche un mari. Elle se fiche de Hess. S'il se trouverait quelque chose de convenable, s'adresser à Madame Gsell, Faubourg St. Antoine.* [Madame Hess is looking for a husband. She is fed up with Hess. If anything suitable turns up, write to Madame Gsell...] There is no hurry, the competition is not great.'[38]

In subsequent letters to Marx, Engels claimed that the good-looking, blond Sibyl, who was the same age as he, 26, had made amorous overtures to him, and over the next two years he kept boasting that she had confided to him 'the most intimate nocturnal secrets of her ménage.' In reports to the Brussels Correspondence Committee and verbally to Marx, Gigot and Stephan Born – the newly arrived 22-year-old printer's apprentice whom he introduced to Communism as well as to the attractions of Paris – he bragged that he had either wholly spurned her best attempts to seduce him, or that he had enjoyed her favours while rejecting her passionately offered love.

Engels's vilification of Hess's mistress would not be worth going into had it not been part of a long-drawn-out campaign of what his modern biographer has termed nothing less than the 'character assassination' of Hess.[39] Conducted for personal reasons, it was enmeshed with a political power struggle for control of the Communist 'party' and its ideology. Engels had been sent to Paris in August 1846 by the Brussels Correspondence Committee on a mission – paid for by his father, who besides sending him a monthly remittance apparently also

965

gave him the money for the journey – to put an end to the influence of Proudhon, Weitling, and the 'true Socialist' Karl Grün over the League of the Just. The workmen and artisans in its ranks – whom Marx and Engels regularly referred to as Straubinger, i.e., 'boors', when not calling them worse – were to be persuaded to accept their own superior intellectual leadership and allow themselves to be guided on history's prescribed path for the proletariat.

Shortly before Engels took Sibyl Pesch to Paris, Hess had written the following lines to Marx: 'With your views on Communist Schriftstellerei [Marx's term for propaganda], as expounded in your letters to Daniels, I am fully in accord.' He added that Communism had, at the beginning, had to take its inspiration from German philosophy, but now it was just as necessary to work out its 'foundations on historic and economic premises' and that he was concentrating on 'economic studies'.

These lines marked Hess's reconciliation of sorts with Marx. He could effect it all the more easily because, for one thing, he had from the beginning recognized Marx as a genius and never questioned his intellectual superiority or meant to displace him; for another, he had made it clear when leaving 'the party' that he was keen to collaborate with Marx, and while he now accepted Marx's principles, time was to show that he maintained his independence of mind and never became a blind Marxist.

For his part, Marx was satisfied to keep Hess in the party. Besides awaiting the fruition of the publishing house project, his own attempts to establish a Correspondence Bureau in Cologne had met with no great success. Hess and D'Ester, on the other hand, together with Gottschalk – another physician and leader of Cologne's Communist Club – took an active part in that summer's election campaign for Cologne's municipal council. In the midst of it, the brutal dispersal by the army of a rowdy group of youngsters at a church fair led to riots, and troops occupied the town's public squares. The ensuing tension between the citizenry and the military was exploited by D'Ester – who, calling himself a 'democrat', was a Communist candidate for the council – and by Hess and Gottschalk to raise the social problem at election meetings. The police also suspected Hess and Gottschalk of using a secret printing press to circulate Socialist propaganda.

Engels in Paris was not at all pleased to hear of the resumption of contacts between Marx and Hess. Commenting on a letter from Hess in which 'the Communist papa sought to re-establish relations', he wrote to the Brussels Correspondence Committee in his report of 16 September:

> It's enough to make one split one's sides. As if nothing had happened
> of course, altogether in dulci jubilo, and moreover altogether the same

old Hess. After the remark that he was to some extent reconciled with 'the party'... comes the following historical note (dated 19 August):

'A few weeks ago we were within a hair's breadth of a bloody riot here in Cologne, large numbers being already armed' (among them certainly not Moses). 'The affair did not come to a head because the military did not put in an appearance (tremendous triumph for Cologne's pint-sized philistine), etc., etc...'

Then he tells of the civic assemblies where 'we', i.e. 'the party' and Mr Moses, 'qua communists, won so complete a victory that we', etc.

As a matter of fact, the public outcry raised at the civic assemblies in Cologne forced the Prussian authorities to set up an inquiry into the army's behaviour. There were demands for an armed citizens' militia to be set up. Seen in retrospect, the Cologne unrest was a prelude to the March revolution which was to rock Berlin less than two years later. D'Ester was elected to Cologne's city council.

Hess's letter quoted by Engels in his above report to the Brussels Correspondence Committee is no longer extant, but according to S. Na'aman, Engels's doctored version of it ridiculed Hess 'without any knowledge of the facts.'[40]

In the aftermath, following the arrest of the anti-Prussian writer Ernst Dronke and of a Paris Communist by the name of Mentel – both of whom had corresponded with Hess – the police, having long suspected the latter of 'destructive tendencies', turned their attention to him. Hess managed to leave Cologne shortly before they searched his father's house. Crossing the French border without a passport, he made his way to Paris.

Marx had notified Engels of Hess's move. He wanted Engels to thrash out his differences with him and the two of them to combat the 'heresies' of Proudhon, Weitling and Grün. Engels, however, was intent on driving a wedge between Hess and Marx, as is evident from the description he sent Marx of his first meeting after Hess arrived in Paris in January 1847:

The worthy man has changed a great deal. His head is adorned with youthful locks, a dainty little beard lends some grace to his angular jaw, a virginal blush hovered about his cheeks, but la grandeur déchue se peignait dans ses beaux yeux [fallen greatness was reflected in his fine eyes] and a strange modesty had come over him.

Here in Paris I have come to adopt a very insolent manner, for bluster is all in the day's work, and it works well with the female sex. But the ravished exterior of that erstwhile world-shaking high-flyer, Hess, all but disarmed me.

Engels seems to have had a healthy respect for Hess, for while falsely continuing to refer to him as a 'true Socialist', he wrote that only his reminding himself that his mission was to combat these utopians restored his courage. 'My treatment of him was so cold and scornful that he will have no desire to return. All I did for him was to give him some good advice about the clap he had brought with him from Germany. He was also a complete fiasco with a number of German painters, some of whom he had known before. Only Gustav Adolph Köttgen has remained faithful to him.'[41]

By mentioning the painter Köttgen, Engels gave away the fact that his self-styled 'insolence' and bluster were his way of covering his own frustration at his inability to detach Hess from Marx. For Köttgen – in a letter signed by Marx, Gigot, Ferdinand Wolff and Engels himself – had in June 1846 been given detailed instructions by the Brussels leadership how the German Communists were to act in the approaching revolution. Köttgen was told that until there was 'a strong and well-organized party', they were to 'behave like Jesuits... support middle class petitions for freedom of the Press, a constitution and so on... To aid the Communist party you should support any policy which will be to our advantage in the long run. And do not be deterred by any stuffy moral scruples about it.'[42]

This was in line with the idea of Marx and his friends that the Communists should help the middle-class liberals to overthrow the feudal aristocracy but to turn upon them once they were in control and to seize power themselves; and Engels's admission that Köttgen had remained loyal to Hess has been seen as evidence that Hess was in Paris on the same 'party' mission as his own. Marx was in fact interested that Hess should stay within the party, rather than become the leader of a potential opposition. And for all Engels's attempts to shake him off, he had no alternative but to have another discussion with him within a month.

There was another reason for Engels's frustration. He had a hard time converting the 'appallingly ignorant' German artisans to his and Marx's new version of Communism. The tailors, tanners and carpenters of the League of the Just 'showed a greater interest in Proudhon's scheme for labour bazaars than in Engels's lectures on history and economics.'[43]

Engels himself had reported in October that 'Weitlingism and Proudhonism' appealed to 'these jackasses, and there is nothing to be done about it.' By the end of the month, the only success he could boast of was that, after furiously haranguing a small group of joiners, he had gained 13 supporters for his definition of Communist principles.

In mid-November or December, he reported to Marx that he had suspended his activities altogether. Following disturbances in the Faubourg Saint-Antoine and clashes with the military, a 'multitude' of the League's members demonstrating against an increase in the price of bread were arrested and interrogated. Engels felt sure that 'some of these numbskulls' had given the police all the information about his subversive agitation. And sick and tired as he was of dealing with these obtuse 'blockheads', he decided to lie low; but making the best of the good life of Paris, he reported to Marx with youthful exuberance that, shadowed by police spies, he frequented the *bals* at the Prado and other music halls and was thankful to the Prefecture for 'some delightful encounters with *grisettes* and for a great deal of pleasure' during what he thought might be his 'last days and nights in Paris' before his expulsion.[44]

In an unexpected development, the London branch of the League of the Just had decided to call an international Communist congress for the summer of 1847. Its leaders, Schapper and Moll, announced this without consulting Marx or the Brussels Correspondence Committee, whom they accused throughout 1846 of 'wanting to establish some kind of intellectual aristocracy [*Gelehrten-Aristokratie*] and rule over the people from your new godly thrones.'[45]

By the end of the year, an exasperated Engels had in fact suggested to Marx that if the boorish London workers – who had earlier ignored an appeal to coordinate their propaganda with Brussels – did not want to have them, they had better leave them to their own devices. At the beginning of 1847, however, Schapper and Moll agreed to cooperate; and in February Moll went to Brussels, and then to Paris, to repair the slight and personally invite Marx and Engels to the proposed congress.

In another development the Central Committee of the League of the Just had in November 1846 – following the police clamp-down on it after the bread riots – been transferred to London. Moll informed Marx and Engels that the proposed congress was designed to reorganize the League of the Just, to iron out differences of views dividing the London branch and factions within the Paris branch, and to formulate its goals. Once these were agreed upon, it planned to send emissaries to strengthen the withering cells established by Weitling in Switzerland and to recruit new ones in Germany and possibly in Sweden.

Marx could hardly refuse the opportunity to influence not only the now 500-strong London branch, but also the Central Committee and, through it, to counteract the confusion of what he called mystical, utopian or 'antiquated and dissident views' in what promised to become an international movement. Marx and Engels therefore joined the League of the Just.

For Engels the spring of 1847 was a time of doldrums. While waiting to attend the London congress in the summer he was so depressed that in March he longed for Marx to come to Paris: 'I have a great desire to go carousing with you,' he wrote. 'If I had an income of 5,000 fr. I would do nothing but work and amuse myself with women until I went to pieces.' But for Sunday excursions and drinking bouts on some evenings with Stephan Born, he complained that there was no one 'to discuss a decent topic with.'[46] His correspondence with Marx was otherwise filled with gossip and frivolous innuendo, principally against Hess but also against others.

Lest this give a wrong impression, it should be noted that at a later date Engels was to establish valuable contacts with such French personalities as Louis Blanc and Ferdinand Flocon, who were to play leading roles in the February 1848 revolution in Paris. But for the moment, he was glad to leave Paris for London, where the international congress of the League of the Just met from 2 to 9 June. As he lacked the money for the journey, Marx did not attend, but he sent his friend Wilhelm Wolff to represent him.

The London congress did not accept the programme Marx and Engels wanted it to adopt, but the Londoners agreed to give up both the ideas they had inherited from Babeuf, via Weitling – of armed revolution by 'putsch, conspiracy' and violence – and all forms of Socialism based on pure sentiment. As a result, the League – which changed its name to The Communist League – abandoned its ideas of universal love. Instead of the old slogan 'All Men are Brothers', the new all-time motto of Communist solidarity – 'Proletarians of all Countries, Unite!' – appeared on the masthead of a periodical it began to issue.

The new statutes of the reorganized League, rather than proclaiming that its aim, as proposed by Engels, was to overthrow the existing order, to abolish private property and create 'a new classless society', said simply: 'The League aims at the abolition of man's enslavement by propagating the theory of the community of goods and by its implementation as soon as possible.'[47]

Although as early as December 1846 Engels, writing from Paris on the basis of his success with 13 joiners, had reported that he had 'triumphed over Grün', in October 1847 – during a second stay in Paris – he was to write that there was 'hellish confusion' among the German artisans and 'we are now only thirty strong.' The fact is that Weitling's followers hated Engels as a rich man's son. More than a year later, in a letter from Paris, Marx told him that the 'blockheads' (whom Engels disdained because none of them 'ever read a book on economics') were still furious with him.

From the London congress Engels went to Brussels. Later in the summer Hess too arrived there from Paris. Early in August, Marx's Brussels Correspondence Committee transformed itself into a secret branch of the Communist League, with himself as its president. At the end of the month a German Workers' Society (*Arbeiterverein*) – on the model of those functioning in London – was legally set up to serve as a front organization for it. Hess, who had likewise joined the Communist League, became its vice-president.

From Marx's viewpoint, the statutes adopted by the London congress represented a compromise. He had accepted it on the basis of a promise that his theory of Communism would be discussed at a second international congress of the League to be held in London before the end of the year. In preparation for it, Schapper and Moll, as though founding a new church, drafted a *Glaubens-bekenntnis* – literally, a 'Confession of Faith', a catechism or credo – and invited the League's London, Paris and Brussels branches to comment on it and to submit their versions of a final Communist programme to be adopted at the second congress in the form of a public manifesto.

According to the Communist League's Rules, the proposals were to be discussed by the communities (cells) forming the rank and file of each local branch. The communities, each comprising a maximum of 12 members, did not know each other. Two to 10 communities constituted a circle, which was the executive organ for all the communities in its district. The executive organ of the whole League was the Central Authority. The League's legislative authority was the congress to be held every year, but all its decisions were to be submitted to the communities for acceptance or rejection.[48]

Hess spent a month in Paris making the rounds of the League's rank-and-file and managed to get his draft adopted for submission to the second London congress as the programme of the Paris communities. He was preparing to return to Brussels when Engels arrived in Paris with a different credo of his own.

Whereas during his first stay in Paris until his departure in June for the first London congress he and Hess had ended up by propagandizing different groups within rival sections of the Paris branch of the League of the Just, as it then was, now the future *Communist Manifesto* was in the making. With the battle for the hearts and minds of the Paris artisans reaching its climax, Engels developed a feverish activity to destroy Hess's influence. One of Marx's and Engels's conditions when joining the reorganized Communist League had been that its institutions be democratized. But with the future of Communism at stake, and in his zeal to have the coming congress adopt his and Marx's brand of it, Engels felt no such scruples.

Compounding his 'character assassination' of Hess with backstage intrigue, he went over the heads of the communities – which had been formally charged with approving any motions – to have his credo sent to London in their name.

In a letter to Marx on 25 October, after blaming Hess for the confusion among the German workers in Paris, Engels gleefully reported: '*Strictly between ourselves*, I have played an infernal trick on Mosi. He had actually put through a delightfully amended confession of faith.' He explained that, having found on his arrival only 30 supporters, 'I at once set up a propaganda committee and I rushed around speechifying. I was immediately elected to the district (i.e., *the circle*).' Dealing with Hess's draft point by point, he had tired out 'the lads' who were its members with so many arguments that in the end they were glad to let him prepare a new draft. This decision, as he italicized the words to Marx in the same letter, had been *'completely unopposed'* and the draft 'will be sent to London *behind the backs of the communities*. Naturally, not a soul must know about it, otherwise we shall all be deposed, and there'll be the devil's own scandal.'[49]

Engels's 'infernal trick' and whole procedure have been seen as setting up a pattern for Marxist methods and tactics of settling internal feuds and ideological schisms behind the united façade of Communist Congresses in Soviet Russia and elsewhere, until well into the 20th century. Before the advent of Krushchev, those engaged in these manoeuvres faced the choice mentioned by Engels of either coming out on top or being 'deposed'.[50]

The concept of the 'symbiosis of ideas' between Hess and Marx seems to have been first used by S. Avineri in 1985 when he noted 'the profound impact Hess's writings had on Marx's intellectual development.'[51] This was nearly a century and a half after Hess had given Marx two articles for the German-French Yearbooks, the second of which – titled 'On the Essence of Money' – Marx, for reasons all the more mysterious since Hess was paid for it, rejected after an 'embarrassing' argument. The title of this essay echoed Feuerbach's 'On the Essence of Christianity', and not by accident. For Hess was extending Feuerbach's concept of man's religious alienation to the social and economic sphere by postulating that a society ruled by Mammon and treating men as worth no more than the product of their labour destroys them as social and human beings. Having adumbrated the idea of social alienation in his earlier *The European Triarchy*, Hess elaborated it more fully in his essay on money. In 1844 Marx made it the central theme of his *Economic and Philosophic Manuscripts*, and in the 20th century the question has been asked to what extent his arguments in the *Manuscripts* were influenced by, or actually borrowed from, Hess's essay, which he had read but rejected.

The issue of the so-called 'symbiosis' between the two was compounded by the fact that while Engels acknowledged Hess in 1843 as the leader of 'philosophical' Communism who had converted both him and Marx to it by demonstrating 'that either all the philosophical efforts of the German nation, from Kant to Hegel, had been useless... or they must end in Communism', Marx himself, in a famous retrospective account of the development of his opinions,[52] omitted any mention of having started out as a philosophical Communist. As neither Marx's *Critique of Hegel's Doctrine of the State* nor his *Economic* nor his *Philosophic Manuscripts* was to be published until the 20th century, 'a whole generation of Marxist theorists knew next to nothing (through no fault of their own) of Marx's early philosophical writings' and were misled to infer 'that Marx had proceeded directly from his discovery of civil society in Hegel' to the construction of mature Marxism.[53]

At the same time, the publication of *The German Ideology* in 1932 was hailed as the first work in which Marx and Engels enunciated the 'scientific' materialist conception of history, or 'dialectical materialism'. Once the term dialectical materialism – which, like Marxism, was bestowed on Communist doctrine by Engels – became the official philosophy of the Soviet Union and Europe's Communist parties, it was to take some time before it was realized that, contrary to the 'myth inspired by Marx and Engels themselves and perpetuated in all "orthodox" Marxist scholarship, both men', under Hess's influence, 'came to Communism out of ethical conviction, not out of scientific discovery.'[54]

As if to bedevil the concept of the Marx-Hess symbiosis, *The German Ideology* contained an indirect criticism of Hess's 'vague and mystical' philosophical Communism. From then on, and for many years thereafter, Engels used such a rich vocabulary of insult and invective when referring to Hess in his correspondence with Marx,[55] that loyalist Marx biographers and historians, following in his footsteps, made it practically a ritual to belittle Hess and reduce his role in the history of Socialism to a marginal one. By the time Avineri introduced the concept of 'symbiosis', the rehabilitation of Hess was in full swing. During the 1960s and 1970s, a number of scholars and biographers variously concluded that Marx's essay 'On the Jewish Question' was inspired by Hess's article 'On the Essence of Money'.[56]

In 1978, however, Julius Carlebach pointed out that, though there were some points of similarity between the essays by Marx and Hess, there was a much stronger case for signs of Hess's influence on Marx's famous *Economic and Philosophic Manuscripts* of 1844. Carlebach juxtaposed a number of points made by Marx in the *Manuscripts* with ideas expressed in Hess's earlier essay on money to show parallels not only in theory but in the actual use of words.

In 1982, in an obvious defence of Marx, S. Na'aman wrote that to bring up the delicate problem of 'influence' or 'plagiarism' was methodologically out of place in the case of a group of radical intellectuals who exchanged ideas 'in endless discussions by day in their places of work and at night in pubs and taverns because the terminology they used became common "party" currency.'[57] Avineri did allow for this factor a few years later, but wrote that 'even so, it cannot be denied that of all his colleagues, it was Hess who influenced Marx more than anybody else' and 'it was to Hess that he owed more than to anybody else his development of social critique.'[58]

Z. Rosen, too, in a study of the intellectual links between Hess and Marx published in 1983, had answered Na'aman's point by remarking that the common 'party' terminology had not prevented modern scholars from 'revealing the radical divergence of conceptions between Marx and Engels in spite of their forty-year-long exchange of ideas.'[59] On the basis of detailed text comparisons, Rosen demonstrated that Hess had an 'enormous' influence on Marx's 'fairly quick' adoption and development of Communism, an influence increasingly reflected in Marx's writings from his *Introduction to the Critique of Hegel*, through *The Economic and Philosophic Manuscripts* and his subsequent *The Holy Family* and *The German Ideology* up to the Marx-Engels *Communist Manifesto*.

Even Marx's 'Theses on Feuerbach', including Thesis 1 ('All social life is essentially practical') and the more famous Thesis 2 would, Rosen pointed out, have been inconceivable without Hess's early-expressed perception of 'social and political practice as an instrument for changing reality.'[60]

Even so, the complex relationship between Marx and Hess was not a one-way street. From the beginning, Hess propagated Communism as a social movement motivated by ethical 'ideas' and the dictates of the heart, as he expressed it. Although he had been one of the earliest to draw attention to the misery of the proletariat, and had characterized its exploitation as 'organized robbery', he had been furious with its presentation – by Lorenz Stein – as a movement of outcasts driven by the primitive 'needs of the stomach' to overthrow society based on property. Hess saw private property as 'the practical realization of egoism', which would gradually have to yield to Communism and a 'whole new relationship to work'.

Unlike Marx, Hess (in the words of Isaiah Berlin) believed that 'social equality was desirable because it was just, not because it was inevitable.' He was out to abolish any kind of 'domination' by the state, by religion or by any class, and to put an end to man's alienation. The letter of reconciliation he addressed to Marx on 28 July 1846, in which he wrote that he agreed with Marx's view that 'it is now necessary to stress the historical and economic foundation of Communism', i.e., 'the needs of the stomach', implies that he had adopted the view that the proletariat was the chosen class which, by emancipating itself, would emancipate mankind. But this did not mean that he had surrendered his mind or the dictates of his heart.

By the end of October 1847, when Engels played his 'infernal trick' on Hess, the February 1848 revolution was only months away. In the same letter of 25–26 October in which Engels wrote to Marx about the 'trick', he informed him that he had been to see Louis Blanc, the French Socialist politician and future member of the Provisional Government.

> He told me a great deal about the underground movement now going
> on among the workers...The workers were more revolutionary than

ever, but had learned to bide their time, no riots, only major coups that would be sure to succeed. The coming revolution, he went on, would be quite different from, and much more drastic than, all previous ones, and it would be sheer madness to keep on thundering only against kings...

Engels also visited Flocon, the editor of the republican *La Réforme* and future Secretary of the Provisional Government. Whereas Engels introduced himself to Louis Blanc as 'coming with a formal mandate from the London, Brussels and Rhineland democrats', to Flocon he chose to pretend to be an Englishman representing the Chartist leader Julian Harney and *The Northern Star*. Flocon knew little about Chartism and happily accepted Engels's offer to write for his paper on English affairs. Engels told Marx that he hoped 'to imprison Flocon still more tightly in our net.' He did in fact, during the following months, contribute 9 articles to *La Réforme*.

Louis Blanc, the only French politician with whom Marx had established mutually cordial relations during the mid-'40, played an important part in his and Engels's plans for the strategy to be pursued by the proletariat in the event of revolution. The Communists being too few to overthrow the bourgeoisie on their own, they must ally themselves with the Chartists in England and with Louis Blanc in France. Not so in Germany. There the bourgeoisie would not support a revolution if it was started by the proletariat. But if the Communists encouraged the bourgeoisie to revolt and helped it into the saddle, it would pay them to keep it in power – until the day when a more developed capitalism invited its own destruction and the proletariat would be strong enough to stage its own revolution and seize the power for itself.

At this very point, a serious rift developed between Marx and Engels on the one hand, and Hess on the other, on the tactics to be pursued by the proletariat, for Hess believed that the German bourgeoisie was too cowardly to revolt with or without the help of the proletariat.

It now remained to be seen whether the 'symbiosis' between Hess and Marx would or would not survive the 2nd congress of the 'Communist' League – to be convened in London on 29 November – whose chief resolution was to charge Marx to draft the final version of its programme and principles in *The Communist Manifesto*.

34

Ferdinand Lassalle and Heine's Inheritance War

'Marx must leave today, and I am simply furious,' Heine had written to Campe on 4 February 1845, a couple of days after Marx's expulsion from Paris. It was not the only reason for Heine's anger, for 1845 had started off for him as badly as it had for Marx. A week before the New Year, his uncle Salomon died in Hamburg at the age of 75. Mourned by the Augsburg *Allgemeine Zeitung* as a philanthropist 'known worldwide' for his many charities, he left, according to the *Journal des Débats*, a fortune of 41 million francs.

Receiving the news a few days later, Heine wrote to his sister Lotte in Hamburg that the death of the man who had 'played a great role in my life' affected him deeply: 'What a heart! What a head!... And how kind he has been to my poor pussycat of a mother... To me he often said harsh things', but 'concerning his last dispositions, I have long been without worry; he said enough to me about it or intimated it clearly.'[1]

At the beginning of January, he received a letter from his cousin Karl, Salomon's son and chief heir, informing him that his father had left him a lump sum of 8,000 Marks in his will. Since 'you have never understood how to handle capital', Karl offered to give him instead 2,000 francs a year, not in perpetuity or as an obligation, but as a gesture of good will. But this hand-out would cease if Heine demanded the 8,000 Marks; and in either case, Cousin Karl stipulated that Heine must undertake not to publish anything about his uncle before submitting it to the family first.[2]

Reeling under the devastating double blow – being deprived of the annual pension of 4,800 francs he had been getting from Salomon (which he had understood would go on until his or Mathilde's death) plus the humiliating proposal to sell his conscience for a pittance and to be placed financially and as a writer under his cousin's tutelage – Heine fainted upon reading the letter.

Modern scholars, noting that Salomon Heine left to his employees gratuities ranging up to 40,000 Marks, have calculated that the original pension Heine expected to get amounted to 'a little over three-hundredths of one percent' of the 15,000,000 francs his cousin Karl had personally inherited; and it has been suggested that Karl and his wife Cécile, in cahoots with his brother-in-law Dr

Adolph Halle, had together persuaded the dying banker that the family must have a lever to protect its reputation against anything his talented but unpredictable nephew might say about him in the Memoirs he might one day publish.[3]

Heine certainly believed that the three had plotted against him. On 8 January, he rejected his cousin's arrogant proposal out of hand, but sent his letter to him in an open envelope to Campe, asking his publisher to make a copy of it for himself before sealing the original and conveying it to his cousin. He wanted Campe to act as his confidential middleman and wrote that he was ready for a 'battle to the death in the courts as well as in the court of public opinion.'[4]

Thus started the 'Inheritance War' that was to preoccupy Heine for the next two years. It was to be fought with no holds barred and at times with the ferocity peculiar to family feuds. Heine threatened Karl with a lawsuit, but he knew that his chances in court were not very promising. For whatever Uncle Salomon had verbally said or 'intimated' to him, he had given him nothing in writing. The only evidence of sorts that Heine finally obtained was a letter from Meyerbeer, in which the composer attested that 'to the best of my memory the late Salomon Heine granted you a pension of 4,000 francs – and not 4,800 – for life. Since I myself, at your request, brought up the matter with him, I do faintly recall the benevolent old gentleman saying that he hoped this pension would protect you in your old age.'[5]

Heine felt stronger in the 'court of public opinion', and almost simultaneously with his approach to Campe he began to mobilize his friends in Germany to start a press campaign that would instil the fear of God in his family. 'Public opinion will easily side with the poet – against the millionaires,' he wrote to Johann Detmold, urging him to attack Uncle Salomon's son-in-law, Dr Adolph Halle. Heine thought that Halle, who presided over Hamburg's Commercial Court, was particularly susceptible to criticism because he hoped to be nominated to the Hamburg Senate.

By 20 January, Detmold (in the *Kölnische Zeitung*) and not many weeks later Ignaz Kuranda (in the widely read periodical *Die Grenzboten*) were variously presenting Dr Halle as a parvenu risen to great riches through his father-in-law's will and pointing a finger at him as the person who might have influenced the old man to leave Heine no more than pin money. The writers wondered, 'How was it that the most distinguished member of the Heine family, the genius whose name will be remembered long after its millions of gold pieces are gone, should have been thrown a bone, and treated like a beggar and a nuisance?'[6]

All this, based on hints thrown out by Heine himself, reflected his feeling that the clique of mediocrities surrounding Uncle Salomon had 'waited twenty years' to satisfy its 'bitter envy of genius' before attacking him 'with outrageous infamy'.

In the battles that followed neither party covered itself with glory. Heine had written to Detmold on 9 January that he was ready to 'throw mud' at his relatives, 'they are not accustomed to it, whereas I can put up with waggon-loads and prosper like a flower on a dung-heap.'[7] He went even further and sent Heinrich Laube, the influential playwright and newspaper editor, two articles for publication in Leipzig. Both were composed by himself, but while the first was 'an attack' upon his family, the second was 'a defence against this attack, which I have made as perfidiously stupid as possible, in the style used by people who defend the rich.' To erase all traces of his authorship, he asked Laube to destroy both manuscripts.

Laube published the first article on 22 February in Brockhaus's *Deutsche Allgemeine Zeitung*; the second appeared in March in *Die Grenzboten*. Heine's justification – to himself and to his friends – for resorting to such methods was that the attempt of his relatives to strangle his voice was tantamount to a 'dastardly assassination'; that his pen was his only weapon; and that he was fighting not only for justice but for his existence and Mathilde's future. Mathilde's reaction to the loss of their pension had been to sit for two days 'stony-faced like a statue by the fireside, without uttering a word.' When she came out of her shock she became all the more vehement, giving Heine not a moment's rest. 'My domestic Vesuvius, which has lain dormant for three years', he wrote to Detmold, 'has begun to spit fire.'[8]

To add to his vexations, the start of the Hamburg 'Inheritance War' coincided with the suppression of the Paris *Vorwärts!* and the persecution of its contributors. Furious as he was at Marx's expulsion, the fact that his own name had been taken off the list of those expelled only after an interpellation in the Chamber of Deputies showed him that political asylum in France was no life insurance. 'My wife is ill, and I'm half-blind,' he wrote to Campe on 4 February. And since his collapse, he suffered from a 'nervous fever'.

The turmoil of the 'Inheritance War' was injurious to his health, but Heine was not one to take things lying down. He had been hurt in his self-esteem and his pride – and by whom? By his own cousin Karl, whose life he had saved at some risk to his own by nursing him through the terrible cholera epidemic of 1831 in Paris, and whose marriage to the lovely Cécile Fould he had later helped to arrange. Disgusted with life and the world, yet determined to fight, Heine wrote, 'Unfortunately, my will is as rigid as that of a madman – that is in my nature.' Madman or not, he alternated between fits of rage and anxiety. But even if his moves were often contradictory, there was a certain strategy to them. The lawyer recommended by Campe had advised that Karl Heine would do everything to avoid being dragged to court. Heine did not agree. Cousin Karl, he wrote to Campe on 4 February, 'is as obdurate as he is uncommunicative.

Unlike his father, who courted public opinion, Karl Heine is completely indifferent to it.' A lawsuit would only make him more stubborn. But Karl 'has three passions: women, cigars and tranquillity.' While he could not take away his cousin's women or his cigars, he could unsettle his peace of mind by keeping his name constantly in the newspapers, writing memoirs and making God and the world his witnesses. The lawsuit, he explained, was only the backdrop for these 'and other tribulations I can think up.'

Indeed, with the articles mentioned appearing one after another between January and March, the first phase of the Inheritance War was hardly played out before the German and European public when Heine launched another move. He sent Campe a power of attorney delegating the publisher to represent all his legal claims in cooperation with the lawyer and at the same time instructed him to obtain from Karl Heine the 8,000 Marks left him in his uncle's will, without prejudice to the chief matter under dispute, the promised life-long pension of which he had been deprived.

On that matter, he was ready for a compromise settlement compatible with his honour. If his full pension of 4,800 francs was restored for life in a legal document, he would promise on his honour never to write anything about his miserable 'pack' of Hamburg relatives. He stressed that, although he would never accept any family censorship, he was ready to reverse himself to this extent and let the whole pack 'enjoy their obscure existence until death confines them to oblivion.'[9]

In April 1845, his cousin Karl duly paid Heine 7,600 Marks – representing the 8,000 left him in his uncle's will, minus 5 per cent inheritance tax. But otherwise he remained unperturbed by press discussion of the affair or personal appeals, and would not budge from his original conditions. A year later, in answer to an intervention by Prince Pückler-Muskau on Heine's behalf, he was still obstinately declaring that 'there are things which must first be wiped out by repentance and good behaviour.' Karl Heine was obviously bent on compelling the rebellious poet to submission as well as humiliating him. His behaviour has been aptly summed up by Jeffrey Sammons:

> The chilly impudence of his letters in the matter is quite stunning when one considers that they were addressed, by a man whose chief accomplishment in life was to have been born to a rich father, to a man who was his cousin, twelve years his senior, and one of the most eminent literary figures in the world... Suppose he had taken the opposite tack and regarded it as an honour to be the friendly patron of Heinrich Heine?... Karl would have come down to posterity as a benefactor of culture, [instead of] a mean-spirited boor.[10]

979

In mid-August, Karl Heine, sticking to his initial offer to give his illustrious cousin 2,000 francs a year as a non-obligatory act of charity so long as he kept silent, sent him this sum. It was less than half the pension Heine had been receiving from his uncle, and the unyielding Karl made no further commitment. By now, 8 months into his campaign, Heine realized that he had landed himself in a war of attrition that was sapping his health. At the beginning of the summer, though half-blind, he had still been socializing with Berlioz, the Princess Belgiojoso, Gautier and others; he had also maintained a vast correspondence and invested some money in railway shares on a tip from Baron Rothschild.

At the beginning of July, however, shortly after he had started a cure at the sulphur baths of Montmorency, he became half-paralyzed and bedridden, with the upper part of his body immobilized. He recovered, and on the 21st, on his feet again but weak, he wrote to Campe that Karl Heine 'has committed a terrible sin against me without even realizing the consequences of his misdeed.' His chief concern was to recover his health, and let his unfinished family feud wait, as he must avoid all excitement and refrain from 'disgusting expectorations'. At the same time, he hoped to start work on the enlarged and improved version of *Atta Troll* – originally serialized in Laube's *Journal for the Elegant World* – which Campe planned to issue in book form. He promised to send him the material soon and remarked that his health was 'by no means as bad as rumoured in Germany', where reports about his deteriorating condition had appeared.

Between July and September of that summer, the Vatican placed Heine's *New Poems* on the Index of Prohibited Books. Translations of his poems continued to appear in Moscow; the *Foreign Quarterly Review* carried an article on his *Germany, A Winter's Tale* and the Dublin University Magazine published excerpts from it. But for occasional trips to Paris – where he met Meyerbeer and obtained the latter's written confirmation of his claim to the full pension – Heine spent all those months at a small country house with a garden at Montmorency, where Mathilde looked after him.

He had not written to Campe since July. On 31 October, a fortnight after he returned to Paris for the winter, he sent an apologetic letter, in which he sought to explain why he had not yet sent the 'long-promised' passages to be inserted in the book version of *Atta Troll*: 'My misfortunes this year have so depressed me that to this day I have been unable to work up the cheerful mood in which the missing passages should be cast... I can no longer deny the wound which has been inflicted upon me, and it will be years before the old humour bubbles forth again.'

His left eye had been shut since January and the right one was 'blurred and lame. I can still write, but cannot read.' He mentioned that practically everyone, including Meyerbeer, had advised him to give in to his cousin's demand that he never write anything about Uncle Salomon; and that all his own appeals to Karl Heine to continue paying him Uncle Salomon's full pension, 'if only as an act of charity for which I will show my gratitude,' had been fruitless. In a significant passage of this letter to Campe he added: 'I am not ready to discuss any further terms – my dignity as an author and the freedom of my pen are at stake, even if for humanitarian reasons I am ready to submit to family considerations.'[11]

With his creativity as well as his health now ruinously affected by this running conflict, a tired Heine was about ready to give up the year-long fight. But some time before the end of 1845, Ferdinand Lassalle, newly arrived in Paris, came to see him. This 20-year-old man, tall, bright, dandyish, fiery and ambitious, had so much firmness of character, compelling logic and fighting spirit that in almost no time, during his relatively short visit, he rekindled Heine's own flagging spirit and made him resume the Inheritance War with renewed energy and vigour.

Lassalle was at the time midway through his final year of studies at Berlin University. The previous year, on his way from Berlin to his native Breslau, he had witnessed Prussia's bloody suppression of the Silesian weavers' strike. But already in 1840, when he was barely 15, he had noted in his diary: 'One's heart cries when one sees what a big jail Germany is, how human rights are trampled underfoot.' Like Hess and Engels, Lassalle was the son of a God-fearing, prosperous merchant. Like them, he had early decided to shun 'a career in the counting-house'. He did not want to become a 'smiling cowardly court flunkey', and swearing to bring 'the annunciation of liberty to all the nations, even if I die in the attempt', he wrote in his diary 4 months after his 15th birthday: 'From Paris, the land of liberty, I shall... send forth the word to all the nations of the earth and the teeth of all the princes shall be set clattering at the news: Their time is up.'[12]

Unlike Hess and Engels, however, Lassalle had doting parents who could deny him nothing. He grew up in a comfortable house, on the ground floor of which – in premises known by their shape as 'the Vault' – his father carried on a wholesale trade in cotton and silks. A precocious boy, he was bored at school, inattentive during lessons, and often played truant, preferring to spend his time in cafés, playing chess, whist or billiards. By the time he was in the fifth form of high school, he had so often forged his mother's, and sometimes his father's, signature on school certificates censuring him for 'bad behaviour' that he felt he was about to be caught. Fearing the consequences and racking his brain as to how to cope with them, he found no better solution than to feign a sudden interest in business and got his adoring father to send him away to the expensive Academy of Commerce in Leipzig before the forgery was discovered.

His father, Hyman Lassal – it was only in Paris that the son adopted the name of Lassalle, to identify himself with a figure of the French Revolution – realized the boy's exceptional intelligence and had decided to help him in every way to achieve the brilliant career for which he seemed destined. The boy was quick to exploit this. He loved his father but, in a reversal of roles, was ultimately to became his educator. The father realized only gradually that he was nursing a rebel at his breast.

At Leipzig, Lassalle had excellent marks, but became the bane of his teachers by delivering 'the most splendid speeches of Robespierre in class. With the fiercest eloquence at my disposal,' he wrote to his father, 'I am doing my best to inflame the cold hearts of the German lads.'

His teachers were hardly enthusiastic. 'A merchant who quotes Socrates and Cicero is sure to go bankrupt sooner or later,' one of them remarked. But a merchant was the last thing Ferdinand wanted to become, and having got himself to Leipzig on false pretenses, he spent much of his time in cafés, inns and the theatre.

He first showed his mettle a year later, when he abruptly returned to Breslau and registered for the final high school examination as an external or 'wild' student at the local Catholic Gymnasium. Being still under 17, he had to obtain a special dispensation from the Ministry of Education, but failed the test. He found out that all the teachers had actually passed him – his Latin, Greek and German essays were the best of the papers submitted – but, much to their shame and embarrassment, the Government Inspector insisted on failing him on the grounds of 'immaturity of character'. One of the reasons given by the Inspector was that, against his father's will, he had changed the plan to study commerce in favour of devoting himself to the sciences.

In an unprecedented step for a pupil, Ferdinand appealed over the heads of the local authorities to the Prussian Minister of Education, Eichhorn. Submitting detailed proofs of what had happened, he challenged the Inspector's decision and cited Martin Luther's change of mind:

> The whole world sees it as a praiseworthy firmness and maturity of character that Luther decided not to sacrifice his favourite study, theology, to the study of law. Why does my preferring the study of the sciences to those of commerce denote an immaturity of character?... And is it so unheard-of that a youth should leave the road planned for him and turn into the direction to which he is drawn by taste and inclination, vocation and feeling?[13]

On 24 August 1842, after reviewing his examination papers and the whole case, Eichhorn granted him permission to take the examination again, not necessarily in Breslau, but 'before any commission of your choosing'. This time Ferdinand passed with flying colours. Having extricated himself from a predicament of his own making – his flight to Leipzig – he enrolled at Breslau University. He was to spend the next 4 years studying there and at Berlin University, in accordance with a well-conceived plan, actually a life-plan, he had formed early on.

In April or May 1841, around his 16th birthday, he had told his father that he was determined to seek a public career and that his vocation would require expensive studies. 'He was surprised', Ferdinand recorded in his diary, 'but said he needed a little while to consider it. I ventured to reply that there was not much to consider, I only wanted his agreement, for nothing would deflect me from my decision.

'It was of course a bit strong of me', he admitted, 'to leave my father no choice in the matter and I had to overcome a little inner struggle.' The young Lassalle knew that his 'tired' father was financially over-burdened by supporting a married daughter and her husband and was waiting for his only son to grow up and take over his wholesale business in Breslau. Yet the boy's firmness of will prevailed over his sympathy for his weary parent, as shown in this conversation with his father:

> Nevertheless, I declared that I had to follow my inclination and unmistakable vocation... He asked what I wished to study. I replied: 'The most comprehensive study in the world, that which is most closely bound up with the interests of mankind, the study of history.' My father asked what I would live on, since in Prussia [as a Jew] I was barred from government posts or a teaching position, and since I did not want to be separated from my parents. My God, as if that was not inevitable and could be helped! Aloud I said only that I would know how to support myself anywhere.
>
> My father asked why I did not want to study medicine or law [two professions accessible to young men of his origin]. 'Doctors and lawyers', I replied, 'are merchants who sell their knowledge. Scholars often do the same... I want to study for the sake of the cause, in order to be effective in it.' These days, I said, a struggle is going on for the noblest ideals of mankind.

Did he think of becoming a poet, his father asked. 'No', Ferdinand Lassalle replied. But there was a new force in the world: public opinion. 'In every country, every nation, men have now risen who fight by the word, fall by the word or achieve victory by it.' The cause, he explained, was the struggle against the existing order. This had not ended with 'the necessarily terrible eruption' of

983

the French Revolution, but continued to be 'waged without cease not by means of crude physical power, but by the power of the mind.

'Later, of course', he added, 'the truth will have to be supported by physical force,' for the crowned heads would not easily abdicate their privileges.

His father was stunned into silence. He came of a learned family in Upper Silesia but, orphaned in his youth, he had worked his way up from scratch to the position of a respected town councillor. Although liberal-minded, and used to surprises from his undisciplined son, he did not relish the idea of his using his gifts to become a revolutionary agitator.

'My father was silent for a long time, and then he said: "My son, I do not deny that there is truth in what you say. But why do you insist on becoming a martyr, you, our only joy, hope and support?..."'

Lassalle pondered his father's words. The answer he entered in his diary in May 1841 gave promise of the man: 'Why? Because God has given me a voice that calls me to the struggle, as well as a fighter's strength and aptitude! Because for a noble cause I am ready both to fight and to suffer. And because I will not deceive God or betray the power given me for a certain purpose. In short, because I cannot do otherwise!'[14]

Besides annoying his teachers in elementary school by his 'forward' manner, young Ferdinand's rebellious temperament had first manifested itself in his reaction to a report on the tortures endured by the Jews of Damascus during the 1840 'blood libel' affair. Furiously he wrote in his diary:

> Was there a revolution more just than that of the Jews of that city,
> if they would rise up, burn Damascus, blow up the towers and kill
> themselves together with their torturers?... Even the Christians won-
> der at the sluggishness of our blood... wonder that we do not rise in
> revolt, in order that we may die on the battlefield, rather than in the
> torture chamber.[15]

But his attachment to the assimilationist Judaism practised by his father was weak, and precisely because the Jews did not revolt but allowed themselves to be treated like pariahs, he there and then decided to embrace the larger cause of humanity. Within months of his emotional outburst, he was fascinated by the ideas of the French Revolution, reading the works of Rousseau and Voltaire and those of Heine and Börne. He loved 'this Heine, he is my second self,' he wrote in his diary about the time when he was reciting the speeches of Robespierre to his classmates in Leipzig. During the general assault on Heine following his sacrilegious memoir on Börne, he published an anonymous article in Heine's defence, challenging his attackers to a duel. None of the readers of the *Breslauer Zeitung* guessed that the challenge came from a 16-year-old boy.

Neither at Breslau University, nor in Berlin, did Ferdinand Lassalle lead a regular student's life. For one thing, having decided on a salvationist role, his mind was focused on a single question, the answer to which was not in the curriculum: How did history work, and how could he insert himself in its movement and play an effective role on the public stage? For another, within a fortnight of having registered for 6 courses at Berlin University, he found out that there was nothing its professors could teach him that he could not more fruitfully study by himself. With extraordinary self-reliance and a certain conceit he wrote to his father on 13 May 1844, 'out of curiosity I shall attend a couple of Schelling's lectures. I expect nothing of him but intuition and mysticism; Trendelenburg offers reflection, the Hegelians only boredom and high-powered trivialities, but no real philosophy.'

Lassalle had discovered philosophy at 18 – or, as he put it in his lordly manner, 'Philosophy came up to me' – during his second year at Breslau University. It opened a new world to him. He continued to frequent saloons and beer cellars, but instead of playing billiards it became his favourite pastime to hold forth on Hegel to groups of admiring fellow-students until late into the night. At the same time, he led several student protests – against the dismissal of one professor and against the derogatory remarks made by another about Feuerbach's philosophy – and was several times jailed in the university *Karzer* for rowdiness.

In Berlin, as if to make up for this unruly period and for all his years as a 'foolish boy', he subjected himself to a rigorous discipline and stuck for about a year to the following schedule:

> I attend only two courses... meaning that I spend only one hour a day at the university. I get up at four in the morning, and study Hegel until nine; at nine I go to the university; at ten I am back, slip into a housecoat... and work without interruption until ten in the evening; at ten I go to sleep... I leave the house only twice a week to have lunch outside. Otherwise I take my meals at home.[16]

Installed in an elegant apartment in Unter den Linden paid for by his father, Lassalle lived at this time a frugal life in stark contrast to his innate love for luxury and, later, a fashionable lifestyle. The only relaxation he allowed himself was to take riding lessons. His father had sent him a whole list of acquaintances to visit, but Ferdinand replied that he had no time to waste on them or their 'sons, doctors and similar rabble. I have much to do. My fingernails are burning.' He was out to master Hegel, and he did so, in the words of his modern biographer, by dint of a phenomenal memory and 'the ability to absorb an enormous amount of knowledge... Soon he surpassed most of his teachers both in erudition as well as in the application of this knowledge.'[17]

If his coffeehouse companions at Breslau had marvelled at his quoting and analyzing the most obscure passages in Hegel by heart, in Berlin – at a soirée in the house of the Berlin banker Joseph Mendelssohn – he was to intervene in a philosophical dispute and to correct the august Alexander von Humboldt himself on a point concerning a statement by Hegel. Whereas Humboldt later that night looked up the passage at home and sent a note to the hostess asking her to inform Lassalle that he had been right, she, thinking that it was an effrontery on the part of a young man to publicly prove the great Humboldt wrong, kept the note to herself. But the story soon made the rounds of Berlin. And even S. Na'aman, in the most comprehensive critical biography of Lassalle, though unsparing in the presentation of his foibles, has rated what he accomplished in one year in Berlin as an 'enormous' achievement, explicable only by the concentrated intensity of his effort.[18]

The ascetic self-discipline of his son during that year of study had made Lassalle's father express the hope that the rowdy Breslau 'chapter' of his life was now over and would not repeat itself. The 19-year-old Ferdinand taught him one better. In his letter of 13 May, he told his father that 'a chapter is only a qualitative phase in the development of the mind... I have now achieved the highest phase and can only develop quantitatively.' Before that, from the day he was born until he went to Leipzig, he had gone through the phase of being 'a foolish boy'; this had been followed by the empty Leipzig phase; as for the last phase, he wrote that 'two and a half years ago I shed my skin for the third time' and went on to declare:

> Philosophy came up to me, and she gave birth to me anew in the spirit. This spiritual rebirth gave me the full absolute powers of the human spirit, the objective substance of morality, of reason, etc.; in short, I became self-comprehending reason, tantamount to self-conscious God in the sense of the mind that comprehends the phenomenon and actualisation of the divine. And he who has been a god will never again be 'a foolish boy'!!!

What Lassalle was telling his father in these and other words was that through philosophy he had matured into a man. Not only that; 'the philosopher appropriates the entire experience of world history from Anno 1 to the present day and makes it his own... He matures in the very process of historic life; he is taught by historic life, that is by God himself. That is how I matured and was taught, basta!'[19]

Hegel and his concept of the hidden absolute Idea governing the actions of men had given the young Ferdinand the key to understanding the process of history. The world was an ever-changing reality made up of an infinite multitude of little facts and occurrences; all these flowed into the wide stream of history; but the man who had the philosophic knowledge of the forces activating history could not only foresee its course, but by his own action become one of the 'waves' influencing this current.

For the youngster who had reached the highest stage of the development of the mind there remained the question how to translate his knowledge into practical action. On 12 June, within a month of his earlier letter to his father, Ferdinand was sending him another with his comments on the Silesian weavers' revolt: 'Have you noticed anything? Do you hear the storm gathering on the horizon? Don't be afraid, it will go away this time, it will pass yet another time – but then all hell will break loose!'

Hegel, in his closing lecture on the history of philosophy, had urged his disciples at all times and everywhere to help the *Zeitgeist* manifest itself. As though echoing him, Ferdinand pointed out to his father: 'You write that we live in agitated times. Yes, very agitated, but thanks be to the Holy Virgin, time has started moving at last, away from the sinful old indolence into which it has fallen.' The hungry weavers' revolt and the increasing social polarization represented at the other end by huge stock exchange speculations were symptoms of the *Zeitgeist*'s moving towards a crisis.

'Or are you really so blind, deaf, stupid and paralyzed in all your senses', he went on, 'not to notice what it all means?' And addressing not only his father but an unseen audience, he concluded:

> Do not be deceived, the beginning of the war between the poor and the rich is terribly close. We are witnessing the first stirrings of Communism which has both theoretically and in practice penetrated our veins. We are witnessing the first birthpangs of an embryo and I ask you, what kind of medics are these who, while the mother is in labour, would firmly block her uterus? Do they believe they will be able to prevent the birth? The child will find its way out – only the mother will be ruined...[20]

During his solitary existence in Berlin, Lassalle continued to use his father as a sounding-board for his ideas. On 6 September, less than three months after he had notified him of the 'birthpangs' of Communism, he sent him another message – to become known as his 'Letter on Industry' – to show him that industrial expansion carried within it the seeds of its own destruction. Reporting on a visit to the 1844 Industrial Exhibition staged at the Arsenal in Berlin, he pointed out ironically that 'industry has removed the weapons from the arsenal to show that the future is one of peace and prosperity, without the exhibitors realizing that the flourishing growth of industry actually presages the approach of the bloodiest war.'

When he emerged from his seclusion and before he left Berlin, the eloquent young Lassalle found ready disciples who, fascinated both by his personality and by the mysteries of the Hegelian dialectics into which he initiated them, fell completely under his spell. In mid-September 1845, some time after he returned to Breslau, Lassalle addressed to them his so-called 'War Manifesto against the World', a letter of some 18 pages when printed.

Between them, the 'Letter on Industry' to his father and the 'War Manifesto' – written a year later – marked Lassalle's transition from theory to practice. They comprised his outline of the fundamental ideas which were later to guide his political action.

'Communism', he postulated, 'requires continuous industrial development,' but not for the same reason that animates industrial expansion in the state based on property. In earlier times the man without property consoled himself for his inability to give external expression to his subjective individuality by devoting his life to God, the commonality, the state. In the bourgeois state which had emerged since the French Revolution, property and money, replacing God and every other value, robbed the poverty-striken proletarian of the little he had and turned him into 'a hollow shell'. Hence the growing disaffection and fury of the toiling masses.

Lassalle acknowledged that industry was one of the essential and creative foundations of the state, but on the negative side property, greed and competition had turned it into 'organized robbery', the war of all against all; and the more it expanded, the greater the misery it created. Communism, too, would promote maximum industrial progress, but would abolish the division of labour which allowed capitalism to rule politics while excluding the labour force which produced its wealth from the political process.

Lassalle, in short, saw in industry a rising 'world power', but one that was only a forerunner of Communism. Industrial expansion, he wrote, 'is grist to our mill'. Instead of an atomized society, Communism would guarantee everyone both property and the possibility of asserting his talent and his subjective individuality, turning him into a full and active participant in the 'organic totality' of a democratic state, a true *citoyen*.

In the diary he had kept for a little over a year until shortly after his 16th birthday, he fixed with remarkable clarity and firmness for his age the aims he wished to pursue in life. He was 7 years younger than Marx, and Engels's junior by 5. In his 1844 'Letter on Industry' and the 1845 'War Manifesto' he achieved for himself single-handedly the same sort of 'self-clarification' which Marx and Engels spent much of their time on in 1845–46 in *The German Ideology*.

'A revolutionary since 1840, and a Socialist since 1844,' as he was later to call himself, Lassalle – against the hypocrisy of the existing propertied state – proclaimed in his 'War Manifesto' that his proposed transformation of it was supported by justice and morality. At the same time, he buttressed it philosophically with the 'almighty power of the mind' and the 'power of the will as its practical executor'. Declaring philosophy to be his only religion, he wrote that the mind or the purposeful 'Idea' had always governed the movement of history, but whereas in the transition from age to age its travail had often foundered on the obstacles of reality, 'now that it has become conscious of its almightiness it must exercise its sovereignty' and he, Lassalle, had the necessary will to lead its effort.

'From head to toe, asleep or awake, I am nothing but will,' he wrote. He had proved it during his ascetic year in Berlin by subjecting his body day and night to the most rigorous discipline commanded by his thought. Armed with the philosopher's faculty of 'seeing through the world situation' and this formidable will, he saw himself as 'lord of the earth, whose breath of fire nothing can resist' and ready to swing the 'weapon of Zeus, the lightning of knowledge' against the god of Mammon.

Like Marx, Lassalle cursed money for standing in the way of man's self-realization. 'The day will come when we shall topple this glowing Moloch and throw his priests after him to be consumed in the flames,' he wrote in the 'War Manifesto'. He and the three disciples to whom it was addressed – Dr Arnold Mendelssohn, a nephew of the banker Joseph Mendelssohn; Alexander Oppenheim, a junior court clerk; and Albert Lehfeldt, a former fellow-student of his – were 'no proletarians. We have all the money we need.' But this, he impressed on them, did not mean that they must wait for the uninformed 'herd' to wake up and start its stampede towards redemption.

As carriers of the 'Idea', morally bound to each other and to no one else in the world, they must 'conquer' money. Unlike Marx, the young Lassalle realized that 'money is the key to the locked reality of the present-day world' and instructed his disciples that 'we must get hold of this key.' Industry was to be beaten with its own weapons, money with money and propaganda too – the 'power of the word', of which he had spoken to his father – required money. For the rest, with his 'knowledge' of the working of the historic process and the 'power of the will as its practical executor', he would provide the necessary leadership.

Lassalle concluded his 'War Manifesto against the World' with the slogan *Vainquons!* and asked his three faithfuls to mark their agreement with his ideas by appending their signatures to it.[21]

Dr Arnold Mendelssohn, whom Lassalle had met in Berlin at the house of his uncle, the banker, was a physician in his early 30s. A grandson of the philosopher Moses Mendelssohn, he was so captivated by Lassalle's personality and his interpretation of the world that in order to be closer to him in Berlin he proposed and arranged that they rent an apartment together. Oppenheim like-wise fell completely in thrall to this domineering young man, and he and Mendelssohn were presently to prove that they were ready to go through fire and water for him.

At the time he wrote the 'War Manifesto', Lassalle was in Breslau working on a study of the philosophy of Heraclitus. As determined as he was to lead a revo-lution, he was no less sure that he would make his name as a scholar. And so he eventually did. Although in November or December, itching for action, he went to Paris and soon afterwards became too busy fighting his first public campaigns to complete his doctoral thesis, his two-volume study, *The Philosophy of Heracli-tus, the Dark One* – when finally published in 1858, after he had years of revolu-tionary activity and a term of political imprisonment behind him – opened to him the doors of Berlin's intellectual élite and its exclusive 'Philosophic Society'.

The purpose of Lassalle's first visit to Paris, where he stayed until the begin-ning of January 1846, was twofold. First and foremost, he wanted to see Heine, of whom, while still a teenager, he had written in his diary that he admired 'the boldness of his ideas and the smashing power of his language, ... to conjure up our gentle longings as well as our furious wrath.'[22] According to a schoolmate at the Leipzig Commercial Academy, his greatest wish at the time 'was to live in Paris by the side of Heine'. But this was also a business trip, connected with his decision that, in order to become a Socialist politician and propagate his ideas with any chance of success, he must get hold of 'money, the key to reality'. Las-salle had a cousin, Ferdinand Friedländer, who was also his brother-in-law, having married Lassalle's elder sister Friederike. This man was a self-taught engineer and something of an adventurer. He had accompanied Prince Des-cazes on his tour of Persia and it was he who in 1840 had furnished Heine with details for his articles on the 'Damascus Affair'. By 1845 Friedländer, who later called himself Chevalier Friedland, had used his technical skill and enterprise to install gas-lighting in Breslau.

Although Lassalle spoke of Communism in 1844–45, he was, after years of friendship and cooperation with Marx, to develop his own concept of industrial Socialism based on the rule of law. Having realized that industry was a 'world power', he not only followed Friedland's efforts with great interest but latched on to them by persuading his father to invest in his next project, which was to install gas-lighting in Prague. Friedland had preceded Lassalle to Paris to discuss the overall financing of this project with the Belgian share company Iris, which had its headquarters in Paris. Either before or during Lassalle's visit, Friedland also persuaded Heine to invest 12,500 francs in the Prague venture.

The handsome and charismatic Lassalle made an extraordinary impression on Heine, almost as though he had seen in him the image of his own youth.

They had much to talk about: literature, philosophy, the Silesian weavers' strike, the Prague gas-lighting project, and possibly also the fate of *Vorwärts!* and the expulsion of Marx, with some of whose writings Lassalle was likely to have been familiar.

Besides feeling so invigorated by Lassalle's company that he took the young man on a tour of the Paris dance-halls and brothels, Heine recognized in him those qualities which within two years were to make him an acclaimed political tribune. The young man undertook to fight for Heine in his Inheritance War all the more eagerly as his championship of the libertarian 'genius' against the aristocracy of money trying to muzzle him had, in the circumstances of the time in Germany, political significance as well as the makings of a case that would propel him on to the public stage.

On 3 January 1846, Heine gave Lassalle a letter of introduction to Varnhagen von Ense in Berlin, in which he wrote of this new 'gladiator' who had offered his services to him: 'My friend, Herr Lassalle, is a young man of quite exceptional intellectual quality. Together with thorough scholarship, wide knowledge and the most acute faculty of perception I have ever encountered he combines an amazing energy of will and aptitude for action.'

Heine's letter to Varnhagen went on:

> Herr Lassalle is a pronounced member of the new generation which wants to know nothing of the renunciation and modesty with which we more or less hypocritically came to terms with our world. This new generation means to enjoy life and show its worth in the open, whereas we of the older generation prostrated ourselves before the invisible; we sought shadowy kisses and the perfume of blue flowers. We renounced much and lamented it, and yet we were perhaps happier than these tough gladiators who so proudly march to death in battle.[23]

If this last sounded like a reservation, it was. Though he admired the fiery youth who combined a passion for action with a cool mind, Heine feared that his daring might ultimately lead to reckless excess. Nevertheless, he could not resist Lassalle's argument that the time for compromise was over. Accordingly, he broke off relations with Meyerbeer – who, while attesting that he had been promised a life-long pension, advocated conciliation – and wrote to Campe that, after a miserable year of 'constant conflict betwwen my heart and mind', he realized that tears and pleas would not move Cousin Karl's inhuman heart, and that instead of 'begging' he must fight for his rights with 'my sword, i.e. my pen.' It was Lassalle who persuaded Heine that, instead of the fruitless press campaign he had conducted through others, he must put on his 'Jacobin cap' and come out to do battle in the open. Preferably, he was to come to Berlin. Heine's arrival there would be a political event.

The ostensible purpose of his visit would be to have his eyes examined by Berlin's famous Dr J.F. Dieffenbach, a pioneer of plastic surgery who had successfully 'rectified' the squinting eyes of more than 200 patients. On 10 January, Heine gave Lassalle a letter of introduction to Dr Dieffenbach, who happened to be an old university pal of his. On the 11th, to make sure he would not be arrested for his many attacks on Prussia and the Prussian king, Heine sent a letter to Alexander von Humboldt, asking him to use his 'high influence' to obtain a safe-conduct for him so that the police would not use the opportunity of so innocent a visit for 'medical consultation' to lay hands on him.

In mid-January Lassalle left for Berlin. Before the month was out he had seen Varnhagen von Ense, obtained Dr Dieffenbach's confident assurance that he 'could repair Heine's health, if he submitted to a cure and diet in Berlin', and passed it on to Humboldt with the further information that Prince Pückler-Muskau was ready to assist him in his effort on behalf of Heine. Humboldt, who meant to take up Heine's plea with the King of Prussia, resented being rushed and replied curtly that 'multiplying' his own 'fearless' intervention would do more harm than good. Lassalle wrote back that it was not for him to reject the Prince's voluntary offer; rather, he had seen it as his duty to pass it on.

But Lassalle did more than that. He had put Heine's case so eloquently to Pückler-Muskau that before the end of January the eccentric but highly placed Prince addressed a personal letter to Karl Heine, the poet's obdurate and close-fisted Hamburg cousin. In the politest style but with firm words he reminded Karl Heine that he was the blood-relative of a genius who, 'for all his occasional wanton excesses', was the pride of Germany. He went on to say that some of the country's 'loftiest minds', men who enjoyed a 'high reputation throughout the world', found it inexplicable that he – 'a double millionaire and the universal heir of one of Germany's most esteemed bankers' – should deny his cousin a niggardly 'few thousand francs' on the formal pretext that the life-long pension promised to him was not mentioned in the testament. Besides appealing to Karl Heine's sense of honour, the Prince, in the most remarkable passage of his letter, wrote that 'thank God, we live in times when neither kings nor millionaires can afford to defy public opinion without detriment to themselves'; and, without mincing his words, he added that he was sure Karl Heine would find the generosity to do justice to his cousin rather than bring down public opprobrium and 'infamy on a house proverbially as rich as the Rothschilds' by forcing a public money collection to be staged in Germany for 'its greatest and wittiest living writer'.[24]

Prince Pückler-Muskau sent this letter in the first instance to Lassalle. He was to make a copy of it and return it with Karl Heine's address. The Prince asked that his letter be kept secret until he got a reply, in case it was effective. But he authorized Lassalle to tell Heine that, if it failed, he was at liberty to publish it.

Significantly, too, Alexander von Humboldt, after speaking to the King, invited Lassalle to his house to hear the result of his intervention. By the end of January 1846, within a fortnight of his arrival, the previously unknown Lassalle had – through Varnhagen, Dieffenbach, Humboldt and Pückler-Muskau – become Heine's delegate and *porte-parole* to a select group of Berlin people.

Heine immediately realized that, in the context of the changing 'contemporary social scene', Prince Pückler's letter represented 'a slap in the face of the parvenu aristocracy of money by one of the last knights of the old aristocracy of birth.' In a letter to Lassalle on 10 February he called it 'a most painful defeat for the bourgeoisie, which will be mocked to boot by the modern opponents of the present rule of Mammon.' Twice he insisted to Lassalle that the Prince's letter 'must be printed'.

Lassalle had by then been informed by Humboldt that his intervention with the King of Prussia had failed. Privately, Humboldt noted that the King was inclined to let bygones be bygones, but the Minister of Police, brandishing a copy of one of Heine's poems lampooning the King, insisted on his arrest for *lèse-majesté* the moment he showed his face in Berlin.[25]

From Karl Heine, Prince Pückler received a barely civil reply rejecting his appeal. There was thus nothing in the way of publishing the letter when Heine wrote to Lassalle on 10 February. Lassalle in fact expected this to be the next step.

In January, however, Heine had drawn a bill of 3,000 francs on his cousin Karl. To his surprise, Karl not only paid it in the first week of February but had since sent him another 1,000 francs. Heine concluded from this that his cousin had been 'shamed' by Prince Pückler's letter to the point of quietly paying him an annual allowance of 4,000 francs.

Lassalle felt that Heine had failed him. The poet had indeed decided, on Varnhagen's advice, to write a conciliatory letter to Cousin Karl, with a view to obtaining a legal assurance that this would be his pension for life. By 7 March, sick in body and soul, he was informing Lassalle that he was forced to 'adjourn any open warfare for some time, because any great emotion now might kill me.' His lips, throat and part of his tongue were paralyzed, 'so that anything I eat tastes like earth.' This, however, had not prevented him from inviting Balzac, Royer, Gautier and a few other Paris celebrities to a dinner party on the 4th in honour of Lassalle's sister, to whom he had taken a special liking.

Heine was very fond of Lassalle, too. Thanking him for his effort, he wrote that 'No one has ever done so much for me' and in an unusual moment of effusion added almost humbly: 'Nor have I ever found in any other but you so much passion united with clairvoyance in action. You have the right to be insolent, the rest of us are but usurpers of that divine right, compared to you I am only a modest fly.'[26]

But he also wondered where his insolence and titanic will might take him. The story that Heine, during one of their first meetings, had told Lassalle that he foresaw a great future for him in Germany, and when asked by Lassalle what he meant replied with a laugh, 'To be killed by one of your own disciples', may be apocryphal. But it expressed Heine's anxiety that the imperious and resolute young man had a dangerous streak in him that would stop at nothing. Heine, at any rate, no longer had the strength to follow this fighter of a new generation onto paths that might put his pension and his peace of mind at risk.

Heine was ultimately to win his Inheritance War, not before giving in to Cousin Karl's demand never to write anything about Uncle Salomon. A letter which Meyerbeer, at Lassalle's urging, addressed to Karl, and Heine's deteriorating health – leading to press reports in August 1846 that he had died and to the publication of sympathetic obituaries – are variously believed to have finally broken down Karl Heine's philistine stubbornness.

Heine was very ill that summer. A cure he had sought in the Pyrenees proved unsuccessful, and Engels, who went to see him shortly after his return to Paris, wrote to Marx on 16 September:

> The poor devil is dreadfully low. He has grown as thin as a rake. The softening of the brain is spreading, and so is the facial paralysis... His intellectual vigour is unimpaired, but his appearance, made stranger still by a greying beard (he can no longer be shaved round the mouth), is enough to plunge anyone who sees him into the depth of depression.[27]

Heine himself believed at the time, as he wrote to Campe, that he had 'at most two years to live in melancholy agony.' One of his eyes was completely shut and the other only half-open, and he could not speak, chew or swallow. But his sense of humour never left him. To the doctor who asked him if he could still whistle he replied: 'Not even at a piece by Scribe!' Before the end of September he drafted a will specifying that, although he was himself 'a Lutheran Protestant (at least officially)', he wished to be buried in Montmartre Cemetery, in Catholic ground, so that Mathilde might be laid to rest next to him.

But Heine had remarkable powers of recovery. His speech returned, and in November he received the visit of Benjamin Lumley, the director of Her Majesty's Theatre in London. Impressed by the success of *Giselle* – the ballet based on a legend published by Heine in his *Elemental Spirits* – Lumley commissioned him to write a Faust ballet. For a first short scenario, 'The Goddess Diana', which Heine knocked off in two hours, Lumley paid him 2,000 francs.

Between spells of illness, Heine then managed to finish the enlarged book version of *Atta Troll. A Summer Night's Dream*, which Campe was to publish in Hamburg in January. Over the next two months of a gloomy and 'terrible' winter, housebound with Mathilde and her parrot, he worked on *The Legend of Doctor Johann Faust*, a pantomime ballet in 5 acts. For this highly original and imaginative work, which combined pagan traditions and modernist erotic anarchy, he was paid an advance of 6,000 francs.

By the beginning of March he was well enough to host a party for Berlioz and other friends, and soon he began to go out again. He called on François Buloz, the director of the *Revue des Deux Mondes*, who had not seen him for some time and was so shocked by his appearance that he wrote on 2 April: 'Heine has one foot in the grave, but he keeps laughing.'

Heine himself wrote to Caroline Jaubert on 13 April that his sunken cheeks, unkempt beard and unsteady gait gave him 'a most killing appearance' to the ladies he passed in the street. 'As a dying man I am a huge success. I devour all hearts, only I cannot digest them.'[28]

Spring brought on a more confident mood. His long and traumatic family conflict was at last over. On 25 February 1847, Karl had paid him a personal visit in Paris and agreed to pay him the full annual pension of 4,800 francs for life. He further, as Heine reported with satisfaction to his mother, 'gave me a solemn promise to pay half that sum to my surviving widow to the end of her days.' By his own peculiar methods, Heine had not only got what he wanted, but the recalcitrant Karl was later to give him large extra sums of up to 10,000 francs.

But Heine paid a heavy price for his victory. Having undertaken not to write anything about his grievances against his cousin's branch of the family, he burned his mother's and sister's letters containing any reference to that matter. But his life-long fury at the censorship, which he had accepted, was to burst forth in poignant verse:

> He who has a heart where love is
> He's already drubbed and downed,
> Half defeated, so I lie here,
> Now completely gagged and bound.
>
> When I die, they'll cut my tongue out
> From a corpse untenanted:
> For they fear I'll come back – talking –
> From the kingdom of the dead.[29]

In February 1846, when Heine had informed Ferdinand Lassalle that he was backing out of his Inheritance War, the young man was already engaged in a new legal and political battle that was to mark the first great 'triumph' of his life and the sensational start of his career as a politician. Although it was ostensibly a marital feud, Lassalle turned the Countess von Hatzfeld's individual case into a general assault on 'all the outrageous injustices of the old world, all the abuses of power and the might of wealth practised against the weak and all those oppressed by the social order' prevailing in Germany.

Years later, recounting the tale of this long struggle, Lassalle compared Count Edmund von Hatzfeldt's treatment of his wife to that of the hero of a cheap novel: 'He tortured and persecuted her... kept her under lock and key in his mountain castles, denied her medical care during her illnesses... and left her without any means of existence while he squandered his vast fortune and his life on the most shameless debauchery.'

By his own account, Lassalle was 'by chance present' when the Countess, at the beginning of 1846, learned of her husband's latest misdeed. Having sent their eldest son to a military academy, and their only daughter to a cloister in Vienna, he now threatened to deprive her of their youngest son Paul, and had sent him a letter saying he would disinherit him unless he secretly left his mother. Paul showed this letter to his mother and Lassalle found her 'dissolved in tears'. He told her that if she was determined 'to win or to die', he would fight for her with all the energy and firmness of his youth. 'Convinced that right was on her side, she had confidence in her own strength and in mine. She accepted my proposal with all her heart.'

> Thereupon I, a young Jew without influence, pitted myself against the most formidable forces – I alone against the world, against the power of rank and the whole aristocracy, against the power of limitless wealth, against the government and against the whole hierarchy of officials, who are invariably the natural allies of rank and wealth, and against every possible prejudice... I had resolved to combat illusion with truth, rank with right, the power of money with the power of the spirit.[30]

Lassalle exaggerated neither Count Edmund's cynical treatment of his wife nor the powers he was taking on. Sophie von Hatzfeldt, who came of a ducal family, had been married at the age of 17 to her cousin Edmund von Hatzfeldt-Wildenburg for reasons of economic convenience, their marriage contract settling an old feud between the family's two lines about the entail of their considerable landed estates. According to one of Lassalle's modern biographers, Count Edmund 'deceived his wife several times a week publicly, and occasionally even in her presence.'[31]

For the past 5 years he had confined her to their castle at Kalkum, ordering her in a letter '(1) not to leave my house and the adjoining gardens without my permission; and (2) not to maintain any written or verbal contacts with friends and people who do not belong to my domestic staff or to your family without my prior knowledge and approval.'[32]

By virtue of his feudal privileges in Prussia's male-dominated society, the Count was not only the lord of his domains but the region's sheriff. Besides being virtually his wife's master as well as her judge, he had high connections at court. On one occasion the Countess is said to have driven off at pistol-point 'an aide-de-camp of the king's who had been sent to get her son for the purpose of putting him away in a military academy.'[33]

Lassalle had first heard of the Countess's plight in January 1846 from a Prussian colonel, Baron Keyerlingk. As it happened, the Countess had recently turned for legal advice to Felix Oppenheim, an assistant judge at the Supreme Court in Berlin. From Oppenheim, a sworn disciple of Lassalle's, one of the three who had signed his 'War Manifesto', he learned that the Countess's highly placed relatives – headed by her eldest brother Hermann Hatzfeldt, Duke of Trachenberg – regarded Edmund as a contemptible lecher, but had always, in order to avoid a public scandal, prevented her from suing for a divorce or taking any steps against him. When Lassalle first approached the Countess he was thus able to tell her: 'You know that you can expect nothing from your relatives. They will, as always, turn against you.'

Furious with her brothers and seeing no other redress against her malevolent husband, the Countess was ready to place her fate in the hands of the eloquent young Lassalle. His first advice to her was to file a suit against her husband's intention to sell one of their estates, on the grounds that – the major part of the family's possessions having been entailed on their eldest son and heir – this would further reduce the small share reserved as the inheritance of the youngest. As though echoing Lassalle's promise that he would fight 'rank with right', the long-humiliated Countess wrote her brother that while she had hitherto 'always submitted to your advice against my better judgment', she would now apply to the courts. 'Perhaps you will notice from my new self-assurance that I am now taking the advice of men who know the law... I am a mother but I am also a human being, and not an object to be exploited by anyone to his profit and advantage.'[34]

In his later account, Lassalle wrote that he acted on the principle enunciated by Robespierre: 'Social oppression exists wherever a single individual is oppressed.' There is no reason to doubt his statement that he undertook to fight for the Countess's rights as 'a single-handed insurrection in a case which was a clear microcosm of all our social ills' or that 'had she not been there, I would have sought another opportunity to manifest my opposition to the world we live in.'[35]

On one occasion, he actually told the Countess that he was 'borrowing her body in the service of an idea of permanent historical importance.' For its sake, he laid aside his doctoral thesis and immersed himself in jurisprudence. With Oppenheim's help he mastered all aspects of the law relating to the Countess's case. Then, together with Oppenheim and his other devotee, Dr Arnold Mendelssohn, he set out for the Rhineland to gather evidence about her husband's extravagant way of life. Lassalle soon found what he needed. He managed to intercept a letter in which Count Edmund assured his new mistress, the Baroness von Meyendorff, that he would do everything 'to get rid' of his wife. With the help of a bribe to one of the Count's staff, Lassalle learned that the Count had not only, 'in the guise of a fictitious debt, signed a bond for an enormous annuity of 25,000 francs to be paid to the Baroness Meyendorff for life by himself and his heirs', but had further undertaken to pay his mistress a penalty of 200,000 francs for any two-months delay in defraying the annual pension.[36]

Besides applying for a divorce on the Countess's behalf, Lassalle prepared a separate lawsuit charging the Count with prodigality for having mortgaged the future of his children. Before proceedings started, Lassalle summoned the Countess from Düsseldorf to Aachen, where her husband was consorting with his mistress. Confronted by his wife, the Count cringed and asked for forgiveness, promised to mend his ways and to cancel the bond to his mistress in the presence of a notary his wife was to bring from Düsseldorf. But when she returned with the notary, he refused to receive them.

At this point, Lassalle learned from one of his spies that the Baroness Meyendorff was on her way to the railway station. Instantly he sent Oppenheim and Mendelssohn to follow her 'to the end of the earth' and to find out as best they could whether or not the Count had cancelled his bond or whatever new arrangement he had made with his mistress. The two managed to catch the same train as Meyendorff, and when she stepped off it at Cologne they followed her and took rooms in the same hotel. Noticing that the Baroness's luggage comprised a small casket of the type used for depositing papers, Oppenheim, convinced that it contained the incriminating bond, stole it, but having no room for it in his travel bag ran with it into Mendelssohn's room.

A grotesque comedy of errors took place. Mendelssohn stuffed the casket into his suitcase, but to make room for it threw out some of his belongings and left them behind when the alarm was given; and the two inexperienced thieves – one an assistant Supreme Court judge and the other a physician – fled in haste in different directions. Mendelssohn boarded a train, but noticing the approach of police and fearing that he had been identified by the clothes left behind at the hotel, jumped from his carriage before the train pulled out of the station. In his flight he abandoned his suitcase as well as Oppenheim's travel bag, which he had grabbed in their rush from the hotel. The upshot was that while Mendelssohn made his escape to Paris, Oppenheim – whose papers were in his bag found on the train – was arrested and charged with the theft of the casket.

The bungled 'casket theft', which occurred on 21 August 1846, produced a sensation in Germany. Its victim, the Baroness Meyendorff, a sister-in-law of a former Russian ambassador to Berlin, was a well-known European society lady. Oppenheim, besides belonging to the judiciary, was the son of one of Germany's most prominent bankers. He had obviously acted on a momentary impulse, having no prior knowledge of the casket nor left room for it in his luggage. Both he and Mendelssohn were older than Lassalle, and their action can only be explained by their zealous devotion to this domineering youth, whom they were eager to help protect the Countess's interests. That Lassalle had neither planned nor ordered the theft is evident from the fact that it robbed his prodigality suit against the Countess's husband of any chance of success. The theft actually saved Count Edmund much embarrassment: the suit against him was dismissed on 28 September as 'insufficiently substantiated'.

With Mendelssohn penniless in Paris and Oppenheim in jail, Lassalle did his utmost to help his two disciples. He sent money to Mendelssohn; asked Alexander von Humboldt to appeal to the King to grant Oppenheim clemency; and mounted a press campaign against Count von Hatzfeldt.

Earlier in the year, in connection with his prodigality suit against the Count, Lassalle had asked Heine for information about the personal life of the Baroness von Meyendorff, who was known to have been a Russian spy in Paris. Heine had replied that such *colportage* belonged in a novel by Eugène Sue and was beneath his dignity. In October, Lassalle proposed that Heine join in his campaign by writing a 'fulminating article against the brutal German feudalism'. This time Heine did not even reply. He was not only shocked by the 'casket theft', but saw in it a fulfilment of his presentiment that Lassalle's 'tenacity of will' would stop at nothing and render him capable of 'murder, forgery, theft'. To Lassalle's father he wrote: 'My heart aches when I see how, for all his many gifts, he may be driven to demonic self-destruction.'

Lassalle, learning from his own sources that Madame Meyendorff was a close friend of that other *grande dame* and former Russian spy, the Princess Lieven (who had since become Guizot's mistress), suspected that Heine did not want to spoil his relations with the French Premier. He had helped Heine to secure his pension and had counted on the influence of his pen in the Hatzfeldt war – which had no smaller, and perhaps greater, social implications than

Heine's Inheritance War. He was stupefied to be forsaken by Heine in a cause which made the comtesse d'Agoult, of whose support Lassalle had not dreamt, publish several articles on the hypocrisy of the German aristocracy.

Accusing Heine of breach of trust, Lassalle in November wrote him a letter which marked the end of their relationship, though not a final break. Lassalle never forgave Heine his defection, but a couple of years later was to visit him in Paris.

Oppenheim was acquitted of the 'casket theft' on 24 November. But this was not the end of the affair. In March 1847 Lassalle was arrested and remanded for trial on the charge of having 'destroyed certain documents' in the Oppenheim case. He was to spend weeks in jail before he was acquitted at the beginning of May. In June, Arnold Mendelssohn returned from Paris to Germany, convinced that since Oppenheim had confessed to the theft and had gone scotfree, he, as a mere accessory to it, had nothing to fear. He was immediately arrested and remanded for trial. On 11 February 1848 he was given a severe sentence of 5 years in prison.

Nine days later Lassalle was arrested in Potsdam and taken to Cologne. While Mendelssohn, thanks to the combined efforts of his family and Alexander von Humboldt, was released almost immediately on condition that he leave not only Germany but Europe and departed via Constantinople for Syria, Lassalle was remanded for trial on the charge of being the 'intellectual instigator' of the casket theft. He was to spend many months in jail.

But Lassalle's fighting spirit thrived on adversity. In and out of jail, he had, since the beginning of 1847, been waging his single-minded war for the 'liberation' of the Countess von Hatzfeldt by launching one lawsuit after another against her husband. With Count Edmund filing some suits of his own, Lassalle's war was to last altogether 8 years and to be fought out in public before 36 tribunals. He was fighting a state system which, to paraphrase one of his modern biographer's view of his actions up to his arrest in February 1848, allowed 'the incredible phenomenon of the culprit of a theft – Oppenheim – being acquitted while his passive accessory is sentenced to five years and then released in the most irregular manner. This was a symptom of the weakness of that state system' which feared Lassalle enough to stage the Mendelssohn trial chiefly for the purpose of implicating him.[37]

Deserted by Heine as well as by Oppenheim since his acquittal, and with Mendelssohn in Paris or in jail and eventually in Syria, Lassalle was able to undertake single-handed the new stage of his war which started in 1847, not only because of his steel-like will and complete identification with the Countess's case, but because as early as the age of 16, when he told his father that 'in every country, every nation, men have now risen who fight by the word, fall by the word or achieve victory by it,' he had realized the power of public opinion.

In one of his 1846 letters to Heine he had written that 'the public triumph of the Countess von Hatzfeldt means to me more than anything that concerns my personal life.' With his usual self-reliance, Lassalle, a self-taught jurist, skilfully invoked every paragraph and sub-paragraph of the existing laws in his fight for 'right' and argued his court cases himself, besides appearing as the Countess's attorney in those he conducted on her behalf.

Sometimes, when he was in jail but due to plead for her, the prison authorities had to escort him day after day to court. He had his speeches printed and published other brochures to a public opinion which by 1847 – with the general European revolution only a year off – was becoming restive in Germany and more receptive than ever.

At the same time, Lassalle was looking after the distraught Countess's finances, as her husband – in spite of their marriage contract which provided for community property – had cut off her means of subsistence. As early as December 1846, she had been reduced to such straits that, to keep her afloat and cover the expenses of legal proceedings and the printing of brochures, Lassalle borrowed money from his father, who reluctantly became involved in his son's appalling affairs.

The tireless Lassalle did even more. He found a benefactor for the Countess in the person of Count Clemens von Westphalen (1805–85), who granted her in February 1847 a substantial loan of 17,000 Thaler without any surety. He was prompted to do so out of human sympathy, after Lassalle had presented him with the documents of the case and a convincing account of the Countess's misfortunes. A leading Catholic, Count von Westphalen wrote to her that, although the young man had tried in vain to convert him to Hegel's philosophy, he had found his acquaintance intellectually most stimulating.

Before his first arrest in March 1847, Lassalle urged Count von Westphalen to use his high influence in Berlin and speak to the President and judges of the High Court of Appeals who were to have the final word on the Countess's prodigality suit and another suit for alimony. Lassalle thought this was justified, because her husband had published a pamphlet in France blackening her reputation and was trying to have it distributed in Germany. When Westphalen remarked on one occasion that the Countess's situation was 'not so bad', Lassalle warned that unless he told His Prussian Majesty and other high personages he knew in Berlin that she was the victim of 'an injustice crying to heaven', he would achieve nothing in the face of the calumnies heaped on her by her husband and circulating among his peers. The magnanimous Westphalen, after failing to persuade Count Edmund to reach a conciliation with his wife, took the young man's high-handed coaching in his stride.

The Hatzfeldt 'war' was also fought out in the corridors of power during the United Diet of representatives of all the provincial assemblies convened by the King in Berlin. Both Westphalen and Count Edmund attended, and each used his influence to win adherents to his camp. Count Edmund, exercising his feudal privileges as lord and sheriff of his estates, had forbidden his wife access to their Schönstein Castle, although it was included in their community property. At Lassalle's suggestion, Westphalen argued to his peers that Count Edmund's shameful behaviour disgraced the entire aristocracy. At the end of June 1847, Lassalle went to Berlin to brief Westphalen before he was to have an audience with the King. Count Edmund also saw the King. On 7 July, Westphalen was to report to the Countess that the King had referred him to Thile (one of his Ministers and confidential advisers), 'who is firmly prejudiced against you.'[38]

Back in May, Lassalle, hardly out of prison after his first acquittal, had begun to foment a revolt against Count Edmund among his own peasants on the Schönstein estate. One day in June he arrived at the castle together with the Countess and her son Paul at the head of several hundred peasants. Count Edmund's armed guards, acting on his instructions, tried to obstruct his wife's passage, but she managed to enter the castle together with Lassalle and her son, only to be forcibly ejected by the Count's guards, lackeys and feudal agents. A stand-off ensued during which this group and a column of peasants who had armed themselves with crowbars from a nearby mine confronted each other menacingly.

Lassalle wrote to his father on 6 July that he had 'never laughed so much as during the eight days we spent on the estate... Not that it was all a laughing matter, for the countess's life and my own would not have been safe had we not been followed everywhere by a bodyguard of 200–400 peasants.' Highlighting the peasants' attachment to the Countess, he added: 'At a word of hers they would have stormed all the count's castles and hung him together with his officials on the highest fir trees! They practically begged for her to utter the command, but she never did.' What made Lassalle laugh was that

> half an hour after midnight, the count's own baronial judge ordered his armed troops (5 gendarmes) to force open the Krottorf castle situated on the same estate and to secure the countess's safe entry. The gendarmes, however, refused to obey. Swinging their sabres, they tried to arrest their own police chief.[39]

He had every reason to be jubilant. At 22, while Germany's liberals and 'democrats' placed high hopes in the 1847 United Diet – expecting that this first representative body assembled in Germany would advise the King to grant a con-stitution – he had rightly assessed that nothing would come of its prolonged sessions. Guided by his revolutionary instinct, he had undermined the Count's authority on his own domains, and by causing confusion and anarchy among his feudal officials, who were actually state officials, he had shown up the growing impotence of the Prussian administration. The authorities were sufficiently embarrassed to refrain from taking any action against their own lackeys, nor did they prosecute the rebellious peasants. Lassalle had further proved his capabil-ity as a popular agitator, and it is likely that this caused the authorities to appre-hend him half a year later in connection with the casket theft.

A few days after his arrest in February 1848, street fighting broke out in Paris. On the 24th, King Louis-Philippe abdicated and a Provisional Government was formed under Lamartine. On the 26th, France declared itself a republic.

Lassalle, who was in prison in Cologne, read a revolutionary manifesto pub-lished by Blanqui in a Paris newspaper, cut it out and pasted it on the wall of his cell. He had become the Countess von Hatzfeldt's attorney and 'general pleni-potentiary'. Several of her lawsuits were pending, and his arraignment on crim-inal charges represented a victory for her husband.

Lassalle, however, welcomed the forthcoming trial. He was determined not only to demonstrate the 'monstrosity' of the charge cooked up against him, but to destroy the Count morally by revealing the full story of his prolonged 'viola-tion of human rights'. Several lawyers tried to dissuade him from this course. They argued that if he kept strictly to the charge of 'intellectual complicity' in the casket theft, he had every chance that the case would be thrown out of court – whereas if he brought in the partisan turmoil of passions kindled by the Hatzfeldt conflict, he risked a 5-year sentence and the loss of his honour.

Overriding their advice, the youngest of the Doctors of Revolution was to turn the criminal proceedings into a political trial and to emerge 5 months later as a hero of the 1848 revolution, more popular at 23 than either Marx or Engels, who in the same month of February published their *Communist Manifesto*. In the course of the revolution, Marx and Lassalle were to become allies.

Marx was not the only man without a country in the aftermath of his expulsion from Paris. In that same month of January 1845 when he had been forced to move to Brussels, the Paris *Gazette des Tribunaux* published the Tsar's decree endorsing a Senate motion to strip Michael Bakunin of the 'rights and digni-ties' of his noble rank and sentencing him – for his refusal to obey an order to return to Russia – to an indefinite period of forced labour in Siberia.

Bakunin's fury at the thought of being banished from Russia and never to see his beloved Premukhino again found a momentary outlet in a letter he published in *La Réforme*. Stating that in Russia 'the law is nothing but the will of the Tsar', he referred to the 'scattered, but extremely significant and multiplying risings of the peasants against their masters', and he warned the Tsar that if his government did not make haste to liberate the people, 'the moment is perhaps not far off when the risings will be merged in a great revolution... and much blood will be spilt.'[40]

Bakunin made this prediction while being completely cut off from events in Russia. Nor did he have any contact with 'the people' either there or in Europe. In the same letter, which appeared on 27 January 1845, he also linked together Russia and Poland for the first time as 'unhappy and oppressed countries' to be saved from their fate by 'democracy'.

During his short stay in Belgium in 1844, Bakunin had met the Polish historian and veteran revolutionary Joachim Lelevel, who lived modestly above the Brussels café where Marx and his cronies now spent some of their evenings. 'Old Lelevel in his blue blouse', as Marx's wife referred to him, represented the best of Polish culture that lay behind his cries for independence. Bakunin, however, showed little interest in the cause of Polish nationalism. But after his piece in *La Réforme* was reproduced in a Polish émigré journal, he was approached by two prominent leaders of the Polish exiles in Paris, Count Adam Czartoryski and the poet Adam Mickiewicz. The Poles, who enjoyed great sympathy in France, were interested in having a Russian ally against their common enemy – the Tsar. But Bakunin found them too immersed in the past sufferings of 'crucified Poland' and given to 'hollow, bombastic' phrases. A 'Russian in spite of everything', he later wrote, 'I ended for the time being my relations with the Poles and saw none of them at all until the spring of 1846.'[41]

Nor would he have anything to do with the 'philistine' Ruge or the German theorists of the League of the Just: 'I kept apart from them and made it clearly known that I would not enter into their Communist union of artisans.'[42]

At the start of the more than two years he spent in Paris, Bakunin had called on George Sand, but for some reason the 'prophetess' in the flesh impressed him less than she had in her novels. He also met Louis Blanc, Pierre Leroux, the abbé de Lamennais and other leading reformers, but soon became disenchanted with France's political and socio-philosophical thinkers and their sundry utopias and panaceas. Proudhon was the only one he respected and continued to see. He lived as a free boarder with the pianist Reichel and his sister; they and the high-living Georg and Emma Herwegh were his only regular company. Occasionally he rubbed shoulders with distinguished foreigners and diplomats at Count Tolstoy's brilliant receptions. These soirées warmed Bakunin's 'petrifying soul'. For he had hardly any real friends in Paris.

He did not exaggerate – or at least not much – when, dwelling on his life in Paris, he was to write in his Confession to Tsar Nicholas I that he found himself in a foreign land, 'in a spiritual atmosphere without any warmth, without family or relatives, without any field of action, without anything to do and without the least hope for something better in the future.'

More than once, depressed by the thought that he would never see Premukhino, his family or his native land again, he asked himself 'whether it wouldn't be better for me simply to throw myself into the Seine and thereby drown this useless and joyless existence.'[43] Like Marx, Bakunin hated his mother. Of the reasons in Marx's case, nothing is known other than her tight-fisted way with money. Bakunin, on the other hand, provided a rare insight into his psychosexual problems in three letters he wrote home between March and May 1845. In these letters, more convincing than the partly dissembling Confession – and entrusted to Russian travellers for safe delivery to his brother Paul and his sister Tatyana at Premukhino – he mentioned his frequent lapses into 'despair' and tried to re-establish his intimacy with these two siblings from whom he had not heard for a couple of years, and in particular with his beloved Tatyana. Guessing that she was as lonely as he and 'that your passionate heart, tortured by its unsatisfied need of love and life, has closed upon itself, and is suffering without end in its proud and inaccessible loneliness', he invited her, the object of his incestual 'love... condemned by the laws' to give 'your grief to me... How I would look after you, if only we could be together, how I would try to set your heart aflame.' He then inquired: 'How's father... Is he still alive?' Having terrorized his father out of his authority and his wits while in Russia, he now called him 'our guardian angel', and wrote: 'Without him, mother would have ruined and corrupted us... mother, for whom I have no feeling in my soul but damnation and the most profound disdain. She is the source of what is unclean in our family. Her presence, her very existence, is an offence to what is sacred.'[44]

In the same letter Bakunin urged his siblings to stick together and pursue their happiness 'in spite of our enemies, or to put it better, our enemy – mother.' More striking, in this very same letter, Bakunin declared that he was 'passionately in love', and mixed up the object of his love by alternately using the pronouns 'she' (a woman) and 'they' (the people):

> I know that they [sic] do care for me a great deal. I want to, I must deserve the love of the one I love, loving her [sic] religiously, that is actively. She is now enslaved by the most terrible, the most shameful slavery, and I must liberate her by struggling against her oppressors, by enflaming in her heart a sense of personal worth, by inspiring in her a need for freedom and a demand for it.

In a letter to Paul written 4 weeks earlier in the spring of 1845, Bakunin likewise identified his mother with 'the enemy'. 'I damn her', he wrote, and had for her 'no other feeling but hatred and the deepest, unmitigated disdain – not for myself, but for you, whom she ruined.' Protesting that he was not 'cruel-hearted', he insisted to his siblings that it was time to give up weak sentimentality and to declare

> implacable war on our enemies, because they are the enemies of all that is human in us, enemies of our dignity, of our freedom... The capacity to hate is inseparable from the capacity to love. We must forgive our enemies only after we have thrown them down and utterly triumphed. But as long as they remain on their feet, no mercy and no respite![45]

The political element in Bakunin's philosophy of violent revolution was always inextricably bound up with the personal. But it was not until 1981 that Arthur Mendel, analyzing the Paris letters Bakunin sent to Paul and Tatyana some 5 years after he had last seen his mother, wrote that it was his own 'oedipal dread' of being drawn into his mother's 'unclean world' that inspired 'such rage, maintained at such intensity over so long a time and distance' and 'such otherwise inexplicable outrage, strong enough to assault "even her existence".'

From Bakunin's associating 'mother' with 'enemies' and his beloved with the 'people' and in his transition, without pause, from the principal 'enemy' (mother) to 'enemies of our dignity' in general – i.e., his various political enemies – Mendel extracted the sexual-incestual roots of his love for the 'people' and ultimately of his anarchism and his apocalyptic vision of the world.

He had announced that vision in *The Reaction in Germany* by predicting an imminent 'storm of destruction' and the 'annihilation of the present political and social world.' For the moment, however, with no cataclysm in sight and no 'field of action' for him, he continued to be preoccupied by his inner problems.

But with his capacity to draw strength from weakness and his conviction that Providence had not chosen him to waste his life, even while withdrawing into his world of fantasies and writing Tatyana (who never answered his letter) that 'nothing is impossible for those with enough will and love' and 'maybe in a few years we will meet in Paris and live together', Bakunin reiterated in the same letter his war cry, 'All or nothing', as a sign of his 'implacable' and unchanged hostility to existing reality.

'A great future awaits me yet,' he had assured his siblings after seeing Paul off at the Dresden railway station. This inner belief never left him, but at the moment he led a bohemian existence, frequented the 'democratic' cafés, and looked for an opportunity for political action.

Such an opportunity presented itself in mid-February 1846, when an insurrection in Cracow – the tiny bit of Polish territory surviving as an independent republic – quickly spread through the rest of Prussian- and Austrian-occupied Poland. It raised high hopes among the Poles in Paris and their French sympathizers. But these were dashed when Austrian and Russian troops occupied Cracow on 12 March.

Although Austria promptly annexed 'free' Cracow, the events there confirmed Bakunin's instinctive realization that the Polish cause had a revolutionary potential and could serve to stir up things in Russia as well. In order to bring himself to the attention of the Poles, 'who had already forgotten about me', Bakunin published an article on 17 March in *Le Constitutionnel*, in which he wrote that the Russian 'oppression of Poland is a disgrace to my country, and its liberation may perhaps mean the liberation of Russia.' He went to the Versailles headquarters of the Polish émigré leaders and offered to assist their cause by stirring a revolt among the Russians in the Tsarist-controlled areas of Poland and Lithuania.

Having no secret network of his own in the areas mentioned, he tried to induce the Poles to put their connections at his disposal by conjuring up before their eyes the vision of a future 'free federated republic of all Slav peoples'. But as nothing came of this project – the 'narrow-minded' Poles had no notion how far they could trust this Russian – he relapsed into prolonged apathy and 'laziness, my primordial national sin'.

'All my life so far', Bakunin observed to his friends, 'has been marked by twists and turns independent of my own intentions. Where will it take me? God knows.' With a self-confessed 'mystic' optimism – 'but who, then, is not a mystic?' – he went on: 'we all of us know practically nothing, we live... surrounded by miracles, by the force of life, and each step of ours can bring them forth.'[46]

Bakunin's doldrums lasted for more than a year and a half, until the Poles unexpectedly provided him with a revolutionary cause and his long-awaited 'chance to act'. But before that happened in November 1847, two of his closest Moscow friends, Herzen and Belinsky, miraculously turned up in Paris.

On 19 January 1847, Alexander Herzen left Russia together with his mother, his wife Nathalie, their three children and an entourage including two family friends and a number of servants. Crossing the border into Prussia on sledges, the party stopped at Königsberg, and after a long journey by post chaise, via Berlin, Cologne, and Belgium, reached Paris on 20 March. Marx and Engels were at that time about to consign *The German Ideology* to the mice; Heine's exhausting Inheritance War had just come to an end; and Ferdinand Lassalle was getting his first taste of jail.

During the past 5 years, Tsar Nicholas I had twice rejected Herzen's request for permission to go abroad. He had finally obtained a passport after a nightmarish wrangle with various arms of the Russian bureaucracy. On one occasion he had arrived in St Petersburg and seen Dubelt, the Director of the 'Third Division' of secret political police, only to be told by the local police chief that his permit 'was valid for leaving Moscow but not for entering Petersburg'. When he took up the matter again with Dubelt, he was given a permit to stay as long as he liked; but when he was about to return to Moscow, the same police chief who had first tried to chase him away refused him a permit to leave. The rigmarole was finally cleared up and 10 days later Herzen returned to Moscow to find a gendarme at his door with a letter from Count Orlov. At his Imperial Majesty's command he was informed that he was relieved from 'police supervision' – which had lasted off and on for 13 years – and had the right to a passport.

To come to Paris from the land of 'absurdity', of 'despotism' and 'official muddle', to open the windows of the Hôtel du Rhin and look out on the Vendôme column and the rue de la Paix, was to the 35-year-old Herzen the fulfilment of a dream he had entertained since childhood:

> I could not stay indoors, I dressed and went out to stroll about at random... to look up Bakunin, Sazonov; here was Rue St. Honoré, the Champs-Elysées – all those names to which I had felt akin for long years... and there was Bakunin himself...
>
> I met him at a street corner; he was walking with three friends and, just as in Moscow, discoursing to them, continually stopping and waving his cigarette. On this occasion the discourse remained unfinished; I interrupted it and took him with me to find Sazonov and surprise him with my arrival.
>
> I was beside myself with happiness.[47]

It was 7 years since Herzen and Bakunin had last seen each other. Though Bakunin struck Herzen as the same garrulous bohemian he had known in Moscow, Herzen himself – according to Annenkov, the ubiquitous observer, who had preceded him to Paris by a year – soon dropped his Moscovite appearance and became, with the help of 'Parisian tailors and other artificers, a perfect Western gentleman with close-cropped hair, an elegant beard and a smart suit-coat draping his shoulders...'[48]

Bakunin and Sazonov were the most prominent radicals of the Russian colony in Paris, and they also had contacts with French Socialists and revolutionaries of virtually every nationality who had found asylum in that city. Herzen, coming from the land where ideas were presented as 'evil intentions', joined their discussions and was carried away to the point where he thought 'that to talk in a café with the historian of the Ten Years' – Louis Blanc – or to meet

Proudhon at Bakunin's lodging was 'something like a promotion, an honour', and a landmark in his political education.

But his intoxication did not last long: 'After the first noisy days in Paris, more serious conversation began, and at once it became evident that we were tuned to very different keys.' Herzen found that the Russians in Paris, deprived of regular contact with the homeland, 'were related to Russia theoretically and from memory.' They had no idea that the Russian intelligentsia were more pre-occupied by the appearance of Gogol's *Dead Souls* than with politics:

> Sazonov and Bakunin... expected to be told about parties, secret soci-
> eties, ministerial crises (under Nicholas!) and the opposition, but I
> told them about professorships, Granovsky's public lectures, Belin-
> sky's articles, and the mood of the students... They had been too
> much separated from Russian life, and had entered too thoroughly
> into the interests of the 'all world' revolution and French problems.[49]

In his memoirs, Herzen surveyed Bakunin's whole career, from his first appear-ance in the youthful circle of Moscow students, through his exploits during the 1848 revolutions – culminating in his arrest in Dresden, 'his trial, imprison-ment, sentence to death, torture in Austria, extradition to Russia', long years in Siberia and his final escape via Japan to San Francisco; and he glorified him as 'one of those individual figures whom neither the contemporary world, nor history can overlook.' But when the two met in Paris, Bakunin was going through his prolonged second doldrums after the Cracow revolution had failed and his offer to the Polish émigré leaders at Versailles to lead a joint Slav revolu-tion had met with no response. Referring to that period, Herzen described Bakunin as having 'within him the germs of a colossal activity for which there was no demand.'

But Bakunin never lost his optimism nor his formidable powers of rhetoric – 'Put him down in any position you like, so long as it is an extreme one', Herzen wrote later, 'and he would have won over the masses and shaken the destinies of nations.' Ever since Bakunin had achieved notoriety in 1842 by predicting (in *The Reaction in Germany*) a continental storm of revolution threatening to engulf 'even Russia', and also through his involvement with the Communist Weitling, Herzen – cooped up under police surveillance in Moscow and engaged in futile literary-philosophical discussions with Granovsky and others – had followed his progress with admiration and no little envy.

For the first time, in his 1845 article in *La Réforme*, Bakunin had informed Western public opinion that the 'innumerable mass' of Russia's peasantry might one day revolt, and had singled out the group in whom Russia's hope for the future lay. While attacking her slavish aristocrats, he had stressed that among them were young nobles of the intelligentsia who, 'closely following the progress of civilisation and freedom in Europe', were striving to cultivate and 'ignite in others' the same aspirations.

When Herzen had read these lines, in which Bakunin postulated in embryo the basic idea later to be taken up by the Russian Narodnik Populists – that of the intelligentsia going down to the people and igniting what Bakunin called its 'democratic instincts' – he had noted in his Moscow diary: 'This is the language of a free man... We are not used to it. We are used to allegories and to bold words *intra muros*.'[50]

About that time, Herzen's Moscow circle of intellectuals had in fact started to drift apart, after years of futile theorizing at soirées and dinner parties. Herzen thus knew that the intelligentsia was far from capable of changing or 'igniting' anything in the Tsarist empire. Hearing Bakunin and Sazonov in Paris in 1847 endlessly discussing the future 'boundaries of Poland and Russia' made him wonder whether they were not living in cloud-cuckoo-land.

Bakunin was all spontaneity. Herzen's was a critical and sceptical nature. But added to their different temperaments was Bakunin's ability to overcome his psychological problems and the terrible 'loneliness' confessed in his last letters to Premukhino, and to hang on to his fantasy of sooner or later producing a Russo-Polish revolution at will. As Arthur Mendel has noted, it is significant that in 1847, while mistrusted and rebuffed by the Poles and with France going through 'a political crisis... he gave his attention not to a real revolution ready to explode on his doorstep' in Paris, but clung to his imaginary Polish-Russian alliance.[51]

Yet this is not to say that Bakunin had lost interest in an 'all world' revolution. He and Herzen were agreed on one point, namely, that Russia, which had no middle class, must at all cost be spared a bourgeois regime of the type which had degenerated into corruption in France. In their discussions, looking for a way to move Russia directly from the nobility to a native variety of Socialism, they were in 1847 actually begetting the populist movement – of which Herzen was later to become the ideologue and Bakunin the conspirator – in the hope that Russia, bypassing the capitalist phase, 'might somehow develop in a way for which there was no precedent in the West, turning the curse of its backwardness into a blessing.'[52]

Though populism as a movement was still a distant prospect, Bakunin had been waiting since 1846 to use Polish nationalism to spark off a revolt against Tsarist despotism and the idea he had ventilated of a 'federation of all Slav peoples' implied in fact that he was already thinking of the grandiose plan he was to launch at a later date: the destruction of the Austrian empire by its Polish, Czech and other Slav minorities.

As for Nicholas Sazonov, he had been one of the 5 students who, in the 1830s, had formed the nucleus of Herzen's idealistic young circle ready 'for every sacrifice' on the model of the Decembrist heroes. But whereas Herzen had been arrested, Sazonov had escaped to Italy. Settling in Paris in 1840, he had since developed extensive contacts with revolutionaries throughout Western Europe. In 1847 he irritated Herzen by his constant talk about an 'imminent' Russian revolution and his confidence that 'one fine evening he would be summoned from his table in the Café Anglais and borne off to govern Russia...'

In June or July 1847 a figure from Herzen's and Bakunin's Moscow debates of earlier years turned up in Paris. Belinsky, Russia's foremost and most ferocious literary and social critic, arrived in a state of acute consumption, looking like the shadow of his former self. He had been ordered by his doctors to take the waters at Salzbrunn in Silesia. His friends took up a subscription to pay for his journey abroad, and Annenkov from Paris, and Turgenev from Berlin, hurried to Salzbrunn to help the invalid and inexperienced traveller, who had never been abroad and spoke neither German nor French. They found him living in a wooden cottage with a little yard on the main street of the town.

It was there that Belinsky, in a fit of energy though weak and racked with coughing, spent three mornings writing his famous letter to Gogol. It was in answer to Gogol's *Selected Passages from a Correspondence with Friends*, a book of humourless homilies in which the author of *The Inspector General* advocated Christian brotherhood and seemed to approve the reactionary state of things in Russia. An angry Belinsky, reminding Gogol that Russia 'has had enough of sermons', wrote:

> She presents the ghastly spectacle of a country where human beings are sold without even that justification of which American plantation lords cunningly avail themselves, by maintaining that a negro is not a human... The most vital national questions in Russia now are the abolition of serfdom, the abolition of corporal punishment, the implementation of at least those laws which already exist.[53]

On Belinsky's arrival in Paris, Herzen came to see him in his hotel. Belinsky read to him a copy of his letter to Gogol. Seizing an opportune moment, Herzen whispered in Annenkov's ear: 'That is a thing of genius – indeed, that, I believe, is his testament.'[54]

Belinsky did not see much of Paris, spending part of his visit in a medical clinic at Passy, and what he saw overwhelmed him. According to Annenkov, Paris struck Belinsky as a quagmire of 'huge dimensions: greed, vice and silliness every bit as much as the cultivation of ideas and knowledge, noble impulses and aspirations.' As for its monuments of culture, museums, lectures, throbbing literary and artistic activities and 'the principles proclaimed to the world' from Paris, all he wanted to know was how 'these beginnings' would affect future generations, and 'the further development of civilization... in short, how great was the sum of universal human hopes borne inside all this visible culture?' He received for the most part optimistic answers, except from Herzen, who, as Annenkov put it, had little faith in the 'capacity for progress' of his contemporaries.[55]

Reunited for one brief summer in Paris, Herzen, Bakunin and Belinsky, the former leaders of Russia's liberal young guard, had some intense discussions before they were to part in the autumn. Bakunin thought that Belinsky should remain in Paris, where he could do more effective work with his pen than in the Russian 'land of censorship'. Herzen and Botkin were of the same opinion. Only Turgenev, during a brief stop in Paris before leaving to pursue his vicarious love of the opera singer Pauline Viardot, remarked that Belinsky was 'too much of a Russsian, and felt like a fish out of water' abroad.

Belinsky did not share Herzen's pessimism about the Russian intelligentsia. Though ill, he still burned with a holy fervour to return to St Petersburg and continue his work among its liberal, democratic elements, the so-called 'Westerners'. Nor was he captivated by Bakunin's optimistic fantasies. He had seen Bakunin master Hegel only to abandon philosophy altogether, and had not changed his opinion about him. Bakunin, he wrote before leaving Paris, 'was born, and will die, a mystic, an idealist, a Romantic; for to renounce philosophy does not change one's nature'.[56]

Belinsky returned to Russia in September. It was there that news of the 1848 revolution in Paris was to reach him. According to Annenkov, he received it 'almost with horror'; Herzen reported that he died (in June) 'taking its glow for the flush of the rising dawn!'[57]

On the day before Belinsky left Paris, Herzen, Bakunin, Sazonov and a few others saw him home in the evening. Herzen, feeling he was pressing Belinsky's hand for the last time, had a lump in his throat as they walked back in silence along the Champs-Elysées. It was at this point that a remark by Sazonov triggered off a clash between 'those who had gone abroad and those who had remained at home.' Sazonov observed that it was a pity that Belinsky had done nothing but journalistic work, 'and under the censorship, too', for with his abilities he might in other circumstances and in other fields have accomplished more.

Herzen, recalling the incident in his memoirs, felt 'vexed and wounded' and burst out:

> But do tell me, please: you now, who are not under the censorship...
> what have you done? Or what are you doing? Surely you don't ima-

gine that walking from one end of Paris to the other every day to talk over the boundaries of Poland and Russia... is doing something? Or that your talks in cafés and at home, where five fools listen to you and understand nothing, while another five understand nothing and talk, is doing something?

'Wait a bit,' a nettled Sazonov interposed, 'you forget our situation.' 'What situation?' said Herzen,

Situations are created. Strong men make themselves acknowledged and force themselves in. One critical article of Belinsky's is of more value for the younger generation than playing at being conspirators and statesmen. You are living in a delirium, walking in your sleep; you're in a perpetual optical illusion with which you deceive your own eyes.

What Herzen had come to object to within three months of his arrival was that 'the severe criticism of their own people' by Sazonov and other Russians 'was transformed into slavish worship of French celebrities.' As the light-hearted Bakunin 'half assented and laughed' at his outburst, Sazonov never forgave him. Sazonov figures in some biographies of Bakunin chiefly for the fact that, having dissipated his fortune on wine and women, he had landed in 1846 in Clichy prison for debt, causing two of his sisters to arrive from Russia, one of whom – like several women before her in Moscow, Switzerland and Paris – immediately fell for Bakunin's charisma in another case of unrequited love.

In an obituary of Sazonov in his memoirs, Herzen was to describe him as a man of 'many capacities and aptitudes' who, in the soul-destroying age of Nicholas, withered away abroad, where his 'immense abilities' were not needed. By implication Bakunin, who in 1847 was likewise an idle man, was to emerge as one of those strong men who create 'situations' or 'force themselves' upon them. At the same time Herzen, keen to assure his early Moscow student circle its rightful place in the history of the Russian revolutionary tradition, wrote in the section devoted to Sazonov: 'We preached the Decembrists and the French revolution, we preached Saint-Simonism... a constitution and a republic. Our propaganda sent down deep roots in all the faculties and extended far beyond the walls of the universities.'[58]

In what may have been a dig at Marx, Herzen, who thought little of his idea of proletarian revolution, added: 'To refuse recognition to men because they have done from inner impulse what others are going to do from necessity is remarkably like the monastic asceticism which only attaches value to repugnant duties.'

Herzen had left Russia with no notion that he would become an émigré for life. Unlike those of the Russian colony in Paris whom he criticized for their fawning attitude towards French celebrities, Herzen was thrilled by the 'quickened pulse' of Paris, which in 1847 was still 'singing Béranger's old songs, but the chorus Vive la réforme! had been unexpectedly changed to Vive la République!', and, in Annenkov's words, rapidly 'turned himself, as had Bakunin, from a gallery spectator into a participant and soloist' in the democratic and social circles of Paris. Like Bakunin, he too amazed such Frenchmen as Proudhon and Michelet, not to mention the German Herwegh and his wife, by his élan, his versatile conversation and wit. Soon he became the centre of a circle of friends and admirers.

Herzen had inherited a substantial fortune on the death of his father and entertained lavishly, but several articles on the radical currents in France which he published in the St Petersburg *Contemporary* caused the Russian government to order his immediate return. When he refused, his and his mother's remaining assets in Russia were confiscated. In October 1847, he temporarily left Paris with his family for Italy, but soon after his return the following May he was able – with the help of the Rothschilds – to recover most of his fortune.

In September 1847, Bakunin was still waiting for his 'chance to act' and dreaming of ways of combining the crisis brewing in France with a Russo-Polish revolt to make an all-European conflagration. He expressed to Herwegh and his wife his feeling that 'soon life will begin for us, and we will again be able to work with the free scope and zeal that all three of us crave.' Revealing how much his violent political fantasies might have been a sublimation of his sexual deficiency, he went on: 'I await my, or, if you will, our communal bride – the revolution. We will be truly happy – that is, we will begin to be our true selves, only when the whole world is engulfed in flame.'[59]

In November, a month or so after Herzen's departure, destiny at last knocked at Bakunin's door in the persons of two young Poles – refugees from Cracow – who invited him to speak at a public gathering to be held in Paris at the end of the month to mark the anniversary of the 1831 Polish rebellion.

Although he was at the time suffering from an illness which had forced him to shave his head, Bakunin accepted with alacrity. Once more he was alone and isolated, both Herzen and Belinsky having downplayed the chances of his fomenting conspiratory action, let alone a revolt, in Russia. But the 'twists and turns' of the 'forces of life', which governed the mystic Bakunin's actions, had worked one of those miracles in which he put his unshakeable faith.

He promptly ordered a wig and worked for three days on the address he delivered on 29 November to an audience of 1,500 Poles and French sympathizers. Declaring that 'the Russian nation speaks through my mouth', he offered the Poles a revolutionary alliance that would bring about the 'liberation of all Slav peoples languishing under a foreign yoke' and the 'final collapse of despotism in Europe.' Attacking the Tsar as 'your oppressor, your bitterest enemy, the personal enemy of Poland, the executioner of so many victims, the man who ravished your liberty, the man who is pursuing you with relentless perseverance, as much through hate and by instinct as through political strategy,' he stunned the audience by highlighting the identity of fate between the Poles and the Russian people. The Tsar, he said, was a German by descent and his government was 'an original combination of Mongol cruelty with Prussian pedantry [which] deprives us of all political rights, including even that natural liberty which the least civilized people enjoy'; and he went on to predict that the reconciliation and joint struggle of Russians and Poles would liberate sixty million people and bring about 'the fall, the definitive collapse of despotism in Russia.'[60]

Bakunin's speech, interrupted by frequent and growing applause, was the first public display of his rousing oratory. The sensation it produced was enhanced when Guizot, under pressure from the Russian ambassador, ordered him on 14 December to be expelled from France. On that same day, *La Réforme* not only published the full text of Bakunin's speech but took the opportunity to attack the government for giving in to foreign intervention.

After he left Paris for Brussels, his expulsion continued to reverberate in France. In December 1847 the campaign of banquets all over France, at which the leaders of the various oposition parties blamed Guizot for the ills of the country, reached its height. Before concluding with the singing of the *Marseillaise*, many of the leaders mentioned the treatment of the Russian aristocrat who had gallantly taken up the cause of the Poles and the sufferings inflicted on them by his own country.

On 4 February 1848, Vavin, the presiding officer of the National Assembly – who had also chaired the Polish gathering addressed by Bakunin – spoke up in his defence. Faced with a growing wave of protests, the French Minister of the Interior, Duchâtel, vaguely hinted at 'serious reasons' for the expulsion, which he could not divulge. At the same time, the Russian Embassy put out rumours to the effect that Bakunin was a Russian agent who had been dismissed because of undisciplined behaviour and fraud. From Brussels, Bakunin challenged Duchâtel 'man to man' to come up with the evidence for his insinuations or to retract them. He received no reply.

The slander that Bakunin was a Russian agent, encouraged by some Poles who mistrusted him from the beginning – and presently to be publicized by Marx as well – was to damage Bakunin's revolutionary aura for many years. But the immediate effect of the hubbub created by his speech and his expulsion from Paris was to make him famous among liberals all over Europe, and notorious to the conservative camp facing them.

In the three and a half years since his short stay in Brussels in 1844, when he had met Lelevel, the Polish historian and revolutionary veteran, a striking change had occurred. More political refugees had since found a haven in Brussels, but of all of them the German group around Marx was the most active.

In August 1847 the Correspondence Committee headed by Marx had reorganized itself to function as a branch of the clandestine Communist League. At the same time its front organization, the Brussels German Workers' Educational Society, of which Moses Hess was vice-president, conducted a regular programme of public lectures and what Marx, in a letter to Herwegh in Paris, called 'debates of a parliamentary nature' as well as social evenings 'with singing, recitation, theatricals and the like' for its 100 members. Since the end of September, Marx had also been able to conduct Communist propaganda in 'a smaller cosmopolitan-democratic society to which Belgians, French, Poles, Swiss and Germans belong.' This was the Association Démocratique, a motley group of Belgian and refugee radicals and liberals who – like the international Fraternal Democrats in London to whom it became affiliated – called for 'the union of all countries'.

'If you come up here again', a satisfied Marx wrote in the same letter to Herwegh, 'you'll find that even in little Belgium more can be done by way of direct propaganda than in big France.'[61] The president of the Association Démocratique was L.L. Jottrand, a radical Belgian lawyer. Marx was one of its two vice-presidents. The other was Lelevel. Marx had not a penny to his name. A trip he had undertaken at the end of September to his sister Sophie in Holland was to yield him (in November) 150 francs from her husband, the attorney Robert Schmalhausen. Though Jenny was in an advanced stage of pregnancy with their third child and sick with worry, Marx was remarking to Herwegh in October that the public activity in the Workers' Educational Society and the Association provided 'an infinitely refreshing stimulus for everyone.'

More important, in September Marx had gained a foothold in a newspaper, the bi-weekly *Deutsche Brüsseler Zeitung*. Its publisher-editor was Adalbert von Bornstedt, a Prussian ex-officer turned journalist, who, although a member of the Communist League and of the Association Démocratique, was suspected of having until recently been a Prussian and Austrian spy. But so long as he was putting at Marx's disposal 'a censorship-free opposition paper of progressive tendencies', Marx – as he explained in another letter to Herwegh – was ready to work with this dubious character and 'cowardly *canaille*', as he privately called him.[62]

Bakunin arrived in Brussels on 19 December. He and Marx inevitably met, for within a week of his arrival Bakunin became a member of the Association Démocratique, at which Marx soon delivered a lecture.

Towards the end of November, Marx had gone to London, where he addressed a banquet of the Fraternal Democrats in memory of the Polish rebellion of 1830. One might have expected, therefore, that the two revolutionary leaders, Marx and Bakunin, who had spent many hours together in Paris in the smoke-filled editorial rooms of *Vorwärts!* in the heady days of 1844, would be all the more keen to resume contact. But Bakunin had recently developed an antipathy to everything German, whether 'Prussian pedantry' or German 'metaphysics and theorizing'. Marx, for his part, took little interest in Bakunin or his new idea that the German-born Tsar, not to mention Prussia and Austria, were the oppressors of 'all the Slavs'. To Marx, the Polish question was one to be resolved in the general salvation of mankind by the victory of the proletariat over the bourgeoisie. Since the conflict between the two 'was most developed in England' – as he told the English Chartists at the 29 November London banquet – their best way of helping the Poles and 'all the oppressed' peoples of Europe was to topple the English bourgeoisie: 'Poland', he said, 'is not to be freed in Poland but in England.'[63]

To Bakunin, on the other hand, the Poles were part of the Slav forces who would regenerate the 'decadent' Western world. In Brussels he met the aging Lelevel again, as well as the leaders of the other factions that divided the small Polish colony in Belgium. On 14 February 1848, in memory of the Decembrist insurrection, Bakunin was invited by Lelevel to deliver a speech at the Association Démocratique. According to his later account (the speech itself has not survived), he spoke of a European revolution and predicted 'the inevitable destruction of the Austrian Empire' by the united Russo-Polish and Slav forces.

Bakunin respected Lelevel's personality, but considered him 'a broken man and a complete nullity in politics'. He also found that the various small clans of émigrés, though 'separately all good Poles, are worthless together as a party.' Whether because of this or because the rumours that he was a Russian agent cast a shadow over his newly achieved fame, nothing came of his plan for an alliance with the Poles.

Altogether, Bakunin had an unhappy time in Brussels. Like Marx, he had no money, and he had to rely on Sazonov's sister Maria Podudensky to come to his rescue. Feeling miserable, and finding that the Association Démocratique too was 'the greatest humbug imaginable', he preferred to frequent a circle of Polish aristocrats and Jesuits who tried to convert him to the Catholic faith: 'Their ladies also concerned themselves about my spiritual salvation. I was greatly entertained in their society.'

As for Marx and the German Communist group in Brussels, Bakunin gave them a wide berth. Before the end of December 1847, hardly arrived in Brussels, he had written in a letter to Herwegh:

> The Germans, those craftsmen Bornstedt, Marx and Engels – especially Marx – are plotting their usual mischief here. Vanity, malice, squabbles, theoretical intolerance and practical cowardice... The single word bourgeois has become an epithet which they repeat ad nauseam, though they themselves are ingrained bourgeois from head to foot.
>
> In a word, lies and stupidity, stupidity and lies. Impossible to breathe freely in such company. I keep away from them...[64]

Bakunin was jealous of Marx, and for good reasons. Marx, besides his circle of 15 to 20 intimates and his troop of 100 followers in the German Workers' Educational Society, had a mouthpiece for recruiting more people to his ideas in the *Deutsche Brüsseler Zeitung*. He was also engaged in co-ordinating the Communist League's branches in London and Paris into a disciplined, if small international organization, and launching a new doctrine upon the world in *The Communist Manifesto*.

But discipline, organizational work and abstract thinking were foreign to Bakunin, who was all impulses, instinct and spontaneous action. Ever since he had learned from Weitling that 'only the people have the audacity to put the arm of destruction to work', Bakunin had been dreaming of reforming the world by enlisting the destructive-creative 'fire of the people'. Christ and Luther, he had written in 1843, 'came from the simple people.' But Bakunin did not know 'the people', nor had he made the slightest effort to meet them.

Bakunin's hour was to come two and a half months after his arrival in Brussels, when the 'February revolution' broke out in Paris. Hastening to the French capital and joining the revolutionary guards and workmen on the barricades, he was at last to make the acquaintance of 'the people', to find his 'bride, the revolution', and to start his legendary career as an international rebel.

But before that happened, during his cheerless days in Brussels he spent much of his time maligning the various Polish leaders to one another. Bakunin was no small intriguer. At that, his strictures about the 'squabbles' going on among Marx and his people were not entirely without foundation. For since the autumn of 1847, Marx and Engels were indeed engaged in a tug-of-war with Bornstedt; Engels's character assassination of Hess had reached a new intensity; and dissensions about the programme and principles of the Communist League threatened to tear apart its various branches. Indeed, they were rife within Marx's Brussels branch itself.

At the beginning of December, Marx, entrusted by the 2nd London Congress with the task of formulating the tenets of the new Communist faith, had won the first stage of a long power struggle. But *The Communist Manifesto* had yet to be written, published and accepted when – within days of Bakunin's end-of-December letter to Herwegh deriding the 'mischief... malice, squabbles,' etc., among the Germans in Brussels – the tension created by these private as well as public ideological conflicts came to a head on New Year's Eve 1848.

35

1848: The Making of *The Communist Manifesto*

Karl and Jenny Marx celebrated New Year's Eve 1848 at a dinner-dance at the 'Le Cygne' (The Swan) restaurant next to the Brussels Town Hall in the Grand' Place. Nearly 100 couples had been invited to the gaily decorated restaurant. The festive programme announced by the organizers – the German Workers' Society – included an after-dinner speech by Marx. Art and politics were to be combined in a 'social political play', actually a dramatic group recital featuring Mme Marx in a prominent role. Moses Hess was to deliver a speech 'to the ladies', and there was to be all-night dancing and merriment.

Karl Marx was almost 30 years old. A slim figure still, of medium height, with athletic shoulders, he had a swarthy face and glowing, or glowering, eyes which struck some of his admirers even then as 'flashing like dark lightning'; and his coal-black hair and full beard already gave his head some of the shaggy look and massive contour which were to coalesce into his final image.

Stephan Born, the young printer's apprentice whom Engels had recruited to his ideas in Paris and used as his right-hand man for propaganda among the workers, had arrived in Brussels in late autumn 1847. He was present at this New Year's Eve celebration – he had in fact written and put together the piece in which Jenny Marx was to appear – and in his memoirs he remarked on her personality and appearance at the time: 'I have seldom known a woman so harmoniously turned out in looks as well as in her heart and spirit and so captivating at the very first glance ...'[1]

Born evoked her in these glowing terms 50 years after his first visit to the Marx home. In Paris, he had often heard Engels heap ridicule on journeymen and manual workers of his own type, and it was with a doubly trepidant heart that he had presented himself to Marx, the master. Relieved by the latter's complimenting him on a brochure he had written and by Jenny's friendly welcome, he may have been carried away by the memory of the 'special interest' she took in him when he was but a diffident, 'hopeful young disciple of her husband's teaching'.

Indeed, he was only 22, and it is to be doubted that, as a wandering apprentice, he had ever before encountered a woman of Jenny's breeding or many lady-like attributes, captivating at first glance. He found the Marxes living 'in a most modest, one might say shabbily furnished, little lodging in a Brussels suburb.' Jenny, though preoccupied by family cares and her children, struck him as completely absorbed in her husband's ideas and totally unlike the type of 'pot-stirring, sock-knitting German Hausfrau.'[2]

She had recently started to attend the weekly social evenings staged by the Workers' Society at The Swan for its members and their wives. While on Sundays and Wednesdays Marx's intellectual associates, and sometimes 'citizen Marx' himself, would enlighten the workers on matters affecting their condition – 'citizen Engels', for instance, briefed them on 'the Stock Exchange as the chief agency where proletarians are made' – Jenny sought to lift their souls and those of their wives by reciting elevating poems and prose pieces. With her pool-like eyes, her calm face, her aristocratic bearing and her fair-haired beauty as yet unravaged as it would be by later miseries, Jenny was sure to attract all the glances at the New Year's Eve party.

Hess, 36 years old and tall, thin, with long locks framing a goateed intellectual's face, was accompanied to the party by his companion, Sibyl Pesch. Although Sibyl was not over-educated, Jenny Marx liked her natural wit and befriended her. But it was Engels, handsome, blue-eyed, with a blond moustache and the 'dashing look of a Guards officer', who sprang a surprise on everyone at The Swan. An early cosmopolitan moving between Manchester, London, Paris and Brussels, Engels had unwisely decided to attend the workers' celebration in company with Mary Burns – the Irish working-girl who had become his mistress in Manchester. He had originally installed Mary and her then 16-year-old sister in a small house in a Manchester suburb he could conveniently visit. She had since joined him in Brussels. This was to be a lifelong liaison – later, when he settled in Manchester, it allegedly included the sister in a convenient *ménage à trois* – but Jenny Marx steadfastly refused to receive Mary Burns and would not acknowledge her existence by so much as a polite nod.

According to Born's account of the party, when he came up to greet Karl and Jenny Marx, with Engels and his mistress apparently not far away, Marx 'gave me to understand by a glance and a significant smile that his wife declined in the most rigorous manner to make the acquaintance of that... damsel.' Because Jenny Marx would not share the head table with Mary Burns, the two couples were to herald the New Year separately, with a 'large hall' between them. Jenny might grace the weekly workers' socials at The Swan with her presence, but she was too wholesome and high-principled ('in matters of dignity and the purity of morals', as Born later put it, 'the noble woman was intransigent') to take any but a dim view of Engels's Irish paramour and his licentious way of living then or later, when – on the death of Mary Burns – her sister Lizzy took her place.

Engels was something of a rake, and his way of bragging even about cheap adventures was distasteful to Jenny. Not many months before the New Year, reporting to Marx that he had run into Hess in a Paris street, he had been unable to stop himself from relating how he had 'left him standing open-mouthed' in mid-sentence while he, Engels, had run off to catch up with two street-bawds 'whom the painter Koerner had just picked up!'

Though he was wont to blurt out such exploits with an exclamation mark and a kind of juvenile satisfaction, Engels was, in his own way, faithful to the Burns sisters – 30 years later he would even marry the second on her death-bed. But Paris, where he lived on his father's cash remittances while trying to convert a couple of hundred 'boorish' workmen to Communism, was full of available girls. His taste was unrefined, he did not break his head over women, and Frau Marx found his cynical, casual treatment of them offensive.

So at the beginning of the dinner at The Swan, Jenny as well as Marx himself publicly snubbed Engels. Marx, bowing to his wife's feelings, sacrificed his friend to her at the banqueting table, as it were. There was, however, little he could have done if he wished to avoid a scene in front of the workers gathered for a night of festivity and good cheer with their intellectual leaders.

To these workers, Engels was the son of the 'great factory lord of Barmen'. Many of them and their solid German wives eyed him with an interest in which there was more mistrust than favour. They felt, in fact, as scandalized by his sinful connection with Mary Burns as Jenny Marx was. This was in the spirit of the age.

Even young Born thought it impolitic and 'insolent' of Engels to flaunt in public his doubly improper alliance with an Ermen & Engels factory girl – just like any rich boss's son satisfying his lust with one of his father's employees. Born felt, or so he wrote afterwards, that Engels should have shown more discretion and known better than to introduce his mistress to a gathering of workers, thereby reminding them of 'the reproach so often made against the rich sons of manufacturers that they took advantage of their position to press the daughters of the people into the service of their pleasures.'[3]

Then too, by New Year's Eve 1848, the strain between Engels and Hess had reached the point of threatening a public scandal. Besides constantly inveighing against Hess and accusing him of preaching the wrong ideas to the German workers in Paris, Engels had frequently boasted – in private letters to Marx as well as in reports to the Communist Correspondence Bureau in Brussels read by others – of having had an affair with Sibyl Pesch, and his bragging had made her the subject of gossip in Brussels's small German colony.

Hess, wrongly suspecting that the rumour-monger was Adalbert von Born-stedt, the publisher of the *Deutsche Brüsseler Zeitung*, resolved to challenge him to a pistol duel. Only the fact that Bornstedt was out of town and the interven-tion of Ferdinand Wolff saved the situation. A member of the Correspondence Bureau, Wolff, known by his nickname 'Red Wolff', contrived to draw up a pro-tocol so phrased as to fob off Hess and satisfy his honour.

Born, who knew of the whole affair, did not mention it in his memoirs. But Engels himself, who left Brussels immediately after the New Year but heard about its outcome from Marx, referred to it with savage and undisguised delight in a letter he sent to him from Paris on 14 January 1848:

> I was enormously tickled by the Mosi business, although annoyed that it should have come to light. Apart from you, no one in Brussels knew of it save Gigot and Lupus – and Born, whom I told about it in Paris once when I was in my cups. Enfin, *c'est égal*. Moses brandish-ing his pistols, parading his horns before the whole of Brussels, and before Bornstedt into the bargain!!, must have been exquisite. Ferdi-nand Wolff's inventiveness over the minutes *m'a fait crever de rire* [made me split my sides laughing] – and Moses believes that!... Only last July here in Paris this Balaam's she-ass [Sibyl Pesch] made me, *in optima forma*, a declaration of love mingled with resignation, and confided to me the most intimate nocturnal secrets of her ménage![4]

If Engels smarted on New Year's Eve under the Marxian insult to his Irish flame, he was far too eager to remain Marx's associate to give any outward sign of it. He had enough sang-froid to mask his feelings, and dance and drink with Mary. Even many years later he would obligingly pack Mary's sister and successor as his mistress off to a pub, in order to clear the coast for a visit by Jenny Marx to his London home.

At The Swan, however, sincerely convinced as he was that Mary Burns was a direct descendant of thepoet Robert Burns, he was all the more incensed to see her being cold-shouldered by Sibyl Pesch. Informed by Marx after the party that Sibyl was furious with him for bringing her into disrepute, he explained his motives in a letter: 'Her rage with me is unrequited love, pure and simple. For that matter, Moses came only second in my thoughts... my first desire being to revenge myself for all the dirty tricks they had played on Mary.'

It would seem that Engels, unable to vent his annoyance at Jenny Marx for being friendly to Hess's mistress while humiliating his own, was taking out at least part of it on Sibyl. And in spite of his denial that his rivalry with Hess had anything to do with it, he cynically concluded his letter to Marx by saying that Hess was perfectly at liberty to avenge himself on all my present, past and future mistresses, and for that purpose I commend to him 1) the Flemish giantess who lives at my former lodgings, 87 Chaussée d'Ixelles au premier... and 2) a Frenchwoman, Mademoiselle Félicie who, on Sunday, the 23rd of this month, will be arriving in Brussels by the first train from Cologne on her way to Paris... Kindly pass on this information to him in order that he may appreciate my honorable intentions. I will give him fair play.[5]

Before the dancing started that night at The Swan, Marx rose to propose a toast in French. According to the *Deutsche Brüsseler Zeitung*, he praised the 'liberal mission of Belgium... a country where freedom of discussion and association' permitted the planting of seeds that would benefit all Europe. There was some irony in this, seeing that the Communist League branch of which he was the president was a secret and subversive organization.

The Polish historian Lelevel then saluted the gathering on behalf of Poland's exiled democrats. Dinner was cleared away and the real party began. There was music and German singing, led by the baritone voice of the printer Karl Wallau. There was dancing under the festooned gas lampoons in the halls of the inn, hung with streamers and gay decorations. There was a hushed interval when Jenny Marx appeared with others in Born's dramatic sketches, earning an ovation.

As for the incidents not mentioned in the newspaper report, but referred to by Engels in his letter of 14 January and later by Born in his memoirs, they showed that the young 'doctors of revolution' were prone to human foibles as strong as their dynamic qualities and their tremendous urge to change the world. For the rest, what happened at The Swan was only the froth of deeper conflicts seething within the Communist League since its first London congress in June 1847. The events of New Year's Eve 1848 were the culmination of a prolonged fight which Marx and Engels had been carrying on with immense energy on several fronts, but at last the famous *Communist Manifesto* was in the making in an atmosphere not lacking touches of Byzantine intrigue.

Europe was on the brink of revolution. On New Year's Eve everyone took its imminent outbreak for granted. In October 1847 Louis Blanc had told Engels in Paris that it would be a more drastic revolution than all previous ones. But the Communist League was at the time in a pitiable state. On 14 September its London Central Authority, waiting since June for its branches in Switzerland, France, Belgium, Germany and Sweden to submit their comments on its proposed draft of a 'Communist Credo' or 'Confession of Faith', complained in a circular that so far it had 'received a definite reply only from the Brussels circle; other places... thanked us for our efforts, made some general comments and no more.'

The Central Authority had sent emissaries to America, Norway, Germany and Holland. In America, it reported, the League was in 'a sad state'. Weitling's arrival had caused discord in the New York branch and after some violent disputes the whole set-up had collapsed. In Germany the Hamburg branch was disaffected and likewise angry at the split caused in the ranks by the persecution of the supporters of Weitling and Grün. In Leipzig some members had defected. Things were more hopeful in Berlin and in Sweden, where its emissary, 'crossing the whole country on foot' with a kitbag of Communist leaflets brought from London, 'distributed them wherever he found German workers.' He was now on his way to Umea and Tornea: 'A Communist emissary among the Lapps!'[6]

In a woeful picture of the Communist League's finances, the Central Authority said that although in London each member paid 3d. a week into an educational fund, it had completely exhausted its resources on the production of a specimen issue of its planned newspaper, *Kommunistische Zeitschrift*. In spite of promises of financial support for the newspaper, the Central Authority noted that, 'apart from the Brussels circle which made a monthly allocation of £1 sterling for printing expenses and 5 francs for propaganda, we have received nothing so far', and appealed to all its branches 'not to leave us in the lurch now.'[7] But as its appeal met with little response, the newspaper's specimen issue was also its last.

While singling out the London branch for its 'remarkable sense of unity' and the Brussels branch for 'working most energetically', the Central Authority spoke of a split in the large Paris branch. Accusing Weitling's supporters of having 'appropriated the whole Paris League's treasury', it further attacked the 'many' Paris supporters of 'Grün's nonsense and Proudhon's most strange ideas. Oddly enough, these people, who are members of the Communist League, seem to reject Communism. They want equality and nothing else.'

Reminding the recalcitrant followers of Weitling that 10 years of moderation, unity and 'brotherly love' preached by the tailor had accomplished 'virtually nothing', the Central Authority declared that 'there is only room for Communists in our League.' Finally, it censored the 'dubious' behaviour of some of its branches in Switzerland, especially that of the Berne community, which had requested and obtained from it 75 francs for producing a Communist newspaper but had used this money 'to print leaflets by Karl Heinzen, who has shown himself to be the bitterest enemy of the Communists.'[8]

Karl Heinzen had been deputy editor of the *Rheinische Zeitung* under Marx until its closure in 1844. He had been in Brussels when Marx arrived there in

February 1845; in protracted discussions, Marx had tried in vain to convert him to Communism. Heinzen – who called himself 'a republican' and later took part in the revolution in Baden – had since gone to Switzerland. On 26 September 1847, less than a fortnight after the Cen-tral Authority's circular, he published an article in the *Deutsche Brüsseler Zeitung* in which, in the name of all German radicals, he accused the Communists of seeking to split the German revolution-ary movement. To the great annoyance of Marx and Engels, Bornstedt, instead of refuting his arguments, prefaced them with an editorial note calling for con-ciliation 'between various shades of German revolutionaries abroad'.

The following day, Engels submitted to Bornstedt the first part of a two-part article, 'The Communists and Karl Heinzen', in which he questioned Hein-zen's qualifications to represent 'the German republicans and democrats' and derided him as 'one of the most ignorant men of this century'. This article, written when the Communist League, within months of its birth, was torn by divisive currents even as its branches were preparing to vote in secret conclaves on a Communist credo or manifesto to be adopted by the forthcoming League's 2nd London congress, marked a new and intensified compaign by Marx and Engels to purge its ranks of all their opponents.

One by one, Bruno Bauer, Ruge, Weitling, Kriege and Grün had been swept aside. In July, Marx had published his anti-Proudhon *Misère de la Philosophie*, in which he announced that only when there were no more classes and class antagonisms 'will social evolutions cease to be political revolutions'. Borrowing a phrase from George Sand, he declared that till then 'the last word of social science' will always be '*Le combat ou la mort; la lutte sanguinaire ou le néant. Ç'est ainsi que la question est invinciblement posée.*'[9] This phrase – 'Combat or death; bloody struggle or extinction. That's the only way the question can be put' – may also be seen as the motto under which, in the autumn of 1847, Marx and Engels turned their fire on the Proudhonists, Grünians and Weitlingians within the ranks of the League's branches, and on anyone who, like Heinzen, ques-tioned their theory of 'scientific Communism'.

Their relentless campaign against Heinzen was to last two months. It had begun in September with Born's being sent from Paris to Switzerland to take up the cudgels against him as well as Weitling's strong supporters in that country. While there, Born had published an anonymous pamphlet, *Heinzen's Idea of the State, a Critique by Stephan*. At the same time, a running feud devel-oped between Engels and Bornstedt over Engels's article, 'The Communists and Karl Heinzen', which Bornstedt at first refused to publish, pleading lack of space. Furious at Bornstedt's breach of his promise to open the paper to their contributions, Engels was further incensed to learn that Bornstedt had orga-nized a banquet at which, on 29 September, the Association Démocratique was to be launched as a European organization in the presence of democrats from several countries. The German Communists in Brussels had not been invited. Engels, rightly suspecting that Bornstedt's large, liberalist federation would eclipse 'our miserable little Workers' Society', packed the foundation banquet with members of the Society and reported to Marx –who was in Holland trying to raise some money from his relatives – that he had managed to have himself elected as one of the vice-presidents of the new organization. Having made sure that the Communists would be represented on the committee of the Association Démocratique, he later ceded his place on it to Marx, who became one of its dominant figures.

Under strong pressure from Marx and Engels, Bornstedt finally published the latter's two-part article on 3 and 7 October. But another clash with Bornstedt followed a couple of weeks later, when he published Heinzen's reply together with a note to the contending parties to 'take their polemic elsewhere' as his newspaper could not afford to publish such long articles.

This time, Marx and Engels hauled Bornstedt before the editorial board, which forced him to publish Marx's reply in full. Thereupon Marx ridiculed Heinzen in an essay of some 12,000 words, 'Moralizing Criticism and Critical Morality', serialized in 5 issues of the *Deutsche Brüsseler Zeitung*. When Heinzen sent a reply from Geneva, a chastised Bornstedt published a note saying that the paper refused to allow him to continue 'his vile private squabble' and would reply to possible public accusations that it denied him the 'free expression of his views' at the proper time and place 'if we deem it necessary.'[10]

In the two months between September and November 1847, during which Marx and Engels virtually wrested control of his paper from Bornstedt and crowned their campaign against Heinzen by closing its columns to him, they wrote between them a dozen articles on a variety of political and economic subjects – from 'The Civil War in Switzerland' to 'The Commercial Crisis in England'. After the still-birth of the London Central Authority's newspaper, the *Deutsche Brüsseler Zeitung* became, in fact if not in name, the Communist League's only mouthpiece.

Besides having won over the London leaders of the Central Authority, Schapper, Moll and Bauer, to their side, Marx and Engels had another advantage. Everything they wrote appeared in several languages, for they had gained outlets for their propaganda in the Paris *La Réforme* and *The Northern Star* of Leeds. Nor was there anyone in the Communist League capable of challenging either the economic foundation of their theories or their historical sweep and polemical talents.

In September, Marx had attended a three-day international congress on free trade which brought to Brussels the editor of *The Economist* as well as 150 leading political economists and manufacturers from England, Holland, Denmark, Italy and Belgium. They all extolled the benefits of free trade, but on the third day the poet and satirist Georg Weerth, who had spent 5 years in England, rose from his seat and, speaking in the name 'of those millions who do not believe that free trade will do wonders for them', warned the assembly: 'You have no longer to fear the Emperor of all the Russias; you dread not an invasion of Cossacks, but if you do not take care, you will have to fear the irruption of your own workmen, and they will be more terrible to you than all the Cossacks in the world.'

Marx had prepared a speech, but was refused the opportunity of delivering it. He meant to surprise the congress by declaring himself in favour of free trade because, by expanding the laws of capitalist production 'upon the territory of the whole earth', it would spread and sharpen the conflicts and antagonisms inherent in capitalism and hasten 'the struggle which will itself lead to the emancipation of the proletarians.'[11]

Although most of the Belgian and foreign newspapers to which Marx offered his speech refused to print it, Engels published it along with Weerth's speech in *The Northern Star*. This was in line with their intensive journalistic propaganda barrage, addressed chiefly to intellectuals. But in the autumn of 1847, Marx and Engels took some decisive political actions towards their aim of forging a small but influential international movement out of the less educated workmen constituting the rank and file of the Communist League.

After disposing of Hess and his supporters in Paris by means of the 'infernal trick' he played against them, Engels made sure that he and nobody else would be the Paris delegate to the 2nd London Congress. He got himself elected on 14 November 'with a big majority' at what he described to Marx as 'an extremely muddled session'. Stephan Born seems to have helped to engineer Engels's election. Come the revolution, the enterprising Born was to anger Marx and Engels by striking out as an independent 'reformer' and launching a trade union movement in Berlin. But in 1847 he was still wholly under the influence of Engels, who used him as his contact man with the workers and journeymen and as his stooge in some of his intrigues. Born, who later emigrated to Switzerland, became a university professor and eventually settled in London, was to write that in 1847, in Paris, he was

> made chairman at a meeting of the secret League [at which] the nomination of a delegate to the London Central Authority came up... Engels wanted the appointment [but] I noticed that it would be very difficult to push through. There was strong opposition against him. I only achieved his election by going against the rules and asking for a

show of hands, not by those who were in favour of his candidacy, but by those who were against him.[12]

'This chairman's trick', as Born called it, 'strikes me today as an abomination. "That was well done," Engels said to me when we went home.'[13] In some accounts the episode related by Born is said to have taken place before Engels attended the *first* London Congress in June 1847. There is, however, more than one reason to support S. Na'aman's opinion[14] that Born chaired the 'muddled session' of 14 November 1847 at which Marx was elected to the 2nd London Congress.

Although Weitling's supporters had been formally expelled from the Communist League since its first London Congress, two of the Paris communities, out of 5 that took part in the vote, opposed Engels's nomination, proposing to send a delegate of their own to the 2nd Congress. They were promptly expelled. And shortly before Engels's arrival in Paris, as he reported to Marx, 'the last of the Grünians were thrown out'. The expulsions were undertaken on the principle that 100 loyal and disciplined members were better than 500 ideologically confused ones.

On 23–24 November, having got himself a mandate from the Paris branch to formulate the basic tenets of 'orthodox' Communism and submit them to the London Congress in its name, Engels wrote to Marx that he had prepared a draft 'catechism' of 25 questions and answers entitled 'Principles of Communism'. Describing it as 'wretchedly worded, in a tearing hurry', he advised Marx that the catechistic form seemed to him unsuitable 'since a certain amount of history has to be narrated in it'. He therefore proposed to call 'the thing' a 'Communist Manifesto'.

With only a week to go before the opening of the London Congress, Engels suggested to Marx from Paris that they meet on the evening of Saturday, 27 November,

> in Ostend, Hotel de la Couronne, just opposite the railway station beside the harbour... If you come by train, which goes between 4 and 5 o'clock, you will arrive approximately at the same time as I... We shall then have time enough to talk things over... and Sunday morning across the water [the Channel].

'This congress', he wrote in the same letter, 'must be decisive,' adding in English the words, which he emphasized, 'As This Time We Shall Have It All Our Own Way.'

As arranged, Marx arrived in Ostend on 27 November in the company of the Belgian Communist Victor Tedesco. They met Engels, and crossed the English

Channel on 29 November. The Communist League being a clandestine organization, Marx arrived in London ostensibly in his capacity as vice-president of the Brussels Association Démocratique and as its delegate to an international meeting of the Fraternal Democrats, organized by the Chartists to mark the anniversary of the Polish uprising of 1830. The meeting took place the evening of Marx's arrival in a hall on Great Windmill Street, in Soho, where the German Workers' Educational Society had its headquarters. This was occasion on which Marx told the assembled Chartists that their victory over the English bourgeoisie would be decisive in 'defeating the entire old society' and that Poland would be freed 'not in Poland but in England.'

Engels and the Chartist leaders George Harney and Ernest Jones also spoke. The next day, in the same building, the 2nd Congress of the Communist League began its secret deliberations. The Congress, presided over by Karl Schapper, with Engels as its secretary, lasted 10 days. According to Engels, Marx 'defended the new theory during fairly lengthy debates' until 'all opposition and doubt were at last overcome.' No record has survived of the arguments and ideas exchanged, but judging by the impression of a participant who later wrote that 'Marx was a born leader of people. His speech was brief, convincing and compelling in its logic. He never said superfluous words; every sentence contained an idea and every idea was an essential link in the chain of his argument,'[15]

Marx dominated the discussions; and the end result showed that, as Engels had forecast, the two of them had it all their own way. Indeed, whereas the League's aim had previously been conceived as the 'diffusion and the most rapid realization of the theory of communal property', Article 1 of the Rules adopted by the Congress stated its objective to be 'the overthrow of the bourgeoisie, the rule of the proletariat, the abolition of the old bourgeois society which rests on the antagonism of classes, and the foundation of a new society without classes and without private property.'[16] And before concluding its sessions on 8 December, the Congress charged Marx with the task of drafting a 'detailed theoretical and practical party programme', to become known as *The Communist Manifesto*.

On 31 December, when the German workers in Brussels and their leaders gathered at The Swan for their New Year's celebration, it was less than three weeks since Marx and Engels (on 13 and 17 December, respectively) had returned from London. Marx had brought back with him, besides Engels's 'Principles of Communism' with its 25 questions and answers, several other drafts of a Communist Manifesto which had been given him by the League's Central Authority. He and his wife were as destitute as ever when – as he began a series of lectures on 'Wages' to the German Workers' Society – he started jotting down notes for the final text. The 150 francs he had received from his Dutch relatives in mid-November had not lasted long. He had gone through the London Congress undeterred by the distress in which he had left Jenny and their children. But it was on his mind, and from London, on the day the Congress disbanded, he had appealed to his Russian friend Paul Annenkov, who was at the time in Paris, for an urgent loan:

> When I set out on this trip... I left my family behind in the most difficult and dire of circumstances. It's not only that my wife and children [Jennychen, Laura and the baby Edgar] were ill. My economic situation just now is so critical that my wife is being veritably harassed by creditors and in the most wretched financial straits.... You would in truth save me from the worst if you could arrange to let my wife have a sum of between 100 and 200 francs. I shall, of course, be unable to pay you until my money matters have been settled with my family.[17]

But Marx had the satisfaction of having launched, with Engels's help, the first international proletarian movement in history. Tireless in their joint effort, their singleness of purpose and ruthless elimination of all opposition had paid off. They knew what they wanted, and Marx was now about to lay down the tenets of modern, 'progressive' and 'scientific' Communism. Although he borrowed a number of points from Engels's draft, it was Marx who wrote most of the *Manifesto* and lent it its historic sweep. Engels was later to write that the 'fundamental proposition... the nucleus of the Manifesto' – the conception of history as a class struggle and the role to be assumed by the proletariat on the stage of history – belonged 'solely and exclusively to Marx'. Marx, on the other hand, acknowledged Engels's part in its gestation and named him as its co-author.

He seems to have promised the Central Authority that he would deliver the *Manifesto* in the course of January 1848, for on the 26th of that month a letter amounting to an ultimatum was received in Brussels: 'The London Central Authority hereby charges the authorities of the Brussels circle to notify K. Marx that, unless the Manifesto of the C[ommunist] Party reaches London by February 1, further measures will be taken against him.' If he did not produce the *Manifesto*, the letter demanded the 'instant return of the documents furnished him by the Congress'.

Marx had thus only started 'packing the power of high explosives' into the *Manifesto* when the New Year's Eve party took place. Threatening 'Communist revolution' and the 'forcible overthrow of the social order', he was to write and rewrite the altogether 9,600 words of the final version through most of January, not knowing that the resulting 23-page pamphlet was to be overtaken by events in the immediate future and to lie about for many decades before going off with the effect of a time-bomb.

Gone were the old slogans of brotherly love, liberty and the like, hitherto invoked by the utopian Socialists in the name of justice and morality. Marx was to serve notice that the indignant, over-exploited proletariat – no longer pleading love, but set on conflict – would henceforth attack the liberty of others in order to gain its own. Conflict meant hatred and class-hatred was necessary to make the working-class aware of its identity, its separate interests and destiny, and to fire 'the proletariat of all lands' to unite in fighting their oppressors and throwing off their chains.

Poor but not meek, the proletariat would inherit the earth. In times to come, *The Communist Manifesto* would be compared by some to 'the Prophecy', and *Das Kapital* to 'the Torah, the Law'; others would mention Jesus as one of Marx's youthful inspirations. But if the proletariat was the new chosen people, it was one not bound by any Covenant with God. Crucified, it would be resurrected – but not under the sign of the cross. Bereft of property and privilege, but achieving consciousness of its power, the proletariat would demolish the whole society based on property and the class-system – and build a new one without a new ruling class.

This was Marx, the full-grown fighter and prophet at 30. Whatever the source of his apocalyptic anger with the existing world, it was barely a dozen years since a romantic, idealistic youth had dedicated to his bride the lines: 'Jenny! If we can but weld our souls together, then I shall contemptuously fling my glove in the face of the world...[and] stride through the wreckage a creator!' Nor can one fail to note that it was not long since he had reached the conclusion that the philosophers had only been interpreting the world; now was the time to change it.

On New Year's Eve, Marx and Engels may have sat at separate tables throughout the evening, but it was Hess, the earliest German Communist, who was the odd man out on that night of music and merriment. As a result of Engels's machinations, Hess's proposed draft of a 'Manifesto' would be lost to history, and the backstage intrigues attending the birth of *The Communist Manifesto* would long remain forgotten behind the folds hiding history's minutiae.

Late in the 20th century, S. Na'aman, after a thorough investigation of the matter, observed that Marx had not been fooled by Engels's October 1847 report to him alleging that Hess had created a 'hellish confusion' in the minds of the ranks of the Paris branch; rather, Marx understood from it that Hess had a greater influence on the Communist German workers in Paris than Engels – who kept referring to him as a 'fallen' hero – was admitting.[18] In short, Engels's own reports signalled to Marx Hess's potential capability of leading an organized opposition to the 'correct' party line.

But this was not the real crux of the ideological-tactical conflict that came to a head between Doctors Marx and Hess by New Year's Eve 1848. That night, with everyone talking of revolution, these two not only disagreed about its prospects, but were at loggerheads over the tactics to be pursued by the proletariat if and when it came. Marx held, as he was to state in the *Manifesto*, that the bourgeoisie, constantly embattled on all sides – 'at first with the aristocracy', later on with those of its own ranks whose interests collided with industrial progress and 'with the bourgeoisie of other countries' – always found itself 'compelled to appeal to the proletariat, to ask for its help, and thus to drag it into the political arena.' The Communists being too few to stage a revolution and overthrow the bourgeoisie by themselves, they must ally themselves with the Chartists in England and with Louis Blanc in France.

Not so in Germany. There, according to Marx's prognosis, the bourgeoisie would not support a revolution if it was started by the proletariat. But if the Communists encouraged the bourgeoisie to revolt and helped it into the saddle, it would pay the workers to keep it in power – until the day when a more developed capitalism invited its own destruction and the success of a working-class revolution was assured. Until then, the proletariat must absolutely stay out of the fray and keep its powder dry.

Hess dissented. 'The German bourgeoisie', he had recently observed in an important article published in 5 instalments by the *Deutsche Brüsseler Zeitung*, was operating 'a modern industry in the bosom of medieval conditions'. It was strong enough to 'curb the feudal passions' of the German rulers, but too weak and 'too cowardly' to stage a revolution. It would never rise or cooperate with the workers. 'The good German burghers hate their feudal oppressors, but they're even more afraid of the oppressed.'

Hess, in short, questioned not only Marx's assumption that, because in the French Revolution the bourgeoisie had united with the workers to displace the feudal aristocracy, it would do so again; but even more his thesis that once it did, it would allow the proletariat to ride to power on its back and instal itself – at the climax of the scenario Marx was to outline in *The Communist Manifesto* – as 'the ruling class'.

Like Marx, Hess held that industrial development, competition and the crises caused by the over-production of goods would ultimately unite the workers against their exploiters. In an original formulation of his own, he pointed out that the problem to be tackled was actually 'under-consumption' due to the fact that the 'masses of the people' were underpaid and impoverished. A proletarian revolution, rather than undercutting production by putting it under communal control, would actually increase production by increasing the purchasing power of the proletarian masses. As for the prospects of revolution, Hess remarked that conditions were not everywhere ripe for it. It was 'not inconceivable' in France, where revolution was always round the corner; it was more likely in industrialized England; and least of all in Germany. If at all, it would come to Germany from the outside, and it would be a proletarian revolution.

In the fifth and last instalment of his long article on the 'Consequences of a Revolution of the Proletariat', Hess forecast that

> the German bourgeoisie will tack about between fear and hope on the quiet ocean of German misery until a storm surges up in the west and the waves of the proletariat foaming up from the depths will break over the monarchy, the aristocracy and the bourgeoisie.[19]

The first instalment had appeared on 10 October, and the last was published on 11 November. The accent placed by Hess on proletarian, not bourgeois, revolution was something of a challenge to Marx's dialectical strategy to goad the bourgeoisie into action and then, after some indefinite period of self-destructive capitalist rule (during which the proletariat would learn how to exercise political power), seize the first opportunity to 'wrest' supremacy.

Hess's views are believed to have by and large reflected those included in his lost draft for a Communist Manifesto, which had been endorsed by the Paris branch. Engels had been sufficiently disturbed by the first two instalments of Hess's serial to write to Marx on 25–26 October: 'What bug has bitten poor Moses that he does not cease to expound his fantasies on the effects of a revolution by the proletariat?' But this nonchalant tone soon gave way to alarm and urgency. Within weeks of cautioning Marx that no one must know about the underhand method whereby he had got their draft of a manifesto approved, Engels was urging Marx to 'put a stop to Moses' chatter'.

Hess, who was in Brussels, had apparently retained a good deal of influence in Paris, for Engels confessed to Marx that Hess's article had caused him enormous trouble with the Paris workers. 'Entire district sittings have been wasted over it, nor is there any possibility of effectively combatting [it] in the communities.'[20]

No one, however – not even Engels, for all his campaign to discredit Hess – could accuse Hess of heresy, for other than his difference with Marx on the point of bourgeois versus proletarian revolution, Hess's ideas in his article remained within the framework of Marx's doctrine on the class-struggle as an inevitable clash of inimical interests, rather than Hess's earlier stock-in-trade of 'ideas' or moral principles. Nevertheless, the difference of their views on the question of bourgeois versus proletarian revolution – like the personal animosi-

ties created by Engels's allegations about his dalliance with Hess's mistress –
had beclouded the New Year's Eve party.

Outwardly, and formally, nothing had changed. Once control of the new
Communist 'Party' had passed into the hands of Marx and Engels, the undemocratic 'tricks' and intrigue accompanying the making of its Manifesto would
hardly bother those of Marx's intimates who knew of them at all.

An exception was Stephan Born. The 'diffident' but intelligent young printer's apprentice – whom Engels had recommended to Marx as 'a fellow most
receptive to our ideas, drum some more into him and he will be quite useful' –
soon realized that the politics of the leaders of the 'party' and would-be creators
of an egalitarian society were in one degree or another ruled by their temperaments and personal ambitions. As a manual worker, Born cared less for the theories of Marx and Engels about 'the remote time when the capitalist world might
disintegrate from within', than about how to influence immediate events. When
the revolution broke out, he was to go to Berlin and to be successful in organizing its workers, on the idea that a trade union movement could ultimately
'become a political power for social reform in a democratized state'. Engels
never forgave Born his independent action and was to accuse him of 'being in
haste to make a political career'.

Before that, on the eve of the revolution, Engels, ebullient after the success
of his manoeuvres, was so eager to get the better of the man he considered his
rival that he was to urge Marx to attack Hess publicly. Simultaneously and on a
separate track, Marx and Engels continued their feud with Bornstedt. Unlike the
personal jealousy animating Engels's campaign against Hess, their conflict with
the newspaper editor was ideologically justified. Bornstedt was found to be in
cahoots not only with Heinzen but with Marx's Paris friend Herwegh. The three
of them planned a grandiose alliance with Germany's 'democrats', and once the
commotion started hoped to establish there – contrary to Marx's strategy – a
'republican' but anti-Communist regime. For falling in with this plan of Herwegh and Heinzen, Bornstedt was to be expelled from the Communist League in
March.

The Communist Manifesto opens with the well-known words: 'A spectre is haunting Europe – the spectre of Communism.' This line had first appeared in Hess's
recent serialized article on 'The Consequences of a Revolution of the Proletariat'. There was no plagiarism in Marx's use of it, for other writers on both
sides of the fence spoke at the time of Communism as a nightmare. Thus George
Sand in March 1848, when she effectively became Minister of Propaganda of the
new French Republic and responsible for its official Bulletins, was to write: 'The
great fear – or pretext – of the aristocracy at this hour is Communism.' Only a

few copies of *The Communist Manifesto* had reached France by that date and it is almost certain that George Sand had not read its opening line.[21]

But some other ideas formulated by Hess in his article were to find their way into the second part of the four-part *Manifesto of the Communist Party*, to use its actual title. Marx alone, however, had the temerity to announce in this document that when 'the proletariat, the lowest stratum of present-day society', bestirred itself to revolt, 'the whole superstructure of official society will be sprung into the air' – i.e., blown to kingdom come! Combined with this, Marx had the philosophic knack of promising that once the proletariat had seized power it would, dialectically as it were, dissolve itself in a classless society.

'Political power', the *Manifesto* declared, was 'merely the organized power of one class for oppressing another'; the struggling proletariat, however, if compelled to 'sweep away by force' the old conditions of production, 'if, by means of a revolution, it makes itself the ruling class... then it will, along with these conditions, have swept away the conditions for the existence of class antagonisms and of classes generally, and will thereby have abolished its own supremacy as a class.'[22]

Far from denying that the bourgeoisie had played a 'revolutionary' role in history, the *Manifesto* wanted to make it clear why the bourgeoisie was the 'ruling class', and why it would be destroyed with its own weapons:

> The bourgeoisie, during its rule of scarce one hundred years, has created more massive and more colossal productive forces than have all preceding generations together. Subjection of Nature's forces to man, machinery, application of chemistry to industry and agriculture, steam-navigation, railways, electric telegraphs, clearing of whole continents for cultivation, canalization of rivers, whole populations conjured out of the ground – what earlier century had even a presentiment that such productive forces slumbered in the lap of social labour?

While fulsomely praising the bourgeoisie's accomplishments, the *Manifesto* damned it to hell at the same time. For if its growing capital and accumulating wealth meant more work, it also meant over-production and ruthless competition, leading to endemic economic crises. The conquest of new markets and the more thorough exploitation of the old ones, or their wholesale liquidation, only paved the way for 'more extensive and more destructive crises'.

Caught in this vicious spiral were the ranks of the proletariat – 'a class of labourers who live only so long as they find work', and must 'sell themselves piecemeal, like a commodity'. Exposed to 'all the fluctuations of the market', this 'special and essential product' of the bourgeoisie – the proletariat – was now the only 'really revolutionary class'. In short, like a sorcerer who has lost control of the forces he has unleashed, modern bourgeois society, with its gigantic means of production and exchange, had with its own hands created its gravediggers.

'The first step in the revolution by the working class', Marx announced in the *Manifesto*, 'is to raise the proletariat to the position of the ruling class.' It was when describing how the new proletarian government would transform society by revolutionizing the existing system of production that a certain similarity between the measures proposed here by Marx and those earlier advocated by Hess in his article in the *Deutsche Brüsseler Zeitung* became noticeable.

Hess had written that one of the first measures would be a partial abolition of private industry. The final objective was its total abolition, but not by 'violent' and sudden nationalization. Rather, the process would be a gradual one, starting with the larger industries, for it would take time 'to change the structure' of society.

Marx wrote in the *Manifesto* that 'the proletariat will use its political supremacy to wrest, by degrees, all capital from the bourgeoisie.' As Marx was the more radical of the two, Hess may have had a moderating influence on him. Hess had stressed that, contrary to fears that proletarian revolution would cause a standstill in production, the new rulers would regard augmenting production as one of their first tasks. Marx likewise hastened to promise that the government would do everything 'to increase the total of productive forces as rapidly as possible.'

Hess had written of 'the imposition of progressive taxes on capital'; Marx, in his Ten Points in the *Manifesto*, stipulated 'a heavy progressive or graduated income tax'. Hess had advocated 'a partial or total abolition of the rights of inheritance'; Marx wrote simply, 'abolition of all rights of inheritance'. Hess: 'Confiscation... of all the property of dukes, priests, noblemen, which becomes ownerless due to the revolution'; Marx: 'Confiscation of property of all emigrants and rebels.' Hess: 'The establishment of large-scale common industries and agricultural enterprises to provide work for all who seek it'; Marx: 'Establishment of industrial armies... combination of agricultural and manufacturing industries.'

Hess attenuated the process of 'uprooting private industry from its very foundation', both to make it less frightening than it might sound and because he considered that to proceed with it overnight was unrealistic. In the first period after the revolution, he had written, 'a considerable number of people will continue to live on the interest of their capital or from the profits of their properties'. With the government transferring taxes to, and otherwise favouring, a strong public industry, the private sector would gradually wither away. As S. Avineri put it in

1985, this approach – designed to signal that the revolution would not be imposed by 'the bayonets of the proletariat' – was ultimately adopted by Marx, with the result that in 'its most amazing feature' *The Communist Manifesto* did not include nationalization of industry, but only of land.[23]

There is little doubt, however, that Hess's lost or suppressed draft of a manifesto may not have stood comparison with the combination of historic breadth, dialectical power of analysis and ringing language which lent force to Marx's call for revolution. At the New Year's party in Brussels, Marx and Engels felt sure that the collapse of the bourgeoisie was close at hand. The discrepancy of views between them and Hess found expression in the *Manifesto*'s declaration that 'the Communists turn their attention chiefly to Germany, because that country is on the eve of a bourgeois revolution... and because the bourgeois revolution in Germany will be but the prelude to a proletarian revolution following immediately upon it.'

So convinced were they of the strength of the German bourgeoisie and its chances of carrying out a victorious revolution in the first instance that on 23 January 1848 – with the first shot yet to be fired – Engels, in an article in the *Deutsche Brüsseler Zeitung*, served notice on 'the gracious masters of capital' that they must rise in arms to rid feudal Germany of kings, barons and clerics. At the same time, 'laying our cards on the table', he informed them in the name of their proletarian ally 'that they will only be working in our interest'. Declaring that they must nonetheless 'conquer, or perish', he notified them with his usual bravado that 'for a reward you will be allowed to rule for a short time', but the proletariat would be waiting for them sword in hand after the feast.

The article, quoting the leitmotiv of Heine's ballad 'Sir Olaf' (*'Ritter Olaf'*), admonished them not to forget one thing: 'The headsman stands at the door!'[24] The events of the revolution, however, were to prove that Hess was right in doubting the revolutionary potential of the 'cowardly' German bourgeoisie. Nor did he believe that the revolution would break out in Germany first.

In *The Communist Manifesto*, Marx took up the reproach that the Communists wished to abolish countries and nationalities: 'The working men have no country. We cannot take from them what they have not got.' The 23-page *Manifesto* contained a summary of Marx's theory of history and other elements of the doctrine he was to spend the rest of his life elaborating.

But when describing the society of the future, it mixed an accurate forecast of the progress of technology with a well-nigh utopian vision of peace on earth:

> National differences and antagonisms between peoples are daily more and more vanishing, owing to the development of the bourgeoisie, to freedom of commerce, to the world market, to uniformity

in the mode of production and in the condition of life corresponding thereto.

The supremacy of the proletariat, Marx promised, 'will cause them to vanish still faster'. Once it had become the ruling class, all national enmities would simply end, together with the cessation of the class-struggle. Marx and Engels were to cling to this view in the face of later developments.

Declaring that the Communists were 'the most advanced and resolute section' of the international proletariat capable of showing it 'the line of march' leading to its ultimate victory, Marx announced in the *Manifesto* that 'the immediate aim of the Communists is... formation of the proletariat into a class, overthrow of the bourgeois supremacy, conquest of political power by the proletariat.'

As mentioned earlier, the organization of 'the working class' as a 'universal union' or party for the purpose of acquiring 'real power' had first been conceived by Flora Tristan in the booklet *Union Ouvrière*, published in Paris in 1843. That year, Hess and Ruge had visited Tristan at her salon in the rue du Bac. Marx, who read her booklet, mentioned her briefly in *The Holy Family*, but never acknowledged the fact that he adopted her formula for the 'self-emancipation' of the proletariat.

In 1844, Tristan set out on a tour of France's chief industrial centres. Urging factory hands everywhere to form a political party and trade unions that would fight for their rights, she advised them in particular to devote some of the 'money power' to be acquired from membership dues to the education of the women because women, being 'in charge of the children male and female', would raise a new generation of educated and intelligent workers of both sexes.

In the course of this exhausting tour she died at the age of 41, and was buried at Bordeaux in November 1844. Of all the writers who were in time to rescue her from oblivion by stressing her tireless feminist and Socialist work – some even placing her at the head of the line that was to produce such revolutionary figures as Clara Zetkin and Rosa Luxemburg – Maximilien Rubel appears to have been the only one who both noted Marx's debt to Flora Tristan and provided an explanation for his failure to acknowledge it. In a little-known essay, Rubel quoted a passage in her diary: 'The Jewish people died in abasement, and Jesus lifted them up. The Christians die today in abasement and Flora Tristan, the first femme forte, will lift them up.' He observed that she had at one time frequented the circle of Enfantin, who made a mystic cult of the 'Female-Mother-Messiah'. Marx, Rubel wrote, 'fully recognized the formidable dynamism' of Flora Tristan's social programme but could not accept, let alone identify with, her invocation of transcendental forces and her apparent self-image as an instrument of the gods.

He adopted her message, even 'made it his own', but purged it of all traces of mysticism and gave it a new formulation equipped with the driving force of historic necessity.[25]

'The Communists', Marx and Engels declared in the *Manifesto*, 'everywhere support every revolutionary movement against the existing social and political order of things' – including 'the Agrarian Reformers in America', the Chartists in England, the Socialists in France, the bourgeois radicals in Switzerland, the nationalist revolutionaries in Poland – as well as 'the democratic parties of all countries.' Whether or not the take-over of the Communist League encouraged them to hope that they would dominate these other parties in time, decades later Lenin was to pronounce a Communist strategy: 'We shall gladly lean for support on other leftist parties – like the rope leaning on the neck of a man about to be hanged.'

The Communist Manifesto was a masterpiece not so much for the truth of some of its generalizations – of which, in spite of its propagandistic purpose, there were quite a few – but for the eloquence of its message to the workers that history was with them. It was a document all the more remarkable because it was written by two young men who were not of proletarian origin. The *Manifesto* included Marx's observation that when a rotten society is in its death-throes 'a small section of the ruling class cuts itself adrift, and joins the revolutionary class.'

Indeed, long after his death, 'Marxism' was to appeal to some of the intellectual élite in many countries as a satisfactory, altruistic, as well as 'scientific', design to change the human condition. The incoherent mass of workers who were less interested in philosophy learned from it that the class struggle was historically inevitable; that they were not only 'the majority' but 'the class that holds the future in its hands', and that in 'a society without classes and without property... accumulated labour, which is capital', could be used to improve their own lives, instead of serving their masters.

The final message of the *Manifesto* that would imprint itself on the minds of generations to come was as clear as it was simple: 'Let the ruling classes tremble at Communist revolution. The proletarians have nothing to lose but their chains. They have a world to win. WORKING MEN OF ALL COUNTRIES, UNITE!'

In *The Communist Manifesto*, Marx, the supposedly dispassionate scholar, combined political-economic theory with the wrath of an Old Testament prophet. But he did not, as it was later said, feel like a new Moses on Mount Sinai 'going to his people, the workers of the world'. This was hardly his conscious self-image. To be sure, he was living up to and acting out the high 'vocation' of serving mankind of which he had spoken in his school-leaving essay; also, he was showing the way to the Promised Land – the new Communist society which, besides enriching and advancing the life of the workers, would ultimately lead to the classless society of the future, a society free of conflicts.

On the eve of 1848, Marx hardly saw himself as a saviour or a new Messiah. As a philosopher, he was far too busy – politically busy, trying to direct an impending revolution from his writing desk – to harbour any such thoughts. Marx saw himself primarily as the great educator of the proletariat. The 'boors' – as he and Engels kept referring to the working plebs of their time – had to be awakened to, and given an understanding of, the role they could, were indeed destined to, play in history.

The *Manifesto* did not present Communism as a new religion. Nor did Marx have to promulgate any new messianic or other faith in explicit words. His announcement that the revolt of the oppressed hosts of the proletariat would rid humanity of the rule of Mammon and every other tyranny, that in the class-less society there would be no more oppressors and oppressed, was enough to cast him in the role of a secular saviour emancipating man from traditional religion, and pointing the way for him to establish the kingdom of heaven on earth – a kingdom in which man made his own fate and did not have to look to heaven for help or consolation.

Marx's metaphysical project of making a better world by producing nothing less than a new type of man who, once in power, would give up its trappings, left the course of the ultimate movement of history – the question how the new society was to function under 'the rule of the proletariat' – in a hazy fog and as open to controversy as the question what paradise looks like.

The 'dictatorship of the proletariat' is nowhere mentioned in *The Communist Manifesto*. That loaded term did not appear in the Marxian vocabulary until March 1850, and its meaning was to become the subject of hot contention throughout the 20th century. All that Marx allowed in the *Manifesto* was that the revolution – ultimately to be staged by the entire proletariat, of which his own Communist League was only the vanguard – was to be the first made on behalf of a majority of the people. It was therefore also to be the last.

Vagueness is of course not incompatible with prophecy, and may sometimes be its complement. If there was a supermundane aspect to Marx's proclamation, it stemmed from his feeling that he knew 'the end of the days' and the fact that, like the will of Jehovah in the Old Testament account – which is 'beyond human verification' and contains 'no forecast that would permit a critical test before the end of historical time' – Marx's Communist programme could not be tested before it was put into effect.[26]

It was this aspect, coupled with the messianist longing in the hearts of men and Marx's prophetic, universalist tone that were to catch the imagination of people and lend the secular *Communist Manifesto* a hallowed gospel-like aura; so much so, that in later days, when Lenin was young, Russian revolutionaries agitating for Marxism would still speak of its aims in such misty terms as 'building a kingdom of justice, a kingdom of truth'.

Marx and Engels, brooking no opposition and increasingly behaving like some papal authority preserving holy writ against blasphemers, ultimately encouraged their image as the founders of a new religion. Fanatic in their hatred of the bourgeoisie and the whole political-social system in which they lived, feeling superior to both the 'enemy' and their own partisans, they gained strength from their single-mindedness in relating absolutely everything to the class struggle, but it also blinded them to all other forces, rational, supra-rational or irrational, that shaped history by causing religious, ethnic or nationalist conflict.

Frock-coated, with a thick black mane, Karl Marx, when carving out the hot angry pages of *The Communist Manifesto* in January 1848, was delineating the exact path the proletariat had to follow to conquer the future. Already in *The German Ideology* he had declared that 'the Communists do not preach morality at all';[27] and Engels was later to write in his and Marx's name that 'we reject every attempt to impose on us any moral dogma whatsoever... Morality has always been a class morality [which] has justified the domination and the interests of the ruling class.'[28]

Marx, about to become the infallible head of a new dogma, rose against monstrous injustice but chose to ignore the possibility that other men might have a developed sense of justice, morality or freedom – in short, a conscience – not influenced by their social condition. In the Communist society of the future there would presumably be a new kind of love – not the love which destroyed families by turning women and children into factory slaves; a new kind of freedom, and not the liberty for some to exploit others; even a new kind of justice, and not the unjust conditions which made the poor and starving commit most of the crimes.

For the rest, bourgeois literati, poets and scientists – and not only merchants and manufacturers – were described in the *Manifesto* as no better than 'paid hirelings of the system'. When he was charged with sedition in Cologne a year later, his acquittal by a bourgeois jury did not change his mind that bourgeois jurors – along with doctors, curates and all the rest of them – might be moved by anything but class considerations.

Carl Schurz, a revolutionary Bonn student who later emigrated to the USA, where he became a Senator and eventually Secretary of the Interior, was present at a democratic conference addressed by Marx a couple of months after he wrote *The Communist Manifesto*. In his memoirs Schurz was to recall the 30-year-old Marx as a figure who attracted general attention, and whose utterances were full of substance and 'meaning, logical and clear'. But, Schurz went on,

> I have never seen a man whose bearing was so provoking and intolerant. To no opinion which differed from his own did he accord the honour of even condescending consideration. Everyone who contradicted him he treated with abject contempt... I remember most distinctly the cutting disdain with which he pronounced the word bourgeois; and as a bourgeois – that is, as a detestable example of the deepest mental and moral degeneracy – he denounced everyone that dared to oppose his opinion.[29]

When Marx later heard of Stephan Born's amazing success in organizing the Berlin workers, he contemptuously dismissed 'Herr Born's idea of modest social reforms'. For Marx thought of revolution in different terms. The revolution he contemplated when he wrote the *Manifesto* was to be 'the greatest political take-over in history', and not a matter of gaining 'a bit of political influence here and there.'

On 6 January 1848, the *Deutsche Brüsseler Zeitung* reported on the New Year's Eve celebration of the German Workers' Society, and highlighted the toast Marx had proposed to Belgian liberalism. The celebration had ended with a 'speech to the ladies' delivered by Hess. After a night of merriment and dancing, Karl and Jenny Marx, Friedrich Engels and Mary Burns, Moses Hess and Sibyl Pesch, heavy with food and drink, made their way through the confetti carpeting the floor of The Swan towards the exit strewn with sawdust. Tired but exuding good fellowship, they parted from each other and the revellers around them to cheerful cries of 'Happy New Year!' When they stepped out into the cold with their ladies and greeted the dawn of 1848 in the Grand'Place of Brussels, it was the last time the three early architects of Communism would ever be seen together.

On 14 January, Engels, who had left Brussels for Paris immediately after the New Year, reported to Marx that things were 'going wretchedly with the [Communist] League here'. Describing the German journeymen who constituted most of its membership as sluggish 'jackasses' who remained devoted to the ideas of Weitling and Proudhon, he wrote that some of them were 'ageing boors, others are aspiring petty bourgeois [and] nothing can be done... I am making one last attempt, and if it doesn't work, I will give up.'

Engels thus admitted the failure of his year-long attempt to carry the Paris branch. He had underhandedly got its leaders to adopt his version of a Communist credo, but the last its rank and file had heard was Hess's version – and

now they refused to rally to a banner in the colour of the Marx-Engels programme, just as it was about to be openly unfurled in the final text of the forthcoming *Communist Manifesto*. Unable to win them over or to rope in the French
democrats either, Engels sounded rather put out, but hoped that the appearance of the *Manifesto* would do the trick.[30]

The February rising of the Paris students and workers was only a month
away when Marx received Engels's letter. As he intensified his labours on the
Manifesto to meet the 1 February deadline given him by the London Central
Authority, he had no idea of the revolution that would spread like a forest fire
from Paris to Prague and from Italy to Hungary, at first bearing out his highest
hopes, only to end in bitter disappointment.

With Engels urging Marx publicly on 14 January to attack Hess or to 'send
him into exile', and seeing that Hess's refusal to abide by their strategy and
tactics seemed indeed unforgivable on the eve of the revolution, it was long
thought that the section of their jointly signed *Manifesto* attacking Germany's
reprehensible 'utopian' or 'true Socialists' was chiefly directed against Hess. The
'true Socialists' were blasted not only for their writings full of 'sorry "eternal
truths", all skin and bone... steeped in the dew of sickly sentiment', but for
being reactionaries whose ethical Socialism 'served the absolute governments as
a welcome scarecrow against the threatening bourgeoisie... just at the time
[when] these same governments dosed the German working-class risings with
floggings and bullets.'[31]

At that, Hess was nowhere mentioned by name in the *Manifesto*. Since to
brand him even by allusion as a reactionary smacked of falsifying history, the
question whether he was really the chief unnamed target of Marx's attack in
this particular section of the *Manifesto* was to exercise scholars until late into
the 20th century. It became all the trickier in 1966, when Edmund Silberner, in
the first modern biography of Hess, wrote that 'clear allusions' in the *Manifesto*
pointed to him. Silberner stressed, however – as did Robert Tucker about the
same time – that Hess had never been a 'true Socialist'. Indeed, Engels admitted as much in a three-line note he wrote before his death, in which he named
Karl Grün – and not Hess – as the chief representative of the 'shabby' group
designated in the *Manifesto* as 'true Socialists'.[32]

But this note was soon forgotten, and Engels's constant mockery of Hess in
his correspondence, followed by the Marxist thinker Georg Lukacz in 1926 dismissing Hess as a tragic figure of a theorist 'brought to ruin by his contact with
materialist dialectic', had the combined effect that for decades thereafter Hess –
in a spate of literature to be produced in East Germany, but not only there – was
disqualified, sometimes in Stalinist fashion, either on the grounds of his 'ethical
utopianism', or his lack of dialectical sharpness and historic perspective.[33]

In fact, Hess was the leader of the school of German philosophical Communism. Marx himself, in his middle age, wrote that when he and Engels set to work on *The German Ideology* in the spring of 1845, 'we resolved... to settle our accounts with our former philosophic conscience.'[34] As Robert Tucker put it, Marx reached the idea of the proletariat by 'the philosophical path' and by 'the doctrine of human self-alienation he had developed under the primary influence of Hegel, Feuerbach and Hess.'[35]

Settling accounts with his own past may of course have made Marx's vituperations against the 'true Socialists' – the label under which he lumped together his rival post-Hegelian German Socialist philosophers – all the more violent. But this does not prove that Hess was the unnamed target of his attack in the *Manifesto*. That question and its twin – whether there was a final rupture between Marx and Hess in 1848 – were laid to rest only in 1982, when S. Na'aman, contesting earlier opinions that there was 'a complete break' between the two and they never resumed relations, emphasized that there was no 'resumption of relations' because relations were never broken off. Na'aman observed that the treatment meted out to Hess after their discord in 1848 was entirely different from Marx's ruthless assault on Proudhon, 'the purging' of Weitling, the liquidation of Grün, Kriege and other dissidents.

Those of them who had been members of the Communist League were simply expelled, and Marx and Engels never again collaborated with the others or any organization to which they belonged. By contrast, Hess was treated like a Communist whose tendencies and capabilities as 'the intellectual head of a potential opposition movement' were 'harmful to the party', one with whom one lives in tension or excludes. 'But no exclusion ever took place.'[36] Indeed, Marx and Hess, during their long years as the frustrated exiles of a failed revolution – Marx in London, and Hess in Geneva and eventually in Paris – kept closely watching and growling at each other. But it is significant that in the autumn of 1867 Hess, always ready to put past feuds and grudges behind him, was to do his utmost in Paris to arrange for Marx's *Das Kapital* to be translated into French. This resulted in a series of discreet and indirect contacts – with Marx's wife writing from London on his behalf to Hess's wife Sibyl. Marx, through another intermediary, hedged his approval of a French translation of *Das Kapital* with so many conditions that nothing came of it at the time.

In 1868, Hess – who had by then helped to found the large German Social Democratic Party – began to attend congresses of the First International, and Marx grudgingly applauded one of his 'excellent' speeches. Not only that, but their joint opposition to the Proudhonists and Bakunin led to a quasi-revival of their 'symbiosis of ideas' – climaxed by Hess's acting on several occasions as

Marx's personal representative when Marx was unable to attend congresses of the International in Brussels or Basle.[37]

On the eve of the 1848 revolution, however, Engels – though unsuccessful in his attempt to persuade Marx to get rid of Hess – had every reason for satisfaction. His year-long 'character assassination' of Hess, mixing ideology with personal vendetta, had by then assured him the coveted seat next to the 'pontiff'.

The reasons why Marx preferred to have Engels by his side were many and varied. Added to his priceless familiarity with factory conditions in both Germany and England, his youthful energy, zeal, polemical and propagandistic talent, not to mention the invaluable financial life-line he was to extend to Marx to his last day and his readiness to serve him loyally in every way, was Engels's boundless optimism, which was to keep up Marx's spirits through his prolonged labours and frequent disappointments.

Henceforth it was no longer Marx alone, but the two of them, against the world. It was a great comfort to Marx to have a lieutenant who not only relieved him of some of his burdens but helped him to clarify his ideas; and a paramount factor in their unique relationship was Engels's complaisant submission to Marx's authority and his readiness to play second fiddle to him. Lest it be thought that this is based on guesswork, the foxy Engels, shortly after Marx's death, was to write with satisfaction and without false modesty: 'All my life I have done what I was cut out for – namely to play second fiddle – and I think that I have done quite well in that capacity. And I have been glad to have had such a wonderful first violin as Marx.'[38]

One of the first people Engels had gone to see on his return to Paris at the beginning of January 1848 was Heinrich Heine. On the 14th he wrote to Marx in Brussels:

> It is nearly all up with Heine. I visited him a fortnight ago and he was in bed, having had a nervous fit. Yesterday he was up but extremely ill. He can hardly manage three steps now; supporting himself against the wall, he crawls from armchair to bed and vice versa. On top of that, the noise in his house, cabinet-making, hammering, etc., is driving him mad.

Heine's physical condition had taken a turn for the worse in September, at the end of a quiet summer he had spent at Montmorency. Installed in a rented house with a large beautiful garden, he hoped that the country air and quiet would calm his nerves. Before leaving Paris he had declared that he wanted to see no more doctors: 'I have noticed that all those who died last winter each had a doctor.'

Mathilde, a country-born girl, happily looked after the flower beds and picked fruit, and on Sundays some of Heine's friends – Théophile Gautier with his mistress; Alphonse Royer with his wife; the journalist Alexandre Weill with the latest Paris gossip and Heinrich Seuffert, the correspondent of the *Augsburger Allgemeine Zeitung* with the latest news from Germany – would come to see them and they would have a champagne party.

In July 1847 Heine had heard from the poet Freiligrath of the foundation of the Communist League in London. Freiligrath further informed him that the 'German West End Communist Society opens its Friday meetings with a prayer-like recital of your Silesian Weavers song.'

While German newspapers that summer carried reports of his death, Heine wrote to his mother on 27 July that he was relatively well and leading a quiet peaceful country existence. Because of his eye trouble he had decided to engage a secretary in the winter. In August he sent greetings to Marx and his wife and said that he hoped to visit them in Brussels. In September the Princess Belgiojoso informed him that she had found a new apartment for him in Paris and would come to Montmorency and tell him the details.

That visit never took place. On 20 September Heine informed her that for the last fortnight he had been unable to walk. His paralysis had suddenly spread to the stomach and legs. He returned to his old Paris quarters in the rue Poissonière. But in October he moved to the apartment the princess had chosen for him in the rue de la Victoire. This soon turned out to be a disaster. 'My infamous landlord', Heine wrote to his mother in the winter, 'has illegally installed his horses directly beneath my bedroom and their all-night stomping robs me of my sleep.'[39]

It was in that noisy apartment that Engels called on him. Heine never revealed his true condition to his mother. Although he wrote that he was spending most days away from home, the last time he had been out was a few days before or after Engels's visit, when, taking a cab to call on Caroline Jaubert, he had himself carried up by his servant to her apartment on the second floor. 'No sooner was he laid on a couch in the salon', she was to write, 'than he was overcome by a terrible cramp which contorted him from head to foot.' Later she learned that the pain of these seizures could only be relieved by the application of hot cones of morphine to the spinal column and that Heine was spending up to 500 francs a year for this calming poison.

The moment he recovered from his seizure, he told Caroline Jaubert that his disease was incurable and that he had come to make her promise that she would never desert him. Then, for comic relief from an embarrassing situation, he joked: 'What a fine hero I should have made for a novelist had I died under your roof...'[40] To add to his troubles, in January Mathilde had some kind of nervous fit, and when she was given a drink she bit the glass and broke it with her teeth, causing Heine no little 'panic' before the splinters were extracted from her mouth. 'Human life so often hangs on a thread,' he wrote to his mother.

At the end of that month they moved to another apartment at 9 rue de Berlin. But Mathilde had barely finished scrubbing and furbishing it when, on 6 February, Heine had to be taken to a private hospital. On the 16th he wrote: 'For the last ten days I have been at my friend Faultrier's *maison de santé*.' Mathilde and her friend Pauline moved in with him. Bedridden, 'unable to walk two steps', yet sometimes driving out in a carriage, Heine was to stay there until the first week of May.

That was his condition when the revolution started in Paris in February.

36

The February Revolution in Paris: 'The Madness of God' Unleashed

In Paris during the morning of Tuesday, 22 February 1848, a column of students and workers began to wind its way from the Panthéon across the Seine to the Madeleine. There were shouts of 'Down with Guizot', and in clashes with troops and sporadic violence 5 people were killed. That evening, the chairs of cafés along the Champs-Elysées were set on fire, but by midnight order seemed to have been restored.

The February revolution which set Europe aflame for the next two years was completely unpremeditated. Originally, on that day 140 opposition deputies were to have staged a political banquet expressing their disgust with the government. Seventy such extra-parliamentary manifestations had been held during the winter, but this was the first to be accompanied by a popular protest march to the banquet hall. Neither Odilon Barrot nor Ledru-Rollin nor Louis Blanc – the leaders of the opposition from Right to Left – had planned a revolution. With Guizot threatening to forbid the whole affair, they had in fact on the 19th tacitly reached a face-saving agreement with the government. The banqueters, accompanied by students and unarmed National Guards, would march to a tent in the Champs-Elysées. A police officer would declare the proceedings illegal. Odilon Barrot would protest the right of public assembly, but would ask the crowd to disperse quietly; the case would then be taken to court.

On Monday the 21st, however, three radical newspapers leaked details of the National Guard's marching orders in the following day's procession. The government promptly banned both the banquet and the procession, on the grounds that for a political committee to call out the Guard was illegal. The opposition leaders, remembering the heavy hand with which Louis-Philippe had suppressed larger insurrections, thereupon cancelled all the proceedings planned for the morrow.

The February revolution was thus launched by students, radical neighbourhood leaders and veteran demonstrators who had either not heard of the cancellation or decided to take things into their own hands. The opposition leaders' loss of control of the situation was matched by miscalculations on the part of the King's men. Having breathed a sigh of relief at the apparent restoration of calm on Tuesday night, they awoke on Wednesday morning to a mounting drama. The people of Paris took to the streets. Barricade after barricade went up, and members of the National Guard were reported to be joining the demonstrators. This was an ominous development, seeing that the part-time National Guard was a governmental organization officered by men of property belonging to the privileged 240,000 entitled to vote and supposed to defend the 'bourgeois monarchy'. Extending the franchise to 9,000,000 other Frenchmen had been the whole object of the reform banquets.

The government had 30,000 regular soldiers waiting in the rain to restore order, but the 75-year-old king, declaring that he had seen enough blood, chose to sacrifice Guizot instead. While Guizot went to the Chamber of Deputies and informed his stupefied majority that they were no longer in power, Molé was appointed Prime Minister in the afternoon. He lasted for exactly 6 hours, during which crowds of workers from the Faubourg Saint-Antoine, waving flags and torches, pressed so close on troops guarding the Foreign Office in the boulevard des Capucines that the soldiers could not fix bayonets. In the ensuing mêlée a shot was fired, and before any one knew it, 50 or so casualties lay on the ground. Both sides recoiled in panic, but the insurgents loaded 16 of their dead on a cart and paraded them by torchlight through Les Halles to the centre of Paris.

At 1 a.m. on Thursday, 24 February, Thiers was summoned to the Tuileries Palace and charged to form a government which, as a sop to the 'reformers' and to save the monarchy, was to include Odilon Barrot, the leader of the Dynastic Left. At dawn, General Bugeaud, the hero of the Algerian war, was placed in command of the regular army. He sent 4 columns from the Tuileries to clear the way to and ensure the safety of such strategic objectives as the Hôtel de Ville, the Panthéon and the Place de la Bastille. They encountered a maze of new barricades, but while the first two objectives were secured, the column working its way towards the Place de la Bastille found its progress barred. The commanding officer sent for instructions to General Bugeaud, but by this time, within an hour or so from the start, King Louis-Philippe – giving in to Thiers and other advisers – had abandoned the whole scheme.

The troops were ordered to return to the Tuileries without firing a shot. The National Guard, this time called out by the government itself, was to take their place in the streets. The hope was that the appearance of the popular citizens' militia and the formation of the new Thiers-Barrot government would pacify the insurgents, and Barrot was sent out to make the announcement. It has been said of this ill-conceived decision that 'the government had mobilized a demonstration against itself.'[1] For although numbers of the National Guard's conservative officers stayed at home, its other ranks, who took over the barricades, saw in the fall of Guizot the prospect of 'reforms' that would give them the vote and a say in the affairs of the country, and so they fraternized with the insurgents.

The result was that some of the retreating army units began to disintegrate. To the amnestied leaders of such secret societies as the Droits de l'Homme, the 'Families' and 'Seasons', on the other hand, the fall of Guizot was a signal that with the smallest violent push they could turn this into a true revolution and topple the monarchy and the whole 'corrupt system'; and the reception Barrot was given was such that he turned on his heels and went home.

At the Tuileries, shortly before noon on Thursday, an alarming report was received that the army in dissolution might not be able to defend the palace. The King mounted his horse and, accompanied by his two sons and a cavalcade of officers, with the diminutive Thiers following on foot, turned out to review his troops drawn up in the courtyard. As he rode down the ranks of the National Guard, two of its legions cried 'Vive le Roi!' but a third broke ranks and shouted 'A bas les ministres! A bas le système!!' Louis-Philippe – without so much as a glance at 4,000 regular troops who were loyal to him – turned his horse and rode back into the palace, where he sank into a chair.

It is not known whether his hesitation to throw in this and other army reserves, which even at this moment could have repulsed the insurgents, was due to a failure of nerve or his abhorrence of bloodshed. General Bugeaud wanted to fight, but was restrained, and the King later rationalized that if he had allowed a bloodbath, he would have been charged with putting his own selfish interests above those of the French people. He accused the government, the opposition and the National Guard of having each 'abdicated' their roles, but gave himself away by saying that he had supported Guizot's anti-reformist policies because to lend his hand to any reform would have meant 'the advent of the opposition, which in turn would have meant war!' The fact is that France had no government; all authority had broken down, and in the general anarchy the police – who knew the names of the leaders of the insurrection and their meeting-places and could easily have arrested them from the start – kept away from the streets.[2]

The culmination of the drama came shortly after noon, when shots were heard at the palace from the Place du Palais Royal. There, some 200 metres away, a large insurgent mob had set fire to a building and was starting to massacre the soldiers defending it. After receiving contradictory advice to abdicate or to hold on to the throne to avoid 'the Republic within the hour', the King turned to Marshals Soult and Gérard and asked: 'Is any defence possible?' Their answer was silence. Louis-Philippe thereupon went to his desk, which had once been Napoleon's, and, declaring that he did not wish 'to spill French blood in vain', wrote that he was abdicating the crown 'in favour of my grand-son the [10-year-old] Comte de Paris.'

Courtiers and politicians left the palace in a panic. The King changed into bourgeois attire and asked for his keys, but in his haste forgot to take any money from the Tuileries treasury. Twelve carriages had been ordered from the royal stables, but due to fighting in the vicinity only two managed to get out and the groom leading them was shot dead before they reached the Tuileries.

The King, with the Queen on his arm mumbling 'treason', walked through the garden to the Place de la Concorde. There, together with their son Mont-pensier and his family, they found themselves surrounded by a dense crowd of spectators while waiting for two one-horse broughams and a cabriolet which their youngest living son, Prince Nemours, had had the foresight to order. A cavalry escort arrived in time to protect the party. The King waved his hat to the crowd and said a few indistinct words. As he mounted the first brougham, an unknown man stepped up and closed the portiere. To the King's thanks, the man replied: 'Don't mention it. I have waited seventeen years for this day.'

The cavalcade disappeared on the road to Saint-Cloud. Left behind in the empty Tuileries were Nemours and his sister-in-law, the widowed duchesse d'Orléans and mother of the Comte de Paris, the heir and king-presumptive, and another younger child. Preparing to face another drama, Nemours had the troops in the courtyard withdraw to the Place de la Concorde, with special orders to a brigade to protect the bridge leading to the Chamber of Deputies in the Palais Bourbon, on the other side of the Seine.

At 1.30 p.m. he escorted the Duchess and her two children to the Chamber, where they took their seats to a burst of applause. It was hoped that parliament, which had legitimized the Orléans branch in 1830, would accept the Duchess (or failing that, Nemours) as Regent for her son.

As Barrot, who had taken over from Thiers as prime minister designate, rose to propose the Regency, the Duchess got up to salute the Assembly, and so, clutching her hand, did the boy-king. Within minutes, however, an armed band of insurgents invaded the hall. The session turned into pandemonium, and the tumult subsided only when Lamartine, the poet-turned-politician, took the rostrum.

'How touching', he said, 'is the spectacle of a majestic princess pleading her cause with her innocent son, coming from a deserted palace to cast herself in the midst of the representatives of the people...' There were cries of 'Very good! very good!' But Lamartine went on to say that, much as he was moved, he felt 'no less respect for this splendid people who have fought to correct a perfidious government... So I demand that a provisional government be set up immediately...[Bravo! Bravo!].' Lamartine had not yet finished speaking when the door of one of the public galleries was forced open with rifle butts and more insurgents stormed into the hall. Amidst the mounting disorder, the parliamentary stenographers assiduously recorded the scene:

(*There are calls for a republic. The duchesse d'Orléans and her children have disappeared. Some of the intruders take over the rostrum.*)

> *Voice from the crowd.* No more Bourbons! – Down with the traitors! A provisional government immediately![3]

In the commotion, the Comte de Paris was separated from his mother. The frightened boy was seized by a National Guard and passed from hand to hand and out through a window to his crying mother. His little brother was picked up from the floor by an usher, who took him home and hid him for two days before returning him to the desolate Duchess. (Nemours had instructed the troops outside the Chamber to defend 'the freedom of deliberations' in the Chamber at all costs, but had not lifted the prohibition to fire.)

Inside the Chamber one of the invaders pointed a rifle at the President, who slid underneath his stand, wildly ringing his bell and declaring the session closed before he fled, as did many others. But the opposition deputies and the armed crowd behind them remained in the hall. Ledru-Rollin, the leader of the moderate republicans, read the names of 6 candidates for a provisional government who were chosen by shouts of 'Yes' or 'No'. Suddenly the voice of the actor Bocage, rising above the tumult, called for Lamartine to lead them to the City Hall, the traditional place for revolutionary rituals.

Shortly after 4 o'clock the newly 'elected' Ministers left the Palais Bourbon, followed by the crowd. 'In the street', as Victor Hugo was to write, they heard the word 'Republic... shouted everywhere, flying from mouth to mouth' and filling the air of Paris. At the Hôtel de Ville, overwhelmed by 'the splendour and terror of their triumph', with 'the noise of the multitude outside sounding like the roar of the ocean... they decreed the Republic without knowing that they were doing anything so momentous,' not before the following exchange:

'Lamartine: We must await the sanction of France... Who knows at present what the people want?

'Ledru-Rollin: I do... What the people want is the Republic at once, the Republic without delay.'[4]

Finally Lamartine wrote on a scrap of paper that 'The Provisional Government of France is the Republican Government', and that the nation would be called upon to ratify its decision. Ledru-Rollin affixed the seal of the City of Paris to it, but forgot to mention the date. Lamartine, Ledru-Rollin and the 4 other Ministers – moderate republicans all – signed it.

Shortly afterwards, in the euphoria of the moment, these electoral reformists agreed to unite with the radical Socialists. To the original list of 6 Ministers were added the names of Louis Blanc; Flocon, of the newspaper *La Réforme*; François Arago; and Albert, the pseudonym of a mechanic representing one of the secret societies.

At the abandoned Tuileries, a huge mob had meanwhile set fire to the throne. The royal apartments were ransacked, the books in the library flung through the windows. The King's armoured car, the famous 'fortress on wheels', was unceremoniously pushed into the Seine, while inside the palace loose women dressed up in court robes and danced on Louis-Philippe's bed and up and down the stairs. The barrels in the cellar had been broached early on, and the orgy of destruction ended only when several drunken revellers were found drowned in the sea of wine which had risen to the upper floors.

The first outbreak of almost 50 revolutions that swept the Continent in 1848 had occurred in January at Palermo when Ferdinand II, the Bourbon King of the Two Sicilies – nicknamed 'Bomba' for his cruel bombardment of Naples – was driven from his throne. But it was the February revolution in Paris, in which 72 soldiers and 289 insurgents were killed, that sparked off the general upheaval. Bakunin had long predicted a European 'storm' and Louis Blanc had predicted to Engels that the coming revolution would be 'much more drastic' than any before. But when it came, the speed of the developments which forced Louis-Philippe to flee to England disguised as 'Mr Smith' surprised all those who had foreseen it, including Blanc and the others who found themselves suddenly in power while Guizot was escaping to Germany pretending to be a servant to a foreign aristocrat. As Béranger, the popular Paris *chansonnier* who had appeared at many of the 'reform' banquets put it: 'We wanted to walk down the staircase, step by step, but were made to jump a whole floor.'

Although Louis-Philippe ostensibly 'lost the throne because 140 of his subjects could not banquet, toast and speechify',[5] an agglomeration of crises – bad harvests, economic slump, widespread unemployment – has been cited among the reasons for his downfall. The revolutionary ferment bubbling beneath the surface of French politics in the 1840s intensified under the rigid and unpopular Guizot, and once it found a spontaneous outlet, the bourgeois monarchy collapsed under the weight of its own misrule.

Few people were more excited by news of the events in Paris than the 'doctors of revolution'. When it all began, Marx in Brussels was attending a dinner at which 100 Belgian and German democrats commemorated the second anniversary of the Cracow uprising with speeches, toasts and singing. He wrote a few months later that 'The February revolution was the beautiful revolution...'

Bakunin was so electrified by the news that on 23 February, the second day of the insurrection, he left Brussels for Paris. The train stopped at the frontier, the railway tracks on the French side having been torn out. Bakunin walked into beflagged Valenciennes and, continuing his journey on foot, reached Paris on the 26th. Years later, still filled with emotion, he described the atmosphere of elation he found in the newly proclaimed Second Republic:

> Not I alone, but everyone was intoxicated. Some from insane fear, others from insane rapture, insane hopes... It was as though the whole world was turned upside down. The improbable became the usual; the impossible, the possible... If someone had come and told us 'God has just chased the devil from the heavens, and proclaimed a republic there' everyone would have believed him and none would have been surprised.[6]

Heine, who had predicted the end of the 'bourgeois comedy' years before it came, had never dreamt that he would be physically involved in it. On the evening of the 23rd, he had driven with Mathilde to his personal physician Dr Gruby. (According to another version they had gone to their home in the rue de Berlin to fetch something.) On the way back to the *maison de santé* in the rue de Lourcines they were caught in the street fighting. The cab was broken up by insurgent workers for use as a barricade. It was only with great difficulty that the invalid Heine and his wife were brought back to the clinic.

He could hardly see, but on 3 March he dictated the first of three articles for the *Augsburger Allgemeine Zeitung*. Praising the heroism of the workers who had braved death without expecting any reward in heaven, he stressed particularly the fact that, although the people had vented their fury at the Tuileries and the Palais Royal – the latter, as well as the Château de Neuilly and a Rothschild mansion full of art treasures had indeed been ransacked in an orgy of destruction lasting nearly a fortnight – there had been no looting. The rich feared for their money, but were surprised that the mob had taken only weapons and food 'by permission' from the royal residences they attacked. At the same time, he expressed a certain sympathy for Louis-Philippe, forced in old age to pick up his wandering staff again and go into exile in foggy England.

Heine was at first in two minds about the revolution. Privately he confessed that he was not a republican. But in his second article – which the *Allgemeine Zeitung* did not publish – he wrote that although 'the victory of the republic was perhaps a logical necessity', the dizzying speed of events made him wonder whether the affairs of this world were 'really guided by reason'. Lamartine, Blanc, Crémieux and the other members of the Provisional Government were all 'great paladins of humanity', but the marriage of convenience between moderate republicans and radical Socialists struck him from the beginning as being flawed by a lack of homogeneity and 'common affinities'. This lack of inner cohesion was indeed to prove fatal to the new government.

On 28 February, Marx, Engels and other leaders of the Association Démocratique in Brussels had sent a message of congratulations to the Provisional Government of the French Republic. In London on that day, *The Communist Manifesto* was finally coming off the press in a Communist printshop operating at 46 Liverpool Street. Its 500 German copies appeared too late to have any influence on the Continent in revolt, nor did the Danish, Swedish, French, Italian and Polish translations, which followed later in the year, play any part. The names of the authors did not appear on the original title-page, which carried only the slogan 'Proletarians of All Countries Unite'.

The Belgian republicans had started preparing an armed uprising, and the German workers too – with money provided by Marx – were beginning to arm. He had recently received 6,000 francs from his mother, representing the remainder of his inheritance. Without thinking of his family's penury or future needs, he 'willingly', as his wife was later to write, gave 5,000 for the purchase of 'daggers, revolvers, etc... In all this', she went on artlessly, 'the government saw conspiracy and criminal plans.' King Leopold, a son-in-law of Louis-Philippe, had indeed proclaimed martial law and there was a general clamp-down on local republicans and foreign agitators. Marx was engaged in a flurry of activity. He had applied to the French Provisional Government for a repeal of his earlier expulsion from Paris. This was immediately granted by Flocon, one of the new Ministers, in a letter of 1 March reading in part: 'Good and loyal Marx,... Tyranny exiled you, now free France opens its door to you and to all those who are fighting for the holy cause, the fraternal cause of all the people.'

The Central Authority of the Communist League in London, upon receiving news of the revolution, decided to move its operations to the Continent and transferred its powers to the Brussels branch. The Brussels group had just met on 3 March, and in a paper signed by Engels, Gigot and Marx, had devolved on Marx 'full discretionary powers to set up a new Central Authority in Paris', when he was handed an order signed by King Leopold giving him 24 hours to leave Belgium.

Later that night, Marx was held for questioning. Jenny, after rushing 'in terrible anxiety' to mobilize the lawyer Jottrand, went to the police headquarters, where she was promptly arrested and thrown into a dark cell with three prostitutes. One of them offered her a place on a hard plank bed:

> I lay down on it. When morning broke, I saw at the window opposite mine, behind iron bars, a cadaverous, mournful face. I recognized our

good old friend Gigot. When he saw me he beckoned to me, pointing downwards. I looked in that direction and saw Karl being led away under military escort.

She was brought before a judge for interrogation and released in the early afternoon. Marx came home a little later. Jenny 'hastily packed my belongings and sold what I could, but left my boxes with all my silver-plates and my best linen in Brussels in charge of the bookseller Vögler.'[7]

They left immediately for Paris with their three children, the youngest of whom was just a year old. After a number of delays and a detour by omnibus at Valenciennes, they took another train and put up in a Paris hotel on 5 March.

Bakunin had by then joined a new National Guard of workers in a barracks near the Luxembourg. The signs of revolution, uprooted pavement stones and smashed omnibuses, were still visible. Bakunin got up at 4 or 5 a.m., and was on his feet all day, taking 'an active, resolute part in all the assemblies, meetings, clubs, marches, demonstrations – in a word, I inhaled the revolutionary atmosphere through all my senses, through my pores.' Occasional visits to his old friend Herwegh were his only distraction. He regarded the revolution 'as a miracle... a feast without beginning or end.' At last he had established an 'electrifying contact' with the people who had 'the audacity to put the arm of destruction to work.' He extolled the heroism of the French workers, these 'simple uneducated people' who combined friendly gaiety with a sense of honour and a 'natural delicacy of behaviour'. But after a time he sobered up.

Caussidière, the new Prefect of Police and commander of the National Guard, did not fail to recognize the anarchist in Bakunin. 'What a man!' he said. 'On the first day of revolution he is a perfect treasure. On the second he ought to be shot.' And Flocon summed up his impression of Bakunin's revolutionary rhetoric and constitutional disinclination to submit to any discipline and organized work by remarking: 'If there were 300 Bakunins, it would be impossible to govern France.'[8]

On 8 March, two days after his arrival, Marx was reconstituting the Central Authority of the Communist League together with Schapper, Moll and Bauer, who had arrived from London. On that day, Engels, who in Brussels was dealing among other things with the liquidation of Marx's household and the dispatch of trunks, reported:

> Splendid news from Germany – in Nassau a revolution completed; in Munich... a full revolt; in Cassel revolution on the doorstep... in western Germany press freedom and National Guard proclaimed... If only Friedrich Wilhelm IV digs his heels in! Then all will be won and in a few months' time we'll have the German Revolution.[9]

On the same day, in Paris, 6,000 excited German workers staged a demonstration for a 'free fatherland'. But Marx was appalled by the way his friend Herwegh meant to ride to fame on their rebellious mood. Before Marx's arrival, the poet had fired a large gathering of artisans and workers with the idea of organizing a German Legion to march into the 'fatherland' and there – in alliance with its non-Communist or anti-Communist democrats and radicals – to proclaim a German Republic. Among others, Herwegh had the support of Dr Ewerbeck and of Börnstein and Bornstedt – the former editors of the Paris *Vorwärts!* and the *Deutsche Brüsseler Zeitung* respectively.

Marx strongly opposed this 'adventurist' plan. Failing to dissuade Herwegh, Marx and his associates founded a German Workers' Club in the hope of mobilizing 300 to 400 workers who would be sent to Germany individually to make Communist propaganda and spread the *Manifesto*. Marx told a public meeting that 'the victory or defeat of revolutionary Europe will depend on the struggle between the proletariat and the bourgeoisie that will soon break out here in Paris,' and advised the German workers not to move but to get ready to 'participate in this armed struggle'. He was booed and accused of being a traitor and a coward.

The Legion began rifle practice at a riding school in the Champs de Mars and Stephan Born was sent to spy on its exercises. The cafés where it met were boycotted by Marx and his friends. But the walls of Paris were soon plastered with posters appealing for 'arms, munitions and money' for Herwegh's crusade: 'Vive la France! Vive Poland! Vive a united republican Germany!'

Contrary to Marx's view that the fate of revolutionary Europe would be decided in Paris, Bakunin, having witnessed 'the birth of a new world', thought that the new French rulers had to be left to the practical job of consolidating their power. He saw no role for himself in that unglamorous work and instinct told him that 'the blaze' was moving elsewhere. In an article he wrote for *La Réforme*, he predicted, in this order, a) the destruction, 'perhaps in less than a year, of the monstrous Austrian Empire'; b) the liberation of Italy from the Austrian yoke; c) the unification of Germany and its proclamation as a republic; d) the return of the Polish democrats to their homeland after 17 years of exile.

He concluded with a flourish: 'The revolutionary movement will only stop when all of Europe, not excluding Russia, is turned into a federal democratic republic. Impossible, they will say? Careful now! That word belongs to yesterday...'[10]

His article had hardly appeared on 13 March when students and workers in Vienna clashed with troops. On the 14th, Metternich, having ruled the Austro-Hungarian empire in the name of the Habsburgs for more than 50 of his 75 years, was making his escape from Vienna in a laundry cart towards exile in

London. On the 15th, Hungary established a constitutional Ministry responsible to its own parliament, severing its link to Austria except for its allegiance to the Emperor. On the 17th, Venice declared itself a republic, and on the 18th, Milan rose in revolt to drive the Austrians from Lombardy in the 'Glorious Five Days'.

Amidst all these eruptions, revolution came to Berlin on 16 April. After two days of popular demonstrations which were brutally dispersed by the army, Friedrich Wilhelm IV – greatly surprised to see his 'beloved' people erecting barricades – promised them freedom of the press and a liberal Prussian and all-German constitution. Later in the day, an incident between two trigger-happy soldiers and a crowd of demonstrators in front of the royal palace escalated into an 8-hour street battle, in which several hundred people were killed.

On the 19th, with outraged Berliners demanding the withdrawal of the troops, the erratic King – to the intense dismay of the army and his own militant brother, who fled for his life – was frightened enough to give in and order his regiments to leave the city. In his patronizing manner, he did so in a proclamation in which he 'pardoned' the citizenry, on condition that they dismantled the barricades. Once Berlin was denuded of troops, a Civil Guard took over and, with arms taken from the unprotected Royal Arsenal, marched into the palace courtyard to parade their dead before the King, who – summoned with his wife to a balcony – was forced to pay his respects to the mutilated bodies of the victims of his army as the name of each was called out.

'Only the guillotine is missing now,' the Queen remarked during this gruesome ceremony. The King never forgot this humiliation, which put the Prussian military monarchy to shame but saved his throne. In Paris, the sensational events in Berlin aroused more excitement among the German émigrés than all the previous revolts in Munich, Cassel, Cologne and western Germany.

On 19 March, Herwegh's 'democratic' German Legion staged an armed march through the streets of Paris, to great applause from the sidewalks. On the 24th, its 2,000 or so men marched off, singing and waving the republican black-red-gold flag, in the direction of the Rhine, to be severely routed – as Marx had foreseen – a month or so later in western Germany.

Bakunin left Paris a week later. Although he supported Herwegh's reckless adventure for its sheer spontaneity, his interest was focused on events in the eastern region of the shaking Austro-Hungarian empire. There its Slav minorities, Poles, Czechs and Croatians, were stirring. In Prussian-held Posen a Polish National Committee had been formed with the tacit consent of the authorities. Suspecting that Prussia's intention was to use the 'Germanized Poles' in a war against Russia, Bakunin decided to go to Posen. Turning the tables upon Prussia, he would get the 'Germanized Poles' to unite with the rest of the liberated

Slavs 'in a war not against the Russian people' but against the Tsar. His plan 'to move nations this way and that' has been called nothing short of megalomania, for he had neither funds nor any new contacts with the Poles.

Money, however, was no problem. The French Provisional Government, busy with its own problems and eager to get rid of foreign agitators, had paid Herwegh's legionaires 50 centimes a day per man for their march to Germany. Flocon gave Bakunin 2,000 francs. Caussidière supplied him with two passports – one in his own name and another in that of an invented Pole, Leonard Neglinski. Thus equipped with two separate identities and still feverish with revolutionary ardour, Bakunin stopped for a while on his way to Posen in Frankfurt, where he met Professor Karl Vogt and other members of the newly convened Pre-Parliament (*Vorparlament*) to the proposed German National Assembly before he continued to Berlin.

There, on 22 April, he was promptly arrested. Since he was now a notorious international conspirator, the Russian as well as the French government kept track of his movements. Informed by them, the Prussian authorities, still shaken by the March uprising in Berlin, handled him like a hot potato. Bakunin was released on his word of honour that he would not go to Posen. His own passport was confiscated; Neglinski's was invalidated for Posen. The Russians were informed that Bakunin was being deported to Cologne. The French were told that he would on no account be handed over to the Russians.

In fact, he was given a third passport in the name of Simon, a Prussian subject, and allowed to proceed to Breslau (Wroclaw), where other revolutionary Poles conducted propaganda against Austria and Russia rather than Prussia. He stopped for a day in Leipzig and upset Arnold Ruge by dragging him to a champagne dinner and making him miss a meeting at which he expected to be elected to the Frankfurt National Assembly. They were still dining when Ruge was informed that another candidate had been elected in his place. Bakunin, having heard from Vogt in Frankfurt of the disunity attending the birth of the National Assembly, told him not to worry: 'The Parliament will produce nothing but rhetoric. After the Slavic Revolution we will compensate you for the ingratitude of the philistine Saxon electors.'

The following morning, 26 April, he left for Breslau.

Marx, too, was being forced to revise his opinion that Paris was the epicentre of the European revolution, and had decided to go to Germany. On one of the first days of April he went to say farewell to Heine at the *maison de santé* in the rue de Fourcine. No record has survived of this visit except that it took place, and for all that is known, Marx may have gone away with the impression that there was no hope for Heine. The following day, he and his family, along with a number of adherents travelling singly or in groups – the journey subsidized by the French Provisional Government – left Paris for Cologne.

Accompanied by Engels, they arrived there on 11 April. While the other Communist returnees went to different places in Germany, each man 'carrying with him the salvation of the world' in the form of *The Communist Manifesto* and a 17-point flysheet entitled 'Demands of the Communist Party in Germany', Marx chose for his base the city where he had first made his name as editor of the *Rheinische Zeitung*. Georg Weerth had told him in a letter that their Cologne friends Drs Daniel and d'Ester were planning to revive this newspaper and that in view of the new press freedom, he could be more effective if he came over 'instead of sitting in Paris'.

While Jenny and her three children were to spend the next three months in Trier, Marx applied to the Cologne authorities for a residence permit and for restoration of his Prussian citizenship. He was granted the first but not the second, and almost immediately became engaged in simultaneous combat on several fronts. On 7 April a Cologne newspaper had carried a notice inviting subscriptions to the revived *Rheinische Zeitung*, signed not by Daniel and d'Ester, but by Hess and Fritz Anneke, a Prussian ex-officer and member of the Communist League. A foundation meeting for the Hess-Anneke project took place on 12 April, the day after Marx's arrival.

A race developed between the two competing groups for the reissue of the paper as the *Neue Rheinische Zeitung*. Hess was in touch with two financiers in Aachen and had enlisted the Communist journalist Louis Heilberg to act as London correspondent and Dr Ewerbeck to cover the Paris scene for the paper. Stephan Born, too, who was at the time in Berlin, was ready to write for Hess's paper. And Hess had a powerful ally in Dr Andreas Gottschalk, the leader of Cologne's Communist League branch and otherwise a physician who, looking for years after the sick and infirm in the city's poorest quarters, had, in spite of being Jewish, achieved an extraordinary popularity among the workers.

On 3 March, together with Anneke and August Willich, another ex-Prussian officer, Gottschalk had organized the greatest mass demonstration before the Berlin revolt, leading a crowd of 4,000 to the town hall square. Gottschalk and Willich broke into the council chamber and presented the city fathers with their demands – universal suffrage, press freedom, a civil guard, state responsibility for employment and education. The army dispersed the crowd outside. Gottschalk, Anneke and Willich were arrested, but released after the victory of the revolution in Berlin.

On 13 April Gottschalk, who was a Communist but not of Marx's denomination, founded a Workers Union which, within the next 10 weeks, recruited no fewer than 8,000 members. It was against this background that the battle for the *Rheinische Zeitung* was fought between the Hess-Anneke-Gottschalk group and Marx and Engels. The promoters of both projects had difficulties in raising the share capital for the newspaper. Marx sent Engels to the Rhineland and other emissaries to various German cities to sell shares and to gauge the possibility of establishing a nation-wide proletarian party. On 25 April, Engels reported to Marx from his native Barmen that 'even the radical bourgeois here see us as their future main enemies and have no intention of putting into our hands weapons which we would very shortly turn against themselves.' Marx had urged him to pump his father, but Engels wrote: 'Sooner than present us with 1,000 Thaler, he would pepper us with a thousand balls of grapeshot.'[11]

Schapper, Wilhelm Wolff and Born – who had variously gone to Mainz, Wiesbaden, Breslau and Berlin – sent back similarly disheartening reports. The 'invasion' from France of Herwegh's Republican Legion and his attempt to assist an uprising in Baden, although defeated, had caused a general change of mood. 'Republic' became a scare-word and Communists the object of public wrath; in all of Frankfurt only two people dared confess that they were Communists, for fear of being stoned to death. The vaunted Communist League branches were in disarray or had simply ceased to exist, and the consensus of all emissaries was that there was not the least chance of organizing a proletarian party.

Gottschalk, whose new Workers Union was going from strength to strength, had already resigned from the disintegrating Communist League. The maintenance of the secret League in the new conditions of press freedom caused a split between Marx and his associates. Marx argued that since propaganda could now be conducted openly the League had become superfluous as a political instrument. Although, as McLellan has remarked, this only 'argued for the continuance of an open Communist League', Marx, in a decision that caused a century-long controversy, cut 'the Gordian knot' and – over the opposition of Schapper and Moll – invoked his discretionary powers and dissolved the League.[12]

He did this all the more readily as by mid-May he and Engels had won the race for the *Neue Rheinische Zeitung* and a platform for propagating their ideas. Although only 13,000 Thaler of the projected capital of 30,000 had been raised, Marx threw in the little that was left of his inheritance money, and they decided to launch the newspaper on 1 June. Hess's project had fallen through at the end of April because of the refusal of his Aachen financiers to grant him absolute editorial freedom.[13]

Simultaneously, and from the very beginning, Marx had engaged in a dispute with Gottschalk, challenging the policy of his 'social and democratic' Workers Union. A quarter of Cologne's artisans and manual workers were unemployed, and the success of Gottschalk's Union has been ascribed to his immense popularity and his skillful representation of their interests. He not only got the municipality to launch a public works programme, but his Union functioned as a political club and also a breeding-ground of trade unionism. Gottschalk divided the Union into occupational sections, and in the prevailing economic crisis of lower wages and lengthened hours these sections had more than enough to do. 'They worked out wage rates, established standards for the working day, busied themselves with conditions of labour. The workers brought their troubles and needs to the Union as though it was omnipotent.'[14]

The difference of views between Marx and Gottschalk came to a head during a violent discussion in May concerning the elections to the Prussian Constituent Assembly and the all-German National Assembly in Frankfurt. Gottschalk was for boycotting both elections on the grounds that the indirect voting system practically disenfranchised the workers in some states. Marx argued that so long as the proletariat did not exist as a mass party it must cooperate with the liberal bourgeoisie in a 'united front' with all democratic elements active in Germany. To Marx, Gottschalk was an ultra-leftist. He sharply criticized him – as he was later to criticize Born's independent activities among the Berlin workers – for 'isolating the proletariat from its allies.'

Gottschalk, on the other hand, had the immediate interests of the workers at heart. Marx and Engels struck him as theorists who cared little for 'the salvation of the oppressed. The distress of the workers, the hunger of the poor have only a scientific doctrinaire interest for them.' At first, Gottschalk had the upper hand, for the majority of the Workers Union sided with him. Six weeks or so later, however, the authorities indirectly cleared the way for Marx to infiltrate the Union by arresting Gottschalk for subversion and keeping him in jail for the next 6 months. By the time he was acquitted the following January, the Union had split in two, and he and Marx were to resume their conflict in changed circumstances.

The first issue of the *Neue Rheinische Zeitung* appeared on 1 June 1848. It was subtitled 'Organ of Democracy', and several pieces of Marx's policy now fell into place. The full title of the dissolved League's recent manifesto was 'Manifesto of the Communist Party'; now, for as long as it was to last, the *Neue Rheinische Zeitung* became 'the party'. In conformity with the programme of action enunciated in the *Manifesto*, Marx and Engels wanted to see the bourgeoisie lifted into the saddle. Under no circumstances did they want the kind of spontaneous proletarian revolt led by Gottschalk. Nor were they interested in trade unions or in petty social improvements. It is a fact that of more than 120 articles they contributed between them to the *Neue Rheinische Zeitung* during 1848 – the majority by Marx, and some 40-odd by Engels – only one dealt with the fate of the working class during the revolution; and it is another little-known fact that, not long after completion of *The Communist Manifesto*, they were trying to suppress it in Germany in order not to estrange the bourgeois financial supporters of their newspaper.[15]

The 17-point 'Demands of the Communist Party' were likewise abandoned. Before returning from the Rhineland and joining Marx again in Cologne on 21 May, Engels had written to him: 'If even a single copy of our 17 points were to circulate here all would be lost for us.'[16]

Since their arrival in Cologne they had been urging the workers to join the 'democratic' societies that sprang up all over Germany. The *Neue Rheinische Zeitung*, planned from the beginning as a national newspaper operating as the left, but not ultra-left, wing of the democratic movement, would give them the necessary guidance. Revolution was a long process of history, and when the time was ripe for the working class to rise under the Communist banner, they would give the signal for it.

For the moment, as Engels was later to sum up the policy of the *Neue Rheinische Zeitung*, to display that banner would have confined them to remaining 'a small sect'. But 'instead of crying in the wilderness', they chose to become 'a great party of action by taking our stand under the banner of democracy (and focusing on two main objectives): a single, indivisible, democratic German republic, and war with Russia which will bring the restoration of Poland.'[17]

In one of its first articles, the paper ridiculed the proceedings of the German National Assembly, or Parlament, which had opened on 18 May in the rotunda of the old Pauluskirche in Frankfurt. This article cost the paper half its 'democratic' shareholders. The great majority of the 830 Deputies assembled in Frankfurt were lawyers, doctors, ministers, civil servants, bankers, merchants and manufacturers and landowners. More than 500 of them – apart from 100 professors, scholars and writers – were university-educated. There had never been 'a more highly educated parliament'. It included no statesmen with practical political experience, nor a single worker, the lower classes being represented by 4 guild-masters and one peasant. The purpose of the Assembly was to draft a progressive constitution for a united Germany, but no one knew how to turn three dozen large and small autocratic German states into a democracy or whether this was to take the form of a monarchy, an empire or a republic. Besides being unable to reach a consensus on its boundaries, the Assembly had no army to enforce its decisions. Nor were Prussia and Austria really ready to be absorbed into a new German nation.

The result was that while one of the Assembly's committees drafted a great constitution for Germany which was never enacted, the so-called Parlament spent its time in long-winded debates and became, in Marx's words, 'a tedious philistine farce'.

War with Russia seemed to Marx the only way of putting an end to all divisions and pumping new life into the hesitant revolution of the German bourgeoisie. Overthrowing the Russian bastion of reaction would topple all the German autocracies at one blow: 'If Germany could be brought to war with Russia, it would be all up with Habsburgs and Hohenzollerns, and the revolution would be victorious all along the line.'[18]

The *Neue Rheinische Zeitung* covered all developments – the Austrian bombardment of Prague, the insurrection of the French workers which led to the bloody 'June Days' in Paris, the second and third revolutions in Vienna and all the fluid events that kept Europe in turmoil during the 14 months of its existence – and linked them in a broad perspective as interactive parts of Europe's revolutionary struggle. Since that struggle was ultimately defeated, the altogether 227 articles Marx and Engels were to contribute to the paper might have mouldered in some Socialist archives had not Lenin come upon them in 1914. Three years before he was to arrive at the Finland Station on the eve of the Bolshevik Revolution, he found in them an 'unsurpassed' model of the revolutionary fighting spirit at its best.

Bakunin, who had stopped in Breslau on his way to Posen, never got there. In May, after suppressing a Polish insurrection in Warsaw, Prussia had withdrawn its support of the Poles in Posen. But the Habsburg Emperor Ferdinand had been forced to leave Vienna, and when Bakunin heard that the Czechs were calling for an all-Slav congress, he hurried to Prague. Arriving there on 3 June, he found himself almost the only Russian in an assembly of Bohemians, Slovaks, Moravians, Poles, Serbs, Croats, Ruthenes and Montenegrins living under Austrian, Russian, Prussian or Turkish rule.

Whereas Marx and Engels wanted a war against Russia in order to save the German revolution, with the liberation of Poland a mere appendix to the plan, Bakunin tried to persuade the dispersed and heterogeneous Slavs to forget their divided national loyalties and conflicting interests and to adopt his pet scheme of a 'great federation of all Slav peoples' aimed at 'the complete destruction of the Austrian Empire', with the liberation of Poland to provide a springboard for propaganda into Russia.

On 12 June, the pan-Slav conference, having considerably toned down the aims of Bakunin's proposed federation (the final resolution spoke only of the 'reorganization of the Austrian Empire'), was closing its sessions, when Czech students and workers started an independent insurrection of their own. The Austrians retaliated heavily during the next few days and on the 17th, Prince Windischgrätz crushed the revolt by bombarding the centre of Prague. Though the other conference delegates had fled the city early on, Bakunin left only on the 18th, not before firing 'a few' rifle shots at the barricades and advising the insurgents 'to overthrow the government in City Hall' and replace it with 'a dictatorial military committee'.

On the same day, Engels in Cologne was publishing an article in the *Neue Rheinische Zeitung*, saying in part:

> The French, even in places where they came as enemies, were able to gain recognition and sympathy. The Germans, however, are recognized nowhere and find sympathy nowhere... What has revolutionary Germany done? It has completely ratified the old oppression of Italy, Poland and now Bohemia too, by the German soldiers.
>
> After all this, are the Germans really asking the Czechs to trust them?...

'The brave Czechs', he went on, 'have been driven into the arms of the Russians by 400 years of German oppression, of which the street battles in Prague are but a continuation. In the great struggle between the West and the East of Europe' – between revolutionary Germany, as he saw it then, and the Russian despotism – 'the Czechs will be the first to be crushed.

'It is the Germans again who will bear the guilt of the downfall of the Czechs. It is the Germans who have betrayed them to the Russians.'[19]

In a follow-up piece two weeks later, Engels again excoriated 'the infamies committed with the aid of Germany in other countries' since the days when it had furnished mercenaries against North Americans fighting the War of Independence:

> Poland has been plundered and dismembered and Cracow throttled with the help of German soldiers; German money and blood have helped to enslave and impoverish Lombardy and Venice [and] to stifle any movement of liberation throughout Italy by means of bayonets, gallows, prisons and galleys.

He blamed the government's foreign policy as well as the German people's 'slavish spirit' in accepting to be tools of the masters 'by divine right' for making the German name abroad detested, cursed and despised.[20]

On 22 June, 5 days after the bombardment of Prague, havoc was loosed in Paris. Since the February days, when the Provisional Government had proclaimed the Republic, the impromptu honeymoon between Lamartine's moderate republicans and Blanc's Socialist radicals had been upset by the result of elections for the National Assembly held in April. Nine million newly enfranchised voters elected almost 500 moderate republicans, 300 Bourbon or Orleanist monarchists and only 100 radicals, showing that France was more conservative than Paris.

The major problem faced by the Provisional Government when it had assumed power in February had been unemployment. By April this had jumped from an original 10,000 to 70,000. Blanc had a famous and daring cure for this – the establishment of cooperative 'social workshops' and factories, initially to be financed by government loans but to be run by the workers themselves, with the profits to be invested in new enterprises. But with the moderate republicans pulling in a different direction, the government had instead launched 'National Workshops', putting the unemployed to work on unproductive road construction jobs at low wages.

In May, following his poor showing in the elections, Blanc was dropped from the government altogether. The number of unemployed kept rising steadily, to 100,000 in May, 120,000 in June. On 15 May several thousand of them, led by the veteran conspirator Auguste Blanqui, stormed the Hôtel de Ville in Paris and proclaimed a new Provisional Government. This insurrection was quickly put down, and Blanqui and other ringleaders were jailed.

On 22 June the government, because of lack of money, announced the termination of the useless National Workshops. An estimated 40,000 Paris workers took to arms. General Louis Cavaignac, like Windischgrätz in Prague, let the insurrection spread before brutally crushing it with guns, razing the most thickly populated district of Paris. Three days of the fiercest street fighting seen in Europe ended with some 10,000 dead and injured. Retribution was fierce, and many of the 11,000 taken prisoner were deported to Algeria.

'The Place de la Bastille is covered with blood and looks more like a slaughterhouse than a battlefield,' Hess reported to a Frankfurt newspaper on 25 June, the last day of the fighting, after visiting the St Denis quarter which had been severely hit. He had ventured into the street in defiance of martial law, as did Herzen and Annenkov on the same day. They were seized by soldiers and interrogated for hours before being released. Hess, who had left Cologne in disgust immediately after the imbroglio between Marx and Gottschalk, went on in his report:

> The social war of the poor against the rich has started in a bloody fashion exceeding the blackest fantasy! There is hardly a doubt that the miserable proletariat will in the end be defeated. Tomorrow Paris will perhaps be quiet again. But what quiet! And what consequences![21]

The June battle of the Paris workers caused Marx and Engels to drop their mask for once and to take up the special cause of the proletariat which they had so far kept out of the *Neue Rheinische Zeitung*. In an article on 'The June Revolution', Marx hailed the heroism of the Paris workers and stressed the historic significance of the uprising in revealing the irreconcilable conflict between capitalism and the proletariat. Passionately he concluded:

> We shall be asked whether we have no tears, no sighs, no words for the victims of the people's rage, for the National Guard, the Mobile Guard, the Republican Guard, the troops of the line.
>
> The reply is this: the state will look after their widows and orphans, decrees will glorify them, solemn funeral processions will inter their remains, the official press will declare them immortal, the European reaction from east to west will pay homage to them. But the plebeians are tortured with hunger, reviled by the press, abandoned by doctors, abused by honest men as incendiaries, galley-slaves, their women and children thrown into still deeper misery, their best sons deported overseas; it is the privilege, it is the right of the democratic press to wind the laurels around their stern and threatening brows.[22]

Engels followed suit with a series of articles, in one of which he compared the uprising of the Paris workers with that of the Roman slaves against their masters and with the 1834 insurrection at Lyons. Contrary to Hess's pessimistic view of its consequences, Engels confidently and/or propagandistically wrote that 'even from a purely military standpoint' the defeated workers had proved that they 'are about to triumph within a fairly short space of time.'[23]

The direct effect of the June insurrection, however, was that before the end of the year Louis Napoleon Bonaparte, the late emperor's nephew, was to be elected President of France by a landslide conservative majority. Another consequence was that in Germany even the most progressive wing of the bourgeoisie were now frightened out of their wits and more than ever determined to go on reforming the monarchy, but to exclude the lower classes from any representation and influence in it.

Instead of the proletariat riding to power on the back of the bourgeoisie, the bourgeoisie exploited the popular unrest to increase its own power.

The fall of the Provisional Government came as no surprise to Heine. Having suspected from the start that it might not last, he was soon comparing its members to 'the amateur actors with whom Shakespeare makes such play in the Midsummer Night's Dream. The miserable wretches had only one fear: that their fooling should be taken seriously, and Snug the joiner proclaimed in advance that he was not really a lion, only a provisional lion.'

The 4 months between the February revolution and the June uprising had brought Heine one disaster after another. Besides his physical discomfort, there was the demoralizing effect of his being 'chained to my couch at a time when everyone else is on his feet and moving.' The February government cancelled the pension he had been receiving from the secret funds of its predecessors, but worse than the financial loss was the exposure in April of the fact that he had been receiving one. This was taken up in Germany and – for all the many statements and explanations he sent out into the world – stained his name. Even the *Augsburger Allgemeine Zeitung*, in what Heine called 'a defence with a bear's paw', suggested that he had not been paid for what he wrote, but for what he did not write.

To add to his discomfiture, in April, while he was still at the *maison de santé*, Campe suddenly broke with him. The publisher had been pressing him to prepare the issue of his *Collected Works* now that the censorship had been lifted in Germany. When Heine, pleading his illness, took his time about it, Campe lost patience. Severing their 20-year-long relationship, he was not to answer Heine's letters for the next three years, leaving the poet in the lurch at a time when 'wounds were kept open on his spine in order to drip morphine directly into them'[24] and when he most needed help.

Campe's behaviour, as Sammons has observed, was particularly puzzling as all his life he 'had been waiting for this moment... the collected edition and the reissue of some of Heine's earlier works... It was as though a quarter century of frustrated energy burst out of him all at once.' To the satirist Georg Weerth, who tried to mediate between the publisher and the poet, Campe gave all sorts of evasive explanations, but allowed that he bore Heine a real grudge: Campe had postponed the christening of his first son and heir for two years since February 1846 because he wanted Heine to be his godfather 'as a token of his firm's link with him for future generations.' With Heine between bouts of illness constantly postponing his visit to Hamburg, he had finally held the christening by proxy in February 1848.

Campe and Heine later made up. Neither of them was an easy man and the upshot of their temporary break was that Heine's *Collected Works* was not to appear until after his death.[25]

On 7 May, after some three months spent at the *maison de santé*, Heine returned to his apartment in the rue de Berlin. Dr Gruby, among whose patients were George Sand, Dumas *père*, Chopin and Liszt, had apparently worked wonders and Heine's condition had improved to the point where he could move his arms and legs. On or about the 15th, he ventured out for a walk. Half-blind, he dragged himself with some difficulty to the Louvre. It was the last time he went out, for he collapsed in front of the Venus de Milo: 'For a long time I lay at her feet and cried so violently that the stones must have had pity on me. Indeed, the goddess gazed at me sympathetically, but so disconsolately as if to say: 'Can't you see I have no arms and can't help?'[26]

Caroline Jaubert, who like 'a good Fairy' kept her promise and visited Heine in the rue de Berlin shortly after the physical collapse from which he was never to recover, ascribed it to his being overcome by the contrast between his one-time Hellenist passion for beauty and his present condition. Heine himself said to her of the armless Venus: 'Her divinity, like my humanity, is reduced by half. And in spite of all mathematical and algebraic rules our two halves cannot make a whole.'[27]

Unable to walk, and having to be carried about 'like a child' from his bed to his easy-chair, Heine did not stay long in the rue de Berlin. During the bloody 'June days' he was living in a quiet house with a garden in Passy, near the Bois de Boulogne. Even dictation, he informed one of his correspondents, was painful because of his half-paralyzed chin, and in a letter to the marquis de Lagrange, inviting him to drop in 'at Passy, Grande-Rue 64', he said that he was 'practicing the miserable métier of a moribund'.[28]

This was written on 23 June, while street fighting was going on half an hour's distance away. While assuring his aging mother in Hamburg that he had passed 'the three terrible days of the great bloodbath' in safety ('The world is full of misfortune and one forgets one's self'), he revealed his true condition in a letter to his sister Charlotte Embden 'so that in case I perish you should not be terribly shocked. I hope, my dear child, that this will not happen so soon; I may have the misfortune of dragging on in my present state for a dozen years.'[29]

He knew that he was dying, but fortunately did not foresee that his agony would last almost 8 years. At the same time, although writing, eating and every move cost him a terrible exertion, he was 'spiritually strong and mentally alert, yes, alert' – as he assured Campe on 9 July 1848 – 'as I have never been before.' In June he had at last sent Campe the requested plan for the edition of his *Collected Works* in 18 volumes. On 9 July he reminded Campe that he was still waiting for an answer. Having no idea as yet how long Campe's silence would last, he sent greetings to 'my young godson' and later wrote some fables to amuse 'our crown prince, the young tsarevich, my future publisher.' He also gave Campe his reaction to the bloody 'June Days': 'About the current events I say nothing; it is universal anarchy, world-huggermugger of God's madness become visible! The old man will have to be locked up if this goes on. It is the fault of the atheists, who have driven him crazy.'[30]

During that month Heine received the news that the German workers in Brussels were singing his songs. At the same time *Les Poésies de Henri Heine*, translated between fits of madness by his talented friend Gérard de Nerval (whose translation of *Faust* had elicited Goethe's enthusiastic admiration), were being serialized in the *Revue des Deux Mondes*. Heine and Nerval spent many hours discussing poetry, and another frequent visitor was Alfred Meissner, a 26-year-old poet from Prague who became Heine's admirer and friend to the end of his life. But, cut off from the world at one of the most eventful times in Europe, Heine found it took a little while to regain his political bearings.

On 29 August he wrote to Jean-Jacques Dubochet, the publisher of the French edition of *Don Quixote*, that in Germany the reaction was gaining the upper hand: 'The so-called "National Party" is incredible. They think only... of rallying the lost tribes under the banner of nationalist Germany.' He feared that they would ultimately demand the return of Alsace and Lorraine. Having once dreamt of a Franco-German reconciliation, he was particularly distressed by the news from the Rhineland:

> The most devoted friends of France, men who have worked for twenty years to destroy the Prussian influence in the Rhenish provinces, today no longer dare to struggle against the wave of nationalism, and have even hoisted the colours of the German Empire.[31]

After Friedrich Wilhelm IV began to insult the Frankfurt National Assembly when not ignoring it, Heine, taking up his old fighting stance, went so far as to devote one of his 'Poems for the Times' to the imaginary guillotining of a king in Germany. The poem, whose title was made up of the dates of the executions of Charles I of England and Louis XVI of France followed by question marks for the putative date of a similar event in Germany, ironically contrasted the French and British lack of sentiment with the German bent for it: whereas Charles was kept awake his last night by the hammering of the scaffold-builders, and Marie Antoinette rode to the guillotine in a cart, the Germans would treat 'their Majesties/With piety and if-you-please' and send them to their execution 'In handsome coach and six'.[32]

On 6 July, the *Neue Rheinische Zeitung* carried a Paris report alleging that George Sand had in her possession papers proving that Bakunin had been, and perhaps still was, in the pay of the Tsarist government and responsible for the arrest of several Poles. To Bakunin, who had arrived in Berlin on the 5th after fleeing the Prague insurrection and a short stop in Breslau, it was a hard blow to read this slander in Germany's foremost 'democratic' paper – and especially painful as rumours that he was a Russian agent had long been circulating in some Polish, French and Belgian circles.

Besides asking George Sand either to produce the evidence or deny the report, he immediately published a denial of his own in Breslau's *Oder-Zeitung*. Marx reprinted it in the *Neue Rheinische Zeitung* on 16 July. On 3 August he also published a letter from George Sand denying that she had any papers incriminating Bakunin. Embarrassed by the fact that he had neglected to check the story with anyone in the first place, Marx added somewhat disingenuously that Sand's letter 'perfectly explained the matter'.

The slander that he was a Russian agent added to Bakunin's depression at the failure of the Prague insurrection and the French and German revolutions. Once more he was 'without money, without friends, openly denounced as a spy, alone in a large city. I had no idea what to do,' he was to write in his Confession to the Tsar. The only thing he had left was his honour, and though he did not know how he 'would live the next day', he swore to fight for it 'until my death would prove to the Poles and Germans that I am no traitor.'[33]

Up to the middle of August there had actually been a great deal of libertarian activity in the Rhineland, much of it stimulated by Marx and the *Neue Rheinische Zeitung*. He had formed a Democratic Society in Cologne to rival Gottschalk's Workers Union. Each held conferences and debates, climaxed by a congress of delegates from almost 100 'Democratic' Clubs in Frankfurt for the purpose of creating a national organization.

Gottschalk, who represented Cologne at this congress some time before his arrest, had proposed as a first step a fusion of his own Workers Union with Marx's Democratic Society and the Union of Employees and Employers. Fearing the preponderance of Gottschalk's stronger Workers Union, Marx refused. But after Gottschalk was jailed, Marx had no problem in assuming the leadership of a steering committee formed by the three bodies.

Though nothing came of the national organization, this committee organized in mid-August the first Rhineland Democratic Congress. Albert Brisbane, of the *New York Daily Tribune*, who saw Marx that year in Cologne, described him as the rising 'leader of a popular movement'. In the midst of this flurry of conferences and congresses, Weitling had returned from America. Addressing Marx's Democratic Society, he advocated a personal dictatorship of the 'most insightful' members of the movement, for the mob never knew where its real interests lay. On 4 August, Marx made short shrift of Weitling by declaring that 'a democratic government composed of the most heterogeneous elements' would exchange ideas and decide on the most effective political programme.[34]

Yet Weitling had touched on a sore point. Of all the 'heterogeneous' elements engaged in the German revolution and pulling this way and that, the workers were the most confused. Few of them had read *The Communist Manifesto* and fewer still understood the role assigned to them in the Marx-Engels strategy of revolution. The *Neue Rheinische Zeitung*, as S. Na'aman has pointed out, covered world events 'from California to Siberia', but showed not the slightest concern for the practical 'self-help' metods of improving the social condition of the workers, such as had brought Gottschalk 8,000 followers in Cologne and were making Born a success in Berlin and Leipzig. When Marx, in Gottschalk's absence, gradually took over his Workers Union, half of its members left.

For the rest, the *Neue Rheinische Zeitung* blasted and mocked everything that happened in Germany. It favoured a united Germany, but ridiculed the Frankfurt Parlament's attempts to work out a constitutional framework for it. The only alternative it offered – war with Russia – frightened its readers. Its last shareholders withdrew their support and the paper was daily threatened with extinction. As Heine had written of Börne's Jacobin 'horse cure', the remedy struck most people as worse than the illness.

It was at this point that Ferdinand Lassalle rose to prominence in Cologne and Düsseldorf, to become Marx's ally and to give the Rhenish freedom movement a new impetus even as the tide was about to turn against the revolution.

Düsseldorf was a chief centre of revolutionary activity in the Rhineland. It had a 'Democratic People's Club', a Committee of Public Safety, and ever since the Prussian King had been alarmed by the March revolt in Berlin an armed Civil Guard moved about town under the wary eyes of his soldiers. There were mass demonstrations against any infringement of liberty, such as the arrest of the poet Freiligrath for publishing a call to arms and for 'red flags on barricades' in the *Neue Rheinische Zeitung*.

An extraordinary figure at these demonstrations was the Countess Sophie von Hatzfeldt. This aristocrat – whose late father, while serving as ambassador to Metternich's Vienna, had coined the reactionary slogan '*il faut terrasser pour toujours le monstre révolutionnaire*' ('we must defeat this revolutionary monster for ever') – declared at a public meeting that she was 'joining the people. I am a proletarian like you.' She attacked the 'aristocratic reaction' which, in the person of her husband, had disrupted her family, robbed her of two of her children as well as her private fortune, and otherwise ruined her life by treating her as a slave.

On 5 August, topping the sensational appearances of the 43-year-old 'red Countess', as she became known, the trial of Ferdinand Lassalle opened before a Cologne jury. He was brought to the court from the jail where he had spent 5 months since his arrest and remand. Reading the newspapers during his confinement and greatly excited by the rapid spread of the revolution to Germany and elsewhere, Lassalle had found an outlet for his energy and revolutionary temperament by continuing from prison the pamphlet war in which he and the Count had been engaged before his arrest. The scandal involving a highly placed person and his wife was eagerly taken up by the newspapers and whipped up public opinion. Since Lassalle turned the Countess's maltreatment by her husband into a political attack on the privileges of Prussia's feudal aristocracy, the *Neue Rheinische Zeitung* reported his fight with more than usual interest.

With the pathos of a great orator and remarkable legal acumen for a self-taught lawyer, Lassalle presented the Countess as 'a victim of her class', abandoned by her own closest kin: 'Where all human rights have been violated and a human being is helplessly forsaken by his or her born protectors – there man's first and last relative must stand up: man.' The prosecution's chief witness was one of Count Hatzfeldt's servants, who claimed to have overheard Lassalle ordering his friend Arnold Mendelssohn to follow the Count's mistress on her travels and to 'get hold in any possible way' of the bond of the annuity he had settled on her, jeopardizing his wife's and children's financial future. Lassalle forced the prosecutor to admit in some embarrassment that the servant had been bribed by the Count's agents and had since opened a shop in Berlin.

The week-long trial culminated in Lassalle's defence speech, which lasted for 6 hours and brought him Varnhagen von Ense's comparison to no one less than Mirabeau. The charge of 'moral complicity', Lassalle declared in court, was unprecedented in Germany, and wherever used had always served as an instrument for proscribing freedom of expression and for 'the political murder' of any opposition. Stressing that he was supposed to have ordered the theft of a document which was not in the casket, while Mendelssohn had been found guilty of stealing the casket for the money it contained, he went on to say that if, immediately after Mendelssohn boarded the train, he had gone to the prosecutor and asked him, 'What crime have I committed?' the latter would have replied: 'That depends on Mendelssohn's action after he reaches his destination. If he steals the object, you are a thief; if he commits a robbery or starts a fire, you will be a robber or an incendiary.' Lassalle then turned to the jury: 'What sort of crime is this whose nature can only be determined 24 hours after its execution, or 24 hours after my supposedly giving the order for it?' Unless, he concluded,

> the state wants to persecute me for my opinions and my conscience, which are not subject to the criminal law, justice must not confuse its realm with that of the police. Suspicion belongs to the preserve of the police, to the empire of the night. Justice must operate in bright daylight on the basis of objective evidence.[35]

Acquitted on 11 August, Lassalle emerged from jail a political and revolutionary hero. Leaving Cologne in the company of the 'red Countess', he arrived in Düsseldorf to a triumphal reception. The people unhitched the horses from their carriage and drew it through the streets to the Countess's residence.

Famous overnight – 'everyone knew who Lassalle was; not everyone knew who Marx was and only few had heard of Engels'[36] – he moved in with her and her youngest son Paul, whose abduction by his father Lassalle had prevented two years earlier and who had testified at the trial in his favour. The Countess's 'proletarian' posture was no pose. After two decades of a troubled life in the bosom of her aristocratic family she had, under the influence of the young Lassalle, become a sincere 'democrat'.

'Democrat' was at the time the cognomen uniting radical revolutionaries, moderate social reformers and republicans of all classes who wanted an end to feudalism. Seeing them all as insurrectionists to whom nothing was sacred, a high Prussian official wrote: *'Gegen Demokraten helfen nur Soldaten*! [Against democrats soldiers are the only remedy!]'. This became the favourite slogan of Prussia's conservatives from the King down.[37]

The day after his release, Lassalle joined Düsseldorf's Democratic Club and Civil Guard, and plunged into their political struggle – which was coordinated with that of Marx and the small 'party' of the *Neue Rheinische Zeitung* in Cologne – at the start of the stormiest period of the revolution in Germany. The chronology of events was as follows:

12 August 1848: The Emperor Ferdinand I returned to Vienna, which had been in the hands of the revolutionaries since May. During his absence at Innsbruck, the Frankfurt National Assembly had chosen the Archduke Johann of Austria as Reichsverweser (Caretaker or Regent) of the hoped-for German empire which was to replace the Bund of more than three dozen separate states. Although Johann's empire was still only a dream – Heine satirized him in a poem as 'John Lackland' (*Hans ohne Land*) – his election was so enthusiastically welcomed by Düsseldorf's 'democratic monarchists' that the Civil Guard fraternized with the Prussian troops in town and invited them to take the oath to the new Regent, symbol of the hope for a united Germany. Friedrich Wilhelm IV promptly forbade his troops to do so. It was the first sign that the King had regained sufficient confidence since the March revolt in Berlin to snub the National Assembly.

16 August: Friedrich Wilhelm IV's visit to Düsseldorf. The disappointed population and the Civil Guard were in no mood to give him a royal reception. The reception staged by the municipality under pressure from the Prussian authorities led to disturbances, in the course of which mud was thrown at the King. Lassalle, who had just been released, was falsely suspected of having organized the protesters.

23 August: Marx left for Vienna and Berlin to raise money for the *Neue Rheinische Zeitung*. In Vienna he addressed its first Workers Union and in Berlin he met such friends as d'Ester, Jung and Köppen and also ran into Bakunin.

Although, as far as is known, their meeting passed off without any friction, 20 years later Bakunin – during his fight with Marx for the International – was to accuse him of malice aforethought in spreading the slander that he was a Tsarist agent.

Marx's fund-raising in Berlin yielded 2,000 desperately needed Thaler, presently to reach the *Neue Rheinische Zeitung* from a group of Polish democrats. From Berlin he went once again to Vienna. His expedition lasted for a month and he had yet to return to Cologne when the Prussian ministry headed by Hansemann resigned and another major crisis followed in short order.

26 August: In defiance of the Frankfurt National Assembly, Prussia signed an armistice with Denmark and agreed to evacuate its troops from Schleswig-Holstein.

4 September: The Frankfurt National Assembly declared the Prussian–Danish armistice invalid.

16 September: The National Assembly reversed itself and by the same slim majority approved the Danish armistice.

As early as 11 September, Lassalle was one of two main speakers at a mass meeting at Neuss at which 10,000 people protested the Danish armistice signed by Prussia at Malmö. This was a slap in the face of the Frankfurt National Assembly, as the King had not bothered even to inform it before concluding the armistice.

The complicated Schleswig-Holstein dispute concerning the two Duchies linking Denmark and Prussia had been brewing since April, when their German populace – to avoid annexation to Denmark – formed a Provisional Government. The Prussian Foreign Minister invited its representatives to Berlin.

This was not enough for the Frankfurt National Assembly, which regarded itself as 'the government of Germany' and wanted nothing less than war with Den-mark. In a moment of enthusiasm the wayward King had ordered Prussian troops into the Duchies, only to regret it almost immediately because Denmark had the strong support of Russia, Britain and France, none of which wanted to see 'the Dardanelles of the North' fall into the hands of what looked like becoming a great united Germany.

The war with Denmark, however, was highly popular. 'Let France', thundered a left-wing member of the Frankfurt Assembly, 'let England, let Russia dare to interfere in our just cause. We shall reply with one and a half million men.' Not only the Frankfurt Assembly was outraged. The Danish armistice caused widespread indignation, presaging as it did the end of the dream of a united Germany, since Friedrich Wilhelm IV was signalling that he did not mean to respect the decisions of the Frankfurt National Assembly.

On 14 September, before the Assembly reversed its decision and while it was still swaying this way and that, Marx (who had returned to Cologne on the 12th) wrote in his newspaper that in Prussia a revolutionary crisis had arisen reminiscent of 1793 in France. He compared the alternatives facing the Assembly with Hobson's choice: 'If [they] decide to reject the armistice they decide their own downfall, like the Girondists of the first revolution... If on the other hand they accept the armistice and place themselves under Prussia's sway, they also decide their own downfall.' Marx was not alone in believing that a second revolution was in the offing in Germany. He hoped that it would lead to 'the unavoidable war with Russia'.

The policy of the *Neue Rheinische Zeitung*, as enunciated by Engels in a recent series of articles, was 'support for a general war of revolutionary Europe against Russia, the backbone of European reaction.' Fought in defiance of Prussia, it would unite Germany and bring down the old order in the process.

16–19 September: Popular revolt in Frankfurt against the National Assembly's capitulation to Prussia in the matter of the Danish armistice.

On the 17th, before news of the Assembly's capitulation and the riots in Frankfurt had reached him, Lassalle went to Cologne and together with Engels addressed another mass demonstration on a meadow at Wörringen, just outside the city. This had been organized by a Public Safety Committee formed in Cologne on the initiative of the *Neue Rheinische Zeitung*. Large Rhine barges flying the red flag had brought 8,000 or more people from all over the province. The meeting adopted a motion calling for a 'democratic social republic, a red republic'. It urged the Frankfurt Assembly to resist any attempt to disperse it by 'the force of bayonets' and assured it that in case of a conflict with Prussia the assembled citizens would 'sacrifice their lives and property' for a united Germany.[38]

Alas, Marx's comparison of the situation with that of revolutionary France in 1793 was greatly exaggerated. Prussians, Austrians, Bavarians and Saxons had yet to decide whether they were a unitary German 'nation', whereas the French in 1793 had already solved that problem. As Golo Mann has put it: 'The Germans in 1848 were not what the French had been in 1793,' and the Prussian, Bavarian and Austrian armies were intact. 'What followed, while not yet the Marxist revolution, was nevertheless a furious popular uprising in Frankfurt.'

There was serious street fighting, and on 18 September the populace – feeling betrayed by the deputies it had elected to the Assembly – lynched two of them. Golo Mann asks,

> What could the unfortunate 'German government' [the Assembly]
> do in these circumstances? Should it wage a people's war against

Denmark, Russia and France in league with those who had just beaten the deputy Prince Lichnovsky to death? It sought protection from the Prussian army... Royal Prussian troops, instead of fighting the Danes, restored order in German Frankfurt.[39]

On 25 September the wave of repression hit Cologne. The police broke up a public meeting in the town square. Schapper and another associate of Marx were arrested. The authorities imposed martial law. The Civil Guard was disarmed; public meetings were forbidden and the *Neue Rheinische Zeitung* was suspended. Warrants were issued for the arrest of Engels and others of the editorial staff. Engels fled to his native Barmen, then to Brussels, and was not to reappear in Cologne for the next three and a half months. The others likewise escaped, one of them hiding with Lassalle and the Countess. In the course of these incidents Marx told the workers to stay put and not start an aimless local revolt which would only 'render us incapable of fighting on the day of decision.'

6 October: Third revolution in Vienna. In March, the Austrian Emperor had granted Hungary's claim of sovereignty over all its lands, including Transylvania and Croatia. In mid-September, however, a Croatian force had invaded Hungary with the help of the Austrian Prince Windischgrätz. The third revolution in 'Red Vienna' was sparked off by the refusal of a regiment to obey orders and march off to crush the successful Hungarian resistance.

The bloody fighting in Vienna lasted three weeks. On its outcome depended the fate of the European revolution. The insurgents stormed the arsenal and the Austrian Minister of War was killed in his office. The Emperor and his court, fleeing Vienna for the second time, left for the fortress town of Olmütz in Moravia. During these weeks the *Neue Rheinische Zeitung*, which started reappearing on 12 October – its staff reduced to Marx, Weerth and the poet Freiligrath who had just been acquitted of high treason – goaded the German 'democrats' to rise in support of Vienna's 'workers, students and intellectuals'. But the Frankfurt National Assembly was guarded by Prussian troops, and no one budged.

31 October: Prince Windischgrätz, assisted by Croatian troops, took Vienna after a three-day siege. The fall of the city to the general who had bombarded Prague was followed by brutal reprisals against all those involved in the insurrection or in Vienna's 'red' administration. Among those summarily executed was Robert Blum, a prominent member of the Frankfurt National Assembly.

On 7 November, in one of the most savage articles published in the *Neue Rheinische Zeitung*, Marx wrote sarcastically: 'Croatian freedom and order won the day and celebrated this victory with arson, rape, looting and other atrocities.' He castigated the treachery of the bourgeoisie and concluded: 'There is only one means by which the murderous death agonies of the old society and the bloody birth throes of the new society can be shortened and concentrated – and that is by revolutionary terror.'[40]

At the beginning of November, following the victory of the Habsburg forces in Vienna, the Hohenzollern king in Berlin felt strong enough to take military action against the Prussian National Assembly which, to his great annoyance, had dropped the title 'King by divine grace' from its proposed constitution. On 9 November the Assembly was ordered out of Berlin, but refused to leave. With the fate of the last revolutionary bastion at stake, Marx advised the Assembly to have the King's ministers arrested for high treason and to proclaim a tax boycott. 'NO MORE TAXES!!!' became the daily slogan beneath the masthead of the *Neue Rheinische Zeitung*.

Marx further appealed to the rest of Germany to go to the assistance of Berlin 'with men and arms'. But on 10 November, General Wrangel with 15,000 troops disarmed Berlin's Civil Guard. Thousands of democrats were arrested. Completing the military putsch or coup d'état, martial law was imposed on the whole of Prussia, and on the 12th the protesting Berlin Assembly was forced at bayonet point to move to a little town in Brandenburg, where it was soon dispersed. On 5 December, instead of the promised constitution granting universal suffrage, the King enforced a constitution of his own, which simply created three categories of propertied voters.

Still Marx did not give up the fight. The Hungarian revolt led by the dynamic Lajosz Kossuth had yet to be subdued and in Rome a popular insurrection on 16 November caused Pope Pius IX to flee the city. On the 18th, Marx published an appeal for a people's levy of all men of military age and for the procurement of 'weapons and munitions through voluntary subscriptions or at the expense of the communes'. He was bent on saving the revolution. So was Lassalle. There is no knowing whether he had read *The Communist Manifesto*, but this young logician quickly grasped the policy of the *Neue Rheinische Zeitung* and fully agreed with Marx's programme and his strategy for social revolution. Both were busy, Lassalle as orator, Marx with his newspaper, 'but they needed few words to understand each other and to drop the third-person *Sie* and adopt the brotherly *Du* in their letters.' They shared a common legacy in Hegel and interpreted their times in the light of his principles, which convinced both of them of the need for revolution.[41]

On 19 November, within a day of Marx's call for a people's levy, Lassalle publicly informed the Frankfurt Assembly that 'the time for passive resistance' was over and urged it in the name of Düsseldorf's Civil Guard and its district militia to issue a call to arms. He formed a committee in Düsseldorf for the procurement of weapons, published subscription lists soliciting money and/or arms for the fight against the government and wrote to the Countess's loyal peasants at the Schönstein estate to hold themselves ready for the day of decision.

Two days later, in a public speech at Neuss, he called on the workers – in line with Marx's strategy – to banish 'any thought of proclaiming a republic, which would be madness in a provincial town... I and my party', he proclaimed, 'stand for social reform.' But the 'social republic' – a term to be used by Marx – was 'for the future'. For the present, all the proletariat wanted was to help the citizenry to 'defend your liberties, your rights, your laws.'

The following day he was arrested and remanded indefinitely for inciting the people to armed revolt against the royal government.

2 December: Ferdinand I abdicated in favour of his nephew Francis Joseph I. This was the result of a plot hatched by the Emperor's sister, the Archduchess Sophia of Bavaria, with the help of Prince Windischgrätz and his brother-in-law Prince Schwarzenberg. These grey-haired leaders of the ultra-reactionary nobility persuaded the feeble-minded Ferdinand to yield his place to Sophia's 20-year-old son. In a secret ceremony at the gloomy old Olmütz castle, the slender, boyish Francis Joseph, who had been recalled from the army, nervously went down on his knees to be crowned by his uncle. Ferdinand stroked his cheek and reassured him: 'Be brave. It's all right.'[42]

The fall of Vienna and the coup which installed Francis Joseph I saved both the Austrian Empire and the Habsburg dynasty at the moment when they were tottering and had been written off. Prince Schwarzenberg became the head of a new government in Vienna and Francis Joseph I, in one of the longest reigns in history, was to rule for the next 68 years until the middle of World War I, provoked two years before his death by the bullet which killed his son at Sarajevo.

As for Prussia, Friedrich Wilhelm IV's constitution of 5 December reduced none of his authority as monarch 'by the grace of God.' And in France, on 10 December, Louis Napoleon Bonaparte – who three decades or so after the defeat of the first Napoleon had put up his candidature as the 'defender of order' – was elected President of France.

In a series of articles summing up the year's events, Marx admitted in December that his faith in a bourgeois revolution had been misplaced. 'The history of the German bourgeoisie as a whole from March to December', he wrote, showed that 'a purely bourgeois revolution and bourgeois rule in the form of a constitutional monarchy is impossible. The only possibility is either a feudal absolutist counter-revolution or a social-republican revolution.'[43] His end-of-the-year message was: 'Working-class revolution in France, world war – that is the agenda for the year 1849.'[44]

Although the alternative to the counter-revolution presented by Marx was 'social-republican', and not 'proletarian' revolution, the *Neue Rheinische Zeitung* now paid more attention to the problems of the workers, the petty bourgeoisie and even the peasants. But this was only a change of tactics. Marx and Engels continued to stick to their grand plan for a war against Russia. They were playing for high stakes. When Marx wrote of world war on 1 January 1849, it was because he realized that every social upheaval on the Continent 'founders on the industrial and commercial world domination of Great Britain... And old England will only be overthrown by a world war,' which alone would enable the Chartist party of English workers to stage 'a successful rising against their gigantic oppressors. The Chartists at the head of the English government – only at that moment does the idea of a social revolution leave the realm of Utopia for that of reality. But every European war which involves England is a world war.'[45]

He predicted that it would start with a working-class revolution in France. Repeating a motto coined by Heine (but in which Heine himself no longer believed), Marx had confidently written on 12 November: 'The Gallic cock will crow again in Paris and awaken Europe.'

At the beginning of 1849, Bakunin was at Koethen, a little town in the German Duchy of Anhalt. He had been on the run since the end of September. Expelled by the Berlin police upon allegations from the Russian Embassy that he was engaged in plotting to assassinate the Tsar, he had shaved off his beard and travelled undetected to Breslau. Within a week, however, he was notified that unless he left Prussian soil he would be turned over to the Russians. He tried Dresden in Saxony, but was allowed to stay no longer than 48 hours. Hunted from pillar to post, he finally hit on the small but independent Duchy of Anhalt, whose exceptionally liberal constitution made it a haven for political exiles and refugees. From mid-October until December, he was later to write, he did nothing but 'hunt rabbits and other wild game. It was for me a period of repose...' Yet it was during this period of inactivity and 'repose' that he wrote his famous *Appeal to the Slavs*.

In this extraordinary document, written with apocalyptic fervour, Bakunin poured out all his frustrations, his 'lost honour' and discreditation as a Tsarist spy, and his shock at the fact that – contrary to his plan of a 'great Federation of all Slav peoples' aimed at 'the complete destruction of the Austrian empire' – the Croatians had actually helped the Austrians to crush the democratic rebellions in Vienna and Milan. The Czech bourgeoisie, too, had silently approved Windischgrätz's slaughter of the Prague students and workers. As one of Bakunin's friends wrote to him from Berlin, the Slavs now appeared as nationalists and 'perfidious crusaders' against democracy.

In his *Appeal to the Slavs*, Bakunin for the first time attacked the bourgeoisie as a counter-revolutionary force. To what extent he was or was not influenced by Marx's sallies at the 'treachery' of the bourgeoisie is a moot point, but he now embraced the cause of the proletariat:

> Two great questions have moved to the forefront from the very first days of the spring! The social question, and that of the independence of all nations, the emancipation of the peoples within and without... The whole world understood that liberty was a lie where a great majority of the population is reduced to a wretched existence, where, deprived of education, of leisure, and of bread, it is condemned to serve as a stepping-stone for the powerful and the rich.

Besides declaring that the solution of the social question required 'the complete overthrow of society', Bakunin proclaimed his faith in a hitherto neglected revolutionary force – the masses of the Russian peasantry. Writing, as he himself admitted, in a state of the 'highest paroxysm' – intensified and 'inflamed by my earlier failures, by my bizarre and intolerable situation and, finally, by the victory of the reaction in Europe'[46] – he warned the 'blind Tsar' that the Russian peasantry concealed in its womb the embryo of a new and unprecedented force,

> a volcanic fire whose explosion will bury beneath tall mounds of lava the well-ordered, artificial gardens of your diplomacy and your reign, shatter your power [and] exterminate it without a trace... Already among the peasant masses of the vast Russian kingdom gigantic craters flare up. Russian democracy with its tongues of fire will devour the state and by its blood-red glow illuminate the whole of Europe.

'I am not afraid of anarchy', Bakunin wrote on 8 December 1848 to Herwegh in Paris. 'I wish it with all my soul.' In announcing his old/new creed of a fire of destruction and postulating that out of 'a sea of blood' in Moscow would come the liberation of all humanity, Bakunin combined his apocalyptic vision of the destruction of 'this old world that is collapsing under the weight of its own injustice' with the promise that from its ruins would arise 'a new world, a real and complete liberation for all individuals as well as all nations, a kingdom of political and social justice, of love and brotherhood, the boundless kingdom of freedom...'[47]

As for the form this kingdom was to take, Bakunin later wrote: 'I wanted a republic. But of what kind? Not a parliamentary republic.' His contempt for representative government and the so-called parliamentary 'balance of powers, where the active forces are so cunningly arranged that not one of them can be effective,' was paralleled only by that later shown by Marx in London when he wrote: 'Being present at sittings of the English Parliament on Monday and

Tuesday, I confess my error in having stigmatized in 1848 the Berlin and Frank-furt Assemblies as the lowest possible expressions of parliamentary life.'

Besides speaking again of revolution in terms of a possessive 'bride' or mis-tress – 'she', he wrote, 'demands that you surrender yourself totally, unreservedly, believing in her and belonging to her completely' – Bakunin in his *Appeal to the Slavs*, drafted and redrafted in French at the very time when the young Francis Joseph was assuming the reign of the Habsburg Empire, was the first of his time to forecast the break-up of that empire into Slav nation states 70 years later.

The German translation of *An Appeal to the Slavs*, from which some of Bakunin's virulent passages against the bourgeoisie had been excised, was pub-lished in Leipzig in pamphlet form. At the end of December he himself moved to Leipzig, where he lived from hand to mouth but managed to arrange for a Polish translation of his pamphlet.

Some 6 weeks later, *An Appeal to the Slavs* was the subject of a searing attack by Engels in the *Neue Rheinische Zeitung*. Engels himself had been on the run since the previous autumn. Having fled Cologne in haste and reached Brussels without a passport and little money, he had been arrested by the Belgians as a simple vagrant and shown across the border into France without further cere-mony. He reached Paris on 5 October, but after a few days – depressed by finding the beautiful city looking 'dead' after the bloody June events – he set out 'one fine morning without any fixed plan' on a walking tour of France. His aim was to reach Switzerland, but 'not by the shortest route', and he spent 5 weeks hiking at his leisure across the countryside and living like a vagabond before reaching Berne via Geneva and Lausanne.

The fact that, instead of staying in Paris or going to London and writing for the *Neue Rheinische Zeitung*, Engels chose to abandon any political activity, dallying in France and later spending another two months in Switzerland, has led his modern biographer to conclude that he apparently 'lost his nerve'.[48] If so, his exhilarating weeks in France certainly did him good. But, in addition to being afraid to return to Cologne or to his shocked parents in Barmen – who had learned from the newspapers of a warrant for his arrest – he seems to have been in the throes of some anxiety that Marx might regard his prolonged absence as desertion. Although at the end of October Marx had sent him 50 Thaler in Geneva, Engels had not a penny to his soul; some time before mid-November Marx expressed his amazement that Engels had not yet received '61 Thaler I sent you ages ago... I further sent 20 Thaler to Gigot and, later, 50 to Dronke for all of you, each time out of my cash box, a total of some 130 Thaler... To suppose that I could leave you in the lurch for even a moment is sheer fantasy. You will always remain my friend and confidant as I hope I will remain yours.'[49]

Deciding 'to face prison in Cologne rather than endure freedom in Switzerland', Engels finally returned to his post at the *Neue Rheinische Zeitung* in mid-January 1849. On the 13th the paper carried an article by him (sent from Switzerland) on the oppression of the Hungarians by the Slavs. In it, and in a follow-up piece on 15 February, he dealt with the grandiose but 'sentimental' plan of 'our friend' Bakunin for Slav unity, called it 'a mere fantasy', and asked how he meant to form 'five-and-a-half million Czechs, Moravians, and Slovaks into one state, and five-and-a-half million Southern Slavs, together with the Slavs of Turkey, into another?'

Giving vent to a veritable phobia, Engels wrote that, 'apart from the Poles, the Russians, and at most the Slavs of Turkey', the others – Czechs, Croats, Serbs, Bosnians, Bulgars, Slovenes and all the rest of them – were backward races, 'the refuse of peoples [*Völkerabfälle*]', unfit for independence. Having never had a history of their own, they had no future.

While rightly observing that the Hungarian revolt was not yet over, he declared that the interests of the revolution justified the use of 'terrorism' against the Slavs of the Austrian Empire and he pronounced the death sentence on them:

> With the first successful revolt of the French proletariat... the Austrian Germans and Magyars will gain their freedom and take a bloody revenge on the Slav barbarians. The general war which will then break out will crush the Slav alliance and annihilate all these small pig-headed nations, erasing their very names.

> The next world war will not only cause reactionary classes and dynasties to disappear from the face of the earth, but also entire reactionary peoples. And that too is an advance.[50]

At the beginning of February, Marx twice had to defend the *Neue Rheinische Zeitung* in the Court of Assizes. On the 7th he appeared together with Engels and Korff, the paper's publisher, to answer charges of having libelled Cologne's Oberprokurator (attorney-general) and the police in an article the previous summer. Addressing the jury, Marx declared that it was the duty of the press to be 'the public watchdog, the omnipresent eye' and jealous guardian of the people's freedom. This required it to denounce not only the rulers but the individuals executing their policies, be they 'this particular gendarme, this Prosecutor, this district administrator.'

Marx had packed the courtroom with Communist supporters. He closed his speech by saying that since the abortive March revolution had 'merely reformed the political summit and left untouched the lower strata supporting it – the old bureaucrats, the old army, the old courts, the old judges born, educated and grown grey in the service of absolutism', the first duty of the press was 'to undermine the entire foundation of the existing political structure.'[51]

The courtroom burst into applause and all three defendants were acquitted.

On the following day, Marx was again in court, this time together with Schapper and their lawyer Schneider. The three had signed the November call to the citizenry to refuse to pay taxes and to offer armed resistance to the government, and were charged with incitement to rebellion. Law, Marx told the jury, 'must be based on society' and express its common interests. 'The Code Napoléon did not produce modern bourgeois society'; bourgeois society found 'its legal expression in the Code.' The National Assembly, expressing the people's will to abolish feudalism, had created a revolutionary situation and no court could judge him by the old laws on a question to be decided by history.

Anti-Prussian sentiment in the Rhineland was still running high. The jury not only acquitted the defendants, but its foreman thanked Marx for his enlightening lecture. Marx was less successful in winning the hearts and full support of either the workers or the Rhineland democratic organizations. Before the end of February, the latent fight for control of Cologne's Workers Union came to a head. Since Gottschalk's arrest the previous summer, the depleted Union had been temporarily run by Moll and Schapper, but after Moll's flight from Cologne in September, Marx had 'provisionally' accepted its presidency. Just before Christmas, however, Gottschalk had emerged from prison as a free man, all the prosecution's efforts to secure his conviction having failed. He resumed the Union's presidency, only to find himself hamstrung by Marx's supporters. On the pretext of preventing disunity, they proposed the adoption of new rules, hedging his authority.

In disgust, Gottschalk left Cologne for Brussels. Schapper became the Union's president. But Gottschalk retained control of the Union's newspaper *Freiheit, Arbeit* through its editor, J. Prinz, who was a friend of his. The Marxists, in a foretaste of later methods, appointed a committee to 'screen' Prinz's activities, but Prinz ignored it and remained unbendingly loyal to Gottschalk.

The elections for the second Prussian National Assembly under the King's 'enforced' new constitution – scheduled for 22 February – found the Workers Union split by the same issue which had divided it in 1848. Gottschalk had at that time pronounced a boycott on the elections to the Frankfurt Assembly, and he was likewise against the new elections. Marx, on the other hand, having as recently as December called for a 'social-republican revolution', now changed his tactics and affirmed that, 'in view of the impossibility of putting one's own principles into effect', the right course was to help the radical democratic bourgeois opposition to win seats in parliament in order to carry on the political fight against feudalism and 'prevent the victory of our common enemy, the absolute monarch.'

Marx's directive to the workers in an article published on 21 February in the *Neue Rheinische Zeitung* was brutally frank:

> Our cry to the workers and petty-bourgeoisie is: you should prefer to suffer in modern bourgeois society, whose industry creates the material conditions for the foundation of a new society that will free you all, rather than step backwards into an obsolete form of society which, under the pretence of saving your classes, will plunge the whole nation back into medieval barbarism.

This elicited the following outcry from Gottschalk in an open letter 'To Herr Karl Marx', published on 25 February: 'Why should we, men of the proletariat, spill our blood [and] plunge deliberately into the purgatory of a decrepit capitalist domination in order to avoid a medieval hell, as you proclaim to us, in order to attain from there the nebulous heaven of your Communist creed?'[52]

This exchange made clear the fundamental difficulty Marx and Engels had in selling their 'scientific' Communism to the proletariat. They looked far into the future, claiming to know the process of history, and reserved for themselves the right to dictate the moves of the proletariat – to suffer while waiting for 'the Gallic cock to crow again', a new revolution in France which, as Marx had recently written, depended in its turn upon the Chartists' seizing power in England and starting a world war.

'Bloodthirsty for philosophical reasons',[53] Marx and Engels in this way – or through the 'war against Russia' constantly advocated by Engels – wanted a world war. Gottschalk, himself an intellectual, called Marx 'a learned sun-god' looking down on the misery and hunger of the workers with a detached 'doctrinaire interest', ready to sacrifice them for the sake of a theory. Like Hess before him, he did not believe that the German bourgeoisie would really stand up and fight, and speaking in the name of 'the revolutionary party', he wrote that 'we can expect nothing from any class except our own.'

Engels, for his part, dismissed Gottschalk as 'a demagogue and hollow-head'. Within one year of its foundation, the originally 8,000-strong Workers Union was riven by these internal dissensions and expired later in 1849 under the blows of the reaction. Dr Gottschalk returned to Cologne during the summer, shortly before a cholera epidemic struck the city. The first, and for a long time the only, physician to venture into the infected slums, he died in September while attending the poor, to be followed to his grave by hundreds of workers.

In February, Marx had had to fend off opposition from his own camp. Joseph Moll returned to Cologne from several months in London with a mandate from its German workers to reconstitute the Communist League. Significantly, he was to do so even without Marx's consent. At a meeting held at the offices of the *Neue Rheinische Zeitung*, Marx firmly rejected the idea (only to reconstitute the League himself two years later).

In the spring, pressure on Marx was mounting. Besides falling out with Moll and other veterans, and being criticized by the radical 'left' wing of the Workers Union, Marx effected another volte-face. After a year's effort to maintain an alliance with the bourgeois democrats and proclaiming that the future government of Germany must be composed of the most 'heterogeneous elements', he suddenly resigned from the Rhineland Committee of Democratic Associations, on the grounds that it contained 'too many heterogeneous elements' to be of any effective use 'to the Cause'. One reason among many that have been cited for his abandoning the precarious coalition with the democrats was his possible fear that he would otherwise lose the support of the impatient workers.

The revolution was not going his way. He was subjected to increasing police harassment and the *Neue Rheinische Zeitung* was on the verge of bankruptcy. Already in mid-November 1848 – at the time when he was coordinating the tax boycott and the 'dispatch of a volunteer corps to Berlin' with Lassalle in Düsseldorf – he had asked the latter privately to send him some money. Lassalle helped him with 200 Thaler. Since then he had been holding the fort by paying printers, compositors, suppliers and distributors from the dwindling remainder of his inheritance.

In the spring of 1849, hoping for world war, yet 'panting for money as doth the hart for cooling streams', he planned to undertake a fund-raising tour of several towns in Germany in an effort to save the newspaper.

During this period, Bakunin was leading a dreary existence in Leipzig. Frequently changing his name and address, he lived in hiding on occasional handouts sent to him from Paris by his pianist friend Reichel. He was down and out, yet with his grand plan for an all-Slav federation against Austria nowhere in sight, he was restlessly engaged in establishing an international conspiratorial network that would undermine Austria from within and turn everything upside down, so that even if his plan foundered, the victorious reactionary government 'would find nothing in place'. One after another he enlisted in his plan two Germans, d'Ester and Hexamer, who had come with him to Leipzig; two young Czech brothers, Gustav and Adolph Straka, whom he 'uprooted' from their studies in the Divinity Faculty of Leipzig University and persuaded, as he confessed, 'to become instruments of my activities in Bohemia';[54] and a number of assorted 'democrats' of different nationalities who met at Leipzig's Golden Cock coffeehouse and discussed revolution.

Bakunin's interest in Bohemia was stirred by the fact that his *Appeal to the Slavs* had been reprinted almost in full in the newspaper of Prague's Slavonic Linden (or 'Lime-Tree') Society. Planning to turn Bohemia into a revolutionary base for inciting the other Slav peoples to action, Bakunin invited a couple of Czech journalists to a conference in Leipzig. Only one, Emmanuel Arnold, came over from Prague for a single day, and to Bakunin's annoyance most of it was wasted by d'Ester and Hexamer's trying to interest him in a 'stupid' project for a German-Slav congress in Leipzig.

Bakunin then privately belaboured Arnold for several hours and, with his hypnotic powers of persuasion, converted him to his scheme of setting up a network of secret societies to plot revolution throughout Bohemia. The plan he outlined to Arnold before sending him back to Prague called for the establishment of three separate groups – one for the petty bourgeoisie, the second for the students, and the third for the peasantry – each to have a different name and to be unaware of the existence of the others. Yet all were to submit to a 'dictatorial' Central Committee

> composed of three, or, at most, five members: myself and Arnold, with the rest to be elected… At the same time a German student from Vienna [was] to organize among the Germans in Bohemia a society of which I should be the secret head, without at first appearing to be part of its Central Committee. If my plan was successful, all the important threads of the movement would be concentrated in my hands and I would be sure that the revolution planned for Bohemia would never stray from the path that I had drafted for it.[55]

In a prototype of Bakunin's later conspiracies, he dispatched the Viennese music student Heimberger to Prague to spy on Arnold and report on his activities. Heimberger went to Prague twice and reported that Arnold had done nothing, but that he had found great admiration for Bakunin everywhere. Thus encouraged, Bakunin shaved off his beard in March and, accompanied by the Straka brothers, went to Prague on an English passport in the name of Anderson. Although he found that the Prague democrats were 'incorrigible chatterboxes' and that 'nothing was ready', Bakunin, who wrote in his Confession to the Tsar, 'I was not born a charlatan, Sire, quite the contrary… I was at one and the same time deceiver and deceived, deceiving myself and others with me', placed fantasy above reality and remained convinced that he 'was not wrong in hoping to find in Bohemia all the necessary factors for a revolution crowned with success.'

From Dresden, where he stopped on his way back from Prague, he sent the Straka brothers 'detailed and complete instructions' to prepare for the revolution

in Prague and Bohemia. In Dresden, he found a friend and supporter in August
Röckel, a former conductor of the Dresden Royal Opera. Sacked because of his
democratic views, Röckel – who had since become a member of the Saxon Chamber of Deputies and the editor of a radical weekly, the *Volksblatt* – offered Bakunin, who was still living under a false name, hospitality and a hiding place in his
house. He also introduced him to his friends, including Richard Wagner, who was
at the time precariously holding on to his position as a conductor of the Dresden
Opera while at the same time – chafing at his dependence on royal patronage –
publishing anonymous articles in favour of a republic.

In the course of April, a long-brewing political crisis in Saxony came to a
head when its king – faced with the threat of a tax-boycott until he accepted
the people's constitutional demands – dissolved the Chamber of Deputies and
appealed to Prussia for military help. Röckel, fearing for his life, sold his furniture, gave some of the resulting money to Bakunin for his Bohemian project
and left for Prague. Bakunin promptly asked him to help with the preparations
for the Bohemian insurrection.

Röckel, however, found that things were not as they had been presented to
him. Czechs, Germans and Hungarians in Bohemia 'glared at each other jeal-
ously, convinced that each would gain from the repression of the other... Rather
than the powerful, widespread organization that Bakunin imagined himself to
be leading... I found scarcely a dozen very young people.'[56]

But whereas Marx and Engels were at this time propagating an equally unrealistic 'clash on German soil' with Russia and advocating world war for philosophical reasons, Bakunin needed a revolution for psychological reasons. As
E.H. Carr put it, 'Bakunin was like a man whose passion for his mistress is
inflamed rather than abated by the discovery of her infidelities.'[57] Aware that he
was 'deceiving myself and others with me', Bakunin realized that his plan for
Bohemia was 'ridiculous', but believed in it because he wanted to. As he later
wrote, 'the demon of destruction had taken hold of me... Instead of countless
obstacles frightening me, they excited my revolutionary thirst, driving me into
tireless and feverish activity. I was doomed to my demise. I foresaw it, and I
rushed towards it joyfully...'[58]

Having no faith in a German revolution, Bakunin took no interest in the
Saxon political crisis. But he found Dresden a lively place and decided to stay
there. On 20 April, upon learning that the Austrian Emperor had turned to the
Tsar for military help against the Hungarian revolt, Bakunin published another
Appeal to the Slavs to unite with the Hungarians and Germans against a Russian
invasion.

A week earlier, on 14 April, Marx had left Cologne on his tour of Northern
Germany and Westphalia to solicit funds for his newspaper. He was to be away

for three weeks, during which time, while Bakunin in Dresden kept his eyes fixed on Bohemia and expected to be summoned to Prague any day, the 1848–49 revolutionary drama, having taken a new turn at the end of March, rapidly moved towards its final act, to decide the fate of both of them and of millions in Europe.

27–28 March 1849: The German National Assembly passed a Constitution and elected Friedrich Wilhelm IV of Prussia 'Emperor of the Germans'.

3 April: Friedrich Wilhelm IV refused to accept the crown from the hands of the people.

The Constitution adopted by the Frankfurt National Assembly was as progressive as could be, guaranteeing individual liberty and equality before the law. On 4 March, in Vienna, the reactionary Prince Schwarzenberg had proclaimed a new constitution decreeing that Austria – including its Hungarian, Croatian and Italian populations – was a territorially indivisible state. The Frankfurt deputies, unwilling to accept Austria's minority nationalities in a 'greater' German state that would be a near-replica of the old German Bund, reacted by declaring that no part of the new united Germany 'shall belong to a state with non-German territories'. This clinched the hitherto unresolved question of the boundaries of the new German Reich. With Austria and the Habsburgs out, the Assembly offered the crown of a smaller but purely German Empire to the Hohenzollern King of Prussia.

Friedrich Wilhelm treated the Assembly's deputation to one of his vague long-winded speeches, so full of contradictions that it took them some time to understand that his answer was 'No'. Privately the King scoffed that the imperial crown offered him by the people was a 'sausage roll', a 'hoop made of mud and wood', a 'pig's crown', a 'crown by grace of butchers and bakers', a 'dog-collar'. He wrote to Ernst Moritz Arndt, 'This [crown] we speak of does not bear the sign of the holy cross, does not press the seal by the grace of God upon the head – it is no crown. [I], the son of more than twenty-four rulers, Electors and kings, will not be made a serf of the revolution.'

He would accept the crown only from princes equal to him in rank. But when the princes of 28 German states declared their readiness to offer it to him, he balked again, for these princes accepted the constitution proposed by the Frankfurt National Assembly. To Friedrich Wilhelm IV this smacked of recognizing the people's sovereignty, and he refused to share his prerogatives with them.

Austria withdrew from the Frankfurt Parlament. The Prussian representatives followed suit and walked out, leaving only a rump Assembly to face the consequences. With the dewy-eyed project of a united Germany thus killed, bitter disillusionment after a year's hopes set in, not only among the radicals but in large sections of the population in several German states, leading to a last spasm.

3–8 May: Revolution in Dresden, suppressed by Prussian troops.

11–13 May: Military revolt in Baden. The Grand Duke of Baden fled.

6 June: The rump German National Assembly moved from Frankfurt to Stuttgart.

18 June: The fewer than 100 remaining deputies of the rump Assembly were dispersed by the King of Württemberg's soldiers.

On 10 May, Marx, having returned from a journey which had yielded practically no funds at all, vented his frustrations and his fury at the Prussian King. In an 'almost hysterical' article, as it has struck some, Marx listed in the *Neue Rheinische Zeitung* the crimes which had accompanied the rise to greatness of the Hohenzollern 'family of corporals', its 'breaches of faith, perfidies', inheritance swindles and its servile obedience to Russian despotism. Yet this was not so hysterical when one considers that in 1847 and 1848 a poem by Heine titled '*Zu Berlin im alten Schlosse*' (In Berlin's Old Castle), in which the Hohenzollerns were presented as sodomites, was published more than once. This was only one of a series of poems in which Heine had been savaging Friedrich Wilhelm IV. In his article on 'The Deeds of the House of Hohenzollern', Marx in fact quoted an earlier poem by Heine, '*Der Wechselbalg*' ('The Changeling'), which described the King as a 'pumpkin-headed child', 'a monster' begot by 'the old sodomite ... on lies and perjury'. The article was to lead to Marx's expulsion.

A week earlier, on 3 May – the day fighting broke out in Dresden, kindling new hopes of a 'second revolution' in Germany – the trial of Ferdinand Lassalle opened before the Düsseldorf Court of Assizes. He had been in custody for more than 5 months since his arrest the day after he had publicly urged the Frankfurt National Assembly to issue a call to arms. Although the charges on which he had been remanded were similar to those against Marx – calling for a tax boycott and 'incitement to arms against the royal authorities' – the Prussian authorities treated them differently. Unlike Lassalle, Marx had refrained from speaking at public demonstrations and the authorities hesitated to stir public opinion by taking any action against the *Neue Rheinische Zeitung*.

Lassalle, because of his involvement in the unsavoury Hatzfeldt family affair, appeared to them to be more vulnerable – and yet a more dangerous agitator because in the mere three months of liberty he had enjoyed between August and November 1848 he had managed to rally Düsseldorf's democrats and workers as well as the peasants of the region into a united revolutionary force.

Marx, who had lost much of the workers' support and was about to sever his ties with the democrats, could not but appreciate this. On 3 January 1849, rallying to Lassalle's defence, he had published in his newspaper Heine's three-year-old letter to Varnhagen extolling Lassalle's exceptional intellect, scholarship and amazing combination of 'energy of will and aptitude for action'.

Joining this testimonial by 'one of Germany's greatest minds', Marx appealed to the Rhenish courts not to allow 'this 24-year-old genius who belongs to our poor country's most talented youth to rot in jail because of his selfless fight for freedom.'

But neither this, nor a petition presented by nearly 3,000 signatories, nor one deputation after another – one of them in March led by Marx – requesting Düsseldorf's Oberprokurator Nicolovius to speed up Lassalle's trial, met with any success. Confined to his cell throughout the dramatic developments which – starting with General Wrangel's occupation of Berlin in December – had culminated in the King's refusal to accept the imperial crown from the people's hands, Lassalle found other outlets for his pent-up energy.

He bullied the warden, insisted that the governor greet him with a civil 'Good morning' when visiting his cell, petitioned the investigating judge to dismiss the case against him out of hand or to release him on bail, and took Nicolovius to task for rejecting his requests for documents, without giving the legal reasons for his refusal. 'We are not living in Turkey', he reminded the prosecutor, 'but in a state which prides itself on its laws.' Besides continuing from prison his unfinished fight for the rights of the Countess Hatzfeldt, he had some of his petitions published in the *Neue Rheinische Zeitung* or printed separately, and otherwise maintained a vast correspondence. On 25 February, when he still hoped to appear before the Assizes in March, he was so confident of the ultimate outcome of the revolution that he wrote to his mother:

> Either Germany will be plunged back for ever into the night of the old conditions – in which case all science will be proved a lie, all philosophy a mere *jeu d'esprit*, Hegel a runaway fool escaped from a madhouse and all history an accident without any thought behind it – or the revolution will soon celebrate a new and decisive triumph.[59]

Before his case finally opened on 3 May, Lassalle wrote his defence speech and had it printed and distributed among his political and other friends. Using the law as a political weapon, he argued in essence that in the March 1848 revolt in Berlin

> the people won a constitutional state. The fundamental principle of a constitutional state is that it is no longer ruled by the will of the monarch but by the general will of the people as expressed by its representatives. In a constitutional state the true regent is the electorate.

It was therefore the Prussian government which, by its military putsch in Berlin and the dispersal of the National Assembly at bayonet point, had committed the most flagrant act of 'high treason'. In these circumstances, he argued, with General Wrangel suddenly turning into 'Prussia's law-giver' and the enforced constitution nothing but a paper monument to 'a King's treachery', the revolution – speaking strictly from a legal viewpoint, even leaving aside human rights and the sovereignty of the people – had become a 'juridical necessity... [and] ringing the alarm bell and calling the people to take up arms and man the barricades was the rightful duty of the citizenry.'

The court, ruling that the advance publication of Lassalle's defence speech violated trial procedure, excluded the public from the courtroom. Knowing that the speech had been read not only by the jury but by a larger public than could fill the courtroom, Lassalle thereupon refused to read his *plaidoyer*. In a short statement reacting to the prosecutor's demand that he be sentenced to 5 years in prison, he asked for his immediate acquittal. The jury, showing no mean civic courage at a time when Prussia was reinforcing its troops in the Rhineland to prevent any flare-up such as had started in Baden and Saxony, brought in a verdict of not guilty.

Nicolovius, however, determined to keep Lassalle in jail, had included in the charge-sheet a second offence, that of calling for 'resistance to state officials'. On this minor and rather ludicrous accusation – already implicit in the main charge of 'resisting the authorities' but subject to judgment only by the criminal court and not the jury – Lassalle was rearrested the day after his acquittal. After another two months in jail he was sentenced on 5 July to 6 months, but released the same day for medical reasons. His imprisonment was deferred until October of the following year, when he was to serve his sentence without deduction of the long months he had already spent in custody.

Although Lassalle's defence speech – containing such phrases as 'Three times more accursed than a foreign despot is the indigenous one who tramples his own country's laws underfoot' – was for decades to be cherished by Germany's workers as a memento of the 'democratic days of 48', his rearrest probably saved him from the blow which was soon to disperse Marx, Engels, Freiligrath and the whole 'party' of the *Neue Rheinische Zeitung* to the four corners of the earth.

Cologne was peaceful on 9 May, when Marx returned from his fund-raising tour. But on the 16th, 5 days after his article on 'The Deeds of the House of Hohenzollern' appeared, he received an order issued from Berlin to leave Prussian soil 'within 24 hours'. The order stated that, not being a Prussian citizen, he had 'disgracefully abused' the hospitality given him by 'inciting contempt for the existing government' and calling for its violent overthrow. Marx barely had time to borrow some money and sell the printing press he owned to pay the typesetters and paper suppliers for the last issue of the paper. Printed in flaming red, it appeared on 19 May. Altogether, Marx had invested in it no less than 7,000 Thaler, of which the smaller portion was his own last cash and the rest borrowed and to keep him in debt for years.

Engels had left on 11 May for Elberfeld, the slummy half of his native twin town of Barmen-Elberfeld. With its unemployed population, it had been taken over by a Committee of Public Safety. Engels was assigned to command a battery of small cannon on the bridge leading to wealthy Barmen and the villas of the factory owners. Legend has it that Engels's bigoted father – the area's textile lord, who was on his way to Sunday church – was shocked to run into his son wearing a red sash which made him conspicuous among the gunners on the bridge. Whether or not this incident really took place, some burghers on the Public Safety Committee were in any case terrified by the young man's reputation as a Communist, and Engels was run out of town.

He returned to Cologne in time to contribute an article to the 'red number' of the *Neue Rheinische Zeitung*. Besides a farewell poem by Freiligrath, the paper's last issue, which is said to have sold 20,000 copies instead of the usual 5–6,000, included an editorial by Marx in which, declaring that 'the royal terrorists, the terrorists by the Grace-and-Law of God are brutal, contemptible and vulgar in practice, cowardly, secretive and deceitful in theory, and dishonourable in both', he promised revenge: 'We also are ruthless, we ask no consideration from you. When our turn comes, we will not conceal our terrorism.'

Jenny Marx, liquidating her household yet again, sold her furniture to avoid its confiscation. The Marxes, with their three children, their maid Lenchen, and Engels, left Cologne on 19 May and went to Frankfurt. There they stayed with their Communist friend Joseph Weydemeyer and his family. Weydemeyer helped Jenny to pawn the silver she had taken along in a borrowed suitcase. With that money she paid the fare for the children and Lenchen to travel to Trier on a visit to her mother. Marx and Engels, having tried to persuade left-wing members of the Frankfurt Parlament to fight for their constitution and if necessary to summon the revolutionary militia fighting in Baden to their aid, went south to meet the leaders of the insurrection in Baden and the Bavarian Palatinate, who had established a provisional government. They tried to convince them to march on Frankfurt and take the National Assembly under their protection – even if not explicitly summoned to do so – against the reactionary government.

It was the last possibility of saving the revolution. But neither the 'Left' in Frankfurt nor the leaders of the democratic militia heeded their advice.

37

The Dispersal of the Doctors of Revolution

On 2 June 1849, four days before the 'rump' German parliament was forcibly moved to Stuttgart, Marx and Engels separated. Engels, deciding to 'gird my sword', went to join the rebels fighting the Prussians in the Bavarian Palatinate. Marx left for Paris, where he took lodgings on the Left Bank under the name of 'Monsieur Ramboz'. A cholera epidemic was raging. 'The sunless heat', wrote Alexander Herzen, who was in the city at the time, 'the frightened, unhappy population and the hearses racing each other to the cemeteries' made it a dismal place. But Marx, resuming contact with old Communist friends like Dr Ewerbeck and the leaders of several secret societies, saw Paris as a 'revolutionary crater', and within a few days of his arrival he was wildly prophesying to Engels in Baden that 'a colossal eruption' was imminent.

A last popular rising did take place in Paris on 13 June, when more than 20,000 workers and others took to the streets unarmed. But they were brutally dispersed by Louis Napoleon Bonaparte's dragoons. Herzen, marching with a crowd of demonstrators, suddenly found himself 'nose to nose' with a snorting horse and a dragoon threatening to strike him with the flat of his sword. On a visit to the Conciergerie, where some of his friends were held, Herzen saw as many as 60 men crowded into one small room, in the middle of which stood a large slop-bucket that was emptied once every 24 hours – and all this in civilized Paris, under the cloud of cholera.[1]

Having no appetite for being locked up there and 'fed on rotten beans and putrid meat', Herzen bought himself a false passport and fled to Geneva. Before leaving, he arranged for his wife Natalie to follow him with Herwegh, whose ridiculous military expedition to 'liberate' Germany had cost him both his revolutionary reputation and his wife's money. Herzen thus unwittingly set the stage for Natalie's romantic love affair with Herwegh, which was to end in tragedy.

One of the first men Marx went to see on his arrival in Paris was Heine, who was also the last person he had visited before leaving the city the previous year. During the 8 weeks Marx was now to spend in Paris he went to see the sick poet three times, alone or in the company of Georg Weerth. Heine had recently affirmed his faith in a personal God and it is not known what he and the atheist Marx discussed. It may have been not only the failure of the attempt to unite Germany under a parliamentary system, but the fact that the Hungarians, who in April had driven the Austrians out of their country and proclaimed an independent republic, were now facing a Russian invasion.

Hungary's revolutionary poet Sàndor Petöfi had dedicated the German translation of his poems to Heine. While he was reading them, the Tsar – like Nikita Krushchev over 100 years later – sent an army to quell the Hungarian revolt just when the Magyars seemed on the point of invading Austria. Petöfi fell in the course of the fighting. 'O Hungary, thy name is like the sound of silver trumpets', Heine was to write of the Magyar fight for freedom against two world powers. In another dramatic event, on 3 July, during Marx's fourth week in Paris, 40,000 French troops dispatched by Bonaparte occupied Rome, heroically defended for a month by Garibaldi, and restored Pope Pius IX. Garibaldi managed an adventurous escape with his Brazilian wife Anita and part of his 6,000-man Legion. And by the 20th, Austrian troops were beginning a long siege of Venice.

As Jenny Marx, with her three children and a fourth on the way, arrived in shuttered, cholera-stricken Paris, Marx wrote to Weydemeyer that he was penniless. Jenny pawned all her jewelry and Marx appealed for help to his friends in Germany.

Fortunately Ferdinand Lassalle, just released from prison after his sentence was deferred, collected a large sum for the Marxes among his Rhenish friends. Lassalle himself, furious at the police for having searched the house of the Countess von Hatzfeldt, also helped, financially and otherwise, one of the editors of Marx's newspaper and other Communists who had been jailed for their agitation in the Rhineland.

- **13 August 1849**: The Hungarian army capitulated to Russian forces at Vilàgos.
- **28 August**: Besieged Venice fell to Austrian troops.

The Hungarians, caught between Austrian regiments in the west and 140,000 Russians pouncing on them from the north, put up a fierce resistance in June and July, but had little chance. After the storming of Budapest and President Kossuth's escape via Turkey to the USA, the capitulation at Vilàgos and the fall of Venice a fortnight later brought the feverish 'Springtime of the Peoples' to an end after 18 fratricidal months. The victors promised clemency to the defeated, but a wave of savage repression followed. In reply to Hungarian pleas for mercy, Prince Schwarzenberg replied: 'A very good idea, but we must have a bit of hanging first.' He did not mention those executed by firing squads. In

Italy the Austrians shot 'Garibaldini' boys captured during their retreat to San Marino. Garibaldi himself again made good his escape with a small band, only to mourn his pregnant wife, who died during their flight.

In Paris, in the course of the arrest and investigation of German radicals who had taken part in the rising of 13 June, the French police discovered the identity of Monsieur 'Ramboz'. On 19 July, Marx had been notified that he and his family must leave Paris within 24 hours. He was not expelled from France, but banished to Morbihan in Brittany. Upon learning that this was one of France's 'most unhealthy coasts, muddy and fever-exhaling', he appealed to the Ministry of the Interior to have the order rescinded. But he obtained only a delay.

Feeling sure that his banishment to 'the Pontine Marshes of Brittany' was a 'cloaked attempt at murder', Marx wrote to Engels on 23 August that he had decided to leave France. With the reactionary regimes restored all over Europe, England loomed as the only country where he might be safe. On the 24th, with the little that remained of the money provided by Lassalle, he left for London, having asked Engels to join him there and 'not to leave me in the lurch'.

He travelled together with a young German revolutionary, Karl Blind, and the two took a room above a coffeehouse in Grosvenor Square. Jenny was allowed to stay in Paris until the lease on their apartment expired on 15 September. Then, with the help of the faithful Lenchen, she packed up her three children and with 100 francs sent by Freiligrath she paid the fare to cross the Channel. Marx was down with 'a kind of cholera' and Jenny, who was 7 months pregnant, arrived sick and exhausted. Weerth installed the family in a boarding house in Leicester Square. Shortly afterwards, they moved to a dingy two-room flat in Chelsea.

There, on 5 November, Jenny gave birth to a boy. As it was Guy Fawkes Day, he was registered as Guy Marx, though his parents called him Guido or Föxchen, which sounded in German like 'Little Fawkes' or 'Little Fox'. The Marxes and their 4 children, each of whom had been born in a different country, were to spend their first winter in London living from hand to mouth in those sleazy two rooms until they were evicted for being £5 behind with the rent.

Engels had no sooner arrived in the Palatinate at the beginning of June than he submitted a two-part article to the official newspaper of its Provisional Government. With his usual cocksureness, he predicted an imminent war – 'in a few weeks, perhaps in a few days' – between 'the massed armies of the republican West and the enslaved East.' The newspaper found the article 'too inflammatory' and published only its first part. Engels thus found that the Palatinate revolution was a 'pothouse' affair, but when he heard that the Prussians were coming, he joined the motley corps of 700–800 insurgents made up of Baden regulars, irregulars and revolutionary volunteers from Germany and a sprinkling of French, Hungarian and Polish workers.

As he wrote to Jenny Marx on 25 July, he took part in 4 engagements: 'The whistle of bullets is an altogether trifling affair. I saw plenty of cowardice during the campaign but there were less than a dozen cases of cowardice in the face of the enemy. I did see plenty of courage that bordered on folly.'[2]

The fighting in the Bavarian Palatinate was only a sideshow compared to the revolt in Baden, in which 45,000 of its fugitive Duke's soldiers, or practically his entire army, had been involved since May. Under the capable command of the Polish revolutionary Ludwig von Mieroslawski, it put up strong resistance to the Prussian forces until the Prussian Crown Prince, with two full army corps and Hessian reinforcements marching through Württemberg, fell upon its flank and forced it to retreat. By mid-July the whole of Baden had been occupied by the overwhelmingly superior Prussian forces, except for the fortress of Rastatt between the Rhine and the Württemberg frontier. By that time, the small force which Engels had joined was wedged in between the Prussians on one flank and the French and Swiss border on the other and could only retreat southwards through the Black Forest. Engels was lucky to cross into Switzerland on 12 July, together with his commander August Willich, the ex-artillery officer whom he knew from Cologne as Gottschalk's ally and whom he described as a brave soldier, though 'a true Socialist'.

Mieroslawski's 6,000 men held out at Rastatt until 23 July. The fall of this fortress marked the end of all the revolts in southwest Germany. Prussian officers at Rastatt, acting in the name of the absentee Duke of Baden, passed draconic sentences on the leaders and participants of the Baden insurrection. Of Willich's smaller force, 28 insurgents were shot and 68 sentenced to long prison terms.

Engels, after dallying for a while in Switzerland, decided to join Marx in London; he embarked at Genoa on the *Cornish Diamond*, which sailed up the Thames on 10 November. Although his parents had sent him money for the journey, his mother wrote on 2 December to tell him not to expect any further support from them 'so long as you pursue a way of life which, to put it mildly, does not meet with our approval.'

Marx and Engels had struggled valiantly to goad the bourgeoisie, not least by means of a war with Russia and 'world war', to overthrow the monarchies, but had failed in their attempt to direct events on the Continent. Nor had the Chartist movement in England, but for a large demonstration in London, fulfilled any of the high hopes Engels had placed in it.

Nonetheless, with the fever of revolution still burning in their minds, they believed, as Marx wrote in letters to Weydemeyer in Frankfurt, that England would be the scene of the next revolutionary 'dance' and that a new and violent crisis was also imminent on the Continent. Immediately upon his arrival in London, Marx, besides joining a committee for the relief of political refugees who were coming in droves, had become occupied with two projects – the reconstitution of the Communist League and the revival of the *Neue Rheinische Zeitung*, this time by its subtitle as a 'Political-Economic Review'. By mid-December arrangements had been made for its publication in Germany, and the first issue appeared in January 1850. Four more issues, written mostly by Marx and Engels, appeared at irregular intervals between the end of March and the end of November, when it collapsed for lack of readers.

The revived Communist League ran into trouble with the arrival in London of August Willich and his election to its Central Committee. Willich, who belonged to the 'left' wing of the Communist movement, wanted action, rather than socio-economic theories, as the basis of political practice. A compromise circular, sent in March to the few local branches left in Germany, stated that in the next revolution the working class should constitute itself as an independent political body and establish 'their own revolutionary workers' governments next to the official government organs.' In a further clause, Marx and Engels, who drafted the circular, wrote that the workers must 'everywhere put up their own candidates beside the democratic candidates, even where they have no prospect whatever of being elected', thus implicitly admitting that their previous policy on this issue had been wrong.

In mid-April a *Société universelle des communistes révolutionnaires* (World Society of Revolutionary Communists) was formed in London. The founding fathers who met to sign its statutes were Marx, Engels and Willich, for the League; two French exiles, Jules Vidil and Adam, who represented Blanqui's insurrectionist movement; and George Harney, the leader of the revolutionary faction of the Chartists. The signatories swore an oath of Communist solidarity to be maintained across national borders. The statutes, drawn up by Willich, proclaimed that the World Society's chief aim was 'the overthrow of all privileged classes, the subjection of these classes to the dictatorship of the proletariat by maintaining the revolution in permanence until the realisation of Communism, which shall be the final organisational form of the human family.'[3]

Neither the Communist League nor the World Society lasted very long. The League split in two in September, disrupted by a fierce squabble between the Marx 'party' and the Willich-Schapper faction – so fierce that Willich and one of Marx's associates fought a duel over it in Ostend, since duelling was outlawed in England. When the Blanquists sided with Willich, Marx severed contact with them and henceforth attacked them as well as Willich. This meant the end of the World Society – no similar Socialist-Communist alliance transcending national frontiers was to arise before the establishment of the First Workers' International.

On 15 September Marx, giving up all predictions of an imminent revolution, transferred the League's Central Committee to Cologne and informed the workers in Germany that they had '15, 20, 50 years of civil war to go through to change the circumstances and fit yourselves for power' and that Louis Blanc's fiasco in France provided the best example of the danger of coming to power too soon.

Marx was now left with no more than 15 to 20 followers in London. In Germany, following an attempt on the life of Friedrich Wilhelm IV and the arrest and trial of a dozen Communists in Cologne, the League was soon to cease its existence. But when the time came, Lenin was to read carefullly the Marx-Engels Circular of March 1850, in which they advocated the establishment of a workers' party 'both clandestine and public', and revolutionary city councils, clubs or armed workers' committees parallel to the official government organs.

The tiny Communist League had done its job. Born out of Weitling's 'League of the Just', and never numbering more than 1,500 or 2,000 members in all its 'international' branches, it was one of the seminal elements out of which – by the cunning of history and Marx's *Communist Manifesto* – the mighty 20th-century Marxist-Leninist state system was to emerge.

On the night of 28–29 August 1849, while Marx, freshly arrived in London, was bedding down for his third night in Grosvenor Square, a detachment of Saxon cavalry set out from Dresden to escort three carriages to Königstein. Each carriage held a fettered prisoner and his two guards. One of the three prisoners, who were locked up towards morning in the rock fortress of Königstein, was Bakunin. The Russian, whose 'demon of destruction' had driven him to 'feverish activity' in connection with an imaginary revolution in Bohemia, had been caught in a real one which had occurred under his very nose in Dresden, and in which he had at first taken no interest.

The Dresden revolution lasted for only 6 days, from 3 to 9 May. Compared to the prolonged military insurrection in Baden, it was a paltry affair; but it will forever be memorable for bringing together two such extraordinary characters as Bakunin and Wagner at a crucial moment of their lives. They were of the same age, Bakunin 35, Wagner 34. The diminutive composer (Wagner was only 162 cm. tall) and the towering Bakunin had first met at August Röckel's house.

On Palm Sunday, 1 April 1849, Bakunin heard Wagner conducting a general rehearsal of Beethoven's Ninth Symphony: 'He came up to me unabashedly in the orchestra', Wagner wrote, 'in order to call out to me that, if all music were to be lost in the coming world conflagration, we should risk our own lives to preserve this symphony.'

In *My Life*, Wagner was to recall the tremendous impression Bakunin made on him:

> Everything about him was on a colossal scale, and he had a strength suggestive of primitive exuberance... At ease when stretched out on [Röckel's] sofa, he could hold forth before a motley group of people on the issues of revolution...

> 'The annihilation of all civilization' was the objective on which he had set his heart... It was necessary, he said, to picture the whole European world, with Petersburg, Paris, and London, transformed into a pile of rubble... The builders of the new world would turn up of their own accord; we had to worry only where to find the power to destroy...

At the same time, Wagner noted that Bakunin was a 'truly likeable and sensitive person'. While preaching horrendous theories of world conflagration, 'he noticed that my eyes were troubling me as a result of the bright light, and despite my protests, held his hand before it to shield me for a full hour.' Wagner often took Bakunin along on his daily walk and more than once invited him to his house for supper. On one occasion, Bakunin made the composer sing and play for him the first scenes of *The Flying Dutchman* and, after listening 'more attentively than anyone else had ever done, he exclaimed "That is terribly beautiful!"'

Yet he rejected all Wagner's attempts 'to acquaint him with my artistic plans more closely. He was not interested in my Nibelung project.' Nor did he want to hear anything about Wagner's conception of the ideal theatre of the future.

Wagner felt drawn to this 'prodigious man' who, in his view, combined 'the purest humanitarian idealism with a savagery utterly inimical to all cultures.' He summed up his relationship with him as 'fluctuating between instinctive horror and irresistible attraction'.[4] It was not only Bakunin's interest in music that drew the two together. As conductor of Dresden's Royal Court Orchestra, Wagner, chafing at his dependence on the King's patronage, had for the past two years been agitating for a reform that would free the theatre of the court's control. Between 1848 and 1850 he completed the preliminary prose sketch for all four parts of the *Ring of the Nibelung*, thus, like Marx in *The Communist*

Manifesto, prefiguring his life's work over the next quarter-century. During the same short span of time, he also published 4 essays, in one of which, not unlike Marx in the *Manifesto*, he fashioned his own type of war machine: *Gesamtkunstwerk der Zukunft* (The Total Art-Work of the Future).

Bakunin's talk of 'fire and destruction' found a ready listener in Wagner, who was to come up with the idea of reforming not only the theatre but the whole outmoded society which acclaimed Meyerbeer's operas by means of a 'world-destroying, world-redeeming' fire cure.

At news of the February revolution in Paris, Wagner had become involved in politics. Even before meeting Bakunin, he had written unsigned subversive articles and caused a public scandal by wondering aloud – in a lecture to a democratic society – whether 'the perfection of social and political conditions' could not be best achieved if the King 'would recognize it as being in his own best interests to establish a truly republican form of government,' and get rid of his court officials.

Before Röckel fled Dresden, Wagner had promised him to continue the publication of the *Volksblatt*, and when the Dresden rising began, he took part in it all the more zealously as he knew that his position as royal Kappelmeister had become untenable.

On 3 May angry crowds in Dresden – outraged at the King of Saxony's dissolution of the Diet and his appeal to Prussia for military help – tried to storm the city arsenal to arm themselves against the expected Prussian 'invaders'. Although 6 civilians and one officer were killed in the attempt, and more wounded, Bakunin did not take seriously the bourgeois restiveness which had been building up in Saxony since the beginning of the week. On that day he was actually about to leave Dresden for Malta with a Greek-Rumanian friend, Prince Ghika. Opinions differ as to whether he decided not to leave because he lacked the money for the fare or because of the influence of friends, who had a 'hard time persuading him to stay'.

It was only on Friday the 4th, after the King had fled and a Provisional Government had been formed, that Bakunin decided 'the movement' had become a revolution. Wagner was on his way to the revolutionary headquarters at the Town Hall when he met Bakunin 'wandering elegantly in a black dress coat' among the barricades. Wagner's active role in the revolution had started with his climbing to the steeple of the Kreuz Church, a practice he repeated daily, not only for the 'sensation of vast delight' at the splendid view and 'the combination of bells and cannon', but in order to survey the gun emplacements. On one occasion he signed an order for hand-grenades and eventually he induced the printer of Röckel's abandoned *Volksblatt* to produce posters exhorting the populace and the Saxon soldiers to oppose the 'foreign' Prussian troops. Since this was to result in a warrant for his arrest for treason, a charge punishable by death, Wagner was to write in his autobiography that 'nobody paid any attention to these posters' – which were actually distributed to all the barricades – 'save the people who subsequently denounced me'; and he otherwise belittled his presence at most revolutionary meetings by writing that he attended them simply as an 'observer' or an 'impassioned spectator at a play'.

Actually, on that Friday, at the Town Hall, Wagner took Bakunin into the inner councils of the Provisional Government formed by three members of the Saxon Chamber of Deputies, K.G. Todt, S.E. Tzschirmer and Otto Heubner (who was also a member of the Frankfurt National Assembly). The three were at a loss what to do. They had been negotiating a truce with members of the Saxon government, who, knowing that Saxon and Prussian troops were on the way, insisted that they and all rebels surrender with their weapons, dismantle the barricades and accept other humiliating terms.

Bakunin told the three 'democratic' but inexperienced leaders of the insurrection that if they wished to avoid a massacre by the approaching Prussian and Saxon troops, they must organize a fighting force and take the offensive. Following his criticism of the amateurish barricades he had seen, the city engineer was sent to reinforce them according to his instructions.

By noon on the 5th, according to Todt's later testimony, Bakunin, having no confidence in the military commander of the rebels – a mercenary ex-colonel in the Greek army named Heinze – had brought in two Polish military advisers, Heltman and Kryzanowski. Establishing his headquarters in the Council Chamber of the Town Hall, 'separated behind a fire screen from the rest of the group', he took over the command of the revolution in practice, if not in name. Although this inevitably led to friction with Heinze – whom he later accused of treason for sending him only 50 men instead of the 300 he had requested for a renewed attempt to capture the arsenal – all accounts agree that during the fierce street fighting that began that night with the arrival of the Prussians, Bakunin behaved with exemplary bravery. On Sunday, the insurgents set fire to Dresden's Opera House. Bakunin's two Polish military advisers fled. When Heubner's two colleagues in the Provisional Government likewise took to their heels, Bakunin went with Heubner to the scene of the fiercest fighting and exhorted the volunteers who had abandoned a barricade or two to retake them.

According to Wagner, Bakunin 'distributed advice in every direction with remarkable sang froid.' Even Marx, no friend of Bakunin, was to write that, while 'the shopkeepers of Dresden' refused to fight, the rebels 'found a capable and cool-headed leader in the Russian Michael Bakunin.'[5] As for the reasons why he threw himself into a revolution in which he did not believe, he told Wagner that he could not abandon the poor 'noble' Heubner to face the music alone, but also that he hoped to use Dresden as a springboard for his Bohemian revolution. He is said, in fact, to have obtained a secret promise from the Provisional Government that, if the revolt was victorious, they would support his pet scheme.

On 7–8 May, in fierce house-to-house fighting, the Prussians prevailed. Heinze was taken prisoner. Other rebels were shot and thrown into the Elbe. Early on the 9th it was all over. The rebels had lost 250 killed and 400 wounded; of the soldiers, over 100 were dead and another 200 injured. The Provisional Government ordered a general retreat to Freiberg, Heubner's home town some 25 km. away.

On Tuesday, at the height of the fighting, Wagner had fled from the centre of Dresden to his home in the remote suburb Friedrichstadt. In *My Life* he was to claim that he made great efforts to return to the barricades, but he was actually in a hurry to pack up house and get away.

On Wednesday morning, Heubner and Bakunin, on their way to Freiberg, met Wagner in a carriage with his wife, their parrot and his dog Peps. In unclear circumstances, which may have been due to the confusion of various militias moving this way and that, Wagner got the wrong impression that the Civil Guard of Chemnitz had been on its way to help the Dresden insurrection but had withdrawn upon hearing that Dresden was lost. Switching carriages to join Heubner and Bakunin on the ride to Freiberg, he told them this, adding that the workers of industrial Chemnitz were sure to supply them with enthusiastic reinforcements for continuing the revolution.

At Freiberg a brief conference took place. Heubner, who was anxious not to expose his battered revolutionary force to new calamities, asked Bakunin for his political views and his opinion on whether or not to give up what might be a hopeless fight. Bakunin answered that he opposed all forms of government, and would not risk his life for any of them. As for the second question, he said that, having gone so far, and after so many lives had been sacrificed, they must go on 'even if only the two of them were to be left', to save at least their honour; otherwise no person would in future have any faith in a revolution.

After a short rest at Freiberg, Heubner and Bakunin, neither of whom had enjoyed a single night's sleep for a week, left for Chemnitz. Relying on Wagner's information, Heubner meant to establish the Provisional Government there with the support of the local populace and 'the many contingents of volunteers purportedly streaming in from all directions', as Wagner disingenuously put it later. Arriving at Chemnitz on the night of 9 May, Heubner and Bakunin were surprised to find no sign or sound of revolution and collapsed exhausted on their beds in a hotel. In the early morning hours, they were arrested by the local authorities in the name of the Government of Saxony.

'Instead of the expected help', Bakunin wrote in his Confession, 'we found treason: the reactionary citizens arrested us in our beds during the night.'[6]

Wagner had prudently left with his wife for Weimar, where he stayed with his friend Liszt. Soon he heard from Dresden that his house had been searched and on 16 May a warrant was issued for his arrest. Fearing that the Weimar authorities would extradite him, he obtained some money from Liszt and, equipped with a false passport, made his way to Switzerland. After a short while he decided to try his luck in Paris. Arriving there on 2 June, during the siege of cholera, he wrote that 'eight days in Paris were enough to convince me of the revolting worthlessness of the Paris Opéra and the whole art business here.' Liszt sent him money for the return fare, and by 6 July Wagner was back in Zürich. Banned from Germany, he was to spend the next 11 years in exile.

Todt and Tzschirmer, who had defected from the Dresden Provisional Government, likewise fled to Switzerland. (Todt died there in 1852, and Tzschirmer returned to Germany after the 1865 amnesty.) Heubner, who together with Bakunin had been shunted for weeks from one prison to another before they were brought to Königstein on the night of 28–29 August, was to pay heavily for having 'nobly' followed Bakunin's advice to stay and fight to the end. The third prisoner, Röckel, had returned to Dresden just before the fall of the city and was captured separately.

The fact that Bakunin had risked his neck for a cause not his own was to make him the hero of many legends. One concerned the burning of Dresden's Opera House, which was attributed by the Prussians to the inspiration of the 'barbarian' Bakunin, although there is no evidence that he had anything to do with it. Another was the famous story spread by Wagner, among others, to the effect that when it became clear that the battle was lost Bakunin proposed to the surviving rebels to blow up their command-post in the Town Hall with themselves in it. There is no concrete proof that Bakunin ever contemplated this suicidal action.

But the fact that he, as well as Heubner and Röckel, were found guilty and sentenced to death in January 1850; the cruel touch which accompanied the Saxon King's clemency in commuting their sentences to life imprisonment without their being told; the drama of 12–13 June, when Bakunin, rudely awakened during the night and driven away, thought he was being taken to his execution only to find himself incarcerated next evening in the Hradcin citadel of Austrian-controlled Prague; the fact that Austria and Russia subsequently vied with one another in demanding his surrender from the Saxons but in a secret deal decided that each should punish him in its turn; the mooted plot by Russian *Carbonari* to rescue him from the Hradcin which caused his transfer in a panic to the fortress town of Olmütz, where he was fettered and chained to the wall of his cell – all this made Bakunin a figure larger than life to both his enemies and his sympathizers. 'Rumours mated and multiplied, compounding themselves into fictions... [Bakunin's] promethean fantasy, until now propagated mainly through his own violent declarations, was becoming a "reality", first in the press, then to the world, and, finally, for history.'[7]

This helps to explain the tranquil, almost resigned mood with which he bore his lot. 'Sick of life' when he had rushed towards his 'demise' at Dresden in spite of foreseeing it (as he was to confess to the Tsar), and sticking it out to the end because it would have been disgraceful to run away, he had been captured in a state of physical and mental exhaustion. But now that he had saved his honour and proved for all the world to see that he had never been a Tsarist agent, he was at peace with himself. The tension between the two sides of his personality, the one that demanded that he assert his manhood by means of power and destruction and the other that always called him to retreat passively into the sanctum of his 'bright inner world' whenever things in the real external world went badly, suddenly abated.

A strange calm bordering on indifference came over him, to the point where he at first refused to help Otto, his Saxon-appointed lawyer, to prepare his defence and then was so laggard about it that Otto wrote it by himself. 'I am well and tranquil. I study mathematics a lot and am reading Shakespeare now and study English,' Bakunin wrote from Königstein to Ruge and others, stressing that he was being treated 'extremely humanely... Thanks to several friends, I have here almost everything that one could desire, within reasonable limits – a comfortable room, books, cigars.'[8]

The books, cigars, as well as money, were sent to him by his friend Reichel and Reichel's sister Mathilda, by Herzen and Emma Herwegh. Bakunin was allowed to correspond with them and also received gifts from anonymous German democrats. But he was not allowed to receive newspapers published since his arrest and when taken out for exercise he was chained to two soldiers.

But this was nothing compared to the hardships he suffered from June 1850 to May 1851 in Prague and in the Olmütz fortress in Moravia. Austria had a long account to settle with him, for in his *Appeal to the Slavs* he had publicly called for its destruction, and Gustav Straka, whom he had sent to Prague to foment revolution, was now a prisoner in the same block of the converted St George monastery on the Hradcin hill. Bakunin was treated like one of Europe's most dangerous conspirators, which may have flattered his ego, but meant in practice that he was denied legal representation, forbidden to send or receive mail, and no longer allowed into the open air; for exercise he was walked up and down a corridor flanked by 6 soldiers, and every 15 minutes, night and day, a guard looked into his cell through the peep-hole.

Providentially, some time during the 9 months of this regime, Captain Franz, the officer in charge of his case, took pity on him and conducted his correspondence for him. Herzen, Herwegh, and some German democrats, including his former lawyer Otto, continued to send him money. As his clothes had remained in Dresden, he was in rags, but he spent most of the money on expensive mathematics books and only the rest on a new night-shirt and some desperately needed food, for the prison rations always left him hungry. Cut off from the world, Bakunin, who had known periods of depression when lonely and isolated in less adverse situations, showed his spirit and a spark of dignity at Olmütz, where, when not chained to the wall, he was subjected to intensive interrogation. Tried by a military court, he insisted that he would only answer questions 'by the officer conducting the inquiry', and that no compulsion would make him break the silence if the officer were changed.

The trial was in fact no more than a ritual. On 15 May 1851, he was found guilty of high treason and sentenced to be hanged. This second death sentence, unlike the first, was promptly commuted to life imprisonment on the same day. By nightfall he had been reduced to a physical wreck, was placed on a special train and dispatched towards the fate worse than death that he had feared throughout most of his imprisonment: the train from Olmütz was headed for the Russian frontier, where he was to be handed over to the Cossacks of the hawk, Tsar Nicholas I.

In the early hours of 17 May, a little over two years after the Dresden revolt, his Austrian fetters were removed. Bakunin jocularly asked if he could keep them as a souvenir but the Austrian guards refused to hand over their imperial government's property. The Russians replaced them with heavier fetters of their own. A detachment of 20 Cossacks and 8 gendarmes then took him by road to St Petersburg. Having been away from Russia for 11 years, the spiritually exhausted man was almost relieved to be back on his native soil, among people who spoke his language.

A week later, he found himself in a cell of the notorious Peter-and-Paul fortress, across the Neva from the Tsar's palace. In Russia he faced no further trial or a third sentence to the gallows, for as early as 1844 he had been sentenced *in contumaciam* to hard labour in Siberia for an indefinite period to be determined by the Tsar. He was thus at the mercy of the despot whom he had declared to be his and Europe's chief enemy. Since the days of Peter the Great, many a Russian had been hanged or tortured to death without trial within the mute precincts of the Peter-and-Paul fortress, and Bakunin had reason to expect the worst.

He was all the more surprised when, in July, Count Orlov appeared in his cell with a message from Nicholas I assuring him that his life was not in danger and urging him to confess his sins to His Majesty, not as a criminal but as if he were writing to a spiritual father-confessor. The result was Bakunin's *Confession*, an extraordinary document to be published only after the Bolshevik Revolution. The Tsar, having shown the same paternalism with which he had extracted penitence from the Decembrist rebels and with the same result, read it with interest, but made a note in the margin saying that this intelligent but 'dangerous young man must be kept shut up'. Then he laid the document aside for the attention of the next tsar. As a result, Bakunin was to languish for three years in the fortress, where the wall of each cell, as later described by Kropotkin, was covered with painted felt and 'five inches of rough linen and yellow printed paper' held by an iron-wire net, making for a kind of double wall 'to prevent the prisoners from speaking with one another by means of taps on the wall.'[9]

In 1854, on the eve of the Crimean War, he was transferred from this 'silent grave' and shut up in the Schlüsselberg fortress. Although Nicholas I died in 1855, Bakunin was kept there for another two years, under the more liberal Alexander II, and then sent into exile for an indefinite period in eastern Siberia. There, he might well have been forgotten among the Tatars had he not, with extraordinary resourcefulness, outwitted the Tsarist empire with all its supervisory machinery, and made a sensational escape.

In London in the spring of 1850, Marx and his family had been brutally evicted from their Chelsea flat. As Jenny wrote to Weydemeyer on 20 May, little Guido-Föxchen was sucking her chafed and bleeding breast when the landlady came in and demanded the rent they owed her:

> As we did not have the money... two bailiffs came and sequestrated all my few possessions – linen, beds, clothes – everything, even my poor child's cradle. They threatened to take everything away in two hours. I would then have to lie on the bare floor with my freezing children and my bad breast. Our friend Schramm, hurrying to town to find help, got into a cab but the horses bolted and he jumped out and was brought bleeding back to the house...

> Finally a friend helped us. He paid our rent and I hastily sold all my beds to pay the chemist, the baker, the butcher and the milkman who suddenly besieged me with their bills.

The Marxes went to a hotel for refugees in Leicester Street, where they stayed until April. Between then and the end of the year, they moved twice again, first to a small two-room flat at 64 Dean Street and then to a slightly larger but equally squalid one at No. 28 in the same street in Soho.

They were to spend the next 6 increasingly wretched years in that area. In the autumn of 1850 Engels, realizing that he must work for a living, took a junior position in the Manchester office of his father's textile firm. For the next 14 years, before the death of his father was to make him a rich man, he earned only around £200 a year. Living a double life as a Communist and a gentleman-merchant maintaining his bachelor apartment and a separate household for his mistress, as well as a horse in a private stable, he was in no position to send Marx more than £1 or £2 from time to time during the financial crises and blows of fate that descended on Karl and Jenny Marx year after year.

On 19 November, a few days after Engels's move to Manchester, the child Guido died suddenly of a convulsive fit. Jenny, who was 6 months pregnant, was devastated, particularly as the sickly infant had known hardly a happy moment during his short life and had 'always been between life and death'. Two years later, Jenny was still blaming the litle angel's death on his drinking only 'torment and sorrow and cares from my breast'.[10]

Shortly before Guido's death, Marx had asked Weydemeyer to sell his wife's silver after redeeming it from the pawnbroker and send him the money. On 8 January 1851 Engels sent Marx £1 to pay the overdue rent, but Marx was now so desperate for money that in March – while engaged in studying the subject of money and currency at the British Museum – he drew an unauthorized bill on his mother in Trier. On 28 March, Jenny gave birth to her fifth child, Franziska. At the same time Lenchen Demuth, the devoted maid and factotum of the Marx household, was secretly pregnant, 'mysteriously' so, as Marx himself used the word when on 31 March he wrote Engels that there was a certain 'mystère' he was going to explain to him in a subsequent letter.

In the event, Marx travelled to Manchester, where on 20 April he confessed to Engels that he was about to become the father of another child. Indeed, on 23 June, less than three months after Jenny was delivered of Franziska, Lenchen was giving birth to an illegitimate son of his. In all the misery about him, and perhaps as a distraction from it, Marx – who described himself to Engels as a 'strong-loined paterfamilias' – had sired this child while Jenny was pregnant. At the time, Jenny was nearly 38, Marx was 34, and Lenchen 28.

By a secret arrangement concluded with Engels during Marx's 6-day April visit to Manchester, the paternity of the boy, Henry Frederick Demuth, was not recorded on the birth certificate. The baby was quickly removed from its mother in Dean Street and passed off as the bastard son of Engels, the debonair bachelor, who assumed all expenses and responsibility for him. Placed in the care of a coachman's family and never told who his father was, Frederick or 'Freddy' Demuth was given a minimum education. He became a common labourer, and eventually a skilled 'engineering worker' in Hackney.

Marx had to keep the secret of his adultery not only to save his marriage but to avoid being confronted with a passage in *The Communist Manifesto* in which, sarcastically debunking 'the bourgeois claptrap' about family mores, children, love and the sanctity of marriage, he had written, 'Our bourgeois, not content with having the wives and daughters of their proletarians at their disposal,... take the greatest pleasure in seducing each other's wives.' Finding no other way to avoid accusations of hypocrisy, he resorted to a common Victorian cover-up.

Jenny is said not to have known of Karl's adultery.[11] In her *Reminiscences*, however, she was to write: 'In the early summer of 1851 an event occurred that I do not wish to relate here in detail, although it greatly increased our worries, both personal and others.' But whether she knew or not, Marx himself, 5 weeks after the 'event', suggested that an atmosphere of hysteria had turned his domestic life into hell:

> Everything at home is in a constant stage of siege. The outbreaks of tears night after night try my nerves and drive me mad. Naturally I cannot do much work. I am sorry for my wife. The main burden falls on her, and *au fond* she is right. *Il faut que l'industrie soit plus productive que le mariage* [Industry must be more productive than marriage]. Despite all this, you will recall that I am by nature *très peu endurant* [very impatient] and even *quelque peu dur* [a little hard] so that from time to time I lose my equanimity.[12]

The next year turned out to be even worse. In February 1851 Marx was confined to his home because he had pawned his winter coat. At Easter little Franziska came down with severe bronchitis. Three days later she died. Like Guido, she was just a little over one year old. Because there was not a farthing in the house her funeral was delayed while a desperate Jenny ran around begging for help, until a friendly French refugee gave her £2 for a coffin.

Jenny was to survive the tragedy of Franziska's death and more births and deaths that succeeded each other in the continually impecunious Marx household. During these wretched years, Marx, in the act of pawning Jenny's Argylls' silver, suffered the embarrassment of being detained by the police on suspicion of having stolen it; and on another occasion, when Jenny was dangerously ill, they did not call a doctor because they had not paid his previous bills.

In January 1855 Jenny gave birth to a daughter, Eleanor, but three months later they were to bury 8-year-old Edgar, the third of their children to die. The loss of the only son he ever acknowledged affected Marx to the point where he confessed to Engels in English that he was 'broken down'. Some 4 months later, he would write to Lassalle: 'Bacon says that really important people have so many relationships to nature and the world, so many objects of interest, that they easily get over any loss. I do not belong to these important people. The death of my child has deeply shattered my heart and brain, and I feel the loss as freshly as on the first day.'[13]

In May 1856 Jenny inherited £156 from a deceased uncle in Scotland. In the summer, while she was visiting Trier with her three surviving daughters, Jenny-chen, Laura and the 18-months-old Eleanor, her ill mother died, leaving her another £120. Following this double windfall, the Marxes moved in October 1856 from unhealthy Soho to a small rented house in the airier district of London near Maitland Park, not far from Hampstead Heath. Redeeming all the linen and other small remains of the Argyll side of her ancestry from the pawn shop, Jenny once again 'had the pleasure of counting the old Scottish damask napkins.'

One would have thought that £270 pounds at that period would last the Marxes for a year, but Jenny's pleasure was short-lived. 'One article after another', she was to write, 'soon had to go back to the pop-house.' They now lived more comfortably, but what with paying off old debts, buying some furniture and the cost of educating Jennychen and Laura, Marx was having difficulties as early as January 1857 paying the rent, and was intimating to Engels that he was actually 'in a more desperate situation than five years ago. I thought I had swallowed the quintessence of muck. *Mais non*. The worst thing is that this crisis is not temporary.'[14]

An ailing and emaciated Jenny, exhausted by grief, worries and 7 pregnancies – the seventh ended in a miscarriage – was by then reduced to a physical and mental wreck. Paradoxically, the brainy Marx, who was later to state that 'the way men produce their means of subsistence conditions their whole social, political and intellectual life', wrote in the above letter that he had 'absolutely no idea' how to cope with his own new domestic crisis. Marx felt for Jenny and gave her all the love he was capable of. He doted on his three bright daughters. Jenny, for her part, while copying his manuscripts and acting as his secretary until Eleanor at 17 or 18 took over, then and later was tortured by the fact that Karl, 'the prop of my life', had to suffer so much from petty worries.

During these unsettling years, Marx developed the first symptoms of the lung congestion, liver inflammation, hemorrhoids and painful furuncles and carbuncles which were to become chronic and to plague him throughout the long years he was eventually to spend on the writing of *Das Kapital*. Remarkably, though, between 1850 and 1856, while often unable to work, either because of Jenny's 'nervous excitement' or his own physical afflictions – and raging at the world and subconsciously at himself for the 'shameful' conditions of their lives – Marx produced his famous pamphlet *The Eighteenth Brumaire of Louis Bonaparte*; wrote a couple of hundred articles on current affairs for the *New-*

York Daily Tribune (some of them actually written by Engels in his name, while some of Marx's own were published by the paper as leaders) and more than 100 for the *Neue Oder-Zeitung*; spent long days at the British Museum researching, and at home late hours at night collating, the material that was to go into the 800-page manuscript of his *Critique of Political Economy*.

At the same time he also achieved his greatest literary success with a series of 6 articles on Lord Palmerston. In May 1855 the London publisher E. Tucker brought out one of these sensational articles – in which he accused the British statesman of being an 'agent' of Russian absolutism – as a pamphlet in *Tucker's Political Fly-sheets*, which sold 15,000 copies and then went into a second edition. At the beginning of 1856, the whole series on Palmerston, which had originally appeared three years earlier in the *New-York Daily Tribune* and in London's *People's Paper*, was reprinted in London's *Free Press* and also issued as a separate pamphlet.

But Marx saw not a penny from these publications. He did not know, and seemed not to want to know, how to make money. 'The writer must earn money in order to be able to live and write, but he must by no means live and write for the purpose of making money,' he had declared in his youth. 'His works are ends in themselves; so little are they a means either for himself or for others that, if necessary, he sacrifices his own existence to their existence...'

Captive to this principle, Marx never once thought of taking any kind of regular job. As early as in 1851, he had expressed his fear that if their endless and ruinous worries about making ends meet continued, 'it will be the end of my wife.'[15] When Jenny was in her early 50s, Marx wrote Engels three letters saying, though not in this order, (a) 'My wife has for years absolutely lost her temper [in English]. She is taking out her miseries, irritations and bad humour on the children and is torturing them to death.'; (b) 'She is very unwell and completely deaf'; (c) 'My wife's nerves are very affected and I fear that things may take a bad end.'[16]

And so it was to be. In 1864, when Marx received the final instalment of his inheritance upon his mother's death, as well as a bounty of £800 bequeathed to him by his friend Wilhelm Wolff, his family was for the first time relieved of financial debts and worries. Nonetheless, the cumulative effect of 20 years of unremitting privation, frequent illnesses, 7 pregnancies, the prostration of seeing three of her children die in a row – and of her continual disappointment at never, until her death in 1881, seeing her husband's indefatigable 'struggle' for the poor and weak crowned with any substantial success – took a heavy toll of Jenny's physical and mental health. An undated letter she sent to Marx while he was in Manchester, some time before Engels moved to London in the 1870s, reveals the state of neurosis and melancholy to which she was sometimes reduced: 'Meanwhile I sit here and go to pieces. Karl, it is now at its worst pitch... I sit here and almost weep my eyes out and can find no help. My head is disintegrating. For 8 days I have kept my strength and now I can no longer...'[17]

'When I see the sufferings of my wife and my own powerlessness,' Marx had written as early as 1852, 'I could rush into the devil's claws.'[18]

Marx's love for his three daughters, whom he entertained with endless games, stories and romps on picnics, has been called 'the most luminous feature' of his otherwise irascible and domineering character. But, determined as he was 'not to allow bourgeois society to turn me into a money-making machine', but to 'follow my goal through thick and thin',[19] he endured every trial, rage and frustration, and went on with his life's work.

In Paris in 1855, Heinrich Heine was at the height of his fame, but no longer able to hold even the telescope through which, from a high, awninged balcony, he had been watching the carriages and the ladies in crinoline passing along the Champs-Elysées.

His latest book of poems and ballads, *Romanzero*, published by Campe in Hamburg, had sold 20,000 copies in 4 months. As if to make up for his cruel three-year-long silence, Campe – after visiting Heine in 1851 and finding that he was as ill as he had claimed – had done this great cycle of poetry proud by issuing it with 'the first illustrated book jacket' in the history of print. It had since been followed by a new edition of Heine's *Religion and Philosophy in Germany*, by his collected political reportage in *Lutezia* and by *Poems 1853 and 1854*.

His youthful *Buch der Lieder* was the first European book to be published in Japan, and with the songs in it constantly reprinted and set to music, Heine was well aware of his future place in German thought and literature, though he did not dream that he would become, as Barker Fairley put it in modern terms, 'possibly the greatest hit in the history of lyrical poetry.'

Admiring letters poured in from all over the world, but he was like a man presented with pots of glory when he could literally not hold a spoon. Since his collapse in front of the Venus de Milo in 1848, he had been dying a slow death, incurable but miraculously alive in spirit on his legendary 'mattress-grave', the two mattresses on the floor on which he preferred to lie – first in the rue d'Amsterdam and since November 1854 on the fifth floor at 3 avenue Matignon, near the Champs-Elysées – rather than on his bed, because he could more easily reach the papers and books spread about him. And from the floor his broad-shouldered mulatto nurse would carry him to his bath or to an armchair when he dictated to a secretary or received visitors.

While the Austrian Emperor now ruled half of Europe more autocratically than Metternich ever had, his eccentric young wife, the Empress Elisabeth, swooned over Heine's bitter-sweet songs. German workers sang his political ditties at secret meetings and on one occasion a men's choir from Cologne, on a concert tour of Paris, came to sing for him settings of his poems.

But Heine, lying 'moribund' for more than 7 years now, sustained only by that irony which made him call himself 'the first mortal to be both dead and alive' and condemned by the high expenses of his medication to earn his living 'on his deathbed', was more concerned with the great ultimate questions. With the monotony of his life during these years interrupted only by Berlioz, Caroline Jaubert, Princess Belgiojoso, Béranger, Gautier, Laube, Fanny Lewald and other selected visitors whom Mathilde admitted to his presence from a stream of curiosity-seekers, he had ample time to wrestle with them; and they plagued him at night when his mind floated, as it were, over his immobilized body.

With Immanuel H. von Fichte, a son of the great philosopher and himself a professor of philosophy, he had long discussions about the immortality of the soul. The Princess Belgiojoso, returned from a pilgrimage to the Holy Land, brought him her personal confessor, Father Caron, in an attempt to convert him to Catholicism and save him from hell. Heine's response was that he believed in no dogma or ritual and that, born as both a Jew and a poet, he needed no intermediary with God. In fact, the cosmopolitan Heine had in 1850, in a letter to Laube, acknowledged a 'personal God who exists outside Nature and man's mind.'

Questioned the same year about his return to Judaism, Heine said to the writer Ludwig Kalish, 'I have not returned to it, since I never left it.... I found my way to God through neither the church nor the synagogue. I introduced myself to Him and was well received. He has cured my soul. I wish he could have done the same for my body.'

Next, the poet who had moved on 'all the dancing-floors of philosophy', repudiated his allegiance to Hegel – whose 'cobwebby dialectic couldn't lure a dog from the hearth, it couldn't kill a cat, how much less a God'[20] – and henceforth, in prose and in verse, he argued with God, sometimes accusing 'the great Author of the universe' of treating him with sheer malice, while acknowledging with mock-humility that the 'Aristophanes of the Heavens' was a superior satirist than he was himself when it came to jesting on a colossal scale.

Flatly denying that his 'return' to God was due to a weakened brain, but claiming on the contrary that suffering had sharpened his understanding of the needs of the individual in a complex world, Heine simply explained in his 1854 *Confessions* that he had found solace in the old Bible which the Jews had saved out of the Roman destruction and carried 'like a portable homeland' through the darkest ages: 'What a book! as great and as wise as the world... It is the book of books...'

Admitting that Moses, because of his prohibition of graven images, had always struck him as an enemy of the arts, Heine wrote now, two years before his death, that what he had failed to see was that Moses the Law-giver was 'himself a great artist... He did not fashion his works from baked bricks and granite like the Egyptians. He took a poor shepherd tribe and from it he created a great immortal, holy people,' that would outlast the centuries better than any monument of bronze or stone.[21]

Describing Moses the Liberator as a revolutionary but practical-minded 'Socialist', Heine observed that at a time when not only the Pharaohs but the philosophical Greeks and the whole ancient world justified slavery, he realized that he could not wipe it out in one day and sensibly ordered every slave to be set free after 6 years. Nor did he reach for the impossible and rashly decree the abolition of property – instead, he sought to bring it into accord with morality by instituting the jubilee year, when all alienated hereditary land reverted to its original owner.[22]

Of the Hellenes, whom he had so admired, Heine wrote: 'I see now that the Greeks were only handsome youths, whereas the Jews were always men, un-yielding men,' mature enough to face up to the woes and problems of the human condition. In an obvious self-projection, Europe's emaciated rebel of all causes expressed his pride in belonging to a martyred people who had 'given the world a God and a morality' and fought on the battlefields of the spirit through 18 centuries of persecution and misery.[23]

Significantly, in his *Confessions* Heine commended to Marx the story of Neb-uchadnezzar, the Babylonian king who 'fell from the height of his self-conceit and ended up crawling like an animal on the ground and eating grass.' He referred to 'my thick-headed friend Marx', and called him a 'godless self-god'.[24] As S.S. Prawer has remarked, 'There is irony here of course, but no sug-gestion that the word "friend" is anything but sincere.' But Heine was too complex a personality – 'complex beyond analysis, the best personification of the jagged modern soul, torn with unanswered questions'[25] – to accept any dogmas like Marx's or to see things in black and white.

In 1854 Campe published the articles Heine had written in Paris during the 1840s. In the dedication to this two-volume collection titled *Lutezia*, Heine wrote that, although these articles had stopped before the February 1848 revo-lution, they had predicted that 'catastrophe with the prophetic pain suffusing the old heroic saga' of the Trojan War, 'where the fire destroying Troy does not constitute the finale, but is heard mysteriously crackling in every verse. I have not described the tempest but the darkly approaching weather clouds carrying it in their bosom.'[26]

But in 1842 Heine had not only forecast the Franco-Prussian war 30 years before it happened; he described it as merely a prelude to a more fantastic drama, that of the class-war that would ultimately lead to 'a European, nay, a world revolution', whose outcome might be 'one fatherland embracing the earth and only one faith', with perhaps 'a single shepherd driving a uniformly shorn, unisonously bleating human herd before him with an iron staff!' Whatever grim forebodings of totalitarianism Heine had when he spoke of a new apocalypse whose writer would have to invent new monsters to depict it, and in the same 1842 article warned 'our grandchildren' that 'the future smells of Russian leather, of blood, of godlessness, of lashes and much hard whipping', he would not, in the face of the 20th-century horrors of Bolshevism, Fascism, Nazism, two World Wars, have had to retract them had he lived today.

By 1855, when dealing with the 'terrible syllogism' presented by Communism in the Preface to the French edition of *Lutezia* (*Lutèce*, which within a dozen years was to go into 9 editions), Heine was terminally ill and his outlook had, if anything, become more pessimistic. With ony a muffled echo of the external world reaching him, he was yet lucid enough to discern trends and events and to express his dread that utilitarian Communism would end all beauty and destroy the achievements of civilization. But he was half-resigned to the prospect that the future belonged to Communism for the simple reason that the old society – unmindful of 'the premise that every man has a right to bread' – deserved to die.

In mid-June, a young lady came to the avenue Matignon and delivered a music score which a Viennese composer had asked her to take to Heine. She was about to leave when Heine called from his room and asked her to come in. The mystery surrounding the stranger, prim, delicate-looking, 27 years old and known chiefly as Camille Selden (the pseudonym under which she later published her memoirs, *Les Derniers Jours de H. Heine*), was of her own creation. Born in Prague, the illegitimate daughter of a Count Nostitz, her name when she met Heine was Elise Krinitz (the name of her adoptive parents). Married off at 18 to a Frenchman who spent her dowry and then got rid of her by interning her under some pretext in a private mental home in London, she lost her speech for a while, but recovered and on her release returned to Paris. Some time after obtaining a divorce, she met Heine's friend Alfred Meissner. He gave her Heine's *Book of Songs*, in which she found solace for her sorrows. Meissner, however, knew her only as 'Margot'. To another friend she was Mlle de Belgern. But it was as Camille Selden that she later won a niche in literary history for the gentle devotion with which she kept Heine's spirit alive at the end of his long struggle with death.

On that first visit, she left after a short conversation about Vienna and the opera, and promised to return. Heine, who 4 years earlier had written in one of the poems in *Romanzero*, 'Just one more time I'd like to cherish / A woman's favours ere I perish,' waited impatiently.

Discovering that she had left her address on the music score, he sent her a letter saying he longed to see her again. Camille Selden replied by messenger within a matter of hours. Her letter bore a seal with the image of a fly. 'La Mouche', as Heine called her from then on, came to him the following day, and after that – except for a short visit abroad – daily during his remaining 9 months. She read to him, looked after his correspondence in lieu of the secretary he had just dismissed, held his hand and otherwise gave the 58-year-old invalid the feeling of savouring love once more.

'Our loathing of everything humdrum, conventional and affected, above all, our whole-hearted devotion to the cult of the beautiful – these became the spiritual bonds uniting us,' she was to write in her memoir of him. Mathilde, for once, suppressed her jealousy. Her better instincts told her to tolerate the intruder whose presence helped to soothe her husband's pains, and on a few occasions she even sent the nurse to fetch her. 'La Mouche', to whom Heine addressed 6 poems, in which he called her 'the passion flower of my lugubrious autumn', was a strange wish-fulfilment and 'almost fairy tale' ending to his life.

Heine died on 17 February 1856. A non-conformist to the end, he had stipulated that neither a Catholic, nor Protestant, nor Jewish minister officiate at his graveside. His last words are said to have been: 'I must write... paper... pencil.' He died a year before the King of Prussia, who had so often been the butt of his satire as the incarnation of all that was wrong-headed in Germany, was forced by 'weakness of the brain' to hand over the reins to his brother, the King and future Emperor Wilhelm I.

Heine was buried in Montmartre Cemetery. Dumas, Gautier, Baudelaire, Mignet and 100 or so friends, not counting Mathilde and 'La Mouche', attended his funeral.

In that same year, Herzen in London celebrated his reunion with the poet Ogarev, the boyhood friend with whom, at the time of the execution of the Decembrists in 1825, he had sworn an oath to fight the Tsarist tyranny. The two had not met since Herzen's departure from Russia in 1847. Ogarev had since been abandoned by his first wife and came to London with a young woman he had married before leaving Russia.

Herzen had arrived in London in 1852, a short but impressive figure with his 'long chestnut hair and beard, small luminous eyes... suave manner and intense power of irony and wit', but a grief-stricken man at 40, as he was then. The debacle of the 1848–49 revolutions, whose bloody suppression he had witnessed in Italy and France, had been capped by the tragedy which was to haunt him for the rest of his life – the seduction of his beloved Natalie by Georg Herwegh, with whom he had formed a friendship bordering on intimacy. Destiny itself seemed to have struck at Herzen, for the public hurt to his honour, not to mention his feelings, caused him by the Natalie-Herwegh affair had been followed by the drowning of his mother and one of his and Natalie's sons in a shipwreck off the French-Italian Riviera, and by Natalie's death shortly after she had returned to him and sent Herwegh packing.

Barely arrived from Switzerland, with few friends in London, Belinsky dead, Ogarev in Russia and Bakunin a prisoner in the Peter-and-Paul fortress, Herzen wrote this lament to Arnold Ruge: 'Happy the men who saved at least their kin. I have lost everything... Beaten in my own home, having gone through terrible and bitter experiences, I drag myself without aim or occupation from one country to another.'[27]

In that same period, however, he started to write the story of his life, an occupation that was to keep him busy, in between his journalistic activities, for the next 15 years and to result in the 4 volumes (in the English version) of his masterpiece, *My Past and Thoughts*. Excerpts from it published in London in 1854 were an immediate success. In 1857 – long before E.H. Carr's classic account of Natalie Herzen's liaison with Herwegh in *The Romantic Exiles* was to appear – Herzen wrote his emotional but personally unsparing 100-page version of his wife's affair with the German poet, but did not allow its full publication during his lifetime. Among the details to be revealed posthumously was an incident which had occurred in 1842, shortly after Herzen had been allowed to return to Moscow from his latest banishment to Novgorod.

Coming home late one night, he fell for the temptations of the pretty serf girl, Katerina, who opened the door for him. Seized by contrition, he confessed his peccadillo to his wife and was surprised by the devastating effect on Natalie: 'Her faith in me was shaken, her idol shattered.' Natalie became a prey to melancholy and fell ill. 'She got over it, but only after she came close to the grave.' Herzen also wrote that he and Natalie eventually became 'wiser and sadder', but the incident marked not only the end of their private dream of otherworldly love, which on their honeymoon in 1838 had made him cry in a fit of ecstasy 'Christ has risen in Vladimir!' but was a portent of the future.

Ogarev had shared the elation of that moment with him. According to Annenkov, it was the soft-souled and incurably Romantic poet who had early inculcated in Herzen – and especially in Natalie – the view that educated people with independent means had the right to live as they pleased, 'ignoring the moral strictures preached by people unacquainted from birth with the charms and pleasures of complete material independence.' Before the Herzens went abroad, Natalie, between the shoals of reality and domestic life, the death of infants and the birth of others, had become bored with the year-long idealistic conversations which led to nothing in their Moscow salon. In the intoxicating atmosphere of Paris, according to Annenkov, she blossomed. She not only became a genuine Parisienne, but longed 'to taste the ambrosia of exalted emotions which few mortals had tried and which romanticism provides for its faithful servants.' In the sophisticated, ingratiating and seductive Herwegh she found her 'dazzling' Lohengrin, only to recoil at his wanton egoism and to be gripped by that 'intense disgust and remorse for everything that had been done' which 'led her to her early grave,'[28]

In July 1857 Herzen launched the Russian-language periodical *Kolokol* (The Bell) in London. Edited jointly by him and Ogarev, it quickly became the most important Russian publication of its kind abroad, and during the 10 years of its existence it made Herzen known as one of the most eminent political figures among Russian 'dissidents' and revolutionary émigrés driven to congregate in the Western capitals after the mid-century. Ogarev, a victim of his own ideal of free love, had not only allowed his unfaithful first wife (Maria Lvovna) to ruin him financially, but for a time had followed her to Rome to live with her and her lover. What happened in London within 6 months of his arrival was hardly surprising. His new young wife, Natalie Tuchova, fell passionately in love with Herzen. Herzen explained their intimacy to his friend as 'a new pledge of our triple union' and the result was a new domestic triangle, with Herzen this time cast in Herwegh's role. Natalie bore Herzen three children, of whom the gentle and tolerant Ogarev assumed formal paternity. Ogarev, who was sterile and sought solace in women, drink and poetry, eventually found a happier love in the arms of an English prostitute whom he picked up in a pub and settled down with.

The remarkable thing is that throughout all of this, and notwithstanding the emotional consequences on the three self-romanticizing Russian principals as well as on Herzen's double set of children, Herzen and Ogarev remained devoted to one another and moved together to Switzerland when *The Bell* transferred its editorial office to Geneva. Having got most of his fortune out of Russia, Herzen was able to disseminate his philosophical and political ideas not only through *The Bell*, whose popularity aroused Marx's envy, but in pamphlets and brochures. Upholding individual liberty, the dignity of man and free will above all else, Herzen, always a sceptic, took a pessimistic view of the values of Western society after the collapse of the 1848 revolutions.

Sharing none of the current notions about 'the process of history', he argued that this process was irrational and not marching towards some determined culmination. There was an interaction between events shaping man and man's role in shaping events; but, he wrote, 'If only people wanted to liberate themselves instead of liberating humanity, how much they would do for the salvation of the world and the liberation of humanity,' more than all 'systems' and dogmas promising an ultimate salvation that would only turn into new tyrannies. He supported every revolutionary cause, but took a dim view of Marx's proletariat as the emancipator of mankind. Like Heine, he felt instinctively that 'Communism will sweep across the world in a violent tempest – dreadful, bloody, unjust, swift; in thunder and lightning amid the fire of the burning palaces, upon the ruin of factories and public buildings the New Commandments will be enunciated'; but he echoed Heine's fear of the excesses of this new 'faith' in the name of which 'the new barbarians' sweeping from the 'garrets and the cellars' would at a command from above unleash a cataclysm in which the just and the unjust would perish. He predicted that after their victory another 'mortal battle will be joined in which Socialism will occupy the place of today's conservatism and will be overwhelmed in a new revolution as yet invisible to us.'[29]

Disillusioned by Western bourgeois-capitalist society and the end of the 1848–49 convulsion in a Walpurgis Night celebrated by the reactionary governments forming an ecumenical police force and abolishing 'safeguards that exist even in backward China and Persia', Herzen was no less disappointed in the liberal camp for having ignited hopes for freedom without putting up a real fight for its proclaimed ideas. Yet his very pessimism about the future of a divided continent, which had yet to solve its social and other problems, led Herzen to turn his eyes back to Russia and to think optimistically that this backward empire with its 'terrible present' might ultimately offer a unique solution.

It was Ferdinand Lassalle who, in 1858, persuaded the reputable Berlin firm of Franz Duncker not only to publish Marx's *Critique of Political Economy* but to offer him the unusually high fee of nearly 200 Thaler, payable in two instalments. Marx laboured hard to divide his unmanageable 800-page manuscript into several books or booklets. In January 1859, when he was ready to send off the first part of it for publication under the above title, he had, as usual, 'not a farthing to mail or insure' his single copy of it, and was forced to apply to Engels for £2 before he was able to dispatch it.

Lassalle had by this time, by dint of his 'tenacity of will bordering on the insane' (as Heine had characterized it), achieved a position such as Marx could only dream of. Fulfilling everything he had promised the Countess Sophie von Hatzfeldt when he was 20, he had won her a divorce from her feudal potentate of a husband, and in 1854, after 36 lawsuits spread over 8 years, he had exhausted Count Edmund to the point where he agreed to restore to his wife a considerable portion of their immense joint fortune.

By the age of 29, rewarded by the Countess with an annual pension of 4,000 Thaler, Lassalle, besides the satisfaction of victory over Prussia's aristocracy and judicial apparatus, was assured of a comfortable, even luxurious, existence for life. He lived with Sophie von Hatzfeldt in Düsseldorf. He had 'rescued' her and restored her self-esteem, and she – being 20 years older than he – had a moderating influence on his fiery temperament. Theirs was to be a unique life-long bond based on absolute mutual trust and equal freedom for each partner. At times it bore the character of a mother-and-son relationship and for a time, in 1855, it became a *ménage à trois* when George Kindworth, a minor diplomat, and his daughter Agnes Denis-Street stayed as house-guests at the Countess's residence. Agnes, who did secretarial work for Lassalle, bore him a daughter, Fernande. Lassalle told the Countess he would raise Fernande as 'a masterpiece of education', but she died as a baby.

A prolonged tour of Constantinople, Smyrna, Damascus and other places in the Orient that Lassalle undertook in 1856 ended his liaison with Agnes, and he and Sophie von Hatzfeldt realized that they could not live without one another. But in 1857 – when Lassalle got the King of Prussia to rescind the edict forbidding him to reside in Berlin – they were forcibly separated because the Queen would not have both him and the 'red Countess' in the capital at the same time. Lassalle had in the meanwhile finished his remarkable study of Heraclitus the Obscure, most of which he had written when he was 20. The first volume was issued by Duncker in November 1857, the second in 1858. Lassalle's reconstruction from fragments left by the Greek philosopher of his whole system on the motion of particles in the universe was a sensational scholarly achievement, which won him immediate acclaim in the highest academic circles from Alexander von Humboldt down.

By the time Marx in 1859 was finally scratching together £2 in order to mail his manuscript to Duncker, Lassalle had been received by acclamation into Berlin's exclusive Philosophic Society. He lived in a splendid apartment in Unter den Linden and entertained Varnhagen von Ense, the writers Ludmilla Assing (who fell in love with him) and Fanny Lewald, the philologist Ardolf Stahr, the conductor Hans von Bülow and his wife, the publisher Duncker (whose wife likewise fell in love with him), his former teacher Professor Böckh and others of Berlin's intellectual elite.

Marx, on the other hand, incensed when Duncker did not reply to his letters, rudely wrote to him on 28 May: 'More than three weeks ago, I received the last three printer's sheets. The corrections that needed to be made could have been done comfortably in one day... I categorically demand that you put an end to these manoeuvres, which appear to me to be highly suspicious.'

Duncker wrote to Marx that he was imagining things, and explained that he had been busy at the Leipzig Book Fair. Marx apologized, but when three weeks passed and nothing happened, he fired off another irate letter threatening Duncker that unless he promptly received the book as well as the remainder of his fee he would publicly attack him.

By this time Duncker had had enough. He replied that the *Critique of Political Economy* had come out on 11 June, enclosed the remaining 90 Thaler due to Marx and added: 'The tone of your letters makes it impossible for me to want to continue our relationship, and, indeed, it makes me almost regret altogether that Lassalle had ever established any contact between us.'

The first volume of Marx's work attracted little attention. The second never appeared. It was to take Marx years, after botching things with the only publisher willing to take a risk on him, to find another. The further books or booklets which he had planned to extract from the mammoth manuscript on which he had struggled for 7 years, never materialized; and whatever the intrinsic interest of the *Critique of Political Economy*, it was eventually to be superseded by *Das Kapital*.

The relations betwen Marx and Lassalle were to last only another couple of years. They reached their first high-point in 1861, when, following Prussia's amnesty of political exiles, Lassalle invited Marx to Berlin, entertained him royally for nearly a month at dinners and gala parties with high society, took him to a ballet performance, for which the Countess von Hatzfeldt got them a box right up against the royal one (to annoy the Prussian King and Queen), and offered to help him resume a political role in Germany as co-editor of a radical daily to be financed by the Countess. The latter impressed Marx as 'a very distinguished lady', intelligent, lively, 'strongly interested in the revolutionary movement, and has an aristocratic *laisser aller*.'

The following year, in London with the Countess on the occasion of the World Fair, Lassalle visited the Marxes, who had pawned everything they possessed to keep up appearances. Lassalle showered Marx's wife and three daughters with gifts, lent him £15, and told Marx that he could draw a bill on him for any amount, provided a third party guaranteed to cover him. Lassalle told him of his plan to launch a political movement in Germany that would incorporate many of Marx's ideas in a form acceptable to the German workers. But Marx, unable to tolerate anyone not inferior – and exasperated to hear that Lassalle was about to complete a 'rapid' study of economics, while he was still labouring on a mass of material on the subject – refused his collaboration. He pocketed Lassalle's £15, drew a bill on him for another £60, and did nothing about the guarantee. When reminded of it, he was offended. A few days before the bill was due in November 1862 he sent Lassalle the money, wrote that he trusted their relationship would 'withstand this shock', but in his spleen cut off all personal relations with him.

This was not the only reason for their rupture. Lassalle admired Marx, but was not intimidated by him. The Berlin newspaper project had come to nothing, partly because Marx's idea (as he wrote to Engels) was to keep Lassalle under 'strict discipline' as an editorial underling; but when he had proposed to invite Engels as co-publisher, Lassalle's rejoinder was: 'Three of us is one too many, unless you and Engels agree to have one vote between you.'

Lassalle had returned from London to find Berlin in the throes of a political crisis. The bourgeois liberals, having gained a majority in the Prussian Chamber, turned down the War Minister's military budget. With Bismarck inaugurating his premiership by governing without a budget, Lassalle adapted Marxism to practical politics and founded the Allgemeiner Deutscher Arbeiterverein, the first German labour movement. Charged with class incitement for his Workers' Programme – which Marx called 'nothing but a bad vulgarization of the Communist Manifesto'[30] – Lassalle got himself acquitted by a brilliant court defence.

Never quite accepting Marx's concentration on 'materialism' to the execution of man's mind and will, he launched a feverish campaign for universal suffrage and direct secret voting, on the idea that once the new working-class party obtained representation 'in all law-making bodies in Germany' it would become a national party capable of attaining power and carrying out a Socialist programme in a future united Germany.

Increasingly affected by an improperly cured syphilis contracted in Paris at the age of 22, Lassalle drove himself indefatigably, and when about to lose his voice had his throat painted with silver nitrate in order to address cheering crowds all over Germany.

He was seconded by Hess, who, arrived from Paris in the wake of the amnesty, saw in him a man 'of the stock of Marx', but less aloof, more charismatic and better able to fire the people. Indeed, Lassalle electrified the German workers with speeches which sounded to them like the trumpet calls of a heroic new Siegfried. Hess stepped in for him when he was unable to appear in Cologne.

Lassalle's Allgemeiner Deutscher Arbeiterverein was the nucleus of the Social-Democratic Party whose mighty growth was to make it Germany's largest political party within a few decades. His contacts with Bismarck, to whom he had sent his Workers' Programme with the remark, 'Here is the constitution of my realm, for which you will perhaps envy me', were watched with horror by Marx. Lassalle's strategy of solving the social-economic problem within the framework of Europe's system of national sovereign states contradicted Marx's vision of the proletariat as the international class that would overthrow all other classes and ultimately dissolve itself in a classless society.

This, and some cruel jokes a jealous Marx traded with Engels in derision of Lassalle's self-assertiveness, was to lead to his vilification by their followers. Late into the 20th century, orthodox Marxist publications would belittle Lassalle as a 'petty-bourgeois Socialist'. Edmund Wilson and Jacques Barzun were among the first to restore Lassalle to his rightful stature. Barzun wrote that he was

> everything that Marx was not – a judicious scholar, an artist, and a man in whom logic and enthusiasm combined with a rare degree of balance. He was above all a born leader of men and a natural master of politics... Whether in the courtroom or on the platform Lassalle's studies in law, history, government and philosophy made him a formidable debater, but they appear at their fullest and maturest in his written works.

> In strong contrast to Marx's crabbed polemics and tortuous erudition, everything in Lassalle is lucid, generous, and orderly... When he borrowed from Marx the doctrine of surplus value to explain the formation of capital he was careful to make full acknowledgment... The conclusion so often insinuated, that Lassalle was a hasty and incomplete popularizer of Marx, is thus groundless, another instance of the desire to rewrite history.[31]

Lassalle's end was as tumultuous as his life. Charged with high treason for attacking Bismarck's policy of 'blood and iron', which was to cause three wars in 7 years, Lassalle was sentenced in Düsseldorf to 12 months' imprisonment, appealed – and got the sentence halved, and then deferred. Seen off by a huge crowd of workers at the railway station, he left for a rest in Switzerland. There fate caught up with him in the person of Helen von Dönninges, the beautiful 21-year-old daughter of a Bavarian diplomat. In Berlin, she had treated Lassalle as her 'lord and master'. In Switzerland she wanted to marry him, but her father – who saw in Lassalle no Siegfried but a radical agitator – was forcibly opposed to this. Lassalle twice refused her offer to elope with him, fearing the scandal would damage his political future. Instead, he delivered her into the hands of her family, fully convinced of his ability to obtain their consent to a proper and honourable marriage.

Baron Dönninges, however, promptly spirited her away. Lassalle moved heaven and earth – mobilizing the Countess von Hatzfeldt, the Bavarian Foreign Minister, Richard Wagner and the Bishop of Mainz, among others – to force

Helen's father to permit him to see her. Always fighting with the law in his hand, he invoked a paragraph against coercion before he obtained the baron's consent.

But the girl never appeared at the proposed tryst. Browbeaten and disconcerted, she informed the over-confident Lassalle that she was going to marry her one-time fiancé, the young Rumanian Prince Racovici. Duelling for his honour in a field near Geneva, Lassalle was felled by Racovici's first bullet and died a few days later in the arms of the Countess von Hatzfeldt.

On 2 September 1864, after a funeral service in Geneva attended by 4,000 mourners, his embalmed remains were placed on a train. Thousands upon thousands attended memorial assemblies as it passed various towns in the Rhineland, until the Prussian police – who had blocked the Countess's intention of publicly exhibiting Lassalle's body, for fear of disturbances – simply confiscated it, rearresting Lassalle, as it were, even after he was dead. He was buried in his native Breslau.

His original gravestone, inscribed 'Lassalle, Thinker and Fighter', was destroyed by the Nazis in 1933. In 1947, after Breslau became Wroclaw, Polish democrats put up a plaque dedicated to the 'Great Socialist'. There is, however, no monument to Lassalle in Germany.[32]

The following lines by Jacques Barzun might well serve as his epitaph:

> If anyone can claim as his own handiwork the transformation of modern Socialist ideas into a truly popular movement, it is the much-reviled Ferdinand Lassalle.
>
> At the age of thirty-nine, after two years' campaigning, he had... [by] his force, magnetism, ingenuity, oratorical power, knowledge of people and of history, created what had never existed before: a party of the Fourth Estate... the party which a decade after Lassalle's death joined the Marx-controlled International to form the great German Social Democratic Party... This party, which forced Bismarck and his successors to steal so much of its thunder, worked presumably in the name of Marx, but actually on Lassallean principles.[33]

As for what drove Lassalle to a senseless duel over a weak-willed girl – the 'gladiator's' indomitable will, pride, conceit, or inability to accept defeat – Heraclitus, his favourite Greek philosopher, had encapsulated it all in around 500 BC in three words:

'CHARACTER IS DESTINY.'

Epilogue

From the 'Doctors' to Lenin

Note: The death of Lassalle in 1864 coincided with the start of the age of Realpolitik. The limited purpose of this Epilogue is to tick off the reactions of the surviving protagonists to the changed European circumstances. The necessarily succinct account traces the Russian tradition of 'direct' violent action, whose methods Lenin was instinctively to adopt even as he made himself accepted as the sole legitimate interpreter of 'Marxism', a term which Marx himself detested.

In June 1861 Michael Bakunin set out on his hazardous escape from Siberia around half the globe to England. First he sailed from Irkutsk down the river Amur for 2,000 miles to the Pacific port of Nikolaevsk. There, defying his official travel permit which allowed him to proceed no further, he talked his way aboard an ocean-going Russian government vessel, the Strelok, then switched to an American sailing boat which it took in tow through the Sakhalin Straits to Japan. At Yokohama, boarding an American steamer, the fugitive Bakunin, finding himself seated at the captain's dinner next to the Russian Consul-General, brazenly engaged him in conversation and intimated that he was on a pleasure trip. Upon being asked whether he was not 'returning home' with a Russian flotilla at anchor in the harbour and about to sail for Nikolaevsk, he said that he wanted to see 'a little more of the country' and would return to Irkutsk via Shanghai and Peking.

The dinner proceeded in an atmosphere of good cheer, and next morning, as the SS Carrington weighed anchor and steamed out into the Pacific, passing the Russian flotilla, Bakunin - 12 years after his capture during the Dresden revolt - was on his way to North America.

Having spent the first 8 of those 12 years in solitary confinement in Austrian and Russian dungeons, Bakunin was an emaciated figure when he started his 'perpetual' banishment to Siberia at Tomsk in 1857. There, as his energies revived, he began to give French lessons, fell in love with one of his students and, though one would have thought he was the last man fit for conjugal life, married this 17-year-old Polish girl, Antonia Kwiatkowski, who was 26 years his junior. She was later to have three children by a friend of his, but Bakunin - whether or not as a substitute for his more dangerous old infatuation with his own sister Tatyana - sincerely loved her; and though he left Antonia behind when he made his escape, he was to fulfil his promise to get her out of Russia.

While he was still at Tomsk, General Nicholas Muraviev, a cousin of his mother, paid him a personal visit, and in January 1859 he was allowed to move with Antonia and her family to Irkutsk, where the general reigned surpreme as Governor-General of Eastern Siberia. Through the influence of his powerful protector, Bakunin was given a well-paid job as a commercial traveller for the Amur Company and in 1860 Muraviev promised to get him a full pardon as well as the right to return to Russia. In January 1861, however, Muraviev was dismissed from his post and Bakunin, deciding not to 'rot away in Siberia', began to plot his escape by persuading a local merchant to advance him 1,000 roubles for a commercial journey along the Amur as far as Nikolaevsk.

Having invented this mission along his exact escape route, Bakunin approached General Korsakov, the new Governor-General, whom he had met more than once in Muraviev's office. Against his word of honour that he would return before the winter, he obtained from Korsakov a letter instructing the captains of all ships on the Amur to give him free passage.

Equipped with this letter, Bakunin, during his month-long trip on the river, had stopped in various places and collected more money from merchants for whom he promised to carry out various business commissions at Nikolaevsk. Luck favours the enterprising, and due to a bureaucratic snafu, a message sent from Irkutsk after his departure warning the maritime authorities that Bakunin was 'a political criminal', had never been passed on to the captain of the Strelok. Having, by his presence of mind, guile, and ingenuity, beaten the supervisory system of the mighty Tsarist empire, Bakunin disembarked from the SS Carrington at San Francisco on 14 October 1861.

Then he changed boats twice to sail through the Isthmus of Panama to New York, and visited Boston before he boarded a ship for the Atlantic crossing to Liverpool. On 27 December 1861, having completed one of the longest escape routes ever, he finally landed like a comet at Orsett House in London, where Herzen and the Ogarevs lived together at the time. They received him like a lost brother.

Bakunin was now almost 47, a huge bearded figure of a man weighing 280 pounds, 'too old only to play', but still burning with fire and 'thirsty for action', as he wrote to George Sand. His arrival in London and the story of his dramatic escape from long prison and exile, prominently featured in two issues of Herzen's Russian journal *The Bell*, followed by the sale of his portrait, stunned Europe. By an unexpected and bizarre chain of developments, Bakunin emerged from the terrible consequences of his spontaneous 1849 action in Dresden, his self-styled 'demise', with a new international reputation.

He was, however, completely ignorant of what had happened in Europe since the 1848-49 revolutions and was shocked to hear that reaction had won everywhere and that, except for some demonstrations in Poland, everything was quiet in Germany, Italy and all over the Continent.

'Then what are we to do?' he asked. 'Must we go to Persia or India to stir things up? It's enough to drive one mad; I cannot sit and do nothing.'[1]

Europe was in fact entering upon the age of Realpolitik. Between 1862, when Bismarck announced his aggressive policy, and January 1871, when he was to crown that policy with the proclamation of the German Empire at Versailles, Europe changed both politically and culturally.

Realpolitik, as defined by the man who coined the term, meant that 'to rule is to exercise power'; that government was best placed in the hands of those who combined 'wealth, opinion and intelligence', and that 'the facts of social reality' were more important in dictating politics than ideas, which were merely 'subjective convictions and served at best to influence public opinion and help one class to succeed the other to political power.'[2]

In 1859, Darwin had presented the world with the first facts supporting his theory of evolution in *On the Origin of Species by Means of Natural Selection*. In the same year Marx, in the Preface to the *Critique of Political Economy*, wrote 'legal relations and the form of the state' were not the result of ideas or 'the general progress of the human mind, but rooted in the material conditions of life', the sum total of which 'Hegel combines under the name of "civil society", that, however, the anatomy of that civil society is to be sought in political economy.'

Turning to his own investigation of political economy, Marx summed up the general result at which he arrived and 'which, once won, served as a guiding thread of my studies', by saying that the economic structure of society and the relations men form in the social production of their lives

> are the real foundation on which rise legal and political superstructures and to which correspond definite forms of social consciousness. The mode of production in material life conditions the social, political and intellectual processes of life. It is not the consciousness of men that determines their being, but, on the contrary, their social being determines their consciousness.

One of Marx's chief conclusions was that when the productive forces of society develop to the maximum they come into conflict with the property relations which hitherto promoted their development. The result is social revolution.[3]

Marx meant to use this 'guiding thread' in his planned series of books on economics. Alas, his *Critique of Political Economy*, the first and only one to appear, aroused so little interest in Germany that, as Marx himself put it, 'not a single rooster crowed over the thing.' Destitute and pressed by debts as he was, Marx was convinced that he was the victim of a 'conspiracy of silence' in Germany -

a conspiracy, as Jenny wrote to Engels, broken 'by a few wretched feuilletons which dealt only with the Preface and not with the content.'[4]

The Preface was indeed the most important part of the book. In August 1859 Engels, in a review of his friend's book published in *Das Volk*, hailed Marx's short general statement in the Preface as the 'revolutionary' discovery of the 'materialist conception of history.' He further proclaimed Marx to be the first thinker who, by applying Hegel's dialectical method to economics, had developed 'a coherent science'.[5]

Das Volk was an obscure journal, but Engels's review was the first augury of his later glorification of Marx as the founder of the 'materialist conception of history' and his ultimately canonizing him as the discoverer of 'the law of development of human history.' It was Engels who first drew Marx's attention to Darwin's *Origin of Species* and the following exchange of letters may throw some light on the germination of the analogy between Marx's and Darwin's respective discoveries of the laws of 'human' and 'organic' history.

Engels to Marx, 12 December 1859: 'Darwin, which I am reading right now, is quite fantastic... There has not been up to now such a wonderful attempt to show evidence of historical development in nature, and never before with such success. One has to take into account of course the clumsy English method.'[6]

Marx to Engels, 19 December 1860: 'In spite of [Darwin's] English ponderousness, this book contains the biological basis of our conceptions.'[7]

Marx to Ferdinand Lassalle, 16 January 1861: 'Darwin's writing is very important and fits in quite conveniently for me as the natural science basis for the historical struggle. One has to take into account of course [his] clumsy English manner of development.'[8]

Marx's literal adoption of Engels's low opinion of Darwin's English method[9] shows perhaps how closely their minds were attuned to each other. But was Marx indeed a Darwinist and 'evolutionist' with a determinist conception of history? This question was to be hotly debated until close to the end of the 20th century, when it would transpire that Marx's conception of history was far less iron-clad and rigid than as presented by Engels.

The axiom enunciated by Marx in 1859 that the bourgeois countries would be struck by revolution at the highest point of their capitalist industrial development - an axiom to be severely tested by the 1917 Bolshevik revolution in Russia, which had hardly reached the apex of industrial development - had been contested early on by Herzen, writing in 1851 that 'the future of Russia lies with the peasant moujik, just as the regeneration of France lies with the workers.'[10]

By 1861 there were nearly 50 million peasant serfs of several kinds in European Russia, out of a total population of 60 millions. If Marx had once extolled the nascent German working class as a 'Cinderella' whose emancipation would ultimately emancipate the world, to Herzen the true 'Cinderella' was Russia's stolid peasantry - tilling the soil of the landlords for so many days in the week and then working the commonly owned open fields in patches periodically allotted by the village assembly to each family according to its size, the number of its working hands and its needs. In Herzen's view these village communes were a rare asset among nations, presenting Russia with a great opportunity, once they were liberated from serfdom, of carrying out a reformist shortcut to Socialism and establishing a society free of capitalist competition and 'proletarian misery' such as Europe's 'noblest minds only dreamed of'.[11]

Herzen in London could not but share the elation which had swept Russia in the spring of 1856, when the new Tsar, Alexander II, not only relaxed press censorship and lifted the restrictions on the number of students in the universities, but began to tackle the immense and complex problem represented by the serfs. As thousands of youths of all classes flocked to the institutions of higher learning, a new era seemed to be dawning. Anyone who was not alive in Russia in 1856, wrote one student, 'does not know what life is.'

A flood of new progressive publications, including a first *Women's Journal*, took their place by the side of the St Petersburg *Contemporary*, the periodical of the intelligentsia, in whose pages Belinsky 'Furioso' had once published his fulminating literary-political articles. His mantle as the director of the social conscience of his generation had now been assumed by a 27-year-old columnist, Nicholas Chernyshevsky, who held an arts degree but combined literary criticism with a revolutionary temperament.

The question on everybody's lips was whether the serfs would be freed 'with land' - to be given up by the nobility - but the Tsar's attempt to persuade the nobles and gentry to be generous in their own interest fell on deaf ears. With the exception of a few 'penitent' souls, the landlords thought that losing their 'baptized property' (the serfs) was sacrifice enough. The Tsar therefore left the task of working out the terms of the emancipation to his bureaucrats.

Finally, in February 1861, Alexander II solemnly set all serfs on state land and several other categories free on more or less convenient terms. But 20 to 23 million serfs of the landlords, or 'bondmen', most of whom were household serfs, were to wait for two years before being freed without land, though they would be offered a chance to acquire the title to it at an exorbitant price - after paying a redemption annuity for 49 years (for plots which were often too small to support a family) plus interest and high taxes to the state.

Thousands of bondmen, who had always felt that they might belong to their masters, 'but the land is ours', took to the roads to plead with the Tsar not to condemn them to pauperism. They were stopped by soldiers, flogged and sent off to Siberia. During the summer rioting, peasants clashed with rural gendarmes and soldiers on 1,200 estates. They suffered 310 casualties, including 140 killed. The bloodshed cast a pall over the new sense of freedom and the 'liberation' of the serfs 4 years before the abolition of slavery in the USA, which might otherwise have set Russia on the road to progress and modernity.

Press and theatre censorship was reimposed. St Petersburg University was closed. Several hundred protesting students were arrested.

During the Tsar's 'honeymoon with the people', Herzen's London *Bell* had enthusiastically hailed Alexander II practically as the first monarch of a soon-to-be Socialist country. By the autumn of 1861, however, when the Tsar forbade the use of the very word 'progress' in official documents and the nature of the 'truncated emancipation' of the peasants sank in, *The Bell* carried a series of articles on 'the new serfdom', each ending with the words: 'The Tsar has deceived the people.' Russian society on the whole, however, as Herzen was to note in his Memoirs, was exhausted by 7 years of fruitless political agitation and wished for nothing but repose.

But the young revolted. Nicholas Chernyshevsky's veiled reaction to the bungled emancipation had been to print a translation of Longfellow's *Poems on Slavery*. Chernyshevsky was aware – without having read Marx – that Western Europe was in the throes of a class struggle which might help to speed events in Russia. But in 1861 he felt that the Tsar had created a revolutionary situation and composed a manifesto 'To the Peasants', urging them to rise in arms and fight for their freedom and their land. Two of his fellow-journalists, Michael Shelgunov and the poet Michael Mikhailov, produced a leaflet, 'To the Young Generation'. Printed by Herzen's press in London and smuggled back into Russia, it declared that 'to slaughter 100,000 landowners' was not too high a price to pay for creating 'a new order unknown even in America.'

The most violent of a spate of underground leaflets was addressed 'To Young Russia' and carried the slogan: 'Get Your Axes!' Composed by 20-year-old Peter Zaichenevsky while he was in jail with other student agitators arrested the previous year for running a 'Sunday school' offering free secular education to workers, it announced the approaching doom of the Romanov dynasty and spoke of marching under the 'red flag' to storm the Winter Palace and to 'exterminate the Tsar and his kin.' Referring to his reactionary supporters as plunderers, it called on the people: 'Kill them in the houses, kill them in the narrow alleys of towns, in the broad avenues of capitals, kill them in the villages and hamlets.'[12]

The bloodthirsty manifesto, which called for a 'Socialist and democratic republic' but left no doubt that it was to be run by a revolutionary dictatorship of the army and the young, was issued in the name of a Central Revolutionary Committee. The Tsarist authorities had no idea that the Committee consisted of exactly 4 students, including Zaichenevsky himself. The incendiary manifesto having been printed by unknown friends of his on a press they had smuggled out of Moscow to a village in the Ryazan province while he was in jail, young Zaichenevsky, whose fantasy of storming the Winter Palace anticipated the 1917 Bolshevik Revolution, got away with a relatively light sentence.

The leaflets produced a rift between Herzen and the young radicals in Russia. While he criticized them for broadcasting their aims in such strident terms 'that liberals and the champions of gradual progress crossed themselves and ran away stopping their ears,' they challenged him to decide between hailing the Tsar as 'Liberator' and attacking his 'phoney' emancipation. Under fire from both Russia's reactionary press and from its ardent radical extremists, Herzen found himself in the predicament of a knight-errant who has lost his way at a crossroads: 'Go to the right, and you will lose your horse, but you will be safe yourself; go to the left, and your horse will be safe, but you will perish; go forward, and everyone will abandon you.'[13]

It was at this point that Bakunin arrived in London. Full of fire and flame, he set out to revolutionize *The Bell*, whose tone was too moderate for his taste. Though Herzen admired Bakunin's audacity, he took a dim view of his impetuousness and his reckless talk of revolution now or never, and kept his hands off the paper. Herzen was above all a champion of individual liberty. Just as he opposed Marx's determinism, feeling that man could 'change the pattern of the carpet' woven by history, so he felt that Bakunin's frivolous passion for all-out destruction as a way of achieving a 'kingdom of freedom' took no account of the fate or liberty of the individual. Both of them, however, were convinced of the revolutionary potential of Russia's moujiks and, sharing the same ultimate goal, they maintained an ambivalent friendship punctuated by frequent arguments, quarrels and reconciliations.

Bakunin helped Herzen to overcome his dilemma by persuading him to go forward from the 'crossroads' and lend his shaken reputation in the homeland to a secret organization, Land and Liberty, which for the first time in Russia attempted to unite the stray radical groups into a national party for the purpose of preparing a revolution. Its founder was N. Serno-Solovievich, a St Petersburg bookseller who, in an anonymous article in *The Bell*, had recently expounded the idea that even a small revolutionary party which had secret cells and cadres among the peasants and soldiery would harass the regime. It might be subject to repression, but history showed that a revolutionary party's 'martyrs' made it stronger in the public eye 'the more it is persecuted.'

The name Land and Liberty was coined by Ogarev to epitomize the two things the Russian people wanted most. Ogarev was more militant than Herzen; conspiracies were Bakunin's element. Herzen was sceptical and hesitated, but in the end he yielded to the arguments of his friends and on 1 March 1862 *The Bell*

announced the formation of Land and Liberty. The leaders of the new organization eventually chose March 1863 as the most propitious date for a Russian peasant rising to coincide with an armed insurrection in Poland that would keep the
Tsar's troops busy in what might become a general European conflict.

In May 1862 a series of mysterious fires in St Petersburg culminated in a blaze
which consumed 2,000 shops and warehouses. Herzen, who had just agreed to
represent Land and Liberty abroad, suspected that the fires had been started by
police agents. The panic-stricken populace, however, vented its fury on Russian
and Polish revolutionary arsonists and blamed Herzen and Bakunin for inspiring
them. A press cartoon showed Herzen at the scene of the conflagration holding
an axe in one hand and a torch in the other, with the caption: 'To Iskander
[Herzen], a ruined people, 28 May 1862'.

The government admitted that the arsonists had not been traced, but in a
series of repressive measures it closed 300 'Sunday schools' throughout Russia
for teaching 'subversive' ideas. The Petersburg Chess Club and its reading rooms
were shut down as a hotbed of radicalism. The publication of *The Contemporary*
was suspended and Chernyshevsky, Serno-Solovievich, Vladimir Obruchev - an
ex-colonel and the son of a general - and 30 others involved in the leaflet campaign were arrested and taken in chains to the Peter-and-Paul fortress, where
they were kept for two years awaiting trial.

The poet Mikhailov had previously been sentenced to 6 years of hard labour
in Siberia. He was to die there within 4, the first martyr of the 1860s. In order
to save Shelgunov, the co-author of 'To the Young Generation', Mikhailov had
assumed sole responsibility for writing and printing it. He was sent to a desolate
area near the Chinese frontier, and being of frail health, did not survive the
unsanitary conditions. Shelgunov was deported in 1863 to Irkutsk and was to
spend 15 years in various parts of Siberia.

During 1862, Herzen and Bakunin in London and the leaders of Land and
Liberty in Russia met on several occasions in secret confabulations with representatives of a Polish National Committee, to synchronize events in the projected Polish insurrection. The Poles were eager to act, but even the impatient
Bakunin joined the leaders of Land and Liberty in advising them that they must
absolutely wait for the set date in March 1863.

The Tsarist Governor of Poland, however, preempted the whole grand
scheme by suddenly ordering a conscription in January, causing the Poles to
revolt prematurely on the 22nd. Bakunin, without waiting for the consequences
- he always, in Herzen's words, 'took the 2nd month of pregnancy for the 9th' -
felt that he must rush to the scene of the fighting in Poland. On 21 February he
left London with a false passport, but all his attempts in Copenhagen and Stock-

holm to establish contact with the Polish National Committee failed. The first European revolution since 1848 created quite a stir on the Continent and Bakunin spent some hectic weeks trying to catch up with a hastily assembled Polish Legion which had sailed from Southend in England for the Baltic, but whose boat was confiscated by the Swedes at Malmö.

In May, under the alias of Professor Henri Soulié, a Canadian scholar, he had a glorious time in Stockholm. Swedish radicals gave a banquet in his honour and he was secretly received in audience by King Charles XV. When the Russian Minister to Stockholm protested that Soulié/Bakunin was a political criminal and should be expelled, the Swedes replied that their democratic public opinion was too 'exercised' over the Polish situation to tolerate his expulsion. But as a sop to the Russians, they published a critical report on his subversive activities in 1848.

By June, however, Land and Liberty's plans for a Russo–Polish revolution had collapsed like a house of cards. None of the Russian troops stationed in Poland joined the insurrection, and the rising of Polish patriots petered out in guerrilla actions. Nor did Russia's peasantry revolt. A small group of Land and Liberty went underground, and the rest disbanded.

A discomfited Bakunin thereupon severed his relations with the Poles and gave up the whole idea of the 'liberation of all the Slavs', which had been his hobby-horse and his obsession. In October, together with his wife Antonia, who had managed to join him from Russia, he left Stockholm for Italy. Travelling in leisurely stages via London, Paris and Switzerland, they arrived there in January 1864, and after stopping on Caprera Island for a three-day visit with Garibaldi, settled in Florence in ostensible retirement.

In the summer of 1864, Chernyshevsky, Obruchev and their fellow prisoners were taken from their fortress cells to a public square in St Petersburg. Like Dostoyevsky before them, they were chained to a pole with the inscription 'State Criminal' on their chests - or, as in the case of Obruchev and other nobles, had to kneel in front of the gallows for a sword to be broken over their heads - while their sentences were read out to a jeering crowd. The pillorying of Chernyshevsky caused indignation among Russia's intelligentsia, and none was more furious or embarrassed than Herzen. For it was a batch of papers sent from his own house in London, which - intercepted by the police - had served as a pretext for Chernyshevsky's arrest in the first place.

Chernyshevsky's 'Appeal to the Peasants' had never been distributed, and all Herzen had written to him was a few lines offering to print *The Contemporary* abroad. The authorities, however, were determined to put an end to Chernyshevsky's wide influence. Sentenced on trumped-up charges, he was to spend 21 years in forced labour, 7 of them in a Siberian silver mine, and the rest in the Arctic region, before he was pardoned and returned to civilization, a broken man.

During his solitary confinement in the Peter-and-Paul fortress (1863–65), he wrote an allegorical novel entitled *What Is to Be Done?*. Portraying a professional revolutionary who steels himself for the 'great battle', the novel ended with a futurist vision of brave new men and emancipated women living in a society of social justice and enjoying all the comforts provided by the progress of science. Although of questionable literary merit, the novel's hidden call for revolution made it the bible of generations of radicals.

Lenin, who was 13 in 1883 when Chernyshevsky returned from the Arctic, was to be so impressed by the novel that he later took its title for the book in which he set out his own version of Marxism-Leninism.

Serno-Solovievich had been seized on the same day as Chernyshevsky, for the confiscated London parcel contained such incriminating items as a letter from Bakunin introducing him to Garibaldi, besides letters to the Armenian poet and nationalist, M.L. Nalbandyan. Serno was kept for interrogation in the Peter-and-Paul fortress until June 1865. Then he, too, was subjected to a mock 'execution' depriving him of his civil rights before he was deported to Irkutsk.

One of the great losers in the aftermath of the 1863 revolution in Poland that never happened was Herzen, who had allowed himself to be dragged into the Land and Liberty conspiracy against his better judgment. The circulation of *The Bell* in Russia dropped from 2,500 copies to 500. In 1865 he stopped its publication in London and moved with the Ogarevs to Switzerland. Travelling with them was the Bakhmetev Fund for revolutionary propaganda, established by Pavel A. Bakhmetev, a wealthy young Russian landowner who had approached Herzen at short notice in 1857 and settled 20,000 francs on him and Ogarev to use for propaganda as they saw fit.[14] On the next day, with his remaining '30,000 francs in gold wrapped up in a thick pocket-handkerchief', he had sailed for the Marquesas Islands.

The Bakhmetev Fund, carefully administered by Herzen and invested in profitable securities, grew steadily. Besides his own fortune, which had enabled him to bear the latest losses incurred by *The Bell*, Herzen thus had the collateral to start a French edition of the paper in Geneva. To his dismay, he received an unfriendly welcome from a small coterie of young alumni of the 1861 university disorders in St Petersburg who had found refuge in the Swiss city. Hardened by their prison experiences in Russia, these radicals looked upon the expatriate millionaire as a 'liberal dinosaur'. Claiming that they were better fit to set the tone for the violent struggle lying ahead, they made no secret of their intention to wrest control of *The Bell* from him and involved him in a public squabble.

Stung by their calling him 'a dead man' and suspecting that their next aim was to lay their hands on the Bakhmetev Fund, Herzen preferred to close down *The*

Bell shortly after its reappearance. Bakunin intervened to point out that whatever the faults of the unprincipled radical youths, they were animated by a passion for justice and freedom, and Herzen, realizing that theirs was the future, soon wrote in an open letter to Ogarev that these stern young 'realists' made him feel that 'our idea will not perish'.

And so it was to be. Herzen completed his rich memoirs, *My Past and Thoughts*, in 1868 and died two years later in Paris. He was buried at Nice next to his wife Natalie. A life-size statue marks his grave. Back in November 1861, during the turmoil caused by the 'truncated emancipation' and the closure of St Petersburg University, he had written to the students: 'Shall I tell you where you should go now?... To the people, to the people... your place is there.' His ideas were to influence Tolstoy, Dostoyevsky and Russia's politically interested intelligentsia, and to make him the progenitor of the Narodnik, or Populist 'go to the people' movement which - under the further influence of the martyred Chernyshevsky - was to sweep the next generation of Russia's youth.

Bakunin was to inspire the extreme radical wing of Populism, not before going through the crowning phase of his career - this time as a genuine political actor in Western Europe capable of challenging Marx's position in the First Working Men's International.

Curiously enough, it was Marx himself who on 3 November 1864 called on Bakunin - who happened to be in London on a short visit - and invited him to join the First International. The two had not met for 16 years. Their relations had been soured by Marx's part in the repeated slander that Bakunin was a Tsarist agent. According to Bakunin, 'We had an explanation. He said he had never done anything against me and had retained great respect for me. I knew that he was lying, but I really no longer bore any grudge against him.'[15]

Marx to Engels on 4 November: '[Bakunin] left for Italy today. I saw him yesterday evening once more. He said that after the failure in Poland he should, in future, confine himself to participation in the Socialist Movement.' In a rare compliment to the Russian or indeed to anyone, Marx added: 'I must say that I liked him very much - better than before. He is one of the few people who I feel, after 16 years, has moved forwards not backwards.'[16]

The International had only recently been founded in London. As Secretary of its governing body, the General Council, Marx was soon to gain control of the European workers movement. He seems to have hoped that Bakunin would help him to win over Garibaldi to Socialism and the International, but he had no idea of the nemesis he was bringing on himself. For Bakunin had no sooner returned to Florence than he established one secret society after another. The World Brotherhood was followed by the International Secret Society for the Liberation of Mankind, and more. Although most of them started as figments of his imagination or remained on paper, he was, like a kind of conjuror, ultimately to make them come to life, to form a 'secret revolutionary international' of his own within the Workers' International.

In October 1865 he moved to Naples, where he lived in a beautiful hilltop villa and enjoyed the patronage of the wealthy and eccentric Princess Zoe Obolensky. Separated from her husband, the Princess supported a whole group of Italian, Polish and other foreign revolutionaries and radicals. According to an eyewitness, when she moved in the summer to the island of Ischia together with her whole retinue, Bakunin 'played providence, arranged promenades and picnics, instructed everybody, issued orders for everybody' and at the same time

> wrote numerous long letters in different languages to the different sections of the World Brotherhood. Everyone obeyed him, and worshipped him with reverence.
>
> He was in fact head and shoulders above those around him and, notwithstanding his benevolence, he had the temperament of a drill-sergeant.[17]

While Bakunin was thus recharging his batteries and beginning to conspire in all directions, Marx in London in 1865 resumed work on *Das Kapital*, the nerve-rending, never-ending magnum opus on which he was to spend the remaining 18 years of his life – driven by the ambition not only to save the proletariat and rouse it to action, but to educate the whole world to his theory that the growing capitalist system was historically and sociologically doomed to ultimate self-destruction. Marx's characteristic way of clarifying and expressing his theories by tearing down those of others in savage polemics has encouraged the image of the fanatical and nasty Marx who, while fighting for the poor and downtrodden, quarreled not only with his true or imaginary foes, but with all his friends, except Heine and of course Engels.

A man of great strengths and many weaknesses, frustrated by decades of living in exile and in 'bourgeois misery', Marx was never more nasty than in 1865. Jealous of the success of Lassalle's Allgemeiner Deutscher Arbeiterverein, he reviled both its dead and living leaders by speaking of the 'stink' left behind by Lassalle, calling the Countess von Hatzfeldt his 'apostolic vicar' and Hess her 'male Pope'. Hess rightly guessed that Marx was out to destroy the new Workers' Party because it refused to submit to him.

Contrasting with this brutal image is that of Marx the warm-hearted paterfamilias romping with his children on Hampstead Heath, inventing mile-long fairy tales for them – 'tell us another mile', they would beg – and stopping to distribute pennies to little street urchins. And superimposed on both is the figure of Marx the solitary philosopher-sage toiling away on *Das Kapital* while his liver was being devoured by chronic inflammation, like his mythological model Prometheus, whose immortal liver was, however, always replenished. Like the Greek demigod who not only brought fire to men but taught them how to use it to build a civilization, Marx stuck to *Das Kapital* because of his hubris in thinking he could build a new world, a new civilization and a breed of new men.

He completed and published only its first volume in 1867, leaving a mass of notes and rough material for another 4 to be edited after his death by Engels and others.[18] In that first volume, generally referred to as *Das Kapital*, Prometheus was used to represent the proletariat chained to capital. Although Marx was obsessed by fear of cancer – his father had died of cancer of the liver – he identified with the suffering proletariat to the point where he felt that it was the economic strain that was eating up his liver. Indeed, every line he wrote was ground out of some painful deprivation of his own. And was he not the victim of the same circumstances as the dispossessed proletarians of this earth? At the same time, as if he were Job ('though I'm less God-fearing'), he was afflicted by a series of recurring plagues – rheumatism, bronchitis, ear infections, pleurisy, boils and irksome carbuncles that robbed him of his sleep and ability to work – and was further troubled by a bad conscience for sacrificing the health and happiness of his wife and daughters to his work and making everyone around him suffer. As he went on exposing the evils of capitalism, his personal venom sounded through the mordant lines about the industrial Moloch immolating the worker on the altar of greedy profit. As he himself put it: 'I hope the bourgeoisie will have reason to remember my carbuncles.' But out of his traumatized days and nights came the epic wrath and force of his promised class-struggle; the savagery of his indictment of capitalism, compared to the universally good Communist society of the future; and the jarring conflict between this ideal and the brutal, hate-instilled deeds the workers must resort to in order to throw off the yoke of their oppressors and inherit the earth.

Although *Das Kapital* at first attracted so little notice that Engels wrote a dozen or so reviews 'from different points of view' and foisted them under different names upon the unsuspecting editors of various journals,[19] it was to magnify Marx's extraordinary intellectual impact on 20th-century thought, politics and history. Capitalism is alive and thriving contrary to one of Marx's fundamental theses, and other flaws in his grand structure – such as its utter disregard of the forces of nationalism– were to become apparent in time.

'The working-men have no country,' Marx and Engels had proclaimed in *The Communist Manifesto*. In 1848 they supported the Poles, Hungarians and Italians as long as they served as a catalyst for revolution. But once the revolution had collapsed, Engels remarked to Marx in 1851 that the Poles were *'une nation foutue'* (a finished nation). He proposed to man their fortresses, especially Posen, with Germans under the pretext of defence, 'to let them stew in their own juice, send them into battle, gobble bare their land, fob them off with promises of Riga and Odessa... A nation which can muster 20,000 to 30,000 men at most is not entitled to a vote.'[20]

While having no use for the Danes or other small nations which, whatever their rights, history or aspirations, were destined 'to perish in the world-wide revolutionary tempest', Marx and Engels favoured large, even colonial nations whose industrial development promised a commensurate potential for revolution. When Bismarck forged the famous Ems telegram, provoking the Franco-Prussian War in 1870, Marx expressed his expectation that a Prussian victory and the unification of Germany would result in 'the ascendancy of the German working class in the world theatre over the French and the preponderance of our theory over Proudhon.'[21]

Marx's doctrine that class alone, and not national, ethnic, cultural or any other bond shaped man's social consciousness and dictated his allegiance was exploded in 1914 when the workers of the various countries marched off enthusiastically to slaughter each other in the First World War. But it was only at the end of the 1980s, when the incipient disintegration of the Soviet Union suddenly revealed that its vast territories teemed with 130 different nationalities – from Abkhazians and Azeris to Tatars and Udmurts, all claiming sovereignty or some form of self-rule - that Marxian scholars seriously began to question his axiomatic idea that proletarians were immune to 'national sentiments'.[22]

The Chechen revolt against Russia, the break-up of Yugoslavia and the flare-up of the Serb-Bosnian-Croat war on the border of Austria and the heartland of Europe underlined the error of Marx's statement in the *Manifesto* that the workers 'have no country'.[23]

Remarkably, Moses Hess had realized as early as 1843, before the 'Springtime of the Peoples', that nationalism was destined to become a factor in modern history. 'Just as humanity cannot be real without distinct individuals', he had written that year, 'so it cannot be real without distinct, specific nations and people. Humanity cannot actualize itself without mediation, it needs the medium of individuality.'[24]

History knew no parallel of a state twice destroyed in antiquity being resurrected when Hess affirmed in 1862 that the Jews with their millennial history had every justification to fight for their rights as a nation just as the Italians, Poles, Greeks and Europe's other oppressed peoples fought for theirs. To Marx and his Communist cronies of old, this was an aberration bordering on absurdity. Hess, however, invoking the Hebrew prophets who had cried out for social justice thousands of years before Marx, effected a synthesis between their message of universal redemption and his modern perception of the dialectical-revolutionary process of history: if the latter strove towards the liberation of the proletariat, it must also, as another step towards a just society, end the Jews' oppressive long exile and alienation from their historic homeland. Hess recalled that back in 1840, under the shock of the 'Damascus Affair', he had wanted 'to give vent to my Jewish feelings in a *cri de coeur*, but this was strangled in my breast by the greater pain awakened in me by the plight of the European proletariat.'[25]

About that time, as it happened, Colonel Charles Henry Churchill, a descendant of the Duke of Marlborough, was writing to Sir Moses Montefiore from Damascus that the days of the Turkish Empire were numbered and the time was ripe for the Jews to 'put their hand to the glorious work of national regeneration.' If they made 'a commencement', the European powers would help them. But it was only in 1859 that Hess's Jewish feelings stirred again.

That year he met Armand Lévy, a third-generation Catholic and revolutionary French Socialist, who, returning from the Crimean War, had brought with him to Paris the mortal remains of Adam Mickiewicz, Poland's national poet and freedom fighter. In the course of their attempts to organize a Polish legion against the Tsar, Mickiewicz, who tended to identify the suffering of the Poles with those of the Jews, had impressed on Lévy, his medical officer and chief aide, the idea that the Jews deserved a place among the nations like any other people.

On his way through the Balkans, Lévy found a large mass of Jews praying to be allowed to return to the Holy Land after their 2,000-year-long exile. Knowing that Turkey, 'Europe's Sick Man', was 'either dying or dead already' – as Tsar Nicholas had put it in the 1840s during a visit to England – Lévy told the Balkan Jewish leaders that redemption was near at hand. The following year Ernest Laharanne, a French officer who had served in Damascus, publicly urged the Jews to seize the initiative and reconstitute their ancient national homeland.[26]

At the same time Garibaldi led his Redshirts in a victorious landing in Sicily, then crossed to Naples and in October proclaimed Victor Emmanuel King of united Italy. With 'self-determination' becoming the call of the day, the Socialist Hess discerned the new drift of history, a drift enabling him to resolve the dilemma between the sorrows of the Jews and the plight of the proletariat which had choked his breast 20 years earlier. Published in Leipzig in 1862, *Rome and Jerusalem*, in which Hess envisioned a Jewish state complete with the 'kibbutz' idea, sold exactly 162 copies. The Jewish circles to whom it was addressed either tried to be more German than the Germans, or put their political trust in the liberal bourgeois state or their faith in the revolutionary movements.

A booklet published by Marx in London in 1860 at his own expense had sold only 80 copies; but this was no consolation to Hess. He joined Lassalle in founding the Allgemeiner Deutscher Arbeiterverein and later represented it at several congresses of the First International. Although at these meetings he sided with

Marx against Bakunin, he never yielded to what he called Marx's 'unfortunate tendency to demand personal subjection.'

The battle between Bakunin and Marx for control of the International began in the wake of a Peace Congress held at Geneva in the autumn of 1867. The Congress was sponsored by such figures as Victor Hugo, Garibaldi, John Stuart Mill and other prominent European 'friends of democracy' for the high purpose of discussing ways of avoiding wars and the establishment of a United States of Europe. Marx had declined to attend, declaring that the Workers' International was enough of a pacifist bulwark. But Bakunin, invited to represent Russia, had arrived from Naples. As he walked up to the platform and Garibaldi rose to embrace him, he received a standing ovation from the 6,000 assembled delegates. In an impassioned speech professing his new Socialist faith, he told the bourgeois audience that they would never get a United States of Europe unless they abandoned nationalism and liberated the working class. Attacking the centralized state, Bakunin declared that every centralized state, no matter how liberal it might be, even if it were a republic, is of necessity an oppressor, exploiting the people in the interest of the privileged class.

Recognized for the first time as a spokesman of European democracy, Bakunin stayed on in Switzerland. Having been elected to the Central Committee of the newly founded League for Peace and Freedom, he turned it into a political lever for infiltrating the Workers' International. He proposed a merger of the two organizations; the League with its revolutionary fire should handle the International's political activities, thus 'getting the power, the entire revolution in our hands', leaving the lacklustre International to deal with economic questions.

When the General Council of the International, on Marx's advice, rejected the proposal, Bakunin founded the Alliance de la démocratie socialiste, which started with 85 members in Switzerland, but soon found more recruits in France and Spain. Persuading a few Swiss leaders of the International to join the Alliance, he then, through one of them (J.P. Becker, an old friend of Marx), boldly applied for its admission into the International as an autonomous body.

Marx and Engels saw through Bakunin's attempt 'to take the workers' movement under his patronage... There would be two General Councils and even two congresses.'[27] But in March 1869 – after Bakunin agreed to disband the Alliance and reconstitute its sections as member groups of the International – Marx himself drafted a resolution accepting this, and they were permitted to retain the name Alliance. Bakunin's Alliance was a master-stroke. He had from the beginning conceived it as a combination of a secret organization with an overlapping public one. Marx and Engels were to discover their error in the autumn, at the 4th Congress of the International scheduled to open at Basle in September 1869.

In London, shortly before the Congress opened, Marx was very proud of the International. Delegates from eleven countries including the USA were to attend. The International boasted of 800,000 members and its newspapers claimed to have 7 million readers. 'Things are on the march', Marx wrote to Engels. 'The next revolution may be nearer than we think, and you and I have this powerful engine in our hand.'

But there was one cloud on the horizon. In Switzerland, Bakunin, while ostensibly making propaganda for the International, had been strenuously converting underpaid foreign construction workers in Geneva and independent-minded village watchmakers of the Jura to his own anarchist ideas. Some of the leaders of the International in Geneva also joined his Alliance, and due to his policy of infiltration several members of his own secret Bureau were commingling with the bosses of 30 Swiss sections of the International.

Together with J.P. Becker, Bakunin sat on the editorial board of the radical newspaper *Egalité*, and he had a further outlet in *Progrès*, a paper put at his disposal by the new Secretary of the Alliance, James Guillaume. He had also established secret branches of the Alliance in Italy and Spain, where the International had none. Although ostensibly complying with the statutes and demands of the International, Bakunin now had within it a 'secret international' of his own, one capable of giving it, as he hoped, a 'revolutionary direction' under his control.[28]

The 4th Congress of the International opened at Basle on 7 September. Marx did not attend in person. He had drafted the General Council's yearly report to the Congress and delegated a German tailor, Eccarius, to speak in his name. Thus Bakunin again stole the limelight when he addressed the 78 delegates present. In an impassioned speech, he moved a resolution demanding that the International adopt forthwith the abolition of inheritance rights in its platform. Eccarius countered with a resolution – prepared by Marx – stating that inheritance rights would disappear in a natural way once private property was abolished, and that Bakunin was raising an artificial issue. But Eccarius could not match Bakunin's eloquence. Bakunin's resolution got 32 votes, Marx's only 19. Although both fell short of the required absolute majority, the outcome was a clear defeat for Marx. Never before had the International failed to act on a recommendation of his – one, moreover, that had been endorsed by the General Council. And Bakunin had proved that he had both the strength and the temerity to challenge Marx. Hess, who was on the Congress executive for Germany, called a plague on both their houses: 'We other Europeans are prepared to suffer neither Russian summary methods... nor Prussian Socialism based on dictatorship.'[29]

Simultaneously with the first round of his power struggle with Marx, Bakunin had become involved in the famous and ultimately fatal Nechaev affair.

Serge Nechaev, a wild and reckless Moscow student of 22, had arrived in Geneva in March 1869 to seek Bakunin's support for a powerful secret society in Russia whose Central Committee he claimed to represent. He pretended to have escaped from the Peter-and-Paul fortress, and Bakunin, seeing in him an image of his younger self, became greatly attached to this 'young fanatic', affectionately calling him 'Boy' (in English) and urging Ogarev to dedicate a poem to him.

Bakunin was a master of make-believe and mystification, but when caught in some exaggeration of fantasy would laugh like a child who meant no harm. Young Nechaev, on the other hand, was a born liar and a ruthless deceiver. The truth was that he belonged to a committee of Moscow students who had been working on a 'Programme of Revolutionary Action'; but the nationwide revolutionary movement he boasted of to Bakunin in Geneva existed only in his dreams and aspirations. He had read both Buonarroti and Bakunin, but although he listened like a good pupil to the latter's anarchist view that the church, the state and all governments were intrinsically evil and dispensable, he had in fact already outdone Bakunin as a prophet of terrorism and sheer violence (of the type practised after World War II by the German Baader-Meinhof Group). Long attributed to Bakunin, the extraordinary *Cetechism of a Revolutionist* - the terrorist's manual to this day - had been composed by Nechaev before he left Moscow. Briefly, the *Catechism* stated that

> honour, feelings, morality do not exist for the professional revolutionary. He must become a nameless tool ready to lie and cheat, to murder, die and send others to their death for the purpose of destroying the fabric of society - for 'the people' to develop a new one that will assure freedom and happiness to the manual workers...
>
> The Russian revolutionist must encourage all evils that will exhaust the people's patience; he must... use blackmail and intimidation even against liberals and associates whom he exploits in the business of simple and total destruction...[30]

There were moments when Bakunin doubted the existence of Nechaev's Committee, but his thrill at taking part in a Russian revolution, even if possibly a fictitious one, was such that he asked no questions. In a bizarre passage he later wrote that, though unsure of the existence of Nechaev's Committee, 'I unconditionally submitted to [its] authority as the sole representative and director of the revolution in Russia.'[31]

And the irresistible Nechaev soon got Bakunin to enlist Ogarev's help in persuading a reluctant Herzen, during a visit to Geneva, to invest 10,000 francs – or half the Bakhmetev Fund – in the young man's dubious revolutionary cause.

In August 1869 Nechaev, equipped with money and revolutionary pamphlets, returned to Moscow and set about creating the mighty secret organization he had bragged about. He managed to establish a number of cells based on the strict discipline of the *Catechism of a Revolutionist*. But it turned out later that in Moscow he let it be believed that he was the International's representative in Russia. Worse, when a fellow-student named Ivanov challenged his credentials, Nechaev simply murdered him. The Tsarist police arrested 300 students. But Nechaev himself, leaving everyone in the lurch – including 4 active accomplices in the murder – escaped to the West.

In January 1870 he reappeared in Geneva. Bakunin, after his triumph at the Basle congress, had retired to Locarno and had started translating Marx's *Das Kapital* into Russian.[32] Delighted to see Nechaev again, he helped to hide the young 'tiger' from the Swiss police and publicly attacked the Russian government and press for calling him a murderer. But Nechaev now showed him a different side of himself.

As a start, Nechaev stopped the translation of *Das Kapital*. Without Bakunin's knowledge he threatened the Russian middleman, Liubavin, who had procured for him an advance of 300 roubles, with every possible violence if he or the St Petersburg publisher claimed it back. Bakunin did not miss the work so much as the outstanding 900 roubles of his fee, which he sorely needed but would now never see. Coming up with one vicious scheme after another, Nechaev next got Bakunin and the now half-senile Ogarev to obtain for him the balance of the Bakhmetev Fund from Herzen's heirs as well as permission from his daughter Tata (Natalie) Herzen to reissue *The Bell*. Nor was his appetite satisfied with this. He also coveted Tata's private fortune; and she was stunned one day when Bakunin advised her to leave herself 'the strictly necessary to live on and give the rest to the common cause.' Tata Herzen was both fascinated and repelled by the demonic Nechaev (the model for the hero of Dostoyevsky's novel *The Possessed*), but drew a distinction between this evil character, whose attempts to draw her into a dark web of conspiracies and intrigue she had to resist, and Bakunin, who protected her from Nechaev's worst excesses, such as a threat to kill her if she ever went back to Russia.[33]

It was only when Nechaev, in short order, refused to have Bakunin as a collaborator on *The Bell*, then stole a box of his correspondence in order to blackmail him, that the older man realized that his adored 'Boy' was applying to him the methods advocated in the *Catechism of a Revolutionist* for the treatment of associates who had lost their usefulness.

In May 1870, G. Lopatin, a well-known Russian radical, came to Geneva for the special purpose of confronting Nechaev. As Lopatin said, in the presence of Bakunin, that Nechaev's 'organization', if he had ever had one, no longer existed and then reeled off details of his machinations and crimes, Nechaev listened in silence. '[Lopatin] triumphed, you retreated before him,' a horrified and hurt Bakunin wrote to Nechaev on 2 June. 'You systematically lied to us. Your whole enterprise was riddled with rotten lies and founded on sand.' After castigating his 'Machiavellian policies and methods of violence' – methods which he had himself preached against enemies, but never against fellow-revolutionaries – Bakunin gave vent in a few sparse words to the full pain inflicted on him by the youth in whom he had seen a model of a Russian revolutionary: 'How deeply, how passionately, how tenderly I loved you and believed in you! You were able, and found it useful, to kill this belief in me...'[34]

Lopatin visited London in July. Marx heard from him of Nechaev's murder of Ivanov, and details of his relations with Bakunin in Switzerland. In letters to all his supporters or correspondents in Europe, Bakunin protested in vain that he was himself the victim of Nechaev's perfidy.

Swiss police and Russian agents had started looking for Nechaev in March 1870. But he kept eluding them for more than two years, throughout the drama of the Franco-Prussian War, the fall of Napoleon III, the proclamation of the republic in Paris under siege, the popular insurrection against the Thiers government and the establishment of the Paris Commune. The revelation that he had posed in Moscow as a representative of the Workers' International shocked Marx, but the news itself was not unwelcome. Gripped for the moment by the events of the civil war in France, Marx stored it away in his mind for use against Bakunin in their next clash.

The civil war in beleagured Paris had started on 18 March 1871. The Provisional Government of Thiers had ordered the National Guard to be disarmed, but the Guardsmen, refusing to hand over the guns bought at their own expense, drove the government from the city instead. The attempt to disarm the Guard was the last straw after Thiers had surrendered Paris, signed away Alsace-Lorraine and started squeezing the people to raise an enormous war indemnity of 5 billion francs imposed by the Prussian victors.

Two days after the week-long May massacre in which the Commune was suppressed, Marx, who had originally supported Bismarck's war but had since protested the Prussian annexation of Alsace-Lorraine, got himself into hot water. In an address to the General Council of the International in London he hailed the heroism of the working men of Paris who had resisted both the German assault and the new tyranny of Thiers's 'government of national defection' in the following terms: 'What elasticity, what a capacity for self-sacrifice in these Parisians!... Working, thinking, fighting, bleeding... to bring about the higher form of emancipation to which society is irresistibly driven by its economic forces... throwing themselves with heroic resolve to their historic mission.'[35]

Marx's justification of the rising and his adoption of its toll of 100,000 Frenchmen killed, maimed or exiled as proof of his class-war theories shocked British public opinion. London's trade unionists were certainly not ready to lay down their lives for some 'historic mission' chosen for them by Marx. With the French press at the same time accusing him of being the 'chief instigator' of the Commune, Marx wrote to his friend Ludwig Kugelmann on 18 June 1871: 'I have the honour to be at this moment the most calumniated man in London.'

The importance of the short-lived Commune was that, for the first time, it had shown that the power of the state could be broken. It drew its support from the patriotism of Paris as much as from social reformism. Most of the Commune's 78 council members were journalists and intellectuals; politically, they were Proudhonists and Blanquists opposed to Marx. Only 21 were workers. But Marx presented the rising as a 'new world-historic phase' in the working-class struggle against capitalism; and by paying open homage to its martyrs he helped, in the words of Isaiah Berlin, 'to create a heroic legend of Socialism.'[36]

Bakunin could more justly claim to have played a part in inspiring the rising of the Paris Commune. In September 1870, shortly after the capitulation of Napoleon III, Bakunin, realizing the potential for revolution in a country 'faced with mortal danger from within and without', had rushed to Lyons. France's second largest city had declared itself an independent republic 9 hours before Paris made the claim. Bakunin arrived to find a newly elected but hesitant Municipal Council. In short order he staged a mass rally, issued a proclamation abolishing the 'governmental machinery of the state' and called for a congress of départements that wished to achieve autonomy and join 'a Revolutionary Federation of Communes'. A few days later, on 28 September, he and a group of supporters forced their way into the Hôtel de Ville, determined to present the Municipal Council with the alternative of either accepting the proclamation or resigning.

The attempted coup ended in a scuffle with two battalions of the National Guard, who evicted Bakunin and his men. Marx may have derided this episode as the comic fiasco it was, but Bakunin's spontaneous initiative and direct action spoke to the hearts of the Proudhonists and Blanquists who in March 1871 hastened to proclaim the Paris Commune. They wanted the metropolis to be an independent republic united in a loose federation with other autonomous French Communes, more or less on the lines proposed by Bakunin.

Italian and Spanish anarchists took up the slogan of 'direct action' and it gradually spread to members of the Workers' International in other countries, who did not want to wait for the 'long struggles' held out by Marx and the historic process. From Belgium and Holland, too, came cries objecting to the London General Council of the International being run by Marx like his personal fief, with the assistance of Engels, a charge supported by the British trade unions.

The 'great battle' between Marx and Bakunin, as Marx's wife called it, was fought out at the next Congress of the Workers' International, which opened at The Hague in September 1872. Marx proposed to expand the General Council's power by permitting it to expel or suspend federal councils as well as individual sections. Bakunin was conspicuous by his absence, having decided not to risk arrest in France or Germany on the way to The Hague. But his Swiss lieutenant James Guillaume told the congress: 'Each member group of the International retains its full and entire liberty to be affiliated with any secret society.' Accusing the General Council of having become a 'private autocracy of a few individuals', Guillaume challenged its power to expel or suspend anyone and proposed that its functions be curtailed to those of a liaison and correspondence bureau – or simply a 'letter-box', as Marx ridiculed the idea.

Twenty Italian sections of the International had chosen a curious way of expressing their solidarity with Bakunin by boycotting the Congress. Their missing votes helped Marx to win a clear majority investing the General Council with the punitive powers he had asked for it. The dirty work of expelling Bakunin was shunted to a Committee of Five which heard evidence in closed sessions from Engels, Guillaume and several Swiss and Spanish delegates. On the basis of information gathered from Bakunin's enemies among the Russian émigrés, Engels accused him of never having dissolved his secret Alliance but of maintaining it as 'an international within the International' in order to dominate and disorganize the latter. But Guillaume truthfully said that he knew nothing of a secret Alliance and two Spaniards explained away a letter in which it was mentioned by saying that it had existed but they were no longer members of it.

So did the Alliance actually exist? The answer is that it existed in Bakunin's head and in the heads of those few initiates in France, Italy, Spain and the Jura with whom he had shared secret codes and false names; but it was not an organization that kept records, membership lists or resolutions. The Committee of Five was therefore forced to note that, though it might have existed, there was 'not sufficient proof' of it.

At this point Marx made an unexpected appearance before the Committee and produced a copy of Nechaev's threatening letter to Liubavin in which he had stopped the translation of *Das Kapital*, allegedly in order to enable Bakunin to pocket the publisher's advance. This letter, Marx later emphasized, 'did the trick'. At his insistence, the previously hesitant Committee now drafted a recommendation that Bakunin, Guillaume and another Swiss be expelled from the International – Bakunin for having 'fraudulently appropriated another man's wealth', and the other two for still belonging to a society called Alliance, of whose existence the Committee itself could find no proof.

So in the end Marx had Bakunin expelled – but on the next day he broke up the International by unexpectedly proposing to transfer the seat of the General Council to New York. Although this move produced general consternation, Marx had actually planned it since the spring. In a letter written on 28 May 1872 he had declared that he could 'no longer afford to combine two sorts of business', namely, theoretical studies and the 'commercial concern [the International]... which has its ramifications all over the world.' Indeed, navigating the International, which was torn by splits and squabbles, had become an increasingly thankless task.

Yet the prime reason for Marx's scuttling the First International was his genuine fear that even those national groups that were nominally loyal to him were about to fall into Bakunin's hands – a fear that materialized quickly enough when the British, Dutch and Belgian sections of it joined a new anti-Marxist International founded in Switzerland by Bakunin's Italian, Spanish and Swiss supporters (in his and Guillaume's presence) on 15 September, within a week of the discordant end of the proceedings at the Concordia dancing hall in The Hague.

Only splinter groups of the First Workers' International survived for a couple of years before they disintegrated. Marx preferred to sabotage and kill the organization which not many years earlier he had called 'this powerful engine in our hands', rather than let it pass into somebody else's, least of all into those of the hated 'fat Russian', Bakunin.

Nechaev, who (when not hiding in Switzerland) had been twice in London and for some time also in Paris, was finally caught in Zurich in August 1872 and handed over to the Russians. At his trial in Moscow he protested against being flogged like a common murderer. As a political émigré he refused to recognize either the court or the Tsar and his laws. At his 'civil execution' in January 1873 he shouted that within three years 'the first Russian guillotine' would dispose of the whole Tsarist camarilla on that very spot. Informed of this, Alexander II changed Nechaev's sentence by a stroke of his pen: instead of being sent to Siberia, he was for prudence's sake to be kept in prison 'for ever'.

He was placed in solitary confinement in a section of the Peter-and-Paul fortress which housed at the time only one other inmate, a lunatic. He was allowed Russian and French books, but was kept strictly incommunicado and it took years before his friends discovered that he was not in Siberia, but in the St Petersburg fortress across the Neva from the Imperial Palace. He smuggled out to them a coded plan for seizing the fortress and setting him free, but this came to nothing because of the assassination of the Tsar in 1881. Nechaev died a year later, aged 35, not before a large number of his guards had been arrested for their alleged part in another plot to help him escape.

At the end of March 1872, the Russian translation of *Das Kapital*, started by Bakunin and completed by the economist N. Danielson, appeared in St Petersburg. To Marx's surprise, not only had the Russian censors passed the book –

on the ground that the menace represented by its 'Socialist character' was offset by the fact that its scientific language made it inaccessible to all but a small readership – but of the 3,000 copies published by Polyakov, 900 had been sold within 6 weeks. Upon learning that most Russian journals and newspapers had favourably discussed his work, which had yet to appear in any of the capitalist countries of the West, Marx wrote to Engels: 'Isn't it an irony of fate that the Russians, whom I have fought for twenty-five-years, always want to be my patrons? They run after the most extreme ideas the West has to offer, out of pure gluttony – just like Herr Bakunin.'

Marx had ridiculed Herzen's early 'discovery' of the Russian moujiks and their village communes as 'a Panslavist attempt to revivify the old, rotten Europe.' Personal rancour and mutual antagonism had kept these two famous expatriates apart in London – Marx on one occasion refusing to attend a Chartist banquet because of Herzen's presence – but when Marx decided to learn Russian with the help of a dictionary, the first thing he practised on was a section of Herzen's Memoirs.

The next thing he read in this manner was The Condition of the Working-Class in Russia by N. Flerovsky.[37] Marx learned from this book that the emancipation of the serfs had 'accelerated the process of dissolution' in Russia to the point of a possible revolution. He praised the author for his 'substantial work', but criticized him for believing that the village communes made Russia a 'perfectible nation'.

According to Marx's wife he had 'begun studying Russian as if it was a matter of life and death' as early as January 1870.[38] This urgency stemmed at least in part from the multiplying signs of possible turmoil in Russia and his eagerness to find out how this bulwark of reaction would behave in a revolution.

Reading some of Chernyshevsky's writings in 1872, Marx was pleased to find in them mention of a developing struggle in Europe between one class which lived 'off the other's labour... the other consisting of ninety percent of the people.'[39] It was, however, to take him years to realize that, much as Chernyshevsky might welcome the collapse of capitalism in Europe, he, like Herzen, had found in the village communes of industrially backward Russia a providential means enabling her to 'leap' over the capitalist stage of maximum industrial exploitation stipulated by Marx as a prerequisite for revolution.

In the spring of 1874 more than 1,000 idealistic Russian youths went to the villages, driven by an urge to help the poor and oppressed. They were heeding not only Herzen's 1861 call to 'go to the people' but a more recent appeal, To the Young Brothers in Russia, published by Bakunin in May 1869. Unlike Herzen, who had dreamt of a Socialist Russia, or others who supported student demonstrations within the bounds of the law, Bakunin advised the students to leave the universities which shackled their minds and stir up a radical upheaval reminiscent of the revolt of peasants and brigands headed in the 17th century by Stenka

Razin. Since it was unlikely 'that there will be another popular hero like Stenka Razin', the educated youth must take on the collective task of liberating the people, not as dictators, but as servants of the cause.

This attempt of the first 'Populist' students to start political agitation in the villages failed, as the peasants proved to trust the Tsar more than they did the students, and over 700 of them, including 158 young women, were arrested. But a few years later Populism received an infusion when the defunct Land and Liberty organization originally founded by Serno-Soloviev was revived by a group of 200 of its veterans who had survived underground. The new Land and Liberty took over the old one's programme of establishing secret cells (consisting of no more than 5 people each) in the regiments and civil service.

It was out of such small groups that kept proliferating, dividing and sometimes reappearing under different names, that Populism slowly developed over the next two decades. Comprising both idealists and realists, their number not exceeding several thousands, the Populist intelligentsia of the 1870s and '80s seriously debated political, social and philosophical issues, including the morality of using force to revolutionize Russia in the best interests of her people, that were to preoccupy the empire's mass parties and their various factions, including that of the Bolsheviks.

In 1873 Peter Lavrov, a member of Land and Liberty and former professor of mathematics who had spent 5 years in prison and exile before escaping abroad, arrived in Zurich and launched a periodical called *Vpered!* (Forward!). As the leader of the moderate wing of Populism, which advocated action within the bounds of the law, Lavrov opposed Bakunin's idea of 'spontaneous' revolution to be sparked off by the deeds of a few, and argued that the Russian intelligentsia must first establish a broad base among the peasantry and educate it to Socialism before instigating a revolution.

Over this issue Zurich, with its swelling colony of Russian students, saw some ugly incidents between Bakuninists and Lavrovists. Zurich was a stronghold of Bakunin and his Russian Brotherhood, whose press in 1873 printed his best-known collection of essays under the title State and Anarchy. When the first issue of Lavrov's *Vpered!* appeared about the same time, Bakunin's entrenched supporters promptly burned copies of it. Soon Lavrov found himself attacked by Peter Tkachev, a former associate of Nechaev. Although not involved in the Ivanov murder, Tkachev had spent 16 months in jail before making his escape to Geneva. Arguing that before long Russia would be so industrialized that the chance of skipping the capitalist stage of revolution would never return, he accused Lavrov of fatally missing this window of opportunity by preaching prolonged educational 'propaganda' among the peasants. To Tkachev, overthrowing Tsarism was a matter of 'now or never' to be taken in hand by a conspiratorial elite.

Lavrov decided to move to London. Tkachev remained in Geneva, but he was not finished with Lavrov, and since the latter developed a close relationship with Marx, both of them were soon to hear from him.

At the end of September 1873, just when things seemed to be going his way, Bakunin sudenly announced his retirement from public life. His victory over Marx had recently been marked by a practically all-European congress of the International adopting new 'anti-authoritarian' (i.e., anarchist) statutes giving its national federations 'complete autonomy', while a congress called by the Marx-supported General Council of New York proved a fiasco.

There was hardly one among the steady influx of Russian students in Switzerland who had not heard of Bakunin, and after talking to him they felt, as one young woman reported, 'convulsed, like the sea after the passage of a steamer.' Prince Kropotkin, the scientist and philosopher, was so impressed during a visit to Switzerland by Bakunin's 'important work in the Jura' that he became an active and life-long anarchist.

Bakunin's renunciation of politics came in the wake of the publication by the *Journal de Genève* of a pamphlet sent to it from London (anonymously) by Engels and Lafargue (Marx's son-in-law), rehashing their version of Bakunin's ruinous influence on the International. In an angry response published on 26 September Bakunin, professing to be 'profoundly disgusted' with Marx's constant slander of him and public life in general, wrote that since he was 60 and not getting any younger, he left it to younger men 'to go on rolling Sisyphus's stone against the triumphant forces of reaction.'

The old warrior was in fact frustrated by his Russian Brotherhood splitting up because of quarrels among his lieutenants. His health too, undermined by years in prison, was swiftly deteriorating. But indications are that his announcement was not unconnected with his having moved in August to an old villa outside Locarno – the Villa Baronata, bought for him by one of his most devoted supporters, Carlo Cafiero, for the express purpose of his redesigning it as a secret revolutionary meeting place, complete with an arms cache, hidden tunnels and escape routes. Bakunin was delighted to hear that, posing as a peaceful Swiss bourgeois gentleman, he was to serve as a 'mask' for the whole undertaking. To believe Guillaume,[40] his letter to the *Journal de Genève* was actually the first gambit in a plan designed to earn him citizenship as a safeguard against expulsion (a dreaded prospect revived by the extradition of Nechaev) while also serving his pose as lord of the Baronata estate.

As for his attacking Marx in that letter, Bakunin still fumed at Marx's exposure of the fact that the secret echelon of his double-layered Alliance - which proposed to build a world free of any authoritarianism - was structured as a dic-

1152

tatorship of one man, 'le citoyen B.'[41] In revenge, Bakunin during the summer, in his *State and Anarchy*, had taken a nasty anti-Semitic swipe at Marx by writing that, 'like Jehovah, the Lord God of his ancestors, he is extremely vain and ambitious, quarrelsome, intolerant and absolutist...'[42]

In this and another of his last works, *The Knouto-Germanic Empire*, published in 1872, Bakunin disputed Marx's thesis that the revolution would come first in the economically most advanced countries. On the contrary, it might erupt like a sudden cataclysm in the non-civilized countries – as it was indeed to do in Russia, China and Vietnam – where the wretched and illiterate masses bore within themselves, 'in their passions, in their instincts, in the miseries of their collective situation all the germs of future Socialism.'

In a remarkable perception of the temptations of power, to which he was himself prone, Bakunin wrote: 'The nature of man is such that, given power over others, he will invariably oppress them... Place the most radical revolutionary upon the all-Russian throne... and within a year he will have become worse than the emperor himself.'[43] And in an equally memorable passage of State and Anarchy he wrote that the revolutionary scenario proposed by Marx in the name of 'science' would be the worst.

Marx's riposte to this and other charges took a curious form. There had been much public mud-slinging between him and the Russian. In 1874, however, when he obtained a copy of *State and Anarchy* in the original Russian, he read it carefully, made long excerpts from it, and took its argument so seriously as to refute it with notes in the margins, notes interspersed with such exclamations as 'Non, mon cher!' as if he were engaged in a mute dialogue with a misguided adversary he had come to respect.

Against Bakunin's charge that he was an authoritarian who meant to impose on the masses the will of a small élite of genuine scientists, Marx wrote that he had never used the term 'scientific Socialism' except in contrast to utopian Socialists who misled the people with their unrealistic fantasies.

Commenting on a passage in which Bakunin had said that, unlike the slow-moving Germans, the 'anarchist' Slav peoples sought their life and freedom not within the state, but 'outside the state... by an all-embracing popular revolt against every state through social revolution', Marx wrote in one of these notes not meant for publication that Bakunin 'would like the European social revolution, whose economic basis is capitalist production, to take place at the level of the Russian or Slav agrarian peoples and pastoral tribes.' And he made a point of noting for the nth time that social revolution was possible 'only where the industrial proletariat under capitalist production has assumed a significant position in the masses.'[44]

Lavrov made Marx's acquaintance shortly after his arrival in London in the spring of 1874. The two met often, and Lavrov's bi-weekly *Vpered!* was to become one of Marx's chief sources of information on Russian politics and literature. Lavrov approved of Marx's ideas as a cure-all for the social ills of the West, but it was to take Marx time to realize that Lavrov saw in capitalist development and the creation of a miserable proletariat an evil which Russia had to avoid like the plague.

When Peter Tkachev had a pamphlet published in London,[45] in which he again chided Lavrov for maintaining that Russia's peasants needed a long preparatory period of indoctrination, Engels took Lavrov's side. Tkachev having written that 'revolutions are prepared by exploiters, capitalists, landowners, priests, police officials... Revolutionaries do not prepare, they make revolutions', Engels publicly dismissed him as a Bakuninist. Tkachev's response was an 'Open Letter to Engels' in which he claimed that Russia would more quickly produce a social revolution than Western Europe because, although she had no proletariat, 'she has no bourgeoisie either'. With the polemic going on into 1875, Marx had Engels lash into Tkachev by writing that he still had 'to learn the ABC of Socialism'.[46]

In a sharp rejoinder to Engels's patronizing remark that he should accept his criticism as well-meant European advice, Tkachev asked him to think what would be the effect produced on Germans 'by a lesson given by a Chinese or Japanese who had by chance learned German but who had never been to Germany... and who had conceived the idea of teaching German revolutionaries, from the height of his Chinese or Japanese majesty, what they ought to do.'[47]

Tkachev was to become the chief theorist of Russian terrorism and the idea of overthrowing Tsarism by means of a coup d'état. Although, and perhaps precisely because, he was one of the few Russians who had read Marx's neglected *Critique of Political Economy,* he too was determined to prevent the growth of capitalism in Russia.

But at the time, he had only a handful of 'Jacobin' followers in Geneva. His radicalism made even Bakunin's partisans recoil and accuse him of trying 'to drag them into the millennium by the scruff of their necks.'[48] And his claim that Russia would have a social revolution before the capitalist West struck Marx and Engels as so much nonsense. For according to their 'ABC of Socialism', it was the industrialized West, led by England, that would show Russia and other countries 'the image of their own future'.

On 21 January 1875, Moses Hess celebrated his 63rd birthday at a dinner followed by a reception in Paris, from which he and his wife had been expelled as enemy aliens at the start of the Franco-Prussian War. They had been allowed to return in December 1871, having spent the interval in Belgium, where Hess published a series of articles that read today like a scenario of World War II and its aftermath. Warning that the new Prussified German Reich would make an all-out attempt to establish German racial hegemony by force of arms, suppressing every freedom and national independence in Europe and putting the clock back by a century, he predicted that Russia, having shaken off Tsarism, would unite with the West to defeat Germany, and the Slavs would eventually march over Prussia's body to recover their former territories 'up to the river Elbe'. Hess, the man of whom it has been said that he was 'more attuned' than Marx to the *Zeitgeist* of the 19th and 20th centuries, then wrote that the Western nations, 'which will include Germany – once it is free from Prussian militarism' – would ultimately form 'a free confederation' and become 'the allies of the United States of America.[49]

Hess nearly died of a stroke at the beginning of March 1875, but recovered briefly and brimmed with satisfaction when the sculptor Paul Kersten read him the draft of the 'Gotha Programme' for the forthcoming union – at a conference to be held in Gotha – of his and Lassalle's Deutscher Allgemeiner Arbeiterverein with the younger Socialist party led by Bebel and Liebknecht.

In London, Marx was at that time preparing his *Critique of the Gotha Programme*. Refusing to have any truck with the Arbeiterverein, he had little popular support in Bismarck's patriotic Germany.

The new men, Liebknecht and Bebel, were associates of Marx, but they had risen in Germany by their own power in elections, and their contacts with him had weakened while they had gone to jail for protesting against the invasion of France. And now Liebknecht (whom Marx had described at one time as his 'only reliable contact in Germany') and Bebel had decided on a joint programme with the Arbeiterverein without even consulting him. Marx was furious.

Scrutinizing the unification programme as if he were the godfather of the new party, Marx - among many critical comments throwing light on what in the mid-20th century the editors of his own works were to call 'scientific Communism'[50] – made the point that it would take time before equality reigned in his Communist state of the future. There would be a transitional period during which 'differences of physical or intellectual ability will continue. Different men doing different labour will create different values – giving them different, not equal rights.' Only a higher phase of Communist society, putting an end to the division of labour and the conflict between physical and mental work, would produce the wealth enabling society to overstep the narrow horizon of bourgeois rights and to proclaim on its banners: 'From each according to his ability, to each according to his needs!'

The most important paragraph in Marx's *Critique of the Gotha Programme*, which he condemned wholesale for being 'tainted through and through' by the ideas of Lassalle, was one in which he said that during the transitional period there would be a 'revolutionary dictatorship of the proletariat'.[51]

Liebknecht did not show Marx's strictures to Bebel and the 'Gotha Programme' was adopted by the eponymous Congress in late May 1875 with only minor alterations. Although Hess did not know this when he died in Paris on 6 April, he felt that the campaign for universal suffrage which he had waged by the side of Lassalle was changing German political life. Indeed, the Social Democratic Party born at Gotha was before long to become the largest of Germany's 6 political parties, garnering 31% of all electoral votes.

The veteran Socialist, one-time apostle of Communism and new-fangled prophet of Zionism never dreamt that these two movements would celebrate their separate triumphs in exactly the same week in 1917 - the former in the Bolshevik Revolution which installed a Marxist-Leninist regime in the Soviet Union, and the latter in the Balfour Declaration, which granted the Jews a national home in Palestine. And it was well beyond his grasp that by the end of the 20th century the Jewish homeland, restored in a unique phenomenon after two destructions and a hiatus of nearly 2,000 years, would have outlasted the former and the collapse of all the statues of Marx, his one-time friend.

Hess was buried (at his request) next to his parents at Deutz, across the Rhine from Cologne, where German Socialists some time later engraved on his tombstone the inscription 'Father of German Social Democracy'. In 1961 the State of Israel transferred his remains and reinterred them at Kinneret, a Socialist kibbutz overlooking Lake Galilee.[52]

At Locarno, in July 1874, the Villa Baronata project had come crashing down on all sides, and throughout 1875 everything Bakunin touched seemed to backfire. First Cafiero, upon finding that Bakunin and the contractor had exhausted his money on road-building, orchards and an extravagant plan to establish a commune that would take some years to become self-supporting, refused any further financing.

To compound matters, Bakunin had made his wife Antonia (who had been in Siberia since 1872) believe that he had bought Baronata with money from his inheritance and now she and her family of 6 (including 3 children and her parents) were on their way to join him at the 'paradise' they thought he had prepared for them. Not having the heart to face her with 'first news of the catastrophe in store', Bakunin signed over Baronata to Cafiero against his promise to care for Antonia and her family 'after my death' and went off to join a group of conspirators planning an insurrection in Bologna.

In Bologna he was given the name 'Tamburini', and spent a week in hiding. But due to the arrest of one of the chief conspirators, the revolution was crushed before it was supposed to start on the night of 7 August, and instead of dying a hero's death Bakunin was led to another hide-out and smuggled out three days later disguised as a country priest carrying a basket of eggs.

At Locarno, Cafiero's men had bluntly told Antonia that Baronata belonged to 'the revolution', and not to her. While she left in a huff, Bakunin, stranded in another corner of Switzerland, was down and out for weeks before Cafiero rescued him with a small sum.

It was a changed Bakunin who eventually arrived at Lugano, where Antonia and the rest of her family had set up a new home. Not only was he chastened by the humiliations he had suffered and the way he had messed up his life, but he seemed physically as well as mentally broken. Under Antonia's care, however, he recovered, and quickly became the centre of a new circle of friends, mostly Italian, French, and Russian political refugees. According to one of them, he would spend the morning meeting them at a café in town, would sleep in the afternoon and at 8 p.m. 'he would appear in Antonia's drawing room and regale her guests with stories of his past exploits. At midnight he retired, and would read or write half the night.'[53]

He had given up any form of political activity because, as he wrote to Ogarev, triumphant 'Bismarckism, i.e., the military, police, and financial monopolies, merged into a single system calling itself the modern state', required fresh young forces to fight it. Already in *State and Anarchy* he had struck a pessimistic note by remarking that 'the masses have left themselves to be profoundly demoralized, subjugated, if not to say castrated by the harmful effects of the civilization of the state.' Now he proclaimed in a letter to Elisée Reclus: 'There remains one hope: world war. These immense militarized states must surely sooner or later destroy each other, devour each other. But what a prospect!'[54]

In February 1875, upon hearing from Antonia's sister Sophia – who had gone to Russia to help him obtain his long-expected inheritance from Premukhino – that his brothers had agreed to let her sell a forest as his part of the inheritance, Bakunin bought the large and handsome Villa Bresso on the outskirts of Lugano. Determined to build a 'paradise' for Antonia on the model of Premukhino, he felled trees, planted new ones and dug trenches. But he used excessive quantities of fertilizer which ruined the soil and made the whole garden look like a desert.

'Before entering paradise one must go through purgatory,' a resigned Bakunin, still hoping that the sale of his Russian forest would make him a rich man, consoled himself as the first of his mortgage payments became due. With the help of Gambuzzi (the father of Antonia's children, who lived in Naples but had a bed reserved for him in her Lugano guest room), he managed to stave off his chief Neapolitan creditor for a while.

In December he finally moved with Antonia and her three children into the Villa Bresso. The day marked the successful accomplishment, against all odds, of the last project he ever embarked on. Alas, at the beginning of May 1876 disaster struck. Sophia returned from Russia with 7,000 roubles. Together with 1,000 she had sent in March, this was all she had obtained for the forest-land representing his entire inheritance. It was much less than either she or Bakunin had expected, and not enough to cover the outstanding part of the mortgage and prevent its foreclosure. After much discussion at a council meeting of the extended family, including Gambuzzi, it was decided that they should all move to the latter's place in Naples.

Antonia left first. Bakunin was to wait in Switzerland until she obtained for him the necessary permission to live in Naples. His health had taken a turn for the worse earlier that spring, but about the same time something good had happened to him. This was the arrival in Lugano of Alexandra Weber, a young Russian student who had Socialist inclinations and, having heard of the famous Bakunin, became a regular visitor at the Villa Bresso. He enjoyed the distraction and relief she brought. 'Suffering kidney, bladder and prostate disorders, he almost never slept and at times did not manage the stairway... The only way he was able to get some relief when the attacks came was by bending, stretched over a table, feet on the ground.'[55]

An Italian working man whom he had met during the Bologna insurrection, and a couple of others who had been fascinated by his tales of revolution, took turns mornings and evenings to help him dress and undress. In a moving account of his fortitude during the closing months of his life, Alexandra Weber noted that in between his physical misery and mental stress he was his usual jocular self. She stressed that although Antonia sometimes treated him with indifference, he was 'an indulgent father to his wife and a gentle grandfather to her children,' with whom he liked to play. When his pains eased he read and wrote, rolled cigarettes, drank huge quantities of tea and talked of dictating his memoirs to Alexandra. But most of all he liked to talk about his childhood and youth at Premukhino. Even the frogs in the Italian garden reminded him of the musical croaking that had filled the air on his father's estate on happy summer evenings. He had never known such happiness again.

On 13 June, a few days after Antonia had left for Naples, Bakunin travelled to Berne to see Dr Vogt about his medical problems. The doctor met him at the station and took him straight to the hospital. He spent the next fortnight there, discussing music and philosophy with his old friend Reichel – 'the world will perish, but the Ninth Symphony will remain,' was one of his last remarks – before his strength gave out.

He died on 1 July 1876, a disillusioned man who left behind a powerful myth of heroic suffering comparable to that inspiring the cult of Che Guevara in our own day. The 1968 revolt of the young led by Daniel Cohn-Bendit and the practically simultaneous American 'counter-culture' had in common the use of violence and other elements of 'direct action' à la Bakunin. In 1971 James Joll, remarking on the ease with which Herbert Marcuse's 'liberating function of negation' was transferable from the philosophical to the practical plane, wrote: 'This is perhaps why it is Bakunin among the classical anarchist thinkers who has most strongly captured the imagination of the contemporary revolutionaries.'[56] Arthur Mendel, pondering the specific question 'why Bakunin's example and words have for so long had so great an influence on the world's intelligentsia,' came up with another explanation: 'One only has to recall those elite rebels of the late 1960s who retreated into peaceful realms' of contemplative beauty,

> while at the same time idolizing the world's most violent revolution-
> ary activists – Ho, Che, Mao – and posting large icons of them on
> their walls... Uncompromising individualists, they demanded com-
> plete freedom for themselves, yet lovingly extolled totalitarian soci-
> eties which made such individualism and such freedom their first
> victims.

Bakunin too, in Mendel's view, wanted most of all 'to remain apart, yet appear to be courageously committed,' a posture allowing him to transmute impotence into omnipotence. Though unmasking Bakunin's heroic performances as 'the-atrical acts', Mendel made an important point by stressing that while the succes-sive secret organizations which Bakunin kept conceiving remained chiefly 'notebook phantasies' whose violent rethoric did little harm, 'it was just such organizational plans as these that were later to be adopted by Lenin and that helped establish the foundations for Soviet party dictatorship.'[57]

With Lassalle, Hess and Bakunin all gone, Marx in 1876 had the field to himself. For the next two years he went on working on Volumes II and III of *Das Kapital*. But having knowingly sacrificed his health, happiness and his whole family to this work, which was posthumously to make him immortal, he gradually let go of it in or about 1878, to spend the remaining 5 years of his life as a gentleman travelling in search of a cure – on the Isle of Wight, in Algiers, at Karlsbad (4 times) and other European watering places. During these years the prophet of wrath and domineering 'self-god' mellowed somewhat. He enjoyed watching the international life at these health resorts and impressed nearly everyone he met with his wide-ranging and witty conversation.

To a lady who in the course of a political discussion wondered who in the future Marxist state would do all the menial jobs and then said to him, 'I cannot imagine you, with your refined tastes and aristocratic manners, living in an egali-tarian society,' Marx is said to have replied: 'Neither can I. Those times will come, but we must by then be gone.'[58]

But Marx was still alive and as alert as ever in 1879, when Peter Tkachev broke away from Land and Liberty in Russia and formed his own clandestine organization –The People's Will – of revolutionaries dedicated to armed combat.

Although Tkachev took some of his ideas from Bakunin, he did not heed Bakunin's call for the destruction of the state and its evils. Rather, the tightly knit and disciplined People's Will aimed at seizing the power concentrated in the state. Having reached the conclusion that in an empire of absolute despotism no social reform could be contemplated unless the despot himself was first removed, Tkachev's latest strategy was to overthrow Tsarism by a military putsch and then to attack the social question. But at the heart of his scheme to save Russia by force was the village commune.

The commune, or *obschina*, was like a lodestar which had drawn Populists of all shadings – the followers of Herzen and Chernyshevsky, Bakuninists and Lavrovists, Westerners, Slavophiles, constitutionalists as well as the radical and moderates of the now split Land and Liberty – to unite around the basic idea that Russia must and could bypass the evils of capitalist exploitation.

Between 1879 and 1881 The People's Will staged 7 attempts on the life of Tsar Alexander II. Six of them failed. But although the active nucleus of The People's Will is said to have consisted of no more than 40 members, they managed to defy and terrorize the forces of the mighty Russian empire; and the seventh attempt was to result in the assassination of the Tsar.

Georgy Plekhanov, one of the leaders of Land and Liberty who opposed this strategy of violence and regicide, watched the constant arrests, executions and serial attentats with horror. As his faction lost ground, he emigrated with a number of his faithfuls to Switzerland, where he discovered Marx's writings and theory of Communism.

Marx himself in 1881, after a decade of studying Russian, was in his old age to find himself desperately trying to puzzle out developments in Russia which threatened to disprove his work and theories of a lifetime. He was drawn into the dispute over Russian revolutionary strategy and tactics in February of that year, when he received a letter from Switzerland. In it Vera Zasulich, a noble-born Russian activist who had joined Plekhanov in Geneva, asked for Marx's authoritative opinion on the question whether her country's village communes could play a role in the development of Socialism: 'We hear it said that the rural commune is an archaic form condemned to perish by history, scientific Socialism and, in short, everything above debate. Those who preach such a view call themselves your disciples par excellence: "Marksists".'

Marx had said nothing about Russia or her communes in *Das Kapital*, and the first Russian 'Marxists' in Switzerland were in a quandary as to how to square their Populist faith in the village people with his exclusive reliance on the industrial proletariat. Zasulich, the heroine of a famous political trial (she had shot the St Petersburg Governor Trepov, and been sensationally acquitted), wanted to know whether it was really 'historically necessary for every country in the world to pass through all the phases of capitalist production.' This was a 'life-and-death question' for her and her comrades, for if the commune was destined to perish all that remained for them was to calculate how many decades or centuries 'it will take capitalism in Russia to reach the level of development in Western Europe.'[59]

But Russia continued to present Marx with a great insoluble enigma. Struggling for three weeks with Zasulich's question, he wrote out 5 drafts before he sent her a sketchy and guarded reply on 8 March. In what Edmund Wilson has called 'perhaps the last vital flicker of his mind,' he wrote that 'my so-called theory' (sic!) limited 'historical inevitability' to Western Europe. The peasant commune, he added, might become the 'fulcrum of Russia's social revival, but one would first have to protect it from the [capitalist] onslaught assailing it from every direction.'[60]

Five days later, Tsar Alexander II was killed in St Petersburg by a terrorist assassin of The People's Will who threw a bomb at his carriage as it was driving along the Catherine Canal. On 11 April Marx wrote to his daughter Jenny(chen) Longuet that Tkachev's men who were on trial in St Petersburg were 'sterling' people: 'Far from preaching tyrannicide as a theory or panacea, they are trying on the contrary to teach Europe that their modus operandi is a specifically Russian, historically inevitable way of action... For this they should not be moralized – for or against – any more than one can moralize the earthquake in Chios.'[61]

Was this just another flicker of his weakening mind, or a dramatic about-face after years of regarding Russia as a 'barbarian' monolith? That it was the latter was the view reached in 1984 by the Japanese scholar Haruki Wada and by Teodor Shani, who wrote, respectively, that Marx had begun to 'perceive the structure unique to backward capitalism'; and that he suddenly realized that industrial England could no longer 'show to the less developed' Russia 'the image of its own future.'[62]

According to the two, Marx's new 'mindset' was the result of his increased contacts with Russian radicals and of the intensive study he devoted to the peasant commune in his drafts of the letter to Zasulich. Wada, though, admitted that by the end of 1881 Marx, whose wife had died, 'was completely exhausted, mentally and physically'. In this condition, in February 1882, he put his signature to some lines in a preface written by Engels to the second Russian edition of *The Communist Manifesto* printed in the same year in Geneva. The lines, differing from his letter to Zasulich, read: 'If the Russian revolution becomes the signal for a proletarian revolution in the West, so that both complement each other, the present Russian common ownership of land may serve as the starting point of Communist development.'[63]

It was a time of great confusion. Within two years of the Tsar's assassination, the active nucleus of The People's Will was wiped out in a massive manhunt. (Tkachev, who never returned to Russia, ended up in a French mental clinic, where he died in 1885.) Plekhanov, who was only 25 but soon to become the founding father of Russian Marxism, published two pamphlets in which –ironically contradicting Marx and Engels – he warned the Populists that the peasant communes offered no way of bypassing the 'historically inevitable' capitalist phase in Russia or anywhere. Plekhanov's band of Marxists in Switzerland was at the time so small that boating with them on the Lake of Geneva he jokingly said: 'Be careful, if we drown, Russian Socialism will perish.'[64]

It was only in the 1890s that Marxism began to spread in Russia and to contend with the Socialist Revolutionary Party. Another offspring of Populism was the Russian Social Democratic Party, which later split into two factions, Mensheviks and Bolsheviks.

Marx died sitting in his chair on 14 March 1883. He was buried on the 17th next to his wife – whose funeral 15 months earlier he had been too ill to attend – in a remote corner of Highgate Cemetery.[65] He had published nothing of importance for more than a decade, but left behind 30,000 pages of notes.

A small group of mourners heard Engels declare at his graveside: 'Just as Darwin discovered the law of development of organic nature, so Marx discovered the law of development of human history.' This law, like the supposedly scientific 'materialist conception of history' – which Engels began to spin in 1859 out of what Marx merely called a 'guiding thread' and then further elaborated in 1878 in his Anti-Dühring and went on propagating after Marx's death[66] – was more of Engels's than Marx's making. Marx used the term 'materialist conception of history' in 1845-46 in *The German Ideology*, but he never followed up with a detailed formulation of it. The only discoveries Marx himself ever took credit for were those he listed in a famous letter under three headings:

> What I did for the first time was show 1) that the existence of classes is simply linked to particular historic phases of the development of production; 2) that the class struggle necessarily leads to the dictatorship of the proletariat; 3) that this dictatorship itself is merely the transition to the abolition of all classes and to a classless society.[67]

Marx also strongly objected to the word 'Marxism', which was originally coined by his Bakuninist and other opponents to deride his theories. Although he more than once denied being a 'Marxist', and half a year before his death let Engels know how much the term sickened him,[68] Engels launched 'Marxism' in 1889 as the over-all name for Marx's teaching because, he limply explained, he could think of 'no other name just as short.'

To the first two generations of Marxists the chief authority on Marx's ideas was Engels. In 1920, in fact, Max Adler called Engels 'the man who perfected and crowned Marxism' by 'systematizing' Marx's thought and enlarging it 'into a world-view.' The later debate on the question whether there was a 'break' between the young and the mature Marx was to culminate a century after his death in scholarly attempts to separate Marx's ideas from those of Engels, his 'co-prophet and intellectual alter ego'. In 1981 Maximilien Rubel, a leading proponent of the 'inner unity' of Marx's thought and of his image as a servant of mankind whose 'utopian-ethical' approach always prevailed over his scientific and rationalist side, wrote that Engels – through various distortions, misunderstandings and omissions in the process of editing Marx's writings – created 'a mythology destined to dominate the history of the 20th century', one that, under the name of 'Marxism', became an authoritarian ideology and 'particularly in its Leninist and Maoist versions... developed a system of state-capitalism combining the traits of the most advanced industrialism with the characteristics of the most inhuman political absolutism.'[69]

In 1984 Bruce Mazlich countered with the argument that Marxism 'changed significantly, not only after Marx, but after Engels, Kautsky, etc., just as Christianity changed after Christ'; and that 'in practice, Marx tended to confuse the party of mankind with himself, and was intolerant of those who did not agree with this identification.'[70]

The debate had by then branched out into such questions as whether 'Leninism would have been inconceivable without Marx',[71] or whether Lenin's totalitarian regime was a 'perversion or misunderstanding of Marxism'. Shortly after David Lovell in 1984[72] and David Conway in 1987 (in *A Farewell to Marx*) had both exonerated Marx of any totalitarian tendencies, the collapse of the Communist-ruled Soviet colossus brought to light a totally new image of a cruel Lenin who, long before Stalin's known crimes and his extermination of whole populations, had instituted terrorism and genocide as Soviet state policy.

In October 1996 Richard Pipes[73] published a series of documents revealing that, as early as in August 1918, less than a year after the Bolshevik seizure of power, Lenin ordered his comrades in the Penza province

> to hang (hang without fail so the people see) no fewer than 100 known
> kulaks, rich men, bloodsuckers; to publish their names; to take from
> them all the grain; to designate hostages... Do it in such a way that for
> hundreds of versts [i.e. hundreds of kilometres] around, the people

will see, tremble, know, shout: they are strangling and will strangle to death the bloodsucker kulaks.[74]

This was only the prelude to another directive a few weeks later in which Lenin set up a commission whose task was 'secretly – and urgently – to prepare the [Red] Terror', which the Soviet government launched in the first week of September 1918.[75]

The most shocking document published by Richard Pipes is Lenin's 'top secret' letter of 19 March 1922 instructing Molotov not only to crush Russia's Orthodox Church and rob it of its sacred vessels and other treasures, but impressing on him that

> It is precisely now, and only now, when in the starving regions people are eating human flesh, and hundreds if not thousands of corpses are littering the roads, that we can (and therefore must) carry out the confiscation of church valuables with the most savage and merciless energy...so as to secure for ourselves a fund of several million gold roubles...(and perhaps several billions) and this can be done successfully only now.

Following the killing of several civilians trying to protect a church at Shuia from soldiers looting it, Lenin in this letter twice stressed that the pillaging of the valuables 'of the richest abbeys, monasteries and churches' must be conducted 'with such brutality [and] merciless determination stopping at nothing' that no one will dare 'even to think of any resistance for decades to come.'

The Politburo was therefore to give a detailed 'directive to the judicial authorities, also verbal', that the trial of the Shuia rebels - to be charged with resisting aid to the hungry - must end 'in no other way than execution by firing squad of a very large number of the most influential and dangerous' clerics and bourgeois reactionaries. For good measure, Lenin added that the more that were executed 'the better'.[76]

According to one estimate, more than 8,000 people were shot as a result of Lenin's letter. Amazingly, this letter was smuggled out of Russia and published in 1970 in Paris, but its authenticity was widely doubted because the cruel streak revealed by Lenin's brutal instruction contradicted the 'soft' image of Lenin the 'democrat' long fostered by some historians in the West. Not before the publication of the letter in April 1990 in the official newspaper Izvestia were these doubts dispelled.

In 1849 Marx, publicly branding the reactionary monarchs of his time as 'royal terrorists' for their brutal suppression of that year's revolutions, had justified the use of the same weapon against them. Promising revenge, he had declared: 'We also are ruthless... When our turn comes we will not conceal our terrorism.' But Marx was a theorist. He never had a state apparatus at his disposal. After writing the above lines in May 1849 he had briefly associated in London with the followers of the French arch-conspirator Blanqui, but had severed relations with them as soon as he realized that all they could think of was to seize 'power at once' by means of conspiracy and incendiary bombs. Marx was against these means for instant revolution. The victory of the reaction in 1848-49 had taught him that it would take decades to educate the proletariat to their 'class interest' and long-term task.

Since then he had discovered that beneath the stark façade of the reactionary Tsarist Empire there functioned a powerhouse of ideas in which serious intellectuals were at work to produce a social model that might enable Russia to show the West the 'image of its future', rather than vice-versa. But there is not a person in the world who can tell exactly at which point in 1881 Marx's mind began to work in flickers, and his private remark to his daughter about the 'sterling' men standing trial in St Petersburg hardly means that he had adopted their 'specifically Russian' modus operandi (i.e. terrorism) into his own programme. It means at most that he had come to realize – as he wrote on 22 February 1881, again privately – that there could be no universal blueprint for revolutions. 'The unique conditions prevailing in each country will directly bring forth the next modus operandi.'[77]

On 29 April, some 6 weeks after the assassination of the Tsar, Marx, congratulating Jennychen on the birth of a fourth son, could not help expressing his *Weltanschauung* by writing: 'Children born today have before them the most revolutionary period which human beings ever had to live in.' But having retired from public life, he went on in the manner of a mere bystander: 'It is not good to be so old that one is capable only of foreseeing and not of seeing.'

Old Marx could hear the hoofbeats of the Horsemen of the Apocalypse, but what he neither saw nor could foresee before he died in 1883 was that in March 1887 a new cell of the decimated People's Will, formed by 7 young idealists, would plot to assassinate the next Tsar. Lenin (then still Vladimir Ilyich Ulyanov) was 17 when his brother Alexander, who was 21, was hanged for taking part in the abortive conspiracy. 'We have never rejected terror on principle,' Lenin wrote in 1901. 'At certain moments of the battle it may even be essential.' To have thought otherwise would have meant to reject his brother's proud stand in court and the tradition of heroic martyrdom which had inspired his small band of conspirators to plan their attempted coup to coincide with the sixth anniversary of the assassination of Alexander III's father.

In Germany, at the turn of the century, even the Marxist wing of the Social Democratic Party, relying on its increasing strength in the Reichstag to achieve democratic parliamentary reforms, had abandoned Marx's concept of the 'dictatorship of the proletariat'. Brooding for 25 years since 1850 over the question how capitalist society was to be transformed into a Communist one, Marx had written in his *Critique of the Gotha Programme* that this period of revolutionary transformation involved a corresponding political period of transition during which the state could be nothing else than a revolutionary dictatorship of the proletariat.

It was for the seventeenth time that he mentioned 'the dictatorship of the proletariat' in one or another context, without ever specifying whether this term implied minority rule by the proletariat under all circumstances, or would allow bourgeois opposition at least in politically advanced 'democratic' countries.[78]

Lenin, a man with a great talent for simplifying things, cut through Marx's ambiguities. When the Austrian Social Democrat Karl Kautsky maintained that by dictatorship Marx had simply meant 'rule' of the proletariat and accused Lenin of wishing to introduce an oligarchic system of goverment like that of 'the Jesuits in Paraguay who had governed the Indians', Lenin replied: 'Dictatorship is an authority relying directly upon force, and not bound by any laws. The revolutionary dictatorship of the proletariat is an authority maintained by the proletariat by means of force over and against the bourgeoisie, and not bound by any laws.[79]

As for the 'broad principles of democracy', this was something the Socialists in Germany – where they enjoyed the privilege of holding public party congresses – could toy with. In Russia, however, where Marxism had come as a godsend to the divided Populist groups operating in secret under the heel of the Tsarist autocracy in the 1890s, they could, in Lenin's words, ill afford such 'luxury'. Alternately, he would later subtly argue that the soviets - or workers', peasants', and soldiers' councils - were 'a higher form of democracy.'

Lenin found little in Marx to tell him how actually to overthrow Tsarism or how to transform Russia on the morrow of a victorious revolution. Characteristically, he did not bother his head with these questions until they required a decision. 'The seizure of power', he wrote in 1917, 'is the point of the uprising. Its political task will be clarified after the seizure,' or as Bertram Wolfe was to paraphrase it,

> Let's take power and then we'll see... [Lenin's] exegesis literally turned Marx on his head until the Marxist view that 'in the last analysis economics determines politics' became the Leninist view that, with enough determination, power itself, naked political power, might succeed wholly in determining economics.[80]

So, was Marx in any way responsible for Lenin's appropriating 'Marxism' while building the first Communist state in history on totalitarian foundations and instituting terrorism as state policy? Marx was by temperament an authoritarian. So was Lenin. Each of them believed that he was an agent of history. As such, each was firmly convinced that he was acting for the future and that he was 'right', and that anyone who disagreed represented the past to be swept away.

But Marx, philosopher of world revolution, was first and foremost a thinker. He was neither a politician, nor an organizer, nor a statesman. At best he was a quasi-politician. Marx's supra-rational urge to make 'the happiness of millions', first expressed when he was 17 and to become the driving force of his search for an ultimate perfect society, bordering on the prophetic and implying a fore-knowledge of the end of history, lent his 'scientific' theories the force of a new faith. Whatever one may think of his programme of salvation, all-out genocidal terrorism of the type instituted by the implacable Lenin – which within half a decade was to cause a total death toll among the peasantry, the workers and the military running into millions – was not part of it.

Lenin, of whom Plekhanov was to say admiringly that he was of the dough of which 'Robespierres are made', was all the things which Marx was not. His great strength lay in the permanent concentration of his mind, energy and will on the ultimate goal. A professional revolutionary skilled in the conspiratorial use of secret codes and invisible ink, he was also a great political manipulator. Consider the psychological advantage he gained when forming his own underground faction in 1903, which in 1912 split away from the Social Democratic Party; he called it the Bolshevik (i.e., the 'Majority') Party, although it had fewer adherents than the rival Mensheviks – a term denoting 'Minority', which automatically stamped them as rebels against the will of the supposed majority.

In laying the theoretical foundation of modern Socialism, Marx had sown the wind. Lenin, stipulating that the dictatorship of the proletariat was the 'very essence of Marx's doctrine', created his own brand of Marxism-Leninism, and riding roughshod over his opponents, imposed it by the force of his personality and inner conviction as the true new gospel not only on his country, but on believers in half the world. In Marx's writings Lenin gleaned the promise of world revolution; but as for the technique of it, he instinctively relied on the methods of the Russian 'revolutionary tradition', that is, on the methods of violent 'direct' action taught by Bakunin, Nechaev and Tkachev. The combination of it all made him the man of destiny who, by his deeds in the First World War, single-handedly changed the course of history for the rest of the 20th century.

At the time of the March 1917 revolution in Russia and the abdication of Tsar Nicholas II, Lenin was in Switzerland. In April, having from the beginning opposed the war, he ordered his Bolshevik organization in Russia not to support Kerensky's Provisional Government but to prepare to topple it. Then, looking for a way of reaching Russia to take charge of events there, he entered into secret negotiations with the German authorities conducting the war against his own country. The upshot, in the words of Winston Churchill, was that the German General Staff 'turned upon Russia the most grisly weapon' by transporting Lenin (and 32 of his comrades) in a special train from Switzerland to Petrograd in exchange for his promise to take Russia out of the war.

Lenin's Bolshevik party in Russia comprised at the time 80,000 organized workers – 'a catalytic drop in the swelling ocean of revolution'[81] – and although acclaimed by his partisans when he stepped off the train in Petrograd, his treasonable action in cahoots with his country's enemies soon forced him to put on a wig and make his escape to Finland aboard a train on which he impersonated an assistant to the engine-driver. From there, in September 1917, he continued to call for revolution and civil war, answering all arguments that this would mean 'rivers of blood' with the justification that the cost of civil war would be incomparably less than the 'rivers of blood' shed by Russian imperialism in its war.

On 20 October he made his way back to Petrograd illegally, in time to appear at the Smolny Bolshevik headquarters and to stage, together with Trotsky, the armed putsch which made him the head of the new revolutionary government. The day was 25 October 1917 by the old Russian calendar still in force (hence the name 'October Revolution', 7 November elsewhere) and by nightfall, reeling with the news that most government buildings, bridges and railway stations had been occupied by 'Red Army' and Bolshevik militia men, Lenin remarked to Trotsky: 'The transition from illegality to power is so abrupt that it makes one dizzy.'

Needless to say, the Bolshevik minority, once in power, suppressed both the Social Revolutionary Party and the Mensheviks, as well as all forms of Populism from which they had themselves sprung. Until Germany's surrender in November 1918, the new 'Marxist-Leninist' Soviet regime was to a large extent financed by the German government.

Later in the 20th century, distinguished men of letters and historians would say that Lenin 'identified history with his will,' or that by virtue of the fact that 'the Communist revolution which he believed himself to be serving was invented, forced through and led by him', Lenin 'was himself an historical force.'[82]

At the beginning of that fateful year, on 30 January, Lenin had written in a letter to his friend and loyal supporter Inessa Armand: 'I continue to be "in love" with Marx and Engels to the point where I will tolerate no defamation of them. These two were really true men! We must learn from them, and never abandon the ground on which they stood.' This strange expression of love stands in stark contrast to Lenin's use and abuse of the malleable term 'Marxism' when building the Soviet 'prototype of all 20th-century totalitarian states', as Richard Pipes has called it, in its name.

With that mighty-looking state gone, capitalism globalized and the class struggle no longer a central issue even in Communist China, there is a natural tendency to write off Marxism for good. But in an unpredictable world still teeming with starving millions in parts of the globe, and given the intellectual and emotional appeal of Marx to so many people over so long a time, no one can say whether the day of this or that brand of Marxism may not come again in one place or another – especially as there will always be those who will argue that the collapse of the USSR was an historic 'catastrophe' not due to any flaw in Marx's theories, but to the Russian attempt to accelerate history.

But rather than speculate about the future, I would point to the 'Pandora effect' of Marx's life-long self-identification with Prometheus which became metaphorically true of him in his after-life. The fire Prometheus stole from heaven made that Titan a benefactor of mankind and the creator of its civiliza-tion. One of Zeus's punishments was to send him the woman Pandora with her vase or jar – wrongly called 'Pandora's Box' – full of diseases and other evils which spread among mankind when she maliciously took off its great lid. But this was not all. According to Hesiod, the theft of fire brought with it the working of metals, which led to the manufacture of weapons, and ultimately to violence and war. In like manner, for decades after the October Revolution the ideas of Marx, the benefactor of mankind, stirred hopes and enthusiasm in the hearts of toiling millions and excited the minds of intellectuals to an extent unimaginable as this century comes to an end.

In Western Europe the 'spectre of Communism' goaded capitalist govern-ments and newly class-conscious but moderate Socialist parties to work out various forms of the welfare state. In Eastern Europe, China, parts of Africa and Latin America, the 'Pandora effect' of Marx's ideas or simulacra of them led to some of the bloodiest upheavals in history.

Marx's endeavour to foist upon the world a salvationist scheme of collective bliss in which the state and all conflicts would 'wither away' failed perhaps chiefly because all such utopian-eschatological visions – predicated as they are on nothing less than a change of human nature – go beyond the borders of empirical research.

The Soviet Union founded by Lenin before he died in January 1924 played a foremost part in beating back Hitler's hordes during World War II, only to col-lapse ultimately under the weight of its own in-built evils.

Appendix

Notes on Marx's Descent from RASHI

The 'Short' Luria Pedigree – Lost, Found and Deciphered. Marx's descent from RASHI, sometimes mooted, but never published in detailed or authenticated form, has been traced in this volume on the basis of the 'short' Luria pedigree compiled by the Alsatian Rabbi Johanan Luria in the 15th century. His 'comprehensive' pedigree – tracing the family's ancestry back to the 2nd-century Talmud sage Johanan Hasandlar – no longer exists. Although reports of it have generated scholarly attempts to reconstruct the long chain connecting the Lurias with figures of antiquity, the 'comprehensive' pedigree is based on tradition, and will not be discussed here.

The 'short' pedigree, tracing the Luria family to RASHI, is another matter. Johanan Luria had inscribed it in a 'book', a term denoting anything from a parchment folio to a prayer book. This is known from a document left by Joseph ben Gershon of Rosheim (1478-1554). In a short *pour-mémoire* written on a special sheet the famous 'commander of all Jewry in the Holy Roman Empire of the German Nation' recorded a meeting with Rabbi Johanan at which the latter showed him the 'book' or document on which he had inscribed his 'short pedigree.' Quoting the text of the inscription, Joseph of Rosheim wrote:

'This I heard from him verbally and then found inscribed in his book: "I, Johanan Luria, son of OT (Our Teacher) Rabbi Aaron, son of OT Rabbi Nethanel, son of OT Rabbi Jehiel, son of OT Rabbi Samson (Shimshon) of Erfurt, son of the Rabbiness Miriam, daughter of OT Shlomo Spira and sister of OT Peretz of Constance. From Shlomo Spira there was no cessation of the Torah among his forefathers' – meaning there was an uninterrupted line of scholars – 'all the way in the line of ascent up to RASHI. This and more: the said Rabbiness Miriam lectured at a yeshivah. For days and years she sat under a marquee, and from behind a curtain, taught Halakha jurisprudence to gifted students. This has come down to me from my forefathers both orally and in writing."'

Following this quotation, Joseph of Rosheim, a man used to handling legal documents and protection letters which he often produced to the Emperors Maximilian I and Charles V in order to remind them that in the original Roman Empire the Jews had enjoyed most of the rights of *cives Romanis*, added meticulously: 'Written from the mouth of OT of genius Rabbi Johanan Luria... I have inscribed it all on this sheet, that it may be remembered forever, from generation to generation.'

Joseph of Rosheim was married to a great-niece of Rabbi Johanan. He was, moreover, himself descended from Shlomo Spira, a fact he mentioned with some pride in detailing his own pedigree.

Read in reverse order, the first part of the pedigree said in effect that the progenitor of all the Lurias, known only by his first name, was Samson (Shimshon) of Erfurt. Born around 1350, and mentioned in the Jews-Book of Erfurt, he later moved to Gotha, where he was appointed regional Rabbi of Turingia and died in 1417. We know today that his Italian great-grandson Aaron, the first to adopt the name Luria, was the father of Johanan, the author of the pedigree. Johanan in turn, through his mother the 'Rabbiness' Miriam Spira and her Trèves ancestors, was the first Luria who could claim descent from RASHI. Rosheim's otherwise authentic copy of the pedigree, however, listed Samson (Shimshon) of Erfurt as 'son of the Rabbiness Miriam.'

But this incongruity attracted no public notice, for Rosheim's *pour-mémoire*, which eventually turned up in the Bodleian Library in a volume – Mss. Bodleian, No. 2240, containing fragments of his Sefer Hamiknah and a Journal of his activities with which it was bound together – was not to be published before the end of the 19th century.

In the 16th century, Johanan Luria's grandson – Shlomo I Hanania ben Aaron II Luria, hereafter referred to as the Rabbi of Worms – received a letter from his famed Polish relative, the MaHarSHaL of Lublin, asking for details of the pedigree. In his reply the Rabbi of Worms, quoting the 'short' pedigree inscribed by his grandfather Johanan in his 'book,' reproduced substantially the same text as Rosheim. The only difference was that in this second version, written in 1556 or possibly 1566, the passage about the Rabbiness Miriam teaching gifted Talmud students 'from behind a curtain' was not attributed to Johanan, the author of the pedigree, but added by the Worms Rabbi from a source of his own.

It was a third version of the 'short' pedigree, penned by the Worms Rabbi's grandson, Aaron III (ben Moshe II Joshua) Luria, which created the enigma about the 'Rabbiness Miriam' Spira's place in the sequence of descent from RASHI. Aaron III Luria was one of the judges of the famous rabbinical court of Frankfurt. Some time before he died in 1613, recalling a visit to his native Worms, he mentioned the exchange of letters between the Worms Rabbi and the MaHarSHaL of Lublin and quoted the text of the 'short' pedigree as transmitted by the former to the latter. Aaron III explained that the 'short' pedigree had come down to his grandfather, the Worms Rabbi, from the lips of the latter's father – Aaron II ben Johanan Luria – that is, from the son of its author, before he died; and he went on to say that his grandfather had in turn communicated it to him before he passed away.

This third version, becoming the first to appear in print when it was published at Fuerth in Germany in 1768, in a book of *responsa* by the MaHarSHaL of Lublin, led researchers down a false trail. For, as in Joseph of Rosheim's (then still unpublished) first version, Samson of Erfurt appeared in it as 'son of the Rabbiness Miriam', who was actually the mother of his great-great-grandson Johanan Luria, the author of the pedigree.

The original of the Worms Rabbi's 16th-century letter to the MaHarSHaL of Lublin had meanwhile (like all the original papers in the case) been lost. A son of the MaHarSHaL, Zeev Wolf Luria, had, however, made a copy of it back in 1596. On this copy subsequent descendants, male or marital, of the main Luria line inscribed their names and parentage, and cousins, uncles and other relatives made altogether nine copies of it for themselves.

The ninth and most important copy, made by Moses Eliezer Beilinson and published in Berlin in 1857 in the Hebrew journal *Hamagid,* included in its reproduction of the Worms Rabbi's letter to the MaHarSHaL the conjunction 'and', which was missing in other copies. The relevant passage read: 'Johanan Luria, son of OT Nethanel, son of OT Jehiel, son of OT Samson (Shimshon) of Erfurt, and son of the Rabbiness Miriam, daughter of OT Shlomo Speyer (Spira), and sister of OT Peretz of Constance. From Shlomo Speyer there was no cessation of the Torah...'

Although a negligent printer left out the name of Johanan's father Aaron and played havoc with this text – it should have read 'Johanan Luria, son of Aaron, son of Nethanel,' etc., – Beilinson's copy, by the introduction of a single vertical stroke (the Hebrew symbol for the vowel oo, which means 'and', so that oo-ben means 'and son'), helped to solve the riddle and confirm the fact that Johanan was the son of Aaron and the Rabbiness Miriam, as becomes evident when the text is spaced in the following manner:

'Johanan Luria, son of OT Aaron – son of OT Nethanel, son of OT Jehiel, son of OT Samson (Shimshon) of Erfurt – and son of the Rabbiness Miriam, daughter of OT Shlomo Speyer (Spira),' etc.

At the bottom of the Worms Rabbi's letter the MaHarSHaL of Lublin, on its receipt in the mid-16th century, had appended a note saying that he knew from his own forefathers 'that our pedigree goes back to RASHI, of blessed memory, as recorded in the yichus letter possessed by those two great luminaries, Rabbi Johanan Luria and his brother, my great-grandfather Rabbi Jehiel (II) Luria, who died at Brisk [Brest-Litovsk] in Lithuania.'

This note, reproduced by Beilinson together with his copy of the Worms Rabbi's letter, publicly confirmed the link between the German and Polish branches of the Luria family. One might have thought that Beilinson's revealing oo–ben solved at least the riddle of the 'Rabbiness Miriam' Spira, by proving that she was the wife of Aaron Luria and the mother of Johanan. But this was not the case.

A bare two years later, in 1859, Aaron III Luria's version of the pedigree, first published at Fuerth in 1768, reappeared in print at Lvov in Poland, in the third edition of the MaHarSHaL's work of *responsa*. It did not contain the vertical stroke turning 'ben' into oo–ben. Nor, to increase the confusion, did Joseph of Rosheim's *pour-mémoire* when it was finally published in 1894 by David Kaufmann, from a copy made by Adolph Neubauer, a bibliographer at Oxford, where he later became a reader and (together with A.E.Cowley) prepared the three-volume *Catalogue of Hebrew Manuscripts in the Bodleian Library*. This oldest and most authentic version of the 'short' pedigree left scholars who had been investigating the Luria pedigree since 1786 none the wiser in figuring out whether Samson (Shimshon) of Erfurt was or was not the 'son of the Rabbiness Miriam'.

With Beilinson's findings seemingly discredited, research into the Luria connection with RASHI continued intermittently into the 20th century. Conducted by scholars who were not looking for Marx's ancestry (while those who were overlooked the fact that his known forefather Katzenellenbogen of Padua was a member of the Luria family and never looked into its history), it gradually fizzled out in speculation and controversial theories. The 'Rabbiness Miriam', especially, remained a mystery, amid conjecture that there might have been two Miriams.

It was only in the late 1970s that Dr Paul Jacobi, subjecting the extant three versions of the 'short' pedigree and the exact devolution and authorship of its nine copies to critical scrutiny, rediscovered the double significance of Beilinson's copy: it was the only one which, besides the telling oo–ben, contained the MaHarSHaL's statement that Jehiel II Luria had possessed a duplicate of his brother Johanan's 'short' pedigree. In a book-length study of the Luria family, Jacobi finally established the correct places of 'Samson (Shimshon) of Erfurt' and the 'Rabbiness Miriam' in the sequence of generations.

But it was not before 1986 or so, after tracing more of RASHI's descendants and finishing two full studies of the enigmatic Miriam's ancestral Trèves and Spira families, that he completed the unravelling of the 'short' pedigree of the Lurias and appended to the volume on them the detailed genealogical charts linking the three families named, through her, to RASHI.

A former Vice-Mayor of Jerusalem and lawyer by profession, Dr Jacobi spent several decades assembling the biographical data of some 400 of Europe's leading Ashkenazi Jewish families – many of them traceable for 15 or more generations, and some through thousands of individuals – in order to puzzle out a striking phenomenon largely neglected by historians. This concerns the 300 years from 1350 to 1650, in the course of which 90 German cities – out of approximately 100 which had any Jewish population worth speaking of – expelled their Jews for long enough periods to rule out any identity between their previous and future Jewish residents. The most glaring example was Cologne, which expelled its Jews in 1424 and did not readmit them until after the annexation of the Rhineland by revolutionary France in 1794.

An overview of Dr Jacobi's immense genealogical material revealed the frequent recurrence during these centuries of a limited number of families – starting with some 80 before 1650 and gradually growing to several hundred – whose scions regularly occupied the chief rabbinical as well as lay leadership positions in almost all major communities of Europe's Ashkenazi world, irrespective of political boundaries.

Impressed by the 'intellectual and material powers of leadership and guidance' stored up by this élite through the centuries, by means (among others) of a 'consciously or instinctively well-pursued marriage policy,' Dr Jacobi applied to these families a process akin to 'Namierization'. That is, he subjected them to the same sort of microscopic scrutiny employed in the 1920s by the late Sir Lewis Namier when, in *The Structure of Politics at the Accession of George III*, he minutely examined the successive composition of Britain's Houses of Parliament (especially the Upper House), going into the family background, marital ties and joint interests, or otherwise, of their membership. But while Namier dealt with the politics of a governing élite, showing *inter alia* how it transformed Britain from a small kingdom into a world empire, Dr Jacobi's research into his '400 families' was merely designed to test the factors that helped an ethnic minority survive under the most adverse circumstances. The conclusion he reached was that their life-force was one of the elements – besides their religion and other obvious factors – which assured the physical survival and spiritual cohesion of Ashkenazi Jewry up to the time of the French Revolution.

At the beginning of 1988, when I first met Dr Jacobi, data condensed from portions of his vast collection were being fed into the computerized Genealogy Centre of the Diaspora House on the Tel Aviv University campus. I am greatly indebted to him for helping me to establish Marx's descent from RASHI and for verifying each of his early and hitherto unknown ancestors by tracing references to them in primary and/or secondary sources, besides providing other valuable data.

In Chapter 29 I have focused on the main figures of Marx's family tree. To fill in the complete line of genealogical succession, it should be noted that RASHI's daughter Jochebed and Meir ben Samuel of Rammerupt, besides producing the four Tosaphists mentioned, also had a daughter, **Hannele**. She married **Samuel ben Simcha** of Vitry-Le-Brulé (today Vitry-en-Perthois, on the Marne). They had a son who was the famous scholar **Isaac II ben Samuel of Dampierre-sur-Aube**, who was recognized by all Franco-German Jewry before he died about 1185 as its chief rabbinical authority. It was a sister of his who married **Jehiel ben Mattathias** (Trèves), a surname bracketed here because his family adopted it only in a later generation.

The founder of the Trèves family was Jehiel's grandfather Moshe – genealogically designated as **Moshe I ben X** –who was a contemporary of RASHI, though younger by one generation.

Little is known of Jehiel's father Mattathias, but Jehiel himself lived in Paris and died there in 1189. His son **Moshe II** was a senior teacher at the increasingly important Talmud academy in Paris, where he died in 1230. Moshe II's son **Joseph ben Moshe** became a rabbi in northern France as well as another famous Tosaphist as RASHI's Talmud commentary continued to generate elaboration upon elaboration for some 200 years. (On the influence of the Tosaphists, including those mentioned, their work and the whereabouts of their MSS, see E.E. Urbach's comprehensive *The Tosaphists: Their History, Writings and Methods* (Hebrew), Bialik Institute, Jerusalem 1955 and later editions.)

A son of Joseph ben Moshe, **Mattathias II ben Joseph**, continued as a rabbi in northern France; another son, **Jehiel II**, also named Sire Vives (Jehiel meaning 'May God Live'), migrated to the Holy Land and died in 1268 at St Jean d'Acre. A third son, **Abraham**, lived first at Troyes and later in Germany. He was the father of **Johanan I ben Abraham Trèves**, born in 1265 and the first of the line to adopt this surname. Trèves is most probably derived from Troyes, RASHI's town, although identified by some with the Italian Treviso, and by others with Trier, Marx's birthplace (called Treveri in Charlemagne's time, and hence Trèves in French). Rabbi Johanan I is known to have lived for a time in Germany, possibly at Trier, but he eventually settled in Provence.

The line continued with **Joseph V Trèves** 'the Great', born around 1305, who became rabbi of Marseilles. Also known as 'the Provencal', he brings us to **Mattathias V ben Joseph Trèves**, born about 1335 in Provence but raised in Barcelona – the first of the Trèves to become Chief Rabbi of France.

As mentioned in Chapter 29, he was succeeded as Chief Rabbi by his son **Johanan Trèves** in 1387. Johanan did not stay in this position long. Following a new expulsion of the Jews in 1394, he moved to Italy, where he died in 1429. He had two sisters who ended up in Germany. One married Raphael Ballin, an ancestor of the modern shipping magnate of the Hamburg-American Line Albert Ballin, who, after trying to prevent the First World War by a naval agreement with England, became one of Kaiser Wilhelm II's chief aconomic advisers.

The second sister married Rabbi **Samuel Spira of Speyer** and moved with him to Heilbronn, there to become, through her son **Shlomo**, the grandmother of the learned 'Rabbiness Miriam', who in her turn effected the alliance with Aaron Luria, the first of his family to bear that name.

In one of his extant papers, Johanan Luria, protesting the arbitrary imposition of the Jew-badge, wrote: 'And if he [the ruler] should command me to carry a stone of ten pounds' weight, I would have to do it. Verily this law is like other laws you impose on us without reason.' In the manuscript of *Meshivat Nefesh* ('Refreshment of the Soul'), four handwritten copies of which have survived – two at Oxford, and the others in Paris and Moscow – Johanan Luria mentioned that he first moved from Heilbronn to Niederheim, but then, being financially well-off, he 'bought a permit' to open a Talmudic academy 'in the Alsatian government city,' as he tersely described it, apparently referring to Colmar or Strasbourg. Some historians, however, believe that by 'government city' he was referring to Ensisheim in upper Alsace – where the Habsburgs had a residence – or Haganau, where the governor of Lower Alsace held office. (See Selma Stern, *Josel von Rosheim*, Stuttgart 1959, p. 23.)

The Polish Lurias: When young, **Moses Isserless** so impressed Lublin's Rabbi Shakhna as a pupil of genius that he gave him his teen-aged daughter in marriage. Some time after the couple moved to Cracow, tragedy struck. In short order Isserless lost his wife when she was 20, as well as his mother and his grandmother, in an epidemic. In 1557 King Sigmund II, over the protests of the clergy, allowed the family to build and dedicate to their memory the synagogue which still stands in Cracow today. Isserless later remarried. His favourite Greek philosopher was Aristotle, whom he studied along with esoteric Kabbalah and works on astronomy, such as Frohbach's *Theorica*, on which he wrote a commentary.

At the same time he revived and adapted the *Shulhan Arukh*, the code of laws and regulations governing the life of the Jews – originally written by a Sephardi rabbi, on the basis of the legal discussions of the Talmud – to bring it in line with the ordinances and practices prescribed by the Franco-German rabbis, so that it became the accepted rulebook for Ashkenazi as well as Sephardi Jews throughout the world.

Prince Radziwill and Saul Wahl-Katzenellenbogen, the titular 'King of Poland' for a day: Prince Radziwill of Poland, stopping in Italy on his return voyage from a pilgrimage to Palestine, is known to have pawned some Holy Land relics with a Venice merchant in 1584. He may have met Saul's father, **Samuel Judah** (1541-1617), who had succeeded the illustrious Katzenellenbogen of Padua as head of the rabbinical court of Venice. According to a family legend, Saul's father advanced the embarrassed prince a generous sum and asked him to look up his son at Brest-Litovsk. Whatever the truth, three years later Radziwill proposed to make **Saul Wahl-Katzenellenbogen** temporary 'King of Poland' during the constitutional deadlock following Stephan Bathory's death. (On the prince's stay in Venice see J.L. Shapiro, *Ancient Jewish Families* (Hebrew), 1991, quoting Warsaw University's Prof. M. Balaban, the late historian of Polish Jewry.)

That Saul's interregum lasted no longer than a day was recorded in 1733 by his grandson in a book manuscript (now at Oxford) and further discussed in detail in an historical study published in London in 1854. The MS at Oxford is *Yesh Manhilim* by Pinhas Katzenellenbogen. Z.H. Edelmann's historical study of Saul Wahl-Katzenellenbogen *Gedullat Sha'ul* (The Greatness of Saul), first published in London in 1854, was reprinted in 1925.

From Nessla Wahl-Katzenellenbogen to Karl Marx: Saul Wahl-Katzenellenbogen died in 1617. His son **Meir** succeeded him as head of the rabbinical court of Brisk (Brest-Litovsk). Since Meir's daughter **Nessla** was to marry a distant kinsman of Cracow, we most turn our sights in that direction. In 1618 **Tanhum Hacohen**, a son of the great scholar Joseph ben Mordecai Gershon Hacohen, died in Cracow. Tanhum's son, **Pessah Judah Hacohen**, moved to Lvov. Although his son **Moshe ben Pessah Judah** preferred to call himself **Kahana** and is quoted in literature by that name, he was a great-grandson of **Joseph ben Mordecai Gershon Hacohen**. Hacohen, Cohen, Kohn, Kahane are variants of the Hebrew name for 'priest,' a name generally used by descendants of the tribe of Aaron.

He married Nessla Wahl-Katzenellenbogen and after serving as rabbi in Slutzk, then Lutzk, he succeeded his wife's father Meir as head of the rabbinical court in Brisk. He and Nessla had a son by the name of **Aaron Jeheskel ben Moshe** who adopted the name of **Lvov**, after the Polish city of his birth. He was first ordinary rabbi in Trier and then from 1692 to 1712 head of the rabbinical court of Westhofen in Alsace. This Aaron Lvov was twice married. His first wife was the daughter of **Isaiah Chaim ben Zwi Spira**, a scion of the great Spira family descended from RASHI; the second wife was a daughter of Gabriel Eskeless of Cracow, who was a descendant of Rabbi Judah Loew, the Golem-maker of Prague.

Aaron Lvov and his first wife (Spira of RASHI decent) had a son **Joshua Heshel Lvov**. Born in Westhofen in 1692, he married Merle, a daughter of Isaac Aaron of Worms, whose family, starting with Israel ben Abraham of Worms, had held the rabbinate of Trier since about 1650.

Joshua Heshel Lvov served for ten years (1723-33) as rabbi of Trier before he was appointed Chief Rabbi of the Duchy of Brandenburg-Ansbach, with residence at Schwabbach. Holding this position for nearly 40 years, he became Germany's oldest rabbi, and being a renowned scholar too, his opinion carried enough weight to be cited in two famous 18th-century rabbinical disputes (the

'Cleves divorce' case and the Emden-Eybeshütz controversy, about which see *Encyclopaedia Judaica*).

Before he died in 1771 he prepared his collected *responsa* for publication under the title *The Face of the Moon*. It should come as no surprise that this manuscript, too – dealing, among other non-lunar matters, with communal taxation and other social and economic questions, and showing a familiarity with German and contemporary ideas of natural science and psychology – should be at Oxford. (The Hebrew title of his book of *responsa* was *Pnei Halevana*, in *Or Hayashar*, No. 32, published in Altona in 1765.)

One of Joshua Heshel's sons, **Moses Lvov**, became Rabbi of Trier in 1764. His daughter Hayya or Eva Lvov (c. 1754-1823) married Karl Marx's grandfather, **Mordecai Halevi Marx** (c. 1743-1804).

In 1788, upon the death of his father-in-law, Mordecai Halevi Marx became the next Rabbi of Trier. Before moving there he had been Rabbi of Sarrelouis, where the two eldest of his 8 children were born – Samuel, who was to succeed him in 1804 as Rabbi of Trier, and Joshua Heshel, who in 1814 began to call himself Heinrich and, after marrying the Dutch-born Henrietta Pressburg, became the father of Karl Marx.

Notes
Bibliography
Index

Notes

NOTES TO CHAPTER 1

(For full titles and other details, see Bibliography)

1. J.M. Thompson, *The French Revolution*, p. 63.
2. See Bernard, p. 171.
3. *Ibidem.*
4. Thompson, *op. cit.*, p. 495.
5. Gershoy, p. 161.
6. Thompson, *op. cit.*, p. 35.
7. Hampson, p. 78; and George Painter, *Chateaubriand*, London 1970, v. 1, p. 120.8. For various accounts of the conversation quoted see, among others, Howarth, Lucas-Dubreton, Beik, and Castillon du Perron.
9. Babeuf's wholesale denunciation of the Committee of Public Safety may have been based on the fact that, whatever his faith in the leaders of the Revolution, including Danton and Robespierre, he could not always suppress an eruption of his feeling that they were all acting to protect the rich, while the hungry and poor had gained nothing from the Revolution.
10. See Thompson, *op. cit.*, p. 361.
11. *The Confessions of Jean Jacques Rousseau*, New York 1945, p. 613.
12. Hampson, p. 37.
13. It is an interesting observation that Saint-Just at the same time foresaw that 'within twenty years the throne might be restored by the fluctuation and the illusions offered to the speculative general will', as was indeed to happen when Napoleon crowned himself Emperor; he, too, claimed to represent the 'general will'.
14. Thompson, *op. cit.*, p. 502.
15. Desanti, p. 27.
16. See R.B. Rose, p. 189.
17. *Ibid.*, p. 195.
18. Babeuf's private papers have long been in Moscow. Pending their possible publication in the wake of recent political changes, it may in fact be said that without Buonarroti there might, figuratively speaking, have been no Babeuf, in the sense that had Buonarroti not published – 34 years after the event – his account of *La Conspiration pour l'Egalité dite de Babeuf*, this last episode of the French Revolution might never have acquired the mythical force it was to exercise on revolutionary minds through most of the nineteenth century.
19. Talmon, *The Origin of Totalitarian Democracy*, p. 199.

NOTES TO CHAPTER 2

1. A bibliography published in 1968 listed 9,768 titles of primary and secondary literature devoted to Heine, whose works had by then been translated into fifty-three languages, under 1,624 titles. Two Heine research institutes in West and East Germany are currently engaged in producing multi-volume (and rival) editions of his poetry, prose and letters, besides pouring out several hundred Heine studies every year, not to mention books and articles by independent authors.
2. The 13 December 1797 birthdate made its appearance in the Düsseldorf Archives in 1809, after its birth and circumcision records had been destroyed. At the request of the authorities, the 75-year-old Rabbi of Düsseldorf, Judah L. Scheuer, reconstructed from memory a list of 30 children born during the preceding 11 years. In this list he placed Heine's birthdate between September 1797 and September 1798.
3. Sammons was of course quoting Leon Edel's famous phrase about Henry James. See Edel, *Literary Biography*, Bloomington, Indiana, 1973.
4. Hirth, I: 210.
5. In 1737 a forced loan of 660,000 guilders was imposed on Vienna's ten richest Jews. Samuel's share was 20,000 guilders, while his brother-in-law Isaac Arnsteiner paid 60,000 guilders. The wealthiest and most famous 'Court Jews' at the time were Samuel Oppenheimer, Samson Wertheimer and Baron Diego Aguilar. In 1742 there were 452 Jews living in Vienna.
6. The note-book Heine discovered as a boy contained only the Chevalier's first diary or travel journal, taking his life-story only as far as 1756. This was published in substance in 1896 by David Kaufmann, an Austro-Hungarian scholar and literary historian. The Chevalier had, however, left behind another diary. On his death this and other papers found their way into the hands of a well-known Cologne collector, Baron von Hupsch. The Baron, some time before he died in 1805, made them over to the Landgrave Ludwig X – who in 1806 (as Ludwig I) became Grand Duke of Hesse-Darmstadt. They were discovered a full century later, in 1905, stored away with the Grand Duke's Baron Hupsch Collection, of which the Darmstadt National and University Library (*Landes und Hochschulbibliothek*) had become the repository. The Darmstadt court librarian, Dr Adolph Schmidt, after cataloguing them, published these 'new finds' in 1912 and called the attention of the 'scientific world' to their importance (once they were properly investigated), to the 'general and cultural history' of the 18th century.

   It was only in 1927 that Dr Schmidt published a fascimile edition of the famous Darmstadt Haggadah, a rare 15th-century manuscript found in the Baron Hupsch collection, but owned by the Chevalier. As far as the life and character of the man himself were concerned, it was not before the 1930s that the Düsseldorf-born journalist and historical writer Fritz Heymann, in a long chapter devoted to 'Der Chevalier von Geldern' in an eponymously titled book, published a series of revelations, from which Heine's mysterious ancestor emerged in an entirely new light as an uncommonly colourful, even forceful, if contradictory, figure – a scholar, mystic and adventurer who had ended up in the curious official position of 'Confidential Magic Councillor and Court Factor' to the Crown Prince of Hesse-Darmstadt. In addition to the Darmstadt papers, Heymann had obtained access to a 'remote private library' and had there discovered a large set of documents and letters proving the Chevalier's involvement with members of the reigning family of Hesse-Darmstadt and a whole group of other rulers of 18th-century Germany's petty states, all of whom had belonged to a secret Order of Knights that believed in alchemy, magic and the occult.

Heymann's book appeared in 1937. Its author having by then had to flee Hitler's Germany to Holland, it was published by the émigré Querido Verlag in Amsterdam. Heymann quoted many letters and documents, but gave no references. He was killed in 1942 at Auschwitz, and the trouble with his fascinating account, from a scholarly viewpoint if no other, was that his unreferenced private sources could not be ascertained.

Finally, after another long hiatus caused by World War II, Dr Rosenthal of Guatemala in 1973, and again in 1975, in a book on Heine and several articles published under the aegis of Düsseldorf's Heinrich-Heine-Institut, solved most of the mystery surrounding the person of the Chevalier. Rosenthal, after making a thorough investigation of the Darmstadt material, established, first, that Heymann's laborious and not unscientific research had to be taken 'quite seriously' and that but for its racy style, occasional poetic licence and some other reservations, his portrait of the Chevalier came 'quite close to the truth' in spite of his pardonable (perhaps forced) unwillingness, given the circumstances at the time he was writing, to reveal his sources.

Secondly, in 1975 Rosenthal published an essay on the Chevalier's relations with 'reigning courts, high state officials and other persons of rank.' This, together with details from the Chevalier's address book, and more items drawn from the Chevalier's correspondence, his sundry passports and laissez-passers, customs receipts, book lists and other papers, has made it possible to put together practically a full picture of his life and activities.

7. It has been calculated that a Jew travelling a distance of 110 miles from Silesia to the Leipzig Fair had to make fourteen different payments at eight stops.

8. Forbidden to settle in Strasbourg or Colmar and to practise any handicraft, the 3,913 Jewish families in Alsace lived in and about the villages and could only engage in cattle-dealing and money-lending on a petty scale, while their scattered communities were themselves heavily in debt because of the manifold individual or collective taxes they had to pay the poll-tax, the royal *vingtième* and *droit de protection* taxes, besides trade-taxes, residence-taxes to the local noblemen, marriage-taxes, and what the historian Heinrich Graetz had called 'contributions to churches and hospitals, war-taxes, and exactions of every sort under other names.' The 480 families permitted to live in Metz, besides carrying a disproportionate one-sixth of the town's total royal taxes, also paid the special Brancas tax – named for the duke of that name to whom Louis XIV had given it as a gift at the beginning of the century – to the amount of a total two million livres before the Revolution was to abolish it as illegal.

NOTES TO CHAPTER 3

1. Because of the absence of records and the manipulations connected with the 'birth date riddle', most birth dates in the Heine family are uncertain. The standard chronology for Heine's life and publications is CHRONIK, according to which Gustav was born in 1805 and Maximilian in 1807, but these dates have been questioned.

2. Heine was later to discuss Agrippa von Nettesheim's theories on black magic and the works of Paracelsus in *Die Romantische Schule* and in a commentary to his *Der Doktor Faust, Ein Tanzpoem*.

3. On Count Stolberg, Hegel, Klopstock, Moser and German reactions to French Revolution see Heer, Hertz, and Harris.

4. Wollner's 1788 Edict, stressing the dominance of 'the Christian religion in its three chief divisions, under which Prussia's monarchy had till now prospered so well,' contrasted so strongly with King Friedrich Wilhelm II's own conduct that even at the time it caused a flood of gibes 'concerning the king, his mistresses and favourites.' HHW, 15: 258.

5. Significantly, Prussia's elder statesman, Evald von Hertzberg, strongly opposed war with France, but was overriden by Friedrich Wilhelm and his new advisers, and dismissed. Bischoffswerder, the King's military expert, admonished Prussian officers not to purchase 'too many horses, the affair will soon be over.' The first threats against France were, as known, uttered by Austria's Leopold II, but he died in February 1792, before the War of the First Coalition actually began. Austria's Chan-

cellor, Kaunitz, opposed it throughout, proposing to let France in her state of revolutionary anarchy wear herself out, and 'like a volcano, bring destruction upon herself.' But his advice was disregarded.

6. The undated visit is described in a contemporary report by one of the Repetenten (i.e., instructors) present, exhibited in Stuttgart in 1970 (on the occasion of the bicentenary of Hegel's birth) and reproduced in Hegel LWW. An extensive account of the Duke's May 1793 visit is to be found in Harris.

7. The two different versions are, respectively, from Raymond Plant, *Hegel*, London 1973 (quoting X. Leon, *Fichte et son temps*, Paris 1922) and Harris. The story of the 'Liberty Tree' appears in most literature on Hegel.

8. According to the records of the Tübingen Stift – quoted in Hegel LWW – Hegel actually left the Seminary on 10 July for Stuttgart, having been permitted to spend the summer at home studying for his theological examination. What is certain in all this is that the Ephor, Christian F. Schnurrer, who in his time had met Rousseau in person, mentioned the (or a) 'Liberty Tree' in a letter to Duke Charles Eugene. According to G. Harris, the Duke was said to maintain a spy or 'gossip' providing him with inside information from the Stift, and in the petty atmosphere of the Duchy Schnurrer constantly had to rebut the most preposterous rumours about his institution circulated by illiberal wags. To underline their absurdity, he wrote the Duke a letter suggesting ironically that next thing they were going to say 'students in the Stift had set up the Liberty Tree before my very eyes.'

9. Having passed his final examination in September 1793 before the Consistory at Stuttgart, and received the Duke's permission to go to Switzerland as a Hofmeister, or private tutor, in the patrician household of a Hauptmann von Steiger – 'on condition that he exercise himself diligently in preaching wherein he is still very weak' – Hegel had moved to Berne in October 1793, and was to spend the next three years there.

10. In the poem 'Jehuda ben Halevy', in Book III of his *Romancero* (in German 'Romanzero'). Judah, or Jehuda or Yehuda Halevi (c. 1075-c. 1140), who practised medicine both at Toledo, under King Alfonso VI of Castile, and in Muslim Cordoba, left a large body of religious, national and secular works. He is most famous for his passionate 'Songs of Zion' and his unusual sea poem. See *Encyclopaedia Judaica* and *The Penguin Book of Hebrew Verse*, London 1981, pp. 106-07 and 333-52.

11. As Prawer has observed, 'we cannot but recall how important the polemic arts were to Heine's own time, what a vital role polemic poetry, the poetry of persuasion, rebuttal, and witty ridicule, played in the art of the Zeitgedicht, the poem treating burning questions of the day, of which Heine had made himself such a master.' See Prawer, *Heine's Jewish Comedy*, pp. 561-78 for the richness of themes concerning poetry, politics, historic fact and legend voven by Heine into this poem; and, of course, the poem itself, in Heine's original *Romanzero*, or, in English, in Draper, pp. 655-77.

12. Opinions quoted in this paragraph: 'Probably not much', Sammons, *op. cit.*, p. 37; 'Jewishness remained a significant factor,' Prawer, *op. cit.*, p. 9; 'Jewish tradition is the key,' Margarita Pazi, in 'Die biblischen und jüdischen Einflüsse in Heines "Nordsee-Gedichten"', *Heine Jahrbuch*, 12 (1973).

13. Cf. Pazi, *ibid.*

14. In his book on Heine as a Jew, Ludwig Rosenthal, distinguishing between Heine's attitude to religion and the influence of his Jewish heritage, has systematically analyzed the sources and relative significance of his Jewish utterances at various periods of his life. He also lists most of the literature on this controversial subject up to 1973.

15. Cf. H. Kohn, 'Goethe and His Time', p. 305.

16. Hampson.

17. Sammons, *Heine*, p. 34, citing Giorgio Tonelli, *Heinrich Heines politische Philosophie (1830-1845)*, Hildesheim and New York 1975.

18. Kohn, *op. cit.*, p. 307. The English translation of Manzoni's stanza is by Edward, Earl of Derby.

19. *Ibid.*, p. 304.

20. See Wadepuhl, pp .20-21. His opinion is shared by many other authors.

21. Reeves, *Heinrich Heine, Poetry and Politics*, pp.32-33. Reeves also has full details of Goethe's 1820 essay and the Kantian quotation which inspired Heine's train of thought.

NOTES TO CHAPTER 4

1. Talleyrand later wrote that 'on someone's advice – I do not know whose – he preferred to stay at my house.' See Bernard, p. 324; Strakhovsky, p. 150; HHW, 17: 489.

2. Strakhovsky, p. 154; Bernard, p. 334.

3. See Strakhovsky, pp. 130-39, and others. Strakhovsky writes that the imperial library did not have a single copy of the Holy Book and that 'Alexander found instead the complete works of Voltaire, Rousseau, Diderot, Montesquieu, Mably, La Fontaine, even the libertine verses of Parny.'

4. L.A.F. de Bourienne, *Mémoire de M. de Bourienne sur Napoléon*, Paris 1830, v. II, p. 243.

5. Markham, p. 64.

6. The Proclamation is quoted from Kobler, who discovered its presumed German text. See also Schwarzfuchs, and Tuchman, *Bible and Sword*. The first to draw attention to the Proclamation in modern times was Philip Guedalla in *Napoleon and Palestine* (reprint of a lecture), London 1925.

7. HHW, 17: 489.
8. Conway, p. 12.
9. The entry in the *Régistre d'inscription des élèves* of the Coblenz Law School for the years 1810-1813 was discovered by Albert Rauch. See his essay in the series of *Schriften* issued by the Karl-Marx-Haus in Trier, No. 14, 1975, p. 3. Dean Lassaulx's list of students was found in the Archives Nationales by Dr Hansgeorg Molitor of Tübingen, *ibid.*, p. 27.
10. Padover, p. 30.
11. Eleanor Marx in *Neue Zeit*, v. I, 1897-98. The two other pictures found on Marx's body and buried with him were those of his wife and his eldest daughter Jenny. Other photographs, however, exist of both of them.
12. 'A born placator,' Catlin, p. 561; 'A touching family sense,' Künzli, p. 75; the other quotations in this paragraph, Berlin, *Karl Marx*.
13. Padover, p. 7.
14. Berlin, *op. cit.*, p. 30.
15. Wolfson, p. 17.
16. *Ibid.*, pp. 12-13.
17. Mazlish, p. 42.
18. McLellan, p. 13.
19. Künzli, p.33. As indicated by its title, *Eine Psychographie*, this massive and thoroughly researched study, analyzing all the elements that went into the making of Marx's persona and the way they came to be reflected in his writings, is the work of a psychiatrist.
20. Wolfson, pp. 12 and 15; Mazlish, pp.43 and 76.
21. Wolfson, p. xiii; Mazlish, pp. 7, 52, 121.
22. More variants and distortions of the names of every member of the family will be found in Albert Rauch's essay in Schriften, No. 14.
23. See Monz, *Karl Marx*, p. 57.
24. 'Only a dozen or so': Zenz, *Trier im 18. Jahrhundert*, p. 101. Writing in 1979, Padover put the number of Jewish families in Trier at 30 to 40.
25. Monz, *op. cit.*, p. 24.
26. Hobsbawn, *The Age of Revolution*, v. I, p. 64.
27. *Ibid.*, v. I, p. 108.
28. Nicolaievsky, p. 2.
29. Letter from Eleanor to Wilhelm Liebknecht, in REM, p. 130.
30. While the warring French took some time to establish a secular, French-type primary and secondary school system, the cloister schools too fell into disarray. As late as 1797, according to a contemporary report, Catholic 'burghers did not know what to do with their children' – and by that time, anyway, Heschel was twenty. Zenz, *op. cit.*, p. 106.
31. Edgar von Westphalen, who knew Marx's father, quoted by B. Nicolaievsky and O. Maenchen-Helfen, in *La Vie de Karl Marx*, Paris 1970, p. 19.
32. See *Henriette Herz, Ihr Leben und ihre Erinnerungen*, Leipzig 1977 (first published 1858).
33. Henriette Herz was an accomplished linguist who spoke (and later taught) more than half a dozen languages, including Greek, Latin, Spanish and Swedish, besides French, English, Italian and German.
34. Golo Mann, *Secretary of Europe*.
35. Margarete Susman, *Frauen der Romantik*, Cologne 1960.
36. Schiller, 'the wrong address:' Heer; 'the things of the spirit' etc.: Margarete Susman, *op. cit.*
37. In a talk with a visiting Heidelberg high-school inspector, whose journal was to be published only in 1976, Kant said that 'so long as the Jews remain Jews and let themselves be circumcised they will ever be more injurious than useful to civic society. As of now they are the vampires of society.'
38. Fichte's article, on the subject of 'Public Opinion and the French Revolution', was published in 1793. See J.G. Fichte, *Schriften zur Revolution*, Frankfurt 1973, p. 86.
39. J.G. Fichte, *Reden an die Deutsche Nation*, Berlin 1846, v. VII, pp. 362ff.
40. Anchel, p. 42.
41. For 'interior policing' and the substance of various petitions see Schwarzfuchs, p. 40 *passim.*, and François Delpech, 'La Révolution et l'Empire' in *Histoire des Juifs en France*, ed. B. Blumenkranz, Toulouse 1972, p. 288. For 'government intervention', see Anchel, p. 238.
42. The Metz community, in debt to the amount of 500,000 livres, was reduced by the emancipation to the absurd straits of asking for a law forbidding anyone to leave the Jewish quarter before he had paid his part of the communal debt.
43. F. Delpech, *op. cit.*, p. 289; and see Schwarzfuchs for a more detailed discussion of the debts and usury problems.
44. Baron de Barante, quoted by Kobler, p. 137.
45. For quotations in this paragraph and for more details of the discussions in the Conseil d'Etat see Kobler, Schwarzfuchs and Delpech. The last two have full bibliographies as well as archival sources.
46. The rabbis acknowledged, however, that 'a Jew who marries a Christian woman does not cease on that account to be considered as a Jew by his brethren, any more than if he had married a Jewess civilly and not religiously.' For the fuller answers see Mendès-Flohr, pp. 116-21.
47. *Ibid.*, p. 102.
48. See Schwarzfuchs, p. 56, and his notes.
49. Diogène Tama, *Procès-Verbaux et decisions du Grand Sanhédrin*, Paris 1807. In translation, F.D. Kirwan, *Transactions of the Paris Sanhedrin*, London 1807; A. Bran, *Gesammelte Aktenstücke und öffentliche Verhandlungen über die Verbesserung der Juden in Frankreich*, Hamburg 1806-07.
50. Kobler, pp. 162-66.
51. See Napoleon, *Correspondance*, v. 13, Paris 1863, pp. 717-19.
52. Kobler, p. 173.
53. Kircher, p. 26, quoting Franz Kobler, *Jüdische*

Geschichte in Briefen aus Ost und West, Vienna 1938.

54. Schwarzfuchs, p. 128.

55. See 'Die Taufe einer Juden-Familie am Vorabend des heiligen Pfingstfestes 1831', etc., on pp. 33-35 of Schriften, No. 14, Trier 1975.

56. Monz, *op. cit.*, p. 271, quoting municipal archives.

57. See Monz, *op. cit.*, pp. 110-15 and his notes.

58. It is not known when and where the two had first met, but their acquaintance, and the match may have been arranged by Heinrich Marx's mother, who now lived in Amsterdam.

59. Monz, *op. cit.*, p. 115.

60. See L. Kochan, 'European Jewry in the 19th and 20th Centuries,' in Kedourie, p. 265.

61. See Rosenthal, p. 102; Kircher, p. 29.

62. Quoted in Brandes, v. III, p. 341.

63. *Ibid.*, v. III, p. 342.

64. Cf. Liptzin, pp. 38, 44.

65. The two parts of the *Eingabe* are preserved in Düsseldorf's Staatsarchiv together with other papers of the 1815-17 Royal Prussian Commission studying 'the civic circumstances of the Jews in the Rhine provinces.' They were published by Adolf Kober in the 1932 Yearbook of Cologne's Historical Society. All quotations from Heinrich Marx's letter and his memorandum are from Kober's essay and appendices in *Jahrbuch des Kölnischen Geschichtsvereins*, v. 14, pp. 111-25

66. Sethe's report and Kircheisen's decision are quoted by Kobler from 'Acta der Immediat-Kommission zu Köln'. Schuckmann's opinion in Monz, *op. cit.*, p. 247.

67. Cf. Monz, *op. cit.*, p. 32: 'Durch die Bestrebungen staatlicherseits, die Juden dem Christentum zuzuführen, wurden die Verhältnisse der Juden auch noch dem Boden des formellen Rechts entrückt und damit der Willkur übergeben.'

68. Künzli, p. 36.

69. Monz, *op. cit.*, p. 32.

70. Monz, *ibid.*, p. 251, and see his remarks.

71. *Ibid.*, p. 248, and more fully in his earlier essay in *Archiv für Sozialgeschichte*, v. VIII, 1968.

NOTES TO CHAPTER 5

1. Strakhovsky, pp. 174, 172.

2. HWW, 17: 496.

3. 'A sort of new code of international law,' Prince Czartoryski's Memoirs, quoted by Sumner, p. 368; 'has been exaggerated,' Seton-Watson, p. 165; 'considerable,' Breunig, p. 134.

4. HWW, 17: 505.

5. See Seton-Watson, pp. 157-59 for details of the Russian constitution he eventually ordered to be drafted, but gave up partly because of his reluctance to fight the 'prejudices against constitutions held by his advisers who strongly attributed to them the evils of the age.'

6. Wadepuhl, p. 28 and Brod, p. 52, respectively.

7. Robertson, p. 8.

8. Letter to Friederike Robert, 12 October 1825, Hirth, I: 233.

9. Heine to Müllner, letter of 30 December 1821, Hirth, I: 35.

10. Klaus H.S. Schulte, '*Das letzte Jahrzehnt von Heinrich Heines Vater in Düsseldorf. Notariatsurkunden uber Samson Heines Geschäfte (1808–1821)*,' HJ 1974, pp. 105-31.

11. *Ibid.*, p. 11.

12. See Monz, *Karl Marx*, pp. 292-94.

13. Padover, p. 26.

14. 'Acta die Regulierung des jüdischen Schuldenwesens betr[effend]', extensively treated by Richard Laufner in Schriften, No. 14, Trier 1975.

15. Eleonore Sterling in *Monumenta Judaica – 2000 Jahre Geschichte und Kultur der Juden am Rhein*, Cologne 1963, p. 294.

16. Cf. Laufner, *op. cit.*, pp. 12 and 17.

17. Heer.

NOTES TO CHAPTER 6

1. Werner, I: 36, 40.

2. See Eberhard Galley, 'Heine und die Burschenschaften,' HJ 1972, p. 70.

3. Werner, I: 44-48.

4. Galley, *op. cit.*, p. 71; and Pierre Grappin, 'Heine's lyrische Anfänge', in Internationaler Heine-Kongress, Düsseldorf 1972, *Referate und Diskusionen* (ed. Manfred Windfuhr), Hamburg, p. 68.

5. Grappin, *ibidem*.

6. Werner, II: 520.

7. Elster, VII: 564.

8. For Karl Daub, see Hegel LWW, p. 188.

9. Elster, VII: 180.

10. Robertson, p. 6.

11. Hegel LWW, pp. 192 and 193.

12. Sammons, p. 81.

13. Letter to Moser, 1 July 1825, and passage in Elster, VII: 255.

14. Lukàcz, pp. 113-18. (Lukàcz's essay was originally written in 1935.)

15. Elster, V: 69.

16. Elster IV: 72.

17. Letter of 24 December 1822 to Karl Immermann.

18. Reeves, *op. cit.*, p. 94, n. 66.

19. Grabbe's remarks about Heine in Werner, I: 74-75; Heine on Grabbe and his mother in Elster VII: 468-69.

20. Letter to Karl Immermann, 4 January 1823.

21. 'Heine und die Burschenschaft', in HJ 1972, p. 73, and see his sources on p. 92.

22. 'Donna Clara' was written in 1823. See its English translation in Draper, p. 115, and his note on p. 855.

23. Christian Ruhs, *Über die Ansprüche der Juden an das deutsche Bürgerrecht* (The Jewish Claim to Citizen Rights in Germany), Berlin 1816. In this and other writings Ruhs claimed that the sufferings of the Fatherland during the

Napoleonic wars had convinced him that 'to develop its national character' Germany must exclude and eliminate all foreign elements. It would have been better if the Jews 'had never settled among us, or that we had more rigorously prevented their immigration and propagation.' As it was, he regarded the measures he proposed as the absolut essential minimum remedy.

24. See Rosenthal, p. 28.
25. On 'God, immortality etc.' see Reissner, p. 70. Reissner quotes his text on 'the totality of Europe' from a 'semi-annual report' Gans delivered verbally to the Society on 28 April 1822. Eduard Krüger, quoting much the same text, refers to three lectures delivered by Gans in the autumn of 1822.
26. Letters to 1) Christian Sethe and 2) Maurice Embden (the fiancé and future husband of his sister Charlotte) on 2 April.
27. Letter to Rudolf Christiani, 7 March 1824.
28. Letter to Wohlwill, 1–7 April 1823.
29. Letters to Embden of 3 May 1823 and of 23 August to Moser.
30. Letters of 7 April, 10 April and 4 May to Wohlwill, Immermann and Julius Schottky, respectively.
31. Letter to Wohlwill, 1–7 April 1823.
32. See Hirth, IV: 66.
33. This statement led more than one scholar, including Jeffrey Sammons, to doubt that Heine had very strong feelings about taking this step, but Sammons himself revised his opinion and in 1979 wrote that he had been 'in error'. Sammons, p. 107.
34. Letter to Moser, 2 February 1824.
35. Letter to Moser, 25 February 1824.
36. Cf. Arendt, *Rachel Varnhagen*, p. 172 and *passim*.

NOTES TO CHAPTER 7
1. Ulam, p. 6.
2. Squire, p. 113.
3. See Venturi, p. 3 and his Russian source on p. 721, n. 6. (4. Squire, *op. cit.*, p. 44 and note 4.
5. Ulam, p. 44 and see his n. 49.
6. *Ibid.*, p. 62.
7. *Ibid.*, p. 55.
8. For Pestel's ideas, and quotations in this and the next paragraph see Venturi, p. 5, and his notes 10 and 11 on p. 722.
9. On Carbonari and possible other influences on Pestel's 'Russian Law' see Venturi, pp. 5 and 722 (n. 12); also Seton-Watson.
10. Ulam, p. 35 and *Encyclopaedia Hebraica*, XII: 988, respectively.
11. See *Encyclopaedia Judaica*, V: 1451 and VI: 713.
12. Dubnow, v. I, pp. 409–13.
13. *Encyclopaedia Judaica*, XIII: 664.
14. See R.B. Rose, p. 342; and Ulam, p. 4.
15. Grey, p. 265.

16. *Ibid.*, p. 266.
17. Squire, p. 116.
18. Grey, p. 268.
19. Squire, pp. 44 and 50–51.
20. *Ibid.*, p. 51, n. 1.
21. *Ibid.*, p. 115.
22. *Ibid.*, pp. 122–23.
23. *Ibid.*, p. 114.
24. Hare, p. 5.
25. Venturi, p. 64.
26. *Ibid.* p. 66.
27. Grey, p. 267.
28. Pestel 'a precursor of Bolshevism': Ulam, p. 4; 'the first act', Pares, p. 332.
29. See, for instance, Confino.

NOTES TO CHAPTER 8
1. Ulam, p. 5.
2. Mendel, p. 8.
3. Bernard, p. 354.
4. Hare, p. 20.
5. Bakunin's full correspondence will be found in Y.M. Steklov (ed.), M.A. Bakunin, *Sobranie sochinenii i pisem, 1828–1876*, Moscow 1934–36 and in A.A. Kornilov, *Molodye gody*, Moscow 1915, which also contains letters from his family and friends. Unless otherwise stated, excerpts from letters in this and subsequent chapters are quoted in the translation offered by Arthur Mendel and/or E.H. Carr in their biographies.
6. Carr, *Michael Bakunin*, p. 7.
7. Letter to his father, 15 December 1837. Steklov, II; 105–06.
8. Kornilov, pp. 36–38.
9. See Kraemer-Badoni, p. 112.
10. Letter to his father, 15 December 1837. (See note 7.)
11. The short account of Herzen's childhood and youth that follows is drawn from MyPaT-(G–H) and MyPaT/DM – both under Abbreviations. For the sake of brevity some conversations have been reproduced in condensed form. Certain sections were published for the first time by M.K.Lemke in his 22-volume *Polnoye sobranie sochinenii i pisem* (Collected Works and Letters), Petrograd 1915–25. This will henceforth be referred to simply as 'Lemke'.
12. On Herzen's father tracing his origins to a boyar of Ivan III see Malia, pp. 9 and 431, n. 2.
13. *Ibid.*, p. 14.
14. Carr, in *The Romantic Exiles*, p. 13: 'He never married her.' Isaiah Berlin, in his Introduction to *My Past and Thoughts*, p. XVII, n. 2: 'There is evidence, although it is not conclusive, that she was married to him according to the Lutheran rite, not recognised by the Orthodox Church.'
15. Malia, p. 14, quoting 'Lemke' and another source.
16. MyPaT(DM): 6–9.

17. *Ibid.*, I: 19.
18. Wilson, p. 266.
19. Cf. Max Nettlau's 'Biographical Sketch of Bakunin', in Maximoff, p. 30.
20. 'Revere their Tsar' and forego 'the chance of seeing any capital in the world:' Letters to his parents (20 September 1831) and to his sisters (Spring 1831). Steklov, I: 52 and 46-47.
21. Letter to his parents, 19 December 1834. *Ibid.*: 155.
22. Letter to his parents, 15 December 1837. Quoted by Carr, *Michael Bakunin*, p. 10.
23. Letter to his parents, May 1833. *Ibid.*
24. Carr, *The Romantic Exiles*, p. 178.
25. *Op cit.*, p. 266.
26. Carr, *Michael Bakunin*, pp. 35-36, and Masters.
27. 'You told me last summer': letter to his relatives (4 November 1842), Steklov, III: 152, quoted by Mendel, p. 178; 'The laws condemn the object of my love': Carr, *Bakunin*, p. 37, quoting Steklov and Kornilov.
28. Tuchmann, *The Proud Tower*, p. 76.
29. See the chapter 'Criticism of Marxism' in Maximoff, pp. 283-88, 363.
30. Excerpts from his letters of 2 March 1830, Spring 1831 and September 1833, Steklov, I: 41, 51, 114.
31. Venturi, p. 36.
32. Kraemer-Badoni, p. 113.
33. Heer, p. 318.
34. Mendel, p. 3.
35. Hare, p. 21.
36. Mendel, p. 3.
37. Carr, *Bakunin*, p. 12.
38. Carr, *The Romantic Exiles*, pp. 180, 181.
39. Letter to his parents, 15 December 1837, Steklov, II: 114-15, 120.
40. Mendel, p. 30.
41. 'Max Nettlau's Biographical Sketch of Bakunin', in Maximoff, p. 30.
42. Carr, *Bakunin*, p. 15.
43. Letters to his brother Paul, 29 March 1845; to his sister Tatyana, 29 June 1845; and to his relatives, 1 May 1845; Steklov, III: 245, 247; pp. 255-56; p. 252.
44. See Wilson, p. 267.
45. Mendel, p. 24, quoting from a letter to his parents, 19 December 1834.
46. *Ibid.*, pp. 24-25 and 30.
47. Letter to his sister Varvara, 24 February 1836, Steklov, I: 207.
48. Carr, *Michael Bakunin*, p. 16, quoting Steklov, *Sobranie.*
49. Letter to his father, 15 September 1837 (Mendel, p. 19).
50. Letters to his parents (28 June 1834) and to the Beyer sisters (11 July 1834). Steklov, I: 134, 138.
51. Letter to his parents, 4 October 1834, Steklov, I: 140.
52. Mendel, p. 446, n. 46, quoting Z. Ralli in *Minuvshie gody*, 1980.

NOTES TO CHAPTER 9

1. Werner, I: 136. Campe's story was first published on Heine's death in 1856 by an anonymous Hamburg correspondent who, in Werner's opinion, probably stylized it.
2. In his essay *Ludwig Markus. A Memorial* (1844), Heine stressed the moral character of 'Little Markus' – a former member of the *Verein* – as against 'the great Gans' and his 'unforgivable felony'. Elster, II: 119.
3. Sammons, p. 98.
4. Letter to Immermann, 14 October 1826.
5. Heine's view of Napoleon in epic Homeric terms was influenced by Count Ségur's *Histoire de Napoléon et de la Grande Armée en 1812*, a book which impressed his as 'an ocean, an Odyssey and Iliad'; his outburst at the British, by Sir Frederick Louis Maitland's account of Napoleon's transportation to St Helena aboard his warship. Heine further read the accounts published between 1822 and 1824 by the Marquis de las Casas (*Mémorial de Ste. Hélène*), dictated by the Emperor; Barry O'Meara's *Napoleon in Exile, a Voice from St Helena*; and Francesco Antommarchi's *Les derniers moments de Napoléon*.
6. Letter to Merckel, 16 November 1826.
7. Sammons, p. 121.
8. Letters of 14 October and 16 November to Immermann and Merckel respectively.
9. Sammons, Vallentin and Wadepuhl respectively.
10. Letter to Christiani, 6 December 1825.
11. Letter to Moser, 9 June 1827.
12. Letter to Friederike Robert, 12 October 1825.
13. Letter of 15 September 1828.
14. Letter of 21 June 1853.
15. Sammons, p. 26. The reference is to Cécile Ney, born in 1867 at Roquencourt, who married the fifth Prince Joachim Napoleon Murat.
16. The biographer mentioned: Wadepuhl, p. 99. For the rest see HSA, 21: 162 and 25: 175 and 234.
17. By Hoffmann and Campe, in *The Book of Songs*.
18. M. Heine, p. 59, and see HSA, 20: 441.
19. Wadepuhl, p. 100.
20. Letter to Moser, 14 April 1828.
21. Letter to Moser in Berlin, 14 April 1828.
22. See Sammons, p. 137, on the 'taboo' on this aspect in Heine discussions in Germany during the 1970s.
23. See Brod, pp. 250-51.
24. Letter to Moser, 6 September 1828.
25. Letter to Johann Herman Detmold, 15 February 1828.
26. Hirth, IV: 182.
27. Quotations from Heine's letters in HSA, 20: 341-59.
28. Werner, I: 176.
29. For details of Gentz's letters to the Varnhagens expressing his admiration for Heine, see HSA, 24K: 62.
30. Sammons, p. 151.

NOTES TO CHAPTER 10

1. Kelly, p. 38.
2. A short description of the ball, and some of the remarks quoted, will be found in Vier, v. I.
3. For Salvandy's remark see *Ibid.*, v, I, p. 123; Pinkney, p. 278; and Howarth, p. 140.
4. For the old and new Paris salons see, besides the memoirs of various hostesses, those of the Austrian diplomat Apponyi. They are more briefly evoked by Vier in his biography of the comtesse d'Agoult and by Lucas-Dubreton. A detailed classification of the salons according to their political allegiance will be found in Kaltenthaler).
5. Wilson, p. 80.
6. Kohn, *Making of the Modern French Mind.*
7. Alem, pp. 45, 58 and *passim.*.
8. Fourier in *L'Inventeur et son siècle*, quoted by Nicholas V. Riasanovsky, p. 113.
9. See Riasanovsky, pp. 32, 39-40 and *passim.*. Fourier is also extensively treated in Manuel.
10. For God's place in Fourier's theories, and his own ambiguity towards Christianity, see Riasanovsky, pp. 100-05 and Desanti, p. 206.
11. On Fourier's attitude to the Jews and on his offer to the Rothschilds, see Poliakov.
12. See, for instance, Ridley.
13. Bernstein.
14. Sternberger, p. 321, n. 5.
15. Brod, pp. 238-39.
16. HSA, 24: 59 and 24 K: 57.
17. Letter to Varnhagen, 21 June 1830.
18. See Werner I: 209 and I: 206 respectively.
19. See his letter to Theodor von Kobbe, HSA, 20: 419.
20. Fejtö, *Heine,* p. 143.
21. 'A literary power in Germany': the writer and literary editor Adalbert von Chamisso in a letter dated 16 September 1830. 'The poet of our age' etc.: J.J. Sachs reporting on a convention of natural scientists in Hamburg whose final session Heine attended in September 1830, see Werner, I: 207-08 and note in II: 544.
22. Butler, p. 95.
23. Sternberger, p. 331.

NOTES TO CHAPTER 11

1. On notices in *Messager* and *Le Globe* see Werner, II: 546 and HSA, 20K: 280 respectively.
2. Chasles later recorded the scene in the *Revue de Paris.* See Werner I: 228-29.
3. Letter to Ferdinand Hiller, 24 October 1832.
4. Letter to Varnhagen, 20 June 1831.
5. On Börne's annoyance see Elster VII: 104; Kolb's letter in Werner, I: 241.
6. Werner, I: 233.
7. Quoted by Booss, p. 75.
8. *Ibid.*, p. 111.
9. Letter to Cotta, 20 January 1832.
10. See Hirth, V: 17 and 25-28; and Booss, pp. 77, 104, 106.
11. Quoted by Alem, p. 70.

12. *Ibid.*, pp. 80-81.
13. Letter to Cotta, 25 January 1832.
14. Elster, VII: 408.
15. Letter received by Varnhagen 22 May 1832.
16. Elster, V: 3-8.
17. *Ibid.*, IV: 208.
18. *Ibid.*, IV: 222-23.
19. Letter to Laube, 10 July 1833.
20. Rahel Varnhagen to Heine, 5 June 1832.
21. In *The History of Religion and Philophy*, which appeared in Germany only in January 1835, but was first published in the *Revue des Deux Mondes* in 1834, under the title 'De l'Allemagne depuis Luther'. Elster IV: 223-24.
22. Hirth V: 25-26.
23. Elster V: 7.
24. Sammons, p. 184.
25. See Werner, I: 338 and his source in II: 560.
26. Elster, V: 135. Johann August Wirth (1799-1848) later made his escape from a German prison to France. In 1848 he was a deputy of the Frankfurt National Assembly.
27. A concise account of the Hambach Festival, complete with sources, will be found in Grab, pp. 79-90.
28. G. Mann, *The History of Germany since 1789*, p. 115.
29. Elster, V: 153.
30. Letter to Friedrich Merckel, 24 August 1832.
31. Concerning Heine's early contacts with La Fayette and Odilon-Barrot, see CHRONIK, pp. 89 and 90 and Hirth, V: 43.
32. Booss, p. 94.
33. Letter to his brother, 21 April 1834.
34. Elster, V: 140.
35. *Ibid.*, V: 132-33, 142.
36. *Ibid.*, V: 92.
37. *Ibid.*, V: 136-37.
38. G. Mann, *op. cit.*, p. 115.
39. Heine on tribune and writer: Elster, V: 142.
40. Sammons, p. 178.
41. Heine's Preface in Elster, V: 11-25.
42. Letter of 28 December 1832.
43. Letter no. 109, bearing the date given.
44. Quotations in this and the next paragraphs on Heine's warning to the French from Elster: IV, pp. 292-96.
45. Elster IV: 204.
46. Jacques Grandjonc, in Kongress, 1972, pp. 166-67.
47. *Psalms*, 137: 'By the rivers of Babylon, there we sat down, yea, we wept when we remembered Zion. We hanged our harps upon the willows in the midst thereof.'
48. Elster, VII: 143-44.
49. Werner, I: 292. Wolff's article was published on 15 May 1835 in Leipzig's *Phoenix.*
50. *Ibid.*, I: 278-83.
51. *Ibid.*, II: 707.
52. Cotta's *Allgemeine Zeitung* and Laube's *Journal for the Elegant World* ('Zeitung für die elegante Welt').
53. Werner, I: 284.

54. See *Ibid.*, I: 275-76, and Hirth, V: 96.
55. Werner, I: 277, II: 326-27, and see Hirth, III: 637.
56. Werner, I: 273.
57. Berlioz to Liszt, 8 February 1838, in Werner, I: 370-71.
58. Werner, I: 289.
59. *Ibid.*, II: 493-94.
60. Musset's poem, 'Sur une morte', was published in the *Revue des Deux Mondes* on 1 October 1842.
61. Elster, IV: 338.
62. Letter of 2 July 1835.
63. See Hirth, V: 142.
64. *Ibid.*, II: 90.
65. Letter of 27 September 1835.
66. See Werner, I: 330, II: 559.
67. Quoting Caroline Jaubert, a friend of Princess Belgiojoso and herself a well-known hostess. Werner, I: 340.
68. Elster IV: 507.
69. See Werner, I: 325-26 and Hirth, V: 178-84.
70. Werner, I: 367 and 370, and II: 565.

NOTES TO CHAPTER 12

1. Monz, p. 128.
2. See Padover, p. 43, and Mazlish, pp. 39-40.
3. Mazlish, p. 7.
4. Eleanor Marx-Aveling, '*Karl Marx - Lose Blätter*' (A Few Stray Notes), in REM
5. McLellan, p. 9, and Monz, p. 297.
6. Cf. Monz, pp. 140-43 and Padover, pp. 29-30.
7. Laufner, *op. cit.*
8. Künzli, p. 58, quoting the director of Trier's Municipal Library, Hubert Schiel; and cf. Monz, p. 243.
9. Künzli, p. 63.
10. *Encyclopaedia Judaica*, VI: 1308-09.
11. Stanley Edgar Hyman, *The Tangled Bank: Darwin, Marx, Frazer and Freud as Imaginative Writers*, New York 1962, p. 143.
12. Monz, p. 174.
13. MEGA 2, III/1: 331.

NOTES TO CHAPTER 13

1. MyPaT(DM): 142-43.
2. *Ibid.*: 157-58.
3. *Ibid.*: 158.
4. *Ibid.*: 164-65.
5. *Ibid.*: 169-70
6. Louis-Philippe's two other sons, Aumale and Montpensier, were 13 and 11 respectively, and thus too young to take part in the review.
7. For this and other examples of incitement by the press see Lucas-Dubreton, pp. 298-323.
8. Prince de Joinville, *Vieux Souvenirs, 1818-1848*, Paris 1894. Quoted in Beik, p. 144.
9. Lucas-Dubreton, p. 327.
10. Hugo, pp. 56-57.
11. Lucas-Dubreton, p. 327.
12. Hugo, p. 58.

13. See Bernstein, pp. 70-76.
14. Lucas-Dubreton, p. 331.
15. *Ibid.*, p. 336.
16. Hugo, p. 76.
17. Quoted in Johnson, p. 165.
18. Lucas-Dubreton, p. 365.
19. See Kennan, pp. 21-22.
20. Sammons, p. 209.

NOTES TO CHAPTER 14

1. MEGA 1, I/1.2: 184-85.
2. Nicolaevsky, p. 18.
3. Quoted by Padover, p. 62, from a scrap of a letter preserved at the International Institute for Social History in Amsterdam.
4. Marx, 'The War in Europe...' in *New-York Daily Tribune*, May 9, 1859.
5. Marx to Ruge, 13 March 1843. MEGA 2, III/1: 45.
6. Monz, pp. 329 and 345.
7. Fragmentary letter of 10 May 1838 and letter of '1839-1840' quoted above. MEGA 2, III/1: 337-38.
8. See Monz, pp. 329-30.
9. According to new material in Monz's *Ludwig Gall, der Sozialreformer aus Trier*.
10. MEGA 2, III/1: 308-09.

NOTES TO CHAPTER 15

1. Quoted by Brown, p. 5.
2. Berlin, *Russian Thinkers*, p. 152.
3. Brown, p. 86.
4. Letter to his sisters, 25 January, 1834. Steklov, I: 122-24. (Hereafter referred to in this section as his 'January 1834 letter to his sisters.')
5. Letter to his family, 23 June, 1834. Steklov, I: 133.)
6. Hare, p. 22.
7. Letters of 11 July and 4 October 1834. Steklov, I: 138 and 141.
8. Mendel, p. 446, quoting Z. Ralli in *Minuvshie gody*, 1980, No. 10.
9. Letter to his father, 15 December 1837. Quoted by Kelly, p. 25.
10. Letter to his sisters, 20 May 1833. Quoted by Kelly, p. 27.
11. Letters to his family, 28 June 1834, and to the Beyer sisters, 11 July 1834. Steklov, I: 134 and 138.
12. Mendel, pp. 30-31, *passim*, and see Kelly.
13. Letter to the Beyer sisters, quoted above.
14. Mendel, p. 79, quoting Belinsky's *Sobranie*, XI.
15. Kornilov, as quoted by Mendel, p. 49.
16. Letter to Efremov, 29 July 1835. Steklov, I: 165-73.
17. Mendel, p. 41, quoting Stankevich's posthumous *Perepiska 1830-1840*, Moscow 1914.
18. Kornilov, pp. 154-55.
19. Steklov, I: 165-73.
20. *Ibid.*: 175.

21. *Ibid.*: 252.
22. Cf. Kelly, pp. 3-4.
23. In this and subsequent letters to the Beyer sisters between 16 March and 3 August 1836 Bakunin shows a growing sense of himself as a Jesus of his time. See Mendel, pp. 62 and 453, n. 31.
24. Stankevich, *Perepiska*, p. 444.
25. Kornilov, pp. 154-55.
26. Letter to Tatyana and Varvara, as quoted by Kelly, p. 37.
27. Brown, p. 61.
28. See Mendel, p. 62 and his sources on p.453.
29. Letters to his brothers 11 September and November 1836. Steklov, I: 351-52 and 354-56.
30. See Brown, p.104.
31. Brown, pp. 66-67.
32. See Hare, pp. 21, 24.
33. See Brown, p. 8.
34. Letter to Alexandra Beyer, March 1836. Steklov, I: 227.
35. Letters to his sister Varvara and to the Beyer sisters, 16 March 1836; letter to Varvara, 17 March 1836. Steklov, I: 240-41 and 244.
36. Letter to Alexandra Beyer, April 1836. *Ibid.*: 226, 276.
37. Brown, p. 11.
38. Quoted in N.D. Brodsky (ed.), *The Early Slavophiles*, Moscow 1910, p. 19.
39. MyPaT(G-H), II: 516-17.
40. For Pushkin and Mandelshtam on Chaadayev, see Victor Terras (ed.), *Handbook of Russian Literature*, New Haven and London 1985, p. 76.
41. MyPaT(G-H), II:. 420, 425.
42. Brown, p. 63, quoting Stankevich's *Perepiska*.
43. *Ibid.*, p. 64, quoting the same source.
44. Letter to Tatyana, 15 April 1836. Steklov, I: 271-72.
45. *Ibid.*, I: 279 (Letter to his sisters Tatyana and Varvara 23 April, 1836), and Kornilov, pp. 214-15.
46. Brown, p. 13.
47. Letter to his sister Varvara, March 1836, Steklov, I: 223-24.
48. See Mendel, pp. 102-03 and his sources.
49. Letter to his father, December 1837, Steklov, II: 128.
50. Letter to Varvara, 23 January, 1837.
51. Letter to the Beyer sisters and their brother Constantine, 22 July 1837. Steklov, II: 44.
52. Bettina, 'the last refuge' etc., Heer, p. 174; ranked with Sand, d'Agoult and George Eliot – by the German cultural historian Hans Meyer.
53. Mendel, p. 79, quoting from Belinsky, *Sobranie*, 11.
54. MyPaT(G-H), II: 411.
55. Kornilov, pp. 256-59.
56. Steklov, I: 354-55.
57. Undated letter to the Beyer sisters. *Ibid.*, I: 295-96.
58. Letter to his sisters, 24 April 1837. *Ibid.*, I: 424.
59. Letter to Varvara, 22 December 1836. *Ibid*, I:376.
60. Mendel, p. 119, n. 32.

NOTES TO CHAPTER 16

1. MEGA 1, I/2: 463.
2. *Ibidem.*
3. *Ibid.*,: 37.
4. *Ibid.*, III/1: 19-20.
5. *Ibid.*, I/2: 582-88.
6. MEGA 2, III/1:. 114.
7. MEGA 1, I/2: 531.
8. *Ibid.*: 128-30.
9. *Ibid.*: 30.
10. *Ibid.*: 25-26.

NOTES TO CHAPTER 17

1. Silberner.
2. Original draft, April 1831, in Hess Bw, p. 48.
3. This and other excerpts from Hess's diary are quoted from Silberner, or from Hess NQHF. The full diary, together with other material by and on Hess, is in the Moscow Institute of Marxism-Leninism. Wolfgang Mönke gives a survey of this material.
4. According to the inscription *Vater der deutschen Sozialdemokratie*, engraved by German Socialists on his tombstone some time between 1875, the year of his death, and 1903.
5. 'The Life and Opinions of Moses Hess', Lucien Wolf Memorial Lecture (Cambridge, 1959) in Isaiah Berlin, *Against the Current, Essays in the History of Ideas*, edited by Henry Hardy, London 1979, pp. 213 and 222.
6. Georg Lukàcs, *Moses Hess und die Probleme der idealistischen Dialektik*, AGS XII, 1926, p. 109; Silberner, p. 653.
7. Avineri, *Moses Hess*, pp. 249 and 253.
8. Hess RJ, p. 39.
9. Avineri, *op. cit.*, p. 253.
10. S. Na'aman, *Emanzipation*, p. 40 and *passim*.
11. Fisch.
12. See his letter to L. Zuntz, May 1829, Hess Bw, pp. 18-19. He is quoting from 'Chapters of the Fathers' (*Avot*), 4:2.
13. Berlin, *Against the Current*, p. 214.
14. Hess Bw, pp. 48-49.
15. Letter to M. Levy, April 1831, Hess Bw, p. 47.
16. *Die Heilige Geschichte der Menschheit. Von einem Jünger Spinoza*, Stuttgart, 1837. Reprinted in Hess PSS.
17. *Ibid.*, p. 62.
18. *Ibid.*, pp. 66-67.
19. *Ibid.*, pp. 51 and 69.
20. *Ibid.*, pp. 72-73.
21. *Ibid.* pp. 67-68; and Silberner, p. 46.
22. Hess Bw, pp. 49-52.
23. Berlin, *Karl Marx*, p. 72.
24. Hess PSS., p. 38.
25. Silberner, p. 11.
26. Avineri, p. 28.
27. NQHF, p. 43.
28. Quoted in Silberner, p. 49.
29. NQHF, pp. 42-43.
30. Hess Bw, pp. 21-22.

31. *Ibid.*, pp. 25-26.
32. *Ibid.*, p. 47. Letter to M. Levy.
33. Hess AS, pp. 86-87.
34. *Prolegomena zur Historiesophie*, Berlin 1838.
35. Hess AS, pp. 92-93.
36. Hess Bw, p. 60.

NOTES TO CHAPTER 18
1. Unless otherwise stated contemporary impressions are quoted from *Berlin*.
2. V.S. Pecherin, quoted in Scheibert.
3. Gans.
4. MEGA 2, III/1: 305.
5. *Ibid.*: 10.
6. *Ibid.*:. 304.
7. *Ibid.*: 303.
8. *Ibidem.*
9. *Ibid.*: 10.
10. *Ibid.*: 307.
11. *Ibid.*: 308-09.
12. *Ibid.*: 10-11.
13. *Ibid.*: 309.
14. MEGA 2, III/1: 15.
15. *Ibidem.*
16. Künzli, pp. 100 and 102-03.
17. *Ibid.*, p. 16.
18. Raddatz, p. 40.
19. MEGA 2, III/1: 319.
20. *Ibid.*:. 324. Letter of 9 December 1837.
21. *Ibid.*: 337. Undated letter, believed to have been written in 1839 or 1840.
22. *Ibid.*: 319.
23. *Ibid.*: 311-12.
24. *Ibid.*: 317-19.
25. Padover, p. 83.
26. *Ibid.*, p. 100.
27. MEGA 1, I/1-2 - Section I, v. 1, 2nd half-volume, p. 222.
28. See the authoritative MEGA 2, III/1: Apparat, p. 736. The father knew on the 17th that Karl was back in Berlin, but due to the son's carelessly omitting his place of residence, he was forced to address his letter to him 'Stralau, no. 4, near Berlin', in the hope that someone would forward it. See MEGA 2, III/1:, 320.
29. The German text of Marx's letter to his father was reprinted in 1927 in MEGA 1, I/1-2: 213-21. Full or partial translations appeared in *Early Texts* (ed. D. McLellan), 1972, pp. 1-10, and Padover, pp. 102-05.
30. Quoted in Kapp, v. II, pp. 624-25.
31. MEGA 2, III/1: 325.

NOTES TO CHAPTER 19
1. On Eleanor's dilemma and on her correspondence with Karl Kautsky and others before publishing the letter in the 1897-98 issue of Stuttgart's *Neue Zeit* see Kapp, v. II, pp. 624-26; on the introduction she wrote, *ibid.*, pp. 737-38, and Padover, p. 101, n. 17.
2. Quotations from the letter are from the full text in MEGA 2, III/1: 323-27.
3. Padover, p. 106.
4. Karl August Varnhagen von Ense, *Tagebücher*, Leipzig 1861, v. I, p. 341.
5. *Friederich der Grosse und seine Widersacher*, Leipzig 1840.
6. Ring, v. I, p. 113.
7. 'Contribution to the Critique of Hegel's Philosophy of Right. Introduction.' *Deutsch-Französische Jahrbücher*, 1844. For full English passage see MER, p. 42.
8. 'Bruno Bauer and Early Christianity' (May 1882), MER, p. 195.
9. Hengstenberg described in Meyer's Lexikon, 1903.
10. Quoted in Nicolaievsky and Maenchen-Helfen, p. 41.
11. Engels in 1886: see MER, p. 223.
12. MEGA 2, III/1: 332-33.
13. *Ibid.*, 290.
14. Blumenberg.
15. Richard Wagner, *Sämtliche Briefe*, Leipzig 1975, v. II, p. 77.
16. MEGA 2, III/1: 328-29.
17. *Ibid.*: 330.
18. *Ibid.*: 331.

NOTES TO CHAPTER 20
1. Elster, VII: 530-31.
2. Letters to Campe, 8 and 14 March 1836; Hirth, II: 119-21.
3. Unless one considers Heine a pathological liar, one cannot ignore the cogency of his remark that to judge a new opera one has to hear it more than once. In fact, as we know from Meyerbeer's diaries, Heine attended a second performance of the opera within the week.
4. Letter to Baron Johann Georg von Cotta (who had succeeded his father as publisher of the *Allgemeine Zeitung*), 29 March 1836; Hirth, II: 125.
5. Hirth, V: 172.
6. Letters to Campe and Lewald, 23 and 25 January 1837 respectively; Hirth, II: 154 and 157-58.
7. Werner, I: 326, 329.
8. *Ibid.*: 325.
9. Hirth, II: 132-33.
10. Letter of 29 August 1837; *Ibid.*, II: 211.
11. The railway shares speculation theory by Wadepuhl in the 1970s; the obligation for a friend or blackmail theory by Vallentin in the 1950s; and the 'made up the whole story' theory by Sammons in 1979.
12. Hirth, II: 154 and 157-58.
13. *Ibid.*, V: 177.
14. Sammons, p. 214.
15. HSA, 25: 20.
16. To Scheible, 24 February 1837, and to Campe, 13 April 1837; Hirth, II: 162-63, 180.
17. *Ibid.*: 180.
18. Cf. Hirth, V: 20.

19. The question is debated in the Babylonian Talmud.
20. Wadepuhl, p. 158; Sammons, pp. 219-20.
21. Letter of 5 August 1837.
22. To Moser, 8 November 1836; Hirth, II: 148.
23. *Ibid.*, V: 184.
24. To Friederike Robert, 12 October 1825; Hirth, I: 233.
25. To Campe, 10 May 1837; *Ibid.*, II: 191.
26. Letter of 1 March 1838; *Ibid.*, II: 240.
27. To Meyerbeer, 24 March 1837; *Ibid.*, II: 247-54.
28. To Lewald, 1 March 1837; *Ibid.*, II: 242.
29. To Meyerbeer, 24 March 1837; see n. 27 above.
30. Hirth, II: 251.
31. 31 March 1838; *ibid.*, II: 257.
32. The letter to Gutzkow, Hirth, II: 277-79. On Heine and the autonomy of art and his playing a role of 'greater significance in the history of aesthetics than [he] himself could possibly have imagined', and on Gautier's affinity with Heine as well as on Victor Cousin's coining *l'art pour l'art*, see Reeves, pp. 173-74 and *passim*.
33. In v. I of his *Gesammelte Werke*, Gutzkow was to write that Heine's Jewishness made his works smell of 'old borrowed clothes'; Hirth, V: 261.
34. Letter to Kolb, 18 August 1938; Hirth, II: 276.
35. 10 May 1837; *Ibid.*, II: 191.
36. ... Mille merci! J'aurais bien voulu vous voir! Les rayons de vos yeux m'auraient fait du bien. Je suis très triste. Vous ne savez pas tous mes malheurs. A l'heure qu'il est je suis atteint d'une cécité physique qui est aussi affligeante que cet aveuglement moral dont je jouis depuis quatre ans et que vous connaissez.

   ... Je vous aime beaucoup, de tout mon coeur, de tous les lambeaux de mon coeur. Si vous êtes libre réjouissez-vous de votre liberté! Moi je suis encore dans les terribles fers, et c'est parce qu'on m'enchaine le soir avec un soin tout particulier que je n'ai pas réussi de vois voir à Paris. Mais quand j'aurais fait mon temps, j'yrai vous rejoindre, et fut-ce au bout du monde...
37. Hirth, V: 259 and *passim*. See also his *Französische Freunde*, pp. 185-210.
38. Sammons, p. 201.
39. Varnhagen on Heine's death, quoted in Werner, I: 220 and II: 667.

NOTES TO CHAPTER 21
1. MyPaT(DM): 192-93.
2. Carr, *The Romantic Exiles*, p. 22.
3. *Ibid.*, p. 19.
4. Herzen's own account of the events briefly related in this section is in MyPaT(G-H). I: 337-447.
5. Carr, *The Romantic Exiles*, pp. 24 and 364.
6. MyPaT(G-H), II: 392 and fragment of a letter quoted in Carr, *op. cit.*, 184.
7. *A Family Drama*, Herzen's version of Natalie's affair with Herwegh will be found in MyPaT (G-H), II: 840-920 and 932-50.

8. MyPaT(G-H), II: 396-98.
9. Quoted in Brown, pp. 75 and 71 in this order.
10. There is some disagreement as to whether Stankevich himself was an irresolute Romantic 'Hamlet,' as E.H. Carr sees him, or whether his 'decision to break the bonds of propriety and "obey his heart" was not necessarily evidence of weakness', but the result of clear reflection in an untenable situation, as Brown has argued. Carr, *Michael Bakunin*, p. 51, and Brown, p. 75.
11. Kornilov, p. 308. Quoted in Mendel, p. 98, and in Brown, pp. 77-78.
12. Annenkov, p. 28.
13. MyPaT(G-H), II: 391.
14. Annenkov, p. 21; and Isaiah Berlin, *Russian Thinkers*, p. 145.
15. Steklov, I: 386-87. (Quoted and italicized in Mendel, p. 85.)
16. *Ibid.*, I: 398 (in Mendel, p. 85).
17. *Ibid.*, I: 398-99 and II: 24: to his siblings, 4 February 1837, and to the Beyer sisters, 24 June 1837 (in Mendel, p. 88).
18. Quoted in Carr, *Bakunin*, p. 52.
19. Steklov, II: 86-88. Letters to Beyer sisters and to his own sisters, both around the middle of December 1837 (in Mendel, p. 98).
20. Cf. Brown, p. 80.
21. *Ibid.*, p. 78.
22. Kornilov, pp. 357-62 (in Mendel, p. 99).
23. Steklov, II: 129-30. Letter to his sisters, 31 December 1837 (in Mendel, p. 101).
24. Matthew, 10: 34-36: 'For I have come to set a man against his father, and a daughter against her mother, and a daughter-in-law against her mother-in-law; and man's foes will be those of his own household.'
25. Steklov, II: 23-182. From letters to the Beyers, December 1837 to May 1838 (in Mendel, p. 104). Emphasis added.
26. See Mendel, p. 105.
27. Carr, *Bakunin*, p. 52.
28. *Ibid.*, pp. 64-65.
29. Steklov, II: 405. Letter to his sisters, 11 February 1838 (in Mendel, p. 103).
30. Bakunin's 'Hegel's Gymnasium Lectures', in Steklov, II. Most passages quoted as rendered by Mendel, a few in Carr's translation.
31. Annenkov, p. 22.
32. Belinsky, *Sobranie*, XI (in Mendel, p. 120).
33. Annenkov, pp. 29-30.
34. Brown, p. 78.
35. Quoted in Mendel, p. 114.
36. Carr, *Bakunin*, p. 69.
37. Belinsky, *Sobranie*, XI: 289-334 (in Mendel, pp. 118-19).
38. Quoted in Carr, *Bakunin*, p. 71.
39. Belinsky, *Sobranie*, XI: 388 (in Mendel, p. 119).
40. *Ibid.*: 282-85, 316-18, 345 (in Mendel, pp. 120-21).
41. Steklov, II: 203-4. Fragment of September 1838 letter to Belinsky (in Mendel, p. 122).

42. See note 40 above.
43. Steklov,II: 195 (in Mendel, p. 112).
44. *Ibid.*, II: 239, 244 (in Mendel, pp. 124-25).
45. Belinsky, *Sobranie*, XI: 443 (in Mendel, pp. 464-65.)
46. Steklov, II: 262. To his sisters, 14 September 1839 (in Mendel, p. 130).
47. For quotations from Bakunin's essay and his 'fateful merger' of Fichte and Hegel see Mendel, pp. 128-30.
48. Kornilov, p. 548 (in Mendel, p. 132).
49. Belinsky, *Sobranie*, XI: 286-88 (Brown, p. 106).
50. Steklov, II: 294-95 (in Mendel, p. 133; in Carr, p. 73)
51. *Ibid.*: 303-04. To his sisters and to Alexandra Beyer (in Mendel, p, 135).
52. Annenkov, p. 22, and MyPaT (G-H): 398.
53. Belinsky, *Sobranie*, XI: 443, 470, 485-86 (in Mendel, p. 134).
54. *Ibidem.*
55. Steklov, II: 392-406 (in Mendel, pp. 137-39 and see Carr, pp. 82-83).
56. *Ibid.*, II: 436, to the Beyer sisters, 29 June 1840; and II: 433, to his sisters and brothers, June 1840 (in Mendel, pp. 143 and 140, respectively).
57. *Ibid.*, II: 434-36 (Mendel, p. 143 and Carr, p. 88).
58. In *Prolegomena zur Historiosophie*, 1838.
59. Steklov, II: 303-04. Letters to Stankevich and the Beyers, February 1840 (in Mendel, pp. 135-36).
60. *Ibid.*, II: 435 and III: 2 (in Mendel, pp. 143 and 148, respectively).
61. *Ibid.*, II: 436 (in Carr, p. 89).
62. *Ibid.*, III: 1-3. Letter to his family, 4 July 1840 (in Mendel, p. 148).
63. Hare, pp. 23-24.
64. Venturi, p. 41.
65. MyPaT(G-H), II: 401.
66. *Ibid.*, II: 402.
67. Quoted in Brown. pp. 107, 109; and in Berlin, *Russian Thinkers*, p.170.
68. Brown, p. 111; Berlin, p. 172.

NOTES TO CHAPTER 22

1. Bernstein, pp. 79-80.
2. Werner, I: 413, 446-47, 465.
3. Hirth, II: 340. Letter to George Sand, 17 March 1840.
4. *Ibid.*, II: 495.
5. Elster, VII: 33-34.
6. *Ibid.*, p. 35.
7. See Prawer, *Heine's Jewish Comedy*, p. 359.
8. Hess to Heine, 19 October 1937. First published by Edmund Silberner in *International Review of Social History*, Amsterdam 1961, pp. 457ff.
9. Werner, I: 432-34.
10. Elster, VI: 149.
11. *Ibidem.*
12. Werner, I: 436-37, quoting Laube's *Erinnerungen*, 1868.

13. Elster VI: 167-68. This was the essence of Heine's warning, which was written in round-about language: 'Today the anvil, tomorrow the hammer!'
14. Elster, VII: 36-37.
15. Articles of 11 June, 25 July and 30 July 1840. Elster, VI: 184-85, 201 and 209-10.
16. *Ibid.*, VI: 203 and 205-06.
17. Lucas-Dubreton, p. 418.
18. *Revue rétrospective ou Archives secrètes du dernier gouvernement*, v.I (1848): 37, 39.
19. Elster, VI: 524-25.
20. Sammons, *op. cit.*, p. VII.
21. Wadepuhl, p. 150.
22. See Michael Werner, 'Heine's französische Staatspension' in HJ, 1977, pp. 134-41.
23. See Lucienne Netter, 'Heine, Thiers et la Presse parisienne', in *Revue d'Allemagne* 4 (1972): 113-53.
24. Werner, *op. cit.*, p. 140, quoting Heine's 1854 'Retrospective Statement' (*q.v.* Elster, VI: 385).
25. Elster, VI: 278, 289.
26. *Ibid.*: 278.
27. *O Dieu! considérez les hommes de ce temps, Aveugles, loin de vous sous tants d'ombres flottants*
28. Breuning, p. 179.
29. Werner, I: 452, quoting Varnhagen von Ense.
30. The original London edition was called *Voyages et aventures de Lord Carisdale en Icarie*. 'To place before the world the example of a great nation having a community of goods', Cabet chose the form of a travel book describing his visit to the utopian island of Icaria in the company of an English nobleman. Icaria took its name from its supposed founder, Icar. Carisdale's role on the fictional journey was to show that even an upper-class Englishman could not resist becoming convinced of the blessings of life in Cabet's ideal society.
31. Elster, VI: 154.
32. Pierre Leroux, *Discours sur la situation actuelle de la société et de l'esprit*, 1841.
33. G, Mann, *The History of Germany since 1789*, p. 121.
34. Quoted in *Preussische Portraits*, Hamburg 1969, p. 146.
35. *Ibidem.*
36. *Ibid.*, p. 147.
37. Quoted in Brandes, v. III, p. 520.
38. *Ibid.*, v. III, pp. 521-22.
39. Letter of 31 March 1841. MEGA 2, III/1: 341.
40. MEGA 2, III/1: 346.
41. *Ibid.*: 340-41, 343, 345-46. Letters of 1 March, 30 March and 5 April 1840.
42. Marx ET, p. 19. Emphasis added.
43. The German title was *Differenz der demokritischen und epikurischen Naturphilosophie*. Marx divided it into two parts, each comprising five sections. Two sections of part I no longer exist. There was also an Appendix, of which only fragments and notes survive.

44. ET, p. 20.
45. *Ibid.*, p. 21.
46. MEGA 2, III/1: 349. Bauer to Marx, 25 July 1840.
47. ET, p. 12.
48. *Ibid.*, p. 13.
49. ET, p. 13 and Prawer, *Karl Marx and World Literature*, p. 23. The fullest English version of Marx's dissertation and his notes will be found in MECW, I. ET contains substantial extracts from the notes as well as the Preface. I have occasionally switched from one to the other, or to passages quoted by other authors, whenever a word or a line seemed a more felicitous rendering of the German original in MEGA 2, I/1.
50. C.M. Bowra, *The Greek Experience*, New York 1959 (paperback reprint), p. 125.
51. Prawer, *op. cit.*, p. 23. See n. 49 above.
52. MECW, I: 103-105 and Padover, pp. 122-24. Italics in Marx's text. Hegel on the 'proofs of the existence of God': lecture delivered by Hegel in the summer of 1829 (*Vorlesungen über die Philosophie der Religion*).

NOTES TO CHAPTER 23

1. Bruno und Edgar Bauer, *Briefwechsel, während der Jahre 1839-1842 aus Bonn und Berlin*, Berlin-Charlottenburg 1844, Aalem 1969, pp. 101-02.
2. Brandes, v. III, p. 532.
3. Grab, *Ein Mann der Marx Ideen gab*, p. 189.
4. *Preussische Portraits, op. cit.*, pp. 143-44.
5. The contemporary was Karl Marx, in a letter of 1843 in which he anticipated Golo Mann's modern characterization of the King as 'the Romantic at odds with his age'.
6. *Ibid.*, MEGA 2, III/1: 357-58. Letter of 12 April 1841.
7. This and the next quote from Marx's dedication: MEGA 1, I/1.1, pp. 6-7.
8. Künzli, *op. cit.*, pp. 111-12.
9. See Monz, *Karl Marx*, p. 284.
10. Letter of 29 May 1840. MEGA 2, III/1: 347-48.
11. MECW, I: 399.
12. Freiligrath's German lines read: '*Der Dichter steht auf einer höhern Warte/Als auf den Zinnen der Partei.*'
13. '*Nur offen wie ein Mann: Für oder wider? / Und die Parole: Sklave oder frei? / Selbst Götter stiegen vom Olymp hernieder / Und kämpften auf der Zinne der Partei.*'
14. Brandes, v. III: 538-39.
15. '*Reisst die Kreuze aus der Erde! / Alle sollen Schwerter werden!*'
16. Elster, VII: 18.
17. *Ibid.*, VII: 137, 139.
18. *Ibid.*, VII: 133-34.
19. Werner, I: 417.
20. Years later, Laube was to claim that before he left Paris Heine had several times told him he was 'erecting the mountain' to go into the Börne book on the subject of the July Revolution: 'These were his last words when I boarded the coach.' It has since been established that this cannot have been true. Laube himself quoted Heine's statement that the July Revolution would require a separate book. Laube left Paris on 4 February 1840, a couple of days after Heine had sent off the original manuscript of the book to Campe. Laube did not know that this MS, the one he had read, was rejected by Campe and that the published version was a new one which Heine sent off only on 18 April 1840. When Laube later saw the Börne book, which instead of a 'mountain' contained the Helgoland Letters, he felt that Heine had been bluffing. Laube's several accounts of this episode also contain other contradictions. See Werner, I: 417, 421-22, and his Notes on pp. 570-71.
21. Elster, VII: 59.
22. *Ibid.*, VII: 99.
23. Letter of 10 July 1833. Hirth, II: 40.
24. Elster, VII: 53.
25. Preface to *Salon I*, Elster IV: 14.
26. In *History of Religion and Philosophy in Germany*, Elster, IV: 294 and 248 in this order. Emphasis added.
27. Elster, VII: 40-41.
28. *Ibid.*, V: 229.
29. *Ibid.*, VII: 124-25.
30. Reissner believes that Heine heard the story of the 'Captive Messiah' in the Society for Jewish Culture in Berlin. Heine's mention of his 1822 visit to Poland would seem to bear that out, for he joined the Society shortly after his return. H.G. Reissner, 'The Tale of the Captive Messiah', in *Der Friede, Idee und Verwirklichung*, Heidelberg 1961.
31. Werner, I: 417.
32. Elster, VII: 143.
33. Enfantin's letter was written on 11 October 1835, two months before Metternich engineered the Bundestag ban on Heine's works and those of the Young Germany writers. See Sternberger, pp. 113, 123.
34. Elster, VII: 143-46.
35. Thomas Mann, *Gesammelte Werke*, Frankfurt 1960, v. X, p. 839.
36. The essay was titled 'Heine and the Consequences' (*Heine und die Folgen*), Vienna and Leipzig 1922, pp. 200-35.
37. H.G. Atkins, *Heine*, London 1929; quoted in Helmut Koopmann, *Heinrich Heine*, Darmstadt 1975, p. 383.
38. MEW, I: 440-441 and *Ergänzungsband* II, p. 118.
39. MEW, XXVII: 441.
40. Hans Kaufmann, 'Die Denkschrift "Ludwig Börne" und ihre Stellung in Heine's Werk', Kongress, pp. 182, 178, in this order.
41. Golo Mann, 'Heine, wem gehört er?' Kongress, p. 19.

42. Werner I: 292, quoting an article published by Wolff in May 1835 in the *Frankfurter Phoenix*.
43. Letter to Ferdinand Friedland. Hirth, II: 361.
44. Direct and indirect quotations from Hirth, V: 315.
45. *Ibid.*, p. 312.

NOTES TO CHAPTER 24

1. Hess AS, pp. 86-87. Emphasis added.
2. *Ibid.*: 92.
3. *Ibid.*: 121.
4. *Ibidem.*
5. *Ibid.*: 110.
6. Hess Bw, pp. 72-73.
7. *Ibid.*: 75-78.
8. MEGA 2, III/1: 364.
9. Hess Bw, pp. 79-80. Emphasis in original.
10. Lovell, p. 23.
11. *Porträts deutsch-jüdischer Geschichte*, herausg. von Thilo Koch, Cologne 1961, p. 67.
12. MEGA 2, III/1: 365.
13. *Ibid.*: 366-68.
14. 'Intellectual rapist': in Carlebach, p. 126. Bauer's description of his method in *Hegels Lehre von der Religion und Kunst*, published anonymously in Leipzig, 1842, p. 41, reprinted by Scientia Verlag, Aalem 1967.
15. Carlebach, p. 127.
16. *Bruno Bauer/Edgar Bauer, Briefwechsel, 1839-1842* (reprint of the original 1844 edition), Scientia Verlag, Aalem 1969, pp. 137-40.
17. MEGA 2 (Apparat), III/1: 751, and Gespräche, I: 4.
18. Carl Josias von Bunsen, *Aus seinen Briefen*, Leipzig 1869, v. II, p. 133.
19. Heine was quoting the Greek author Ctesias of Cnidus (5th-century BC); Elster, VII: 101.
20. Letter to Kolb, 3 July 1841. Hirth, II: 389-90.
21. *Ibid.*: 393.
22. Werner, I: 489, and letter to Campe of 9 September 1841, Hirth, II: 411.
23. Vallentin, pp. 217, 219.
24. Hirth, II: 410, 411, 414. Emphasis added.
25. To Alexandre Weill, 26 August 1841. *Ibid.*: 407.
26. Kornilov, p. 667 (in Brown, p. 81).
27. Steklov, III: 9. To his siblings, 9 August 1840 (quoted in Mendel, p. 151).
28. *Ibid.*, III: 31-34. Letter of 23 October 1840 (in Mendel, p. 152).
29. Kornilov, *Gody stranstvii M. Bakunin*, pp. 51-52 (in Mendel, p. 467).
30. *Ibid.*
31. Letter to his sisters, quoted in Kelly, p. 80.
32. Steklov, III: 38. Letter of 16 November 1840 (in Mendel, p. 152).
33. Varnhagen von Ense, *op. cit.*, v. I, pp. 232, 263.
34. Steklov, III: 85-86. Letter to his sisters, January 1841 (in Mendel, p. 153).
35. To his brother Nicholas, 29 March 1841. *Ibid.*: 52-56 (in Mendel, pp. 158-59).

36. Venturi, p. 43.
37. Steklov, III: 35-36. Letter to his childhood governess, Julie Nindel, 29 October 1840 (in Mendel, p. 151).
38. *Ibid.*, III: 45. Letter to his brother Paul, January 1841 (in Mendel p. 157).
39. This was a shortened title, the original having been *Hallische Jahrbücher für deutsche Kunst und Wissenschaft*. In spite of its title, it was a monthly publication.
40. Steklov, III: 47 (in Mendel p. 156).
41. *Ibid.*, III: 60 (in Mendel p. 157).
42. *Ibid.*, III: 31-32. Letter of 23 October 1840 (in Mendel, p. 155).
43. Mendel, p. 156.
44. Werder's thoughts 'seldom strayed beyound the classroom', Carr, *Bakunin*, p. 95; an 'undistinguished man', Kelly, p. 76.
45. Steklov, III: 62-63. Letter of 22 October 1841 (in Mendel, pp. 164-65, and Kelly, p. 90).
46. *Ibid.*, III: 61. Letter to his family, 19 September 1841 (in Mendel, p. 159).
47. Félicité de Lamennais, *Paroles d'un croyant*, Paris 1834, pp. 49-56.
48. 'Liberty...has to be seized', etc. and Harold Laski quoted in Howarth, pp. 169-70.
49. Steklov, III: 63-78. Four letters variously addressed to Premukhino and to Varvara and Paul in Dresden between 22 October and 15 November 1841 (in Mendel, p. 166).

NOTES TO CHAPTER 25

1. Engels's description, written at the end of November, was to appear in an anonoymous article (sgd. Fr. Oswald) titled *Schelling über Hegel* (Schelling on Hegel), and published in the Hamburg *Telegraph* in mid-December 1841. MEGA 1, I/2: 173-80.
2. *'Schelling und die Offenbarung'* (sgd. Fr. Oswald) was published by Robert Binder in Leipzig in March 1842. MEGA 1, I/2,: 181-227.
3. Letter of 21 June 1840. Bruno Bauer/Edgar Bauer, *Briefwechsel 1839-1842*, p. 88.
4. Wilfrid Blunt, *On Wings of Song: Felix Mendelssohn*, p. 220.
5. Heinz und Gudrun Becker (ed.), *Giacomo Meyerbeer: Briefwechsel und Tagebücher*, III: 368 (hereafter Meyerbeer BW).
6. *Ibid.*, III: 727.
7. Letter of 5 January 1840. Bruno Bauer/Edgar Bauer, *op. cit.*, p. 30.
8. MECW, I: 106.
9. Silberner, pp. 98, 97 in that order.
10. *Ibid.*, p. 99.
11. Hess Bw, p. 85.
12. *Ibid., p.* 81.
13. *Ibid.*, p. 83.
14. From the *Berlinische Nachrichten von Staats- und gelehrten Sachen*; in Meyerbeer BW, III: 730-31.
15. MEGA 2, III/1: 226-28.

16. *Ibid.*: 369.
17. *'Bemerkungen über die neueste preussische Zensurinstruktion'*, MEGA 2, I/1: 97-120.
18. Hess Bw, p. 90.
19. Letters of 12 March and 27 May 1842. Hess Bw, pp. 93 and 95.
20. *Ibid.*: 95.
21. *'Die Kommunisten in Frankreich'*, *Rheinische Zeitung*, 21 April 1842.
22. See Zamoyski, p. 203.
23. Elster, VI: 294-300.
24. Johnson, p. 66.
25. Lucas-Dubreton, p. 437.
26. Collins, pp. 96-97; and see Howarth, p. 280.
27. Alexandre Auguste Ledru-Rollin, in an election speech, July 1841. Quoted in Beik, p. 156.
28. Howarth, p. 269.
29. Condensed from *The German Ideology*. For Bauer as an 'intellectual rapist', see Carlebach, p. 126 and note on p. 395.
30. MECW I: 385.
31. Quoted in McLellan, *Karl Marx*, p. 43.
32. MECW, I: 387.
33. MEGA 2, I/1 Apparat: 998-99.
34. MEGA 2, I/1: 121-69.
35. MEGA 1, 1/2: 229-49.
36. Written in June-July 1842 and published in Zurich in December. MEGA, I/2: 252-81.

NOTES TO CHAPTER 26
1. Marx's article in MEGA 2, I/1: 172-90.
2. MECW, I: 389.
3. MEGA 2, III/1: 351.
4. Blumenberg, p. 39.
5. MEW, XXIX: 653-54.
6. MECW, I: 390.
7. *Ibidem.*
8. Howarth, p. 285.
9. Lucas-Dubreton, p. 443.
10. See Johnson, p. 439 and Breunig, p. 228.
11. Elster, VI: 279.
12. *Ibid.*, VI: 314-15.
13. *Ibid.*, VI: 316-17.
14. *Ibid.*, VI: 324-25.
15. Letter of 7 November 1842. Hirth II: 439.
16. Sammons, *op.cit.*, p. 269; Robertson, p. 24.
17. Quoted in Carr, *Bakunin*, p. 102.
18. *Bakunin: Selected Writings* (ed. and introduced by Arthur Lehning), New York 1974, pp. 41, 45, 52 and 56. The English version of 'The Reaction in Germany', trans. by Mary Barbara Zeldin, was first published in *Russian Philosophy*, v. I (eds. J.M. Edie, J.P. Scanlan and Zeldin), Chicago 1965.
19. *Ibid.*, p. 56.
20. Hess AS, p. 86.
21. Steklov, III: 63 (in Mendel, p. 166.)
22. *Ibidem.*
23. *Bakunin: Selected Writings*, p. 43.
24. *Ibid.*, pp. 48-49.
25. Hare, p. 24.
26. *Ibid.*, p. 53.

27. Quoted in Hare, pp. 23-24, and in Kelly, p. 96.
28. Kelly, p. 95.
29. Mendel, p. 172.
30. *Ibid.*, pp. 168, 172.
31. Kelly, pp. 94 and 97.
32. Letter of 4 November 1842, Steklov, III: 151 (in Mendel, p. 176).
33. *Ibid.*, III: 98 (in Mendel, p. 183).
34. *Ibid.*, III: 117-18. Quoted in Carr, *Bakunin*, p. 102.
35. Steklov, III: 109-10 (in Mendel, p. 178).
36. Letter of December 1841. Quoted in Kelly, p. 95.
37. Some of it was destroyed by Bakunin and his friends because of its subversive character, and some was unearthed only long after his death.
38. *Bakunin: Selected Writings*, pp. 57-58.

NOTES TO CHAPTER 27
1. Letter to Auerbach, 19 June 1843. Hess Bw, p. 103
2. Marx ro Oppenheim. MEGA 1 I/2: 280.
3. Lorenz von Stein, *Der Sozialismus und Kommunismus des heutigen Frankreichs. Ein Beitrag zur Zeitgeschichte*, Leipzig 1842.
4. Karl Grün, in *Neue Anekdota*, Darmstadt 1845.
5. ET, pp. 44, 47-48.
6. Engels himself, in an article published on 18 November 1843 in Robert Owen's *New Moral World*, called Hess 'the first Communist' in Germany. MEGA 1, II/635.
7. See Silberner, pp. 115-17.
8. *Ibid.*, p. 121.
9. An excellent brief survey of the literature on the relations between Hess and Marx will be found in Rosen, pp. 95-111.
10. Avineri, *Moses Hess*, p. 16.
11. Quoted by Ellen Moers in *George Sand in Her Own Words* (ed. Joseph Barry), London and New York 1979, p. xxv.
12. MEGA 1, I/1.1: 304.
13. ET, pp. 49-51.
14. MEGA 1, I/1.2: 282-84.
15. MECW, I: 393-95.
16. Silberner, pp. 166-71.
17. MEW, *Ergänzungsband*, I: 419 (italics in original).
18. MEGA 1, I/2: 152, 153.
19. Ernst von der Heide, who wrote under the pseudonym of Karl Grün, later translated Proudhon's *Misère de la Philosophie* into German. In defence of Grün, Proudhon was to write to Marx the famous sentence: 'Let us not become the leaders of a new intolerance.'
20. K. Heinzen in his memoirs (*Erlebtes*, Boston 1874). MEGA 1, I/2: 151.
21. MECW, I: 396-98. In part I have preferred Padover's translation in *Karl Marx*, p. 149.
22. *Anekdota zur neuesten deutschen Philosophie und Publicistik*, Zurich and Winthertur 1843.
23. MECW, I: 398-99.
24. MEGA 2, III/1: 396-97.

25. MECW, I: 399.

26. EW, p. 200.

27. Article of 18 November 1843. MEGA 1, I/2: 447.

28. Letter to the Herweghs, 19 September 1847. Steklov, III: 265 (in Mendel, p. 267.)

NOTES TO CHAPTER 28

1. 8 January 1843. Steklov, III: 172 (in Mendel, p. 184).

2. Mendel, p. 169.

3. Letter of 9 October 1842. Steklov, III: 133 (in Mendel, p. 176).

4. Letter of 4 November 1842. Steklov, III: 148-53. Emphasis added. English translation partly in Mendel, partly in Carr.

5. Letters of 10 and 20 February 1843 to Paul and his sisters. Steklov, III: 181 and 186.

6. Letter to Paul, 12 February 1843 and various letters to his sisters between February and May that year. *Ibid.*, III: 181-83 *et seqq.*

7. Venturi, p. 44; Carr, *Bakunin*, p. 111; MyPaT (G-H), II: 492; Kelly, p. 110.

8. Letter to his relatives, May 1843. Steklov, III: 220.

9. Letters of 11 and 19 March 1843.

10. Carr, *Bakunin*, pp. 119-20.

11. Bakunin, *Communism*, June 1843 (quoted in Mendel, pp. 190-91, and in Kelly, p. 115).

12. Hare, p. 25.

13. Letter to Ruge, May 1843. Steklov, III: 228.

14. Letter to his brother Paul, 29 March 1845. Steklov, III: 247, and see Mendel's comment on p. 199: 'Even the Soviet editor of Bakunin's letters, who strains mightily to preserve an image of normality and rationality in his notes on Bakunin, concludes that he is talking abnout his love for the "people".'

15. Mendel, p. 208.

16. Letters of 9 October and 7 April 1842, in that order. Steklov, III: 123-24 and 122. Also in Mendel, p.179.

17. Letter of 1 May 1845, *ibid.*, III: 251.

18. Letter of 29 March 1845, *ibid.*, III: 247.

19. Carr, *Bakunin*, pp. 7-8.

20. Mendel, pp. 198, 208.

21. Hare, p. 25.

22. For the full letter in English see EW, pp. 200-06 and ET, pp. 74-79.

23. See Bernstein. According to Andreas , Schapper was at the barricades by accident or as a personal combatant, but may have given Engels the impression that the League as a whole took part in the insurrection. Engels wrote his account, '*Zur Geschichte des Bundes der Kommunisten*', in 1885, when introducing a new edition of Karl Marx's '*Enthüllungen über den Kommunisten-Prozess zu Köln*'.

24. The original titles of Weitling's two publications were *Die Menschheit, wie sie ist und wie sie sein sollte* and *Garantien der Harmonie und Freiheit.*

25. Bluntschli, pp. 91-92.

26. *Ibid.*, p. 11.

27. *Ibid.*, pp. 49-50 and 64. Emphasis in original.

28. Hess AS, pp. 138, 136-37, in this order. Emphasis in original.

29. Bluntschli, pp. 62, 64.

30. Bluntschli, *Denkwürdigkeiten aus meinem Leben*, 1884, p. 341.

31. Ewerbeck, Seiler and Becker to Weitling between February and May 1843. Bluntschli, *Die Kommunisten...*, pp. 106, 113, 118, 186.

32. Quoted in Barnikol, pp. 131-32.

33. *Ibid.*, pp. 122-23.

34. *Ibid.*, p. 131.

35. EW, p. 206.

36. *Ibid.*, pp. 207-08 and ET, p. 81.

37. EW, p. 58.

38. *Ibid.*, pp. 62-63.

39. *Ibid.*, pp. 98, 107-08, and ET, p. 81.

40. Marx in 1873, harking back to his 1843 Hegel Critique in an Afterword to the first volume of *Das Kapital*, 2nd ed. Marx and Engels, *Selected Works*, Moscow 1962, v. I, p. 436. However, the simile about Hegel's treating society 'like a stepmother' was coined by Engels in *Die Zukunft* in 1869.

41. J.M. Jost, *Neuere Geschichte der Israeliten 1815-1845*, Berlin 1846, pp. 295-96

42. Becker, p. 21

43. MECW, I: 400

44. EW, pp. 212-17

45. EW, pp. 221, 220 in this order

46. 'Engels, Feuerbach and the End of Classical German Philosophy', in *Neue Zeit* (1886), Nos. 4 and 5

47. EW, p. 233

48. 'Die Fähigkeit der heutigen Juden und Christen frei zu werden', published in *Einundzwanzig Bogen aus der Schweiz*, ed. Georg Herwegh, Zurich 1843.

49. EW, pp. 235-41

50. Künzli, p. 203

NOTES TO CHAPTER 29

1. Mazlish, p. 74.

2. Carlebach, p. 178.

3. Edmund Silberner, 'Was Marx an Anti-Semite?', in *Historia Judaica*, XI, 1 (April 1949): 27. Silberner was at the time teaching at Princeton University.

4. 'On The Jewish Question', Marx EW: 238-39.

5. Silberner, *op. cit.*, p. 37.

6. Mazlish, pp. 7, 17.

7. *Ibid.*, pp. 146-47.

8. Heer, p. 112, and *cf.* Padover, p. 3.

9. Pearl, p. 10.

10. Cf. Kadourie, p. 175.

11. For the text of the full note see Pearl. One or two other unfinished tractates were completed by RASHI's disciples and his grandsons.

12. According to another theory held by some genealogists, it was a daughter of Rabbi Yom

Tov of Falaise - and thus a great-granddaughter of RASHI by way of Miriam, and not Jochebed - who married Jehiel ben Mattathias (Trèves). The proponents of this theory cite in its support a tradition prevailing in the family of Gabriel Riesser, the famous spokesman of the 1848-49 Frankfurt National Assembly and champion of German-Jewish emancipation. I shall not go into this dispute, for in either case it was a granddaughter of RASHI whose alliance with the Trèves leads to the Luria family.

13. In 1755 Hirsch 'Hijman' or Hyman Pressburg represented Hungary's Jews in the matter of the so-called 'tolerance' tax. Otherwise he was a Purveyor to the Vienna Mint. Married to Tamar Randel, a daughter of Rabbi Elia Ellenbogen, he died in 1773.

14. Indeed, the genealogical chart of Karl Marx circulated by the Study Centre in Trier connects Hirsch 'Hijman' with Isaac Pressburg merely by a horizontal bracket, indicating presumed paternity; and a note in small print at the top of the chart contains the reservation that Isaac Pressburg was 'most likely' the son of Hirsch Pressburg.

15. The statue built by Ladislav Saloun shows a young girl reaching up to the towering figure of the 'Exalted Rabbi' to offer him a rose. It immortalizes the legend that the Angel of Death, helpless against the MaHaRaL's otherworldly powers and unable to get at his soul, hid himself in a rose which the Rabbi's daughter innocently offered, and which the old man knowingly accepted in order not to hurt her feelings.

16. Jorge Luis Borges, in his poem 'The Golem', had 'Judah Lion' create his 'doll' and 'explain the universe to him,' and then wondered philosophically: 'Who can tell us what God felt / As he gazed on His rabbi in Prague?'

17. Norbert Wiener, *God and Golem*, Cambridge, MA, 1964.

18. The meeting was recorded by the rabbi's son-in-law, who was present, and by his student David Gans (who drew maps for Tycho Brahe). Between them they noted that it dealt with 'secret things', that the Emperor's reception of Judah Loew was 'warm and gracious', and that the two spoke 'face to face' as equals.

19. Sherwin.

20. *Netzach Israel* ('The Eternity of Israel'), Prague 1599, London 1960; Jerusalem, 1964; and in vol. 6 of the MaHaRaL's collected writings, *Kol Sifrei MaHaRaL Mi-Prag*, 12 vols, New York 1969. Two of the MaHaRaL's manuscripts are in the Bodleian Library, Oxford.

21. Buber, *On Zion*, p. 77.

22. Steiner remarked that Marx's wish to see the Jews 'dissolve' themselves in 'the anonymity of mankind' could be seen as 'a parodistic inversion' of the prophetic image of the redemption of all men at the end of days. George Steiner, *op. cit.*, p. 75.

23. Marx, 'The Eighteenth Brumaire of Louis Bonaparte', in Robert C. Tucker (ed.), *The Marx-Engels Reader*, pp. 594-95.

24. Pierre Grimal, *Dictionary of Classical Mythology*, Harmondsworth 1991.

25. Ludwig Feuerbach, *The Essence of Christianity*, 2nd ed. (tr. Marian Evans), London 1893, p. 298 (originally *Das Wesen des Christentums*, 1841).

26. Poliakov, p. 422.

27. See Feuerbach's letter of 21 October 1851 in his *Sämtliche Werke* (ed. W. Bolin), 1904; new ed. by H.M. Sass, Stuttgart 1964, v. 13, p. 189.

28. MECW, VI: 631. Minutes of Marx's report to the London German Workers' Educational Society on 30 November 1847.

29. Marx to Engels, 10 May 1861, MEW, V: 94.

30. Carlebach, *op. cit.*, pp. 152-53.

31. Berlin, *Karl Marx*, p. 100.

32. Otto Rühle, *Karl Marx*, New York 1929, p. 377.

33. N. Rotenstreich, 'For and Against Emancipation: The Bruno Bauer Controversy', Yearbook of the Leo Baeck Institute, 4 (1959): 26.

34. Padover, p. 167; Mazlish, pp. 75-76.

35. Padover, p. 171.

36. Wolfson, pp. 76, 92.

37. Blumenberg, p. 58.

38. T. Lessing, *Der Jüdische Selbsthass*, Berlin 1930.

39. *Kritische Geschichte der Nationalökonomie und des Sozialismus*, Berlin 1875, p. 574.

40. *Geschlecht und Charakter*, Vienna/Leipzig 1903.

41. See *Encyclopaedia Judaica*, XI: 50.

42. The first two articles appeared on 9 and 22 September 1855; the third on 4 January 1856. Marx started writing for the *New-York Daily Tribune* in 1851. In the course of 1853 and 1854, the paper published about 120 articles signed by him (though some were actually written by Engels). In July 1855, Marx's name disappeared from the columns of the paper, and his articles from then on bore a byline identifying him as one of the paper's foreign correspondents.

43. Silberner, *op. cit.*, p. 33.

44. For a discussion of the three articles under review see also Arthur Prinz, 'New Perspectives on Marx as a Jew', in Yearbook of the Leo Baeck Institute, 15 (1970), pp. 109-10.

45. Künzli, p. 212.

46. *Ibid.*, pp. 202, 212.

47. *Ibid.*, p. 213, quoting Jolande Jacobi's *Die Psychologie von C.G. Jung*, Zürich 1959.

48. *Ibidem.*

49. Berlin, *op. cit.*, p. 269.

50. Künzli, p. 305.

51. See the poems 'Invocation of One in Despair' and 'Human Pride' in MECW, pp. 563-64 and 584-85.

52. Letters to Engels of 18 June 1862, 5 January 1882 and 14 August 1879.

53. Letter of 22 February 1858.

54. Künzli, p. 306.
55. EW, p. 209.
56. Tucker, p. 144.
57. Künzli, pp. 512 and 560.
58. *Ibid.*, pp. 565-66.
59. *Ibid.*, p. 560.
60. *Ibid.*, pp. 371-73.
61. Avineri, *The Social and Political Thought of Karl Marx*, p. 144.
62. MEW, VII: 79.
63. Silberner, *op. cit.*, pp. 46-48.
64. Carlebach, p. 324.
65. Kapp, v. II, pp. 510-11.
66. *Ibid.*, p. 514.
67. *Ibid.*, p. 260.
68. Quoted in Carlebach, p. 317.
69. Heer, p. 112.
70. For Hitler's August 1920 speech see R.H. Phelts (ed.), 'Hitlers "Grundlegende" Rede über den Antisemitismus', *Vierteljahrshefte für Zeitgeschichte*, 16 (4), 1968, pp. 414-15.
71. Silberner's 52-page English essay, 'Was Marx an Anti-Semite?', became Chapter 8 of his German book *Sozialisten zur Judenfrage*, published in 1962. Quotations here are from the original essay in *Historia Judaica*, v. XI (April 1949): 15 and 52.
72. *Proverbs*, 18:21.
73. Padover, p. 648; Mazlish, p. 176.

NOTES TO CHAPTER 30

1. Elster, VI: 409.
2. Its title was 'Towards A Critique of Hegel's Philosophy of Right. Introduction'.
3. *The Holy Family*, p. 125.
4. EW, p. 244.
5. *Ibid.*, pp. 244-45. Italics in the original. Translation slightly adapted from Louis S. Feuer (ed.), *Marx & Engels; Basic Writings on Politics and Philosophy*, London 1984.
6. EW, pp. 245, 249.
7. Mazlish, p. 79.
8. EW, p. 244.
9. *Ibid.*, p. 256.
10. *Ibid.*, pp. 244, 257.
11. *Ibid.*., pp. 256-57. Emphasis in original.
12. For Heine on opium, see Elster, VII: 116; for Hess, AS: 149.
13. See Lovell, *Marx's Proletariat*, p. 8.
14. EW, p. 207.
15. Künzli, p. 637, quoting *Exodus*, 6:9: 'But they hearkened not unto Moses for anguish of spirit, and for cruel bondage.'
16. Georg Herwegh's letters, edited by his son Marcel, as quoted in *Gespraeche*, I: 20.
17. To Feuerbach, Kreuznach, 3 October 1843. MECW, III: 349-50.
18. Ruge's proposal to Marx in MEGA 1, I(2): 315; Emma Herwegh's reaction in *Gespraeche*, I: 20.
19. Tucker, p. 113.
20. Marx to Fröbel in Zurich. MECW, III: 351-53.
21. Ruge to Marx, 1 December 1843. MEGA 2, III/1: 422.

22. Heine to Campe, 29 December 1843. Hirth, II: 496 ff.
23. Letters in German, Zentralarchiv, Abt. Merseburg. Quoted in Silberner, p. 179.
24. Hess AS, p. 87.
25. Marx to Ruge, May and September 1843. EW, pp. 206-07.
26. Letter to Auerbach, 19 June 1843. Hess Bw, pp. 102-03.
27. Engels in 'Progress of Social Reform on the Continent', published in November 1843 in Robert Owen's *New Moral World*.
28. Jenny Marx, 'Short Sketch of an Eventful Life' (1865), in REM, p. 222.
29. Ruge to his mother, 19 May 1844, in *Gespraeche*, I: 27-28.
30. Quoted in Carr, *The Romantic Exiles*, p. 56.
31. Ruge to the publisher F.G. Duncker, 29 August 1844, *Gespraeche*, I: 30.
32. Ruge to Feuerbach. *Ibid.*, I: 23-24.
33. From Herwegh's letters, *op. cit.*, I: 20.
34. See Padover, p. 177.

NOTES TO CHAPTER 31

1. Cf. Sammons, p. 261.
2. Published in the *Revue des Deux Mondes*, 15 September 1854.
3. See Fejtö, an early exponent of this trend, p. 256; and Sammons, *op. cit.*, p. 261: 'At times Heine has been maneuvered into the role of John the Baptist to Marx's Christ.'
4. Reeves, *Heinrich Heine: Poetry and Politics*, p. 153.
5. William Rose, *Heinrich Heine*; 'more recent authorities': see Sammons, *op. cit.*, p. 262.
6. Written on 30 March 1855. Elster, VI: 572. *Lutèce* was a two-volume collection of the articles published by Heine in the *Augsburger Allgemeine Zeitung* between 1840 and 1844.
7. *Ibid.*, VI: 572-73.
8. *Ruge's Briefwechsel und Tagebuchblätter aus dem Jahren 1825-80*, Berlin 1886, II: 346.
9. Letter of 1 February 1845. MECW, XXXVIII: 21.
10. Letter to Mathilde, 31 October 1843. Hirth, II: 477.
11. *Ibid.*: 490.
12. Sammons, *op. cit.*, p. 268.
13. German original in Elster, II: 429-30; English in CPHH, p. 482.
14. See Ross Atkinson, 'Irony and Commitment in Heine's *Deutschland ein Wintermärchen*', *Germanic Review*, v. 50, May 1975; Sammons, *op. cit.*; and Robertson.
15. Rose, p. 62.
16. *Ibid.*, p. 68.
17. Letters to Campe (17 April 1844) and to Kolb (12 April 1844), Hirth, II: 506, 504.
18. To Campe (5 June 1844) and to Johann Herman Detmold (14 September 1844). *Ibid.*: 516, 538.
19. He stressed this point again in a letter written

later in 1844 to Caroline Jaubert. To Marx, 21 September 1844; to Jaubert, 16 December 1844. Hirth, II: 542, 557.
20. Elster, VI: 572.
21. *Ibid.*, VI: 573.
22. 'Communism, Philosophy and Clerisy', 15 June 1843. *Ibid.*, VI: 419.
23. Written on 30 March 1855. Elster, VI: 573.
24. Th. Creizenach, 'Mitteilungen über Heine', 19 April 1856, in *Frankfurter Museum*, No. 16, p. 123. Quoted in *Begegnungen*, p. 551.
25. Elster, IV: 157.
26. *Ibid.*, V: 327 and 329.
27. Hal Draper's translation in CPHH, pp. 550-51; one line omitted.
28. From Hamburg, 21 September 1844. Hirth, II: 543.
29. Karl Kautsky, 'Heine und Marx' (based on information from Eleanor Marx-Aveling) in *Die Neue Zeit*, XIV, 1895/96, v. I, No. 1, p. 16.

NOTES TO CHAPTER 32
1. Jenny to Karl Marx in Paris, 21 June 1844. MEGA 2, III/1: 428.
2. EW, p. 281.
3. See Avineri, *Hegel's Theory...*, p. 154.
4. *Ibidem.*
5. In *An Inquiry into the Nature and Causes of the Wealth of Nations.*
6. Schulz's book, published in 1843 in Zurich, was titled *The Movement of Production (Die Bewegung der Produktion)*. On Schulz see Grab, *Ein Mann der Marx Ideen gab.*
7. EW, p. 359.
8. *Ibid.*, p. 326.
9. *Ibid.*, pp. 356-57.
10. EW, pp. 378-79.
11. *Timon of Athens*, Act. IV, Scene 3.
12. EW, p. 377.
13. McLellan, *Karl Marx*, p. 264.
14. Quoted in Padover, pp. 176-77.
15. *Ibid.*, p. 430.
16. Letters of mid-August and of 4-7 August 1844. MEGA 2, III/1: 441-42 and 439.
17. Jenny Marx, *op. cit.*, p. 228.
18. Mazlish, p. 87.
19. Künzli, pp. 581-87.
20. Marx to Sigfried Meyer, 10 April 1867. MEW, XXXI: 542.
21. Künzli, p. 588.
22. Ruge to Ludwig Feuerbach, in *Gespraeche*, I: 23.
23. EW, p. 379.
24. EW, p. 348.
25. MECW, IV: 36-37.
26. Engels, 'The Burial of Karl Marx,' in *Der Sozialdemokrat*, 22 March 1883.
27. Conway, pp. 80-81.
28. See Meyerbeer, *Briefwechsel und Tagebücher* (ed. Hans and Gudrun Becker), III: 767.
29. Draper, CPHH, p. 544.
30. EW, pp. 402 and 416-17.
31. *Ibid.*, p.420.
32. A point noted by Maximilien Rubel, 'Socialism and the Commune' in E. Kamenka (ed.), *Paradigm for Revolution?*, p. 46 and by Lovell, *Marx's Proletariat*, p. 99.
33. EW, p. 415.
34. Jacques Grandjonc at an International Heine Congress. Kongress, p. 167.
35. EW, pp. 415-16.
36. Quoted in Sagarra, p. 397.
37. Ruge to his mother, 19 May 1844, *Gespraeche*, I: 26, 27.
38. Letter of 11-18 August 1844. MEGA 2, III/1: 440.
39. Belinsky to Annenkov in 1840. See Annenkov, p. 27.
40. Heinrich Börnstein, *Fünfundsiebzig Jahre in der Alten und Neuen Welt. Memoiren eines Unbedeutenden*, 2nd ed., Leipzig 1884, v. I, pp. 350-53.
41. *Ibidem.*
42. Marx to Schweitzer. *Marx-Engels Selected Works*, Moscow 1935, v. I, p. 392.
43. Bakunin wrote this in 1871 in an essay on his personal relations with Marx. Quoted in English in Carr, *Bakunin*, pp. 129-30.
44. This scene, related by Vogt to Herzen and to find its way into most Socialist literature, did not, according to some accounts, take place in 1844, but in 1847. See Herzen, MyPaT(DM): 422.
45. Written in 1870. Quoted in Dolgoff, p. 25.
46. *Gespraeche*, I: 39.
47. *Ibid.*, II: 709-10.
48. Letter of September 1843. EW, p. 209.
49. See Theodore Zeldin, *Politics and Anger (France 1848-1945)*, Oxford 1975, pp. 106-07.
50. Letter of 9 March 1847. MECW, XXXVIII: 115.
51. Catlin, p. 565.
52. Letter of 19 November 1844.
53. Engels to Marx, 22 February - 7 March, 1845. MECW, XXXVIII: 22.
54. Wilson, p. 147; Künzli, p. 375.
55. Engels, *Ludwig Feuerbach and the End of Classical German Philosophy*, Moscow 1950 (German original: Stuttgart 1880.)
56. 'London Letters' (*Briefe aus London*), published in the *Schweizerischer Republikaner*, 27 May 1843.
57. Henderson, v. 1, p. 27.
58. Engels to Marx, early October 1844. MECW, XXXVIII: 6.
59. Letters of 4-7 and 11-18 August 1844. MEGA 2, III/1: 439-42.
60. To Charlotte Embden, 29 December 1844. Hirth, II: 564.
61. Letters of 14 and 20 September 1844. Hirth, II: 538, 542.
62. Heine's letter to Marx in Hirth, II: 541-43, and see his *Confessions*, Elster, VI: 44-45.
63. In *Die Neue Zeit*, v. 14 (1895-96), p. 17.
64. MECW, XXXVIII: 8.
65. McLellan, *Karl Marx*, p. 133.

NOTES TO CHAPTER 33

1. To Marx, on or about 20 January 1845. MECW, XXXVIII: 19-20.
2. To Marx, 22 February-7 March 1845, *ibidem*.
3. Hess to Marx in Paris, 3 July, 1844. MEGA 2, III/1: 434.
4. Silberner, p. 211.
5. Letter of 22 February-7 March 1845, MECW, XXXVIII: 23.
6. Engels to Marx, 17 March 1845, *Ibid.*: 28-30.
7. Padover, p. 225.
8. McLellan, *Karl Marx*, p. 138.
9. Heer, p. 139.
10. Letter on or about 20 January 1845. MECW, XXXVIII: 16.
11. Henderson, v. I, p. 30.
12. Quoted in Nicolaievsky, p. 120.
13. Friedrich Engels, *The Festival of Nations in London*. MECW, VI: 12-13.
14. *Ibid.*, p. 5.
15. Padover, p. 238.
16. Marx to Proudhon, 5 May 1846. MECW, XXXVIII: 38-39.
17. To Marx, 6 May 1846. Hess Bw, p. 153.
18. Arthur P. Mendel (ed.), in his Introduction to Annenkov, p. IX.
19. Quoted in Hunt, v. I, pp. 155-56.
20. Hess Bw, pp. 150-51.
21. Karl Marx, Herr Vogt, MEW, XIV: 439.
22. McLellan, *op. cit.*, p. 157, n. 4.
23. *Correspondance de J.P. Proudhon*, Paris 1875, v. II, pp. 198-202.
24. MECW, XXXVIII: 39-40.
25. Quoted in Silberner, p. 252. Grün's lecture was delivered on 28 April 1844 at Bielefeld.
26. Hess Bw, p. 155.
27. *Ibid.*, p. 157.
28. Marx to Weydemeyer, 14-16 May 1846. MECW, XXXVIII: 41-42.
29. Marx in 1859 in the preface to *A Contribution to the Critique of Political Economy*.
30. MECW, V: 38.
31. *Ibid.*: 6-8.
32. Weydemeyer and Marx were eventually reconciled and Weydemeyer became a member of the Communist League before he emigrated in 1851 to the USA. In New York he founded the journal *The Revolution* which propagated Marx's ideas. He served as a brigadier general in the Union army during the Civil War. See Padover, pp. 203-04.
33. Marx to Engels in Paris, 15 May 1847. MECW, XXXVIII: 117-18.
34. Hess was referring to Engels's mistress Mary Burns. Hess Bw, p. 157.
35. MECW, V: 491.
36. Hess's essay was 'Dr Georg Kuhlmann of Holstein or The Prophecy of True Socialism', *Ibid.*, pp. 531-39.
37. Engels to Marx, 27 July, and Engels and Marx to Hess in Cologne 27-29 July 1846. MECW, XXXVIII: 46, 47.
38. MEGA 1, Part III, 1: 27.
39. Henderson, v. I, p. 89.
40. S. Na'aman, in his 1982 biography of Hess, p. 210.
41. Engels to Marx in Brussels, 15 January 1847. MECW, XXXVIII: 108.
42. Marx to Köttgen, 15 June 1846. MEW, IV: 21 ff.
43. Henderson, v. I, pp. 96-97.
44. MECW, XXXVIII: 89-91.
45. Shapper to Marx, 6 June 1846. Andreas, quoted here from the German edition, 1968, 1: 347.
46. To Marx, 9 March 1847. MECW, XXXVIII: 115.
47. See Andreas.
48. Rules of the Communist League. MECW, VI: 585-86.
49. Engels to Marx, 25 October 1848. MECW, XXXVIII: 138-39.
50. Cf. Raddatz, *Karl Marx*, p. 126.
51. Avineri, *Moses Hess*, p. 115.
52. Preface to his *Critique of Political Economy*, 1859.
53. Lucio Colletti in *Introduction to Marx*, EW, p. 8; and Tucker, p. 106.
54. Hunt, v. I, p. 131.
55. *Gespraeche*, II: 714.
56. See Silberner (1966), Tucker (1951), D. McLellan (1969 and 1973).
57. S. Na'aman, *Emanzipation und Messianismus*, p. 133.
58. Avineri, *op. cit.*, p. 133.
59. Rosen, p. 9.
60. *Ibid.*, p, 134 and *passim*.

NOTES TO CHAPTER 34

1. Hirth, II: 564.
2. Letter of 30 December 1844, HSA, 26: 123-24.
3. Cf. Sammons, *op. cit.*, p. 279, and Na'aman, *Lassalle*, p. 61.
4. Letter To Campe, 8 January and 4 February 1845. Hirth, III; 3.
5. Meyerbeer to Heine, undated, written some time before 31 October 1845. HSA, 26: 138.
6. Hirth, VI: 9-12.
7. Hirth, III: 5.
8. *Ibid.*: 6.
9. Letter of 4 February 1844. *Ibid*: 14-21.
10. Sammons, *op. cit.*, pp. 279-80.
11. Hirth, III: 29-31.
12. Diary, 23-24 July and 26 August 1840. All Diary entries are from Ferdinand Lassalles, *Tagebuch* (ed. Paul Lindau), Breslau 1891.
13. Uexküll, p. 38.
14. Diary, April or May 1841.
15. *Ibid.*, 21 May 1840.
16. Letter to his father, 13 May 1844. *Ferdinand Lassalle, Nachgelassene Briefe und Schriften*, ed. Gustav Mayer (6 vols), Stuttgart-Berlin 1921-25, v. I, p. 87.
17. Uexküll, p. 38.

18. Na'aman, *op. cit.*, p. 28.
19. Mayer, *Lassalle Nachlass*, v. I, pp. 89-90.
20. *Ibid.*, pp. 101-02.
21. 'Letter on Industry', *Ibid.*, pp. 114-136, 'War Manifesto', pp. 213-31.
22. Diary, 9 September 1840.
23. Hirth, III: 36.
24. Pückler to Karl Heine, 28 January 1846. Hirth, VI: 35-37.
25. The poem involved was 'The New Alexander', of which the Police Minister sent Humboldt a copy on 28 January 1846. *Ibid.*: 30.
26. *Ibid.*, II: 47, 67.
27. MECW, XXXVIII: 65.
28. Hirth, III: 107.
29. German original in Elster, II: 108, English in Draper, CPHH, pp. 88-89.
30. From his famous 40-page letter to Sophie Sontzeff, a Russian-born lady whom he wished to marry. Hans Feigl (ed.), *Ferdinand Lassalle: Reden und Schriften, Tagebuch, Seelenbeichte*, Vienna 1911, p. 102 and *passim*.
31. Uexküll, p. 75.
32. *Ibid.* (condensed from his letter of 22 September 1840).
33. Wilson, p. 234.
34. Mayer, *Lassalle Nachlass*, v. IV, pp. 2f.
35. Letter to Sophie Sontzeff. Feigl, *op. cit.*, p. 101.
36. Lassalle to Humboldt, 25 October 1846. Mayer, *op. cit.*, v. II, p. 279.
37. Cf. Na'amann, *Lassalle*, p. 109.
38. Mayer, *op. cit.*, v. I, p. 338.
39. For a detailed account and analysis of the episode see S. Na'aman, *op. cit.*, pp. 106-07.
40. Steklov, III: 241-42.
41. Quoted in Mendel, p. 196.
42. *Ibidem.*
43. Bakunin, 'Confession'. Steklov, IV: 111, 115 (in Mendel, p. 196).
44. Letter of 1 May 1845. Steklov, III: 251-52. Carr mentions three letters but quotes only a short section of one of them. The longer extracts that follow here are from Mendel's *Bakunin*, pp. 197-99.
45. Letters to Paul, 29 March 1845 and April 1843. Steklov, III: 247, and 203-04.
46. Letter to Annenkov and other friends. In *The Extraordinary Decade*, pp. 182-83, Annenkov dated this letter 'October 1847', though it appears from the context that it was written from Brussels after Bakunin's expulsion from Paris in mid-December 1847.
47. Herzen, MyPaT (DM): 323-24.
48. Annenkov, p. 164.
49. MyPaT (G-H), II: 961.
50. Quoted in Venturi, p. 49.
51. Mendel, p. 202.
52. Cf. Yarmolinsky, p. 173; and . Venturi, p. 50.
53. Quoted in E. Lampert, *Studies in Rebellion*, London 1957.
54. Annenkov, p. 224.
55. *Ibid.*, p. 230.
56. Belinsky, *Pisma* (Letters), III: 328.
57. Annenkov, p. 232; Herzen, MyPaT (DM): 245.
58. See the chapter on N.I. Sazonov in MyPaT (G-H), II.
59. To Georg and Emma Herwegh, 6 September 1847. Steklov, III: 265.
60. Dolgoff, p. 60.
61. Marx to Georg Herwegh, 26 October 1847. MECW, XXXVIII: 141.
62. Marx to Georg Herwegh, 8 August 1847. MEW, XXVII: 467.
63. MECW, VI: 389.
64. Quoted with slight variations in most works on Bakunin and/or Marx. Given here from Carr's *Bakunin*, p. 146 and Venturi, p. 52.

NOTES TO CHAPTER 35

1. Stephan Born, *Erinnerungen eines Achtundvierzigers*, Leipzig 1898. Quoted in *Gespraeche*, I: 76-77.
2. *Ibidem.*
3. *Ibid.*, p. 81.
4. Engels to Marx. Paris, 14 January 1848. MECW, XXXVIII: 153.
5. *Ibidem.*
6. The Central Authority to the League, in MECW, VI: 603-04.
7. *Ibid.*: 604-09.
8. *Ibid.*: 610.
9. *Ibid.*: 212. The phrase Marx borrowed from George Sand appeared in her *Jean Ziska. Episode de la guerre des hussites*. Introduction.
10. Heinzen's reply to Engels was published in the DBZ on 21 October 1847. Marx's lengthy essay appeared on 18 and 31 October, and was continued on 11, 18 and 25 November, MECW, VI: 682.
11. Weerth's and Marx's speeches as reported by Engels in *The Northern Star*. MECW, VI: 285, 290.
12. MECW, XXXVIII: 138-39.
13. Stephan Born, *op. cit.*, quoted in *Gespraeche*, I: 74.
14. Na'aman, *op. cit.*, p. 220.
15. Friedrich Lessner, 'Vor 1848 und nachher', Wien 1898, pp. 109, 154-60.
16. *Rules of the Communist League*, London, 8 December 1847. MECW, VI: 633.
17. MECW, XXXVIII: 150-51.
18. Na'aman, *op. cit.*
19. Hess's article in Hess AS: 193-205. A comprehensive English summary of the article will be found in Avineri, *Moses Hess*.
20. MECW, XXXVIII: 146.
21. See *George Sand in Her Own Words*, *op. cit.*, p. 373.
22. The first English version of *The Communist Manifesto* appeared in London in 1850. Many other translations were published in the 20th century in various Englisn anthologies and collections of Marx's and Engels's writings. The quotations in this chapter are taken mostly from v. 6 of the 40-volume MECW

(Marx and Engels: Collected Works) which – published in Moscow, London and New York in 1975-84 under the aegis of the Moscow Institute of Marxism-Leninism – may be regarded as the 'authorized' English version of their writings.

23. Avineri, *op. cit.*, p. 152 and his *Social and Political Thought of Karl Marx*, p. 206.

24. Engels, 'The Movements of 1847'. MECW, VI: 528-29.

25. Maximilien Rubel, *Flora Tristan et Karl Marx*, Paris 1946.

26. Cf. Wolfson, p. 223.

27. MECW, V: 247.

28. Louis Feuer, *op. cit.*, pp. 312-13.

29. Schurz, *Reminiscences*, London 1909, v. I, pp. 138f.

30. MECW, XXXVIII: 153.

31. MECW, VI: 512.

32. For Engels's note, appended to the 1890 German edition of the *Manifesto*, see MECW, VI: 513.

33. For a review of the anti-Hess literature see Rosen.

34. Marx in the Preface to his *A Contribution to the Critique of Political Economy*, published in London in 1859. See *The Portable Karl Marx*, selected and introd. by Eugene Kamenka, Harmondsworth 1983, p. 161.

35. Silberner, p. 282; Tucker, p. 113.

36. Na'aman, *Emanzipation und Messianismus*, p. 227.

37. See Avineri, *Moses Hess*, p. 244.

38. Engels to Johann Philipp Becker, 15 October 1884. Eleanor Marx, REM, p. 188.

39. Letter of 19 January 1848. Hirth, III: 130.

40. Werner, II: 99-100.

NOTES TO CHAPTER 36

1. Johnson, p. 258.

2. Lucas-Dubreton, p. 643.

3. Condensed from the report in the *Moniteur officiel* of 25 February 1848. See Beik, pp. 179-86.

4. Victor Hugo, *Things Seen* (ed. and trans. by David Kimber, Intro. by Joanna Richardson), Oxford 1964, pp. 192-94.

5. Béranger in Lucas-Dubreton, p. 643; 'could not banquet', etc. in Johnson, p. 261. For the various reasons that led to the February rising, see also Howarth; Breunig; and Zeldin.

6. Marx in an article in the *Neue Rheinische Zeitung*, 29 June 1848; Bakunin in his Confession to the Tsar, *Steklov*, IV: 122-23.

7. Jenny Marx, *op. cit.*, pp. 133-34.

8. Herzen, MyPaT (G-H), III: 1353; Carr, *Bakunin*, p. 150.

9. MECW, XXXVIII: 159-60.

10. Steklov, III: 294-96.

11. MECW, XXXVIII: 172-73.

12. For the controversy about Marx's dissolution of the Communist League see McLellan, *op.*

cit., p. 197 and Nicolaievsky and Maenchen-Helfen, *op. cit.*, pp. 414-17.

13. *Ibid.*, p. 185.

14. Nicolaievsky and Maenchen-Helfen, *op. cit.*, p. 169.

15. Feuer, *op. cit.*, p. 29.

16. Letter of 25 April 1848. MECW, XXXVIII: 173.

17. Engels, 'Marx und die Neue Rheinische Zeitung.' 13 March 1884. MEW XXI: 15-19 (condensed).

18. *Ibid.*, p. 22.

19. Marx, *The Revolutions of 1848* (*Political Writings*, v. I, ed. David Fernbach, Harmondsworth 1978, pp. 126-27).

20. Engels, 'Germany's Foreign Policy', in *Neue Rheinishe Zeitung*, 3 July 1848. MECW, VII: 165-66.

21. Quoted in Silberner, p. 291.

22. Marx, *The Revolutions of 1848* (see n. 19 above), pp. 129-34.

23. Engels, 'The 23rd of June'. MECW, VII: 130, 164.

24. Sammons, *op. cit.*, p. 304.

25. *Ibid.*, p. 303; on Georg Weerth's mediation, see Hirth, VI: 72.

26. Elster, I: 487.

27. Werner, II: 116.

28. Hirth, III: 147.

29. *Ibid.*: 148 (to his mother, 26 June) and 145 (to his sister, 12 June 1848).

30. *Ibid.*, III: 151.

31. *Ibid.*: 152-53.

32. Elster, II: 201-02.

33. Steklov, IV: 161-63. Mendel, pp. 220-21.

34. Report in *Der Wächter am Rhein*, Cologne, 23 August 1848, reproduced by H. Meyer in *Historische Zeitschrift*, December 1951, p. 524.

35. Oncken, pp. 109-13.

36. Na'aman, *op. cit.*, p. 114.

37. The official was Wilhelm von Merckel. See Uexküll, p. 61.

38. MECW, VII: 586-87.

39. G. Mann, *The History of Germany*, pp. 178-79.

40. MECW, VII: 503-06.

41. Uexküll, p. 62.

42. E. Taylor, pp. 84-85.

43. Marx, 'The Bourgeoisie and the Counter-Revolution,' MEW, VI:124.

44. *Ibid.*: 149.

45. Marx, 'The Revolutionary Movement', MEW, VI: 149.

46. Steklov, III: 335-36, 340.

47. *Ibid.*, III: 49, 360 and 362 (in Mendel, pp. 224-25).

48. Henderson, v. I, p. 149.

49. MECW, XXXVIII: 177-79.

50. Engels, 'The Magyar Struggle' and 'Democratic Pan-Slavism', in Karl Marx, *The Revolutions of 1848, op. cit.*, v. I, pp. 213-45.

51. Marx, Speech in his defence, MEW, VI: 232.

52. Quoted in Wilson, p. 171. Nicolaievsky, p. 199.

53. G. Mann, *op. cit.*, p. 177.

54. Confession to the Tsar, Steklov, IV: 168.
55. *Ibid.*: 177–78.
56. A. Röckel, *Sachsens Erheburg und das Zucht-haus zu Waldheim*, Frankfurt 1865, pp. 144–45.
57. Carr, *Bakunin*, p. 106.
58. Confession to the Tsar. Steklov, IV: 180.
59. Quoted in Oncken, p. 73.

NOTES TO CHAPTER 37

1. Herzen, MyPaT(DM): 357.
2. W.O. Henderson (ed.), *Engels: Selected Writings*, Harmondsworth 1967, pp. 128–29.
3. MEW, VII: 553.
4. Wagner, *My Life* (transl. Andrew Gray, ed. Mary Whittall), Cambridge 1983, pp. 384–88.
5. Marx in the *New-York Daily Tribune*, 2 October 1852. Quoted in Dolgoff (ed.), p. 31.
6. Confession to the Tsar, Steklov, IV: 205.
7. Mendel, p. 240.
8. To Ruge, 15 October 1849; to Adolf Reichel 9 December 1849. Steklov, IV: 11–12 and 17.
9. Peter Kropotkin, *In Russian and French Prisons*, New York 1971, pp. 92–96.
10. Jenny to Weydemeyer, 20 May 1850 and to Adolph Cluss, 15 October 1852.
11. It was only after she and Marx were dead that Engels, in 1895, shortly before his own death, confessed to their youngest daughter Eleanor that Freddy was her half-brother. The secret of Marx's paternity and the relevant documents were first published in 1962 by Blumenberg, pp. 115f.
12. Letter to Engels, 31 July 1851. MEW, XXVII: 536.
13. Letter of 28 July 1855. MEW, XXVIII: 617.
14. Letter to Engels, 20 January 1857, MEW, XXIX: 97.
15. Marx to Weydemeyer, 2 August 1851.
16. Letters of 13 November 1863, 8 May 1863 and 20 November 1861. Quoted in Künzli, pp. 319–20.
17. *Ibid.*, pp. 320–21.
18. MEW, XXVIII: 161f.
19. Written in 1859 and quoted in Wilson, pp. 208–09.
20. Preface to the second edition of *History of Religion and Philosophy*.
21. Elster, 7: 54–55.
22. *Ibid.*: 60.
23. *Ibid.*: 55–56.
24. *Ibid.*: 53.
25. Liptzin, p. 68.
26. Elster, 6: 159.
27. Quoted in Venturi, p. 90.
28. Annenkov, pp. 188–91.
29. Herzen, *From the Other Shore & The Russian People and Socialism* (tr. Moura Budberg), Oxford 1979, pp. 128, 148.
30. Marx to Engels, 28 January 1863.
31. Barzun, pp. 190, 192.
32. See Uexküll, p. 7.
33. Barzun, pp. 190–91.

NOTES TO EPILOGUE

1. Carr, *Bakunin*, p. 239.
2. The concept of Realpolitik was launched by August Ludwig von Rochau in *Grundsätze der Realpolitik*, a widely read book published in Germany in 1853. Cf. Hajo Holborn, *Deutsche Geschichte in der Neuzeit*, Frankfurt 1981, v. II, p. 348.
3. R. Tucker (ed.), *The Marx-Engels Reader*, p 4.
4. Padover, p. 322.
5. MEW, XXX: 469, 471, 474.
6. Marx-Engels *Briefwechsel*, Berlin 1949, v. II, p. 547.
7. MEW, XXX: 131.
8. MEW, XXX: 578.
9. In the German original Engels had written '*plumpe*' (for clumsy). Marx writing to Lassalle wrote *grob* which in German means clumsy or coarse.
10. Herzen, *From the Other Shore...*, *op. cit.*, p. 190.
11. 'Cinderella's dowry' and 'Europe's noblest minds': see Yarmolinsky, pp. 90, 82, respectively.
12. *Ibid.*, p. 112.
13. Herzen, MyPaT (G-H), III: 1310.
14. *Ibid.*, III: 1344–1347.
15. Quoted in Masters, p. 163.
16. *Ibid.*; see also Carr, *Bakunin*, p. 206.
17. Quoted in Carr, *op. cit.*, p. 317.
18. Two other volumes of text were only published posthumously between 1905 and 1910 and two volumes of notes only in 1954.
19. For Engels's 'unscrupulous stratagem' see Henderson, v. II, pp. 404–06.
20. Engels from Manchester to Marx in London, 23 May 1851, MEW, XXXVIII: 363–65.
21. Marx to Engels, 20 July 1870, MEW, XXIII: 5.
22. Cf. Lovell, *Marx's Proletariat*, pp. 140, 179.
23. S. Avineri in *Haaretz* (23 March 1990, Hebrew).
24. Hess in the *Kölnische Zeitung*, 14 October 1843.
25. *Rome and Jerusalem*, p. 240.
26. Laharanne in his pamphlet *On The Oriental Question*, published in Paris in 1860, advocated the establishment of three states - Egyptian, Arab and Jewish - in the area from the Suez to Izmir.
27. Engels to Marx, 18 December 1868.
28. Quoted in Mendel, p. 309.
29. Quoted in Silberner, p. 602.
30. An excellent summary of *The Catechism of a Revolutionary* appeared in Wilson, pp. 276–77. Wilson, however, thought that it was composed jointly by Nechaev and Bakunin. This has since been disproved.
31. Quoted in Mendel, p. 317.
32. On the eve of their fight Marx had sent him an inscribed copy of it, and in spite of their antagonism, Bakunin had earlier translated *The Communist Manifesto*.
33. For a full account of (and previously unpublished documents on) relations between these three protagonists see Confino.

34. *Ibid.*, p. 275.
35. *The Civil War in France*, read by Marx to the General Council on 30 May 1871, issued the same year as a brochure in English and German, reprinted in 1891 in Berlin. Russian translation edited by Lenin, published in 1905, Odessa. See Tucker, *The Marx-Engels Reader*, pp. 618-52.
36. Berlin, *Karl Marx*, pp. 258-59.
37. Flerovsky was the pseudonym of V.V. Bervi, who in 1861 had proposed to the Tsar that the redemption payments of the bondmen be borne by the entire population. For this he had been confined to a lunatic asylum for half a year. In the 1870s he was sentenced to long-term confinement in northern Russia.
38. Rubel/Manala (ed.), *Marx without Myth*, p. 252.
39. *Ibid.*, p. 278; and see Ulam, p. 118.
40. Guillaume later wrote that during a prolonged stay in Berne with his influential friend Dr Vogt, Bakunin had tried to find out the chances of his obtaining Swiss citizenship 'in return for a public assurance that he would henceforth take no part in any revolutionary agitation.'
41. See Mendel, p. 307, on the Central Bureau at the top of this secret echelon being elected by its founding members, who before returning to their countries, 'delegated their powers to citizen B.'
42. Bakunin in his book *Gossudarstvemmost i Anarchiya* (State and Anarchy), Geneva 1873. Quoted in Padover, p. 180.
43. Quoted in Mendel, p. 426.
44. See Rubel/Manale, pp. 292-93.
45. *The Aims of Revolutionary Propaganda in Russia*, London 1874.
46. MEW, XVIII: 557.
47. Engels's articles published in *Der Volksstaat*, 16-21 April 1875; 'He still has to learn the ABC of Socialism', in MEW, XVIII: 557; for Tkachev's reply to Engels, see Venturi, pp. 415-16.
48. *Ibid.*, p. 205.
49. *Le Peuple belge* (Brussels), 2 March 1871; quoted in Silberner, pp. 630-31.
50. See MEW, XII, n. 127.
51. Quoted with abbrevations from Tucker, *The Marx-Engels Reader*, pp. 525-42.
52. The remains of Hess's parents were transferred together with his. The tombstone with the inscription '*Vater der deutschen Sozialdemokratie*', which survived the Nazi period, remained in its place at Cologne's old Jewish cemetery at Deutz. Silberner, pp. 644-50.
53. Arthur Arnoud, a refugee from the Paris Commune, quoted in Carr, *Bakunin*, pp. 477-78.
54. Quotations in Mendel, pp. 403, 412, 413.
55. Mendel, p. 414.
56. David Apter and James Joll (eds.), *Anarchism Today*, London 1971.
57. Mendel, pp. 424, 432.
58. Franziska Kugelmann in Mohr und General, *Erinnerungen an Marx und Engels*, Berlin 1964, p. 288.
59. Zasulich's letter dated 16 February 1881 in Shanin, pp. 98-99.
60. MEW, XXXV: 167.
61. *Ibid.*: 178.
62. Shanin, p. 18; and see Wada's essay on 'Marx and Revolutionary Russia', in the same volume, pp. 40-71.
63. MEW, IV: 576.
64. Quoted in Yarmolinsky, p. 338.
65. It was only in 1956 that his grave was moved to its present site and his cast-iron head surmounting a marble block was erected on the initiative of the then USSR.
66. See Engels, 'Appendix on Historical Materialism' in v. III of *Das Kapital* and 'Letters on Historical Materialism' in Tucker, *The Marx-Engels Reader*, pp. 760-68.
67. Marx to Joseph Weydemeyer, 5 March 1852, MEW, XXVIII: 507-08.
68. '"Marxists" and "anti-Marxists", both kinds have done their best to spoil my stay in France,' Marx to Engels, 20 September 1882, MEW, XXXV: 100.
69. *Rubel on Karl Marx*, p. 14.
70. Mazlish, *The Meaning of Karl Marx*, Oxford 1984, pp. 162 and 163.
71. Avineri, *The Social and Political Thought of Karl Marx*, p. 258.
72. Lovell, *From Marx to Lenin*, p. 197.
73. Pipes, *The Unknown Lenin*.
74. *Ibid.*, p. 50 (Document 24).
75. *Ibid.*, pp. 55-56 (Document 28).
76. *Ibid.*, pp. 151-54 (Document 94).
77. Marx to the Dutch Socialist Ferdinand D. Nieuwenhuis. Quoted in Padover, pp. 459-60.
78. For Marx's use of the 'dictatorship of the proletariat' concept or slogan see Hunt, v. I.
79. Karl Kautsky in *Dictatorship of the Proletariat*, 1918. Lenin's reply in the pamphlet *Kautsky the Renegade and Proletarian Revolution*.
80. Bertram D. Wolfe, *Three Who Made a Revolution*, London 1984, pp. 336-37.
81. Sumner, p. 49.
82. See Wilson, p. 451, and G. Mann, *The History of Germany*, p. 261.

Bibliography

Primary Sources and Abbreviations

A. Marx and Engels: Collected Works and Correspondence

In the spring of 1991 the Moscow Institute of Marxism-Leninism (MIML) and the International Institute for Social History in Amsterdam set up a joint editorial board of Western and Soviet scholars charged with the task of compiling a full and definitive critical 'Marx-Engels' edition. No such complete and objective edition exists to date, but this does not mean that the basic writings of the fathers of Marxism are not currently available. It only means that, until the internationally supervised edition of up to 100 projected volumes is ever completed, Eugene Kamenka's 1983 advice to students 'to move from one extant edition to the other, to consult single volumes, to make use of several languages' continues to hold good.

MEGA 1 *Marx-Engels Historisch-Kritische Gesamtausgabe.*
Started in 1927 and published on behalf of the MIML in Frankfurt and Berlin, vols. I–II were edited by David Ryazanov. When he was sent into exile (to die in a Stalinist prison), vols. III, IV, V, VI were edited by V. Adoratsky. In 1935, after 13 volumes - including two half-volumes - had appeared, publication was discontinued.
MEGA 1, I/1.1 stands for Section I, v. 1, 1st half-volume of this edition;
MEGA 1, I/1.2 for Section I, v. 1, 2nd half-volume;
MEGA 1, I/2 for Section 1, v. 2, followed in each case by the page number.

MEGA 2 *Marx-Engels Gesamtausgabe.*
Early in the 1970s the MIML and the East German Institute of Marxism-Leninism launched an ambitious project for a 100-volume 'Marx-Engels' edition (50 of text and 50 of notes and apparatus). Starting in 1972, several score volumes, not all of them in consecutive order, of the German edition (known as MEGA 2), were published by Dietz Verlag, Berlin, before the unification of Germany. The closure of the Institute in East Berlin caused this valuable edition too to be discontinued.
MEGA 2, III/1 stands for Section III, v. 1 of this edition.

MEW *Marx-Engels Werke.*
An earlier joint enterprise of the MIML and the East German Institute - started in 1956 by Dietz Verlag - was stopped in 1968 before the launching of the MEGA 2 project. This consists of 39 volumes, plus two volumes of supplements and one of index. Though incomplete, it remains one of the basic sources for the assorted writings of Marx and Engels and for some 1,600 letters exchanged by them between 1844 and Marx's death in 1883.

Marx and Engels as Seen by Their Contemporaries

Gespraeche *Gespraeche mit Marx und Engels* (ed. Hans Magnus Enzensberger), 2 vols., Frankfurt 1973.
REM *Reminiscences of Marx and Engels*. (Abridged version: *Marx and Engels through the Eyes of Their Contemporaries*), Moscow 1972.
Schriften *Schriften aus dem Karl-Marx-Haus*. Essays on aspects of Marx's life and work, issued periodically in Trier.

Marx-Engels Collections in English

MECW *Marx-Engels: Collected Works*. Forty volumes - published jointly by Lawrence & Wishart Ltd., London, International Publishers Co. Inc., New York, and Progress Publishers, Moscow - have appeared since this 50-volume project was launched in 1975 in collaboration with the MIML. This is the largest collection of Marx-Engels material published so far in English, some of it for the first time.

Single Volumes in English (Short List)

ET *Marx, Early Texts* (transl. and ed. by D. McLellan), Oxford 1972.
EW *Marx, Early Writings* (introd. by L. Colletti, transl. by R. Livingstone and G. Benton), Harmondsworth/New York, 1975, 1977.
Grund *Marx, Grundrisse; Foundations of the Critique of Political Economy* (transl. with foreword by M. Nicolaus), Harmondsworth/New York 1973, 1974, 1977.
MER *Marx-Engels on Religion* (introd. by R. Niebuhr), New York 1969.
MESC *Marx-Engels, Selected Correspondence* (transl. by I. Lasker, ed. S.W. Ryazanskaya), Moscow 1975.
PKM *The Portable Karl Marx* (selected, transl. in part and with an ntroduction by Eugene Kamenka), Harmondsworth/New York 1983.

To mention but a few of the innumerable other one-volume or small collections, there is *Marx's Selected Writings* (ed. Bottomore/Rubel), Harmondsworth/New York 1956; Selections from Marx's articles in the *New York Daily Tribune* will be found in S. Avineri, *Marx on Colonialism and Modernization*, Garden City, N.Y. 1969; *Capital* is available in 3 vols. in the Pelican Marx Library, which has also published 3 vols. of his *Political Writings* (including 'The Revolutions of 1848', 'Surveys from Exile' and 'The First International and After'), Harmondsworth/New York 1973, 1978; S.K. Padover's 7-volume *Karl Marx Library*, New York 1971-77, includes some of the same as well as a volume each on *Marx on Freedom of the Press and Censorship, On*

Education, Women and Children and *On History and People*; E. Fischer has presented *Marx in His Own Words*, London 1970; and finally, there is Robert C. Tucker, *The Marx-Engels Reader*, New York 1978, offering a chronological selection of the whole range of their writings.

B. Heine: Poems, Prose, Collected Works and Correspondence

Heinrich Heine, *Sämtliche Schriften* (ed. K. Briegleb and others), 6 vols. in 7, Munich 1968-76.
Chronik F. Mende, *H. Heine: Chronik seines Lebens und Werkes* (a practically daily record of his literary and other activities), Berlin-DDR 1970.
DA *Heinrich Heine, Historisch-kritische Gasamtausgabe der Werke*, also known as West German or 'Düsseldorf Ausgabe' (ed. M. Windfuhr and others). Started in 1973 and completed in 1997: 16 volumes in 23 (including supplements, index etc.), Hamburg.
Elster *Heines Sämtliche Werke* (ed. Ernst Elster), 7 vols., Leipzig and Vienna 1887-90. Still useful.
Hirth *Heinrich Heine, Briefe* (ed. F. Hirth), 6 vols., Mainz 1950-51.
HJ *Heine-Jahrbuch*, issued annually since 1962 under the aegis of the Heinrich-Heine-Institut in Düsseldorf.
HSA *Heinrich Heine Säkularausgabe*. 27 vols. of this East German edition sponsored from Weimar by the Nationale Forschungs- und Gedenkstätten der klassischen deutschen Literatur were published in East Berlin and simultaneously by the Centre National de la Recherche Scientifique in Paris between 1975 and 1984.
KAUF *Heinrich Heine, Sämtliche Werke: Kritische Ausgabe* (ed. Hans Kaufmann), 14 vols., Munich 1964.
Kongress *Internationaler Heine-Kongress, Düsseldorf 1972, Referate und Diskussionen* (on the occasion of the 175th anniversary of his birthday, ed. Manfred Windfuhr), Hamburg 1973.
Werner 'Begegnungen mit Heine', in *Fortführung von H.H. Houbens 'Gespräche mit Heine'* (ed. Michael Werner), 2 vols., Hamburg 1973.

Heine in English
CPHH *The Complete Poems of Heinrich Heine*: A Modern English Version by H. Draper, Boston 1982. The first English rendition of Heine's entire poetic output.
HPP *Heine's Prose and Poetry* (intro. E. Rhys), London 1966.
HHPP *Heinrich Heine, Poetry and Prose* (ed. J. Hermand and R.C. Holub, foreword by A. Kazin), New York 1982.
HHSW *Heinrich Heine, Selected Works* (transl. and ed. H.M. Mustard, poetry transl. M. Knight), New York 1973.
P&B *Poems and Ballads* (transl. E. Lazarus), New York 1950.
Poems L. Untermeyer, *The Poems of Heinrich Heine* (a selection), London 1938.
Reed T.J. Reed, *Deutschland: A not so sentimental journey*, London 1986. An excellent translation of Heine's famous 'Deutschland, ein Wintermärchen').
Sword *The Sword and the Flame: Selections from Heinrich Heine's Prose* (ed. Alfred Werner), New York 1960.

Hess: Works and Correspondence
Hess AS Moses Hess, *Ausgewählte Schriften* (ed. H. Lademacher), Cologne 1962.
Hess Bw *Moses Hess Briefwechsel* (ed. Edmund Silberner, with Werner Blumenberg), The Hague 1959.
Hess INV Edmund Silberner, *The Works of Moses Hess: An Inventory of his Signed and Anonymous Publications, Manuscripts and Correspondence*, Leiden 1958. Supplemented by the same author in 'Zur Hess Bibliographie' in *Archiv für Sozialgeschichte*, vols. VI-VII, Amsterdam 1966-67, pp. 241-314.
Hess NQHF Wolfgang Mönke (ed), 'Neue Quellen zur Hess-Forschung,' in *Abhandlungen der Deutschen Akademie der Wissenschaften zu Berlin*, Jg. 1964, No. 1, Akademie-Verlag, Berlin-DDR. This contains extracts from Hess's diary as well as from his MSS and his correspondence with Marx, Engels, Weitling, Ewerbeck and others.
Hess PSS Moses Hess, *Philosophische und sozialistische Schriften 1837-1850* (ed. A. Cornu and W. Mönke), Berlin DDR 1961. (2nd enlarged edition, Vaduz 1980).
Hess RJ Moses Hess, *Rom und Jerusalem*, Leipzig 1862. Modern edition in Hess AS. English: *Rome and Jerusalem* (ed. and transl. M. Waxmann), New York 1943.
Note: As is evident from the above, no complete edition of Moses Hess's writings exists, nor has his diary been published in full.

Other Abbreviations
AGS Archiv für die Geschichte des Sozialismus u. der Arbeiterbewegung, Hrsg. Carl Grünberg, 1910-30.
Hegel LWW *Hegel Katalog 1770-1970, Leben, Werk, Wirkung*. Catalogue of contemporary reports and documents exhibited in 1970 in Stuttgart, on the bicentenary of Hegel's birth.
HHW *The Historians' History of the World* (26 vols. plus Index), The Encyclopaedia Britannica Co., 5th ed., London/ New York 1926.
MyPaT(G-H) *My Past and Thoughts, The Memoirs of Alexander Herzen* (transl. C. Garnett, revised H. Higgens, intro. Isaiah Berlin), 4 vols., New York 1968.
MyPaT(DM) *My Past and Thoughts, The Memoirs of Alexander Herzen*, one-volume edition of the above (abridged with a preface and notes by D. Macdonald), London 1974.

General Bibliography
Jean-Pierre Alem, *Enfantin, Le Prophète aux Sept Visage*, Paris 1963.
R. Anchel, *Napoléon et les Juifs*, Paris 1928.
Bert Andreas, *Documents Constitutifs de la Ligue des Communistes (On the Foundation of the Communist League)*, bilingual French-German edition, Hamburg 1968 and Paris 1972.
P.V. Annenkov, *The Extraordinary Decade* (ed. Arthur Mendel, transl. R. Titunik), Ann Arbor, MI 1968.
Rodolphe Apponyi, *Vingt-cinq ans à Paris (1826-1850)*, Paris 1913-26.
Hannah Arendt, *Elemente und Ursprünge Totaler Herrschaft*, Frankfurt-am-Main 1955.

Rachel Varnhagen: The Life of a Jewess (transl. Richard and Clara Winston), London 1957.

S. Avineri, *The Social and Political Thought of Karl Marx*, Cambridge 1968.

Hegel's Theory of the Modern State, Cambridge 1972.

Moses Hess: Prophet of Communism and Zionism, New York 1985.

The Making of Modern Zionism, London 1981.

E. Barnikol, *Weitling der Gefangene und seine Gerechtigkeit*, Kiel 1929.

Jacques Barzun, *Darwin, Marx, Wagner*, Chicago 1985.

E. Bauer, *Bruno Bauer und seine Gegner*, Berlin 1842.

Heinz Becker, *Der Fall Heine-Meyerbeer*, Neue Dokumente revidieren ein Geschichtsurteil, Berlin 1958.

Paul H. Beik, *Louis-Philippe and the July Monarchy*, Princeton 1965.

H. Ben-Israel, *English Historians on the French Revolution*, Cambridge 1968.

Berlin: Neun Kapitel Seiner Geschichte, Berlin 1960.

Isaiah Berlin, *Karl Marx, His Life and Environment*, Oxford 1963.

Russian Thinkers (ed. Henry Hardy and Aileen Kelly, intro. A. Kelly), London 1978.

Against the Current, Essays in The History of Ideas (ed. with a bibliography by H. Hardy, intro. R. Hausheer), London 1979.

J.F. Bernard, *Talleyrand: A Biography*, London 1973.

Samuel Bernstein, *Auguste Blanqui and the Art of Insurrection*, London 1971.

G. Bertier de Sauvigny, *The Bourbon Restoration*, Philadelphia 1966.

R.J. Bezucha, *The Lyon Uprising of 1834, Social and Political Conflict in the early July Monarchy*, Cambridge MA 1974.

Werner Blumenberg, *Karl Marx in Selbstzeugnissen und Bilddokumenten*, Hamburg 1962, 1973.

Wilfrid Blunt, *On Wings of Songs, A Biography of Felix Mendelssohn*, New York 1974

J.C. Bluntschli, *Die Kommunisten in der Schweiz*, Zurich 1843.

H. Böll, 'Karl Marx - ein deutscher Jude verändert die Welt', in *Porträts zur deutsch-jüdischen Geistesgeschichte*, Cologne 1961.

Rutger Booss, *Ansichten der Revolution, Paris-Berichte deutscher Schriftsteller nach der Juli-Revolution 1830: Heine, Börne u.a.*, Cologne 1977.

J.L. Borges, *A Personal Anthology* (ed. and foreword by A. Kerrigan), London 1968.

Georg Brandes, *Hauptströmungen der Literatur des Neunzehnten Jahrhunderts*, 3 vols., Berlin 1924.

W. Brazill, *The Young Hegelians*, New Haven 1970.

Charles Breunig, *The Age of Revolution and Reaction, 1789-1850* (The Norton History of Modern Europe, v. IV), New York 1977.

Bernhard Brilling, *Beiträge zur Geschichte der Juden in Trier*, Trierisches Jahrbuch 1958.

Max Brod, *Heinrich Heine, The Artist in Revolt* (transl. Joseph Witriol), London 1956.

Edward J. Brown, *Stankevich and his Moscow Circle, 1830-1840*, Stanford 1966.

Martin Buber, *On Zion, The History of an Idea* (transl. S. Godmann), London 1973.

Paths of Utopia (transl. R.F.C. Hull), London/ Boston 1958, 1960.

R. Burnand, *La Vie quotidienne en France en 1830*, Paris 1943.

E.M. Butler, *The Saint-Simonian Religion in Germany: A Study of the Young German Movement*, Cambridge 1926.

Julius Carlebach, *Karl Marx and the Radical Critique of Judaism*, London 1978.

E.H. Carr, *Michael Bakunin*, London 1937, 1975.

The Romantic Exiles, London 1933, 1949

Marguerite Castillon du Perron, *Louis-Philippe et la Révolution française*, Paris 1984.

George Catlin, *The Story of the Political Philosophers*, New York 1939.

S.C.G. Charlety, *Histoire du Saint-Simonisme (1825-1864)*, Paris 1931.

M. Cherniavsky, *Tsar and People, Studies in Russian Myths*, New Haven 1961.

Irene Collins, *The Government and the Newspapers in France 1814-1881*, Oxford 1959.

Michael Confino (ed.), *Daughter of a Revolutionary: Natalie Herzen and the Bakunin-Nechayev Circle* (transl. Hilary Sternberg and Lydia Bott), London 1974.

David Conway, *A Farewell to Marx*, Harmondsworth/New York 1989.

Duff Cooper, *Talleyrand*, London 1964.

M. Davis (ed.), *Israel, Its Role in Civilization*, New York 1956.

Dominique Desanti, *Les Socialistes de L'Utopie*, Paris 1970.

W. Dilthey, *Die Jugendgeschichte Hegels*, Berlin 1905.

Doctrine Saint-Simonienne, Exposition par Bazard, Au nom du Collège, en 1829 et 1830. In English: *The Doctrine of Saint-Simon: An Exposition* (transl. with notes and introduction by G.G. Iggers), New York 1972.

Sam Dolgoff (ed.), *Bakunin on Anarchy*, New York 1972.

Hal Draper, *Karl Marx's Theory of Revolution* (v. I: State and Bureaucracy; v. II, The Politics of Social Classes), New York/ London 1977, 1978.

J. Droz, *Europe between Revolutions 1815-1848*, Glasgow 1967.

Simon Dubnow, *Nationalism and History* (ed. and intro. Koppen S. Pinson), New York 1970.

B. Fairley, *Heinrich Heine: An Interpretation*, Oxford 1954.

François Fejtö, *Heine, A Biography* (transl. Mervyn Savill), London 1846.

Harold Fisch, *The Zionist Revolution, A New Perspective*, London 1978.

R.H. Foerster, *Die Rolle Berlins im Europäischen Geistesleben*, Berlin 1968.

W.B. Gallie, *Philosophers of Peace and War*, Cambridge 1978.

Eduard Gans, *Rückblicke auf Personen und Zustände*, Berlin 1836.

A.G. Garrone, *Philippe Buonarroti et les révolutionnaires du XIXe siècle*, Paris 1975.

L. Gershoy, *The French Revolution and Napoleon*, New York 1964.

P. Geyl, *Napoleon: For and Against*, London 1949.

B. Gille, *La Banque en France au XIXe siècle*, Paris, 1970.

Walter Grab, *Ein Mann der Marx Ideen Gab*, Düsseldorf 1979.

Heinrich Heine als politischer Dichter, Heidelberg 1982.

Deutsche Aufklärung u. Juden-Emanzipation, 1979 International Symposium, Tel Aviv University Institute for German History.

C. Grana, *Bohemian Versus Bourgeois Society*, New York 1964.

J. Grandjonc, *Marx et les Communistes allemands à Paris, Vorwärts, 1844*, Paris 1974.

Ian Grey, *The Romanovs, The Rise and Fall of a Russian Dynasty*, New York 1970.

R. Grimsley, *The Philosophy of Rousseau*, Oxford 1973.

R.W. Gutman, *Richard Wagner, The Man, His Mind, His Music*, New York 1968.

W. Gössmann (ed.), *Geständnisse: Heine im Bewusstsein heutiger Autoren*, Düsseldorf 1972.

Norman Hampson, *The First European Revolution, 1776-1815*, London/New York 1969.

Richard Hare, *Portraits of Russian Personalities between Reform and Revolution*, Oxford 1959.

G. Harris, *Hegel's Development: Toward The Sunlight*, Oxford 1971.

Johan Y. Hasslin (ed.), *Berlin*, Munich 1955.

H. Hatfield, *Clashing Myths in German Literature from Heine to Rilke*, Cambridge MA 1974.

J.C. Hauschild/M. Werner, *'Der Zweck des Lebens ist das Leben selbst': A Heine Biography*, Cologne 1997.

Friedrich Heer, *Europe, Mother of Revolutions* (transl. Charles Kessler and Jenneta Adcock), London 1971. (Original German version, *Europa, Mutter der Revolutionen*, Stuttgart 1974).

S.J. Heims, *John von Neuman and Norbert Wiener*, Cambridge MA 1982.

Maximilian Heine, *Erinnerungen an Heinrich Heine*, Berlin 1866.

W.O. Henderson, *The Life of Friedrich Engels*, 2 vols., London 1976.

F.O. Hertz, *The Development of the German Public Mind*, 2 vols., London 1957, 1962.

A. Hertzberg, *The French Emancipation and the Jews*, New York 1968.

F. Heymann, *Der Chevalier von Geldern*, Amsterdam 1937, first published in Germany, Berlin 1963 and reprinted Königstein 1985.

E.G. Hobsbawm, *The Age of Revolution: Europe 1789-1848*, London 1962.
The Age of Capital, 1848-1875, London 1976.

H. Holborn, *A History of Modern Germany*, vols. II (1648-1840) and III (1840-1945), Princeton 1969 and 1982.

Sidney Hook, *From Hegel to Marx* (2nd ed.), Ann Arbor, MI, 1962.

A. Horne, *Napoleon, Master of Europe*, London 1979.

T.E.B. Howarth, *Citizen-King, The Life of Louis-Philippe, King of the French*, London 1961, 1962.

Victor Hugo, *Things Seen* (ed. and transl. by David Kimber), Oxford 1964.

R.N. Hunt, *The Political ideas of Marx and Engels* (2 vols.), London 1975, 1984.

E. Hyams, *Proudhon, His Revolutionary Life, Mind and Work*, London 1979.

Douglas Johnson, *Guizot, Aspects of French History, 1787-1874*, London/Toronto 1963.

Z.A. Jordan, *The Revolution of Dialectical Materialism*, New York 1967.

Albert Kaltenthaler, *Die Pariser Salons als europäische Kulturzentren unter besonderer Berücksichtigung der deutschen Besucher, 1815-1848*, Munich 1960.

H.E. Kaminski, *Michel Bakounine, La Vie d'un Révolutionnaire*, Paris 1938.

W. Kanowsky, *Vernunft und Geschichte, Heinrich Heines Studium als Grundlegung seiner Welt- und Kunstanschauung*, Bonn 1975.

D. Kaufmann, *Aus Heinrich Heines Ahnensaal*, Breslau 1896.

Yvonne Kapp, *Eleanor Marx* (2 vols.: *Family Life* and *The Crowded Years*), London 1972, 1976.

E. Kedourie (ed.), *The Jewish World, Revelation, Prophecy and History*, London/New York 1979.

Alison Kelly, *Michael Bakunin, A Study in the Psychology and Politics of Utopianism*, Oxford 1982.

Linda Kelly, *The Young Romantics*, Paris 1827-37, London 1976.

George F. Kennan, *The Marquis de Custine and his Russia in 1839*, Princeton 1971.

S. Kent, *Electoral Procedure under Louis-Philippe*, New Haven 1937.

Hartmut Kircher, *Heinrich Heine und das Judentum*, Bonn 1973.

Adolf Kober, 'Karl Marx's Vater und das napoleonische Ausnahmegesetz gegen die Juden 1808',

Jahrbuch des Kölnischen Geschichtsverein, Band 14, 1932.

Franz Kobler, *Napoleon and the Jews*, New York 1976.

Hans Kohn, *Making of the Modern French Mind*, New York 1955. 'Goethe and His Time', in *Der Friede: Idee und Verwiklichung/ The Search for Peace/ Festgabe für Adolf Leschnitze* (a bilingual collection of essays in German and English ed. by E. Fromm, H. Herzfeld & K. Grossmann), Heidelberg 1961.

Rudolph Kraemer-Badoni, *Anarchismus, Geschichte und Gegenwart einer Utopie*, Vienna-Munich-Zurich 1970.

L. Kreutzer, *Heine und der Kommunismus*, Göttingen 1970.

E. Krüger, Heine und Hegel: Dichtung, Philosophie und Politik bei Heinrich Heine, Kronberg 1977

J.A. Kruse, *Heines Hamburger Zeit*, Hamburg 1972.

Ich Narr des Glücks: Heinrich Heine 1797-1856, Stuttgart 1997.

A. Künzli, *Karl Marx: Eine Psychographie*, Vienna-Frankfurt-Zürich 1966.

H. Lamm, *Karl Marx 1818-1968*, Mainz 1968.

R.W. Leonhardt (ed.), *Heinrich Heine 1797-1856*, Hamburg 1972.

Solomon Liptzin, *The English Legend of Heinrich Heine*, New York 1954.

David W. Lovell, *From Marx to Lenin, An evaluation of Marx's responsibility for Soviet authoritarianism*, Cambridge 1984.

Marx's Proletariat, The Making of A Myth, London/New York 1988.

Jean Lucas-Dubreton, *Louis-Philippe*, Paris 1938.

Georg Lukàcs, *Deutsche Realisten des 19. Jahrhunderts*, Berlin 1952.

D. McLellan, *Marx: His Life and Thought*, London 1973.

D. McLellan (ed.), *Marx: the First Hundred Years*, London 1983.

Isabel de Madariaga, *Russia in the Age of Catherine the Great*, London 1981.

D. Magashak, *Turgenev, A Life*, London 1959.

Martin Malia, *Alexander Herzen and the Birth of Russian Socialism, 1812-1855*, Cambridge MA 1961.

Golo Mann, *Secretary of Europe. The Life of Friedrich Gentz* (transl. William H. Hoglom), New Haven 1946.

The History of Germany since 1789 (transl. Marian Jackson), London 1968.

Thomas Mann, *Wagner und Unsere Zeit - Aufsätze, Betrachtungen, Briefe*, Berlin 1963.

Frank E. Manuel, *The Prophets of Paris*, Cambridge MA 1962.

P. Mariel, *Les Carbonari*, Paris 1973.

F. Markham, *Napoleon*, New York 1963.

Anthony Masters, *Bakunin, the Father of Anarchism*, London 1974.

André Maurois, *Lélia, The Life of George Sand* (transl. Gerald Hopkins), New York 1953.

J.P. Maximoff (ed.), *The Political Philosophy of Bakunin: Scientific Anarchism*, New York 1953.

Bruce Mazlish, *The Meaning of Karl Marx*, Oxford 1984.

Arthur P. Mendel, *Michael Bakunin: Roots of Apocalypse*, New York 1981.

P.R. Mendès-Flohr and J. Reinharz (ed.), *The Jew In The Modern World: A Documentary History*, Oxford 1980.

G. Meyerbeer, *Briefwechsel und Tagebücher* (3 vols.), Berlin 1970. Enlarged edition, including vols. IV and V, 1985-99.

H. Monz, *Karl Marx, Grundlagen der Entwicklung zu Leben und Werk*, Trier 1973.

Ludwig Gall, der Sozialreformer aus Trier, Trier 1983.

S. Na'aman, *Emanzipation und Messianismus: Leben und Werk des Moses Hess*, Frankfurt 1982.

Lassalle, Hannover 1970.

Heine und Lassalle: Ihre Beziehungen im Zeichen der Dämonie des Geldes. Sonderdruck aus dem Archiv für Sozialgeschichte, Band 4, Hanover 1964.

B. Nicolaievsky and O. Maenchen-Helfen, *Karl Marx, Man and Fighter* (transl. Gwenda David and Eric Mosbacher), London 1936 (Penguin ed. 1976).

Friedrich Nietzsche, *The Birth of Tragedy* and *The Case of Wagner* (transl. with commentary by Walter Kaufmann), New York 1967.

Basic Writings of Nietzsche (transl. and ed., with commentaries by Walter Kaufmann), New York 1968.

B. Ollman, *Alienation, Marx's Conception of Man in Capital Society*, Cambridge 1976.

Hermann Oncken, *Ferdinand Lassalle. Eine politische Biographie*, Stuttgart/Berlin 1920.

S.K. Padover, *Karl Marx, An Intimate Biography*, New York 1978.

Bernard Pares, *A History of Russia*, New York 1965.

R. Payne (ed.), *The Unknown Marx*, New York 1971, London 1972.

Chaim Pearl, *Rashi*, London 1988.

David H. Pinkney, *The French Revolution of 1830*, Princeton 1972.

R. Pipes, *Russia under the Old Regime*, London 1974.

The Unknown Lenin, From The Secret Archive, New Haven and London 1996.

Léon Poliakov, *The History of Antisemitism* (v. III: *From Voltaire to Wagner*, transl. M. Kochan), New York 1975.

S. Posener, *Adolphe Crémieux*, New York 1940.

S.S. Prawer, *Heine's Jewish Comedy: A Study of his Portraits of Jews and Judaism*, Oxford 1983.

Heine, The Tragic Satirist: A Study of the later Poetry 1827-1856, Cambridge 1961.

Karl Marx and World Literature, Oxford 1978.

A.M. Prinz, 'Myths, Facts and Riddles about the Literary Estate of Karl Marx', in *Der Friede: Idee und Verwiklichung/ The Search for Peace...* (See under H. Kohn)

Fritz J. Raddatz, *Karl Marx, Eine politische Biographie*, Hamburg 1975.

Heine, Ein deutsches Märchen, Hamburg 1977.

Taubenherz und Geierschnabel: Heinrich Heine, eine Biographie, Weinheim 1997.

Nigel Reeves, *Heine and the Young Marx*, Oxford 1972.

Heinrich Heine, Poetry and Politics, Oxford 1974.

M. Reich-Ranicki, *Der Fall Heine*, Stuttgart 1997.

H.G. Reissner, *Eduard Gans, Ein Leben im Vormärz*, Tübingen, 1965.

Nicholas V. Riasanovsky, *The Teaching of Charles Fourier*, Berkeley 1969.

N. Rich, *The Age of Nationalism and Reform, 1850-1890*, New York 1970.

Jasper Ridley, *Garibaldi*, London 1974.

Max Ring, *Erinnerungen*, Berlin 1898.

J. Ritter, *Hegel und die französische Revolution*, Cologne 1957.

Ritchie Robertson, *Heine*, London 1988.

R.B. Rose, *Gracchus Babeuf, The First Revolutionary Communist*, Stanford 1978.

William Rose, *Heinrich Heine: Two Studies of his Thought and Feeling* (Heine's Political and Social Attitude. Heine's Jewish Feeling), Oxford 1956.

The Early Love Poetry of Heinrich Heine: An Inquiry into Poetic Inspiration, Oxford 1962.

Zwi Rosen, *Moses Hess und Karl Marx. Ein Beitrag zur Entstehung der Marxschen Theorie*, Hamburg 1983.

Ludwig Rosenthal, *Heinrich Heine als Jude*, Berlin/Frankfurt 1973.

Maximilien Rubel, with Margaret Manale, *Marx Without Myth. A Chronological Study of His Life and Work*, Oxford 1975.

Rubel on Karl Marx, Five Essays (ed. Joseph O'Malley and Keith Algozin), Cambridge 1981.

Eda Sagarra, *A Social History of Germany 1648-1914*, London 1976.

J.L. Sammons, *Heinrich Heine, A Modern Biography*, Princeton 1979.

A.I. Sandor, *The Exile of Gods: Interpretation of a Theme, and a Technique in the Works of Heinrich Heine*, The Hague 1967.

Peter Scheibert, *Von Bakunin zu Lenin, Geschichte der russischen revolutionären Ideologien 1840-1895*, Leiden 1956, 1970.

H. Schnee, *Die Hoffinanz und der moderne Staat* (6 vols.), Berlin 1963, 1965.

G.G. Scholem, *Major Trends in Jewish Mysticism*, London 1955.

Simon Schwarzfuchs, *Napoleon, the Jews and the Sanhedrin*, London 1979.

M. Seliger, *The Marxist Conception of Ideology*, Cambridge 1977.

Hugh Seton-Watson, *The Russian Empire 1801-1917*, Oxford 1967.

Teodor Shanin, *Late Marx and the Russian Road*, London 1984.

B.L. Sherwin, *Mystical Theology and Social Dissent: The Life and*

Works of Judah Loew of Prague, London/Toronto 1982.

Edmund Silberner, *Moses Hess. Geschichte seines Lebens*, Leiden 1966.

A.B. Spitzer, *Old Hatreds and Young Hopes*, Cambridge MA 1971.

P.S. Squire, *The Third Department: The Establishment and Practices of the Political Police in the Russia of Nicholas I*, Cambridge 1968.

E. Sterling (and others), *Monumenta - 2000 Jahre Geschichte und Kultur der Juden am Rhein*, Cologne 1963.

Er ist wie Du, Aus der Frühgeschichte des Antisemitismus in Deutschland 1815-1850, Munich 1956

Dolf Sternberger, *Heinrich Heine und die Abschaffung der Sünde*, Hamburg and Düsseldorf 1972.

L.I. Strakhovsky, *Alexander I of Russia, The Man Who Defeated Napoleon*, New York 1947.

H. Stuke, *Philosophie der Tat* (Industrielle Welt 3, Schriftenreihe des Arbeitskreises fur moderne Sozialgeschichte), Stuttgart 1963.

B.S. Sumner, *Survey of Russian History*, London 1961.

Margarete Susman, *Frauen der Romantik*, Cologne 1960.

J.L. Talmon, *The Origin of Totalitarian Democracy*, London 1952/ New York 1965.

Romanticism and Revolt, Europe 1815-1848, London/New York 1969.

Diogène Tama, *Procès-Verbaux et décisions du Grand Sanhédrin* (transl. with Preface by F.D. Kirwan and published in London in 1807 as *Transactions of the Paris Sanhedrim* [sic] or *Acts of The Assembly of Israelitish Deputies*), Farnborough, England, 1971.

C. Taylor, *Hegel*, Cambridge 1975.

Edmond Taylor, *The Fall of the Dynasties, The Collapse of The Old Order 1905-1922* New York 1963.

J.M. Thompson, *The French Revolution*, Oxford 1944.

To The Happy Few, Selected Letters of Stendhal (transl. N. Cameron, intro. Emmanuel Boudot-Lamotte), New York 1955.

Henri Troyat, *Catherine The Great*, London 1979, 1981.

Barbara Tuchman, *Bible and Sword*, New York/ London 1957.

The Proud Tower, New York/ London 1967.

Robert C. Tucker, *Philosophy and Myth in Karl Marx*, Cambridge 1961.

Gosta v. Uexküll, *Ferdinand Lassalle in Selbstzeugnissen und Bilddokumenten*, Reinbek bei Hamburg 1974.

Adam B. Ulam, *Russia's Failed Revolutions: From the Decembrists to the Dissidents*, London 1981.

Louis Untermeyer, *Heinrich Heine: Paradox and Poet*, New York 1937.

Antonina Vallentin, *Heine, Poet in Exile*, New York 1956.

F. Venturi, *Roots of Revolution: A History of the Populist and Socialist Movements in Nineteenth Century Russia* (trans. Francis Haskell, intro. Isaiah Berlin), London 1960.

Jacques Vier, *La Comtesse d'Agoult et son Temps*, Paris 1955.

D. Villiers (ed.), *Next Year in Jerusalem: Jews in the 20th Century*, London 1976.

B. Wachstein, 'Die Abstammung von Karl Marx', in *Festskrift*, Copenhagen 1923.

W. Wadepuhl, *Heinrich Heine, Sein Leben, Seine Werke*, Munich 1977.

Norbert Wiener, *God and Golem*, Cambridge MA.

Edmund Wilson, *To the Finland Station*, New York 1940.

M. Windfuhr, *Heinrich Heine, Revolution und Reflexion*, Stuttgart 1969.

C. Wittke, *The Utopian Communist: A Biography of Wilhelm Weitling, Nineteenth Century Reformer*, Baton Rouge 1950.

Murray Wolfson, *Marx: Economist, Philosopher*, London 1982.

Avraham Yarmolinsky, *Road to Revolution: A Century of Russian Radicalism*, Princeton 1986.

A. Zamoyski, *Chopin, A Biography*, London 1979.

Theodore Zeldin, *France 1848-1945: Ambition and Love*, Oxford 1979.

Emil Zenz, *Trier im 18. Jahrhundert 1700-1794*, Trier 1981.

Chronik der Stadt Trier, 2000 Jahre Berichte in Bildern, Trier 1985.

Index